FEATURES AND BENEFITS
Mathematics: Applications and Connections, Course 2

1. **NCTM Standards** As the correlation on pages **T19-T20** shows, strict a
   Standards in developing this program. Also see **the Scope** and Sequenc

2. **Applications/Connections** Because the ability to grasp concepts and s ̲ ̲ ̲ ̲ ̲ ̲ ̲ ̲ ̲ ̲ ̲ced when they
   are tied to applications, nearly every lesson opens with an application that connects the content to the
   students' real world. See page 48. Other features that relate to this issue are the *Teen Scene* (page
   79), *Did You Know?* (page 11), *When am I ever going to use this?* (page 29), *chapter openers* (pages
   46-47), and the *Extended Projects Handbook* (pages 562-571).

   Connections to *algebra* (page 28), *measurement* (page 78), *statistics* (page 98), *probability* (page 157)
   and *geometry* (page 194) also enhance learning, as well as increase the students' interest.

3. **Problem Solving** The ongoing attention to problem solving is evidenced by the inclusion of *Problem
   Solving and Applications* in every set of exercises (exercises 31-34 on page 139). *Critical Thinking*
   exercises add to this focus on problem solving (exercise 33 on page 139), as do the *Data Search* exercises (exercise 10 on page 7). The *Problem-Solving Strategy* lessons give students the opportunity to
   build a repertoire of strategies (pages 142-144). The *Decision Making* lessons add another dimension as they connect the mathematics to the students' real-life experiences as consumers (pages 148-
   149).

4. **Mathematics Labs** These optional hands-on activities give students the opportunity to discover
   mathematical concepts by working cooperatively with a partner or a group. Some serve as a preview
   of the lesson that follows (page 223); others act as a lesson follow-up (page 232). The *Mini-Labs* also
   afford students this opportunity within lessons (page 298).

5. **Algebra/Geometry** Because algebraic concepts and skills are introduced early and are reinforced
   and extended throughout the three courses, students will be better prepared for first-year algebra
   (page 28). Similarly, the integration of geometry will help to prepare students for high school geometry (page 243).

6. **Review** To maintain prior-taught skills and concepts, a *Mixed Review* is included in each set of exercises, and each of these problems is referenced to the related lesson (exercises 37-41 on page 134).
   The *Look Back* feature also relates to review, as it guides students to the related help on previously-
   learned concepts (page 146).

7. **Technology** To help prepare students to function in a high tech environment, instruction on the role
   of the calculator and computer as problem-solving tools is integrated throughout (pages 96-97, 133,
   and exercise 51 on page 135). Graphing Calculator and Spreadsheet activities in the *Technology
   Activities* strengthen this focus (pages 644-648).

8. **Teacher Support** The Teacher's Wraparound Edition makes it easy for you to organize, present and
   enhance the content. The extensive set of resource materials helps you increase each student's chance
   for success. See pages 10-15 in the brochure that follows.

The First Mathematics Program Developed Exclusively for Middle School Students

MATHEMATICS
Applications and Connections
Course 3

MATHEMATICS
Applications and Connections
Course 2

MATHEMATICS
Applications and Connections
Course 1

Meets NCTM Standards

GLENCOE

- Glencoe's *Mathematics: Applications and Connections* is the first series of mathematics textbooks developed specifically for the middle school. Not just an extended elementary program, the three courses of the *Mathematics: Applications and Connections* series address not only content areas, but also the unique developmental needs and personal interests of your middle school students.

- The program features an in-depth, integrated preparation for algebra, with fresh, attractive textbooks that appeal to rapidly maturing middle school students. The texts contain lessons that cover the content in greater depth and features that are relevant to the experiences and concerns of your middle school students.

Glencoe Presents a Middle School Mather
Prepares Your Students for Algebra and G

Table of Contents

- Most mathematics textbooks used at this level present each lesson in a two-page format. In *Mathematics: Applications and Connections*, the length of each lesson is determined by the content presented. Skills and concepts are tied to applications that are part of the students' real world or to connections with other mathematics topics and technology. Each chapter places a strong emphasis on problem-solving skills.

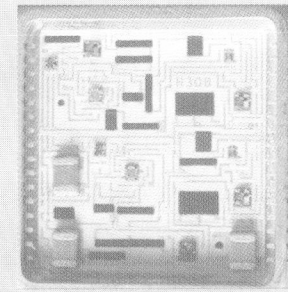

tics *Program That* metry.

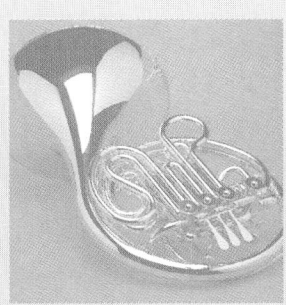

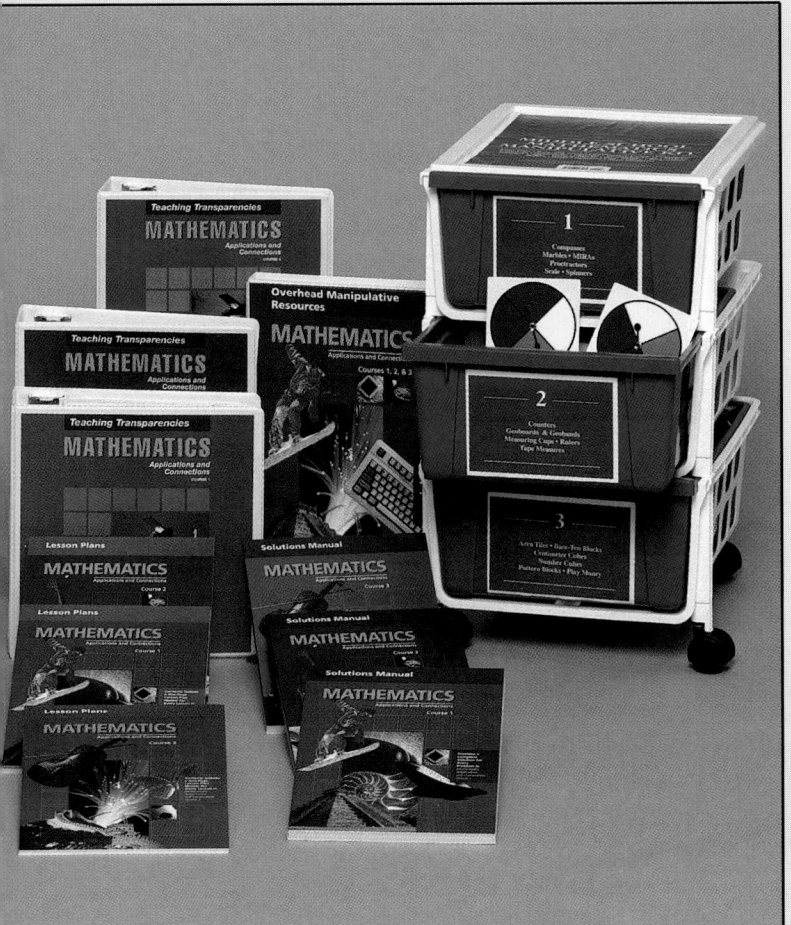

A Real-World Emphasis Makes Mathematics Meaningful for Today's Students

Mathematics: Applications and Connections Answers the Real-Life Question, "Why Do I Have to Learn Math?"

Some of your students may not believe that mathematics has very much to do with their everyday lives. *Mathematics: Applications and Connections* can help you change that attitude. The combination of content and meaningful applications helps your students learn that understanding mathematics will aid them in becoming problem solvers in other areas of life as well. In *Mathematics: Applications and Connections*, your students come to understand mathematics within the context of real-life situations and through the integration of mathematical content.

APPLICATIONS tie mathematics to the real world and give reasons to learn mathematics.

WHEN AM I EVER GOING TO USE THIS? connects mathematics to situations young people encounter each day and to real-life careers.

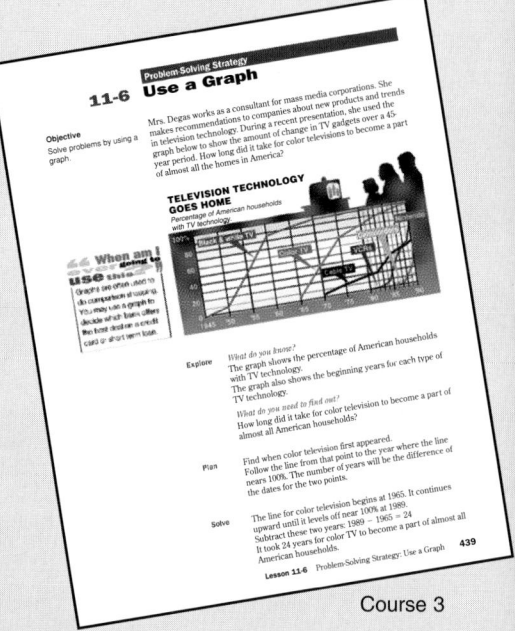

Course 3

Examples *Connection*

4 **Algebra** Write x^3 as a product.

The base is x. The exponent 3 means x is used 3 times.

$$x^3 = x \cdot x \cdot x$$

5 **Algebra** Write $a \cdot a \cdot a \cdot a$ using exponents.

a is a base. Since a is a factor 4 times, the exponent is 4.

$$a \cdot a \cdot a \cdot a = a^4$$

6 **Algebra** Evaluate n^4 if $n = 3$.

$n^4 = 3^4$ *Replace n with 3.*

3 $\boxed{y^x}$ 4 $\boxed{=}$ 81

Course 2

CONNECTIONS to algebra, geometry, measurement, probability, and other topics illustrate how various areas of mathematics are interrelated.

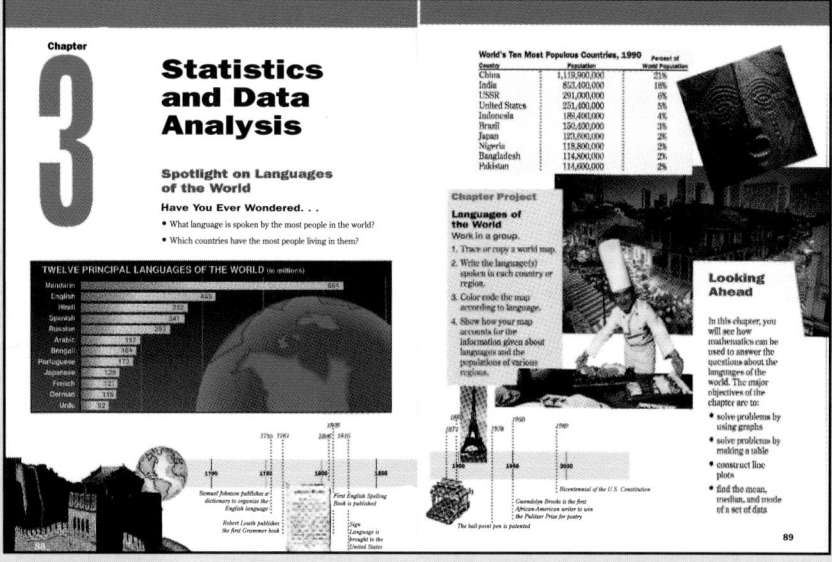

Course 2

CHAPTER OPENERS begin with a Spotlight focusing on topics of interest to your middle school students. Every Spotlight includes "Have You Ever Wondered..." questions, fascinating facts and data, a timeline or comic, a Chapter Project, and a concise chapter preview.

Stimulating Problems and Relevant Applications Integrate Mathematics into the Rapidly Changing World of the Middle School Student

Mathematics: Applications and Connections is jam-packed with opportunities for problem solving. As a teacher, you know that solving classroom problems doesn't prove mastery. Your students must be able to use what they've learned beyond the classroom setting. *Mathematics: Applications and Connections* places heavy emphasis on the development of critical thinking skills, strategies, applications to the real world, and connections to other mathematics and non-mathematics disciplines.

Course 1

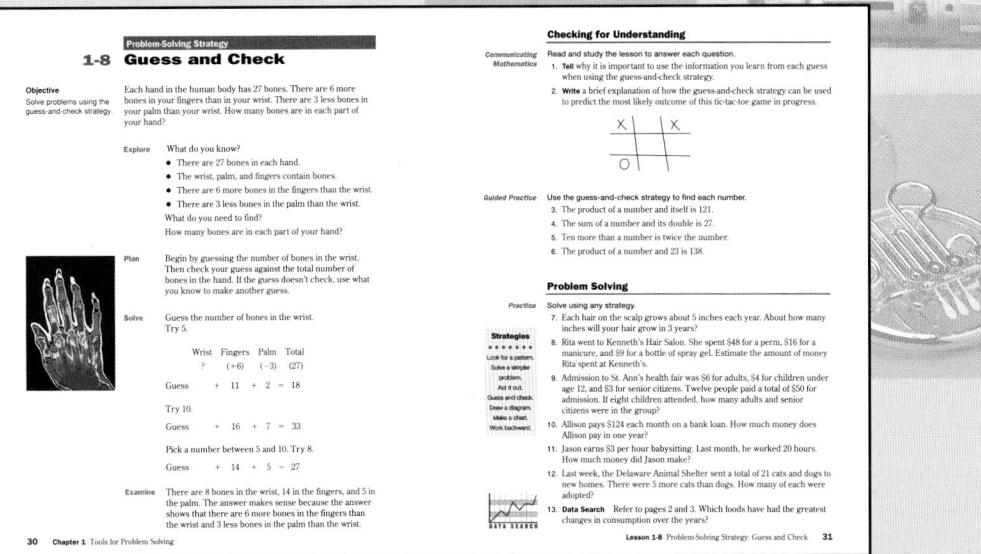

PROBLEM-SOLVING STRATEGY LESSONS include a variety of problem-solving options for students. Students learn that there are many valid ways to approach mathematical problems.

DECISION-MAKING LESSONS present situations that enable students to connect mathematics to their real-life experiences as consumers and citizens.

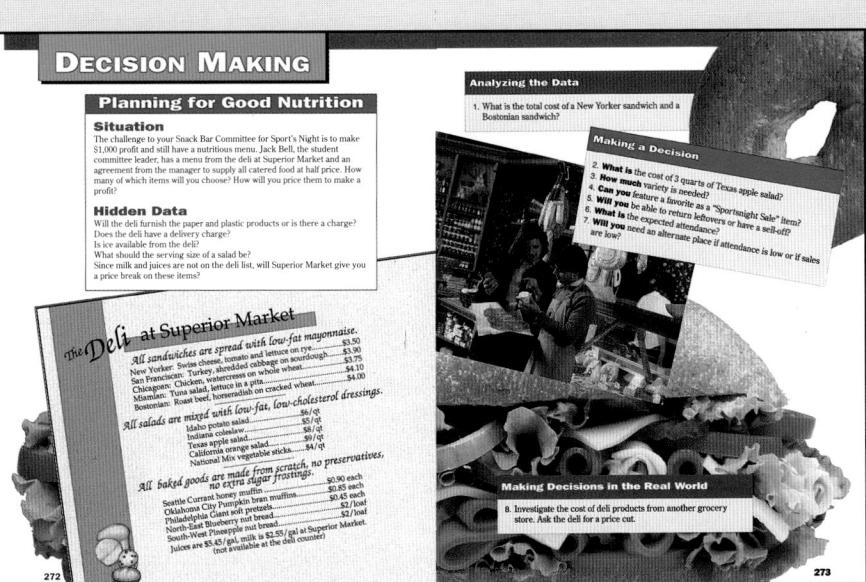

Course 2

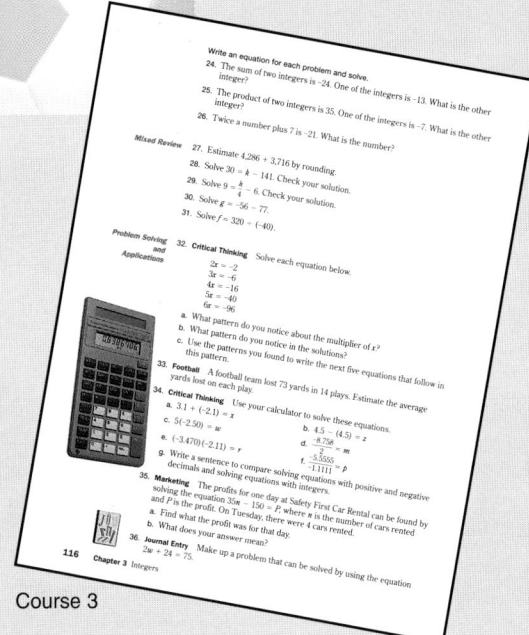

Course 3

CRITICAL THINKING exercises challenge students to develop and apply higher-order thinking skills.

PROBLEM SOLVING AND APPLICATIONS in each lesson directly link mathematics to real-world situations and to art, history, science, and other subject areas.

Mathematics: Applications and Connections Prepares Students for the Future Through Its Attention to Technology.

Technology is built-in through **COMPUTER CONNECTIONS** exercises, labs, examples, and features that increase your students' proficiency in using calculators and computers (data bases and spreadsheets).

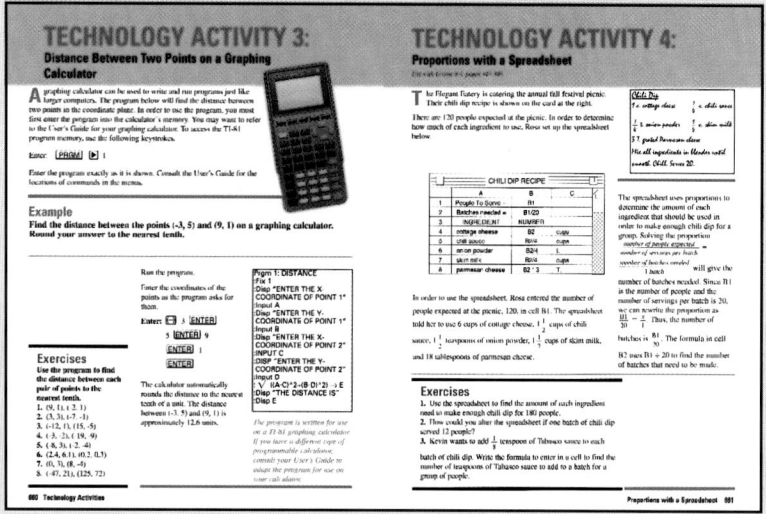

Course 3

TECHNOLOGY ACTIVITIES in the Student Edition allow students to explore mathematics with graphing calculators or spreadsheets. Complete step-by-step instructions guide students through the activities.

INTERACTIVE MATHEMATICS TOOLS provide an opportunity to use a Macintosh computer to explore and discover mathematical concepts. This multimedia software allows students to interact with the computer screen to manipulate mathematical models. The computer activities are designed around lessons, Mathematics Labs, and Mini-Labs in the student text.

Course 1

Calculator Hint
· · · · · · · · · · ·
Many calculators have a key labeled y^x. This key allows you to compute exponents very quickly. Suppose you want to find 16^5.

16 y^x 5 $=$

1048576

The result appears immediately.

CALCULATOR HINTS offer tips for solving problems.

Mathematics: Applications and Connections Teaches Students to Communicate Their Understanding of Mathematical Concepts

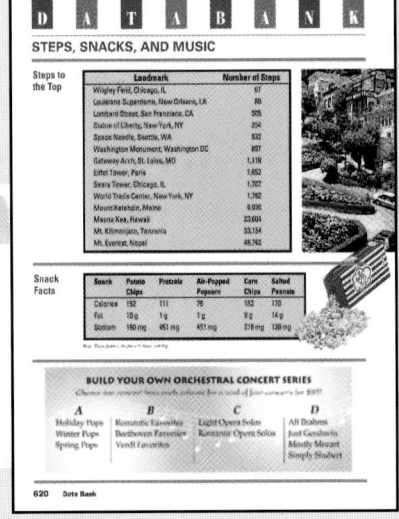

Mathematics: Applications and Connections offers a myriad of opportunities for your students to become active participants in learning mathematics.

TEEN SCENES feature interesting tidbits about math-related topics that are of interest to middle school students, such as teen spending habits.

TEEN SCENE

The custom of sending valentine cards and gifts began in the 16th century. Many believe the valentine was the first of all greeting cards.

Course 1

The **DATA SEARCH QUESTIONS** and **DATA BANK** give students the opportunity to explore real-world data. In each chapter, students will use the information provided in the Data Bank to answer questions they care about.

46. Data Search Refer to page 620. In which landmark do you climb about 650 feet to get to the top?

Course 1

DATA BANK
STEPS, SNACKS, AND MUSIC

Course 1

The **MIDDLE SCHOOL MATHEMATICS MANIPULATIVE KIT** offers the tools students need to work with the Mathematics Labs and the Mini-Labs. A Teacher's Guide provides a correlation to the Student Edition.

COMMUNICATING MATHEMATICS exercises are included in **Checking for Understanding**. They give students the opportunity to clarify their thinking about mathematical concepts. Students are asked to respond verbally, in writing, or through the use of pictures, symbols, graphs, or models.

GUIDED PRACTICE is an in-class activity that allows students the opportunity to check their understanding of lesson concepts before they begin **INDEPENDENT PRACTICE** homework.

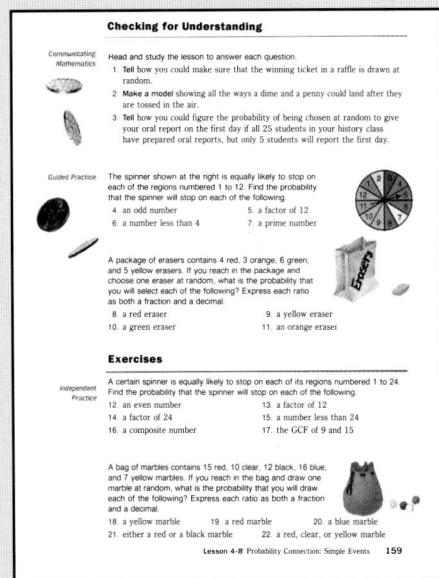

Course 2

Checking for Understanding

Communicating Mathematics Read and study the lesson to answer each question.
1. **Tell** how you could make sure that the winning ticket in a raffle is drawn at random.
2. **Make** a model showing all the ways a dime and a penny could land after they are tossed in the air.
3. **Tell** how you could figure the probability of being chosen at random to give your oral report on the first day if all 25 students in your history class have prepared oral reports, but only 5 students will report the first day.

Guided Practice The spinner shown at the right is equally likely to stop on each of the regions numbered 1 to 12. Find the probability that the spinner will stop on each of the following.
4. an odd number
5. a factor of 12
6. a number less than 4
7. a prime number

A package of erasers contains 4 red, 3 orange, 6 green, and 5 yellow erasers. If you reach in the package and choose one eraser at random, what is the probability that you will select each of the following? Express each ratio as both a fraction and a decimal.
8. a red eraser
9. a yellow eraser
10. a green eraser
11. an orange eraser

Exercises

Independent Practice A certain spinner is equally likely to stop on each of its regions numbered 1 to 24. Find the probability that the spinner will stop on each of the following.
12. an even number
13. a factor of 12
14. a factor of 24
15. a number less than 24
16. a composite number
17. the GCF of 9 and 15

A bag of marbles contains 15 red, 10 clear, 12 blue, 16 blue, and 7 yellow marbles. If you reach in the bag and draw one marble at random, what is the probability that you will draw each of the following? Express each ratio as both a fraction and a decimal.
18. a yellow marble
19. a red marble
20. a blue marble
21. either a red or a black marble
22. a red, clear, or yellow marble

Lesson 4-8 Probability Connection: Simple Events **159**

Mathematics: Applications and Connections Provides Opportunities for Students to Engage in Cooperative Learning Activities.

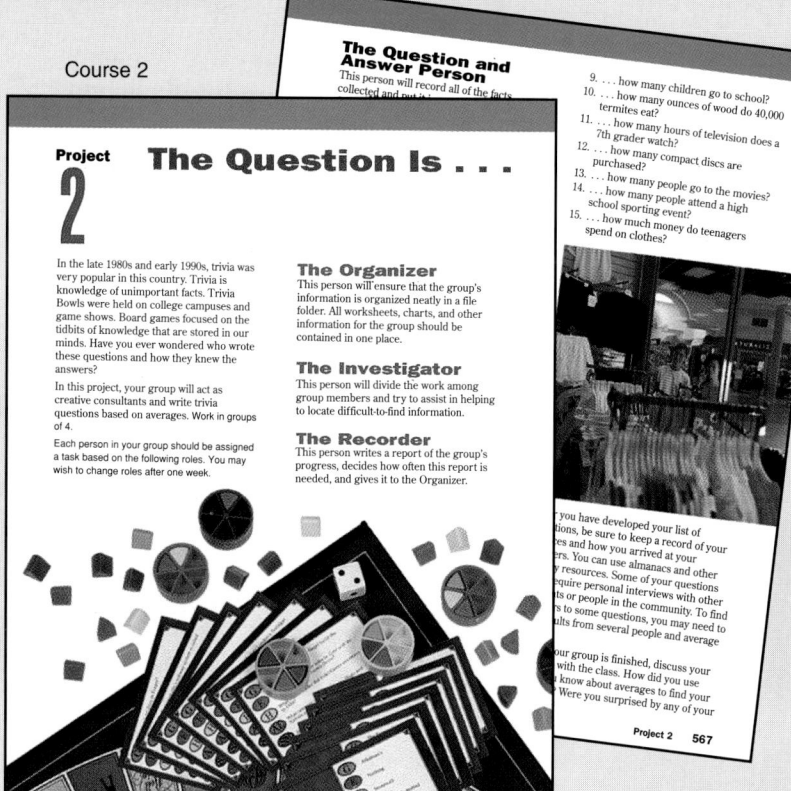

Course 2

Project 2 — The Question Is . . .

In the late 1980s and early 1990s, trivia was very popular in this country. Trivia is knowledge of unimportant facts. Trivia Bowls were held on college campuses and game shows. Board games focused on the tidbits of knowledge that are stored in our minds. Have you ever wondered who wrote these questions and how they knew the answers?

In this project, your group will act as creative consultants and write trivia questions based on averages. Work in groups of 4.

Each person in your group should be assigned a task based on the following roles. You may wish to change roles after one week.

The Organizer
This person will ensure that the group's information is organized neatly in a file folder. All worksheets, charts, and other information for the group should be contained in one place.

The Investigator
This person will divide the work among group members and try to assist in helping to locate difficult-to-find information.

The Recorder
This person writes a report of the group's progress, decides how often this report is needed, and gives it to the Organizer.

The Question and Answer Person
This person will record all of the facts collected and put it . . .

9. . . . how many children go to school?
10. . . . how many ounces of wood do 40,000 termites eat?
11. . . . how many hours of television does a 7th grader watch?
12. . . . how many compact discs are purchased?
13. . . . how many people go to the movies?
14. . . . how many people attend a high school sporting event?
15. . . . how much money do teenagers spend on clothes?

. . . you have developed your list of . . . tions, be sure to keep a record of your . . . and how you arrived at your . . . You can use almanacs and other . . . resources. Some of your questions . . . quire personal interviews with other . . . or people in the community. To find . . . to some questions, you may need to . . . ults from several people and average . . .

. . . ur group is finished, discuss your . . . with the class. How did you use . . . know about averages to find your . . . Were you surprised by any of your . . .

Project 2   567

An **EXTENDED PROJECTS HANDBOOK** in the Student Edition provides opportunities for your students to work together on intriguing long-tern projects.

Course 2

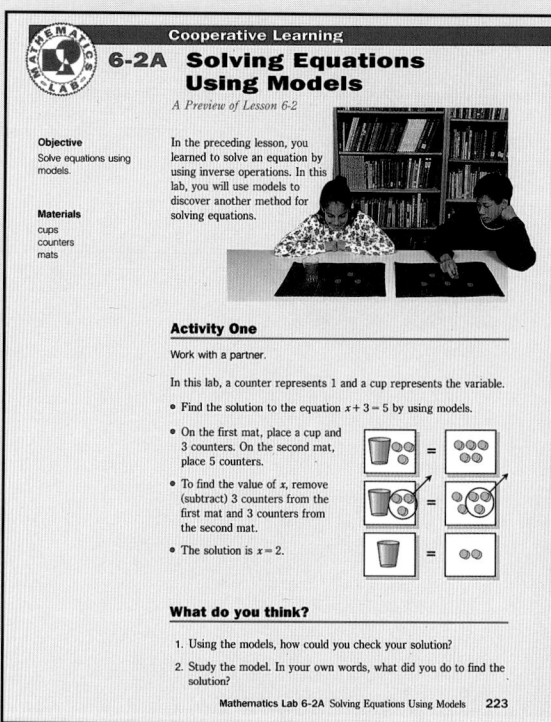

Cooperative Learning
6-2A Solving Equations Using Models
A Preview of Lesson 6-2

Objective
Solve equations using models.

Materials
cups
counters
mats

In the preceding lesson, you learned to solve an equation by using inverse operations. In this lab, you will use models to discover another method for solving equations.

Activity One

Work with a partner.

In this lab, a counter represents 1 and a cup represents the variable.

- Find the solution to the equation $x + 3 = 5$ by using models.
- On the first mat, place a cup and 3 counters. On the second mat, place 5 counters.
- To find the value of x, remove (subtract) 3 counters from the first mat and 3 counters from the second mat.
- The solution is $x = 2$.

What do you think?

1. Using the models, how could you check your solution?
2. Study the model. In your own words, what did you do to find the solution?

Mathematics Lab 6-2A Solving Equations Using Models   223

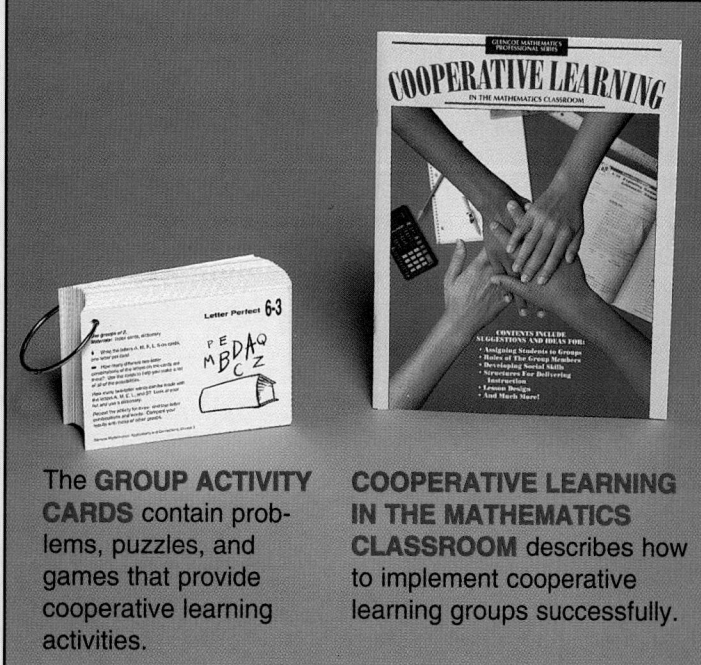

The **GROUP ACTIVITY CARDS** contain problems, puzzles, and games that provide cooperative learning activities.

COOPERATIVE LEARNING IN THE MATHEMATICS CLASSROOM describes how to implement cooperative learning groups successfully.

MATHEMATICS LABS and **MINI-LABS** give students the opportunity to investigate and discover concepts by working in cooperative groups or on their own.

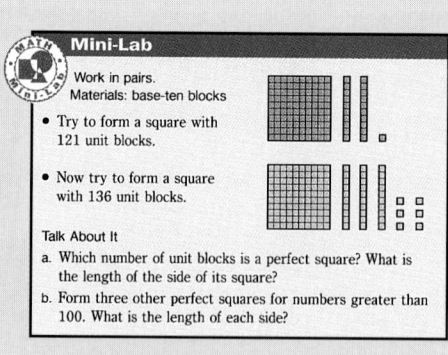

Mini-Lab

Work in pairs.
Materials: base-ten blocks

Course 2

- Try to form a square with 121 unit blocks.
- Now try to form a square with 136 unit blocks.

Talk About It
a. Which number of unit blocks is a perfect square? What is the length of the side of its square?
b. Form three other perfect squares for numbers greater than 100. What is the length of each side?

The Program Offers a Variety of Tools for Review and Assessment

STUDY GUIDE AND REVIEW, a section at the end of each chapter, presents review from a variety of perspectives; for example, Communicating Mathematics, Self Assessment, Applications and Problem Solving, Curriculum Connection Projects, and a bibliography called Read More About It.

Course 1

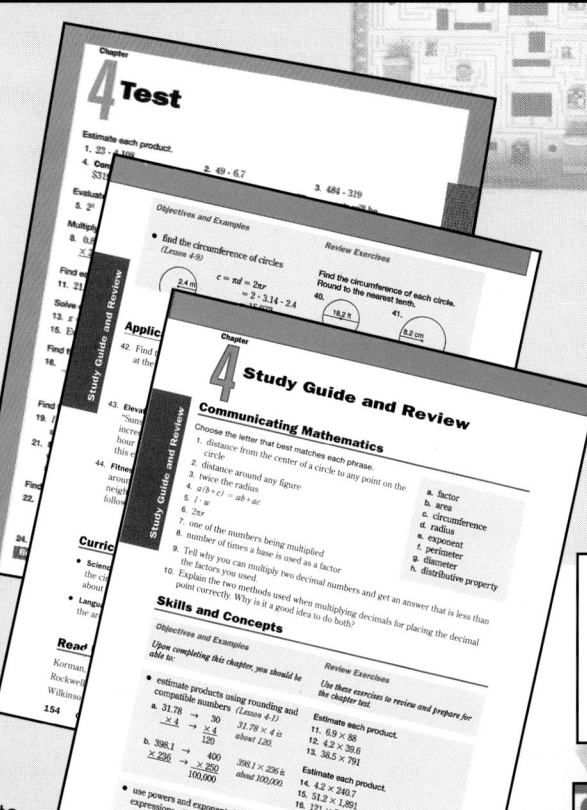

LOOKBACK

You can review bar graphs on pages 47 and 48.

Course 1

LOOK BACK guides students to pages where they may review previously learned concepts.

CHAPTER TESTS and **ACADEMIC SKILLS TESTS** provide ways to gauge students' understanding of concepts and applications.

Course 3

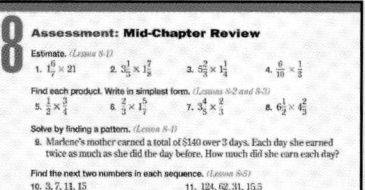

Mixed Review   30. Use mental math to find 320

31. Solve $12 = \frac{a}{14} + 10$. Check y *(Lesson 2-7)*

32. Solve $r + (-125) = 483$. Che *(Lesson 3-9)*

33. **Statistics**   Would a pet stor location to find a representa

Course 1

JOURNAL ENTRY questions ask your students to record their thoughts about the mathematics they're learning.

14. **Journal Entry**   In this course, you will be required to keep a journal. Write two or three sentences in your journal that describe what you expect to learn in this course.

Course 3

8 **Assessment: Mid-Chapter Review**

Continual review keeps concepts fresh. **MIXED REVIEWS** and **ASSESSMENT: MID-CHAPTER REVIEWS** help your students retain what they've learned. Each problem is referenced to the related lesson so students can find help.

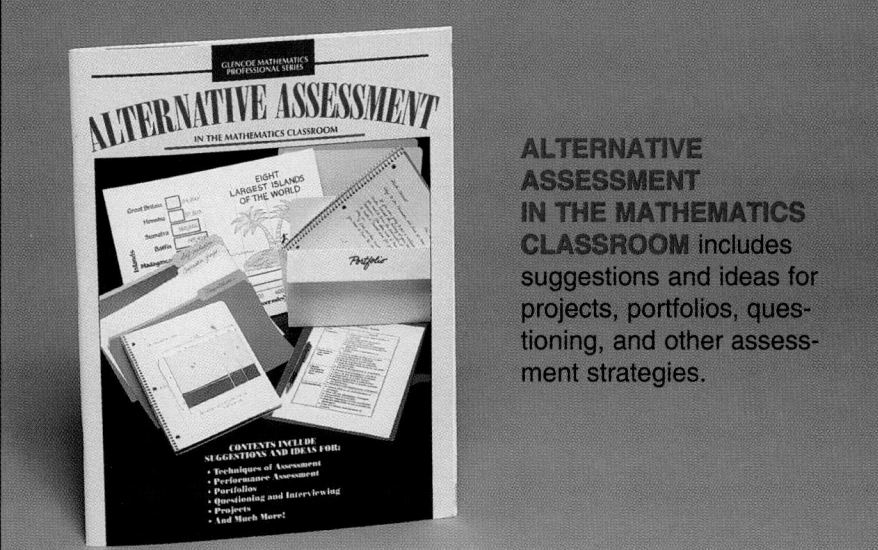

ALTERNATIVE ASSESSMENT IN THE MATHEMATICS CLASSROOM includes suggestions and ideas for projects, portfolios, questioning, and other assessment strategies.

PORTFOLIO SUGGESTIONS ask students to select a sample of their work to demonstrate what they have learned.

Course 2

 53. **Portfolio Suggestion**   A portfolio contains representative samples of your work, collected over a period of time. Begin your portfolio by selecting an item that shows something you learned in this chapter.

FORMAL ASSESSMENT TOOLS
Evaluation Masters
Test and Review Generators
Performance Assessment Booklet

Mathematics: Applications and Connections Puts Innovative Teaching Strategies Right in the Palm of Your Hand

The **TEACHER'S WRAPAROUND EDITION** provides you with unique teaching strategies. This makes it possible for you to reach your teaching goals and to create the environment most conducive to learning.

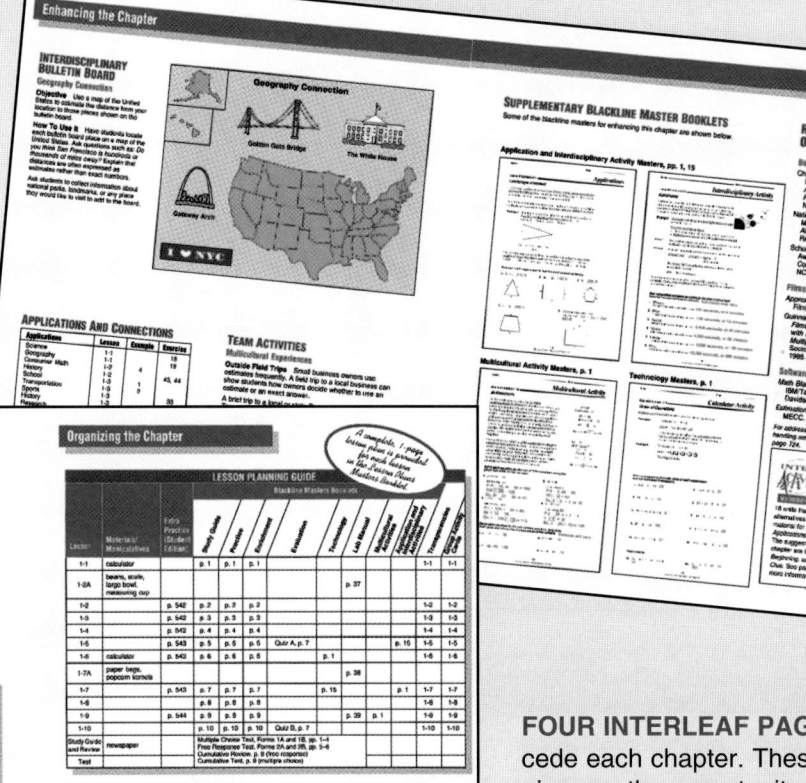

FOUR INTERLEAF PAGES precede each chapter. These pages give you the opportunity to preview the chapter and its objectives, to organize the content with the help of a planning chart, and to examine the suggestions for enhancing the chapter content.

Team Teaching

Inform the other teachers on your team that your students are studying decimals. Suggestions for curriculum integration are:

Social Studies: statistical analysis

Physical Education: measuring speed, distance

Science: life science and astronomical measurements (scientific notation); formulas in physical science; weather

TEAM TEACHING offers suggestions on how to integrate mathematics with other disciplines.

Multicultural Education

Mathematicians are not in total agreement as to the origin of our common numerals. Most believe that the symbols we use today originated in India, made their way to Iraq sometime in the eighth century, and then spread to Europe.

MULTICULTURAL EDUCATION highlights how other people and cultures have influenced mathematics or presently use it.

A carefully designed **THREE-STEP TEACHING APPROACH** gives you the tools you need to **FOCUS**, **TEACH**, and **PRACTICE/APPLY**.

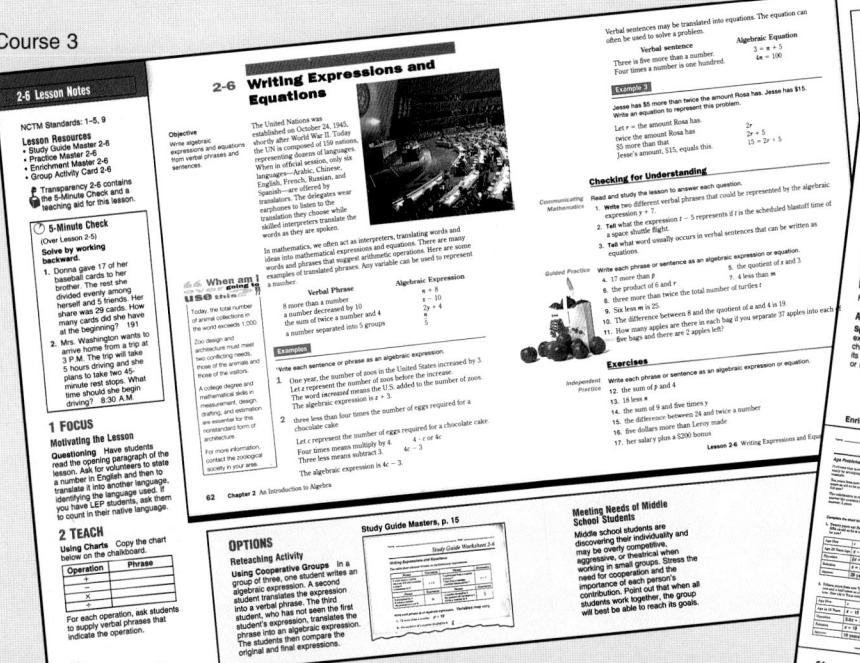

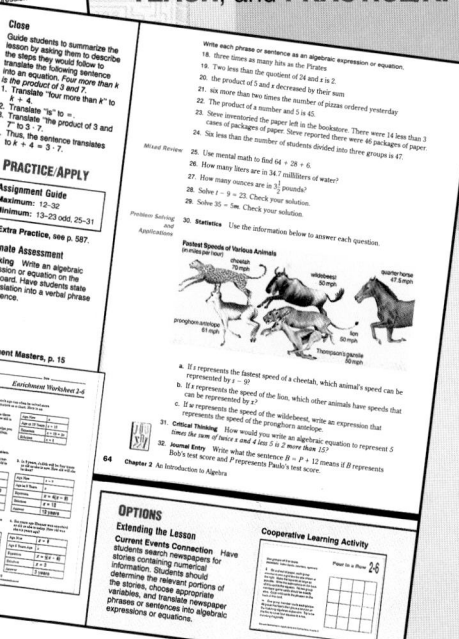

MEETING NEEDS OF MIDDLE SCHOOL STUDENTS offers ways to prepare your students for later mathematics courses, to maintain their interest and curiosity and to tailor material to meet their developmental stages and personal concerns.

Course 2

Bell Ringer

Write on the chalkboard:
The height of a tall tree might be:
12.2 ft   122.2 ft   1,222.2 ft
122.2 ft

Ask students which answer is the most reasonable. Have them work with partners to write a 5-item quiz similar to the sample. Have students provide answers to their items.

BELL RINGERS are problems or activities you can utilize before presenting the lesson or whenever you have a few extra class minutes.

Course 2

Limited English Proficiency

Focus on the term *estimation*. Ask students to describe situations that involve making estimates, such as estimating a length of time, a weight, a height, and so on. Then introduce the terms *clustering, front-end,* and *compatible*. Give examples of everyday meanings of these terms.

LIMITED ENGLISH PROFICIENCY features methods to reach and teach students for whom English is not their primary language.

Course 2

Gifted and Talented Needs

Have students work with partners. Ask them to list situations in which it makes better sense to round numbers down and situations in which it is most reasonable to round numbers up. Have students justify their choices.

GIFTED AND TALENTED NEEDS suggests ways to keep these students motivated and challenged.

Course 1

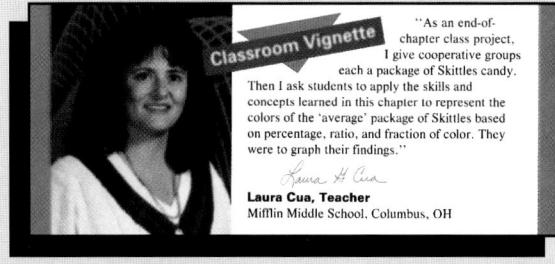

"As an end-of-chapter class project, I give cooperative groups each a package of Skittles candy. Then I ask students to apply the skills and concepts learned in this chapter to represent the colors of the 'average' package of Skittles based on percentage, ratio, and fraction of color. They were to graph their findings."

Laura H. Cua

Laura Cua, Teacher
Mifflin Middle School, Columbus, OH

CLASSROOM VIGNETTES provide teacher-proven tips for planning and enhancing your lessons.

Outstanding Teacher Resources Offer an Abundance of Options to Complement Your Individual Teaching Style

From initial lesson plans to assessment, Glencoe's exciting selection of resource materials helps you increase each student's chance for success in mathematics.

TECHNOLOGY

TECHNOLOGY MASTERS contain calculator and computer activities for each chapter that show your students how to use these tools to solve problems.

INTERACTIVE MATHEMATICS TOOLS MULTIMEDIA SOFTWARE, available in Macintosh format, helps students gain mathematical power through highly interactive activities that combine video, sound, animation, graphics, and text.

Windows and CD-Rom formats are being planned.

A **TEACHER'S GUIDE FOR SOFTWARE RESOURCES** describes how to use the most popular commercially available software with every lesson in Courses 1-3. Included are a detailed correlation, suggested activities, an annotated bibliography, and a list of computers on which the software runs.

GRAPHING CALCULATORS IN THE MATHEMATICS CLASSROOM demonstrates how to use Texas Instruments and Casio graphing calculators to explore various topics in mathematics.

ASSESSMENT

EVALUATION MASTERS for each chapter offer multiple-choice and free-response tests, quizzes, and cumulative reviews.

The **PERFORMANCE ASSESSMENT BOOKLETS** contain open-ended assessment items and a scoring rubric for each chapter.

The **PLACEMENT /DIAGNOSTIC TEST** booklet is designed to aid with the placement of students in Pre-Algebra, Algebra 1, Algebra 1 in Two Years, and Integrated Mathematics, Course 1.

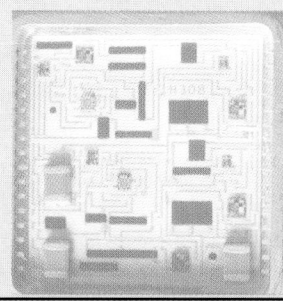

MEETING INDIVIDUAL NEEDS

ALTERNATIVE ASSESSMENT IN THE MATHEMATICS CLASSROOM includes suggestions and ideas for projects, portfolios, questioning, and other assessment strategies.

The **TEST AND REVIEW GENERATOR**, available in IBM, Apple, and Macintosh versions, allows you to use pre-prepared tests or to create your own tests, quizzes, and worksheets.

PRACTICE MASTERS contain additional exercises for reinforcing important mathematics skills. The Practice Workbook is a consumable version of the Practice Masters.

ENRICHMENT MASTERS extend the main ideas of each chapter through the use of stimulating and thought-provoking puzzles and games.

STUDY GUIDE MASTERS offer a brief explanation along with examples and exercises on the main concept in each lesson.

SPANISH RESOURCES provides Spanish translations of chapter tests from the Evaluation Masters. Also, the lesson objectives and glossary are provided in Spanish.

Outstanding Teacher Resources Offer an Abundance of Options to Complement Your Individual Teaching Style

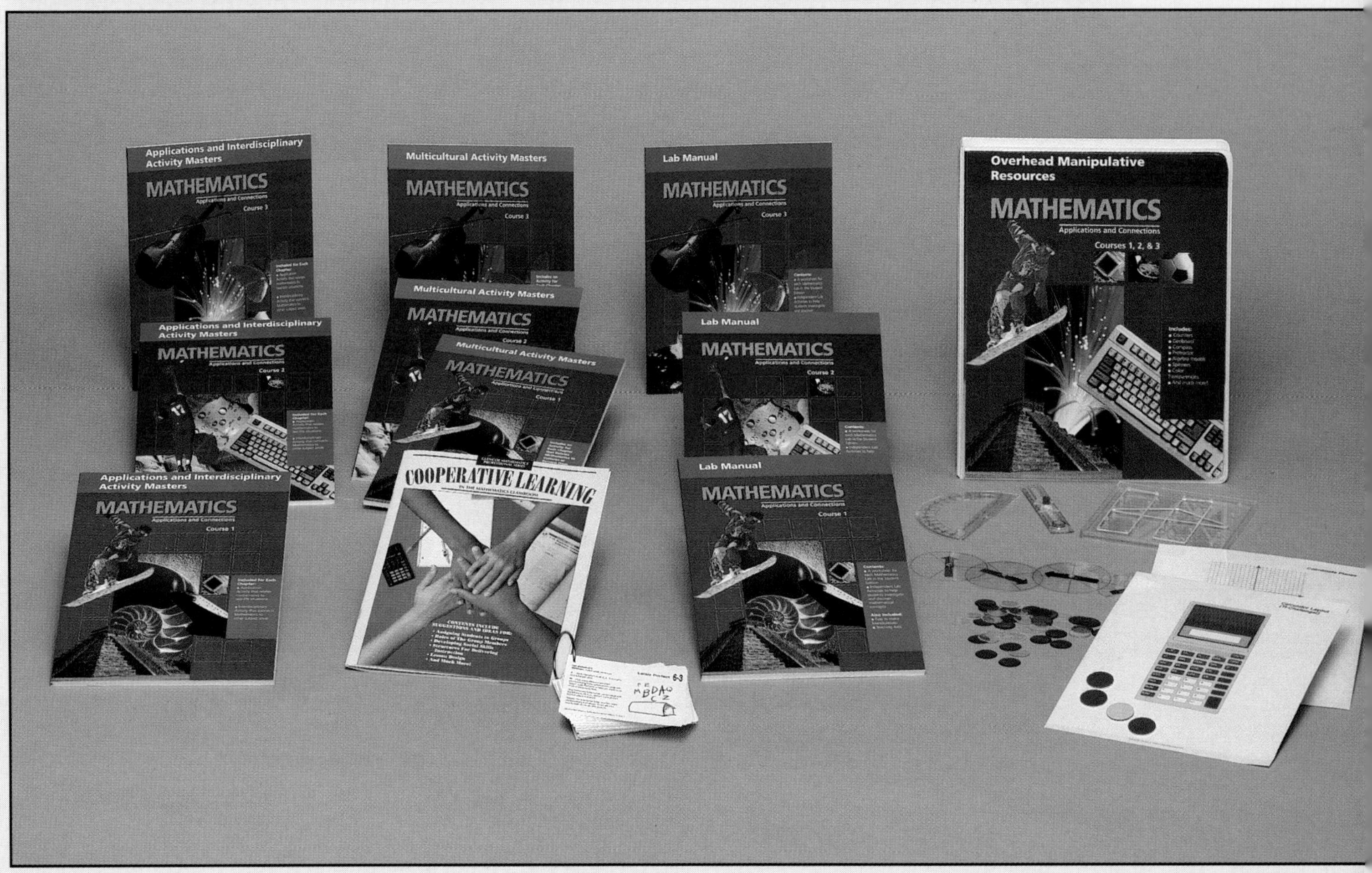

The **INTERACTIVE MATHEMATICS** units present cooperative learning activities that can be used to enhance the program. Each Teacher's Wraparound Edition contains references to the 18 units.

APPLICATIONS

APPLICATIONS AND INTERDISCIPLINARY ACTIVITY MASTERS accent the relationships among mathematics, the real world, and other disciplines.

MULTICULTURAL ACTIVITY MASTERS present a cross-cultural spectrum of historical situations that invite students to solve problems.

COOPERATIVE LEARNING

GROUP ACTIVITY CARDS are problems, puzzles, and games that provide cooperative learning activities.

COOPERATIVE LEARNING IN THE MATHEMATICS CLASSROOM describes how to successfully implement cooperative learning groups.

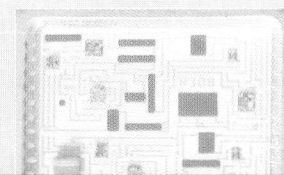

HANDS-ON ACTIVITIES

The **LAB MANUAL** contains pages of activities and easy-to-make manipulatives to augment chapter content. Recording sheets that correspond to each mathematics lab in the student texts are also included.

The **MIDDLE SCHOOL MATHEMATICS MANIPULATIVE KIT** offers the tools students need to work with the Mathematics Labs and the Mini-Labs. A Teacher's Guide provides a correlation to the Student Edition.

The **OVERHEAD MANIPULATIVE RESOURCES** contain manipulatives, such as algebra titles, counters, spinners, and special transparencies that can be used with an overhead projector. A Teacher's Guide provides activities and teaching suggestions.

TRANSPARENCIES

Each **TRANSPARENCY PACKAGE** contains over 150 full-color teaching transparencies, one for each lesson and chapter opener. A Teacher's Guide provides suggestions and extension activities.

PLUS

The **SOLUTIONS MANUAL** provides a complete solution for every problem in the Student Edition.

LESSON PLANS include easy-to-use formats that help you plan challenging daily lessons.

INVOLVING PARENTS AND THE COMMUNITY IN THE MATHEMATICS CLASSROOM presents suggestions on how parents and the community can be active participants in supporting mathematics instruction.

At Last! A Mathematics Course Designed Specifically for Your Middle School Students

Glencoe's three course series, *Mathematics: Applications and Connections,* integrates strong mathematics content with real-life activities that are relevant and meaningful to the experience of the early teenager. Your students will learn how the world of mathematics is intertwined with the world they live in and why mathematics is important in daily life.

The Student Edition is supported by an unparalleled Teacher's Wraparound Edition and extensive Teacher's Classroom Resources that combine to offer the most comprehensive, yet manageable, approach to teaching mathematics in the middle

COMPONENTS

Title	Course 1	Course 2	Course 3
Student Edition	0-02-824623-3	0-02-824624-1	0-02-824625-X
Teacher's Wraparound Edition	0-02-824626-8	0-02-824627-6	0-02-824628-4
Teacher's Classroom Resources	0-02-824629-2	0-02-824630-6	0-02-824631-4
Practice Masters	0-02-824614-4	0-02-824615-2	0-02-824616-0
Enrichment Masters	0-02-824617-9	0-02-824618-7	0-02-824619-5
Study Guide Masters	0-02-824620-9	0-02-824621-7	0-02-824622-5
Evaluation Masters	0-02-824605-5	0-02-824606-3	0-02-824607-1
Technology Masters	0-02-824608-X	0-02-824609-8	0-02-824610-1
Lab Manual	0-02-824611-X	0-02-824612-8	0-02-824613-6
Multicultural Activity Masters	0-02-824595-4	0-02-824596-2	0-02-824597-0
Applications and Interdisciplinary Activity Masters	0-02-824598-9	0-02-824599-7	0-02-824601-2
Solutions Manual	0-02-824602-0	0-02-824603-9	0-02-824604-7
Spanish Resources	0-02-824586-5	0-02-824587-3	0-02-824588-1
Lesson Plans	0-02-824589-X	0-02-824590-3	0-02-824591-1
Practice Workbook	0-02-824592-X	0-02-824593-8	0-02-824594-6
Performance Assessment	0-02-824455-9	0-02-824454-0	0-02-824453-2
Placement/Diagnostic Tests			0-02-824764-7
Interactive Mathematics Tools, Macintosh	0-02-824167-3	0-02-824172-X	0-02-824170-3
Transparency Package	0-02-824632-2	0-02-824633-0	0-02-824745-0
Test and Review Generator IBM	0-02-824746-9	0-02-824749-3	0-02-824752-3
Apple	0-02-824747-7	0-02-824750-7	0-02-824753-1
Macintosh	0-02-824748-5	0-02-824751-5	0-02-824754-X
Teacher's Guide for Software Resources	0-02-824583-0	0-02-824583-0	0-02-824583-0
Overhead Manipulative Resources	0-02-824584-9	0-02-824584-9	0-02-824584-9
Middle School Mathematics Manipulative Kit	0-02-824465-6	0-02-824465-6	0-02-824465-6
Alternative Assessment in the Mathematics Classroom	0-02-824381-1	0-02-824381-1	0-02-824381-1
Cooperative Learning in the Mathematics Classroom	0-02-824071-5	0-02-824071-5	0-02-824071-5
Involving Parents and the Community in the Mathematics Classroom	0-02-824369-2	0-02-824369-2	0-02-824369-2
Graphing Calculators in the Mathematics Classroom	0-02-824176-2	0-02-824176-2	0-02-824176-2

For more information contact your nearest regional office or call 1-800-334-7344

1. **Northeast Region**
   GLENCOE
   17 Riverside Drive
   Nashua, NH 03062
   603-880-4701
   800-424-3451
   CT, MA, ME, NH, NY, RI, VT

2. **Mid-Atlantic Region**
   GLENCOE
   5 Terri Lane, Suite 5
   Burlington, NJ 08016
   609-386-7353
   800-553-7515
   DC, DE, MD, NJ, PA

3. **Atlantic-Southeast Region**
   GLENCOE
   Brookside Park
   One Harbison Way, Suite 101
   Columbia, SC 29212
   803-732-2365
   800-732-2365
   KY, NC, SC, VA, WV

4. **Southeast Region**
   GLENCOE
   6510 Jimmy Carter Boulevard
   Norcross, GA 30071
   404-448-7493
   800-982-3992
   AL, FL, GA, TN

5. **Mid-America Region**
   GLENCOE
   4635 Hilton Corporate Drive
   Columbus, OH 43232
   614-759-6600
   IN, MI, OH, WI

6. **Mid-Continent Region**
   GLENCOE
   846 East Algonquin Road
   Schaumburg, IL 60173
   708-397-8448
   800-762-4876
   IA, IL, KS, MN, MO, ND, NE, SD

7. **Southwest Region**
   GLENCOE
   320 Westway Place, Suite 550
   Arlington, TX 76108
   817-784-2100
   800-828-5096
   NM, OK, AR, MS, LA

8. **Texas Region**
   GLENCOE
   320 Westway Place, Suite 550
   Arlington, TX 76108
   817-784-2100
   800-828-5096
   TX

9. **Western Region**
   GLENCOE
   610 East 42nd, # 102
   Boise, ID 83714
   208-378-4002 & 4004
   800-452-6126
   Includes Alaska
   AK, AZ, CO, ID, MT, NV, OR, UT, WA, WY

10. **California Region**
    GLENCOE
    15319 Chatsworth Street
    P.O. Box 9609
    Mission Hills, CA 91346
    818-898-1391
    800-432-9534
    CA, Includes Hawaii

Glencoe Catholic School Region
GLENCOE
25 Crescent Street, 1st Floor
Stamford, CT 06906
203-964-9109
800-551-8766

Canada
Maxwell Macmillian Canada
1200 Eglinton Avenue, East
Suite 200
Don Mills, Ontario M3C 3N1
Telephone:416-449-6030
Telefax: 416-449-0068

Overseas
Macmillian/McGraw-Hill
International
10 Union Square East
New York, NY 10003
Telephone: 212-353-5700

GLENCOE
McGraw-Hill

MA 90889-2
4-94

MATHEMATICS

Applications and Connections

Course 2

GLENCOE

Macmillan/McGraw-Hill

New York, New York   Columbus, Ohio   Mission Hills, California   Peoria, Illinois

Send all inquiries to:
Glencoe Division, Macmillan/McGraw-Hill
936 Eastwind Drive
Westerville, Ohio 43081

ISBN: 0-02-824624-1 (Student Edition)
ISBN: 0-02-824627-6 (Teacher's Wraparound Edition)

1 2 3 4 5 6 7 8 9 10 RRD-WLH-P 03 02 01 00 99 98 97 96 95 94

Dear Students, Teachers, and Parents,

Middle school students are special! That's why we've written the first and only middle school mathematics program in the United States designed specifically for you. The layout of Mathematics: Applications and Connections will delight your eyes. And the exciting content will hold your interest and show you why you need to study mathematics every day.

Please look carefully as you page through the text. Right away, you'll notice the variety of ways mathematics content is presented to you. You'll see the many connections made among mathematical topics and note how mathematics naturally fits into other subject areas and with technology.

You will note that content for each lesson is clearly labeled up front. And you'll appreciate the easy-to-follow lesson format. It introduces each new concept with an interesting application followed by clear examples.

Each day, as you read the text and complete the activities, you'll see the practical value of mathematics. You'll quickly grow to appreciate how often mathematics is used in real-world situations that relate directly to your life. If you don't already realize the importance of mathematics in your life, you soon will!

Sincerely, The Authors

Kay McClain

Linda Dritsas

Patricia Frey-Mason

David D. Molina

Beatrice Moore-Harris

Jack M. Ott

Ron Pelfrey

Barbara D. Smith

Patricia S. Wilson

iii

William Collins teaches mathematics at James Lick High School in San Jose, California. He has served as the Mathematics Department Chairperson at James Lick and Andrew Hill High Schools. He received his B.A. from Herbert H. Lehman College and is a Masters candidate at California State University, Hayward. Mr. Collins has been a consultant for the National Assessment Governing Board. He is a member of the National Council of Teachers of Mathematics and is active in several professional mathematics organizations at the state level. Mr. Collins is currently a mentor teacher for the College Board's EQUITY 2000 Consortium in San Jose, California.

Linda Dritsas is the Mathematics Coordinator for the Fresno Unified School District in Fresno, California. She also taught at California State University at Fresno for two years. Ms. Dritsas received her B.A. and M.A. (Education) from California State University at Fresno. Ms. Dritsas has published numerous mathematics workbooks and other supplementary materials. She has been the Central Section President of the California Mathematics Council and is a member of the National Council of Teachers of Mathematics and the Association for Supervision and Curriculum Development.

Patricia Frey-Mason is the Mathematics Department Chairperson at the Buffalo Academy for Visual and Performing Arts in Buffalo, New York. She received her B.A. from D'Youville College in Buffalo, New York, and her M.Ed. from the State University of New York at Buffalo. Ms. Frey-Mason has published several articles in mathematics journals. She is a member of the National Council of Teachers of Mathematics and is active in other professional mathematics organizations at the state, national, and international levels. Ms. Frey-Mason was named a 1991 Woodrow Wilson Middle School Mathematics Master Teacher.

Arthur C. Howard is Consultant for Secondary Mathematics at the Aldine School District in Houston, Texas. He received his B.S. and M.Ed. from the University of Houston. Mr. Howard has taught in grades 7–12 and in college. He is Master Teacher in the Rice University School Mathematics Project in Houston. Mr. Howard is also active in numerous professional organizations at the national and state levels, including the National Council of Teachers of Mathematics. His publications include curriculum materials and articles for newspapers, books, and *The Mathematics Teacher*.

Kay McClain received her B.A. from Auburn University and her Educational Specialist degree from the University of Montevallo. She is currently working on a Ph.D. at Vanderbilt University. While a teacher at Mountain Brook Middle School in Birmingham, Ms. McClain received a Presidential Award for Excellence in the Teaching of Mathematics. She is a Woodrow Wilson fellow and an active member of the National Council of Teachers of Mathematics.

David D. Molina is a professor at Trinity University in San Antonio, Texas. He received his M.A. and Ph.D. in Mathematics Education from the University of Texas at Austin. Dr. Molina has been a speaker both at national and international mathematics conferences. He has been a presenter for the National Council of Teachers of Mathematics, as well as a conductor of workshops and in services for other professional mathematics organizations and school systems.

Beatrice Moore-Harris is the EQUITY 2000 Project Administrator and former Mathematics Curriculum Specialist for K-8 in the Fort Worth Independent School District in Fort Worth, Texas. She is also a consultant for the National Council of Teachers of Mathematics. Ms. Moore-Harris received her B.A. from Prairie View A & M University in Prairie View, Texas. She has also done graduate work there and at Texas Southern University in Houston, Texas, and Tarleton State University in Stephenville, Texas. Ms. Moore-Harris is active in many state and national mathematics organizations. She also serves on the Editorial Board of NCTM's *Mathematics and the Middle Grades* journal.

Ronald S. Pelfrey is the Mathematics Coordinator for the Fayette County Public Schools in Lexington, Kentucky. He has taught mathematics in Fayette County Public Schools, with the Peace Corps in Ethiopia, and at the University of Kentucky in Lexington, Kentucky. Dr. Pelfrey received his B.S., M.A., and Ed.D. from the University of Kentucky. He is also the author of several publications about mathematics curriculum. He is an active speaker with the National Council of Teachers of Mathematics and is involved with other local, state, and national mathematics organizations.

Barbara Smith is the Mathematics Supervisor for Grades K-12 at the Unionville-Chadds Ford School District in Unionville, Pennsylvania. Prior to being a supervisor, she taught mathematics for thirteen years at the middle school level and three years at the high school level. Ms. Smith received her B.S. from Grove City College in Grove City, Pennsylvania and her M.Ed. from the University of Pittsburgh in Pittsburgh, Pennsylvania. Ms. Smith has held offices in several state and local organizations, has been a speaker at national and state conferences, and is a member of the National Council of Teachers of Mathematics.

Jack Ott is a Professor of Mathematics Education at the University of South Carolina in Columbia, South Carolina. He has also been a consultant for numerous schools in South Carolina as well as the South Carolina State Department of Education and the National Science foundation. Dr. Ott received his A.B. from Indiana Wesleyan University, his M.A. from Ball State University, and his Ph.D. from The Ohio State University. Dr. Ott has written articles for *The Mathematics Teacher* and *The Arithmetic Teacher* and has been a speaker at national and state mathematics conferences.

Jack Price has been active in mathematics education for over 40 years, 38 of those in grades K-12. He is currently the Co-Director of the center for Science and Mathematics Education at California State Polytechnic University at Pomona, California, where he teaches mathematics and methods courses for preservice teachers and consults with school districts on curriculum change. Dr. Price received his B.A. from Eastern Michigan University, and has a Doctorate in Mathematics Education from Wayne State University. He is president of the National Council of Teachers of Mathematics and is an author of numerous mathematics instructional materials.

Patricia S. Wilson is an Associate Professor of Mathematics Education at the University of Georgia in Athens, Georgia. Dr. Wilson received her B.S. from Ohio University and her M.A. and Ph.D. from The Ohio State University. She has received the Excellence in Teaching Award from the College of Education at the University of Georgia and is a published author in several mathematics education journals. Dr. Wilson has taught middle school mathematics and is currently teaching middle school mathematics methods courses. She is on the Editorial Board of the *Journal for Research in Mathematics Education,* published by the National Council of Teachers of Mathematics.

Elaine Ivey
Mathematics Teacher
Adams Junior High School
Tampa, Florida

Donna Jamell
Mathematics Teacher
Ramsey Junior High School
Fort Smith, Arkansas

Augustus M. Jones
Mathematics Teacher
Tuckahoe Middle School
Richmond, Virginia

Marie Kasperson
Mathematics Teacher
Grafton Middle School
Grafton, Massachusetts

Larry Kennedy
Mathematics Teacher
Kimmons Junior High School
Fort Smith, Arkansas

Patricia Killingsworth
Math Specialist
Carver Math/Science Magnet
   School
Little Rock, Arkansas

Al Lachat
Mathematics Department
   Chairperson
Neshaminy School District
Feasterville, Pennsylvania

Kent Luetke-Stahlman
Resource Scholar Mathematics
J. A. Rogers Academy of Liberal
   Arts & Sciences
Kansas City, Missouri

Dr. Gerald E. Martau
Deputy Superintendent
Lakewood City Schools
Lakewood, Ohio

Nelson J. Maylone
Assistant Principal
Maltby Middle School
Brighton, Michigan

Irma A. Mayo
Mathematics Department
   Chairperson
Mosby Middle School
Richmond, Virginia

Daniel Meadows
Mathematics Consultant
Stark County Local School
   System
Canton, Ohio

Dianne E. Meier
Mathematics Supervisor
Bradford Area School District
Bradford, Pennsylvania

Rosemary Mosier
Mathematics Teacher
Brick Church Middle School
Nashville, Tennessee

Judith Narvesen
Mathematics Resource Teacher
Irving A. Robbins Middle School
Farmington, Connecticut

Raymond A. Nichols
Mathematics Teacher
Ormond Beach Middle School
Ormond Beach, Florida

William J. Padamonsky
Director of Education
Hollidaysburg Area School
   District
Hollidaysburg, Pennsylvania

Delores Pickett
Instructional Supervisor
Vera Kilpatrick Elementary
   School
Texarkana, Arkansas

Thomas W. Ridings
Team Leader
Gilbert Junior High School
Gilbert, Arizona

Sally W. Roth
Mathematics Teacher
Francis Scott Key Intermediate
   School
Springfield, Virginia

Dr. Alice W. Ryan
Assistant Professor of Education
Dowling College
Oakdale, New York

Fred R. Stewart
Supervisor of
   Mathematics/Science
Neshaminy School District
Langhorne, Pennsylvania

Terri J. Stillman
Mathematics Department
   Chairperson
Boca Raton Middle School
Boca Raton, Florida

Marty Terzieff
Secondary Math Curriculum
   Chairperson
Mead Junior High School
Mead, Washington

Tom Vogel
Mathematics Teacher
Capital High School
Charleston, West Virginia

Joanne Wilkie
Mathematics Teacher
Hosford Middle School
Portland, Oregon

Larry Williams
Mathematics Teacher
Eastwood 8th Grade School
Tuscaloosa, Alabama

Deborah Wilson
Mathematics Teacher
Rawlinson Road Middle School
Rock Hill, South Carolina

Francine Yallof
Mathematics Teacher
East Middle School
Brentwood, New York

Table of Contents

High Interest Features
Did You Know?
5, 11, 40, 54, 67, 79
Teen Scene
79
When Am I Ever Going To Use This?
29, 61
Save Planet Earth
31
Cultural Kaleidoscope
74
Journal Entry
10, 13, 35, 53, 66, 77

Chapter 3

Statistics and Data Analysis

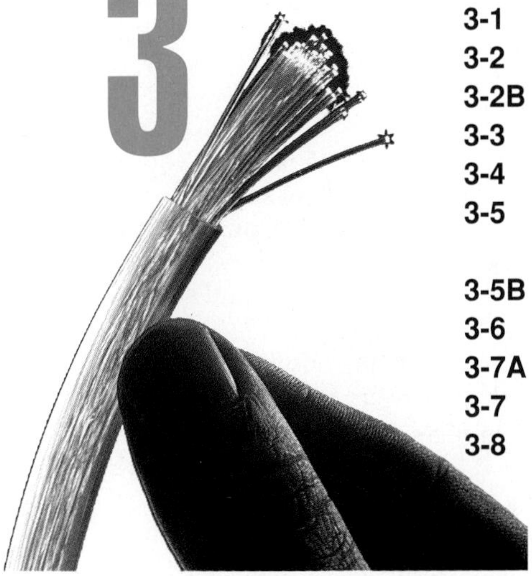

Chapter 4

Patterns and Number Sense

High Interest Features

Teen Scene
90, 158

Did You Know?
93, 102, 109, 113, 136, 150, 164

When Am I Ever Going To Use This?
98, 145

Save Planet Earth
119, 160

Journal Entry
100, 115, 119, 135, 153, 156

Mini-Labs
145, 158, 166

Applications and Connections

Have you ever asked yourself this question?

"When am I ever going to use this stuff?"

It may be sooner than you think! Here are two of the many ways this textbook will help you answer that question.

Applications

You'll find mathematics in all of the subjects you study in school and in your life outside of school. Lesson 1-9 on page 32, gives you good tips on saving our Earth while learning about powers and exponents. In Lesson 3-3 on page 98, range and scale are applied to talking on the phone.

These and other applications provide you with fascinating information that connects math to the real world and other school subjects and gives you a reason to learn math.

On pages 649–652, you will find a **Data Bank.** You'll have the opportunity to use the up-to-date information in it to answer questions throughout the book.

The **Extended Projects Handbook** consists of interesting long-term projects that involve issues in the world around you.

Five **Decision Making** features further enable you to connect math to your real-life experience as a consumer.

Connections

You'll discover that various areas of mathematics are very much interrelated. For example, Lesson 5-8 on page 201 shows one way in which fractions and probability are connected. **Connections** to algebra, geometry, statistics, measurement, probability, and number theory help show the power of mathematics.

The **Mathematics Labs** and **Mini-Labs** also help you connect what you've learned before to new concepts. You'll use counters, measuring tapes, and many other objects to help you discover these concepts.

x

Chapter 5

Applications with Fractions

Chapter 6

An Introduction to Algebra

High Interest Features

Cultural Kaleidoscope
181

Teen Scene
182, 229

When Am I Ever Going To Use This?
194, 236

Did You Know?
200, 207, 233, 238

Save Planet Earth
222

Journal Entry
177, 185, 196, 227, 235, 245

Mini-Lab
182, 197

Chapter 7

Integers

Chapter 8

Investigations in Geometry

High Interest Features

Did You Know?
259, 263, 297, 303

When Am I Ever Going To Use This?
268, 308

Cultural Kaleidoscope
276

Teen Scene
278, 307

Journal Entry
256, 258, 289, 300, 305, 329

Mini-Labs
298, 314, 321

Chapter

9

Area

Chapter

10

Surface Area and Volume

High Interest Features

Did You Know?
338, 360, 378

Teen Scene
348, 388

When Am I Ever Going To Use This?
366, 383

Cultural Kaleidoscope
386

Journal Entry
340, 353, 358, 380, 400

Mini-Labs
338, 351, 383, 395

Technology

Labs, examples, computer-connection problems, and other features help you become an expert in using computers and calculators as problem-solving tools. You'll also learn how to read data bases, use spreadsheets, and use BASIC and LOGO programs. On many pages, **Calculator Hints** and printed keystrokes illustrate how to use a calculator.

Here are some highlights.

TV Stations

The number of television stations an average U.S. household receives.

- 27 — 1990
- 25 — 1988
- — 1986
- 19 — 1984
- 17

☐ = 3 stations

The **Technology Activities** allow you to use a graphing calculator and spreadsheets as tools for learning and doing mathematics.

Chapter 11

Ratio, Proportion, and Percent

Chapter 12

Applications with Percent

High Interest Features

Did You Know?
411, 417, 462

When Am I Ever Going To Use This?
426, 465

Save Planet Earth
443

Teen Scene
445, 470

Cultural Kaleidoscope
458

Journal Entry
416, 435, 439, 461, 473, 481

Mini Labs
427, 433, 437, 444, 459, 476

Chapter 13

Discrete Math and Probability

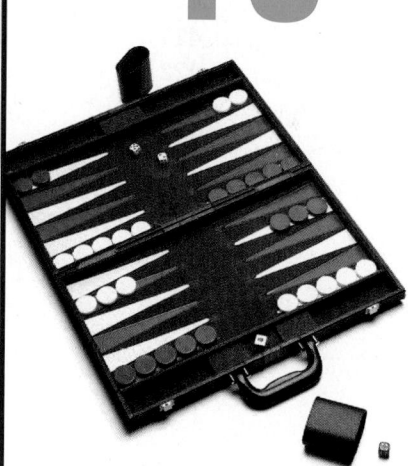

Chapter 14

Functions and Graphs

High Interest Features

Teen Scene
497, 536

When Am I Ever Going To Use This?
500, 548

Did You Know?
506, 518, 540, 546

Save Planet Earth
520

Cultural Kaleidoscope
534

Journal Entry
499, 509, 513, 542, 545, 550

Mini-Labs
493, 500

Setting The Scene

To help chart their journeys, wise travelers consult a map before they begin. Just as maps lead travelers to their destinations, the script on the next five pages points out the ways that you use the mathematics in this text in your daily lives.

Narrator:
Toshio, Shanita, Erin, and Jason are all friends who listen to radio station WXYZ.

Toshio:
Hey, you guys, did you hear about the contest on WXYZ?

Erin:
Yeah, they're advertising it like crazy. To win, you've got to guess the number of songs the station will play next month. The winner gets 5,000 bucks!

Jason:
Man, just think what $5,000 would buy. I'd get the biggest, baddest game machine they sell.

Shanita:
I'd go on a serious shopping spree!

Erin:
Oh, come on, you guys. All it takes to win a contest is luck.

Toshio:
Well, maybe, but I'd still like to enter the contest.

Shanita:
What are you gonna do, stay by the radio every day and night counting the songs they play?

Toshio:
No way!...But you know, that's not such a bad idea.

Erin:
Maybe we can all work together to figure out a plan. Then we could split the money.

Shanita:
I could go for that—that's $1.250! So what's the plan?

Erin:
Why don't we each take an hour this week and count the songs they play?

Jason:
Yeah, we can listen at different times and compare our results.

xvii

Setting The Scene

OVERVIEW

Objective   Use statistics and probability to predict the winning answer to a radio contest question.

Summary

Students read a script that involves four students who are trying to win a radio contest. The students use statistics and probability to better their chances of winning. This script demonstrates how decisions can be made by using statistics and probability.

Time Required

2 days

Materials Needed

calculators

Key Terms

average
bar graph
compares
line graph
typical

TEACHING NOTES

Select five students to take the roles in the toolkit script: Narrator, Toshio, Erin, Jason, and Shanita. Have these students read the script. Stop the class on page xix and have your students work in groups to determine the friends' chances of winning and whether they have a good plan. You may want to have the groups share their ideas before you continue the reading of the script.

WRITING PROMPTS

When the students have finished reading through the script, you may want to have your students write to the following prompts.
- *How do you use mathematics to make decisions?*
- *What problem-solving strategies and/or mathematical tools did the characters in the script use?*

Toshio:

But who's gonna listen in the middle of the night? or during school?

Shanita:

I know a way. I can program my tape recorder to tape for an hour and listen to it later.

Erin:

That's good. Maybe we can tape the whole week!

Jason:

No way! Do you know how many hours of tape that is?

Toshio:

Let's see: 24 hours times 7 days is 168 hours. There's no way we could buy that much tape.

Erin:

Okay, okay, bad idea. But maybe we could tape a few hours and use those as a sample.

Jason:

You know, they probably play more songs at some times than at others. Like, there's probably a big difference between the number of songs they play in the middle of the night and what they play in the morning when people are driving to work.

Shanita:

Let's divide up the week so we each listen for 6 hours.

Narrator:

Each student listens to WXYZ for 6 separate hours at various times during the week. They then count the number of songs that were played. Their results are shown below.

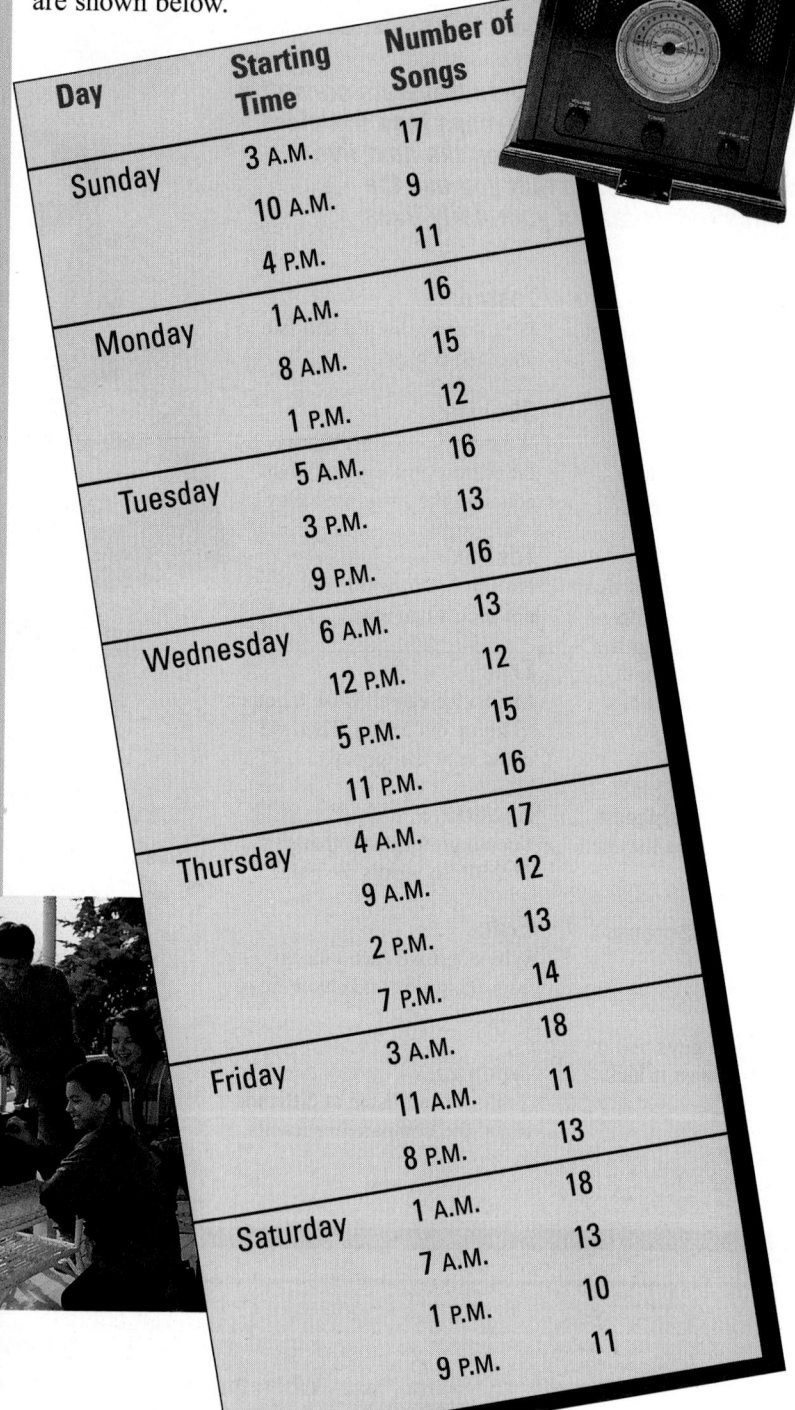

Day	Starting Time	Number of Songs
Sunday	3 A.M.	17
	10 A.M.	9
	4 P.M.	11
Monday	1 A.M.	16
	8 A.M.	15
	1 P.M.	12
Tuesday	5 A.M.	16
	3 P.M.	13
	9 P.M.	16
Wednesday	6 A.M.	13
	12 P.M.	12
	5 P.M.	15
	11 P.M.	16
Thursday	4 A.M.	17
	9 A.M.	12
	2 P.M.	13
	7 P.M.	14
Friday	3 A.M.	18
	11 A.M.	11
	8 P.M.	13
Saturday	1 A.M.	18
	7 A.M.	13
	1 P.M.	10
	9 P.M.	11

and determine whether or not the students have a good plan. How would you use these data to predict the number of songs played next month?

Narrator:

The students meet again to discuss their next move.

Shanita:

Well, now that we have a list, what do we do with it?

Toshio:

Since there are four of us and we each recorded six hours, we have twenty-four hours of songs. That's a typical day. Let's just multiply our number by 31 days to get a final count.

Jason:

No. This doesn't represent a typical day. It's just data from selected times during the week.

Erin:

That's right. On some days, they play a lot of songs, and on other days, they don't play as many.

Shanita:

I'll draw a line graph that shows the average number of songs played each hour by day of the week.

Average Songs Played Per Hour

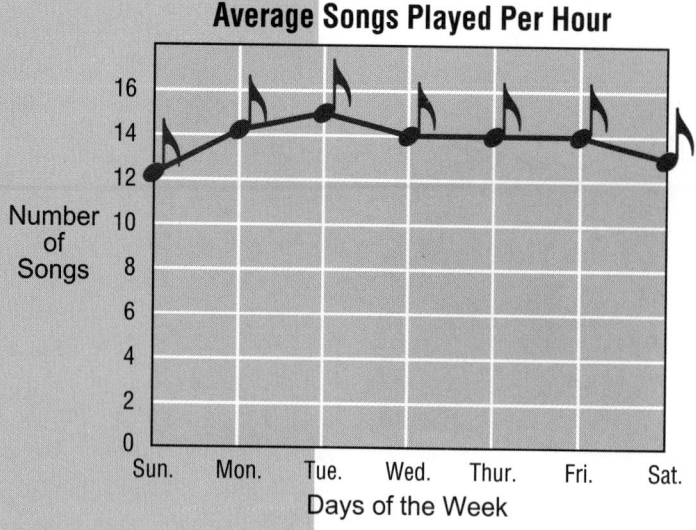

Number of Songs

Days of the Week

Jason:
I told you so. Look at the weekends; they play fewer songs. But I also think the times of day are important.

Erin:
I'll make a bar graph that compares the average number of songs played during the day and at night.

Average Songs Played During the Day (6 A.M.– 6 P.M.) and at Night (6 P.M.– 6 A.M.)

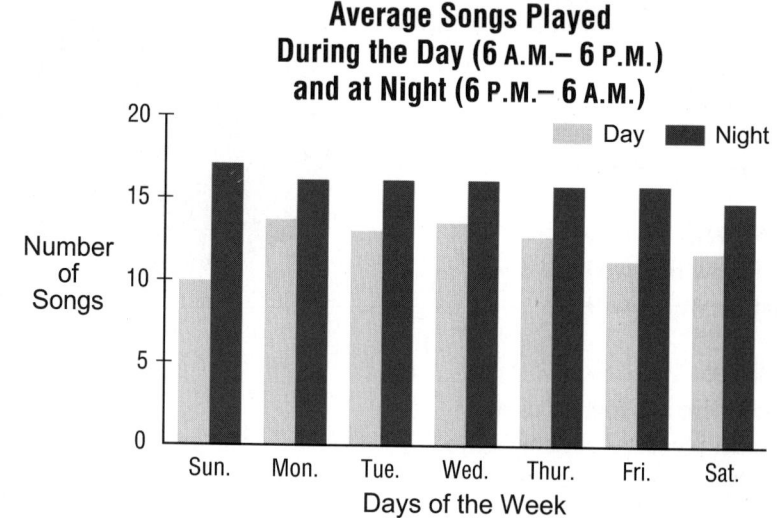

☐ Day ■ Night

Number of Songs

Days of the Week

The Most Music Machine

Toshio:
So the station does play more songs at night than during the day.

Jason:
I'll make a chart to find the average number of songs played on weekdays in the morning, afternoon, evening, and at night.

Day	M	Tu	W	Th	F	Avg.
Night	1 A.M.	5 A.M.	6 A.M.	4 A.M.	3 A.M.	16
Morning	8 A.M.		12 P.M.	9 A.M.	11 A.M.	12.5
Afternoon	1 P.M.	3 P.M.	5 P.M.	2 P.M.		13.3
Evening		9 P.M.	11 P.M.	7 P.M.	8 P.M.	14.8

Sousing the numbers from the chart, the average for any weekday is

$$\frac{16 + 12.5 + 13.3 + 14.8}{4} \text{ or } 14.2.$$

Erin:

Let's see—14.2 songs per hour times 24 hours is about 341 songs played each weekday.

Toshio:

The average number of songs played each hour on Saturday was 13 and 12.3 on Sunday. I'll multiply each number by 24 hours. On Saturdays, they play an average of 312 songs and on Sundays, they play an average of about 295 songs.

Jason:

Now we've got to figure out how many weekends and weekdays there'll be next month. Who's got a calendar?

Shanita:

I have one in my notebook. There will be 4 Saturdays, 4 Sundays, and 23 weekdays next month.

Jason:

Okay, Let's figure out the total number of songs played: 23 weekdays times 341 songs is 7,843 songs; 4 Saturdays times 312 songs is 1,248 songs; 4 Sundays times 295 songs is 1,180 songs. So, the total is 7,843 + 1,248 + 1,180 or 10,271

Erin:

No wonder they call themselves "The Most Music Machine!" I would never have guessed that high.

Shanita:

Let's hope nobody else does, either!

Narrator:

WXYZ played 10,283 songs that month. Since no one else even came close, the students won the contest.

This concludes Setting the Scene. Throughout this text, you will encounter new ways to make mathematics real to you. From time to time, read through this script to remind yourself how relevant mathematics can be in your life.

MATHEMATICS
Applications and Connections

TEACHER'S HANDBOOK

NEW DIRECTIONS IN MIDDLE SCHOOL MATHEMATICS.

Middle school teachers can testify to the fact that students in this age group are a unique bunch: They are energetic and enthusiastic, yet easily bored. They may behave as children one day and as young adults the next. These students want and need structure and security. They yearn for independence from parents, yet desire their protection. Each day they struggle to find their place in their peer groups, in their schools and communities, and in the world.

Decisions made by middle school students about what and how they study can dramatically affect their futures. Our research with middle school students revealed two not-so-surprising facts:

- **Most middle school students do not believe that mathematics has much to do with their everyday lives.**

- **Most middle school students see little or no connection between mathematics and other subjects they study.**

To convince them otherwise, an effective middle school mathematics program for the 1990s must embrace the concepts of understanding, problem solving, and conjecturing about mathematical concepts in an active classroom environment that capitalizes upon the innate enthusiasm of students in this age group.

TABLE OF CONTENTS

We at Glencoe are firmly convinced that our program, **Mathematics: Applications and Connections**, makes it easier for teachers to help their students develop a positive attitude about mathematics. Each lesson reflects the following major goals.

ENGAGE STUDENTS IN MATHEMATICS.
Students must be convinced that mathematics belongs to them and is not solely the property of the teacher or the textbook. Our program accomplishes this by providing historical and cultural perspectives to mathematics, using multiple representations for concepts, allowing students to make decisions, and avoiding trivial, unrealistic contexts for presenting mathematics. It provides challenging tasks supported by interesting, relevant information that enables students to be active participants in mathematics.

HELP STUDENTS EXPAND AND APPLY THEIR MATHEMATICAL SKILLS.
Students must be taught to integrate the compartmentalized pieces of mathematics they learned in elementary school. For mathematics to be meaningful to them, they must learn to organize information, interpret data, communicate quantitatively, make conjectures, and solve problems. Our program helps students apply their mathematics and see it and technology as useful tools in their lives.

PREPARE STUDENTS FOR FURTHER STUDY IN MATHEMATICS.
To succeed now and in the future, all students must learn to generalize (algebra), think spatially (geometry), and reason probabilistically (probability, statistics). **Mathematics: Applications and Connections** is designed to prepare all students for the study of higher mathematics, by making sure they possess understanding as well as proficiency.

You will see that **Mathematics: Applications and Connections** meets these three goals and captures the essence of the NCTM Standards. The program provides the tools teachers need to help middle school students see, understand, and appreciate the connection between mathematics and real life. In every lesson, students at all levels repeatedly receive this message: "Math is for everyone . . . You can do it . . . You'll use it every day."

BRIDGING

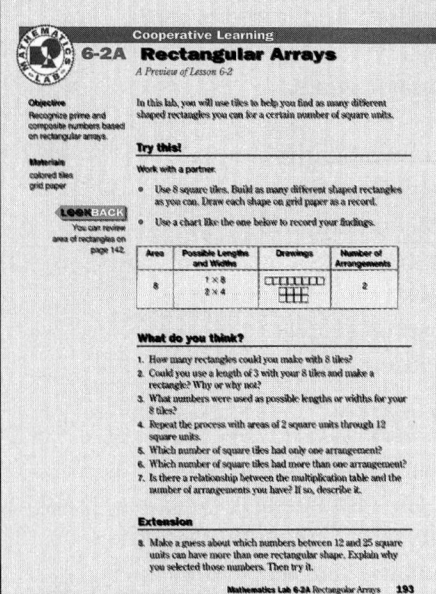

Course 1, p. 193

Course 2, p. 145

An examination of the mathematics textbooks for grades 6-8 of any K-8 elementary program shows that the vast majority of content focuses on review of previously-learned skills, ideas, and concepts. In fact, research shows that only about 35% of the material in the books is "new" content. Unfortunately, when these same students enter Algebra 1 class, the opposite is true. About 90% of the content is new. Suddenly—and with little warning and less preparation—they are bombarded with new ideas, new concepts, and new skills. It's no wonder that so many Algebra 1 students feel overwhelmed!

Glencoe's Middle School Mathematics program provides a more in-depth and integrated preparation for Algebra 1 and Geometry than a K-8 elementary program.

Mathematics: Applications and Connections prepares all students for success in Algebra 1 and Geometry. How? By introducing a variety of new concepts not found in traditional K-8 math curricula, and by integrating them appropriately into all three programs. For example, integers are introduced in Chapter 12 of Course 1, in Chapter 7 of Course 2, and in Chapter 3 of Course 3. Because algebra and geometry are introduced early in all three courses—and because both are reinforced throughout middle school— students are much better prepared to take these courses in high school.

Mathematics Labs and Mini-Labs help students discover concepts on their own.

Research shows that learning is more meaningful when students discover new concepts on their own. **Mathematics Labs** in ***Mathematics: Applications and Connections*** give students hands-on experience, with a partner or group, in discovering mathematics concepts for themselves.

Students may also participate in shorter **Mini-Labs** in which they investigate mathematical concepts within a lesson.

THE GAP

The **Overhead Manipulative Resources** includes transparencies and translucent objects such as counters, a geoboard, and a safety compass that can be used by the teacher or students to demonstrate concepts. A complete Teacher's Guide, correlated to the Mathematics Labs and Mini-Labs, provides suggestions for demonstrations using these resources.

The **Middle School Mathematics Manipulative Kit** offers the tools students need to work through the Mathematics Labs and Mini-Labs. A Teacher's Guide provides a correlation to all student editions.

experiences— regardless of the age of the student or the subject matter. It has also been proven that students master difficult learning tasks more readily when cooperative strategies are used.

Group Activity Cards featuring interesting problems, puzzles, and games, and more detailed cooperative learning activities are important components of *Mathematics: Applications and Connections.*

Effective cooperative learning groups share these characteristics:

1. Students must perceive that they "sink or swim together."

2. Students are responsible for everyone else in the group, as well as themselves, in learning the assigned material.

3. Students must see that they all have the same goal, that they need to divide up the tasks and share the responsibility equally, and that one evaluation or reward will apply to all members of the group.

Keep in mind that cooperative learning does not just "happen." The first few days may be tumultuous as students learn the rules. Be patient and keep at it!

> "Hands-on, experiential learning in which students take an active role and assume responsibility for their own learning is an integral part of the instructional practices of this program."
>
> **Beatrice Moore-Harris, Author**

Middle School Mathematics Manipulative Kit

Cooperative learning groups help students with academic achievement, self-esteem, and socialization

Studies show that cooperative learning experiences are more effective than competitive or individual learning

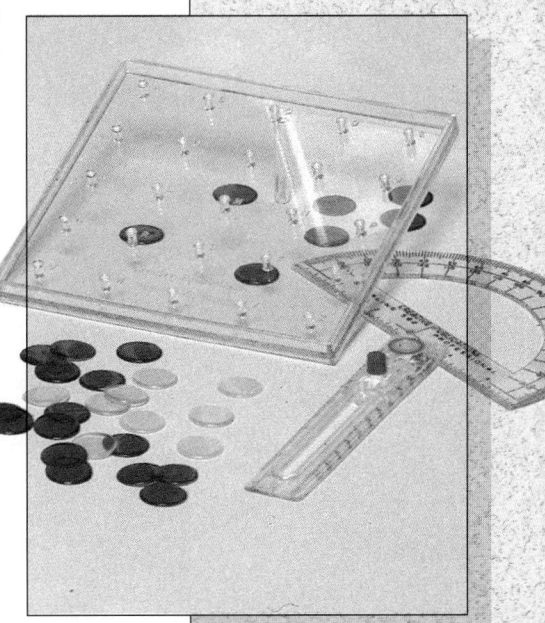

Overhead Manipulative Resources

MOTIVATING
MIDDLE SCHOOL STUDENTS

"Why do I have to study this?"
"When are we ever going to use it?"

As a middle school mathematics teacher, you have probably heard these questions from your students many times. Although they may be couched as complaints, the questions are certainly legitimate.

We at Glencoe realize that effective programs that really motivate middle school students must have more than strong content—although solid content is certainly important. The curriculum must also be interesting and must demonstrate the usefulness of mathematics in a way that relates to students' interests.

Because it highlights issues and situations that are of interest to middle school students, *Mathematics: Applications and Connections* does just that. Rather than simply present content-specific material, the program involves students in problems and situations that are current and real—and that demonstrate a practical purpose for mathematics.

> ## "THE CURRICULUM MUST GO BEYOND THE BASICS — TO BE RELEVANT, IT MUST BE OF INTEREST TO STUDENTS AND EMPHASIZE THE USEFULNESS OF MATHEMATICS."
>
> ### RON PELFREY, AUTHOR

For example, in Course 1, Lesson 6-5, real data about M & M's, is used to illustrate simplifying fractions. In Course 2, Lesson 1-3, students use estimation to find the number of pictures artists drew each day to create the first Mickey Mouse cartoon. And in Course 3, Lesson 10-7, students make a circle graph based on attendance statistics at four major theme parks.

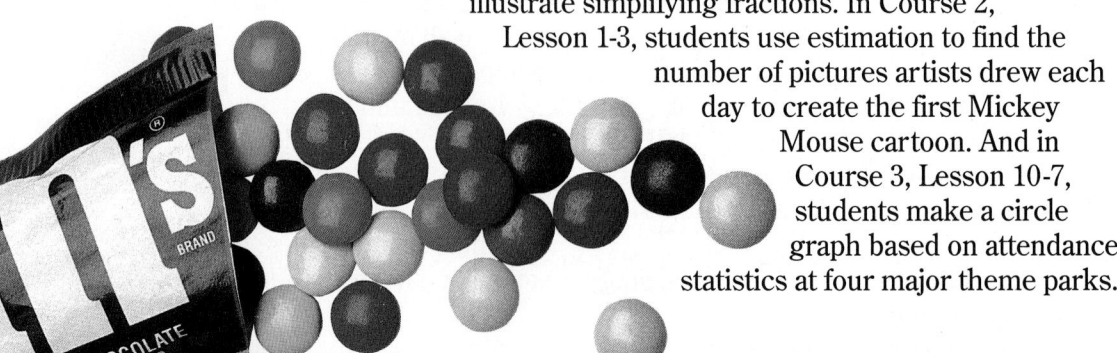

TEEN SCENE

When the first two-piece swimsuit was seen at the beach, it was named for the shock it caused. Bikini is the name of an island in the Pacific Ocean where the hydrogen bomb was first tested.

Course 2, p. 278

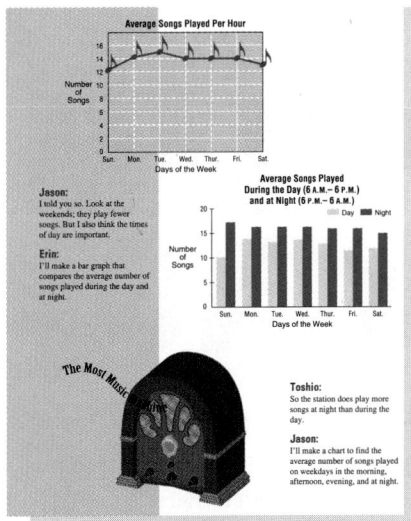

Course 2, p. xx

"When am I ever going to use this?"

A photojournalist's ability to perceive the significant in a fraction of a second and to use the camera with such speed and precision is a great creative gift. To be a good photographer, you also need to have good mathematical skills to estimate distance, calculate F-stop settings, and crop photos.

For more information, contact:
Associated Press
50 Rockefeller Plaza
New York, NY 10020

Course 3, p. 196

Mathematics: Applications and Connections is clearly a student-centered text.

At the beginning of each course, students are invited to act out a script called **Setting the Scene**. Students are placed in a real-life situation that requires the use of mathematics and makes it real to them. For example, in Course 2, students estimate how many songs a radio station plays in a month in order to win a contest.

Teen Scene provides tidbits of information to capture students' interest.

When Am I Ever Going To Use This? helps you answer that age-old question.

Save Planet Earth features environmental issues that focus on how students can make a difference.

Save Planet Earth

Start Your Own Club Students are making a significant contribution to saving our planet. Clintion Hill was a sixth-grade student when he organized an environmental activists' club at his school in New Hope, Minnesota. His enthusiasm and concern about the deteriorating environment motivated other students to become involved and help save the planet.

After Clinton's death in 1989, his parents, William and Tessa Hill, established a club called Kids for Saving Earth (KSE). Today there are over 3,600 KSE clubs in schools around the country.

How You Can Help
- Start a KSE Club in your school. For more information and a monthly newsletter, write to KSE Clubs, P.O. Box 47247, Plymouth, Minnesota 55447-0247.
- Organize and implement a recycling program in your school.

Course 1, p. 513

DEVELOPING PROBLEM SOLVING

According to the NCTM Standards, "Problem solving is the process by which students experience the power and usefulness of mathematics in the world around them. It is also a method of inquiry and application . . . to provide a consistent context for learning and applying mathematics. Problem situations can establish a 'need to know' and foster the motivation for the development of concepts." In response to the Standards, the authors of ***Mathematics: Applications and Connections*** made problem solving the central theme of their program. Here's how:

The first chapter of all courses is titled "Tools for Problem Solving."

Problem-Solving Strategy lessons present opportunities to solve nonroutine problems.

Frequent **Problem-Solving Hints** suggest using problem-solving strategies to investigate and understand mathematical content and apply strategies to new problem situations.

Applications opening nearly every lesson provide students with fascinating information that connects mathematics to the real world and give students a reason to learn mathematics.

Problem Solving examples give students the opportunity to study completely worked-out application problems in real-life fields, such as marketing and the environment.

Connection examples integrate one area of mathematics, such as geometry, with another, such as algebra.

Critical Thinking exercises give students practice in developing and applying higher-order thinking skills.

Mathematics becomes a vital force in the lives of middle school students as their eyes are opened to the relationship between mathematics and sports, shopping and other teen interests. They "take ownership" of their skills by writing their own problems and presenting class projects connected to real life.

(Lesson 7-3)

Problem Solving
and
Applications

42. **Personal Finance** Rosa opened a checking account with a balance of $150. She wrote a check for $87.

    a. Write an addition sentence to represent this situation.

    b. How much money remained in the account?

43. **Space Travel** During a space shuttle launch, a maneuver is scheduled to begin at T minus 75 seconds, which is 75 seconds before liftoff. The maneuver lasts 2 minutes. At what time will this maneuver be complete?

44. **Critical Thinking** Jack made up a game of darts using the target at the right. Each person throws three darts. The score is the sum of the numbers in the regions that the darts hit. If all the darts hit the target, list all possible scores.

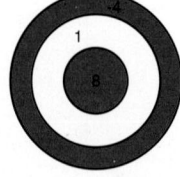

266   **Chapter 7** Integers

> "Problem solving is an integral component of this program. It requires students to think critically, examine new concepts, and then extend or generalize what they already know."
>
> Linda Dritsas, Author

MATHEMATICS: APPLICATIONS AND CONNECTIONS LINKS PRACTICAL PROBLEM SOLVING TO STUDENTS' REAL-LIFE INTERESTS

Specific features of the program that foster problem solving include:

Problem Solving and Applications exercises in each lesson directly link mathematics to real-world fields like engineering, and to art, history, science, and other subjects.

Five **Decision Making** lessons in each of Courses 1-3 provide students with opportunities to connect mathematics to their real-life experience as consumers and citizens.

The **Extended Projects Handbook** provides opportunities for your students to work together on intriguing long-term projects.

A **Data Bank** in the back of each text provides up-to-date information and statistics. Students refer to it to answer **Data Search** questions that appear throughout the student edition.

Course 1, p. 244

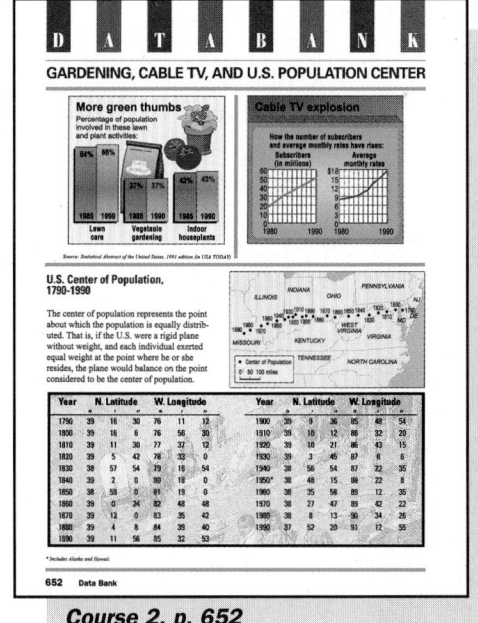

Course 2, p. 652

Course 3, p. 576

INCORPORATING TECHNOLOGY INTO YOUR CLASSROOM

According to figures from the U.S. government, by the year 2000, seven out of ten jobs will be related to computers, electronics, and high technology. Clearly, technology is changing the workplace and the home at an increasingly rapid pace. Without technical mathematical skills, today's students will have little or no chance of finding good jobs.

Using technology in your classroom can open up many ideas and opportunities. It is up to you to decide how to present and use technology in your classroom. Many of the standard teaching techniques, such as using cooperative groups, are appropriate but there are also new ways of teaching that are appropriate when using technology in your classroom. For example, you can assign lab partners in each class. Each pair of students would then work together whenever technology is used. This can also be used if you have a limited supply of equipment.

Mathematics: Applications and Connections provides many different ways for your students to prepare to function in a high-tech environment. Practice with computers, calculators, and spreadsheets is designed to enhance — not replace — students' practice with pencil-and-paper exercises, estimation, mental math, and other important tried-and-true techniques.

35. Computer Connection The BASIC program below will compute the circumference of a circle with a given diameter.

```
10 PRINT "WHAT IS THE DIAMETER?"
20 INPUT D
30 C = 3.14 * D
40 PRINT C
```

Course 2, p. 200

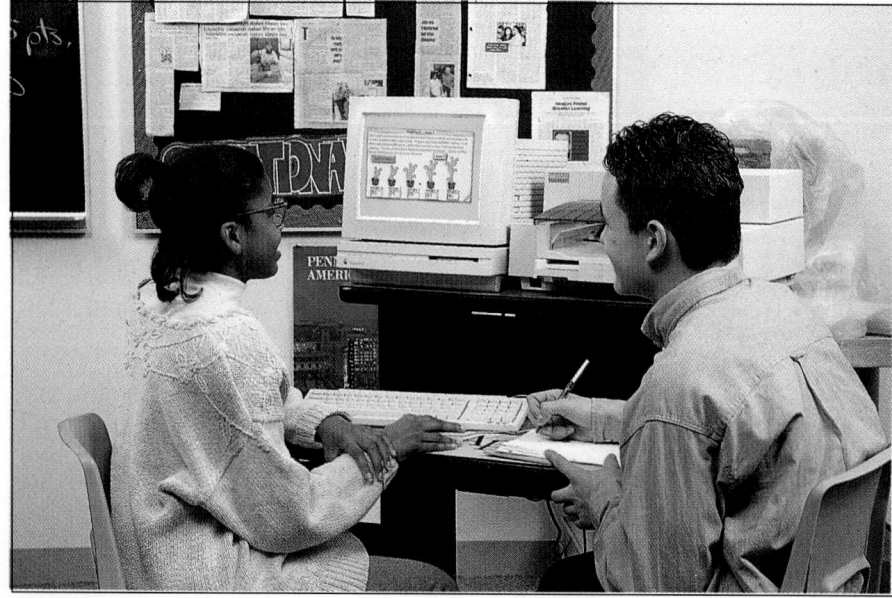

Computer Connection exercises increase students' proficiency in using computers to solve problems.

The Mathematics Lab shown at the right highlights the use of **Spreadsheets** as a problem-solving tool.

Frequent **Calculator Hints** and printed keystrokes illustrate for students how to use a calculator.

Five or six **Technology Activities** are provided in each text to give students the opportunity to work with graphing calculators and more spreadsheets. References to these activities are made throughout the student edition.

The **Interactive Mathematics Tools** multimedia software, available in Macintosh format, helps students gain mathematical power through highly interactive activities that combine video, sound, animation, graphics, and text.

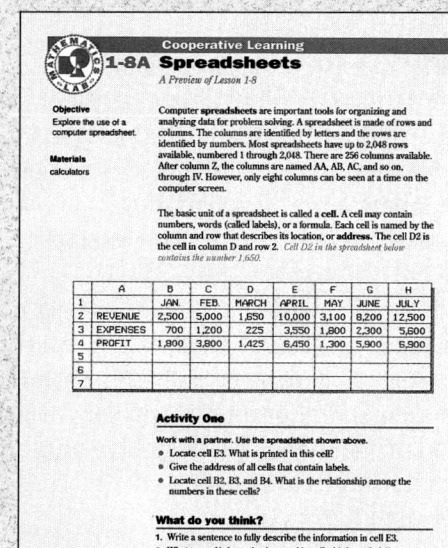
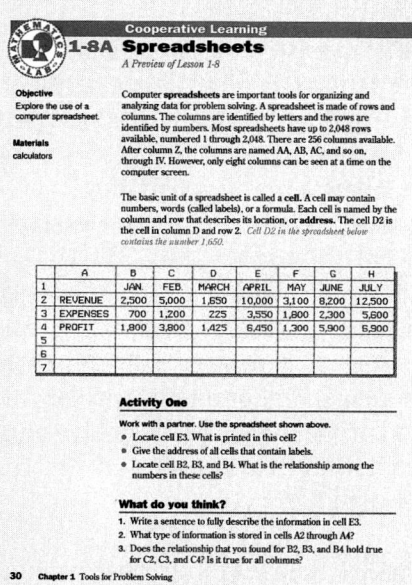

Course 3, pp. 30-31

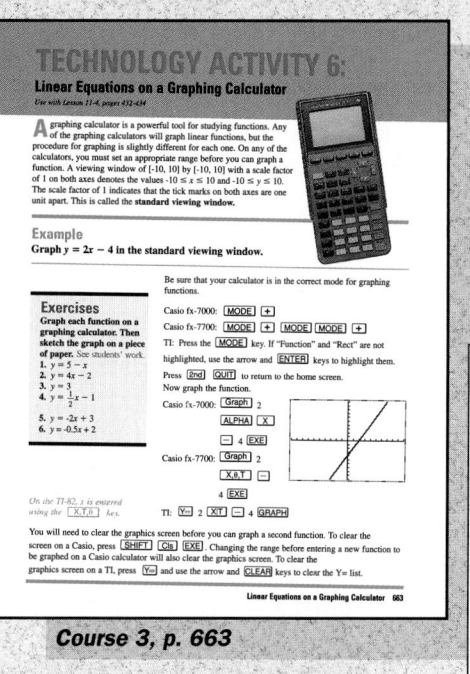

Course 3, p. 663

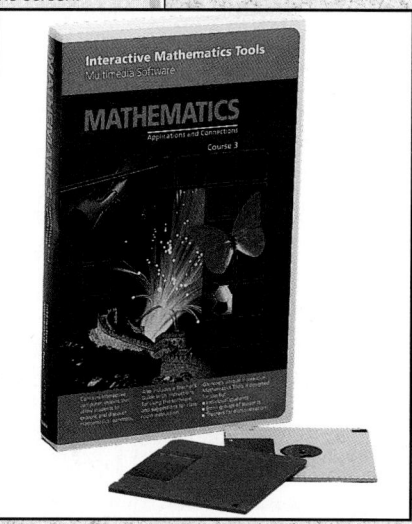

Course 1, p. 281

Interactive Mathematics Tools

In **Mathematics: Applications and Connections**, assessment goes far beyond requiring students to exhibit simple recall of facts and algorithms. In addition, they are expected to organize information, apply previously-learned information to new situations, explain why something is true, and make conjectures based on gathered evidence.

The following program features and components help students to assess themselves and guide teachers in assessment.

OPEN-ENDED PROBLEMS Most real-world problems do not have a single correct solution. Instead, there are usually many appropriate options. To help prepare students to become smart citizens, wise consumers, and good decision-makers, the text presents a variety of open-ended problems that require students to work cooperatively, think critically, and propose multiple feasible solutions to problems. The **Decision-Making** features help teachers to assess students' reasoning skills and evaluate their abilities to work effectively in groups.

JOURNALS Besides direct observation, another effective assessment method is to regularly read students' daily journals in which they are required to record and reflect upon what they have learned. **Journal Entries** throughout the student editions provide students with prompts for journal writing.

PORTFOLIOS Another way to assess students' understanding is to periodically review their portfolios. The portfolios should contain work that is representative of their growth as a learner. **Portfolio Suggestions** appear as appropriate throughout the student editions.

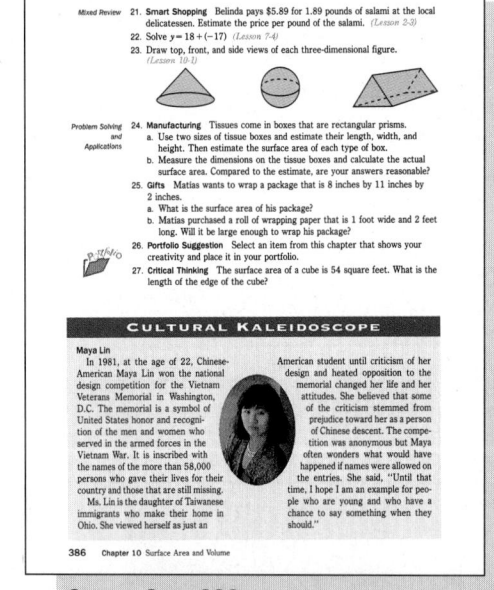

Course 2, p. 386

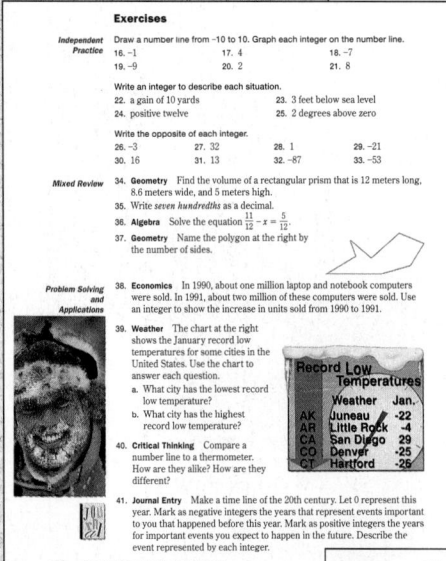

Course 1, p. 422

26. **Portfolio Suggestion** Select an item from this chapter that shows your creativity and place it in your portfolio.

27. **Critical Thinking** The surface area of a cube is 54 square feet. What is the length of the edge of the cube?

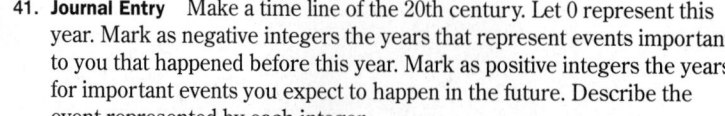

41. **Journal Entry** Make a time line of the 20th century. Let 0 represent this year. Mark as negative integers the years that represent events important to you that happened before this year. Mark as positive integers the years for important events you expect to happen in the future. Describe the event represented by each integer.

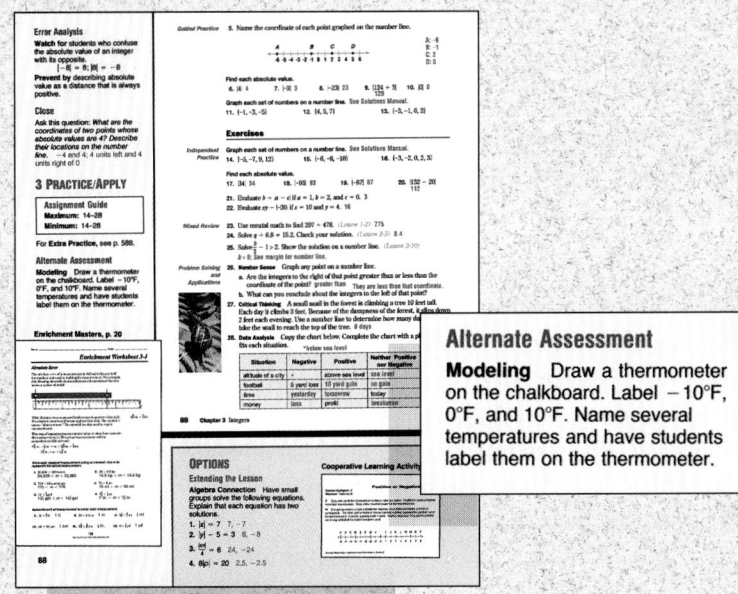

Error Analysis

Watch for students who confuse the absolute value of an integer with its opposite.

$|-8| = 8; |8| = -8$

Prevent by describing absolute value as a distance that is always positive.

Close

Ask this question: *What are the coordinates of two points whose absolute values are 4? Describe their locations on the number line.* −4 and 4; 4 units left and 4 units right of 0

3 PRACTICE/APPLY

Assignment Guide
Maximum: 14–28
Minimum: 14–28

For **Extra Practice,** see p. 588.

Alternate Assessment

Modeling Draw a thermometer on the chalkboard. Label −10°F, 0°F, and 10°F. Name several temperatures and have students label them on the thermometer.

Enrichment Masters, p. 20

Enrichment Worksheet 3-1

88

Guided Practice 5. Name the coordinate of each point graphed on the number line. A: −6 B: −1 C: 2 D: 5

Find each absolute value.
6. $|4|$ 4 7. $|-3|$ 3 8. $|-23|$ 23 9. $|124 + 5|$ 129 10. $|0|$ 0

Graph each set of numbers on a number line. See Solutions Manual.
11. {−1, −3, −5} 12. {4, 5, 7} 13. {−3, −1, 0, 2}

Exercises

Independent Practice Graph each set of numbers on a number line. See Solutions Manual.
14. {−5, −7, 9, 12} 15. {−6, −8, −10} 16. {−3, −2, 0, 2, 3}

Find each absolute value.
17. $|34|$ 34 18. $|-93|$ 93 19. $|-87|$ 87 20. $|132 - 20|$ 112

21. Evaluate $b + |a - c|$ if $a = 1$, $b = 2$, and $c = 0$. 3
22. Evaluate $xy - |-30|$ if $x = 10$ and $y = 4$. 10

Mixed Review 23. Use mental math to find 297 + 478. (Lesson 1-2) 775
24. Solve $q + 6.8 = 15.2$. Check your solution. (Lesson 2-3) 8.4
25. Solve $\frac{b}{2} - 1 > 2$. Show the solution on a number line. (Lesson 2-10) $b > 6$; See margin for number line.

Problem Solving and Applications 26. **Number Sense** Graph any point on a number line.
a. Are the integers to the right of that point greater than or less than the coordinate of the point? greater than
b. What can you conclude about the integers to the left of that point? They are less than that coordinate.

27. **Critical Thinking** A small snail in the forest is climbing a tree 10 feet tall. Each day it climbs 3 feet. Because of the dampness of the forest, it slips down 2 feet each evening. Use a number line to determine how many da[ys it will] take the snail to reach the top of the tree. 8 days

28. **Data Analysis** Copy the chart below. Complete the chart with a p[hrase that] fits each situation. *below sea level

Situation	Negative	Positive	Neither Positive nor Negative
altitude of a city	*	above sea level	sea level
football	5 yard loss	10 yard gain	no gain
time	yesterday	tomorrow	today
money	loss	profit	breakeven

88 Chapter 3 Integers

OPTIONS

Extending the Lesson

Algebra Connection Have small groups solve the following equations. Explain that each equation has two solutions.
1. $|x| = 7$ 7, −7
2. $|y| - 5 = 3$ 8, −8
3. $\frac{|w|}{4} = 6$ 24, −24
4. $5|p| = 20$ 2.5, −2.5

Cooperative Learning Activity

Alternate Assessment

Modeling Draw a thermometer on the chalkboard. Label −10°F, 0°F, and 10°F. Name several temperatures and have students label them on the thermometer.

Course 3, p. 88

DAILY ASSESSMENT The Teacher's Wraparound Edition contains an alternate assessment option for most lessons. Students' understanding can be evaluated through writing, modeling, or speaking activities. These provide methods for providing immediate feedback as well as motivation for students who are usually most eager to show what they know.

PERFORMANCE ASSESSMENT To determine what students know and what they can apply, they should be presented with authentic problem-solving situations. The **Performance Assessment Booklets** contain student assessment items for each chapter, as well as scoring rubrics.

Alternative Assessment in the Mathematics Classroom, one of the booklets in Glencoe's Mathematics Professional Series, contains further information and activities to help you implement other types of evaluation strategies.

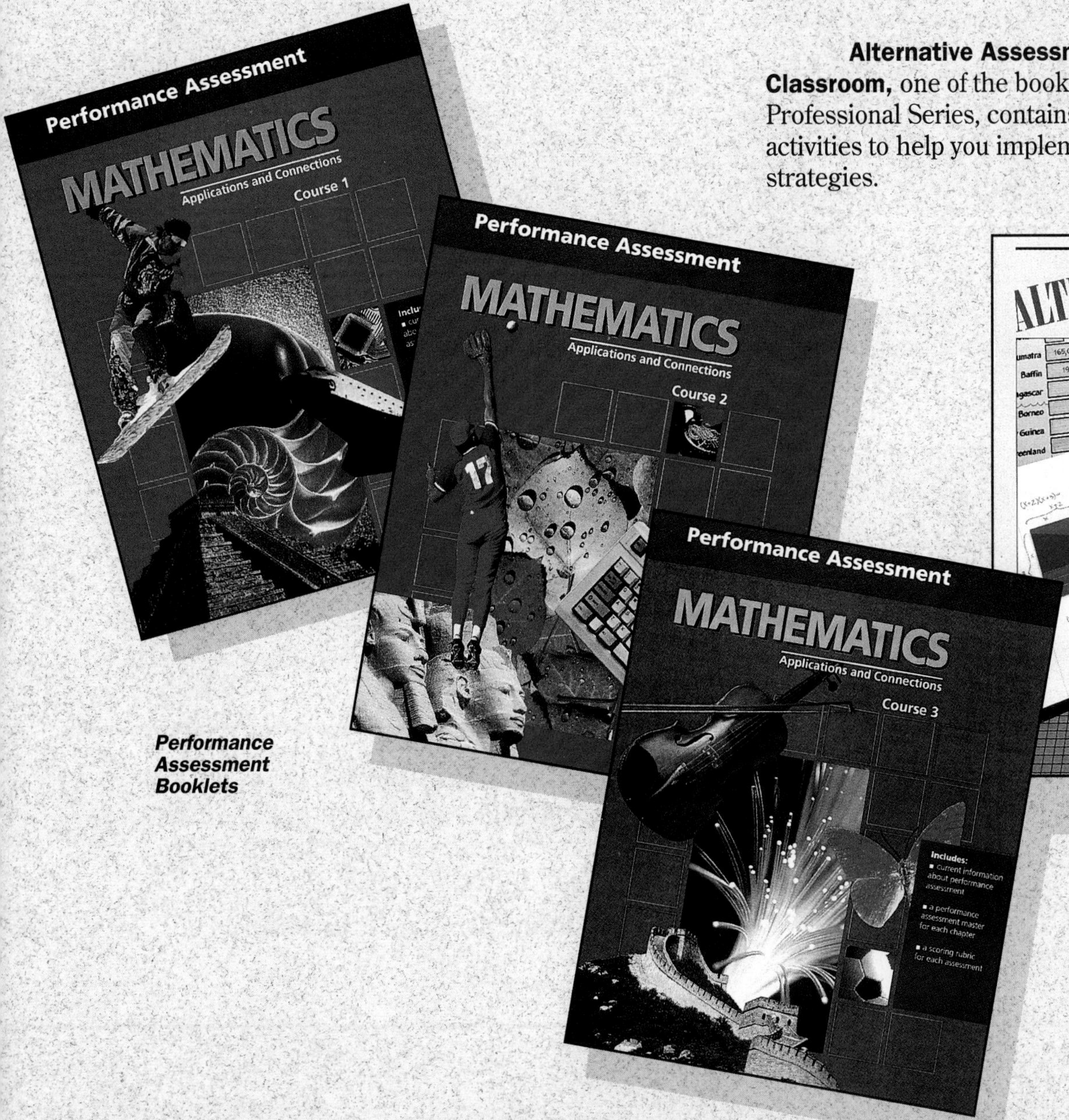

Performance Assessment Booklets

Alternative Assessment in the Mathematics Classroom

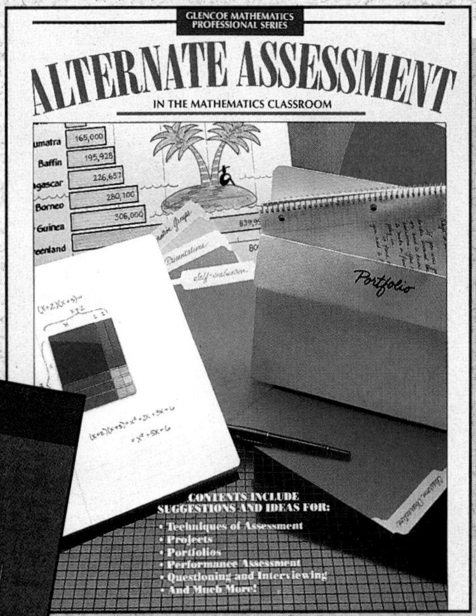

Integrating the 3 R's
Reading, Writing, and 'Rithmetic

Besides being articulate speakers and fluent writers, today's and tomorrow's citizens must be able to interpret data, express mathematical ideas verbally and in writing, organize information in tables, and draw graphs and diagrams.

Mathematics: Applications and Connections provides abundant opportunities for students to develop and integrate their communication skills through modeling, speaking, writing, and showing what they have learned.

Every exercise set begins with **Communicating Mathematics**. These in-class exercises help develop students' understanding through writing, talking, modeling, drawing, and so on.

Checking for Understanding

Communicating Mathematics

Read and study the lesson to answer each question.

1. **Show** two methods to solve $x = -15 + 23$.
2. **Tell** how you know the sign of the sum of two integers with different signs.
3. **Tell** how you know whether to add or subtract the absolute values to find the sum of two integers. Give examples.
4. **Write** the addition sentence shown by each model.

a.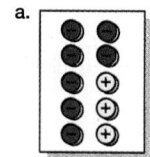
b.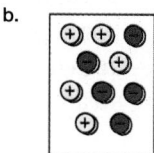
c.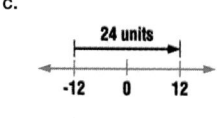

Course 3, p. 93

Journal Entries throughout the text give students a chance to reflect upon and record their understanding of the mathematical content.

Portfolio Suggestions offer ways for students to organize representative work samples that can be used for assessment and to show their growth.

 26. **Journal Entry** Collect data by measuring the playing surface of a court or playing field at your school. Make and label a scale drawing of it. What is its area?

Course 2, p. 245

 23. **Portfolio Suggestion** Select an item from this chapter that you feel shows your best work and place it in your portfolio. Explain why you selected it.

Course 1, p. 176

"The ability to read, listen, think creatively, and communicate about problem situations, mathematical representations, and the validation of solutions will help students to develop and deepen their understanding of mathematics."

- NCTM Curriculum and Evaluation Standards, 1989

A MULTICULTURAL PERSPECTIVE ON MATHEMATICS

The United States has become an increasingly multicultural society, and schools clearly reflect our country's diversity. There is a growing emphasis on educating students to understand, respect, and appreciate the differences among the many cultures that contribute to the wonderful diversity of our country and the world.

In **Mathematics: Applications and Connections**, students learn that mathematics has been shaped by the contributions of many cultures. From the ancient Egyptians, who used the "Pythagorean" theorem 1,500 years before Pythagoras, to the ancient Chinese, who calculated the value of π to ten places 1,200 years before the Europeans, the history of mathematics was molded—and continues to be developed— by persons of many cultures.

The multicultural focus of **Mathematics: Applications and Connections** helps to educate students about these important multicultural issues: that there is strength in diversity; that it is important to respect the rights of all persons and groups; and that social justice and equal opportunity must be made available to all people.

Numerous lessons, examples, and exercises contain applications that highlight multicultural experiences in mathematics.

Cultural Kaleidoscopes introduce students to persons from various cultures in the past and present who have been successful in their careers.

Multicultural Activity Masters contains one multicultural activity for each chapter in each course.

Each *Teacher's Wraparound Edition* contains suggestions in the interleaf as well as with individual lessons for incorporating a multicultural perspective in the classroom.

13-1 Counting Outcomes

Objective
Count outcomes using a tree diagram or the Fundamental Principle of Counting.

Words to Learn
outcome
tree diagram
Fundamental Principle of Counting

The games you played in Mathematics Lab 13-1A involved counting outcomes by listing them. In this lesson you will learn two other ways to count outcomes.

The Hopi Indians invented a game of chance called Totolospi. This game was played with three cane dice, a counting board inscribed on stone, and a counter for each player. Each cane die can land round side up (R) or flat side up (F). In Totolospi for two players, each player places a counter on the nearest circle. The moves of the game are determined by tossing the three cane dice.

504   Chapter 13 Discrete Math and Probability

Course 3, p. 504

Problem Solving

Practice   Solve. Use any strategy.

Strategies
Look for a pattern.
Solve a simpler problem.
Act it out.
Guess and check.
Draw a diagram.
Make a chart.
Work backward.

6. Find the number of line segments determined by six points on a line.
7. Gloria made enough money with her computer graphics to buy a new printer. She told Al and Sue who each let two of their computer network friends know ten minutes later. If the news spread like this every ten minutes, how many people knew by the end of the hour?
8. Complete the pattern 100, 98, 94, _?_, 80, _?_.
9. You plant 10 hyacinths in exactly 5 rows. There are 4 bulbs in each row. Draw a diagram of your garden.
10. This pattern is known as Pascal's Triangle. Find the pattern and complete the 6th and 7th rows.

1st row   1
2nd row   1   1
3rd row   1   2   1
4th row   1   3   3   1
5th row 1   4   6   4   1

11. A college student sent home this letter.   SEND
If each letter stands for one digit 0-9,   + MORE
how much money did he ask for?   MONEY
12. Complete the chart on page 274.
13. **Data Search** Refer to page 651. If the actual temperature is 15 degrees Fahrenheit, how much colder does it feel when the wind increases from 5 mph to 10 mph?

CULTURAL KALEIDOSCOPE

Pat Neblett
If children are our future, Pat Neblett wants to make sure that they know and understand different cultures. With $2,000, the former real estate agent founded Tuesday's Child Books in 1988 from her Randolph, Massachusetts home. She began selling African-American books through direct mail catalogs. Now most of her business comes from sales to schools. The titles have expanded to include children's books about Asians,

276   Chapter 7 Integers

Course 2, p. 276

CULTURAL KALEIDOSCOPE

Pat Neblett
If children are our future, Pat Neblett wants to make sure that they know and understand different cultures. With $2,000, the former real estate agent founded Tuesday's Child Books in 1988 from her Randolph, Massachusetts home. She began selling African-American books through direct mail catalogs. Now most of her business comes from sales to schools. The titles have expanded to include children's books about Asians,

Hispanics, Native Americans, and minority groups in the United States. Neblett carries more than 300 titles. She reads each book herself to ensure that the content positively reinforces a child's self-worth.

Sales have increased from $7,000 in her first year to a projected $25,000 in 1991. She plans to open her own retail store if her business continues to grow.

276   Chapter 7 Integers

Meeting Individual Needs

Mathematics: Applications and Connections provides outstanding teacher resources specifically tailored for middle school teachers and students. The program offers an abundance of options and suggestions for creating an environment that is most conducive to learning. They include:

Meeting Needs of Middle School Students provides ways to prepare students for later mathematics courses, to maintain their interest and curiosity, and to tailor material to meet their developmental stages and personal concerns.

Limited English Proficiency features methods to reach and teach students for whom English is a secondary language.

Gifted and Talented Needs suggests ways to keep these students motivated and challenged.

Team Teaching offers suggestions on how to integrate mathematics with other disciplines.

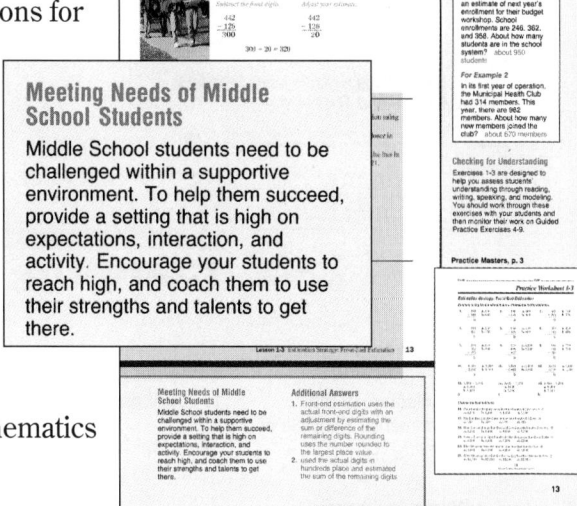

Meeting Needs of Middle School Students

Middle School students need to be challenged within a supportive environment. To help them succeed, provide a setting that is high on expectations, interaction, and activity. Encourage your students to reach high, and coach them to use their strengths and talents to get there.

Course 1, p. 13

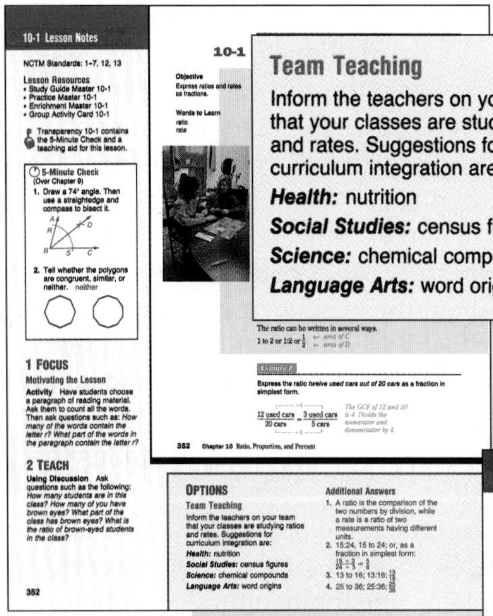

Team Teaching

Inform the teachers on your team that your classes are studying ratios and rates. Suggestions for curriculum integration are:

Health: nutrition
Social Studies: census figures
Science: chemical compounds
Language Arts: word origins

Course 1, p. 352

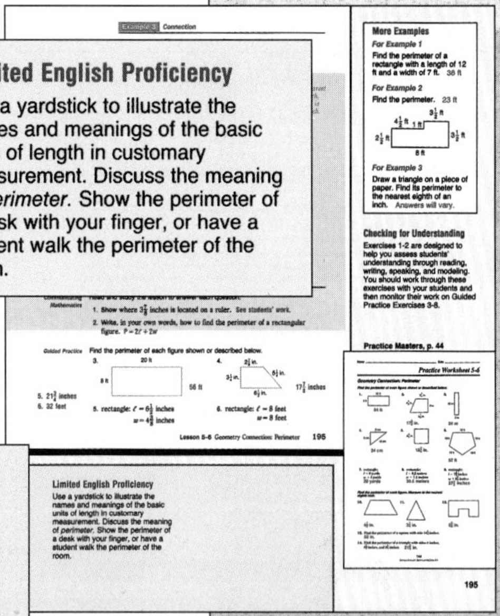

Limited English Proficiency

Use a yardstick to illustrate the names and meanings of the basic units of length in customary measurement. Discuss the meaning of *perimeter*. Show the perimeter of a desk with your finger, or have a student walk the perimeter of the room.

Course 2, p. 195

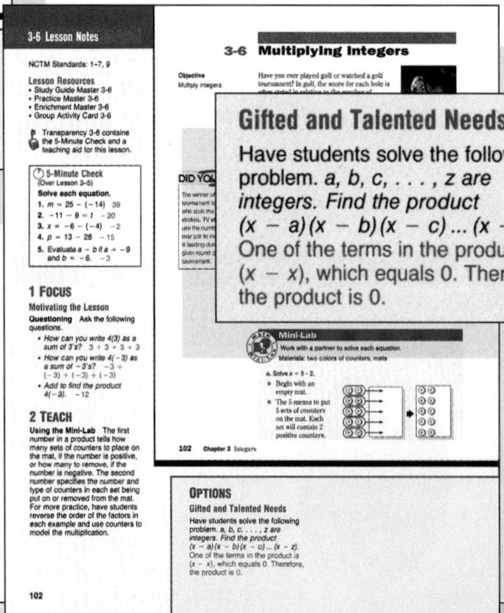

Gifted and Talented Needs

Have students solve the following problem. *a, b, c, . . . , z are integers. Find the product $(x - a)(x - b)(x - c) ... (x - z)$.* One of the terms in the product is $(x - x)$, which equals 0. Therefore, the product is 0.

Course 3, p. 102

When children enter 6th grade, for a variety of reasons, it may become difficult for parents to remain on top of what's going on at school. The curricula grow more specialized, the typical middle school child becomes more independent of his or her parents, and multiple teachers replace the sole or primary teacher of the elementary school years.

When parents do have the opportunity to meet with teachers, they often ask what they can do to motivate their children. Here are some ideas to share with parents. Developed by Reginald Clark of the Academy for Educational Development in Washington, D.C., they are designed to foster positive attitudes and boost learning.

- Share the fact that there is an inverse correlation between excessive TV viewing and high achievement in school.
- Suggest that they discuss school, education, careers, life skills, etiquette, rules, and expectations with their children.
- Explain that it's important for them tell stories, recount experiences, and share problem-solving strategies with their children.
- Stress the importance of seeing to it that their children complete homework assignments.
- Urge them to provide time, space, and materials, needed for homework, reading, and hobbies.
- Remind them how important it is to listen to their children read and/or to read to their children.

FOSTERING COMMUNITY INVOLVEMENT

If your school does not have a formal community information program, suggest that one be established. Send photos and press releases to your local newspaper to inform the community about the exciting things your students are learning.

Have a "math career day" and invite local business people to describe to students how they use math in their jobs.

Set up a "shadow day" in which students spend a half-day "shadowing" people in the community who use math in their careers.

Find out about—or implement your own—math fairs and competitions that give your students a chance to shine in the "outside world."

Involving Parents and the Community in the Mathematics Classroom, one of the booklets in Glencoe's Mathematics Professional Series, presents additional suggestions on how parents and the community can be active participants in supporting mathematics instruction.

INVOLVING PARENTS AND THE COMMUNITY

CLASSROOM RESOURCES APPROPRIATE FOR FAMILIES

Some of the Teacher's Classroom Resources that accompany *Mathematics: Applications and Connections* are appropriate for parents and children to use together.

Study Guide Masters offer a brief explanation, examples, and exercises of the main concept in each lesson.

Enrichment Masters provide stimulating and thought-provoking puzzles, games, and extensions.

Multicultural Activity Masters present a cross-cultural spectrum of multicultural settings as a basis for problem solving.

Applications and Interdisciplinary Activity Masters accent the relationships among mathematics, the real world, and other disciplines.

Interactive Mathematics
An Alternate Approach

Interactive Mathematics: Activities and Investigations offers an innovative, alternative approach to teaching and learning middle school mathematics. Each of the 18 units that make up this comprehensive, activity-based program may be used an alternative for supplement to chapters in ***Mathematics: Applications and Connections.***

Each unit involves students working together in cooperative group settings to discover mathematical concepts and to apply them in real-life situations. Hands-on activities dealing with issues that are vital and interesting to middle school students assure high student involvement.

As a teacher, you assist individual students and groups with the problems they're attempting to solve, and you help your students construct the concepts that lead to mathematical understanding. You guide your students as they are transformed from passive learners to active, involved mathematics explorers.

Units of ***Interactive Mathematics: Activities and Investigations*** are referenced as appropriate in the teacher's chapter interleaf pages of ***Mathematics: Applications and Connections.*** The unit titles and mathematical focus of each are a follows:

Unit	Title	Mathematical Focus
1	From the Beginning	Building Math Power
2	A Million to One	Number Sense
3	Just the Right Size	Scale Drawings and Proportional Reasoning
4	Through the Looking Glass	Spatial Visualization
5	Get A Clue	Logical Reasoning
6	The Road Not Taken	Graph Theory and Networks
7	Take It From the Top	Building Math Power
8	Data Sense	Statistics and Data Analysis
9	Don't Fence Me In	Area and Perimeter
10	Against the Odds	Probability
11	Cycles	Algebra Patterns
12	Treasure Island	Geometry and Measurement
13	Start Your Engines	Building Math Power
14	Run for Cover	Surface Area and Volume
15	On the Move	Graphing and Functions
16	Growing Pains	Linear and Exponential Growth
17	Infinite Windows	Fractals and Chaos Theory
18	Quality Control	Applied Data Analysis

MEETING THE NCTM STANDARDS

Mathematics: Applications and Connections is an integrated, three-year Middle School Mathematics Program.

Mathematics: Applications and Connections thoroughly integrates all thirteen curriculum standards outlined in the NCTM Standards. The standards listed below are for grades 5-8. See page 65 of the Standards.

STANDARD 1: *Mathematics as Problem Solving*
Course 1   (Chapters 1–14)
4-37, 44-71, 78-107, 116-121, 124-151, 160-162, 165-166, 168-183, 190-223, 232-264, 274-291, 293-303, 310-341, 350-379, 386-413, 420-451, 460-489, 496-521
Course 2   (Chapters 1–14)
4-41, 48-83, 90-119, 128-167, 174-213, 220-245, 254-289, 296-329, 336-367, 376-404, 410-447, 454-483, 492-525, 532-555
Course 3   (Chapters 1–14)
4-37, 44-79, 86-119, 128-167, 174-205, 212-247, 256-293, 304-335, 338-371, 380-415, 422-457, 464-493, 502-535, 542-565

STANDARD 2: *Mathematics as Communication*
Course 1   (Chapters 1–14)
4-37, 44-71, 78-107, 116-121, 124-151, 160-183, 190-223, 232-264, 274-303, 310-341, 350-379, 386-413, 420-451, 460-489, 496-521
Course 2   (Chapters 1–14)
4-41, 48-83, 90-119, 128-167, 174-213, 220-245, 254-289, 296-329, 336-367, 376-404, 410-447, 454-483, 492-525, 532-555
Course 3   (Chapters 1–14)
4-37, 44-79, 86-119, 128-167, 174-200, 202-205, 212-247, 256-293, 304-335, 338-371, 380-415, 422-457, 464-493, 502-535, 542-565

STANDARD 3: *Mathematics as Reasoning*
Course 1   (Chapters 1–14)
4-37, 44-71, 78-107, 116-121, 124-151, 160-183, 190-223, 232-264, 274-291, 293-303, 310-341, 350-379, 386-413, 420-451, 460-489, 496-521
Course 2   (Chapters 1–14)
4-41, 48-83, 90-119, 128-167, 174-213, 220-245, 254-289, 296-329, 336-367, 376-404, 410-447, 454-483, 492-525, 532-555
Course 3   (Chapters 1–14)
4-37, 44-79, 86-119, 128-167, 174-205, 212-247, 256-293, 304-335, 338-371, 380-415, 422-457, 464-493, 502-535, 542-565

STANDARD 4: *Mathematical Connections*
Course 1   (Chapters 1–14)
4-37, 44-71, 78-107, 116-121, 126-133, 135-151, 160-183, 190-192, 194-201, 204-223, 232-248, 250-264, 274-277, 280-291, 293-303, 310-317, 321-323, 326-329, 331-339, 352-357, 359-379, 386-402, 404-413, 420-425, 427-445, 448-451, 462-465, 467-470, 473-477, 480-489, 496-521
Course 2   (Chapters 1–14)
4-41, 48-83, 90-119, 128-167, 174-213, 220-245, 254-289, 296-329, 336-367, 376-404, 410-447, 454-483, 492-525, 532-555
Course 3   (Chapters 1–14)
4-37, 44-79, 86-119, 128-167, 174-179, 181-205, 212-247, 256-293, 304-335, 338-371, 380-415, 422-457, 464-493, 502-535, 542-565

STANDARD 5: *Number and Number Relationships*
Course 1   (Chapters 1–14)
25-26, 30-31, 35-37, 47-52, 57-71, 78-107, 116-121, 124-131, 134-144, 149-151, 160-183, 190-192, 194-196, 199-223, 232-243, 246-248, 250-264, 274-303, 310-323, 326-329, 331-339, 350-358, 361-379, 388-402, 404-413, 420-445, 448-451, 460-489, 498-501, 506-517, 519-521
Course 2   (Chapters 1–14)
4-41, 48-83, 90-95, 99-119, 128-167, 174-213, 220-245, 254-289, 296-300, 306, 311-316, 319-323, 336-367, 381-404, 410-447, 454-483, 492-525, 532-555
Course 3   (Chapters 1–14)
4-14, 17-37, 51-72, 86-94, 98-119, 128-138, 141-161, 164-167, 212-247, 256-258, 262-267, 270-277, 284-290, 304-309, 317-335, 338-360, 364-371, 380-397, 400-415, 425-434, 446-449, 451-457, 464-467, 491-493, 519-520

STANDARD 6: *Number Systems and Number Theory*
Course 1   (Chapters 1–14)
27-29, 32-34, 44-46, 50-56, 61-63, 78-107, 116-121, 124-131, 134-144, 146-151, 160-173, 177-183, 190-192, 194-223, 232-243, 246-248, 250-264, 274-303, 310-323, 326-329, 331-339, 352-358, 361-379, 388-402, 404-413, 420-445, 448-451, 460-489, 498-501, 506-517, 519-521
Course 2   (Chapters 1–14)
4-41, 48-83, 90-95, 99-119, 128-167, 174-213, 220-245, 254-289, 296-300, 306, 311-316, 319-323, 336-367, 381-404, 410-447, 454-483, 492-525, 532-555
Course 3   (Chapters 2, 3, 6–8)
77-79, 95-105, 212-217, 219-240, 259-261, 304-306, 310-313

STANDARD 7: *Computation and Estimation*
Course 1   (Chapters 1–14)
4-37, 47-51, 53-67, 94-107, 116-121, 124-137, 139-144, 149-151, 160-173, 177-183, 190-192, 194-201, 204-206, 221-223, 232-248, 250-264, 274-303, 310-323, 326-329, 331-339, 352-379, 386-402, 404-413, 420-445, 448-451, 460-489, 496-504, 506-517, 519-521
Course 2   (Chapters 1–14)
4-26, 28-41, 54-69, 71-83, 90-95, 99-100, 104-112, 116-119, 129-167, 174-188, 191-213, 220-222, 225-231, 233-240, 243-245, 263-266, 268-276, 278-289, 319-323, 336-342, 344-367, 381-404, 411-420, 422-447, 454-483, 497-515, 517-520, 522-525, 532-534, 536-554
Course 3   (Chapters 1–14)
4-37, 44-79, 86-119, 128-135, 145-167, 176-179, 181-190, 192-200, 212-217, 219-244, 256-275, 278-293, 304-335, 338-371, 380-402, 406-415, 422-430, 432-457, 464-469, 475-493, 504-530, 533-535, 543-563

STANDARD 8: *Patterns and Functions*
Course 1   (Chapters 1–14)
15-17, 50-51, 57-71, 116-121, 129-131, 139-151, 163-164, 190-196, 221-223, 287-291, 293-296, 331-333, 340-341, 359-363, 371-373, 391-397, 411-413, 426, 435-451, 462-465, 478-489, 496-517, 519-521
Course 2   (Chapters 4, 7, 14)
129-144, 274-276, 278-280, 287-289, 547-550
Course 3   (Chapters 1–14)
30-34, 44-47, 60-66, 139-144, 149-150, 155-158, 159-161, 164-167, 181-182, 191-195, 202-205, 212-214, 218-223, 230-232, 236-240, 256-258, 270-277, 282-283, 307-309, 314-326, 332-335, 350-352, 361-371, 391-392, 422-457, 515-520

STANDARD 9: *Algebra*
Course 1   (Chapters 1–14)
22-24, 27-29, 32-34, 53-71, 106-107, 116-121, 126-131, 135-137, 139-144, 146-151, 160-162, 171-173, 177-181, 190-192, 194-196, 207-212, 219-220, 250-252, 257-260, 280-286, 289-291, 293-302, 326-329, 355-357, 361-363, 368-370, 374-379, 388-397, 404-413, 420-445, 448-451, 460-475, 478-489, 498-501
Course 2   (Chapters 1–14)
27-41, 58-59, 61-63, 132-139, 204-206, 220-237, 241-245, 259-261, 263-266, 268-271, 278-289, 297-300, 306, 313-316, 321-323, 383-386, 394-397, 402-404, 417-420, 422-429, 465-468, 476-483, 497-499, 535-554
Course 3   (Chapters 1–14)
44-56, 60-79, 86-119, 176-179, 183-190, 197-200, 215-217, 221-232, 236-238, 256-267, 270-275, 278-281, 284-293, 310-316, 319-322, 332-335, 344-349, 353-363, 365-371, 380-390, 400-402, 406-415, 422-438, 442-457, 464-467, 487-490, 542-563

STANDARD 10: *Statistics*
Course 1   (Chapters 1–14)
4-7, 9-11, 20-21, 27-29, 32-34, 53-71, 87-90, 94-97, 103-107, 116-121, 126-133, 135-141, 146-148, 168-170, 194-196, 199-201, 204-206, 216-223, 244-245, 249-252, 257-260, 274-277, 289-291, 297-299, 314-317, 364-365, 368-379, 398-399, 420-425, 431-434, 440-445, 476-477, 483-489, 496-501, 506-509, 518-521
Course 2   (Chapters 3–14)
90-119, 164-167, 220-222, 233-235, 281-282, 313-316, 319-320, 444-447, 462-464, 469-473, 506-509, 543-554
Course 3   (Chapters 1–14)
30-31, 62-64, 86-88, 128-161, 164-167, 181-182, 239-244, 338-341, 344-349, 393-396, 403-405, 431, 439-441, 533-535

STANDARD 11: *Probability*
Course 1   (Chapters 1–4, 12, 14)
32-34, 57-63, 87-90, 124-125, 132-133, 420-422, 496-521
Course 2   (Chapters 4, 5, 9, 13)
157-160, 201-203, 363-367, 492-505, 510-513, 517-520, 522-525
Course 3   (Chapters 6, 12, 13)
233-235, 464-467, 502-509, 512-518, 521-532

STANDARD 12: *Geometry*
Course 1   (Chapters 4–14)
32-34, 85-93, 106-107, 135-137, 139-151, 160-162, 171-173, 190-193, 199-201, 210-212, 232-243, 246-248, 253-256, 274-279, 284-291, 310-341, 350-363, 371-373, 377-379, 386-413, 420-422, 431-434, 440-451, 467-470, 483-489, 506-517, 519-521
Course 2   (Chapters 5–14)
32-35, 38-41, 51-53, 194-200, 241-245, 296-318, 321-329, 338-367, 376-386, 389-404, 411-413, 422-425, 469-473, 476-478, 536-539, 551-555
Course 3   (Chapters 2–14)
8-14, 26-28, 35-37, 54-56, 73-76, 106-110, 117-119, 174-205, 218, 224-226, 230-235, 272-275, 278-290, 304-306, 308-309, 317-335, 342-343, 353-371, 391-396, 403-405, 425-427, 432-438, 442-457, 464-490, 542

STANDARD 13: *Measurement*
Course 1   (Chapters 1–14)
4-11, 18-19, 32-34, 79-86, 91-97, 100-102, 106-107, 119-121, 126-128, 139-151, 160-162, 171-176, 190-192, 199-201, 207-218, 232-243, 246-248, 253-256, 261-264, 274-291, 300-303, 310-323, 326-329, 337-339, 352-357, 359-363, 371-373, 377-379, 386-402, 404-413, 420-422, 435-437, 443-445, 448-451, 467-470, 487-489, 506-517
Course 2   (Chapters 2–14)
78-80, 142-144, 238-240, 344-367, 398-401, 417-420, 422-425, 433-435, 454-456
Course 3   (Chapters 1–14)
22-29, 77-79, 86-88, 91-101, 117-119, 174-180, 183-191, 196, 201, 227-229, 245-247, 256-258, 278-287, 342-343, 356-371, 393-397, 403-405, 470-473, 478-481, 486, 491-493

Communication, cooperative learning, connections among disciplines, applications, calculator, computer, and the use of manipulatives are integrated throughout the mathematical content as appropriate.

Problem Solving

Course	1	2	3
Develop a plan			
Strategies			
Guess and Check			
Classifying Information			
Use a Graph			
Make a Table			
Determine Reasonable Answers			
Use a Formula			
Solve a Simpler Problem			
Choose the Method of Computation			
Make a List			
Eliminate Possibilities			
Find a Pattern			
Use Logical Reasoning			
Draw a Diagram			
Make a Model			
Work Backward			
Use an Equation			
Act It Out			
Use the Pythagorean Theorem			
Use a Venn Diagram			
Factor Polynomials			
Analyzing and Making Decisions			
Finding and classifying information			
Interpreting data			
Making predictions based on data			

Estimation and Mental Math

Course	1	2	3
Estimation			
Rounding whole numbers			
Rounding decimals			
Strategies for estimating			
rounding			
front-end			
patterns			
compatible numbers			
choosing the computation method			
capture-recapture			
use fractions, decimals, & percents interchangeably			
Estimating with whole numbers			
sums & differences			
products & quotients			
Estimating with decimals			
sums & differences			
products & quotients			

Estimation and Mental Math (cont.)

Course	1	2	3
Estimating with fractions			
sums & differences			
products & quotients			
Estimating percent			
Estimating with Geometry			
angle measures			
area, volume			
Estimating square roots			
Mental Math			
Strategies			
using properties			
patterns			
compatible numbers			
compensation			
choosing the computation method			
Solving equations mentally			

Decimals

Course	1	2	3
Understanding the concept			
Reading & writing			
Decimal place value			
Comparing and ordering			
Rounding			
Relating decimals & fractions			
Relating decimals, ratios, & percents			
Operations with Decimals			
Adding & subtracting			
Multiplying: by a whole number			
two decimals			
Dividing: by a whole number			
by powers of 10			
by a decimal			
with zeros in the quotient			
Estimating sums & differences			
Estimating products & quotients			
Scientific notation			
Terminating, repeating			

Number Theory

Course	1	2	3
Reading and writing whole numbers			
Place value of whole numbers			
Place value of decimals			
Compare & order whole numbers			
Compare & order decimals			
Compare & order fractions			
Compare & order integers			
Compare & order rationals			

■ Introduce

▨ Develop

☐ Reinforce/Integrate

Communication, cooperative learning, connections among disciplines, applications, calculator, computer, and the use of manipulatives are integrated throughout the mathematical content as appropriate.

Number Theory (cont.)	Course	1	2	3
Compare & order irrationals				
Rounding whole numbers				
Rounding decimals				
Rounding fractions				
Positive exponents				
Negative exponents				
Greatest Common Factor (GCF)				
Least Common Multiple (LCM)				
Divisibility rules				
Prime and composite numbers				
Prime factorization				
Relative primes				
Scientific notation				
Square roots				
Relating fractions and decimals				

Fractions		1	2	3
Fraction concepts				
Writing mixed numbers as fractions				
Mixed numbers and improper fractions				
Equivalent fractions				
Comparing & order fractions				
Simplifying fractions				
LCD				
Rounding & estimating fractions				
Operations with fractions				
Adding & subtracting				
Subtracting with renaming				
Multiplying & dividing				
Estimating sums & differences				
Estimating products & quotients				
Relating fractions & decimals				

Geometry		1	2	3
Lines				
Constructions				
congruent lines				
perpendicular lines				
parallel lines				
segment bisectors				
Angles				
classify and measure angles				
sum of angle measures				
constructions				
congruent angles				
angle bisectors				
Tesselations				
Identify polygons				
Classify triangles and quadrilaterals				

Geometry (cont.)	Course	1	2	3
Construct polygons				
Symmetry				
Identify congruent figures & similar figures				
Corresponding parts of similar polygons				
Translations, reflections, & rotations				
Identify & draw three-dimensional figures				
Relationships in a right triangle				
Pythagorean Theorem				

Measurement		1	2	3
Metric System				
use units of length, capacity, & mass				
change units within the metric system				
Customary System				
use customary units of measurement				
convert within the customary system				
Precision and significant digits				
Measuring perimeter/circumference				
Measuring area				
of irregular figures				
of rectangles				
of parallelograms				
of triangles				
by connecting algebra & geometry				
of circles				
of a trapezoid				
Measuring surface area				
of rectangular prisms				
of triangular prisms				
of cylinders				
of spheres				
Measuring volume				
of rectangular prisms				
of cylinders				
of pyramids and circular cones				
of spheres				
Relating surface area & volume				

Probability		1	2	3
Making predictions using a sample				
Conducting Experiments				
simple event				
independent events				
dependent events				
using area models				
experimental probability				
tree diagrams				
Fundamental Principle of Counting				
permutations & combinations				

■ Introduce
▨ Develop
□ Reinforce/Integrate

Communication, cooperative learning, connections among disciplines, applications, calculator, computer, and the use of manipulatives are integrated throughout the mathematical content as appropriate.

Statistics

	Course 1	2	3
Recording & interpreting data			
organizing data into a table	▓	▓	
constructing graphs	▓	▓	
constructing line plots		▓	
constructing stem-and-leaf plots		▓	
constructing histograms			▓
constructing box-and-whisker plots			▓
constructing scatter plots			▓
Interpret data			
mean, median, & mode	▓	▓	
range & quartiles		▓	
misleading graphs & statistics		▓	
making predictions from statistics	▓	▓	

Ratio, Proportion, & Percent

	Course 1	2	3
Ratio			
Understanding concept of ratio	▓	▓	
Reading and writing ratios	▓	▓	
Equal ratios	▓	▓	
The Golden Ratio			▓
Proportion			
Understanding concept of proportion	▓	▓	
Solving proportions	▓	▓	
Scale drawings	▓	▓	
Similar figures	▓	▓	
Dilations		▓	
Indirect measurement		▓	
Tangent, sine, & cosine ratios			▓
Percent			
Understanding the concept of percent	▓	▓	
Writing fractions & decimals for percent	▓	▓	
Finding percent of a number	▓	▓	
Percents greater than 100%, less than 1%		▓	
Percent one number is of another		▓	
Finding number when percent is known		▓	
Estimating percents	▓	▓	
Discount		▓	
Sales tax		▓	
Simple interest		▓	
Percent of change		▓	

Algebra

	Course 1	2	3
Properties			
of whole numbers			▓
of rational numbers			▓
Integers			
Read & write integers	▓	▓	
Graphing integers on the number line	▓	▓	

Algebra (cont.)

	Course 1	2	3
Absolute value		▓	▓
Compare and order integers	▓	▓	
Add & subtract integers	▓	▓	
Multiply & divide integers	▓	▓	
Rational numbers			
Identify and simplify rational numbers			▓
Scientific notation		▓	▓
Rational numbers as decimals			▓
Compare and order rational numbers			▓
Solve equations with rational number solutions			▓
Real Numbers			
Identify & classify real numbers			▓
Negative exponents		▓	▓
Square roots			▓
Irrational numbers			▓
Density property			▓
Patterns, Functions, Expressions, & Equations			
Recognize and extend sequences	▓	▓	
Fibonacci Sequence			▓
Pascal's Triangle			▓
Function tables	▓	▓	
Linear functions			▓
Order of operations	▓	▓	
Evaluate algebraic expressions	▓	▓	
Solve two-step equations		▓	
Solve equations			
with integer solutions		▓	
with two variables		▓	
Write algebraic expressions from verbal phrases	▓	▓	
Identify and solve inequalities	▓	▓	
Graphing			
Points on a coordinate plane	▓	▓	
Functions		▓	
Equations		▓	
Transformations on a coordinate plane	▓	▓	
Irrational numbers on a number line			▓
Linear functions			▓
Quadratic functions			▓
To solve systems of equations			▓
Slope			▓
Polynomials			
Represent & simplify polynomials			▓
Add, subtract, & multiply polynomials			▓
Factor polynomials			▓
Multiply binomials			▓

▓ Introduce

▓ Develop

☐ Reinforce/Integrate

BIBLIOGRAPHY

Publications

Azzolino, Agnes, *How to Use Writing to Teach Mathematics*, Keyport, NJ: Mathematical Concepts, 1987.

California State Department of Education Task Force on Middle Grade Education, *Caught in the Middle*, California State Department of Education, Sacramento, CA, 1987.

Carnegie Council on Adolescent Development, *Turning Points*, Washington, DC, 1989.

Cuevas, Gilbert J., *Mathematics Learning in English as a Second Language*, Journal for Research in Mathematics Education, XV (March 1984) 134-144.

Farrell, Margaret A., ed., *Imaginative Ideas for the Teacher of Mathematics, Grades K-12: Ranucci's Reservoir*, Reston, VA: NCTM, 1988.

Jamski, William D., ed., *Mathematical Challenges for the Middle Grades*, Reston, VA: NCTM, 1990.

Johnson, David W. and Roger T. Johnson, *Cooperation and Competition, Theory and Research*, Edina, MN: Interaction Book Co., 1989.

Kagan, Spencer, *Cooperative Learning, Resources for Teachers*, Laguna Niguel, CA: Resources for Teachers, 1989.

Mathematical Sciences Education Board and National Research Council, *Everybody Counts: A Report to the Nation on the Future of Mathematics Education*, Washington, DC: National Academy Press, 1989.

National Council of Teachers of Mathematics, *Curriculum and Evaluation Standards for School Mathematics*, Reston, VA: NCTM, 1989.

_____, *Mathematics for the Middle Grades (5-9), 1982 Yearbook*, Reston, Va:NCTM, 1982.

_____, *Professional Standards for Teaching Mathematics*, Reston, VA: NCTM, 1991.

Paulos, John A., *Innumeracy: Mathematical Illiteracy and Its Consequences*, New York, NY: 1988.

Skolnick, Joan, Carol Langbort, and Lucille Day, *How to Encourage Girls in Math and Science: Strategies for Parents and Educators*, Englewood Cliffs, NJ: Prentice Hall, 1982

Slavin, Robert, *Cooperative Learning, Student Teams, 2nd ed.*, Washington, DC: National Education Association, 1987.

Thompson, Robert G., *Practical BASIC for Teachers*, Columbus, OH: Merrill, 1985.

Thornton, Carol Z., et al., *Teaching Mathematics to Children with Special Needs*, Menlo Park, CA: Addison-Wesley, 1983.

Trafton, Paul R., and Albert P. Shulte, ed., *New Directions for Elementary School Mathematics*: 1989 Yearbook, Reston, VA: NCTM, 1989.

William T. Grant Foundation Commission on Work, Family and Citizenship, *The Forgotten Half: Pathways to Success for America's Youth and Young Families*, Washington, DC: 1988.

Computer Software

Coordinate Math, (Apple II), MECC

Data Models, (Macintosh), Wings for Learning/Sunburst

How the West Was One + Three x Four, (Apple II, Macintosh, IBM/Tandy), Wings for Learning/Sunburst

Keep Your Balance, (Apple II), Wings for Learning/Sunburst

Math Tutor: Fractions Part I, Fractions Part II, (Apple II, IBM/Tandy), Scholastic Inc.

Tobbs Learns Algebra, (Apple II), Wings for Learning/Sunburst

Films/Videotapes

Algebra for Everyone, Reston, VA: NCTM, 1991.

Guinness World Records Math Filmstrips: Problem Solving with Addition, Subtraction, Multiplication, and Division, Chicago, IL: Society for Visual Education, 1985.

Mathematics: Making the Connection, Reston, VA: NCTM, 1991.

Statistics: Understanding Mean, Median, and Mode, Bloomington, IN: Agency for Instructional Technology, 1987.

The Theory of Pythagoras, Reston, VA: NCTM, 1988.

Volume and Capacity, Los Angeles, CA: Oxford Films, 1974.

Addresses of Software Companies

Gamco Industries, P.O. Box 1862C9, Big Spring, TX 79721-1911, 800/351-1404

IBM, 4111 Northside Pwky NW, P.O. Box 2150, Atlanta, GA 30055, 800/IBM-2468

MECC, 6160 Summit Drive North, Minneapolis, MN 55430-4003, 800/685-MECC

Scholastic Inc., P.O. Box 7502, Jefferson City, MO 65102, 800/541-5513

Wings for Learning/Sunburst, 101 Castleton Street, Pleasantville, NY 10570, 800/338-3457

COURSE PLANNING GUIDES

The charts below give suggested time schedules for three Options: I, II, and III, and for two types of grading periods, 6-week and 9-week.

Option I covers Chapters 1-12. It allows extra time for longer lessons and for reteaching and review. Option II covers Chapters 1-13. Option III covers Chapters 1-14. This option is intended for students who master concepts quickly and retain skills well. Generally, one day is allotted for each lesson, Chapter Study Guide and Review, and Chapter Test.

Note that the total days suggested is 165 days which is considerably less than the number of days most school districts are in session. This is to allow the teacher flexibility in planning due to shortened class periods because of outside activities, bad weather days, or any other similar circumstances.

Course Planning Guide 6-Week Grading Period

Grading Period	Option I Chapter	Option I Days	Option II Chapter	Option II Days	Option III Chapter	Option III Days
1	1	15	1	14	1	13
	2	14	2	13	2	12
					3	3
					(Lessons 3-1 to 3-2B)	
2	3	13	3	12	3	8
	4	16	4	14	(Lesson 3-3 to end)	
					4	14
					5	6
					(Lesson 5-1 to 5-6)	
3	5	16	5	14	5	7
	6	11	6	11	(Lesson 5-7 to end)	
			7	4	6	10
			(Lessons 7-1 to 7-4)		7	10
					(Lessons 7-1 to 7-9)	
4	7	14	7	9	7	3
	8	13	(Lesson 7-5A to end)		(Lesson 7-10 to end)	
			8	13	8	12
			9	6	9	12
			(Lessons 9-1 to 9-6)			
5	9	14	9	6	10	10
	10	11	(Lesson 9-7A to end)		11	13
			10	11	12	5
			11	10	(Lessons 12-1 to 12-5)	
			(Lessons 11-1A to 11-8)			
6	11	15	11	4	12	6
	12	13	(Lesson 11-9 to end)		(Lesson 12-6 to end)	
			12	12	13	12
			13	12	14	9
Total Days		165		165		165

Course Planning Guide 9-Week Grading Period

Grading Period	Option I Chapter	Option I Days	Option II Chapter	Option II Days	Option III Chapter	Option III Days
1	1	15	1	14	1	13
	2	14	2	13	2	12
	3	13	3	12	3	11
					4	5
					(Lessons 4-1A to 4-4)	
2	4	16	4	14	4	9
	5	16	5	14	(Lesson 4-5 to end)	
	6	11	6	11	5	13
			7	4	6	10
			(Lessons 7-1 to 7-4)		7	10
					(Lessons 7-1 to 7-9)	
3	7	14	7	9	7	3
	8	13	(Lesson 7-5A to end)		(Lesson 7-10 to end)	
	9	14	8	13	8	12
			9	12	9	12
			10	7	10	10
			(Lessons 10-1A to 10-5)		11	4
					(Lessons 11-1A to 11-3B)	
4	10	11	10	4	11	9
	11	15	(Lesson 10-6 to end)		(Lesson 11-4 to end)	
	12	13	11	14	12	11
			12	12	13	12
			13	12	14	9
Total Days		165		165		165

1 Tools for Problem Solving

Previewing the Chapter

This chapter explores several **problem-solving strategies,** as well as the mental-math strategies of compensation and estimation. It also provides four lessons that focus on algebraic concepts and applications. The problem-solving strategies examined are using a four-step plan, choosing a method of computation, and solving problems by classifying information. The estimation strategies presented are front-end estimation and using compatible numbers. Students finish the chapter by exploring algebraic ideas and tools—order of operations, variables and expressions, and powers and exponents. They use these concepts to help them evaluate expressions and to solve equations mentally.

Lesson	Lesson Objectives	NCTM Standards	State/Local Objectives
1-1	Solve problems using the four-step plan.	1–7, 13	
1-2	Estimate sums and differences using rounding.	1–5, 7	
1-3	Estimate products and quotients using patterns.	1–5, 7	
1-4	Use estimation to determine whether answers to problems are reasonable.	1–5, 7	
1-5	Solve problems by choosing estimation, mental math, paper and pencil, or calculator.	1–5, 7	
1-6	Solve problems by classifying information.	1–4, 7	
Decision Making	Planning a flower garden.	1–5, 7	
1-7	Evaluate expressions using the order of operations.	1–5, 7, 9	
1-8A	Model algebraic expressions.	1–5, 9	
1-8	Evaluate numerical and simple algebraic expressions.	1–5, 7, 9	
1-9	Use powers and exponents in expressions.	1–5, 9, 12	
1-9B	Describe a spreadsheet.	1–5	
1-10	Solve equations using mental math.	1–4, 7, 9	

A complete, 1-page lesson plan is provided for each lesson in the Lesson Plans Masters Booklet.

LESSON PLANNING GUIDE

Lesson	Materials/ Manipulatives	Extra Practice (Student Edition)	Study Guide	Practice	Enrichment	Evaluation	Technology	Lab Manual	Multicultural Activities	Application and Interdisciplinary Activities	Transparencies	Group Activity Cards
			Blackline Masters Booklets									
1-1			p. 1	p. 1	p. 1						1-1	1-1
1-2		p. 572	p. 2	p. 2	p. 2						1-2	1-2
1-3		p. 572	p. 3	p. 3	p. 3						1-3	1-3
1-4		p. 572	p. 4	p. 4	p. 4						1-4	1-4
1-5	calculator		p. 5	p. 5	p. 5	Quiz A, p. 7					1-5	1-5
1-6			p. 6	p. 6	p. 6						1-6	1-6
1-7	calculator	p. 573	p. 7	p. 7	p. 7			p. 1			1-7	1-7
1-8A	counters, cups							p. 36				
1-8	cups, counters	p. 573	p. 8	p. 8	p. 8		p. 15			p. 1	1-8	1-8
1-9	calculator	p. 573	p. 9	p. 9	p. 9		p. 1	p. 37			1-9	1-9
1-9B								p. 38				
1-10		p. 574	p. 10	p. 10	p. 10	Quiz B, p. 7				p. 15	1-10	1-10
Study Guide and Review			Multiple Choice Test, Forms 1A and 1B, pp. 1–4 Free Response Test, Forms 2A and 2B, pp. 5–6 Cumulative Review, p. 8 (free response)									
Test			Cumulative Test, p. 9 (multiple choice)									

Pacing Guide: Option I (Chapters 1–12) - 15 days; Option II (Chapters 1–13) - 14 days; Option III (Chapters 1–14) - 13 days
You may wish to refer to the complete **Course Planning Guides** on page T25.

OTHER CHAPTER RESOURCES

Student Edition
Chapter Opener, pp. 2–3
Mid-Chapter Review, p. 19
Decision Making, pp. 22–23
Portfolio Suggestion, p. 35
Save Planet Earth, p. 37

Manipulatives
Overhead Manipulative Resources
Middle School Mathematics Manipulative Kit

Software/Technology
Interactive Mathematics Tools (Macintosh)
Test and Review Generator (IBM, Apple, Macintosh)
Teacher's Guide for Software Resources

Other Supplements
Transparency 1–0
Performance Assessment, pp. 1–2
Glencoe Mathematics Professional Series
Lesson Plans, pp. 1–12

INTERDISCIPLINARY BULLETIN BOARD

Geography Connection

Objective Draw a road map with driving distances in miles; formulate and solve problems by using information from a map.

How To Use It Have students use information in a road atlas to make a driving-distances map and then use the map to write problems for classmates to solve. Problems should involve travel times between cities. They may also involve time-zone data.

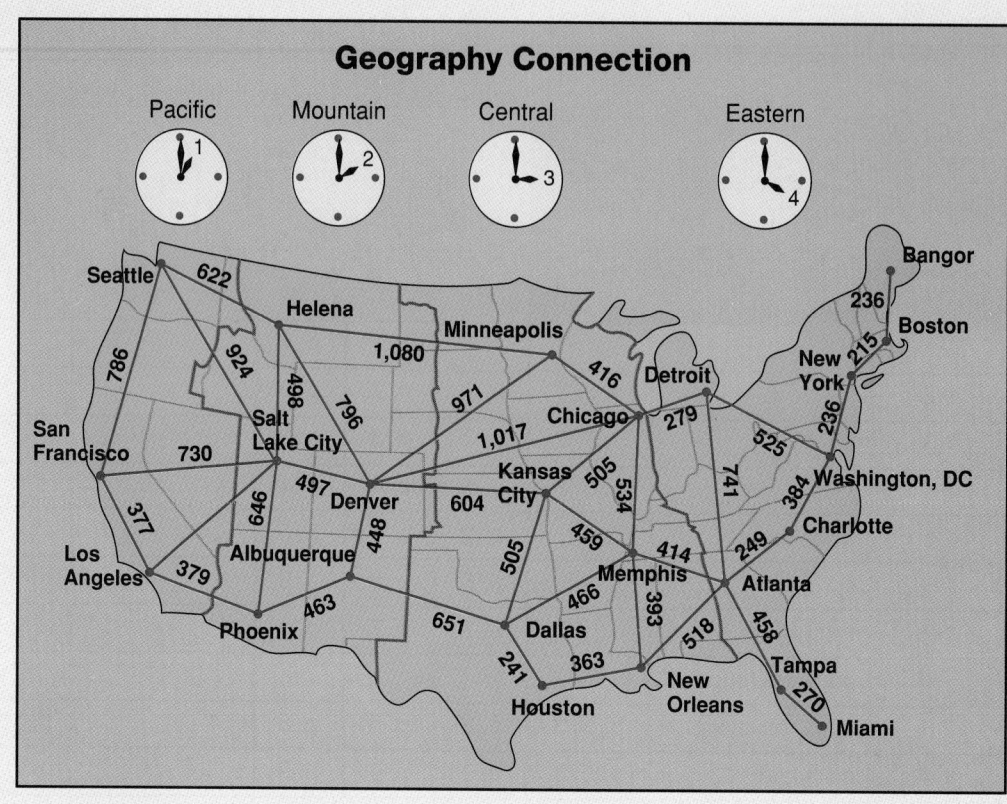

Geography Connection

APPLICATIONS AND CONNECTIONS

Applications	Lesson	Example	Exercise
Travel	1-1		4
Sports	1-1		6, 7
Smart Shopping	1-1		9
Transportation	1-1		11
Baseball	1-1		12
Smart Shopping	1-2		29, 31
Clubs	1-2		30
Air Travel	1-3	3	
Art	1-3		40
Travel	1-3		41
Animals	1-3		42
Smart Shopping	1-4	2	
Games	1-4		41
Smart Shopping	1-7		47
Computer	1-7		49
Nature	1-8		32
Aeronautics	1-8		33
Entertainment Industry	1-9		54–56
Health	1-10	2	
Travel	1-10		18
Nutrition	1-10		52
Connections			
Algebra	1-9	4, 5, 6	38–43
Geometry	1-9		50
Number System	1-9		51
Geometry	1-10		53

TEAM ACTIVITIES

Multicultural Experiences

Outside Field Trips A brief trip to a restaurant can be helpful in giving students practice estimating lunch prices and in using mental math strategies to determine actual costs.

A visit to a car dealership can provide the opportunity for students to see how the total cost of a new car is determined not only by the stated price but also by factors such as optional features and taxes.

In-Class Speakers Ask a buyer for a supermarket to make a presentation on the factors that affect the quantities of products he or she orders for the supermarket's shelves.

Invite a manager of a health club to speak to the class about considerations that are taken into account in planning schedules and ordering equipment.

SUPPLEMENTARY BLACKLINE MASTER BOOKLETS

Some of the blackline masters for enhancing this chapter are shown below.

Application and Interdisciplinary Activity Masters, pp. 1, 15

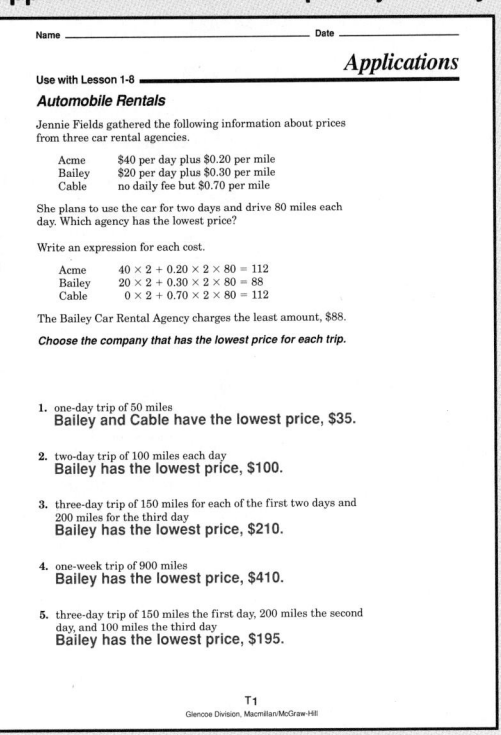

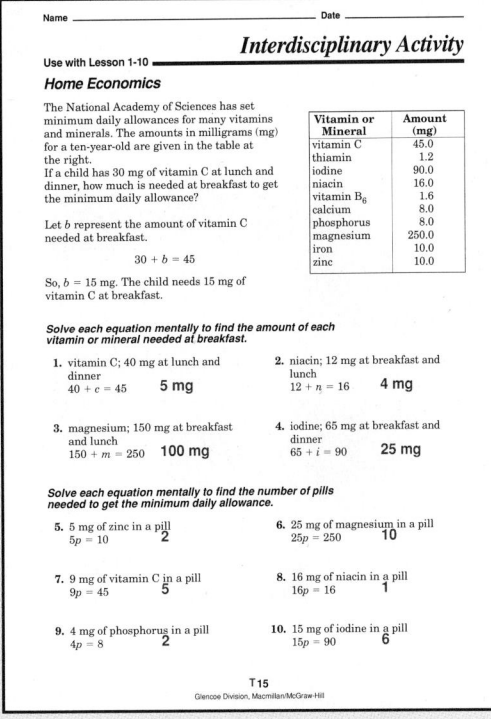

Multicultural Activity Masters, p. 1

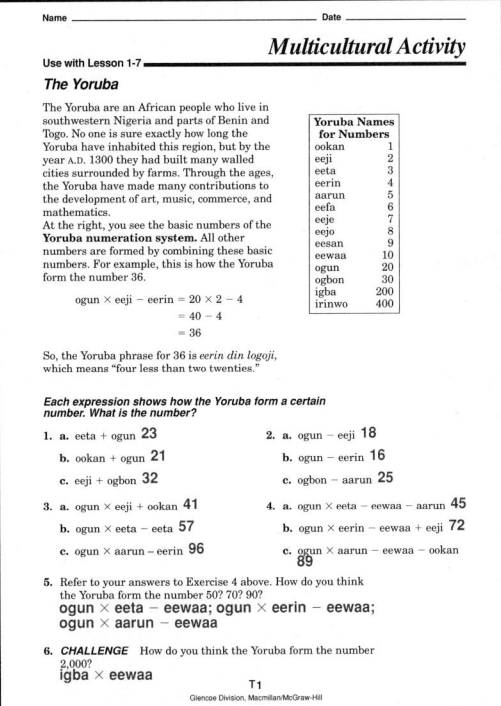

Technology Masters, p. 1

RECOMMENDED OUTSIDE RESOURCES

Books/Periodicals

Krulik, Stephen, and Jesse A. Rudnick, *A Sourcebook for Teaching Problem Solving,* Newton, MA: Allyn and Bacon, Inc., 1984.

National Council of Teachers of Mathematics, *The Ideas of Algebra, K–12, 1988 Yearbook,* Reston, VA: NCTM, 1988.

Schoen, Harold and Marilyn Aweng, *Estimation and Mental Computations,* 1986 Yearbook, NCTM, 1986.

Films/Videotapes/Videodiscs

Approximating and Estimating, Films Inc., 1971.

Guinness World Records Math Filmstrips: Problem Solving with Addition, Subtraction, Multiplication, and Division, Society for Visual Education, 1985.

Software

Estimation: Quick Solve I, Estimation: Quick Solve II, (Apple II), MECC

EduCalc, (Apple II), Houghton Mifflin Co.

For addresses of companies handling software, please refer to page T24.

Glencoe's *Interactive Mathematics: Activities and Investigations* consists of 18 units that may be used as alternatives or supplemental material for *Mathematics: Applications and Connections.* The suggested unit for this chapter is Unit 7, *Take It From the Top.* See page T18 for more information.

This two-page introduction to the chapter provides a visual, relevant way to engage students in the mathematics of the chapter. Questions are included that help students see the need to learn the mathematics in the chapter. Data in charts and graphs provide statistical information that students can analyze and interpret at this point as well as later in the chapter. The Chapter Project provides an activity that applies the mathematics of the chapter.

MAKING MATHEMATICS RELEVANT

Spotlight on Skiing

Students can apply the mathematics of this chapter to the topic of skiing. Concepts include the estimation strategies of front-end estimation and using compatible numbers, the mental-math strategy of using compensation, and the problem-solving strategies of choosing a computation method and classifying data.

Chapter

Tools for Problem Solving

Spotlight on Skiing

Have you ever wondered . . .

- How much lift tickets would cost for two adults for a three-day weekend if one lift ticket costs $25 per day?

- Why high mountains are covered in snow? Because the temperature falls 41° every time the height increases by 3,280 feet. What is the temperature on top of a mountain that is 10,000 feet high if the temperature at the foot of the mountain is 95°?

SNOW PLACES IN THE U.S.
1989 Total Snowfall

Anchorage, Alaska	68.5 inches
Juneau, Alaska	98.2 inches
Flagstaff, Arizona	96.4 inches
Denver, Colorado	59.8 inches
Sault St. Marie, Michigan	116.4 inches
Mt. Washington, New Hampshire	254.8 inches

2

"Have You Ever Wondered?" Answers
- Tickets would cost $150.
- The temperature would be about 30° below zero.

Have students examine the table on page 2 and locate the places listed on a map. Ask them how they think the snowfall in those places compares with the snowfall where they live. Is it the case that the amount of snowfall rises as you travel further north?   No. For example, the snowfall in Anchorage, the northernmost location, is less than that of Flagstaff, the southernmost location.

Data Search

A question related to these data is provided in Lesson 1-7, page 26, Exercise 46.

CHAPTER PROJECT

Students should work in small groups to complete the project. A call or visit to a travel agency might prove helpful, as would a visit to a store selling ski clothing and equipment.

If students live in an area where skiing is not found, suggest that they plan another type of recreational activity. Have the groups provide a written summary of their findings and recommendations and make a presentation to the class.

Chapter Project

Skiing
Work in a group.

1. Plan a ski weekend with your group. Choose a couple of locations and compare the costs of transportation, lodging, ski-lift tickets, and food at each location. Check with travel agents, airlines, newspapers, ski magazines, and so on.

2. Find out the cost of buying or renting clothes, accessories, and equipment.

3. What factors might affect the cost of your trip?

4. Estimate the total cost of your trip.

5. Choose the most reasonable location.

6. Compare your information with that of other groups. Is there a significant price difference in your ski weekends?

Looking Ahead

In this chapter, you will see how mathematics can be used to answer the questions about skier spending.

The major objectives of this chapter are to:

● solve problems using the four-step plan

● use estimation to solve problems

● use the order of operation

● solve algebraic expressions

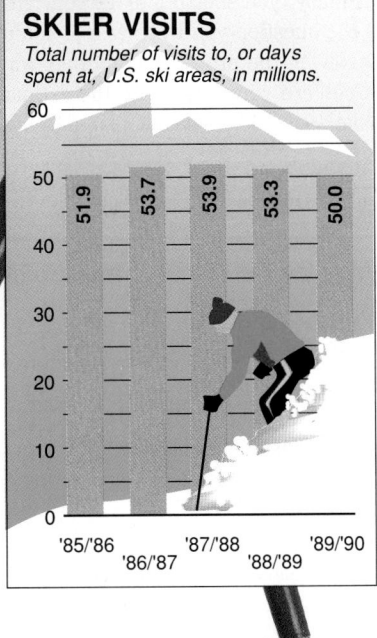

SKIER VISITS
Total number of visits to, or days spent at, U.S. ski areas, in millions.

60 —

50 — 51.9 | 53.7 | 53.9 | 53.3 | 50.0

40 —

30 —

20 —

10 —

0 —

'85/'86   '86/'87   '87/'88   '88/'89   '89/'90

3

Chapter Opener Transparency

Transparency 1-0 is available in the Transparency Package. It provides another full-color, motivating activity that you can use to capture students' interest.

NCTM Standards: 1–7, 13

Lesson Resources
- Study Guide Master 1-1
- Practice Master 1-1
- Enrichment Master 1-1
- Group Activity Card 1-1

 Transparency 1-1 contains the 5-Minute Check and a teaching aid for this lesson.

⏱ 5-Minute Check

Replace each __?__ with <, >, or = to make each sentence true.

1. 4 hours __?__ 200 minutes
   >

2. 150 minutes __?__ 3 hours
   <

3. 300 seconds __?__
   5 minutes   =

4. 2.5 days __?__ 54 hours
   >

5. 4 months __?__ 130 days
   <

---

1 FOCUS

Motivating the Lesson

Situational Problem Have students solve the following problem. *Kim ran for 0.7 hour, Will ran for 40 minutes, and Jerome ran for 1,925 seconds. How can you determine who ran for the longest time?*

2 TEACH

Using Calculators Have students work with a partner to write a key sequence for solving the lesson's opening problem. Include the steps needed to check whether an answer is reasonable. Have the pairs of students compare their results.

1-1 A Plan for Problem Solving

Objective

Solve problems using the four-step plan.

In the news, you have often heard of people who are millionaires or billionaires. You know that they are very rich, but just how rich are they?

One way to understand the size of a million is to find how many days it would take you to count to one million. You can use a four-step plan to solve this and other problems. The four steps are described below.

1. **Explore** The plan begins with understanding the problem. You need to know what information you have and need and what is asked.

2. **Plan** After understanding the problem, you should develop a plan to solve it. There are many ideas or strategies you can use. You will learn many of these in this book. It is usually helpful to make an estimate.

3. **Solve** Then you carry out your plan. If the plan does not work, try another—and another.

4. **Examine** Finally, you should look at your answer to see whether it answers the question you were asked. You may also check your answer by solving the problem in another way by using a different strategy. Compare your answer to the estimate. If the answer doesn't make sense, make a new plan and try again.

Example 1

Let's try the four-step plan with the opening problem.

Explore *What is given? What do you know?*

- There are 60 seconds in a minute.
- There are 60 minutes in an hour.
- There are 24 hours in a day.
- Assume that it takes 1 second to say a number.

What is asked?

- How many days will it take you to count to one million?

OPTIONS

Bell Ringer

Elena's bank has been charging her 10¢ for every check she writes plus a monthly service charge of $2. It will now charge a $3 service fee every month and 7¢ per check. The bank officer tells Elena these changes will save her money. How many checks must Elena write in a month for this to be so?   at least 34 checks

Plan   Since you have assumed it takes 1 second to say a number, it will take 1,000,000 seconds to count to one million. To find the number of days it takes to count to one million, first find out how many seconds there are in a day. To do this, change days to hours, hours to minutes, and minutes to seconds. Then divide to find the number of days it takes to count to one million.

Solve
- Change days to minutes.

$$24 \;\boxed{\times}\; 60 \;\boxed{=}\; \mathsf{1440} \quad \textit{minutes in one day}$$

    ↑ *hours in a day*   ↑ *minutes in an hour*

- Change minutes to seconds.

$$1440 \;\boxed{\times}\; 60 \;\boxed{=}\; \mathsf{86400} \quad \textit{seconds in one day}$$

    ↑ *minutes in a day*   ↑ *seconds in a minute*

- Divide to find the number of days it takes to count to one million.

$$1000000 \;\boxed{\div}\; 86400 \;\boxed{=}\; \mathsf{11.574074} \quad \textit{days}$$

    ↑ *count*   ↑ *seconds in a day*

- It would take *about* $11\frac{1}{2}$ days to count to one million. That means not sleeping, not eating, not doing anything except counting.

Examine   Is your answer reasonable? You can check division by multiplying.

$$11.574074 \;\boxed{\times}\; 86400 \;\boxed{=}\; \mathsf{999999.99} \quad \checkmark$$

Example 2

The trans-Alaska pipeline can deliver about two million barrels of oil a day. The 810-mile trip from Prudhoe Bay to Valdez in Alaska takes about five days. How many miles a day is this?

Explore   You need to find the number of miles traveled in one day. You know the trip is 810 miles long and the trip takes 5 days.

Lesson 1-1 A Plan for Problem Solving   **5**

5

Exercises 1-3 are designed to help you assess students' understanding through reading, writing, speaking, and modeling. You should work through these exercises with your students and then monitor their work on Guided Practice Exercises 4-5.

Close

Guide students to summarize how they can use the 4-step plan to solve a problem. Then ask them to formulate a problem based on information from their daily lives. Have students use the 4-step plan to solve each other's problems.

3 PRACTICE/APPLY

Assignment Guide
Maximum: 6–13
Minimum: 6–13

Practice Masters, p. 1

Name _____ Date _____

Practice Worksheet 1-1

A Plan for Problem Solving

Solve each problem.

1. **Sports** "Go Dogs, Go Dogs, Go, Go, Go." is a cheer for the Bulldogs' basketball team. If 15 cheerleaders yell the cheer 5 times, how many times is "Go" said?

   Explore: 15 cheerleaders yell cheer 5 times. How many times do they say "Go?"

   Plan: 5 "Go's" in one cheer. 5 × 5 is number of "Go's" for one cheerleader. 5 × 5 × 15 is total number of "Go's".

   Solve: 5 × 5 = 25 "Go's" per cheerleader. 25 × 15 = 375 "Go's" altogether.

   Examine: Seems like a lot of "Go's". Use 5 × 5 × 10 to estimate 5 × 5 × 15. The product 250 is close to 375.

2. **Cooking** A can of orange juice concentrate holds 12 ounces. If you mix it with 3 cans of water, how big a pitcher do you need to hold it all?

   Explore: One can holds 12 ounces. Mix it with 3 cans of water (12 ounces each). Pitcher has to be as big as water plus concentrate.

   Plan: 4 cans, 12 ounces each. 4 × 12 gives total amount of orange juice after mixing.

   Solve: 4 × 12 = 48 ounces of juice. I need a pitcher that holds at least 48 ounces of liquid.

   Examine: 12 oz + 12 oz + 12 oz + 12 oz = 48 oz

T1
Glencoe Division, Macmillan/McGraw-Hill

6

Plan	To find the number of miles the oil travels in one day, divide 810 by 5.

Estimate. $500 \div 5 = 100$
              $1,000 \div 5 = 200$

The answer should be between 100 and 200.

Solve	Now solve. $810 \div 5 = 162$

The oil travels 162 miles a day.

Examine	Is your answer reasonable? Remember you can use multiplication to check division: $162 \times 5 = 810$.

You can also examine the problem mentally. If the trip were made in 10 days, the oil would move 81 miles daily. So in five days (half the time), it would move twice as far or 162 miles.

Remember to compare your answer to the estimate to see if your answer is reasonable.

Checking for Understanding

Communicating Mathematics

Read and study the lesson to answer each question.

1. **Tell** why it is important to plan before solving a problem. **See margin.**

2. **Tell** two reasons for including the *Examine* step. **See margin.**

3. **Write** in your own words:
   a. what to do if your first plan does not work. **Make a new plan and solve again.**
   b. how you know it did not work. **The answer is not reasonable.**

Guided Practice

4. **Travel**   The Masons traveled 753 miles to the Great Smoky Mountains for their vacation. They took a different route home and traveled 856 miles. How many miles did they travel in all? **1,609 miles**

5. **Gardening**   Three garden hoses are joined together to reach a flower bed. Two hoses are 25 feet each and one is 50 feet. Will the combined length reach 92 feet? **yes**

OPTIONS

Meeting Needs of Middle School Students

Many middle school students can appreciate exaggeration and satire. So, when possible, try to include elements of humor in the word problems you present. Do not discourage students from doing the same and from using their imagination when they formulate their own problems.

Additional Answers

1. You need to determine how all the facts are related and what strategy to use to solve the problem.

2. You need to know whether your solution answers the question being asked and whether the solution makes sense.

Exercises

6. **Sports** Hank Aaron is the all-time home run leader of major league baseball with 755 home runs. In 1966 and 1967 alone, he hit a total of 83 home runs. If he hit 44 home runs in 1966, how many home runs did he hit in 1967? **39 home runs**

7. **Sports** There will be 460 people at the sports award banquet. If each table seats 8 people, how many tables are needed? **58 tables**

8. **Critical Thinking** Find the least four-digit number that is divisible by 2, 5, and 9. **1,080**

DATA SEARCH

9. **Smart Shopping** David saw an advertisement for piano lessons at $15.95 per lesson. How much will 12 lessons cost? **$191.40**

10. **Data Search** Refer to page 649. Approximately how much popcorn was sold in the years 1990 to 1992? **about 3 billion pounds**

11. **Transportation** Nine school buses serve Maplewood Middle School. The buses travel a total of 4,482 miles in one school week. How many miles does each bus travel weekly? **498 miles**

12. **Baseball** The table at the right gives the highest number of home runs hit in each year during the 1970s in either the National or American Leagues. What is the total number of home runs hit by the leaders during this time? **429 home runs**

Year	HR	Year	HR
1970	45	1975	38
1971	48	1976	38
1972	40	1977	52
1973	44	1978	40
1974	36	1979	48

13. **Mathematics and Media** Read the following paragraph.

> In 1906, R. Fessenden made the first radio transmission of human speech. How is sound transmitted by radio? Sound waves consist of air which is compressed and then expanded. A microphone changes the sound waves into electrical signals, and a transmitter produces radio waves which can carry the sound signals. An aerial radiates the radio waves into the air which can be received by a radio with an antenna. A speaker in the radio converts the radio waves back into sound waves.

In 1989, 343 million radios were in use in the home, 131.4 million in cars, 37.8 million in trucks and vans, and 20.8 million at work. *About* how many radios were in use? **Sample answer: about 530 million radios**

Lesson 1-1 A Plan for Problem Solving   **7**

Extending the Lesson

Mathematics and Media Remind students that many people were responsible for developing technical improvements in radio transmission during the early part of this century. These include Lee de Forest, who invented the audion, which allowed radio waves to be amplified, and Edwin H. Armstrong, whose research made long-range radio reception practicable.

Cooperative Learning Activity

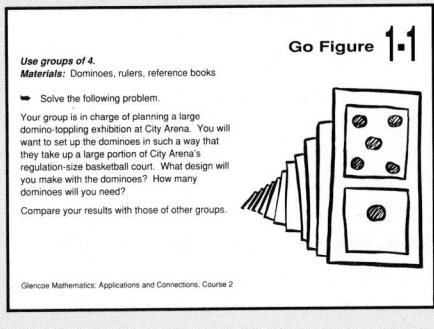

Go Figure 1·1

Use groups of 4.
Materials: Dominoes, rulers, reference books

➡ Solve the following problem.

Your group is in charge of planning a large domino-toppling exhibition at City Arena. You will want to set up the dominoes in such a way that they take up a large portion of City Arena's regulation-size basketball court. What design will you make with the dominoes? How many dominoes will you need?

Compare your results with those of other groups.

Glencoe Mathematics: Applications and Connections, Course 2

Alternate Assessment

Writing Have students work with a partner. One student formulates a multi-step problem *without* numbers. The other student writes how he or she would solve the problem using the 4-step plan. Then students switch roles.

Enrichment Masters, p. 1

Name _____ Date _____

Enrichment Worksheet 1-1

Bargain Hunt

Use the For Sale signs on this page to solve each problem. If information you need is not given, write "cannot be solved."

2 for $5
JIGSAW PUZZLES
Regularly $3.49 each

1. Kiko works Saturday mornings at the videotape store. She bought ten videotapes on sale and used a $10 employee discount coupon to help pay for the tapes. How much did she spend it all? **$81.90**

2. Toni Sue bought six handbags at the store that is going out of business. How much did she spend for each handbag? **$5.00**

Save! Sweatshirts $9.99 each Regularly $11.99

3. Sid earned $40 working after school. How much money will he have left if he buys a sweatshirt and four jigsaw puzzles? **$20.01**

Videotapes!!! **5 for $45.95!**

4. Suzette bought six jigsaw puzzles and a model airplane kit. How much change did she receive from a $20 bill? **$1.01**

This Week Only!
Model Airplane Kits $3.99
Reg. $4.99–$24.99

5. Last week Norrine bought a model airplane kit for $18.67. How much would she have saved if she had waited until this week to buy the kit? **$14.68**

6. How much would you save if you bought three sweatshirts and two jigsaw puzzles? **$7.98**

Going Out of Business
Handbags — 3 for $15

T 1
Glencoe Division, Macmillan/McGraw-Hill

1-2 Using Rounding

NCTM Standards: 1–5, 7

Lesson Resources
• Study Guide Master 1-2
• Practice Master 1-2
• Enrichment Master 1-2
• Group Activity Card 1-2

 Transparency 1-2 contains the 5-Minute Check and a teaching aid for this lesson.

⏱ 5-Minute Check
(Over Lesson 1-1)

Use the 4-step plan to solve each problem.

1. Phyllis joined speaker wires together so that the speakers to her stereo would reach into her living room. She used pieces that were 22 feet, 17 feet, and 31 feet long. Will the combined length reach 80 feet? Explain. no; 22 + 17 + 31 = 70, 70 < 80

2. Buses will be used to take 288 students to a play. If a bus has room for 40 passengers, how many buses will be needed? 8 buses

3. Pat and Mei began work at the same time. It took Mei 110 minutes to mow the lawn, while Pat took $1\frac{3}{4}$ hours to paint the fence. Who finished first? Pat

1 FOCUS

Motivating the Lesson

Activity Provide students with a price list from a music store or a video store. Have them use estimation to choose 4 items that would cost between $50 and $75 in total. Ask students to explain how they estimated the total cost of their purchase.

Objective
Estimate sums and differences using rounding.

The Journalism Department of Ross Middle School is saving to buy a computer for producing the school newspaper. Rob is the chairperson of the fund-raising committee. The computer store gave Rob a price list for the type computer needed. About how much money will the committee need to raise?

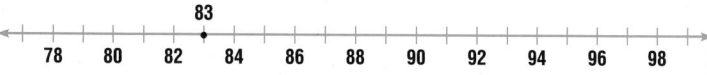

```
COMPUTER                    687.00
VGA MONITOR                 197.90
CD ROM                      217.90
PRINTER & PRINTER CARD      222.99
SOFTWARE                     82.59
```

$687.00 ⟶ $700
197.90 ⟶ 200
217.90 ⟶ 200
222.99 ⟶ 200
+ 82.59 ⟶ + 100
$1,400

You can estimate the money needed by using rounding. In this situation, round the numbers to the nearest hundred. Then add mentally.

The fund-raising committee needs to raise about $1,400 to buy the computer.

Let's review the rules for rounding.

Examples

1 Round 83 to the nearest ten.

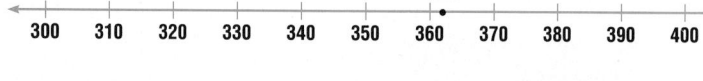

Look at the digit to the right of the tens place. Since 3 < 5, the digit in the tens place stays the same. 83 rounded to the nearest ten is 80.

2 Round 362 to the nearest hundred.

Look at the digit to the right of the hundreds place. Since 6 > 5, round the digit in the hundreds place up. 362 rounded to the nearest hundred is 400.

Estimation Hint
••••••••••••••
Sometimes it makes more sense to round each number in a sum or difference to its greatest place value and then add or subtract. For example, to estimate 1,836 + 429 + 213 + 1,208, add: 2,000 + 400 + 200 + 1,000. The estimate is 3,600.

OPTIONS

Reteaching Activity

Using Models Have students use place-value models to model addends or numbers being subtracted. For example, in Exercise 4, they can first add the hundreds squares, then adjust by adding the tens strips.

Study Guide Masters, p. 2

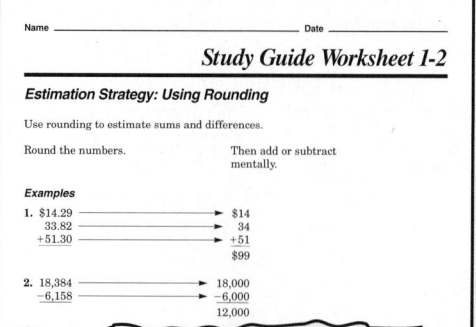

Name _____ Date _____

Study Guide Worksheet 1-2

Estimation Strategy: Using Rounding

Use rounding to estimate sums and differences.

Round the numbers.   Then add or subtract mentally.

Examples

1. $14.29 ⟶ $14
   33.82 ⟶ 34
   +51.30 ⟶ +51
   $99

2. 18,384 ⟶ 18,000
   −6,158 ⟶ −6,000
   12,000

Estimation provides a quick answer when an exact number is not necessary. You can also estimate to check the reasonableness of an answer.

Example 3

Consumer Math   Suppose you stopped at the local market to pick up the ingredients for tonight's family dinner. You purchase some vegetable oil, chicken, bacon, and green pepper. The register tape for your purchase is shown below. Is the total reasonable?

```
Lucky Markets
   June 10

Oil         2.55
Chicken     5.47
Bacon       2.15
Gr pepper   1.09
TOTAL      11.26
```

Round each item to the nearest dollar amount.

$2.55 rounds to $3.
$5.47 rounds to $5.
$2.15 rounds to $2.
$1.09 rounds to $1.

The total bill should be about $3 + $5 + $2 + $1 or $11. Therefore, a total of $11.26 is reasonable.

Checking for Understanding

Communicating Mathematics

Read and study the lesson to answer each question.

1. **Write** two reasons you might use estimation. **See margin.**
2. **Tell** how you would round 677 to the nearest ten using the number line below. **See margin.**

<------+------>

3. **Show** how you would use rounding to find the difference between 764 and 189. **See margin.**

Guided Practice

Estimate using rounding. **Sample answers are given.**

4. 532 + 625 + 419 **1,500**
5. 927 − 618 **300**
6. 427 + 962 + 520 **1,900**
7. 8,429 − 6,258 **2,000**
8. $35.80 + $29.90 + $41.90 **$110**
9. 15,734 − 3,212 **13,000**
10. 3,624 + 521 + 8,201 **12,300**
11. 680 − 83 **600**

12. Kelly's Family Restaurant offers a Healthy Start Breakfast Special. The menu items and the number of calories are shown in the chart at the right. About how many calories are there in the meal? **600 calories**

Menu Item	Calories
Fresh Fruit Salad	50
Nonfat-Strawberry Yogurt	190
Whole-wheat English Muffin	218
Skim Milk	90

Lesson 1-2 Estimation Strategy: Using Rounding   **9**

Limited English Proficiency

Review the meaning of each place value position. List a group of numbers on the chalkboard and have students come up and circle the digits that are in the ones, tens, hundreds, and thousands places.

Additional Answers

1. It provides a quick answer when an exact number is not necessary and it allows you to check the reasonableness of an answer.
2. 677 is closer to 680 than to 670.
3. Round 764 to 800 and round 189 to 200. Then subtract mentally. 800 − 200 = 600

---

2 TEACH

Using Cooperative Groups

Work through the opening problem with students. Then provide groups with a supermarket price list. Have one group member choose a list of items to buy. Then have two other students in the group use rounding to estimate total cost.

More Examples

For Example 1

Round 62 to the nearest 10.

Since 2 < 5, round to 60.

For Example 2

Round 558 to the nearest hundred.

558 is closer to 600 than it is to 500. So round to 600.

For Example 3

Estimate the sum $4.77 + $2.02 + $8.38 + $7.12. about $22

Practice Masters, p.2

Name _____   Date _____

Practice Worksheet 1-2

Estimation Strategy: Using Rounding

Use rounding to estimate.   Limit student time for estimation worksheets. Accept all reasonable estimates.

1. 5,823 + 3,246   **9,000**
2. 3,298 + 2,049   **5,000**
3. 6,934 + 6,841   **14,000**
4. 2,910 + 1,208   **4,000**
5. 8,592 − 6,228   **3,000**
6. 5,249 − 1,004   **4,000**
7. 9,981 − 7,378   **3,000**
8. 6,938 − 2,180   **5,000**
9. 12,890 − 3,348   **10,000**
10. 14,888 − 7,491   **8,000**
11. 19,482 − 13,088   **6,000**
12. 37,890 − 14,529   **23,000**
13. 9,399 − 5,094   **4,000**
14. 7,930 − 892   **7,000**
15. 72,917 − 2,847   **70,000**
16. 5,023 + 2,285 + 1,529   **9,000**
17. 4,298 + 5,841 + 6,294   **16,000**
18. 8,914 + 846 + 2,912   **13,000**
19. $5.25 + $2.19 + $3.98   **$11**
20. $9.17 + $0.49 + $3.47   **$12**
21. $7.45 + $2.91 + $1.23   **$11**
22. $3.98 + $2.98 + $1.98   **$9**
23. $8.45 − $3.29   **$5**
24. $15.69 − $8.29   **$8**
25. the difference of 9,208 and 4,100   **5,000**
26. the sum of 48,939 and 45,230   **94,000**
27. the sum of 65,903 and 3,893   **70,000**
28. the sum of 81,360 and 390   **81,000**
29. the sum of $6.23, $8.49 and $1.12   **$15**
30. the difference of $17.33 and $12.15   **$5**
31. the sum of $12.03 and $2.19   **$14**
32. the difference of $19.34 and $0.19   **$19**
33. the sum of 42,990 and 39,349   **82,000**
34. the difference of 88,888 and 34,840   **55,000**

T2
Glencoe Division, Macmillan/McGraw-Hill

Checking for Understanding

Exercises 1-3 are designed to help you assess students' understanding through reading, writing, speaking, and modeling. You should work through these exercises with your students and then monitor their work on Guided Practice Exercises 4-12.

Close

Have students explain the strategy of using rounding to estimate as if to someone who has never heard of it.

3 PRACTICE/APPLY

Assignment Guide

Maximum: 13–33

Minimum: 13–23 odd, 25–32

For **Extra Practice**, see p. 572.

Alternate Assessment

Writing Provide students with a consumer catalogue. Have them create estimation problems from the catalogue items.

Enrichment Masters, p. 2

Exercises

Independent Practice

Estimate by rounding.

13. $4,522 + 6,059$ **11,000**

14. $7,247 - 4,126$ **3,000**

15. $15,923 - 6,782$ **9,000**

16. $8,723 - 5,247$ **4,000**

17. $6,522 + 493 + 8,026$ **15,000**

18. $5,278 + 4,258 + 6,233$ **15,000**

19. $\$6.68 + \$9.00 + \$2.42$ **\$18**

20. $65,378 - 23,753$ **41,000**

21. Estimate the sum of 6,015 and 2,843. **9,000**

22. Estimate the difference of 4,963 and 519. **4,400**

23. Estimate the difference of 37,444 and 13,127. **24,000**

24. Estimate the sum of 3,988 and 12,019. **16,000**

Mixed Review

25. *True* or *False:* In the four-step plan, the *Solve* step comes last. *(Lesson 1–1)* **false**

26. **Travel** A bicyclist planning a 1,800-mile trip decides that he can ride 15 miles per hour for 6 hours each day. How many days will it take for him to complete the trip? *(Lesson 1–1)* **20 days**

27. **Smart Shopping** At the grocery store, Jeanne is deciding between purchasing a 50-ounce bottle of shampoo priced at 10¢ per ounce and a 30-ounce bottle priced at 20¢ per ounce. Which bottle will cost more? *(Lesson 1–1)* **30-ounce bottle; $6 as opposed to $5**

28. **Music** A popular rock band is putting together a new CD. They can use up to 60 minutes of music. They have selected 6 songs that are each 4 minutes long and 8 songs that are each 5 minutes long. Will all of their selections fit on the CD? *(Lesson 1–1)* **no**

Problem Solving and Applications

29. **Education** Georgia Institute of Technology and Georgia State University are in Atlanta, Georgia. The enrollment at Georgia Tech is 12,891, and the enrollment at Georgia State is 24,101. Estimate how many more students attend Georgia State than Georgia Tech. **about 10,000 students**

30. **Clubs** The Band Boosters sold 5,720 boxes of cookies the first week of the fund-raiser to buy new band uniforms. 6,147 boxes were sold in the second week. *About* how many boxes of cookies were sold in the first two weeks? **about 12,000 boxes**

31. about 9,200 stations

31. **Broadcasting** 2,496 radio stations in the United States specialize in country music. There are 2,307 adult contemporary stations, 1,220 religious stations, 972 top 40 stations, 723 oldies stations, 491 album rock stations, 488 talk stations, and 460 news stations. *About* how many radio stations are there in the United States?

32. Sample answer: 975 + 864

32. **Critical Thinking** Given the digits 4, 5, 6, 7, 8, and 9, and using each digit only once, form two three-digit numbers that give you the greatest sum.

33. **Journal Entry** In this course, you will be required to keep a journal. Write two or three sentences in your journal that describe what you expect to learn in this course. **See students' work.**

OPTIONS

Extending the Lesson

Generalizing Ask students how they can increase the degree of accuracy in the rounding strategy for making estimates. Have them give an example. Round to thousands instead of ten-thousands: **23,**107 + **21,**216 $\longrightarrow$ **44,000**

Cooperative Learning Activity

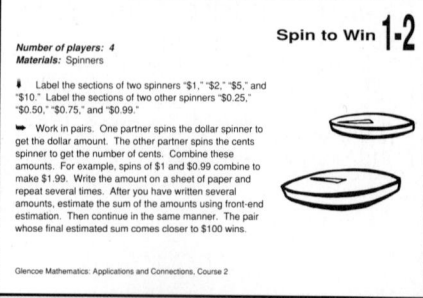

Spin to Win 1-2

Number of players: 4
Materials: Spinners

♦ Label the sections of two spinners "$1," "$2," "$5," and "$10." Label the sections of two other spinners "$0.25," "$0.50," "$0.75," and "$0.99."

➥ Work in pairs. One partner spins the dollar spinner to get the dollar amount. The other partner spins the cents spinner to get the number of cents. Combine these amounts. For example, spins of $1 and $0.99 combine to make $1.99. Write the amount on a sheet of paper and repeat several times. After you have written several amounts, estimate the sum of the amounts using front-end estimation. Then continue in the same manner. The pair whose final estimated sum comes closer to $100 wins.

Glencoe Mathematics: Applications and Connections, Course 2

1-3 Using Patterns

Objective

Estimate products and quotients using patterns.

The city of Lillehammer, Norway, hosted the 1994 Winter Olympic Games. The organizers constructed the Olympic facilities with the heritage of the country and the Games in mind. The Gjovick Olympic Cavern Hall, which was the site of the hockey competition, was literally carved out of Hovdetoppen Mountain. 29,000 truckloads of rock were removed to build the arena. If a truck holds about 5 cubic yards of rock, about how many cubic yards of rock were removed?

We need to estimate the product of 29,000 and 5. You can use patterns to estimate products. Round factors to their greatest place value position. Do not change any factors that contain only 1 digit. Then multiply by multiples of 10, 100, or 1,000.

DID YOU KNOW

Building the Olympic hockey arena underground had many advantages. For one, valuable land space was saved. Also, the constant temperature underground saves energy on heating and cooling.

Now estimate $29,000 \times 5$.

Step 1 Round 29,000 to 30,000.
Step 2 Look for a pattern. Solve mentally.

$3 \times 5 = 15$
$30 \times 5 = 150$
$300 \times 5 = 1,500$
$3,000 \times 5 = 15,000$
$30,000 \times 5 = 150,000$

About 150,000 cubic yards of rock were removed to build Gjovik Olympic Cavern Hall.

Examples

1 Estimate $2,268 \times 6$.

    Step 1 Round 2,268 to 2,000.

    Step 2 Look for a pattern Solve mentally.

    $2 \times 6 = 12$
    $20 \times 6 = 120$
    $200 \times 6 = 1,200$
    $2,000 \times 6 = 12,000$

    $2,238 \times 6$ is about 12,000.

2 Estimate 21×404.

    Step 1 Round 21 to 20. Round 404 to 400.

    Step 2 Look for a pattern. Solve mentally.

    $20 \times 4 = 80$
    $20 \times 40 = 800$
    $20 \times 400 = 8,000$

    21×404 is about 8,000.

Lesson 1-3 Estimation Strategy: Using Patterns **11**

OPTIONS

Reteaching Activity

Using Applications Have students use estimation to find the approximate annual salary needed to earn $1,100,000 in several lifetime careers, such as 22 years, 34 years, and 45 years.

Study Guide Masters, p. 3

Name _____ Date _____

Study Guide Worksheet 1-3

Estimation Strategy: Using Patterns

You can use patterns to estimate products and quotients mentally.

Example 1 Estimate 289×7.
  Step 1 Round 289 to 300.
  Step 2 Look for a pattern and solve mentally.

    $3 \times 7 = 21$
    $30 \times 7 = 210$
    $300 \times 7 = 2,100$
    289×7 is about 2,100.

Example 2 Estimate $5,712 \div 73$.
  Step 1 Round 73 to 70 and round 5,712 to 5,600 since 56 is divisible by 7.
  Step 2 Solve mentally.

    $5,600 \div 7 = 800$
    $5,600 \div 70 = 80$
    $5,712 \div 73$ is about 80.

Estimate using patterns. Answers may vary. Accept all reasonable estimates.

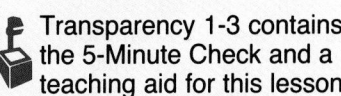
NCTM Standards: 1–5, 7

Lesson Resources
• Study Guide Master 1-3
• Practice Master 1-3
• Enrichment Master 1-3
• Group Activity Card 1-3

Transparency 1-3 contains the 5-Minute Check and a teaching aid for this lesson.

⏱ 5-Minute Check
(Over Lesson 1-2)

Estimate. Use rounding estimation.

1. $298 + 519 + 774$
  1,600

2. $\$46.59 + \$8.75 + \$12.29$ $68

3. $5,649 - 3,118$ 3,000

4. $55,463 - 17,295$
  41,000

5. Ed bought groceries for $4.99, $2.05, $8.79, and $12.45. The total on the register tape was $46.73. Is the total reasonable? Explain.   no; The sum is *about* $28.

---

1 FOCUS

Motivating the Lesson

Situational Problem Ask students to determine which store has the better price for Dog Yummies. Have them explain their strategy.

• Al's Market sells 5 pounds for $14.88.

• Alice's Market sells 12 pounds for $45.95.

2 TEACH

Using Charts Have students refer to the chart on a state road map that shows the distances between major cities. Then have them choose two cities and estimate the number of hours to travel between them at 28 mi/h, 39 mi/h, and 47 mi/h.

11

More Examples

For Example 1

Estimate 381 × 4.   1,600

For Example 2

Estimate 731 × 8.   5,600

For Example 3

Today, most large passenger jets can easily make the 4,800-kilometer flight across the Atlantic Ocean in about 7 hours. *About* how fast do these planes travel in kilometers per hour?   700 km/h

Checking for Understanding

Exercises 1-2 are designed to help you assess students' understanding through reading, writing, speaking, and modeling. You should work through these exercises with your students and then monitor their work on Guided Practice Exercises 3-17.

You can also use patterns to estimate quotients. To do this, round the divisor to its greatest place-value position. Then replace the dividend with a number that you know will divide easily.

Example 3   *Problem Solving*

Entertainment   The first Mickey Mouse animated film, *Steamboat Willie*, was released in 1928. Ub Iwerks drew the 14,400 pictures in the film in just 24 days! *About* how many pictures did he draw per day?

We need to estimate 14,400 ÷ 24.

Step 1   Round 24 to 20. *Round divisor to its greatest place value.*

Step 2   Round 14,400 to 14,000, since you know 14 is divisible by 2.

Step 3   Use the pattern to divide mentally.

$$14 \div 2 = 7$$
$$140 \div 20 = 7$$
$$1,400 \div 20 = 70$$
$$14,000 \div 20 = 700$$

Ub Iwerks drew *about* 700 pictures a day. That's a lot of pictures!

Checking for Understanding

Communicating Mathematics

Read and study the lesson to answer each question.

1. **Tell** how you would use patterns to estimate 54 × 689.   **See margin.**

2. **Write** the number to which you would round 4,234 to estimate the quotient 4,234 ÷ 7. Explain your answer.   **See margin.**

Guided Practice

Estimate using patterns.   **Sample answers are given.**

3. 3 × 57   **180**   4. 2 × 8,192   **16,000**   5. 5 × 42   **200**   6. 8 × 18   **160**

7. 86 × 4   **360**   8. 678 × 9   **6,300**   9. 377 × 4   **1,600**   10. 4 × 784   **3,200**

11. 622 ÷ 5   **120**   12. 389 ÷ 2   **200**   13. 186 ÷ 4   **50**   14. 731 ÷ 7   **100**

15. 3,568 ÷ 5   **800**   16. 6,104 ÷ 6   **1,000**   17. 7,837 ÷ 4   **2,000**

Exercises

Independent Practice

Estimate using patterns.   **Sample answers are given.**

18. 129 × 3   **300**   19. 695 × 8   **5,600**   20. 41 × 207   **8,000**   21. 105 ÷ 4   **25**

22. 123 ÷ 6   **20**   23. 78 × 42   **3,200**   24. 778 ÷ 8   **100**   25. 6,321 × 7   **4,200**

26. 9,465 ÷ 3   **3,000**   27. 1,041 ÷ 4   **250**   28. 459 × 62   **30,000**

29. Estimate 792 times 9.   **7,200**

30. Estimate the quotient of 6,152 and 58.   **100**

OPTIONS

Gifted and Talented Needs

Have students work in groups to make up a game for two or more players that requires using patterns to make estimates. The game should use a number cube or a spinner as a way to choose divisors. It should also have a chart or other way to show a range of dividends and a way to keep score.

Additional Answers

1. Round 54 to 50 and 689 to 700.
   50 × 7 = 350
   50 × 70 = 3,500
   50 × 700 = 35,000

2. Sample answer: 4,200; 42 is easily divisible by 7.

Mixed Review

31. **Sports** A baseball stadium holds 20,000 people. If 3,650 people can be seated in the bleachers, how many seats are available in the rest of the stadium? *(Lesson 1-1)* **16,350 seats**

32. **Construction** A new highway under construction requires 4 tons of concrete for every 2 miles of road. How many tons of concrete will be needed to build 100 miles of the highway? *(Lesson 1-1)* **200 tons**

33. Use rounding to estimate the sum of 3,425 and 6,243. *(Lesson 1-2)* **9,000**

34. **Summer Camp** A total of 486 campers are expected to arrive at Camp Miami. If 269 have already arrived, *about* how many campers are still expected? Use rounding to estimate. *(Lesson 1-2)* **200 campers**

35. about $2,800

35. **Banking** Anthony has a savings account that currently has a balance of $2,346.21. He deposits a check in the amount of $521.19. *About* how much money is in his account now? Use rounding to estimate. *(Lesson 1-2)*

Problem Solving and Applications

7. about 3,000
3. about 40 times as tall

36. **Art** In a wheat field near Duns, Scotland, a reproduction of Vincent van Gogh's *Sunflowers* was created with 250,000 plants and flowers. The "painting" covered a 46,000-square foot area. *About* how many flowers and plants were planted per square foot? **about 5 flowers and plants**

37. **Animals** An elephant in a zoo will eat 57 cabbages in a week. *About* how many cabbages does an elephant eat in a year?

38. **History** On July 4, 1986, the restored Statue of Liberty was dedicated with concerts, ethnic festivals, fireworks, and the swearing in of 25,000 new American citizens. The statue is 305 feet 1 inch tall from the base of the pedestal to the top of the torch. The statue's index finger is 8 feet long. *About* how many times taller is the statue than the finger is long?

39. **Money** The average 13- to 15-year-old received $15 a week in allowance in 1992. About how much allowance money did the average teen receive in one year? **about $750**

40. **Travel** Big Ben is the largest bell in the clock located in London's Houses of Parliament. The bell weighs about 27,000 pounds. This is about 68 times as much as the hammer that strikes the bell weighs. *About* how much does that hammer weigh? **about 400 pounds**

41. **Critical Thinking** Kara has budgeted $60 a month to pay for a new computer. She is trying to decide between two similar computers at MicroMax. One computer costs $789 over 12 months, and the other costs $829 over 16 months. Which computer can Kara afford? **$829 computer**

42. **Journal Entry** According to a recent magazine, "The average American eats 10 cans of tuna a year." How do you think they arrived at this estimate? Find other estimates in a newspaper or magazine and describe how you think being able to estimate products and quotients will be useful to you as you read. **See students' work.**

Lesson 1-3 Estimation Strategy: Using Patterns　**13**

Extending the Lesson

Consumer Connection Students have learned that they can use patterns to estimate quotients. Have students give an example, using prices from a store's advertisement or price list, of how they can also use this strategy to estimate *products*.

Cooperative Learning Activity

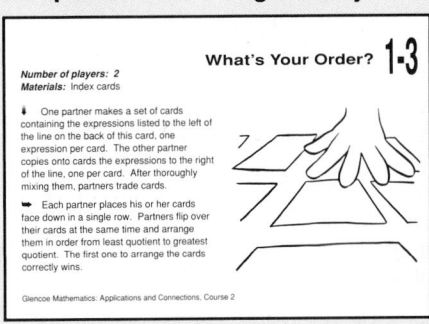

What's Your Order? 1-3

Number of players: 2
Materials: Index cards

One partner makes a set of cards containing the expressions listed to the left of the line on the back of this card, one expression per card. The other partner copies onto cards the expressions to the right of the line, one per card. After thoroughly mixing them, partners trade cards.

Each partner places his or her cards face down in a single row. Partners flip over their cards at the same time and arrange them in order from least quotient to greatest quotient. The first one to arrange the cards correctly wins.

Glencoe Mathematics: Applications and Connections, Course 2

Error Analysis

Watch for students who correctly identify a pattern, but then divide incorrectly.

Prevent by having students check their answers for reasonableness, then check with a calculator.

Close

Have students each write two word problems, each of which could be solved by using patterns to estimate quotients.
One problem should involve a 1-digit divisor and the other a 2-digit divisor.

3 PRACTICE/APPLY

Assignment Guide
Maximum: 18–42
Minimum: 19–29 odd, 37–41

For **Extra Practice,** see p. 572.

Alternate Asssessment

Writing Have students write a description of the difference between the two estimation strategies they have used, estimation by rounding and estimation by patterns.

Enrichment Masters, p. 3

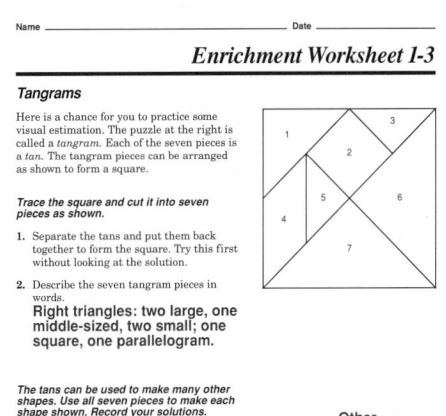

Name _____ Date _____

Enrichment Worksheet 1-3

Tangrams

Here is a chance for you to practice some visual estimation. The puzzle at the right is called a *tangram*. Each of the seven pieces is a *tan*. The tangram pieces can be arranged as shown to form a square.

Trace the square and cut it into seven pieces as shown.

1. Separate the tans and put them back together to form the square. Try this first without looking at the solution.

2. Describe the seven tangram pieces in words.
Right triangles: two large, one middle-sized, two small; one square, one parallelogram.

The tans can be used to make many other shapes. Use all seven pieces to make each shape shown. Record your solutions.

Other arrangements are possible.

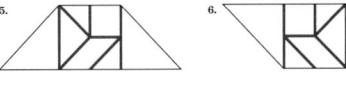

T 3
Glencoe Division, Macmillan/McGraw-Hill

1-4 Determine Reasonable Answers

NCTM Standards: 1–5, 7

NCTM Standards: 1–5, 7

Lesson Resources
• Study Guide Master 1-4
• Practice Master 1-4
• Enrichment Master 1-4
• Group Activity Card 1-4

 Transparency 1-4 contains the 5-Minute Check and a teaching aid for this lesson.

⏱ 5-Minute Check
(Over Lesson 1-3)

Estimate using patterns.

1. 538 ÷ 9   60
2. 331 ÷ 42   8
3. 2,688 ÷ 8   300
4. 4,177 ÷ 70   60
5. 5,924 ÷ 30   200

1 FOCUS

Motivating the Lesson

Questioning Ask students if they have ever found a mistake on a store receipt. How did they determine that a mistake had been made?

2 TEACH

Using Cooperative Groups
Before going over the introductory problem and the examples, have students work in pairs to estimate the answers to 12 + 72 + 92 + 119 and 1,993 ÷ 61. Have them discuss the estimation strategies they used. Then have students use a calculator to find the exact answers.

Objective
Use estimation to determine whether answers to problems are reasonable.

Dylan earns $4.25 an hour working weekends as a waiter at The Ice Cream Dream. After he had been working there 6 months, the manager gave Dylan a $0.35 per hour raise. Dylan used a calculator to determine that if he works 12 hours a week, his weekly pay will increase by $42.00. Is this answer reasonable?

Using a calculator is a fast and simple way to do calculations. But sometimes hitting the wrong key, misentering the numbers, or misunderstanding the order in which the calculator completes calculations can cause errors. Being able to determine if an answer you find on a calculator is reasonable is an important skill.

You can use estimation to determine if an answer is reasonable. If the estimate is close to the answer found on the calculator, the calculator answer is probably correct.

Estimate the amount of increase Dylan's raise should provide each week. Since we are finding a product, using a pattern to estimate is appropriate.

Step 1   Round 12 to 10.

Step 2   Round $0.35 to 0.4.

Step 3   Look for a pattern. $10 \times 4 = 40$
Solve mentally. $10 \times 0.4 = 4$

Dylan's raise should increase his pay by about $4 per week. So his calculation of a $42.00 increase is not reasonable.

Example 1

Simone got an answer of 6.15 when she divided 4,182 by 680 on her calculator. Is this answer reasonable?

Step 1   Round 680 to 700.

Step 2   Round 4,182 to 4,200.

Step 3   Look for a pattern. $42 \div 7 = 6$
Solve mentally. $420 \div 70 = 6$
$4,200 \div 700 = 6$

Yes, 6.15 is a reasonable answer.

OPTIONS

Reteaching Activity

Using Applications Tell students that they have received $50 as a birthday gift. Have them choose items from advertisements in a newspaper or catalog and estimate the cost of the items to determine if they will have enough money to buy the items.

Study Guide Masters, p. 4

Name _____ Date _____

Study Guide Worksheet 1-4

Problem-Solving Strategy: Determine Reasonable Answers

You can use estimation to determine whether an answer is reasonable.

Example   Kevin got an answer of 3,311 when he used his calculator to multiply 43 and 77. Is this answer reasonable?

Use a pattern to estimate the product 43 × 77.

Step 1   Round 43 to 40 and 77 to 80.
Step 2   Look for a pattern.
Solve mentally.

$4 \times 8 = 32$
$40 \times 8 = 320$
$40 \times 80 = 3,200$

Finding an estimate to determine if a calculation is reasonable can be helpful in everyday situations.

Example 2 *Problem Solving*

Smart Shopping Kim bought a pair of sunglasses, two rolls of film, and a bottle of sunscreen to take on her vacation. The sunglasses were $15.79, the film was $2.29 per roll, and the sunscreen was $3.69. The cashier asked for $24.06. Is that total reasonable?

Estimate the sum to determine if the total from the cashier is reasonable.

Round each number to the nearest dollar.

$15.69	→	$16.00
2.29	→	2.00
2.29	→	2.00
+ 3.69	→	+ 4.00
		$24.00

Yes, the cashier's total is reasonable.

Checking for Understanding

Communicating Mathematics

Read and study the lesson to answer each question.

1. **Explain** how you could use estimation to determine if an answer you found with a calculator is reasonable. **See margin.**

2. **Tell** of a situation where you think estimating to check the reasonableness of an answer will be helpful to you. **See students' work.**

3. **Tell** where you think Dylan make a mistake in calculating his weekly pay raise. **See margin.**

Guided Practice

Determine whether the answers shown are reasonable.

4. $669 + 217 = 776$ **no**

5. $35 + 82 + 110 = 227$ **yes**

6. $4,982 \times 11 = 54,802$ **yes**

7. $11,472 \times 8 = 910,776$ **no**

8. $12,324 \div 52 = 112$ **no**

9. $81,576 \div 792 = 103$ **yes**

10. You need to buy 3 cans of tuna fish at 69¢ each, a box of crackers at $1.99, and a gallon of milk at $2.19 for dinner tonight. Should you take $5.00 or $10.00 with you to the store? **$10.00**

Exercises

Independent Practice

Determine whether the answers shown are reasonable.

11. $921 + 1,193 = 2,114$ **yes**

12. $974 + 601 = 1,125$ **no**

13. $1,923 - 411 = 1,412$ **no**

14. $\$15.29 - \$3.88 = \$11.41$ **yes**

Lesson 1-4 Problem-Solving Strategy: Determine Reasonable Answers **15**

Gifted and Talented Needs

Present the following problem to a group of students. Then ask them to create mental-math problems similar to it for use in a future math contest.

Charlotte received $12 from her mother and $10.50 from her father to spend at the street fair. Charlotte bought lunch for $4.82 and a T-shirt for $14.28 and had $1.20 when she returned home. Is this reasonable? no

Additional Answers

1. Use patterns or rounding to estimate the answers. Then calculate. If the calculated answer is close to the estimate, then the answer is probably correct.

3. The answer Dylan got is about ten times the actual answer. He probably misplaced the decimal point when he used the calculator.

Close

Have students explain why being able to estimate to determine reasonableness is important.

3 PRACTICE/APPLY

Assignment Guide
Maximum: 11–35
Minimum: 11–25 odd, 27–35

For **Extra Practice,** see p. 572.

Alternate Assessment

Writing   Have students write a word problem that requires determining if an answer is reasonable. Have students exchange problems and solve.

Enrichment Masters, p. 4

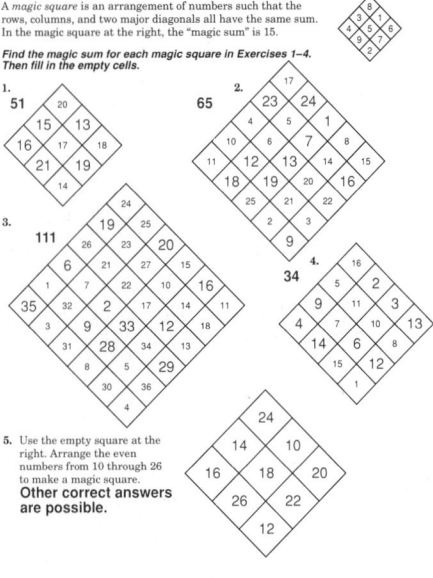

15. $740 \times 9 = 6,660$ **yes**
16. $1,539 \times 88 = 105,432$ **no**
17. $\$44.98 \times 12 = \$639.76$ **no**
18. $9,101 - 109 = 8,992$ **yes**
19. $109 + 8,802 = 9,411$ **no**
20. $\$0.88 \times 144 = \$189.72$ **no**
21. $4,104 \div 18 = 228$ **yes**
22. $\$14.16 \div \$0.59 = 24$ **yes**
23. $105,336 \div 198 = 532$ **yes**
24. $1,921 + 5,992 + 308 = 8,641$ **no**
25. $\$6.59 + \$3.19 + \$5.59 + \$0.77 = \$19.16$ **no**
26. $137,294 - 19,247 = 118,047$ **yes**

Mixed Review   27. **Sports**   A triathalon competition consists of running 10 miles, bicycling 35 miles, and swimming 3 miles. How many miles will each athlete travel during the competition? *(Lesson 1–1)* **48 miles**

28. **Politics**   A total of 326 members of the U.S. House of Representatives voted on a budget bill. If 212 of them voted against the bill, *about* how many representatives voted in favor of the bill? Use rounding to estimate. *(Lesson 1–2)* **about 100 members**

29. Estimate $4,391 + 7,887$ by rounding. *(Lesson 1–2)* **about 12,000**

30. **Exercise**   Each year the average American walks 1,250 miles. *About* how many miles does he or she walk in a day? Use patterns to estimate. *(Lesson 1–3)* **about 3 miles per day**

34. yes;
$5 \times 400 = 2,000$

31. **Medicine**   Dr. Mudd spends about 17 minutes with each patient she sees. *About* how many patients should the office manager schedule for an 8-hour work day? Use a pattern to estimate. *(Lesson 1–3)* **about 24 patients**

Problem Solving and Applications   32. **Employment**   When Hernan received his work schedule for the week, he multiplied the 21 hours he was scheduled to work by his wage of $4.75 per hour. His calculator showed that his pay for the week should be $82.50. Is this answer reasonable? **no; $20 \times 5 = 100$**

33. **Community Service**   There were four drop-off centers for the community food drive. One center collected 2,629 cans of food, the second collected 2,892 cans, the third collected 4,429 cans, and the fourth collected 3,298 cans. The newsletter editor reported that over 13,000 cans of food were collected. Is this answer reasonable? **yes; $3,000 + 3,000 + 4,000 + 3,000 = 13,000$**

34. **Money**   A magazine article on saving money suggested that people cut $5 a day from their spending to save $1,825 in a year. Is this reasonable?

35. **Critical Thinking**   Tamoko read the article below the sports section of the local newspaper. Do all of the numbers in the article seem reasonable to you?

> **Madison, Wis.** - Marcus Cox, a fifth-year senior from Columbus, Georgia, continues to start at fullback for Wisconsin's unbeaten football team.
>
>   Cox caught three passes for 87 yards last week as Wisconsin knocked off Air Force, 24–12.
>
>   For the season, Cox has caught seven passes for 118 yeards (16.9 yards per reception). He has also rushed for 63 yards on 29 carries (5.2 yards per carry).
>
>   Wisconsin meets North Carolina in Madison this Saturday.

no; 63 yards in 29 carries is about 2 yards per carry, not 5.2

16   Chapter 1 Tools for Problem Solving

OPTIONS

Extending the Lesson

Consumer Connection   Present the following situation. *You receive your menu at a restaurant and you make your selection. Should you overestimate or underestimate the total bill to make sure that you have enough money?*
Explain.   **overestimate; you are less likely to be short of money**

Cooperative Learning Activity

1-5 Choose the Method of Computation

Objective

Solve problems by choosing estimation, mental math, paper and pencil, or calculator.

Ms. Meadows gave her class this problem. Choose five digits. Use all five digits to make a two-digit number and a three-digit number that when multiplied have the greatest product possible.

Which method of computation would you use to solve this problem? You can use estimation, mental math, pencil and paper, or calculator.

Explore What do you know?

You can use any five digits. You need to make a two-digit and a three-digit number, using all the digits you chose.

What are you trying to find?

Which pair of numbers has the greatest product?

Plan Use the chart below to help you decide which method of computation to use.

Do you
need an exact — no → Estimate.
answer?

|
yes
↓

Do you   Are   Are
see a   — no →   there   — no →   there
pattern or   simple   large
number   calculations   numbers
fact   to do?   or many
                                                        calculations?

| | |
yes   yes   yes
↓   ↓   ↓

Use mental math.   Use paper   Use a
                          and pencil.   calculator.

Since you need an exact answer and you need to multiply all the number pairs, use a calculator.

Lesson 1-5 Problem-Solving Strategy: Choose the Method of Computation   **17**

Study Guide Masters, p. 5

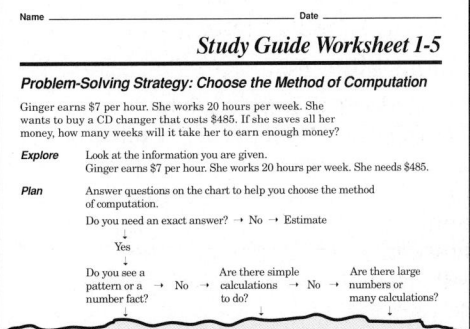

Name _____ Date _____

Study Guide Worksheet 1-5

Problem-Solving Strategy: Choose the Method of Computation

Ginger earns $7 per hour. She works 20 hours per week. She wants to buy a CD changer that costs $485. If she saves all her money, how many weeks will it take her to earn enough money?

Explore Look at the information you are given.
Ginger earns $7 per hour. She works 20 hours per week. She needs $485.

Plan Answer questions on the chart to help you choose the method of computation.

Do you need an exact answer? → No → Estimate
↓
Yes
↓
Do you see a   Are there simple   Are there large
pattern or a → No → calculations → No →   numbers or
number fact?   to do?   many calculations?
↓   ↓   ↓

Lesson Resources
• Study Guide Master 1-5
• Practice Master 1-5
• Enrichment Master 1-5
• Evaluation Master, Quiz A, p. 7
• Group Activity Card 1-5

 Transparency 1-5 contains the 5-Minute Check and a teaching aid for this lesson.

⏱ 5-Minute Check
(Over Lesson 1-4)

Determine whether the answers shown are reasonable.

1. $88 + 53 = 141$ yes
2. $811 - 74 = 687$ no
3. $294 \times 19 = 5{,}106$ no
4. You bought three cans of juice for 89¢ each. Is $3.37 a reasonable total?   no

---

1 FOCUS

Motivating the Lesson

Questioning Ask students to read the opening problem. Ask them to guess whether the greatest possible product would be less than 100,000 if all 5 digits may be the same.   yes; 999×99 is less than 1000×100.

2 TEACH

Using Problem Solving Begin by discussing with students the ways in which each computation method is useful. Then discuss strategies they could use to solve the problem, such as making and using an organized list, accounting for all possibilities, guessing and checking, and looking for a pattern using simpler numbers.

Solve · Let's choose the digits 1, 2, 3, 4, and 5. Place the 5 and 4 in the greatest place-value positions of both numbers. Keep track of the products.

521 ⊠ 43 ⊟ 22403
531 ⊠ 42 ⊟ 22302
532 ⊠ 41 ⊟ 21812
432 ⊠ 51 ⊟ 22032
431 ⊠ 52 ⊟ 22412 ✓
421 ⊠ 53 ⊟ 22313

The two-digit and three-digit numbers that have the greatest product from the numbers 1, 2, 3, 4, and 5 are 431 and 52.

Examine · Products with the 5 and 4 in the same number are less than any of the products in the *Solve* step.

541 ⊠ 32 ⊟ 17312
54 ⊠ 321 ⊟ 17334

Checking for Understanding

Communicating Mathematics

Read and study the lesson to answer each question.

1. **Tell** how to use the chart to help you choose a method of computation. See margin.

2. **Write** a sentence explaining how you know when estimation is an acceptable method for solving a problem. **See margin.**

3. **Model** your own chart for choosing a method of computation. **See Solutions Manual.**

Guided Practice

Read each situation. Write *exact* if the number must be figured exactly and *estimate* if the number can be approximate.

4. amount earned for babysitting **exact**

5. attendance at a baseball game **estimate**

6. grocery bill as you place items in the cart **estimate**

7. amount of money you give the cashier for groceries **exact**

8. amount of change from a purchase **exact**

9. average number of cars produced in 5 years **estimate**

18 **Chapter 1** Tools for Problem Solving

18

Problem Solving

Practice   Choose the method of computation. Then solve.

10. Max needs to buy four markers to make posters for a social studies project. He has $4. Does he have enough money if each marker is 89¢? **yes**

11. A trip from Des Moines to Chicago is 360 miles. If 10 gallons of gasoline are used, how many miles per gallon is this? **36 miles per gallon**

Strategies
• • • • • • • • •
Look for a pattern.
Solve a simpler problem.
Act it out.
Guess and check.
Draw a diagram.
Make a chart.
Work backward.

12. A student council convention had 4,293 students registered. The convention manager had to assign 537 students per hotel. To how many different hotels did the manager have to assign the students? **8 hotels**

NATIONAL STUDENT COUNCIL CONVENTION

13. Choose five digits. Use the five digits to form a two-digit and a three-digit number so that their product is the least product possible. Use each digit only once.

13. Sample answer for 1, 2, 3, 4, 5: 245×13

14. During a political campaign, each of 256 persons donated $100. How much money was donated? **$25,600**

15. The Mediterranean Sea is an almost completely closed sea of about 900,000 cubic miles of water. Water entering at the Strait of Gibraltar takes about 150 years to flush through the sea. *About* how many cubic miles of water clear the sea in a day? **about 16 cubic miles**

---

1 Assessment: Mid-Chapter Review

1. **Health** Do you know how much blood is in your body? To find the approximate number of quarts, divide your weight by 30. *(Lesson 1-1)*
   Sample answer: 120 pounds ÷ 30 = 4 quarts

Estimate using rounding. *(Lesson 1-2)* **Sample answers given.**

2. $4{,}251 + 822 + 1{,}089$ **6,000**
3. $6{,}743 - 3{,}221$ **4,000**

Estimate using patterns. *(Lesson 1-3)*

4. Estimate the quotient of 4,932 and 79. **60**
5. Estimate the quotient of 5,378 and 61. **90**

Determine whether the answers shown are reasonable. *(Lesson 1-4)*

6. $53 + 27 = 80$ **yes**
7. $400 - 184 = 188$ **no**
8. $\$6.96 \div 12 = \$0.58$ **yes**

9. **Sports** The distance between successive bases on a baseball diamond is 27.43 meters. *About* how far does a player run when hitting a home run? *(Lesson 1-5)* **108 meters**

Extending the Lesson

Using More Than One Method
Have students formulate a problem for others to solve that involves more than one step, and for which it is reasonable to use more than one computation method. Ask each problem writer to compare the methods he or she had in mind with those used by the problem solver.

Cooperative Learning Activity

Flights of Fancy 1-5

Use groups of 2.

▪ Each group member copies the problems below onto a sheet of paper.

▪ The table on the back of this card shows the air distances between certain world cities. The distances are given in statute miles (a statute mile is a mile in the air). You will need to refer to the table to solve the problems below. Try to be the first to solve all of the problems.

1. Which would be a longer flight: Chicago to New York to Paris or Chicago to Los Angeles to Honolulu?
2. Suppose that every Monday morning you fly from Los Angeles to San Francisco and that every Friday night you fly back to Los Angeles. If you do this every week for one year, how many miles will you have flown?
3. If you are flying in an airplane that flies about 600 miles per hour, about how long will a flight from San Francisco to Tokyo be?

Glencoe Mathematics: Applications and Connections, Course 2

Close
Have students list the four computation methods shown and describe how each could be useful. Have them give examples.

3 PRACTICE/APPLY

Assignment Guide
Maximum: 10–15
Minimum: 10–15
All: Mid-Chapter Review

Alternate Assessment
Writing Have students use newspaper ads or store fliers to write four problems—one that they would solve using each of the computation methods given. Ask them to justify their choices.

Enrichment Masters, p. 5

Name _____ Date _____

Enrichment Worksheet 1-5

Estimation Afloat

The puzzle on this page is called an *acrostic*. To solve the puzzle, work back and forth between the paragraph and the puzzle box. For example, the first word of the paragraph begins with the letter R. It should be written above 29 in the paragraph, and in Box 29 below.

Some Advice About Problem Solving:

R E A D the problem to K N O W what information
29 17 33 1   35 3 9 31

you have. Sometimes there will be A missing F A C T.
    27   12 6 26 4

You C A N then explore different methods of solution.
34 13 22

You might use B O T H a calculator and paper and pencil.
32 24 11 20

As you work A T finding a S O L U T I O N,
21 15   5 2 8 10 19 7 30 28

it's better to proceed carefully rather than to H U R R Y.
16 25 14 18 23

A Problem Solving Strategy You Might Use on the Water:

1 D	2 O	3 N	4 '	5 T	6 S	7 A	8 I L
9 O	10 U T	11	12 F	13 A	14 R	15 T	16 H E R
	19 T	20 H	21 A	22 N	23 Y	24 O	25 U
26 C	27 A	28 N	29	30 R	31 O W	32 B	33 A C K

T5
Glencoe Division, Macmillan/McGraw-Hill

NCTM Standards: 1–4, 7

Lesson Resources
• Study Guide Master 1-6
• Practice Master 1-6
• Enrichment Master 1-6
• Group Activity Card 1-6

 Transparency 1-6 contains the 5-Minute Check and a teaching aid for this lesson.

🕐 5-Minute Check
(Over Lesson 1-5)

Choose the method of computation. Then solve.
Sample methods given.

1. Each of 212 persons contributed $50 to the zoo. How much money was contributed? **$10,060; mental math**

2. The drive from Albuquerque to Flagstaff is 330 miles. If 15 gallons of gasoline are used, how many miles per gallon is the car getting? **22; paper and pencil.**

Practice Masters, p. 6

Name _____ Date _____

Practice Worksheet 1-6

Problem-Solving Strategy: Classify Information

If the problem has enough facts, solve it. If not, write the missing facts.

1. A package of three compact discs costs $22.95. How much does each disc cost? **$7.65**

2. The Martino family drove 350 miles on a full tank of gasoline. What was the average miles per gallon of gasoline? **You need to know how many gallons of gasoline the tank holds.**

3. Justin sits three rows behind Mark, and Mark sits next to Frances. If Frances sits in the front row, in which row does Justin sit? **fourth**

4. Twelve people shared a giant submarine sandwich during a party. The sandwich cost $30. What was the cost per person? **$2.50**

5. Pencils sell for $0.15 each, and pens sell for $0.49 each. How much do 12 pencils cost? **$1.80**

6. Jennifer and her girlfriends bought a pizza. Each girl paid $2.00. How much did the pizza cost? **You need to know how many girls there were altogether.**

7. The top sports show in the 1990–91 season was Super Bowl XXV, with two out of every five TV households watching it. How many households watched the show? **You need to know what the total number of TV households was.**

8. Jocelyn paid $3.00 for a pair of socks and seven times as much for a pair of shoes. Her brother also bought socks and shoes but paid twice as much for each. How much money did they spend altogether? **$72.00**

T 6
Glencoe Division, Macmillan/McGraw-Hill

20

1-6 Classify Information

Objective
Solve problems by classifying information.

The husbands—a doctor, dentist, and artist—and their wives—a physicist, architect, and professor—sit side by side in one row at the theater. No two husbands and no two wives sit together, and no wife sits next to her husband. The names are Jan, Joy, Jill, Bob, Bart, and Brad. (The names and occupations are in no special order.)

The dentist occupies one of the middle seats, and he is sitting next to Joy. Bob sits at one end of the row next to the artist's wife. How are the husbands and wives seated?

Sometimes it helps to classify information when you are deciding how to solve a problem.

Explore   What do you know?
• Six adults sit in a row.
• Men and women sit alternately.
• No husband and wife sit together.
• The dentist is in a middle seat next to Joy.
• Bob sits on an end next to the artist's wife.

What are you trying to find?
How are the husbands and wives seated?

Plan   Let's start with Bob, the artist's wife, the dentist, and Joy since we know where they are sitting.

Solve   Bob sits on one end next to the artist's wife.   → Bob, artist's wife

Alternate seating puts the dentist in the middle seat and next to Joy.   → Bob, artist's wife, dentist, Joy

Husbands and wives do not sit together. The remaining husband is the artist since his wife is next to Bob. For this same reason, the dentist's wife must be at the end of the row. Joy must be Bob's wife. Therefore, Bob must be the doctor.

20   **Chapter 1** Tools for Problem Solving

OPTIONS

Reteaching Activity

Using Problem Solving When students are asked to solve problems for which they must decide which information is relevant, they may find it helpful to first rewrite the question and then list the pertinent data.

Study Guide Masters, p. 6

Name _____ Date _____

Study Guide Worksheet 1-6

Problem-Solving Strategy: Classify Information

Noteworthy events in the early history of Massachusetts include: the Pilgrims landing at Plymouth in 1620, the founding of Harvard College in 1636, the Boston Massacre in 1770, and the Boston Tea Party in 1773. How many years before the Boston Tea Party was Harvard College founded?

Explore   What do you know?
• Pilgrims landed at Plymouth in 1620.
• Harvard was founded in 1636.
• The Boston Massacre was in 1770.
• The Boston Tea Party was in 1773.

What are you trying to find?
How many years before the Boston Tea Party Harvard College was founded.

Plan   Classify the information.

The seating arrangement is as follows.

doctor, artist's wife, dentist, doctor's wife, artist, dentist's wife

Examine   Look at the seating arrangement above. No husband or wife sat together and each person is seated according to the clues.

The wives' occupations and the names except for Bob and Joy were extra information.

Checking for Understanding

Communicating Mathematics   Read and study the lesson to answer each question.

1. **Tell** how to identify extra information in a problem. **See Solutions Manual.**

2. **Write** a sentence explaining what you do if a problem does not have enough information. **See Solutions Manual.**

Guided Practice   If the problem has enough facts, solve it. If not, write the missing facts.

3. Forty videos rent at the same price. How much will it cost to rent all forty videos? **not enough facts; the cost of each video**

4. There are 10 CDs in a box. They sell for $13.65 each. How much will 3 CDs cost? **$40.95**

5. Ned says his birthday is on a Tuesday this year. Bill says it's on Monday. Ron says it was on Thursday last year. What day is Ned's birthday? **not enough facts; whether or not it is a leap year**

Problem Solving   6. not enough facts; which pizza they ordered

9. not enough facts; which socks he bought
Practice   If the problem has enough facts, solve it. If not, write the missing facts.

6. Five girls share a pizza. The large size costs $9.60. The medium size costs $6.25. How much did each girl pay?

7. Dan bought a burger for $2.95 and an apple juice for $0.79. How much change did he get from a $5 bill? **$1.26**

8. First class stamps sell for $0.29. Postcard stamps sell for $0.19. How much do 25 first class stamps cost? **$7.25**

9. Socks cost $4 a pair for striped tops and $3 a pair for solid tops. Paul bought 3 pairs of socks. How much did he spend?

10. Jan has $10.56. Pat has twice as much except for one cent less. How much do they have in all? **$31.67**

Strategies
• • • • • • • • •
Look for a pattern.
Solve a simpler problem.
Act it out.
Guess and check.
Draw a diagram.
Make a chart.
Work backward.

Lesson 1-6 Problem-Solving Strategy: Classify Information   **21**

Extending the Lesson

Using Cooperative Groups Have groups prepare problem-solving tests for classmates. Each test should include problems that contain just the right amount of information, problems with extra facts, problems with not enough facts, and some with both extra facts and not enough facts.

Cooperative Learning Activity

Jumpy Coinage 1-6

Use groups of 2.
Materials: Play money

● Arrange eight coins as shown in the figure below.

➡ The object of this game is to transform eight coins arranged as shown below into four stacks of two coins each in four turns. On each turn, you must move one coin to the left or to the right so that it jumps two other coins. These two coins may be stacked or side by side. The sum of the amounts in the four stacks you make must be $0.82.

(penny) (nickel) (dime) (quarter) (penny) (nickel) (dime) (quarter)

Glencoe Mathematics: Applications and Connections, Course 2

NCTM Standards: 1–5, 7

Objective Analyze data and make a decision.

1 FOCUS

Introducing the Situation

Have groups of students begin by sharing experiences they have had either ordering items from catalogues or planting bulbs in a garden. Guide them to discuss costs and related considerations. As they work through the lesson, one group member should record responses to questions raised about overall costs, about the location and size of the garden, and about the type and number of bulbs to buy. Students can do this by following the lesson, question by question.

2 TEACH

Using Applications Provide students with real seed catalogues so that they can see the variety of factors to consider when placing an order. These include additional costs, package sizes in which seeds are sold, and delivery times. Guide students to see that in the real world, garden planners must answer questions similar to those presented in this lesson.

Analyzing the Data

Have students explain how to use the map. Then ask them how they will figure out whether they can plant a "spring bloom" for each student in the school.

Planning a Flower Garden

Situation

Suppose the Booster Club at your school is arranging a Spring Surprise. There are 12 of you in the club and you have $158 in the treasury. Do you have enough money and people to plant enough bulbs near the school's front entrance to make a big splash of color in the spring?

Hidden Data

Will you need to add any nutrients to the soil at planting time?
How many bulbs are needed?
What will be the cost of shipping and handling for ordering the bulbs?
How much will the sales tax be, if applicable?

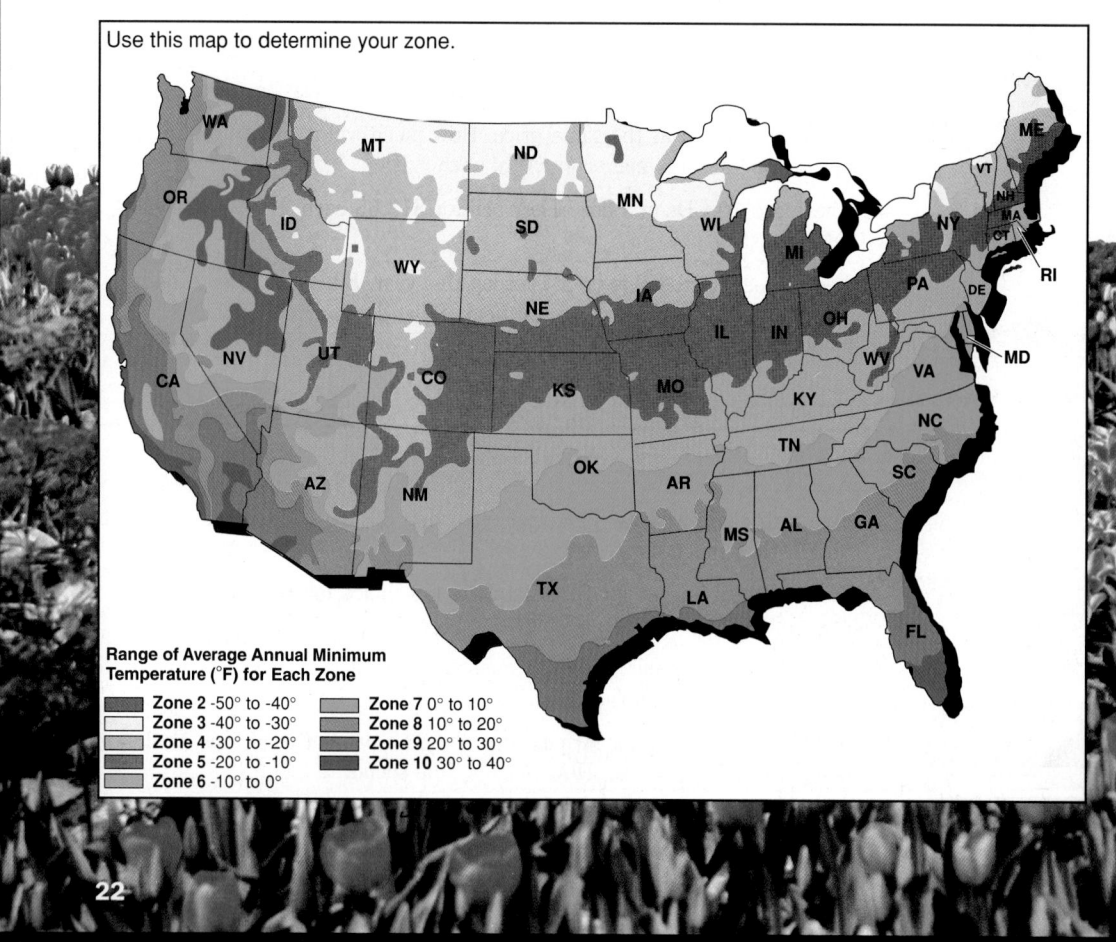

Use this map to determine your zone.

Range of Average Annual Minimum Temperature (°F) for Each Zone

Zone 2 -50° to -40°	**Zone 7** 0° to 10°
Zone 3 -40° to -30°	**Zone 8** 10° to 20°
Zone 4 -30° to -20°	**Zone 9** 20° to 30°
Zone 5 -20° to -10°	**Zone 10** 30° to 40°
Zone 6 -10° to 0°	

22

TOTAL OF GOODS		ADD:
Up to $20	Calculate	$3.00
$20.01—$40	Charges	$4.00
$40.01—$60	For EACH	$6.00
$60.01—$80	Delivery	$7.00
$80.01—$100	to EACH	$9.00
$100.01—$250	Separate	$13.00
Over $250	Address	$20.00

Analyzing the Data

1. What zone is your area in?
2. Which variety of bulbs are compatible with your climate?

Narcissus Collection

Bulb size 12 to 15 cm
White, Blush, Yellow; hardy in zones 4 to 8. Southwinds Mix; hardy in zones 9 and 10. Shipped late September through October.
Sets of 50 bulbs

Blush #22...........$30
Yellow #24..........$25
White #28...........$29
Southwinds
   Mix #20..........$28

Crocus for Naturalizing

Bulb size 10 cm
Light shade or full sun
Variegated colors; hardy in zones 3 to 8
Shipped in October

50 bulbs #91......$15
100 bulbs #95....$27

Tulip Mixture

SAVE

Bulb size 12 cm
Suitable for cutting
Mix of four colors; hardy in zones 3 to 8
Shipped in October

32 bulbs #71......$18
60 bulbs #75......$32

Lily Bed Low
(plant 20 cm apart)

Bulb size 14 cm
Will not need staking
Multicolored hardy in zones 3 – 10
Shipped in October

40 bulbs #206.....$34
80 bulbs #205.....$60

Making a Decision

3. **Who is** going to weed the garden each year?
4. **How will** the garden be cared for after the bulbs bloom and die each year?
5. For the amount of money the club spends, how many years do you expect the garden to bloom?
6. **Would your club** want to promote this Spring Surprise with a spring bloom for each student? teacher? staff member?

Making Decisions in the Real World

7. **Research** the cost of materials from a nearby nursery for both outside bulbs and inside bulbs.

23

Checking for Understanding

Have groups of students prepare a list of the issues they must face as they go about planning their flower garden. Ask them also to present strategies for resolving the issues. Ask a representative of each group to explain how they chose the order in which the issues on their list are to be resolved. Encourage groups to revise their plan as they hear the issues and strategies of the other groups.

3 PRACTICE/APPLY

Making a Decision

Have a student go to the front entrance of your school to report on its suitability for planting. If it is not suitable, have the class suggest another garden site, either on the school grounds or inside the building. If there is no feasible area for planting bulbs on school property, assign students the task of finding a neighborhood location that would be suitable for a garden.

Making Decisions in the Real World

Tell students to imagine that they are going to buy a plant for their room at home. Ask them to describe where they will put the plant together with the light and heat it will get. Then have them visit a nursery or plant store to find the names of three plants that would grow well under those conditions. Students should also find the costs and care required for each plant. Have them also record their findings and present a short report accompanied by a chart.

Additional Answer

1.–6. Answers will vary.

NCTM Standards: 1–5, 7, 9

Lesson Resources
- Study Guide Master 1-7
- Practice Master 1-7
- Enrichment Master 1-7
- Multicultural Activity, p. 1
- Group Activity Card 1-7

 Transparency 1-7 contains the 5-Minute Check and a teaching aid for this lesson.

🕐 5-Minute Check
(Over Lesson 1-6)

If the problem has enough facts, solve it. If not, write the missing facts.

1. Maria bought a pizza slice for $1.30 and a glass of orange juice for $0.80. How much change did she get from a $10 bill? $7.90

2. One kind of greeting card costs $2.50 while a second costs $1.00. Phil bought 5 of these cards. How much did he spend?   needs number of each kind bought

---

1 FOCUS

Motivating the Lesson

Situational Problem   Present the following problem: *Use five 2's to make the number 1. You may use the symbols $+$, $-$, $\times$, and $\div$ as well as parentheses.*

2 TEACH

Using Discussion   Have students compare the following:

$$4 + (2 + 12)$$
$$4 + (2 \times 12)$$
$$4 \times (2 + 12)$$
$$(4 \times 2) \times 12$$

In which expression(s) will the value change if the parentheses are dropped? $4 \times (2 + 12)$

Under what conditions can parentheses always be omitted?   whenever only addition or only multiplication is involved

---

1-7 Order of Operations

Objective
Evaluate expressions using the order of operations.

Words to Learn
order of operations

Sarah and Erick are photographers on the middle school yearbook. Erick found 2 rolls of film with 36 exposures each and 3 rolls of film with 24 exposures each in the supply cabinet. How many photos can they take before they have to buy more film?

First they make an estimate.

$$2 \times 36 \quad \rightarrow \quad 2 \times 40 \text{ or } 80$$
$$3 \times 24 \quad \rightarrow \quad 3 \times 20 \text{ or } 60$$

They can take about $80 + 60$ or 140 photos before they have to buy more film.

Sarah and Erick then decide to use a calculator to find the exact number of photos. They each use a different calculator. Here are the results.

Sarah: 2 ⊠ 36 ⊞ 3 ⊠ 24 🟰 **144**

Erick: 2 ⊠ 36 ⊞ 3 ⊠ 24 🟰 **1800**

Which answer is correct? Sarah reasons that 144 is correct because it is close to the estimate.

To make sure that expressions like $2 \times 36 + 3 \times 24$ have only one value, mathematicians have agreed on the following **order of operations.** Grouping symbols, such as parentheses, are used to change the order of operations.

Order of Operations	1. Do all operations within grouping symbols first. 2. Do multiplication and division from left to right. 3. Do addition and subtraction from left to right.

Calculator Hint
• • • • • • • • • • • • •
To see whether your calculator follows the order of operations, enter

2 ⊞ 5 ⊠ 3.

If your calculator displays 17, your calculator follows the order of operations.

Some calculators are programmed to follow the order of operations. In the situation described above, Sarah's calculator follows the order of operations. You may want to try the problem shown above with your calculator to determine whether it follows the order of operations.

Example 1

Evaluate $(5 + 4) \div 3$.

$(5 + 4) \div 3 = 9 \div 3$ *Add 5 and 4 since they are in parentheses.*
$ = 3$ *Divide by 3.*

Interactive Mathematics Tools

This multimedia software provides an interactive lesson that is tied directly to Lesson 1-7. Students will explore the order of operations.

Study Guide Masters, p. 7

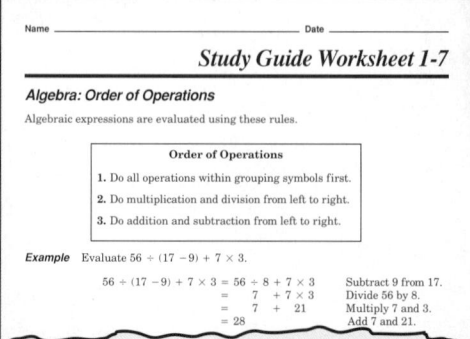

Name _____   Date _____

Study Guide Worksheet 1-7

Algebra: Order of Operations

Algebraic expressions are evaluated using these rules.

Order of Operations
1. Do all operations within grouping symbols first.
2. Do multiplication and division from left to right.
3. Do addition and subtraction from left to right.

Example   Evaluate $56 \div (17 - 9) + 7 \times 3$.

$$56 \div (17 - 9) + 7 \times 3 = 56 \div 8 + 7 \times 3 \qquad \text{Subtract 9 from 17.}$$
$$= 7 + 7 \times 3 \qquad \text{Divide 56 by 8.}$$
$$= 7 + 21 \qquad \text{Multiply 7 and 3.}$$
$$= 28 \qquad \text{Add 7 and 21.}$$

There are other ways to indicate multiplication, besides using the symbol ×. One way is to use a raised dot.

$$3 \cdot 5 \boxed{\text{means}} \!\!\!\!> \ 3 \times 5$$

Another way is to use parentheses.

$$2(4 + 5) \boxed{\text{means}} \!\!\!\!> \ 2 \times (4 + 5)$$

Example 2

Evaluate $3(4 + 7) - 5 \cdot 4$.

$3(4 + 7) - 5 \cdot 4$	$= 3(11) - 5 \cdot 4$	*Add 4 and 7.*
	$= 33 - 5 \cdot 4$	*Multiply 3 and 11.*
	$= 33 - 20$	*Multiply 5 and 4.*
	$= 13$	*Subtract 20 from 33.*

Checking for Understanding

Communicating Mathematics

Read and study the lesson to answer each question.

1. **Show** that $3(4 + 5)$ is equal to $3(4) + 3(5)$. **See Solutions Manual.**

2. Sample answer: $6(5 + 2)$

2. **Write** an expression in which you should add first.

3. **Tell** which operation you should do first in the expression $6(3 + 7)$. Explain. **Addition; order of operations states all operations within grouping symbols are computed first.**

Guided Practice

4. multiplication
5. addition
6. subtraction

Name the operation that should be done first.

4. $3 + 5 \cdot 6$ 5. $10 - (3 + 4)$ 6. $4 + 2(8 - 6)$
7. $(17 + 3) \div (4 + 1)$ 8. $12 - 3(4)$ 9. $4(6 + 4) \div 2$
   addition   **multiplication**   **addition**

Evaluate each expression.

10. $3 + 5 \cdot 4$ **23**   11. $(12 - 4) \div 2$ **4**   12. $5 \cdot 8 - 3 \cdot 4$ **28**
13. $3 \cdot 4(5 - 3)$ **24**   14. $14 - 8 \div 8$ **13**   15. $4(10 + 8) \div 6$ **12**

Exercises

Independent Practice

16. multiplication
17. subtraction

Name the operation that should be done first.

16. $12 - 3 \cdot 4$ 17. $7 + 3(5 - 2)$ 18. $(8 + 3) - 5$ **addition**
19. $5 + 3(4)$ 20. $(8 - 4) \div 2$ 21. $7 \times 9 - (4 + 3)$
    multiplication   **subtraction**   **addition**

Evaluate each expression.

22. $7 \cdot 3 + 8 \cdot 2$ **37**   23. $(8 - 2) \div 3$ **2**   24. $5 - 3 + 1$ **3**
25. $16 \div 4 \cdot 2$ **8**   26. $12 - 8 \div 4 + 6$ **16**   27. $24 \div (7 - 3)$ **6**
28. $14 - (19 - 19)$ **14**   29. $25 \div (9 - 4)$ **5**   30. $84 - 28 \div (4 \cdot 7)$ **83**
31. $2(14 - 9) - (17 - 14)$ **7**   32. $(26 - 9) - 4 \times 3$ **5**
33. $3(24 - 7) - 2 \cdot 13$ **25**   34. $16(2 - 1) \div 2 + 2$ **10**
35. $(81 + 19) \div 25 + 5$ **9**   36. $82 - 43 - 6 \div 6$ **38**

Lesson 1-7 Order of Operations   **25**

More Examples

For Example 1
Evaluate $(6 + 2) \div 4$.   2

For Example 2
Evaluate $4(3 + 5) - 2 \cdot 7$.   18

Checking for Understanding

Exercises 1-3 are designed to help you assess students' understanding through reading, writing, speaking, and modeling. You should work through these exercises with your students and then monitor their work on Guided Practice Exercises 4-15.

OPTIONS

Reteaching Activity

Using Manipulatives Have groups of students use differently colored counters to model the expression in the lesson opener. Then have them use the counters to evaluate the expressions in Examples 1 and 2. They should write an explanation for each step in the process.

Practice Masters, p. 7

Have students work in a group to create expressions for others in the group to evaluate. Some students may use calculators, others manipulatives.

3 PRACTICE/APPLY

Assignment Guide
Maximum: 16–49
Minimum: 17–39 odd, 41–48

For **Extra Practice,** see p. 573.

Alternate Assessment

Speaking   Have students tell the order of operations to follow when evaluating an expression. Ask them to tell in their own words why it is important to have an order of operations.

Enrichment Masters, p. 7

Name _____   Date _____

Enrichment Worksheet 1-7

Nested Expressions

Sometimes more than one set of parentheses are used to group the quantities in an expression. These expressions are said to have "nested" parentheses. The expression below has "nested" parentheses.

$(4 + (3 \cdot (2 + 3)) + 8) \div 9$

Expressions with several sets of grouping symbols are clearer if brackets such as [ ] or braces such as { } are used. Here is the same example written with brackets and braces.

$[4 + \{3 \cdot (2 + 3)\} + 8] \div 9$

To evaluate expressions of this type, work from the inside out.

$[4 + \{3 \cdot (2 + 3)\} + 8] \div 9 = [4 + \{3 \cdot 5\} + 8] \div 9$
$= [4 + 15 + 8] \div 9$
$= 27 \div 9$
$= 3$

Evaluate each expression.

1. $3 + [(24 \div 8) \cdot 7] - 20$ **4**

2. $[(16 - 7 + 5) \div 2] - 7$ **0**

3. $[2 \cdot (23 - 6) + 14] \div 6$ **8**

4. $50 - [3 \cdot (15 - 5)] + 25$ **45**

5. $12 + [28 - \{2 \cdot (11 - 7)\} + 3]$ **35**

6. $[75 \div 3 \cdot \{(17 - 9) \div 2\}] \cdot 2$ **174**

Evaluate each expression.

7. $20 + [3 \cdot \{6 + (56 \div 8)\}]$ **59**

8. $[4 + \{5 \cdot (12 - 5)\} + 15] \cdot 10$ **540**

9. $[15 \cdot \{(38 - 26) \div 4\}] - 15$ **30**

10. $[\{34 + (6 \cdot 5)\} \div 8] + 40$ **48**

T 7
Glencoe Division, Macmillan/McGraw-Hill

Copy each sentence below. Use your calculator to determine where to insert parentheses to make each sentence true. You may use the parentheses keys.

37. $(16 + 5) \times 4 \div 2 = 42$

38. $64 \div (8 + 24) - 1 = 1$

39. $(36 \div 3 - 9) \div 3 = 1$

40. $18 \div (24 - 18) - 3 = 0$

Mixed Review

41. **Production**   Soft drink cans can be filled by a machine on a production line at a rate of 8 cans per minute. How many cans can be filled during an 8-hour shift? *(Lesson 1-1)* **3,840 cans**

42. **Consumer Math**   A new car has a sticker price of $16,150. The tax to be paid on this amount is $1,035. About how much is the total cost of the car? Use rounding. *(Lesson 1-2)* **about $17,000**

43. Use patterns to estimate $1,243 \div 310$. *(Lesson 1-3)* **about 4**

44. Determine whether $394 + 21 = 431$ is reasonable. *(Lesson 1-4)* **no**

45. **Health**   Stephan weighed 204 pounds before starting a new diet plan. After 4 weeks on the diet, he weighed 186 pounds. Stephen wrote his friend that he lost 18 pounds. Is that answer reasonable? *(Lesson 1-4)* **yes**

Problem Solving and Applications

46. **Data Search**   Refer to pages 2 and 3. *About* how much more snow fell in Sault St. Marie, Michigan, than in Anchorage, Alaska, in 1989? **about 47 inches**

47. **Smart Shopping**   At a local coffee house, coffee can be purchased by the pound. Megan buys 3 pounds of Mexican coffee priced at $5 per pound. Nick buys 7 pounds of Spanish coffee priced at $9 per pound. How much more did Nick spend than Megan? **$48**

48. **Critical Thinking**   In a collection of nickels and quarters, there are four more nickels than quarters. If the coins are worth $5.60, how many quarters are there? **18 quarters**

COMPUTER CONNECTION

49. **Computer Connection**   BASIC is a computer language that can be used to program a computer. The chart at the right shows the BASIC notation for the operations we use in mathematics. The BASIC computer language also follows the order of operations. Evaluate these expressions that are written in BASIC notation.

Operation	Mathematics	BASIC
Addition	+	+
Subtraction	−	−
Multiplication	×	*
Division	÷	/

a. $2 * 5 + 9$ **19**

b. $25 + 5 - 10$ **20**

c. $40/10 * 8$ **32**

d. $(19 + 17)/12$ **3**

e. $12/(31 - 2 * 15)$ **12**

f. $3 * 5 * 15$ **225**

OPTIONS

Extending the Lesson

Business Connection   Taxis usually charge a certain price for the first part of a trip, perhaps $\frac{1}{5}$ of a mile, and then a price per fraction of a mile for the rest of the trip. Have students use the rates of a local taxi company to estimate the cost of a trip from the school to the nearest airport.

Cooperative Learning Activity

Status Quo or No? **1-7**

Number of players: 2
Materials: Index cards, spinner

▸ Copy onto cards the number sentences listed on the back of this card. Shuffle the cards and place them face down in a pile. Label equal sections of a spinner "Change" and "No Change." Determine which partner will go first.

▸ The first partner selects a card and spins the spinner. If the spinner points to "No Change," the first partner evaluates the expression on the card and writes the value. If the spinner points to "Change," the other partner can try to rewrite the expression, using the same numbers and symbols, to decrease the value of the expression. Partners take turns drawing a card and spinning until all the cards are used. Both partners then find the sum of the values of their expressions. The winner is the partner with the greater sum.

Glencoe Mathematics: Applications and Connections, Course 2

1-8A Algebra: Variables and Expressions

A Preview of Lesson 1-8

Objective
Model algebraic expressions.

Materials
counters
cups

The phrase *the sum of four and some number* is an algebraic expression. This phrase contains a *constant* that you know, 4, and an unknown value "some number."

- You can use counters to represent 4 and a cup to represent the unknown value.

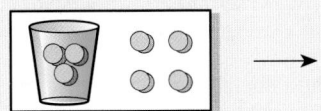

- Any number of counters may be in the cup. Suppose you put 3 counters in the cup. Instead of an unknown value, you know the cup has a value of 3. When you empty the cup and count all the counters, the expression has a value of 7.

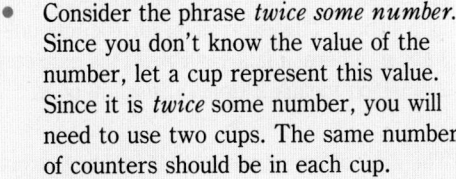

- Consider the phrase *twice some number*. Since you don't know the value of the number, let a cup represent this value. Since it is *twice* some number, you will need to use two cups. The same number of counters should be in each cup.

Try this!

Work in groups of three.

Model each phrase with cups and counters. Then put four counters in each cup. How many counters are there in all? Record your answer by drawing pictures of your models.

1. the sum of 3 and a number 7
2. three times a number 12
3. 5 more than a number 9
4. five times a number 20

5. The cup represents the variable or the unknown quantity.

What do you think?

5. Write a sentence to describe what the cup represents.
6. Write a sentence that explains why $x + 4$ is called an algebraic expression. It expresses an unknown quantity.

Mathematics Lab 1-8A Algebra: Variables and Expressions   **27**

Interactive Mathematics Tools

This multimedia software provides an interactive lesson that is tied directly to Lesson 1-8A. Students will use cups and counters to explore expressions.

Lab Manual, p. 36

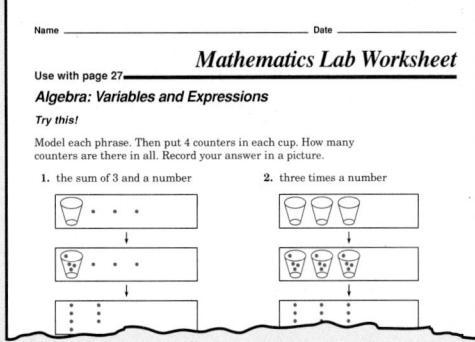

Name _____   Date _____

Mathematics Lab Worksheet

Use with page 27

Algebra: Variables and Expressions

Try this!

Model each phrase. Then put 4 counters in each cup. How many counters are there in all. Record your answer in a picture.

1. the sum of 3 and a number
2. three times a number

NCTM Standards: 1–5, 9

Management Tips

For Students Provide groups of students with cups and counters or other small objects that are uniform in size.

For the Overhead Projector *Overhead Manipulative Resources* provides appropriate materials for teacher or student demonstration of the activities in this Mathematics Lab.

1 FOCUS

Introducing the Lab

Ask students the meaning of *phrase* and *expression*. Then discuss with them how using algebraic expressions to represent unknown quantities can be an effective problem-solving strategy.

2 TEACH

Using Applications To help students understand the concept of an unknown value, have them write expressions to match the expressions in the Try This section. For example, for "5 more than a number," students might write *5 more laps than last week*."

Lab Manual You may wish to make copies of p. 36 of the *Lab Manual* for students to use as a recording sheet.

3 PRACTICE/APPLY

Using Models Have students make up situations containing unknown values. Then have other students interpret the situations as algebraic expressions and model the expressions using the counters and cups.

Close

Have students work in pairs. One student gives a phrase for the other to represent as an algebraic expression using models. Then switch roles. Check that the models match the expressions.

27

1-8 Variables and Expressions

NCTM Standards: 1–5, 7–9

Lesson Resources
- Study Guide Master 1-8
- Practice Master 1-8
- Enrichment Master 1-8
- Technology Master, p. 15
- Application Master, p. 1
- Group Activity Card 1-8

 Transparency 1-8 contains the 5-Minute Check and a teaching aid for this lesson.

🕐 5-Minute Check
(Over Lesson 1-7)

Evaluate each expression.
1. $15 - 3 \cdot 2$ 9
2. $25 \div (10 - 5)$ 5
3. $12 \div 3 + 1$ 5
4. $3(5 + 4) - 4 \times 2$ 19
5. $(24 + 36) \div 12 + 7$ 12

1 FOCUS

Motivating the Lesson

Activity Place 18 pennies on one pan of a two-pan balance and three empty cans on the other pan. From a jar of pennies have students find the number of pennies that should be placed in each cup to get the scale to balance. Each cup must have the same number of pennies. Repeat the activity with 12 pennies and 33 pennies.

2 TEACH

Using Computers You may wish to use the idea of spreadsheets at the start of the lesson to introduce variables and evaluate algebraic expressions. Discuss with students how varying one figure, either the quantity or unit price, will affect the total according to a recognizable pattern. Discuss ways that businesses use spreadsheets.

Objective
Evaluate numerical and simple algebraic expressions.

Words to Learn
variable
algebra
algebraic expression
evaluate

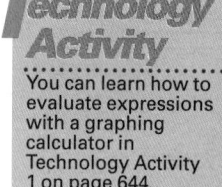

Technology Activity
You can learn how to evaluate expressions with a graphing calculator in Technology Activity 1 on page 644.

Tammy charges $2 per hour for babysitting. If she babysits for one hour, she makes $1 \times \$2$ or \$2. If she babysits for two hours, she makes $2 \times \$2$ or \$4. The amount she makes increases with the number of hours she babysits.

You can make a table to show the pattern between the number of hours spent babysitting and the amount earned.

Number of Hours	Amount Earned
0	$\$2 \times 0 = \$0$
1	$\$2 \times 1 = \$2$
2	$\$2 \times 2 = \$4$
3	$\$2 \times 3 = \$6$
4	$\$2 \times 4 = \$8$

In the table above, notice that the amount earned per hour is constant, \$2, but the number of hours varies. You can use a placeholder, or **variable,** to represent the number of hours spent babysitting. The expression for the amount earned is $\$2 \times \blacksquare$ or $\$2 \times n$, where n is a variable. This expression can also be written as $2n$, which means 2 times the value of n.

The area of mathematics that involves expressions that have variables is called **algebra.** The expression $2n$ is called an **algebraic expression** because it contains variables, numbers, and at least one operation.

You can **evaluate** an algebraic expression by replacing the variable with a number and then finding the value of the numerical expression. Consider the expression $2n$. How much money will Tammy earn if she babysits for 6 hours?

First use cups and counters to find the solution.

Place six counters in each cup.

The solution is 12.

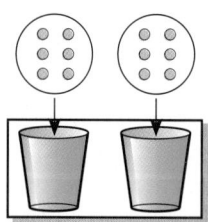

OPTIONS

Limited English Proficiency

Have students work with a partner. Taking turns, one writes an algebraic expression for the other to read orally. Both students then evaluate the expression together.

You can also solve this problem algebraically.

$$2n = 2 \times 6 \qquad \text{\textit{Replace n with 6.}}$$
$$= 12 \qquad \text{\textit{Tammy will earn \$12.}}$$

Example 1

Evaluate $x + y + 4$ if $x = 7$ and $y = 11$.

$$x + y + 4 = 7 + 11 + 4 \qquad \text{\textit{Replace x with 7 and y with 11.}}$$
$$= 18 + 4 \qquad \text{\textit{7+ 11+ 18}}$$
$$= 22 \qquad \text{\textit{18+ 4= 22}}$$

To make sure everyone understands the language of mathematics, mathematicians agree on standard notation for multiplicaton and division with variables.

$3a$ [means] $3 \times a$, or $3 \cdot a$, or $(3)(a)$

rs [means] $r \times s$

$4cd$ [means] $4 \times c \times d$

$\frac{m}{2}$ [means] $m \div 2$

When am I ever going to use this?

The expression $110 + \frac{A}{2}$ is used to estimate a person's normal blood pressure. A stands for the person's age.

Estimate the normal blood pressure of an 18-year-old.

$$110 + \frac{18}{2} = 119$$

The blood pressure of an 18-year-old is *about* 119.

Examples

2 Evaluate $5a + 3b$ if $a = 7$ and $b = 2$.

$$5a + 3b = 5(7) + 3(2) \qquad \text{\textit{Replace a with 7 and b with 2.}}$$
$$= 35 + 6 \qquad \text{\textit{Multiply.}}$$
$$= 41 \qquad \text{\textit{Add 35 and 6.}}$$

3 Evaluate $\frac{ab}{3}$ if $a = 7$ and $b = 9$.

$$\frac{ab}{3} = \frac{(7)(9)}{3} \qquad \text{\textit{Replace a with 7 and b with 9.}}$$
$$= \frac{63}{3} \qquad \text{\textit{Multiply 7 and 9.}}$$
$$= 21 \qquad \text{\textit{Divide 63 by 3.}}$$

4 Use a calculator to evaluate $\frac{x}{y} + 50$ if $x = 12$ and $y = 2$.

$$\frac{x}{y} + 50 = \frac{12}{2} + 50 \qquad \text{\textit{Replace x with 12 and y with 2.}}$$

12 [÷] 2 [+] 50 [=] 5b

Lesson 1-8 Algebra Connection: Variables and Expressions   **29**

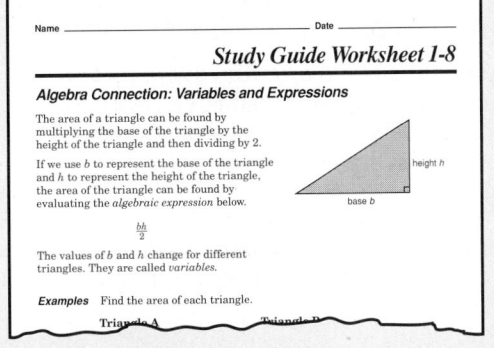

Error Analysis

Watch for students who incorrectly evaluate expressions by performing operations out of order.

Prevent by reviewing the order of operations with those students and having them read the expressions aloud to clearly identify each operation in the order in which it occurs.

Close

Have students write and evaluate an algebraic expression for the word phrase "the cost of five roses at $6 each and three tulips at $2 each." $5 \cdot 6 + 3 \cdot 2 = 36$

3 PRACTICE/APPLY

Assignment Guide

Maximum: 16–34
Minimum: 17–27 odd, 28–34

For **Extra Practice,** see p. 573.

Practice Masters, p. 8

Name _____ Date _____

Practice Worksheet 1-8

Algebra Connection: Variables and Expressions

Evaluate each expression if x = 5, y = 4, and z = 3.

1. $x + 3$ **8**   2. $z - 3$ **0**   3. $10 - z$ **7**

4. $13 + y$ **17**   5. $x + z$ **8**   6. $y + z$ **7**

7. $y + 3 - z$ **4**   8. $x - 2 + z$ **6**   9. $x - x + 4$ **4**

10. $x - y + 8$ **9**   11. $xy - 2$ **18**   12. $xz - 4$ **11**

13. $yz + 10$ **22**   14. $yz - 10$ **2**   15. $xz + 4$ **19**

Evaluate each expression if a = 8, b = 4, and c = 2.

16. $a + b + c$ **14**   17. $4b + a$ **24**   18. $cb - a$ **0**

19. $\frac{a}{b} + 5$ **7**   20. $3bc$ **24**   21. $\frac{a}{b} + c$ **4**

22. $\frac{2a}{4} - b$ **0**   23. $3(b + a) - c$ **34**   24. $2b - 3c$ **2**

25. $\frac{2b}{c}$ **4**   26. $\frac{6(a+c)}{b}$ **15**   27. $b(b + a) - b$ **44**

Evaluate each expression if a = 12, b = 3, c = 4, m = 9, and n = 3.

28. $\frac{m}{n} + 6$ **9**   29. $1mn$ **27**   30. $\frac{a}{c} - b$ **0**

31. $\frac{3n}{m} + 4$ **5**   32. $3(n + n) - m$ **9**   33. $4c - 3b$ **7**

34. $10 - \frac{2m}{n}$ **4**   35. $\frac{3(b+c)}{b+c}$ **3**   36. $b(c - b) + c$ **7**

T8
Glencoe Division, Macmillan/McGraw-Hill

30

Checking for Understanding

Communicating Mathematics

Read and study the lesson to answer each question.

1. **Write** two different expression that mean the same as $4x$. **$4 \cdot x$ and $x + x + x + x$**

2. **Write** an expression that means the same as $5 \div a$. **$\frac{5}{a}$**

3. **Tell,** in your own words, the difference between numbers and variables. **Numbers have a known value while variables are letters representing unknown values.**

Guided Practice

Evaluate each expression if $x = 6$, $y = 4$, $a = 3$, $b = 2$, and $c = 7$.

4. $x + 2$ **8**   5. $y - 3$ **1**

6. $9 - c$ **2**   7. $14 + y$ **18**

8. $x + y$ **10**   9. $a + b$ **5**

10. $c + 8 - a$ **12**   11. $y - 1 + x$ **9**

12. $x - y + 3$ **5**   13. $a - b + 5$ **6**

14. $ab - 1$ **5**   15. $xy - 4$ **20**

Exercises

Independent Practice

Evaluate each expression if $a = 6$, $b = 3$, and $c = 2$.

16. $a + b + c$ **11**   17. $3a + b$ **21**   18. $ab - c$ **16**

19. $\frac{a}{c} + 4$ **7**   20. $2ab$ **36**   21. $\frac{a}{b} + c$ **4**

22. $\frac{2a}{3} - c$ **2**   23. $2(a + b) - c$ **16**   24. $2a - 3b$ **3**

25. $5 - \frac{2b}{c}$ **2**   26. $\frac{6(a+c)}{b}$ **16**   27. $c(b + a) - a$ **12**

Mixed Review

28. **Consumer Math** Jackie receives a paycheck stating that her total pay, before taxes, for 52 hours of work amounts to $353. About how much is her hourly wage? Use patterns. *(Lesson 1-3)* **about $7 per hour**

29. **Music** Tanya owns 95 CDs. She added the information to a list of valuables for her insurance agent. Each disc is worth about $15. Is $2,100 a reasonable estimate of the value of the CDs? *(Lesson 1-4)* **no**

30. Mr. Jackson plans to walk 14 miles a week. How many more miles does Mr. Jackson have to walk? If the problem has enough facts, solve it. If not, write the missing facts. *(Lesson 1-6)* **missing fact: the number of miles he has walked**

31. Evaluate the expression $24 - 12 \div 3 \cdot 5 + 6$. *(Lesson 1-7)* **10**

OPTIONS

Bell Ringer

On a trip to the city, Ann spent half of her money on the train ticket. She then spent half of what she had left on a taxi ride. When she got out of the taxi, she bought juice for $1. When she met her friend, she had only $2 left. Ask students how how much money Ann brought with her that day. **$12**

32. **Nature** You can estimate the temperature in degrees Fahrenheit by counting the number of times a cricket chirps in one minute, dividing it by 4, and then adding 37.

    a. Write an expression for temperature using this information. Let c represent the number of chirps per minute. $c \div 4 + 37$

    b. Find the temperature if a cricket chirps 104 times in one minute. **63°F**

33. **Aeronautics** An aircraft is said to travel at Mach 2 if it travels at twice the speed of sound, Mach 3 if it travels at 3 times the speed of sound, and so on.

    a. If the speed of sound is about 740 mph, write an expression to indicate the speed an aircraft travels in terms of its Mach number. Let m represent the Mach number. **740 m**

    b. Find the speed of an aircraft traveling at 5 times the speed of sound. **3,700 mph**

34. **Critical Thinking** Demarcus and Latisha are remodeling the bathroom in their apartment. Latisha is installing 9-inch square ceramic tiles on the wall while Demarcus is installing 12-inch square vinyl tiles on the floor.

    a. How often will the seams line up along an 8-foot wall if they both begin at the left edge of the wall? **twice**

    b. How far is each common seam line from the left edge? **3 feet and 6 feet**

Save Planet Earth

The Ozone Layer
The ozone layer is a thin layer of gas located miles above our heads. It filters out damaging radiation from the sun. Chemicals such as chlorofluorocarbons (CFCs) can destroy the ozone by drifting upward into the atmosphere from our homes, factories, and cities.

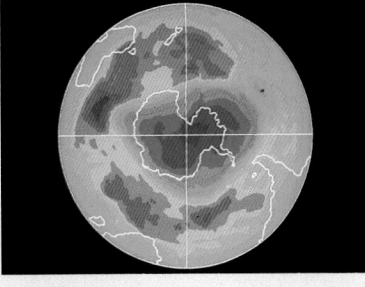

Styrofoam, which is often injected with gases used with CFCs, is a threat to the ozone layer, as well as marine life and our already-full landfills.

How You Can Help
Avoid foam packaging in picnic goods, fast food restaurants, and egg cartons.

Lesson 1-8 Algebra Connection: Variables and Expressions   **31**

Extending the Lesson

Save Planet Earth Explain to students that styrofoam is not biodegradable, that is, it will not decompose in a reasonably short period of time.

Cooperative Learning Activity

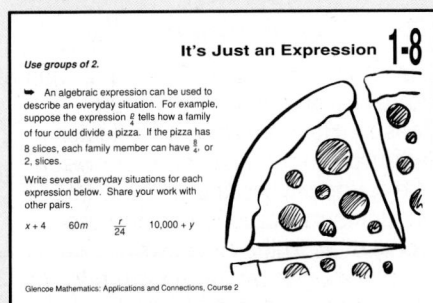

It's Just an Expression 1-8

Use groups of 2.

➡ An algebraic expression can be used to describe an everyday situation. For example, suppose the expression $\frac{p}{8}$ tells how a family of four could divide a pizza. If the pizza has 8 slices, each family member can have $\frac{8}{4}$, or 2, slices.

Write several everyday situations for each expression below. Share your work with other pairs.

$x + 4$ $60m$ $\frac{r}{24}$ $10,000 + y$

Glencoe Mathematics: Applications and Connections, Course 2

Enrichment Masters, p. 8

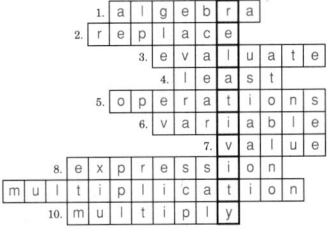

Name _____ Date _____

Enrichment Worksheet 1-8

Albert Einstein's Famous Theory

When you have solved the puzzle below, the letters in the heavy black boxes will spell the name of an important scientific theory proposed by Albert Einstein. His theory relates mass and energy.

Use these clues to complete the puzzle below.

1. A language of symbols.
2. To evaluate an expression, you _____ the variable with a number.
3. To find a specific numerical value for an algebraic expression.
4. An expression must contain at _____ one operation as well as variables or numbers.
5. The order of _____ helps you to know which operation to do first when evaluating an expression.
6. A symbol that stands for an unknown quantity.
7. The worth of something.
8. You call $2a + 3b$ an algebraic _____.
9. The process of finding the product of two numbers is called _____.
10. In an algebraic expression, you should _____ or divide before you add or subtract.

1. a l g e b r a
2. r e p l a c e
3. e v a l u a t e
4. l e a s t
5. o p e r a t i o n s
6. v a r i a b l e
7. v a l u e
8. e x p r e s s i o n
9. m u l t i p l i c a t i o n
10. m u l t i p l y

T8
Glencoe Division, Macmillan/McGraw-Hill

Lesson Resources
- Study Guide Master 1-9
- Practice Master 1-9
- Enrichment Master 1-9
- Technology Master, p. 1
- Lab Manual, p. 37
- Group Activity Card 1-9

 Transparency 1-9 contains the 5-Minute Check and a teaching aid for this lesson.

🕐 5-Minute Check
(Over Lesson 1-8)

1. Evaluate $n + m + 5$ if $m = 2$ and $n = 8$.   15

2. Evaluate $4x + 3y$ if $x = 4$ and $y = 6$.   34

3. Evaluate $\frac{cd}{4}$ if $c = 3$ and $d = 8$.   6

4. Evaluate $\frac{a}{b} + 30$ if $a = 18$ and $b = 9$.   32

5. Use the information on page 31 about cricket chirps to find the temperature in degrees Fahrenheit if a cricket chirps 96 times in one minute.   61

1 FOCUS

Motivating the Lesson

Situational Problem Ask students to suppose that they were going to trace their ancestors back for 5 generations. Assuming that each of their two parents had two parents, each of whom had two parents, and so on, ask them to figure out how many of their ancestors were in the fifth generation preceding theirs.

1-9 Powers and Exponents

Objective
Use powers and exponents in expressions.

Words to Learn
factors
exponent
base
powers
cubed
squared

Do you want to do your part to save Earth? Here is something all Americans can do to help save our planet. We could save 150,000 trees every year, if just 100,000 people would stop delivery of junk mail to their homes.

Numbers such as 100,000 can be written as $10 \cdot 10 \cdot 10 \cdot 10 \cdot 10$. When two or more numbers are multiplied, these numbers are called **factors** of the product. When the same factor is used, you may use an **exponent** to simplify the notation.

$$100,000 = \underbrace{10 \cdot 10 \cdot 10 \cdot 10 \cdot 10}_{5 \text{ factors}} = 10^{\overset{\textstyle 5}{\underset{base}{}}} \leftarrow exponent$$

The common factor is called the **base.** Numbers expressed using exponents are called **powers.**

The powers 2^3, 4^2, and 5^4 are read as follows.

2^3	**two to the third power, or two cubed**
4^2	**four to the second power, or four squared**
5^4	**five to the fourth power**

Examples

1 Write 3^4 as a product.

The base is 3. The exponent 4 means 3 is used 4 times.

$3^4 = 3 \cdot 3 \cdot 3 \cdot 3$

2 Write $2 \cdot 2 \cdot 2 \cdot 2 \cdot 2$ using exponents.

2 is a base. Since 2 is a factor 5 times, the exponent is 5.

$2 \cdot 2 \cdot 2 \cdot 2 \cdot 2 = 2^5$

The *order of operations* now must include exponents.

Order of Operations	1. Do all operations within grouping symbols first.
	2. Evaluate all powers before other operations.
	3. Do multiplication and division from left to right.
	4. Do addition and subtraction from left to right.

OPTIONS

Limited English Proficiency

Have students work in small groups to review the vocabulary in the lesson. Have them pay particular attention to the distinction between the terms *power* and *exponent*. LEP students can practice saying the phrase "*m* to the nth power," substituting different numbers for the base and exponent each time.

Additional Answers

1. Sample answer: Exponents allow large numbers to be represented by a simpler notation.

2. Sample answer: A power is a product of equal factors. It has a base (the common factor) and an exponent (the number of times the factor occurs).

3. The pattern is that the number of zeros following the 1 is the same as the exponent of the base, 10. Thus, $10^5 = 100,000$.

Evaluate powers as follows.

Example

3   Evaluate 5^3.

$$5^3 = 5 \cdot 5 \cdot 5$$
$$= 125$$

Calculator Hint

• • • • • • • • • • • •

Many calculators have a 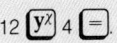 key. This key allows you to compute exponents. Suppose you want to find 12^4. Press

12 $\boxed{y^x}$ 4 $\boxed{=}$.

The answer, 20,736, is displayed immediately.

Examples   *Connection*

4   **Algebra**   Write x^3 as a product.

The base is x. The exponent 3 means x is used 3 times.

$$x^3 = x \cdot x \cdot x$$

5   **Algebra**   Write $a \cdot a \cdot a \cdot a$ using exponents.

a is a base. Since a is a factor 4 times, the exponent is 4.

$$a \cdot a \cdot a \cdot a = a^4$$

6   **Algebra**   Evaluate n^4 if $n = 3$.

$$n^4 = 3^4$$ *Replace n with 3.*

3 $\boxed{y^x}$ 4 $\boxed{=}$ 81

Checking for Understanding

Communicating Mathematics

Read and study the lesson to answer each question.

1. **Tell** why exponents are useful. **See margin.**
2. **Tell**, in your own words, what powers are. Use the terms *factor, base,* and *exponent*. **See margin.**
3. **Write** one or two sentences that explain the pattern used when you find the product of 10^5 mentally. **See margin.**

Guided Practice

Write each power as a product of the same factor.

4. 2^4 $2 \cdot 2 \cdot 2 \cdot 2$
5. 7^5 $7 \cdot 7 \cdot 7 \cdot 7 \cdot 7$
6. 12^3 $12 \cdot 12 \cdot 12$
7. 9^7 $9 \cdot 9 \cdot 9 \cdot 9 \cdot 9 \cdot 9 \cdot 9$

Write each product using exponents.

8. $6 \cdot 6 \cdot 6$ 6^3
9. $15 \cdot 15 \cdot 15 \cdot 15$ 15^4
10. $a \cdot a \cdot a \cdot a \cdot a \cdot a$ a^6

Evaluate each expression.

11. 5^4 625
12. 2^6 64
13. 4^4 256
14. 8^3 512

Lesson 1-9 Algebra Connection: Powers and Exponents   **33**

Watch for students who multiply the base by the exponent to find the value of the expression.

Prevent by having students write exponential expressions as expanded products prior to writing the standard form.

Close

Have students explain what an exponential expression is, including an explanation of each key term, as if to a person who has never seen exponents.

3 PRACTICE/APPLY

Assignment Guide
Maximum: 16–57
Minimum: 17–43 odd, 44–56

For **Extra Practice,** see p. 573.

Practice Masters, p. 9

Name _____ Date _____

Practice Worksheet 1-9

Algebra: Powers and Exponents

Write each power as a product.

1. 5^4 $5 \cdot 5 \cdot 5 \cdot 5$ 2. 3^5 $3 \cdot 3 \cdot 3 \cdot 3 \cdot 3$ 3. 8^4 $8 \cdot 8 \cdot 8 \cdot 8$

4. 15^4 $15 \cdot 15 \cdot 15 \cdot 15$ 5. 6^7 $6 \cdot 6 \cdot 6 \cdot 6 \cdot 6 \cdot 6 \cdot 6$ 6. n^4 $n \cdot n \cdot n \cdot n$

Write each product using exponents.

7. $8 \cdot 8 \cdot 8$ 8^3 8. $12 \cdot 12 \cdot 12 \cdot 12 \cdot 12$ 12^6 9. $m \cdot m \cdot m \cdot m$ m^4

10. $3 \cdot 3 \cdot 3$ 3^3 11. $1 \cdot 1 \cdot 1 \cdot 1 \cdot 1$ 1^5 12. $r \cdot r \cdot r \cdot r \cdot r \cdot r$ r^6

Evaluate each expression.

13. 3^2 9 14. 3^3 27 15. 2^5 32

16. 0^6 0 17. 12 squared 144 18. 3 to the fourth power 81

19. In 1970, the government spent about 9×10^9 dollars on child nutrition (including school lunches). In 1979, the amount was up to about 4×10^{10} dollars. How much did the government spend on child nutrition in 1979? $40,000,000,000

Use a calculator to determine whether each sentence is true or false.

20. $4^5 > 5^4$ true 21. $6^5 = 5^8$ false 22. $5^4 = 10^2$ false

Evaluate each expression.

23. y^2 if $y = 9$ 81 24. m^6 if $m = 3$ 729

25. x^5 if $x = 10$ 100,000 26. z^4 if $z = 6$ 1,296

27. x^3 if $x = 6$ 216 28. y^5 if $y = 7$ 16,807

T9
Glencoe Division, Macmillan/McGraw-Hill

---

15. **Fitness** In one year, Americans spent $1,410,000,000 on home exercise equipment. Out of this money, Americans spent about 10^8 dollars on weight sets. About how much money did Americans spend on weight sets? $100,000,000

Exercises

Independent Practice

Write each power as a product.

16. 4^5 $4 \cdot 4 \cdot 4 \cdot 4 \cdot 4$ 17. 9^3 $9 \cdot 9 \cdot 9$ 18. 3^4 $3 \cdot 3 \cdot 3 \cdot 3$ 19. n^9 $n \cdot n \cdot n \cdot n \cdot n \cdot n \cdot n \cdot n \cdot n$

Write each product using exponents.

20. $7 \cdot 7 \cdot 7 \cdot 7$ 7^4 21. $12 \cdot 12$ 12^2 22. $x \cdot x \cdot x \cdot x \cdot x$ x^5

Evaluate each expression.

23. 7^2 49   24. 1^{12} 1   25. 3^5 243   26. 6^3 216

27. 3^4 81   28. 11^2 121   29. 9^2 81   30. 13^1 13

32. 512

31. 6 squared 36   32. 8 to the third power   33. 5 cubed 125

34. Given that $2^5 = 32$, find 2^6 mentally. 64

Use a calculator to determine whether each sentence is *true* or *false*.

35. $3^7 > 7^3$ true   36. $12^4 = 182$ false   37. $6^3 < 4^4$ true

Algebra Evaluate each expression.

38. n^3 if $n = 4$ 64   39. m^4 if $m = 5$ 625

40. x^6 if $x = 1$ 1   41. r^2 if $r = 11$ 121

42. s^4 if $s = 3$ 81   43. t^7 if $t = 2$ 128

44. about 30 miles per gallon

Mixed Review

44. Use patterns to estimate how many miles per gallon a car gets if it travels 295 miles and uses 9 gallons of gasoline. *(Lesson 1-3)*

45. Determine whether $37 \div 5 = 7.4$ is reasonable. *(Lesson 1-4)* yes

46. Evaluate the expression $36 + 9 \div 3$. *(Lesson 1-7)* 39

47. **Smart Shopping** Packages of pencils come with 12 pencils. Pens are packaged 10 to a pack. To start the school year, Susan buys 3 packages of pencils and 2 packages of pens. What is the total number of pens and pencils she buys? *(Lesson 1-7)* 56 pens and pencils

48. **Algebra** Evaluate the expression $2x + 3(x + y) - xy$ if $x = 10$ and $y = 2$. *(Lesson 1-8)* 36

OPTIONS

Team Teaching

Inform other teachers on your team that your classes are studying exponents. Suggestions for curriculum are:

Science: space exploration; creation of solar system, Earth, evolution of life on Earth

Social Studies: population statistics, values of products and services on both a national and global scale

49. **Animals** It is believed that a dog ages 7 human years for every calendar year that it lives. *(Lesson 1-8)*

a. Write an expression for determining a dog's age in human years. Let y represent the number of calendar years the dog has lived. **7y**

b. Find the human age of a dog that has lived for 12 calendar years. **84 years old**

Problem Solving and Applications

50. **Geometry** To find the volume of a cube, you find the cube of the length of one edge. Find the volume of a cube with an edge of six inches. **216 cubic inches**

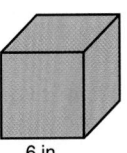

6 in.

51. **Number System** The base-ten number system uses powers of ten to express numbers. For example, 1 quintillion is the number expressed as a 1 followed by 18 zeros. How would this number be expressed as a power with a base of 10? 10^{18}

52. **Critical Thinking** Based on the pattern shown at the right, write a convincing argument that any number, besides 0, raised to the 0 power equals 1. Use the $\boxed{y^x}$ key on a calculator to see what happens. **See margin.**

$$2^4 = 16$$
$$2^3 = 8$$
$$2^2 = 4$$
$$2^1 = 2$$
$$2^0 = ?$$

53. **Portfolio Suggestion** A portfolio contains representative samples of your work, collected over a period of time. Begin your portfolio by selecting an item that shows something you learned in this chapter. **See students' work.**

Entertainment Industry Use the graph below for Exercises 54–56.

54. a. In which state was the most money spent?

54a. California

b. *About* how much money was spent? **$4,000,000,000,000**

55. *About* how much more money was spent filming on location in New York than in Massachusetts? **$999,800,000,000**

56. *About* how much money did film and television companies spend shooting on location in these five states? **$5,000,900,000,000**

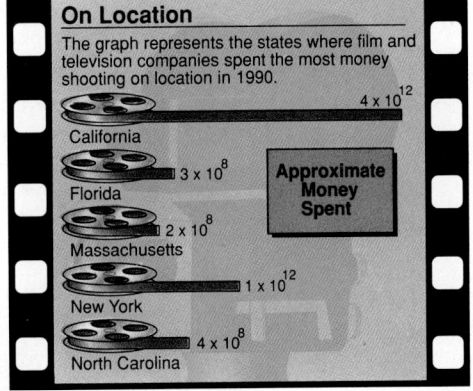

On Location

The graph represents the states where film and television companies spent the most money shooting on location in 1990.

California — 4×10^{12}
Florida — 3×10^8
Massachusetts — 2×10^8
New York — 1×10^{12}
North Carolina — 4×10^8

Approximate Money Spent

57. **Journal Entry** Why do you think expressions like 10^5 are written with exponents? **See students' work**

Lesson 1-9 Algebra Connection: Powers and Exponents **35**

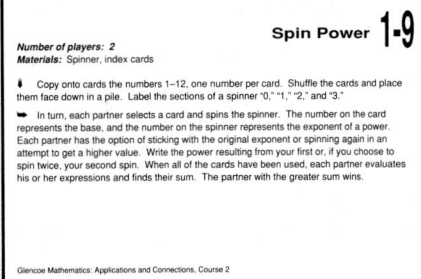

Enrichment Masters, p. 9

35

Management Tips

For Students   Have students work with partners and encourage them to discuss their formulas and results with other groups.

For the Overhead Projector
Overhead Manipulative Resources provides appropriate materials for teacher or student demonstration of the activities in this Mathematics Lab.

1 FOCUS

Introducing the Lab

Discuss the uses of spreadsheets with students. Ask them to suggest additional uses. If possible, use a computer to demonstrate the ease and speed with which a computer spreadsheet tabulates data.

2 TEACH

Using Applications   Suggest to students that they choose other topics of interest for their spreadhsheets, such as a record of batting averages, TV-watching hours, or money saved or spent.

1-9B Spreadsheets

A Follow-Up of Lesson 1-9

Objective
Describe a spreadsheet.

Words to Learn
spreadsheet
cell

A **spreadsheet** is a computer program that organizes numerical data into rows and columns. It is used for computing calculations and making overall adjustments based on new data.

Most spreadsheets can be as large as 999 rows long and 127 columns wide. The spreadsheet below shows data of test results for four students.

	A STUDENT	B TEST 1	C TEST 2	D TEST 3	E TOTAL	F AVERAGE
1	M. JONES	85	83	90	258	86
2	A. SMITH	91	95	87		
3	C. MAYO	77	89	92		
4	D. WHITE	100	68	93		

Each section of a spreadsheet is called a **cell**. A cell can contain data, labels, or formulas. The first cell in the upper left-hand corner is called cell A1. The cell directly to the right in column B and row 1 is called B1. The cell below that is B2. You can enter information in a spreadsheet one cell at a time.

To perform a calculation, you need to enter a formula in a cell. A formula can contain constant values, operations, and cell locations. Besides + (addition) and − (subtraction), the following operations can also be used: * (multiplication), / (division), and ^ (exponentiation).

What do you think?

Work with a partner. Use the spreadsheet on the previous page.

2. Add the scores in columns B, C, and D that correspond with the same row in cell E.

1. What test score is stored in cell C4? **68**
2. How are the totals in column E found? **See Solutions Manual.**
3. Copy and complete the spreadsheet on page 36.
4. What formula might you enter in cell E2 to find the total test scores for A. Smith? **B2 + C2 + D2**
5. What formulas might you enter in cells F2 to F4 to find the average test scores? $\frac{B2 + C2 + D2}{3}$, $\frac{B3 + C3 + D3}{3}$, $\frac{B4 + C4 + D4}{3}$
6. What formula might you enter in cell F5 if you wanted to find out the average test score of the four students? $\frac{F1 + F2 + F3 + F4}{4}$

	A	B	C
1	CITY	MILES WIDE	MILES LONG
2	EVERYWHERE		
3	NOWHERE	5	

Use the spreadsheet above to answer each of the following.

7. Cell B2 contains the formula B3 ^ 3. Find the value that would be in cell B2. **125**
8. What value would be in cell C3, if the cell contained the formula (B2 + B3) ^ 2? **16,900**
9. What value would be in cell C2, if the cell contained the formula (C3/130) ^ 2? **16,900**

Extension

10. Create a spreadsheet that computes a table of squares and cubes of numbers. **See Solutions Manual.**

Mathematics Lab 1-9B Spreadsheets   **37**

Using Questioning   Ask students questions similar to those in the first "What Do You Think?" section in order to make sure that they understand how to read a spreadsheet.

Close

Have students explain how a spreadsheet helps them to use data. Then ask them to describe how they would design a simple spreadsheet to keep track of the weekly hours of workers in a supermarket.

OPTIONS

Lab Manual   You may wish to make copies of the blackline master on p. 38 of the *Lab Manual* for students to use as a recording sheet.

Lab Manual, p. 38

Name _____   Date _____

Mathematics Lab Worksheet

Use with pages 36-37

Spreadsheets

What do you think?

1. The test score __68__ is stored in cell C4.

2. Add the scores in columns B, C, and D for rows 1, 2, 3, and 4

3.

1		B Test 1	C Test 2	D Test 3	E Total	F Average
	M. Jones	85	83	90	258	86
	A. Smith	91	95	87	**273**	**91**
	C. Mayo	77	89			

NCTM Standards: 1–4, 7, 9

Lesson Resources
- Study Guide Master 1-10
- Practice Master 1-10
- Enrichment Master 1-10
- Evaluation Master, Quiz B, p. 7
- Interdisciplinary Master, p. 15
- Group Activity Card 1-10

 Transparency 1-10 contains the 5-Minute Check and a teaching aid for this lesson.

🕐 5-Minute Check
(Over Lesson 1-9)

1. Write 4^5 as a product of the same factor.
   $4 \cdot 4 \cdot 4 \cdot 4 \cdot 4$

2. Write $3 \cdot 3 \cdot 3 \cdot 3 \cdot 3 \cdot 3$ using exponents. 3^6

Evaluate each expression.

3. 6^3 216
4. 12^5 248,832
5. n^4 if $n = 3$ 81

---

1 FOCUS

Motivating the Lesson

Activity   Have students remove and add weights or objects to one pan of a two-pan scale. Then have them tell how to keep the scale in balance.

2 TEACH

Using Models   Have students continue to use the two-pan scale to connect the idea of equal weights on a scale that is in balance with the concept of equal values on opposite sides of a true equation.

1-10 Solving Equations Mentally

Objective
Solve equations using mental math.

Words to Learn
equation
solve
solution

The __?__ Ocean is on the east coast of the United States. You cannot determine whether this sentence is true or false until you fill in the blank. If you say Atlantic, the sentence is true. If you say Pacific, the sentence is false.

An **equation** is a sentence in mathematics that contains an equal sign.

$45 + 12 = 67$ This sentence is false.

$32 - 10 = 22$ This sentence is true.

The equation $f + 9 = 16$ contains a variable. This equation is neither true nor false until f is replaced with a number. You **solve** the equation when you replace the variable with a number that makes the equation true. Any number that makes the equation true is called a **solution**. The solution to $f + 9 = 16$ is 7 because $7 + 9 = 16$.

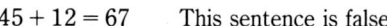

Example 1

Which of the numbers 8, 9, or 10 is the solution of $9 + t = 18$?

Replace t with 8.	Replace t with 9.	Replace t with 10.
$9 + t = 18$	$9 + t = 18$	$9 + t = 18$
$9 + 8 \stackrel{?}{=} 18$	$9 + 9 \stackrel{?}{=} 18$	$9 + 10 \stackrel{?}{=} 18$
$17 \neq 18$	$18 = 18$	$19 \neq 18$
This sentence is false.	This sentence is true.	This sentence is false.

The solution is 9.

The equation in the example above was solved by replacing the variable, t, with each number until a true sentence was found.

OPTIONS

Multicultural Education

Historically, different cultures have had their own ways of using symbols in algebraic expressions and equations. For example, to write equations, the ancient Chinese used a system of sticks placed in squares within a board.

Estimation Hint

• • • • • • • • • • • • •

Since 1940 + 20 = 1960, the answer should be close to the year 1960.

DID YOU KNOW

The toothbrush is thought to have been invented in China in the late 1400s. It may have been made of hog's hair.

Example 2 *Problem Solving*

Health The first toothbrush with nylon bristles was produced in 1938 in the United States. It was called Dr. West's Miracle Tuft Toothbrush. The first electric toothbrush was made by the Squibb Company 23 years later. What year did the first electric toothbrush makes its appearance?

Let y represent the year the electric toothbrush was invented. You need to solve the equation $y - 1938 = 23$ to find y. Start by making a guess. Replace y in the equation with your guess and see if the resulting equation is true. Do this until you find the value of y that makes the equation true.

We guessed 1968 first. Then we guessed 1958 followed by 1961.

$$y - 1938 = 23 \qquad\qquad y - 1938 = 23 \qquad\qquad y - 1938 = 23$$
$$1968 - 1938 \stackrel{?}{=} 23 \qquad 1958 - 1938 \stackrel{?}{=} 23 \qquad 1961 - 1938 \stackrel{?}{=} 23$$
$$30 \neq 23 \qquad\qquad\quad 20 \neq 23 \qquad\qquad\quad 23 = 23$$

This sentence is false.   This sentence is false.   This sentence is true.

The solution is 1961. The first electric toothbrush made its appearance in 1961.

Some equations can be solved mentally by using basic facts or arithmetic skills you already know well.

Examples

3 Solve $12m = 120$ mentally.

$$12 \cdot 10 \stackrel{?}{=} 120 \qquad \textit{You know } 12 \cdot 10 = 120.$$
$$120 = 120$$

The solution is 10. The value of m is 10.

4 Solve $b = \dfrac{56}{7}$ mentally.

$$8 \stackrel{?}{=} \dfrac{56}{7} \qquad \textit{You know that } \dfrac{56}{7} = 8.$$
$$8 = 8$$

The solution is 8. The value of b is 8.

Lesson 1-10 Algebra Connection: Solving Equations Mentally   **39**

Teaching Tip Some students may realize that when solving an equation they are actually solving a related number sentence. You may want to have students demonstrate this fact using one of the Guided Practice exercises.

More Examples

For Example 1

Which of the numbers 7, 8, or 9 is the solution of $6 + r = 14$?   8

For Example 2

Columbus landed in the West Indies in 1492. Sixty-five years later the equals sign appeared in the first algebra book that was published in English. In what year did the equals sign make its appearance? 1557

For Example 3

Solve $11m = 132$ mentally. 12

For Example 4

Solve $t = \dfrac{84}{7}$ mentally.   12

Reteaching Activity

Using Connections Using an overhead projector, write an equation that involves coins, such as $n + \$0.10 = \$0.25$. Have students use actual coins to model the equation. Ask students to choose the coins that will make the equation true. Emphasize that n represents the value of the coins needed.

Study Guide Masters, p. 10

Name _____ Date _____

Study Guide Worksheet 1-10

Algebra Connection: Solving Equations Mentally

An equation is a mathematical sentence that contains an equal sign.

Example   Phil can address 50 envelopes in an hour. How long will it take him to address 300 envelopes?

Let h represent the number of hours. The problem may be represented by $50 \times h = 300$.

$$50 \times h = 300$$
$$50 \times 6 \stackrel{?}{=} 300$$
You know that $50 \times 6 = 300$.
The solution is 6.
It will take Phil 6 hours to address 300 envelopes.

Name the number that is a solution for the equation.

Checking for Understanding

Exercises 1-3 are designed to help you assess students' understanding through reading, writing, speaking, and modeling. You should work through these exercises with your students and then monitor their work on Guided Practice Exercises 4-18.

Close

Have students make up a word problem that can be solved by writing and solving an equation. Then have them give their problem to a classmate to solve.

40

Checking for Understanding

Communicating Mathematics
1. to know if your answer is reasonable

Read and study the lesson to answer each question.

1. **Tell** why it is important to estimate when solving problems mentally.
2. **Write** a definition of *solution*. **A solution is any number that makes an equation true.**
3. **Tell** the solution of $4c = 12$. **c = 3**

Guided Practice

Tell whether the equation is *true* or *false* using the given value of the variable.

4. $j + 4 = 14; j = 18$ **false**
5. $p - 8 = 19; p = 27$ **true**
6. $10k = 200; k = 20$ **true**
7. $t \div 7 = 49; t = 7$ **false**

Name the number that is a solution of the given equation.

8. $q + 8 = 21; 12, \underline{13}, 14$
9. $d - 14 = 27; 39, 40, \underline{41}$
10. $9 \cdot 9 = r; \underline{81}, 82, 83$
11. $x \div 5 = 4; 10, \underline{20}, 30$

Solve each equation.

12. $3x = 21$ **7**
13. $g + 12 = 30$ **18**
14. $13 \cdot 11 = k$ **143**
15. $25 + 19 = a$ **44**
16. $n \div 4 = 20$ **80**
17. $c - 10 = 27$ **37**

18. **Travel** If it takes you 5 hours to travel 250 miles in a car, what is the average speed of the car? Use the equation $250 = 5r$ where r is the average speed of the car. **50 mph**

Exercises

Independent Practice

Name the number that is a solution of the given equation.

19. $a + 15 = 19; 4, 5, 6$
20. $b - 13 = 29; \underline{40}, 41, 42$
21. $11e = 77; 6, 7, 8$
22. $v \div 10 = 4; \underline{20}, 30, 40$
23. $33 + t = 51; 18, 19, \underline{20}$
24. $13 \cdot 9 = g; \underline{107}, 117, 127$
25. $w \div 12 = 8; 96, \underline{97}, 98$
26. $51 - 24 = b; \underline{17}, 27, 37$

Solve each equation.

27. $x + 35 = 91$ **56**
28. $m + 18 = 24$ **6**
29. $c - 15 = 71$ **86**
30. $15r = 105$ **7**
31. $\frac{n}{8} = 6$ **48**
32. $17y = 1,615$ **95**
33. $a - 75 = 98$ **173**
34. $d + 25 = 80$ **55**
35. $z \div 14 = 8$ **112**
36. $9g = 108$ **12**
37. $r - 29 = 117$ **146**
38. $\frac{f}{3} = 61$ **183**
39. $\frac{s}{6} = 12$ **72**
40. $234 - 89 = h$ **145**
41. $43 + z = 65$ **22**

OPTIONS

Gifted and Talented Needs

Have students work with a partner to construct a cross-number puzzle whose answers are the solutions to equations. Clues can be given as equations or as sentences. Have students share their puzzle with other students.

42. A number plus four is eight. What is the number? Use the equation
$b + 4 = 8$. **4**

43. A number less three is 14. Find the number. Use the equation $p - 3 = 14$. **17**

44. The product of a number and 6 is 84. What is the product? Use the equation
$6s = 84$. **14**

45. The quotient of a number and 22 is 7. Find the number. Use the equation
$e \div 22 = 7$. **154**

Mixed Review   46. Determine whether $163 + 75 = 438$ is reasonable. *(Lesson 1-4)* **no**

47. **Decorating**   Wallpaper for a bedroom costs $16 per roll for the walls and
$9 per roll for the border. If the room requires 12 rolls of paper for the
walls and 6 rolls for the border, compute the total cost for the decorating
job. *(Lesson 1-7)* **$246**

48. *True* or *False:* If $m = 2$ and $n = 3$, then $m + n = mn$. *(Lesson 1-8)* **false**

49. **Food Industry**   Pierre runs a pizza
parlor. His daily cost of operating the
parlor consists of a constant cost of $75
for rent, employee wages, and utilities
plus $1 for every pizza he makes.

   a. Write an expression for Pierre's total
   daily cost. Let n represent the
   number of pizzas Pierre makes during
   the day. **$75 + ($1)n**

   b. Find Pierre's total cost for a day during which he makes 45 pizzas.
   (Lesson 1-8) **$120**

50. Write the following product using exponents: $4 \cdot 4 \cdot 4 \cdot 4$. *(Lesson 1-9)* **$4^4$**

51. Find the number of seconds in 60 hours. *(Lesson 1-9)* **216,000 seconds**

*Problem Solving
and
Applications*   52. **Nutrition**   Suppose you eat 2 tablespoons of peanut butter a day. Two
tablespoons of peanut butter provides you with 8 grams of protein. If you
need 44 grams of protein a day, how many more grams of protein are
required? **36 grams**

53. **Geometry**   The perimeter of a square is four
times the length of one of its sides. What is
the perimeter of a square whose side has a
length of 21 centimeters? **84 cm**

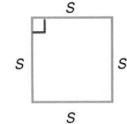

54. **Critical Thinking**   Consider the equation $0 + b = c$. What can you say about
the values of b and c? **They are equal.**

Lesson 1-10 Algebra Connection: Solving Equations Mentally   **41**

Extending the Lesson

Consumer Connection   Have
students solve the following problem.
*A tape player and a car radio cost
$340 together. Speakers cost $65
each. The tape player costs 3 times
as much as the radio. What does the
radio cost?*   **$85**

Cooperative Learning Activity

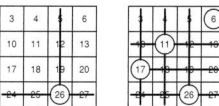

Gone Fishing 1-10

Number of players: 2
Materials: Index cards

⬥ Copy onto cards the numbers and equations shown on the back of this card. Decide
which partner will be the dealer.

➡ The dealer shuffles the cards and deals five to himself or herself and five to his or her
partner. The dealer then places the remaining cards face down in a pile. Each partner
removes any pairs from his or her hand. (A pair is an equation and its solution.) In turn,
partners try to make additional pairs by asking each other questions about the cards they are
holding. If you guess a card in your partner's hand, take the card, remove the pair from your
hand, and ask another question. If you do not guess correctly, take a card from the pile. If
you can form a pair using the card you selected from the pile, remove the pair from your
hand. The partner with the most pairs is the winner.

Glencoe Mathematics: Applications and Connections, Course 2

The Chapter Study Guide and Review begins with a section on Communicating Mathematics. This includes questions that review the new terms and concepts that were introduced in the chapter.

Then, the Skills and Concepts presented in the chapter are reviewed using a side-by-side format. Encourage students to refer to the Objectives and Examples on the left as they complete the Review Exercises on the right.

The Chapter Study Guide and Review ends with problems that review Applications and Problem Solving.

Chapter

1 Study Guide and Review

Study Guide and Review

Communicating Mathematics

Choose the correct term to complete the sentence.

1. The first step of the four-step plan is ___?___. **explore**

2. Front-end estimation is a process that can be used to estimate the ___?___ of two values. **sum**

3. The expression $3x - 4$ is called an ___?___. **algebraic expression**

4. Order of operations states that ___?___ precedes addition and/or subtraction. **multiplication**

5. In the expression 4^3, 4 is called the ___?___. **base**

6. In your own words, explain what should be done during the examine step of the four-step plan. **Check to see if your solution answers the question and if your solution makes sense.**

equation
exponent
solution
explore
product
sum
algebraic expression
multiplication
base

Self Assessment

Objectives and Examples	Review Exercises
Upon completing this chapter, you should be able to:	Use these exercises to review and prepare for the chapter test.
• solve problems using the four-step plan *(Lesson 1-1)* The four steps are *Explore, Plan, Solve* and *Examine*.	Use the four-step plan to solve. 7. A car traveling 60 mph will travel how far in 7 hours? **420 miles** 8. Ann starts the day with $100. If she spends $35 at the mall, how much is left for groceries? **$65**
• estimate sums and differences using rounding *(Lesson 1-2)* Estimate $8,324 + 6,936$. $\begin{array}{rr} 8,324 & 8,000 \\ +\,6,936 & +\,7,000 \\ \hline & 15,000 \end{array}$	Estimate using rounding. 9. $16,327 + 8,102$ **24,000** 10. $43,212 - 21,605$ **21,000** 11. $864 - 219$ **700** 12. $3,986 + 4,627$ **9,000** 13. $236,549 + 86,333$ **330,000**

Classroom Vignette

"In conducting in-services, I suggest that teachers use one form of the chapter test (in the Evaluation Masters booklet) as a pre-test for the next chapter. Pre-testing serves as a diagnostic tool that can identify a student's strengths and weaknesses and can provide valuable information for teacher planning."

Beatrice Moore-Harris

Beatrice Moore-Harris
Author

Objectives and Examples

Review Exercises

- estimate quotients using patterns *(Lesson 1-3)*

  Estimate $1,457 \div 33$.

  $1,457 \div 33 \rightarrow 1,500 \div 30 = 50.$
  $1,457 \div 33$ is about 50.

Estimate using patterns. **Sample answers are given.**
14. $987 \div 11$ 90
15. $12,042 \div 62$ 200
16. $1,100 \div 12$ 100
17. $6,350 \div 92$ 70
18. $254,102 \div 512$ 500

- use estimation to determine whether answers are reasonable *(Lesson 1–4)*

  Is $347 + 28 = 375$ reasonable?

  $\begin{array}{rr} 347 & 350 \quad \textit{Round} \\ + \ 28 & + \ 30 \\ \hline & 380 \end{array}$

  Yes, the answer is reasonable.

Determine whether the answers shown are reasonable.
19. $37 + 86 = 193$ no
20. $148 - 63 = 85$ yes
21. $1,840 \div 5 = 308$ no
22. $95 \times 118 = 14,210$ no
23. $\$0.94 \times 14 = \$13.16$ yes

- evaluate expressions using the order of operations *(Lesson 1-7)*

  Evaluate $3(9 + 7) - 4 \div 2 + 3$.

  $\begin{aligned} 3(9 + 7) &- 4 \div 2 + 3 \\ &= 3(16) - 4 \div 2 + 3 \\ &= 48 - 2 + 3 \\ &= 49 \end{aligned}$

Evaluate each expression.
24. $3 + 7 \cdot 4 - 6$ 25
25. $8(16 - 5) - 6$ 82
26. $12 - 18 \div 9$ 10
27. $83 + 3(4 - 2)$ 89
28. $75 \div 3 + 6(5 - 1)$ 49
29. $10(12 - 2) \div 10$ 10

- evaluate numerical and simple algebraic expressions *(Lesson 1-8)*

  Evaluate $6x - xy + y$ if $x = 10$, $y = 3$.

  $\begin{aligned} 6x - xy + y &= 6(10) - (10)(3) + 3 \\ &= 60 - 30 + 3 \\ &= 33 \end{aligned}$

Evaluate each expression if $p = 12$, $q = 3$, and $r = 5$.
30. $p + q - r$ 10
31. $\frac{p + q}{r}$ 3
32. $3(p + q) - r$ 40
33. $6qr - p$ 78
34. $25 - 2(p - 2q)$ 13

- use powers and exponents in expressions *(Lesson 1-9)*

  $2^5 = 2 \cdot 2 \cdot 2 \cdot 2 \cdot 2 = 32$

Evaluate each expression.
35. 10^3 1,000   36. 3^6 729
37. 15 squared 225   38. y^4 if $y = 4$ 256

- solve equations using mental math *(Lesson 1-10)*

  Solve $3s = 36$.

  You know that $3 \cdot 12 = 36$. So, the value of s is 12.

Solve each equation using mental math.
39. $t - 12 = 35$ 47
40. $8x = 88$ 11
41. $\frac{m}{4} = 16$ 64
42. $28 + r = 128$ 100

Chapter 1 Study Guide and Review   **43**

You may wish to use a Chapter Test from the Evaluation Masters booklet as an additional chapter review. The two free-response forms are shown below. One of the two multiple-choice forms is shown on the next page.

Evaluation Masters, pp. 5–6

Name _____ Date _____

Form 2A _____ *Chapter 1 Test*

Estimate. Use rounding.

1. $12,833 - 8,675$ 1. __4,000__
2. $5,285 + 6,287 + 7,244$ 2. __18,000__
3. sum of 2,899 and 11,208   3. __14,000__
4. difference of 8,742 and 5,336   4. __4,000__

Estimate. Use patterns.

5. $798 \div 4$ 6. $5,807 \times 30$ 5. __200__
     6. __180,000__

Determine whether the answers shown are reasonable.

7. $397 + 598 = 995$ 8. $702 - 96 = 606$ 7. __yes__
9. The sum of 55 and 348 is 503.   10. The difference of 916 and 586 is 330.   8. __yes__
     9. __no__
     10. __yes__

Evaluate each expression.

11. $36 \div (8 - 5)$ 12. $(44 + 55) \div 9 + 9$ 11. __12__

Evaluate each expression if a = 8, b = 4, and c = 2.

13. $2b - c$ 14. $3(a + b) - c$ 12. __20__
15. Write 7^4 as a product.   13. __6__
16. Write $11 \cdot 11$ using exponents.   14. __34__

Evaluate.
     15. __$7 \cdot 7 \cdot 7 \cdot 7$__

17. 10^4 18. 9 squared   16. __11^2__
     17. __10,000__

Solve each equation.
     18. __81__

19. $16x = 144$ 20. $l - 39 = 128$ 19. __9__
21. $29 + z = 117$ 22. $\frac{m}{7} = 22$ 20. __167__

Solve each problem.
     21. __88__

23. Will $50.00 buy a pair of running shoes at $46.95 and a pair of socks at $4.00?   22. __154__
24. In the 1986–1987 and 1987–1988 seasons, Larry Bird scored 4,351 points in basketball for the Boston Celtics. In the 1986–1987 season, he scored 2,076 points. How many more points did he score in the 1987–1988 season?   23. __No__
25. There are 10 audio-tape cassettes in a package for $15.95. How much will 40 cassettes cost?   24. __199__
     25. __$63.80__

BONUS Evaluate $2(5 - 2) \div ((6 - 3)6)$.   __$\frac{1}{3}$__

5

Glencoe Division, Macmillan/McGraw-Hill

Name _____ Date _____

Form 2B _____ *Chapter 1 Test*

Estimate. Use rounding.
     1. __12,000__

1. $24,856 - 12,978$ 2. __18,000__
2. $6,186 + 4,389 + 8,347$ 3. __14,000__
3. sum of 9,175 and 4,893   4. __5,000__
4. difference of 7,931 and 3,275   5. __54,000__

Estimate. Use patterns.
     6. __90__

5. $6,308 \times 9$ 6. $8,219 \div 88$ 7. __no__

Determine whether the answers shown are reasonable.
     8. __yes__

7. $4.79 + $1.41 = $6.90   8. $712 - 189 = 523$ 9. __yes__
9. The sum of 178 and 33 is 211.   10. The difference of 896 and 438 is 458.   10. __yes__

Evaluate each expression.
     11. __1__

11. $(25 - 9) - 5 \times 3$ 12. $(19 - 7) \div 3 + 9$ 12. __13__

Evaluate each expression if a = 10, b = 6, and c = 4.
     13. __8__

13. $3b - a$ 14. $2(b + c) - a$ 14. __10__
15. Write 6^5 as a product.   15. __$6 \cdot 6 \cdot 6 \cdot 6 \cdot 6$__
16. Write $11 \cdot 11 \cdot 11 \cdot 11$ using exponents.   16. __11^4__

Evaluate.
     17. __1,728__

17. 12^3 18. 4 squared   18. __16__

Solve each equation.
     19. __100__

19. $64 = l - 36$ 20. $19p = 171$ 20. __9__
21. $m + 41 = 80$ 22. $\frac{r}{3} = 35$ 21. __39__

If the problem has enough facts, solve it. If not, write the missing facts.
     22. __105__

23. Sanchez bought a sandwich for $3.95 and an orange juice for $0.75. How much change did he get from a $10 bill?   23. __$5.30__
24. The distance between successive bases on a baseball diamond is about 27.43 meters. About how far does a player run when hitting a double?   24. __about 55 m__
25. A VCR and a television set each cost the same. What is the total cost for the two items?   25. __The costs are missing.__

BONUS Evaluate $2[2(6 + 3) \div (6 - 3)2]$.   __6__

6

Glencoe Division, Macmillan/McGraw-Hill

Applications and Problem Solving

Choose the method of computation. Then solve.

43. Use all five even digits to form a two-digit number and a three-digit number which will yield the smallest possible product. *(Lesson 1-5)* **$20 \times 468 = 9,360$**

If the problem has enough facts, solve it. If not, write the missing fact.

44. **Seating** Anna, Barbara, Conchita, Doris, and Emma sit around a circular table. No two girls whose names begin with adjacent letters of the alphabet sit next to each other at the table. Emma sits on the right of Conchita. Where do the others sit? *(Lesson 1-6)*
Sample answer: Conchita, Emma, Barbara, Doris, Anna

45. **Business** A house painter finds that he needs 30 minutes to set up his equipment before painting and then 5 minutes for every square foot that he paints. Write an expression for the total time the painter needs. Let *n* represent the number of square feet he paints. *(Lesson 1-8)* **$30 + 5n$**

Curriculum Connection Projects

- **Language Arts** Write ten sentences in which the word *variable* is used as an adjective. Make a crossword puzzle or word search from the ten nouns *variable* describes.

- **Health** Learn an emergency procedure such as CPR or the Heimlich maneuver with a friend. Write steps for demonstrating your procedure to the class.

Read More About It

DeJong, Meindert. *The Wheel on the School.*
Smullyan, Raymond. *Alice in Puzzle-Land.*
Packard, Edward. *The Cave of Time.*

1. The Lewis Middle School Band is planning a bus trip to a band competition. There are 138 members in the band and each bus will hold 32 people. How many buses are needed for the trip? **5 buses**

Estimate. **Sample answers are given.**

2. $6,394 + 2,412$ **8,700**   3. $13,986 - 2,667$ **11,300**   4. $1,812 \div 94$ **20**

5. **Fast Food**   On a given day, a fast-food restaurant sold 1,545 ounces of cola, 1,239 ounces of lemon-lime drink, and 482 ounces of root beer. Estimate the total amount of soft drinks that were sold. **Sample answer: 3,100 ounces**

Determine whether the answers shown are reasonable.

6. $85 + 29 = 114$ **yes**   7. $8,799 \div 247 = 3.5$ **no**   8. $356 - 198 = 158$ **yes**

Choose the method of computation. Then solve.

9. Use all five odd digits to form a two-digit number and a three-digit number which will yield the largest possible product. $93 \times 751 = 69,843$

10. not enough facts; cost of student tickets

If the problem has enough facts, solve it. If not, write the missing fact.

10. **Sales**   Adult tickets for the fair are $5. Bob collected $100 for a total of 30 adult and student tickets. How many of each kind did Bob sell?

11. Name the operation to be done first in the expression $26 + 12 \div 3$. **division**

Evaluate.

12. $13 + 2 \cdot 4 - 6$ **15**   13. $5 + \frac{2mn}{4}$ if $m = 6$ and $n = 3$ **14**   14. b^3 if $b = 3$ **27**

15. **Animals**   Heather left her dog and cat at a kennel for 3 nights each. The kennel charges $8 per night for the dog and $5 per night for the cat. Compute Heather's total bill. **$39**

16. **Dessert**   Johnson's Real Ice Cream charges 25¢ for a cone and 75¢ for each scoop of ice cream added to the cone. Write an expression for the cost of an ice cream cone if n represents the number of scoops on it. **0.25 + 0.75n**

Solve.

17. $6a = 72$ **12**   18. $\frac{x}{8} = 100$ **800**   19. $p + 13 = 25$ **12**   20. $35 - m = 19$ **16**

Bonus   Find the last digit of 5^{10} without computing. **5**

Using the Chapter Test

This page may be used as a chapter test or another chapter review.

Evaluation Masters, pp. 1–2

Name _____ Date _____

Form 1A _____ *Chapter 1 Test*

1. Estimate $6,235 + 2,505$. Use rounding.
   A. 12,000   B. 10,000   C. 9,000   D. 8,000   1. __C__

2. Estimate $7,623 - 4,317$. Use rounding.
   A. 11,900   B. 3,000   C. 4,000   D. 5,300   2. __C__

3. Estimate the difference of 28,624 and 14,219.
   A. 14,000   B. 16,000   C. 4,400   D. 42,800   3. __A__

4. Estimate 551×6. Use patterns.
   A. 8,000   B. 3,600   C. 4,000   D. 3,000   4. __B__

5. Estimate the quotient of 9,497 and 28. Use patterns.
   A. 90   B. 900   C. 300   D. 30   5. __C__

6. Is $68 + 41 = 109$ reasonable?
   A. yes   B. no   6. __A__

7. Is $795 - 698 = 107$ reasonable?
   A. yes   B. no   7. __B__

8. Evaluate $5 \cdot 7 + 9 \cdot 6$.
   A. 480   B. 176   C. 54.72   D. 89   8. __D__

9. Evaluate $10 + (72 + 28) \div 50$.
   A. 12   B. 2.2   C. 14   D. 20   9. __A__

10. Evaluate $15(4 - 1) \div 5 + 5$.
    A. 6   B. 14   C. 4.5   D. 41   10. __B__

11. Evaluate $81 \div 9 + 33 - 5$.
    A. 757   B. 2   C. 37   D. 3   11. __C__

12. Evaluate $a + b - c$ if $a = 8$, $b = 3$, and $c = 5$.
    A. 6   B. 16   C. 0   D. 10   12. __A__

13. Evaluate $3ab$ if $a = 8$ and $b = 3$.
    A. 27   B. 14   C. 15   D. 72   13. __D__

14. Evaluate $\frac{3a}{4} - c$ if $a = 8$ and $c = 6$.
    A. 2   B. 0   C. 1   D. $\frac{3}{4}$ 14. __B__

15. Write 7^3 as a product.
    A. $3 \cdot 3 \cdot 3$ B. $7 \cdot 7$
    C. $3 \cdot 3 \cdot 3 \cdot 3$ D. $7 \cdot 7 \cdot 7$ 15. __D__

1
Glencoe Division, Macmillan/McGraw-Hill

Name _____ Date _____

Chapter 1 Test, Form 1A (continued)

16. Write $8 \cdot 8 \cdot 8 \cdot 8$ using exponents.
    A. 4^8 B. 8^8 C. 8^4 D. 4^4 16. __C__

17. Evaluate 2^6.
    A. 12   B. 64   C. 32   D. 26   17. __B__

18. Solve $m - 16 = 53$.
    A. 69   B. 37   C. 213   D. 848   18. __A__

19. Solve $17k = 153$.
    A. 170   B. 136   C. 2,601   D. 9   19. __D__

20. Solve $\frac{e}{8} = 16$.
    A. 2   B. 128   C. 8   D. 28   20. __B__

21. Solve $16 + y = 64$.
    A. 48   B. 4   C. 80   D. 1,204   21. __A__

22. The Donovans traveled 850 miles to New York City to attend a wedding. They took a different route home and traveled 915 miles. How many more miles did they travel on the way home?
    A. 915 mi   B. 65 mi   C. 135 mi   D. 75 mi   22. __B__

23. Use each of the digits 5, 6, 7, 8, and 9 once to form a two-digit number and a three-digit number that when multiplied have the least product possible. What is this product?
    A. 44,184   B. 39,463   C. 39,372   D. 39,273   23. __D__

24. Four boys share a large pizza. The medium size costs $6. The large size costs more than the medium size. How much did each boy pay?
    A. $1.50   B. $1.25
    C. $1.75   D. missing facts   24. __D__

25. Cal has $8.75. Len has three times as much except for $10 less. How much money does Len have?
    A. $8.25   B. $16.25
    C. $17   D. missing facts   25. __B__

BONUS   Solve $\frac{k}{3} = \frac{2}{9}$.   __B__

A. $\frac{2}{27}$ B. $\frac{2}{3}$ C. $1\frac{1}{2}$ D. $13\frac{1}{2}$

2
Glencoe Division, Macmillan/McGraw-Hill

Test and Review Generator software is provided in Apple, IBM, and Macintosh versions. You may use this software to create your own tests or worksheets, based on the needs of your students.

The **Performance Assessment Booklet** provides an alternate assessment for evaluating student progress. An assessment for this chapter can be found on pages 1–2.

2 Applications with Decimals

Previewing the Chapter

This chapter investigates operations with decimals and some of its many applications. Students compare, order, and round decimals, and estimate sums, differences, products, and quotients of decimals. They explore the use of powers of ten as a mental math strategy, and also work with scientific notation. Students also use estimation to determine reasonable answers in the **problem-solving strategy** lesson.

Lesson	Lesson Objectives	NCTM Standards	State/Local Objectives
2-1	Compare and order decimals.	1–6	
2-2	Round decimals.	1–6	
2-3	Estimate with decimals.	1–7	
2-4A	Multiply decimals using models.	1–7	
2-4	Multiply decimals.	1–7, 9	
2-5	Multiply decimals mentally by powers of ten.	1–7, 9	
2-6	Express numbers greater than 100 in scientific notation and vice versa.	1–7	
2-7A	Divide decimals using models.	1–6	
2-7	Divide decimals.	1–7, 9, 13	
2-8	Round decimal quotients to a specified place.	1–6, 13	
2-9	Change metric units of length, capacity, and mass.	1–5, 7, 13	
2-10	Determine whether answers are reasonable.	1–5, 7, 13	

Organizing the Chapter

LESSON PLANNING GUIDE

Lesson	Materials/Manipulatives	Extra Practice (Student Edition)	Blackline Masters Booklets									
			Study Guide	Practice	Enrichment	Evaluation	Technology	Lab Manual	Multicultural Activities	Application and Interdisciplinary Activities	Transparencies	Group Activity Cards
2-1		p. 574	p. 11	p. 11	p. 11						2-1	2-1
2-2		p. 574	p. 12	p. 12	p. 12			p. 39			2-2	2-2
2-3		p. 575	p. 13	p. 13	p. 13						2-3	2-3
2-4A	decimal models markers							p. 40				
2-4		p. 575	p. 14	p. 14	p. 14					p. 2	2-4	2-4
2-5		p. 575	p. 15	p. 15	p. 15	Quiz A, p. 16	p. 16				2-5	2-5
2-6		p. 576	p. 16	p. 16	p. 16						2-6	2-6
2-7A	decimal models markers							p. 41				
2-7	calculator	p. 576	p. 17	p. 17	p. 17		p. 2		p. 2		2-7	2-7
2-8	calculator	p. 576	p. 18	p. 18	p. 18						2-8	2-8
2-9		p. 577	p. 19	p. 19	p. 19					p. 16	2-9	2-9
2-10			p. 20	p. 20	p. 20	Quiz B, p. 16					2-10	2-10
Study Guide and Review			Multiple Choice Test, Forms 1A and 1B, pp. 10–13 Free Response Test, Forms 2A and 2B, pp. 14–15 Cumulative Review, p. 17 (free response)									
Test			Cumulative Test, p. 18 (multiple choice)									

Pacing Guide: Option I (Chapters 1–12) - 14 days; Option II (Chapters 1–13) - 13 days; Option III (Chapters 1–14) - 12 days
You may wish to refer to the complete **Course Planning Guides** on page T25.

OTHER CHAPTER RESOURCES

Student Edition
Chapter Opener, pp. 46–47
Mid-Chapter Review, p. 66
Cultural Kaleidoscope, p. 74
Portfolio Suggestion, p. 74

 Manipulatives
Overhead Manipulative Resources
Middle School Mathematics Manipulative Kit

 Software/Technology
Interactive Mathematics Tools (Macintosh)
Test and Review Generator (IBM, Apple, Macintosh)
Teacher's Guide for Software Resources

Other Supplements
Transparency 2-0
Performance Assessment, pp. 3–4
Glencoe Mathematics Professional Series Lesson Plans, pp. 13–24

INTERDISCIPLINARY BULLETIN BOARD

Science Connection

Objective Use decimals and scientific notation to describe data about space.

How To Use It Have students research amazing facts about astronomy to add to the bulletin board. Ask them to display their data using scientific notation when it is appropriate.

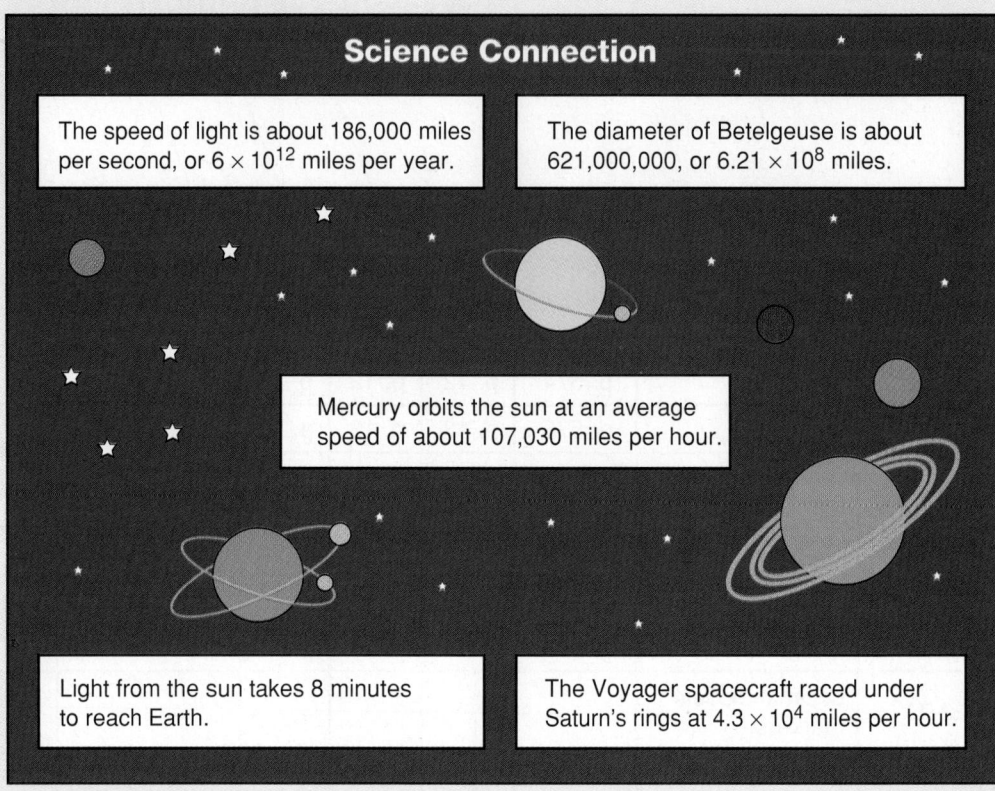

Science Connection

The speed of light is about 186,000 miles per second, or 6×10^{12} miles per year.

The diameter of Betelgeuse is about 621,000,000, or 6.21×10^8 miles.

Mercury orbits the sun at an average speed of about 107,030 miles per hour.

Light from the sun takes 8 minutes to reach Earth.

The Voyager spacecraft raced under Saturn's rings at 4.3×10^4 miles per hour.

APPLICATIONS AND CONNECTIONS

Applications	Lesson	Example	Exercise
Weather	2-1		38
Sports	2-1		39
Measurement	2-2		39, 41
Consumer Math	2-3		42
Geography	2-3		43
Animals	2-4	1	
Biology	2-4		42
Currency			43
Geology	2-5		30
History	2-5		31
Computer	2-5		33
Astronomy	2-6	3	42
Geography	2-6		41
Sports	2-7	3	
Animals	2-7		48
Science	2-7		49
Sports	2-8	1	
Astronomy	2-8	2	
Buildings	2-8		28
Geography	2-8		29
Photography	2-10		12
Connections			
Geometry	2-2	3	
Algebra	2-4	2	
Geometry	2-9		38

TEAM ACTIVITIES

Multicultural Experiences

Outside Field Trips A trip to a planetarium will show students an everyday use of decimal numbers, particularly those written in scientific notation.

A visit to a drug store or supermarket provides an opportunity for students to compare measure of metric mass and capacity.

In-Class Speakers Ask a track coach to visit the class and show how an understanding of decimals is needed to distinguish between many sports statistics such as racing times and points for gymnastics events.

Ask a pharmacist to visit and talk about how he or she uses metric measures nearly exclusively to fill prescriptions.

SUPPLEMENTARY BLACKLINE MASTER BOOKLETS

Some of the blackline masters for enhancing this chapter are shown below.

Application and Interdisciplinary Activity Masters, pp. 2, 16

Name _____ Date _____

Applications

Use with Lesson 2-4

Agriculture

To determine the income from their farm this year, the Ferrells need to know four things:

- what crops they will plant
- how many acres they will plant
- how much of the crop they can grow on an acre (the "yield")
- how much money they will receive for the crop

1990 yields and prices for various crops are given below. In the table, bu. stands for bushel.

Crop	Yield	Income
Corn	116.2 bu./acre	$2.25/bu.
Wheat	39.5 bu./acre	$2.61/bu.
Soybeans	34.0 bu./acre	$5.75/bu.
Rice	2.85 ton/acre	$142.00/ton
Sorghum	11.2 bu./acre	$2.05/bu.

Example How much income would the Ferrells receive for harvesting 250 acres of corn?

250 acres × 116.2 bushels/acre = 29,050

They expect to harvest 29,050 bushels of corn. At $2.25/bu., they expect their income to be
29,050 × $2.25 = $65,362.50

How much would the Ferrells receive for harvesting the following grains?

1. 260 acres of wheat
$26,804.70

2. 2,000 acres of rice
$809,400

3. 900 acres, half in wheat and half in sorghum
$46,392.75 + $10,332 = $56,724.75

4. 600 acres, twice as much in corn as in soybeans
$104,580 + $39,100 = $143,680

T 2
Glencoe Division, Macmillan/McGraw-Hill

Name _____ Date _____

Interdisciplinary Activity

Use with Lesson 2-9

Civics

If you own a house, you will probably have to pay taxes to the city or county in which it is located. Most cities give your house an "assessed value" and then charge you a certain amount of money per $100 of assessed value.

Example Find the taxes you would pay on a house assessed at $77,250 and having a tax rate of $2.1315 per $100 of assessed value.

Step 1 Find how many hundreds of dollars in $77,250.
$77,250 ÷ $100 = 772.5

Step 2 Find their taxes. Use a calculator.
2.1315 × 772.5 = 1,646.58375
The taxes on the $77,250 house are $1,646.58.

Estimate the taxes you would pay for houses with these conditions. Round dollar amounts as shown in the example.

1. a house assessed at $82,350 with a tax rate of $1.9235 per $100
$1,584.00

2. a house assessed at $109,200 with a tax rate of $0.8605 per $100
$939.67

3. a house assessed at $133,050 with a tax rate of $2.4009 per $100
$3,194.40

4. a house assessed at $25,120 with a tax rate of $0.8291 per $100
$208.27

5. a house assessed at a half million dollars with a tax rate of $1.0988 per $100
$5,494.00

T 16
Glencoe Division, Macmillan/McGraw-Hill

Multicultural Activity Masters, p. 2

Name _____ Date _____

Multicultural Activity

Use with Lesson 2-7

Teiji Takagi

Japanese mathematician Teiji Takagi (1875–1960) made significant contributions both to mathematical research and to the teaching of mathematics. As a researcher, he was responsible for revolutionary advances in the field of mathematics known as *algebraic number theory*. As a professor at Imperial University in Tokyo, he wrote several mathematics textbooks that became widely used throughout Japan. He also wrote several popular books that stimulated interest in mathematics among the general public.

Takagi's research centered on the mathematical structure that is called a **group.** An example of a group is shown in the table at the right. Here you see an operation ⊕ defined on the set of numbers {1, 2, 3, 4, 5, 6}. To perform this operation on two numbers in the set, you find the first number in the left column, then find the second number in the top row. For example, the shading in the table shows that 2 ⊕ 5 = 1.

⊕	1	2	3	4	5	6
1	2	3	4	5	6	1
2	3	4	5	6	1	2
3	4	5	6	1	2	3
4	5	6	1	2	3	4
5	6	1	2	3	4	5
6	1	2	3	4	5	6

Use the table above to find the value of each expression.

1. 4 ⊕ 5 **3**   2. 5 ⊕ 1 **6**   3. 6 ⊕ 2 **2**   4. 5 ⊕ 5 **4**

5. (3 ⊕ 5) ⊕ 2 **4**   6. 3 ⊕ (1 ⊕ 6) **4**

Tell whether each statement is true or false.

7. 2 ⊕ 5 = 5 ⊕ 2 **true**   8. 4 ⊕ 3 = 3 ⊕ 4 **true**

9. (1 ⊕ 2) ⊕ 3 = 1 ⊕ (2 ⊕ 3) **true**   10. 5 ⊕ (1 ⊕ 4) = (5 ⊕ 1) ⊕ 4 **true**

11. Find the value of each expression. What do you observe?
  a. 1 ⊕ 6 **1** b. 2 ⊕ 6 **2** c. 3 ⊕ 6 **3** d. 4 ⊕ 6 **4** e. 5 ⊕ 6 **5** f. 6 ⊕ 6 **6**
  When you perform the operation n ⊕ 6, the result is n.

12. In the group shown on this page, the operation ⊕ is sometimes referred to as *clock arithmetic*. Can you explain why? **The results are the same as if you were adding hours on a "six-hour clock,"** like the one shown at the right.

T 2
Glencoe Division, Macmillan/McGraw-Hill

Technology Masters, p. 16

Name _____ Date _____

Computer Activity

Use with Lesson 2-5

Multiplying by a Power of Ten

The program below will give you ten multiplication problems involving decimals and powers of ten. When prompted, write down the product as a decimal. The program will tell you if you are right or wrong. It will also give your score on the ten-question quiz it gives you.

	Problem Given	Your Answer	Your Score Out of 10:
1.			
2.			
3.			
4.			
5.			
6.			
7.			
8.			
9.			
10.			

TYPE
```
NEW
10   PRINT "MENTAL MULTIPLICATION"
20   FOR K = 1 TO 10
30   LET A = INT (RND(1) * 10000 + 1) / 100
40   LET B = INT (RND(1) * 5 + 1)
50   LET C = 10 ^ B
60   PRINT "MULTIPLY "; A; "BY "; C
70   INPUT W
80   IF ABS (W - A * C) < 0.1 THEN 110
90   PRINT "SORRY. NOT CORRECT."
100  GOTO 120
110  S = S + 1: PRINT "GOOD JOB!"
120  NEXT K
130  PRINT "YOU GOT "; S; "/10 ANSWERS CORRECT!"
140  END
```

T 16
Glencoe Division, Macmillan/McGraw-Hill

RECOMMENDED OUTSIDE RESOURCES

Books/Periodicals

Bitter, G. and J. Mikesell, *Sourcebook for Teachers Using the TI-12 Math Explorer Calculator,* Menlo Park, CA: Addison-Wesley, 1989.

Lewis, Anne C., *Making it in the Middle,* New York, NY: The Edna McConnell Clark Foundation, 1990.

Films/Videotapes/Videodiscs

Let's Go Metric, Teaching Resources Films, 1974.

Powers of Ten, Santa Monica, CA: Pyramid Film, 1968.

Weight and Mass, Oxford Films, 1974.

Software

IBM MathConcepts Series, Level III and Level IV, (IBM/Tandy), IBM

For addresses of companies handling software, please refer to page T24.

This two-page introduction to the chapter provides a visual, relevant way to engage students in the mathematics of the chapter. Questions are included that help students see the need to learn the mathematics in the chapter. Data in charts and graphs provide statistical information that students can analyze and interpret at this point as well as later in the chapter. The Chapter Project provides an activity that applies the mathematics of the chapter.

MAKING MATHEMATICS RELEVANT

Spotlight on Clubs and Recreation

The table and graph on page 46 use decimals to show relationships among clubs and social activities. Students will encounter many applications involving decimals in this chapter, including comparing, ordering, and operating with decimals.

Using the Timeline

Ask students (a) which event on the timeline occurred nearest to the turn of the last century and (b) which event happened during the administration of President John F. Kennedy. Then have students tell between which two events shown on the timeline their grandparents were in seventh grade.   (a) Wright Brothers' flight; (b) Peace Corps established

---

Chapter

2

Applications with Decimals

Spotlight on Clubs and Recreation

Have You Ever Wondered . . .

● How many people in the United States spend their free time by joining clubs or volunteering?

● How the number of boy scouts compares with the number of girl scouts?

Here are some of the most popular associations that Americans join:	membership in milions
American Association of Retired Persons	28.0
American Automobile Association	29.0
American Bowling Congress	3.3
American Farm Bureau Federation	3.3
Boy Scouts of America	4.8
4-H Program	4.8
Girl Scouts of the U.S.A.	3.1
National Committee to Preserve Social Security and Medicare	5.0
National Geographic Society	10.5

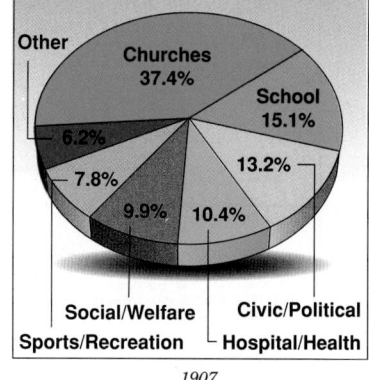

Americans Volunteer

Other — Churches 37.4%
School 15.1%
6.2%
13.2%
7.8%
9.9% 10.4%
Social/Welfare   Civic/Political
Sports/Recreation — Hospital/Health

GIRL SCOUTS

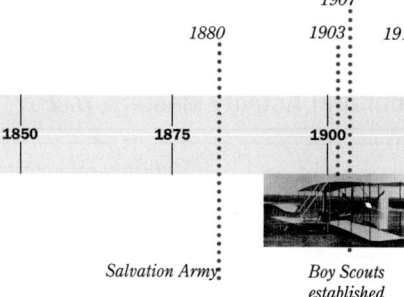

1907
1880   1903 1912

1850   1875   1900   1925

Salvation Army   Boy Scouts   Girl Scouts
                  established   established

46

"Have You Ever Wondered?" Answers

● Large numbers of people across the country belong to various organizations.

● The number of boy scouts is about 1.5 as great as the number of girl scouts.

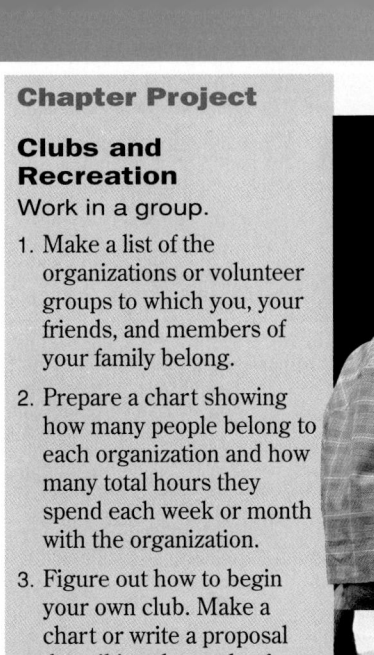

Chapter Project

Clubs and Recreation

Work in a group.

1. Make a list of the organizations or volunteer groups to which you, your friends, and members of your family belong.

2. Prepare a chart showing how many people belong to each organization and how many total hours they spend each week or month with the organization.

3. Figure out how to begin your own club. Make a chart or write a proposal describing the goals of your club, its expenses, and its sources of income.

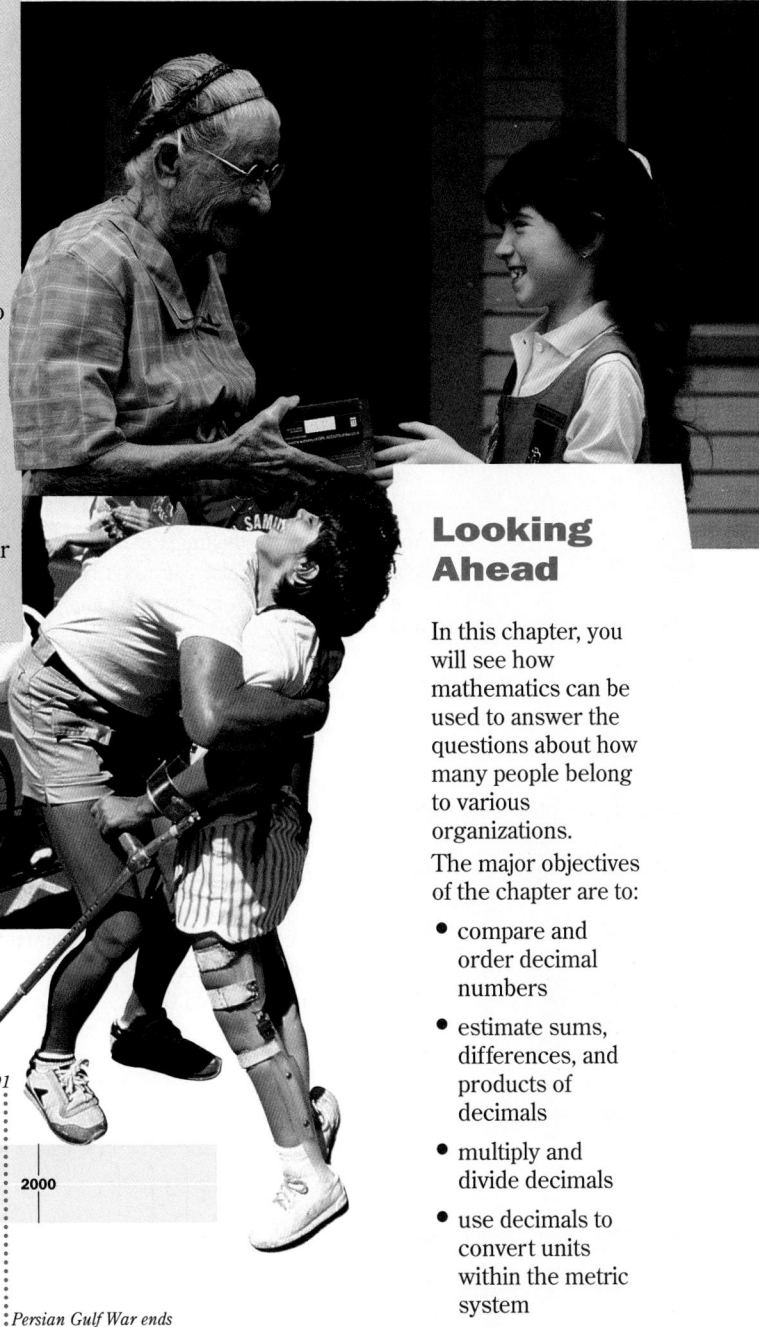

Looking Ahead

In this chapter, you will see how mathematics can be used to answer the questions about how many people belong to various organizations.

The major objectives of the chapter are to:

- compare and order decimal numbers

- estimate sums, differences, and products of decimals

- multiply and divide decimals

- use decimals to convert units within the metric system

1950s   *1961*   *1991*

1950   **1975**   **2000**

Peace Corps established

Persian Gulf War ends

47

Lesson Resources
- Study Guide Master 2-1
- Practice Master 2-1
- Enrichment Master 2-1
- Group Activity Card 2-1

 Transparency 2-1 contains the 5-Minute Check and a teaching aid for this lesson.

⏱ 5-Minute Check
(Over Chapter 1)

1. Estimate 14,924 + 5,032 using front-end estimation. 19,900

2. Estimate 4,719 ÷ 64

   Sample: 80

3. Evaluate the expression $18 - (7 \times 2) + 5$. 9

4. Evaluate $\frac{ab}{4}$ if $a = 6$ and $b = 12$. 18

1 FOCUS

Motivating the Lesson

Questioning Ask students to read the opening paragraph of the lesson. Ask them whether they should use estimation in order to choose the fast-food meal containing fewer calories.
Sample answer: Both meals are "about" 80 calories per ounce. To obtain a more useful answer it is better to keep the decimal amounts.

2 TEACH

Using Discussion Guide students to see the advantage of comparing decimals by comparing the digits in each place-value position. Ask students why they must be sure to align decimal points, and why they start at the left when comparing the digits.
so that digits compared have the same place value; to find as quickly as possible the greatest place value for which the compared digits are different

48

2-1 Comparing and Ordering Decimals

Objective
Compare and order decimals.

Are you hungry for a Quarter Pounder® with Cheese or are you having a Big Mac® attack? A McDonald's® Quarter Pounder® with Cheese contains 76.7 calories per ounce, and a Big Mac® contains 83.3 calories per ounce. The Big Mac® contains more calories per ounce. When you use words like *more, less,* or *equal to,* you are comparing numbers.

You can compare decimals like 76.7 and 83.3 using a number line. To graph these decimals, you need to locate the number on the number line and draw a dot at that point.

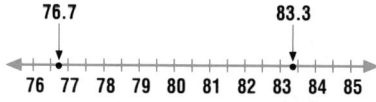

On a number line, numbers to the right are greater than numbers to the left.

Say: 83.3 *is greater than* 76.7.   **Write:** 83.3 > 76.7

OR

Say: 76.7 *is less than* 83.3.   **Write:** 76.7 < 83.3

You can also compare decimals by comparing the digits in each place-value position. The place-value chart below tells the position of each digit in the number 125.0674.

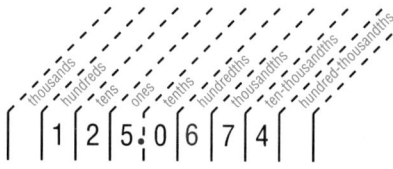

The digit 6 is in the hundredths position. This digit and its place-value position name the number six hundredths, 0.06.

To compare two decimals, align the numbers by their decimal points. Start at the left and compare the digits in each place-value position. Compare as with whole numbers.

48   **Chapter 2** Applications with Decimals

OPTIONS

Reteaching Activity

Using Applications Use the newspaper to find common baseball statistics such as batting averages. Some students can easily understand that a batting average of 0.324 is greater than one of 0.299 and may thus be guided to see that comparing batting averages is actually comparing decimals.

Study Guide Masters, p. 11

Name _____ Date _____

Study Guide Worksheet 2-1

Comparing and Ordering Decimals

Which is greater, 36.74 or 36.704?

You can compare the decimals on a number line.
Numbers to the right are greater than numbers to the left.

36.70 36.71 36.72 36.73 36.74

You can also compare decimals by comparing the digits in each place-value position.

Find the first place in which the digits are different.	Compare the digits.	The decimal with the greater digit is greater.
36.704 36.74	0 is less than 4. 0 < 4	36.704 < 36.74

1 Compare 24.9 and 25.3.

24.9 In the tens place, the digits are the same.

25.3 In the ones place, 4 < 5. So, 24.9 < 25.3.

You can check this by graphing 24.9 and 25.3 on a number line.

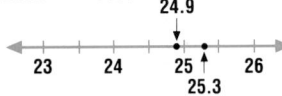

Since 24.9 is to the left of 25.3, 24.9 < 25.3.

2 Compare 0.43 and 0.4.

0.43 In the ones and tenths place,
0.4   the digits are the same.

To compare in the hundredths place, annex a zero to 0.4 to make it 0.40.

Annexing zeros to the right of a decimal produces *equivalent* decimals.

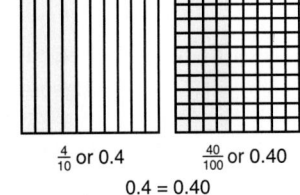

$\frac{4}{10}$ or 0.4 $\frac{40}{100}$ or 0.40

0.4 = 0.40

Now compare the   0.4**3**
hundredths place.   0.4**0**   *In the hundredths place, 3 > 0.*

So, 0.43 > 0.4.

Checking for Understanding

Communicating Mathematics

Read and study the lesson to answer each question.

1. **Draw** a place-value chart for 840.107. **See Solutions Manual.**

2. **Tell** a friend how comparing decimals is similar to and different from comparing whole numbers. **See margin.**

3. **Show** how you would compare 0.3 and 0.003. **Compare 0.300 to 0.003.**

Guided Practice

For number lines to Exercises 4–6,
Draw a number line to show which decimal is greater. see Solutions Manual.

4. 0.56, 0.51 >   5. 1.22, 1.02 >   6. 0.97, 1.06 <

Replace each ● with <, >, or =.

7. 2.15 ● 2.05 >   8. 7.9 ● 7.9 =   9. 1.3 ● 1.31 <

Exercises

For number lines to Exercises 10–15, see Solutions Manual.

Independent Practice

Draw a number line to show which decimal is greater.

10. 0.31, 0.33 <   11. 0.23, 0.29 <   12. 1.4, 1.04 >

13. 1.037, 1.009 >   14. 5.23, 5.0066 >   15. 2.5, 2.49 >

Lesson 2-1 Comparing and Ordering Decimals   **49**

Team Teaching

Inform the other teachers on your team that your students are studying decimals. Suggestions for curriculum integration are:

Social Studies: statistical analysis

Physical Education: measuring speed, distance

Science: life science and astronomical measurements (scientific notation); formulas in physical science; weather

Interactive Mathematics Tools

This multimedia software provides an interactive lesson that is tied directly to Lesson 2–1. Students will use changeable models to explore fractions.

More Examples

For Example 1

Compare 34.7 and 32.9.
34.7 > 32.9

For Example 2

Compare 0.52 and 0.5.
0.52 > 0.5

Teaching Tip Before assigning the exercises, remind students that the symbols > and < always point to the *lesser* number.

Checking for Understanding

Exercises 1-3 are designed to help you assess students' understanding through reading, writing, speaking, and modeling. You should work through these exercises with your students and then monitor their work on Guided Practice Exercises 4-9.

Additional Answer

2. In both cases you compare digits in the same place-value position. However, with decimals you may have to annex zeros in order to compare.

Practice Masters, p. 11

Error Analysis

Watch for students who incorrectly use the $>$ and $<$ symbols.

Prevent by reinforcing the fact that just as the $>$ and $<$ symbols always point to the lesser number, their open sides always face the greater number.

Close

Have each student, working with a partner, write three decimal numbers that the other must order from least to greatest. Have students check each other's work.

3 PRACTICE/APPLY

Assignment Guide
Maximum: 10–39
Minimum: 11–31 odd, 33–39

For **Extra Practice,** see p. 574.

Alternate Assessment

Speaking Have students verbalize a step-by-step procedure for comparing decimals.

Enrichment Masters, p. 11

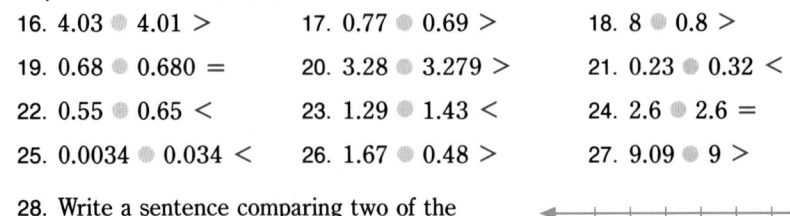

Replace each ● with $<$, $>$, or $=$.

16. 4.03 ● 4.01 $>$ 17. 0.77 ● 0.69 $>$ 18. 8 ● 0.8 $>$

19. 0.68 ● 0.680 $=$ 20. 3.28 ● 3.279 $>$ 21. 0.23 ● 0.32 $<$

22. 0.55 ● 0.65 $<$ 23. 1.29 ● 1.43 $<$ 24. 2.6 ● 2.6 $=$

25. 0.0034 ● 0.034 $<$ 26. 1.67 ● 0.48 $>$ 27. 9.09 ● 9 $>$

28. Write a sentence comparing two of the numbers shown on the number line.
Sample answer: 0.30 $<$ 0.50

Order each set of numbers from least to greatest.

29. 5.13, 5.07, 5.009
    5.009, 5.07, 5.13

30. 0.9, 0.088, 1.02, 0.98
    0.088, 0.9, 0.98, 1.02

31. 0.087, 0.901, 2, 1.001
    0.087, 0.901, 1.001, 2

32. 12.3, 12.008, 1.273, 12.54
    1.273, 12.008, 12.3, 12.54

Mixed Review
33. $10,000 ÷ 40 = $250

33. Use patterns to estimate the quotient of $9,850 and 36. *(Lesson 1–3)*

34. **Algebra** Evaluate the expression $6mn + n ÷ m$ if $m = 4$ and $n = 20$. *(Lesson 1–8)* **485**

35. Carla is 6 years old and is 12 years younger than Maria. How old is Maria? *(Lesson 1–10)* **Maria is 18 years old.**

36. Add 82,998 and 3,700 mentally. *(Lesson 1–4)* **86,698**

Problem Solving and Applications

37. **Critical Thinking** The numbers 999, 463, 208, and 175 are in order from greatest to least. Place decimal points in each number so that the resulting decimal will be in order from *least* to *greatest*. Do not rearrange the numbers. **0.999, 4.63, 20.8, 175.**

38. (a) 29.13 mm,
    29.97 mm,
    30.22 mm,
    30.53 mm,
    31.01 mm,
    (b) 31.01 mm

38. **Weather** A barometer is an instrument that measures atmospheric pressure in terms of millimeters of mercury. The higher the mercury rises in the tube, the higher the atmospheric pressure is.
    a. Order the following barometer readings from least to greatest:
       29.97 mm, 30.22 mm, 29.13 mm, 30.53 mm, 31.01 mm.
    b. At which barometric reading is the atmospheric pressure the greatest?

39. **Sports** The chart below shows the winning scores in the 1988 Olympic women's balance beam.
    a. Rank the scores in order from 1 to 4. The highest score gets a rank of 1. **See the chart.**
    b. Whose score(s) was higher than 19.875? **Daniela**
    c. Whose score(s) was lower than 19.875? **Phoebe and Gabriela**
    d. Whose score was higher, Gabriela's or Phoebe's? **They are tied.**

Women's Balance Beam	Points
Phoebe Mills **3**	19.837
Daniela Silivas **1**	19.924
Gabriela Potorac **3**	19.837
Elena Shoushounova **2**	19.875

50   **Chapter 2** Applications with Decimals

50

OPTIONS

Extending the Lesson

Decimals and Fractions Aaron, Julio, and Carla were comparing fossil finds. Aaron found a bone that weighed 0.64 pound, Julio a 0.6-pound bone, and Carla a $\frac{5}{8}$-pound bone. Ask students how they could determine which bone was the heaviest. **Change $\frac{5}{8}$ to a decimal; compare the decimals.**

Cooperative Learning Activity

Places in the Chart 2-1

Number of players: 4
Materials: Spinner, large sheet of paper, index cards

● Draw a place-value chart showing thousands place through ten-thousandths place. Make sure that an index card with the shorter sides at the bottom and top will fit in each place. Label the sections of a spinner with the digits 0–9. Make two sets of cards containing the digits 0–9. (Turn the cards as indicated above.)

➤ Work in pairs. Decide which pair will go first. One partner in the first pair spins the spinner. The partners then decide where on the chart to place the card showing this number. Once a card has been placed on the chart, it cannot be moved. Taking turns at the spinner, the partners continue, until all the places on the chart have been filled. The other pair repeats the procedure but tries to form a greater number than the first pair's. Play several rounds.

Glencoe Mathematics: Applications and Connections, Course 2

2-2 Rounding Decimals

Objective
Round decimals.

Engineers hope that one day soon they can build a roller coaster that will travel 100 miles per hour. Right now one of the fastest roller coasters in the world is The Beast at King's Island in Ohio. Its top speed is 64.77 miles per hour. What is its top speed rounded to the nearest whole number?

On the number line, the graph of 64.77 is closer to 65 than 64. To the nearest whole number, 64.77 rounds to 65.

64.77
64   65

You can round to any place-value position without using a number line.

Rounding Decimals	Look at the digit to the right of the place being rounded. • The digit remains the same if the digit to the right is 0, 1, 2, 3, or 4. • Round up if the digit to the right is 5, 6, 7, 8, or 9.

Examples

1 Round 1.84 to the nearest tenth.

1.84 → *The digit to the right of 8 (tenths place) is 4. So, 8 remains the same.* → 1.8

1.84 rounded to the nearest tenth is 1.8.

2 Round 14.295 to the nearest hundredth.

14.295 → *The digit to the right of 9 (hundredths place) is 5. So, 9 rounds up.* → 14.30

14.295 rounded to the nearest hundredth is 14.30.

Lesson 2-2 Rounding Decimals **51**

OPTIONS

Reteaching Activity

Using Models Reinforce the concept of rounding by having students use a number line to round several additional numbers to the nearest whole number and to the nearest tenth.

Study Guide Masters, p. 12

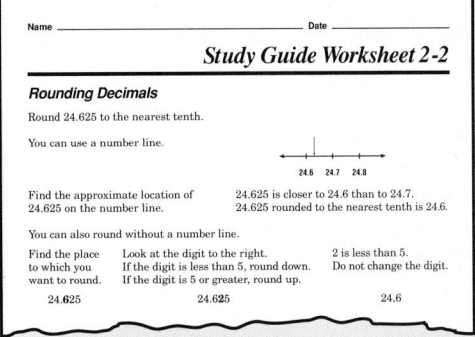

Name _____ Date _____

Study Guide Worksheet 2-2

Rounding Decimals

Round 24.625 to the nearest tenth.

You can use a number line.

24.6 24.7 24.8

Find the approximate location of 24.625 on the number line. 24.625 is closer to 24.6 than to 24.7. 24.625 rounded to the nearest tenth is 24.6.

You can also round without a number line.

| Find the place to which you want to round. | Look at the digit to the right.
If the digit is less than 5, round down.
If the digit is 5 or greater, round up. | 2 is less than 5.
Do not change the digit. |
| 24.625 | 24.625 | 24.6 |

2-2 Lesson Notes

NCTM Standards: 1–6

Lesson Resources
• Study Guide Master 2-2
• Practice Master 2-2
• Enrichment Master 2-2
• Lab Manual, p. 39
• Group Activity Card 2-2

Transparency 2-2 contains the 5-Minute Check and a teaching aid for this lesson.

⏱ 5-Minute Check
(Over Lesson 2-1)

Replace each • with <, >, or = to make a true sentence.

1. 3.06 • 3.08   <

2. 1.34 • 0.86   >

3. 7 • 0.7   >

Order each set of numbers from least to greatest.

4. 0.5, 0.55, 0.05, 0.505
0.05, 0.5, 0.505, 0.55

5. 0.076, 1, 0.76, 1.007
0.076, 0.76, 1, 1.007

---

1 FOCUS

Motivating the Lesson

Activity Write the following headlines on the chalkboard:
2.2 BILLION SOLD.
EASTMAN RUNS 100 IN 9.141 SECONDS.
LIGHTS PLACED EVERY 10.5 FEET.
ESTATE WORTH 55.5 MILLION.
Ask students to decide which of these statements contain exact numbers and which are probably estimates. Have them explain their reasoning. Answers will vary.

2 TEACH

Using Connections Discuss with students how rounding decimals is similar to rounding whole numbers. Then provide students with supermarket receipts. Ask them to round amounts to the nearest dollar *and* to the nearest dime.

Checking for Understanding

Exercises 1-3 are designed to help you assess students' understanding through reading, writing, speaking, and modeling. You should work through these exercises with your students and then monitor their work on Guided Practice Exercises 4-15.

Practice Masters, p. 12

Name _____ Date _____

Practice Worksheet 2-2

Rounding Decimals

Round each number to the place indicated. Draw a number line to support your decision.

1. 0.235; Round to the nearest tenth.   **0.2**

2. 3.492; Round to the nearest hundredth.   **3.49**

3. 8.0769; Round to the nearest thousandth.   **8.077**

Round each number to the underlined place-value position.

4. 9.4   **9**
5. 17.145   **17.15**
6. 0.392   **0.4**
7. 19.3208   **19.32**
8. 0.0063   **0.006**
9. 16.742   **16.7**
10. 6.13982   **6.1398**
11. 0.336   **0.34**
12. 1.873   **1.87**
13. 0.892   **0.9**
14. 0.444   **0.44**
15. 67.903   **67.9**
16. 84.590   **85**
17. 5.129806   **5.130**
18. 99.105   **100**
19. 62.017   **60**
20. 0.129866   **0.1**
21. 37.09   **40**

22. Draw a number line to show that, when rounded to the nearest whole number, 9.8 rounds to 10.

23. The Sears Tower, the world's tallest building, is 1,454 feet tall. Round this height to the nearest 100 feet.   **1,500 ft**

24. In 1990, the population of St. Louis, Missouri, was 396,685. Round this number to the nearest ten thousand and to the nearest hundred thousand. How do the numbers compare?   **400,000; 400,000; they are equal**

T 12
Glencoe Division, Macmillan/McGraw-Hill

Example 3 *Connection*

Geometry   There are some numbers that are not exact. Pi (π), which is a number used to find the area of a circle, is such a number. Pi is 3.1415926. . . . Round pi to the nearest hundredth.

First write pi to the thousandths place: 3.141.

3.141   →   *The digit to the right of 4 (hundredths place) is 1.*   →   3.14
So, 4 remains the same.

3.1415926 . . . rounded to the nearest hundredth is 3.14.

Checking for Understanding

Communicating Mathematics

Read and study the lesson to answer each question.

1. **Tell** why you can ignore all the digits to the right of 7 when you are rounding 6.37215 to the nearest tenth. **See margin.**

2. **Tell**, using the number line below, to what whole number you would round 14.37. **14**

   14.37

   13   14   15   16

3. **Show** how 9.1651 rounds to 9.2 on a number line. **See margin.**

Guided Practice

Round each number to the place indicated. Draw a number line to support your decision. **For number lines to Exercises 4–7, see Solutions Manual.**

4. 0.315 · Round to the nearest tenth. **0.3**
5. 0.2456   Round to the nearest hundredth. **0.25**
6. 7.0375   Round to the nearest thousandth. **7.038**
7. 17.499   Round to the nearest tenth. **17.5**

Round each number to the underlined place-value position.

8. 8.2 **8**
9. 12.1256 **12.13**
10. 23.09 **23**
11. 0.238 **0.24**
12. 16.4875 **16.5**
13. 0.218 **0.22**
14. 709.0921 **709.1**
15. 0.08541 **0.085**

Exercises

Independent Practice

Round each number to the underlined place-value position.

16. 23.48 **23**
17. 0.37 **0.4**
18. 0.789 **0.79**
19. 0.96 **1.0**
20. 1.572 **1.57**
21. 0.163 **0.2**
22. 0.0084 **0.008**
23. 15.451 **15.5**

OPTIONS

Gifted and Talented Needs

Have students work with partners. Ask them to list situations in which it makes better sense to round numbers down and situations in which it is most reasonable to round numbers up. Have students justify their choices.

Additional Answers

1. All numbers between 6.37000 . . . and 6.37999 . . . (inclusive) round to 6.4 to the nearest tenth. So the digits to the right of 7 can be ignored.

3.

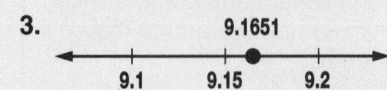

9.1651

9.1   9.15   9.2

Round each number to the underlined place-value position.

24. 3.1$\underline{4}$53 **3.15**   25. 4.52$\underline{9}$88 **4.530**   26. 0.4$\underline{4}$5 **0.45**   27. 0.$\underline{7}$87 **0.8**

28. $\underline{3}$8.56 **40**   29. 5$\underline{9}$.61 **60**   30. 0.5$\underline{5}$5 **0.6**   31. 1.7$\underline{0}$4 **1.70**

32. The height of the world's tallest mountain, Mt. Everest, is 29,067 feet. Round this height to the nearest thousand feet. **29,000**

33. Draw a number line to show how 3.67 rounds to 4. **See margin.**

Mixed Review   **34. $750**
34. Use rounding to estimate the sum of $179 + $213 + $355. *(Lesson 1-2)*

35. Juanita is preparing for her birthday party. She buys 2 boxes of cookies containing 24 cookies each and 3 packages of brownies containing 15 brownies each. Find the total number of dessert items she has bought. *(Lesson 1-7)* **93 items**

36. Evaluate 4^3. *(Lesson 1-9)* **64**

37. Solve $\frac{x}{6} = 3$ mentally. *(Lesson 1-10)* **18**

38. Order 6.32, 8.75, 9, 10.29, 8.78, and 9.15 from least to greatest. *(Lesson 2-1)* **6.32, 8.75, 8.78, 9, 9.15, 10.29**

Problem Solving and Applications

39. **Measurement**   Barry is using a ruler marked in centimeters to measure the length of the ribbon at the right.

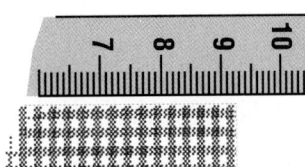

  a. To the nearest centimeter, what is the length of the ribbon? **9 cm**

  b. To the nearest tenth of a centimeter, what is the length of the ribbon?
     9.2 cm

40. **Critical Thinking**   In certain everyday situations, it is best to round *all* numbers up. What are some situations in which this might happen?
    Sample answer: When buying items you don't want to run out of, such as paint or lumber.

41. **Measurement**   A gill is a unit of capacity that is equal to one-fourth of a pint. It has a volume of 7.2187 cubic inches. To the nearest hundredth of a cubic inch, what is its volume? **7.22 in³**

42. **Journal Entry**   Why do people use rounded numbers, even when they know the exact amount? For example, why would you tell a friend you live about a mile from school, even if you knew that you actually lived 1.1 miles from school? **Sample answer: It is simpler.**

Lesson 2-2 Rounding Decimals   **53**

Extending the Lesson

Using Number Sense   Have students write both the least and greatest numbers, expressed in thousandths, that round to 5.5, when rounded to the nearest tenth, and round to 5.48, when rounded to the nearest hundredth. Ask students to explain how they solved the problem and to make up others like it to challenge classmates.   5.475; 5.484; Problems will vary.

Cooperative Learning Activity

Rounding Race 2-2

Number of players: 2
Materials: Large sheet of paper, yardstick, counters, spinner

• On a large sheet of paper (or several sheets taped together), copy the two lines shown below. Make sure that you can fit a counter on each tick mark. Label the sections of one spinner "1," "2," "3," and "5." This spinner is for the digits in ones place. Label the sections of another spinner with the digits 0–9. This spinner stands for the digits in tenths place.

► Each partner places a counter on the first tick mark of one of the side-by-side lines. Decide which partner goes first. In turn, each partner spins both spinners, rounds the resulting decimal to the nearest whole number, and moves his or her counter forward by this number of tick marks. Try to be the first to move your counter past the last tick mark.

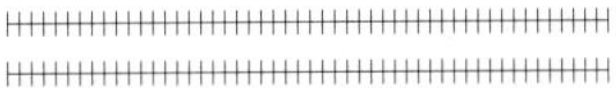

Glencoe Mathematics: Applications and Connections, Course 2

Close
Have students round the number 25.6271 to the nearest whole number, tenth, hundredth, and thousandth.   26; 25.6; 25.63; 25.627

3 PRACTICE/APPLY

Assignment Guide
Maximum: 16–42
Minimum: 17–33 odd, 34–41

For **Extra Practice**, see p. 574.

Alternate Assessment

Speaking   Have students explain why 12.803 rounded to the nearest hundredth is *not* 12.8. Ask them to give the correct answer.
12.8 is not a number expressed in hundredths; 12.80

Additional Answer
33.

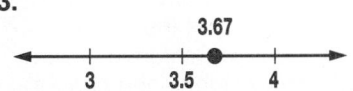

3.67

3   3.5   4

On the number line, 3.67 is closer to 4 than to 3.

Enrichment Masters, p. 12

Name _____   Date _____

Enrichment Worksheet 2-2

Record-Breaking Rides
Round each decimal to the nearest tenth. Then use the letter to show its location on the number lines below.

Letter	Decimal	Letter	Decimal	Letter	Decimal	Letter	Decimal
A	0.41	G	0.738	M	0.067	S	7.72
A	3.316	H	6.252	N	2.909	T	4.11
A	7.28	H	4.236	N	0.98	T	7.78
B	6.71	I	4.99	O	2.475	T	3.86
E	4.377	L	3.752	O	2.68	T	6.181
E	6.93	L	1.82	P	5.06	U	1.23
E	5.43	M	1.365	R	5.707	U	3.639
E	6.646	M	2.103	S	3.08	V	4.667
						X	1.608

Located in Cedar Point Park, Sandusky, Ohio, this roller coaster has the highest vertical drop.

This Japanese roller coaster is one of the tallest in the world. It is 246 feet tall.

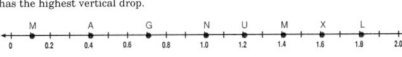

This large, looping roller coaster is found at Six Flags Magic Mountain in Valencia, California.

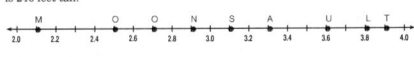

With a run of 1.4 miles, this roller coaster at Kings Island near Cincinnati, Ohio, may be the longest in the world.

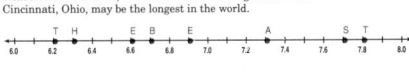

T12
Glencoe Division, Macmillan/McGraw-Hill

53

Lesson Resources
- Study Guide Master 2-3
- Practice Master 2-3
- Enrichment Master 2-3
- Group Activity Card 2-3

 Transparency 2-3 contains the 5-Minute Check and a teaching aid for this lesson.

🕐 **5-Minute Check**
(Over Lesson 2-2)

Round each number to the underlined place-value position.

1. 4.2<u>6</u>82   4.27
2. 0.<u>6</u>45   0.6
3. 0.6<u>6</u>6   0.67
4. <u>6</u>4.77   60
5. At 14,494 feet, Mount Whitney is the tallest peak in California. Round this height to the nearest hundred feet.   14,500 feet

---

1 FOCUS

Motivating the Lesson

Activity On the chalkboard, make a long list of prices to look like a receipt from a drugstore or supermarket. Ask students to describe a strategy they can use to make a reasonable estimate of the sum of the prices. Then have them apply and compare their strategies.

2 TEACH

Using Discussion Some students may be reluctant to make estimates using the methods presented, thinking that only exact answers are acceptable. Discuss situations in which estimates are more useful or descriptive than exact answers.

2-3 Estimating with Decimals

Objective
Estimate with decimals.

Words to Learn
clustering

In a recent year, some of the busiest airports in the United States were Dallas/Fort Worth, San Francisco, Los Angeles, Hartsfield in Atlanta, John F. Kennedy (JFK) in New York, and O'Hare in Chicago. *About* how many millions of passengers use these airports in one year?

Airport	Passengers (in millions)
Dallas/Fort Worth	47.6
Hartsfield, Atlanta	43.3
JFK, New York City	30.3
Los Angeles	45
O'Hare, Chicago	59.1
San Francisco	29.9

To solve this problem, you can use *rounding* to estimate the answer. To estimate by rounding, round each addend to its greatest place-value position. Then complete the operation.

$$
\begin{array}{rcr}
47.6 & \rightarrow & 50 \\
43.3 & \rightarrow & 40 \\
30.3 & \rightarrow & 30 \\
45.0 & \rightarrow & 50 \\
59.1 & \rightarrow & 60 \\
+29.9 & \rightarrow & +\ 30 \\
\hline
& & 260
\end{array}
$$

There are *about* 260 million passengers using these airports in one year.

DID YOU KNOW

260 million passengers . . . that's more than the population of the United States. It must be noted, though, that many of these passengers are probably repeat passengers. That is, the same person uses these airports several times a year.

Examples

1 Estimate the difference of 16.295 and 8.762.

$$
\begin{array}{rcr}
16.295 & \rightarrow & 16 \\
-\ 8.762 & \rightarrow & -\ 9 \\
\hline
& & 7
\end{array}
$$
  The difference is *about* 7.

2 Estimate the product of 34.9 and 48.3.

$$
\begin{array}{rcr}
34.9 & \rightarrow & 30 \\
\times 48.3 & \rightarrow & \times\ 50 \\
\hline
& & 1{,}500
\end{array}
$$
  The product is *about* 1,500.

You can also use **clustering** to estimate sums. Clustering is used in addition situations if the numbers seem to be clustered around a common quantity.

OPTIONS

Limited English Proficiency

Focus on the term *estimation*. Ask students to describe situations that involve making estimates, such as estimating a length of time, a weight, a height, and so on.

Example 3 *Problem Solving*

Homework Latricia used a calculator to solve a math homework problem. She added 32.8, 29.7, 34.1, 30.9, 27.5, and 33.6 and got 157.9. Check the reasonableness of her answer using clustering.

All the numbers are clustered around 30. There are six numbers. So, the sum is *about* 30×6, or 180.

157.9 is not very close to 180. Latricia may have made an error in entering the numbers. She should add the six numbers again.

You can review estimation using rounding on page 8.

You can use rounding to estimate a sum or a product.

Examples

Estimate using rounding.

4 Estimate the sum of 5.82, 2.19, 8.1, and 6.05.

$$
\begin{array}{rcr}
5.82 & \rightarrow & 6 \\
2.19 & \rightarrow & 2 \\
8.1 & \rightarrow & 8 \\
+\ 6.05 & \rightarrow & +\ 6 \\
\hline
& & 22
\end{array}
$$

The estimate is 22.

5 Estimate $23.9 - 11.4$.

$$
\begin{array}{rcr}
23.9 & \rightarrow & 24 \\
-11.4 & \rightarrow & -11 \\
\hline
& & 13
\end{array}
$$

The estimate is 13.

You can review using patterns on page 11.

You can use patterns to estimate quotients.

Example 6

Divide 0.59 by 2.3.

$$2.3\overline{)0.59} \quad \rightarrow \quad 2\overline{)0.6}^{\,0.3} \qquad \text{The quotient is } about\ 0.3.$$

Checking for Understanding

Communicating Mathematics

Read and study the lesson to answer each question.

1. **Tell** why estimation is helpful when using a calculator to solve math problems. **Sample answer: to help you catch errors in entering the numbers**

2. See margin.
2. **Tell** whether you agree or disagree with the following statement and why.
   An estimate is a good way to answer the opening question of this lesson.

3. **Write** a sentence describing when it makes sense to use the clustering method to estimate a sum. **when the numbers seem to be clustered around a common quantity**

Lesson 2-3 Estimating with Decimals **55**

More Examples

For Example 1

Use rounding to estimate the difference of 14.388 and 9.563. about 4

For Example 2

Estimate the product of 28.7 and 62.6 about 1,800

For Example 3

Toby added 18.45, 22.5, 20.77, 19.05, 24.1, and 17.64 on a calculator and got an answer of 162.61. Check the answer using clustering. about 6 × 20, or 120

For Example 4

Estimate the sum of 6.27, 3.4, 7.8 and 8.75. 26

For Example 5

Estimate 34.8 − 13.5. 21

For Example 6

Use a pattern to divide 3.7 by 6.4. about 0.6

Checking for Understanding

Exercises 1-3 are designed to help you assess students' understanding through reading, writing, speaking, and modeling. You should work through these exercises with your students and then monitor their work on Guided Practice Exercises 4-16.

Additional Answer

2. Answers will vary. Sample answer: Since a precise number is not needed, an estimate is an acceptable form for the answer.

Reteaching Activity

Using Cooperative Groups Have students use the topic of buying items in a store to formulate problems involving addition, subtraction, multiplication, and division of decimals. Have students, as a group, investigate which estimation strategies or combination of strategies provide the most useful answers to the problems. Have them share their findings.

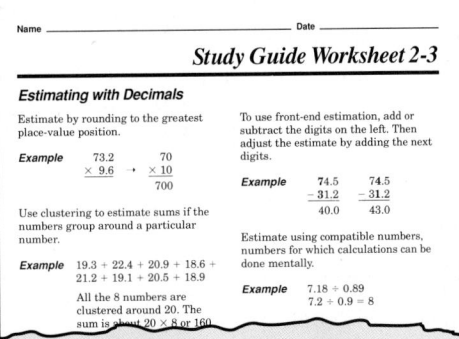

Study Guide Masters, p. 13

Name _____ Date _____

Study Guide Worksheet 2-3

Estimating with Decimals

Estimate by rounding to the greatest place-value position.

Example
$$
\begin{array}{r}
73.2 \\
\times\ 9.6
\end{array}
\rightarrow
\begin{array}{r}
70 \\
\times\ 10 \\
\hline
700
\end{array}
$$

Use clustering to estimate sums if the numbers group around a particular number.

Example $19.3 + 22.4 + 20.9 + 18.6 + 21.2 + 19.1 + 20.5 + 18.9$

All the 8 numbers are clustered around 20. The sum is about 20×8 or 160.

To use front-end estimation, add or subtract the digits on the left. Then adjust the estimate by adding the next digits.

Example
$$
\begin{array}{r}
74.5 \\
-31.2 \\
\hline
40.0
\end{array}
\qquad
\begin{array}{r}
74.5 \\
-31.2 \\
\hline
43.0
\end{array}
$$

Estimate using compatible numbers, numbers for which calculations can be done mentally.

Example $7.18 \div 0.89$
$7.2 \div 0.9 = 8$

55

Error Analysis

Watch for students who always use rounding to estimate, even when another strategy may make more sense.

Prevent by presenting students with a situation in which rounding is not an appropriate strategy. An example is deciding whether a five-dollar bill will pay for purchases of $1.19, $1.20, $1.21, and $1.18. The amounts cluster around $1.20. Thus, 4 × $1.20, or $4.80 is less than $5.00

Close

Have students describe the difference between using clustering and using rounding to estimate sums. Ask them to explain how to use a pattern to estimate quotients.

3 PRACTICE/APPLY

Assignment Guide

Maximum: 17–43
Minimum: 17–33 odd, 35–39, 41

For **Extra Practice,** see p. 575.

Practice Masters, p. 13

Name _____ Date _____

Practice Worksheet 2-3

Estimating with Decimals

Estimate by rounding.

1. 5.98
   +9.82
   ‾‾16‾‾

2. 8.2
   ×9.1
   ‾‾72‾‾

3. 6.8)49.42
   7

Estimate by clustering.

4. 71.1 + 69.8 + 70.9
   210

5. 6.8 + 7.3 + 7.1
   21

6. 15.2 + 14.9 + 14.8
   45

Estimate by using front-end estimation.

7. 8.71
    6.43
   +5.98
   ‾‾21‾‾

8. 12.76
    10.91
     9.23
   +13.25
   ‾‾46‾‾

9. 16.19
    −2.18
   ‾‾14‾‾

Estimate by using compatible numbers.

10. 7.2)84.1 12

11. 29.8)986.24 33

12. 6.3)89.92 15

Estimate. Use an appropriate strategy. Accept all reasonable estimates.

13. $9.82
     8.71
    +6.18
    ‾$25‾

14. 2.4
    +8.87
    ‾‾11‾‾

15. 29.53
    −18.12
    ‾‾12‾‾

16. 8.9
    ×6.1
    ‾54‾

17. 27.2
    ×9.7
    ‾270‾

18. 5.3)39.61 8

19. 3.1 + 2.9 + 2.87 + 3.3 12

20. 81.2 + 79.9 + 80.22 240

21. 30.2)119.1 4

T13
Glencoe Division, Macmillan/McGraw-Hill

Estimate by rounding.

4.   9.56
   + 5.34
   ‾‾15‾‾

5. 23.84
   + 12.13
   ‾‾30‾‾

6.   6.8
   × 3.7
   ‾‾28‾‾

7.   7
   9.3)65.48

Estimate by clustering.

8. 56.9 + 63.2 + 59.3 + 61.1
   4(60) = 240

9. 18.4 + 22.5 + 20.7
   3(20) = 60

Estimate by using rounding.

10. 32.6
     56.2
   + 71.9
   ‾160‾

11. 13.21
    − 8.23
    ‾‾5‾‾

12. 9.34
   + 3.18
   ‾‾12‾‾

Estimate by using patterns.

13. 2.6)8.99 3

14. 38.1)984.76 25

15. 6.8)40.79 6

16. **Games** You are watching Wheel of Fortune and the letters R, S, T, N, and L are chosen to solve the puzzle. Use the table at the right to estimate what percent of the time at least one of these letters would appear in the puzzle. 7 + 6 + 11 + 7 + 3 = 34 → 34%

Percentage That Each Letter Is Used.					
A	8.2	J	0.1	S	6.0
B	1.4	K	0.4	T	10.5
C	2.8	L	3.4	U	2.5
D	3.8	M	2.5	V	0.9
E	13.0	N	7.0	W	1.5
F	3.0	O	8.0	X	0.2
G	2.0	P	2.0	Y	2.0
H	5.3	Q	0.1	Z	0.07
I	6.5	R	6.8		

Exercises

Estimate. Use an appropriate strategy. Sample answers given.

17. $3.27
    6.75
   + 8.56
   ‾$19‾

18. 19.5
   +56.13
   ‾‾75‾‾

19. 34.3
   −18.9
   ‾‾10‾‾

20. 67.86
   −24.35
   ‾‾50‾‾

21. 7.5
   ×8.4
   ‾64‾

22. 26.3
   × 9.7
   ‾260‾

23. 8.1)73.8
    9

24. 18.4)41.7
    2

25. 121.5
   +487.8
   ‾600‾

26. $76.22
   − 47.34
   ‾$30‾

27. 32.5
   ×81.4
   ‾2,400‾

28. 11.4)35.7 3

29. 50.4 + 51.1 + 48.9 + 49.5 200

30. 9.9 + 10.0 + 10.3 + 11.1 40

31. 100.5 + 97.8 + 101.6 + 100.2 + 99.3 + 99.1 600

32. Estimate the quotient of 119 and 23. 120 ÷ 20 = 6

33. Estimate the product of 72 and 99. 7,200

34. Estimate the difference of 69.4 and 16.2. 50

56 Chapter 2 Applications with Decimals

OPTIONS

Bell Ringer

Write on the chalkboard:
The height of a tall tree might be:
12.2 ft 122.2 ft 1,222.2 ft
122.2 ft

Ask students which answer is the most reasonable. Have them work with partners to write a 5-item quiz similar to the sample. Have students provide answers to their items.

35. **Sports** Min has a collection of 269 baseball cards. He trades 25 of them to a friend for an autographed baseball. Min says he has 214 cards left in his collection. Is this reasonable? *(Lesson 1-4)* **no**

36. **Algebra** Write an expression that represents a $500 donation plus $5 for every event. Let *n* represent the number of events. *(Lesson 1-8)* **500 + 5*n***

37. Solve $m + 18 = 33$ *(Lesson 1-10)* **15**

38. Replace the ● in the following sentence with <, >, or =. 0.2 ● 0.214 *(Lesson 2-1)* **<**

39. **Outdoor Exercise** A ski resort advertises a new cross country ski trail that is 5.673 miles long. To the nearest 0.1 mile, what is the length of the trail? *(Lesson 2-2)* **5.7 miles**

40. **Critical Thinking** Using rounding, an estimate of $11 + 38$ is 50 and an estimate of $14 + 44$ is 50. Which estimate is closest to the exact sum? Why? **11 + 38; because one number rounds up and one rounds down.**

41. **Land Speed** In 1910, the land speed record was 131.72 miles per hour. In 1970, it was 622.29 miles per hour. About how many times faster was the speed in 1970? **about 5 times faster**

42. **Consumer Math** The menu at the right appears at the snack counter of a local movie theater. Use estimation to answer each question.

Popcorn . . . . sm.	$1.69
. . . . lg.	$2.79
Nachos w/cheese	$2.29
Soft drinks . . . . sm.	$0.95
. . . . med.	$1.35
. . . . lg.	$1.95

    a. *About* how much do a small popcorn and 2 medium soft drinks cost? **$4.50**

    b. Is $4.00 enough to buy nachos with cheese and a small soft drink? **yes**

    c. Is $3.21 the correct change from $5.00 for a large popcorn? **no**

43. **Geography** The table at the right shows the length in miles of the three longest rivers in the world. *About* how many miles long are the three rivers? **about 12,000 miles**

    Longest Rivers
    This graph shows the longest rivers in the world. Their lengths are shown in thousands of miles.

Nile	4.132
Miss./Mo./Red Rock	3.9
Amazon	3.83

Extending the Lesson

Using Menus Provide copies of a take-out menu from a local restaurant. Have pairs of students pretend that they have a certain amount of money to spend. Have them use the menu to choose meals they could order without spending more than they have.

Cooperative Learning Activity

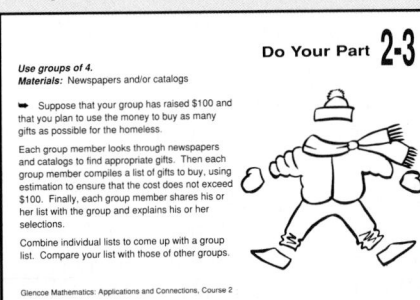

Do Your Part 2-3

Use groups of 4.
Materials: Newspapers and/or catalogs

➡ Suppose that your group has raised $100 and that you plan to use the money to buy as many gifts as possible for the homeless.

Each group member looks through newspapers and catalogs to find appropriate gifts. Then each group member compiles a list of gifts to buy, using estimation to ensure that the cost does not exceed $100. Finally, each group member shares his or her list with the group and explains his or her selections.

Combine individual lists to come up with a group list. Compare your list with those of other groups.

Glencoe Mathematics: Applications and Connections, Course 2

---

1 FOCUS

This lesson is optional. If your students need practice in the addition and subtraction of decimals, you may wish to devote a whole class period to this lesson. However, if your students are proficient in this skill and/or can use a calculator to perform it, you may wish to omit the lesson.

2 TEACH

Using Connections Focus on how adding and subtracting decimals is similar to adding and subtracting whole numbers. Remind students that even whole numbers can be represented using decimal points. Ask them where these decimal points are. Then emphasize two distinctions—aligning decimal points prior to computing, and annexing zeros when necessary in subtraction. Encourage students to use estimation strategies they have learned to estimate sums or differences prior to computing.

Review

Addition and Subtraction of Decimals

Objective

Add and subtract decimals.

This page and the next provide a review of addition and subtraction of decimals. To add or subtract decimals, align the decimal points. Then start at the right and add or subtract the numbers in each place-value position. Annex zeros when necessary.

Examples

1 Add $0.75 + 0.82$.

Estimate: $0.8 + 0.8 = 1.6$

Align the decimal points.	*Add the hundredths.*	*Add the tenths.*
0.75	0.75	$\overset{1}{0.75}$
$\underline{+0.82}$	$\underline{+0.82}$	$\underline{+0.82}$
	7	1.57

Compare to the estimate.

2 Add $1.73 + 24 + 2.236$.

Estimate: $2 + 24 + 2 = 28$

$\begin{array}{r} 1.730 \\ 24.000 \\ +\ 2.236 \end{array}$ *Align the decimal points. Annex zeros so each addend has the same number of decimal places.* $\begin{array}{r} 1.730 \\ 24.000 \\ +\ 2.236 \\ \hline 27.966 \end{array}$

3 Subtract $4.285 - 2.51$.

Estimate: $4 - 3 = 1$

$\begin{array}{r} 4.285 \\ -2.510 \end{array}$ *Align the decimal points. Annex a zero.* $\begin{array}{r} \overset{3\ \ 12}{4.\cancel{2}85} \\ -2.510 \\ \hline 1.775 \end{array}$ *Subtract in each place-value position.*

4 Subtract $2.23 - 0.497$.

Estimate: $2 - 0.5 = 1.5$

$\begin{array}{r} 2.230 \\ -0.497 \end{array}$ *Align the decimal points. Annex a zero. Then subtract.* $\begin{array}{r} \overset{1\ 111210}{2.2\cancel{3}\cancel{0}} \\ -0.497 \\ \hline 1.733 \end{array}$

OPTIONS

Reteaching Activity

Using Models Provide graph paper from which students are to cut out two 10×10 large-square sheets, each of which is assigned a value of one. Explain why each small square represents $\frac{1}{100}$, or 0.01. Have students shade 75 small squares of one of the large-square sheets and 82 small squares of the second sheet. Then have them count the total number of shaded squares (157) and interpret the result. Finally, have them compare their result with Example 1.

Exercises

Independent Practice

Add or subtract.

1. 2.3 +4.1 6.4	2. 0.37 +0.55 0.92	3. 0.67 −0.43 0.24	4. 42.76 −31.59 11.17
5. $6.78 + 4.99 $11.77	6. 8 +6.76 14.76	7. 8.267 −6.52 1.747	8. 17.6 − 4.739 12.861
9. 67.4 8.05 +105.3 180.75	10. 5.124 32.45 + 8.6 46.174	11. 18 − 9.36 8.64	12. 7.63 −3.009 4.621 37.632

13. 6.6 + 4.58 **11.18**   14. 5.77 − 2.374 **3.396**   15. 86.332 − 48.7

16. 0.563 + 5.8 + 6.89 **13.253**   17. 23.4 + 9.865 + 18.26 **51.525**

Solve each equation.   **13.59**   **19.64**

18. $r = 0.32 + 8.99$ **9.31**   19. $32.45 − 18.86 = m$ 20. $a = 12 + 7.64$ **12.43**

21. $t = 34.6 − 23.88$ **10.72** 22. $6.2 + 8.57 = y$ **14.77** 23. $c = 26.13 − 13.7$

24. $d = 45.1 + 16 + 8.091$ **69.191**   25. $f = 9.32 + 7.06 + 12.221$ **28.601**

26. Find the difference of 156.003 and 89.42 **66.583**

27. Find the sum of 67.03 and 100.97. **168**

Problem Solving and Applications

28. **Critical Thinking** How is subtraction of decimals similar to subtraction of whole numbers? How is it different?

28. Sample answer: You subtract in each place-value position; you must line up the decimal points and might have to annex zeros.

29. **Algebra** The equation $5.7 − n = 2.06$ can be solved by solving the related sentence $5.7 − 2.06 = n$. What is the value of n? **3.64**

30. **Sports** In the 1984 Olympic games, Edwin Moses of the United States won the 400-meter hurdles with a time of 47.75 seconds. In the 1988 games, another American, Andre Phillips, won the 400-meter hurdles in 47.19 seconds. How much faster was Phillips than Moses? **0.56 seconds**

31. **Statistics** According to a 1989 projection, there will be 131.2 million males and 137.1 million females in the United States in the year 2000. What will be the total population of the United States in the year 2000? **268.3 million people**

Review: Addition and Subtraction of Decimals   **59**

More Examples

For Example 1

Add 0.67 + 0.94. 1.61

For Example 2

Add 1.59 + 16 + 3.418.
21.008

For Example 3

Subtract 5.374 − 3.42.
1.954

For Example 4

Subtract 2.34 − 0.587.
1.753

Close

Have students use Olympic track records from an almanac to write a word problem that can be solved by adding decimals and a word problem that can be solved by subtracting decimals.

3 PRACTICE/APPLY

Assignment Guide
Maximum: 1–31
Minimum: 1–31 odd

Alternate Assessment

Speaking Have students explain to classmates procedures for adding and subtracting decimals.

Extending the Lesson

Using Number Sense Have students create either missing-digit exercises or magic squares that involve addition and subtraction of decimals. Ask students to solve each other's puzzles.

Interactive Mathematics Tools

This multimedia software provides an interactive lesson that is tied directly to Lesson 2–3B. Students will use decimal grids to explore multiplication of decimals.

Management Tips

For Students Provide graph paper with which students can mark off a number of 10 × 10 grids, each representing 1 whole.

For the Overhead Projector *Overhead Manipulative Resources* provides appropriate materials for teacher or student demonstration of the activities in this Mathematics Lab.

1 FOCUS

Introducing the Lab

Tell students that each large 10 × 10 grid represents 1 whole. Ask them how they would use the model to show numbers less than or greater than one.

2 TEACH

Using Critical Thinking Provide several multiplications of decimal numbers for students to model. Ask them what they notice about products of two decimals, if both are less than 1. Ask them what they can say about the product of two decimals when one is less than 1 and the other is greater than 1. Ask them what they can predict about the product of two decimals if both are greater than 1. It is less than either factor; It is less than one factor but greater than the other; It will be greater than either factor.

3 PRACTICE/APPLY

Using Applications Have groups of students write word problems to match some of the exercises in the *What Do You Think* section.

Close

Have students describe how they can use the models to show the product of two decimals.

Additional Answer

2. **a.** 1, 0, 1 **b.** 1, 1, 2 **c.** 1, 1, 2
   d. 1, 1, 2 **e.** 1, 0, 1 **f.** 1, 1, 2

2-4A Multiplication with Decimal Models

A Preview of Lesson 2-4

Objective
Multiply decimals using models.

Materials
decimal models
markers

Multiplication of decimals is similar to multiplication of whole numbers. You can multiply decimals using a decimal model.

Try this!

Work in groups of two.

- Model 0.4×0.6 by shading 4 tenths and 6 tenths as shown.

- What is the product? Tell how you figured it out. **0.24; The product is shown where two colors overlap to make the third color.**

- Model 1.3×0.9 by shading 13 tenths and 9 tenths as shown using two decimal models.

- What is the product? Tell how you figured it out. **1.17; The third color represents the product.**

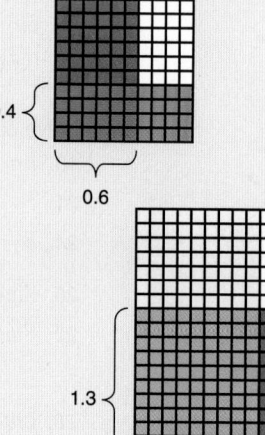

What do you think?   See Solutions Manual for models.

1. Use decimal models to show each product. **c. 1.12** **f. 0.11**
   a. 0.3×3 **0.9**   b. 0.7×0.5 **0.35**   c. 1.4×0.8
   d. 0.2×0.9 **0.18**   e. 0.6×2 **1.2**   f. 1.1×0.1

2. Tell how many decimal places there are in each factor and in each product in Exercise 1. **See margin.**

3. How does the number of decimal places in a product relate to the number of decimal places in the factors? **The sum of the number of decimal places in the factors is the number of decimal places in the product.**

Extension

4. Use what you have learned in this lab to find the product of 1.3 and 1.8. **2.34**

Interactive Mathematics Tools

This multimedia software provides an interactive lesson that is tied directly to Lesson 2-4A. Students will use decimal grids to explore multiplication of decimals.

Lab Manual, p. 40

Name _____ Date _____

Mathematics Lab Worksheet

Use with Lesson 2-2

Rounding Decimals

materials: centimeter ruler

Measure each line segment to the nearest whole centimeter.

8 cm _____

9 cm _____

7 cm _____

7 cm _____

8 cm _____

2-4 Multiplying Decimals

Objective
Multiply decimals.

Do you know that math and music are related? All sound is caused by vibrations. The number of vibrations per second determines the pitch of the sound. The more vibrations per second the higher the pitch. The number of vibrations per unit of time is called frequency. The frequency of any note multiplied by 1.06 gives the frequency of the note one-half step higher.

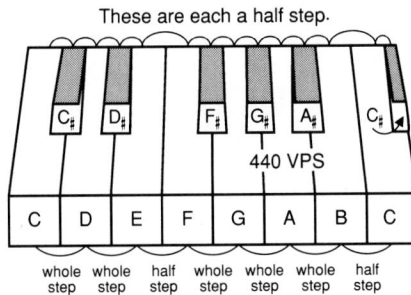

These are each a half step.

Read A♯ as "A sharp."

The frequency of A is 440 vibrations per second. What is the frequency of A♯ (one-half step higher)? To find the frequency of A♯, multiply 440 by 1.06.

Use estimation to help place the decimal point in the product.
Estimate: $1.06 \times 440 \rightarrow 1 \times 440 = 440$

$$
\begin{array}{r}
440 \\
\times\, 1.06 \\
\hline
26\,40 \\
440\,0 \\
\hline
466.40
\end{array}
$$

Since the estimate is 440, place the decimal point so the answer is in the 400s.
Compared to the estimate of 440, the answer 466.4 is reasonable.

The frequency of A♯ is 466.4 vibrations per second.

There is another way to find the product of two decimals.
Look at the table below.

Factors and Product	Decimal Places in Factors	Decimal Places in Product
5 ⊠ 0.7 ▭ 3.5	0, 1	1
0.5 ⊠ 0.7 ▭ 0.35	1, 1	2
0.5 ⊠ 0.07 ▭ 0.035	1, 2	3

This table gives the number of decimal places in each factor and the number of places in the product. The number of decimal places in the product is the sum of the number of decimal places in the factors.

Lesson 2-4 Multiplying Decimals **61**

❝When am I ever going to use this?❞

Multiplying decimals is an important concept in the banking industry.

Suppose you deposited $125.50 into an account. After 6 months, you had 1.04 times as much money in the account. How much money is in the account?

125.50×1.04
$= 130.52

OPTIONS

Reteaching Activity

Using Models Some students may need further exploration using 10×10 grids to understand that the product of two decimals may be less than either of the factors, in between the two factors, or greater than either factor.

Study Guide Masters, p. 14

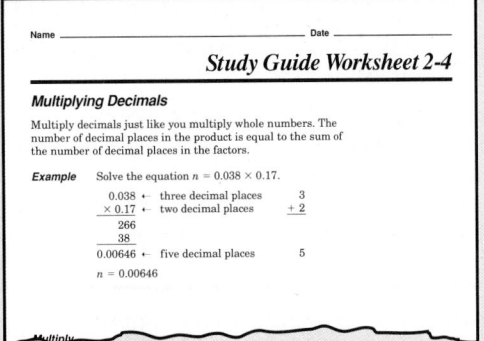

Name _____ Date _____

Study Guide Worksheet 2-4

Multiplying Decimals

Multiply decimals just like you multiply whole numbers. The number of decimal places in the product is equal to the sum of the number of decimal places in the factors.

Example   Solve the equation $n = 0.038 \times 0.17$.

$$
\begin{array}{r}
0.038 \\
\times\, 0.17 \\
\hline
266 \\
38 \\
\hline
0.00646
\end{array}
$$

← three decimal places   3
← two decimal places   + 2
← five decimal places   5

$n = 0.00646$

2-4 Lesson Notes

NCTM Standards: 1–7, 9

Lesson Resources
• Study Guide Master 2-4
• Practice Master 2-4
• Enrichment Master 2-4
• Application Master, p. 2
• Group Activity Card 2-4

Transparency 2-4 contains the 5-Minute Check and a teaching aid for this lesson.

⏱ 5-Minute Check
(Over Lesson 2-3)

Estimate. Use an appropriate strategy. All answers are samples.

1. 31.4 + 28.3 + 33.28 + 29.7   120; clustering
2. 22.97 ÷ 4.025   6
3. $57.79 − $32.88   30; rounding
4. 8.2 + 2.7 + 3.6 + 12.5   28; rounding
5. 28.9 × 42.3   1,200; rounding

1 FOCUS

Motivating the Lesson

Questioning Ask students to read the opening paragraphs of the lesson. Ask the following questions:

• *Should you find an exact answer or an estimate?* exact answer
• *What would you do to find the frequency of B (two half-steps higher than A)?* Multiply. 440 × 1.06 × 1.06

2 TEACH

Using Discussion Discuss some of the special cases of multiplying decimals, such as when to affix zeros to the right of the decimal point in the product, as in the result of multiplying 0.2 by 0.3.

Animals A snail moves at a speed of about 0.005 kilometers per hour. To find out how far it can travel in a half hour (0.5 hour), multiply 0.005 and 0.5.

$$
\begin{array}{rl}
0.005 & \textit{three decimal places} \\
\times\ \ 0.5 & \textit{one decimal place} \\
\hline
0.0025 & \textit{four decimal places} \quad \textit{Is the answer reasonable?}
\end{array}
$$

Check with a calculator: 0.005 ⊠ 0.5 ⊟ **0.0025**

A snail can travel 0.0025 kilometers in a half hour.

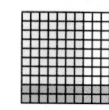 LOOKBACK

You can review evaluating expressions on page 28.

Algebra Evaluate $2.5 \cdot a$ if $a = 0.7$.

$$
\begin{aligned}
2.5 \cdot a &= 2.5 \cdot 0.7 \quad \textit{Replace a} \\
&= 1.75 \qquad\quad \textit{with 0.7.}
\end{aligned}
$$

$$
\begin{array}{rl}
2.5 & \textit{one decimal place} \\
\times\ 0.7 & \textit{one decimal place} \\
\hline
1.75 & \textit{Count two decimal places} \\
& \textit{from the right.}
\end{array}
$$

Checking for Understanding

Communicating Mathematics

Read and study the lesson to answer each question.

1. See students' work.

2.

1. **Tell** in your own words why the number of decimal places in the product of two decimals is equal to the sum of the decimal places in the factors.

2. **Write** the multiplication sentence for the model at the right.
   $0.2 \times 0.7 = 0.14$

3. **Make a model** to show why $0.1 \times 0.1 = 0.01$. **See Solutions Manual.**

Guided Practice

Place the decimal point in each product.

4. $1.32 \times 4 = 528$
   5.28
5. $0.7 \times 1.1 = 077$
   0.77
6. $5.48 \times 3.6 = 19728$
   19.728

Multiply.

7. 0.4
   × 0.7
   0.28
8. 3.4
   × 7.8
   26.52
9. 0.15
   × 1.23
   0.1845
10. 11.5
    × 0.47
    5.405

11. 0.45×0.02
    0.009
12. 8.32×0.064
    0.53248
13. 1.9×0.6
    1.14

14. Evaluate $1.4 \cdot x$ if $x = 0.9$. 1.26

15. Evaluate $4.2 \cdot y$ if $y = 3.6$. 15.12

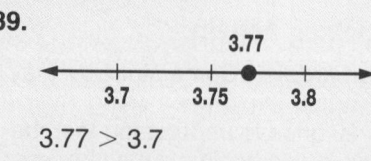

Exercises

Independent Practice

Multiply.

16. 0.2
 $\times\ 6$
 1.2

17. 0.3
 $\times 0.9$
 0.27

18. 0.45
 $\times 0.12$
 0.0540

19. 0.0023
 $\times\ 32$
 0.0736

20. 10.1×9 **90.9**
21. 4.5×0.34 **1.53**
22. 0.0023×0.35
23. 6.78×1.3 **8.814**
24. 1.5×2.7 **4.05**
25. 0.25×36.3 **9.075**

22. 0.000805

Solve each equation.

26. $p = 0.45 \times 0.02$ **0.009**
27. $5.1 \times 4.3 = g$ **21.93**
28. $r = 0.08 \times 1.9$ **0.152**
29. $0.25 \times 0.0004 = t$ **0.0001**
30. $b = 0.4 \times 3$ **1.2**
31. $m = 1.17 \times 0.09$ **0.1053**

Evaluate each expression if $a = 0.6$ and $b = 3.1$.

0.00589

32. $0.32 \cdot b$ **0.992**
33. $a \cdot 1.2$ **0.72**
34. $12.4 \cdot a$ **7.44**
35. $b \cdot$ **0.0019**

36. **Animals** A giant tortoise can travel at a speed of about 0.2 kilometers per hour. At this rate, how far can it travel in 1.75 hours? **0.35 km**

Mixed Review

37. Use patterns to estimate $\$1.19 \div 16$. *(Lesson 1-3)* **\$0.06**
38. Evaluate b^5 if $b = 2$. *(Lesson 1-9)* **32**
39. Draw a number line to show which is greater, 3.77 or 3.7. *(Lesson 2-1)* **See margin.**
40. Round 26.394 miles to the nearest mile. *(Lesson 2-2)* **26 miles**
41. Find the difference of 5.8 and 3.59. *(Lesson 2-3)* **2.21**

Problem Solving and Applications

42. **Biology** The Marshall Island goby, the world's smallest fish, measures 0.47 inch. The striped bass, an American sport fish, is about 25.5 times longer. How long is the bass? **11.985 inches**

43. **Currency** On October 2, 1991, the Japanese yen was worth 0.0075 United States dollars. At that time, how much was 450 yen worth in United States dollars? **\$3.375**

44. **Critical Thinking** Make up a problem in which the factors each have two decimal places, but the product has only three. **Sample answer: $0.45 \times 0.12 = 0.054$**

45. **Mathematics and Time** Read the following paragraphs.

> Throughout history, people have measured the passing of time by observing natural events like the succession of days and nights, different positions of the sun in the sky, the phases of the moon, or the tides. In 3500 B.C., the first measuring device appeared in Egypt. It was called a *clepsydrae* ('klep-sə-drə), or water clock.
>
> Today, time is measured with great precision. We use watches with hands, digital watches, and chronometers to regulate time.

Earth revolves around the sun in 365.24 days. How many days does it take Earth to revolve 12 times? **4,382.88 days**

Lesson 2-4 Multiplying Decimals **63**

Extending the Lesson

Mathematics and Time To correct for the small difference between 365 days and 365.24 days, a leap year of 366 days is interposed every four years except in years such as 1900 that are divisible by 100 but not by 400. (The years 1600 and 2000 are leap years.) The rule thus adjusts for the fact that $3 \times 365 + 366$ is slightly greater than 4×365.24.

Cooperative Learning Activity

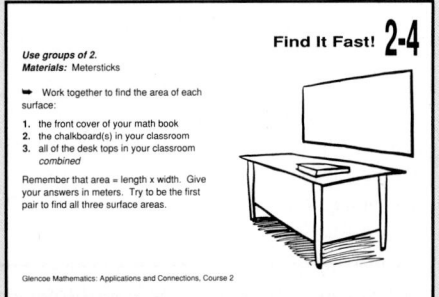

Find It Fast! **2-4**

Use groups of 2.
Materials: Metersticks

► Work together to find the area of each surface:

1. the front cover of your math book
2. the chalkboard(s) in your classroom
3. all of the desk tops in your classroom combined

Remember that area = length x width. Give your answers in meters. Try to be the first pair to find all three surface areas.

Glencoe Mathematics: Applications and Connections, Course 2

2-5 Powers of Ten

NCTM Standards: 1–7, 9

Lesson Resources
- Study Guide Master 2-5
- Practice Master 2-5
- Enrichment Master 2-5
- Evaluation Master, Quiz A, p. 16
- Technology Master, p. 16
- Group Activity Card 2-5

 Transparency 2-5 contains the 5-Minute Check and a teaching aid for this lesson.

🕐 5-Minute Check
(Over Lesson 2-4)

Multiply.

1. $\begin{array}{r} 0.43 \\ \times 0.6 \end{array}$ 0.258

2. 8.8×0.28 2.464

3. 0.0052×0.09
0.000468

4. Solve: $r = 0.61 \times 0.02$
0.0122

Evaluate each expression if $a = 0.7$ and $b = 2.5$.

5. $0.5 \cdot a$ 0.35

6. $b \cdot 0.003$ 0.0075

---

1 FOCUS

Motivating the Lesson

Situational Problem Ask students how they would determine the length of the Amazon River, which is 3.9×10^3 miles long.

2 TEACH

Using Connections Elicit from students the fact that the number 10 in the opening paragraph is called the *base*, and the raised "5" is an *exponent*, indicating that 10 is a factor 5 times. Emphasize the relationship between the power of 10 and the number of zeros in the standard form of the number. Have students use this relationship to continue the table through 10^9.

Objective

Multiply decimals mentally by powers of ten.

How far away is the moon? Scientists have calculated it to be 2.39×10^5 miles from Earth. You can multiply 2.39 and 10^5 to find the number of miles.

$$2.39 \times 10^5 = 2.39 \times 100,000$$

2.39 ⊗ 100000 ⊜ **239000.**

The moon is 239,000 miles from Earth.

How can you find the product of a power of 10, like 10^5, and another number without using a calculator or paper and pencil?

Consider the following products. Look for a pattern.

Decimal		Power of Ten		Product
2.39	×	10^0 (or 1)	=	2.39
2.39	×	10^1 (or 10)	=	23.9
2.39	×	10^2 (or 100)	=	239
2.39	×	10^3 (or 1,000)	=	2,390
2.39	×	10^4 (or 10,000)	=	23,900

Note that as the decimal is multiplied by greater powers of 10, the decimal point in the product is farther to the right of the original position. Study the last two columns. The exponent in the power of 10 and the number of places the decimal point moved to the right are the same.

You can use this pattern to multiply mentally.

Mental Math Hint
••••••••••••

You can also determine the number of places the decimal point moves to the right by counting the number of zeros in the power of ten. That is, in Example 2, you can see that there are three zeros in 1,000, so you will move the decimal point three places to the right.

Examples

1 Multiply 0.34 and 10^4 mentally.
$$0.34 \times 10^4 = 3,400.$$

Move the decimal point 4 places to the right.

The solution is 3,400.

2 Solve $c = 13.1 \times 1,000$.
$$\begin{aligned} c &= 13.1 \times 1,000 &\textit{Rename} \\ &= 13.1 \times 10^3 &\textit{1,000 as } 10^3. \\ &= 13,100. \end{aligned}$$

Move the decimal point 3 places to the right.

The solution is 13,100.

OPTIONS

Reteaching Activity

Using Games Each player rolls a die twice to get the tens and units digit of a number. A third roll is taken as either 1) the exponent for a power of 10 or 2) the tenths place of the number. With option 2, a fourth roll is required, for the exponent. Example: 1, 4, 6 to get 14×10^6; Option 2: 1, 4, 6, 5 to get 14.6×10^5. The player with the greatest number wins.

Study Guide Masters, p. 15

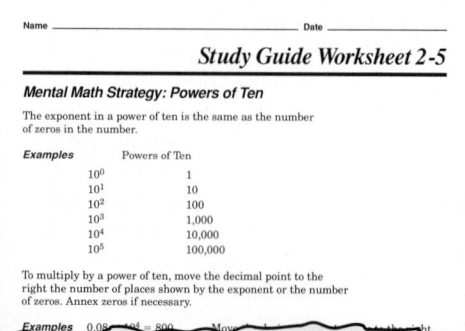

Name _____ Date _____

Study Guide Worksheet 2-5

Mental Math Strategy: Powers of Ten

The exponent in a power of ten is the same as the number of zeros in the number.

Examples   Powers of Ten

10^0	1
10^1	10
10^2	100
10^3	1,000
10^4	10,000
10^5	100,000

To multiply by a power of ten, move the decimal point to the right the number of places shown by the exponent or the number of zeros. Annex zeros if necessary.

Examples   0.08 ___ ___ = 800

For answers to Exercises 1–2, see margin.
Checking for Understanding

Communicating Mathematics

Read and study the lesson to answer each question.

1. **Tell** a classmate how you would solve $x = 2.378 \times 100$ mentally.

2. **Show** the steps you would take to multiply 100×0.28 using paper and pencil. Compare it to solving the problem mentally.

Guided Practice

Choose the correct product mentally.

3. 2.34×100; 0.0234 or 234 **234**

4. 0.8×10^0; 8 or 0.8 **0.8**

5. 0.028×10^2; 2.8 or 28 **2.8**

6. 1.4×10^5; 140,000 or 14.07 **140,000**

Multiply mentally.

7. 12.53×10 **125.3**

8. $0.605 \times 1,000$ **605**

9. 3.159×100 **315.9**

Solve each equation.

10. $n = 2.031 \times 10^4$ **20,310**

11. $a = 0.78 \times 10^2$ **78**

12. $1.32 \times 10^3 = x$ **1,320**

Exercises

Independent Practice

Multiply mentally.

13. 0.05×100 **5**

14. 4.527×10^0 **4.527**

15. $2.78 \times 1,000$ **2,780**

16. 5.492×10^4 **54,920**

17. 0.925×100 **92.5**

18. 99.44×10^2 **9,944**

Solve each equation.

19. $c = 0.78 \times 1,000$ **780**

20. $m = 11.23 \times 10^5$ **1,123,000**

21. $6.894 \times 1,000 = k$ **6,894**

22. $28.1 \times 100 = b$ **2,810**

23. $t = 9.3 \times 1,000$ **9,300**

24. $3.76 \times 10^6 = y$ **3,760,000**

25. Suppose a can of soup costs 73¢. If you purchase 100 cans to donate to the Food Bank, what will the cost be? **$73.00**

Mixed Review

26. Estimate the sum of 1,237 and 896. *(Lesson 1-2)* **2,000**

27. Order 3, 0.3, 3.33, 0.33, 0.03, 3.03 from least to greatest. *(Lesson 2-1)* **0.03, 0.3, 0.33, 3, 3.03, 3.33**

28. Round 63.2765 to the nearest whole number. *(Lesson 2-2)* **63**

29. **Travel** At one point during Manuel's summer trip, he drove 356.5 miles in 6.3 hours. Estimate Manuel's speed. *(Lesson 2-3)* **60 mph**

Problem Solving and Applications

30. **Geology** In 1872, Yellowstone National Park became the first national park in the United States. It is noted for its hot springs that erupt through the surface of Earth forming geysers. The park has about 2,000 hot springs. If 0.1 of these are geysers, how many geysers are in the park? **200 geysers**

Lesson 2-5 Mental Math Strategy: Powers of Ten **65**

Gifted and Talented Needs

Challenge students to work with partners to devise a mental math strategy for multiplying a decimal by multiples of powers of 10, such as 40, 500, 5,000, and so on. Have them share their results with others.

Additional Answers

1. Move the decimal point in 2.378 two places to the right.

2.
$$\begin{array}{r} 0.28 \\ \times\,1.00 \\ \hline 28.00 \end{array}$$
Mental solution: Move the decimal point in 0.28 two places to the right. The result is the same.

Close

Have students explain how to use mental math to express the number 0.205 × 10⁴ in standard form. **Move the decimal point 4 places to the right; 2,050**

3 PRACTICE/APPLY

Assignment Guide
Maximum: 13–34
Minimum: 13–25 odd, 26–32
All: Mid-Chapter Review

For **Extra Practice,** see p. 575.

Alternate Assessment

Writing Have students work with partners to make a simple cross-number puzzle with clues that involve multiplying decimals and powers of 10. Answers should be in standard form.

32. When multiplying by powers of 10, the number increases. When dividing by powers of 10, the number decreases.

31. **History** During the seventeenth century, the Spanish used a coin called the *real*. A real was equal to $0.125 in today's U.S. currency. If you had 100 reals, how much money did you have in U.S. currency? **$12.50**

32. **Critical Thinking** Explain why the decimal point moves right when multiplying by powers of ten and why the decimal point moves left when dividing by powers of ten.

COMPUTER CONNECTION

33. **Computer Connection** The BASIC computer language uses a special notation, E, for powers of 10. For example, the notation 2.4E3 means 2.4×10^3. Write the number represented by each of the following.
   a. 1E6 1×10^6 b. 6.07E2 6.07×10^2 c. 3.9256E7 3.9256×10^7

34. **Journal Entry** When do you think you will use what you have learned about multiplying by powers of ten mentally? **See students' work.**

2 Assessment: Mid-Chapter Review

Replace each ● with <, >, or =. *(Lesson 2-1)*
   1. 0.28 ● 0.028 **>**   2. 1.32 ● 1.320 **=**   3. 3.25 ● 3.2 **>**

Round each number to the underlined place-value position. *(Lesson 2-2)*
   4. 0.49 **0.5**   5. 6.52 **6.5**   6. 0.997 **1.00**   7. 3.124 **3.1**

Estimate. *(Lesson 2-3)*

8.	9.	10.	11.
43.67	$6.23	2.8	5.7)43.9
+ 17.32	− 4.09	× 8.2	**7**
60	**$2**	**24**	

12. Estimate the sum of 71.28, 68.4, 70.73, 69.45, and 73.21. *(Lesson 2-3)* **350**

Multiply. *(Lesson 2-4)*

13.	14.	15.	16.
0.7	6.4	5.32	0.87
× 0.9	× 5.8	× 4.1	× 16
0.63	**37.12**	**21.812**	**13.92**

17. **Postage** Mr. Jackson buys 1,000 stamps for his business. If each stamp cost 29¢, how much did he spend altogether? *(Lesson 2-5)* **$290**

OPTIONS

Extending the Lesson

Using Critical Thinking Ask students whether a pattern emerges when numbers are multiplied by decimal powers of 10, such as 0.1, 0.01, 0.001, and so on. Have them investigate to find out. Challenge students to use a pattern to figure out a way to multiply by decimal powers of 10 using mental math.

Cooperative Learning Activity

It's All in the Notation 2-5

Number of players: 3
Materials: Index cards, spinner

● Copy onto cards the numbers on the back of this card. Shuffle the cards and place them face down in a pile. Label the sections of a spinner "10," "10," "10," "10," "10," and "10."

➡ One group member turns over a card and spins the spinner. The other group members compete to tell what number results in the number on the card when multiplied by the power on the spinner. Trade roles after every five rounds.

Glencoe Mathematics: Applications and Connections, Course 2

2-6 Scientific Notation

Objective

Express numbers greater than 100 in scientific notation and vice versa.

Words to Learn

scientific notation

DID YOU KNOW

Mercury takes only 88 Earth days to make one trip around the sun. However, it rotates slowly on its axis. One day on Mercury is about 59 Earth days long.

Did you know that the planet Mercury was named after the Roman wing-footed messenger of the gods? The planet was so named because of the speed it travels. Mercury orbits the sun at 30 miles per second while Earth orbits the sun at only 18.5 miles per second. Mercury is about 36,000,000 miles from the sun and is the closest planet to the sun.

Large numbers like 36,000,000 can be expressed in scientific notation.

A number in **scientific notation** is written as the product of a number greater than or equal to 1 and less than 10 and a power of ten. The power of ten is written with an exponent. To find the exponent, count the number of places the decimal point was moved in the original number.

Write 36,000,000 in scientific notation.

3.6000000   *Move the decimal point to get a number between 1 and 10.*

3.6×10^7 *The decimal point was moved 7 places.*

Mercury is about 3.6×10^7 miles from the sun.

Examples

1   Write 347,000 in scientific notation.

3.47000   *Move the decimal point to get a number between 1 and 10.*

3.47×10^5 *The decimal point was moved 5 places.*

2   The planet Mars is an average distance of 141,710,000 miles from the sun. Express this number in scientific notation.

1.41710000   *Move the decimal point to get a number between 1 and 10.*

1.4171×10^8 *The decimal point was moved 8 places.*

Notice that the number in Example 2 has more digits to the right of the decimal point than the numbers in other examples. Usually, the decimal part of a number written in scientific notation is rounded to the hundredths place.

$1.4171 \times 10^8 \rightarrow$ The distance from Mars to the Sun is about 1.42×10^8 miles.

Lesson 2-6 Scientific Notation   **67**

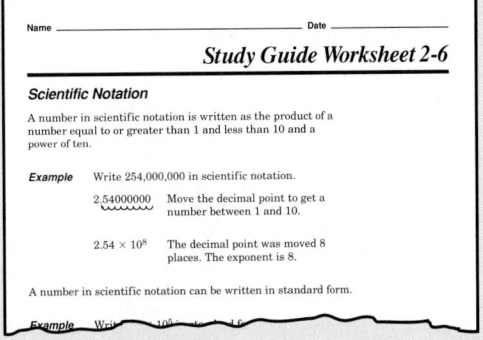

Study Guide Masters, p. 16

Name _____ Date _____

Study Guide Worksheet 2-6

Scientific Notation

A number in scientific notation is written as the product of a number equal to or greater than 1 and less than 10 and a power of ten.

Example   Write 254,000,000 in scientific notation.

2.54000000   Move the decimal point to get a number between 1 and 10.

2.54×10^8 The decimal point was moved 8 places. The exponent is 8.

A number in scientific notation can be written in standard form.

Example   Write ___ $10^?$ ___

NCTM Standards: 1–7

Lesson Resources
- Study Guide Master 2-6
- Practice Master 2-6
- Enrichment Master 2-6
- Group Activity Card 2-6

 Transparency 2-6 contains the 5-Minute Check and a teaching aid for this lesson.

⏱ 5-Minute Check
(Over Lesson 2-5)

Multiply mentally.

1. 0.06×100 6
2. 3.192×10^3 3,192
3. $83.11 \times 1,000$ 83,110
4. Solve: $n = 42.4 \times 10^5$ 4,240,000
5. Suppose a can of peaches costs $0.59. What would 1,000 cans cost? $590

1 FOCUS

Motivating the Lesson

Situational Problem Write 6,000,000,000,000,000,000 on the chalkboard. Ask students to give a name for this number (6 quintillion). Ask them what kinds of things numbers this large might describe. (As a guide, the number of words printed since the Gutenberg bible is more than 10^{16}.) Ask them how they could write numbers like this in a more compact form.

2 TEACH

Using Charts Use a chart to list the numbers presented in the lesson in standard form as well as in scientific notation. Have students use an almanac or other source to add other astronomical measurements to the chart.

Checking for Understanding

A number that is in scientific notation can be written in standard form when necessary.

Example 3 *Problem Solving*

Astronomy The diameter of Jupiter is 1.43×10^5 kilometers. The diameter of Earth is 1.28×10^4 kilometers. How much greater is Jupiter's diameter?

Write the numbers in standard form.
$1.43 \times 10^5 = 1.43 \times 100,000 = 143,000$
$1.28 \times 10^4 = 1.28 \times 10,000 = 12,800$

The difference is $143,000 - 12,800$ or $130,200$ kilometers. Jupiter's diameter is 130,200 kilometers greater than Earth's.

Checking for Understanding

Communicating Mathematics

Read and study the lesson to answer each question.

1. **Show** how you would determine which is greater: 25,200 or 1.75×10^5. $1.75 \times 10^5 = 175,000$; $175,000 > 25,200$

2. **Show** a classmate how to write 5,280, the number of feet in a mile, in scientific notation. 5.28×10^3

Guided Practice

Write each number in scientific notation.

3. 890 8.9×10^2

4. 4,300 4.3×10^3

5. 6,235 6.235×10^3

6. 52,000 5.2×10^4

7. 820,000 8.2×10^5

8. 126,400,000 1.264×10^8

Write each number in standard form.

9. 9.87×10^3 9,870

10. 6×10^2 600

11. 1.75×10^4 17,500

12. 2.3×10^4 23,000

13. 4.95×10^8 495,000,000

14. 0.57×10^6 570,000

Exercises

Independent Practice

Write each number in scientific notation.

15. 7,500 7.5×10^3

16. 8,450 8.45×10^3

17. 40,700 4.07×10^4

18. 630,000 6.3×10^5

19. 400,000 4×10^5

20. 32,000,000 3.2×10^7

21. 7,900,000 7.9×10^6

22. 558,000 5.58×10^5

23. 160,000,000 1.6×10^8

Write each number in standard form.

24. 5×10^3 5,000

25. 1.42×10^4 14,200

26. 4.2×10^2 420

27. 5.47×10^5 547,000

28. 9.5×10^6 9,500,000

29. 2.71×10^7 27,100,000

30. 8.08×10^3 8,080

31. 6.024×10^8 602,400,000

32. 5.75×10^4 57,500

33. The circulation of *'Teen* magazine is about 1,100,000. Write this number in scientific notation. 1.1×10^6

34. **History** In 1989, 4.056×10^5 people immigrated to the United States from Mexico. Write this number in standard form. **405,600 people**

Mixed Review

35. **Hobby** Last year Gene had 237 baseball cards. He collected another 78 cards this year. Is a total of 315 cards reasonable? *(Lesson 1-4)* **yes**

36. Evaluate $100 \div 10 + 2 \cdot 6 \div 4$. *(Lesson 1-7)* **13**

37. The quotient of a number and 8 is 14. Find the number. *(Lesson 1-10)* **112**

38. **Math** Carissa solved a difficult math problem in 7.9 minutes. Ted took 2.3 times longer to solve the same problem. How long did it take Ted to solve the problem? *(Lesson 2-4)* **18.17 minutes**

39. Multiply 1,000 and 18.7. *(Lesson 2-5)* **18,700**

Problem Solving and Applications

40. **Critical Thinking** Order from least to greatest: 8.35×10^2, 5.29×10^3, 5.29×10^4; 8.35×10^2; 9.05×10^3; 5.29×10^3. 9.05×10^3, 5.29×10^4

41. **Geography** Mauna Kea, a Hawaiian mountain, would be 3.35×10^4 feet tall if its height was measured from the ocean floor. Mt. Everest, the highest mountain in the world, is about 29,000 feet tall.

   a. If Mt. Everest were next to Mauna Kea on the ocean floor, which would be taller? **Mauna Kea**

   b. How much taller would it be? **4,500 feet**

42. **Astronomy** The closest approach of a planet to the sun is called its *perihelion*. In 1991, Pluto was near its perihelion, which is 2,762,000,000 miles. At the same time, Neptune's perihelion was 2.766×10^9 miles. At that time in history, which of these planets was the ninth (and outermost) planet? **Neptune**

43. **Data Search** Refer to page 46. Order from greatest to least the nine organizations that have the most members. **See margin.**

"I introduce the use of negative exponents as an extension of this lesson. Students don't need an understanding of integers, and the concept is connected to decimals which is what this chapter is about."

Mary anne Hardy

Maryanne Hardy, Teacher
Brown Middle School, Madison, CT

Close
Have students design a flow chart for converting a number in standard form to scientific notation.

3 PRACTICE/APPLY

> **Assignment Guide**
> **Maximum:** 15–43
> **Minimum:** 15–33 odd, 35–42

For **Extra Practice,** see p. 576.

Alternate Assessment

Writing Tell students that the speed of sound at sea level is about 7.61×10^2 miles per hour. Ask them to write the speed in standard form. Tell them the speed of light is about 186,000 miles per second. Ask them to write that number in scientific notation. **761 mi/h; 1.86×10^5 mi/s**

Enrichment Masters, p. 16

Name _____   Date _____

Enrichment Worksheet 2-6

The Speed of Light

Light travels at approximately 186,000 miles per second. You can use the formula below to find how long it takes light to travel from one place to another.

$$\frac{distance}{speed\ of\ light} = time$$

For example, the sun is about 9.3×10^7 miles from Earth. If a gigantic explosion were to occur on the sun, how long would it take to see it from Earth?
To find the answer, divide.

$$\frac{93,000,000}{186,000} = 500 \quad \leftarrow \text{Write } 9.3 \times 10^7 \text{ as } 93,000,000.$$

It would take about 500 seconds to see the explosion.

Now you need to change seconds to minutes, since minutes is a more sensible unit for time in this case.
To change seconds to minutes, divide.

$$\frac{500}{60} \quad \rightarrow \quad 60\overline{)500} \atop {480 \atop 20}$$

It would take about 8 minutes to see the explosion from Earth.

Compute each amount of time it takes for light to travel to Earth from each place. Then change seconds to a sensible unit.

	Location	Closest Distance to Earth	Time (in seconds)	Time (in a sensible unit)
1.	moon	2.2×10^5 mi	1 s	1 s
2.	Mars	3.46×10^7 mi	186 s	3 min
3.	Venus	2.57×10^7 mi	138 s	2 min
4.	Jupiter	3.67×10^8 mi	1,973 s	33 min
5.	Pluto	2.67×10^9 mi	14,355 s	4 h
6.	nearest star	2.48×10^{13} mi	133,333,333 s	4 y

T16
Glencoe Division, Macmillan/McGraw-Hill

Management Tips

For Students Have groups of students mark off a number of 10 × 10 grids on graph paper. Ask them to use pencils as they shade squares to model the division process.

For the Overhead Projector
Overhead Manipulative Resources provides appropriate materials for teacher or student demonstration of the activities in this Mathematics Lab.

1 FOCUS

Introducing the Lab

Remind students how they used 10 × 10 grids to model multiplication of decimals. Ask students to suggest ways to use the same model to show division of a decimal by a decimal.

2 TEACH

Using Questioning Ask students what each small square and each column of small squares represents. Then ask students how they can determine the total number of squares to be shaded, and the number of columns to shade. hundredths; tenths; number of hundredths in dividend; number of tenths in divisor

3 PRACTICE/APPLY

Using Critical Thinking Ask students to explain why it can become impractical to use models to divide decimals. Sample answer: a very large number of squares may be needed

Close

Have students work with partners. Each writes a decimal division for the other to model. Have students explain their methods.

2-7A Division with Decimal Models

A Preview of Lesson 2-7

Objective
Divide decimals using models.

Materials
decimal models
markers

Division can be thought of as putting a collection of objects into equal groups. You can show division of decimals using a decimal model.

Try this!

Work with a partner.

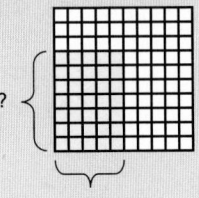

- Model 0.35 ÷ 0.5 by shading 35 squares such that 5 columns of squares are shaded.
- How can you write the 35 squares as a decimal? **0.35**
- How many squares are in each column? **7**
- Write the squares in each column as a decimal. **0.7**

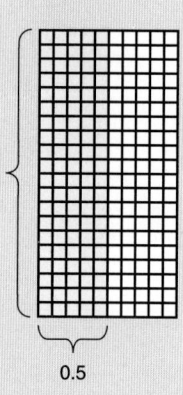

- Model 1 ÷ 0.5 by shading 100 squares such that 5 columns of squares are shaded. To do this, you will need two decimal models.
- What is the quotient? Tell how you figured it out. **2; There are two groups of ten in each column.**

What do you think?

1. True or False? The examples show that decimal division is similar to whole-number division. **True**
2. Explain how the decimal models show each quotient.
   a. 0.35 ÷ 0.5   b. 1 ÷ 0.5   **See students' wo**
3. Use decimal models to show each quotient. **See Solutions Manual.**
   a. 0.25 ÷ 0.5   b. 2 ÷ 0.8   c. 0.6 ÷ 0.2
4. When a whole number is divided by a decimal less than 1, as in **Greater; Y** 2 ÷ 0.5, is the quotient greater or less than the divisor? Why? **are dividin into groups of less than the divisor, so there will be more than 1 grou**

Extension

5. Predict the quotient of 1 ÷ 0.25. **4**

OPTIONS

Lab Manual You may wish to make copies of the blackline master on p. 41 of the *Lab Manual* for students to use as a recording sheet.

Lab Manual, p. 41

Name _____ Date _____

Mathematics Lab Worksheet

Use with page 70

Division with Decimal Models

Try this!

35 squares can be written as the number ____0.35____ .

There are ____7____ squares in each column.

The squares in each column can be written as the number ____0.7____

1 ÷ 0.5 = ____2____ , because the column of the decimal model is

20 squares and two decimal models are needed for this quotient.

What do you think?

1. True The dividend is shaded. It is the product of the divisor and quotient.

2-7 Dividing Decimals

Objective
Divide decimals.

Leonardo Da Vinci was an artist, scientist, and inventor. But he is best known as an artist. He was born in Italy in 1452. His most famous painting is the Mona Lisa. The painting hangs in the Louvre Museum in Paris, France. It has a width of 0.5 meters and an area of 0.4 square meters. What is the height of the Mona Lisa?

You can use a decimal model to find the height. Shade 40 squares so that 5 columns of squares are shaded. The height is 0.8 meters.

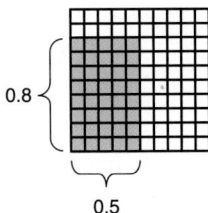

You can also solve this problem by dividing the area by the width: $0.4 \div 0.5$.

Estimate: $\frac{1}{2} \div \frac{1}{2} = 1$

0.4 $\boxed{\div}$ 0.5 $\boxed{=}$ $\boxed{0.8}$

The height of the painting is 0.8 meters.

To divide two decimals using paper and pencil, it is best to change the divisor to a whole number by moving the decimal point to the right. You must also move the decimal point in the dividend the same number of places to the right. Study the models on the next page to see how this works.

Lesson 2-7 Dividing Decimals   **71**

2-7 Lesson Notes

NCTM Standards: 1–7, 9, 13

Lesson Resources
- Study Guide Master 2-7
- Practice Master 2-7
- Enrichment Master 2-7
- Multicultural Activity, p. 2
- Technology Master, p. 2
- Group Activity Card 2-7

 Transparency 2-7 contains the 5-Minute Check and a teaching aid for this lesson.

🕐 5-Minute Check
(Over Lesson 2-6)

Write each number in scientific notation.

1. 6,700,000 6.7×10^6

2. 80,300 8.03×10^4

Write each number in standard form.

3. 4×10^7 40,000,000

4. 2.7×10^4 27,000

5. The population of a city is about 2,900,000. Write this number in scientific notation. 2.9×10^6

1 FOCUS

Motivating the Lesson

Questioning   Have students read the opening paragraph. Then ask them how they could solve the problem without using a decimal model. Have them describe any difficulties they might encounter when they use paper and pencil to solve the problem.

OPTIONS

Gifted and Talented Needs

Ask students what they can say about the relationship between the quotient and the dividend when the divisor is less than 1. Ask them to write a word problem that can be solved by dividing by a number less than 1.   The quotient will always be greater than the dividend. Problems will vary.

Using Discussion Have students discuss why, when changing the divisor to a whole number by moving the decimal point to the right, they must also move the decimal point in the dividend the same number of places to the right. They should understand that doing so amounts to multiplying each number by the same multiple of 10. The two models on pages 71 and 72 illustrate that the quotient (the height of the column) remains constant when both the divisor (the column width) and dividend (total area) are multiplied by 10.

More Examples

For Example 1

$0.13\overline{)0.364}$ 2.8

For Example 2

Solve $n = 0.6 \div 0.05$.   12

For Example 3

A dolphin can swim at a speed of about 37 miles per hour. The fastest human swimmer can reach a speed of about 5.2 miles per hour. About how many times faster than humans are dolphins?   about 7.12 times faster

---

Checking for Understanding

Exercises 1-4 are designed to help you assess students' understanding through reading, writing, speaking, and modeling. You should work through these exercises with your students and then monitor their work on Guided Practice Exercises 5-16.

Additional Answer

1. A keying error may produce an "exact" answer that is completely unreasonable. If the answer has first been estimated, then the error is not likely to be accepted as correct.

Change 0.5 to 5 and 0.4 to 4 by multiplying by 10 (moving the decimal point one place to the right.)

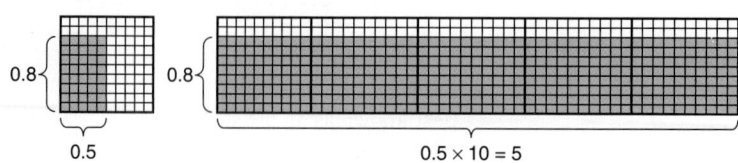

$$0.4 \div 0.5 = 0.8 \qquad\qquad 4 \div 5 = 0.8$$

Notice that the answer is the same for both models. So dividing 0.4 by 0.5 has the same result as dividing 4 by 5.

When you are using paper and pencil to find a quotient, the divisor is usually changed to a whole number. Of course, the dividend must be changed in the same way.

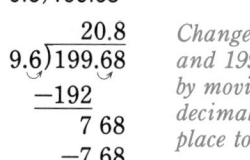

Estimation Hint
• • • • • • • • • • • •
In Example 1, use patterns to estimate
$199.68 \div 9.6$.
$200 \div 10 = 20$

Examples

1 $9.6\overline{)199.68}$

$$
\begin{array}{r}
20.8 \\
9.6\overline{)199.68} \\
-192 \\
\hline
7\ 68 \\
-7\ 68 \\
\hline
0
\end{array}
$$

Change 9.6 to 96 and 199.68 to 1,996.8 by moving both decimal points one place to the right.

2 Solve $n = 0.7 \div 0.05$.

$$
\begin{array}{r}
14 \\
0.05\overline{)0.70} \\
-5 \\
\hline
20 \\
-20 \\
\hline
0
\end{array}
$$

Annex a zero. Why?

Example 3 *Problem Solving*

Sports In 1991, American sprinter Carl Lewis set a world record of 9.86 seconds for the 100-meter dash. A honeybee can fly the same distance in 20.706 seconds. How many times faster than a honeybee is Carl Lewis?

We need to divide 20.706 by 9.86.
Estimate: $20 \div 10 = 2$.

$$
\begin{array}{r}
2.1 \\
986.\overline{)2070.6} \\
-1972 \\
\hline
98\ 6 \\
-98\ 6 \\
\hline
0
\end{array}
$$

Change 9.86 to 986 and 20.706 to 2,070.6.

Carl Lewis is 2.1 times faster than a honeybee.

OPTIONS

Reteaching Activity

Using Manipulatives Have students use centimeter cubes to model division of decimals. For example, an individual cube can represent 0.1 and a stack of 10 cubes can represent 1. Ask students how they would model $7.5 \div 1.5$.

Study Guide Masters, p. 17

Name _____   Date _____

Study Guide Worksheet 2-7

Dividing Decimals

To divide by a decimal, change the divisor to a whole number.

Example $0.5194 \div 0.49$

$$
\begin{array}{r}
1.06 \\
0.49.\overline{)0.51.94} \\
49 \\
\hline
294 \\
294 \\
\hline
0
\end{array}
$$

Change 0.49 to 49. Move the decimal point two places to the right.

Move the decimal point in the dividend the same number of places to the right.

Divide as with whole numbers.

Without finding each quotient, change each problem so that the divisor is a whole number.

Checking for Understanding

Communicating Mathematics

Read and study the lesson to answer each question.

1. **Write** one or two sentences explaining why you should estimate before using a calculator. **See margin.**

2. **Write** the division sentence for the model at the right.
   0.63 ÷ 0.9 = 0.7

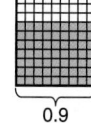
0.9

3. **Make a model** to show $0.56 \div 0.7$. **See Solutions Manual.**

4. **Tell** a friend why $4.4 \div 0.8$ and $44 \div 8$ have the same quotient. **Multiplying both the dividend and divisor by 10 does not change the quotient.**

Guided Practice

Without finding or changing each quotient, change each problem so that the divisor is a whole number.

5. $0.36 \div 0.4$ **3.6 ÷ 4**   6. $1.05 \div 0.7$ **10.5 ÷ 7**   7. $4.4 \div 1.1$ **44 ÷ 11**

8. $2.94 \div 0.084$ **2,940 ÷ 84** 9. $1.89 \div 0.9$ **18.9 ÷ 9**   10. $50.4 \div 0.56$
                                                                          5,040 ÷ 56

Divide.

11. $3 \div 0.6$ **5**   12. $4.2 \div 1.2$ **3.5**   13. $0.084 \div 0.056$ **1.5**

14. $0.287 \div 0.035$ **8.2**   15. $51 \div 0.8$ **63.75**   16. $0.245 \div 0.7$ **0.35**

Exercises

Independent Practice

Without finding or changing each quotient, change each problem so that the divisor is a whole number.
                                                    68,130 ÷ 3
17. $0.82 \div 0.4$ **8.2 ÷ 4**   18. $68.13 \div 0.003$ 19. $2.6 \div 1.3$ **26 ÷ 13**

20. $0.00945 \div 0.021$ 21. $1.488 \div 3.1$ 22. $14.42 \div 0.206$
    9.45 ÷ 21   **14.88 ÷ 31**   **14,420 ÷ 206**

Divide.

23. $0.6\overline{)4.8}$ **8**   24. $0.7\overline{)0.21}$ **0.3**   25. $0.5\overline{)35}$ **70**

26. $1.6\overline{)0.768}$ **0.48** 27. $0.53\overline{)74.2}$ **140** 28. $0.075\overline{)0.345}$ **4.6**

29. $9\overline{)8.19}$ **0.91**   30. $1.2\overline{)108}$ **90**   31. $7.5\overline{)0.345}$ **0.046**

32. Find the quotient of 6.51 and 0.7. **9.3**

33. Find the quotient of 0.89 and 1.78. **0.5**

Solve each equation.

34. $3.68 \div 0.92 = p$ **4**   35. $f = 0.4664 \div 5.3$ **0.088**

36. $1.25 \div 5 = s$ **0.25**   37. $a = 7.56 \div 0.63$ **12**

38. $0.42 \div 3.5 = w$ **0.12**   39. $n = 2.04 \div 0.6$ **3.4**

40. $17.94 \div 2.3 = m$ **7.8**   41. $c = 2.665 \div 4.1$ **0.65**

Lesson 2-7 Dividing Decimals   **73**

Error Analysis

Watch for students who misplace the decimal point in the quotient because they did not multiply the dividend by the same power of ten they used to multiply the divisor.

Prevent by reviewing the procedure for moving the decimal point to the right, and by having students estimate the quotient first.

Close

Have students use paper and pencil to find the cost of a gallon of gasoline at a gasoline station where a sale of 6.8 gallons cost a customer $8.77.   about $1.29

3 PRACTICE/APPLY

Assignment Guide
Maximum: 17–50
Minimum: 17–41 odd, 42–50

For **Extra Practice,** see p. 576.

Alternate Assessment

Speaking   Have students tell the steps in the process of dividing a decimal by a decimal.

Practice Masters, p. 17

Name _____ Date _____

Practice Worksheet 2-7

Dividing Decimals

Without finding each quotient, change each problem so that the divisor is a whole number.

1. $0.84 \div 0.2$ 2. $1.02 \div 0.3$ 3. $3.9 \div 1.3$
   8.4 ÷ 2   **10.2 ÷ 3**   **39 ÷ 13**

4. $13.6 \div 0.003$ 5. $1.622 \div 1.4$ 6. $0.00025 \div 0.035$
   13,600 ÷ 3   **16.22 ÷ 14**   **0.25 ÷ 35**

Divide.

7. $0.5\overline{)9.5}$ 8. $0.8\overline{)0.048}$ 9. $0.4\overline{)82}$
   19   **0.06**   **205**

10. $3.5\overline{)2.38}$ 11. $0.62\overline{)600.16}$ 12. $0.015\overline{)0.06}$
    0.68   **968**   **4**

13. $1.4\overline{)121.8}$ 14. $8\overline{)0.0092}$ 15. $0.38\overline{)760.38}$
    87   **0.00115**   **2,001**

Solve each equation.

16. $7.8 \div 2.6 = k$ 17. $3.92 \div 0.08 = m$ 18. $s = 149.73 \div 0.23$
    3   **49**   **651**

19. $v = 155 \div 0.1$ 20. $c = 1,098 \div 6.1$ 21. $3,633.4 \div 3.7 = d$
    1,550   **180**   **982**

22. $903.6 \div 25.1 = n$ 23. $363.6 \div 5 = r$ 24. $2.004 \div 0.2 = b$
    36   **72.72**   **10.02**

25. $w = 84.7 \div 3.85$ 26. $165.2 \div 8.26 = t$ 27. $29.28 \div 1.22 = s$
    22   **20**   **24**

T17
Glencoe Division, Macmillan/McGraw-Hill

42. **Mileage**   Susannah has 2 gallons of gasoline left in her car. Her car averages 15 miles per gallon. If Susannah's home is 32 miles away, will she make it home before she runs out of gasoline? *(Lesson 1-1)* **no**

43. **Algebra**   Evaluate $3x - y \div 6$ if $x = 4$ and $y = 12$. *(Lesson 1-8)* **10**

44. **Consumer Math**   A survey of the weekly average amount spent on groceries for a family of four is $147.2653. Find the weekly average to the nearest cent. *(Lesson 2-2)* **$147.27**

45. Estimate 21.7×6.3. *(Lesson 2-3)* **120**

46. Write 635,000 in scientific notation. *(Lesson 2-6)* **6.35×10^5**

47. **Currency**   All currency bills (paper money) in the United States, no matter what their value is, are the same size. A currency bill has an area of about 15.86 square inches and a length of about 6.1 inches. What is the width of a currency bill? **2.6 inches**

48. **Animals**   A blue whale, the largest creature ever to live on Earth, can weigh 153.26 tons.
    a. An eighteen-wheel semitractor trailer fully loaded, can weigh 48.5 tons. How many times heavier is the blue whale? **3.16 times heavier**
    b. How many times heavier than *you* is the blue whale? **Answers will vary.**

49. **Science**   The bacterium *E. coli* has a diameter of 0.001 millimeter. The head of a pin has a diameter of 1 millimeter. How many bacteria *E. coli* could fit across the head of a pin? **1,000 bacteria**

50. **Critical Thinking**   Place a decimal point in each of the numbers 11,008 and 256 such that their quotient will be 430. **Sample answer: $1,100.8 \div 2.56 = 430$**

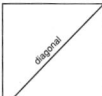

51. **Portfolio Suggestion**   Select one of the assignments from this chapter that you found especially challenging. Place it in your portfolio. **See students' work.**

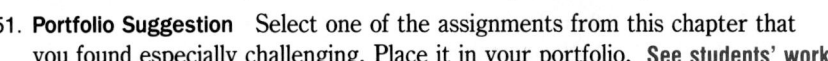

CULTURAL KALEIDOSCOPE

Benjamin Banneker

Benjamin Banneker (1731–1806) was a mathematician, an astronomer, a compiler of almanacs, an inventor, a writer, and a very important African-American intellectual.

In 1761, he attracted attention by building a wooden clock that kept precise time. In 1773, Banneker began astronomical calculations and accurately predicted a solar eclipse which occurred in 1789.

Appointed to the District of Co-

lumbia Commission by President George Washington in 1790, he helped to survey Washington D.C. He published almanacs annually from 1791 to 1802 and sent his first one to Thomas Jefferson, then United States Secretary of State. Banneker, who opposed war and slavery, worked very hard to try to bring about better conditions for African-Americans.

74   **Chapter 2** Applications with Decimals

Enrichment Masters, p. 17

Name _____ Date _____

Enrichment Worksheet 2-7

Diagonals and Altitudes

In these activities, you will use decimals to describe two different geometric relationships.

1. The *diagonal* of a square connects opposite corners. Measure one side and the diagonal of this square to the nearest tenth of a centimeter.   **4.0 cm; 5.7 cm**

2. On a separate sheet of paper, draw squares of various sizes. Use your squares to complete this table.
   Answers will vary.

Length of Side				
Length of Diagonal				

3. Describe the relationship between the diagonal of a square and its side.   **The length of the diagonal is about 1.4 times the length of a side.**

4. An *equilateral triangle* has three sides of the same length. The *altitude* of the triangle connects one corner with the middle of the opposite side. Measure one side and the altitude of this equilateral triangle to the nearest tenth of a centimeter.   **4.0 cm; 3.5 cm**

5. On a separate sheet of paper, draw equilateral triangles of various sizes. Use your figures to complete this table.
   Answers will vary

Length of Side				
Length of Altitude				

6. Describe the relationship between the altitude of an equilateral triangle and its side.
   The length of the altitude is about 0.87 times the length of one side.

T17
Glencoe Division, Macmillan/McGraw-Hill

OPTIONS

Extending the Lessons

Cultural Kaleidoscope   Point out to students that Banneker used his knowledge of mathematics to create his inventions and perform his astronomical calculations.

Cooperative Learning Activity

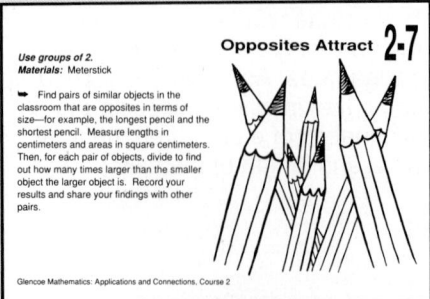

Use groups of 2.
Materials: Meterstick

Opposites Attract 2-7

➡ Find pairs of similar objects in the classroom that are opposites in terms of size—for example, the longest pencil and the shortest pencil. Measure lengths in centimeters and areas in square centimeters. Then, for each pair of objects, divide to find out how many times larger the larger object is. Record your results and share your findings with other pairs.

Glencoe Mathematics: Applications and Connections, Course 2

2-8 Rounding Quotients

Objective
Round decimal quotients to a specified place.

Marisa and three of her friends ordered a large pizza for $13.89. To find out how much each of them owes, they divide $13.89 by 4.

Estimate: $12 ÷ 4 = $3

13.89 ⊡ 4 ⊟ **3.4725**

Since the smallest unit of money is a penny ($0.01), they round the quotient to two decimal places.

3.4725 → 3.48   *When a quotient involves money, it is usually rounded up.*

Each person should pay $3.48.

There are other situations, besides money, when it is useful to round quotients.

Calculator Hint
••••••••••••
Some calculators round and some calculators truncate results. *Truncate* means to cut off at a certain place-value position, dropping the digits that follow. Does your calculator round or truncate results?

| **Example 1** | *Problem Solving* |

Sports A table tennis table has an area of 4.165 square meters, while a tennis court has an area of 260.76 square meters. How many times larger is the tennis court than the table to the nearest hundredth?

To solve, divide 260.76 by 4.165.

Estimate: 240 ÷ 4 = 60

260.76 ⊡ 4.165 ⊟ **62.607443**

≈   62.61   *Round to the nearest hundreth.*

≈ *means "is approximately equal to"*

The tennis court is about 62.61 times larger than the table tennis table.

Sometimes, it is helpful to round a quotient that is very large to the greatest place-value position of the whole number.

Lesson 2-8 Rounding Quotients   **75**

OPTIONS

Reteaching Activity

Using Applications Have groups of students use a take-out menu from a fast food restaurant as if to order lunch. Tell them that the group members will share the cost equally. Ask them to add to figure out the total cost for lunch and to divide, using rounding, to determine what each student should pay.

Study Guide Masters, p. 18

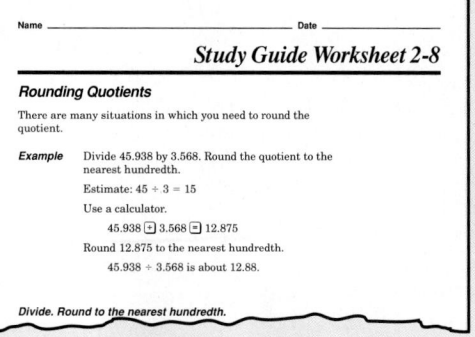

2-8 Lesson Notes

NCTM Standards: 1–6, 13

Lesson Resources
• Study Guide Master 2-8
• Practice Master 2-8
• Enrichment Master 2-8
• Group Activity Card 2-8

Transparency 2-8 contains the 5-Minute Check and a teaching aid for this lesson.

⏱ 5-Minute Check
(Over Lesson 2-7)
Divide.
1. 0.7)‾4.2   6
2. 0.25)‾0.625   2.5
3. Find the quotient of 1.856 and 0.2.   9.28

Solve each equation.
4. 26.5 ÷ 0.5 = t   53
5. p = 0.72 ÷ 0.009   80

1 FOCUS

Motivating the Lesson

Situational Problem Ask students how they would determine which store has better prices for used paperback books—Wilson's, which sells 5 paperbacks for $6.49, or Stern's, which sells 3 for $3.87.

2 TEACH

Using Critical Thinking Have students suggest everyday situations in which rounding quotients is necessary or makes better sense than finding exact answers. Ask them why they think it is reasonable to round up quotients involving amounts of money. Have them support their opinions with examples.

76

More Examples

For Example 1

Pat's bedroom has an area of 156.25 square feet, while her cat usually sleeps in a box with an area of 6.875 square feet. How many times larger is Pat's room than the cat's box to the nearest hundredth?   about 22.73 times larger

For Example 2

The length of a year on Neptune is equal to 164.8 Earth years. The length of a year on Jupiter is 11.86 Earth years. How many times longer is a Neptune year than a Jupiter year? about 14 times longer

Checking for Understanding

Exercises 1-2 are designed to help you assess students' understanding through reading, writing, speaking, and modeling. You should work through these exercises with your students and then monitor their work on Guided Practice Exercises 3-12.

Practice Masters, p. 18

Name _____ Date _____

Practice Worksheet 2-8

Rounding Quotients

Divide. Round to the nearest tenth.

1. $0.8\overline{)32.6}$
   40.8
2. $3.1\overline{)82.56}$
   26.6
3. $0.06\overline{)12.8884}$
   214.8

Divide. Round to the nearest hundredth.

4. $0.04\overline{)0.00086}$
   0.02
5. $3.9\overline{)4.686}$
   1.20
6. $14\overline{)68.6352}$
   4.90

7. $0.06\overline{)268}$
   4,466.67
8. $6.9\overline{)0.682}$
   0.10
9. $0.029\overline{)0.8732}$
   30.11

Divide. Round to the greatest place-value position of the quotient.

10. $0.9\overline{)34,521.9}$
    40,000
11. $3.4\overline{)86,487.36}$
    30,000
12. $0.09\overline{)42,854.2}$
    500,000

Divide. Round up to the next cent.

13. $4\overline{)\$68.23}$
    $17.06
14. $24\overline{)\$182.51}$
    $7.61
15. $19\overline{)\$98.63}$
    $5.20

T 18
Glencoe Division, Macmillan/McGraw-Hill

Example 2 *Problem Solving*

Astronomy Ceres, one of the largest known asteroids, is 690.4 kilometers in diameter. Jupiter, the first planet beyond the asteroid belt, has a diameter of 142,748.8 kilometers. How many times longer is Jupiter's diameter than Ceres' diameter?

To find out, divide 142,748.8 by 690.4.

Estimate: $140,000 \div 700 = 200$

142748.8 ÷ 690.4 = 206.762457

≈ 200 *Round to the nearest hundred.*

Jupiter's diameter is *about* 200 times longer than Ceres'.

Checking for Understanding

Communicating Mathematics

Read and study the lesson to answer each question.

1. **Write** one or two sentences that explain how to round the quotient of a money problem. **See Solutions Manual.**

2. **Write** an example of a division problem involving very large quantities that requires rounding to the greatest place-value position. **See Solutions Manual.**

Guided Practice

Divide. Round to the nearest tenth.

3. $0.7\overline{)29.3}$
   41.9
4. $2.6\overline{)56.38}$
   21.7
5. $0.04\overline{)15.999}$
   400.0

Divide. Round to the greatest place-value position of the quotient.

6. $0.14\overline{)56,382.9}$
   400,000
7. $1.8\overline{)26,788.13}$
   10,000
8. $0.09\overline{)25,788.89}$
   300,000

Divide. Round up to the next cent.

9. $6\overline{)\$8.25}$
   $1.38
10. $15\overline{)\$168.57}$
    $11.24
11. $23\overline{)\$48.98}$
    $2.13

12. Round the quotient of 14.85 and 0.023 to the nearest hundredth. 645.65

Exercises

Independent Practice

Divide. Round to the nearest hundredth.

13. $0.03\overline{)0.00775}$ 0.26
14. $2.2\overline{)6.329}$ 2.88
15. $13\overline{)56.728}$ 4.36

76   **Chapter 2** Applications with Decimals

Classroom Vignette

"Students brought several different calculators to class and, using the 'Calculator Hint', determined whether each one rounded or truncated the results. The students also determined what percent rounded and what percent truncated. Then they discussed the value and disadvantages of each kind."

Marshalyn E. Baker

Marshalyn Baker, Teacher
Williams Junior High School, Oakland, ME

Divide. Round to the greatest place-value position of the quotient.

16. $0.9\overline{)32{,}567.1}$
40,000

17. $2.31\overline{)123{,}678.55}$
50,000

18. $5.6\overline{)5{,}498.21}$
1,000

Divide. Round up to the next cent.

19. $0.05\overline{)\$45.67}$
$913.40

20. $6.3\overline{)\$89.73}$
$14.25

21. $0.4\overline{)\$74.23}$
$185.58

22. Round the quotient of $7.69 and 5 to the nearest cent. **$1.54**

23. Round the quotient of 7,180,000 and 2.05 to its greatest place-value position. **4,000,000**

Mixed Review

24. Estimate the number of inches in 2,573 feet. *(Lesson 2-3)* **about 30,000 inches**

25. **Pets** Steve has two dogs. Rex is 1.7 years old and Lady is 2.5 times older. How old is Lady? *(Lesson 2-4)* **4.25 years old**

26. Write 3.075×10^4 in standard form. *(Lesson 2-6)* **30,750**

27. **Smart Shopping** A jar of peanut butter holds 39 ounces and costs $1.95. What is the cost per ounce in cents? *(Lesson 2-7)* **$0.05 per ounce**

Problem Solving and Applications

28. **Buildings** Each story in an office building is about 3.66 meters tall. Find the height in stories of each of the structures.
    a. Great Pyramid of Cheops **40**
    b. Gateway Arch **52**
    c. Statue of Liberty **25**

29. **Geography** Alaska, the largest state in the United States, has an area of 1,478,458 square kilometers. Rhode Island, the smallest state in the United States, has an area of 2,732 square kilometers. How many times larger is Alaska? **about 541 times larger**

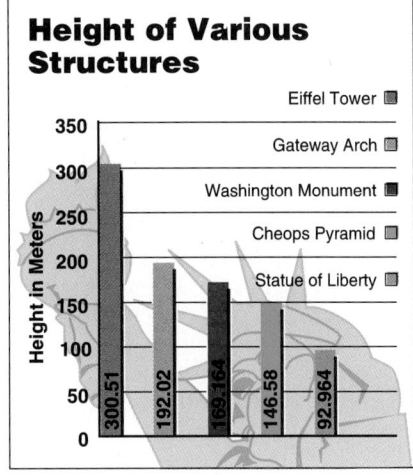

Height of Various Structures

- Eiffel Tower
- Gateway Arch
- Washington Monument
- Cheops Pyramid
- Statue of Liberty

Height in Meters

300.51 192.02 169.164 146.58 92.964

30. **Critical Thinking** Write a division problem where the quotient rounded to the nearest tenth and the quotient truncated to the tenths place are the same. Write a division problem where they are different.
    Sample answers: $10.6 \div 2 = 5.3$; $15.1 \div 2 = 7.6$

31. **Journal Entry** Name three situations that require division and state how you would round each quotient. Explain. **See students' work.**

Lesson 2-8 Rounding Quotients   **77**

Extending the Lesson

Have students create a cross-number puzzle for others to solve. Clues should include division of decimals, division with rounding of quotients, and equations and word problems involving decimal division.

Cooperative Learning Activity

Stocking Up **2-8**

Number of players: 3
Materials: Spinner

Label the sections of a spinner "0.5," "0.75," "0.89," "0.95," "1," and "2."

Suppose your group owns $15 worth of stock in a company. This means that each group member's share is currently worth $5.

Group members take turns spinning the spinner. After each spin, multiply the number on the spinner and the amount of money the stock is worth. For example, the stock might be worth 0.89 x $15 = $13.35 after the first spin. After you have determined the new worth of your stock, divide by 3 to find out how much each group member's share is now worth.

After the first round, each group member decides before each spin whether to continue or to "cash in" his or her stock. Of course, whenever a group member decides to quit, the value of the group's stock decreases by the value of his or her share.

Try to have the most valuable share after a maximum of twenty spins.

Glencoe Mathematics: Applications and Connections, Course 2

Enrichment Masters, p. 18

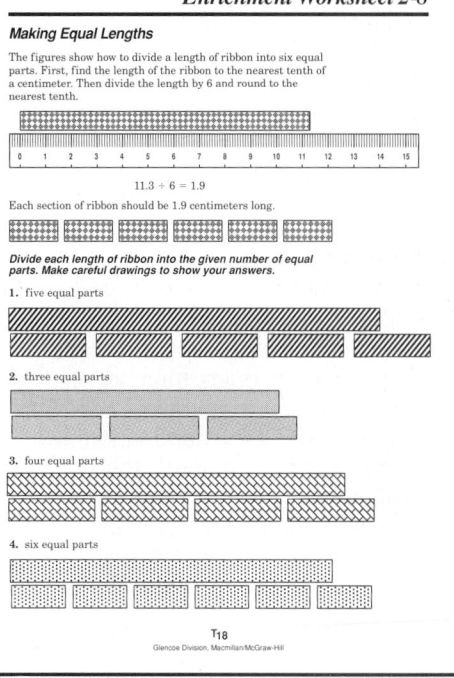

Name _____ Date _____

Enrichment Worksheet 2-8

Making Equal Lengths

The figures show how to divide a length of ribbon into six equal parts. First, find the length of the ribbon to the nearest tenth of a centimeter. Then divide the length by 6 and round to the nearest tenth.

$11.3 \div 6 = 1.9$

Each section of ribbon should be 1.9 centimeters long.

Divide each length of ribbon into the given number of equal parts. Make careful drawings to show your answers.

1. five equal parts

2. three equal parts

3. four equal parts

4. six equal parts

T18
Glencoe Division, Macmillan/McGraw-Hill

Close

Have students explain how they would use division with rounding to determine how much larger the diameter of one planet is than the diameter of another. **Answers should include rounding the quotient to its greatest place.**

3 PRACTICE/APPLY

Assignment Guide
Maximum: 13–31
Minimum: 13–23 odd, 24–30

For **Extra Practice**, see p. 576.

Alternate Assessment

Writing Have students write two problems for classmates to solve—one in which the quotient should be rounded up to the next cent, and one in which it must be rounded to its greatest place-value position. Students should provide solutions to their problems.

2-9 The Metric System

NCTM Standards: 1–5, 7, 13

Lesson Resources
- Study Guide Master 2-9
- Practice Master 2-9
- Enrichment Master 2-9
- Interdisciplinary Master, p. 16
- Group Activity Card 2-9

 Transparency 2-9 contains the 5-Minute Check and a teaching aid for this lesson.

⏱ 5-Minute Check
(Over Lesson 2-8)

1. Divide and round to the nearest hundredth:
   0.09⟌6.09   67.67

2. Divide and round to the greatest place-value position of the quotient:
   2.4⟌326,652.22
   100,000

3. Divide and round up to the next cent: 0.6⟌$38.56
   $64.27

4. Round the quotient of $8.45 and 9 to the nearest cent. $0.94

1 FOCUS

Motivating the Lesson

Activity   Have students describe a distance in the classroom that is about 5 m long, name something in the classroom that weighs about 5 kg, and draw a picture of a container with a capacity of about 1 L. Repeat the activity at the conclusion of the lesson.

2 TEACH

Using Connections   When discussing metric measurements with students, guide them to recognize that the prefixes *kilo, hecto, deka, deci, centi,* and *milli* apply to all metric units, and always have the same meaning. Focus on the meanings of the most frequently encountered prefixes, *kilo, centi,* and *milli*.

Objective
Change metric units of length, capacity, and mass.

Words to Learn
meter
metric system
gram
liter

Sound travels at about 343 meters per second in air. In water, sound travels about 1.435 kilometers per second. Does sound travel faster in air or water? One way to find out is to change 1.435 kilometers per second to meters per second.

Both the measurements above are based on the **meter** (m), which is the basic unit of length in the **metric system.** A meter is about the distance from the floor to a doorknob.

All units of length in the metric system are defined in terms of the meter. A prefix is added to indicate the decimal place-value position of the measurement. Study the chart below.

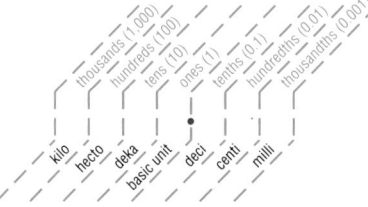

Notice that each place value is 10 times the place value to its right.

Notice that the value of each metric prefix is 10 times the value of the prefix to its right.

One way to solve the problem above is to change 1.435 kilometers to meters. Since 1 km = 1,000 m, multiply by 1,000.

$1.435 \times 1,000 = 1,435$

Sound travels 1,435 meters per second in water.

Since $1,435 > 343$, sound travels faster in water than in air.

Mental Math Hint
• • • • • • • • • • • • •
To multiply or divide by a power of ten, you can move the decimal point.

This diagram can help you change metric units.

MULTIPLY to change from longer units to shorter units.

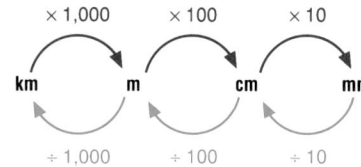

DIVIDE to change from shorter units to longer units.

OPTIONS

Reteaching Activity

Using Number Sense   To provide a different perspective, you may wish to have students convert among metric units by always multiplying rather than by choosing between multiplying and dividing. When converting to larger units, students can multiply by 0.1, 0.01, 0.001, and so on.

Study Guide Masters, p. 19

Name _____   Date _____

Study Guide Worksheet 2-9

The Metric System

The metric system is a base-10 system. The meter is the basic unit of length. The liter is the basic unit of capacity. The gram is the basic unit of mass.

Prefix	Meaning	Length	Capacity	Mass
kilo-	1,000	kilometer (km)	kiloliter (kL)	kilogram (kg)
	1	meter (m)	liter (L)	gram (g)
centi-	0.01	centimeter (cm)	centiliter (cL)	centigram (cg)
milli-	0.001	millimeter (mm)	milliliter (mL)	milligram (mg)

Units may be changed by multiplying or dividing by multiples of 10.

TEEN SCENE

Weather forecasters use instruments such as thermometers, rain gauges, or a barometer to measure weather.

But did you know that human hair can be used to measure humidity? Hair expands in moist air and shrinks as it dries out. The change in length and in humidity can be measured using a hair hygrometer.

Examples

1 0.9 cm = ▓ mm

To change from centimeters to millimeters, multiply by 10 since 1 cm = 10 mm.

$0.9 \times 10 = 9$
$0.9 \text{ cm} = 9 \text{ mm}$

2 4,500 m = ▓ km

To change from meters to kilometers, divide by 1,000 since 1 km = 1,000 m.

$4,500 \div 1,000 = 4.5$
$4,500 \text{ m} = 4.5 \text{ km}$

The **gram** (g) is the basic unit of mass in the metric system. *Mass* is the amount of matter that an object contains. A thumbtack has a mass of about one gram. You will notice that kilogram, gram, and milligram are related in a manner similar to kilometer, meter, and millimeter.

Examples

3 2,647 g = ▓ kg

To change from grams to kilograms, divide by 1,000 since 1 kg = 1,000 g.

$2,647 \div 1,000 = 2.647$
$2,647 \text{ g} = 2.647 \text{ kg}$

4 6 g = ▓ mg

To change from grams to milligrams, multiply by 1,000 since 1 g = 1,000 mg.

$6 \times 1,000 = 6,000$
$6 \text{ g} = 6,000 \text{ mg}$

The **liter** (L) is the basic unit of capacity in the metric system. *Capacity* is the amount of dry or liquid material an object can hold. Soft drinks often come in a 2-liter plastic container. You will notice that kiloliter, liter, and milliliter are related in a manner similar to kilometer, meter, and millimeter.

Examples

5 0.8 L = ▓ mL

Multiply by 1,000 since 1 L = 1,000 mL.

$0.8 \times 1,000 = 800$
$0.8 \text{ L} = 800 \text{ mL}$

6 862 L = ▓ kL

Divide by 1,000 since 1 kL = 1,000 L.

$862 \div 1,000 = 0.862$
$862 \text{ L} = 0.862 \text{ kL}$

Lesson 2-9 Measurement Connection: The Metric System **79**

More Examples

For Example 1
0.8 cm = __?__ mm   8

For Example 2
3,700 m = __?__ km   3.7

For Example 3
3,429 g = __?__ kg   3.429

For Example 4
8 g = __?__ mg   8,000

For Example 5
0.4 L = __?__ mL   400

For Example 6
628 mL = __?__ L   0.628

Checking for Understanding

Exercises 1-2 are designed to help you assess students' understanding through reading, writing, speaking, and modeling. You should work through these exercises with your students and then monitor their work on Guided Practice Exercises 3-13.

Practice Masters, p. 19

Name _____   Date _____

Practice Worksheet 2-9

The Metric System

Complete.

1. 470 mm = **47** cm
2. 63.5 km = **63,500** m
3. 612 g = **0.612** kg
4. 12.8 g = **12,800** mg
5. 8 L = **8,000** mL
6. 68.2 kg = **68,200** g
7. 0.8 L = **800** mL
8. 65 km = **65,000** m
9. 30 g = **0.03** kg
10. 368 mL = **0.368** L
11. 84 cm = **840** mm
12. 15.4 cm = **0.154** m
13. 43 m = **4,300** cm
14. 92 kg = **92,000** g
15. 3 L = **3,000** mL
16. 24 cm = **0.24** m
17. 9 m = **900** cm
18. 53 km = **53,000** m
19. 9.5 kg = **9,500** g
20. 1.5 L = **1,500** mL
21. 9,876 g = **9.876** kg
22. 1.1 m = **110** cm
23. 2.3 mm = **0.23** cm
24. 6,200 cm = **62** m
25. How many milliliters are in 0.09 liters?   90
26. How many centimeters are in 9.02 kilometers?   902,000
27. How many millimeters are in 4.2 kilometers?   4,200,000
28. How many milligrams are in 0.012 kilograms?   12,000

T19
Glencoe Division, Macmillan/McGraw-Hill

Classroom Vignette

"To help students remember the place-value position of metric prefixes I provide students the following mnemonic.

'King Henry Died Drinking Chocolate Milk'.
(kilo-, hecto-, deka-, deci-, centi-, milli-)"

Diane Hilt

Diane Hilt, Teacher
Faith Middle School, Fort Benning, GA

79

Close

First have students explain why they cannot perform a conversion such as kilometers to milliliters or centigrams to liters. Then have each student provide a partner with measurements in meters, grams, and liters. The partner then rewrites the measurements in both greater and smaller units.

3 PRACTICE/APPLY

Assignment Guide

Maximum: 14–38
Minimum: 15–31 odd, 32–38

For **Extra Practice,** see p. 577.

Alternate Assessment

Writing Have a group of students create a matching puzzle that consists of a list of units of measurement in the left column of a page and equivalent units of measurement listed in random order in the right columns of the page. The remaining students must match the pairs of equivalent measures.

Enrichment Masters, p. 19

Checking for Understanding

Communicating Mathematics

Read and study the lesson to answer each question.

1. **Tell** how you know when to multiply or divide when you are converting measures. **See Solutions Manual.**
2. **Tell** how the metric system and decimals are similar. **Both are based on 10.**

Guided Practice

Complete.

3. 550 mm = ▓ cm **55**   4. 43.8 km = ▓ m **43,800**   5. 814 g = ▓ kg **0.814**
6. 16.5 g = ▓ mg **16,500**   7. 5 L = ▓ mL **5,000**   8. 32 L = ▓ mL **32,000**
9. 89 km = ▓ m **89,000**   10. 67.1 kg = ▓ g **67,100**   11. 0.6 L = ▓ mL **600**

12. How many grams are in 1.01 kilograms? **1,010 grams**
13. How many centimeters are in 0.56 meter? **56 cm**

Exercises

Independent Practice

Complete.   22. **620,000**

14. 234 mm = ▓ cm **23.4**   15. 5.8 m = ▓ cm **580**   16. 13.2 cm = ▓ m **0.132**
17. 0.9 cm = ▓ mm **9**   18. 46 km = ▓ m **46,000**   19. 6,700 m = ▓ km **6.7**
20. 567 mg = ▓ g **0.567**   21. 80 g = ▓ kg **0.080**   22. 0.62 kg = ▓ mg
23. 73.8 kg = ▓ g **73,800**   24. 24.7 g = ▓ mg **24,700**   25. 8.1 L = ▓ mL **8,100**
26. 329 mL = ▓ L **0.329**   27. 47 L = ▓ kL **0.047**   28. 0.52 kL = ▓ mL
                                                                    520,000

29. How many milliliters are in 0.07 liters? **70 mL**
30. How many centimeters are in 6.302 kilometers? **630,200 cm**
31. How many milligrams are in 0.014 kilograms? **14,000 mg**

Mixed Review

32. Evaluate 2^8. *(Lesson1-9)* **256**
33. Which is greater, 3.19 or 3.1? *(Lesson 2-1)* **3.19**
34. Solve the equation $16.2 \div 2.5 = n$. *(Lesson 2-7)* **6.48**
35. **Advertising** A 30-second advertisement on a local television station during prime time costs the advertiser $1,280. To the nearest cent, how much does the ad cost per second? *(Lesson 2-8)* **$42.67 per second**

                                                        See Solutions Manual.

Problem Solving and Applications

36. **Research** Look up the *metric system* in your school library. What are the meanings of the prefixes: micro-, tera-, giga-, and nano-?
37. **Critical Thinking** Order from least to greatest. **3.4 cm, 53.25 mm, 0.49 m,** 0.0031 km   **0.0031 km** 3.4 cm   53.25 mm   0.49 m
38. **Geometry** In order for three numbers to represent the measures of the sides of a triangle, the sum of any two numbers must be greater than the third. Could 1.3 centimeters, 9.5 millimeters, and 0.127 meters be the lengths of the sides of a triangle? Draw a diagram to explain your answer.
                                                        No; see Solutions Manual.

OPTIONS

Extending the Lesson

Using Sensible Measures Have students make up a multiple-choice quiz for classmates to test their understanding of *length, mass,* and *capacity* in the metric system. Questions should be like the following, and in a similar format:
A bowling ball might have a mass of ____?

6 mg   6 g   6 kg   6 kg

Cooperative Learning Activity

Use groups of 2.
Materials: Metersticks, index cards

Mystery Measurements **2-9**

♦ Working alone, secretly measure four objects in the classroom. Then write the name of each object on a card. Finally, write the length of each object in *kilometers* on another card. Keep a record of your measurements on a separate sheet of paper.

➡ Shuffle your cards and then exchange cards with your partner. Try to be the first to correctly match each object with its measure.

Glencoe Mathematics: Applications and Connections, Course 2

2-10 Determine Reasonable Answers

Objective
Determine whether answers are reasonable.

Megan has $80 to spend on clothes for school. After looking at sale ads in the newspaper, she decides that she will buy 2 pairs of jeans for $29.99 each and 2 belts for $8.18 each. She thinks that she would have $10.00 left to buy hair accessories. Does this seem reasonable?

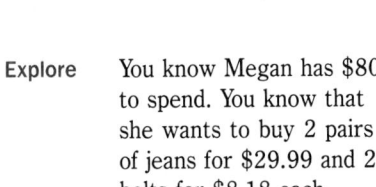

Explore   You know Megan has $80 to spend. You know that she wants to buy 2 pairs of jeans for $29.99 and 2 belts for $8.18 each.

You want to find out whether it is reasonable for Megan to have $10 left to buy hair accessories.

Plan   Estimate to find the total amount Megan will spend. Then determine if she has enough money left for hair accessories.

Solve

$30.00	*Round $29.99 to $30.00.*
30.00	
10.00	*Round $8.18 to $10.00*
+ 10.00	
$80.00	

$80.00	
− 80.00	
$ 0.00	It is not reasonable for Megan to have $10 left for hair accessories.

Examine   You can use a calculator to see how much Megan will actually have left.

2 ⊠ 29.99 ⊟ STO 2 ⊠ 8.18 ⊞ RCL ⊟ 76.34

C/CE 80 ⊟ 76.34 ⊟ 3.66

Lesson 2-10 Problem-Solving Strategy: Determine Reasonable Answers   **81**

NCTM Standards: 1–5, 7, 13

Lesson Resources
- Study Guide Master 2-10
- Practice Master 2-10
- Enrichment Master 2-10
- Evaluation Master, Quiz B, p. 16
- Group Activity Card 2-10

 Transparency 2-10 contains the 5-Minute Check and a teaching aid for this lesson.

🕐 5-Minute Check
(Over Lesson 2-9)
Complete.
1. 440 mm = ? cm   44
2. 54 km = ? m   54,000
3. 22.6 g = ? mg
   22,600
4. 6.1 L = ? mL   6,100
5. How many centimeters are in 4.036 km?
   403,600 cm

1 FOCUS
Motivating the Lesson

Situational Problem   Provide students with a copy of the following passage. Ask them to place decimal points in each of the numbers so that the measurements make sense. *Li looked around the classroom. She estimated the ceiling height to be about 582 meters and the length of the room to be about 155,000 centimeters. She estimated that the football player she saw stretching on the field outside weighed about 757 kilograms.*

2 TEACH

Using Applications   Have students review a menu from a local restaurant. Then have them decide whether it seems reasonable to be able to pay for an appetizer, entree, dessert, and drink with a $20 bill and have enough left over for a $3 tip.

OPTIONS
Reteaching Activity

Using Problem Solving   Guide students, working with partners, to choose strategies for solving problems like those in the lesson but using simpler numbers.

Study Guide Masters, p. 20

Name _____ Date _____

Study Guide Worksheet 2-10

Problem-Solving Strategy: Determine Reasonable Answers

Hot dogs cost $3.89 for a package of 8. Hot dog buns cost $1.29 for a package of 6. Kathy thinks the $30 she has is enough to pay for 48 hot dogs and 48 buns. Does this seem reasonable? Explain.

Explore   What do you know?
You know that 8 hot dogs cost $3.89 and 6 buns cost $1.29.

You know Kathy wants to buy 48 hot dogs and 48 buns.
What do you want to know?
You want to know if $30 is enough to pay for 48 hot dogs and 48 buns.

Plan   Estimate to find the cost of 48 hot dogs and 48 buns. Then decide if $30 is enough.

Solve   Find the number of packages of hot dogs needed. 48 ÷ 8 = 6
Round $3.89 to $4. $4 × 6 = $24

Checking for Understanding

Communicating Mathematics

Read and study the lesson to answer each question.   **See margin.**

1. **Tell** another strategy you could have used to solve the problem on page 81.

2. **Write** a problem with an unreasonable answer and ask a classmate to explain why they think the answer is unreasonable. **See students' work.**

Guided Practice   Solve.

3. Mr. Eldridge eats food that has 2,755 calories in an average day. When he multiplied the number of calories he eats per day by the number of days in a week, the calculator showed 192,850. Is this answer reasonable? Explain. **No; $3,000 \times 7 = 21,000$.**

4. At the Book Fair, Brian wants to buy 2 science fiction books for $2.95 each, 3 magazines for $2.95 each, and 1 bookmark for $0.39. Does he need to bring $15 or $20 with him? **$20**

5. Vinney's Video Haven is selling 3 blank video tapes for $14.96. Carlene says she can get 9 tapes for under $40. Is her answer reasonable? **no**

Problem Solving

Practice   Solve using any strategy.

6. New car carriers deliver new cars from the loading dock at the auto plant to car dealerships. Each truck can carry about 20,000 pounds of weight. If an economy-sized car weighs about 2,330 pounds, what is a reasonable number of cars that could be transported on one truck? **8 cars**

7. The trail up to the top of Pike's Peak is about 22 miles long. The Arnold family drove about one third of the way. Did they drive about 7 miles or 17 miles? **7 miles**

8. Felicia's vacation lasted 8 days and 7 nights. She spent $95 per night for the hotel and $30 per day for food. How much did she spend on food and lodging? **$905**

9. In the 1992 Olympics, Gail Devers ran the 100-meter dash in 10.82 seconds. Round this decimal to the nearest tenth of a second. **10.8 seconds**

10. Suppose a flask contains 750 milliliters of an acid. A chemist pours 0.5 liters of the acid into a solution. How many milliliters are left in the flask? **250 mL**

11. The width of the continental shelf along West Africa varies. It is about 4.5 miles wide in the Gulf of Guinea and only 2.5 miles wide off Angola. What is the average width of those two readings? **3.5 miles**

82   Chapter 2 Applications with Decimals

12. **Photography** A paramecium that is 0.25 millimeters long is magnified to 60 millimeters for a science book photograph. How many times larger is the paramecium in the photo than the actual paramecium? **240 times**

13. During one 20-game span of the Los Angeles Lakers, Magic Johnson scored 498 points and James Worthy scored 425 points. Find the total points scored together by both athletes. **923 points**

14. Suppose a relative matches your age with dollars on your birthday. You are 13. How much money have you been given over the years by this relative? **$91**

15. Al Johnson is measuring an exterior wall of the family room in order to paint it. There is one large window and a door on that wall. Al multiplies the width times the height of the wall and gets 240 square feet. The paint label says a quart covers 100 square feet. How much paint should he buy? **3 quarts**

16. Ms. Francis drove her car 427 miles on 15.8 gallons of gasoline.
    a. To the nearest mile, how many miles per gallon does her car get? **27 miles per gallon**
    b. What was the cost of gasoline at $1.439 per gallon? **$22.74**

17. **Data Search** Refer to page 649. What was the change in the number of Boy Scouts from 1980 to 1990? **increase of 1.1 million**

18. Peta places a long distance phone call to her grandparents in California and talks for 45 minutes. The phone company bills the call at a rate of $0.10 per half-minute. How much does the call cost Peta? **$9**

19. The average adult male weighs 162 pounds. The average adult cat weighs 10 pounds. *About* how many times heavier is a man than his cat? **about 16 times**

Lesson 2-10 Problem-Solving Strategy: Determine Reasonable Answers **83**

Extending the Lesson

Consumer Have students use the numbers 15, 57, 3, 9, 100, 2 and 43 and any dollar signs they need to write a paragraph describing a purchase of five items in a store. Then ask students to make up problems like the one on page 81 for others to solve.

Cooperative Learning Activity

Materials: Index cards, spinners

Don't Be Unreasonable **2-10**

● Copy onto cards the amounts shown on the back of this card, one per card. Shuffle the cards and divide them evenly. Label the sections of a spinner $10, $15, $25, $50, $75, $100, $200, $500.

● Each partner places a card face up. Then one partner spins the spinner. Each partner writes the number of items you could buy at the price shown on the card with the amount of money shown on the spinner. Check the reasonableness of each other's answers. Continue in this way, taking turns at the spinner, until all of the cards have been played. Try to "purchase" more items than your partner by the end of the game.

Glencoe Mathematics: Applications and Connections, Course 2

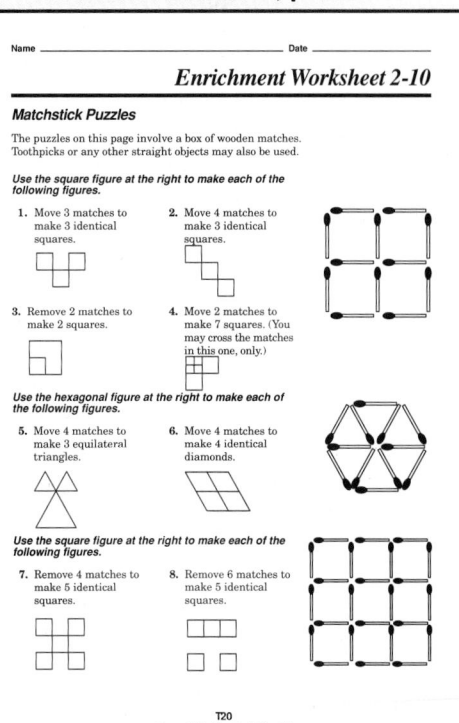

Using the Chapter Study Guide and Review

The Chapter Study Guide and Review begins with a section on Communicating Mathematics. This includes questions that review the new terms and concepts that were introduced in the chapter.

Then, the Skills and Concepts presented in the chapter are reviewed using a side-by-side format. Encourage students to refer to the Objectives and Examples on the left as they complete the Review Exercises on the right.

The Chapter Study Guide and Review ends with problems that review Applications and Problem Solving.

Additional Answers

7. 3.04, 3.15, 3.7, 3.9, 4.2
8. 0.06, 0.159, 1.4, 1.59, 15.91
9. 0.015, 0.105, 0.149, 0.15, 0.501
10. 15.09, 15.99, 16, 16.03, 16.3
11. 0.257, 2.04, 2.046, 25.7, 26.04

Chapter 2

Study Guide and Review

Communicating Mathematics

Choose the correct term or number to complete the sentence.

1. The number 0.04 is (less, greater) than 0.041.
2. When rounding decimals, the digit in the place being rounded should be rounded up if the digit to the right is a (4, 7).
3. The number of decimal places in the product when multiplying decimals is the (sum, product) of the number of places in the factors.
4. In scientific notation, a number is written as a (sum, product) of a decimal number and a power of ten.
5. The basic unit of mass in the metric system is the (gram, meter).
6. In your own words, explain the relationship between a meter and a centimeter. **Sample answer: A centimeter is $\frac{1}{100}$ of a meter.**

Self Assessment

Objectives and Examples	*Review Exercises*
Upon completing this chapter, you should be able to:	*Use these exercises to review and prepare for the chapter test.*
• compare and order decimals *(Lesson 2-1)* Order the following decimals from least to greatest. 3.2, 0.4, 0.43, 3.5, 4 0.4, 0.43, 3.2, 3.5, 4 **For answers to Exercises 7–11, see margin.**	Order each set of decimals from least to greatest. 7. 4.2, 3.9, 3.15, 3.04, 3.7 8. 15.91, 1.59, 0.159, 0.06, 1.4 9. 0.15, 0.149, 0.105, 0.015, 0.501 10. 16.3, 16.03, 16, 15.99, 15.09 11. 26.04, 25.7, 0.257, 2.046, 2.04
• round decimals *(Lesson 2-2)* Round 237.359 to the nearest tenth. The digit to the right of the 3 in the tenths place is 5, so round up. 237.359 → 237.4	Round each number to the underlined place-value position. 12. 5.75 **6** 13. 13.274 **13.27** 14. 129,342 **129,000** 15. 0.076 **0.1** 16. 81.349 **81.3** 17. 257.196 **257.20** 18. 200,543 **200,000** 19. 0.0015 **0.002**

Objectives and Examples

- estimate with decimals *(Lesson 2-3)*

  You can use rounding, clustering, or patterns to estimate sums, differences, products, and quotients of decimals.

Review Exercises

Estimate.

20. $13.72 + 12.07$ **25**

21. $243.46 + 112.3$ **350**

22. $25.73 - 2.19$ **23**

23. 11.75×3.13 **36**

24. $72.4 \div 9.3$ **8**

25. $150.96 \div 4.76$ **30**

- multiply decimals *(Lesson 2-4)*

$$\begin{array}{r} 3.2 \\ \times 0.6 \\ \hline 1.92 \end{array}$$

  1 decimal place
  1 decimal place
  Count 2 decimal places from the right.

Multiply.

26. 2.6×3.7 **9.62**

27. 0.13×2 **0.26**

28. 12.5×0.0017 **0.02125**

29. 7.5×3.03 **22.725**

30. 1.001×0.4 **0.4004**

- multiply decimals mentally by powers of ten *(Lesson 2-5)*

  $100 \times 2.3 = 230$

Multiply.

31. 13.7×10^3 **13,700**

32. $0.0065 \times 10,000$ **65**

33. 6.37×10 **63.7**

34. 128.63×10^2 **12,863**

- express numbers greater than 100 in scientific notation and vice versa *(Lesson 2-6)*

  $256,000 = 2.56 \times 10^5$

  $6.79 \times 10^7 = 67,900,000$

Write each number in scientific notation.

35. $6,000$ **6×10^3**

36. $459,000,000$ **4.59×10^8**

Write each number in standard form.

37. 1.37×10^4 **13,700**

38. 9.99×10^6 **9,990,000**

- divide decimals *(Lesson 2-7)*

$$\begin{array}{r} 12.6 \\ 3.6)\overline{45.36} \\ -36 \\ \hline 9\,3 \\ -7\,2 \\ \hline 2\,16 \\ -2\,16 \\ \hline 0 \end{array}$$

Divide.

39. $12 \div 1.2$ **10**

40. $8.4 \div 0.2$ **42**

41. $0.0036 \div 0.9$ **0.004**

42. $1.47 \div 0.06$ **24.5**

43. $5 \div 0.005$ **1,000**

44. $0.002 \div 0.01$ **0.2**

Chapter 2 Study Guide and Review **85**

You may wish to use a Chapter Test from the Evaluation Masters booklet as an additional chapter review. The two free-response forms are shown below. One of the two multiple-choice forms is shown on the next page.

Evaluation Masters, pp. 14-15

Name ______________ Date ______________

Form 2A — *Chapter 2 Test*

Order each set of numbers from least to greatest.

1. 0.68, 1.01, 0.99, 0.7
2. 10.44, 1.173, 10.4, 10.006

Round each number to the underlined place-value position.

3. 215.0<u>1</u>8
4. 0.<u>6</u>941
5. 1<u>0</u>.096
6. 3.<u>0</u>512

Estimate. Use an appropriate strategy.

7. 8.76 + 6.74
8. 12.31 − 9.33
9. 32.8 × 49.3
10. 4.2)0.78

Multiply or divide.

11. 3.9 × 10,000
12. 6.4 × 0.003
13. 0.00029×10^7
14. 0.6)5.4
15. How many dimes are there in $45.00?

Change from standard form to scientific notation or vice-versa.

16. 4.09×10^3
17. 795

Complete.

18. 2.93 L = ■ mL
19. 432 g = ■ kg
20. Divide 0.04)0.0853. Round to the nearest hundredth.
21. During a twelve-week period, Raman saved $10.25 per week. Estimate the amount he saved in twelve weeks.
22. To make punch, Lawrence mixes 3 L of lemon soda with 2,800 mL of orange juice. How many liters of punch does this make?
23. The O'Sullivans spend $127.75 a year for a daily newspaper. They receive it 365 days a year. How much does one paper cost?
24. Jerry hiked 4 fewer miles than Raul. If Jerry hiked 13.3 miles, how many miles did Raul hike?
25. Claudia bought 3 pounds of peanuts for $5.97, 2 packages of cheese crackers for $5.98, and 2 bags of corn chips for $2.98. Should she expect to pay about $10, $15, or $20 at the checkout?

BONUS What is the difference between 1.73×10^4 and 1.73×10^3?

Answers:
1. 0.68, 0.7, 0.99, 1.01
2. 1.173, 10.006, 10.4, 10.44
3. 215.02
4. 0.7
5. 10
6. 3.1
7. about 16
8. about 3
9. about 1,500
10. about 0.2
11. 39,000
12. 0.0192
13. 2,900
14. 9
15. 450
16. 4,090
17. 7.95×10^2
18. 2,930
19. 0.432
20. 2.13
21. about $120
22. 5.8 L
23. 35¢
24. 17.3 mi
25. $15

15,570

14
Glencoe Division, Macmillan/McGraw-Hill

Name ______________ Date ______________

Form 2B — *Chapter 2 Test*

Order each set of numbers from least to greatest.

1. 1.53, 1.74, 0.91, 0.9
2. 6.55, 7.501, 6.0, 7.032, 6.01

Round each number to the underlined place-value position.

3. 8<u>5</u>.97
4. 0.1<u>2</u>4
5. 6.<u>1</u>501
6. 2.56<u>9</u>1

Estimate. Use an appropriate strategy.

7. 42.89 − 10.16
8. 9.31 + 8.75
9. 22.7 × 56.2
10. 3.3)0.89

Multiply or divide.

11. 100,000 × 1.6
12. 4.7 × 0.005
13. 0.00303×10^8
14. 0.7)8.4
15. How many nickels are there in $35.00?

Change from standard form to scientific notation or vice-versa.

16. 8.9×10^5
17. 214

Complete.

18. 301 g = ■ kg
19. 0.75 L = ■ mL
20. Divide 0.07)0.389. Round to the nearest hundredth.
21. Ben bought 18 yards of fabric to make draperies. The fabric cost $5.35 a yard. Estimate the cost of the fabric.
22. Chico made 4 L of punch for a party. If he served 3,250 mL of punch, how many liters of punch were left?
23. Kari works 12 hours a week. She earns $5.25 an hour. How much does she earn in two weeks?
24. Mr. Tsao needs a 45.5-centimeter piece of molding. How many centimeters remain after he cut off the end of a 1-meter piece of molding?
25. Vicki vacationed for 7 days and 6 nights. She spent $98 a night for the hotel and $40 a day for food. How much did she spend on food and lodging?

BONUS Use scientific notation to show the product of 1.73×10^{20} and 1.73×10^6.

Answers:
1. 0.9, 0.91, 1.53, 1.74
2. 6.0, 6.01, 6.55, 7.032, 7.501
3. 86
4. 0.12
5. 6.2
6. 2.569
7. about 32
8. about 18
9. about 1,200
10. about 0.3
11. 160,000
12. 0.0235
13. 303,000
14. 12
15. 700
16. 890,000
17. 2.14×10^2
18. 0.301
19. 750
20. 5.56
21. about $100
22. 0.75 L
23. $126
24. 54.5 cm
25. $868

2.9929×10^{26}

15
Glencoe Division, Macmillan/McGraw-Hill

Objectives and Examples	*Review Exercises*
• round decimal quotients to a specific place *(Lesson 2-8)* 1.25 ÷ 4 = 0.3125 Rounded to the nearest tenth, 0.3125 is 0.3.	Divide. Round to the indicated place-value position. 45. 3.5 ÷ 1.3 to the nearest tenth. **2.7** 46. 14.78 ÷ 2.6 to the nearest whole number. **6**
• change metric units of length, capacity, and mass *(Lesson 2-9)* 1.39 kg = ■ g Multiply by 1,000 since 1 kg = 1,000 g. 1.39 kg = 1,390 g	Complete. 47. 27 mm = ■ m 48. 3.9 mg = ■ g 49. 6.85 km = ■ m 50. 3.3 mL = ■ L 51. 16 cm = ■ mm 52. 0.04 kL = ■ L 53. 43 g = ■ kg 54. 3.9 kL = ■ mL **For answers to Exercises 47-54, see margin.**

Applications and Problem Solving

55. **Smart Shopping** Thomas' Apple Orchard is selling apple cider in 34.7-ounce bottles for $2.08. Thomas' competitor is selling 24.6-ounce bottles of cider for $1.99. Who is selling at the lower price per ounce? Round to the nearest cent. *(Lesson 2-8)* **Thomas is lower at 6¢/oz.—competitor is 8¢/oz.**
56. **Remodeling** Anna needs 1.2×10^3 square feet of carpeting to carpet her new house. Write this number in standard form. *(Lesson 2-6)* **1,200 square feet**
57. When Kevin divided 78,278.2 by 1,547, the calculator displayed 506. Is this a reasonable answer? *(Lesson 2-10)* **no**

Curriculum Connection Projects

- **Geography** List the populations of the ten largest and ten smallest countries in the world. Rewrite each population as a power of ten. **See margin.**
- **Physical Education** Work with two friends to measure, to the nearest tenth of a meter, how far a person travels while performing a cartwheel. Find how many cartwheels must be performed to travel 1.5 kilometers.

Read More About It

McGraw, Eloise. *The Money Room.*
Simon, Seymour. *The Paper Airplane Book.*
Sachar, Louis. *Sideways Arithmetic from Wayside School.*

Additional Answers

47. 0.027
48. 0.0039
49. 6,850
50. 0.0033
51. 160
52. 40
53. 0.043
54. 3,900,000

2 Test

Order each set of decimals from least to greatest.

1. 12.6, 4.3, 8.7, 4, 12.06
   4, 4.3, 8.7, 12.06, 12.6

2. 0.07, 0.7, 0.71, 1.07, 1.71
   0.07, 0.7, 0.71, 1.07, 1.71

Round each number to the underlined place-value position.

3. 13.2̲75 **13.28**
4. 0.0̲76 **0.1**
5. 12̲,436 **12,000**
6. 0̲.995 **1**

7. The average attendance at a game during the football season was 2,176.34. Round to the nearest person. **2,176**

Estimate.

8. 27.34 + 12.95 **40**
9. 236.95 − 107.07 **100**
10. 23.6 × 2.95 **60**
11. 11.1)142.6 **14**
12. 91.6 × 7.999 **720**

13. **Earning Money** During a two-week period, Hiroko worked 89.7 hours. Her hourly wage is $6.85. Estimate the amount earned. **about $630**

Multiply or divide.

14. 0.3 × 8 **2.4**
15. 5.5 × 0.004 **0.022**
16. 6.7 × 1,000 **6,700**
17. 0.0047 × 10⁵ **470**
18. 3,003 × 100 **300,300**
19. 0.4)4.8 **12**
20. 0.24)0.0072 **0.03**
21. 0.0016)64 **40,000**

22. **Pets** Alicia's cat Felix weighed 0.95 pounds at birth. On his first birthday, Felix weighed in at 9.2 times his birth weight. What was Felix's weight on his first birthday? **8.74 pounds**

23. How many pennies are there in $36.00? **3,600 pennies**

Change from standard form to scientific notation or vice versa.

24. 23,000 **2.3 × 10⁴**
25. 632 **6.32 × 10²**
26. 8.03 × 10⁴ **80,300**
27. 1.6349 × 10³ **1,634.9**

28. **Child Care** The Wests spend $3,575 per year on day care for their daughter Lisa. Lisa actually is in day care 245 days per year. What is the cost per day? Round to the nearest cent. **$14.59 per day**

Complete.

29. 1.62 L = ■ mL **1,620 mL**
30. 243 g = ■ kg **0.243 kg**
31. 0.09 km = ■ mm **90,000 mm**

32. **Party Time** To mix a punch, Yolanda starts with 4 liters of ginger ale and adds 2,650 milliliters of cranberry juice.
    a. How many liters are in the punch bowl when the punch is complete? **6.65 L**
    b. How many 200-mL glasses of punch can be served? **about 33**

33. **Smart Shopping** Teresa bought 3 pounds of apples for $2.89, 2 pounds of carrots for $1.79, and 4 avocados for $0.99 cents each. Should she expect to pay about $5 or $10 at the checkout?. **$10**

Bonus How many times greater is 1.73 × 10²⁰ than 1.73 × 10⁶?
1 × 10¹⁴ or 100,000,000,000,000

Using the Chapter Test

This page may be used as a chapter test or another chapter review.

Evaluation Masters, pp. 10-11

Name _____ Date _____

Form 1A *Chapter 2 Test*

1. Order 0.8, 0.07, 1.03, and 0.87 from least to greatest.
   A. 0.07, 0.8, 1.03, 0.87 B. 0.07, 0.8, 0.87, 1.03
   C. 1.03, 0.87, 0.8, 0.07 D. 0.07, 0.87, 0.8, 1.03 **1. B**

Round each number to the underlined place-value position.

2. 8,205.6
   A. 8,206 B. 8,200 C. 8,210 D. 8,205 **2. C**

3. 1.2431
   A. 1.243 B. 1.250 C. 1.241 D. 1.24 **3. D**

Estimate. Use an appropriate strategy.

4. 9.39 + 5.81
   A. 15 B. 14 C. 16 D. 13 **4. A**

5. 16.42 − 9.75
   A. 7 B. 6 C. 5 D. 8 **5. B**

6. 4.87 × 49.7
   A. 200 B. 20 C. 250 D. 25 **6. C**

7. 6.1)71.77
   A. 11 B. 10 C. 13 D. 12 **7. D**

Multiply or divide.

8. 4.6 × 0.24
   A. 11.04 B. 1 C. 110.4 D. 1.104 **8. D**

9. 0.032 × 23
   A. 0.736 B. 73.6 C. 7.36 D. 736 **9. A**

10. 0.53 × 0.003
    A. 0.00122 B. 0.0016 C. 0.0015 D. 0.00159 **10. D**

11. 1.78 × 2.5
    A. 4.45 B. 6 C. 4 D. 0.445 **11. A**

12. 0.0793 × 10⁶
    A. 793 B. 0.0008 C. 79,300 D. 7,930 **12. C**

13. 1.3)169
    A. 130 B. 13 C. 1.3 D. 0.13 **13. A**

14. 0.8)0.048
    A. 0.05 B. 6 C. 0.06 D. 0.6 **14. C**

10
Glencoe Division, Macmillan/McGraw-Hill

Name _____ Date _____

Chapter 2 Test Form 1A (continued)

15. Find the quotient when 7.83 is divided by 0.9.
    A. 7.8 B. 78 C. 780 D. 8.7 **15. D**

16. How many nickels are there in $25.50?
    A. 510 B. 500 C. 5,100 D. 51 **16. A**

17. Divide 0.075)0.341. Round to the nearest hundredth.
    A. 4.25 B. 4.55 C. 4.54 D. 4.26 **17. B**

18. Write 498,000 in scientific notation.
    A. 49.8 × 10⁴ B. 4.98 × 10⁶
    C. 4.98 × 10⁵ D. 0.498 × 10⁶ **18. C**

19. Write 2.04 × 10⁴ in standard form.
    A. 20,400 B. 2,040 C. 204 D. 204,000 **19. A**

20. Complete 0.75 L = ■ mL.
    A. 75 B. 750 C. 7,500 D. 7.5 **20. B**

21. Complete 7,462 g = ■ kg.
    A. 74.62 B. 0.7462 C. 746.2 D. 7.462 **21. D**

22. A beaker contains 625 milliliters of water. A chemist pours 0.25 liters of the water into a solution. How many milliliters are left in the beaker?
    A. 375 B. 600 C. 2,500 D. 250 **22. A**

23. Lee buys 100 postcards for his business. If each postcard costs 19¢, how much did he spend?
    A. $1.90 B. $19 C. $190 D. $19.90 **23. B**

24. A giant tortoise can travel at a speed of about 0.2 kilometers per hour. At this rate, how far can it travel in 2 hours 30 minutes?
    A. 0.5 m B. 12.5 m C. 12.5 km D. 0.5 km **24. D**

25. The trail up to the top of Pike's Peak is about 23 miles long. The Kalman family drove about three quarters of the way. About how many more miles must they drive to reach the top?
    A. 4 B. 8 C. 6 D. 14 **25. C**

BONUS It is about 2.39 × 10⁵ miles from Earth to our moon, and about 9.3 × 10⁷ miles from Earth to the sun. How many times farther is it to the sun than to the moon?
    A. 389 B. 186 C. 4 D. 18.6 **A**

11
Glencoe Division, Macmillan/McGraw-Hill

Test and Review Generator software is provided in Apple, IBM, and Macintosh versions. You may use this software to create your own tests or worksheets, based on the needs of your students.

The **Performance Assessment Booklet** provides an alternate assessment for evaluating student progress. An assessment for this chapter can be found on pages 3–4.

3 Statistics and Data Analysis

Previewing the Chapter

This chapter focuses on statistics—the collecting, organizing, and summarizing of data. Students interpret bar, line, and circle graphs, find ranges and scales, and make line plots and stem-and-leaf plots. They also work with three statistical measures of central tendency: the mean, median, and mode. Students use graphs to make predictions and examine ways in which graphs can mislead. In the two **problem-solving strategy** lessons, students solve problems by interpreting graphs and by organizing data in a table.

Lesson	Lesson Objectives	NCTM Standards	State/Local Objectives
3-1	Solve problems by interpreting bar graphs, line graphs, and circle graphs.	1–15, 10	
3-2	Solve problems by organizing data in a table.	1–5, 7, 10	
3-2B	Work with a database.	1–4, 10	
3-3	Choose appropriate scales and intervals for data.	1–5, 7, 10	
3-4	Construct line plots.	1–5, 7, 10	
3-5	Find the mean, median, and mode of a set of data.	1–5, 7, 10	
3-5B	Use mean, median, and mode to describe students in your school.	1–5, 7, 10	
3-6	Construct stem-and-leaf plots.	1–5, 7, 10	
3-7A	Use mode, median, and mean to make predictions.	1–5, 7, 10, 13	
3-7	Make predictions from graphs.	1–5, 7, 8, 10	
3-8	Recognize when statistics and graphs are misleading.	1–5, 7, 10	

Organizing the Chapter

A complete, 1-page lesson plan is provided for each lesson in the Lesson Plans Masters Booklet.

LESSON PLANNING GUIDE

| Lesson | Materials/ Manipulatives | Extra Practice (Student Edition) | Blackline Masters Booklets | | | | | | | | | |
			Study Guide	Practice	Enrichment	Evaluation	Technology	Lab Manual	Multicultural Activities	Application and Interdisciplinary Activities	Transparencies	Group Activity Cards
3-1			p. 21	p. 21	p. 21				p. 3		3-1	3-1
3-2			p. 22	p. 22	p. 22						3-2	3-2
3-2B								p. 42				
3-3		p. 577	p. 23	p. 23	p. 23						3-3	3-3
3-4		p. 577	p. 24	p. 24	p. 24	Quiz A, p. 25	p. 17			p. 3	3-4	3-4
3-5	calculator	p. 578	p. 25	p. 25	p. 25		p. 3			p. 17	3-5	3-5
3-5B	pencil, paper markers, ruler							p. 43				
3-6		p. 578	p. 26	p. 26	p. 26						3-6	3-6
3-7A	popcorn, pencil, paper							p. 44				
3-7	magazines and newspapers	p. 578	p. 27	p. 27	p. 27						3-7	3-7
3-8	newspaper or magazines		p. 28	p. 28	p. 28	Quiz B, p. 25					3-8	3-8
Study Guide and Review			Multiple Choice Test, Forms 1A and 1B, pp. 19–22 Free Response Test, Forms 2A and 2B, pp. 23–24 Cumulative Review, p. 26 (free response)									
Test			Cumulative Test, p. 27 (multiple choice)									

Pacing Guide: Option I (Chapters 1–12) - 13 days; Option II (Chapters 1–13) - 12 days; Option III (Chapters 1–14) - 11 days
You may wish to refer to the complete **Course Planning Guides** on page T25.

OTHER CHAPTER RESOURCES

Student Edition
Chapter Opener, pp. 88–89
Portfolio Suggestion, p. 106
Mid-Chapter Review, p. 107
Save Planet Earth, p. 119
Academic Skills Test, pp. 124–125

 Manipulatives
Overhead Manipulative Resources
Middle School Mathematics Manipulative Kit

 Software/Technology
Interactive Mathematics Tools (Macintosh)
Test and Review Generator (IBM, Apple, Macintosh)
Teacher's Guide for Software Resources

Other Supplements
Transparency 3-0
Performance Assessment, pp. 5–6
Glencoe Mathematics Professional Series
Lesson Plans, pp. 25–35

INTERDISCIPLINARY BULLETIN BOARD

Architecture Connection

Objective Create a stem-and-leaf plot to display data from a table.

How To Use It Have students do research to find the heights in feet and in stories of well-known buildings other than those shown at the right, as well as buildings in your area. Have them add the information to the bulletin board. Ask them to make a stem-and-leaf plot to display the data. Have them write a summary of what the plot shows.

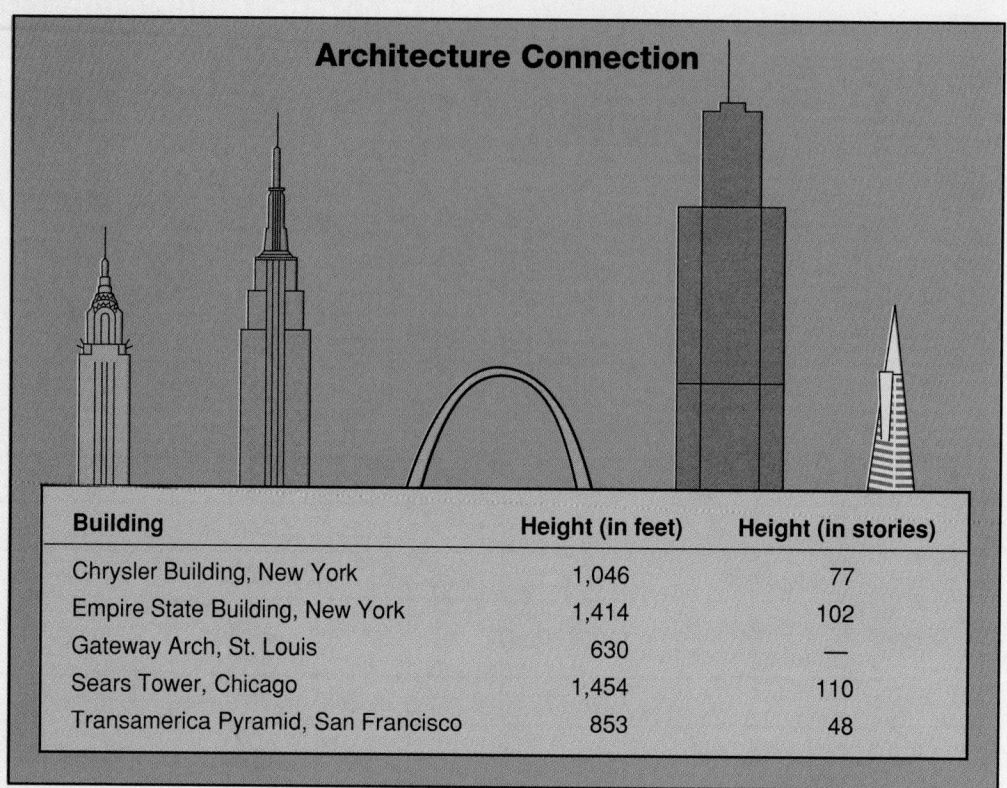

Architecture Connection

Building	Height (in feet)	Height (in stories)
Chrysler Building, New York	1,046	77
Empire State Building, New York	1,414	102
Gateway Arch, St. Louis	630	—
Sears Tower, Chicago	1,454	110
Transamerica Pyramid, San Francisco	853	48

APPLICATIONS

Applications	Lesson	Example	Exercise
Reading	3-2		12
History	3-3		24
Television	3-3		25
Computer	3-4		18
Business	3-5	2	16
Sports	3-5		13
Weather	3-5		15
Sports	3-6		13
Health	3-7	1	
Business	3-7	2	
Sports	3-7		9
Business	3-8	1	
Human Resources	3-8	2	
Entertainment	3-8		10
Advertising	3-8		11

TEAM ACTIVITIES

Multicultural Experiences

Outside Field Trips A trip to a TV newsroom or offices of a newspaper can be helpful in showing students how people working in media create and make extensive use of graphs and statistics.

A visit to the office of your local congressional representative might be helpful in pointing out to students how people in public office use statistics to guide their actions and help them make decisions.

In-Class Speakers Invite a coach or a statistician for a local sports team or from a newspaper or magazine to demonstrate how coaches and managers often analyze statistics when they determine strategies.

Ask a local store or restaurant owner to talk to your students about ways in which he or she uses statistics both to decide what items to order and to determine the size of the order.

SUPPLEMENTARY BLACKLINE MASTER BOOKLETS

Some of the blackline masters for enhancing this chapter are shown below.

Application and Interdisciplinary Activity Masters, pp. 3, 17

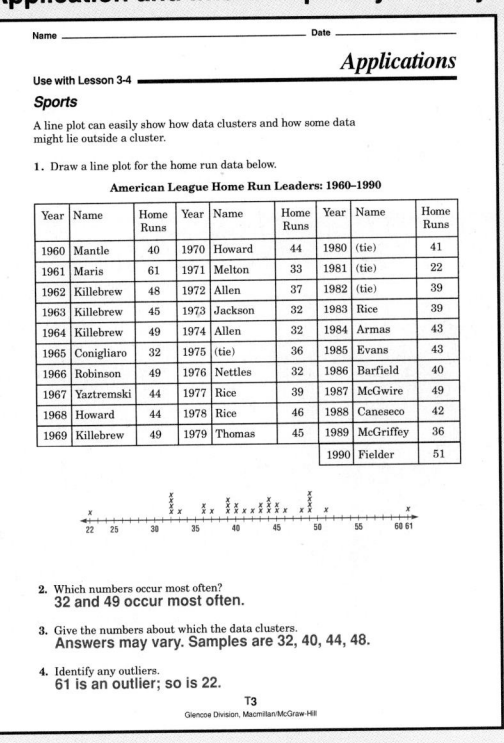

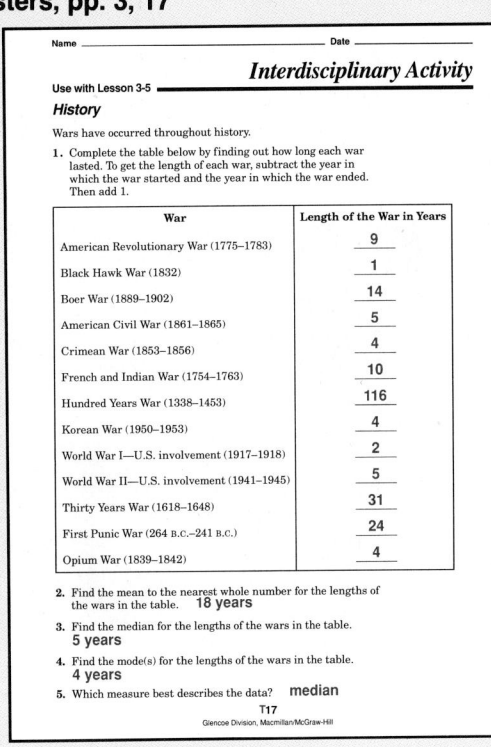

Multicultural Activity Masters, p. 3

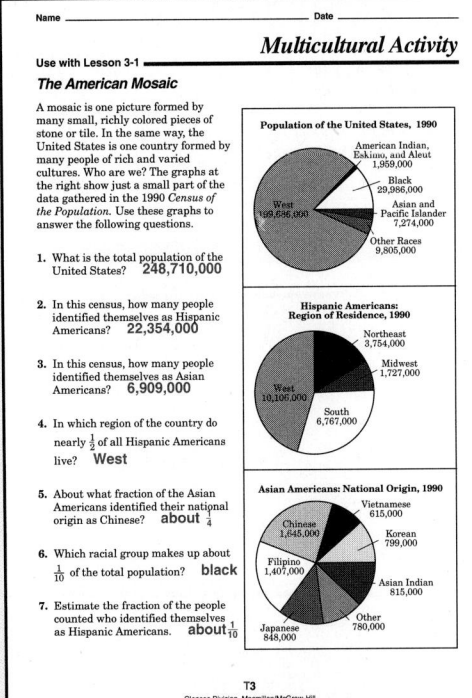

Technology Masters, p. 3

RECOMMENDED OUTSIDE RESOURCES

Books/Periodicals

Curcio, Frances, *Developing Graph Comprehension: Elementary and Middle School Activities,* Reston, VA: NCTM, 1989.

Jaffe, A.J., and Herbert F. Spirer, *Misused Statistics: Straight Talk for Twisted Numbers,* New York, NY: Marcel Dekker, Inc., 1987.

Films/Videotapes/Videodiscs

Black Mathematicians, Montclair, NJ: Mathematical Symposium, 1989.

Statistics: Understanding Mean, Median, and Mode, Agency for Instructional Technology, 1987.

Software

Statistics Workshop, (Macintosh), Wings for Learning/Sunburst

Bank Street School Filer, (Apple II), Wings for Learning/ Sunburst

For addresses of companies handling software, please refer to page T24.

 Glencoe's *Interactive Mathematics: Activities and Investigations* consists of 18 units that may be used as alternatives or supplemental material for *Mathematics: Applications and Connections.* The suggested units for this chapter are Unit 8, *Data Sense,* and Unit 18, *Quality Control.* See page T18 for more information.

88d

This two-page introduction to the chapter provides a visual, relevant way to engage students in the mathematics of the chapter. Questions are included that help students see the need to learn the mathematics in the chapter. Data in charts and graphs provide statistical information that students can analyze and interpret at this point as well as later in the chapter. The Chapter Project provides an activity that applies the mathematics of the chapter.

MAKING MATHEMATICS RELEVANT

Spotlight on Languages of the World

Students can use the graphing and table-making skills of this chapter to compare the sizes of populations that speak particular languages. This is illustrated in the graph on page 88. The mean, median, and mode can be applied to the table of ten most populous countries on page 89.

Using the Timeline

Have students find the copyright date of their dictionary at home or of one in their classroom or school library. Ask them to indicate approximately where this date would fit on the timeline.

Chapter

3

Statistics and Data Analysis

Spotlight on Languages of the World

Have You Ever Wondered. . .

- What language is spoken by the most people in the world?
- Which countries have the most people living in them?

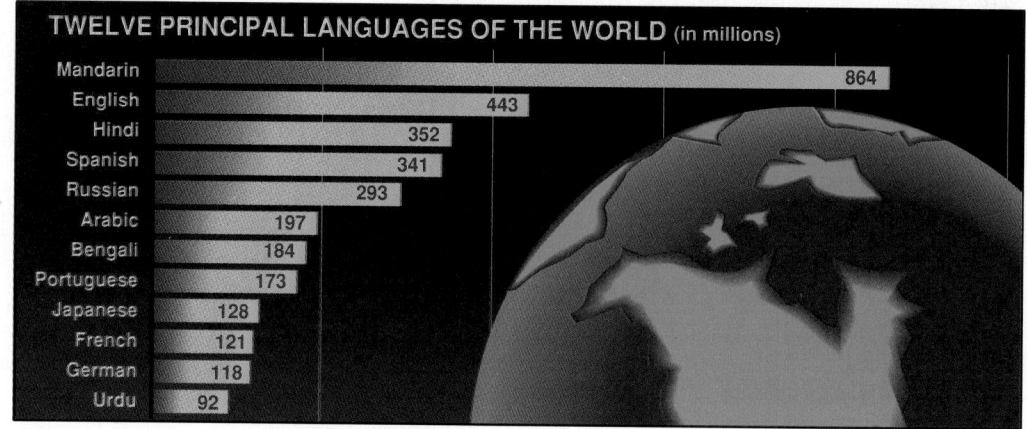

TWELVE PRINCIPAL LANGUAGES OF THE WORLD (in millions)

Language	Millions
Mandarin	864
English	443
Hindi	352
Spanish	341
Russian	293
Arabic	197
Bengali	184
Portuguese	173
Japanese	128
French	121
German	118
Urdu	92

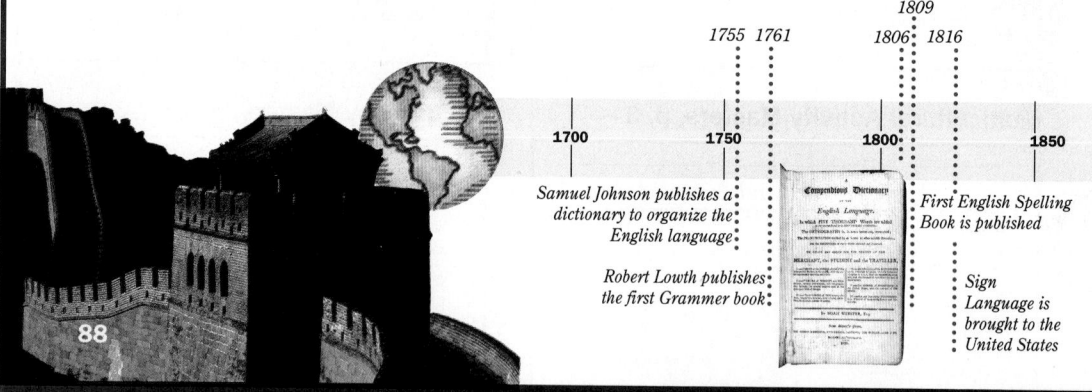

1755   1761   1806   1809   1816

1700   1750   1800   1850

Samuel Johnson publishes a dictionary to organize the English language

Robert Lowth publishes the first Grammer book

First English Spelling Book is published

Sign Language is brought to the United States

88

"Have You Ever Wondered?" Answers

- Mandarin is the most widely spoken language in the world.
- China is the most populous country, followed closely by India. Help students make the connection between China and the Mandarin language.

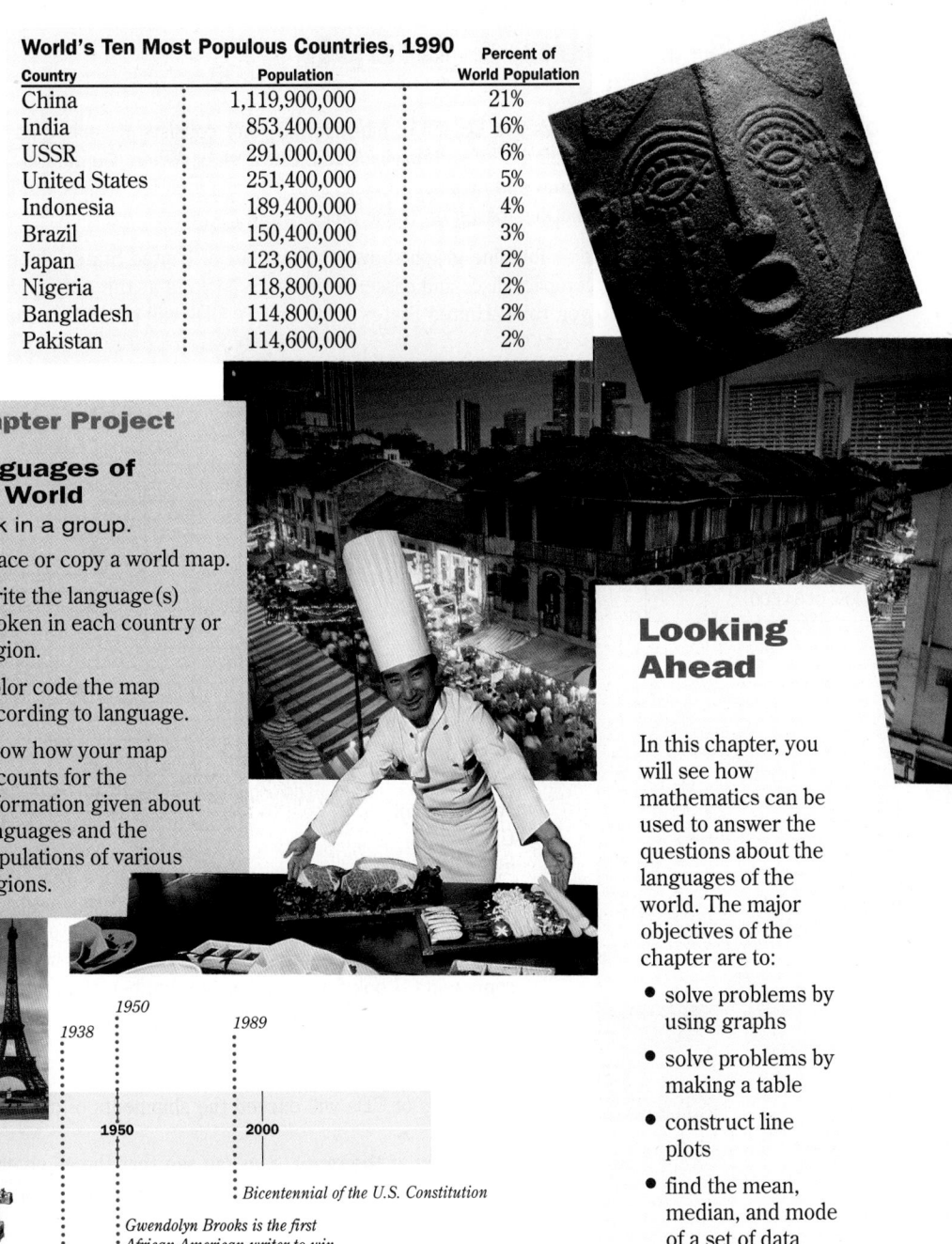

World's Ten Most Populous Countries, 1990

Country	Population	Percent of World Population
China	1,119,900,000	21%
India	853,400,000	16%
USSR	291,000,000	6%
United States	251,400,000	5%
Indonesia	189,400,000	4%
Brazil	150,400,000	3%
Japan	123,600,000	2%
Nigeria	118,800,000	2%
Bangladesh	114,800,000	2%
Pakistan	114,600,000	2%

Chapter Project

Languages of the World

Work in a group.

1. Trace or copy a world map.

2. Write the language(s) spoken in each country or region.

3. Color code the map according to language.

4. Show how your map accounts for the information given about languages and the populations of various regions.

1889
1874
1950
1938
1989

1900
1950
2000

Bicentennial of the U.S. Constitution

Gwendolyn Brooks is the first
African-American writer to win
the Pulitzer Prize for poetry

The ball-point pen is patented

Looking Ahead

In this chapter, you will see how mathematics can be used to answer the questions about the languages of the world. The major objectives of the chapter are to:

- solve problems by using graphs

- solve problems by making a table

- construct line plots

- find the mean, median, and mode of a set of data

89

DATA ANALYSIS

Challenge students to determine what intervals would make sense to use if they were to make a bar graph to display the population data in the table on page 89. Ask them how many times as high as the bar for Pakistan, the bar for China would have to be.   about 10 times

Data Search

A question related to these data is provided in Lesson 3-5, page 107, Exercise 18.

CHAPTER PROJECT

Provide students with a world map that is easily traceable. Direct them to sources such as encyclopedias to find the major languages spoken in various countries. Guide students to make the connection that a language spoken in a highly populated region will be among the world's languages with the largest number of speakers.

Chapter Opener Transparency

Transparency 3-0 is available in the Transparency Package. It provides another full-color, motivating activity that you can use to capture students' interest.

NCTM Standards: 1–5, 10

Lesson Resources
- Study Guide Master 3-1
- Practice Master 3-1
- Enrichment Master 3-1
- Multicultural Activity, p. 3
- Group Activity Card 3-1

 Transparency 3-1 contains the 5-Minute Check and a teaching aid for this lesson.

⏱ 5-Minute Check
(Over Chapter 2)

1. Order the following set of numbers from least to greatest. 3.4, 11.8, 4, 1.28, 0.98   0.98, 1.28, 3.4, 4, 11.8

2. Round 12.375 to the underlined place.   12.4

Multiply or divide.

3. 0.6×7.003 4.2018

4. $0.012 \overline{)0.072}$ 6

5. Write 31,000 using scientific notation.
3.1×10^4

---

1 FOCUS

Motivating the Lesson

Situational Problem Tell students that the population of Phoenix, Arizona is growing while the population of Detroit, Michigan is decreasing. Ask them how they can predict the year in which the population of Phoenix will pass that of Detroit.

2 TEACH

Using Discussion Discuss with students the differences in the type of data represented by each of the three kinds of graphs presented in the lesson. Ask students which of the graphs is most effective for showing changes over time, which is best for comparing quantities, and which shows how a whole is divided into parts.   line graph; bar graph; circle graph

---

3-1 Use a Graph

Objective
Solve problems by interpreting bar graphs, line graphs, and circle graphs.

Statistics is a branch of mathematics that consists of collecting, organizing, and summarizing numerical facts. When the data is collected and displayed in a graph, you can look for trends and make predictions based on these facts.

The double-line graph shows the number of United States shipments of compact discs and cassette tapes. By looking at the graph, when do you think United States shipments of CDs will exceed that of cassettes?

TEEN SCENE

In 1975, over 257,000 shipments of record albums were sent to retailers. By 1989, that number hit a 15-year low of 34,600.

Explore What do you know?
You know the number of cassette tapes and CD shipments as shown on the graph.

What are you trying to find?
You are trying to predict when shipments of CDs will exceed that of cassettes.

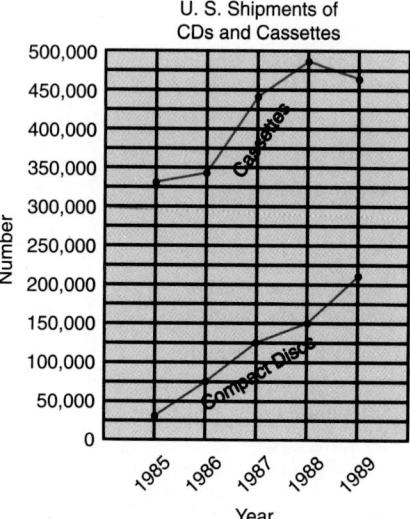

U. S. Shipments of CDs and Cassettes

Plan Study the graph. Determine what each of the lines represents. Look for trends in the number of shipments from 1985 to 1989. When did cassette shipments start to decline?

Next extend the lines mentally to predict when the shipments of CDs will exceed the shipments of cassettes.

Solve By looking at the graph, you can see that the shipments of cassettes begins to decline in 1988 and the shipments of CDs have steadily risen since 1985. You can predict that CD shipments will exceed the shipment of cassettes in about 3 years or in 1992.

OPTIONS

Reteaching Activity

Using Applications Have students keep track of the amount of time in a one-week period that they spend sleeping, eating, being at school, doing homework, watching television, or doing any other daily activity. Then have students work with partners to make double-bar graphs to compare the results.

Study Guide Masters, p. 21

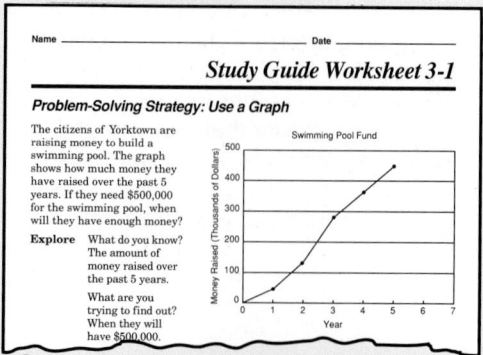

Name _____ Date _____

Study Guide Worksheet 3-1

Problem-Solving Strategy: Use a Graph

The citizens of Yorktown are raising money to build a swimming pool. The graph shows how much money they have raised over the past 5 years. If they need $500,000 for the swimming pool, when will they have enough money?

Swimming Pool Fund

Explore What do you know?
The amount of money raised over the past 5 years.

What are you trying to find out?
When they will have $500,000.

Examine Copy the graph. Extend the lines and the horizontal and vertical scales to see when the lines cross.

Example

The double-graph shows the number of degrees earned for various years during a 30-year period. Were there more advanced degrees in 1969–70 or 1989–90?

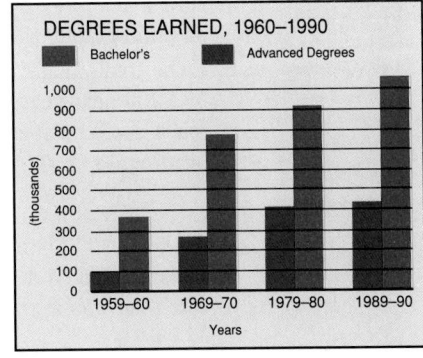

DEGREES EARNED, 1960–1990

The key, below the title of the graph, shows that the blue bars represent the number of advanced degrees earned. Locate the bars for 1969–70 and 1989–90. In 1969–70, about 275,000 advanced degrees were earned. In 1989–90, about 425,000 advanced degrees were earned. So, about 150,000 more advanced degrees were earned in 1989–90 than in 1969–70.

Checking for Understanding

Communicating Mathematics

Read and study the lesson to answer each question.

1. **Tell** why different colors are used to show data in a double-line graph.

1. To make the graph easier to read

2. **Write** a sentence explaining why you might display data on a graph rather than in a chart. **A graph is quicker and easier to read than a chart.**

Guided Practice

Solve. Use the line graph.

3. About how many more women worked as temporary employees in 1986 than in 1982?

3. 400 thousand women

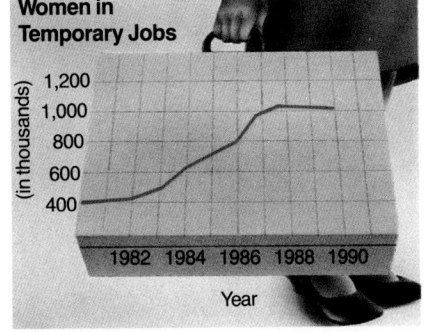

Women in Temporary Jobs

4. In what year were there the greatest number of temporary employees? **1988**

5. The economic recession was the cause of the drop in temporary jobs in 1990. Given the steady growth since 1982, do you think the number of temporary jobs will continue to decline? Why? **Sample answer: Yes, until the recession ends.**

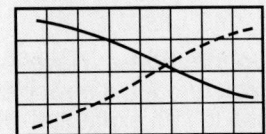

Lesson 3-1 Problem-Solving Strategy: Use a Graph **91**

Gifted and Talented Needs

On the chalkboard, sketch the double-line graph at the right. Ask students to sketch the graph, and then to describe information that might look something like this if it were displayed on a double line graph. Challenge them to draw and label scales for each axis and to give a title to their graph.

Sample answer: The rising curve represents a nation's average real income over a 50-year period. The falling curve represents the same nation's per capita share of the national debt.

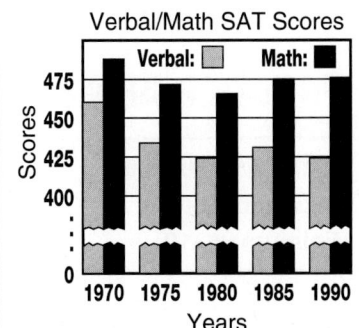
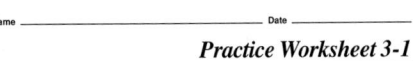
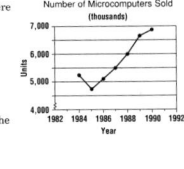
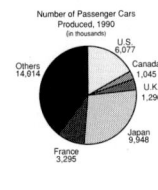

Problem Solving

Practice Solve. Use the circle graph.

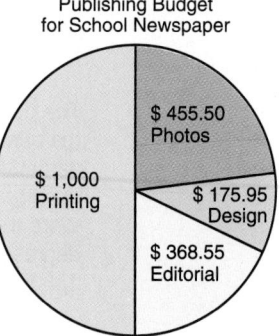

Publishing Budget for School Newspaper

$455.50 Photos
$1,000 Printing
$175.95 Design
$368.55 Editorial

6. What part of the budget is spent on printing? $\frac{1}{2}$

7. How much more money is spent on photography than design? **$279.55**

8. If the total budget is increased by $200 next year, about how much could be spent on printing? **$1,100**

Solve. Use any strategy.

9. Melanie made a display with 66 cat food cans. She put 1 less can in each row than was in the row below. How many cans were in the bottom row? **11 cans**

10. Ilsa bought 6 rolls of film on sale for $28.13. She took 216 photos on her vacation. If each roll had the same number of exposures, how many photos did she get from each roll of film? **36 photos**

11. Danny bought a new pair of athletic shoes for $55.59, a new sweatshirt for $24.87, and sweat pants for $34.99. Did he spend more or less than $100? **more**

12. Alaska, the largest U.S. state, has an area of 1,478,458 square kilometers. Rhode Island, the smallest, has an area of 2,732 square kilometers. How many times larger is Alaska? **541.2 times larger**

13. **Data Search** Refer to page 649. In 1990, how many people participated in volleyball, basketball, or bowling? **89.6 million**

14. There were 12 more seventh graders at the pep rally than sixth graders. There were 178 sixth and seventh graders at the rally. How many seventh graders went to the pep rally? **95 seventh graders**

92   **Chapter 3** Statistics and Data Analysis

OPTIONS

Extending the Lesson

Making Connections Have students look through a newspaper or magazine to find examples of double-line or bar graphs. Ask them to summarize the information the graph shows, including any trends they can notice. Ask students to share their findings with the class.

Cooperative Learning Activity

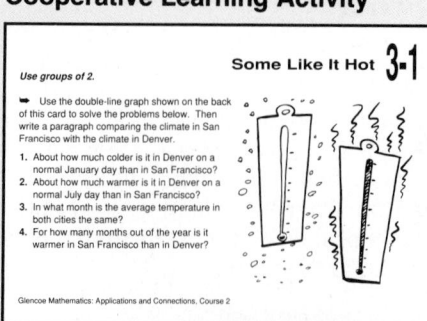

Some Like It Hot **3-1**

Use groups of 2.

➡ Use the double-line graph shown on the back of this card to solve the problems below. Then write a paragraph comparing the climate in San Francisco with the climate in Denver.

1. About how much colder is it in Denver on a normal January day than in San Francisco?
2. About how much warmer is it in Denver on a normal July day than in San Francisco?
3. In what month is the average temperature in both cities the same?
4. For how many months out of the year is it warmer in San Francisco than in Denver?

Glencoe Mathematics: Applications and Connections, Course 2

Problem-Solving Strategy

3-2 Make a Table

Objective
Solve problems by organizing data in a table.

Words to Learn
frequency table

Team 7-A is studying a unit on communication. They learned that Alexander Graham Bell patented the telephone in 1876. They decided to take a survey to find out how many classmates on Team 7-B knew the year that Bell patented the telephone. The class wanted to organize the data in a way that made it easy to study the results.

Mr. Kim's class organized the data in a **frequency table.**

DID YOU KNOW

In 1884, Bell Telephone Company set up the first long distance telephone line between Boston and New York. It used copper wire instead of iron, which allowed the signals to travel farther.

Year	Tally	Frequency
1825					3
1850	⊮||||	9
1854	⊮|	6
1862	⊮|||	8
1876				2
1898	⊮	5

Explore What do you know?
You know how each person responded.
What are you trying to find?
You are trying to find the number of people that knew the year the telephone was patented.

Plan Study the frequency table that Mr. Kim's class made. A tally has been marked for each response, and the frequency is the sum of the tally marks.

Solve The frequency table shows that only 2 people surveyed knew the year the telephone was patented.

Examine Read down the column marked Year until you find 1876. Read across the row, 1876, until you find the frequency column that shows the number of responses is 2.

Lesson 3-2 Problem-Solving Strategy: Make a Table   93

OPTIONS

Reteaching Activity

Using Discussion Talk about the purpose of each column in the frequency table, paying particular attention to the reason for having a tally column. Guide students to see that using tally marks is an organized way to record information as it is being received. Ask students to describe the relationship between the Tally and Frequency columns.

Study Guide Masters, p. 22

Name _____ Date _____

Study Guide Worksheet 3-2

Problem-Solving Strategy: Make a Table

Members of the seventh grade class were surveyed to determine when to hold the winter dance. On what date should the dance be held?

Explore What do you know?
You know how each person responded.

What are you trying to decide?
You are deciding on what date to hold the dance.

Dates Reported			
Dec 9	Dec 2	Dec 9	Dec 8
Dec 2	Dec 9	Dec 8	Dec 9
Dec 9	Dec 2	Dec 9	Dec 1
Dec 2	Dec 9	Dec 9	Dec 9
Dec 8	Dec 2	Dec 9	Dec 1
Dec 2	Dec 9	Dec 2	Dec 9
Dec 8	Dec 9		

Plan Make a frequency table.

Solve The frequency table shows that the greatest number of people want to

Date	Tally	Frequency
Dec 1	||	2
Dec 2	⊮|||	8

3-2 Lesson Notes

NCTM Standards: 1–5, 7, 10

Lesson Resources
• Study Guide Master 3-2
• Practice Master 3-2
• Enrichment Master 3-2
• Group Activity Card 3-2

Transparency 3-2 contains the 5-Minute Check and a teaching aid for this lesson.

⏱ 5-Minute Check
(Over Lesson 3-1)

The graph below shows daily high and low temperatures in one city for one week.

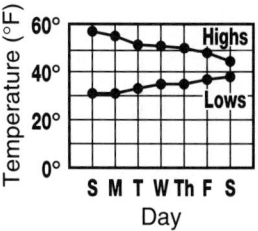

1. Which day had the lowest high temperature?
   Saturday

2. Summarize the information shown in the graph. Sample answer: The differences in high and low temperatures are decreasing as high temperatures are dropping and low temperatures are rising.

1 FOCUS

Motivating the Lesson

Activity Have students name their favorite movie of all time. Ask them how they would design a table to record this information.

2 TEACH

Using Cooperative Groups
Have groups design a frequency table to record the number of times they blink in one minute. Have them first guess the number of blinks. Then have them do the experiment and fill in the table.

93

Checking for Understanding

Exercises 1-2 are designed to help you assess students' understanding through reading, writing, speaking, and modeling. You should work through these exercises with your students and then monitor their work on Guided Practice Exercises 3-4.

Practice Masters, p. 22

You can make a frequency table using data from a survey or questionnaire.

Example

Rosita asked all the students in her seventh-grade math class to vote for their favorite amusement park out of Disneyland (DL), Dollywood (DW), or Six Flags (SF.)

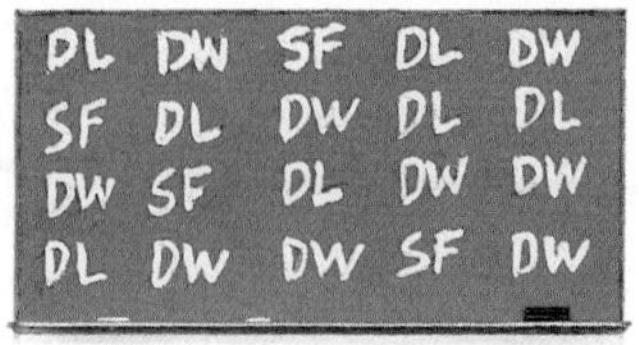

DL DW SF DL DW
SF DL DW DL DL
DW SF DL DW DW
DL DW DW SF DW

To make a frequency table:
- Draw a table with three columns.
- In the first column, list the items in the set of data.
- In the second column, tally the data.
- In the third column, write the frequency or number of tallies.

Park	Tally	Frequency
Disneyland	||||| ||	7
Dollywood	||||| ||||	9
Six Flags	||||	4

Checking for Understanding

Communicating Mathematics

Read and study the lesson to answer each question.

1. **Tell** why it is important to be able to organize data. **so other people can understand it**

2. **Write** a sentence about what each column represents in the frequency table above. **1st column—different possibilities; tally-mark when it happens; frequency—how many times the event occurs.**

Guided Practice

3. Copy the table and complete the frequency column.

Heights of Junior High Students

HEIGHT(cm)	TALLY	FREQUENCY
145			1
150							5
155												10
160			1
165								6
170					3

4a.

Age	Tally	Freq.
21				2
22		0
23		0
24			1
25								6
26							4
27		0
28		0
29		0
30					3

4. The ages of guests at a birthday party are given at the right.
   a. Make a frequency table.
   b. What age was the most common at the party? **25**

25	21	30	24
26	26	21	30
25	25	26	25
30	25	25	26

Classroom Vignette

"I took my class to the local cemetery to gather information about the early settlers of our area. Students then organized the data and illustrated it in graphs."

Sue Gould

Sue Gould, Teacher
Clear Creek Middle School, Idaho Springs, CO

Problem Solving

Practice   Solve using any strategy.

5. Make a frequency table for the data at the right. **See margin.**
   a. Which time appeared the most often? **30 seconds**
   b. Which time appeared the least often? **60 seconds**

Lengths of TV Commercials (in seconds)						
30	30	10	20	60	10	10
30	60	10	20	20	30	30
20	10	60	20	30	30	30

Answers will vary.

6. **Collect Data**   Take a survey of your classmates' favorite television show.
   a. Organize the data in a frequency table.
   b. Which television show was picked as a favorite the most often?

7. The price of a T-shirt is $15.00 plus $0.62 sales tax. How much would 6 shirts cost? **$93.72**

   $59.00

8. Dina rented 20 movies at $2.95 each. How much did she spend on rentals?

9. An elevator sign reads "DO NOT EXCEED 2,500 POUNDS." How many people each weighing about 150 pounds can be in the elevator at the same time? **16 people**

10. Marco bought 6 tickets to the circus. He gave the cashier $170 and received $8 in change. How much did one ticket cost? **$27.00**

11. Choose five digits. Use the five digits to form a two-digit and a three-digit number so that their product is the least product possible. **Sample answer for 1, 2, 3, 4, 5: 245 × 13**

12. **Reading**   Chuck is reading a book that has 16 chapters. Each chapter has 28 pages. How many pages does the book have? **448 pages**

13. **Mathematics and Telecommunications**   Read the following paragraphs.

In 1966, it was first suggested to use fiber optic cables instead of copper wires to carry telephone conversations. Pulses of light are used to transmit calls down the fiber optic cables.

Fiber optic cable is made up of strands of glass. Each strand is the width of a human hair. Light is beamed into the inner core, bouncing along it. Thousands of telephone calls can be carried at the same time in each strand of glass.

The fibers in a cable are bundled. If each fiber is 0.0005 inch thick, how thick is a bundle of 3,000 fibers? **1.5 inches**

Lesson 3-2 Problem-Solving Strategy: Make a Table   **95**

95

NCTM Standards: 1-4, 10

Management Tips

For Students Have students work with partners to work through this lab. Provide pairs of students with other examples of data bases to examine. Encourage groups to work together if it helps them understand the new terms and concepts and to apply them to the sample company provided.

For the Overhead Projector
Overhead Manipulative Resources provides appropriate materials for teacher or student demonstration of the activities in this Mathematics Lab.

1 FOCUS

Introducing the Lab

Ask students if they have ever seen or used a data base. Have those who have done so share what they know with classmates. Then ask students how a data base is like a frequency table, and to describe ways in which it is different. Sample answer: It is a table that lists data in an organized form; it contains many more kinds of information than a frequency table.

Cooperative Learning

3-2B Data Base

A Follow-Up of Lesson 3-2

Objective
Work with a data base.

Words to Learn
data base
file
record
fields

A **data base** is a collection of data organized for rapid search and retrieval, usually by a computer. A company's data base is one of its most valuable resources. A data base computer program can assist a company in analyzing the past and making projections for the future.

A data base is organized into files. A **file** is a collection of data about a particular subject. The subject, or sub unit within the file, is called a **record.** For example, in a sales file that contains data about a company's sales, you may find records about the individual salesperson or company.

The first step in creating a data base file is to specify its structure. Name the file and then describe the elements, or **fields** within each record. A field name can be up to 10 characters. It must start with a letter and include no spaces between the characters. For each field, you must specify its name, the type of data it will contain (character, C, or numeric, N), the size of each field, and, if numeric, how many decimal places the field contains.

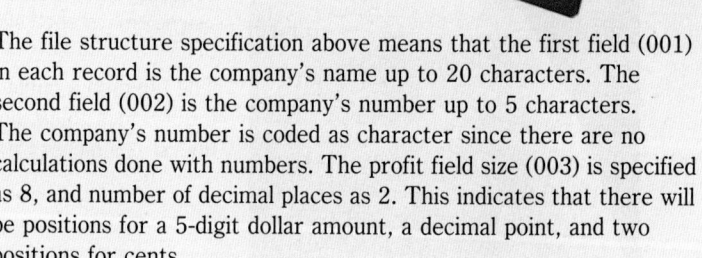

Field	Specifications
001	Name,C,20
002	Number,C,5
003	Profit,N,8,2

The file structure specification above means that the first field (001) in each record is the company's name up to 20 characters. The second field (002) is the company's number up to 5 characters. The company's number is coded as character since there are no calculations done with numbers. The profit field size (003) is specified as 8, and number of decimal places as 2. This indicates that there will be positions for a 5-digit dollar amount, a decimal point, and two positions for cents.

Try this!

2. information about the company's sales system

3. name file and describe elements

Work with a partner.

1. What does a file in a data base contain? **records about a particular subject**

2. What information would you expect to find in a sales file?

3. How do you enter a field structure?

4. Explain why you cannot use the format, 001 Customer Name,C,20 to specify a field? **contains more than 10 characters**

Consider the following data base.

```
CUSTOMER        CUSTOMER   TERRITORY   DATE    ORDER    AMOUNT
NAME            NUMBER                         NUMBER
NEWPORT RENTAL   54213        15       112091   11340   8000.00
DOLLAR FURNITURE 15682        10       111891   11289    792.00
SERVICE STAR     38900        12       112091   11300   3000.00
NEWPORT RENTAL   54213        15       111791   11250    400.00
CITY LIMITS      80087        11       111891   11280     10.00
EVERY STEP       18851        13       112191   11450    350.00
DOLLAR FURNITURE 15682        10       112291   11560   1000.00
DOLLAR FURNITURE 15682        10       112091   11301    850.00
EVERY STEP       18851        13       111991   11299    985.00
DOLLAR FURNITURE 15682        10       112391   11600     50.00
```

What do you think?  5. See margin.

5. How many fields does this data base contain? What are they?

6. How many records does the data base contain? **10**

7. What is the largest number that can be entered in the amount field? **99999.99**

8. How would you use this data base to predict sales for each company over a period of time? **See margin.**

9. How would you use the data base to predict sales for a specific territory? **See margin.**

Extension

See students' work.

10. Create your own data base. Write a short paragraph describing the type of information it contains, how many fields there are, and what the field specifications are.

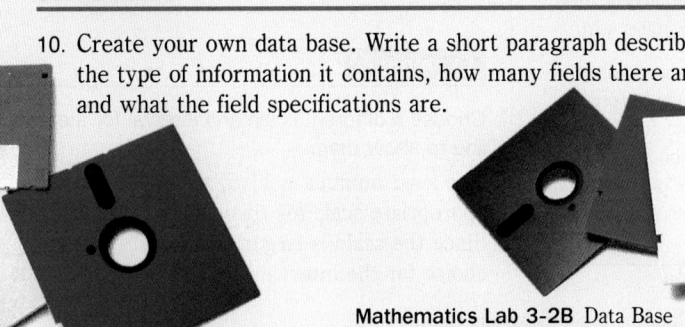

Mathematics Lab 3-2B Data Base **97**

Using Connections Have students record the new vocabulary from this lesson in their notebooks in an organized manner. Have them describe or give an example for each term introduced. After completing the *Try This!* activity, students should compare data bases with other students and discuss how to improve them, if possible.

3 PRACTICE/APPLY

Using Discussion Discuss student answers to the *What Do You Think?* questions as a whole class.

Close

Have students suggest how using a data base might help a local business. Have students follow up by calling or visiting the store and asking the owners how they use a data base, or if they don't, why they don't.

Additional Answers

5. 6; customer name, customer number, territory, date, order number, amount

8. Review the sales figures for each company over the period of time. Note the rate of increase or decrease. From this, predict future sales.

9. Review the sales figures for the territory over a period of time and note the rate of increase or decrease. From this, predict future sales for the territory.

OPTIONS

Lab Manual You may wish to make copies of the blackline master on p. 42 of the *Lab Manual* for students to use as a recording sheet.

Lab Manual, p. 42

Name _____ Date _____

Mathematics Lab Worksheet

Use with pages 96–97

Data Base

What do you think?

1. A file in a data base contains a collection of data records about a particular subject.

2. A sales file would contain data about a company's sales system.

3. Specify its name, whether it contains character or numeric data, its size, and whether it contains decimal places.

4. The phrase customer name consists of more than 10 characters. Also, spaces are not allowed.

What do you think?

NCTM Standards: 1–5, 7, 10

Lesson Resources
- Study Guide Master 3-3
- Practice Master 3-3
- Enrichment Master 3-3
- Group Activity Card 3-3

 Transparency 3-3 contains the 5-Minute Check and a teaching aid for this lesson.

◷ 5-Minute Check
(Over Lesson 3-2)

The number of absences from class during January are shown below.

```
0 1 2 0 0 0 4 0
0 0 0 3 1 0 0 0
1 1 3 1 2 2 2 0
```

1. Make a frequency table.

Number	Tally	Fre-quency
0	ⅬⅡⅠⅠ ⅬⅡⅠⅠ	10
1	ⅬⅡⅠⅠ	5
2					3
3				2
4			1

2. What is the most common number of absences? 0

3. What is the least common number of absences? 4

1 FOCUS

Motivating the Lesson

Situational Problem Luisa wants to record on a number line the number of hours her classmates spend watching TV during the school week. How can she find the range? How will she choose an appropriate scale and reasonable intervals for the data?

3-3 Range and Scales

Objective
Choose appropriate scales and intervals for data.

Words to Learn
range
scale
interval

Telecommunications Professional

Telecommunications have brought the world closer together by electronically communicating information by fax, telex, cellular phone, electronic mail, and on-line data bases.

Careers for computer programmers and systems analysts are expected to grow by 50% within the next decade. A technical background in mathematics and computer programming is essential in this field.

For more information, contact the National Telecommunications and Information Administration, Dept of Commerce, 14th St., Washington, DC 20230.

How much time do you spend talking on the phone in one week? Is it hours, minutes, or seconds? The average number of hours a teenager spends talking on the telephone is two hours a day. Girls are likely to talk a half hour more than boys.

Susan Ching asks 11 of her classmates how many hours they spent on the phone last week. She records the data in the table at the right. To analyze this data, she needs to find an appropriate scale and intervals for the data.

Number of Hours on the Telephone			
Sue	15	Lyn	17
Bob	11.5	Kathy	16
Tim	14	John	12
Joe	11.5	Carole	14
Pete	13	Ida	13.5
Jill	16.5		

First, Susan finds the range of the data. The **range** is the difference between the greatest number and the least number in the set of data.

The range is $17 - 11.5$ or 5.5

greatest number ↗   ↖ *least number*

Next she chooses a scale for the number line. The **scale** must include numbers from 11.5 to 17; that is all data points. So, Susan decides on a scale of 11 to 18. This scale will allow her to plot all the data she has collected.

She then decides on the interval. The **intervals** separate the scale into equal parts. Since the data is grouped closely together, she decides on an interval of 1.

```
←——|——|——|——|——|——|——|——|——→
   11 12 13 14 15 16 17 18
```

There is more than one correct way you can choose the scale and interval for the same data.

Example 1

Choose a different scale and interval for the data above. Draw a number line to show them.

The least number is 11.5, and the greatest number is 17. Another appropriate scale for this data is 10 to 20.
Since the scale is larger, a good choice for the interval is 2.

```
←——|——|——|——|——|——→
  10 12 14 16 18 20
```

OPTIONS

Reteaching Activity

Using Cooperative Groups Have students use a small set of closely-clustered data that the group has collected, such as the length in centimeters of their pencils. Have them work with a partner to find the range of the data and to choose a scale and interval for the number line.

Study Guide Masters, p. 23

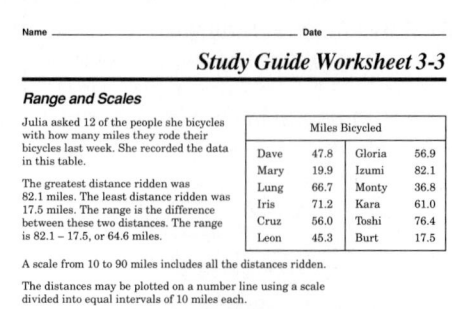

Name _____ Date _____

Study Guide Worksheet 3-3

Range and Scales

Julia asked 12 of the people she bicycles with how many miles they rode their bicycles last week. She recorded the data in this table.

Miles Bicycled			
Dave	47.8	Gloria	56.9
Mary	19.9	Izumi	82.1
Lung	66.7	Monty	36.8
Iris	71.2	Kara	61.0
Cruz	56.0	Toshi	76.4
Leon	45.3	Burt	17.5

The greatest distance ridden was 82.1 miles. The least distance ridden was 17.5 miles. The range is the difference between these two distances. The range is 82.1 − 17.5, or 64.6 miles.

A scale from 10 to 90 miles includes all the distances ridden.

The distances may be plotted on a number line using a scale divided into equal intervals of 10 miles each.

Checking for Understanding

Communicating Mathematics

Read and study the lesson to answer each question.

1. **Tell**, in your own words, how to find the range, the scale, and the interval for a set of data. **See Solutions Manual.**

2. **Tell** the advantages and disadvantages of the two different scales and intervals used for the data on p. 98. **See Solutions Manual.**

3. **Draw** a number line that shows a scale of 0 to 50 and intervals of 5.

0 5 10 15 20 25 30 35 40 45 50

Guided Practice

Name the scale and intervals of each number line.

4. **2 to 10, 2**
5. **1 to 21, 4**
6. **50 to 70, 5**
7. **100 to 160, 20**

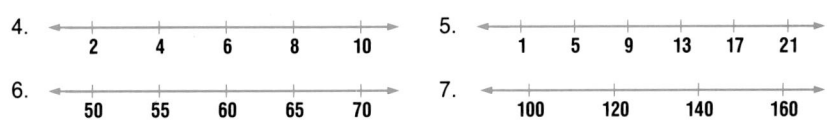

4. 2 4 6 8 10
5. 1 5 9 13 17 21
6. 50 55 60 65 70
7. 100 120 140 160

Find the range for each set of data. Choose two different scales and intervals for each set of data. Draw two number lines to show each. **See Solutions Manual.**

8. 3, 7, 1, 9, 3, 5 **8**

9. 14, 19, 4, 0, 13, 8, 2 **19**

10. 25, 75, 50, 34, 56 **50**

11. 785, 900, 456, 832, 678 **444**

12. 4.5, 2.3, 4.5, 7.8, 5.5, 5.1, 3.9 **5.5**

Exercises   For number lines for Exercises 13–18, see Solutions Manual.

Independent Practice

Find the range for each set of data. Choose an appropriate scale and intervals. Draw a number line to show the scale and intervals.

13. 2, 6, 8, 9, 12, 4 **10**

14. 9, 0, 18, 19, 2, 9, 8, 13, 4 **19**

15. 20, 60, 30, 80, 90, 120, 40 **100**

16. 6.4, 4.2, 3.6, 2.4, 5.0 **4**

17. 200; 600; 300; 800; 900; 1,200; 400 **1,000**

18. 14.5, 18.2, 21.6, 18.8, 17.3, 14.1 **7.5**

19a. Sample answer: 30–150, 20

19. Scott has been taking bowling lessons. His scores for the first ten games are 36, 54, 72, 89, 90, 110, 146, 134, 140, and 145.
    a. Find a scale and intervals to graph the scores.
    b. Draw a number line to show them.

    30 50 70 90 110 130 150

Mixed Review

20. **Home Economics** To make a new dress, Melissa buys 4 yards of cotton fabric at $5 a yard and 2 yards of lace at $3 a yard. What is the total cost for the fabric and lace she purchases? *(Lesson 1-7)* **$26.00**

Lesson 3-3 Range and Scales   **99**

Limited English Proficiency

Review the mathematical meanings of the vocabulary used in the lesson: *range, scale,* and *interval.* Record data on a number line to help students with limited English proficiency understand how the meanings of these words are related.

Interactive Mathematics Tools

This multimedia software provides an interactive lesson that is tied directly to Lesson 3-3. Students will use changeable histograms to explore data.

Using Questioning To help students understand the relationship between the range of data and the scale and intervals to use, ask questions such as: *How would you find the range of student ages in your school? How will you decide on a scale?*

More Examples

For the Example

Choose another scale and interval for the data in the opening situation in the text. Draw a number line to show them.   Sample answer:

10 11 12 13 14 15 16 17 18 19

Checking for Understanding

Exercises 1-3 are designed to help you assess students' understanding through reading, writing, speaking, and modeling. You should work through these exercises with your students and then monitor their work on Guided Practice Exercises 4-12.

Practice Masters, p. 23

Name _____   Date _____

Practice Worksheet 3-3

Range and Scales

Name the scale and intervals of each number line.

1. 3 6 9 12 15 18 21
   scale: 3 to 21; interval: 3

2. 100 110 120 130
   scale: 100 to 130; interval: 10

3. 75 80 85 90 95
   scale: 75 to 95; interval: 5

4. 96 98 100 102 104
   scale: 96 to 104; interval: 2

Find the range for each set of data. Choose two different scales and intervals for each set of data. Draw two number lines to show each.   Accept all justifiable answers.

5. 8, 2, 6, 10, 3, 4 **range: 8**
   scale: 0 to 10; interval: 2
   scale: 2 to 10; interval 1

6. 10, 15, 0, 13, 13, 17, 5 **range: 17**
   scale: 0 to 20; interval: 2
   scale: 0 to 18; interval: 3

7. 70, 33, 61, 20, 20, 54 **range: 52**
   scale: 0 to 100; interval: 10
   scale: 15 to 70; interval: 5

8. 664, 320, 500, 500, 425 **range: 344**
   scale: 200 to 800; interval: 100
   scale: 300 to 700; interval: 50

Find the range for each set of data. Choose an appropriate scale and intervals. Draw a number line to show the scale and intervals.   Accept all justifiable answers.

9. 1, 5, 9, 12, 12, 4, 7 **range: 11**
   scale: 0 to 12; interval 1

10. 27, 22, 19, 21, 12, 15, 11 **range: 16**
    scale: 10 to 30; interval: 5

11. 55, 59, 53, 95, 98, 76 **range: 45**
    scale: 50 to 100
    interval: 10

12. 400; 1,200; 800; 900; 1,100 **range: 800**
    scale: 400 to 1,200
    interval: 100

T23

Glencoe Division, Macmillan/McGraw-Hill

Error Analysis

Watch for students who confuse the range of the set of data with the scale for the number line.

Prevent by reminding students to determine the range first, by finding the difference between the greatest and least numbers in the data. Then choose the scale.

Close

Have students write a short explanation of the connection between the range of a set of data and the scale and intervals to use when presenting the data.

3 PRACTICE/APPLY

Assignment Guide
Maximum: 13–26
Minimum: 13–25

For **Extra Practice,** see p. 577.

Alternate Assessment

Writing Have students gather a set of data related to a daily experience, such as the number of hours spent on reading. Ask them to write the range and to determine a reasonable interval.

Enrichment Masters, p. 23

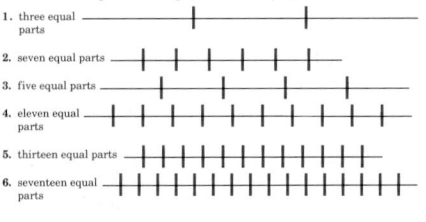

Name _____ Date _____

Enrichment Worksheet 3-3

Dividing a Line Segment into Equal Parts

Notice in the drawing at the right how the parallel lines divide segment *AB* and segment *AC* into equal parts. This property of parallel lines can be used to divide any segment into any number of equal parts. Follow these steps to divide the segment at the right below in five segments each the same length.

Step 1   Lay a sheet of notebook paper over the line segment. Line up one edge with the left endpoint of the segment.

Step 2   Hold the notebook paper at the left endpoint and then turn it until the fifth line of the paper touches the right endpoint of the segment.

Step 3   On the notebook paper, place a dot at each point where the line segment touches a line on the notebook paper. There should be six dots.

Step 4   Fold the notebook paper just above the six dots. Then use it to mark the divisions on the line segment.

Divide each line segment into the given number of equal parts.

1. three equal parts
2. seven equal parts
3. five equal parts
4. eleven equal parts
5. thirteen equal parts
6. seventeen equal parts

T23
Glencoe Division, Macmillan/McGraw-Hill

100

21. **Physical Fitness** Ed completes an obstacle course in 6.9 minutes. It takes Andre 1.4 times longer to complete the course. How long does it take Andre to complete the course? *(Lesson 2-4)* **9.66 minutes**

22. Complete the sentence 2.33 km = ▓ m. *(Lesson 2-9)* **2,330 meters**

Problem Solving and Applications

23. **Critical Thinking** Given a set of data, can there be more than one range? More than one scale? More than one interval? Explain your reasoning for each answer.

23. Range must remain constant; scale and interval can vary somewhat depending on an individual's choice.

24. **History** The table at the right shows the length of reign of the 11 most recent rulers of England and Great Britain.

a. Which ruler had the shortest reign? **Edward VIII**

b. Draw a number line with an appropriate scale and intervals for this data.

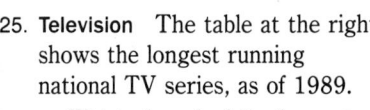

Ruler	Reign (years)
George I	13
George II	33
George III	59
George IV	10
William IV	7
Victoria	63
Edward VII	9
George V	25
Edward VIII	1
George VI	15
Elizabeth II	41*

* as of 1993

25. **Television** The table at the right shows the longest running national TV series, as of 1989.

a. Which show had the longest running time? **Walt Disney**

b. Draw a number line with an appropriate scale and intervals for the number of seasons.
Sample answer:

Program	Number of Seasons	Years
Walt Disney	33	1954–86
Ed Sullivan	24	1948–71
60 Minutes	21	1968–
Gunsmoke	20	1955–75
Red Skelton	20	1951–71
Meet the Press	18	1947–65
What's My Line?	18	1950–67
Lassie	17	1954–71
Lawrence Welk	17	1955–71

26. **Journal Entry** Take a survey of ten of your classmates to find the number of hours each person spends on the phone in a week. **See students' work.**

a. Find the range.

b. Choose an appropriate scale and intervals.

c. Draw a number line.

d. How does your number line compare with Susan Ching's number line on page 98?

100   **Chapter 3** Statistics and Data Analysis

OPTIONS

Extending the Lesson

Graphing Connection Ask students to suggest other ways of representing a set of data, for example by using graphs. Have them suggest kinds of graphs they could make that would require them to figure out the range, scale, and interval of the data being recorded.
Answers will vary. Sample: sales figures; bar graph, line graph

Cooperative Learning Activity

Spontaneous Generation **3-3**

Use groups of 4.
Materials: Masking tape, yardstick, spinners, index cards

▲ Label the sections of two spinners with the digits 0–9. Use masking tape to make a line on the floor that is a little more than 6 feet long. Create a number line by making arrowheads at both ends of the line. Make a tick mark at the left end. Then place tick marks every 6 inches.

● Decide which spinner stands for tens place and which stands for ones place. Then, two group members at a time, spin the spinners to generate at least 10 two-digit numbers. Use cards to show how you would label your number line to plot the data your group generated. What scale will you choose? what interval?

Generate at least three sets of data, changing the labels on the number line for each data set if necessary.

Glencoe Mathematics: Applications and Connections, Course 2

3-4 Line Plots

Objective
Construct line plots.

Words to Learn
line plot
outlier
cluster

Have you ever curled up with a good book on a rainy day? For many people, reading is very enjoyable and relaxing.

Meredith conducted a survey of her classmates to determine how many books each student read last month. The results are shown at the right.

Number of Books	
Emilio—1	Marna—2
Jeremy—4	Bruce—3
Alicia—2	Jana—1
Wai—2	Rick—5
Daniel—0	Scott—2
Charo—3	Ellen—10
Sarah—1	Enrique—2
Bret—3	Mark—0
Mika—1	Kathleen—2
Julie—5	Sei—2

One way to organize this data is to present it on a number line. A **line plot** is a picture of information on a number line.

- First draw a number line. Find the range of the data and determine a scale and intervals.

  The least number of books is 0, and the greatest number is 10. The range is 10 − 0 or 10. You can use a scale of 0 to 10 and an interval of 2 to draw the number line. Other scales and intervals could also be used.

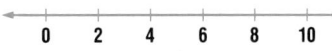

- Put an "x" above the number that represents the number of books each student read. If the number is odd, place the "x" halfway between the appropriate notches.

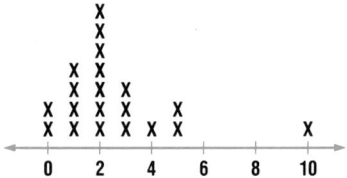

This statistical graph is called a line plot.

You can make some observations about the data from the line plot above.
- The number that occurs most frequently is 2.
- The number 10 is far apart from the rest of the data. It is called an **outlier.**
- There seems to be a **cluster** of data between 1 and 3. Data that are grouped closely together are called a cluster.

Lesson 3-4 Line Plots **101**

OPTIONS

Reteaching Activity

Using Applications Have students work in groups to record the number of times each student blinks in 1 minute. Have students make a table and a line plot for the set data they have collected.

Study Guide Masters, p. 24

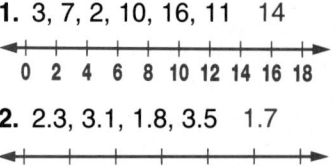

Name _____ Date _____
Study Guide Worksheet 3-4

Line Plots

Darrell surveyed some kennels to find the cost of grooming his dog. The prices given were: $25.00, $27.00, $32.00, $22.00, $43.00, $28.00, $18.00, $24.00, $25.00, $27.00, $30.00, $24.00, $22.00, $30.00, $12.00, $25.00, and $20.00.

Darrell made a line plot to organize the data on a number line. First he found the range of the data: $43.00 − $12.00 = $31.00. He chose a scale of $10.00 to $45.00 to include all of the data and an interval of $5.00 to separate the data into 7 sections. He drew an x to represent each price. For prices between marked intervals he estimated to position the x.

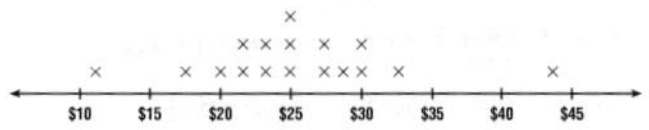

The data is grouped or clustered between $20 and $30. The $43 price is far outside...

3-4 Lesson Notes

NCTM Standards: 1–5, 7, 10

Lesson Resources
- Study Guide Master 3-4
- Practice Master 3-4
- Enrichment Master 3-4
- Evaluation Master, Quiz A, p. 25
- Technology Master, p. 17
- Application Master, p. 3
- Group Activity Card 3-4

 Transparency 3-4 contains the 5-Minute Check and a teaching aid for this lesson.

⏱ 5-Minute Check
(Over Lesson 3-3)

Find the range for each set of data. Choose an appropriate scale and intervals. Draw a number line to show the scale and intervals. Sample number lines are shown.

1. 3, 7, 2, 10, 16, 11   14

2. 2.3, 3.1, 1.8, 3.5   1.7

3. 16.2, 18.6, 17.3   2.4

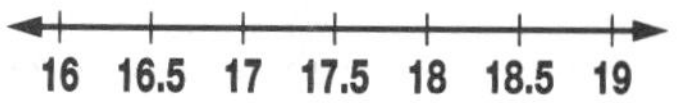

1 FOCUS

Motivating the Lesson

Questioning Ask students to read the lesson's opening paragraphs and to review the table Meredith made. Ask the students to describe both the advantages and disadvantages of displaying data in a table.

2 TEACH

Using Critical Thinking Have students work with partners to write questions about the line plot constructed from the reading survey. For example, can any conclusions be drawn concerning the time spent on reading?

101

More Examples

For the Example

The table shows the winning times in seconds for the 400-meter run in the Olympic Games from 1920 to 1992. Draw a line plot of these data.

Year	Time	Year	Time
1920	49.6	1960	44.9
1924	47.6	1964	45.1
1928	47.8	1968	43.8
1932	46.2	1972	44.7
1936	46.5	1976	44.3
1948	46.2	1980	44.6
1952	45.9	1984	44.3
1956	46.7	1988	43.9
		1992	43.5

```
    ×
    × ×
    × × ×
    × × × ×
    × × × × ×        ×
 +--+--+--+--+--+--+--+--+--+-->
 43 44 45 46 47 48 49 50 51
```

Checking for Understanding

Exercises 1-4 are designed to help you assess students' understanding through reading, writing, speaking, and modeling. You should work through these exercises with your students and then monitor their work on Guided Practice Exercises 5-8.

Practice Masters, p. 24

DID YOU KNOW

The presidential candidates in 1928 were Herbert Hoover and Alfred E. Smith. In 1992, they were George Bush and Bill Clinton.

Example 1

The table at the right shows the voter turnout for presidential elections from 1928 to 1992. Draw a line plot of this data.

The least percent is 50.2, and the greatest is 62.8. You can round to the nearest whole percent to graph them more easily. An appropriate scale for this graph is 50 to 63 with an interval of 1.

Unlike a line graph, a line plot does not need to start at zero.

Year	Voter Turnout
1928	51.8%
1932	52.6
1936	56.8
1940	58.8
1944	56.1
1948	51.1
1952	61.6
1956	59.4
1960	62.8
1964	61.9
1968	60.9
1972	55.2
1976	53.5
1980	52.6
1984	53.1
1988	50.2
1992	55.9

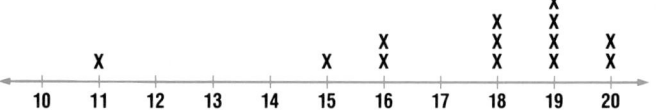

```
                X
                X           X          X          X
   X  X  X  X  X  X  X  X    X       X  X  X
 --+--+--+--+--+--+--+--+--+--+--+--+--+-->
  50 51 52 53 54 55 56 57 58 59 60 61 62 63
```

Checking for Understanding

Communicating Mathematics

Read and study the lesson to answer each question.

1. **Tell** the advantage of using a line plot instead of a table to display data. **Sample answer: it's easier to spot trends**

2. **Write** the definition of an outlier. **a number that is far apart from the rest of the data**

3. **Write** the outliers and clusters, if any, for the line plot below. **outliers—11, clusters—18 to 20**

```
                                            X
                                   X     X
                             X     X  X  X
        X              X  X  X  X  X  X  X
 --+--+--+--+--+--+--+--+--+--+--+-->
  10  11  12  13  14  15  16  17  18  19  20
```

4. **Draw** a line plot that shows ten items of data. The scale should be 10 to 50 with an interval of 5. Eight of the ten items should be from 25 through 35. **See margin.**

Guided Practice

Make a line plot for each set of data. Circle any outliers on the line plot.

5. 3, 5, 4, 5, 9, 10, 2, 4, 3, 12, 6, 4

6. 50, 45, 35, 40, 40, 30, 55, 35, 45, 35

7. 110, 115, 114, 106, 101, 119, 108, 102, 111, 114

8. Make a line plot of the test scores: 100, 89, 88, 84, 90, 97, 100, 89, 90, 90, 73, 91, 83, 95. Name any outliers and clusters.

For answers to Exercises 5–8, see Solutions Manual

OPTIONS

Gifted and Talented Needs

Have students work with partners to construct bar graphs using data provided in the lesson. Ask the students to compare their bar graphs with their line plots of the same data. Ask them to tell which way of visualizing the data is more useful and to explain why they think so.

Additional Answers

4.
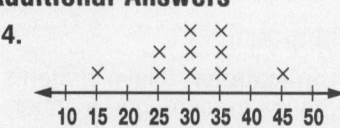

```
              × ×
           × × ×
     ×     × × ×       ×
 --+--+--+--+--+--+--+--+--+-->
  10 15 20 25 30 35 40 45 50
```

17. a. It shows data measures as column heights.
    b. It shows the frequency of a data measure using crosses rather than a vertical scale.
    c. line plot

Exercises

For answers to Exercises 9–12, see Solutions Manual.

Independent Practice

Make a line plot for each set of data. Circle any outliers on the line plot.

9. 36, 45, 42, 16, 41, 30, 38, 52, 32, 33

10. 340, 500, 600, 640, 730, 520, 600, 560, 490, 670

11. 1983, 1980, 1976, 1985, 1984, 1989, 1990, 1985, 1987, 1976, 1988, 1986

12. 3.2, 3.6, 3.7, 4.0, 3.8, 3.3, 3.2, 3.0, 4.0, 3.6, 3.2

13. See Solutions Manual.

13. Ruth wanted the best price on her favorite shampoo. She found the following prices at different stores: $2.40, $2.35, $2.50, $2.25, $3.00, $2.75, $2.40, $2.10, $2.50.

a. Make a line plot of the data.

b. What did Ruth find out about the prices?

Mixed Review

14. **Travel** The Jones' drove 274 miles one day and 304 miles the next day. *About* how far did they travel in two days? Use front-end estimation. *(Lesson 1-2)* **570 miles**

15. Find the range and appropriate scale and interval for the following data:
3, 17, 21, 19, 36, 15, 12, 9.
Draw a number line to show the scale and interval.
(Lesson 3-3) **Sample answer: scale = 0–40; interval = 5; range = 33. See Solutions Manual for number line.**

Problem Solving and Applications

18. Sample answer: Most students eat fast food 2 to 4 times a month, but a few eat fast food as often as 10 times a month.

16. **Collect Data** Conduct a survey of your classmates to determine how many books each student read last month. **See students' work.**

a. Make a line plot of the data.

b. Write a sentence that compares this line plot to the one on page 101.

17. **Critical Thinking** Compare a line plot to a bar graph. **See margin.**

a. How is a line plot like a bar graph?

b. How is it different?

c. Which is easier to construct?

 COMPUTER CONNECTION

18. **Computer Connection** Marcos asked 15 of his classmates how many times they bought food from a fast-food restaurant last month. He entered the data in a computer and made a line plot of the data. What conclusions can you make from this line plot? *Hint: Look for outliers and clusters.*

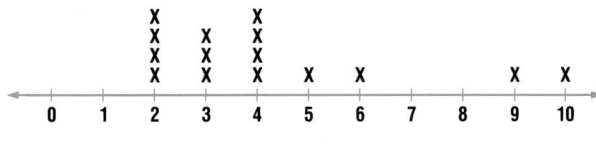

Lesson 3-4 Line Plots **103**

Extending the Lesson

Statistical Connection Have students examine the line plots they have made. Ask them to describe what limitations line plots have. Have them suggest data for which a line plot would *not* be an effective form of visual representation. **Sample answers: For wide ranges, line plots are awkward to use. Line plots do not show time change, so "increase in car sales" would not work.**

Cooperative Learning Activity

Use groups of 4.
Materials: Masking tape, yardstick, index cards, counters, spinner

Counter Plot 3-4

▮ Label the sections of a spinner with the digits 0–9. Use masking tape to make a number line on the floor. Make a line that is a little less than 5 feet long, and then add arrowheads to both ends. Make a tick mark at the left end and place tick marks every 6 inches. Using index cards, label the tick marks 0–9.

▮ In turn, each group member spins the spinner and places a counter above the number line to show the result. Each group member should have at least two spins. Which digit occurs most frequently on your line plot? Is there an outlier? a cluster?

Compare your results with those of other groups.

Glencoe Mathematics: Applications and Connections, Course 2

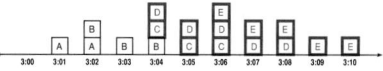
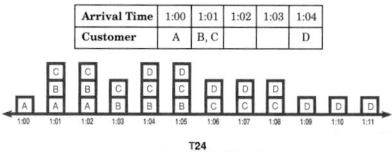
103

NCTM Standards: 1–5, 7, 10

Lesson Resources
- Study Guide Master 3-5
- Practice Master 3-5
- Enrichment Master 3-5
- Technology Master, p. 3
- Interdisciplinary Master, p. 17
- Group Activity Card 3-5

 Transparency 3-5 contains the 5-Minute Check and a teaching aid for this lesson.

⏱ 5-Minute Check
(Over Lesson 3-4)

Make a line plot for each set of data. Circle any outliers on the line plot.

1. 4, 6, 4, 5, 6, 6, 3, 11, 6, 7

2. 20, 25, 15, 30, 35, 20, 25, 15, 25, 30

3. 85, 75, 80, 55, 70, 70, 70

1 FOCUS

Motivating the Lesson

Situational Problem A clothing store owner is studying her sales records before placing an order with the manufacturer for more tops. She must decide which style of top to order from 20 available styles. Ask students whether she should use the mode, the median, or the mean of the most recent sales figures to help her decide.

3-5 Mean, Median, and Mode

Objective
Find the mean, median, and mode of a set of data.

Words to Learn
mean
median
mode
average

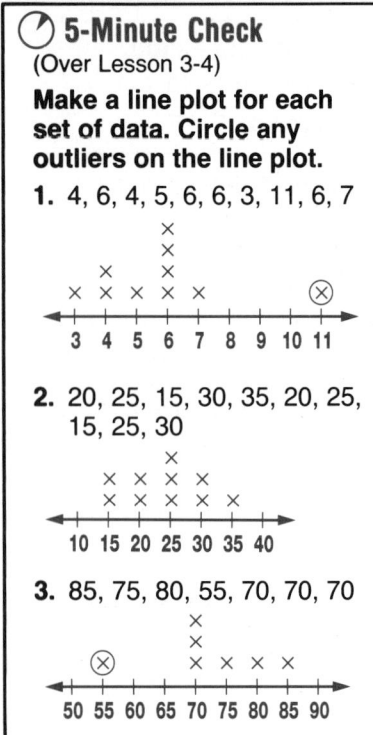

Suppose you are watching the movie *Home Alone* on TV and it is interrupted by commercials that seem to go on forever. You decide to time the length of the next 15 commercials to find out the average length of a commercial. The times, written to the nearest 10 seconds, are listed below.

10 60 20 20 30 20 40 20
40 50 30 10 60 20 50

In mathematics, there are three common ways to describe the data: the mode, the median, and the mean.

Mode	The mode of a set of data is the number or item that appears most often.

A line plot of the commercial lengths can quickly give you the mode.

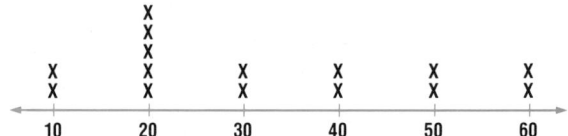

The mode is 20 because 20 occurs most often.

Median	The median is the middle number in a set of data when the data are arranged in numerical order.

The median can also be found by looking at the line plot. Since there are 15 numbers in the data set, the eighth number is the median. The median is 30.

Mean	The mean of a set of data is the arithmetic average.

The mean, or arithmetic **average,** is what people usually are talking about when they say "average." It is found by adding the numbers in the data set and then dividing by the number of items in the set.

Classroom Vignette

"Working in pairs, students measured and recorded each others' foot length, arm length, finger length, and wrist, head, and neck circumference. Then they chose one of these measures and presented a summary of the whole class using a line plot and/or a stem-and-leaf plot."

Janice Loraw

Janice Loraw, Teacher
Donegal Middle School, Marietta, PA

$$\text{mean} = \frac{(10 + 10 + 20 + 20 + 20 + 20 + 20 + 30 + 30 + 40 + 40 + 50 + 50 + 60 + 60)}{15}$$

$$= \frac{480}{15} \text{ or } 32$$

The mean is 32. Note that the mode, the median, and the mean are *not* the same for this set of data.

Example 1

Mental Math Hint
• • • • • • • • • • • • •
If the number of data is even, the set has two middle numbers. In that case, the median is the mean of the two numbers. Just think "what number is halfway between."

Joe's mathematics test scores for the first half of the year are 60, 93, 99, 72, 80, 96, 95, 91. Find the mode, median, and mean.

There is no mode because each score occurs only once. To find the median, arrange the numbers in numerical order: 60, 72, 80, 91, 93, 95, 96, 99. Since there are 8 numbers, the median is the mean of the fourth and fifth numbers, 91 and 93.

$$\text{median} = \frac{91 + 93}{2} \qquad \text{The median is 92.}$$

To find the mean, calculate the arithmetic average.

$(\boxed{\text{(}}\; 60 \;\boxed{+}\; 72 \;\boxed{+}\; 80 \;\boxed{+}\; 91 \;\boxed{+}\; 93 \;\boxed{+}\; 95 \;\boxed{+}\; 96 \;\boxed{+}\; 99 \;\boxed{\text{)}}\; \boxed{\div}\; 8$

$\boxed{=}\; 85.75 \qquad$ The mean is about 86.

In Example 1, if Joe wants to brag about his scores, he would probably use the median, 92. When his mathematics teacher computes his grade, she will probably use the mean, 86.

Example 2 *Problem Solving*

Business A survey was conducted by a bedding firm to determine the average number of hours people sleep each night. The bedding firm wants to use this information to convince people that they should buy a good mattress since they spend a lot of time sleeping.

Number of Hours	Number of People
5	4
6	10
7	35
8	35
9	16

a. Determine the mode, median, and mean of the data.
b. Which number would the bedding firm probably use? Why?

Since the 35 people sleep 7 hours and 35 people sleep 8 hours, there are two modes, 7 and 8.

One hundred people were surveyed, so the median is the mean of the two middle numbers, 8 and 8. The median is 8 hours.

$$\text{mean} = \frac{4(5) + 10(6) + 35(7) + 35(8) + 16(9)}{100}$$

$$= \frac{749}{100} \text{ or } 7.49 \qquad \text{The mean is 7.49 hours.}$$

The bedding firm would use the median because it shows the greatest number of hours spent sleeping.

2 TEACH

Using Communication Before students have read the lesson, discuss with them the meaning of the word "average" as it is used in daily situations. Have them give examples of how statements using the word "average" can be interpreted in different ways. You may wish to start the discussion by writing the phrase "average amount of homework" on the chalkboard. Ask students what "average" might mean in that phrase. Then discuss the meaning assigned to the word on the first page of the lesson.

More Examples

For Example 1

Alonzo's science test scores for the second half of the year are 70, 85, 76, 81, 97, 85, and 88. Find the mode, median, and mean.   mode: 85; median: 85; mean: about 83

For Example 2

Mrs. Martinez wants to present her class with its scores on a recent test using the average that puts the score results in the best light. Four students scored 82, three scored 84, one scored 94, five scored 80, one scored 73, one scored 97, and two scored 78. Determine the mode, median and mean of the scores. Which statistic should Mrs. Martinez use, the mode, the median, or the mean? Explain.   80, 82, 82.4; the mean, since it is the greatest number

---

Reteaching Activity

Using Applications List on the chalkboard travel times to school that day for about 10 students. Have students arrange the data from least to greatest. Discuss what is meant by *mode,* comparing it with the common usage of the term. Then introduce *median* as the middle-most number in the list. Have students use calculators to find the mean.

Study Guide Masters, p. 25

Name _____ Date _____

Study Guide Worksheet 3-5

Mean, Median, and Mode

To find the mean, or arithmetic average, of a set of numbers, find the sum of the numbers and divide by the number of items in the set.

To find the median of a set of numbers, arrange the numbers in order from least to greatest and find the middle number.

To find the mode of a set of numbers, find the number or item that appears most often.

Length of Nine Ladybugs (in inches)		
0.30	0.28	0.34
0.32	0.30	0.31
0.34	0.34	0.30

Example Find the mean, median, and mode of the ladybug lengths.

Mean: $\frac{0.30 + 0.28 + 0.34 + 0.32 + 0.30 + 0.31 + 0.34 + 0.34 + 0.30}{9}$

The mean is about 0.31 inches.

Median: 0.28, 0.30, 0.30, 0.30, 0.31, 0.32, ...

Checking for Understanding

Exercises 1-2 are designed to help you assess students' understanding through reading, writing, speaking, and modeling. You should work through these exercises with your students and then monitor their work on Guided Practice Exercises 3-5.

Close

Have students distinguish among the three measures of central tendency—the mode, the median, and the mean. Ask them to explain how to find each.

3 PRACTICE/APPLY

Assignment Guide
Maximum: 6-18
Minimum: 7-12, 14-17
All: Mid-Chapter Review

For **Extra Practice,** see p. 578.

Practice Masters, p. 25

Name _____ Date _____

Practice Worksheet 3-5

Mean, Median, and Mode

Order the data from least to greatest. Then find the mode(s), median, and mean.

1. 31, 18, 19, 18, 18, 17, 12 **12, 17, 18, 18, 18, 19, 31 mode: 18; median: 18; mean: 19**

2. 5, 0, 9, 9, 3, 0, 5, 5, 4 **0, 0, 3, 4, 5, 5, 5, 9, 9 mode: 5; median: 5; mean: 4.4**

3. 81, 81, 83, 84, 83, 85, 86 **81, 81, 83, 83, 84, 85, 86 modes: 81, 83; median: 83; mean: 83.3**

4. 77, 70, 65, 62, 65, 80, 85 **62, 65, 65, 70, 77, 80, 85 mode: 65; median: 70; mean: 72**

Find the mode(s), median, and mean for each set of data.

5. 5, 6, 3, 9, 0, 4, 1, 2, 7 **mode: none; median: 4; mean: 4.1**

6. 9, 9, 3, 2, 8, 7, 1, 1, 8 **modes: 1, 8, and 9; median: 7; mean: 5.3**

7. 24, 33, 43, 44, 23, 41, 40 **mode: none; median: 40; mean: 35.4**

8. 77, 76, 55, 76, 66, 58, 55 **modes: 76, 55; median: 66; mean: 66.1**

9. 3.8, 4.2, 4.0, 4.2, 4.2 **mode: 4.2; median: 4.2; mean: 4.1**

10. 8.1, 9.0, 9.1, 8.4, 8.4, 8.4, 8.4 **mode: 8.4; median: 8.4; mean: 8.5**

11. 1,220, 1,440, 1,220, 1,660, 1,660 **modes: 1,220, 1,660; median: 1,440; mean: 1,440**

12. 3,200, 3,100, 3,100, 3,000, 3,300 **mode: 3,100; median: 3,100; mean: 3,140**

Use the table at the right to answer the following.

13. Find the mode(s), median, and mean of the five countries' military research and development spending. **mode: $3.5 billion; median: $3.5 billion; mean: $9.2 billion**

14. Find the mode, and mean of the countries' civilian research and development spending. **mode: none; median: $26.1 billion; mean: $34.52 billion**

Money spent on Research and Development in Selected Countries (Billions of Dollars)		
Country	Military	Civilian
United States	37.3	79.4
United Kingdom	3.5	8.5
France	3.5	14.6
West Germany	1.4	26.1
Japan	0.3	44.0

T25
Glencoe Division, Macmillan/McGraw-Hill

106

Checking for Understanding

Communicating Mathematics

Read and study the lesson to answer each question.

1. **Tell**, in your own words, how you would find each of the following from a set of data. **See margin.**
   a. the median, if there is an odd number of items.
   b. the median, if there is an even number of items

2. **Show** a set of data that meets each condition. **Sample answers given.**

   a. 1 mode   b. 2 modes   c. no mode
      2, 2, 3   1, 2, 2, 4, 4   1, 2, 3, 4

Guided Practice

Order the data from least to greatest. Then find the mode(s), median, and mean.

3. 13, 17, 20, 18, 17, 15, 12   **12, 13, 15, 17, 17, 18, 20 ; 17, 17, 16**

4. 3, 4, 7, 6, 5, 7, 8, 2   **2, 3, 4, 5, 6, 7, 7, 8 ; 7, 5.5, 5.25**

5. 90, 92, 94, 91, 90, 94, 95, 98   **90, 90, 91, 92, 94, 94, 95, 98 ; 90 and 94, 93, 93**

Exercises

Independent Practice

Find the mode(s), median, and mean for each set of data.

6. 1, 5, 8, 3, 5, 4, 6, 2, 3, 7   **3 and 5, $4\frac{1}{2}$, $4\frac{2}{5}$**

7. 56, 75, 65, 57, 76, 66, 65, 64   **65, 65, $65\frac{1}{2}$**

8. 8.9, 8.0, 9.0, 9.1, 9.3, 9.4   **none, 9.05, 8.95**

9. 1,755; 1,780; 1,755; 1,805; 1,805   **1,755 and 1,805 : 1,780 : 1,780**

10. Your math teacher makes a frequency table of students' test scores on the last test. Find the mode, median, and mean of these scores.
    85 and 100, 95, 92.7

Test Score	Tally	Number
100	ⅢⅢ	5
95					3
90				2
85	ⅢⅢ	5

Mixed Review

11. Express 32,500 in scientific notation. *(Lesson 2-6)* **3.25×10^4**

12. Make a line plot for the following data: 21, 19, 16, 21, 20, 19, 18, 21, 19. Circle any outliers. *(Lesson 3-4)* **See margin.**

Problem Solving and Applications

13. **Sports** The scores of the winning teams of the Super Bowl from 1981 to 1990 are 27, 26, 27, 38, 28, 46, 39, 42, 20, and 55.
    a. Make a line plot. **See margin.**
    b. Find the mode, median, and mean. **27, 33, 34.8**

14. **Portfolio Suggestion** Select your favorite word problem from this chapter and place it in your portfolio. Attach a note explaining why it is your favorite. **See students' work.**

106   **Chapter 3** Statistics and Data Analysis

OPTIONS

Team Teaching

Inform the other teachers on your team that your classes are studying measures of central tendency. Suggestions for curriculum integration are:

Health: average height gains

Social Studies: average family size, population, work day

Science: average temperatures

Additional Answers

1. List in ascending order. Choose the middle number. Find the mean of the two middle numbers.

12.
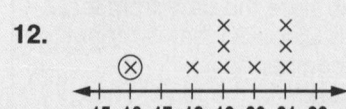

13. a.
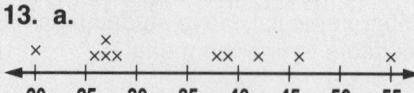

15. **Weather** The high temperatures for the first week of school were 84, 87, 89, 81, 83, 80, and 89.

    a. Find the mode, median, and mean. **89, 84, 84.7**

    b. Which number would you use to emphasize how hot it was? **the mode, 89**

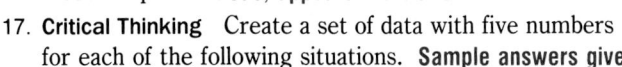

16. **Business** The manager of The Foot Locker keeps a record of the sizes of each athletic shoe sold. Which number is probably most useful: the mean, median, or mode? Explain. **mode, appears most often**

17. **Critical Thinking** Create a set of data with five numbers for each of the following situations. **Sample answers given.**

    a. The mode, median, and the mean are the same. **1, 2, 2, 2, 3**

    b. The mean is greater than the median. **1, 2, 3, 10, 11**

    c. The mean is not equal to one of the numbers in the set. **4, 5, 7, 8**

18. **Data Search** Refer to pages 88 and 89. What is the total number of Arabic-speaking people and Portuguese-speaking people? **370 million**

---

3 Assessment: Mid-Chapter Review

Use the line graph to answer the question.

1. Was the median age of the U.S. population greater or less than 25 in 1970? *(Lesson 3–1)* **greater**

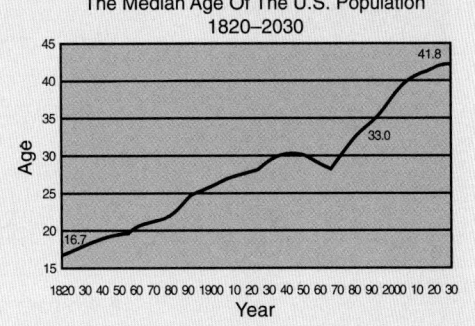

The Median Age Of The U.S. Population 1820–2030

The scores on a 20-point quiz are given at the right. **See margin.**

11	19	16
19	17	20
15	13	16
20	18	19
15	14	18
17	18	15
18	17	14

2. Make a frequency table for this set of data. *(Lesson 3–2)*

3. What is the range of the data? *(Lesson 3–3)* **9**

4. Make a line plot of the data. *(Lesson 3–4)* **See margin.**

5. Find the mode, median, and mean. *(Lesson 3–5)* **18, 17, 16.6**

6. Which number best describes the data, mode, median, or mean? Explain. *(Lesson 3–5)* **mean, It includes all scores.**

Extending the Lesson

Using Critical Thinking Have students write three problems involving averages of sets of data, one for which the mode is the most descriptive measure, one for which the median is most descriptive, and one for which the mean is the most descriptive measure. Have students solve each other's problems.

Cooperative Learning Activity

Get the "Write" Description 3-5

Use groups of 2.
Materials: Centimeter grid paper

• Collect as many pencils as you can from the classroom.

→ Lining up the erasers with the bottom line of the grid paper, arrange the pencils in order from least length to greatest length. Use the grid paper to determine each length. Then find the mode, median, and mean of the lengths.

Compare your results with those of other pairs.

Glencoe Mathematics: Applications and Connections, Course 2

Alternate Assessment

Writing Have students create a set of data using information from their daily lives. Have them find the mode(s), median, and mean of the data.

Additional Answers

2.

Score	Tally	Freq.
11	I	1
12		0
13	I	1
14	II	2
15	III	3
16	II	2
17	III	3
18	IIII	4
19	III	3
20	II	2

4.

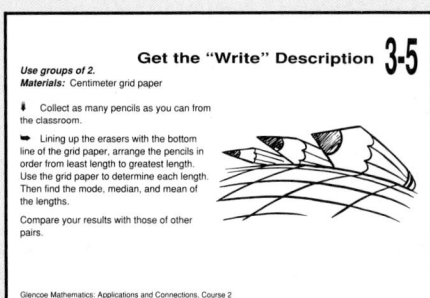

Enrichment Masters, p. 25

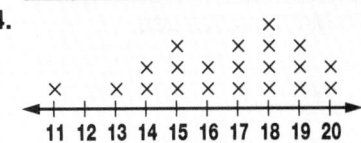

Name _____ Date _____

Enrichment Worksheet 3-5

Quartiles

The median is a number that describes the "center" of a set of data. Here are two sets with the same median, 50, indicated by ○.

25   30   35   40   45   (50)   55   60   65   70   75

0   10   20   30   40   (50)   60   70   80   90   100

But, sometimes a single number may not be enough. The numbers shown in the triangles can also be used to describe the data. They are called *quartiles*. The lower quartile is the median of the lower half of the data. It is indicated by ▽. The upper quartile is the median of the upper half. It is indicated by △.

Circle the median in each set of data. Draw triangles around the quartiles.

1. 29   52   44   37   27   46   43   60   31   54   36

2. 1.7   0.4   1.4   2.3   0.3   2.7   2.0   0.9   2.7   2.6   1.2

3. 1,150   1,600   1,450   1,750   1,500   1,300   1,200

4. 5   2   9   7   9   3   7   8   7   2   5   6   9   5   1

Use the following set of test scores to solve the problems.

71   57   29   37   53   41   25   37   53   27
62   55   75   48   66   53   66   48   75   66

5. Which scores are "in the lower quartile"? **25, 27, 29, and 37**

6. How high would you have to score to be "in the upper quartile"? **66 or higher**

T25
Glencoe Division, Macmillan/McGraw-Hill

NCTM Standards: 1–5, 7, 10

Management Tips

For Students Provide each group with only the data they will use. Group members should share the tasks of making the frequency table or line plot and finding the three measures of average. As a group, they should decide which measure best describes the data.

For the Overhead Projector
Overhead Manipulative Resources provides appropriate materials for teacher or student demonstration of the activities in this Mathematics Lab.

1 FOCUS

Introducing the Lab

Ask students what they think it means when someone is described as an "average" person. Explain to students that they are going to work together to identify what an "average" student in their class would be like.

2 TEACH

Using Discussion List on the chalkboard all the questions students suggest for identifying the "average" student. Encourage the class to discuss the list in order to produce a final set of ten questions that will elicit the most useful information.

3 PRACTICE/APPLY

Using Critical Thinking Ask students to suggest uses for the information they have compiled. Then have them tell how survey results might be used by groups having a special interest, for example, by politicians, business people, and unions.

Close

Have students write an outline of the steps they followed to determine what it means to be "average" in their class.

Cooperative Learning

3-5B Are You Average?

A Follow-Up of Lesson 3-5

Objective
Use mean, median, and mode to describe students in your school.

Materials
pencil
paper
markers
ruler

How would you describe an "average" student in your school? The average student in your school may vary quite a bit from the average student in another. In this lab, you will find out what the average student in your math class is like.

Try this!

Work together as a class.

- List at least ten questions you would like to ask to find out what the average student is like. For example:

  What is your height in inches?
  What is your age in months?
  How many children are in your family?
  What is your favorite TV program?

- Prepare a survey with your ten questions. Each student in the class should complete the survey.

Work in groups of three.

- Each group should take at least two of the questions and compile the data in a frequency table or on a line plot.
- Find the mode, median, and mean. Decide which one best describes the data.

Work together as a class.

- Compile the results of all the groups.
- Prepare a poster that describes the "average" student in the classroom.

What do you think?

1. Which did you use for your data: mode, median, or mean? Explain why. **mode, outliers throw off mean**
2. If you surveyed students in another class, would you expect the same results? Why or why not? **no, could be older or younger group and that would change answers**

Extension

3. Run a contest in your school. Find the student that best meets the description of the "average" student.
   See students' work.

OPTIONS

Lab Manual You may wish to make copies of the blackline master on p. 43 of the *Lab Manual* for students to use as a recording sheet.

Lab Manual, p. 43

Name _____ Date _____

Mathematics Lab Worksheet

Use with page 108

Are You Average?

Try this!

List the ten questions. Answers will vary.

1. _____
2. _____
3. _____
4. _____
5. _____
6. _____
7. _____

3-6 Stem-and-Leaf Plots

Objective
Construct stem-and-leaf plots.

Words to Learn
stem-and-leaf plot
stem
leaf

DID YOU KNOW

Theodore Roosevelt was William McKinley's vice president. When McKinley was killed in 1901, Roosevelt assumed the presidency. At age 42, he was the youngest person to serve as president.
John F. Kennedy, however, was the youngest person to be *elected* president. He was 43 when he took office.

Did you know that Theodore Roosevelt was the youngest United States president to be sworn into office? He was 42 years old. He served as president from 1901–1909.

The oldest president to be sworn into office was Ronald Reagan. He was 69 years old. He served as president from 1981–1989.

As of 1994, there had been 42 presidents. The ages of each United States president when sworn into office are listed at the right.

57	61	57	57	58	57	61	54
68	51	49	64	50	48	65	52
56	46	54	49	50	47	55	55
54	42	51	56	55	51	54	51
60	62	43	55	56	61	52	69
64	46						

When there are many numbers in a set of data, one way to show the data and make it easy to read is to construct a **stem-and-leaf plot.**

- Find the least number and the greatest number in the data set above. The greatest number, 69, has a 6 in the tens place and the least number, 42, has a 4 in the tens place.

- Draw a vertical line and write the digits in the tens places from 4 through 6 to the left of the line. The tens digits form the **stems.**

  4 |
  5 |
  6 |

- The units digits are written to the right of the line.

  4 | 98697236
  5 | 7778741026405541651415 62
  6 | 1184502194

  The units digits form the **leaves.**

- Rewrite the units digits in each row from the least to greatest.

  4 | 23667899
  5 | 00111122444455555666677778
  6 | 0111244589

- Include an explanation.

  4 | 2 means 42.

OPTIONS

Reteaching Activity

Using Manipulatives Have students use place-value models to model data that consists of two-digit numbers that you provide. Have students record the numbers of ten strips they use in the stems column of the stem-and-leaf plot, and the number of ones squares in the leaves column.

Study Guide Masters, p. 26

Name _____ Date _____

Study Guide Worksheet 3-6

Stem-and-Leaf Plots

The chart below shows the number of home runs Hank Aaron hit by year.

Home Runs Hit by Hank Aaron											
Year	1954	1955	1956	1957	1958	1959	1960	1961	1962	1963	1964	1965
Home Runs	13	27	26	44	30	39	40	35	45	44	24	32
Year	1966	1967	1968	1969	1970	1971	1972	1973	1974	1975	1976	
Home Runs	44	39	29	44	38	47	34	40	20	12	10	

A stem and leaf plot of the data is shown below.

The tens digits are the stems.   1 | 0 2 3
The ones digits are the leaves.

NCTM Standards: 1–5, 7, 10

Lesson Resources
- Study Guide Master 3-6
- Practice Master 3-6
- Enrichment Master 3-6
- Group Activity Card 3-6

 Transparency 3-6 contains the 5-Minute Check and a teaching aid for this lesson.

⏱ 5-Minute Check
(Over Lesson 3-5)

Find the mode(s), median, and mean for each set of data.

1. 2, 6, 5, 6, 7, 8, 3, 2, 6
   mode: 6; median: 6; mean: 5

2. 54, 73, 63, 55, 74, 64, 62, 63   mode: 63; median: 63; mean: 63.5

3. 1,255; 1,280; 1,305; 1,305; 1,255   modes: 1,255; 1,305; median: 1,280; mean: 1,280

1 FOCUS

Motivating the Lesson

Questioning Have students read the first three paragraphs of the lesson and, without reflecting, quickly decide whether most newly inaugurated presidents have been in their 40's, 50's or 60's. Record the student responses on the chalkboard. Later in the lesson, compare the responses to the answer revealed by the stem-and-leaf plot.

2 TEACH

Using Discussion Have students measure one another's heights in centimeters. Then have them make a stem-and-leaf plot of the data. Discuss advantages of stem-and-leaf plots with students, focusing on how the plots make it easy to find outliers and data that form in a cluster. The mode(s), and median are also easily found.

More Examples

For the Example

High temperatures (°F) on a December day for 17 southwestern cities are 54°, 67°, 64°, 61°, 70°, 65°, 72°, 63°, 49°, 58°, 60°, 48°, 68°, 77°, 69°, 65°, 82°. In which interval (0°–9°, 10°–19°, and so on) do most of the temperatures fall?
60°F–69°F

Teaching Tip Before doing the *Checking for Understanding*, point out to students that a stem-and-leaf plot is most useful for displaying data within a reasonably narrow range of stem values that you want to display in its entirety. Ask for examples of such data.

Checking for Understanding

Exercises 1-2 are designed to help you assess students' understanding through reading, writing, speaking, and modeling. You should work through these exercises with your students and then monitor their work on Guided Practice Exercises 3-6.

Practice Masters, p. 26

Name _____ Date _____

Practice Worksheet 3-6

Stem-and-Leaf Plots

Determine the stems for each set of data.

1. 44, 32, 77, 44, 31, 45, 79, 34, 35, 66, 55 **stem: 3 to 7**

2. 56, 48, 90, 69, 82, 91, 44, 55, 60, 72 **stem: 4 to 9**

3. 5, 3, 33, 58, 22, 39, 40, 38, 22, 57, 29 **stem: 0 to 5**

4. 20, 13, 15, 6, 16, 29, 24, 22, 21, 20, 18, 3, 22 **stem: 0 to 2**

5. 89, 134, 79, 65, 85, 132, 101, 88, 100 **stem: 6 to 13**

6. 94, 68, 90, 35, 84, 92, 103, 88, 91, 80 **stem: 3 to 10**

Make a stem-and-leaf plot for each set of data.

7. 18, 67, 35, 20, 45, 55, 69, 23, 34, 58, 61, 43, 56, 63, 29, 32

```
          1 | 8
          2 | 039
          3 | 245
          4 | 35
1|8 means  5 | 568
18         6 | 1379
```

8. 82, 91, 80, 105, 113, 104, 83, 90, 84, 91, 109, 112, 100, 92, 85, 92, 92

```
           8 | 02345
           9 | 011222
          10 | 0459
          11 | 23
8|0 means 80
```

9. $1.13, $1.25, $1.19, $1.32, $1.25, $1.50, $1.45, $1.48, $1.52, $1.19

```
           $1.1 | 399
           $1.2 | 55
           $1.3 | 2
$1.1|3 means $1.4 | 58
$1.13      $1.5 | 02
```

10. $0.89, $1.12, $0.92, $1.28, $1.25, $1.02, $1.13, $1.02, $1.01, $1.10, $1.14, $1.23

```
           $0.8 | 9
           $0.9 | 2
           $1.0 | 122
           $1.1 | 0234
$0.8|9 means $0.89  $1.2 | 358
```

Use the stem-and-leaf plot to answer the following.

11. How many zero-degrees days does the coldest metropolitan area in the United States have in a year? **54 zero-degree days**

12. What is the range of the zero-degree day data? **23 days**

Number of zero-degrees days per year in the eight coldest metropolitan areas of the United States
3 | 1345
4 | 1
5 | 114
3|1 means 31 zero-degree days per year.

T26
Glencoe Division, Macmillan/McGraw-Hill

110

It is easy to see now that most of the presidents were between 50 and 58 years when they were sworn into office. What other things can you find out quickly from the stem-and-leaf plot?

Example 1

Low temperatures on a March day for 19 midwestern cities are 34°, 57°, 56°, 27°, 58°, 46°, 53°, 28°, 34°, 9°, 56°, 57°, 45°, 34°, 29°, 52°, 57°, 57°, 8°. In which interval (0°–9°, 10°–19°, and so on) do most of the temperatures fall?

Make a stem-and-leaf plot.

The tens digit of a single-digit number is 0. So the stems start with 0 and end with 5. Include 1 as a stem even though none of the numbers have a 1 in the tens place.

```
0 | 89
1 |
2 | 789
3 | 444
4 | 56
5 | 236677778
5 | 2 means 52°.
```

Most of the temperatures fall in the 50°–59° interval.

The mode, median, and any outliers can easily be found using a stem-and-leaf plot. For the data above, the mode is 57°, the median is 46°, and the outliers are 8° and 9°.

Checking for Understanding

Communicating Mathematics

Read and study the lesson to answer each question.

1. **Tell** whether you would make a stem-and-leaf plot if you had five numbers in your set of data. Explain. **No; They should be used for many numbers.**

2. **Discuss**, in a small group, some conclusions you can draw from the stem-and-leaf plot of the presidents' ages on page 109. Do you think that the next president will be over 70 years old when he or she is sworn into office? Why or why not? **See students' work.**

Guided Practice

Determine the stems for each set of data.

3. 28, 22, 41, 39, 26, 33, 17, 14, 22, 56, 44 **1, 2, 3, 4, 5**

4. 42, 33, 9, 21, 7, 11, 14, 6, 40, 5, 9, 5 **0, 1, 2, 3, 4**

5. 100, 132, 135, 92, 86, 136, 106, 89, 128, 112 **8, 9, 10, 11, 12, 13**

110 Chapter 3 Statistics and Data Analysis

OPTIONS

Meeting Needs of Middle School Students

To help your students organize their study of statistics, encourage them to set aside a special section of their notebook for examples of the different graphs, tables, plots, and other statistical measures that they are learning about.

6. a.
```
1 | 6
2 | 359
3 | 2556
4 | 15
5 |
6 | 7
1 | 6 means
16 years.
```

6. The ages of eleven people randomly surveyed in the Paramount Theater are 23, 67, 45, 35, 16, 25, 29, 35, 41, 36, and 32.
   a. Make a stem-and-leaf plot of this data.
   b. How many people are under 30 years old? **4**
   c. In which age group do most of the people fall? **30's.**

Exercises

Independent Practice

Make a stem-and-leaf plot for each set of data.

7. 58, 27, 34, 53, 24, 36, 38, 20, 43, 45, 54, 78, 35, 36, 47, 58

8. $0.83, $0.94, $0.54, $0.92, $0.85, $0.54, $0.96, $0.89, $0.75, $1.17
   Hint: Think of $0.54 as 54¢.

7.
```
2 | 047
3 | 45668
4 | 357
5 | 3488
6 |
7 | 8
2 | 7 means
27.
```

The stem-and-leaf plot at the right shows the high temperatures for the first 14 days of January in Buffalo, New York.

```
0 | 6
1 | 1145899
2 | 3556
3 | 36
1 | 1 means 11°.
```

9. What were the highest and lowest temperatures? **36°, 6°**

10. In which interval do most of the temperatures lie? **10–19°**

Mixed Review

11. **Algebra** Evaluate $3a - 2b + 6(a - b)$ if $a = 14$ and $b = 2$. *(Lesson 1-8)* **110**

12. Find the mean, median, and mode for this set of data. $10, $18, $15, $6, $13, $12, $10 *(Lesson 3-5)* **$12, $12, $10**

Problem Solving and Applications

8.
```
$ .5 | 44
  .6 |
  .7 | 5
  .8 | 359
  .9 | 246
 1.0 |
 1.1 | 7
 .5 | 4 means
 $.54.
```

13. **Sports** The table at the right shows the points scored by each player in a high school basketball game.
    a. Make a stem-and-leaf plot of this data.
    b. How many players scored over 10 points? **3**
    c. Find the mode, median, and mean of the points scored. Which one best describes the data? **2 & 4, 5, 7.8; median**

Player	Points
Bill	6
Alonso	4
Gary	15
Rich	3
Leroy	11
Javier	22
Ed	2
Mike	9
Doug	4
Andy	2

13. a.
```
0 | 2234469
1 | 15
2 | 2
1 | 5 means
15 points.
```

14. **Collect Data** Ask 15 of your friends how much change they have in their wallets or pockets. **See students' work.**
    a. Make a stem-and-leaf plot of this data.
    b. How many of your friends have more than 50¢?
    c. Write a sentence that describes the shape of the stem-and-leaf plot.

15. **Critical Thinking** How is a stem-and-leaf plot like a bar graph? **The length of each row of numbers are like the length of bars on a graph.**

Lesson 3-6 Stem-and-Leaf Plots **111**

Extending the Lesson

Science Connection Have students use the newspaper to find yesterday's high and low temperatures for 15 cities in the United States. Ask students to make a double stem-and-leaf plot for this data. Tell them that in a double stem-and-leaf plot, one column of stems has a column of leaves on its left and one on its right.

Cooperative Learning Activity

Number of players: 2
Materials: Spinners

Leaf It to Me 3-6

▲ Label the sections of two spinners with the digits 0–9. Decide which spinner will be spinner A and which will be spinner B. For one partner, spinner A gives digits in tens place and spinner B gives units digits. For the other partner, spinner A gives units digits and spinner B gives digits in tens place.

▲ Each partner makes the "stem" portion of a stem-and-leaf plot by writing the digits 0–9 in a single column and drawing a vertical line to the right. Both partners then spin the spinners at the same time. Each partner records the resulting two-digit number on his or her stem-and-leaf plot. The first partner to write five leaves beside any stem wins the round. Play several rounds.

Glencoe Mathematics: Applications and Connections, Course 2

Close

Have students compare a stem-and-leaf plot with a line plot. Ask them to describe what they have in common and explain how they are different.

3 PRACTICE/APPLY

Assignment Guide
Maximum: 7–15
Minimum: 7–15

For **Extra Practice**, see p. 578.

Alternate Assessment

Modeling Have students use an almanac to find the heights, in feet, of the 10 tallest buildings in a city in the United States. Have them display the data in a stem-and-leaf plot.

Enrichment Masters, p. 26

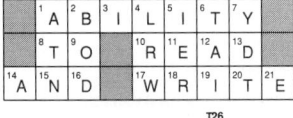

Name _____ Date _____

Enrichment Worksheet 3-6

Who Needs Statistics?

The puzzle on this page is called an *acrostic*. To solve the puzzle, work back and forth between the words and the puzzle box below.

Use the clues to write the missing letters in each word. The missing letters are used to finish the quotation at the bottom of the page.

1. mark useful for taking surveys   T A L L Y
2. type of line used to graph data   N U M B E R
3. what you use a graph to organize   D A T A
4. far out from the rest of the data   O U T L I E R
5. half the data are above this   M E D I A N
6. where you would expect to find the median of a set of data   M I D D L E
7. where the leaves are in a stem-and-leaf plot   R O W S

Statistical thinking will one day be as necessary for efficient citizenship as the . . .

A B I L I T Y
T O   R E A D
A N D   W R I T E

H.G. Wells

T26
Glencoe Division, Macmillan/McGraw-Hill

NCTM Standards: 1–5, 7, 10, 13

Management Tips

For Students You may find it more manageable and time-saving to have only about 15 students grab handfuls of popcorn. Have paper plates or a large plastic bag available so that students can either eat or discard the counted popcorn.

For the Overhead Projector *Overhead Manipulative Resources* provides appropriate materials for teacher or student demonstration of the activities in this Mathematics Lab.

1 FOCUS

Introducing the Lab

Before students grab handfuls of popcorn, challenge each to guess how many kernels he or she can hold. Once students have their handfuls, ask them to estimate how many kernels they have. Students can compare their initial guesses with actual results.

2 TEACH

Using Discussion Have the groups discuss the advantages and disadvantages of each method of data presentation before choosing one to use. Ask students to explain why one presentation seems more effective than the others.

3 PRACTICE/APPLY

Using Critical Thinking Ask students whether any of the results surprised them, and if so, to explain why. Have students formulate another question that might be asked in this part of the lab.

Close

Have students suggest a way to present the data that would be an *ineffective* way to present the data about popcorn. Ask them to explain why it would not work well in this case.

3-7A How Much Is a Handful?

A Preview of Lesson 3-7

Objective
Use, mode, median, and mean to make predictions.

Materials
popcorn
pencil
paper

Jeremy and his older brother ask their mother if they can have some popcorn. She says, "Only one handful apiece." How much is a handful? Will Jeremy and his older brother get the same amount of popcorn?

In this lab, we will predict how many popped kernels are in a handful.

Try this!

- Each student should grab a handful of popped popcorn.
- Count the number of popped kernels in each handful and have one person write the numbers on the board.

Work in groups of three.
- Find the mode, median, and mean of the data.
- Choose one of the following ways to present the data: frequency table, bar graph, line graph, line plot, or stem-and-leaf plot.
- Display your data presentation to the rest of the class. Explain.

What do you think? For answers to Exercises 1–3, see students' work.

1. Which number (mode, median, or mean) best describes the data?
2. Which data presentation seemed most effective? Why?
3. Predict how many popped kernels would be in a handful for a student your age who is not in your class.

Extension For answers to Exercises 4–5, see students' work.

4. Randomly choose 10 students that are not in your math class and have them grab a handful of popcorn. Compare their handfuls with your prediction.
5. Do you think you could use your findings to predict a handful for an adult? Randomly choose 10 adults and have them grab a handful of popcorn. Compare their handfuls with your data.

OPTIONS

Lab Manual You may wish to make copies of the blackline master on p. 44 of the *Lab Manual* for students to use as a recording sheet.

Lab Manual, p. 44

Name _____ Date _____

Mathematics Lab Worksheet

Use with page 112 _____

How Much Is a Handful?

Try this! Answers may vary.

The number of popped kernels in my handful is _____.

For the class, the mode is _____, the median is _____, and the mean is _____.

Present the data to the class. Answers may vary.

3-7 Making Predictions

Objective

Make predictions from graphs.

At Disney World, in Epcot's Future World, visitors were shown a short video and asked to answer questions about space travel. A computer then counted the responses and displayed them on a video screen. The responses of one set of visitors are shown at the right.

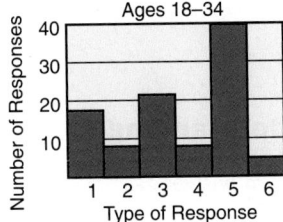

Where would you like to visit?
(Responses are out of 100)

	AGES			
	18-34	35-49	50-64	65+
1. A floating space station	17	27	32	33
2. A lunar base	8	9	9	9
3. A Martian settlement	22	16	17	14
4. Jupiter or Saturn	8	4	5	5
5. Another solar system	40	36	29	21
6. No response	5	8	8	18

A bar graph of the responses for ages 18–34 is shown below.

LOOK BACK

You can review bar graphs and line graphs on page 90.

If 100 others in the same age group were asked the same questions, how do you think they would respond? What if 200 others were asked the same questions?

You can use graphs to make predictions about how other people, similar to the ones in the survey, would respond to a given question.

You can use line graphs to predict future events.

DID YOU KNOW

Science experiments are often used to make predictions. For example, if you measure the growth of a bean plant for 10 days and record the results, you can make a prediction about what the growth will be on the 14th day.

Example 1 *Problem Solving*

Health Yoko has been walking a mile each morning before school. She has recorded her times on a line graph. If she continues to walk each day, what do you think her time will be in 5 more days? Use the graph to make your prediction.

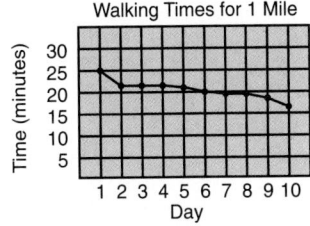

Because the line graph is sloping downward, you could predict that her times will probably continue to decrease each day. A good prediction would be 15 minutes. Do you think her time will continue to decrease indefinitely? Why or why not?

Lesson 3-7 Making Predictions **113**

OPTIONS

Reteaching Activity

Using Applications Have students record the time of sunrise for 5 consecutive days. Then have them construct a line graph to show the data. Next, ask them to discuss any trend in sunrise times the graph suggests. Finally, ask students to explain how they can use the graph to predict what time the sun will rise tomorrow and on a day next week.

Study Guide Masters, p. 27

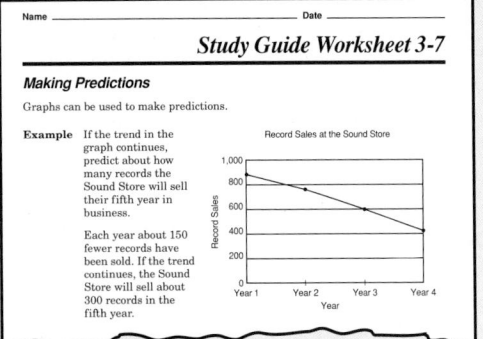

NCTM Standards: 1–5, 7, 8, 10

Lesson Resources
- Study Guide Master 3-7
- Practice Master 3-7
- Enrichment Master 3-7
- Group Activity Card 3-7

 Transparency 3-7 contains the 5-Minute Check and a teaching aid for this lesson.

🕐 5-Minute Check
(Over Lesson 3-6)

1. **Make a stem-and-leaf plot for these data:**

46, 37, 32,	3	2 3 7 9
51, 48, 44,	4	0 4 6 8
33, 54, 39,	5	1 4 6 9
40, 56, 59		5|1 means 51.

The stem-and-leaf plot below shows the heights, in stories, of the 15 tallest buildings in a city.

2	7 8
3	2 2 3 7 9
4	0 1 1 3 5 8
5	2 4

5|2 means 52.

2. **How tall is the tallest building?** 54 stories

3. **In which 10-story interval do most of the buildings lie?** 40–49 stories

1 FOCUS

Motivating the Lesson

Activity Have students list the number of hours of TV they watched on each of the last 5 nights. Have each student make a bar graph from his or her data. Ask them how they can predict their TV viewing from their graph.

2 TEACH

Using Applications Suggest ways that people make predictions based on information in graphs. For example, discuss how urban planners might use graphs showing population trends.

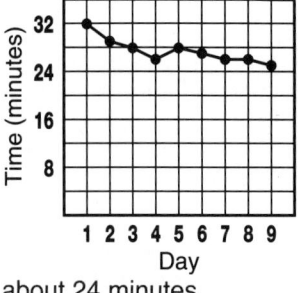
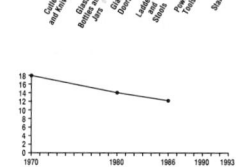
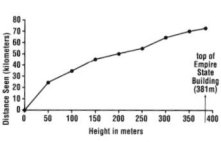
Line graphs can also be used to make decisions.

Example 2 *Problem Solving*

Business The manager of a McDonald's® restaurant wants to determine when extra help is needed. She makes a line graph of the number of orders placed each hour.

If extra help is needed whenever the number of orders in one hour exceeds 60, during which hours would the manager need extra help?

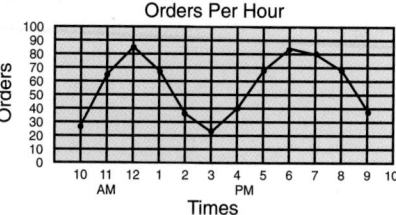

Orders Per Hour

The line graph goes above 60 between 11:00 A.M. and 2:00 P.M. and between 5:00 P.M. and 9:00 P.M. These are the times when extra help would be needed.

Checking for Understanding

Communicating Mathematics

Read and study the lesson to answer each question.

1. **Tell** three ways graphs can be used to make predictions. **Answers will vary.**

2. **Draw** a bar graph of the responses of the 35–49 age group in the Disney World example on page 113. **See Solutions Manual.**

Guided Practice

3. On the day before class elections, 100 students were asked who they would choose for class president. The graph at the right shows the results. Who do you think will win? **Ana**

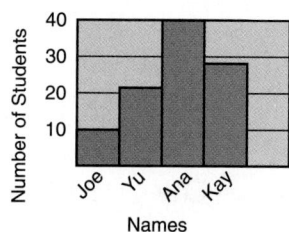

Names

4. The line graph at the right shows the number of TV stations an average U.S. household receives. How many TV stations per household would you predict in 1992? **about 30**

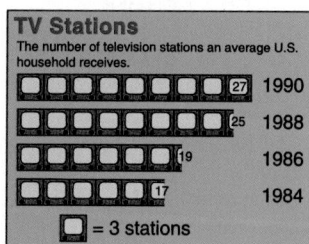

114 **Chapter 3** Statistics and Data Analysis

OPTIONS

Multicultural Education

Since Jesse Owens won the 100-meter dash in the 1936 Olympics, African-Americans have dominated this event. Have students use data from an almanac to make a line graph showing winning times in this event, from Owen's time of 10.3 seconds through Carl Lewis's 1988 winning time of 9.92 seconds. Have them use their graphs to predict the winning time 20 years from now.

Exercises

5. A shoe store needs to know how many shoes of each color to order. The graph at the right shows how many of each color were sold last month. Based on the graph, for which color should they order the most?
black

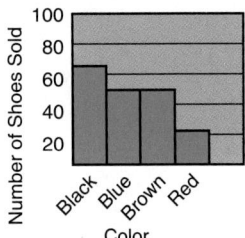

6. George has been practicing basketball free throws. What do you predict his percent will be on day 14? **about 60%**

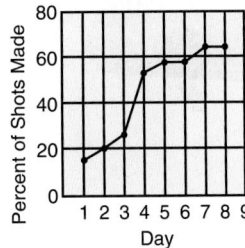

Mixed Review

7. Order 25.9, 21.6, 23, 30.2, and 27.4 from least to greatest. *(Lesson 2-1)*
21.6, 23, 25.9, 27.4, 30.2

8.
```
6 | 0
7 | 256
8 | 1368
9 | 14
6 | 0 means 60.
```

8. **Final Exams** An American History class gets the following grades on their final exam: 83, 76, 91, 88, 72, 60, 75, 86, 94, 81. Construct a stem-and-leaf plot for this set of data. *(Lesson 3-6)*

Problem Solving and Applications

9. **Sports** The graph at the right shows the attendance at professional baseball games from 1977 to 1990.

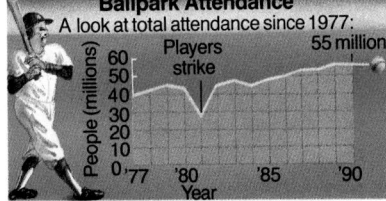

a. Based on the graph, what do you predict the attendance to be in 1995?

9.a. **About 60 million**

b. What other factors, besides the graph, would you want to take into consideration when making your prediction? **Sample answer: popularity of baseball compared to other sports**

10. **Critical Thinking** If you were the restaurant manager in Example 2, would you use the graph shown to predict the extra help needed on a holiday? Why or why not? **no; the graph doesn't say anything about holidays**

11. **Journal Entry** Collect at least three graphs from magazines and newspapers from which you could make a prediction. Include these in your journal. Write a statement about your predictions for each graph. **Answers will vary.**

Lesson 3-7 Making Predictions **115**

Extending the Lesson

Business Connections Have students work with partners. Each pair of students should choose a local store and draw a bar graph or line graph to show its customer traffic either by the hour or within time periods. They should formulate problems that can be solved by making predictions. Students should use reasonable data, or even ask the store for actual information.

Cooperative Learning Activity

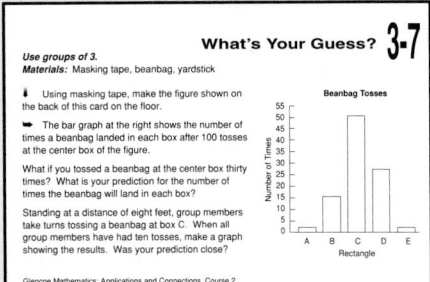

Checking for Understanding

Exercises 1-2 are designed to help you assess students' understanding through reading, writing, speaking, and modeling. You should work through these exercises with your students and then monitor their work on Guided Practice Exercises 3-4.

Close

Have students explain how a librarian can use a graph to predict how many books will be taken out on a Friday. **by using a bar graph showing books taken out on past Fridays**

3 PRACTICE/APPLY

Assignment Guide
Maximum: 5-11
Minimum: 5-10

For **Extra Practice,** see p. 578.

Alternate Assessment

Writing Have students explain how they could use a graph to predict the time the sun will rise and set one month from today.

Enrichment Masters, p. 27

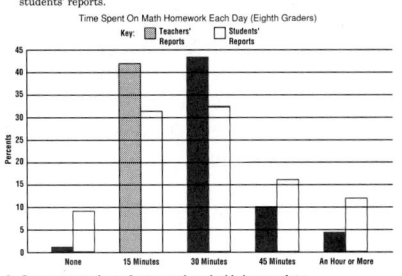

115

NCTM Standards: 1–5, 7, 10

Lesson Resources
- Study Guide Master 3-8
- Practice Master 3-8
- Enrichment Master 3-8
- Evaluation Master, Quiz B, p. 25
- Group Activity Card 3-8

 Transparency 3-8 contains the 5-Minute Check and a teaching aid for this lesson.

⏱ 5-Minute Check
(Over Lesson 3-7)

1. The graph shows how many of each size were sold at a clothing store last week. Based on the graph, which size should the store order the least of? size XL

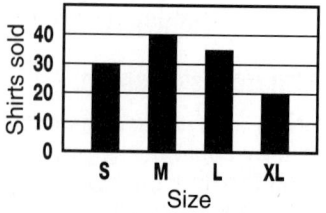

2. Lucinda has been doing sit-ups. How many do you predict she will do on day 10? about 40

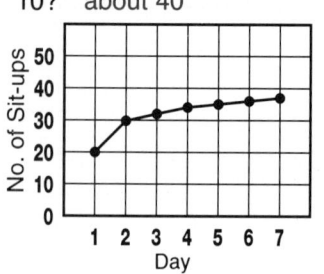

1 FOCUS

Motivating the Lesson

Situational Problem Ask students what may be misleading about the following advertisement. *90% of all dentists agree—Sparkle works best!*

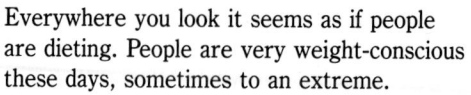

3-8 Misleading Statistics

Objective
Recognize when statistics and graphs are misleading.

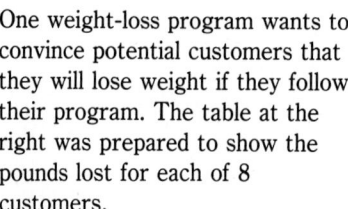

Everywhere you look it seems as if people are dieting. People are very weight-conscious these days, sometimes to an extreme.

As a result of this increasing weight-consciousness, weight-loss programs have become big business.

One weight-loss program wants to convince potential customers that they will lose weight if they follow their program. The table at the right was prepared to show the pounds lost for each of 8 customers.

Customer	Number of Pounds Lost
Bob	25
Karen	34
Patty	29
Rosa	21
Mike	35
Betty	28
Chun	32
Linda	24

Did the company only give the weight lost by the 8 people who lost the most weight? How long did it take these people to lose the weight? How much did they weigh when they started the program? What else might be *misleading* about this data?

When you are given insufficient background information or an incomplete picture of the data, the data may be misleading.

Example 1 *Problem Solving*

Business Both line graphs below show monthly CD (compact discs) sales for one year at Barnie's Music Barn. Which graph could be misleading?

LOOK BACK
You can review scales on page 96.

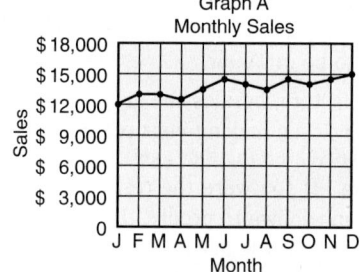

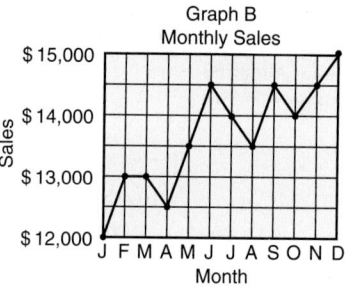

Both graphs show the same data, but they look very different. Graph B could be misleading because the vertical scale on the graph does not begin with zero.

OPTIONS

Team Teaching

Inform the other teachers on your team that your classes are studying misleading statistics. Suggestions for curriculum integration are:

Social Studies: population or business trends

Language Arts: writing advertisements

Health: interpreting weight-loss program results

Additional Answer

1. Sample answers: Outlier may distort the data; Data may be inaccurate; Data may be incomplete.

Example 2 *Problem Solving*

Human Resources A company is interviewing people for a job opening. Mr. Eckert, a prospective employee, is told that the mean annual salary is $47,050. Study the table of salaries below. Do you think Mr. Eckert would make $47,050 as a beginning employee?

Position	Number of Employees	Annual Salary
President	1	$400,000
Vice President	2	$100,000
Sales Person	10	$ 25,000
Clerical Person	7	$ 13,000

Mr. Eckert would probably not make $47,050. The very high salaries of the president and vice presidents make this statistic misleading.

 **LOOKBACK**

You can review outliers on page 101.

Whenever there are outliers in the data, the mean is not a good way to describe the data. Which number would be a better way to describe the salaries above? **median**

Checking for Understanding

Communicating Mathematics

Read and study the lesson to answer each question.

1. **Tell**, in your own words, three ways data can be misleading. **See margin.**

2. **Tell** which graph in Example 1 the manager of Barnie's Music Barn might prefer to use to show the owner of the store that sales are increasing? **B, although it does not give an accurate picture of what is going on.**

Guided Practice

3. A; it makes the scores look higher.

Rosio wants to show her parents that her math test scores have really improved.

3. Which graph below would she probably show them? Why?

4. How is the graph at the left misleading? **It starts at 80 instead of 0.**

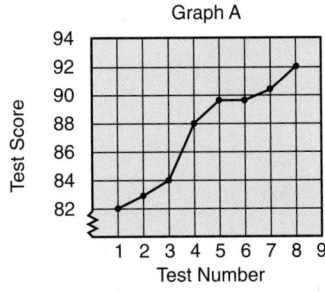

Graph A

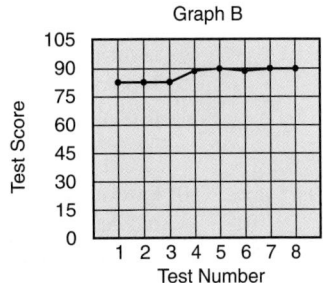

Graph B

---

2 TEACH

Using Critical Thinking Bring in and display an ad on a self-help program, for example, on weight loss. Have students suggest ways in which the ad may be misleading. Guide students to see whether enough information is given and whether there are any hidden facts.

More Examples

For Example 1

Both line graphs show boat sales at Milly's Marina in thousands of dollars. Which graph could be misleading?

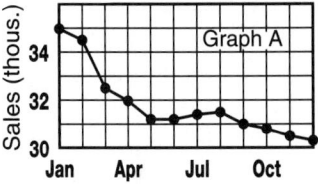

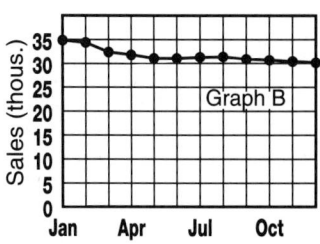

either; Accept answers students can justify.

For Example 2

Two hundred students at King School have raised money for the library.

Money Raised	Number of Students
$50	12
$40	18
$30	22
$20	28
$10	33
$5	87

For this set of data, which statistic is misleading, the mode, median, or mean? Why? mean; The data are skewed by the outliers. Most students raised $5.

Checking for Understanding

Exercises 1-2 are designed to help you assess students' understanding through reading, writing, speaking, and modeling. You should work through these exercises with your students and then monitor their work on Guided Practice Exercises 3-5.

3 PRACTICE/APPLY

Assignment Guide

Maximum: 6–13
Minimum: 6–12

Alternate Assessment

Writing Have students draw a misleading graph or write a misleading advertisement. Have them exchange ads and graphs, examine the one they receive, and explain why it is misleading.

Practice Masters, p. 28

Name _____ Date _____

Practice Worksheet 3-8

Misleading Statistics

1. A company that sells computer diskettes wants to encourage customers to buy more by showing how much the price drops as you buy more diskettes.
   a. Which graph below would they print in their catalog? **Graph B**
   b. How is the graph at the right misleading? **The vertical scale does not begin with zero.**

2. Tina weighs herself every month. Her weights for the last year, in order, are 75, 75, 77, 76, 77, 78, 80, 80, 81, 82, 83, 83.
   a. Draw two line graphs of this data, one with a vertical scale of 0 to 100 and the other with a vertical scale of 75 to 83.
   b. What conclusion might you make from the first graph? **Tina is gaining a little bit of weight.**
   c. What conclusions might you make from the second graph? **Tina is gaining a lot of weight.**

3. The incomes of the families in a small mill town are listed in the chart at the right.
   a. Find the mode, median, and mean of the data. **mode: $0 median: $20,000 mean: $33,987**
   b. Which number is misleading? **mean**
   c. Which would most accurately describe the data? **median**

Income (to nearest $10,000)	Number of Families
$2,000,000	1
$ 200,000	2
$ 40,000	30
$ 30,000	30
$ 20,000	20
$ 10,000	30
$ 0	40

4. A television commercial says *9 out of 10 doctors recommend Blyer's Aspirin.* Do you think this survey is reliable? Why or why not? **The survey is not reliable because it says nothing about which doctors were surveyed or exactly what questions they were asked.**

T 28
Glencoe Division, Macmillan/McGraw-Hill

118

---

5. A school newspaper reporter randomly stops 50 students leaving gym class and asks them if they thought there was enough time between classes. Forty-five students said that there was not enough time. Do you think this survey reflects the opinions of all students? Why or why not? **No; this is not a representative group.**

Exercises

Independent Practice

6. a. See margin.

6. b. All his scores are very good.

6. Tei's history test scores, in order, are 89, 87, 90, 92, 95, 97, 99, and 100.
   a. Draw two line graphs of this data, one with a vertical scale of 0 to 100 and the other with a vertical scale of 80 to 100.
   b. What conclusion might you make from the first graph?
   c. What conclusion might you make from the second graph? **His scores aren't all good.**

7. One hundred teenagers were asked how much spending money they get from their parents each week.

Amount of Money	Number of Teenagers
$25	8
$20	16
$15	10
$10	21
$ 5	45

   a. Find the mode, median, and mean of the data. **$5, $10, $11.05**
   b. Which number is misleading? **mean**
   c. Which would most accurately describe the data? **median**

Mixed Review

8. Evaluate 5^4. *(Lesson 1-9)* **625**

9. The bar graph shows responses to the question, "What is your favorite type of music?" Of which type of music will a music store probably sell the most? *(Lesson 3-8)* **rock**

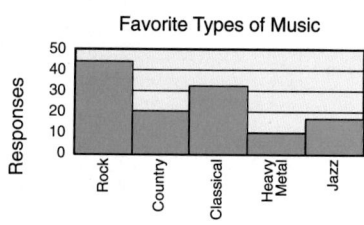

Favorite Types of Music

Problem Solving and Applications

10. **Entertainment** A movie advertisement says "Thousands of people rate this movie as the BEST MOVIE OF THE YEAR." What kind of information would you want to know before believing that this movie really is the best one of the year? **Sample answer: how many people they questioned**

OPTIONS

Gifted and Talented Needs

Write the following table on the chalkboard.

Store	Pet-Care Videos Sold
Pat's Pets	132
Pilar's Pets	223
Pete's Pets	288
Penny's Pets	94
Pearl's Pets	305

Have students use the information in the table to make two graphs—one in which they show sales data accurately, and one as if they work for Pearl and want to show that she outsells the others by a huge margin.

For answers to Exercises 11a–d, see Solutions Manual.

11. **Advertising** Super Sandwiches, a new fast-food restaurant, wants to promote its products. Super Burgers have 540 calories and 25 grams of fat. Super Dogs have 235 calories and 43 grams of fat.

Select data from the chart at the right to compare with the Super Burgers and Super Dogs. Draw bar graphs that will promote Super Burgers and Super Dogs as healthier food in each of the following areas.

Item	Calories	Fat (gm)
HAMBURGERS		
Burger King Whopper	660	41
Jack-in-the-Box Jumbo Jack	538	28
McDonald's Big Mac	591	33
Wendy's Old Fashioned	413	22
SANDWICHES		
Roy Rogers Roast Beef	356	12
Burger King Chopped-Beef Steak	445	13
Hardee's Roast Beef	251	17
Arby's Roast Beef	370	15

a. Super Burgers: calories
b. Super Burgers: fat
c. Super Dogs: calories
d. Super Dogs: fat

12. No, it doesn't matter if the number is real low or just a little low: 0, 10, 11, 12, 13 same as 9, 10, 11, 12, 13.

12. **Critical Thinking** Do outliers affect the *median* of a set of data? Give several examples to support your answer.

13. **Journal Entry** Find at least four newspaper or magazine ads. Describe how each one might be misleading. **See students' work.**

Save Planet Earth

Garbage in Schools The amount of trash created in schools has grown steadily over the last 10 years as cafeterias have switched to paper and throwaway plastic instead of conventional tableware, glass, or reusable plastic. In schools around the country, napkins, plates, cups, forks, knives, and spoons are tossed into the garbage thousands of times per day.

How You Can Help

- Take lunch to school in reusable containers instead of bags, plastic wrap, and waxed paper.
- Work with your student council or parent-teacher organization to reduce the amount of garbage your school produces.

  a. Stop using throwaway dishes for regular school meals.
  b. Put uneaten food in a separate garbage can. The waste can be composted and used as fertilizer.

Lesson 3-8 Misleading Statistics **119**

Additional Answer

6. a.

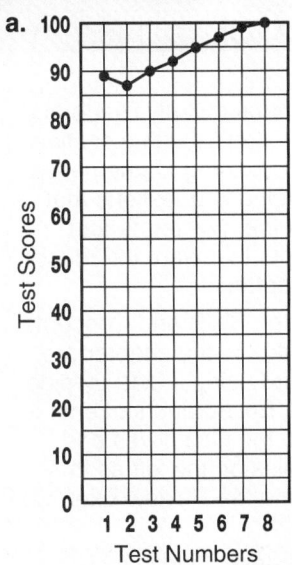

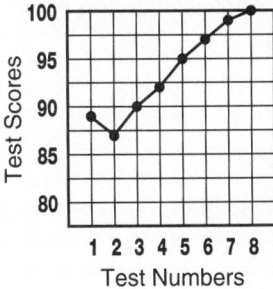

Enrichment Masters, p. 28

Name _____ Date _____

Enrichment Worksheet 3-8

Misleading Dissections

Dissection puzzles involve cutting one figure into parts so that the parts can be rearranged to form a second figure.

1. Copy the Greek cross and cut it into 5 pieces as shown. Then rearrange the pieces to form a square.

2. Rearrange the 4 pieces shown to form a square. Does this square have the same area as the one in Exercise 1? **yes**

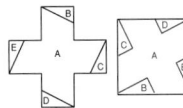 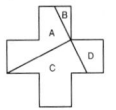

Some dissection puzzles involve vanishing squares. Here are two puzzles of this type. Your job is to explain what happens to the "disappearing" square. In Exercises 3 and 4, use the figure below.

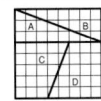

3. The rectangle below has an area of 65 square units, but the area of the square is only 64 square units.

The pieces actually overlap along the diagonal lines.

4. The square has area 64 square units, but the area of the new figure is only 63 square units.

There is a slight overlap along the diagonal.

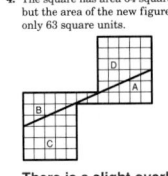

T28
Glencoe Division, Macmillan/McGraw-Hill

Extending the Lesson

Save Planet Earth You may wish to turn a class project into a demonstration of the amount of garbage your school produces and its effect on the landfill space in your community.

Cooperative Learning Activity

We Just Disagree 3-8

Use groups of 2.
Materials: Number cubes

◆ Decide which partner's number cube stands for a digit in tens place and which stands for a digit in ones place. Toss both number cubes and write the resulting two-digit number. Find a total of 5 two-digit numbers in this way.

☛ The partner with the tens number cube draws a line graph in which the variation in the numbers from toss to toss seems very slight. The partner with the ones number cube draws a line graph in which there appears to be a great variation in the numbers from toss to toss.

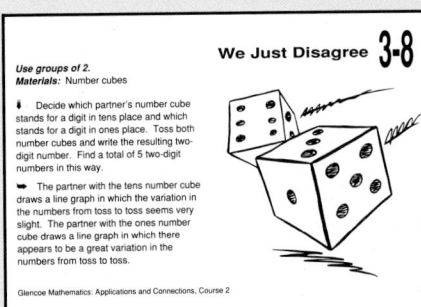

Glencoe Mathematics: Applications and Connections, Course 2

The Chapter Study Guide and Review begins with a section on Communicating Mathematics. This includes questions that review the new terms and concepts that were introduced in the chapter.

Then, the Skills and Concepts presented in the chapter are reviewed using a side-by-side format. Encourage students to refer to the Objectives and Examples on the left as they complete the Review Exercises on the right.

The Chapter Study Guide and Review ends with problems that review Applications and Problem Solving.

Study Guide and Review

Chapter

3 Study Guide and Review

Communicating Mathematics

State whether each sentence is *true* or *false*. If false, replace the underlined word to make the sentence true.

1. The <u>scale</u> of a set of data is the difference between the greatest number and the least number. **false; range**

2. It is possible to have more than one choice of <u>interval</u> for a set of data. **true**

3. An <u>outlier</u> is a number that differs greatly from the rest of the data. **true**

4. The <u>median</u> of a set of data is the number or item that appears most often. **false; mode**

5. In a stem-and-leaf plot, the units digits form the <u>stems</u>. **false; leaves**

6. In your own words, describe a situation for which the mean would not be the best way to describe the average of a set of data. **When there are outliers.**

Self Assessment

Objectives and Examples	Review Exercises
Upon completing this chapter, you should be able to:	*Use these exercises to review and prepare for the chapter test.*

• choose appropriate scales and intervals for graphs *(Lesson 3-3)*

Find the range and appropriate scale and interval for the data 11, 24, 2, and 26. Draw a number line.

range = 26 − 2 = 24
scale = 0 to 30, interval of 5

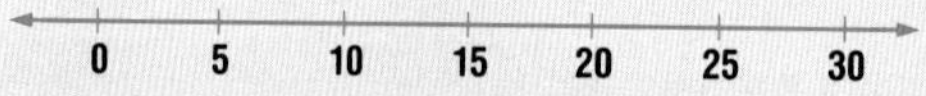

Find the range for each set of data. Choose an appropriate scale and interval. Then draw a number line to show the scale and intervals.

7. 3, 12, 1, 43, 25, 16
8. 75, 150, 100, 400, 550
9. 2.3, 11.9, 7.6, 1.3, 4.8
10. 35,000, 24,500, 53,000, 18,500
For answers to Exercises 7-10, see Solutions Manual.

• construct line plots *(Lesson 3-4)*

Make a line plot and circle any outliers for the data 5, 7, 3, 8, 3, 2, 8, 4, 15.

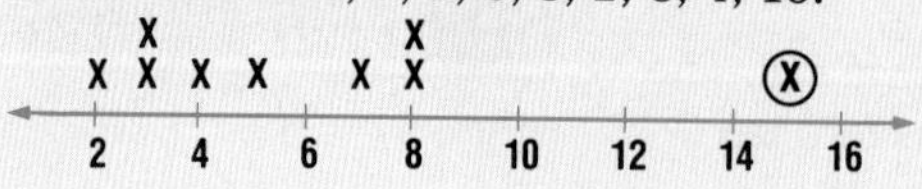

Make a line plot for each set of data. Circle any outliers.

11. 10, 12, 10, 8, 13, 10, 8, 22
12. 7.9, 8.3, 10.2, 8.7, 8.3, 3.8
13. 1,550, 1,700, 1,625, 1,590, 1,655, 1,780, 1,760, 1,575
For answers to Exercises 11-13, see Solutions Manual.

Objectives and Examples	Review Exercises

Objectives and Examples

- find the mean, median, and mode for a set of data *(Lesson 3-5)*

21, 18, 19, 20, 23, 19, 20, 19

$$mean = \frac{21+18+19+20+23+19+20+19}{8}$$

$$= 19.875$$

median = 19.5   mode = 19

Review Exercises

Find the mode(s), median, and mean for each set of data.

14. 2, 3, 4, 3, 4, 3, 8, 7, 2 3, 3, 4
15. 24, 26, 18, 23, 31 none, 24, 24.4
16. 89, 76, 93, 100, 72, 86, 74 none, 86, 84.3
17. 54,000, 49,000, 112,000, 89,000, 76,000, 65,000 none; 70,500; 74,166.7

- construct stem-and-leaf plots *(Lesson 3-6)*

49, 58, 42, 63, 55, 42, 59, 44

```
4 | 2249
5 | 589      4 | 2 means 42.
6 | 3
```

Make a stem-and-leaf plot for each set of data.

18. 75, 61, 83, 99, 78, 85, 87, 92, 77, 78, 60, 53, 87, 89, 91, 90
19. $0.29, $0.54, $0.31, $0.26, $0.38, $0.46, $0.23, $0.21, $0.32, $0.37
For answers to Exercises 18-19, see Solutions Manual.

- make predictions from graphs *(Lesson 3-7)*

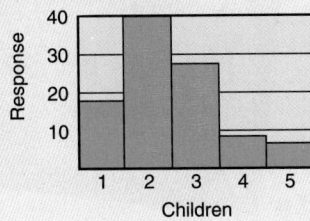

The most common response to the question "How many children are in your family?" will be 2.

Predict the answer in the following situation.

20. Isabel displayed her salary for the last five years in the line graph below. Predict her salary after three more years. **between $35,000 and $40,000**

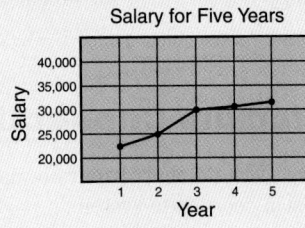

- recognize when statistics and graphs are misleading *(Lesson 3-6)*

When you are given insufficient background information or an incomplete picture of the data, the data may be misleading.

Identify the part of the following situation which could be considered misleading.

21. The mean score on a math exam is 81.6. The set of test scores is 89, 92, 87, 86, 95, 93, 29. **The 29 brought the mean down; the other six scores were well above 81.6.**

Study Guide and Review

You may wish to use a Chapter Test from the Evaluation Masters booklet as an additional chapter review. The two free-response forms are shown below. One of the two multiple-choice forms is shown on the next page.

22. Use the graph on page 107. The United States Bureau of the Census projects that the median age of the population will be 41.8 years in the year 2030. How much higher is that than in 1980? *(Lesson 3-1)* **11.8 years**

23. Use the graph on page 107. Was the median age of the U.S. population greater or less than 25 in 1940? *(Lesson 3-1)* **less than**

24. Use the frequency table on page 94. What was the most common height of junior high students? *(Lesson 3-2)* **155 cm**

25. **After-School Jobs** Eight students were asked their hourly wage at their after-school jobs. The following data resulted. $3.65, $4.15, $3.90, $4.25, $3.90, $4.00, $4.50, $3.80 Find the mode, median, and the mean. *(Lesson 3-5)* **$3.90, $3.95, $4.02**

26. **Television** A survey of the number of minutes a junior high student watches TV on a school day produced the following data.

95, 85, 69, 75, 90, 45, 92, 65, 50, 40, 75

Make a stem-and-leaf plot for the data. *(Lesson 3-6)* **4 | 5 means 45 minutes.**

4	05
5	0
6	59
7	55
8	5
9	025

Curriculum Connection Projects

- **History** Write a short paper on mathematician René Descartes and the Cartesian coordinate system.

- **Current Events** Read and interpret today's graph from the front page of the *USA Today* newspaper.

Read More About It

Martin, Susan. *I Sailed With Columbus.*
Belton, John and Cramblit, Joella. *Dice Games.*
Kohn, Bernice. *Secret Codes and Ciphers.*

122 **Chapter 3** Study Guide and Review

Evaluation Masters, pp. 23–24

Name _____ Date _____

Form 2A _____ *Chapter 3 Test*

Use the frequency table for Exercises 1-2.

Grade 7 Students	
Weight (kg)	Tally
40	III
45	IIII I
50	IIII IIII
55	III
60	III
65	I

1. How many students were 50 kilograms or more? **1. 17**
2. What is true about the mean, median, and mode? **2. They are equal.**

Find the range for each set of data.

3. 16, 8, 23, 19, 11, 20, 5, 29, 33 **3. 28**
4. 8.6, 9.1, 10.0, 4.5, 7.9, 11.7, 2.0 **4. 9.7**
5. Rita's grades on five Spanish tests were 96, 84, 79, 81, and 70. Find an appropriate scale and interval. Draw a number line to show them. **5.** Sample answer: 70 80 90 100

Make a line plot for each set of data. Circle any outliers.

6. 45, 70, 62, 65, 66, 62 **6.**
7. 3, 6, 7, 6, 4, 5, 6, 4 **7.**

Find the mode(s), median, and mean for each set of data.

8. 6, 11, 40, 11, 5, 2, 9, 12, 12 **8. 11, 12; 11; 12**
9. 60, 68, 64, 60, 63, 60, 67, 73, 58, 60, 49 **9. 60; 60; 62**
10. 1.4, 1.2, 1.0, 1.0, 1.6, 0.8, 1.6, 1.2, 1.0 **10. 1.0; 1.2; 1.2**
11. Make a stem-and-leaf plot for the set of data: 96, 109, 77, 76, 85, 83, 93, 106 **11.**

Larry Bird scored 27, 33, 18, 32, 35, 22, 31, 39, 28, and 26 points in ten games.

12. Make a stem-and-leaf plot of these data. **12.**
13. About how many points might you expect Larry Bird to score in a game? **13.** Sample answer: Between 25 and 35

The graph at the right shows the men's shirt sales for the month of March.

14. Which were the two most popular neck sizes? **14. 15, 15½**
15. Which number would be the most useful in deciding which sizes to order when the new styles come out: mean, median, or mode? **15. mode**

BONUS In your own words, describe the mean. Then explain how it is different from the median.

Sample answer: The mean is the sum of the numbers divided by the number of numbers. It differs from the median in that it does not have to be a member of the set of numbers.

23
Glencoe Division, Macmillan/McGraw-Hill

Name _____ Date _____

Form 2B _____ *Chapter 3 Test*

Scores on a ten-question quiz are shown at the right.

Reading Quiz	
Score	Tally
2	II
3	IIII
4	I
5	IIII
6	II
7	IIII II
8	III
9	III
10	I

1. How many students scored better than 6? **1. 14**
2. How many students scored below the mode and the median? **2. 13**

Find the range for each set of data.

3. 105, 116, 125, 131, 79, 79, 106, 116 **3. 52**
4. 2.4, 2.3, 2.9, 2.4, 2.3, 3.1, 2.4, 2.7 **4. 0.8**
5. Sonja's golf scores for five rounds were 88, 83, 87, 80, and 90. Find an appropriate scale and interval. Draw a number line to show them. **5.**

Make a line plot for each set of data. Circle any outliers.

6. 0, 2, 1, 0, 2, 3, 2, 1, 3, 4, 3, 4, 7 **6.**
7. 15, 20, 20, 17, 17, 19, 18, 19, 18, 19, 18, 17 **7.**

Find the mode(s), median, and mean for each set of data.

8. 23, 22, 22, 24, 23, 19, 25, 21, 20 **8. 22, 23; 22; 22.1**
9. 7.8, 9.3, 8.8, 8.4, 9.0, 6.7, 8.2, 5.6, 8.6 **9. none; 8.4; 8.0**
10. 414, 387, 455, 508, 432, 545, 387, 431, 527 **10. 387; 432; 454**

Make a stem-and-leaf plot for each set of data in Exercises 11 and 12.

11. 30, 41, 27, 18, 22, 19, 37, 22, 26 **11.**
12. 5, 12, 17, 20, 26, 29, 35, 35, 3, 12, 17, 20, 26, 29, 35 **12.**
13. At Prep Textiles, 6 employees earn $20,000, 3 earn $32,000, and 2 earn $62,500. List the salaries in a frequency table.

Salary	Frequency
$20,000	6
$32,000	3
$62,500	2

13.

14. Find the mean, median, and mode of the salaries. **14. $31,000; $20,000; $20,000**
15. Which number(s) would you use to best describe the salaries: mean, median, or mode? Explain. **15.** The median or mode because the two $62,500 salaries are twice as large as the mean.

BONUS Make up a set of data with at least 9 items that have the same number for the mean, median, and mode.

Sample: 1, 2, 3, 4, 4, 4, 5, 6, 7

24
Glencoe Division, Macmillan/McGraw-Hill

Study Guide and Review

3 Test

The median age will be about 60.

1. Use the graph on page 107. Based on the data presented in the line graph, predict what the graph will show by the year 3000.

2. Use the frequency table on page 94. How many more students were taller than 155 centimeters? **10 students**

For answers to Exercises 3-8, see Solutions Manual.
Find the range for each set of data. Choose an appropriate scale and interval. Then draw a number line to show the scale and intervals.

3. 2, 7, 26, 19   4. 8.9, 6.3, 10.3

5. Ann's grades on six French tests are 95, 76, 82, 90, 71, and 80. Find an appropriate scale and interval. Draw a number line to show them.

Make a line plot for each set of data. Circle any outliers.

6. 72, 76, 75, 72, 80, 55   7. 3.2, 7.2, 3.7, 3.3

8. **Family Tree** Mrs. Hanna has 5 children whose ages are 32, 20, 19, 17, and 22. Make a line plot and make a conclusion about the differences in ages.

Find the mode(s), median, and mean for each set of data.

9. 4, 6, 11, 7, 4, 11, 4
4, 6, 6.7

10. 12.4, 17.9, 16.5, 10.2
none, 14.45, 14.25

Make a stem-and-leaf plot for each set of data.

11. 37, 59, 26, 42, 57, 53, 31, 58 **See Solutions Manual.**

12. $0.46, $0.59, $0.42, $0.69, $0.55, $0.48, $0.66, $0.43 **See Solutions Manual.**

13. **Employment** The line graph at the right shows the percent of women holding jobs outside the home from 1975–1990. In which year were the most number of women working outside the home? **1990**

Women in Jobs

14. Using the graph at the right, predict the percent of women who will hold jobs outside the home in the year 2000. **45-50%**

15. The prices of 50 pairs of shoes at a local shoe store are recorded in the table at the right.
a. Find the mode, median, and mean. **$20, $30, $27.20**
b. Which average would the manager prefer to quote to a cost-conscious customer? **mode**

Price	Pairs
$10	6
$20	17
$30	15
$40	9
$50	3

Bonus What effect does an outlier have on the range of a set of data?
It makes the range greater.

This page may be used as a chapter test or another chapter review.

Evaluation Masters, pp. 19–20

Form 1A — *Chapter 3 Test*

Ricardo made a circle graph to show how he spent his time.

1. What fraction of the day is spent sleeping? A. 1/12 B. 1/4 C. 1/3 D. 1/8 — **C**
2. How much more time is spent in school than in sports? A. 1 hour B. 6 hours C. 2 hours D. 4 hours — **D**
3. What fraction of the day is spent in school or sleeping? A. 1/12 B. 1/2 C. 1/2 D. 2/8 — **A**

The scores for a 30-point test are shown at the right. Make a frequency table.
25 17 25 17 28 / 25 25 28 25 17 / 21 24 30 21 30 / 26 23 28 21 20 / 19 25 19 24 21

4. What is the frequency of the score that appeared the most often? A. 4 B. 6 C. 5 D. 7 — **B**
5. If 19 is the lowest passing score, how many scores are passing scores? A. 20 B. 15 C. 22 D. 19 — **C**
6. Name the scale of the number line. A. 12 B. 39 C. 27 D. 15 — **D**
7. Name the interval of the number line. A. 2 B. 3 C. 1 D. 4 — **B**
8. Find the range of 3, 4, 2, 8, 7, 5, and 6. A. 2 B. 5 C. 35 D. 6 — **D**

Use the line plot to answer Exercises 9 and 10.
9. Name the outlier in the line plot. A. 0 B. 8 C. 4 D. 2 — **A**
10. Name the cluster in the line plot. A. between 0 and 4 B. between 0 and 8 C. between 4 and 8 D. between 0 and 6 — **C**
11. Find the mode(s) of 22, 25, 27, 28, 30, 27, and 23. A. 30 B. 25 C. 23 D. 27 — **D**
12. Find the median of 15, 19, 20, 21, 22, 24, and 24. A. 21 B. 20 C. 15 D. 24 — **A**
13. Find the mean of 31, 25, 20, 18, 22, and 28. A. 22 B. 24 C. 144 D. 25 — **B**

19
Glencoe Division, Macmillan/McGraw-Hill

Chapter 3 Test, Form 1A (continued)

14. Which digit in the numbers 59, 68, 67, 65, 53, 64, 65, and 70 would not appear as a leaf when drawing a stem-and-leaf plot? A. 0 B. 9 C. 2 D. 5 — **C**

The stem-and-leaf plot at the right shows the scores on a science test.
5 | 024
6 | 133
7 | 28999
8 | 13899
9 | 447

15. Name the highest score on the test. A. 96 B. 100 C. 94 D. 97 — **D**
16. Name the score that appears the most. A. 79 B. 97 C. 89 D. 98 — **A**

On the day before class elections, 50 students were asked who they would choose for the class treasurer. The graph at the right shows the results.

17. Who do you think will win the election? A. Kit B. Al C. Mel D. Tu — **C**
18. Who is most likely to lose the election? A. Kit B. Al C. Mel D. Tu — **B**

Employee salaries at a company are shown in the frequency table at the right.

Salary	Number
$100,000	1
$75,000	2
$50,000	3
$24,000	15
$12,000	6

19. Which average best represents the data in the frequency table? A. mean B. mode or median C. median D. mode — **B**
20. What number best describes the data? A. $30,815 B. $24,000 C. $18,000 D. $21,000 — **B**

BONUS What is the best description for the average employee at ACE Electronics?

ACE Electronics	Paul Liang	Joseph Foley	Susan Keveney	Jenny Lincoln	Raman Sharma
Age	28	33	37	32	35
Salary	$13,000	$26,500	$65,000	$35,000	$48,000
Height (cm)	155	159	164	158	149
Favorite Entertainment	reading	sports	sports	theater	movies

A. 33 years; $38,000; 157 cm; theater
B. 32 years; $34,700; 159 cm; sports
C. 33 years; $35,000; 157 cm; sports
D. 34 years; $34,700; 158 cm; reading

— **C**

20
Glencoe Division, Macmillan/McGraw-Hill

Test and Review Generator software is provided in Apple, IBM, and Macintosh versions. You may use this software to create your own tests or worksheets, based on the needs of your students.

The **Performance Assessment Booklet** provides an alternate assessment for evaluating student progress. An assessment for this chapter can be found on pages 5–6.

Academic Skills Test

Chapter

3 Academic Skills Test

Directions: Choose the best answer. Write A, B, C, or D.

1. Three tablecloths are sewn together end-to-end to make one long tablecloth. The tablecloths are about 48 inches, 64 inches, and 54 inches long. What is the combined length?

   D

   A 102 in. B 112 in.
   C 118 in. D 166 in.

2. 182×6 is about

   B

   A 6,000 B 1,200
   C 1,080 D 600

3. $2,396 \div 42$ is about

   B

   A 600 B 60
   C 80   D 5

4. To mentally add 106 and 255, you can

   D

   A add 6 to each addend.
   B add 100 and 250.
   C subtract 6 from each addend.
   D add 100 and 261.

5. What is the value of $x + y + 5$ if $x = 6$ and $y = 15$?

   C

   A 21 B 25
   C 26 D none of these

6. Which is equivalent to 3^6?

   D

   A 36
   B 18
   C $6 \cdot 6 \cdot 6$
   D $3 \cdot 3 \cdot 3 \cdot 3 \cdot 3 \cdot 3$

7. What is the value of $3[2(23 - 11) - (3 + 9)]$?

   B

   A 12 B 36
   C 60 D 133

8. Which is a true statement?

   A

   A $7.2 > 0.72$
   B $3.91 < 3.9$
   C $0.489 > 4.81$
   D $0.35 < 0.202$

9. Which is correct for rounding to the nearest tenth?

   B

   A 0.56 rounds to 0.5
   B 0.95 rounds to 1.0
   C 1.205 rounds to 1.3
   D 0.4173 rounds to 0.42

10. $3.1 \times 2.5 =$

    B

    A 77.5 B 7.75
    C 7.5   D 0.75

11. Earth is about 93,000,000 miles from the sun. How is this written in scientific notation?

    B

    A 93×10^6
    B 9.3×10^7
    C 9.3×10^8
    D 0.93×10^8

12. Tomato juice is priced at three cans for $2.39. To the nearest cent, what is the cost of one can?

    C

    A $0.08 B $0.79
    C $0.80 D $1.20

13. Suppose you need 0.65 liters of water
B   for a science experiment but the
    container is measured in milliliters.
    How much water do you need?

    A 6,500 milliliters
    B 650 milliliters
    C 65 milliliters
    D 0.00065 milliliters

14.   Average Height for Adolescents

A
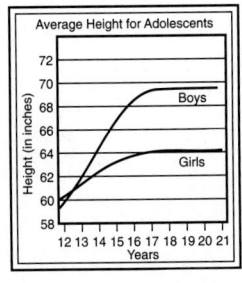

    At age 16, about how much taller is
    the average boy than the average
    girl?

    A 4 in.   B 6 in.
    C 63.5 in.   D 67.5 in.

15. About what is the range of boys'
B   heights shown in the graph in
    question 14?

    A 9 years   B 10 in.
    C 21 years   D 69.5 in.

16. The line plot shows how far in
C   kilometers some students live from
    school. How many students are
    represented in the plot?

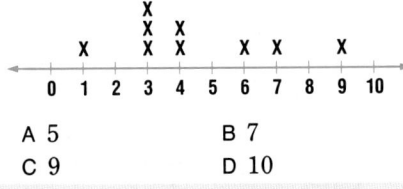

    A 5   B 7
    C 9   D 10

Test-Taking Tip

Most standardized tests have a time
limit, so you must budget your time
carefully. Some questions will be much
easier than others. If you cannot
answer a question within a few minutes, go on to the next one. If there is
still time left when you get to the end
of the test, go back to the questions
that you skipped.

Do not wait until the night before taking a test to review. Allow yourself
plenty of time to review the basic skills
and formulas which are tested.

17. Use the data in question 16. What is
B   the median distance?

    A about 3 km   B about 4 km
    C about 5 km   D about 9 km

18. In a stem-and-leaf plot of the data
C   below, what numbers would be used
    for the stems?

    Height in Inches

52	75	49	51	57	66	69
58	59	62	61	61	73	68
76	74	78	49			

    A 0–9   B 1–9
    C 4–7   D none of these

19. Use the graph in question 14. About
D   how much can a 13-year-old girl expect
    to grow in the next two years?

    A 63 in   B 61.5 in.
    C 4 in.   D 1.5 in.

20. A business had weekly profits of $5,000,
C $3,000, $2,000, $2,500, and $5,000.
    Which "average" might be misleading?

    A mean   B median
    C mode   D none of these

Chapter 3 Academic Skills Test   **125**

4 Patterns and Number Sense

Previewing the Chapter

This chapter explores several aspects of number theory including divisibility, prime and composite numbers, and factorization. Also studied are geometric and arithmetic sequences, factors and multiples, fractions, relationships between fractions and decimals, and probability of simple events. *Make a list* is the **problem-solving strategy** lesson. It explores the Fibonacci sequence of numbers.

Lesson	Lesson Objectives	NCTM Standards	State/Local Objectives
4-1A	Discover the factors of the whole numbers 1–30.	1–6	
4-1	Use divisibility rules.	1–8	
4-2	Find the prime factorization of a composite number.	1–9	
4-3	Recognize and extend sequences.	1–8	
4-3B	Recognize the amount of change in arithmetic and geometric sequences.	1–5, 7, 8	
4-4	Solve problems by making an organized list.	1–8, 13	
4-5	Find the greatest common factor of two or more numbers.	1–7	
Decision Making	Sponsor a retirement center.	1–4, 7	
4-6	Express fractions in simplest form.	1–7	
4-7	Express terminating decimals or fractions and express fractions as decimals.	1–7	
4-8	Find the probability of a simple event.	1–5, 7, 11	
4-9	Find the least common multiple of two or more numbers.	1–7	
4-10	Compare and order fractions by first writing them as equivalent fractions with a common denominator.	1–7, 10	

Organizing the Chapter

A complete, 1-page lesson plan is provided for each lesson in the Lesson Plans Masters Booklet.

LESSON PLANNING GUIDE

Lesson	Materials/ Manipulatives	Extra Practice (Student Edition)	Blackline Masters Booklets: Study Guide	Practice	Enrichment	Evaluation	Technology	Lab Manual	Multicultural Activities	Application and Interdisciplinary Activities	Transparencies	Group Activity Cards
4-1A	30 pieces of tagboard numbered individually from 1 to 30							p. 45				
4-1	calculator	p. 579	p. 29	p. 29	p. 29						4-1	4-1
4-2	calculator	p. 579	p. 30	p. 30	p. 30						4-2	4-2
4-3		p. 579	p. 31	p. 31	p. 31				p. 4	p. 4	4-3	4-3
4-3B	calculator graph paper notebook paper							p. 46				
4-4	calculator		p. 32	p. 32	p. 32						4-4	4-4
4-5	4 colored pencils	p. 580	p. 33	p. 33	p. 33	Quiz A, p. 34					4-5	4-5
4-6		p. 580	p. 34	p. 34	p. 34		p. 18				4-6	4-6
4-7	calculator	p. 580	p. 35	p. 35	p. 35		p. 4	p. 47			4-7	4-7
4-8	2 number cubes	p. 581	p. 36	p. 36	p. 36					p. 18	4-8	4-8
4-9	calculator	p. 581	p. 37	p. 37	p. 37						4-9	4-9
4-10		p. 581	p. 38	p. 38	p. 38	Quiz B, p. 34					4-10	4-10
Study Guide and Review	telephone book, auto repair manual		Multiple Choice Test, Forms 1A and 1B, pp. 28-31 Free Response Test, Forms 2A and 2B, pp. 32-33 Cumulative Review, p. 35 (free response) Cumulative Test, p. 36 (multiple choice)									
Test												

Pacing Guide: Option I (Chapters 1–12) - 16 days; Option II (Chapters 1–13) - 14 days; Option III (Chapters 1–14) - 14 days
You may wish to refer to the complete **Course Planning Guides** on page T25.

OTHER CHAPTER RESOURCES

Student Edition
Chapter Opener, pp. 126–127
Mid-Chapter Review, p. 153
Save Planet Earth, p. 160
Portfolio Suggestion, p. 163

Manipulatives
Overhead Manipulative Resources
Middle School Mathematics Manipulative Kit

Software/Technology
Interactive Mathematics Tools (Macintosh)
Test and Review Generator (IBM, Apple, Macintosh)
Teacher's Guide for Software Resources

Other Supplements
Transparency 4-0
Performance Assessment, pp. 7–8
Glencoe Mathematics Professional Series
Lesson Plans, pp. 36–47

INTERDISCIPLINARY BULLETIN BOARD

Journalism Connection

Objective   Determine what fraction of a newspaper consists of news.

How To Use It   Have students display a 1- or 2-page spread of a local newspaper on the bulletin board. Ask them to determine what fraction of a page of newsprint is used for news, and what fraction is for other information such as advertising, photos, art, graphs, tables, and cartoons related to news items. Have students repeat the process for other pages or papers. Encourage students to look for other ways to use fractions to analyze the pages.

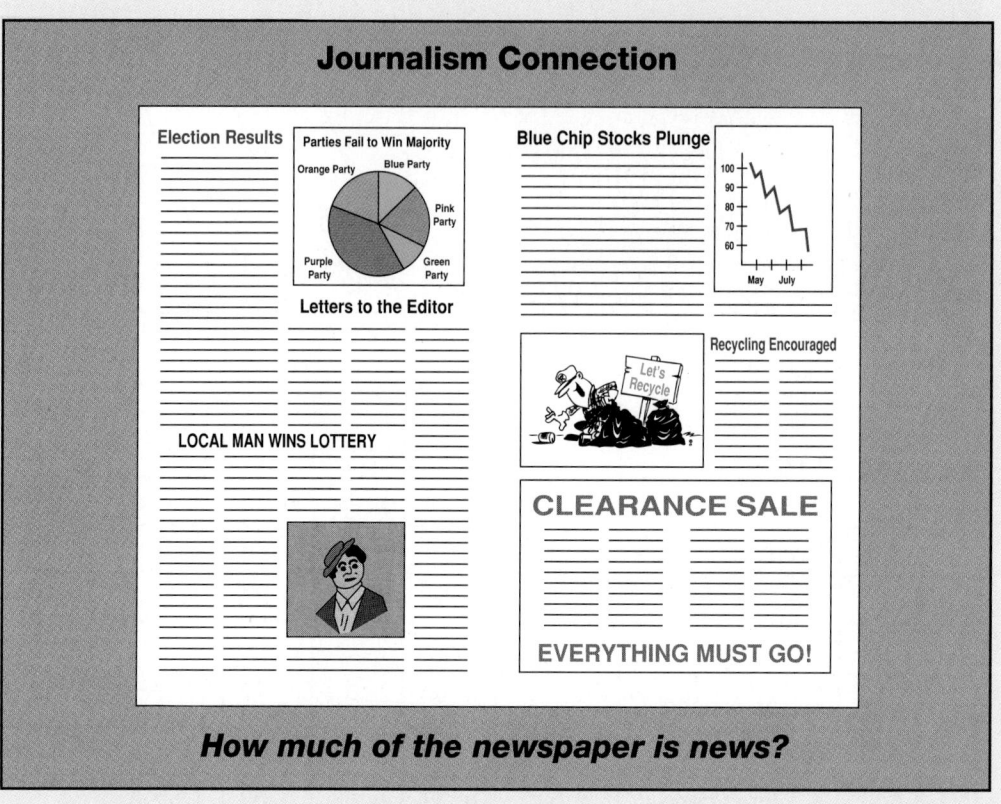

How much of the newspaper is news?

APPLICATIONS AND CONNECTIONS

Applications	Lesson	Example	Exercise
History	4-1		36
School	4-1		37
Business	4-2		42
Computer	4-2		51
Health	4-3		31
Geography	4-4		6
Science	4-4		10
School	4-5		32
School	4-6		33
Sports	4-6		34
Taxes	4-7		48
Business	4-8	2	
Health	4-9		27
Scheduling	4-9		28
Sports	4-10	3	
Civics	4-10		42
Connections			
Algebra	4-2	3	35, 36
Number Sense	4-2		43, 44
Measurement	4-4		13
Number Sense	4-5		33
Statistics	4-7		45
Number Sense	4-8		29, 30
Number Sense	4-9		29, 30
Statistics	4-10		40, 41

TEAM ACTIVITIES

Multicultural Experiences

Outside Field Trips   Visit a hardware store and talk with someone there about how fractions and decimals are involved in the design and purchase of measuring devices, tools, and other hardware.

Go with the class to a factory that manufactures scales, or visit a supermarket, fish market, or butcher store to find out more about how scales differ from one another in function and accuracy.

In-Class Speakers   Ask a health care professional to come in and talk about how he or she uses estimation when providing patient care.

Invite a musician to discuss the relationship between fractions and notes on the musical scale.

SUPPLEMENTARY BLACKLINE MASTER BOOKLETS

Some of the blackline masters for enhancing this chapter are shown below.

Application and Interdisciplinary Activity Masters, pp. 4, 18

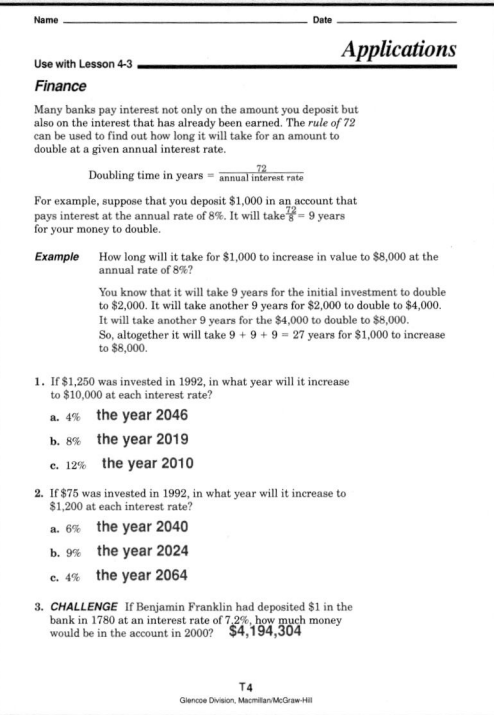

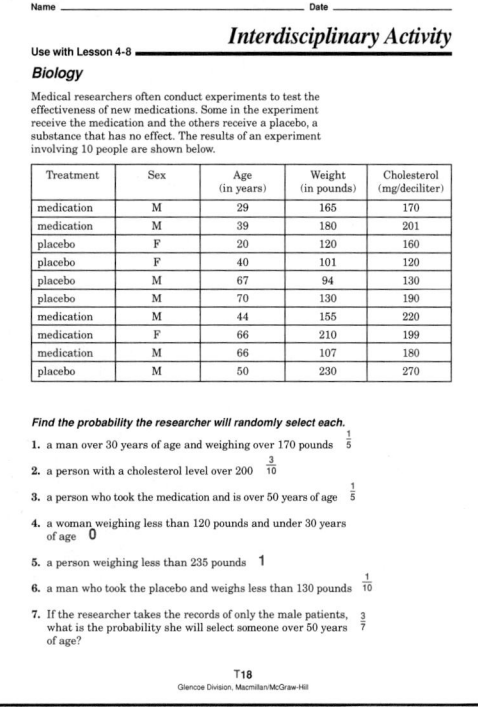

Multicultural Activity Masters, p. 4

Technology Masters, p. 18

Chapter

4

Patterns and Number Sense

Spotlight on Forestland

Have You Ever Wondered. . .

- Where most of the forestland in the United States is located?

- How many forest fires each year are caused by people?

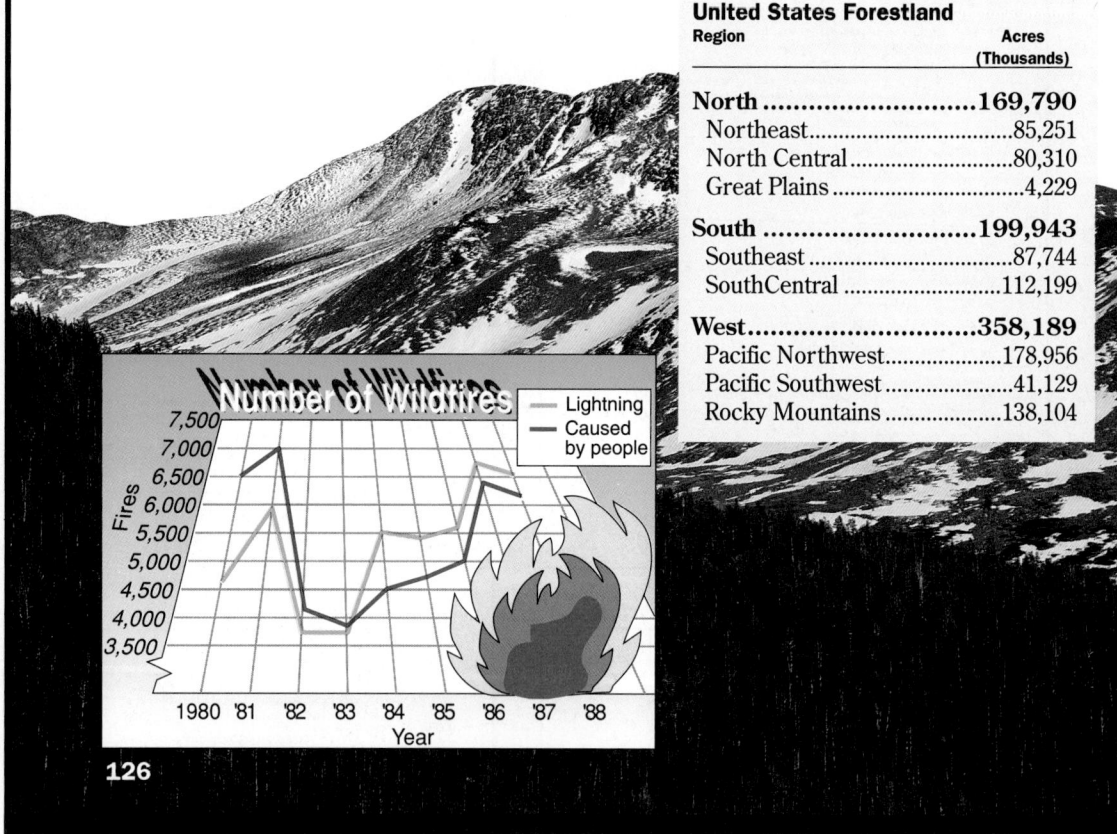

Number of Wildfires

United States Forestland

Region	Acres (Thousands)
North	**169,790**
Northeast	85,251
North Central	80,310
Great Plains	4,229
South	**199,943**
Southeast	87,744
SouthCentral	112,199
West	**358,189**
Pacific Northwest	178,956
Pacific Southwest	41,129
Rocky Mountains	138,104

126

Looking Ahead

In this chapter, you will see how patterns play an important role in mathematics.

The major objectives of the chapter are to:

- find prime factorization of a composite number

- solve problems by making an organized list

- find the greatest common factor or least common multiple of two or more numbers

- compare and order fractions and decimals

Calvin and Hobbes
by Bill Watterson

127

NCTM Standards: 1–6

Management Tips

For Students In this exploration, the number of students specified, 30, is chosen because it is rich in factors (1, 2, 3, 5, 6, 10, 15, 30). However, this fact should not be an impediment to your using more or fewer students, if you prefer.

For the Overhead Projector *Overhead Manipulative Resources* provides appropriate materials for teacher or student demonstration of the activities in this Mathematics Lab.

1 FOCUS

Introducing the Lab

Ask students to suppose that a group of 30 students was going to be divided into a number of teams of equal size to compete in a science fair. Ask them how the organizers can decide upon the possible size of the teams.

2 TEACH

Using Communication Point out to students that there will be one person between "every second student," two people between "every third student," three between every fourth, and so on.

3 PRACTICE/APPLY

Using Critical Thinking Before counting to record the answers to questions in the Applications section, have students predict the answers to those questions. Ask them to explain their predictions.

Close

Ask students to explain the connection between the numbers 2 through 30 and the cards with the fewest and most numbers written on them. Ask them to explain the relationship between the greatest number of numbers on a card (8, on card 30) and "divisibility with no remainder."

4-1A Exploring Factors

A Preview of Lesson 4-1

Objective
Discover the factors of the whole numbers 1–30.

Materials
Thirty pieces of tagboard numbered individually from 1 to 30.

Try this!

- In order around the classroom, give thirty students each a number card from 1 to 30.
- **Step 1** Have each of these students stand up and write the number 1 on the back of his or her card.
- **Step 2** Have every second student, beginning with the student holding the "2" card, sit down and write the number 2 on the back of his or her card.
- **Step 3** Have every third student, beginning with the student holding the "3" card, stand up or sit down (depending on whether the student is already sitting or standing) and write the number 3 on the back of his or her card.
- Continue this process for each of the remaining numbers, until the thirtieth student has stood up or sat down and written the number 30 on the back of his or her card.

What do you think?

1. Make a conjecture about the numbers written on the back of each number card. **Numbers on back are factors of the numbers on the front.**

2. Use your conjecture to predict the numbers that would be written on the back of number cards from 31 to 35. **See Solutions Manual.**

Applications

3. Which number cards have exactly two numbers on the back? **2, 3, 5, 7, 11, 13, 17, 19, 23, 29**
4. Which card has the fewest numbers on the back? **1**
5. Which cards have the most numbers on the back? **24 and 30**
6. What number cards are held by those students standing at the end of the activity? **1, 4, 9, 16, 25**

Extension

7. Suppose there were 100 students holding number cards. Predict which number cards would be held by students standing at the end of the activity and write a statement explaining why. **1, 4, 9, 16, 25, 36, 49, 64, 81, 100; Perfect square numbers because there is an odd number of factors**

OPTIONS

Lab Manual You may wish to make copies of the blackline master on p. 45 of the *Lab Manual* for students to use as a recording sheet.

Lab Manual, p. 45

Name _____ Date _____

Mathematics Lab Worksheet

Use with page 128

Exploring Factors

What do you think?

1. The numbers written on the back of each number card are the factors of that number.

2. 31: 1, 31   32: 1, 2, 4, 8, 16, 32
   33: 1, 3, 11, 33   34: 1, 2, 17, 34
   35: 1, 5, 7, 35

Applications

3. The number cards with exactly two numbers on the back are

4-1 Divisibility Patterns

Objective
Use divisibility rules.

Words to Learn
divisible
factor

Chapter 4 p 129

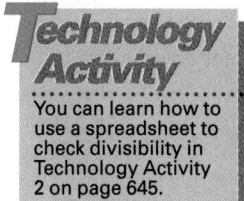

Technology Activity
You can learn how to use a spreadsheet to check divisibility in Technology Activity 2 on page 645.

Suppose you are baby-sitting for your neighbor's three children. To avoid arguments while the children color pictures, you decide to divide up the box of 48 crayons. Can you divide the crayons evenly among the three children?

$48 \div 3 = 16$ Since the quotient is a whole number, we say 48 is **divisible** by 3 or 3 is a **factor** of 48.

Thus, the crayons can be evenly divided with each child receiving 16 crayons.

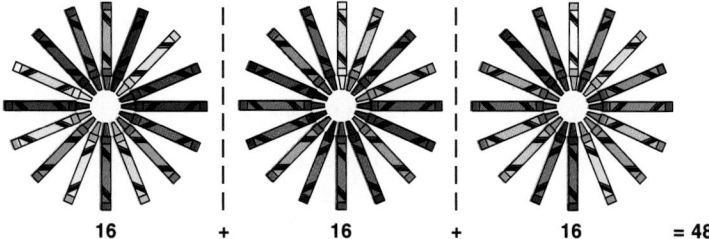

16   +   16   +   16   = 48

Mental Math Hint

The divisibility rule for 2 can be used to determine whether an even number is also divisible by 4. Mentally divide your even number by 2. If the quotient is also even, your number is divisible by 4.

48 is also divisible by 1, 2, 3, 4, 6, 8, 12, 16, 24, and 48.

In order to quickly check the divisibility of large numbers, you can use the following rules of divisibility.

A number is divisible by:

2   if the digit in the ones place is even.

3   if the sum of the digits is divisible by 3.

4   if the number formed by the last two digits is divisible by 4.

5   if the digit in the ones place is 5 or 0.

6   if the number is divisible by both 2 and 3.

9   if the sum of the digits is divisible by 9.

10   if the digit in the ones place is 0.

Lesson 4-1 Divisibility Patterns   **129**

NCTM Standards: 1–8

Lesson Resources
• Study Guide Master 4-1
• Practice Master 4-1
• Enrichment Master 4-1
• Group Activity Card 4-1

 Transparency 4-1 contains the 5-Minute Check and a teaching aid for this lesson.

🕐 5-Minute Check
(Over Chapter 3)

1. Find the range, mode(s), median, and mean for the following set of data: 62, 66, 65, 62, 70, 45
   range: 25; mode: 62; median: 63.5; mean: $61\frac{2}{3}$

2. Make a stem-and-leaf plot for the following set of data: 113, 103, 105, 96, 97, 129, 116

9	6 7
10	3 5
11	3 6
12	9

   11| 3 means 113.

1 FOCUS

Motivating the Lesson

Questioning   Have students read the opening paragraph. Ask them how they could tell whether 48 is divisible by numbers other than 3.   Sample answer: by guessing and checking other numbers to see whether they divide evenly into 48

2 TEACH

Using Discussion   Review the divisibility rules with students, guiding them to see how knowing these rules can help them use mental math. You may wish to introduce the rule for divisibility by 8: A number is divisible by 8 if the number formed by its last 3 digits is divisible by 8.

Teaching Tip   Point out to students another way to tell whether a number is divisible by 9—if the sum of its digits add to 9 or to a multiple of 9.

1   Determine whether 126 is divisible by 2, 3, 4, 5, 6, 9, or 10.

> 2:   The ones digit, 6, is even, so 126 is divisible by 2.
>
> 3:   The sum of the digits, 9, is divisible by 3, so 126 is divisible by 3.
>
> 4:   The number formed by the last two digits, 26, is not divisible by 4, so 126 is not divisible by 4.
>
> 5:   The ones digit is not 5 or 0, so 126 is not divisible by 5.
>
> 6:   The number is divisible by both 2 and 3, so 126 is divisible by 6.
>
> 9:   The sum of the digits, 9, is divisible by 9, so 126 is divisible by 9.
>
> 10:   The ones digit, 6, is not 0, so 126 is not divisible by 10.

2   Use your calculator to determine whether 397 is divisible by 7.

$$397 \; \boxed{\div} \; 7 \; \boxed{=} \; 56.714286$$

Since the quotient is not a whole number, 397 is not divisible by 7.

3   Find a number that is divisible by 3, 9, 5, and 10.

The ones digit must be 0 in order for the number to be divisible by 10 (which means the number will also be divisible by 5), and the sum of the digits must be divisible by 9 (which means the sum is also divisible by 3).

The numbers 1,260, 9,990, 333,000, and 123,210 are just a few of the numbers that meet these requirements.

Checking for Understanding

Communicating Mathematics

Read and study the lesson to answer each question.   Because 5 is a factor of 10.

1. **Tell** why every number that is divisible by 10 is also divisible by 5.

2. **Draw** pictures showing how 48 dots can be equally divided into 4 rows, 6 rows, or 8 rows. **See Solutions Manual.**

3. **Tell** what the figure at the right suggests about the divisibility of the number 15. **It is not divisible by 4.**

4. **Tell** how to pick a number that is divisible by 3 but not divisible by 9. Then give two examples of such a number. **Sum of digits is divisible by 3 but not 9; 6, 12**

OPTIONS

Team Teaching

Inform the other teachers on your team that your classes are studying patterns and number sense. Suggestions for curriculum integration are:

Science: patterns in nature, for example, plant reproduction

Social Studies: presidential and congressional election years

Additional Answers

9. 2, 3, 4, 5, 6, 9, 10
10. 2, 4
11. 5
12. 2, 3, 4, 5, 6, 9, 10
13. 2, 3, 4, 6, 9
14. None
36. 1820, 1840, 1860, 1880, 1900, 1920, 1940, 1960, 1980

Using the divisibility rules or your calculator, determine whether the first number is divisible by the second number.

5. 113; 3 **no**   6. 2,357,890; 10   7. 81,726,354; 9   8. 7,538; 4 **no**
yes   **yes**

Using the divisibility rules, determine whether each number is divisible by 2, 3, 4, 5, 6, 9, or 10. **For answers to Exercises 9-14, see margin.**

9. 180   10. 364   11. 95,455
12. 1,260   13. 31,212   14. 1,837

Exercises

Independent Practice

Determine whether the first number is divisible by the second number.

15. 813; 3 **yes**   16. 5,112; 6 **yes**   17. 2,115; 6 **no**
18. 7,770; 10 **yes**   19. 3,308; 4 **yes**   20. 2,927; 9 **no**

Determine whether each number is divisible by 2, 3, 4, 5, 6, 9, or 10.

21. 510 **2, 3, 5, 6, 10**   22. 1,455 **3, 5**   23. 101 **none**
24. 6,600 **2, 3, 4, 5, 6, 10**   25. 775 **5**   26. 3,770 **2, 5, 10**

For Exercises 27-31, sample answers are given.
Name two numbers that are divisible by both of the given numbers.

27. 2, 5 **10, 20**   28. 4, 9 **36, 72**   29. 3, 10 **30, 60**   30. 4, 5 **20, 40**   31. 6, 5
30, 60

Mixed Review

32. Estimate 365 ÷ 38. *(Lesson 1-3)* **about 10**

33. Round 0.006 to the hundredths place. *(Lesson 2-2)* **0.01**

34. Choose an appropriate scale and interval for the following data. Then draw a number line to display the scale and interval. 35, 42, 18, 25, 32, 47, 34 *(Lesson 3-3)* **See margin.**

35. **Statistics** Dave Smith reports that the average income for the five people who work in his department is $29,080. The five individual salaries are $26,700, $23,500, $24,800, $28,300, and $42,100. Why could the average quote be considered misleading? *(Lesson 3-8)* **$42,100 is considerably higher than all the other salaries.**

Problem Solving and Applications

36. **History** Thomas Jefferson was elected president of the United States in 1800. The United States holds a presidential election every 4 years. Which presidential election years since 1800 were divisible by 10? **See margin.**

37. **School** Mr. Variety has arranged the desks in his classroom in different ways, but he is always careful to have the same number of desks in each row. He can arrange the desks in 3 rows, 4 rows, and 6 rows. What is the fewest number of desks in his classroom? **12 desks**

38. **Critical Thinking** Are all numbers that are divisible by 9 also divisible by 3? Are all numbers that are divisible by 3 also divisible by 9? Give an argument or a counterexample to support your answer.

38. Yes, 3 is a factor of 9. Therefore, it must be a factor also; no, 12.

Lesson 4-1 Divisibility Patterns **131**

Checking for Understanding

Exercises 1–4 are designed to help you assess students' understanding through reading, writing, speaking, and modeling. You should work through these exercises with your students and then monitor their work on Guided Practice Exercises 5–14.

Close

Have students write a problem for a classmate to solve by applying divisibility rules for 3 and 4.

3 PRACTICE/APPLY

Assignment Guide
Maximum: 15–38
Minimum: 15–31 odd, 32–38

For **Extra Practice,** see p. 579.

Alternate Assessment

Writing Have students write a rule for a number that is divisible by 2, 3, 4, 6, and 10. It ends in 0, the sum of the digits is divisible by 3, and its last two digits form a multiple of 4.

Enrichment Masters, p. 29

Name _____ Date _____

Enrichment Worksheet 4-1

Perfect Numbers

A positive integer is *perfect* if it equals the sum of its factors that are less than the integer itself.

If the sum of the factors (excluding the integer itself) is greater than the integer, the integer is called *abundant*.

If the sum of the factors (excluding the integer itself) is less than the integer, the integer is called *deficient*.

The factors of 28 (excluding 28 itself) are 1, 2, 4, 7, and 14. Since 1 + 2 + 4 + 7 + 14 = 28, 28 is a perfect number.

Complete the chart to classify each number as perfect, abundant, or deficient.

	Number	Divisors (Excluding the Number Itself)	Sum	Classification
1.	14	1, 2, 7	10	deficient
2.	6	1, 2, 3,	6	perfect
3.	12	1, 2, 3, 4, 6	16	abundant
4.	20	1, 2, 4, 5, 10	22	abundant
5.	10	1, 2, 5	8	deficient

Show that each number is perfect.

6. 496
$1 + 2 + 4 + 8 + 16 + 31 + 62 + 124 + 248 = 496$

7. 8,128
$1 + 2 + 4 + 8 + 16 + 32 + 64 + 127 + 254 + 508 + 1,016 + 2,032 + 4,064 = 8,128$

8. **CHALLENGE** 33,550,336
$1 + 2 + 4 + 8 + 16 + 32 + 64 + 128 + 256 + 512 + 1,024 + 2,048 + 4,096 + 8,191 + 16,382 + 32,764 + 65,528 + 131,056 + 262,112 + 524,224 + 1,048,448 + 2,096,896 + 4,193,792 + 8,387,584 + 16,775,168 = 33,550,336$

T29
Glencoe Division, Macmillan/McGraw-Hill

Extending the Lesson

Using Number Sense Have students experiment to find out whether a number can have an odd number of factors. Yes. For example, all perfect squares have an odd number of factors.

Additional Answer
34.

```
 |--+--+--+--+--+--+--+--|
15  20  25  30  35  40  45  50
```

Cooperative Learning Activity

Use groups of 3.
The Possibility of Divisibility 4-1
Materials: Number cubes, spinner

◆ Decide which number cube will stand for digits in hundreds place, which number cube will stand for digits in tens place, and which number cube will stand for digits in ones place. Label equal sections of a spinner "1," "2," "3," "4," "5," "6," "9," and "10." Write these same numbers as headings on a sheet of paper.

➡ Each group member tosses a number cube at the same time. One group member then spins the spinner. If the three-digit number resulting from tossing the number cubes is divisible by the number on the spinner, write the number under the matching heading. Continue in the same way, taking turns at the spinner, until you have written at least one example of a three-digit number under each heading.

Glencoe Mathematics: Applications and Connections, Course 2

Lesson Resources
• Study Guide Master 4-2
• Practice Master 4-2
• Enrichment Master 4-2
• Group Activity Card 4-2

 Transparency 4-2 contains the 5-Minute Check and a teaching aid for this lesson.

⏱ 5-Minute Check
(Over Lesson 4-1)

Determine whether the first number is divisible by the second number.

1. 724; 3   no

2. 4,118; 4   no

Determine whether each number is divisible by 2, 3, 4, 5, 6, 9, or 10.

3. 620   2, 4, 5, 10

4. 4,254   2, 3, 6

5. Choose two numbers that are divisible by both 6 and 9.   Sample answer: 18, 36

---

1 FOCUS

Motivating the Lesson

Questioning   Ask students to explain how to determine whether a number is prime. Ask them to figure out whether 201 is a prime number, and to explain their strategy for doing so.   Sample answer: no; 201 is divisible by 3 ($= 2 + 0 + 1$).

2 TEACH

Using Discussion   Work through Example 1 with students step by step. Then encourage them to suggest other ways to arrive at the same set of prime factors. Have students put their solution steps on the chalkboard, and ask them to explain their methods. Repeat the process with another composite number.

4-2 Prime Factorization

Objective
Find the prime factorization of a composite number.

Words to Learn

prime number
composite numbers
prime factorization
factor tree

Did you know that on average a hen lays 300 eggs per year? That is 25 dozen eggs. The numbers 25 and 12 are factors of 300 because $25 \times 12 = 300$. Just as 300 can be written as 25×12, the numbers 25 and 12 can also be written as the products of a pair of factors: $5 \times 5 = 25$ and $3 \times 4 = 12$. We could also have chosen $2 \times 6 = 12$.

For some numbers, the only product that can be written is 1 times the number itself. These numbers are called **prime numbers.**

A prime number is a whole number greater than 1 that has exactly two factors, 1 and itself. 2, 5, 11, and 17 are examples of prime numbers.

Notice that 0 and 1 are neither prime nor composite numbers.

Numbers that have more than two factors, such as 12 and 25, are called **composite numbers.** A composite number is a whole number greater than 1 that has more than two factors.

The Fundamental Theorem of Arithmetic states that every composite number can be written as the product of prime numbers in exactly one way if you ignore the order of the factors. This product is called the **prime factorization** of the number. Looking again at the number 300, let's write its prime factorization.

The figure formed by the steps of the factorization of 300 is called a factor tree.

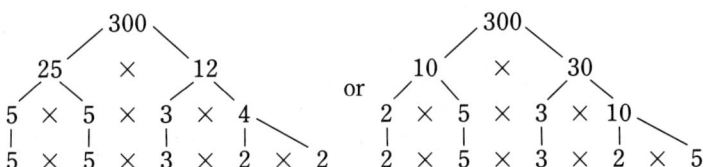

Since 2, 3, and 5 are prime numbers, then $2 \times 2 \times 3 \times 5 \times 5$ or $2^2 \times 3 \times 5^2$ is the prime factorization of 300.

Example 1

Use a factor tree to find the prime factorization of 630.

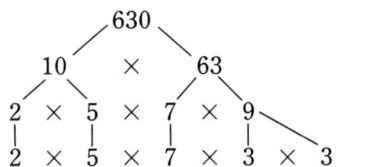

630 is divisible by 10.

The prime factorization of 630 is $2 \times 3^2 \times 5 \times 7$.

Classroom Vignette

"For an extension activity, two number cubes are labeled 4 through 9 while a third number cube is labeled 1 through 6. Students toss the cubes, multiply two of the numbers, and either add or subtract the third. If the result is a prime number, a point is scored. First player to score 5 points wins."

Arneta Brown

Arneta Brown, Teacher
Barrett Middle School, Columbus, OH

Example 2

Use your calculator to find the prime factors of 132.

$$132 \;\boxed{\div}\; 2 \;\boxed{=}\; \text{66} \;\boxed{\div}\; 2 \;\boxed{=}\; \text{33} \;\boxed{\div}\; 3 \;\boxed{=}\; \text{11}$$

The prime factorization of 132 is $2^2 \times 3 \times 11$.
Thus, the prime factors are 2, 3, and 11.

Example 3 *Connection*

Algebra Evaluate the expression $n^2 + n + 11$ for $n = 0, 1, 2,$ and 3 to find four prime numbers.

$n = 0$:	$n = 1$:	$n = 2$:	$n = 3$:
$0^2 + 0 + 11$	$1^2 + 1 + 11$	$2^2 + 2 + 11$	$3^2 + 3 + 11$
$= 0 + 0 + 11$	$= 1 + 1 + 11$	$= 4 + 2 + 11$	$= 9 + 3 + 11$
$= 11$	$= 13$	$= 17$	$= 23$

The numbers 11, 13, 17, and 23 are prime. *See Exercise 35 for more about the expression $n^2 + n + 11$.*

Checking for Understanding

Communicating Mathematics

Read and study the lesson to answer each question.

1. **Tell** why 1 is neither a prime number nor a composite number. **by definition**

2. **Tell** why 0 is neither a prime number nor a composite number. **by definition**

3. **Tell** why $2^4 \times 15$ is not the prime factorization of 240. **15 is not prime.**

4. **Draw** a figure showing 21 dots in a rectangular array. (In a rectangular array, each row has the same number of dots and each column has the same number of dots.) What does this show? **See margin.**

5. **Draw** a figure showing 11 dots in a rectangular array. What do you discover? **See margin.**

Guided Practice

Determine whether each number is composite or prime.

6. 15   7. 29   8. 333   9. 552
   composite   prime   composite   composite

Use a factor tree to find the prime factorization of each number.

10. 252   11. 66   12. 880   13. 270   14. 144
   $2^2 \times 3^2 \times 7$ $2 \times 3 \times 11$ $2^4 \times 5 \times 11$ $2 \times 3^3 \times 5$ $2^4 \times 3^2$

Use your calculator to find the prime factors of each number. Then write the prime factorization of each number.

15. 88   16. 146   17. 221   18. 250   19. 300
   $2^3 \times 11$ 2×73 13×17 2×5^3 $2^2 \times 3 \times 5^2$

Lesson 4-2 Prime Factorization   **133**

133

Watch for students who stop factoring before all the factors are prime numbers.

Prevent by having students make and refer to a list of prime numbers as a guide, and to circle each prime factor as it appears in the factor tree.

Close

Have students explain how to find the prime factors of a number and to demonstrate their method by finding the prime factors of 456. $2^3 \times 3 \times 19$

3 PRACTICE/APPLY

Assignment Guide
Maximum: 20–51
Minimum: 21–35 odd, 37–41, 45–47

For **Extra Practice**, see p. 579.

Practice Masters, p. 30

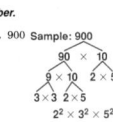

Name _____ Date _____

Practice Worksheet 4-2

Prime Factorization

Determine whether each number is composite or prime.

1. 18 composite   2. 31 prime   3. 434 composite

4. 97 prime   5. 111,111 composite   6. 4,293 composite

Use a factor tree to find the prime factorization of each number.

7. 280 Sample: 280   8. 92 Sample: 92   9. 900 Sample: 900
$2^3 \times 5 \times 7$ $2^2 \times 23$ $2^2 \times 3^2 \times 5^2$

Use your calculator to find the prime factors of each number. Then write the prime factorization of each number.

10. 66   11. 306   12. 2,475
$2 \times 3 \times 11$ $2 \times 3^2 \times 17$ $3^2 \times 5^2 \times 11$

13. 196   14. 2,400   15. 1,024
$2^2 \times 7^2$ $2^5 \times 3 \times 5^2$ 2^{10}

16. 225   17. 187   18. 170
$3^2 \times 5^2$ 11×17 $2 \times 5 \times 17$

Find the missing factor.

19. $3^2 \times 5 \times \blacksquare = 315$ 7   20. $2^4 \times \blacksquare \times 7 = 1,008$ 3^2

21. $3^3 \times \blacksquare = 135$ 5   22. $2^2 \times 3^2 \times \blacksquare = 252$ 7

23. $5^2 \times \blacksquare = 275$ 11   24. $3^3 \times 5^2 \times \blacksquare = $ 11

T30
Glencoe Division, Macmillan/McGraw-Hill

134

Exercises

Independent Practice

Determine whether each number is composite or prime.

20. 75   21. 17   22. 6,453   23. 10,101
    composite   prime   composite   composite

Write the prime factorization of each number.

24. 72   25. 1,260   26. 625   27. 1,300   28. 221
    $2^3 \times 3^2$ $2^2 \times 3^2 \times$ 5^4 $2^2 \times 5^2 \times 13$ 13×17
    5×7

Use your calculator to find the prime factors of each number. Then write the prime factorization of each number.

29. 90   30. 121   31. 175   32. 236   33. 320
    $2 \times 3^2 \times 5$ 11^2 $5^2 \times 7$ $2^2 \times 59$ $2^6 \times 5$

34. Find the missing factor: $2^3 \times \blacksquare \times 3^2 = 360$. **5**

35. **Algebra** Find the least whole number n for which the expression $n^2 + n + 11$ is not prime. **10**

36. **Algebra** Is the value of $2a + 5b$ prime or composite if $a = 3$ and $b = 5$? **prime**

Mixed Review

37. Evaluate $2m + 4(m - n) + mn$ if $m = 10$ and $n = 3$. *(Lesson 1-8)* **78**

38. Compute mentally $0.045 \times 1,000$. *(Lesson 2-5)* **45**

39. Divide 1.08 by 1.2. *(Lesson 2-7)* **0.9**

40. **Statistics** During the first two weeks of the new semester, Mrs. Jing keeps track of the attendance in her history class. Construct a stem-and-leaf plot for the following attendance data. 27, 31, 25, 19, 41, 32, 34, 36, 33, 31. *(Lesson 3-6)* **See Solutions Manual.**

41. Use the divisibility rules to determine whether 135 is divisible by 2, 3, 4, 5, 6, 9, or 10. *(Lesson 4-1)* **135 is divisible by 3, 5, and 9.**

For Exercises 42a, b, and e, sample answers are given.

Problem Solving and Applications

42. **Business** Andre is designing cartons to ship cans of gourmet pecans. The height, width, and length of the cartons must be measured in whole cans. For example, a carton could be 3 cans high, 4 cans wide, and 2 cans long. Such a carton would contain $2 \times 3 \times 4$, or 24 cans of pecans.

a. List two other ways to arrange 24 cans. $2 \times 2 \times 6; 1 \times 3 \times 8$

b. List three ways to arrange 36 cans in a carton. $2 \times 3 \times 6; 2 \times 2 \times 9; 3 \times 3 \times 4$

c. In how many different ways could you arrange 30 cans? **5 ways**

d. How would you arrange 29 cans? $1 \times 1 \times 29$

e. From his research, Andre knows that shipping from 30 to 35 cans is cost-effective. What number and arrangement of cans would you recommend be shipped in each carton? **Sample answer: 32; $2 \times 4 \times 4$**

OPTIONS

Gifted and Talented Needs

Tell students that in the 18th century Christian Goldbach made some conjectures about prime numbers, one of which is that every even number greater than 2 can be expressed as the sum of two prime numbers. Have students verify that this holds true for numbers through 50.

Interactive Mathematics Tools

This multimedia software provides an interactive lesson that is tied directly to Lesson 4-2. Students will use changeable grids to explore the factors of integers.

43.
a. $4 = 2 \cdot 2$
$9 = 3 \cdot 3$
$16 = 2 \cdot 2 \cdot 2 \cdot 2$
$25 = 5 \cdot 5$
$36 = 2 \cdot 2 \cdot 3 \cdot 3$
$49 = 7 \cdot 7$
$64 = 2 \cdot 2 \cdot 2 \cdot 2 \cdot 2 \cdot 2$
b. Squares of prime numbers have only two factors in their prime factorization.
c. See students' work; the hypothesis holds.

43. a. Number Sense Determine the prime factorization for each of the following square numbers: 4, 9, 16, 25, 36, 49, 64.
   b. What pattern do you notice?
   c. Test your hypothesis on 81, 100, and 121.

44. Number Sense Will the sum of any two prime numbers be prime? Justify your answer. **No; 11 + 23 = 34, 34 is not prime.**

45. Critical Thinking Numbers that can be represented by a triangular arrangement of dots, such as those below, are called **triangular** numbers.

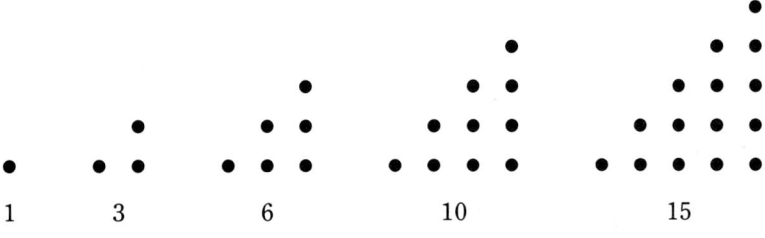

| 1 | 3 | 6 | 10 | 15 |

Determine the prime factorization for the first ten triangular numbers and describe the pattern. **See margin.**

46. Using the square at the right, multiply the middle number by 9. What does this product represent? Explain. **sum of all numbers**

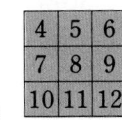

4	5	6
7	8	9
10	11	12

47. Jenny found a pair of prime numbers, 5 and 7, that differed by 2. These numbers are called **twin primes.** Find all the twin primes that are less than 100. **3, 5; 5, 7; 11, 13; 17, 19; 29, 31; 41, 43; 59, 61; 71, 73**

48. Number Sense Find the least 3-digit number that has 2, 3, 5, and another prime number as its prime factors. **210**

49. Number Sense Name two numbers that have exactly twelve factors, including 1 and the number itself, and are divisible by both 5 and 7. **6,125; 8,575**

50. Journal Entry How do you go about finding the prime factorization of a number? Do you follow a set pattern or use guess and check? **See students' work.**

51. Computer Connection Many formulas have been tried to see whether they generate prime numbers. The computer program below will evaluate the expression $n^2 + n + 17$ for $n = 0, 1, 2, \ldots, 20$. Run the program and identify each number from the output as prime or composite. **See Solutions Manual.**

```
10  FOR N = 0 TO 20
20  P = N^2 + N + 17
30  PRINT N, P
40  NEXT N
```

Lesson 4-2 Prime Factorization   **135**

Extending the Lesson

Using Relatively Prime Numbers Tell students that two numbers that have no common factors other than 1 are *relatively prime.* Ask them to determine whether numbers have to be prime in order to be relatively prime. **No.**
Examples: 15 and 16

Cooperative Learning Activity

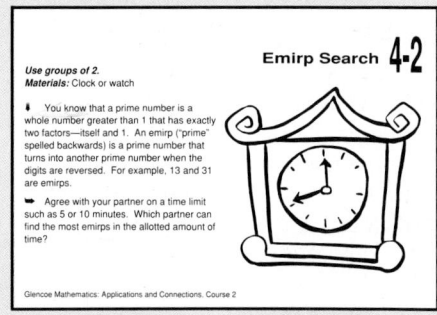

Emirp Search **4-2**

Use groups of 2.
Materials: Clock or watch

You know that a prime number is a whole number greater than 1 that has exactly two factors—itself and 1. An emirp ("prime" spelled backwards) is a prime number that turns into another prime number when the digits are reversed. For example, 13 and 31 are emirps.

Agree with your partner on a time limit such as 5 or 10 minutes. Which partner can find the most emirps in the allotted amount of time?

Glencoe Mathematics: Applications and Connections, Course 2

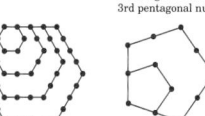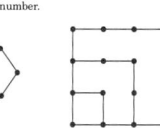
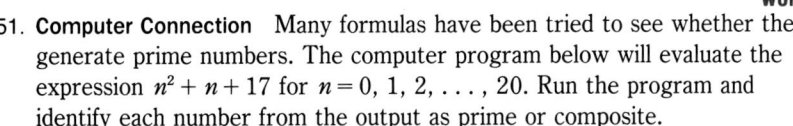
135

NCTM Standards: 1–8

Lesson Resources
- Study Guide Master 4-3
- Practice Master 4-3
- Enrichment Master 4-3
- Multicultural Activity, p. 4
- Application Master, p. 4
- Group Activity Card 4-3

 Transparency 4-3 contains the 5-Minute Check and a teaching aid for this lesson.

5-Minute Check
(Over Lesson 4-2)

Determine whether each number is composite or prime.

1. 65   composite
2. 161   composite

Write the prime factorization for each number.

3. 54 2×3^3
4. 1,400 $2^3 \times 5^2 \times 7$
5. Use your calculator to find the prime factors of 198 and then write its prime factorization.
   $2 \times 3^2 \times 11$

1 FOCUS

Motivating the Lesson

Activity   Ask students to think of a sequence from everyday life, such as exercise routines. List students' ideas on the chalkboard. Then ask students whether the pattern of a plant's growth can realistically be described as a sequence. Have them justify their answers.

4-3 Sequences

Objective
Recognize and extend a pattern for sequences.

Words to Learn
sequence
terms
arithmetic
  sequence
geometric
  sequence

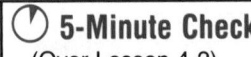 **DID YOU KNOW**

A Sequoia tree starts out as a seed weighing $\frac{1}{100}$ of an ounce. It increases its weight 100,000,000,000 times and can grow as tall as 340 feet.

The bamboo plant is the fastest-growing plant in the world. One bamboo plant was observed to have grown 36 inches in 24 hours. If the plant grew at a constant rate during the 24 hours, how many inches would the bamboo plant have grown after 8 hours?

Making a table or organized list can help you discover a pattern.

Since the plant grew 36 inches in 24 hours and it is assumed to have grown at a constant rate, it was growing $36 \div 24$, or 1.5 inches per hour.

Hours	1	2	3	4
Growth in inches during each hour	1.5	1.5	1.5	1.5
Total growth in inches after the hour	1.5	3.0	4.5	6.0

By studying the sequence of numbers in the last row of the table, you can identify a pattern and then use the pattern to find the growth after 8 hours. A **sequence** of numbers is a list in a specific order. The numbers in the sequence are called **terms.**

Since the growth each hour is a constant 1.5 inches, you can find the growth at the end of any hour by multiplying the number of hours by 1.5.

$$8 \times 1.5 = 12$$

The bamboo plant grew 12 inches in 8 hours.

If you can always find the next term in the sequence by adding the same number to the previous term, the sequence is called an **arithmetic sequence.**

$$3, \quad 6, \quad 9, \quad 12, \quad 15, \dots$$
$$+3 \;\; +3 \;\; +3 \;\;\; +3$$

OPTIONS

Limited English Proficiency

Review the new vocabulary. Have students enter and define the words in their vocabulary lists. Focus on the difference between the mathematical meanings of *terms, arithmetic* and *geometric* and the more familiar everyday meanings.

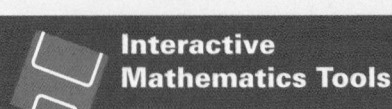 **Interactive Mathematics Tools**

This multimedia software provides an interactive lesson that is tied directly to Lesson 4–3. Students will extend arithmetic and geometric sequences.

Example 1

Identify the pattern in the sequence 3, 8, 13, 18, 23, . . . and describe how the terms are created. Then find the next three terms.

$$3, \quad 8, \quad 13, \quad 18, \quad 23, \ldots$$
$$+5 \quad +5 \quad +5 \quad +5$$

This is an arithmetic sequence in which each term after the first is created by adding 5 to the previous term.

$$23 + 5 = 28 \qquad 28 + 5 = 33 \qquad 33 + 5 = 38$$

The next three terms are 28, 33, and 38.

If you can always find the next term in the sequence by multiplying the previous term by the same number, the sequence is called a **geometric sequence.**

$$3, \quad 9, \quad 27, \quad 81, \ldots$$
$$\times 3 \quad \times 3 \quad \times 3$$

Example 2

Identify the pattern in the sequence 64, 32, 16, 8, . . . and describe how the terms are created. Then find the next three terms.

$$64, \quad 32, \quad 16, \quad 8, \ldots$$
$$\times \frac{1}{2} \quad \times \frac{1}{2} \quad \times \frac{1}{2}$$

This is a geometric sequence in which each term after the first is created by multiplying the previous term by $\frac{1}{2}$.

$$8 \times \frac{1}{2} = 4 \qquad 4 \times \frac{1}{2} = 2 \qquad 2 \times \frac{1}{2} = 1$$

The next three terms are 4, 2, and 1.

There are many sequences that are neither arithmetic nor geometric.

Lesson 4-3 Sequences **137**

2 TEACH

Using Charts Use charts to help show the pattern in real-life sequences students have identified. Be sure students understand that an arithmetic sequence is generated by adding the *same* number to each successive term and a geometric sequence generated by multiplying successive terms by the *same* number.

More Examples

For Example 1

Identify the pattern in the sequence 4, 11, 18, 25, 32, ... Then find the next three terms.   Pattern: add 7; 39, 46, 53

For Example 2

Identify the pattern in the sequence 729, 243, 81, 27, ... Then find the next three terms.   Pattern: multiply by $\frac{1}{3}$; 9, 3, 1

For Example 3

Identify the pattern in the sequence 1, 4, 8, 13, 19, ... Then find the next three terms.   Pattern: add 3, add 4, add 5, and so on; 26, 34, 43

Checking for Understanding

Exercises 1–4 are designed to help you assess students' understanding through reading, writing, speaking, and modeling. You should work through these exercises with your students and then monitor their work on Guided Practice Exercises 5–13.

Reteaching Activity

Using a Model Have students use number lines drawn on graph paper to plot the opening arithmetic sequence and others. Have them connect the terms to show the distance between them. In this way, students can visualize the distinction between sequences that are arithmetic and those that are not.

Study Guide Masters, p. 31

Name _____ Date _____

Study Guide Worksheet 4-3

Sequences

A sequence of numbers is a list in a specific order. The numbers in the sequence are called terms.

A sequence is an arithmetic sequence if you can find the next term by adding the same number to or subtracting the same number from the previous term.

Examples 7, 11, 15, 19, 23, . . .   The next term can be found by adding 4 to the previous term.

The next three numbers in the sequence are 27, 31, and 35.

76, 73, 70, 67, 64, . . .   The next term can be found by subtracting 3 from the previous term.

The next three numbers in the sequence are 61, 58, and 55.

137

138

Close

Have students tell whether the following sequence is arithmetic, geometric, or neither, and to explain their answer: 6, 12, 24, 42, 66, ... **neither; Consecutive terms are not found by adding the same number to the previous term, or by multiplying it by the same number.**

3 PRACTICE/APPLY

Assignment Guide
Maximum: 14–34
Minimum: 15–27 odd, 28–34

For **Extra Practice,** see p. 579.

Alternate Assessment

Speaking Have students explain how to find the pattern in an arithmetic sequence and in a geometric sequence. **Determine the difference between consecutive terms; determine the factor by which neighboring terms are related.**

Practice Masters, p. 31

Name _____ Date _____

Practice Worksheet 4-3

Sequences

Identify the sequence as arithmetic, geometric, or neither. Then find the next three terms.

1. 6, 12, 18, 24, . . .
arithmetic;
30, 36, 42

2. 1, 4, 16, 64, . . .
geometric;
256; 1,024; 4,096

3. 18, 9, $\frac{9}{2}, \frac{9}{4}, . . .$
geometric;
$\frac{9}{8}, \frac{9}{16}, \frac{9}{32}$

4. 2, 9, 7, 14, 12, 19, . . .
neither;
17, 24, 22

5. 9, 18, 27, 36, 45, . . .
arithmetic;
54, 63, 72

6. 0.2, 0.4, 0.8, 1.6, . . .
geometric;
3.2, 6.4, 12.8

7. 3, 1, $\frac{1}{3}, \frac{1}{9}, \frac{1}{27}, . . .$
geometric;
$\frac{1}{81}, \frac{1}{243}, \frac{1}{729}$

8. 1, 4, 9, 16, 25, . . .
neither;
36, 49, 64

9. 0, 16, 32, 48, 64, . . .
arithmetic;
80, 96, 112

10. 1.2, 2.3, 3.4, 4.5, . . .
arithmetic;
5.6, 6.7, 7.8

11. 1, 5, 25, 125, . . .
geometric;
625; 3,125; 15,625

12. 210, 211, 213, 216, . . .
neither;
220, 225, 231

Create a sequence using each of the given rules. Provide at least four terms for each sequence beginning with the given number. State whether the sequence is arithmetic, geometric, or neither.

13. Add 0.4 to each term; 8
8, 8.4, 8.8, 9.2;
arithmetic

14. Multiply the previous number by 3; 5   5, 15, 45, 135;
geometric

15. Multiply the previous number by $\frac{1}{2}$; 42
42, 21, $\frac{21}{2}, \frac{21}{4}$; geometric

16. Add 0.3 to the first term, 0.5 to the next term, 0.7 to the next term, and so on; 10   10, 10.3, 10.8, 11.5; neither

T 31
Glencoe Division, Macmillan/McGraw-Hill

138

Example 3

Identify the pattern in the sequence 1, 4, 9, 16, 25, . . . and describe how the terms are created. Then find the next three terms.

The terms are squares of the numbers 1, 2, 3, 4, 5, ... That is,

1, 4, 9, 16, 25, . . . can be written as $1^2, 2^2, 3^2, 4^2, 5^2, ...$

This is neither an arithmetic nor geometric sequence.

The next three terms are $6^2, 7^2, 8^2,$ or 36, 49, 64.

Checking for Understanding

Communicating Mathematics
Read and study the lesson to answer each question. **For answers to Exercises 1-4, see margin.**

1. **Tell** why the sequence in Example 3 is neither arithmetic nor geometric.
2. **Draw** a model using dots for each number in the sequence 1, 3, 5, 7, 9, . . . to show that the sequence is arithmetic.
3. **Tell** how to find the next term in the sequence 0, 3, 8, 15, 24, 35, ...
4. **Write** a rule for generating a sequence of your own. Then have a classmate try to create the sequence using only the first number and your rule. **For answers to Exercises 5-10, see margin.**

Guided Practice
Describe the pattern in each sequence. Identify the sequence as arithmetic, geometric, or neither. Then find the next three terms.

5. 7, 14, 21, 28, 35, 42, . . .
6. 2, 6, 18, 54, . . .
7. 0, 1, 3, 6, 10, 15, . . .
8. 15, 30, 45, 60, . . .
9. 1, 6, 4, 9, 7, 12, 10, . . .
10. 9, 3, 1, $\frac{1}{3}, \frac{1}{9}, . . .$

For answers to Exercises 11-13, see margin.
Create a sequence using each of the given rules. Provide at least four terms for each sequence beginning with a number of your choice. State whether the sequence is arithmetic, geometric, or neither.

11. Add 3 to each term.
12. Multiply each term by $\frac{1}{3}$.
13. Add 0.1 to the 1st term, add 0.2 to the 2nd term, add 0.3 to the 3rd term, and so on.

Exercises

Independent Practice
Identify each sequence as arithmetic, geometric, or neither. Then find the next three terms in each sequence. **A; 0.9,**

14. 0.1, 0.3, 0.5, 0.7, . . . **1.1, 1.3**
15. 2, 1, 0.5, 0.25, . . . **G; 0.125, 0.0625, 0.03125**
16. 12, 17, 22, 27, . . . **A; 32, 37, 42**
17. 1, 2.1, 3.2, 4.3, . . . **A; 5.4, 6.5, 7.6**
18. 100, 101, 103, 106, 110, . . . **N; 115, 121, 128**
19. 4, 1, $\frac{1}{4}, \frac{1}{16}, . . .$ **G; $\frac{1}{64}, \frac{1}{256}, \frac{1}{1,024}$**
20. 0, 17, 34, 51, . . . **A; 68, 85, 102**
21. 11, 22, 33, 44, . . . **A; 55, 66, 77**
22. 1, 2, 2, 3, 3, 3, 4, 4, 4, 4, . . . **N; 5, 5, 5**
23. 1, 8, 27, 64, . . . **N; 125, 216, 343**

138   Chapter 4 Patterns and Number Sense

OPTIONS

Gifted and Talented Needs

Write the first four square numbers on the chalkboard, as shown at the right. Have students describe the pattern determined by the shapes, and continue it to determine the tenth square number in the sequence. **The difference between successive pairs of neighboring terms increases by 2 each time; tenth term: 100**

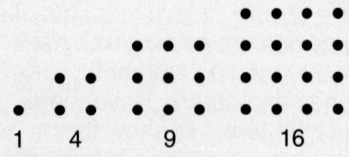

1   4   9   16

Create a sequence using each of the given rules. Provide at least four terms for each sequence beginning with the given number. State whether the sequence is arithmetic, geometric, or neither. **For answers to Exercises 24-26, see Solutions Manual.**

24. Add 0.6 to each term; 10.

25. Square consecutive odd integers; 1.

26. Add $\frac{1}{2}$ times to each term; 12

Mixed Review

27. Solve mentally $3y = 63$. *(Lesson 1-10)* **21**

28. **Science Experiment** Juan's science experiment requires 2.3 mL of sodium. How many liters of sodium are required? *(Lesson 2-9)* **0.0023 L**

29. **Statistics** Find the mean, median, and mode for the following set of data. 3, 5, 2, 3, 3, 4, 3, 2, 2. *(Lesson 3-5)* **3, 3, 3**

30. Use a factor tree to find the prime factorization of 630. *(Lesson 4-2)* $2 \times 3^2 \times 5 \times 7$

Problem Solving and Applications

31. **Health** Sara has decided to start an exercise program and she knows that it is important to begin gradually. She plans to begin by working out for 5 minutes and then double her exercise time each day for 1 week. Write a sequence showing the length of time she exercises each day. Is her plan reasonable? Why or why not? **5, 10, 20, 40, 80, 160, 320; no, 320 min = $5\frac{1}{3}$ h**

32. See Exercise 45 on page 135. Write a sequence formed by the first eight triangular numbers. Write a rule for generating the sequence. **See Solutions Manual.**

33. **Critical Thinking** A magic square is a number square in which the rows, columns, and diagonals all have the same sum. Make a magic square by using the sequence 2.3, 3.2, 4.1, 5, ... Find the pattern and write the first nine terms. Then place the terms in the appropriate squares. **See Solutions Manual.**

?	?	?
?	?	?
?	?	?

34. **Mathematics and Science** Read the following paragraph.

There are more than 335,000 kinds of plants. The simplest plants are algae. Some algae are simply single cells, which reproduce themselves by splitting in two. Others, including seaweed, are much bigger. Fungi are plants that cannot make their own food, so they feed on rotting or dead matter.

The giant kelp seaweed is found in the Pacific Ocean. One plant grows 3 feet the first two days. If it continues to grow at the same rate, what would be the length of the seaweed at the end of 80 days? **120 feet**

Lesson 4-3 Sequences   **139**

Extending the Lesson

Mathematics and Science
Encourage students to find the pattern in the exercise. Have them set up the expression $3 + 78 \times 1.5$ to find the solution.

Cooperative Learning Activity

Sequence of Events **4-3**

Number of players: 5
Materials: Index cards

• Copy onto one set of cards the digits 1-9. Copy onto a second set the "rules" for sequence building shown on the back of this card. Shuffle each set separately and place the cards face down in two piles. Arrange four chairs in a row and number them 1-4. Place a fifth chair facing the other four.

• One group member sits facing the other four. The group member in chair 1 looks at the top card from each pile and then passes the rule card down the row. After the group member in chair 1 reads his or her number aloud, each of the others, in turn, applies the rule to the previous number and tells the next number in the sequence. The fifth group member tries to guess the fifth number in the sequence and the rule.

Continue in the same manner, trading roles each time, until all group members have had a chance to guess the rule.

Glencoe Mathematics: Applications and Connections, Course 2

Enrichment Masters, p. 31

Name _____ Date _____

Enrichment Worksheet 4-3

Nested Magic Squares

A magic square is a square arrangement of numbers in which the sum of the numbers in every row, column, and diagonal is the same number. The numbers 1 through 49 can be arranged to make *three nested* magic squares. First, the large 7-by-7 outer square is magic. Remove its border and you get a 5-by-5 magic square. Finally, remove the border again to get a 3-by-3 magic square.

In the figure below, insert the rest of the numbers 1 through 49 to make three nested magic squares.

46	1	2	3	42	41	40
45	35	13	14	32	31	5
44	34	28	21	26	16	6
7	17	23	25	27	33	43
12	20	24	29	22	30	38
11	19	37	36	18	15	39
10	49	48	47	8	9	4

T31
Glencoe Division, Macmillan/McGraw-Hill

NCTM Standards: 1–5, 7, 8

Management Tips

For Students Have students work individually, but encourage them to help each other interpret the directions and to compare their results.

For the Overhead Projector
Overhead Manipulative Resources provides appropriate materials for teacher or student demonstration of the activities in this Mathematics Lab.

1 FOCUS

Introducing the Lab

To spark student interest in geometric sequences, ask them to suppose they are offered a one-month job. The pay is to be either $50 a day or a penny the first day, 2¢ on the second, 4¢ on the third, 8¢ on the fourth, and so on. Ask them which way they would prefer to be paid. Have them confirm their decisions by direct calculation. $50 a day produces $1,500 in a 30-day month. By doubling the number of pennies each day, you receive over $5 million on the last day alone.

Cooperative Learning

4-3B Exploring Geometric and Arithmetic Sequences

A Follow-Up of Lesson 4-3

Objective
Recognize the amount of change in arithmetic and geometric sequences.

Materials
calculator
notebook paper
graph paper

In business, science, sports, and our daily lives, we can see patterns of growth. Two common patterns are arithmetic sequences and geometric sequences.

Activity One

- Fold a piece of notebook paper in half and record the number of layers of paper. (See the table below.)
- Shade one side of the folded paper.
- Open the piece of paper and record the fractional part of the paper that is *not* shaded. Refold the piece of paper.
- Fold your paper in half again so the unshaded side is on the outside and record the number of layers of paper.
- Shade one side of the folded paper.
- Open the piece of paper and record the fractional part of the paper that is *not* shaded. Completely refold the paper.
- Continue folding, shading, and recording until you can no longer fold your paper (at least five folds).

Number of Folds	Layers of Paper	Fraction of Paper Unshaded
1	2	$\frac{1}{2}$
2	4	$\frac{1}{4}$
3	8	
4		
⋮		

What do you think?

1. Examine the sequence of numbers in the "Layers" column of your table. Is this sequence arithmetic or geometric? **geometric**

2. Study the sequence in the "Fraction" column. Is this sequence arithmetic or geometric? **geometric**

Activity Two

Imagine continuing the paper-folding process from Activity One forever. Assuming that your unfolded sheet of notebook paper is 0.002 inches thick, make a table similar to the one below for the first five folds.

Number of Folds	Thickness of the Folded Paper	
	In Layers	In Inches
1	2	0.004
2	4	0.008
3	8	
⋮		

What do you think?

14 folds is 32.768 in., 15 folds is 65.536 in., and 16 folds is 131.072 in.
3. How many folds would it take until the paper is as tall as you?

4. One mile is 5,280 feet. How many folds would it take until the folded paper is one mile tall? **25 folds**

5. How would your data change if you were folding the paper into thirds instead of halves? **increase faster**

Extension

6. a. Write the first ten terms of the geometric sequence 3, 9, 27, . . . , which is created by multiplying the previous number by 3. **See margin.**
   b. Write the sequence of numbers formed by ones digits of successive terms in the sequence. **See margin.**

   c. What pattern do you see? **repeats 3, 9, 7, 1**

   d. Find the sum of the digits for each term in the sequence created in part a. **See margin.**

   e. Which sums are divisible by 3? **all of them**

   f. Which sums are divisible by 9? Describe the pattern. **all but the first**

Mathematics Lab 4-3B Exploring Geometric and Arithmetic Sequences **141**

2 TEACH

Using Communication Point out to students that when they fold the paper in half, they must shade one of the two back-to-back sheets of paper, *not* the left or right side of one of the sheets.

3 PRACTICE/APPLY

Using Number Sense In Activity One, have students identify the factor in each geometric sequence. In Activity Two, discuss with students why it will be impossible for the paper to fold into the heights described despite the geometric sequence that defines the increasing width of the paper.

Close

Have students describe the difference between an arithmetic and a geometric sequence. Ask them to give an example of each.

Additional Answers

6a. 3; 9; 27; 81; 243; 729; 2,187; 6,561; 19,683; 59,049
  b. 3, 9, 7, 1, 3, 9, 7, 1, 3, 9
  d. 3, 9, 9, 9, 9, 18, 18, 18, 27, 27

Lab Manual, p. 46

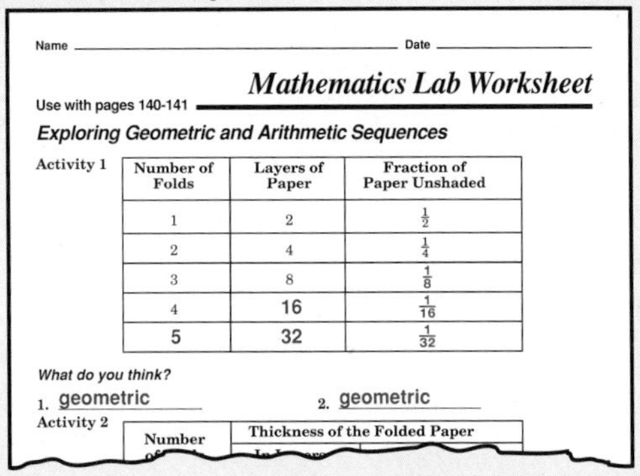

| | Date |
| Name | |

Mathematics Lab Worksheet

Use with pages 140-141

Exploring Geometric and Arithmetic Sequences

Activity 1

Number of Folds	Layers of Paper	Fraction of Paper Unshaded
1	2	$\frac{1}{2}$
2	4	$\frac{1}{4}$
3	8	$\frac{1}{8}$
4	16	$\frac{1}{16}$
5	32	$\frac{1}{32}$

What do you think?
1. **geometric**   2. **geometric**

Activity 2

| Number of Folds | Thickness of the Folded Paper |
| | In Layers |

NCTM Standards: 1–8, 13

Lesson Resources
- Study Guide Master 4-4
- Practice Master 4-4
- Enrichment Master 4-4
- Group Activity Card 4-4

 Transparency 4-4 contains the 5-Minute Check and a teaching aid for this lesson.

🕐 5-Minute Check
(Over Lesson 4-3)

Identify each sequence as arithmetic, geometric, or neither. Then find the next three terms in each sequence.

1. 0.2, 0.3, 0.5, 0.8, . . .
neither; 1.2, 1.7, 2.3

2. 72, 63, 54, 45, . . .
arithmetic; 36, 27, 18

3. $\frac{1}{5}, \frac{1}{10}, \frac{1}{20}, \frac{1}{40}, \cdots$
geometric; $\frac{1}{80}, \frac{1}{160}, \frac{1}{320}$

---

1 FOCUS

Motivating the Lesson

Activity Have students do research to find out more about Leonardo Fibonacci and his sequence. See whether they can discover any applications of the sequence in nature and in music.

2 TEACH

Using Problem Solving
Discuss the problem-solving strategy of making an organized list. Guide students to see that they can use this strategy to organize information in a way that can help them account for all possibilities while avoiding repetitions. For example, write the names of 5 students on the chalkboard. Ask the class to list all possible 3-person debating teams that can be formed from this group.

4-4 Make a List

Objective
Solve problems by making an organized list.

Leonardo Fibonacci, a mathematical genius during the Middle Ages, is best known for a sequence of numbers. Fibonacci introduced his sequence by making up a story. The story begins on January 1 with one pair of rabbits named A that live in a pen.

On February 1, a pair of bunnies named B is born. *Now there are 2 pairs of rabbits: 1 adult pair and 1 baby pair.*

By March 1, the original parents have had another pair of bunnies and the original bunnies have grown into adult rabbits. *Now there are 3 pairs of rabbits: 2 adult pairs and 1 baby pair.*

The pattern continues. Find the pattern.

Explore
What do you know?
You know that:
    On January 1, there is 1 pair of rabbits in a pen.
    On February 1, there are 1 pair of rabbits and 1 pair of bunnies.
    On March 1, there are 2 pairs of rabbits and 1 pair of bunnies.
    On April 1, the pattern continued.

What are you trying to find?
You are trying to find the pattern.

Plan
Make an organized list. Use A for adult pairs of rabbits and B for pairs of bunnies. Organize a list of the number of As, Bs, and total pairs. Use this to find a pattern.

Solve

Date													Number of As	Number of Bs	Total
1/1						A							1	0	1
2/1				B			A						1	1	2
3/1			A		B			A					2	1	3
4/1		B	A		A	B		A					3	2	5
5/1	A	B	A	B		A	A	B	A				5	3	8
6/1	B	A	A	B	A	A	B	A	B	A	A	B A	8	5	13

OPTIONS

Reteaching Activity

Using Models Use counters to help students visualize the Fibonacci sequence and other sequences.

Study Guide Masters, p. 32

Name _____ Date _____

Study Guide Worksheet 4-4

Problem-Solving Strategy: Make a List

Mrs. Nitobe bought four rose bushes. Their flowers are red, yellow, white, and pink. She wants to plant the bushes in a row in front of her house. In how many different ways can she arrange the bushes in a row if she does not want to plant the red bush next to the pink bush?

Explore What do you know?
There are four bushes: red, yellow, white, and pink. Mrs. Nitobe does not want to plant the red next to the pink.

What do you want to find?
how many ways the bushes can be planted in a row if the red bush is not next to the pink bush

Plan Make an organized list. Find all the possible arrangements. Then eliminate the arrangements in which the red and pink bushes are next to each

You can see a pattern in each of the columns. Look at the numbers in column A.

1, 1, 2, 3, 5, 8, . . . is the **Fibonacci sequence.**

The terms are called Fibonacci numbers. For discussion purposes, we will label each term as F1, F2, and so on.

F1 = 1, F2 = 1, F3 = 2, F4 = 3, F5 = 5, F6 = 8, . . .

By looking at each of the columns, you can see that F1 + F2 = F3, F2 + F3 = F4, F3 + F4 = F5, F4 + F5 = F6, and so on.

Examine After the first two terms, 1 and 1, of the Fibonacci sequence, the sum of each two consecutive terms gives the next term.

$$1 + 1 = 2 \qquad 1 + 2 = 3 \qquad 2 + 3 = 5 \qquad 3 + 5 = 8$$

Checking for Understanding

Communicating Mathematics Read and study the lesson to answer each question.

13, 8, 21

1. **Tell** the next three numbers on page 142 for columns A, B, and Total.

2. a. **Write** in your own words how to extend the list on page 142 through July 1. **See margin.**

   b. **Show** the list on page 142 completed through July 1. **See Solutions Manual.**

Guided Practice Solve by making a list.

3. List the first 20 Fibonacci numbers. **See margin.**

4. Refer to the list on page 142. What is the relationship between the numbers under *Total* and the numbers under *Number of As?* **See margin.**

Problem Solving

Practice Solve using any strategy.

5. Explore the Fibonacci sequence using your calculator to complete the table.

   a. Write the first 10 terms of the Fibonacci sequence. Divide each term by the succeeding term. Round to the nearest thousandth. **See margin.**

   b. In your own words, describe the pattern of quotients. **See margin.**

Term	Quotient
1	—
1	$1 \div 1 = 1$
2	$1 \div 2 = 0.5$
3	$2 \div 3 = 0.667$
⋮	⋮

Lesson 4-4 Problem-Solving Strategy: Make a List **143**

Bell Ringer

Have students research to find what a golden rectangle is, and how the ratio of its length to its width is related to Fibonacci's sequence. Ask students to look around the classroom for examples of golden rectangles. Suggest that they measure with centimeter rulers to check their conjectures.

Sides are in the approximate ratio 1:1.6; Consecutive terms in the Fibonacci sequence approximate the same ratio.

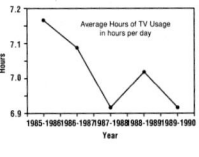
143

Close

Have students summarize the lesson by explaining how to use a list to find terms in a sequence.

3 PRACTICE/APPLY

Assignment Guide
Maximum: 5–14
Minimum: 5–14

Alternate Assessment

Writing Have students investigate the Fibonacci sequence to find a fraction or decimal that describes the relationship between successive terms. Each term is about 1.6, or $1\frac{3}{5}$ as great as the previous one.

Additional Answers

5a. Quotients of successive terms: 1, 0.5, 0.667, 0.6, 0.625, 0.615, 0.619, 0.618, 0.618

b. The quotient approaches approximately 0.618.

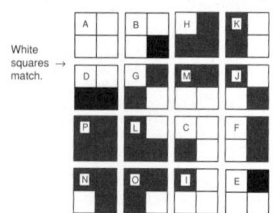
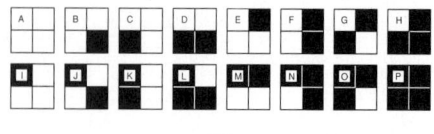
144

Strategies

Look for a pattern.
Solve a simpler problem.
Act it out.
Guess and check.
Draw a diagram.
Make a chart.
Work backward.

6. **Geography** Mount Everest, the tallest mountain on Earth, is 8,872 meters tall. The tallest mountain on Mars is Olympus Mons, which is 23,775 meters tall. How much taller is Olympus Mons than Mount Everest? **14,903 meters taller**

7. Jo sees that every third Fibonacci number is even ($F_3 = 2$, $F_6 = 8$, $F_9 = 34$). Find F_{30}. **832,040**

8. John took a bag of cookies to the school play rehearsal. Half were given to the actors and five to the director of the play. That left John with 15 cookies. How many cookies did he take to rehearsal? **40 cookies**

9. Find two numbers so that, when added together, they equal 56 and, when multiplied, they equal 783. **27, 29**

10. **Science** Telephone calls travel through optical fibers at the speed of light, which is 186,000 miles per second. A millisecond is 0.001 of a second. How far can your voice travel over an optical line in 1 millisecond? **186 miles**

11. Are there any perfect squares (for example: $4 \times 4 = 16$) or perfect cubes (for example: $4 \times 4 \times 4 = 64$) in the first 12 terms of the Fibonacci sequence? If so, name them. **yes; 1, 144; 1, 8**

12b. added squared Fibonacci number to previous squared Fibonacci number starting with the second term

12. Sarah is experimenting with the Fibonacci numbers. She has these numbers on her paper.

a. Describe the pattern in the second column. **squared Fibonacci numbers**

b. Tell what she did to get the pattern in the third column.

1	1	
1	1	2
2	4	5
3	9	13
5	25	34
8	64	89
13	169	...

13. **Data Search** Refer to page 650. Draw the next figure in each of the three series and find the number for each figure. **See Solutions Manual.**

14. **Aircraft** A Boeing 747 Jumbo Jet, the largest capacity jetliner, is 70.51 meters long. The Stits Skybaby, the smallest fully functional aircraft, is only 2.794 meters long. How many Skybabies, set end-to-end, would it take to equal the length of the 747? **about 25 Skybabies**

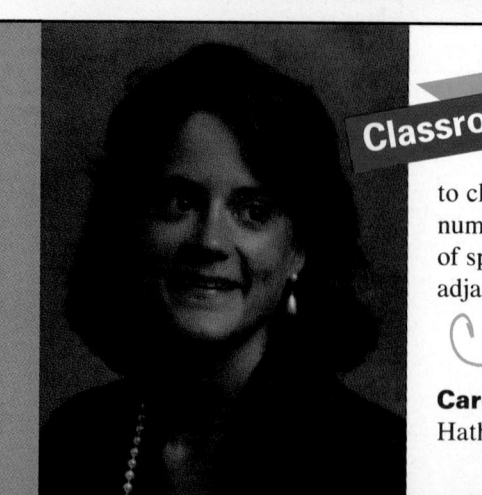

Classroom Vignette

"To show students how Fibonacci numbers exist in nature, I bring pineapples and pine cones to class and have students count the spirals. The number of spirals going clockwise and the number of spirals going counterclockwise are usually adjacent Fibonacci numbers."

Caroline Harrison

Caroline Harrison, Teacher
Hathaway Brown School, Shaker Heights, OH

4-5 Greatest Common Factor

Objective

Find the greatest common factor of two or more numbers.

Words to Learn

greatest common factor (GCF)

Eratosthenes, a Greek mathematician, lived during the 3rd century B.C. One of his many contributions is a device, now generally known as the *sieve of Eratosthenes,* which can be used to find prime numbers.

By using the sieve to find prime numbers, you can discover the **greatest common factor** of two or more numbers. The greatest common factor (GCF) of two or more numbers is the greatest number that is a factor of each number.

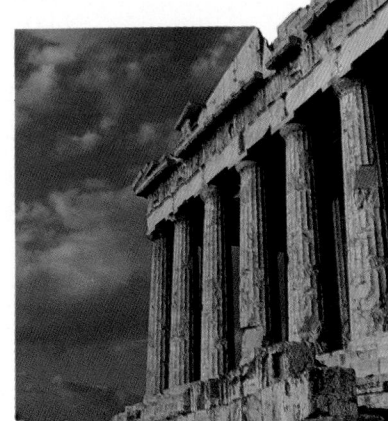

Mini-Lab

Work with a partner.
Materials: 4 colored pencils

- Copy the array of numbers shown at the right.
- Use a different colored pencil for each step below.

	2	3	4	5	6	7	8	9	10
11	12	13	14	15	16	17	18	19	20
21	22	23	24	25	26	27	28	29	30
31	32	33	34	35	36	37	38	39	40
41	42	43	44	45	46	47	48	49	50

Follow this "sieve" process.

Step 1 Circle 2, the first prime number. Cross out every second number after 2.

Step 2 Circle 3, the second prime number. Cross out every third number after 3.

Step 3 Circle 5, the third prime number. Cross out every fifth number after 5.

Step 4 Circle 7, the fourth prime number. Cross out every seventh number after 7.

Talk About It

a. In the process, 30 was crossed off when using which primes? **2, 3, 5**

b. In the process, 42 was crossed off when using which primes? **2, 3, 7**

c. What prime factors do 30 and 42 have in common? What composite factor do they have in common? **2, 3; 6**

d. What is the greatest common factor of 30 and 42? **6**

"When am I ever going to use this?"

Health Care Professional

There are many career options in this field from home health care aides to highly trained nurses and physicians.

In addition to specific training, health care workers need to have estimation and problem solving skills.

For more information contact:
National Health Council
350 Fifth Avenue,
Suite 1118
New York, NY 10118

4-5 Lesson Notes

NCTM Standards: 1-7

Lesson Resources

- Study Guide Master 4-5
- Practice Master 4-5
- Enrichment Master 4-5
- Evaluation Master, Quiz A, p. 34
- Group Activity Card 4-5

Transparency 4-5 contains the 5-Minute Check and a teaching aid for this lesson.

5-Minute Check

(Over Lesson 4-4)

1. Find the Fibonacci number for F28. 317,811
2. What is the greatest common factor of the Fibonacci numbers F6 and F12? 8

1 FOCUS

Motivating the Lesson

Situational Problem Ask students to explain how they would find the greatest common factor of 8 and 12. Ask them to explain whether the same method is practical for finding the GCF of 36 and 212.

2 TEACH

Using the Mini-Lab Have students explain why crossing out the numbers in each step is a way of finding prime numbers. Then ask them to suggest what Step 5 might be, if the array were increased to include numbers through 200. Crossing out multiples leaves prime numbers; circle 11 and cross out every 11th number after it.

Teaching Tip As students do Example 2, make sure they understand why they write $3 \times 3 \times 5$ and not $3 \times 3 \times 3 \times 5 \times 5$ or 3×5 to find the GCF.

OPTIONS

Reteaching Activity

Using Models Help students find prime factors by having them complete partially completed factor trees. In addition, review divisibility rules, and encourage students to use calculators to find factors.

Study Guide Masters, p. 33

Name ______ Date ______

Study Guide Worksheet 4-5

Greatest Common Factor

The greatest common factor (GCF) of two or more numbers is the greatest number that is a factor of each number. One way to find the GCF is to list the factors of each number and then choose the greatest of the common factors.

Example Find the GCF of 72 and 108.

factors of 72: 1, 2, 3, 4, 6, 8, 9, 12, 18, 24, 36, 72
factors of 108: 1, 2, 3, 4, 6, 9, 12, 18, 27, 36, 54, 108

common factors: 1, 2, 3, 4, 6, 9, 12, 18, 36

The GCF of 72 and 108 is 36.

Another way to find the GCF is to write the prime factorization of each number. Then identify all common prime factors and find their product.

More Examples

For Example 1

Find the GCF of 36 and 48 by listing the factors of each number.   GCF = 12

For Example 2

Find the GCF of 160 and 550 by writing the prime factorization of each number.   GCF = 10

For Example 3

Find the GCF of 450, 552, and 207 by writing the prime factorization of each number.   GCF = 3

Checking for Understanding

Exercises 1–3 are designed to help you assess students' understanding through reading, writing, speaking, and modeling. You should work through these exercises with your students and then monitor their work on Guided Practice Exercises 4–13.

Practice Masters, p. 33

Name _____ Date _____

Practice Worksheet 4-5

Greatest Common Factor

Find the GCF of each set of numbers by listing the factors of each number.

1. 12, 18
   Factors of 12:
   1, 2, 3, 4, 6, 12
   Factors of 18:
   1, 2, 3, 6, 9, 18
   GCF: 6

2. 16, 30
   Factors of 16:
   1, 2, 4, 8, 16
   Factors of 30:
   1, 2, 3, 5, 6, 10
   15, 30
   GCF: 2

3. 44, 153
   Factors of 44:
   1, 2, 4, 11, 22, 44
   Factors of 153:
   1, 3, 9, 17, 51,
   153
   GCF: 1

List the common prime factors for each pair of numbers. Then write the GCF.

4. $80 = 2^4 \times 5$
   $110 = 2 \times 5 \times 11$
   Common prime factors: 2, 5
   GCF: 10

5. $42 = 2 \times 3 \times 7$
   $49 = 7 \times 7$
   Common prime factor: 7
   GCF: 7

6. $16 = 2^4$
   $48 = 2^4 \times 3$
   Common prime factors: 2^4
   GCF: 16

Find the GCF of each pair of numbers by writing the prime factorization of each number.

7. 35, 85
   35   85
   5×7 5×17
   Common prime factor: 5
   GCF: 5

8. 40, 100
   40   100
   4×10 10×10
   2×2 2×5 2×5 2×5
   Common prime factors: 2, 2, 5
   GCF: 20

9. 42, 23
   42   23
   2×21 23×1
   3×7
   Common prime factor: none
   GCF: 1

Find the GCF of each set of numbers.

10. 66, 72
    6

11. 144, 72
    72

12. 9, 11
    1

13. 720, 480
    240

14. 90, 130
    10

15. 12, 33
    3

16. 6, 9, 12
    3

17. 10, 20, 35
    5

18. 64, 80, 120
    8

T33
Glencoe Division, Macmillan/McGraw-Hill

146

One of the following two methods is usually used to find the greatest common factor (GCF) of two or more numbers.

Method 1: List the factors of each number. Then identify the common factors and choose the greatest of these common factors, the GCF.

LOOKBACK

You can review prime factorization on page 132.

Method 2: Write the prime factorization of each number. Then identify all common prime factors and find their product, the GCF.

Examples

Problem-Solving Hint
● ● ● ● ● ● ● ● ● ● ● ●
Make a list.

1 Find the GCF of 45 and 54 by listing the factors of each number.

factors of 45: **1**, **3**, 5, **9**, 15, 45
factors of 54: **1**, 2, **3**, 6, **9**, 18, 27, 54

common factors: 1, 3, 9

Thus, the GCF of 45 and 54 is 9.

2 Find the GCF of 180 and 675 by writing the prime factorization of each number.

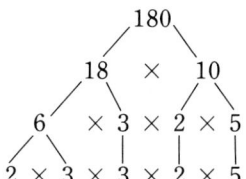 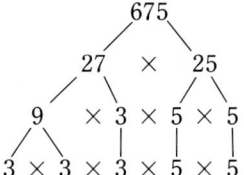

common prime factors: 3, 3, 5

Thus, the GCF of 180 and 675 is $3 \times 3 \times 5$ or 45.

3 Find the GCF of 510, 714, and 306 by writing the prime factorization of each number.

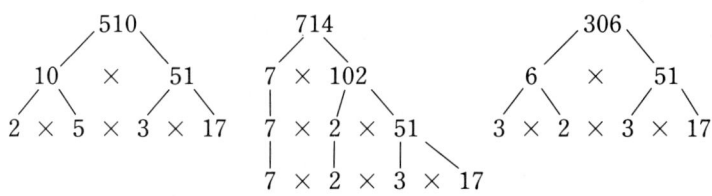

common prime factors: 2, 3, 17

Thus, the GCF of 510, 714, and 306 is $2 \times 3 \times 17$ or 102.

OPTIONS

Bell Ringer

The difference between two 2-digit numbers is the square of their GCF. The sum of the digits of both numbers is the same. What are the numbers?   51 and 60

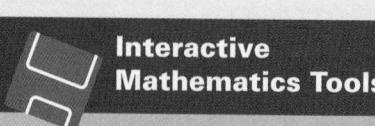

Interactive Mathematics Tools

This multimedia software provides an interactive lesson that is tied directly to Lesson 4–5. Students will use changeable grids to determine the greatest common factor of two integers.

Checking for Understanding

Communicating Mathematics

Read and study the lesson to answer each question.

1. **Write** all the common factors of 12 and 20. Which is the greatest common factor? **1, 2, 4; 4**

2. **Draw** factor trees for 210 and 150, and then circle the common factors. What is the GCF of 210 and 150? **See Solutions Manual.**

3. **Tell** why the GCF of 56 and 140 is *not* 14, even though $56 = 14 \times 4$ and $140 = 14 \times 10$. **See Solutions Manual.**

Guided Practice

Find the GCF of each pair of numbers by listing the factors of each number.

4. 16, 36 **4**   5. 12, 30 **6**   6. 33, 121 **11**   7. 28, 84 **28**

List the common prime factors for each pair of numbers. Then write the GCF.

8. $60 = 2^2 \times 3 \times 5$
    $105 = 3 \times 5 \times 7$ **3, 5; 15**

9. $36 = 2^2 \times 3^2$
    $27 = 3^3$ **3, 3; 9**

Find the GCF of each pair of numbers by writing the prime factorization of each number.

10. 45, 75 **15**   11. 100, 30 **10**   12. 12, 78 **6**   13. 39, 91 **13**

Exercises

Independent Practice

Find the GCF of each set of numbers.

14. 360, 540 **180**   15. 132, 108 **12**   16. 120, 72 **24**   17. 14, 33 **1**

18. 18, 54 **18**   19. 20, 30 **10**   20. 16, 28 **4**   21. 8, 9 **1**

22. 6, 8, 12 **2**   23. 10, 15, 20 **5**   24. 18, 42, 60 **6**   25. 54, 90, 126 **18**

26. Name two different pairs of numbers whose GCF is 28. **See Solutions Manual.**

Mixed Review

27. Jamie Hyatt has 12 gallons of gasoline in her car. She needs to drive 465 miles to a business meeting. Her car averages 37 miles per gallon. Can Jamie make the trip without stopping for gasoline? *(Lesson 1-1)* **no**

28. Estimate 23.69 divided by 4.05. *(Lesson 2-3)* **about 6**

29. **Statistics** Construct a line plot for 76, 65, 82, 93, 75, 72, 81, and 90. *(Lesson 3-4)* **See Solutions Manual.**

30. Describe the pattern and find the next three terms for the sequence 13, 26, 52, 104, . . . *(Lesson 4-3)* **multiply by 2; 208, 416, 832**

Problem Solving and Applications

31. In the sequence 15, 30, 45, 60, 75, . . . , what is the GCF of all the numbers in the sequence? **15**

32. **School** A band director chooses to have the band march on and off the field in a rectangular array. She likes to have at least 3 rows. On a piece of graph paper, sketch all the possible rectangular arrays for 48 musicians. **See Solutions Manual.**

33. **Number Sense** Can the GCF of a set of numbers be greater than any one of the numbers? Explain. **See Solutions Manual.**

34. **Critical Thinking** A set of numbers whose GCF is 1 are *relatively prime*. Find the two least composite numbers that are relatively prime. **4, 9**

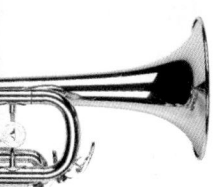

Lesson 4-5 Greatest Common Factor   **147**

Extending the Lesson

Using Another Method Tell students that another way to find the GCF of two numbers is to divide the greater one by the lesser one, and then divide the divisor by the remainder, repeating the process until the remainder is 0. The GCF will be the last divisor. This process is called the Euclidean Algorithm. Have students try this method with a few pairs of numbers.

Cooperative Learning Activity

Prime Time 4-5

Use groups of 2.
Materials: Spinners

✦ Label equal sections of one spinner "Factor" and "No Factor." Label equal sections of a second spinner "2," "3," "5," "7," "11," "37."

➡ In turn, each partner spins the first spinner described above. If the spinner points to "Factor," spin the second spinner and write the resulting number. If the spinner points to "No Factor," you do not spin the other spinner and you do not write a factor for the round. Continue until each partner has spun the first spinner ten times. Then each partner multiplies the factors he or she has written, and the partners find the greatest common factor for the resulting products by multiplying the common prime factors.

Glencoe Mathematics: Applications and Connections, Course 2

Error Analysis

Watch for students who find the prime factors of two numbers, but use them incorrectly to find the GCF.

Prevent by having students circle all the *common* prime factors of the two numbers and then multiply them.

Close

Have students find the GCF of 200 and 144 first by listing factors and then by writing the prime factorization of each number.   **GCF = 8**

3 PRACTICE/APPLY

Assignment Guide

Maximum: 14–34

Minimum: 15–25 odd, 27–34

For **Extra Practice**, see p. 580.

Alternate Assessment

Speaking Have students explain how to find the GCF of two numbers if they know the prime factors of each.   **Multiply the common factors.**

Enrichment Masters, p. 33

NCTM Standards: 1–4, 7

Objective Analyze data and make a decision.

1 FOCUS

Introducing the Situation

Have groups of students begin by sharing experiences they have had ordering catalogue items. Have them discuss the various expenses, options, shipping considerations, and any hidden data or costs involved. As they work through the lesson, a group member should record their responses to the questions raised, including any new questions that come up.

2 TEACH

Using Applications Provide students with actual catalogues so that they can see the variety of factors to consider when ordering. Guide students to see that people purchasing from catalogues must answer questions similar to those presented in this lesson.

Analyzing the Data

Ask students which is more expensive per pound, a 5-pound 3 BOX CLUB or a 7-pound DELUXE 3 BOX CLUB.   DELUXE

Checking for Understanding

Have each group prepare an ordered list of the questions they have about planning their fruit purchase, and their strategies for answering them. Ask a representative of each group to explain how they prioritized their list. Encourage groups to revise their plan as they hear the questions and methods of the other groups.

Sponsoring a Retirement Center

Situation

Suppose your student body voted unanimously to sponsor the Crown Retirement Center this year. For most of the year, you scheduled in-house activities with music, writers and readers, and parties. There are two trips scheduled for outside the retirement center, but some of the patients can't leave. What activities will you plan for them to make February and August special? Since the student body has $650 in their treasury, Meg suggests that they order fruit from the Big Bounty Catalogue.

Hidden Data

There are shipping and handling charges when ordering from a catalogue. There may be reduced prices or club prices. You may need to watch the quantity on membership prices.

To avoid long distance charges, see if there is an 800 number for toll-free calling.

Big Bounty Catalogue's Fruit of the Month Club

January Crisp Valley Apples	$19.99	**3 BOX CLUB** (Jan., Feb., Mar.)	**$53.99**
February Sumptuous Grapefruit	19.99		
March Lucious Large Oranges	20.99	**5 BOX CLUB** (3 box plus June, Aug.)	**85.99**
April Exotic Pineapple	22.99		
May Maypole Apples	21.99	**8 BOX CLUB** (5 box plus May, July , Oct.)	**145.99**
June Plumet Plums	20.99		
July Golden Tangerines	22.99	**12 BOX CLUB** (All 12 boxes shown)	**210.99**
August Natural Nectarines	21.99		
September Russet Pears	20.99		
October Blue Giant Grapes	21.99	Each box is approximately 5 pounds.	
November Best Bosc Pears	19.99		
December Japanette Apples	23.99		

Deluxe Clubs
Each box is approximately 7 pounds.

3 BOX CLUB....... **$82.99**
5 BOX CLUB........ **111.99**
8 BOX CLUB....... **162.99**
12 BOX CLUB...... **229.99**

Giant Party Drums -
Giant pears and apples, cookies, candies, corn puffs, cheeses, and nuts: ORDER ANY TIME.

$7\frac{1}{2}$ gal. drum, about 10 lb.....**$60.00**
4 gal. drum, about $5\frac{1}{2}$ lb......**$40.00**

Standard Delivery Charge	
Merchandise Total	Add
Up to $25.00	$3.95
$25.01-$50.00	$5.95
$50.01-$100.00	$9.95
$100.01-$150.00	$14.95
$150.01-$200.00	$19.95
$200.01-$250.00	$24.95
$250.01-$400.01	$29.95

We will compute all applicable state and local taxes.

Analyzing the Data

1. What is the standard delivery charge for a 3 BOX CLUB?
2. What is the standard delivery charge for a DELUXE 12 BOX CLUB?
3. What other items can be ordered besides the BOX CLUB?

Making a Decision

4. **Can you** find a club item for February and August?
5. **Would you** buy extra items to have the club selections?
6. **Is there** a charge for state and local taxes?
7. **Can you** order gifts for less than one per person?
8. **Can you** order one large gift that all patients can share?
9. **Did you** check with the nursing home staff for patient diet information?

Making Decisions in the Real World

10. **Request** special prices for your school project from local shops in return for advertising possibilities.
11. **Find** the cost of buying separate items and packaging them at school.

149

---

3 PRACTICE/APPLY

Making a Decision

Ask students to list any other questions they have or matters they will have to consider before choosing what to buy.

Making Decisions in the Real World

Tell students to imagine that they are going to buy in quantity from a local merchant's catalogue. Have them visit the store and speak with the owner about arrangements that might lower the cost of the purchase. Before they visit the store, students should think of ways a purchase at a lower price would benefit both the school and the business. If they have a plan for providing advertising, students should write out the plan and present it to the store owner. Students should report to the class with the results of their transaction with the store.

Answers
1. $9.95
2. $24.95
3. individual types of fruit, giant party drums
4.–9. Answers will vary.

Lesson Resources
- Study Guide Master 4-6
- Practice Master 4-6
- Enrichment Master 4-6
- Technology Master, p. 18
- Group Activity Card 4-6

Transparency 4-6 contains the 5-Minute Check and a teaching aid for this lesson.

⏱ 5-Minute Check
(Over Lesson 4-5)

Find the GCF of each set of numbers.

1. 8, 28 4
2. 36, 60 12
3. 124, 280 4
4. 26, 65, 117 13
5. What is the GCF of all the numbers in the sequence 12, 24, 36, 48, . . . ? 12

---

1 FOCUS

Motivating the Lesson

Activity Tell students that out of 276 passes thrown, a quarterback completed 168. Ask them to write a fraction in simplest form to express this statistic. $\frac{14}{23}$

2 TEACH

Using Communication Talk with students about how it is possible to express an idea in many ways, some simpler than others. Using students' suggestions, list on the chalkboard different ways of saying something without changing the meaning. Then discuss with students the terminology *reduced form* and *simplest form* when applied to a fraction such as $\frac{1}{2}$. Ask them why *reduced form* could be misleading. Sample answer: The word *reduced* suggests that the value of the fraction has diminished.

4-6 Fractions in Simplest Form

Objective
Express fraction in simplest form.

Words to Learn
simplest form

DID YOU KNOW

The Appalachian dulcimer is an American variety of the zither. Various forms of the zither were played in Europe during the 18th century. The Swedish *hummel*, the Norwegian *langleik*, and the French *épinette des Vosges* are but a few of the regional forms of the zither.

A dulcimer is a stringed musical instrument that produces a soft, melodic sound. The most common dulcimer in the United States is the Appalachian dulcimer. It is used to play a variety of folk music. Music is produced by strumming or hammering the strings. When struck, a string vibrates and produces a specific tone. For example, when middle C is played, the string vibrates at a frequency of 256 vibrations per second, producing the tone for middle C. The tone for the next higher C is produced by a frequency of 512 vibrations per second.

Can you express the fractions $\frac{256}{512}$ in simplest form? A fraction is in **simplest form** when the GCF of the numerator and denominator is 1.

To express a fraction in simplest form:

- find the greatest common factor (GCF) of the numerator and denominator,
- divide the numerator and the denominator by the GCF, and
- write the resulting fraction.

To simplify $\frac{256}{512}$, first find the GCF of 256 and 512 by listing the factors of each number.

factors of 256: 1, 2, 4, 8, 16, 32, 64, 128, 256
factors of 512: 1, 2, 4, 8, 16, 32, 64, 128, 256, 512

The GCF of 256 and 512 is 256.

$$\frac{256}{512} = \frac{256 \div 256}{512 \div 256} = \frac{1}{2}$$

OPTIONS

Gifted and Talented Needs

Ask students to provide examples of situations that can be expressed by fractions in which it makes more sense or is more useful *not* to use the simplest form of the fraction.
Sample answer: When writing a check, one writes, for example "Twenty six and $\frac{25}{100}$ dollars."

If the numerator and denominator do not have any common factors other than 1, then the fraction is in simplest form.

Examples

Express each fraction in simplest form.

1 $\frac{36}{54}$

Since $36 = 2 \times 2 \times 3 \times 3$ and $54 = 2 \times 3 \times 3 \times 3$, the GCF of 36 and 54 is $2 \times 3 \times 3$ or 18.

Now divide the numerator and denominator by using the GCF.

$$\frac{36}{54} = \frac{36 \div 18}{54 \div 18} = \frac{2}{3}$$

2 $\frac{45}{75}$

Since $45 = 3 \times 3 \times 5$ and $75 = 3 \times 5 \times 5$, the GCF of 45 and 75 is 3×5 or 15.

$$\frac{45}{75} = \frac{45 \div 15}{75 \div 15} = \frac{3}{5}$$

3 $\frac{17}{35}$

Since $35 = 5 \times 7$ and 17 is prime, 17 and 35 have no common factors greater than 1. Therefore, $\frac{17}{35}$ is in simplest form.

For answers to Exercises 1-3, see margin.

Checking for Understanding

Communicating Mathematics Read and study the lesson to answer each question.

1. **Tell** how to determine if a fraction is in simplest form.
2. **Tell** why $\frac{13}{17}$ is in simplest form, but $\frac{2}{4}$ is not in simplest form.
3. **Tell** why the method shown below does not produce an equivalent fraction in simplest form.

$$\frac{35}{45} = \frac{3\cancel{5}}{4\cancel{5}} = \frac{3}{4}$$

Guided Practice Express each fraction in simplest form.

4. $\frac{15}{35}$ $\frac{3}{7}$
5. $\frac{150}{350}$ $\frac{3}{7}$
6. $\frac{25}{45}$ $\frac{5}{9}$
7. $\frac{99}{66}$ $\frac{3}{2}$
8. $\frac{81}{90}$ $\frac{9}{10}$
9. $\frac{44}{160}$ $\frac{11}{40}$
10. $\frac{64}{80}$ $\frac{4}{5}$
11. $\frac{300}{400}$ $\frac{3}{4}$
12. Write two different fractions that can be expressed in simplest form as $\frac{5}{7}$.
   Sample answers: $\frac{25}{35}$, $\frac{15}{21}$

More Examples

Express each fraction in simplest form.

For Example 1

$\frac{28}{49}$ $\frac{4}{7}$

For Example 2

$\frac{50}{80}$ $\frac{5}{8}$

For Example 3

$\frac{13}{40}$ is in simplest form

Checking for Understanding

Exercises 1–3 are designed to help you assess students' understanding through reading, writing, speaking, and modeling. You should work through these exercises with your students and then monitor their work on Guided Practice Exercises 4–12.

Additional Answers

1. It is in simplest form, if the GCF is 1.
2. The GCF of 13 and 17 is 1 while the GCF of 2 and 4 is 2.
3. The GCF of 35 and 45 is 5. Divide 35 and 45 both by 5 to get $\frac{7}{9}$, not $\frac{3}{4}$.

Reteaching Activity

Using Manipulatives Have students use fraction strips to model different ways of expressing a fraction, such as $\frac{4}{8}$. Have them express that fraction in simplest form.

Study Guide Masters, p. 34

Name ______ Date ______

Study Guide Worksheet 4-6

Fractions in Simplest Form

A fraction is in simplest form when the greatest common factor (GCF) of the numerator and the denominator is 1.

Example Express $\frac{36}{54}$ in simplest form.

factors of 36: 1, 2, 3, 4, 6, 9, 12, 18, 36
factors of 54: 1, 2, 3, 6, 9, 18, 27, 54
The GCF of 36 and 54 is 18.

$\frac{36}{54} = \frac{36 \div 18}{54 \div 18} = \frac{2}{3}$ Divide the numerator and denominator by the GCF.

The GCF of 2 and 3 is 1.
The simplest form of $\frac{36}{54}$ is $\frac{2}{3}$.

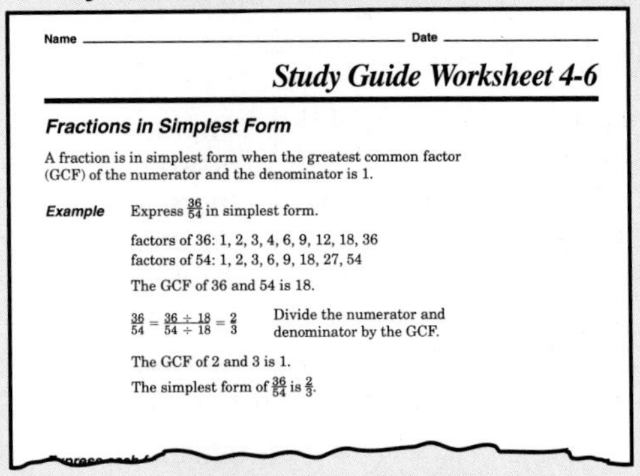

Close

Have students write a fraction in simplest form that expresses the number of days per month that they have school this month and that they will have next month.

3 PRACTICE/APPLY

Assignment Guide
Maximum: 13–39
Minimum: 13–27, odd, 29–38
All: Mid-Chapter Review

For **Extra Practice,** see p. 580.

Alternate Assessment

Speaking   Have students explain why the fraction $\frac{17}{30}$ is expressed in simplest form, and why the fraction $\frac{12}{30}$ is not.   **The GCF of 17 and 30 is 1. The GCF of 12 and 30 is 6.**

Practice Masters, p. 34

152

Exercises

Independent Practice   Express each fraction in simplest form.

13. $\frac{16}{32}$ $\frac{1}{2}$ 14. $\frac{50}{75}$ $\frac{2}{3}$ 15. $\frac{250}{450}$ $\frac{5}{9}$ 16. $\frac{42}{72}$ $\frac{7}{12}$

17. $\frac{27}{33}$ $\frac{9}{11}$ 18. $\frac{120}{100}$ $\frac{6}{5}$ 19. $\frac{49}{63}$ $\frac{7}{9}$ 20. $\frac{9}{123}$ $\frac{3}{41}$

21. $\frac{56}{128}$ $\frac{7}{16}$ 22. $\frac{125}{625}$ $\frac{1}{5}$ 23. $\frac{22}{33}$ $\frac{2}{3}$ 24. $\frac{20}{36}$ $\frac{5}{9}$

Write three different fractions that can be expressed in simplest form as each of the following. **For Exercises 25–28, sample answers are given.**

25. $\frac{2}{3}$ $\frac{4}{6}, \frac{6}{9}, \frac{8}{12}$ 26. $\frac{3}{10}$ $\frac{6}{20}, \frac{9}{30}, \frac{12}{40}$ 27. $\frac{3}{4}$ $\frac{6}{8}, \frac{9}{12}, \frac{12}{16}$ 28. $\frac{5}{6}$ $\frac{10}{12}, \frac{15}{18}, \frac{20}{24}$

Mixed Review   29. Is $234 \div 7 = 3.7$ reasonable? *(Lesson 1-4)* **no**

30. Divide 0.81 by 0.3 *(Lesson 2-7)* **2.7**

31. **Statistics**   Refer to the graph in Exercise 5 on page 115. Which color of shoe would you consider to be the least popular? *(Lesson 3-7)* **red**

32. Find the greatest common factor of 72 and 270. *(Lesson 4-5)* **18**

Problem Solving and Application   33. **School**   Clark Middle School has 525 girls and 600 boys. Express the number of girls as a fraction of the total student population. Write the fraction in simplest form. $\frac{525}{1,125} = \frac{7}{15}$

34. **Sports**   Kara has won 24 of her 30 tennis matches during the tennis season.
    a. In simplest form, what fraction of her matches has she won? $\frac{24}{30} = \frac{4}{5}$
    b. In simplest form, what fraction of her matches has she lost? $\frac{6}{30} = \frac{1}{5}$

35. **Daily Living**   Jacob made the following table showing how he spends his day. Find the fraction of the day he spends on each activity.
    a. Express all fractions in simplest form.

Activity	Number of Hours	
Sleeping	8	$\frac{1}{3}$
Eating	2	$\frac{1}{12}$
Dressing & bathing	1	$\frac{1}{24}$
School	7	$\frac{7}{24}$
Studying	3	$\frac{1}{8}$
Swim practice	2	$\frac{1}{12}$
Miscellaneous	1	$\frac{1}{24}$

    b. Make a table for your day. Include at least six activities. **See students' work**

OPTIONS

Bell Ringer

Have students explain what is inaccurate about the following advertisers' claims.

1. *All shirts at only a fraction of the list price.*   The fraction might be $\frac{99}{100}$.

2. *Putting it as simply as we can, 15 out of every 20 customers come back.* $\frac{15}{20} = \frac{3}{4}; \frac{3}{4}$ is simpler.

36. **Critical Thinking** Ling read 125 pages of his 300-page book.
   a. What fraction of his book has he read? $\frac{5}{12}$
   b. If Ashley has read the same fraction of her 240-page book, how many pages has she read? **100 pages**

Solve. Use the chart at the right.

37. Suppose a female, age 13, took in 2,000 calories in one day. What fraction, in simplest form, of the recommended daily calories did she take in? $\frac{10}{11}$

38. Suppose a male, age 25, took in 3,600 calories in one day. What fraction, in simplest form, represents the amount he took in compared to the recommended daily calories? $\frac{4}{3}$

Recommended Daily Calories (moderately active person)		
	Females	Males
Age	Calories	Calories
11–14	2,200	2,700
15–18	2,100	2,800
19–22	2,100	2,900
23–50	2,000	2,700
51+	1,800	2,400

39. **Journal Entry** Could a fraction have more than one simplest form? Explain your answer. **No; once GCF of numerator and denominator is 1, there is no other simplest form.**

4 Assessment: Mid-Chapter Review

Determine whether the first number is divisible by the second number. *(Lesson 4-1)*

1. 811; 5 **no**   2. 392; 4 **yes**   3. 5,739; 3 **yes**   4. 3,025; 9 **no**

Write the prime factorization for each number. *(Lesson 4-2)*

5. 28 $2^2 \times 7$ 6. 57 3×19 7. 72 $2^3 \times 3^2$ 8. 108 $2^2 \times 3^3$

Identify each sequence as arithmetic, geometric, or neither. Then find the next three terms in each sequence. *(Lesson 4-3)*

9. 12, 19, 26, 33, . . .   10. 3, 15, 75, 375, . . .   11. 16, 2, $\frac{1}{4}$, $\frac{1}{32}$, . . .
   A; 40, 47, 54   **G; 1,875, 9,375, 46,875**   **G;** $\frac{1}{256}, \frac{1}{2,048}, \frac{1}{16,384}$

Solve by making a list. *(Lesson 4-4)*

12. Show that the sum of the first ten Fibonacci numbers is divisible by 11. Then show that the sum of the second through the eleventh terms is also divisible by 11. *Recall the sequence: 1, 1, 2, 3, 5, 8, 13, 21, ...* $\frac{143}{11} = 13$; $\frac{231}{11} = 21$

Find the GCF of each set of numbers. *(Lesson 4-5)*

13. 12, 56 **4**   14. 110, 215 **5**   15. 88, 383 **1**   16. 35, 72 **1**

Express each fraction in simplest form. *(Lesson 4-6)*

17. $\frac{18}{63}$ $\frac{2}{7}$ 18. $\frac{7}{98}$ $\frac{1}{14}$ 19. $\frac{228}{336}$ $\frac{19}{28}$ 20. $\frac{120}{35}$ $\frac{24}{7}$

Lesson 4-6 Fractions in Simplest Form   **153**

Extending the Lesson

Using Number Sense Have students work with a partner to make up a 5-question True/False quiz for classmates. All answers must be explained. Provide the following as a sample:

4 hours is $\frac{1}{4}$ of a day.

Cooperative Learning Activity

Fraction Match **4-6**

Number of players: 2
Materials: Index cards

• Copy onto cards the fractions shown on the back of this card, one fraction per card. Then shuffle the cards and place them face down in rows of four.

➡ In turn, each partner flips over two cards. Remove pairs of cards showing equivalent fractions from the game and turn nonmatching cards—cards showing fractions that are not equivalent—face down again. Either partner who finds a match continues until two nonmatching cards are flipped over. The partner with more pairs of equivalent fractions at the end of the game is the winner.

Glencoe Mathematics: Applications and Connections, Course 2

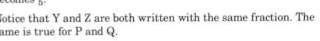

Lesson Resources

- Study Guide Master 4-7
- Practice Master 4-7
- Enrichment Master 4-7
- Technology Master, p. 4
- Lab Manual, p. 47
- Group Activity Card 4-7

 Transparency 4-7 contains the 5-Minute Check and a teaching aid for this lesson.

🕐 5-Minute Check
(Over Lesson 4-6)

Write each fraction in simplest form.

1. $\frac{14}{28}$ $\frac{1}{2}$
2. $\frac{75}{125}$ $\frac{3}{5}$
3. $\frac{20}{33}$ $\frac{20}{33}$
4. $\frac{12}{135}$ $\frac{4}{45}$
5. Write three different fractions that can be expressed as $\frac{4}{5}$ in simplest form. Sample answer: $\frac{8}{10}, \frac{12}{15}, \frac{20}{25}$

---

1 FOCUS

Motivating the Lesson

Activity Ask students to suggest situations for which they would want to express a fraction as a decimal, or to express a decimal as a fraction. Have students discuss the responses. Sample answers: as a decimal—for ease of comparison, as in sports statistics; as a fraction—for impact, as in advertising

2 TEACH

Using Calculators Once you are convinced students understand how to express a fraction as a decimal, encourage them to work more efficiently by using calculators to find decimal answers.

4-7 Fractions and Decimals

Objective

Express terminating decimals as fractions and express fractions as decimals.

Words to Learn

terminating decimal
repeating decimal

Are you a "lefty?" President Clinton, Paul McCartney, and Martina Navratilova are all left-handed. Actually, about 3 out of every 25 people are left-handed. The fraction $\frac{3}{25}$ can be expressed as a decimal.

There are two methods for expressing a fraction as a decimal.

Method 1: Find an equivalent fraction with a denominator of 10, 100, or any other power of 10. This equivalent fraction can easily be expressed as a decimal.

$$\overset{\curvearrowright \times 4}{\frac{3}{25}} = \frac{12}{100} = 0.12 \atop \curvearrowright \times 4$$

Method 2: A fraction indicates division. Divide the numerator of the fraction by the denominator.

$$\frac{3}{25} \;\rightarrow\; 25\overline{)3.00}^{\;0.12} \quad\text{or}\quad 3 \boxed{÷} 25 \boxed{=} \;\text{0.12}$$

This method may be more efficient than Method 1.

Examples

1 Express $\frac{33}{500}$ as a decimal by finding an equivalent fraction with a denominator of 10, 100, or 1,000.

$$\overset{\curvearrowright \times 2}{\frac{33}{500}} = \frac{66}{1,000} = 0.066 \atop \curvearrowright \times 2$$

2 Express $\frac{7}{8}$ as a decimal by dividing the numerator of the fraction by the denominator.

$$\frac{7}{8} \;\rightarrow\; 8\overline{)7.000}^{\;0.875} \quad\text{or}\quad 7 \boxed{÷} 8 \boxed{=} \;\text{0.875}$$

In both of these examples, the result is a **terminating decimal**. Every terminating decimal can be written as a fraction with a denominator of 10, 100, 1,000, and so on. Examples 3–5 involve fractions whose decimal equivalent is a **repeating decimal**. A repeating decimal is a decimal whose digits repeat forever.

OPTIONS

Reteaching Activity

Using Models Use hundreds squares and tens strips to show the relationship between fractions and decimals. Each square represents $\frac{1}{100}$ and each strip, $\frac{1}{10}$.

Study Guide Masters, p. 35

Name _____ Date _____

Study Guide Worksheet 4-7

Fractions and Decimals

To express a fraction as a decimal, divide the numerator of the fraction by the denominator.

Example Express $\frac{3}{8}$ as a decimal.

$$8\overline{)3.000}^{\;0.375} \qquad \frac{3}{8} = 0.375$$

A decimal like 0.375 is a terminating decimal. The decimal equivalents for some fractions are repeating decimals rather than terminating decimals. Use a bar to indicate the digits that repeat.

Examples Express $\frac{5}{12}$ as a decimal.   Express $\frac{13}{33}$ as a decimal.

$$12\overline{)5.00000}^{\;0.41666} = 0.41\overline{6} \qquad 33\overline{)13.000000}^{\;0.393939\ldots} = 0.\overline{39}$$

Express each fraction as a decimal using division.

3 $\frac{2}{3}$

Pencil and paper

$$\begin{array}{r} 0.666... \\ 3)\overline{2.000} \\ -1\ 8 \\ \hline 20 \\ -18 \\ \hline 2 \end{array}$$

We will continue to get a remainder of 2.

Calculator

$2 \boxed{\div} 3 \boxed{=} \boxed{0.6666667}$

A calculator can only show a certain number of digits. Even though the digit 6 will repeat forever, the calculator may round the final digit to 7.

Use a bar to indicate that the digit 6 repeats. So, $\frac{2}{3} = 0.\overline{6}$.

4 $\frac{5}{6}$

$5 \boxed{\div} 6 \boxed{=} \boxed{0.8333333}$

$\frac{5}{6} = 0.8\overline{3}$

5 $\frac{23}{99}$

$23 \boxed{\div} 99 \boxed{=} \boxed{0.2323232}$

$\frac{23}{99} = 0.\overline{23}$.

You can also express decimals as fractions. Express the decimal as a fraction with a denominator of the power of 10 indicated by the place value of the final digit of the decimal. Simplify the fraction.

$$0.12 = \frac{12}{100} = \frac{3}{25} \qquad \textit{The GCF of 12 and 100 is 4.}$$

Examples

Express each decimal as a fraction.

6 0.45

Write as a fraction. $\qquad 0.45 = \frac{45}{100}$

Simplify. $\qquad\qquad\quad = \frac{9}{20} \qquad$ *The GCF of 45 and 100 is 5.*

7 0.8

$0.8 = \frac{8}{10}$ or $\frac{4}{5}$

8 0.125

$0.125 = \frac{125}{1,000}$ or $\frac{1}{8}$

1. You can multiply each numerator and denominator by 2 to get a fraction whose denominator is 10.

Checking for Understanding

Communicating Mathematics

Read and study the lesson to answer each question.

1. **Tell** how you know that $\frac{1}{5}, \frac{2}{5}, \frac{3}{5},$ and $\frac{4}{5}$ will all be terminating decimals.

2. **Tell** why 0.45 and 0.450 can be represented by the same fraction. Can 0.450 and 0.045 be represented by the same fraction? Why or why not? **See margin.**

Lesson 4-7 Fractions and Decimals **155**

More Examples

For Example 1

Express $\frac{27}{500}$ as a decimal by finding an equivalent fraction with a denominator of 10, 100, or 1,000. 0.054

For Examples 2–5

Express $\frac{5}{8}$ as a decimal. 0.625

Express $\frac{1}{3}$ as a decimal. $0.\overline{3}$

Express $\frac{1}{6}$ as a decimal. $0.1\overline{6}$

Express $\frac{21}{99}$ as a decimal. $0.\overline{21}$

For Examples 6–8

Express each decimal as a fraction.

0.65 $\frac{13}{20}$ 0.6 $\frac{3}{5}$ 0.875 $\frac{7}{8}$

Checking for Understanding

Exercises 1–2 are designed to help you assess students' understanding through reading, writing, speaking, and modeling. You should work through these exercises with your students and then monitor their work on Guided Practice Exercises 3–17.

Practice Masters, p. 35

Name _____ Date _____

Practice Worksheet 4-7

Fractions and Decimals

Express each fraction as a decimal by finding an equivalent fraction with a denominator of 10, 100, or 1,000.

1. $\frac{3}{5}$
$\frac{6}{10} = 0.6$

2. $\frac{19}{20}$
$\frac{95}{100} = 0.95$

3. $\frac{22}{250}$
$\frac{88}{1000} = 0.088$

Express each fraction as a decimal by dividing. Use bar notation if necessary.

4. $\frac{23}{50}$
0.46

5. $\frac{17}{30}$
0.5$\overline{6}$

6. $1\frac{5}{8}$
1.625

Express each fraction as a decimal. Use bar notation if necessary.

7. $\frac{19}{25}$
0.76

8. $\frac{7}{12}$
0.58$\overline{3}$

9. $\frac{14}{110}$
0.1$\overline{27}$

10. $\frac{45}{180}$
0.25

11. $\frac{24}{40}$
0.6

12. $\frac{7}{8}$
0.875

Express each decimal as a fraction in simplest form.

13. 0.08
$\frac{2}{25}$

14. 0.225
$\frac{9}{40}$

15. 3.8
$3\frac{4}{5}$

16. 8.875
$8\frac{7}{8}$

17. 11.325
$11\frac{13}{40}$

18. 0.78
$\frac{39}{50}$

19. 1.375
$1\frac{3}{8}$

20. 14.74
$14\frac{37}{50}$

21. 0.29
$\frac{29}{100}$

T35
Glencoe Division, Macmillan/McGraw-Hill

Multicultural Education

Baseball batting averages are found by dividing the number of hits by the number of times at bat, and are expressed as decimals in thousandths. First baseman Buck Leonard of the Homestead Grays played in 5 consecutive Negro League All Star Games from 1937 to 1941. During that time, he had a combined average of 0.350. Ask students to guess how many times Leonard was at bat, and how many hits he had. 7 hits, 20 at-bats

Additional Answer

2. $0.45 = \frac{45}{100}$, $0.450 = \frac{450}{1,000} = \frac{45}{100}$; no; $0.450 = \frac{450}{1,000}$, $0.045 = \frac{45}{1,000}$, $\frac{450}{1,000} \neq \frac{45}{1,000}$

Watch for students who choose the incorrect power of 10 when writing a decimal as a fraction.

Prevent by having students read the decimal aloud so that they can hear the correct power of 10.

Close

Have students write a fraction to describe how far they have reached in a book they are reading. Then have them express that number as a decimal.

3 PRACTICE/APPLY

> ### Assignment Guide
> **Maximum:** 18–50
> **Minimum:** 19–41 odd, 43–49

For **Extra Practice,** see p. 580.

Alternate Assessment

Writing Have students express each of the following fractions as a decimal and order them from least to greatest: $\frac{5}{8}, \frac{2}{3}, \frac{7}{16}, \frac{5}{6}, \frac{7}{10}$ and $\frac{3}{4}$. 0.625, 0.666 . . . , 0.4375, 0.8333 . . . , 0.7, 0.75; $\frac{7}{16}, \frac{5}{8}, \frac{2}{3}, \frac{7}{10}$, $\frac{3}{4}, \frac{5}{6}$

Enrichment Masters, p. 35

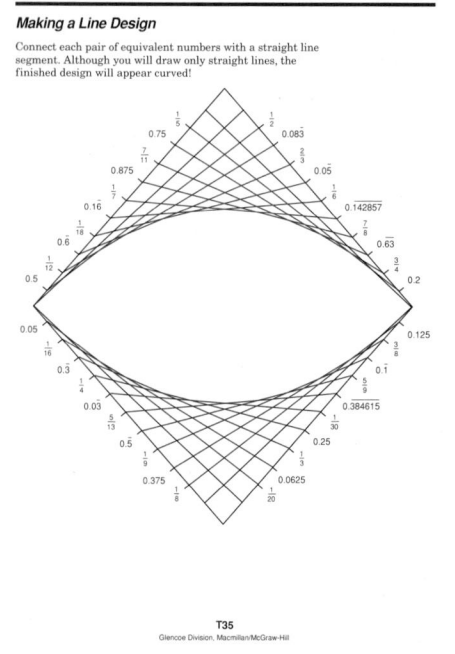

Name _____ Date _____

Enrichment Worksheet 4-7

Making a Line Design

Connect each pair of equivalent numbers with a straight line segment. Although you will draw only straight lines, the finished design will appear curved!

T35
Glencoe Division, Macmillan/McGraw-Hill

Guided Practice Express each fraction as a decimal by finding an equivalent fraction with a denominator of 10, 100, or 1,000.

3. $\frac{4}{5}$ 0.8 4. $\frac{17}{50}$ 0.34 5. $\frac{6}{25}$ 0.24 6. $\frac{7}{250}$ 0.028 7. $\frac{56}{50}$ 1.12

Express each fraction as a decimal by dividing. Use bar notation if necessary.

8. $\frac{14}{25}$ 0.56 9. $\frac{7}{40}$ 0.175 10. $1\frac{3}{8}$ 1.375 11. $\frac{7}{9}$ $0.\overline{7}$ 12. $\frac{4}{11}$ $0.\overline{36}$

Express each decimal as a fraction in simplest form.

13. 0.85 $\frac{17}{20}$ 14. 0.625 $\frac{5}{8}$ 15. 0.50 $\frac{1}{2}$ 16. 0.83 $\frac{83}{100}$ 17. 0.075 $\frac{3}{40}$

Exercises

Independent Practice Express each fraction as a decimal. Use bar notation if necessary.

18. $\frac{8}{25}$ 0.32 19. $\frac{11}{20}$ 0.55 20. $\frac{8}{250}$ 0.032 21. $\frac{6}{50}$ 0.12 22. $\frac{12}{200}$ 0.06

23. $\frac{14}{16}$ 0.875 24. $\frac{7}{12}$ $0.58\overline{3}$ 25. $\frac{3}{8}$ 0.375 26. $\frac{17}{25}$ 0.68 27. $\frac{8}{11}$ $0.\overline{72}$

28. $\frac{2}{3}$ $0.\overline{6}$ 29. $\frac{20}{30}$ $0.\overline{6}$ 30. $\frac{34}{125}$ 0.272 31. $\frac{7}{8}$ 0.875 32. $\frac{15}{9}$ $1.\overline{6}$

Express each decimal as a fraction in simplest form.

33. 0.09 34. 0.64 35. 0.375 36. 8.407 37. 2.5

38. 0.10 39. 0.48 40. 0.540 41. 12.205 42. 21.48

For answers to Exercises 33-42, see Solutions Manual.

Mixed Review 43. Evaluate 3^4. *(Lesson 1-9)* 81

0.22, 0.23, 1.6, 2.29, 2.3, 23

44. Order from least to greatest: 2.3, 0.23, 23, 1.6, 2.29, 0.22. *(Lesson 2-1)*

45. **Statistics** Angela collects the following heights (in inches) from the girls in her gym class: 62, 58, 68, 63, 64, 56, 65, 61, 70. Find the mean and the median height. *(Lesson 3-5)* 63, 63

46. Use a factor tree to find the prime factorization of 245. *(Lesson 4-2)* 5×7^2

47. Express $\frac{39}{81}$ in simplest form. *(Lesson 4-6)* $\frac{13}{27}$

Problem Solving and Applications 48. **Taxes** A mill is a unit of money that is used in assessing taxes. One mill is $\frac{1}{1,000}$ of a U.S. dollar or $\frac{1}{10}$ of a cent. Use these facts to copy and complete the following table.

	0.75	0.375	0.1	1,500	125	0.001
Mills	1,000	750	375	100	?	?	1
U.S. Dollars	1	?	?	?	1.50	?	?
Cents	100	?	?	?	?	12.5	?

75 37.5 10 150 0.125 0.1

49. **Critical Thinking** Which of the fractions, $\frac{1}{2}, \frac{1}{3}, \frac{1}{4}, \frac{1}{5}, \frac{1}{6}, \frac{1}{7}, \frac{1}{8}$, and $\frac{1}{9}$, are terminating decimals and which are repeating? **See Solutions Manual.**

50. **Journal Entry** Use long division to express $\frac{1}{9}$ and $\frac{2}{9}$ as decimals. Then, predict the decimal equivalents of $\frac{3}{9}, \frac{4}{9}, \frac{5}{9}, \frac{6}{9}, \frac{7}{9}$, and $\frac{8}{9}$. Use your calculator to check your predictions. Write a paragraph comparing your predictions to the decimals computed using your calculator. $0.\overline{1}, 0.\overline{2}, 0.\overline{3}, 0.\overline{4}, 0.\overline{5}, 0.\overline{6}, 0.\overline{7}, 0.\overline{8}$; See students' work.

156 Chapter 4 Patterns and Number Sense

OPTIONS

Extending the Lesson

Using Connections Have students explain how they would express a mixed number as a decimal.

Cooperative Learning Activity

Decimal Bingo 4-7

Number of players: 4 or more
Materials: Counters

⬥ Each group member copies a 4 x 4 grid on a separate sheet of paper. Be sure that a counter will fit in each box. Each group member then writes the following decimals in the boxes (in any order) to create a card for bingo.

0.155	0.95	0.875	0.044
0.24	0.145	0.4	0.085
0.125	0.082	0.074	0.325
0.625	0.13	0.035	0.75

No two group members should have exactly the same bingo card. Copy onto cards the fractions on the back of this card. Shuffle the cards and place them face down in a pile.

➡ In turn, each group member flips over a card, and all the group members place a counter on the equivalent decimal on their bingo cards. The first group member with four counters in any row, column, or diagonal is the winner.

Glencoe Mathematics: Applications and Connections, Course 2

4-8 Simple Events

Objective

Find the probability of a simple event.

Words to Learn

event
probability
random

Your school is raffling off a bicycle to raise money for new gym equipment. A total of 500 raffle tickets were sold. If your family bought 10 of the tickets, what is the probability that your family will win the bicycle?

The **event,** or specific outcome, we are interested in is your family winning the bicycle.

Probability	**In words:** The probability of an event is the ratio of the number of ways an event can occur to the number of possible outcomes.
	In symbols: $P(\text{event}) = \dfrac{\text{number of ways event occurs}}{\text{number of possible outcomes}}$

Outcomes occur at **random** if each outcome is equally likely to occur. Since the winning raffle ticket will be drawn at random,

$$P(\text{your family winning}) = \frac{\text{number of ways your family can win}}{\text{number of ways one ticket can be drawn}}$$

$$= \frac{10}{500} \qquad \textit{Your family has 10 tickets.}$$
$$\textit{500 tickets were sold.}$$

$$= \frac{1}{50} \qquad \textit{Express the fraction in simplest form.}$$

Thus, your family has a 1-in-50 chance of winning the bicycle. This probability can also be expressed as the decimal 0.02.

Example 1

You can review prime numbers on page 132.

Find the probability of drawing a card with a prime number on it from a deck of cards numbered 1 to 24.

$$P(\text{prime}) = \frac{\text{number of ways of drawing a card with a prime number}}{\text{number of ways a card can be drawn}}$$

$$= \frac{9}{24} \qquad \textit{The primes are 2, 3, 5, 7, 11, 13, 17, 19, and 23.}$$
$$\textit{There are 24 cards.}$$

$$= \frac{3}{8} \qquad \textit{The GCF of 9 and 24 is 3.}$$

The probability of drawing a card with a prime number is $\frac{3}{8}$ or 0.375.

4-8 Lesson Notes

NCTM Standards: 1–5, 7, 11

Lesson Resources
• Study Guide Master 4-8
• Practice Master 4-8
• Enrichment Master 4-8
• Interdisciplinary Master, p. 18
• Group Activity Card 4-8

 Transparency 4-8 contains the 5-Minute Check and a teaching aid for this lesson.

⏱ 5-Minute Check
(Over Lesson 4-7)

Express each fraction as a decimal.

1. $\frac{6}{25}$ 0.24

2. $\frac{3}{8}$ 0.375

3. $\frac{7}{11}$ $0.6\overline{36}$

Express each decimal as a fraction in simplest form.

4. 0.08 $\frac{2}{25}$

5. 6.148 $6\frac{37}{250}$

1 FOCUS

Motivating the Lesson

Situational Problem On the chalkboard, write the statements listed below, along with others. Have students categorize each as *certain*, *likely*, *unlikely*, or *impossible*.

• It will be dark tonight.
• A spaceship will land in Miami this year.
• There will be a flood somewhere this year.
• A scientist will clone a unicorn in 1998.

OPTIONS

Limited English Proficiency

Review the new vocabulary with students and have them add the terms to their list. Introduce the concept of "equally likely outcomes" by spinning a spinner or flipping a coin, and having students tell or demonstrate what is likely to occur.

Using the Mini-Lab Before students do the activity, ask them to predict which sum or sums will occur most often and which will occur least often. Have them compare their results with their predictions as well as with the theoretical probabilities. Ask them to try to explain any discrepancies.

More Examples

For Example 1

Find the probability of drawing a red card from a shuffled deck containing 10 red cards, 10 black cards, and 5 yellow cards.

$\frac{2}{5}$

For Example 2

Gary's Gas Station is having a contest. Every customer who buys gas gets a ticket with a number on it. Each week, a winning ticket is drawn and the winner gets a free tank of gas. This week, 220 people bought gas each day. Opal bought gas twice. What is the probability that she will win the free fill-up?

$\frac{2}{1,540}$, or about 0.0013

Checking for Understanding

Exercises 1–3 are designed to help you assess students' understanding through reading, writing, speaking, and modeling. You should work through these exercises with your students and then monitor their work on Guided Practice Exercises 4–11.

Additional Answer

f. $\frac{1}{36}, \frac{1}{18}, \frac{1}{12}, \frac{1}{9}, \frac{5}{36}, \frac{1}{6}, \frac{5}{36}, \frac{1}{9}, \frac{1}{12}, \frac{1}{18}$, $\frac{1}{36}$

158

Madonna's real name is Madonna Louise Veronica Ciccone.

Example 2 *Problem Solving*

Business Burger House is having a contest. Each time you visit, you can place your name in a barrel. Each week they will draw one winner who will receive a $20 gift certificate. Burger House serves about 450 customers per day every day of the week. Lisa has put her name in the barrel twice this week. What is the probability that she will win? Assume half of the customers put their name in the barrel.

First find the total number of cards in the barrel for one week. Then divide by the number of cards that Lisa placed in the barrel.

number of cards: 450 $\boxed{\div}$ 2 $\boxed{\times}$ 7 $\boxed{=}$ **1575**
number of cards with Lisa's name on them: 2

$$P(\text{Lisa}) = \frac{\text{number of cards with Lisa's name}}{\text{number of cards in the barrel}}$$

$$= \frac{2}{1,575}$$

$$= \frac{2}{1,575} \qquad 2 \boxed{\div} 1575 \boxed{=} \mathbf{0.0012698}$$

The probability of Lisa's name being drawn is $\frac{2}{1,575}$ or about 0.0013.

 **Mini-Lab**

Work with a partner.
Materials: two number cubes

- Roll the number cubes 100 times.
- Make a frequency table and record the sum of the numbers on the two cubes.
- Copy and complete the table at the right. The table shows the sum of the numbers rolled on two cubes.

Number Cube A

		1	2	3	4	5	6
Number Cube B	1	2	3	4	5	6	7
	2	3	4	5	6	7	8
	3	4	5	6	7	8	9
	4	5	6	7	8	9	10
	5	6	7	8	9	10	11
	6	7	8	9	10	11	12

Talk About It

a. What patterns do you see in the table? **See students' work.**
b. What is the most frequent sum in the table? **7**
c. What sum(s) did you roll most frequently? **See students' work.**
d. What is the least frequent sum in the table? **2, 12**
e. What sum(s) did you roll least frequently? **See students' work.**
f. There are 36 entries in the table and the number 6 is shown in five of them. This means that the probability of rolling a sum of 6 using two number cubes is $\frac{5}{36}$ or $0.13\overline{8}$. Find the probability for rolling each sum from 2 to 12. **See margin.**
g. Describe how your actual results of rolling the number cubes compare to the probabilities found in part f. **See students' work.**

OPTIONS

Reteaching Activity

Using Models Using counters of one color, ask students for the probability of randomly choosing one counter of that color. Then repeat the process with two counters of one color and two of another, then three of one color, one of the other, and so on, until students explore the range of probabilities from 1 to 0.

Study Guide Masters, p. 36

Name _____ Date _____

Study Guide Worksheet 4-8

Probability Connection: Simple Events

If you roll a cube with the numbers 1 through 6 on the faces, there are six possible outcomes: 1, 2, 3, 4, 5, and 6. Each of the outcomes is equally likely to occur. A particular outcome, such as rolling a 5, is an event. Probability is the chance that the event will occur.

Probability = $\frac{\text{number of ways an event can occur}}{\text{number of possible outcomes}}$

Rolling a 5 can occur 1 way out of 6 possible outcomes. $P(5) = \frac{1}{6}$.

Example Suppose Ping-Pong balls numbered 1 through 25 are placed in a box and one is drawn without looking. Find each probability.

probability of drawing a 12:
$P(12) = \frac{\text{number of ways 12 can occur}}{\text{number of possible outcomes}} = \frac{1}{25}$

Checking for Understanding

Communicating Mathematics

Read and study the lesson to answer each question.

1. **Tell** how you could make sure that the winning ticket in a raffle is drawn at random. **See students' work.**

2. **Make a model** showing all the ways a dime and a penny could land after they are tossed in the air. **See margin.**

3. **Tell** how you could figure the probability of being chosen at random to give your oral report on the first day if all 25 students in your history class have prepared oral reports, but only 5 students will report the first day.
Find $\frac{\text{number of students to report the first day}}{\text{number of students in class}}$ or $\frac{5}{25}$.

Guided Practice

The spinner shown at the right is equally likely to stop on each of the regions numbered 1 to 12. Find the probability that the spinner will stop on each of the following.

4. an odd number $\frac{1}{2}$ 5. a factor of 12 $\frac{1}{2}$

6. a number less than 4 $\frac{1}{4}$ 7. a prime number $\frac{5}{12}$

A package of erasers contains 4 red, 3 orange, 6 green, and 5 yellow erasers. If you reach in the package and choose one eraser at random, what is the probability that you will select each of the following? Express each ratio as both a fraction and a decimal.

8. a red eraser $\frac{2}{9}$, $0.\overline{2}$ 9. a yellow eraser $\frac{5}{18}$, $0.27\overline{7}$

10. a green eraser $\frac{1}{3}$, $0.\overline{3}$ 11. an orange eraser $\frac{1}{6}$, $0.16\overline{6}$

Exercises

Independent Practice

A certain spinner is equally likely to stop on each of its regions numbered 1 to 24. Find the probability that the spinner will stop on each of the following.

12. an even number $\frac{1}{2}$ 13. a factor of 12 $\frac{1}{4}$

14. a factor of 24 $\frac{1}{3}$ 15. a number less than 24 $\frac{23}{24}$

16. a composite number $\frac{7}{12}$ 17. the GCF of 9 and 15 $\frac{1}{24}$

18. $\frac{7}{60}$, $0.11\overline{6}$

19. $\frac{1}{4}$, 0.25

20. $\frac{4}{15}$, $0.2\overline{6}$

21. $\frac{9}{20}$, 0.45

22. $\frac{8}{15}$, $0.53\overline{3}$

A bag of marbles contains 15 red, 10 clear, 12 black, 16 blue, and 7 yellow marbles. If you reach in the bag and draw one marble at random, what is the probability that you will draw each of the following? Express each ratio as both a fraction and a decimal.

18. a yellow marble   19. a red marble   20. a blue marble

21. either a red or a black marble   22. a red, clear, or yellow marble

Lesson 4-8 Probability Connection: Simple Events   **159**

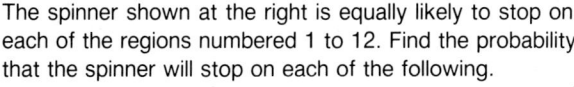

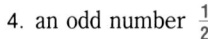

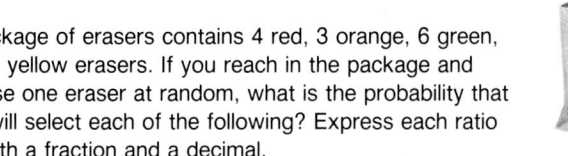

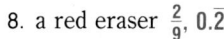

Additional Answer

2.
Dime	Penny
H	H
H	T
T	T
T	H

3 PRACTICE/APPLY

Assignment Guide
Maximum: 12–31
Minimum: 13–21 odd, 23–26, 27–31 odd

For **Extra Practice**, see p. 581.

Alternate Assessment

Modeling   Have students draw a spinner with 8 sectors of equal size, each with a number on it, designed so that the probability of spinning an even number is 0.25. Sample answer: use two even numbers and six odd numbers.

Practice Masters, p. 36

Name _____ Date _____

Practice Worksheet 4-8

Probability Connection: Simple Events

The spinner shown at the right is equally likely to stop on each of its regions numbered 1 to 16. Find the probability that the spinner will stop on each of the following.

1. an even number $\frac{1}{2}$ 2. a prime number $\frac{3}{8}$

3. a factor of 10 $\frac{1}{4}$ 4. a number less than 7 $\frac{3}{8}$

5. a composite number $\frac{5}{8}$ 6. the GCF of 10 and 15 $\frac{1}{16}$

A bag of marbles contains 3 yellow, 6 blue, 7 green, 12 white, and 8 black marbles. If you reach into the bag and draw one marble at random, what is the probability that you will draw each of the following? Express each ratio as both a fraction and a decimal.

7. a yellow marble $\frac{1}{12}$, 0.083   8. a white marble $\frac{1}{3}$, 0.3   9. a blue marble $\frac{1}{6}$, $0.1\overline{6}$

10. either a black or a blue marble $\frac{7}{18}$, 0.38   11. a green, white, or blue marble $\frac{25}{36}$, 0.694

A package of candy contains 14 cherry, 16 orange, 10 lemon, and 10 lime flavored candies. If you reach into the package and draw one piece of candy at random, what is the probability that you will draw each of the following? Express each ratio as both a fraction and a decimal.

12. a lemon candy $\frac{1}{5}$, 0.2   13. an orange candy $\frac{8}{25}$, 0.32   14. a cherry candy $\frac{7}{25}$, 0.28

15. an orange or lemon candy $\frac{13}{25}$, 0.52   16. a lime, lemon, or cherry candy $\frac{17}{25}$, 0.68

17. any candy 1   18. a candy that is not lemon, lime or cherry $\frac{8}{25}$, or 0.32

T36
Glencoe Division, Macmillan/McGraw-Hill

159

23. Evaluate $2(3 + 5) \div 4 - 2$. *(Lesson 1-7)* **2**

24. **Smart Shopping** Suzanne buys 3.5 yards of fabric for $7.52. Find the price per yard rounded to the nearest cent. *(Lesson 2-8)* **$2.15**

25. Compute mentally 314×0.001. *(Lesson 2-5)* **0.314**

26. Express $\frac{4}{9}$ as a decimal. *(Lesson 4-7)* **$0.\overline{4}$**

Problem Solving and Applications

27. All the factors of 36 are written on separate cards. If you randomly choose a card, what is the probability of choosing a prime number? **$\frac{2}{9}$**

28. **School** The students and faculty at South High School are selling 1,000 raffle tickets for $5 each. The prize is a new television set.

    a. If you spend $20 on tickets, what is the probability that you will win? **$\frac{1}{250}$**

    b. How many tickets would you have to buy so that your probability of winning would be greater than your probability of losing? How much would it cost? **501; $2,505**

29. **Number Sense** Describe an event that has a probability of 1. **29. an event that will definitely happen**

30. **Number Sense** Describe an event that has a probability of 0.

31. **Critical Thinking** If you know the probability of an event is 0.32, how can you determine the probability of the event *not* occurring? Explain.

30. an event that will definitely not happen

31. $1 - 0.32 = 0.68$; Probability of event happening plus probability of event not happening always equals 1.

Save Planet Earth

SAVE THE PLANET • SAVE THE PLANET

Test the Water The investigation of the White House drinking water in 1991 has led many Americans to worry about the safety of their drinking water. A 1990 EPA study estimated that at least one of six Americans drinks water containing an unacceptable amount of lead.

This may be a problem in school buildings as well. The solder that connects pipes in most plumbing systems is about 50% lead. In addition, many drinking fountains contain lead-lined cooling tanks or pipes. The longer the water sits unused in the lead fountains or pipes, the more lead may dissolve into it.

How You Can Help

- Let the water run before taking a drink.
- Ask school officials to check for lead in the drinking water and change the piping as necessary.
- Contact the EPA's toll-free drinking water hot line at 1-800-426-4791 for more information on water-testing.

Enrichment Masters, p. 36

Name _____ Date _____

Enrichment Worksheet 4-8

Coin-Tossing Experiments

If a coin is tossed 3 times, there are 8 possible outcomes. They are listed in the table below.

Number of Heads	0	1	2	3
Outcomes	TTT	HTT	HHT	HHH
		THT	THH	
		TTH	HTH	

Once all the outcomes are known, the probability of any event can be found. For example, the probability of getting 2 heads is $\frac{3}{8}$. Notice that this is the same as getting 1 tail.

1. A coin is tossed 4 times. Complete this chart to show the possible outcomes.

Number of Heads	0	1	2	3	4
Outcomes	TTTT	HTTT	HHTT	THHH	HHHH
		THTT	HTHT	HTHH	
		TTHT	THHT	HHTH	
		TTTH	TTHH	HHHT	
			THTH		
			HTTH		

2. What is the probability of getting all tails? $\frac{1}{16}$

3. Now complete this table. Make charts like the one in Exercise 1 to help find the answers. Look for patterns in the numbers.

Number of Coin Tosses	2	3	4	5	6	7	8
Total Outcomes	4	8	16	32	64	128	256
Probability of Getting All Tails	$\frac{1}{4}$	$\frac{1}{8}$	$\frac{1}{16}$	$\frac{1}{32}$	$\frac{1}{64}$	$\frac{1}{128}$	$\frac{1}{256}$

4. What happens to the number of outcomes? the probability of all tails? **It is doubling; it is halving.**

T36
Glencoe Division, Macmillan/McGraw-Hill

OPTIONS

Extending the Lesson

Save Planet Earth Ask students to find out what the effects are of having too much lead in the drinking water. Have them explain why it is important to have such water tested.

Cooperative Learning Activity

Bag It 4-8

Use groups of 4.
Materials: Index cards, paper bag

▶ Write the numbers 1–20 on cards, one number per card, and put the cards in a paper bag. Make a frequency table like the one shown on the back of this card.

▶ In turn, each group member selects a card, records the outcome in the table, and returns the card to the bag. After the experiment has been performed twenty times, write the number of times a number greater than 12 was selected as the numerator of a fraction with a denominator of 20. Express this fraction as a decimal. Then use the following formula to find the theoretical probability of drawing a number greater than 12:

$P(\text{drawing a number} > 12) = \frac{\text{number of ways to draw number} > 12}{\text{number of possible outcomes}}$

Did your experimental results come close to the theoretical probability you computed?

Glencoe Mathematics: Applications and Connections, Course 2

4-9 Least Common Multiple

Objective

Find the least common multiple of two or more numbers.

Words to Learn

multiple
least common multiple (LCM)

Presidents of the United States are elected to four-year terms. United States Senators are elected to six-year terms. In 1988, a presidential election year, Robert Byrd of West Virginia was reelected to the United States Senate. If he continues to run for reelection each time his term expires, in what year will he again campaign during a presidential election year?

	+6	+6	+6	
Byrd Reelection	1988	1994	2000	2006
Presidential Election	1988	1992	1996	2000
	+4	+4	+4	

The next presidential election year that is also a possible election year for Senator Byrd is the year 2000.

When you multiply a number by the whole numbers 0, 1, 2, 3, 4, and so on, you get **multiples** of the number. The **least common multiple (LCM)** of two or more numbers is the least of the common positive multiples of all the numbers. The least common multiple of 4 years and 6 years is 12 years.

One of the following two methods is usually used to find the least common multiple of two or more numbers.

Method 1: List several multiples of each number. Then identify the common multiples and choose the least of these common multiples, the LCM.

Method 2: Write the prime factorization of each number. Identify all common prime factors. Then find the product of the prime factors using each common prime factor only once and any remaining factors. The product is the LCM.

Example 1

Problem-Solving Hint
••••••••••••••
Make a list.

Find the LCM of 8 and 12 by listing the multiples of each number.

multiples of 8: 8, 16, **24**, 32, . . . _Zero is a multiple of every number._
multiples of 12: 12, **24**, 36, 48, . . .

The LCM of 8 and 12 is 24.

Lesson 4-9 Least Common Multiple   **161**

OPTIONS

Reteaching Activity

Using Connections Use coins, such as quarters and dimes, to show how the same money amounts can be made with different numbers of either coin. Guide students to see that since $0.50 is the _smallest_ amount of money that can be put together with either only quarters _or_ only dimes, this number is the LCM of 10 and 25.

Study Guide Masters, p. 37

Name _____ Date _____

**Study Guide Worksheet 4-9**

Least Common Multiple

A multiple of a number is the product of that number and any whole number. The least nonzero multiple of two or more numbers is the least common multiple (LCM) of the numbers.

Example   Find the least common multiple of 15 and 20.

positive multiples of 15:   15, 30, 45, 60, 75, 90, 105, 120 . . .
positive multiples of 20:   20, 40, 60, 80, 100, 120, 140 . . .
The LCM of 15 and 20 is 60.

Prime factorization can also be used to find the LCM.

Example   Find the LCM of 8, 12, and 18.

8 = 2 × 2 × 2   Find the prime factors of each number.
12

NCTM Standards: 1–7

Lesson Resources

• Study Guide Master 4-9
• Practice Master 4-9
• Enrichment Master 4-9
• Group Activity Card 4-9

 Transparency 4-9 contains the 5-Minute Check and a teaching aid for this lesson.

⏱ 5-Minute Check
(Over Lesson 4-8)

A certain spinner is equally likely to stop on each of its regions numbered 1–20. Find the probability that the spinner will stop on each of the following.

1. an odd number $\frac{1}{2}$

2. a number greater than 15 $\frac{1}{4}$

3. a factor of 20 $\frac{3}{10}$

4. a prime number $\frac{2}{5}$

5. the GCF of 15 and 20 $\frac{1}{20}$

1 FOCUS

Motivating the Lesson

Situational Problem   Present the following situation: _Starting at the beginning of a block, Art, Bonita, and Connie are each delivering a limited number of fliers to the houses. Art drops off a flier to every second house, Bonita gives one to every third house, and Connie delivers to every fourth house. Which house first gets all three fliers?_

2 TEACH

Using Models   In Example 2, follow this scheme.

2	10	12	15	Divide by 2.
2	5	6	15	Divide by 2.
3	5	3	5	Divide by 3.
5	5	1	5	Divide by 5.
	1	1	1	All ones. Stop.

LCM = 2 × 2 × 3 × 5, or 60

161

More Examples

For Example 1

Find the LCM of 8, 10, and 12 by writing the prime factorization of each number. 120

For Example 2

Mentally compute the LCM of 4, 5, and 8 by listing multiples. 40

For Example 3

Use your calculator to find the LCM of 54 and 16. 432

Teaching Tip Encourage students to use mental math or calculators to get the LCM by finding multiples. Have them start with multiples of the greatest number they are examining.

Check for Understanding

Exercises 1–2 are designed to help you assess students' understanding through reading, writing, speaking, and modeling. You should work through these exercises with your students and then monitor their work on Guided Practice Exercises 3–10.

Practice Masters, p. 37

Name _____ Date _____

Practice Worksheet 4-9

Least Common Multiple

Find the LCM of each set of numbers by listing the multiples of each number.

1. 75, 25
75: 75, 150
25: 25, 50, 75
LCM: 75

2. 40, 50
40: 40, 80, 120, 160, 200
50: 50, 100, 150, 200
LCM: 200

3. 2, 4, 5
2: 2, 4, 6, 8, 10, 12, 14, 16, 18, 20
4: 4, 8, 12, 16, 20
5: 5, 10, 15, 20
LCM: 20

Find the LCM of each set of numbers by writing the prime factorization.

4. 4, 8, 10
$4 = 2^2$
$8 = 2^3$
$10 = 2 \times 5$
LCM: 40

5. 11, 8, 22
$11 = 11$
$8 = 2^3$
$22 = 2 \times 11$
LCM: 88

6. 39, 9, 117
$39 = 3 \times 13$
$9 = 3^2$
$117 = 3^2 \times 13$
LCM: 117

Find the LCM of each set of numbers.

7. 4, 12
12

8. 15, 12
60

9. 156, 13
156

10. 250, 30
750

11. 3, 4, 13
156

12. 200, 18
1,800

13. 4, 10, 12
60

14. 48, 16, 3
48

15. 66, 55, 44
660

16. 70, 90
630

17. 29, 58, 4
116

18. 6, 15, 20
60

19. 18, 54
54

20. 30, 65
390

21. 180, 252
1,260

T37
Glencoe Division, Macmillan/McGraw-Hill

162

Examples

Notice that a factor need only appear in one prime factorization for it to be used to compute the LCM.

2 Find the LCM of 10, 12, and 15 by writing the prime factorization of each number.

$10 = 2 \times 5$
$12 = 2 \times 2 \times 3 = 2^2 \times 3$
$15 = 3 \times 5$

The LCM of 10, 12, and 15 is $2^2 \times 3 \times 5$ or 60.

3 Mentally compute the LCM of 5, 6, and 10 by listing multiples.

Think: The positive multiples of 10 are 10, 20, 30, 40, ...

Ask: What is the least of these multiples that is divisible by both 5 and 6? It's 30.

So, the LCM of 5, 6, and 10 is 30.

4 Use your calculator to find the LCM of 63 and 14.

Write the multiples of the greater number, 63: 63, 126, 189, . . .
Find the least multiple that is divisible by 14:

$$63 \boxed{\div} 14 \boxed{=} 4.5 \qquad 126 \boxed{\div} 14 \boxed{=} 9 \checkmark$$

Thus, the LCM of 63 and 14 is 126.

1. A multiple should have all the prime factors of each number; 216.
Checking for Understanding

Communicating Mathematics Read and study the lesson to answer each question.

1. **Tell** why the LCM of 24 (which is $2^3 \times 3$) and 54 (which is 2×3^3) must have factors of 2^3 and 3^3. What is the LCM of 24 and 54?

2. **Write** a description of the types of problems where you could easily find the LCM mentally. **small numbers and powers of 5**

Guided Practice Find the LCM for each set of numbers by listing the multiples of each number.

3. 60, 12 **60**   4. 30, 15 **30**   5. 2, 3, 5 **30**   6. 20, 30, 50 **300**

Find the LCM of each set of numbers by writing the factorization of each number.

7. 6, 12, 18 **36**   8. 17, 6, 34 **102**   9. 22, 11, 4 **44**   10. 35, 25, 49 **1,225**

162   Chapter 4 Patterns and Number Sense

OPTIONS

Bell Ringer

On a store's 100th anniversary, every person who enters gets a pin. Every fourth person gets a mug. Every tenth person gets perfume. Every 25th person gets an umbrella, and every 75th person gets a free dinner. Ask students which shopper will be the first to get all 5 gifts? Which will be the second? 300th shopper, 600th shopper

Additional Answer

25. 0 | 2 5 9
1 | 0 2 3 6 7
2 | 3 5 5
3 | 1
2 | 3 means 23.

Exercises

Independent Practice

Find the LCM of each set of numbers. **18. 3,750**

660

11. 3, 15 **15**   12. 16, 176 **176**   13. 4, 10, 9 **180**   14. 55, 44, 33

15. 24, 12, 6 **24**   16. 42, 16, 7 **336**   17. 300, 18 **900**   18. 625, 30

19. 60, 80 **240**   20. 12, 15 **60**   21. 6, 9, 12 **36**   22. 10, 12, 15 **60**

Mixed Review

23. Estimate the sum of 125 and 2,347. *(Lesson 1-2)*   **about 2,460**

24. Multiply 2.6 by 3.15. *(Lesson 2-3)*

8.19

25. **Statistics**   Construct a stem-and-leaf plot for the following data: 12, 17, 23, 5, 9, 25, 13, 16, 2, 25, 31, 10. *(Lesson 3-6)*   **See margin.**

26. **Probability**   Ryu purchases 5 tickets in support of a raffle to raise money for intramural sports at his high school. A total of 500 tickets are sold. One ticket is to be selected to win the grand prize, which is a season pass to the Washington Redskins football games. What is the probability that Ryu will win the season pass? *(Lesson 4-8)* $\frac{1}{100} = 0.01$

Problem Solving and Applications

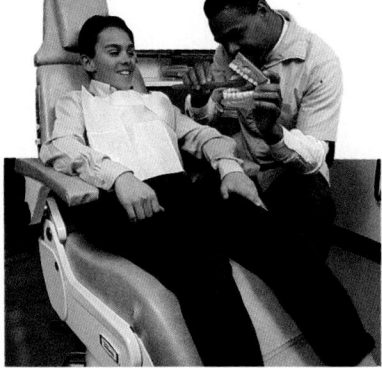

27. **Health**   Robbie visits the dentist every 6 months. He sees his optometrist every 18 months and gets a physical for football every August 1. If he schedules all his appointments on August 1 this year, in how many years will they all fall on August 1 again? **3 years**

28. **Scheduling**   Sam, Lilly, and Tom were hired to work a regular schedule in the evenings at the library, which is open every day. They each started work on the same day, but they did not work the same evening again until 30 days later. Sam and Lilly worked the same evening every 6 days, and Sam and Tom worked the same evening every 10 days. If Sam worked every second day, what schedules did Lilly and Tom have?

28. Lilly every third day, Tom every fifth day

29. **Number Sense**   When will the LCM of two numbers be one of the numbers? **when the smaller number is a factor of the larger number**

30. when the two numbers are relatively prime

30. **Number Sense**   When will the LCM of two numbers be their product?

31. **Critical Thinking**   Write a set of three numbers whose LCM is the product of the numbers. **Sample answer: 10, 13, 21**

32. **Portfolio Suggestion**   Review the items in your portfolio. Make a table of contents of the items, noting why each item was chosen. Replace any items that are no longer appropriate. **See students' work.**

Lesson 4-9 Least Common Multiple   **163**

Extending the Lesson

Using Connections   Have students find the LCM and GCF for two numbers. Then have them find the product of the two numbers as well as the product of their GCF and LCM. Ask students what they notice. Ask them to investigate further, using other pairs of numbers. Ask students what conclusions, if any, they can draw.   **product of the two numbers = product of GCF and LCM**

Cooperative Learning Activity

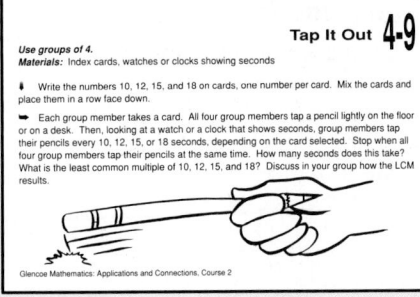

Tap It Out 4-9

Use groups of 4.
Materials: Index cards, watches or clocks showing seconds

♦ Write the numbers 10, 12, 15, and 18 on cards, one number per card. Mix the cards and place them in a row face down.

♦ Each group member takes a card. All four group members tap a pencil lightly on the floor or on a desk. Then, looking at a watch or a clock that shows seconds, group members tap their pencils every 10, 12, 15, or 18 seconds, depending on the card selected. Stop when all four group members tap their pencils at the same time. How many seconds does this take? What is the least common multiple of 10, 12, 15, and 18? Discuss in your group how the LCM results.

Glencoe Mathematics: Applications and Connections, Course 2

Close

Have students explain how to find the LCM of a set of numbers. List multiples, choose the least of the common ones; use the product of their prime factors, with each such factor appearing the maximum number of times it appears in any of the numbers.

3 PRACTICE/APPLY

Assignment Guide
Maximum: 11–32
Minimum: 11–21 odd, 23–32

For **Extra Practice,** see p. 581.

Alternate Assessment

Writing   Have students use the method they find most reasonable to find the LCM of 4, 8, and 12. Sample answer: 24; use mental math to list multiples

Enrichment Masters, p. 37

Name _____   Date _____

Enrichment Worksheet 4-9

A Cross-Number Puzzle

Use the clues at the bottom of the page to complete the puzzle. You are to write one digit in each box.

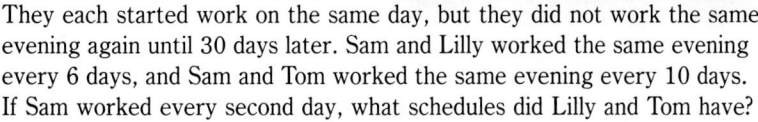
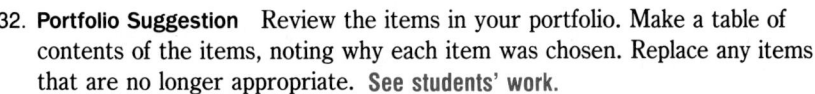

Across

C Largest number less than 200 that is divisible by 29
E Square of first prime greater than 20
F Sum of first seven Fibonacci numbers
H Next term in sequence 61, 122, 244, 488
J Greatest common factor of 141 and 329
K The eighth power of 2
L Least common multiple of 2, 7, and 13
M Numerator of fraction equal to 0.8125
N Least common multiple of 86 and 5
O Smallest prime greater than 60
P Largest two-digit prime

Q Next term in sequence 4, 15, 26, 37
R Largest two-digit composite less than 40

Down

B Smallest number divisible by 3 and 5
D The sixth power of 4
G Least common multiple of 2 and 179
H The number of two-digit positive integers
I Smallest number over 600 divisible by 89
L Smallest three-digit number divisible by 13
M The smallest two-digit prime number
N Largest prime factor of 82
O Perfect square between 60 and 70
P Largest two-digit number divisible by 3

T37
Glencoe Division, Macmillan/McGraw-Hill

Lesson Resources
- Study Guide Master 4-10
- Practice Master 4-10
- Enrichment Master 4-10
- Evaluation Master, Quiz B, p. 34
- Group Activity Card 4-10

 Transparency 4-10 contains the 5-Minute Check and a teaching aid for this lesson.

⏱ 5-Minute Check
(Over Lesson 4-9)

Find the LCM for each set of numbers.

1. 3, 12   LCM = 12
2. 10, 12   LCM = 60
3. 6, 9, 15   LCM = 90
4. 225, 30   LCM = 450
5. 8, 12, 16   LCM = 48

1 FOCUS

Motivating the Lesson

Situational Problem   Tell students that in a basketball game, Margaret made 4 of 5 free throws and Sabrina made 12 of 16. Ask them which girl made a greater fraction of her shots.

2 TEACH

Using the Mini-Lab   After working through the Mini-Lab with students, have students use a Venn diagram to show (A) students in the art club, (B) students in the baking club, (C) students in the chess club, (D) students in both the art and baking club, (E) students in both the baking and chess clubs, and (F) students in all three clubs.

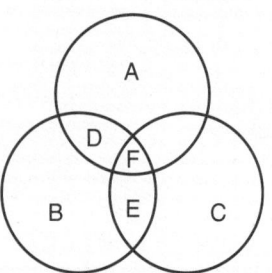

164

4-10 Comparing and Ordering Fractions and Decimals

Objective
Compare and order fractions by first writing them as equivalent fractions with a common denominator.

Words to Learn
common denominator
least common denominator (LCD)

Calculator Hint
••••••••••••
You can compare $\frac{30}{35}$ and $\frac{42}{48}$ on a calculator by using cross products.

30 ⊠ 48 🟰 **1,440**

35 ⊠ 42 🟰 **1,470**

Since 1,440 is less than 1,470, $\frac{30}{35} < \frac{42}{48}$.

DID YOU KNOW

One-fourth of U.S. schools include geography in their curriculum.

In Ms. Mapp's geography class, Laura has earned 30 points out of a possible 35 points on tests, projects, and oral reports. In English class she worked hard writing her short story and book report, earning 42 out of a possible 48 points. In which class has Laura earned a greater portion of the possible points?

That is, which fraction is greater, $\frac{30}{35}$ or $\frac{42}{48}$?

One way to compare these two fractions is to first write each fraction in simplest form.

$$\frac{30}{35} = \frac{6}{7} \qquad \frac{42}{48} = \frac{7}{8}$$

To compare $\frac{6}{7}$ and $\frac{7}{8}$, rewrite each fraction using the same denominator. Then you need only compare the numerators.

A **common denominator** is a common multiple of the denominators of two or more fractions. The **least common denominator (LCD)** is the least common multiple (LCM) of the denominators of two or more fractions.

To rewrite $\frac{6}{7}$ and $\frac{7}{8}$ with the same denominators, first find the LCD by listing the multiples of each denominator.

multiples of 7: 7, 14, 21, 28, 35, 42, 49, **56**, . . .
multiples of 8: 8, 16, 24, 32, 40, 48, **56**, . . .

The LCD of the fractions $\frac{6}{7}$ and $\frac{7}{8}$ is 56, since 56 is the LCM of 7 and 8. So, rewrite each fraction using a denominator of 56.

$$\frac{6}{7} = \frac{6 \times 8}{7 \times 8} = \frac{48}{56} \qquad \frac{7}{8} = \frac{7 \times 7}{8 \times 7} = \frac{49}{56}$$

Now, compare $\frac{49}{56}$ and $\frac{48}{56}$. Since 49 > 48, then $\frac{49}{56} > \frac{48}{56}$, and Laura has earned a greater portion of the possible points in English than in geography.

OPTIONS

Gifted and Talented Needs

Ask students what happens to the value of a fraction if the same nonzero number is added to its numerator and denominator.   Its value increases.

Three strategies can be used to compare fractions. The first strategy was used on the previous page.

1. Express each fraction in simplest form. Then write equivalent fractions using the LCD.
2. Consider each fraction in relationship to the nearest whole number.
3. Express each fraction as a decimal.

Examples

1 Compare $\frac{7}{15}$ and $\frac{4}{10}$ by writing equivalent fractions using the least common denominator.

The LCM of 15 and 10 is 30.

$$\frac{7}{15} = \frac{7 \times 2}{15 \times 2} = \frac{14}{30} \qquad \frac{4}{10} = \frac{4 \times 3}{10 \times 3} = \frac{12}{30}$$

Since $\frac{12}{30} < \frac{14}{30}$, then $\frac{4}{10} < \frac{7}{15}$.

2 The diameter of an Oreo® cookie is $1\frac{3}{4}$ inches long. The diameter of an Archway® gingersnap cookie is $1\frac{3}{16}$ inches long. Which cookie has the longer diameter?

Since both diameters are at least one inch long, we will compare only the fractions. Let's use strategy 2.

$\frac{3}{16}$ is nearest to 0. $\frac{3}{4}$ is nearest to 1.

So, $\frac{3}{4} > \frac{3}{16}$ and $1\frac{3}{4} > 1\frac{3}{16}$.

The Oreo® cookie has the longer diameter.

Example 3 *Problem Solving*

Sports   Kiesha was proud that her soccer team had won 7 of their 10 matches. Her cousin wrote her a letter announcing that his team had won 11 of their 16 matches. Whose team won a greater fraction of their matches?

Since $\frac{7}{10}$ and $\frac{11}{16}$ are already in simplest form and yet are still difficult to compare, express each fraction as a decimal and then compare (strategy 3).

$$7 \boxed{\div} 10 \boxed{=} 0.7 \qquad\qquad 11 \boxed{\div} 16 \boxed{=} 0.6875$$

Since $0.7 > 0.6875$, then $\frac{7}{10} > \frac{11}{16}$ and Kiesha's team won a greater fraction of their matches.

Lesson 4-10 Comparing and Ordering Fractions and Decimals   **165**

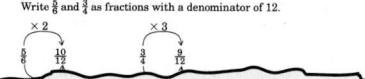

Have students write a problem that classmates can solve by comparing and ordering fractions.

3 PRACTICE/APPLY

Assignment Guide

Maximum: 11–46

Minimum: 11–33 odd, 35–39, 41–45

For **Extra Practice,** see p. 581.

Alternate Assessment

Speaking Have students explain a method for writing three fractions in order from least to greatest. Ask them to demonstrate their method.

Practice Masters, p. 38

Name _____ Date _____

Practice Worksheet 4-10

Comparing and Ordering Fractions and Decimals

Find the LCD for each pair of fractions.

1. $\frac{4}{7}, \frac{3}{5}$ 2. $\frac{5}{12}, \frac{7}{24}$ 3. $\frac{6}{28}, \frac{3}{7}$
   35   24   28

4. $\frac{7}{15}, \frac{1}{4}$ 5. $\frac{7}{11}, \frac{3}{5}$ 6. $\frac{5}{17}, \frac{7}{8}$
   60   55   136

7. $\frac{5}{12}, \frac{7}{10}$ 8. $\frac{15}{16}, \frac{1}{4}$ 9. $\frac{5}{8}, \frac{3}{8}$
   60   16   40

10. $\frac{5}{16}, \frac{3}{32}$ 11. $\frac{7}{13}, \frac{1}{3}$ 12. $\frac{7}{9}, \frac{13}{27}$
   32   39   27

Complete with <, >, or = to make a true statement.

13. $\frac{3}{4}$ ___ $\frac{3}{5}$ 14. $\frac{5}{8}$ ___ $\frac{4}{7}$ 15. $\frac{4}{9}$ ___ $\frac{9}{14}$
   >   >   <

16. $\frac{7}{11}$ ___ $\frac{9}{12}$ 17. $\frac{7}{10}$ ___ $\frac{3}{5}$ 18. $\frac{7}{12}$ ___ $\frac{3}{8}$
   <   >   >

19. $\frac{3}{8}$ ___ $\frac{2}{3}$ 20. $\frac{21}{30}$ ___ $\frac{17}{20}$ 21. $\frac{8}{13}$ ___ $\frac{7}{19}$
   <   <   >

22. $\frac{1}{8}$ ___ $\frac{1}{7}$ 23. $\frac{2}{3}$ ___ $\frac{3}{2}$ 24. $\frac{5}{24}$ ___ $\frac{4}{12}$
   >   <   =

T 38
Glencoe Division, Macmillan/McGraw-Hill

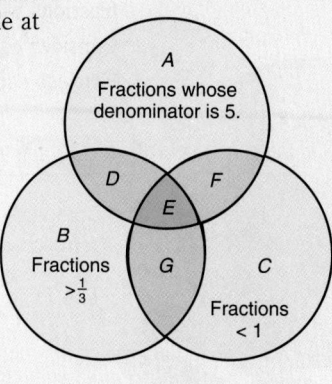

Mini-Lab

Work with a partner.

The figure below is called a **Venn diagram.** The circle at the lower left contains all fractions greater than $\frac{1}{3}$. The circle at the lower right contains all fractions less than 1. Thus the region labeled G, where only these two circles overlap, contains all fractions that are greater than $\frac{1}{3}$ *and* less than 1.

A Fractions whose denominator is 5.

B Fractions $> \frac{1}{3}$

C Fractions < 1

Talk About It

a. Write a description of the fractions contained in each of regions A through F. **See margin.**

b. For each of regions A through F, name a fraction that would be located in that region. **Sample answers:** $\frac{1}{5}, \frac{3}{2}, \frac{1}{4}, \frac{4}{5}, \frac{4}{5}, \frac{4}{5}, \frac{1}{2}$

c. Identify the region where each of the following fractions would be located. **See margin.**
   $\frac{1}{5}, \frac{2}{9}, \frac{8}{5}, \frac{7}{8}, \frac{12}{7}, \frac{4}{5}, \frac{1}{3}, \frac{3}{3}$

d. Which regions contain an infinite number of fractions? a finite number of fractions? no fractions? **A, B, C, D, F, G; E; none**

Checking for Understanding

Communicating Mathematics

Read and study the lesson to answer each question.

1. **Write** a problem that involves comparing fractions and state the strategy that would be easiest to use to make the comparison. **See students' work.**

2. **Tell** how you can use a calculator to compare fractions. **Use a calculator to change each fraction to a decimal. Then compare the decimals.**

Guided Practice

Find the LCD for each pair of fractions.

3. $\frac{5}{9}, \frac{7}{12}$ 36   4. $\frac{7}{5}, \frac{14}{11}$ 55   5. $\frac{3}{13}, \frac{4}{26}$ 26   6. $\frac{6}{7}, \frac{13}{16}$ 112

Replace each ● with < or > to make a true statement.

7. $\frac{5}{8}$ ● $\frac{2}{3}$ <   8. $\frac{9}{13}$ ● $\frac{14}{20}$ <   9. $\frac{5}{9}$ ● $\frac{8}{15}$ >   10. $\frac{3}{4}$ ● $\frac{7}{8}$ <

166   Chapter 4 Patterns and Number Sense

OPTIONS

Bell Ringer

Ask students to write an explanation, including an example, of how to find a fraction between any two fractions. Sample answer: Rewrite the fractions with a common denominator. Then form a new fraction with this denominator and a numerator between the other two numerators.

Exercises

Independent Practice

Find the LCD for each pair of fractions.

11. $\frac{2}{5}, \frac{2}{6}$ 30
12. $\frac{4}{5}, \frac{8}{9}$ 45
13. $\frac{5}{4}, \frac{9}{8}$ 8
14. $\frac{11}{16}, \frac{3}{4}$ 16

15. $\frac{3}{10}, \frac{1}{3}$ 30
16. $\frac{7}{8}, \frac{23}{24}$ 24
17. $\frac{13}{17}, \frac{3}{4}$ 68
18. $\frac{2}{3}, \frac{19}{27}$ 27

19. $\frac{1}{6}, \frac{2}{15}$ 30
20. $\frac{3}{10}, \frac{1}{12}$ 60
21. $\frac{6}{7}, \frac{15}{21}$ 21
22. $\frac{4}{5}, \frac{6}{8}$ 40

Replace each ● with $<$, $>$, or $=$ to make a true statement.

23. $\frac{8}{13}$ ● $\frac{8}{17}$ $>$
24. $\frac{17}{20}$ ● $\frac{36}{50}$ $>$
25. $\frac{45}{90}$ ● $\frac{15}{30}$ $=$
26. $\frac{4}{3}$ ● $\frac{8}{7}$ $>$

27. $\frac{4}{5}$ ● $\frac{6}{7}$ $<$
28. $\frac{1}{3}$ ● $\frac{3}{5}$ $<$
29. $\frac{5}{6}$ ● $\frac{7}{8}$ $<$
30. $\frac{5}{8}$ ● $\frac{4}{7}$ $>$

31. $\frac{3}{10}$ ● $\frac{1}{5}$ $>$
32. $\frac{4}{7}$ ● $\frac{5}{8}$ $<$
33. $\frac{5}{12}$ ● $\frac{3}{8}$ $>$
34. $\frac{2}{9}$ ● $\frac{5}{14}$ $<$

Mixed Review

35. Evaluate $15(xy) - (x + y)$ if $x = 4$ and $y = 1$. *(Lesson 1-8)* **55**

36. **Sports** During a basketball game, it is announced that the attendance for the game is 10,300. Express the attendance in scientific notation. *(Lesson 2-6)* **1.03×10^4**

37. **Statistics** Choose an appropriate scale and interval for the following set of data. Then construct a number line displaying the scale and interval. 1.2, 3.4, 2.7, 4.3, 1.9, 2.5, 3.7, 1.8 *(Lesson 3-3)* **See Solutions Manual.**

38. Find the prime factorization of 255. *(Lesson 4-2)* **$3 \times 5 \times 17$**

39. Find the least common multiple of 27 and 30. *(Lesson 4-9)* **270**

Problem Solving and Applications

Statistics Jolie's math class uses cooperative learning groups to study mathematics. Each group keeps score based on points earned out of number of points attempted. Find the median score for each group by ranking the scores from least to greatest and locating the middle score.

40. **Group 1:** $\frac{3}{7}, \frac{4}{8}, \frac{4}{7}, \frac{5}{8}, \frac{5}{6}$
$\frac{3}{7}, \frac{4}{8}, \frac{4}{7}, \frac{5}{8}, \frac{5}{6}$. $\frac{4}{7}$

41. **Group 2:** $\frac{7}{10}, \frac{8}{9}, \frac{4}{6}, \frac{9}{11}, \frac{7}{9}$
$\frac{4}{6}, \frac{7}{10}, \frac{7}{9}, \frac{9}{11}, \frac{8}{9}$. $\frac{7}{9}$

42. **Civics** Amy and Jose are handing out pamphlets urging people to register to vote. Amy has delivered 72 pamphlets of the 108 pamphlets assigned to her. Jose has delivered 84 pamphlets of the 126 pamphlets assigned to him. Which student has completed more of the assignment? **See margin.**

43. **Critical Thinking** When is the least common denominator of two fractions equal to one of the denominators? Give two examples. **See Solutions Manual.**

44. **Number Sense** Which fraction is nearest to 2? Explain why. $1\frac{15}{16}, \frac{63}{32}, \frac{17}{8}$ **See margin.**

45. **School** If the brass section makes up $\frac{4}{9}$ of the marching band and the woodwind section makes up $\frac{2}{7}$, which section is larger? **brass section**

46. **Data Search** Refer to pages 126 and 127. **a. See margin.**
   a. What fraction of the U.S. forestland is in the West? North? South?
   b. Is there a greater portion of forestland in the North or in the South? **South**

Lesson 4-10 Comparing and Ordering Fractions and Decimals **167**

Extending the Lesson

Business Ask students to tell what is wrong with the following advertisement: *Store-wide Sale! Save $\frac{1}{2}, \frac{1}{3}, \frac{1}{5}$ and even more than that!* Fractions are in decreasing order.

Cooperative Learning Activity

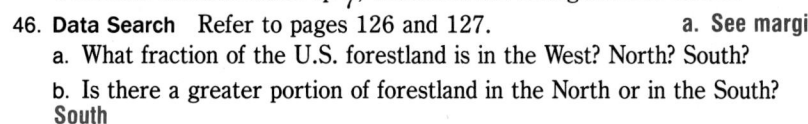

Dare to Compare 4-10

Use groups of 2.
Materials: Spinners

● Label equal sections of one spinner with the following numbers: 2, 5, 6, 8, 9, 13. You will use these numbers as the numerators of fractions. Label equal sections of a second spinner with the following numbers: 15, 16, 17, 18, 19, 20. You will use these numbers as the denominators of fractions.

➡ In turn, each partner spins both spinners and writes the resulting fraction. The partner with the greater fraction wins the round. Play at least seven rounds.

Glencoe Mathematics: Applications and Connections, Course 2

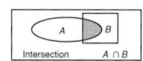 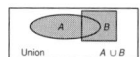
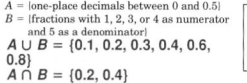 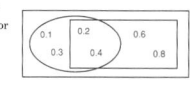

The Chapter Study Guide and Review begins with a section on Communicating Mathematics. This includes questions that review the new terms and concepts that were introduced in the chapter.

Then, the Skills and Concepts presented in the chapter are reviewed using a side-by-side format. Encourage students to refer to the Objectives and Examples on the left as they complete the Review Exercises on the right.

The Chapter Study Guide and Review ends with problems that review Applications and Problem Solving.

Chapter

4 Study Guide and Review

Study Guide and Review

Communicating Mathematics

Choose the correct term or number to complete each sentence.

1. The number 72 is said to be divisible by 8 because the quotient is a(n) __?__ of 72. **factor**

2. A(n) __?__ number is a whole number greater than 1 that has exactly two factors, 1 and itself. **prime**

3. Every composite number can be written as the __?__ of at least two prime numbers. **product**

4. In a geometric sequence, you can always find the next term by __?__ the previous term by the same number. **multiplying**

5. A fraction is in simplest form when the GCF of the numerator and the denominator is __?__. **1**

6. The __?__ is the least common multiple of the denominators of two or more fractions. **LCD**

7. In your own words, explain the difference between a terminating decimal and a repeating decimal. **Terminating decimals end while repeating decimals repeat the same digit or digits forever.**

GCF
adding
factor
multiple
10
whole number
prime
sum
LCM
1
composite
LCD
product
multiplying

Self Assessment

Objectives and Examples	Review Exercises
Upon completing this chapter, you should be able to:	*Use these exercises to review and prepare for the chapter test.*

• use divisibility rules *(Lesson 4-1)*
  Determine whether 336 is divisible by 2, 3, 4, 5, or 6.

  2: The ones digit, 6, is even, so 336 is divisible by 2.

  3: The sum of the digits, 12, is divisible by 3, so 336 is divisible by 3.

  4: The number formed by the last two digits, 36, is divisible by 4, so 336 is divisible by 4.

  5: The ones digit is not 5 or 0, so 336 is not divisible by 5.

  6: The number is divisible by both 2 and 3, so 336 is divisible by 6.

Determine whether each number is divisible by 2, 3, 4, 5, 6, 9, or 10.

8. 221 **none** 9. 1,225 **5**

10. 630 **2, 3, 5, 6, 9, 10** 11. 1,300 **2, 4, 5, 10**

12. 828 **2, 3, 4, 6, 9** 13. 707 **none**

14. 452 **2, 4** 15. 594 **2, 3, 6, 9**

16. 255 **3, 5** 17. 93 **3**

168 Chapter 4 Study Guide and Review

Objectives and Examples

- find the prime factorization of a composite number *(Lesson 4-2)*

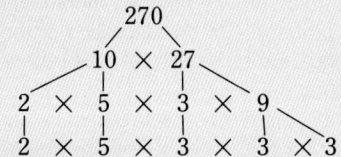

270
10 × 27
2 × 5 × 3 × 9
2 × 5 × 3 × 3 × 3

The prime factorization of 270 is $2 \times 3^3 \times 5$.

- recognize and extend sequences *(Lesson 4-3)*

32, 16, 8, 4, 2, . . . is a geometric sequence created by multiplying the previous term by $\frac{1}{2}$. The next three terms are $1, \frac{1}{2}, \frac{1}{4}$.

- find the greatest common factor of two or more numbers *(Lesson 4-5)*

$45 = ③ \times 3 \times ⑤$
$75 = ③ \times 5 \times ⑤$

The GCF of 45 and 75 is 3×5 or 15.

- express fractions in simplest form *(Lesson 4-6)*

Write $\frac{45}{81}$ in simplest form.

$\frac{45}{81} = \frac{45 \div 9}{81 \div 9} = \frac{5}{9}$ *The GCF of 45 and 81 is 9.*

- express terminating decimals as fractions and express fractions as decimals *(Lesson 4-7)*

$\frac{6}{20} = \frac{30}{100} = 0.30$

$\frac{1}{6} \rightarrow 6\overline{)1.000} \rightarrow 0.1\overline{6}$
$\underline{-6}$
$\quad 40$
$\quad \underline{-36}$
$\quad\quad 40$

$0.32 = \frac{32}{100} = \frac{8}{25}$ *The GCF of 32 and 100 is 4.*

Review Exercises

Write the prime factorization of each number.

18. 1,000 $2^3 \times 5^3$ 19. 144 $2^4 \times 3^2$
20. 950 $2 \times 5^2 \times 19$ 21. 77 7×11
22. 96 $2^5 \times 3$ 23. 300 $2^2 \times 3 \times 5^2$
24. 2,800 $2^4 \times 5^2 \times 7$ 25. 1,450 $2 \times 5^2 \times 29$

Identify each sequence as arithmetic, geometric, or neither. Then find the next three terms. **For answers to Exercises 26–29, see margin.**

26. 16, 21, 26, 31, 36, . . .   see margin.
27. 1, 4, 16, 64, 256, . . .
28. 0, 2, 6, 12, 20, 30, . . .
29. 10, 100, 1,000, 10,000, . . .

Find the GCF of each set of numbers.

30. 36, 81 9   31. 40, 65 5
32. 252, 336 84   33. 57, 240 3
34. 56, 280, 400 8

Express each fraction in simplest form.

35. $\frac{56}{70}$ $\frac{4}{5}$ 36. $\frac{250}{750}$ $\frac{1}{3}$
37. $\frac{26}{39}$ $\frac{2}{3}$ 38. $\frac{60}{18}$ $\frac{10}{3}$
39. $\frac{77}{121}$ $\frac{7}{11}$ 40. $\frac{57}{95}$ $\frac{3}{5}$

Express each fraction as a decimal and express each decimal as a fraction in simplest form.

41. $\frac{10}{25}$ 0.4   42. 0.36 $\frac{9}{25}$
43. $\frac{3}{8}$ 0.375   44. 1.25 $1\frac{1}{4}$
45. $\frac{5}{9}$ $0.\overline{5}$ 46. $\frac{33}{300}$ 0.11

Chapter 4 Study Guide and Review   **169**

Additional Answers

26. Add 5 to previous term; arithmetic; 41, 46, 51
27. Multiply previous term by 4; geometric; 1,024   4,096   16,384
28. Add 2 to the first term, 4 to the second term, 6 to the third term, and so on; neither; 42, 56, 72
29. Multiply previous term by 10; geometric; 100,000   1,000,000   10,000,000

Evaluation Masters, pp. 32–33

170

Objectives and Examples	Review Exercises

- **find the probability of a simple event** *(Lesson 4-8)*
  When a die is rolled,
  $P(\text{odd}) = \frac{3}{6}$
  $= \frac{1}{2}$ or 0.5

A bag contains 6 red, 3 pink, and 3 white bows. If you draw a bow at random, what is the probability of drawing each of the following? Express each ratio as both a fraction and a decimal.
47. red $\frac{1}{2} = 0.5$ 48. either red or white $\frac{3}{4} = 0.75$

- **find the least common multiple of two or more numbers** *(Lesson 4-9)*
  $4 = 2 \times 2 = 2^2$
  $18 = 2 \times 3 \times 3 = 2 \times 3^2$
  The LCM of 4 and 18 is $2^2 \times 3^2$ or 36.

Find the LCM of each set of numbers.
49. 6, 15 30   50. 42, 56 168
51. 16, 40 80   52. 15, 125, 600 3,000
53. 21, 81, 147 3,969   54. 48, 81, 270 6,480

- **compare and order fractions** *(Lesson 4-10)*
  $\frac{5}{9} = \frac{10}{18}$ $\frac{4}{6} = \frac{12}{18}$
  Since $10 < 12$, then $\frac{5}{9} < \frac{4}{6}$.

Replace each ● with < or > to make a true statement.
55. $\frac{2}{3}$ ● $\frac{3}{4}$ <   56. $\frac{11}{12}$ ● $\frac{8}{9}$ >
57. $\frac{3}{8}$ ● $\frac{5}{12}$ <   58. $\frac{7}{10}$ ● $\frac{13}{25}$ >

Applications and Problem Solving

59. Find the greatest common divisor of the twelfth and fifteenth terms of Fibonacci sequence, 1, 1, 2, 3, 5, 8, 13, 21, ... *(Lesson 4-4)* 2

60. **School** Beth scored 21 out of 25 on her spelling test. Ted scored 37 out of 40 on his test. Who scored higher? *(Lesson 4-10)* Ted

Curriculum Connection Projects

- **Communications** Open a telephone book ten times at random and write down the page numbers. Find the prime factors for each page number listed.
- **Automotive** Check auto repair manuals to find the cylinder firing sequences for three different 6-cylinder cars.

Read More About It

Cooper, Clare. *Ashar of Qarius.*
Pluckrose, Henry. *Know About Patterns.*
Charosh, Mannis. *Mathematical Games for One or Two.*

4 Test

Determine whether each number is divisible by 2, 3, 4, 5, 6, 9, or 10.

1. 639 **3, 9**

2. 2,350 **2, 5, 10**

Write the prime factorization of each number.

3. 250 2×5^3

4. 1,296 $2^4 \times 3^4$

5. 2,400 $2^5 \times 3 \times 5^2$

6. Find two terms in the Fibonacci sequence that are divisible by the seventh term.
1, 1, 2, 3, 5, 8, 13, . . . **F14 = 377, $\frac{377}{13}$ = 29; F21 = 10,946, $\frac{10,946}{13}$ = 842**

Identify each sequence as arithmetic, geometric, or neither. Then find the next three terms.

7. 9, 15, 21, 27, 33, . . . **add 6; A; 39, 45, 51**

8. 2, 6, 18, 54, 162, . . . **multiply by 3; G; 486, 1,458, 4,374**

9. **Savings** Elena plans to open a savings account with $50 from her January paycheck and then increase the amount she deposits by $5 each month. How much will Elena deposit from her April check? **$65**

Find the GCF of each set of numbers.

10. 52, 100 **4**

11. 95, 150, 345 **5**

Express each fraction in simplest form.

12. $\frac{33}{55}$ **$\frac{3}{5}$**

13. $\frac{24}{64}$ **$\frac{3}{8}$**

14. $\frac{60}{135}$ **$\frac{4}{9}$**

15. **Vacation** Mina spent 8 of her 14 vacation days in Florida. Express this fraction of her vacation in simplest form. **$\frac{4}{7}$**

Express each fraction as a decimal and each decimal as a fraction in simplest form.

16. $\frac{28}{70}$ **0.4**

17. 0.32 **$\frac{8}{25}$**

18. $\frac{4}{20}$ **0.2**

The spinner shown at the right is equally likely to stop on each of the regions. Find the probability that the spinner will stop on each of the following.

19. a prime number **$\frac{1}{2}$**

20. a factor of 24 **$\frac{3}{4}$**

Find the LCM of each set of numbers.

21. 8, 28 **56**

22. 14, 21, 27 **378**

Replace each   with < or > to make a true statement.

23. $\frac{5}{8}$ $\frac{12}{20}$ **>**

24. $\frac{12}{15}$ $\frac{9}{12}$ **>**

25. **Civics** On election day in a small town, 175 of the 200 registered Republicans voted, and 160 of the 200 registered Democrats voted. Which party had the better turnout? **Republicans**

Bonus Why is 2 the only even prime number? **All other even numbers have 2 as a factor and therefore they have more than two factors.**

This page may be used as a chapter test or another chapter review.

Evaluation Masters, pp. 28–29

Name _____ Date _____

Form 1A _____ *Chapter 4 Test*

1. Which number is a factor of 8,358?
   A. 5   B. 6   C. 10   D. 9   1. **B**

2. Which number is not a factor of 60,070?
   A. 5   B. 2   C. 10   D. 6   2. **D**

3. Find the prime factorization of 18.
   A. $2 \cdot 2 \cdot 3$ B. $3 \cdot 6$ C. $2 \cdot 3 \cdot 3$ D. $3 \cdot 3 \cdot 3$ 3. **C**

4. Find the prime factorization of 42.
   A. $2 \cdot 3 \cdot 7$ B. $3 \cdot 3 \cdot 7$ C. $3 \cdot 14$ D. $2 \cdot 5 \cdot 5$ 4. **A**

5. Find the prime factorization of 81.
   A. $3 \cdot 3 \cdot 3$ B. $3 \cdot 5 \cdot 7$ C. $3 \cdot 3 \cdot 3 \cdot 3$ D. $3 \cdot 3 \cdot 9$ 5. **C**

6. Find the next term in the sequence 72, 66, 60, 54, . . .
   A. 52   B. 48   C. 50   D. 58   6. **B**

7. Find the sixth term in the sequence 16, 4, 1, $\frac{1}{4}$, . . .
   A. $\frac{1}{64}$ B. $\frac{1}{16}$ C. $\frac{1}{32}$ D. $\frac{1}{12}$ 7. **A**

8. Find the GCF of 48 and 56.
   A. 336   B. 4   C. 8   D. 9   8. **C**

9. Find the GCF of 8, 20, and 36.
   A. 2   B. 4   C. 6   D. 8   9. **B**

10. Express $\frac{36}{60}$ in simplest form.
    A. $\frac{9}{15}$ B. $\frac{18}{30}$ C. $\frac{12}{20}$ D. $\frac{3}{5}$ 10. **D**

11. Express $\frac{99}{81}$ in simplest form.
    A. $\frac{11}{9}$ B. $\frac{33}{27}$ C. $\frac{11}{10}$ D. $\frac{27}{33}$ 11. **A**

12. Express $\frac{32}{72}$ in simplest form.
    A. $\frac{16}{36}$ B. $\frac{8}{18}$ C. $\frac{4}{9}$ D. $\frac{18}{8}$ 12. **C**

13. Express $\frac{13}{20}$ as a decimal.
    A. 6.5   B. 0.35   C. 0.65   D. 0.56   13. **C**

14. Express 0.125 as a fraction in simplest form.
    A. $\frac{1}{5}$ B. $\frac{1}{6}$ C. $\frac{5}{8}$ D. $\frac{1}{8}$ 14. **A**

Name _____ Date _____

Chapter 4 Test Form 1A (continued)

15. Express $\frac{11}{12}$ as a decimal.
    A. 0.92   B. 0.916   C. 0.9166   D. $0.91\overline{6}$ 15. **D**

A bag contains 4 blue, 5 red, 1 green, and 2 white marbles. If you draw a marble at random:

16. What is the probability of drawing a blue marble?
    A. $\frac{5}{12}$ B. $\frac{1}{4}$ C. $\frac{1}{12}$ D. $\frac{1}{3}$ 16. **D**

17. What is the probability of drawing a marble that is not red?
    A. $\frac{7}{12}$ B. $\frac{5}{12}$ C. $\frac{1}{4}$ D. $\frac{1}{3}$ 17. **A**

18. Find the LCM of 12 and 16.
    A. 24   B. 192   C. 48   D. 96   18. **C**

19. Find the LCM of 10, 12, and 18.
    A. 2   B. 18   C. 2,160   D. 180   19. **D**

Replace each ● to make a true statement.

20. $\frac{6}{7}$ ● $\frac{3}{5}$
    A. >   B. <   C. =   D. +   20. **A**

21. $\frac{3}{2}$ ● $\frac{4}{3}$
    A. >   B. <   C. =   D. ×   21. **A**

22. $\frac{7}{12}$ ● $\frac{5}{8}$
    A. >   B. <   C. =   D. –   22. **B**

23. In the Fibonacci sequence, 1 is a perfect cube. What is the only other perfect cube in the first twelve terms?
    A. 27   B. 64   C. 8   D. 2,197   23. **C**

24. The sixth Fibonacci number is:
    A. 2   B. 5   C. 13   D. 8   24. **D**

25. Carlos plans to open a savings account with $100 from his March paycheck and then increase the amount he deposits by $100 each month. How many months will it take for Carlos to have $600 in deposits in his account?
    A. July   B. 3   C. 4   D. 6   25. **B**

BONUS Find the next two terms of the sequence 65, 62, 57, 50, 41, 30, . . .
    A. 17, 2   B. 19, 4   C. 16, 1   D. 16, 3   **A**

Test and Review Generator

software is provided in Apple, IBM, and Macintosh versions. You may use this software to create your own tests or worksheets, based on the needs of your students.

The **Performance Assessment Booklet** provides an alternate assessment for evaluating student progress. An assessment for this chapter can be found on pages 7–8.

5 Applications with Fractions

Previewing the Chapter

This chapter focuses first on operations with fractions and then on curriculum connections in fields such as geometry and probability. Specifically, perimeter and circumference are studied using fractional numbers, as is the topic of expected value. Properties of real numbers, such as the associative properties of addition and of multiplication, are also explored using fractions. Attention is paid also to real-life applications of fractions such as unit pricing, cooking, meteorology, and recreation. Students explore the **problem-solving strategy** of solving problems by using estimation to eliminate possibilities.

Lesson	Lesson Objectives	NCTM Standards	State/Local Objectives
5-1	Change mixed numbers to improper fractions and vise versa.	1–7	
5-2	Estimate sums, differences, products, and quotients of fractions and mixed numbers.	1–7	
5-3	Add and subtract fractions.	1–7, 13	
5-4	Add and subtract mixed numbers with unlike denominators.	1–7, 13	
5-5A	Find the product of fractions by using models.	1–6	
5-5	Multiply fractions and mixed numbers.	1–7, 9, 13	
5-6	Find perimeter using fractional measurements.	1–7, 12, 13	
5-7	Find the circumference of circles.	1–7, 9, 12, 13	
5-8	Find expected value of outcomes.	1–5, 7, 11	
5-9	Use addition, multiplication, and distributive properties to solve problems mentally.	1–7, 9	
5-10	Divide fractions and mixed numbers.	1–7, 13	
5-10B	Find unit price.	1–7, 13	
5-11	Solve problems by using estimation to eliminate possibilities.	1–5, 7, 8	

Organizing the Chapter

A complete, 1-page lesson plan is provided for each lesson in the Lesson Plans Masters Booklet.

LESSON PLANNING GUIDE

Lesson	Materials/ Manipulatives	Extra Practice (Student Edition)	Blackline Masters Booklets									
			Study Guide	Practice	Enrichment	Evaluation	Technology	Lab Manual	Multicultural Activities	Application and Interdisciplinary Activities	Transparencies	Group Activity Cards
5-1	circle models	p. 582	p. 39	p. 39	p. 39						5-1	5-1
5-2		p. 582	p. 40	p. 40	p. 40						5-2	5-2
5-3	fraction models calculator	p. 582	p. 41	p. 41	p. 41		p. 19				5-3	5-3
5-4	calculator	p. 583	p. 42	p. 42	p. 42						5-4	5-4
5-5A	fraction circles sheets of paper							p. 48 p. 49				
5-5		p. 583	p. 43	p. 43	p. 43						5-5	5-5
5-6		p. 583	p. 44	p. 44	p. 44	Quiz A, p. 43				p. 19	5-6	5-6
5-7	metric ruler, string, circular objects of various sizes, calculator	p. 584	p. 45	p. 45	p. 45		p. 5				5-7	5-7
5-8	calculator, die		p. 46	p. 46	p. 46					p. 5	5-8	5-8
5-9		p. 584	p. 47	p. 47	p. 47						5-9	5-9
5-10		p. 584	p. 48	p. 48	p. 48				p. 5		5-10	5-10
5-10B	play money sheets of paper							p. 50				
5-11			p. 49	p. 49	p. 49	Quiz B, p. 43					5-11	5-11
Study Guide and Review			Multiple Choice Test, Forms 1A and 1B, pp. 37–40 Free Response Test, Forms 2A and 2B, pp. 41–42 Cumulative Review, p. 44 (free response)									
Test			Cumulative Test, p. 45 (multiple choice)									

Pacing Guide: Option I (Chapters 1–12) - 16 days; Option II (Chapters 1–13) - 14 days; Option III (Chapters 1–14) - 13 days

You may wish to refer to the complete **Course Planning Guides** on page T25.

OTHER CHAPTER RESOURCES

Student Edition
Chapter Opener, pp. 172–173
Cultural Kaleidoscope, p. 181
Mid-Chapter Review, p. 193
Portfolio Suggestions, pp. 193, 209

 Manipulatives
Overhead Manipulative Resources
Middle School Mathematics Manipulative Kit

 Software/Technology
Interactive Mathematics Tools (Macintosh)
Test and Review Generator (IBM, Apple, Macintosh)
Teacher's Guide for Software Resources

Other Supplements
Transparency 5-0
Performance Assessment, pp. 9–10
Glencoe Mathematics Professional Series Lesson Plans, pp. 48–60

INTERDISCIPLINARY BULLETIN BOARD

Social Studies Connection

Objective Use fractions to determine the weight of various categories of television programming.

How To Use It Have students use a TV programming guide to figure out what kinds of programs appear most frequently on TV during particular viewing times. Have different groups choose blocks of time, such as 2–6 P.M., 7–11 P.M., weekend afternoons, and so on. Each group places a picture of a large TV set on the bulletin board, labels it by the viewing time it represents, and divides the picture by the fraction of viewing time for categories of programming such as talk shows, drama, sports, news, and variety programs.

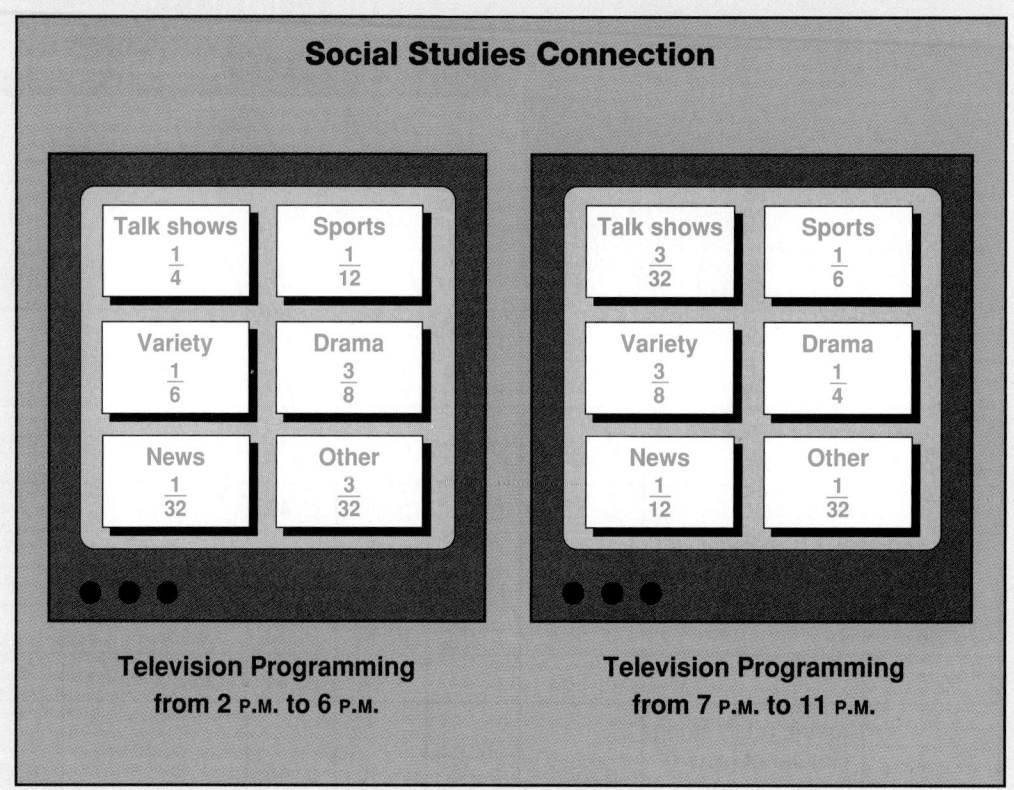

Social Studies Connection

Television Programming from 2 P.M. to 6 P.M.

Talk shows $\frac{1}{4}$	Sports $\frac{1}{12}$
Variety $\frac{1}{6}$	Drama $\frac{3}{8}$
News $\frac{1}{32}$	Other $\frac{3}{32}$

Television Programming from 7 P.M. to 11 P.M.

Talk shows $\frac{3}{32}$	Sports $\frac{1}{6}$
Variety $\frac{3}{8}$	Drama $\frac{1}{4}$
News $\frac{1}{12}$	Other $\frac{1}{32}$

APPLICATIONS AND CONNECTIONS

Applications	Lesson	Example	Exercise
Business	5-1		55
Music	5-1		56
Journalism	5-1		57
Smart Shopping	5-2		65
Construction	5-2		64
History	5-2		65
Movies	5-3	3	
Energy	5-3		29
Home Economics	5-3		30
Television	5-4		40
Sports	5-4		41
Landscaping	5-5		33
Coin Collecting	5-5		34
Landscaping	5-6		21
Recreation	5-7		33
Computer	5-7		35
Recreation	5-7		36
Games	5-8	X	
Science	5-8		15
Cooking	5-9		28
Food	5-10	4	
Housing	5-10		43
Connections			
Measurement	5-6	3	
Geometry	5-8		14
Geometry	5-9		29

TEAM ACTIVITIES

Multicultural Experiences

Outside Field Trips A trip to a fabric store can be helpful in showing students how operations with fractions is an everyday part of buying and selling fabric.

A visit to a brokerage house or stock exchange can be useful for showing students the essential part played by fractions in the minute-by-minute stock transactions that take place.

In-Class Speakers Ask a caterer, an author of a cookbook, or a parent who has had experience cooking for large groups, to talk with students about how operations with fractions and making estimates with fractions is an essential part of planning the number and size of the servings for a recipe.

Invite someone involved in carpentry to talk with students about how he or she works with fractional amounts on the job.

SUPPLEMENTARY BLACKLINE MASTER BOOKLETS

Some of the blackline masters for enhancing this chapter are shown below.

Application and Interdisciplinary Activity Masters, pp. 5, 19

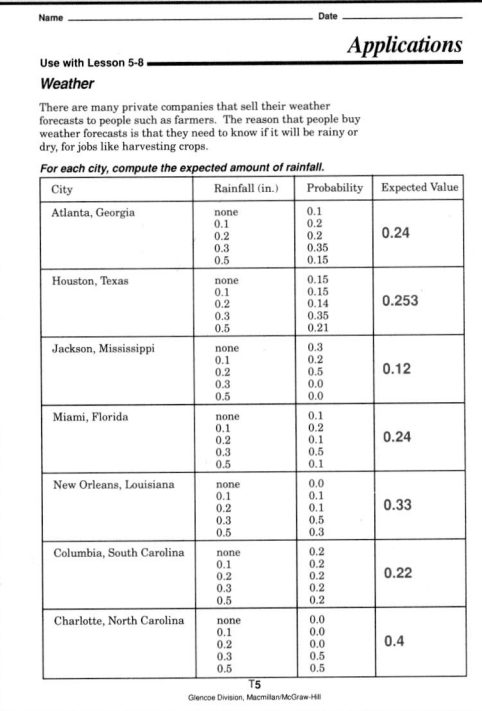

Multicultural Activity Masters, p. 5

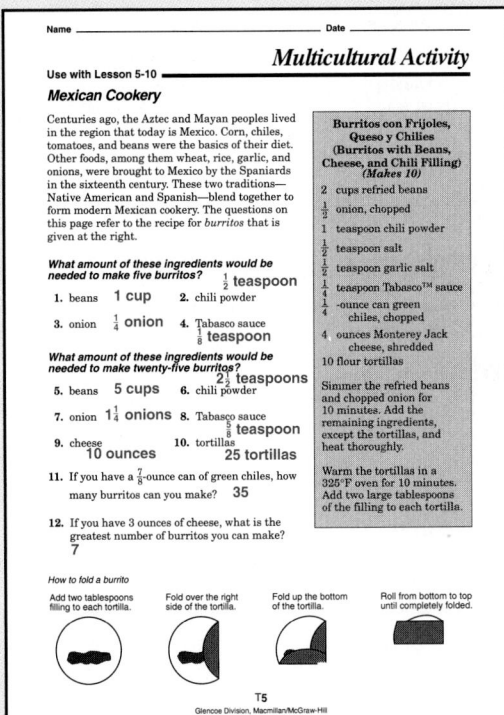

Technology Masters, p. 5

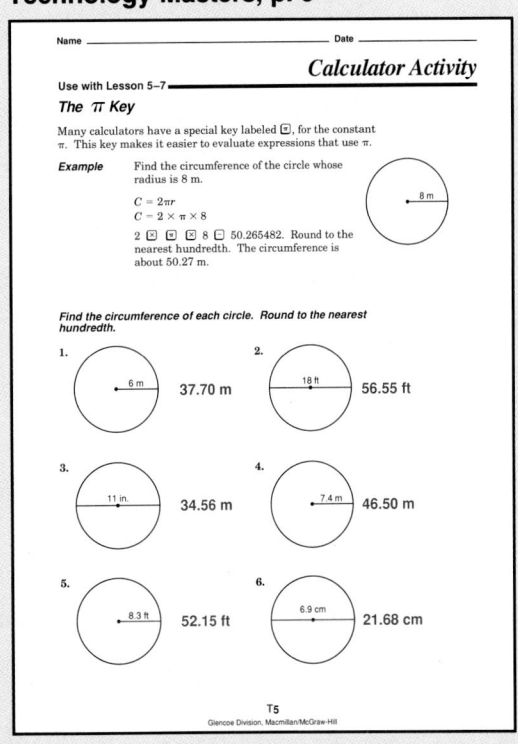

RECOMMENDED OUTSIDE RESOURCES

Books/Periodicals

National Council of Teachers of Mathematics, *Curriculum and Evaluation Standards for School Mathematics,* Reston, VA: NCTM, 1989.

Schulte, Albert P., ed., *Teaching Statistics and Probability,* 1981 Yearbook, NCTM, 1981.

Films/Videotapes/Videodiscs

Probability, Wilmette, IL: Films Inc., 1970.

The Story of Pi, Reston, VA: NCTM, 1989.

Software

Fractions: Addition and Subtraction; Multiplication and Division, (Apple II, IBM/Tandy), Gamco Industries

IBM Geometry Series, Geometry One: Foundations, (GeoDraw), (IBM/Tandy), IBM

For addresses of companies handling software, please refer to page T24.

This two-page introduction to the chapter provides a visual, relevant way to engage students in the mathematics of the chapter. Questions are included that help students see the need to learn the mathematics in the chapter. Data in charts and graphs provide statistical information that students can analyze and interpret at this point as well as later in the chapter. The Chapter Project provides an activity that applies the mathematics of the chapter.

MAKING MATHEMATICS RELEVANT

Spotlight on Business

An understanding of operations with fractions, particularly adding, subtracting, and multiplying fractions, is essential for digesting data about stock market transactions and interpreting the columns of stock prices in the financial pages.

Using the Timeline

Ask students to interview older members of their family to find out how the stock market crash of 1929 affected the lives of their families then and thereafter. Have students ask their families how life in the Great Depression that followed the crash compared with life during the recession of the early 1990s. Have students share their findings with classmates.

Chapter

5

Applications with Fractions

Spotlight on Business

Have You Ever Wondered. . .

- What it means when a news reporter says that IBM closed at $94\frac{3}{8}$, down $3\frac{1}{2}$?

- How newspapers, radio stations, and movie theaters can be different divisions of the same industry?

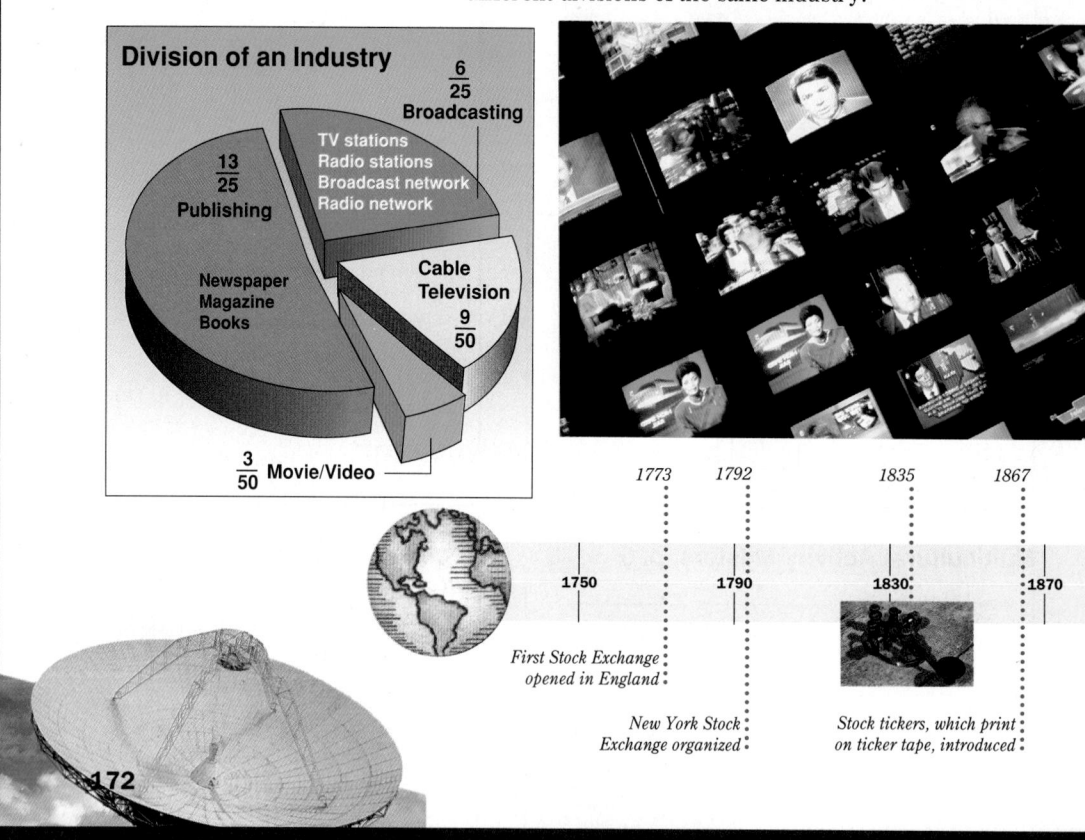

Division of an Industry

$\frac{6}{25}$ **Broadcasting**

$\frac{13}{25}$ **Publishing**

TV stations
Radio stations
Broadcast network
Radio network

Newspaper
Magazine
Books

Cable Television $\frac{9}{50}$

$\frac{3}{50}$ **Movie/Video**

1773 1792 1835 1867

1750 1790 1830 1870

First Stock Exchange opened in England

New York Stock Exchange organized

Stock tickers, which print on ticker tape, introduced

172

"Have You Ever Wondered?" Answers

- The closing number is the price per share at the end of the trading day. "Down $3\frac{1}{2}$" means that the price per share has gone down that amount since the previous day's closing price.

- The media industry is fractioned into smaller segments.

Chapter Project

Business

Work in a group.

1. Use the financial pages of a newspaper to choose four stocks. In a table, keep track of your stocks for one month on a daily basis.

2. Note which stocks increased and decreased overall.

3. Pretend that you bought 100 shares of each of the four stocks. If you sold them all at the end of the month, would you have gained or lost money?

4. To calculate price, multiply the number of shares by the closing price. Compare the price on the first day with that on the last day.

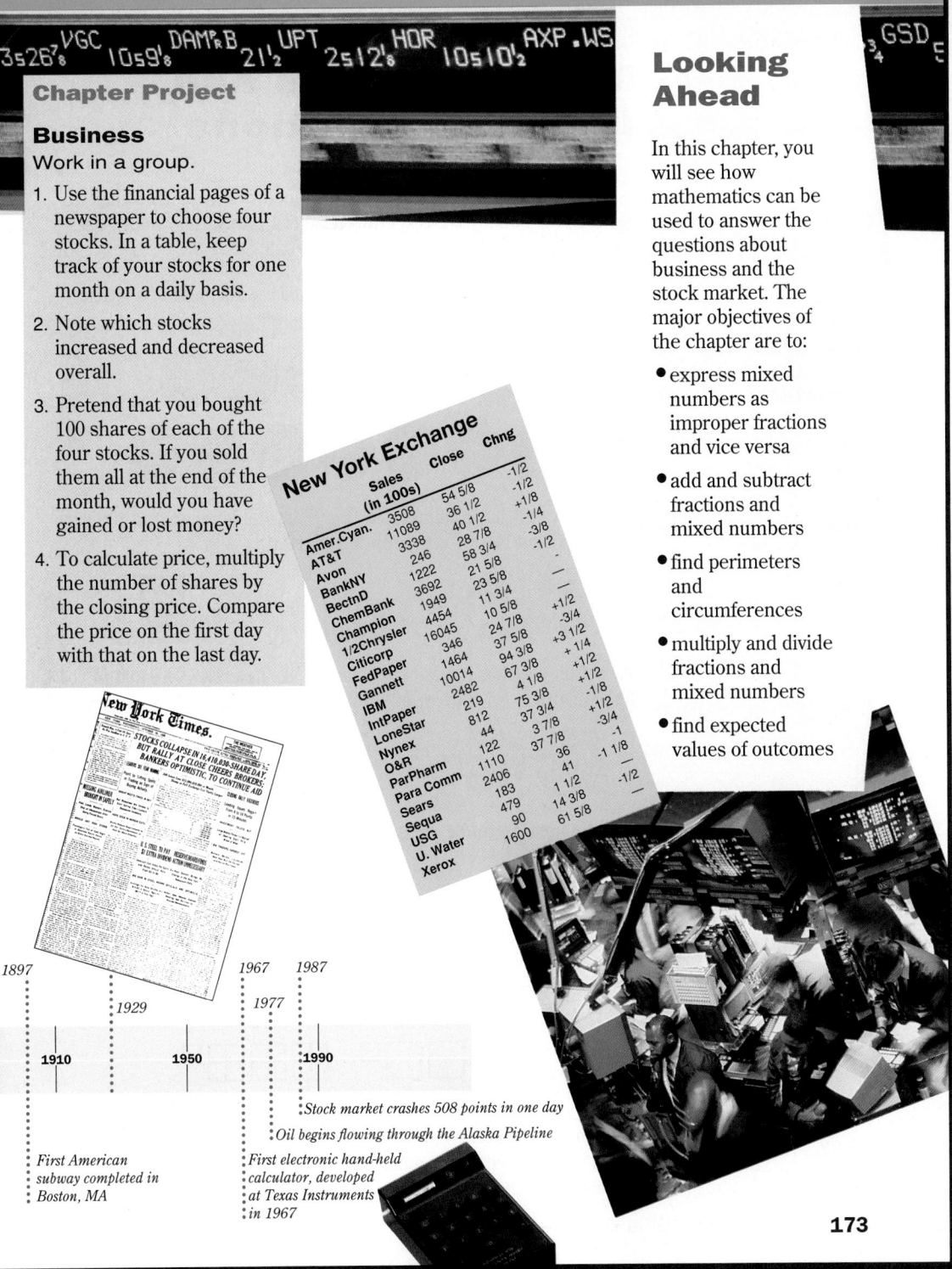

Looking Ahead

In this chapter, you will see how mathematics can be used to answer the questions about business and the stock market. The major objectives of the chapter are to:

- express mixed numbers as improper fractions and vice versa

- add and subtract fractions and mixed numbers

- find perimeters and circumferences

- multiply and divide fractions and mixed numbers

- find expected values of outcomes

New York Exchange	Sales (In 100s)	Close	Chng
Amer.Cyan.	3508	54 5/8	-1/2
AT&T	11089	36 1/2	-1/2
Avon	3338	40 1/2	+1/8
BankNY	246	28 7/8	-1/4
BectnD	1222	58 3/4	-3/8
ChemBank	3692	21 5/8	-1/2
Champion	1949	23 5/8	—
1/2Chrysler	4454	11 3/4	+1/2
Citicorp	16045	10 5/8	-3/4
FedPaper	346	24 7/8	-3 1/2
Gannett	1464	37 5/8	+ 1/4
IBM	10014	94 3/8	+1/2
IntPaper	2482	67 3/8	-1/8
LoneStar	219	4 1/8	-1/2
Nynex	812	75 3/8	+1/2
O&R	44	37 3/4	-3/4
ParPharm	122	3 7/8	-1
Para Comm	1110	37 7/8	-1 1/8
Sears	2406	36	-1/2
Sequa	183	41	
USG	479	1 1/2	
U. Water	90	14 3/8	
Xerox	1600	61 5/8	

Stock market crashes 508 points in one day

Oil begins flowing through the Alaska Pipeline

First American subway completed in Boston, MA

First electronic hand-held calculator, developed at Texas Instruments in 1967

1897 1967 1987
1929 1977
1910 1950 1990

173

DATA ANALYSIS

Discuss the information in the circle graph with students. Have them choose a local media business such as a magazine or newspaper or a TV or radio station and find out about its ownership and affiliations.

Data Search

A question related to these data is provided in Lesson 5-2, page 181, Exercise 68.

CHAPTER PROJECT

Help students to understand how to interpret the stock price columns in the financial pages. During the four weeks the groups follow the fortunes of their stocks, display the daily financial page on the bulletin board. Help students prepare a table in which they record the necessary information about each stock. You may find it useful to have students practice multiplying mixed numbers before they calculate gains and losses. At the end of the time period, have each group prepare a written report describing its results.

Chapter Opener Transparency

Transparency 5-0 is available in the Transparency Package. It provides another full-color, motivating activity that you can use to capture students' interest.

Lesson Resources
- Study Guide Master 5-1
- Practice Master 5-1
- Enrichment Master 5-1
- Group Activity Card 5-1

 Transparency 5-1 contains the 5-Minute Check and a teaching aid for this lesson.

🕐 5-Minute Check
(Over Chapter 4)

1. Determine whether 530 is divisible by 2, 3, 4, 5, 6, 9, or 10.   divisible by 2, 5, 10

2. Identify the sequence as arithmetic, geometric, or neither. Then find the next three terms. 4, 12, 36, 108, . . . geometric; 324, 972, 2,916

3. Express $\frac{33}{60}$ in simplest form. $\frac{11}{20}$

4. Express 0.45 as a fraction in simplest form. $\frac{9}{20}$

5. Find the LCM for 8, 12, and 20.   120

1 FOCUS

Motivating the Lesson

Questioning   Ask students to write, to the nearest quarter of an hour, the number of hours of sleep they got on the previous night both as a mixed number and as an improper fraction.

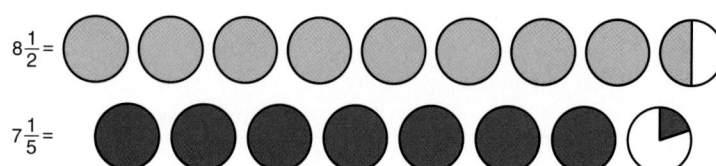

5-1 Mixed Numbers and Improper Fractions

Objective

Change mixed numbers to improper fractions and vice versa.

Words to Learn

mixed number
proper fraction
improper fraction

How much sleep do you get at night? Doctors recommend that we get 8 to $8\frac{1}{2}$ hours of sleep. The average American, however, gets only $7\frac{1}{5}$ hours.

Mixed numbers such as $8\frac{1}{2}$ and $7\frac{1}{5}$ indicate the sum of a whole number and a fraction.

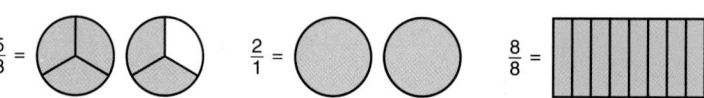

A fraction that has a numerator less than the denominator like each of those given below, is a **proper fraction.**

$$\frac{1}{5} = \qquad \frac{1}{2} = \qquad \frac{2}{3} = $$

A fraction that has a numerator that is greater than or equal to the denominator is an **improper fraction.** Here are three examples.

$$\frac{5}{3} = \qquad \frac{2}{1} = \qquad \frac{8}{8} = $$

Mixed numbers can be written as improper fractions, as shown below.

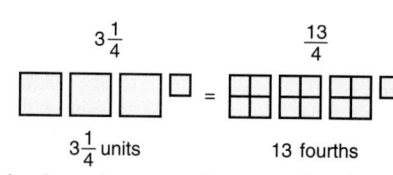

$2\frac{1}{2}$ $\frac{5}{2}$

$2\frac{1}{2}$ units   5 halves

$3\frac{1}{4}$ $\frac{13}{4}$

$3\frac{1}{4}$ units   13 fourths

To change a mixed number to an improper fraction, multiply the whole number and the denominator. Then add the numerator. Write the sum over the denominator.

OPTIONS

Bell Ringer

Have students invent a game in which they use from 10 to 20 index cards, each cut in half, with each half containing a mixed number or the equivalent improper fraction. The game, which may be in the *Concentration* format, should involve matching pairs of equivalent numbers.

 **Interactive Mathematics Tools**

This multimedia software provides an interactive lesson that is tied directly to Lesson 5-1. Students will use models to represent fractions as in the introductory example.

Change each mixed number to an improper fraction.

1 $2\frac{1}{2}$

$$2\frac{1}{2} = \frac{(2 \times 2) + 1}{2}$$

$$= \frac{5}{2}$$

2 $3\frac{2}{5}$

$$3\frac{2}{5} = \frac{(5 \times 3) + 2}{5}$$

$$= \frac{17}{5}$$

A whole number can be changed to an improper fraction.

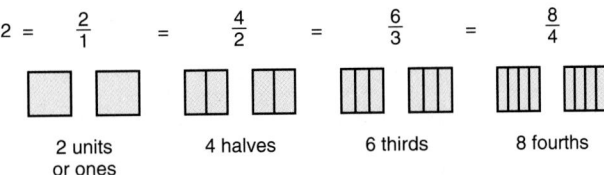

$2 = \frac{2}{1} = \frac{4}{2} = \frac{6}{3} = \frac{8}{4}$

| 2 units or ones | 4 halves | 6 thirds | 8 fourths |

An improper fraction can be changed to either a whole number or a mixed number.

$\frac{7}{2}$ $3\frac{1}{2}$

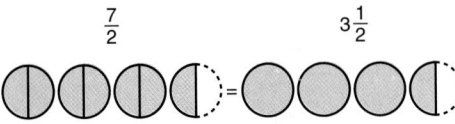

To change an improper fraction to a whole number or a mixed number, divide the numerator by the denominator.

Change each improper fraction to a mixed number in simplest form or a whole number.

3 $\frac{23}{4}$

$$4\overline{)23} \rightarrow 5\frac{3}{4}$$
$$\underline{20}$$
$$3$$

So, $\frac{23}{4} = 5\frac{3}{4}$.

4 $\frac{21}{7}$

$$7\overline{)21} \rightarrow 3$$
$$\underline{21}$$
$$0$$

So, $\frac{21}{7} = 3$.

Lesson 5-1 Mixed Numbers and Improper Fractions   **175**

---

2 TEACH

Using Manipulatives Have students use fraction strips to model mixed numbers. For example, have students use halves to model $2\frac{1}{2}$, then ask them how many halves are equivalent to $2\frac{1}{2} \times 5$. Have students model other mixed numbers and improper fractions involving fourths, sixths, eighths, and so on.

More Examples

Change each mixed number to an improper fraction.

For Examples 1 and 2

$3\frac{1}{2} = \underline{?}$ $\frac{7}{2}$

$4\frac{3}{5} = \underline{?}$ $\frac{23}{5}$

Change each improper fraction to a mixed number in simplest form or a whole number.

For Examples 3 and 4

$\frac{22}{3} = \underline{?}$ $7\frac{1}{3}$

$\frac{24}{6} = \underline{?}$ 4

Checking for Understanding

Exercises 1-3 are designed to help you assess students' understanding through reading, writing, speaking, and modeling. You should work through these exercises with your students and then monitor their work on Guided Practice Exercises 4-21.

Error Analysis

Watch for students who multiply the whole number by the numerator and then add the denominator when changing a mixed number to an improper fraction.

Prevent by using fraction strips to model the correct procedure—multiplying the whole number by the denominator and adding the numerator.

Reteaching Activity

Using Manipulatives Have students work with partners or in small groups. Provide each group with an inch ruler and ask students to locate a mixed number, such as $5\frac{1}{2}$ inches, and write it as an improper fraction. Then have them count 15 one-eighth-inch spaces and name that length as a mixed number. Have students repeat the process with other numbers.

Study Guide Masters, p. 39

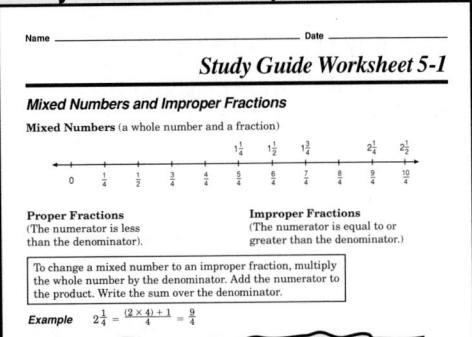

Name _____ Date _____

Study Guide Worksheet 5-1

Mixed Numbers and Improper Fractions

Mixed Numbers (a whole number and a fraction)

Proper Fractions
(The numerator is less than the denominator).

Improper Fractions
(The numerator is equal to or greater than the denominator.)

To change a mixed number to an improper fraction, multiply the whole number by the denominator. Add the numerator to the product. Write the sum over the denominator.

Example $2\frac{1}{4} = \frac{(2 \times 4) + 1}{4} = \frac{9}{4}$

Close

Have students explain how they would change $12\frac{3}{4}$ to an improper fraction, and $\frac{28}{5}$ and $\frac{32}{8}$ to whole or mixed numbers.

3 PRACTICE/APPLY

Assignment Guide
Maximum: 22–60
Minimum: 23–47 odd, 49–54, 55–59 odd

For **Extra Practice,** see p. 582.

Alternate Assessment

Writing Have each student work with a partner. Each writes a series of mixed numbers and improper fractions. They exchange papers and change each mixed number to an improper fraction and each improper fraction to a mixed number. Each checks the other's work.

Practice Masters, p. 39

Name _____ Date _____

Practice Worksheet 5-1

Mixed Numbers and Improper Fractions

Identify each number as a proper fraction, an improper fraction, or a mixed number.

1. $\frac{2}{3}$ proper fraction
2. $2\frac{3}{9}$ mixed number
3. $\frac{17}{12}$ improper fraction

Change each improper fraction to a mixed number in simplest form or a whole number.

4. $\frac{8}{5}$ $1\frac{3}{5}$
5. $\frac{30}{6}$ 5
6. $\frac{27}{2}$ $13\frac{1}{2}$
7. $\frac{21}{3}$ 7
8. $\frac{18}{5}$ $3\frac{3}{5}$
9. $\frac{41}{6}$ $6\frac{5}{6}$
10. $\frac{14}{3}$ $4\frac{2}{3}$
11. $\frac{29}{4}$ $7\frac{1}{4}$
12. $\frac{108}{9}$ 12

Change each mixed number or whole number to an improper fraction.

13. $2\frac{3}{4}$ $\frac{11}{4}$
14. $1\frac{2}{5}$ $\frac{7}{5}$
15. $5\frac{1}{3}$ $\frac{16}{3}$
16. $3\frac{5}{9}$ $\frac{32}{9}$
17. 6 $\frac{6}{1}$
18. $7\frac{1}{2}$ $\frac{15}{2}$
19. 23 $\frac{23}{1}$
20. $4\frac{9}{13}$ $\frac{61}{13}$
21. $3\frac{7}{10}$ $\frac{37}{10}$

T39
Glencoe Division, Macmillan/McGraw-Hill

176

Checking for Understanding

Communicating Mathematics

Read and study the lesson to answer each question.

1. **Make a model** to show the meaning of $\frac{7}{4}$. See margin.

2. **Write,** in your own words, how to change a mixed number to an improper fraction. **Multiply the denominator and whole number. Then add the numerator. Write the sum over the denominator.**

3. **Tell** what number this model represents. $\frac{7}{3}$

Guided Practice

Identify each number as a proper fraction, an improper fraction, or a mixed number.

4. $\frac{7}{3}$ improper
5. $2\frac{1}{3}$ mixed number
6. $\frac{3}{8}$ proper
7. $\frac{4}{4}$ improper
8. $\frac{15}{11}$ improper

Complete the diagram to change each number to an improper fraction or a mixed number.

9. $\frac{7}{2}$ = ◯◯◯◖ = ◯ _?_ _?_ ◖ = $3\frac{1}{2}$ See margin.

10. $2\frac{3}{4}$ = ◯◯◔ = ⊕ _?_ _?_ = $\frac{11}{4}$ See margin.

11. $\frac{5}{3}$ = ▥▯ = ▨▯ = _?_ $1\frac{2}{3}$

Change each improper fraction to a mixed number in simplest form or a whole number.

12. $\frac{9}{2}$ $4\frac{1}{2}$
13. $\frac{12}{4}$ 3
14. $\frac{14}{6}$ $2\frac{1}{3}$
15. $\frac{7}{7}$ 1
16. $\frac{45}{10}$ $4\frac{1}{2}$

Change each mixed number or whole number to an improper fraction.

17. $1\frac{7}{8}$ $\frac{15}{8}$
18. $2\frac{3}{4}$ $\frac{11}{4}$
19. $3\frac{3}{1}$
20. $4\frac{5}{9}$ $\frac{41}{9}$
21. $13\frac{2}{3}$ $\frac{41}{3}$

Exercises

Independent Practice

Identify each number as a proper fraction, an improper fraction, or a mixed number.

22. $\frac{9}{9}$ improper
23. $2\frac{6}{7}$ mixed number
24. $\frac{8}{9}$ proper
25. $\frac{5}{3}$ improper
26. $6\frac{1}{3}$ mixed number

OPTIONS

Gifted and Talented Needs

Write $13 \div 4$ on the chalkboard. Tell students that three possible answer forms include (a) $3\frac{1}{4}$, (b) 3 R 1, and (c) 4. Challenge them to write a problem for which each answer form makes the most sense.

Samples: (a) You saw a 13-foot board into 4 equal lengths. How long is each length? (b) You divide your collection of 13 videos equally among 4 of your friends. How many do you give to each friend? (c) Thirteen girls are being driven to their basketball game. Four can fit in a car. How many cars are needed?

Change each improper fraction to a mixed number in simplest form or a whole number.

27. $\frac{9}{7}$ $1\frac{2}{7}$ 28. $\frac{7}{4}$ $1\frac{3}{4}$ 29. $\frac{12}{5}$ $2\frac{2}{5}$ 30. $\frac{8}{8}$ 1   31. $\frac{20}{8}$ $2\frac{1}{2}$

32. $\frac{17}{5}$ $3\frac{2}{5}$ 33. $\frac{6}{2}$ 3   34. $\frac{21}{9}$ $2\frac{1}{3}$ 35. $\frac{26}{6}$ $4\frac{1}{3}$ 36. $\frac{23}{7}$ $3\frac{2}{7}$

Change each mixed number or whole number to an improper fraction.

37. $3\frac{4}{5}$ $\frac{19}{5}$ 38. $2\frac{2}{3}$ $\frac{8}{3}$ 39. 5 $\frac{5}{1}$ 40. $6\frac{1}{4}$ $\frac{25}{4}$ 41. $3\frac{7}{8}$ $\frac{31}{8}$

42. $2\frac{2}{9}$ $\frac{20}{9}$ 43. $4\frac{3}{8}$ $\frac{35}{8}$ 44. $3\frac{6}{7}$ $\frac{27}{7}$ 45. $2\frac{7}{10}$ $\frac{27}{10}$ 46. $3\frac{5}{12}$ $\frac{41}{12}$

47. Change $5\frac{4}{7}$ to an improper fraction. $\frac{39}{7}$

48. Change $\frac{27}{6}$ to a mixed number in simplest form. $4\frac{1}{2}$

Mixed Review

49. Use rounding to estimate $12,768 − $3,428. *(Lesson 1-2)* **$10,000**

50. **Pets** Tom's dog Echo will stay for 7.5 minutes after Tom issues the command "stay." Kathy's dog Sam will stay for 2.3 times longer than Echo. How long will Sam stay? *(Lesson 2-4)* **17.25 minutes**

51. Divide $0.0081 \div 0.09$. *(Lesson 2-7)* **0.09**

52. **Statistics** Draw a number line to show the scale and interval for test scores of 76, 85, 99, 45, 82, 70, and 94. *(Lesson 3-3)* **See Solutions Manual.**

53. Find the next three terms in the following sequence. 2, 5, 12.5, 31.25, . . . *(Lesson 4-3)* **78.125, 195.3125, 488.28125**

54. Order $\frac{1}{2}$, $\frac{7}{8}$, $\frac{1}{16}$, $\frac{5}{6}$, and $\frac{2}{3}$ from least to greatest. *(Lesson 4-10)* $\frac{1}{16}$, $\frac{1}{2}$, $\frac{2}{3}$, $\frac{5}{6}$, $\frac{7}{8}$

Problem Solving and Applications

55. **Business** Ruth's Cafe sold 28 pieces of apple pie today. If each piece was an eighth of a pie, how many apple pies did they sell? $3\frac{1}{2}$ **pies**

56. **Music** How many whole notes are there in eight quarter notes? *Hint: quarter means $\frac{1}{4}$.* **2 whole notes**

57. **Journalism** Ren sold ten quarter-page ads for the school newspaper. How many pages of advertisement did she sell? $2\frac{1}{2}$ **pages**

58. **Coin Collection** Elise has $10 worth of quarters and Juan has $10 in half-dollar coins. Which one has the greatest number of coins? **Elise**

59. **Critical Thinking** If $5 + \frac{1}{4}$ can be written as the improper fraction $\frac{21}{4}$, how would you write $c + \frac{1}{4}$ as an improper fraction? $\frac{4c + 1}{4}$

60. **Journal Entry** Use circle models to show that $1\frac{3}{4} = \frac{7}{4}$. **See Solutions Manual.**

Lesson 5-1 Mixed Numbers and Improper Fractions   **177**

Extending the Lesson

Logical Thinking Challenge students to write the number 9 as *both* an improper fraction and a mixed number. Answers will vary; sample: $8\frac{9}{9}$; $\frac{18}{2}$

Cooperative Learning Activity

Fashioning Models 5-1

Use groups of 4.
Materials: 3-inch by 12-inch strips of paper, colored pencils, ruler, index cards

● Decide who will model halves, thirds, fourths, and sixths. Make the halves models by cutting each of twelve 3-inch by 12-inch paper strips into two equal pieces; the thirds models by cutting each of eight paper strips into three equal pieces; the fourths models by cutting each of six paper strips into four equal pieces; and the sixths models by cutting each of four paper strips into six equal pieces. Using a different color pencil than the other group members, color your fraction models.

Copy onto cards the numbers 7, 9, 10, 12, 13, 15, 17, 23.

➡ In turn, each group member selects a card. The number on the card tells the number of pieces each group member needs to use to model an improper fraction. Each group member models and writes the improper fraction, and then models and writes the improper fraction as a whole number or mixed number.

Glencoe Mathematics: Applications and Connections, Course 2

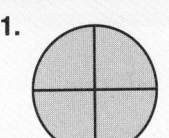 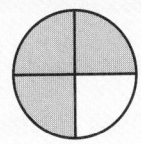

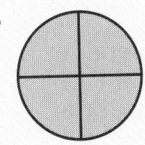 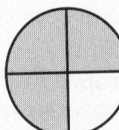

NCTM Standards: 1–7

Lesson Resources
- Study Guide Master 5-2
- Practice Master 5-2
- Enrichment Master 5-2
- Group Activity Card 5-2

Transparency 5-2 contains the 5-Minute Check and a teaching aid for this lesson.

⏱ 5-Minute Check
(Over Lesson 5-1)

Identify each number as a proper fraction, an improper fraction, or a mixed number.

1. $\frac{5}{3}$ improper fraction

2. $4\frac{1}{8}$ mixed number

Change each improper fraction to a mixed number in simplest form or a whole number.

3. $\frac{17}{6}$ $2\frac{5}{6}$

4. $\frac{15}{5}$ 3

Change each mixed number or whole number to an improper fraction.

5. $5\frac{5}{8}$ $\frac{45}{8}$

6. 6   Sample answer: $\frac{36}{6}$

---

1 FOCUS

Motivating the Lesson

Situational Problem Tell students that Kareem bought $\frac{3}{4}$ pounds of apples, $\frac{15}{16}$ pounds of bananas, and $\frac{7}{8}$ pounds of grapes. Ask them how they would use estimation to determine whether Kareem bought more or less than two pounds of fruit.

5-2 Estimating with Fractions

Objective
Estimate sums, differences, products, and quotients of fractions and mixed numbers.

Marie plans to make three loaves of banana bread. The recipe for a single loaf calls for $1\frac{3}{4}$ cups of flour. To make sure she has enough flour before starting, she estimates how much flour will be needed for all three loaves. Marie estimates the product of 3 and $1\frac{3}{4}$.

To estimate the sum, difference, or product of mixed numbers, round each mixed number to the nearest whole number.

$$3 \times 1\frac{3}{4} \;\rightarrow\; 3 \times 2 = 6$$

Marie will need *about* six cups of flour.

Example 1

Estimate the sum of $6\frac{1}{2}$ and $2\frac{1}{3}$.

$$6\frac{1}{2} + 2\frac{1}{3} \;\rightarrow\; 7 + 2 = 9$$ *When a mixed number contains $\frac{1}{2}$, the number is rounded up.*

$6\frac{1}{2} + 2\frac{1}{3}$ is *about* 9.

Estimation Hint
• • • • • • • • • • • •
A fraction is close to 1 when the numerator and denominator are close in value. A fraction is close to $\frac{1}{2}$ when the numerator is about half of the denominator. A fraction is close to 0 when the numerator is much smaller than the denominator.

To estimate the sum or difference of proper fractions, round each fraction to 0, $\frac{1}{2}$, or 1, whichever is closest.

Examples

2 Estimate $\frac{3}{8} + \frac{6}{7}$.

$$\frac{3}{8} + \frac{6}{7} \;\rightarrow\; \frac{1}{2} + 1 = 1\frac{1}{2}$$

$\frac{3}{8} + \frac{6}{7}$ is *about* $1\frac{1}{2}$.

$\frac{3}{8}$ is about $\frac{1}{2}$; $\frac{6}{7}$ is about 1.

3 Estimate $\frac{4}{5} - \frac{1}{2}$.

$$\frac{4}{5} - \frac{1}{2} \;\rightarrow\; 1 - \frac{1}{2} = \frac{1}{2}$$

$\frac{4}{5} - \frac{1}{2}$ is *about* $\frac{1}{2}$.

$\frac{4}{5}$ is about 1.

178   Chapter 5 Applications with Fractions

OPTIONS

Team Teaching

Inform the other teachers on your team that your classes are studying operations with fractions. Suggestions for curriculum integration are:

Science: chemistry

Home Economics: recipes, sewing

Art: graphic design

Physical Education: field-event heights or lengths

Social Studies: population changes, travel times, economics

You can also use patterns to estimate with fractions.

LOOKBACK You can review using patterns on page 11.

Examples

Estimate each product or quotient.

4 $\frac{1}{3} \times 14$ *$\frac{1}{3} \times 14$ means $\frac{1}{3}$ of 14.*

$\frac{1}{3}$ of 14 $\rightarrow$ $\frac{1}{3}$ of 15 or 5 *15 is divisible by 3.*

$\frac{1}{3}$ of 14 is *about* 5.

5 $34\frac{3}{4} \div 5\frac{1}{2}$

First, round $5\frac{1}{2}$ to 6. Then replace the dividend with a number that is easy to divide mentally.

$34\frac{3}{4} \div 5\frac{1}{2} \rightarrow 34\frac{3}{4} \div 6$

$\rightarrow 36 \div 6$ or 6 *36 is divisible by 6.*

$34\frac{3}{4} \div 5\frac{1}{2}$ is *about* 6.

Checking for Understanding

Communicating Mathematics

Read and study the lesson to answer each question.

1. **Tell** whether each point marked on the number line is closest to 0, $\frac{1}{2}$, or 1. **0, $\frac{1}{2}$, $\frac{1}{2}$, 1**

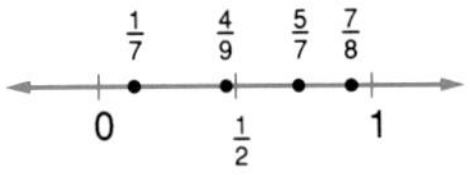

1/7
4/9
5/7
7/8
0
1/2
1

2. **Write** how you would use rounding to estimate $\frac{1}{2} + \frac{5}{6}$. **$\frac{1}{2} + 1 = 1\frac{1}{2}$**
3. **Tell** how you would use patterns to estimate $\frac{1}{4} \times 21$. **$\frac{1}{4} \times 20 = 5$**

Guided Practice

Round each fraction to 0, $\frac{1}{2}$, or 1.

4. $\frac{11}{12}$ **1**
5. $\frac{1}{6}$ **0**
6. $\frac{3}{5}$ **$\frac{1}{2}$**
7. $\frac{3}{4}$ **1**
8. $\frac{2}{3}$ **$\frac{1}{2}$**

Round to the nearest whole number.

9. $5\frac{3}{4}$ **6**
10. $9\frac{1}{6}$ **9**
11. $2\frac{1}{2}$ **3**
12. $4\frac{1}{8}$ **4**
13. $6\frac{3}{4}$ **7**

Estimate. Tell which strategy you used. **Sample answers are given.**

14. $\frac{1}{2} + \frac{7}{8}$ **$1\frac{1}{2}$; rounding**
15. $\frac{3}{8} - \frac{1}{10}$ **$\frac{1}{2}$; rounding**
16. $5\frac{1}{3} - 2\frac{3}{4}$ **2; rounding**
17. $\frac{3}{4} \times 11$ **9; patterns**
18. $\frac{1}{8} \times \frac{3}{4}$ **$\frac{1}{8}$; patterns**
19. $\frac{4}{5} \div \frac{7}{8}$ **1; rounding**

2 TEACH

Using Number Sense To help students check that their estimates of sums and differences make sense, have them use number sense to determine the two whole numbers between which the answer will fall.

More Examples

For Example 1

Estimate the sum of $5\frac{3}{4}$ and $7\frac{4}{5}$. **14**

For Example 2

Estimate $\frac{2}{5} + \frac{7}{8}$. **$1\frac{1}{2}$**

For Example 3

Estimate $\frac{5}{6} - \frac{1}{2}$. **$\frac{1}{2}$**

Estimate each product or quotient.

For Example 4

$\frac{1}{4} \times 19$ **5**

For Example 5

$41\frac{3}{8} \div 6\frac{1}{6}$ **7**

Checking for Understanding

Exercises 1-3 are designed to help you assess students' understanding through reading, writing, speaking, and modeling. You should work through these exercises with your students and then monitor their work on Guided Practice Exercises 4-19.

Reteaching Activity

Using Manipulatives Provide number lines or fraction strips to help students round mixed numbers to the nearest whole number by using visual estimation. Similarly, have them use the manipulatives to round proper fractions to the nearest 0, $\frac{1}{2}$, or 1.

Study Guide Masters, p. 40

Name ____________ Date ________

Study Guide Worksheet 5-2

Estimating with Fractions

Use rounding or patterns to estimate with fractions.

Rounding: For mixed numbers, round to the nearest whole number.

$4\frac{1}{6} + 3\frac{7}{8} \rightarrow 4 + 4 = 8$

$4\frac{1}{6} + 3\frac{7}{8}$ is about 8.

For proper fractions, round to 0, $\frac{1}{2}$ or 1.

$\frac{11}{12} - \frac{4}{9} \rightarrow 1 - \frac{1}{2} = \frac{1}{2}$

$\frac{11}{12} - \frac{4}{9}$ is about $\frac{1}{2}$.

Compatible Numbers: $\frac{1}{4} \times 19\frac{1}{2} \rightarrow \frac{1}{4} \times 20 = 5$

20 is divisible by 4.

$\frac{1}{4} \times 19\frac{1}{2}$ is about 5.

$29\frac{1}{3} \div 3\frac{9}{10} \rightarrow 28 \div 4 = 7$

28 is divisible by 4.

Close

Have students choose a whole number. Ask them to write four pairs of fractions or mixed numbers, each of which, when its members are rounded and then either added, subtracted, multiplied, or divided, yields an estimate equal to the number chosen.

3 PRACTICE/APPLY

Assignment Guide
Maximum: 20–68
Minimum: 21–53 odd, 55–66

For **Extra Practice,** see p. 582.

Alternate Assessment

Speaking   Have students explain how estimating with fractions is similar to and different from estimating with whole numbers and decimals.

Practice Masters, p. 40

Name _____ Date _____

Practice Worksheet 5-2

Estimating with Fractions

Round each fraction to 0, $\frac{1}{2}$, or 1.

1. $\frac{7}{12}$ $\frac{1}{2}$ 2. $\frac{1}{8}$ 0   3. $\frac{9}{10}$ 1

4. $\frac{13}{14}$ 1   5. $\frac{4}{7}$ $\frac{1}{2}$ 6. $\frac{1}{10}$ 0

Round to the nearest whole number.

7. $1\frac{7}{8}$ 2   8. $3\frac{1}{2}$ 4   9. $9\frac{9}{10}$ 10

10. $5\frac{1}{7}$ 5   11. $7\frac{1}{4}$ 7   12. $6\frac{6}{8}$ 7

Estimate. Tell which strategy you used.

13. $\frac{3}{4} + \frac{1}{6}$ 1
rounding

14. $\frac{1}{2} \times 19$ 10
compatible
numbers

15. $5\frac{1}{3} - \frac{1}{4}$ 5
rounding

16. $32\frac{1}{4} \div 2\frac{1}{8}$ 16
rounding

17. $9\frac{3}{5} - 3\frac{1}{2}$ 6
rounding

18. $3\frac{2}{8} \times 1\frac{3}{5}$ 4
rounding

19. $\frac{9}{10} - \frac{5}{20}$ 1
rounding

20. $12 \div 2\frac{5}{8}$ 4
rounding

21. $2\frac{1}{7} + 5\frac{9}{10}$ 8
rounding

22. $\frac{1}{2} \times 19\frac{3}{4}$ 10
compatible
numbers

23. $33\frac{1}{4} + 3\frac{1}{8}$ 11
rounding

24. $10\frac{1}{7} - 4\frac{3}{8}$ 6
rounding

T40
Glencoe Division, Macmillan/McGraw-Hill

180

Exercises

Independent Practice

Round each fraction to 0, $\frac{1}{2}$, or 1.

20. $\frac{1}{8}$ 0   21. $\frac{4}{5}$ 1   22. $\frac{2}{5}$ $\frac{1}{2}$ 23. $\frac{5}{6}$ 1   24. $\frac{1}{4}$ $\frac{1}{2}$

25. $\frac{1}{7}$ 0   26. $\frac{11}{12}$ 1   27. $\frac{3}{10}$ $\frac{1}{2}$ 28. $\frac{5}{12}$ $\frac{1}{2}$ 29. $\frac{9}{10}$ 1

Round to the nearest whole number.

30. $7\frac{1}{3}$ 7   31. $4\frac{1}{10}$ 4   32. $6\frac{7}{8}$ 7   33. $3\frac{1}{2}$ 4   34. $1\frac{3}{8}$ 1

35. $5\frac{3}{4}$ 6   36. $10\frac{4}{9}$ 10   37. $8\frac{7}{12}$ 9   38. $11\frac{2}{3}$ 12   39. $7\frac{5}{12}$ 7

Estimate.

40. $\frac{1}{3} + \frac{1}{8}$ $\frac{1}{2}$ 41. $\frac{5}{8} - \frac{1}{12}$ $\frac{1}{2}$ 42. $\frac{3}{4} - \frac{2}{5}$ $\frac{1}{2}$

43. $4\frac{1}{4} + 3\frac{4}{5}$ 8   44. $9\frac{7}{8} - 2\frac{3}{4}$ 7   45. $3\frac{1}{3} \times 2\frac{2}{3}$ 9

46. $5\frac{5}{7} \times 8\frac{2}{3}$ 54   47. $21\frac{1}{2} \div 1\frac{3}{4}$ 11   48. $13\frac{1}{6} \div 4\frac{1}{8}$ 3

49. $\frac{1}{2} \times 17$ 8   50. $18 \div \frac{3}{8}$ 36   51. $\frac{7}{8} \times \frac{3}{5}$ $\frac{1}{2}$

52. Estimate the product of $\frac{1}{4}$ and $\frac{2}{9}$. **0**

53. Estimate the quotient of $2\frac{4}{5}$ and $\frac{7}{8}$. **3**

54. Estimate the quotient of $\frac{3}{5}$ and $\frac{7}{12}$. **1**

Mixed Review 55. Compute the sum of 65 and 59 mentally to see if they are equal to 136. *(Lesson 1-4)* **no, 124**

56. Evaluate $5(6 + 3) \div (3 + 2)$. *(Lesson 1-7)* **9**

57. Estimate the difference of 14.82 and 5.13. *(Lesson 2-3)* **15 − 5 = 10**

58. Express 36 milliliters as liters. *(Lesson 2-9)* **0.036 liters**

59. **Attendance**   The number of students who missed school during the past three weeks at Lincoln Junior High are 3, 15, 24, 0, 31, 14, 7, 9, 10, 13, 4, 9, 3, 8, and 1. Make a stem-and-leaf plot for the data. *(Lesson 3-6)*   **See margin.**

60. Write the prime factorization for 36. *(Lesson 4-2)* **2² · 3²**

61. Express $3\frac{5}{8}$ as an improper fraction. *(Lesson 5-1)* **$\frac{29}{8}$**

Problem Solving and Applications 62. **Smart Shopping**   Kenny bought a tomato for a chef's salad he is making. The tomato he chose weighed 7 ounces. If tomatoes cost 90¢ a pound, *about* how much did Kenny pay for the tomato? *Hint: 1 pound = 16 ounces.*
45¢

OPTIONS

Gifted and Talented Needs

Have students work in small groups. One marks off a floor distance in the classroom or elsewhere. The others must visually estimate a fraction of that distance, such as $\frac{1}{3}$ or $\frac{3}{4}$. The closest estimate wins. Students should repeat the activity, taking turns marking, measuring, and estimating.

Additional Answer

59.
```
0 | 0 1 3 3 4 7 8 9 9
1 | 0 3 4 5
2 | 4
3 | 1
```

2 | 4 means 24.

It will be greater.

63. **Critical Thinking** If the dividend in a division problem is rounded up and the divisor is rounded down, what is the effect on the quotient?

64. **Construction** For a new home, a carpenter is building a built-in bookcase with eight shelves that are $3\frac{1}{2}$ feet long each. *About* how many shelves can he cut from a 12-foot board? **about 3**

65. **History** In 1986, *Voyager* became the first plane to fly nonstop around the world without refueling in midair. *Voyager* weighed 2,000 pounds, but at take-off it carried *about* $3\frac{1}{2}$ times its weight in fuel. *About* how many pounds of fuel did *Voyager* carry at take-off? **7,000 pounds**

66. **Travel** Tim Brody traveled from New York to Chicago to visit his cousin. His car's odometer read 48,297 when he left for Chicago and 50,000 when he returned home. *About* how many miles did he travel? **about 2,000 miles**

67. **Baking** Suppose a cookie recipe called for $2\frac{1}{2}$ cups of flour and $1\frac{2}{3}$ cups of sugar. *About* how many cups of dry ingredients are in the recipe? **about 5 cups**

68. **Data Search** Refer to pages 172 and 173. What fraction of the media industry is made up of publishing and cable television? $\frac{7}{10}$

CULTURAL KALEIDOSCOPE

Fannie Merrit Farmer

The printing press revolutionized cooking by making cookbooks widely available. The first known cookbook was printed in 1485. It was produced by an Italian who recorded recipes for marzipans and other sweets.

One of the most successful and popular cookbooks of all time was produced in the United States in 1896, when Fannie Farmer took on the editorship of *The Boston Cooking-School Cook Book.* She was the first to standardize the methods and measurements of her recipes. Before then, most recipes were written with vague directions such as "a pinch of salt," "a handful of flour," and "a dash of pepper."

Lesson 5-2 Estimating with Fractions **181**

Extending the Lesson

Cultural Kaleidoscope Ask students what might happen to the cooked recipe if measurements were not standardized. Discuss why cooks use a measuring cup and a knife to level off the ingredients in each cup.

Cooperative Learning Activity

Everything in Its Place **5-2**

Use groups of 4.

- Work in pairs. Each pair copies onto a sheet of paper the figure on the back of this card.
- Each pair rounds the following fractions to the nearest whole number.

$\frac{7}{8}$	$2\frac{3}{4}$	$3\frac{1}{2}$	$5\frac{1}{16}$
$16\frac{4}{9}$	$29\frac{3}{5}$	$1\frac{2}{3}$	$6\frac{11}{12}$
$41\frac{5}{6}$	$5\frac{9}{10}$	$8\frac{2}{5}$	$10\frac{1}{8}$
$12\frac{4}{7}$	$25\frac{5}{9}$	$15\frac{6}{29}$	$19\frac{5}{7}$

Try to be the first pair to write the estimated whole numbers in the blanks so that the total sum of the sums, differences, products, and quotients is 100.

Glencoe Mathematics: Applications and Connections, Course 2

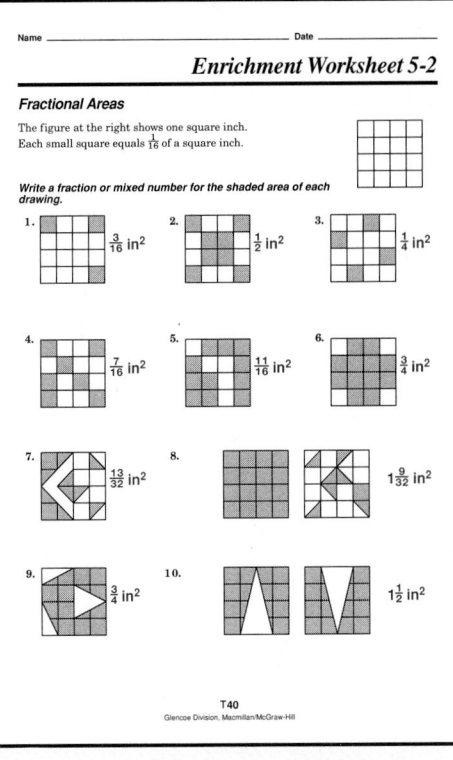

NCTM Standards: 1–7, 13

Lesson Resources
- Study Guide Master 5-3
- Practice Master 5-3
- Enrichment Master 5-3
- Technology Master, p. 19
- Group Activity Card 5-3

 Transparency 5-3 contains the 5-Minute Check and a teaching aid for this lesson.

⏱ 5-Minute Check
(Over Lesson 5-2)

Round each fraction to 0, $\frac{1}{2}$ or 1.

1. $\frac{2}{7}$ $\frac{1}{2}$ 2. $\frac{7}{8}$ 1

Round to the nearest whole number.

3. $8\frac{5}{8}$ 9

Estimate. Sample strategies are given.

4. $\frac{1}{5} + \frac{5}{6}$ 1 (round to 0 and 1)

5. $4\frac{3}{8} \times 3\frac{1}{4}$ 12 (round to nearest whole number)

6. $23\frac{1}{8} \div 3\frac{1}{3}$ 8 (use compatible numbers)

1 FOCUS

Motivating the Lesson

Situational Problem Survey students to find out what fraction of the class is wearing black pants. Write the fraction in simplest form. Next find out what fraction of the class is wearing blue pants. Write it in simplest form. Then ask students how they could determine the fraction of the class that is wearing either black pants *or* blue pants.

5-3 Adding and Subtracting Fractions

Objective
Add and subtract fractions.

Teen Scene

You can help prevent the greenhouse effect by using public transportation and avoid using hair spray, deodorant, and air freshener in aerosol cans.

The greenhouse effect is a concern of many people today. Some scientists claim that industrial gases emitted into the atmosphere are slowly causing the Earth's temperature to rise. This temperature increase may lead to unusual weather patterns which could eventually threaten crops, wildlife, and our very existence.

Carbon dioxide gas is said to be responsible for $\frac{1}{2}$ of the greenhouse effect. Chlorofluorocarbons are said to account for another $\frac{1}{6}$ of it. Together, how much are these two gases responsible for the greenhouse effect? You need to find the sum of $\frac{1}{2}$ and $\frac{1}{6}$.

To find the sum or difference of numbers, the units of measure must be the same.

Mini-Lab

Work with a partner.

Materials: fraction models

- To add 3 oranges and 2 apples, the common unit of measure is fruit.

  3 oranges + 2 apples → 3 fruits + 2 fruits = 5 fruits

- To find the difference of 1 yard and 2 feet, the common unit of measure is feet.

  $$1 \text{ yd} - 2 \text{ ft} = 3 \text{ ft} - 2 \text{ ft} = 1 \text{ ft}$$

- To add $\frac{1}{2}$ and $\frac{1}{4}$, the common unit of measure is fourths.

$$\frac{1}{2} + \frac{1}{4} \quad \blacktriangleright \quad \frac{2}{4} + \frac{1}{4} = \frac{3}{4}$$

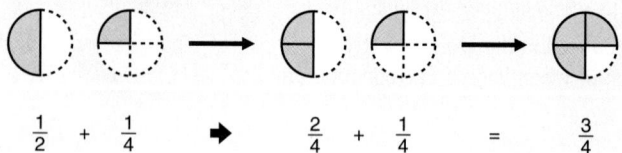

Classroom Vignette

"I model adding and subtracting fractions with Cuisenaire Rods. It's easier for my students to understand than fraction circles because I use the rods all year long."

Karey Killion

Karey Killion, Teacher
Westbridge Middle School, Grand Island, NE

Talk About It

a. Name a unit of measure that would allow 4 cats and 3 dogs to be added. Find the sum. **animals; 7 animals**

b. Write a subtraction problem with two different units of measure so that the difference is 10 inches. **See margin.**

c. Name a unit of measure that would allow $\frac{1}{2}$ and $\frac{1}{3}$ to be subtracted. What is the difference? **sixths; $\frac{1}{6}$**

d. What conclusion can you draw about units of measures for fractions that are to be added or subtracted? **They must be the same.**

Now solve the problem at the beginning of this lesson.

$$\frac{1}{2} + \frac{1}{6} \rightarrow \frac{3}{6} + \frac{1}{6} = \frac{4}{6} \text{ or } \frac{2}{3}$$

The denominator names the units to be added. The common unit is sixths.

Carbon dioxide gas and chlorofluorocarbons are responsible for about $\frac{2}{3}$ of the greenhouse effect.

Adding and Subtracting Fractions with Unlike Denominators	To add or subtract fractions: 1. Rename the fractions with a common denominator as necessary. 2. Add or subtract the numerators. 3. Simplify.

The least common multiple (LCM) can be used to rename fractions for addition and subtraction.

LOOK BACK

You can review LCM on page 161.

Example 1

Find $\frac{5}{8} - \frac{1}{6}$. Write the difference in simplest form.

Estimate: $\frac{1}{2} - 0 = \frac{1}{2}$

$$\begin{array}{l} \frac{5}{8} \\ -\frac{1}{6} \\ \hline \end{array} \quad \rightarrow \quad \begin{array}{l} 8 = 2 \times 2 \times 2 \text{ and } 6 = 2 \times 3 \\ \text{The LCM of 8 and 6 is} \\ 2 \times 2 \times 2 \times 3 \text{ or } 24. \\ \frac{5 \times 3}{8 \times 3} = \frac{15}{24} \text{ and } \frac{1 \times 4}{6 \times 4} = \frac{4}{24} \end{array} \quad \rightarrow \quad \begin{array}{l} \frac{15}{24} \\ -\frac{4}{24} \\ \hline \frac{11}{24} \end{array}$$

So, $\frac{5}{8} - \frac{1}{6} = \frac{11}{24}$.

Lesson 5-3 Adding and Subtracting Fractions **183**

Interactive Mathematics Tools

This multimedia software provides an interactive lesson that is tied directly to Lesson 5-3. Students will use models to add fractions.

2 TEACH

Using the Mini-Lab Have students write other fraction subtraction and addition examples for their partners to solve by using fraction models. Students should name the common unit measure.

Teaching Tip Before beginning the examples, review the relationship between adding fractions and finding the LCM. Review ways to find the least common denominator of two fractions.

More Examples

Add or subtract. Write each sum or difference in simplest form.

For Example 1
$\frac{7}{8} - \frac{1}{3}$ $\frac{13}{24}$

For Example 2
$\frac{3}{5} + \frac{5}{6}$ $\frac{43}{30}$ or $1\frac{13}{30}$

For Example 3
A school ordered uniforms for its football team. One-fourth of the uniforms had numbers between 10 and 20 inclusive and $\frac{5}{12}$ had numbers between 21 and 40 inclusive. What part of the team uniforms had numbers from 10 to 40?
$\frac{2}{3}$ of the uniforms

Checking for Understanding

Exercises 1-3 are designed to help you assess students' understanding through reading, writing, speaking, and modeling. You should work through these exercises with your students and then monitor their work on Guided Practice Exercises 4-9.

Reteaching Activity

Using Manipulatives Have students find common denominators, then use fraction strips to show equivalent fractions.

Additional Answer

Talk About It
b. Sample answer:
1 ft. − 2 in. = 10 in.

183

Error Analysis

Watch for students who add or subtract both the numerators and the denominators.

Prevent by stressing that they should add numerators only, and place that sum above the common denominator of the two fractions.

Close

Have students write two word problems, one that can be solved by adding fractions, and one that can be solved by subtracting fractions. Have students exchange papers and solve each other's problems.

3 PRACTICE/APPLY

Assignment Guide
Maximum: 10–32
Minimum: 11–23 odd, 25–29, 31

For **Extra Practice,** see p. 582.

Practice Masters, p. 41

Name _____ Date _____

Practice Worksheet 5-3

Adding and Subtracting Fractions

Add or subtract. Write each sum or difference in simplest form.

1. $\frac{1}{7}$ $\frac{4}{7}$
   $+\frac{3}{7}$

2. $\frac{3}{4}$ $\frac{1}{2}$
   $-\frac{1}{4}$

3. $\frac{11}{12}$ $\frac{7}{12}$
   $-\frac{1}{3}$

4. $\frac{8}{15}$ $\frac{2}{15}$
   $-\frac{2}{5}$

5. $\frac{17}{25}$ $\frac{49}{50}$
   $+\frac{3}{10}$

6. $\frac{7}{8}$ $1\frac{13}{24}$
   $+\frac{2}{3}$

7. $\frac{6}{7}$ $\frac{5}{7}$
   $-\frac{1}{7}$

8. $\frac{9}{10}$ $1\frac{1}{10}$
   $+\frac{1}{5}$

9. $\frac{2}{3}$ $1\frac{11}{21}$
   $+\frac{6}{7}$

10. $\frac{11}{15}+\frac{3}{5}$ $1\frac{1}{3}$

11. $\frac{4}{5}-\frac{1}{10}$ $\frac{7}{10}$

12. $\frac{17}{18}-\frac{2}{9}$ $\frac{13}{18}$

13. $\frac{3}{4}+\frac{1}{9}$ $\frac{31}{36}$

14. $\frac{7}{8}-\frac{1}{3}$ $\frac{13}{24}$

15. $\frac{7}{9}+\frac{1}{3}$ $1\frac{1}{9}$

16. $\frac{3}{4}-\frac{2}{5}$ $\frac{7}{20}$

17. $\frac{2}{5}+\frac{12}{13}$ $1\frac{21}{65}$

18. $\frac{3}{20}+\frac{3}{10}$ $\frac{9}{20}$

T41
Glencoe Division, Macmillan/McGraw-Hill

184

Example 2

Find $\frac{7}{9}+\frac{5}{12}$. Write the sum in simplest form.

Estimate $1+\frac{1}{2}=1\frac{1}{2}$

$\frac{7}{9}$ $\rightarrow$ $9=3\times3$ and $12=2\times2\times3$
The LCM of 9 and 12 is
$2\times2\times3\times3$ or 36. $\rightarrow$ $\frac{28}{36}$

$+\frac{5}{12}$ $\frac{7\times4}{9\times4}=\frac{28}{36}$ and $\frac{5\times3}{12\times3}=\frac{15}{36}$ $+\frac{15}{36}$

$\frac{43}{36}$

Rename $\frac{43}{36}$ as $1\frac{7}{36}$. So, $\frac{7}{9}+\frac{5}{12}=1\frac{7}{36}$.

Example 3 *Problem Solving*

Movies For the movie *The Wizard of Oz*, the wardrobe department had to make emerald green costumes for the residents of Emerald City. One-third of the shoes and stockings dyed for the movie were for the gentlemen and their wives, and $\frac{4}{15}$ were for the shopkeepers and their wives. What part of the shoes and stockings dyed for the movie were for the gentlemen and their wives and for the shopkeepers and their wives?

> **Calculator Hint**
> ● ● ● ● ● ● ● ● ● ● ● ● ●
> You can add and subtract fractions using a calculator. To find $\frac{1}{3}+\frac{4}{15}$, enter:
>
> 1 [/] 3 [+] 4 [/]
> 15 [=] 9/15.
>
> To get the answer in simplest form, press [Simp] [=] until N/D → n/d no longer appears on the screen.

We need to add $\frac{1}{3}$ and $\frac{4}{15}$.

Estimate: $\frac{1}{2}+0=\frac{1}{2}$

$\frac{1}{3}$ $\rightarrow$ $15=5\times3$
The LCM of 3 and 15 is 3×5 or 15. $\rightarrow$ $\frac{5}{15}$

$+\frac{4}{15}$ $\frac{1\times5}{3\times5}=\frac{5}{15}$ $+\frac{4}{15}$

$\frac{9}{15}$

Rename $\frac{9}{15}$ as $\frac{3}{5}$.

Three-fifths of the dyed shoes and stockings were for the gentlemen and their wives and the shopkeepers and their wives.

Checking for Understanding

Communicating Mathematics

Read and study the lesson to answer each question.

1. **Tell** why you must have a common denominator to add or subtract fractions. **See margin.**

2. **Tell** what is a common unit of measure that can be used to add 1 yard and 8 inches. **inches**

3. **Draw** a circle diagram that shows $\frac{1}{2}+\frac{1}{3}=\frac{5}{6}$. **See margin.**

184   **Chapter 5** Applications with Fractions

OPTIONS

Bell Ringer

Provide students with examples of how ancient Egyptians used hieroglyphics to write unit fractions. On the chalkboard, write the chart shown at the right. Challenge students to create their own symbols for fractions. Ask them to make up problems using these symbols for others to solve.

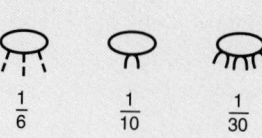

$\frac{1}{2}$ $\frac{1}{3}$ $\frac{1}{4}$

$\frac{1}{6}$ $\frac{1}{10}$ $\frac{1}{30}$

Add or subtract. Write each sum or difference in simplest form.

4. $\frac{1}{5}$

    $+\frac{2}{5}$ $\frac{3}{5}$

5. $\frac{2}{6}$

    $-\frac{1}{6}$ $\frac{1}{6}$

6. $\frac{3}{8}$

    $-\frac{1}{12}$ $\frac{7}{24}$

7. $\frac{3}{4} + \frac{7}{20}$ $1\frac{1}{10}$

8. $\frac{9}{10} - \frac{1}{6}$ $\frac{11}{15}$

9. $\frac{7}{15} + \frac{5}{9}$ $1\frac{1}{45}$

Exercises

Add or subtract. Write each sum or difference in simplest form.

10. $\frac{2}{9}$

    $+\frac{4}{9}$ $\frac{2}{3}$

11. $\frac{2}{4}$

    $-\frac{1}{4}$ $\frac{1}{4}$

12. $\frac{5}{8}$

    $-\frac{1}{2}$ $\frac{1}{8}$

13. $\frac{3}{5}$

    $+\frac{1}{15}$ $\frac{2}{3}$

14. $\frac{4}{5}$

    $-\frac{1}{6}$ $\frac{19}{30}$

15. $\frac{3}{7}$

    $+\frac{4}{5}$ $1\frac{8}{35}$

16. $\frac{5}{8} - \frac{5}{12}$ $\frac{5}{24}$

17. $\frac{5}{9} + \frac{5}{6}$ $1\frac{7}{18}$

18. $\frac{3}{7} + \frac{9}{14}$ $1\frac{1}{14}$

19. $\frac{4}{15} + \frac{9}{10}$ $1\frac{1}{6}$

20. $\frac{7}{11} - \frac{1}{4}$ $\frac{17}{44}$

21. $\frac{19}{24} - \frac{1}{4}$ $\frac{13}{24}$

22. Find the sum of $\frac{8}{9}$ and $\frac{7}{15}$. $1\frac{16}{45}$

23. Find the difference of $\frac{5}{8}$ and $\frac{5}{36}$. $\frac{35}{72}$

24. Find the sum of $\frac{11}{12}$ and $\frac{9}{20}$. $1\frac{11}{30}$

25. **Statistics** Find the mean, median, and mode for 12, 18, 25, 38, 44, and 49. *(Lesson 3-5)* **31, 31.5, no mode**

26. **Statistics** Make a line plot for $150, $1,200, $475, $235, $895, $1,075, and $390. Circle any outliers. *(Lesson 3-4)* **See margin.**

27. Find the least common multiple for 16 and 20. *(Lesson 4-9)* **80**

28. Estimate $1\frac{7}{12} \times 12\frac{1}{5}$. *(Lesson 5-2)* **2 × 12 = 24**

29. **Energy** Cars use about $\frac{4}{9}$ of the energy consumed by the transportation industry. Buses and trains use $\frac{1}{6}$. How much more energy is used by cars than by buses and trains? $\frac{5}{18}$

30. **Home Economics** Mrs. Keaton used $\frac{1}{4}$ pound of cheddar and $\frac{1}{3}$ pound of monterey jack cheese to make nachos. How much cheese did she use in all? $\frac{7}{12}$ **pound**

31. **Critical Thinking** Does $\frac{3}{4} + \frac{7}{8} - \frac{5}{6} = \frac{7}{8} + \frac{5}{6} - \frac{3}{4}$? Explain.
    No. Associative and commutative properties do not hold for subtraction.

32. **Journal Entry** Write a sentence or two in your journal about when being able to add and subtract fractions is useful in your everyday life.
    See students' work.

Lesson 5-3 Adding and Subtracting Fractions   **185**

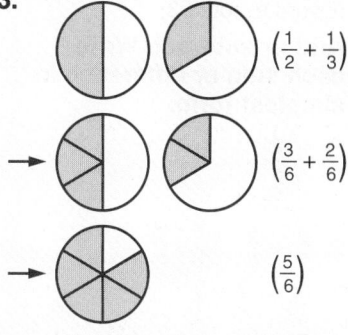
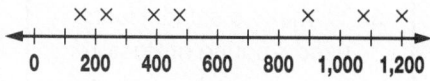
185

Lesson Resources
- Study Guide Master 5-4
- Practice Master 5-4
- Enrichment Master 5-4
- Group Activity Card 5-4

 Transparency 5-4 contains the 5-Minute Check and a teaching aid for this lesson.

⏱ 5-Minute Check
(Over Lesson 5-3)

Add or subtract. Write each sum or difference in simplest form.

1. $\frac{3}{8}$
   $+\frac{5}{8}$ 1

2. $\frac{2}{9} + \frac{3}{5}$ $\frac{37}{45}$

3. $\frac{9}{10} - \frac{3}{4}$ $\frac{3}{20}$

4. Find the sum of $\frac{11}{12}$ and $\frac{5}{9}$. $1\frac{17}{36}$

5. To make a salad, Henry used $\frac{3}{4}$ pound of Boston lettuce, and $\frac{2}{3}$ pound of red lettuce. How much did he use in all? $1\frac{5}{12}$ lb

---

1 FOCUS

Motivating the Lesson

Questioning Have students read the opening paragraph. Ask them how adding mixed numbers will be similar to adding fractions and how it will be different.

2 TEACH

Using Discussion Focus on two key elements of adding and subtracting mixed numbers—the need to find common denominators, and the need to rename in subtraction, when necessary. Have students compare this renaming with renaming in subtraction of whole numbers.

5-4 Adding and Subtracting Mixed Numbers

Objectives
Add and subtract mixed numbers with unlike denominators.

Did you know that you can make your own window-washing solution that is environmentally safe? Just mix the four ingredients at the right in a large bucket.

$1\frac{1}{3}$ cups ammonia

$\frac{1}{4}$ cup baking soda

$1\frac{1}{2}$ cups vinegar

2 gallons water

What is the total amount of ammonia and vinegar used? Find the sum of $1\frac{1}{3}$ and $1\frac{1}{2}$.

Adding and Subtracting Mixed Numbers	To add or subract mixed numbers: 1. Add cr subtract the fractions. If necessary, rename the fractions first. 2. Add or subtract the whole numbers. 3. Rename and simplify.

To find the total amount of ammonia and vinegar used, add $1\frac{1}{3}$ and $1\frac{1}{2}$.

Estimate: 1 + 2 = 3

$$1\frac{1}{3} \atop +1\frac{1}{2} \qquad \rightarrow \qquad \text{\textit{Use the LCM of 2 and 3 to rename }} \frac{1}{3} \text{\textit{ as }} \frac{2}{6} \text{\textit{ and }} \frac{1}{2} \text{\textit{ as }} \frac{3}{6}. \qquad \rightarrow \qquad \begin{array}{r} 1\frac{2}{6} \\ +1\frac{3}{6} \\ \hline 2\frac{5}{6} \end{array}$$

The total amount of ammonia and vinegar used is $2\frac{5}{6}$ cups.

Calculator Hint
••••••••••••••
You can add and subtract mixed numbers using a calculator. To find $18\frac{3}{4} + 13\frac{5}{6}$, enter:

18 [Unit] 3 [/] 4
[+] 13 [Unit] 5
[/] 6 [=] [Ab/c]

32 7/12.

To get the answers in simplest form, press [Simp] [=]

until N/D → n/d no longer appears on the screen.

Examples

Add or subtract. Write each sum or difference in simplest form.

1 $8\frac{3}{4} - 2\frac{5}{12}$

Estimate: 9 − 2 = 7

$$\begin{array}{r} 8\frac{3}{4} \\ -2\frac{5}{12} \end{array} \rightarrow \begin{array}{r} 8\frac{9}{12} \\ -2\frac{5}{12} \\ \hline 6\frac{4}{12} \text{ or } 6\frac{1}{3} \end{array}$$

2 $18\frac{3}{10} + 13\frac{5}{6}$

Estimate: 18 + 14 = 32

$$\begin{array}{r} 18\frac{3}{10} \\ +13\frac{5}{6} \end{array} \rightarrow \begin{array}{r} 18\frac{9}{30} \\ +13\frac{25}{30} \\ \hline 31\frac{34}{30} \end{array}$$

OPTIONS

Reteaching Activity

Using Manipulatives Provide pairs of students with inch rulers to use as number lines. Have them use the rulers to model addition of mixed numbers by locating the first addend and then *counting on*. They can model subtraction by locating the first mixed number and then *counting back*.

Study Guide Masters, p. 42

Name _____ Date _____

Study Guide Worksheet 5-4

Adding and Subtracting Mixed Numbers

To add or subtract mixed numbers:
1. Add or subtract the fractions. Rename if necessary.
2. Add or subtract the mixed numbers.
3. Rename and simplify.

Examples

1. $14\frac{1}{2} \rightarrow 14\frac{3}{6} \rightarrow 14\frac{3}{6} \rightarrow 14\frac{3}{6}$
   $+18\frac{2}{3} \quad +18\frac{4}{6} \quad +18\frac{4}{6} \quad +18\frac{4}{6}$
   $\qquad\qquad\qquad\qquad\qquad\quad \frac{7}{6} \qquad 32\frac{7}{6} = 33\frac{1}{6}$

2. $21 \rightarrow 20\frac{6}{6} \rightarrow 20\frac{6}{6} \rightarrow 20\frac{6}{6}$
   $-12\frac{5}{6} \quad -12\frac{5}{6} \quad -12\frac{5}{6} \quad -12\frac{5}{6}$

$$31\frac{34}{30} = 31 + \frac{34}{30}$$
$$= 31 + 1\frac{4}{30}$$
$$= 32\frac{4}{30} \text{ or } 32\frac{2}{15}$$

When you subtract two mixed numbers where the fraction in the first mixed number is less than the fraction in the second mixed number, you need to rename the first mixed number before subtracting.

Example 3

Find $3\frac{1}{3} - 1\frac{2}{3}$.

$\frac{1}{3}$ is less than $\frac{2}{3}$, so you need to rename $3\frac{1}{3}$.

Think: $3\frac{1}{3} = 2\frac{\square}{3}$

Use circle diagrams.

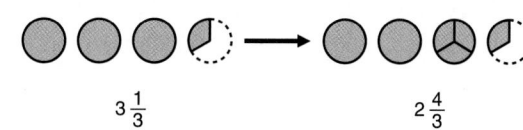

$3\frac{1}{3}$ $2\frac{4}{3}$

Now find the difference.

$$2\frac{4}{3}$$
$$-1\frac{2}{3}$$
$$\overline{1\frac{2}{3}}$$ So, $3\frac{1}{3} - 1\frac{2}{3} = 1\frac{2}{3}$.

Checking for Understanding

Communicating Mathematics

Read and study the lesson to answer each question. **For answers to Exercises 1–2, see margin.**

1. **Show** that $2\frac{1}{4} = 1\frac{5}{4}$ using circle models.

2. **Show** that $\frac{10}{3} = 3\frac{1}{3}$ using circle models.

Guided Practice

Complete.

3. $5\frac{1}{6} = 4\frac{\square}{6}$ 7

4. $3\frac{10}{7} = 4\frac{\square}{7}$ 3

5. $8\frac{3}{5} = 7\frac{\square}{5}$ 8

6. $2\frac{12}{9} = \square\frac{1}{3}$ 3

Add or subtract. Write each sum or difference in simplest form.

7. $5\frac{1}{8} + 3\frac{3}{8}$ $8\frac{1}{2}$

8. $6\frac{5}{6} - 2\frac{1}{3}$ $4\frac{1}{2}$

9. $3\frac{1}{2} - 1\frac{3}{4}$ $1\frac{3}{4}$

10. $7\frac{5}{6} + 9\frac{3}{8}$ $17\frac{5}{24}$

11. $4 - 2\frac{3}{15}$ $1\frac{4}{5}$

12. $13\frac{7}{8} + 15\frac{7}{10}$ $29\frac{23}{40}$

Lesson 5-4 Adding and Subtracting Mixed Numbers   **187**

Meeting Needs of Middle School Students

To foster supportive involvement with adults, have students and their parents or older family members work together to solve problems based on information from their daily lives. Suggest that they formulate and solve mixed number problems related to VCR programming, cooking, carpentry and home repair, sewing, and so on.

Additional Answers

1.

2.

187

Close

Have students explain how to subtract mixed numbers with renaming, as if to a student who has missed the lesson.

3 PRACTICE/APPLY

Assignment Guide
Maximum: 13–42
Minimum: 13–33 odd, 35–42

For **Extra Practice,** see p. 583.

Alternate Assessment

Writing Ask students to write and solve two problems involving mixed numbers, one in which renaming is necessary and one in which it is not. Have students present the solutions in simplest form.

Independent Practice

Complete.

13. $6\frac{1}{2} = 5\frac{\square}{2}$ 3
14. $3\frac{6}{4} = 4\frac{\square}{2}$ 1
15. $9\frac{9}{8} = 10\frac{\square}{8}$ 1
16. $6\frac{1}{2} = 5\frac{\square}{2}$ 3

17. $4\frac{5}{6} = 3\frac{\square}{6}$ 11
18. $7\frac{14}{10} = 8\frac{\square}{10}$ 4
19. $12\frac{9}{5} = \square\frac{4}{5}$ 13
20. $9\frac{2}{3} = \square\frac{5}{3}$ 8

Add or subtract. Write each sum or difference in simplest form.

21. $3\frac{1}{6} + 5\frac{1}{6}$ $8\frac{1}{3}$
22. $8\frac{7}{9} - 3\frac{1}{9}$ $5\frac{2}{3}$
23. $7\frac{3}{8} + 4\frac{7}{8}$ $12\frac{1}{4}$

24. $9\frac{4}{5} - 2\frac{3}{10}$ $7\frac{1}{2}$
25. $5\frac{5}{6} - 3\frac{2}{3}$ $2\frac{1}{6}$
26. $3\frac{7}{12} + 8\frac{3}{4}$ $12\frac{1}{3}$

27. $6\frac{13}{15} - 2\frac{3}{5}$ $4\frac{4}{15}$
28. $7\frac{3}{8} + 9\frac{1}{6}$ $16\frac{13}{24}$
29. $8\frac{3}{4} - 1\frac{7}{10}$ $7\frac{1}{20}$

30. $4\frac{3}{10} - 1\frac{3}{4}$ $2\frac{11}{20}$
31. $13\frac{1}{8} - 1\frac{7}{10}$ $11\frac{17}{40}$
32. $3\frac{1}{6} + 5\frac{1}{2} + 2\frac{7}{8}$ $11\frac{13}{24}$

33. Find the difference of $7\frac{1}{3}$ and $3\frac{5}{9}$. $3\frac{7}{9}$
34. Find the sum of $5\frac{7}{12}$ and $6\frac{5}{8}$. $12\frac{5}{24}$

Mixed Review

35. **Measurement** Find the number of feet in 3 yards. *(Lesson 1-9)* **9 feet**
36. Multiply 0.00003×10^6. *(Lesson 2-6)* **30**
37. Find the next three terms in the following sequence: 22.5, 25, 27.5, 30, ... *(Lesson 4-4)* **32.5, 35, 37.5**

38. **Travel** Don drove to an out-of-town business meeting. It took $11\frac{4}{5}$ hours. About how many hours did he drive? *(Lesson 5-1)* **12 hours**

39. Add $\frac{5}{6}$ and $\frac{2}{3}$. *(Lesson 5-3)* $1\frac{1}{2}$

Problem Solving and Applications

40. **Television** A video tape will record 6 hours in the EP mode. Mike has recorded $2\frac{5}{6}$ hours of a baseball game. He wants to record $3\frac{1}{2}$ hours more on the same tape. Can he do this? Explain your answer. **No; $3\frac{1}{2} + 2\frac{5}{6} = 6\frac{1}{3}$.**

41. **Sports** Sergei Bubka, a pole vaulter from the former Soviet Union, has set several world records in pole vaulting. Use the graph at the right to find the difference between his world record vault in 1988 and his world record vault in August 1991. $1\frac{3}{4}$ **inches**

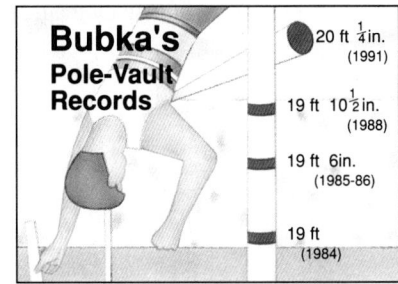

Bubka's Pole-Vault Records

20 ft $\frac{1}{4}$ in. (1991)

19 ft $10\frac{1}{2}$ in. (1988)

19 ft 6 in. (1985-86)

19 ft (1984)

42. **Critical Thinking** A string is cut in half and one half is used to bundle newspapers. Then one fifth of the remaining string is cut off and used to tie a balloon. The piece left is 8 feet long. How long was the string originally? **20 ft**

Enrichment Masters, p. 42

Name _____ Date _____

Enrichment Worksheet 5-4

Arithmetic Sequences of Fractions

Each term in an *arithmetic* sequence is created by adding or subtracting the same number to the term before. The number added or subtracted is called the *common difference.*

The sequence below is an increasing arithmetic sequence with a common difference of $\frac{1}{4}$.
$\frac{1}{8}, \frac{3}{8}, \frac{5}{8}, \frac{7}{8}, 1\frac{1}{8}$

Below is a decreasing arithmetic sequence with a common difference of $1\frac{1}{8}$.
$7\frac{3}{8}, 6\frac{5}{8}, 5\frac{5}{8}, 4, 2\frac{3}{8}$

Write the common difference for each arithmetic sequence.

1. $\frac{1}{2}, \frac{5}{8}, \frac{3}{4}, \frac{7}{8}, 1, 1\frac{1}{8}$ $\frac{1}{8}$
2. $1\frac{1}{4}, 3\frac{3}{4}, 6\frac{1}{4}, 8\frac{3}{4}$ $2\frac{1}{2}$

3. $4\frac{1}{2}, 4\frac{2}{5}, 4\frac{3}{10}, 4\frac{1}{5}$ $\frac{1}{10}$
4. $11, 9\frac{2}{3}, 8\frac{1}{3}, 7, 5\frac{2}{3}$ $1\frac{1}{3}$

Write the next term in each arithmetic sequence.

5. $\frac{3}{8}, \frac{5}{8}, \frac{7}{8}, 1\frac{1}{8}, 1$ $1\frac{1}{12}$

6. $\frac{13}{20}, \frac{11}{20}, \frac{9}{20}, \frac{7}{20}$ $\frac{1}{4}$

7. $5\frac{1}{6}, 5\frac{7}{10}, 6\frac{5}{6}, 6\frac{7}{10}$ $7\frac{5}{6}$
8. $4\frac{1}{12}, 3\frac{3}{4}, 2\frac{7}{12}, 1\frac{1}{12}$ $\frac{3}{12}$, or $\frac{1}{4}$

Write the first five terms in each sequence.

9. This increasing sequence starts with $\frac{1}{6}$ and has a common difference of $1\frac{1}{5}$.
$\frac{1}{6}, 1\frac{11}{30}, 2\frac{17}{30}, 3\frac{23}{30}, 4\frac{29}{30}$

10. This decreasing sequence starts with $6\frac{1}{3}$ and has a common difference of $\frac{3}{4}$.
$6\frac{1}{3}, 5\frac{7}{12}, 4\frac{5}{6}, 4\frac{1}{12}, 3\frac{1}{3}$

T42
Glencoe Division, Macmillan/McGraw-Hill

188

OPTIONS

Extending the Lesson

Using Patterns Have students write the next three numbers in each sequence. Then ask them to make up sequences of their own for others to continue.

1. $2\frac{1}{4}, 3\frac{3}{4}, 5\frac{1}{4}, \ldots$ $6\frac{3}{4}, 8\frac{1}{4}, 9\frac{3}{4}, \ldots$

2. $20\frac{1}{3}, 17\frac{2}{3}, 15, \ldots$ $12\frac{1}{3}, 9\frac{2}{3}, 7, \ldots$

Cooperative Learning Activity

So Shoe Me! **5-4**

Use groups of 4.
Materials: Rulers

♦ Read the following passage.

There are several different ways to compute shoe sizes. The modern "English" method works like this: The smallest size is size 0, which is a shoe with a length of 4 inches. You add $\frac{1}{3}$ inch to get the next larger size. Sizes run from 0 to 13 and then start over again at 1. About three hundred years ago, English shoe sizes were computed differently. In those days, size 0 was 5 inches long, and you added $\frac{1}{4}$ inch to get the next larger size.

➡ Each group member finds the length in inches of one of his or her own shoes and determines his or her modern English shoe size. Each group member then answers the following question: Suppose that you could travel back in time to the England of three hundred years ago and that you want to buy a pair of fashionable shoes. If you ask for your modern English shoe size, will the shoes you get be too big or too small? How much too big or too small?

Glencoe Mathematics: Applications and Connections, Course 2

5-5A Multiplying Fractions and Mixed Numbers

A Preview of Lesson 5-5

NCTM Standards: 1–6

Management Tips

For Students Have each group of students work together to do all three activities and then answer the questions. Students should draw the circle models with reasonable care so that they can be re-used. Allow a full class period.

For the Overhead Projector *Overhead Manipulative Resources* provides appropriate materials for teacher or student demonstration of the activities in this Mathematics Lab.

Objective
Find the product of fractions by using models.

Materials
fraction circles
sheets of paper

As in multiplication of whole numbers, multiplication of fractions and mixed numbers represents repeated addition.

The product $a \times b$ means a sets of size b. You can show this by making a model. Consider 3×2.

$$\underset{\substack{\text{number} \\ \text{of sets}}}{3} \quad \times \quad \underset{\substack{\text{size of} \\ \text{each set}}}{2} \quad \rightarrow$$

set 1 + set 2 + set 3 →

Therefore, $3 \times 2 = 6$.

You can make a model to show $3 \times \frac{1}{2}$ by using fraction circles. Use 3 sheets of paper to represent 3 sets. Put a half circle in each set. Find the product.

$$\underset{\substack{\text{number} \\ \text{of sets}}}{3} \quad \times \quad \underset{\substack{\text{size of} \\ \text{each set}}}{\frac{1}{2}} \quad \rightarrow$$

$\frac{1}{2}$ 1 set + $\frac{1}{2}$ 1 set + $\frac{1}{2}$ 1 set →

Therefore, $3 \times \frac{1}{2} = 1\frac{1}{2}$.

1 FOCUS

Introducing the Lab

Before students begin *Activity One,* point out that just as they used fraction circles to model addition of fractions, they can use them to model repeated addition, or multiplication.

Activity One

Work in groups of three.

- Make a model to show the product of $4 \times \frac{1}{3}$ by using fraction circles and sheets of paper.

What do you think?

1. How many sheets of paper were needed? **4**
2. What part of a circle did each sheet of paper contain? $\frac{1}{3}$
3. What is the product? $\frac{4}{3}$ or $1\frac{1}{3}$
4. How is this model similar to or different from the model for whole numbers? **You must piece the fractions together.**
5. Repeat Activity One for $2 \times \frac{3}{4}$, $5 \times \frac{2}{3}$, and $6 \times \frac{3}{8}$. **See Solutions Manual.**

Mathematics Lab 5-5A Multiplying Fractions and Mixed Numbers   **189**

2 TEACH

Using Cooperative Groups
Although only one student needs to draw and cut the models, group members should work together to determine what their model should look like and how to use it to show the multiplication. If appropriate, encourage groups to show other products using fraction circles. Challenge advanced groups to model the multiplication of two mixed numbers, such as $2\frac{1}{2} \times 1\frac{3}{4}$.

3 PRACTICE/APPLY

Using Critical Thinking Ask students to identify the relationship between the first factor in the multiplication and the number of sheets of paper needed to make the model.

Close

Have students explain how to use fraction circles to model multiplication of fractions. Then ask them to model the solution to the following problem: *It takes Karen $\frac{3}{4}$ hour to complete a puzzle. At that rate, how long will it take her to complete 4 puzzles?* 3 hours

190

Activity Two

- Make a model to show the product of $2\frac{1}{2} \times \frac{1}{2}$. Use $2\frac{1}{2}$ sheets of paper to represent $2\frac{1}{2}$ sets. Put a half circle on each full sheet of paper to represent $\frac{1}{2}$. Since a full sheet contains $\frac{1}{2}$, put $\frac{1}{4}$ on the half sheet of paper. Then find the product.

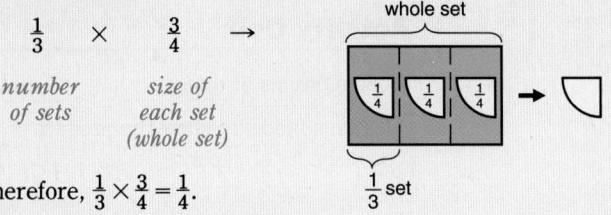

$$2\frac{1}{2} \quad \times \quad \frac{1}{2} \rightarrow$$

number of sets   *size of each set*

Therefore, $2\frac{1}{2} \times \frac{1}{2} = 1\frac{1}{4}$.

- Make a model to show the product of $1\frac{1}{2} \times \frac{2}{3}$.

What do you think?

6. a. What part of a circle should the full sheet of paper contain? $\frac{2}{3}$
   b. What part of a circle should the half sheet of paper contain? $\frac{1}{3}$

7. What is the product? 1

8. Repeat this activity for $2\frac{1}{2} \times \frac{1}{4}$. **See Solutions Manual.**

Activity Three

- Make a model to show the product of $\frac{1}{3} \times \frac{3}{4}$. Use a full sheet of paper to represent one set. Since a full sheet contains $\frac{3}{4}$, put $\frac{1}{4}$ on the one-third sheet. Now find the product.

$$\frac{1}{3} \quad \times \quad \frac{3}{4} \rightarrow$$

number of sets   *size of each set (whole set)*

whole set

$\frac{1}{3}$ set

Therefore, $\frac{1}{3} \times \frac{3}{4} = \frac{1}{4}$.

- Make a model to show $\frac{1}{3} \times \frac{3}{8}$.

What do you think?

9. a. What part of a sheet of paper is needed? $\frac{1}{3}$
   b. What part of a circle does the one-third sheet of paper contain? $\frac{1}{8}$

10. What is the product? $\frac{1}{8}$

11. Repeat this activity for $\frac{1}{2} \times \frac{2}{4}$ and $\frac{1}{3} \times \frac{6}{8}$. **See Solutions Manual.**

OPTIONS

Lab Manual You may wish to make copies of the blackline master on p. 48 of the *Lab Manual* for students to use as a recording sheet.

Lab Manual, p. 48

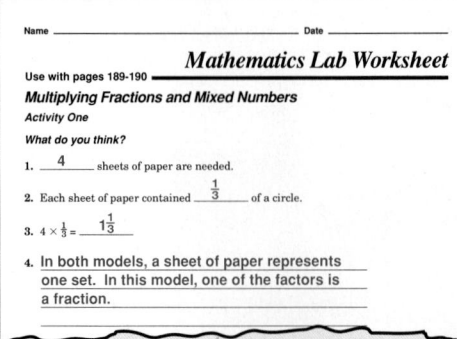

Name _____ Date _____

Mathematics Lab Worksheet

Use with pages 189–190

Multiplying Fractions and Mixed Numbers

Activity One

What do you think?

1. ____4____ sheets of paper are needed.

2. Each sheet of paper contained ____$\frac{1}{3}$____ of a circle.

3. $4 \times \frac{1}{3} =$ ____$1\frac{1}{3}$____

4. In both models, a sheet of paper represents one set. In this model, one of the factors is a fraction.

5-5 Multiplying Fractions and Mixed Numbers

Objective

Multiply fractions and mixed numbers.

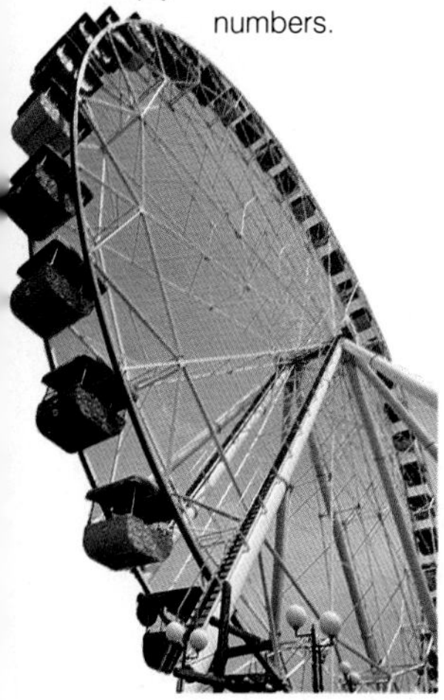

MegaCorp purchased land that is $\frac{2}{3}$ mile long and $\frac{1}{2}$ mile wide. How many square miles is the land?

Draw a model of a square mile. Divide the length in thirds and the width in halves. If the land is $\frac{2}{3}$ mile long and $\frac{1}{2}$ mile wide, then its area is $\frac{2}{6}$ or $\frac{1}{3}$ of a square mile.

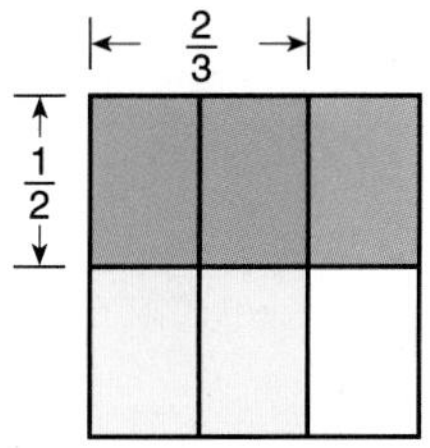

2/3
1/2

You also get $\frac{1}{3}$ if you multiply the fractions.

$$\frac{2}{3} \times \frac{1}{2} = \frac{2 \times 1}{3 \times 2} = \frac{2}{6} \text{ or } \frac{1}{3}$$

The area of the land will be $\frac{1}{3}$ square mile.

Multiplying Fractions	**In Words:** To multiply fractions, multiply the numerators and then multiply the denominators.
	Arithmetic $\frac{1}{4} \times \frac{1}{2} = \frac{1}{8}$ **Algebra** $\frac{a}{b} \times \frac{c}{d} = \frac{ac}{bd}$

Example 1

Find $\frac{2}{3} \times \frac{3}{4}$.

$$\frac{2}{3} \times \frac{3}{4} = \frac{6}{12} = \frac{1}{2}$$

2 × 3, *3 × 4*

$\frac{2}{3}$ × $\frac{3}{4}$ → *number of sets* , *size of set*

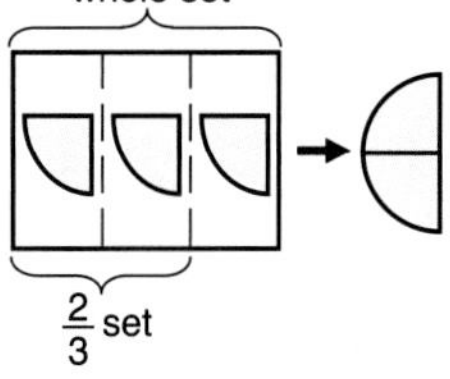

whole set
2/3 set

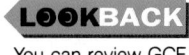

Estimation Hint

Estimate $\frac{2}{3} \times \frac{3}{4}$.

Round $\frac{2}{3}$ to $\frac{1}{2}$ and $\frac{3}{4}$ to 1.

$\frac{1}{2} \times 1 = \frac{1}{2}$

When the numerator and denominator of either fraction have a common factor, you can simplify before you multiply.

Examples

Multiply.

2 $\frac{3}{4} \times \frac{5}{6}$

Estimate: 1 × 1 = 1 — *The GCF of 3 and 6 is 3.*

$$\frac{3}{4} \times \frac{5}{6} = \frac{\overset{1}{\cancel{3}}}{4} \times \frac{5}{\underset{2}{\cancel{6}}} = \frac{5}{8}$$

Divide 3 and 6 by 3.

3 $\frac{6}{25} \times \frac{5}{8}$

Estimate: $0 \times \frac{1}{2} = 0$ — *The GCF of 6 and 8 is 2.*

$$\frac{6}{25} \times \frac{5}{8} = \frac{\overset{3}{\cancel{6}}}{\underset{5}{\cancel{25}}} \times \frac{\overset{1}{\cancel{5}}}{\underset{4}{\cancel{8}}} = \frac{3}{20}$$

The GCF of 25 and 5 is 5.

LOOKBACK

You can review GCF on page 145.

OPTIONS

Reteaching Activity

Using Manipulatives Some students may be confused by the fact that the product of two fractions is less than either factor. Have such students continue to use fraction circles or work with grids and cross-hatching to model the multiplication. Begin with simpler multiplications such as $\frac{1}{2} \times \frac{2}{3}$ and $\frac{1}{4} \times \frac{4}{5}$.

Study Guide Masters, p. 43

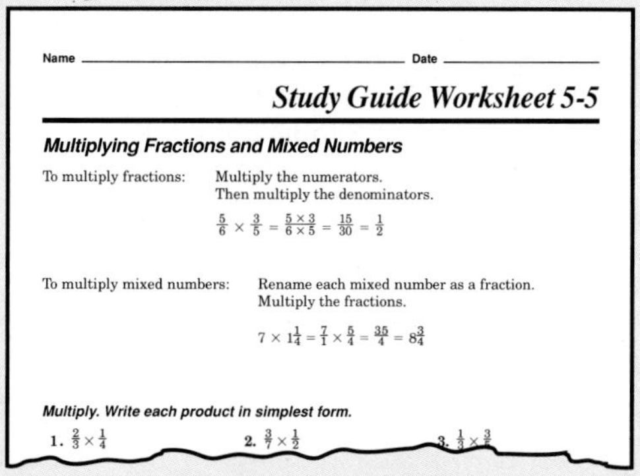

Name ____ Date ____

Study Guide Worksheet 5-5

Multiplying Fractions and Mixed Numbers

To multiply fractions: Multiply the numerators. Then multiply the denominators.

$\frac{5}{6} \times \frac{3}{5} = \frac{5 \times 3}{6 \times 5} = \frac{15}{30} = \frac{1}{2}$

To multiply mixed numbers: Rename each mixed number as a fraction. Multiply the fractions.

$7 \times 1\frac{1}{4} = \frac{7}{1} \times \frac{5}{4} = \frac{35}{4} = 8\frac{3}{4}$

Multiply. Write each product in simplest form.

1. $\frac{2}{3} \times \frac{1}{4}$ 2. $\frac{3}{7} \times \frac{1}{2}$ 3. $\frac{1}{3} \times \frac{3}{}$

5-5 Lesson Notes

NCTM Standards: 1-7, 9, 13

Lesson Resources

- Study Guide Master 5-5
- Practice Master 5-5
- Enrichment Master 5-5
- Group Activity Card 5-5

Transparency 5-5 contains the 5-Minute Check and a teaching aid for this lesson.

5-Minute Check

(Over Lesson 5-4)

Complete.

1. $4\frac{1}{6} = 3\frac{\square}{6}$ 7
2. $7\frac{2}{5} = 6\frac{\square}{5}$ 7

Add or subtract. Write each sum or difference in simplest form.

3. $3\frac{2}{3} + 5\frac{1}{3}$ 9
4. $6\frac{5}{8} + 8\frac{5}{6}$ $15\frac{11}{24}$
5. $7\frac{1}{5} - 2\frac{1}{2}$ $4\frac{7}{10}$

1 FOCUS

Motivating the Lesson

Questioning Have students read the opening paragraphs. Then have them suppose that the site in question was $1\frac{2}{3}$ miles long and $\frac{1}{2}$ mile wide. Ask them to explain how they would find the area of the site without a model.

2 TEACH

Using Discussion Have students discuss any prior knowledge they have about the procedure for multiplying fractions and mixed numbers. Ask students to explain the advantage of simplifying fractions before multiplying.

Multiplying Mixed Numbers	To multiply mixed numbers, rename each mixed number as an improper fraction. Multiply the fractions.

Example 4

Find $2 \times 2\frac{1}{4}$.

Estimate: $2 \times 2 = 4$

$2 \times 2\frac{1}{4} = 2 \times \frac{9}{4}$

$= \frac{2}{1} \times \frac{9}{4}$

$= \frac{9}{2}$ or $4\frac{1}{2}$

Checking for Understanding

Communicating Mathematics

Read and study the lesson to answer each question.

1. **Draw** a model using sets to show what $2\frac{1}{2} \times \frac{2}{3}$ means. **See margin.**

2. **Tell** how to multiply fractions.   **Multiply the numerators and then multiply the denominators.**

Guided Practice

Multiply. Write each product in simplest form.

3. $\frac{3}{5} \times \frac{1}{2}$ $\frac{3}{10}$

4. $\frac{2}{3} \times \frac{5}{6}$ $\frac{5}{9}$

5. $\frac{2}{3} \times \frac{3}{8}$ $\frac{1}{4}$

6. $2 \times \frac{3}{4}$ $1\frac{1}{2}$

7. $2\frac{1}{2} \times 2\frac{2}{3}$ $6\frac{2}{3}$

8. $1\frac{1}{6} \times \frac{3}{7} \times \frac{1}{3}$ $\frac{1}{6}$

9. $\frac{4}{5} \times \frac{1}{8}$ $\frac{1}{10}$

10. $4 \times \frac{2}{5}$ $1\frac{3}{5}$

11. $3\frac{1}{4} \times 2\frac{2}{3}$ $8\frac{2}{3}$

Exercises

Independent Practice

Multiply. Write each product in simplest form.

12. $\frac{1}{8} \times \frac{3}{4}$ $\frac{3}{32}$

13. $\frac{1}{5} \times \frac{1}{2}$ $\frac{1}{10}$

14. $\frac{1}{4} \times \frac{4}{5}$ $\frac{1}{5}$

15. $\frac{3}{8} \times \frac{4}{5}$ $\frac{3}{10}$

16. $\frac{3}{7} \times \frac{2}{3}$ $\frac{2}{7}$

17. $\frac{4}{5} \times \frac{1}{8}$ $\frac{1}{10}$

18. $\frac{5}{6} \times \frac{3}{5}$ $\frac{1}{2}$

19. $\frac{3}{5} \times \frac{10}{21}$ $\frac{2}{7}$

20. $\frac{4}{9} \times \frac{2}{3}$ $\frac{8}{27}$

21. $\frac{1}{2} \times \frac{5}{8}$ $\frac{5}{16}$

22. $\frac{3}{7} \times \frac{5}{6}$ $\frac{5}{14}$

23. $\frac{5}{9} \times \frac{9}{10}$ $\frac{1}{2}$

24. $3\frac{2}{3} \times 9$ 33

25. $1\frac{4}{7} \times 4\frac{2}{3}$ $7\frac{1}{3}$

26. $5\frac{1}{3} \times \frac{4}{5}$ $4\frac{4}{15}$

27. Find the product of $4\frac{1}{2}$ and $1\frac{1}{3}$. 6

28. Find the product of 3 and $2\frac{1}{7}$. $6\frac{3}{7}$

OPTIONS

Gifted and Talented Needs

Ask students to compare the size of the product and the size of the factors when (a) both factors are fractions and (b) both factors are mixed numbers.   (a) The product is less than either factor; (b) The product is greater than both factors.

Additional Answer

1.

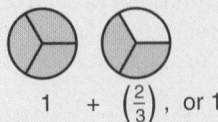

whole set $\left(\frac{2}{3}\right)$

$2\frac{1}{2}$ sets

$1 + \left(\frac{2}{3}\right)$, or $1\frac{2}{3}$

Mixed Review

29. Evaluate $3m + 4(p + m) - 2mnp$ if $m = 2$, $n = 3$, and $p = 1$. *(Lesson 1-8)* **6**

30. **Income** The mean income for a group of accountants was $26,266.67. The incomes were $17,500, $26,100, $19,800, $23,400, $21,300, and $49,500. In what way is the mean misleading? *(Lesson 3-8)* **See margin.**

31. 2, 3, 4, 5, 6, 10

31. Tell whether 240 is divisible by 2, 3, 4, 5, 6, 9, or 10. *(Lesson 4-1)*

32. Find the sum of $6\frac{3}{4}$ and $9\frac{7}{8}$. *(Lesson 5-4)* **$16\frac{5}{8}$**

Problem Solving and Applications

33. **Landscaping** A brick is about $2\frac{1}{4}$ inches thick, and the mortar joint is about $\frac{1}{2}$ inch thick. If six layers of brick are to be laid around a new flower bed, about how high will the wall be? **16 inches**

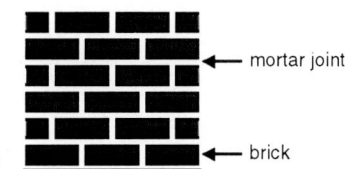

← mortar joint

← brick

34. **Coin Collecting** Susan B. Anthony was a leader in the women's suffrage movement. In 1979, the United States honored her efforts by minting a special one-dollar coin with her portrait on the front. The coin is $\frac{3}{4}$ copper and $\frac{1}{4}$ nickel. It weighs $8\frac{1}{2}$ grams. How many grams of copper are in each coin? **$6\frac{3}{8}$ grams**

35. **Critical Thinking** Observe that $3 \times \frac{1}{3} = 1$, $4 \times \frac{1}{4} = 1$, and $9 \times \frac{1}{9} = 1$. What number times $1\frac{1}{2}$ equals one? times $2\frac{1}{2}$? **$\frac{2}{3}, \frac{2}{5}$**

36. **Portfolio Suggestion** Select an item from this chapter that you feel shows your best work and place it in your portfolio. **See students' work.**

---

5 Assessment: Mid-Chapter Review

Change each mixed number to an improper fraction. *(Lesson 5-1)*

1. $2\frac{1}{2}$ **$\frac{5}{2}$**   2. $4\frac{2}{3}$ **$\frac{14}{3}$**   3. $3\frac{1}{3}$ **$\frac{10}{3}$**   4. $5\frac{4}{5}$ **$\frac{29}{5}$**

Estimate. *(Lesson 5-2)*

5. $\frac{3}{4} + \frac{1}{8}$ **1**   6. $\frac{5}{6} - \frac{1}{5}$ **$\frac{1}{2}$**   7. $4\frac{1}{6} \times 5\frac{1}{3}$ **20**

8. **Machinery** A steel rod has a diameter of $\frac{3}{4}$ inch. It must be made into a $\frac{9}{16}$-inch rod to fit on a tractor. How much must the diameter be reduced? *(Lesson 5-3)* **$\frac{3}{16}$ inch**

Add or subtract. Write each sum or difference in simplest form. *(Lesson 5-4)*

9. $8\frac{3}{8} + 6\frac{5}{6}$ **$15\frac{5}{24}$**   10. $2\frac{1}{4} - 1\frac{5}{8}$ **$\frac{5}{8}$**   11. $8\frac{7}{9} + 1\frac{1}{3}$ **$10\frac{1}{9}$**

Multiply. Write each product in simplest form. *(Lesson 5-5)*

12. $\frac{3}{8} \times \frac{2}{5}$ **$\frac{3}{20}$**   13. $\frac{5}{9} \times \frac{3}{7}$ **$\frac{5}{21}$**   14. $\frac{4}{5} \times \frac{5}{6}$ **$\frac{2}{3}$**

Lesson 5-5 Multiplying Fractions and Mixed Numbers   **193**

Extending the Lesson

Cooking Have students use a cookbook to find a recipe for a dessert they would want to make. Ask them to rewrite the recipe, giving the amount of each ingredient that will be needed to serve the class.

Additional Answer

30. It is higher because of the outlier, $49,500.

Cooperative Learning Activity

From Top to Bottom 5-5

Number of players: 4
Materials: Index cards, spinner

▸ Copy onto a large sheet of paper (or several sheets taped together) the game board shown on the back of this card. Be sure that you can place an index card above and below each fraction bar. Make two sets of cards containing the numbers 1–12, one number per card. Shuffle each set of cards. Label equal sections of a spinner "Numerator" and "Denominator."

▸ Work in pairs. Each pair divides a set of cards evenly. Then one partner from each pair spins the spinner. The spinner tells whether each partner's cards should be placed in the numerator or the denominator. The other partner in each group places his or her cards on the game board to complete each fraction. Each partner finds the product space of the numbers on his or her cards, writes the product on a blank card, and places it in the product space on the game board. Finally, partners show the solution in simplest form. The pair with the greater product wins the round. Play several rounds.

Glencoe Mathematics: Applications and Connections, Course 2

Error Analysis

Watch for students who "simplify" two numerators or denominators before multiplying fractions.

Prevent by reminding students that they simplify fractions by dividing a numerator and a denominator by their GCF. "Simplifying" in any other way may change the value of the fractions.

Close

Have students describe how multiplying mixed numbers is related to multiplying fractions.

3 PRACTICE/APPLY

Assignment Guide
Maximum: 12–35
Minimum: 13–27 odd, 29–35
All: Mid-Chapter Review

For **Extra Practice**, see p. 583.

Alternate Assessment

Speaking Have students write a fraction that represents the number of yards of fabric needed for 6 costumes if each costume requires $3\frac{1}{4}$ yards.   **$19\frac{1}{2}$ yd**

Enrichment Masters, p. 43

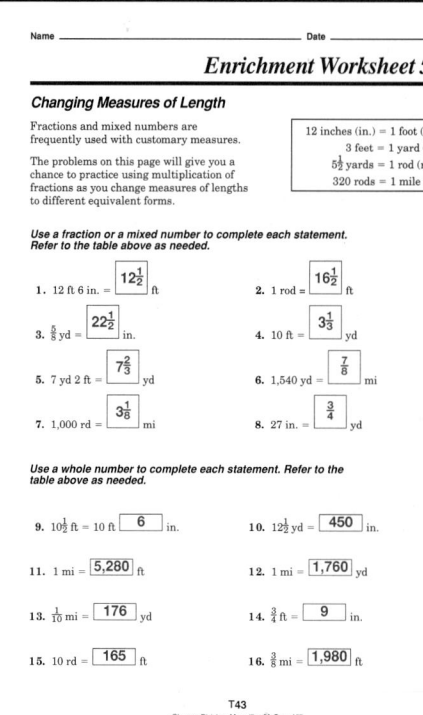

Name _____   Date _____

Enrichment Worksheet 5-5

Changing Measures of Length

Fractions and mixed numbers are frequently used with customary measures.

The problems on this page will give you a chance to practice using multiplication of fractions as you change measures of lengths to different equivalent forms.

12 inches (in.) = 1 foot (ft)
3 feet = 1 yard (yd)
$5\frac{1}{2}$ yards = 1 rod (rd)
320 rods = 1 mile (mi)

Use a fraction or a mixed number to complete each statement. Refer to the table above as needed.

1. 12 ft 6 in. = $\boxed{12\frac{1}{2}}$ ft   2. 1 rod = $\boxed{16\frac{1}{2}}$ ft

3. $\frac{5}{8}$ yd = $\boxed{22\frac{1}{2}}$ in.   4. 10 ft = $\boxed{3\frac{1}{3}}$ yd

5. 7 yd 2 ft = $\boxed{7\frac{2}{3}}$ yd   6. 1,540 yd = $\boxed{\frac{7}{8}}$ mi

7. 1,000 rd = $\boxed{3\frac{1}{8}}$ mi   8. 27 in. = $\boxed{\frac{3}{4}}$ yd

Use a whole number to complete each statement. Refer to the table above as needed.

9. $10\frac{1}{2}$ ft = 10 ft $\boxed{6}$ in.   10. $12\frac{1}{2}$ yd = $\boxed{450}$ in.

11. 1 mi = $\boxed{5,280}$ ft   12. 1 mi = $\boxed{1,760}$ yd

13. $\frac{1}{10}$ mi = $\boxed{176}$ yd   14. $\frac{3}{4}$ yd = $\boxed{9}$ in.

15. 10 rd = $\boxed{165}$ ft   16. $\frac{3}{8}$ mi = $\boxed{1,980}$ ft

T43
Glencoe Division, Macmillan/McGraw-Hill

NCTM Standards: 1–7, 12, 13

Lesson Resources
- Study Guide Master 5-6
- Practice Master 5-6
- Enrichment Master 5-6
- Interdisciplinary Master, p. 19
- Evaluation Master, Quiz A, p. 43
- Group Activity Card 5-6

 Transparency 5-6 contains the 5-Minute Check and a teaching aid for this lesson.

🕐 5-Minute Check
(Over Lesson 5-5)

Multiply. Write each product in simplest form.

1. $\frac{2}{5} \times \frac{1}{2}$ $\frac{1}{5}$

2. $\frac{2}{3} \times \frac{5}{8}$ $\frac{5}{12}$

3. $6 \times 2\frac{3}{4}$ $16\frac{1}{2}$

4. $2\frac{1}{4} \times 1\frac{1}{6}$ $2\frac{5}{8}$

5. $2\frac{4}{7} \times \frac{8}{9}$ $2\frac{2}{7}$

1 FOCUS

Motivating the Lesson

Situational Problem Draw an outline of the classroom floor on the chalkboard. Ask students to describe ways to figure out the distance around this floor.

2 TEACH

Using Connections Have students use inch rulers and yardsticks to measure the perimeter of some objects and regions within the classroom. Have them estimate before measuring. Encourage students to look for shapes other than rectangles for which perimeter formulas could be developed.

5-6 Perimeter

Objective
Find perimeter using fractional measurements.

Words to Learn
perimeter

Mr. Kirby has a pond he uses for irrigation and fishing. He wishes to fence the field around the pond to protect small children that have moved to the neighborhood. How much fencing does he need?

Mr. Kirby needs to know the distance around his field. The distance around a geometric figure is called its **perimeter.**

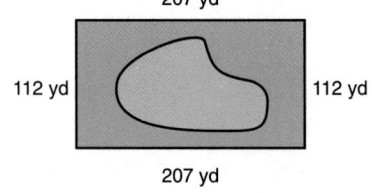

To find the perimeter, P, of the field, Mr. Kirby adds the measures of the sides.

$P = 207 + 112 + 207 + 112$
  $= 638$ Mr. Kirby needs 638 yards of fencing.

Perimeter of a Rectangle	**In Words:** The perimeter of a rectangle is the sum of the measures of the sides.
	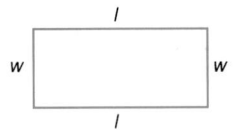 **In symbols:** $P = \ell + w + \ell + w$ $P = 2\ell + 2w$

💬 When am I ever going to use this?

Suppose you wanted to frame a 6-inch × 7-inch cross-stitch design with a 2-inch mat around the needlework. What is the perimeter of the frame you will need?
at least 34 in.

Examples

1 Find the perimeter of a rectangle with a length of 7 feet and a width of 4 feet.

$P = 2\ell + 2w$
  $= 2(7) + 2(4)$ *Replace ℓ with 7 and w with 4.*
  $= 14 + 8$
  $= 22$ The perimeter is 22 feet.

2 Find the perimeter of the figure at the right.

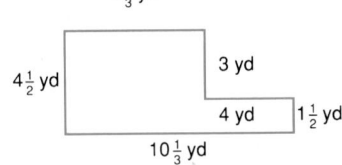

Estimate:
$5 + 10 + 2 + 4 + 3 + 6 = 30$

$P = 4\frac{1}{2} + 10\frac{1}{3} + 1\frac{1}{2} + 4 + 3 + 6\frac{1}{3}$
  $= 29\frac{2}{3}$ The perimeter is $29\frac{2}{3}$ yards.

OPTIONS

Reteaching Activity

Using Manipulatives Have students use a ruler to cut out thin strips of cardboard with which to lay out a rectangle. Students can find the perimeter of the figure by placing the cardboard strips end-to-end in a line and measuring them. They can see that the sum of the sides is the perimeter.

Study Guide Masters, p. 44

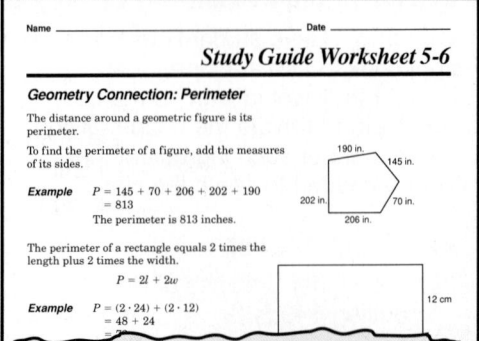

Name _____   Date _____

Study Guide Worksheet 5-6

Geometry Connection: Perimeter

The distance around a geometric figure is its perimeter.

To find the perimeter of a figure, add the measures of its sides.

Example $P = 145 + 70 + 206 + 202 + 190$
        $= 813$
The perimeter is 813 inches.

The perimeter of a rectangle equals 2 times the length plus 2 times the width.

$P = 2l + 2w$

Example $P = (2 \cdot 24) + (2 \cdot 12)$
        $= 48 + 24$

Example 3 *Connection*

Measurement Find the perimeter of the rectangle. Measure to the nearest eighth inch.

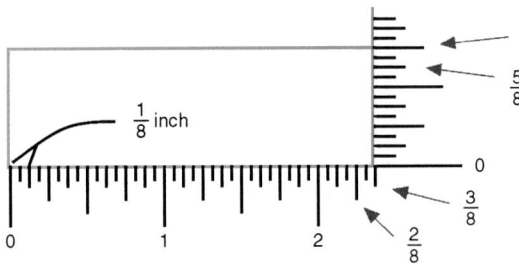

To the nearest eighth inch, the width is $\frac{6}{8}$ or $\frac{3}{4}$ inch.

To the nearest eighth inch, the length is $2\frac{3}{8}$ inches.
Estimate: $2 + 1 + 2 + 1 = 6$

$$P = 2\ell + 2w$$

$= (2 \times 2\frac{3}{8}) + (2 \times \frac{3}{4})$	*Replace ℓ with $2\frac{3}{8}$ and w with $\frac{3}{4}$.*
$= (2 \times \frac{19}{8}) + (2 \times \frac{3}{4})$	*Change $2\frac{3}{8}$ to $\frac{19}{8}$.*
$= \frac{38}{8} + \frac{6}{4}$	*Multiply within each set of parentheses.*
$= \frac{38}{8} + \frac{12}{8}$	*Change $\frac{6}{4}$ to $\frac{12}{8}$.*
$= \frac{50}{8}$	*Add.*
$= 6\frac{2}{8}$ or $6\frac{1}{4}$	The perimeter is $6\frac{1}{4}$ inches.

Checking for Understanding

Communicating Mathematics

Read and study the lesson to answer each question.

1. **Show** where $3\frac{7}{8}$ inches is located on a ruler. **See students' work.**

2. **Write**, in your own words, how to find the perimeter of a rectangular figure. **$P = 2\ell + 2w$**

Guided Practice

Find the perimeter of each figure shown or described below.

3.

20 ft
8 ft
56 ft

4.
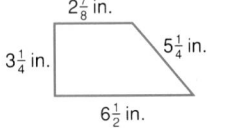
$2\frac{7}{8}$ in.
$3\frac{1}{4}$ in.
$5\frac{1}{4}$ in.
$6\frac{1}{2}$ in.
$17\frac{7}{8}$ inches

5. $21\frac{3}{4}$ inches
6. 32 feet

5. rectangle: $\ell = 6\frac{1}{2}$ inches
   $w = 4\frac{3}{8}$ inches

6. rectangle: $\ell = 8$ feet
   $w = 8$ feet

Lesson 5-6 Geometry Connection: Perimeter   **195**

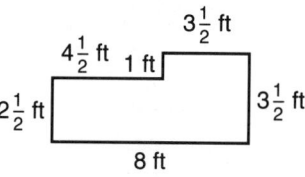
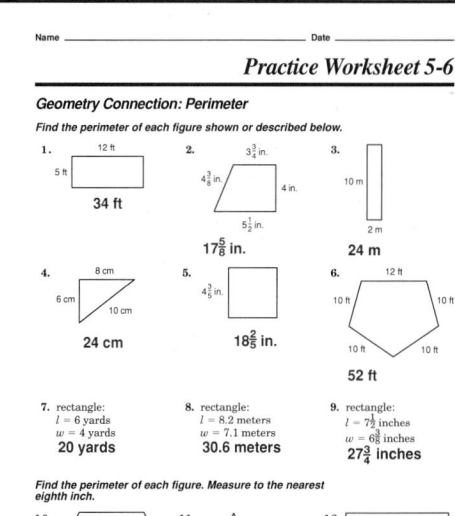

Classroom Vignette

"To assess students, they were asked to make rectangles that had a perimeter of 24 inches. Some made their rectangles with tape on the floor while others constructed them on paper. Some had only whole number dimensions while others included the use of fractions and mixed numbers."

Joy A. Metzger

Joy Metzger, Teacher
Buckeye Valley Middle School, Radnor, OH

Close

Have students write a word problem, the solution to which involves finding the perimeter of a shape or region.

3 PRACTICE/APPLY

Assignment Guide
Maximum: 9–23
Minimum: 9–22

For **Extra Practice,** see p. 583.

Alternate Assessment

Writing Have students explain how they could find the perimeter of the figure in Example 2 by using the formula for the perimeter of a rectangle. **by repositioning the 3-yd and 4-yd segments to obtain the following figure:**

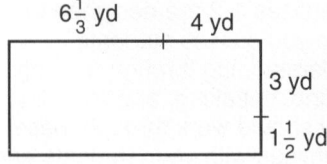

Enrichment Masters, p. 44

Name _____ Date _____

Enrichment Worksheet 5-6

Musical Notation

Music is written on parallel lines. Vertical lines divide the music into measures. This piece of music has 5 measures.

The fraction at the beginning of the music, $\frac{4}{4}$, shows that there are 4 beats in a measure (the numerator). The denominator, 4, shows that the quarter note gets 1 beat.

The sample shows three kinds of notes.

𝅗𝅥 This is a half note. It gets two beats.

♩ This is a quarter note. It gets one beat.

♪ This is an eighth note. It gets one-half of a beat.

1. Now, you be the music writer! Complete this composition using quarter, half, and eighth notes. Make sure that each measure has a total of four beats. **Answers will vary.**

2. Ask a friend who plays a musical instrument to play your composition for you.
Answers will vary.

T 44
Glencoe Division, Macmillan/McGraw-Hill

196

Find the perimeter of each figure. Measure to the nearest eighth inch.

7.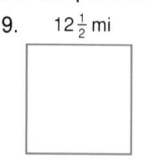
$3\frac{1}{4}$ inches

8.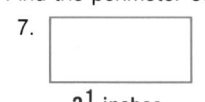
$2\frac{3}{4}$ inches

Exercises

Independent Practice Find the perimeter of each figure shown or described below.

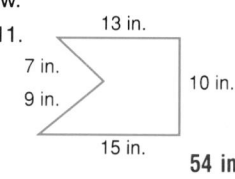

9. $12\frac{1}{2}$ mi   **50 mi**

10. 20 ft / 16 ft / 20 ft   **56 ft**

11. 13 in. / 7 in. / 9 in. / 10 in. / 15 in.   **54 in**

12. rectangle: $\ell = 5$ yards
$w = 2$ yards **14 yards**

13. rectangle: $\ell = 3.5$ miles
$w = 1.7$ miles **10.4 miles**

14. Find the perimeter of a square with side 15 yards. **60 yards**

15. Find the perimeter of a rectangle with length $13\frac{1}{2}$ feet and width $7\frac{3}{4}$ feet.
$42\frac{1}{2}$ feet

Find the perimeter of each figure. Measure to the nearest eighth inch.

16.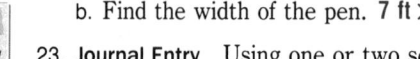
$3\frac{1}{8}$ inches

17.
$3\frac{1}{2}$ inches

Mixed Review 18. **Money** Jill has a total of $76.89 in pennies. How many pennies does she have? *(Lesson 2-5)* **7,689 pennies**

19. Express $\frac{18}{24}$ in simplest form. *(Lesson 4-6)* **$\frac{3}{4}$**

20. Find $\frac{5}{9} \times \frac{3}{4}$. *(Lesson 5-5)* **$\frac{5}{12}$**

Problem Solving and Applications

21b. 103 bushes

21. **Landscaping** Mrs. Knowles plans to plant azalea bushes across the back and down two sides of her yard. Her lot is 100 feet wide and 160 feet deep.
a. Draw and label a diagram of Mrs. Knowles' yard. **See Solutions Manual.**
b. How many bushes will she need to buy if she plants them 4 feet apart?

22. **Critical Thinking** Khoa has 36 feet of fencing for a rectangular dog pen. He plans to use 22 feet of the garage wall for one side of the pen.
a. Draw and label a diagram of the pen. **See Solutions Manual.**
b. Find the width of the pen. **7 ft × 22 ft**

23. **Journal Entry** Using one or two sentences, describe a situation where you needed to find the perimeter of an object. **Sample answer: wallpaper border around bedroom**

OPTIONS

Extending the Lesson

Real Estate Have students use graph paper to sketch a floor plan of their ideal apartment or one-story house. Encourage them to include any extravagance they wish. All floor plans should include measurements. Have students exchange completed plans, and then determine the perimeter of each other's homes.

Cooperative Learning Activity

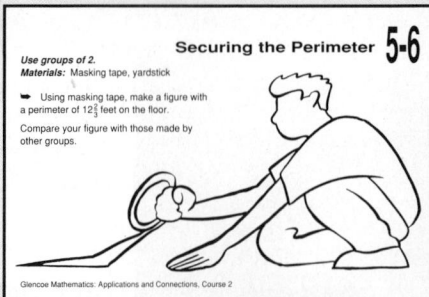

Use groups of 2.
Materials: Masking tape, yardstick

Securing the Perimeter 5-6

➡ Using masking tape, make a figure with a perimeter of $12\frac{5}{6}$ feet on the floor.

Compare your figure with those made by other groups.

Glencoe Mathematics: Applications and Connections, Course 2

5-7 Circles and Circumference

Objective

Find the circumference of circles.

Words to Learn

circle
center
diameter
radius
circumference

Today, you don't need a watchdog to watch your house. A robot can do that for you! A recently developed robot, 2 feet high and shaped like a dome, can roam around your house and "watch" for intruders. If anything moves within a 30-foot radius of the robot, the robot will detect this motion and send a silent alarm to the local police. What is the circumference of the circle the robot guards? *This question will be answered on page 198.*

Let's study some terms and properties related to circles. A **circle** is the set of all points in a plane that are the same distance from a given point called the **center.**

The **diameter (d)** of a circle is the distance across the circle through its center. The **radius (r)** of a circle is the distance from the center to any point on the circle. The **circumference (C)** of a circle is the distance around the circle.

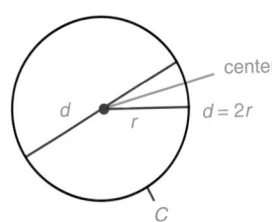

Mini-Lab

Work with a partner.
Materials: metric ruler, string, circular objects of various sizes

- Find a circular object.
- Use a metric ruler to measure the diameter of your circular object. Record your finding.
- Wrap a string around the circular object once. Mark the string where it meets itself.
- Lay the string out straight and measure the length of the string with your ruler. Record your finding. This is the circumference of the circle.
- Divide the circumference by the diameter. Record your answer.
- Repeat this activity with circular objects of various sizes.

Lesson 5-7 Geometry Connection: Circles and Circumference **197**

OPTIONS

Multicultural Education

As in some other early societies, mathematicians in ancient China searched for the value of π. As early as 3,200 years ago, they are known to have used the value 3. The most accurate Chinese measurement obtained before modern times was that of Tsu Ch'ung-chih, who established a value of about 3.1415926.

5-7 Lesson Notes

NCTM Standards: 1–7, 9, 12, 13

Lesson Resources
- Study Guide Master 5-7
- Practice Master 5-7
- Enrichment Master 5-7
- Technology Master, p. 5
- Group Activity Card 5-7

Transparency 5-7 contains the 5-Minute Check and a teaching aid for this lesson.

⏱ 5-Minute Check
(Over Lesson 5-6)

Find the perimeter of each figure shown or described below.

1. $9\frac{1}{2}$ in.   2.   12 in.

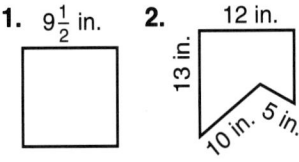

  38 in.   49 in.

3. l = 2.5 meters
   w = 3.8 meters   12.6 m

4. Find the perimeter of a square with a side 12 inches long.   48 in.

5. Find the perimeter of any rectangular object in the classroom. Measure to the nearest eighth of an inch.

1 FOCUS

Motivating the Lesson

Situational Problem Tell students that Inez takes her dog to the park on an 18-foot leash. Ask them how they could determine the greatest distance the dog can run in one circle around Inez.

2 TEACH

Using the Mini-Lab First have students guess what their findings will be prior to measuring. After they conclude the activity, ask them how the wheel of a bicycle is related to a spoke. Then ask students to suggest ways to use their conclusions about the relationship between diameter and circumference to design a measuring device to find the length of their school building.

More Examples

For Example 1

Find the circumference of a circle with a diameter of 42 inches. Use $\frac{22}{7}$ for π. about 132 in.

For Example 2

Find the circumference of a circle with a radius of 6.6 meters. Use 3.14 for π. about 41.45 meters

---

Teaching Tip Before assigning the Independent Practice, ask students when it would make better sense to use $\frac{22}{7}$ for π than 3.14. when the radius or diameter is a multiple of 7

Checking for Understanding

Exercises 1-4 are designed to help you assess students' understanding through reading, writing, speaking, and modeling. You should work through these exercises with your students and then monitor their work on Guided Practice Exercises 5-14.

198

Talk About It

a. Compare your results. What do you find? $\frac{C}{d} = \pi$

b. How is the circumference related to the diameter? $C = \pi d$

The Greek letter π is used to represent the circumference divided by the diameter $\left(\frac{C}{d}\right)$. Often used approximations for π are 3.14 and $\frac{22}{7}$.

Formulas for Circumference of a Circle	**In words:** The circumference of a circle is equal to π times its diameter or π times twice the radius. (The diameter is twice the radius.)
	In symbols: $C = \pi d$ $C = 2\pi r$

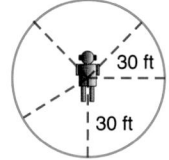

Now let's solve the problem given at the beginning of the lesson. Find the circumference of the circle the robot guards. Since you know the radius, use the formula $C = 2\pi r$.

$C = 2\pi r$ $\approx$ means "approximately equal to."
$C \approx 2 \times 3.14 \times 30$ Use 3.14 for π. Replace r with 30.
$C \approx 188.4$

The robot guards a circle with a circumference of about 188.4 feet.

Examples

1 Find the circumference of a circle with a diameter of $10\frac{1}{2}$ inches. Use $\frac{22}{7}$ for π.

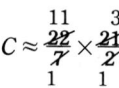

$C = \pi d$

$C \approx \frac{22}{7}\left(10\frac{1}{2}\right)$ *Estimate: $3 \times 11 = 33$*

$C \approx \frac{\overset{11}{\cancel{22}}}{\underset{1}{\cancel{7}}} \times \frac{\overset{3}{\cancel{21}}}{\underset{1}{\cancel{2}}}$

$C \approx 33$ The circumference is about 33 inches.

2 Find the circumference of a circle with a radius of 8.5 meters.

$C = 2\pi r$ *Estimate: $2 \times 3 \times 9 = 54$*
$C \approx 2\pi(8.5)$
$2\ \boxed{\times}\ \boxed{\pi}\ \boxed{\times}\ 8.5\ \boxed{=}\ \mathtt{53.407075}$
$C \approx 53.4$ The circumference is about 53.4 meters.

OPTIONS

Reteaching Activity

Using Manipulatives Provide students with compasses, rulers, and string with which to draw circles. Then measure each circle to find the relationship between the radius and diameter and the circumference of the circle.

Study Guide Masters, p. 45

Name _____ Date _____

Study Guide Worksheet 5-7

Circles and Circumference

A circle is all of the points in a plane that are the same distance from a given point called the center.

The diameter (d) is the distance across the circle through its center.

The radius (r) is the distance from the center to any point on the circle.

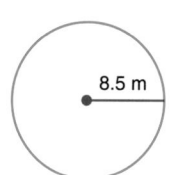

The circumference (C) is the distance around the circle.

If the diameter of a circle is 7.5 inches, what is its circumference?

$C = \pi d$ Circumference = π times the diameter
$C \approx 3.14 \times 7.5$ 3.14 is an approximation for π
$C \approx 23.55$ The circumference of the circle is about 23.55 inches.

Checking for Understanding

Communicating Mathematics

Read and study the lesson to answer each question.

1. **Write** the steps taken in finding the circumference of a circle whose diameter is 25 feet. **Multiply 25 by π.**

2. **Write** *an estimate* for the circumference of a circle with a diameter of 5 inches. **15 inches**

3. **Tell** two numbers that are approximations of π. **3.14; $\frac{22}{7}$**

4. **Tell** how to find the circumference of a circle. **Multiply the diameter by π.**

Guided Practice

Find the circumference of each circle. **7. 28.26 yd 8. 37.68 cm**

5. 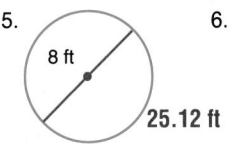 8 ft **25.12 ft**

6. 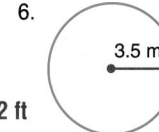 3.5 m **21.98 m**

7. 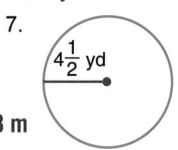 $4\frac{1}{2}$ yd

8. 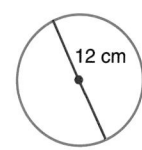 12 cm

9. $d = 14$ in. **43.96 in.**

10. $r = 3.2$ m **20.096 m**

11. $r = 10\frac{1}{2}$ in. **65.94 in.**

12. $d = 6.5$ in. **20.41 in.**

13. What is the radius of a circle whose diameter is 6 meters long? **3 meters**

14. What is the diameter of a circle whose radius is 7.5 meters long? **15 meters**

Exercises

Independent Practice

Find the circumference of each circle. **17. 29.83 km 18. 38.308 m**

15. $1\frac{3}{4}$ ft **10.99 ft**

16. 0.5 mi **3.14 mi**

17.  9.5 km

18. 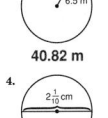 12.2 m

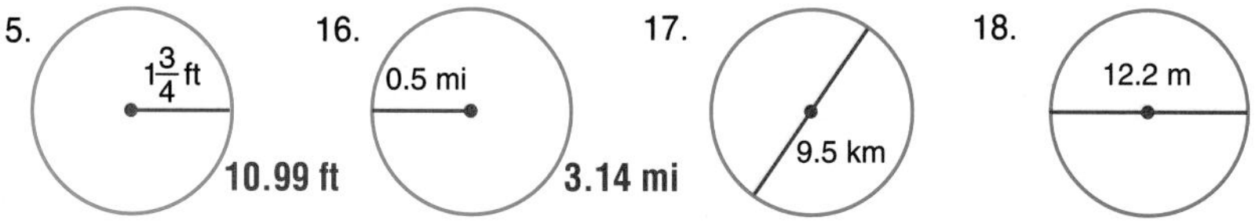

19. 55 mi
20. $4\frac{5}{7}$ in.
21. 9.42 km
22. 18.84 cm

19. $d = 17\frac{1}{2}$ mi

20. $r = \frac{3}{4}$ in.

21. $r = 1.5$ km

22. $d = 6$ cm

23. $r = 6.2$ cm **38.936 cm**

24. $d = 4.5$ yd **14.13 yd**

25. $d = 8\frac{3}{4}$ ft **$27\frac{1}{2}$ ft**

26. $r = 1\frac{1}{3}$ yd **$8\frac{8}{21}$ yd**

27. What is the diameter of a circle whose radius is 13 feet? **26 feet**

28. Find the circumference of a circle whose radius is 6.5 inches. **40.82 inches**

Mixed Review

29. **Packaging** If 2,365 light bulbs are packaged in cases of 12, *about* how many cases of bulbs are there? *(Lesson 1-3)* **about 200 cases**

30. Order 3.4, 2.6, 3.8, 1.9, 2.3, and 3.6 from least to greatest. *(Lesson 2-1)* **1.9, 2.3, 2.6, 3.4, 3.6, 3.8**

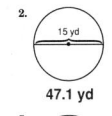

Lesson 5-7 Geometry Connection: Circles and Circumference **199**

Limited English Proficiency

Introduce the terms *circle, circumference, diameter,* and *radius.* Using a clearly-labeled diagram, name and point to each part of the circle, or identify the parts using a real-life example, such as a bicycle wheel.

199

31. Express $\frac{7}{8}$ as a decimal. *(Lesson 4-7)* **0.875**

32. **Carpentry** The deck on Jack's house is $25\frac{4}{5}$ feet long and $12\frac{1}{2}$ feet wide. One length of the deck is against the house. How many feet of wood does Jack need to buy to build a railing around the deck. *(Lesson 5-6)* **$50\frac{4}{5}$ feet**

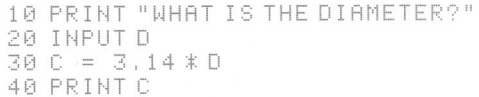

Problem Solving and Applications

33. 200.96 inches or about 17 feet

34. $5\frac{1}{3}$ times

33. **Recreation** The pedals on a bicycle of the 1870s were on the front wheel. For speed, the front wheel was large, with a diameter of about 64 inches. The back wheel was about 12 inches. How far did a cyclist travel each time the pedals made a complete turn?

34. **Critical Thinking** In Exercises 33, how many times does the back wheel go around for each complete turn of the front wheel?

35. **Computer Connection** The BASIC program below will compute the circumference of a circle with a given diameter.

```
10 PRINT "WHAT IS THE DIAMETER?"
20 INPUT D
30 C = 3.14 * D
40 PRINT C
```

35b. When the diameter is doubled, the circumference doubles.

a. Run the program for diameters of 2, 4, 8, 16, 32, and 64 units. **6.28, 12.56, 25.12, 50.24, 100.48, 200.96**

b. Write a sentence that describes how the circumference changes when the diameter is doubled.

36. **Data Search** Refer to page 650. What part of the juice we drink is apple, grape, or blends? $\frac{1}{4}$

37. **Mathematics and Cycling** Read the following paragraphs.

The Tour de France is considered to be the world's most important bicycle race. It was established in 1903 by Henri Desgrange, a French cyclist and journalist.

The annual race involves 120 or more professional contestants and covers about 2,500 miles of flat and mountainous country, mostly in France and Belgium. The bicycle and the rider with the lowest total time for all stages at the completion of the race is the winner.

a. The longest race ever held was in 1926. It covered 3,562 miles and took 3 weeks to complete. If the cyclists rode one third of the race in the first week, how many miles did they travel? **about 1,187 miles**

b. The diameter of a bicycle wheel is 28 inches. How far will you travel after 1 complete turn of the wheel? **87.92 inches or about 7 feet**

Enrichment Masters, p. 45

Name _____ Date _____

Enrichment Worksheet 5-7

A Circle Puzzle

The circle at the right has been divided into ten pieces. Notice that the vertical diameter is marked off into four congruent segments.

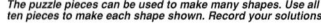

Trace the circle and cut it into ten parts to make a set of puzzle pieces.

1. Separate the pieces and put them back together to form the circle. Try this first without looking at the solution.

The puzzle pieces can be used to make many shapes. Use all ten pieces to make each shape shown. Record your solutions.

2.  3.  4.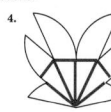

5.  6.

7.  8.

T45
Glencoe Division, Macmillan/McGraw-Hill

200

OPTIONS

Extending the Lesson

Mathematics and Cycling Have students use $\frac{22}{7}$ for π in Exercise 37b. Then have them check their answer using the π key on their calculator.

Cooperative Learning Activity

String Thing 5-7

Number of players: 2
Materials: String, scissors, compass, index cards

Cut two 1-meter-long pieces of string.

In this game, the sum of the circumferences of circles you draw cannot exceed 1 meter. In each round, each partner writes on a card the measure of the radius of a circle. Since the sum of the circumferences cannot exceed 1 meter, you cannot write a radius length that is greater than 15.9 centimeters (the circumference of a circle with a radius of 15.9 centimeters is about 1 meter). Both partners flip their cards over at the same time. Then, using the same center, both partners draw on a sheet of paper a circle with the radius length shown on their cards. Each partner takes a string, measures the circumference of his or her circle with the string, and then cuts off the length of the circumference. The partner with the larger circle wins the round, provided that this partner has enough string to measure the circumference of the circle. Try to win more rounds than your partner before you run out of string.

Glencoe Mathematics: Applications and Connections, Course 2

5-8 Expected Value

Objective
Find expected value of outcomes.

Words to Learn
expected value

The Boy Scouts are having a fund-raiser for camp. They are selling 400 tickets for $1 each. The prizes are one $80-bicycle, two $20-Walkman stereos, and ten $4-theater passes.

Dawn wants to know whether buying a fund-raiser ticket is wise. To do so, she calculates the expected value of her ticket. The **expected value** is the long-term average of what she could expect to win by repeatedly buying a ticket.

LOOKBACK

You can review probability on page 157.

To find the expected value, she first needs to find the probability of winning each prize.

$P(\text{bicycle}) = \frac{1}{400}$ *number of bicycle-winning tickets*
                                total number of tickets

$P(\text{Walkman}) = \frac{2}{400}$ *number of Walkman winning-tickets*
                                total number of tickets
             $= \frac{1}{200}$

$P(\text{theater passes}) = \frac{10}{400}$ *number of theater-winning tickets*
                                    total number of tickets
                   $= \frac{1}{40}$

Next she needs to find the probability of *not* winning a prize.

$P(\text{not winning}) = \frac{387}{400}$ *number of nonwinning tickets*
                                 total number of tickets

Using these probabilities, she can find the expected value of a fund-raiser ticket. The expected value is found by multiplying each probability by the value of that prize and then adding these products together.

Calculator Hint

To change $\frac{80}{400}$ to a decimal, press

$80 \div 400 =$

0.20

$$80\left(\tfrac{1}{400}\right) + 20\left(\tfrac{1}{200}\right) + 4\left(\tfrac{1}{40}\right) + 0\left(\tfrac{387}{400}\right) = \tfrac{80}{400} + \tfrac{20}{200} + \tfrac{4}{40} + 0$$
$$= 0.20 + 0.10 + 0.10 + 0$$
$$= 0.40$$

The expected value of a ticket is 40¢. That means that if Dawn buys one ticket after another, she could expect to win an average of 40¢ in prizes per ticket. Since this is less than the cost of a ticket, Dawn believes the ticket is *not* a good buy. But she is happy to help the Boy Scouts anyway because they will make a profit of $1.00 − $0.40 or $0.60 per ticket.

Lesson 5-8 Probability Connection: Expected Value   **201**

OPTIONS

Reteaching Activity

Using Reasoning Simplify the Example by assuming that only the $1 sector pays off. Then each spin is worth $1\left(\tfrac{1}{4}\right)$ dollars. Similarly, if only the $2 sector pays off, each spin is worth $2\left(\tfrac{1}{8}\right)$ dollars. The value of the game if both sectors pays off is $1\left(\tfrac{1}{4}\right) + 2\left(\tfrac{1}{8}\right)$. Extend the reasoning to all four sectors.

Study Guide Masters, p. 46

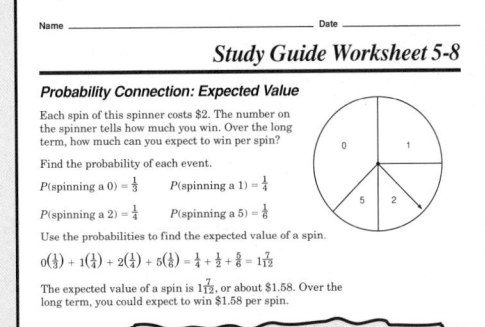

Name _____ Date _____

Study Guide Worksheet 5-8

Probability Connection: Expected Value

Each spin of this spinner costs $2. The number on the spinner tells how much you win. Over the long term, how much can you expect to win per spin?

Find the probability of each event.

$P(\text{spinning a } 0) = \tfrac{1}{3}$ $P(\text{spinning a } 1) = \tfrac{1}{4}$

$P(\text{spinning a } 2) = \tfrac{1}{4}$ $P(\text{spinning a } 5) = \tfrac{1}{6}$

Use the probabilities to find the expected value of a spin.

$0\left(\tfrac{1}{3}\right) + 1\left(\tfrac{1}{4}\right) + 2\left(\tfrac{1}{4}\right) + 5\left(\tfrac{1}{6}\right) = \tfrac{1}{4} + \tfrac{1}{2} + \tfrac{5}{6} = 1\tfrac{7}{12}$

The expected value of a spin is $1\tfrac{7}{12}$, or about $1.58. Over the long term, you could expect to win $1.58 per spin.

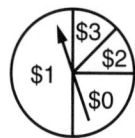
Checking for Understanding

Example *Problem Solving*

Games   Barry's hometown of Bucyrus, Ohio, holds a bratwurst festival each year. One of the games at the festival is called Spin-O-Rama. Each spin costs $1. The number on the spinner tells you how much you win. Is this game a good buy?

First find the probability of each event.

P(spinning a 0) $= \frac{1}{2}$

P(spinning a 1) $= \frac{1}{4}$

P(spinning a 2) $= \frac{1}{8}$

P(spinning a 3) $= \frac{1}{8}$

Now find the expected value of a spin.

$$0\left(\frac{1}{2}\right) + 1\left(\frac{1}{4}\right) + 2\left(\frac{1}{8}\right) + 3\left(\frac{1}{8}\right) = \frac{1}{4} + \frac{1}{4} + \frac{3}{8}$$

$$= \frac{7}{8}$$

Calculator Hint

● ● ● ● ● ● ● ● ● ● ● ● ●

To change $\frac{7}{8}$ to a decimal, press

7 [÷] 8 [=] 0.875

The expected value of a spin is $\frac{7}{8}$ of a dollar or about 88¢. That means that if you play the game over and over, you could expect to win an average of 88¢ per spin. Since this is less than the cost of a spin, the game is *not* a good buy. However, many people will play anyway to try to beat "the odds."

Checking for Understanding

Communicating Mathematics

Read and study the lesson to answer each question.

1. **Write**, in your own words, how you would find the expected value of a raffle ticket.   **probability × value of prize**

2. **Tell** how knowing the expected value of an event helps you to make a good buy.   **Buy something with a high expected value.**

Guided Practice

Use Spinner A to find each of the following.

3. P(spinning a 0) $\frac{1}{2}$
4. P(spinning a 1) $\frac{1}{4}$
5. P(spinning a 2) $\frac{1}{4}$

Spinner A

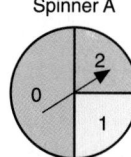

6. If the number on the spinner tells the number of dollars you win, find the expected value of a spin.   **$0.75**

7. Over the long-term, would you expect to win, lose, or break even if each spin costs 50¢?   **win**

Exercises

Independent Practice

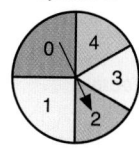

Use Spinner B to answer each of the following.

8. If the number on the spinner tells the number of dollars you win, find the expected value of a spin. **$1.75**

9. Over the long term, would you expect to win, lose, or break even if each spin cost $2? **lose**

10. What should each spin cost to be a fair game (you have an equal chance of winning or losing)? **$1.75**

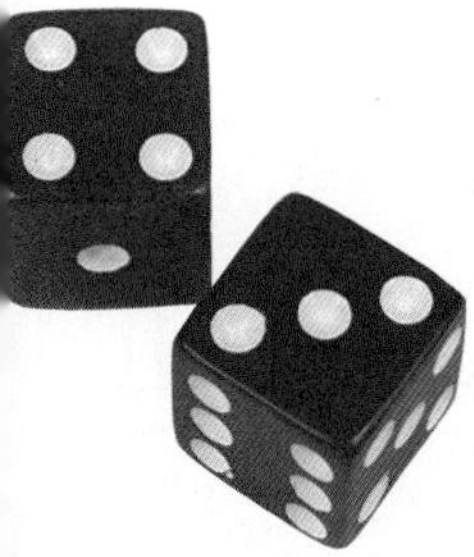

Spinner B

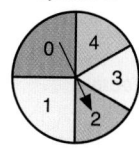

Use a die to answer each of the following.

11. If the number on the die tells the number of dollars you win, find the expected value of a roll. **$3.50**

12. Would you play the game if each roll costs $2? Why or why not? **Yes; you should win money.**

Mixed Review

13. Coke, Pepsi, Slice

14. $30\frac{9}{14}$ inches

13. **Statistics** The bar graph at the right displays the responses to the question "What is your favorite soft drink?" Which soft drinks should the manager of the local grocery always keep in stock? *(Lesson 3-7)*

Favorite Soft Drinks

Responses	
40	
30	
20	
10	

7 Up, Coke, Pepsi, Root Beer, Slice

Soft Drinks

14. **Geometry** Find the circumference of a circle having a radius of $4\frac{7}{8}$ inches. *(Lesson 5-7)*

Problem Solving and Applications

15. **Science** Use the table below to determine the expected number of girls in a family having three children. Leave your answer as a mixed number. **$1\frac{1}{2}$ girls**

number of girls	0	1	2	3
probability	$\frac{1}{8}$	$\frac{3}{8}$	$\frac{3}{8}$	$\frac{1}{8}$

16. **Critical Thinking** If the numbers were rearranged on Spinner C as shown at the right, would the expected value in Exercise 8 increase, decrease, or remain the same? Explain your answer. **The expected value of Spinner C is $2.25. Since $2.25 > $1.75, the expected value increases.**

Spinner C

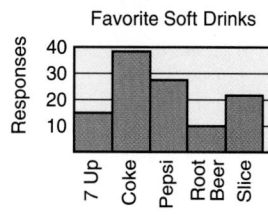

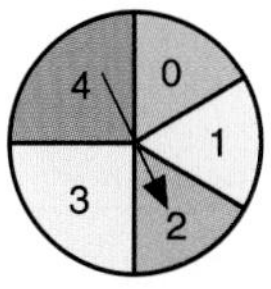

Lesson 5-8 Probability Connection: Expected Value **203**

Extending the Lesson

Attendance The following chart shows the pattern of attendance at baseball games.

Attendance	Weather	Probability
20,000	Cold	0.16
26,000	Cloudy	0.32
35,000	Moderate	0.39
31,000	Hot	0.13

Ask students to find the expected value of the attendance per game.

Cooperative Learning Activity

Raff It Up **5-8**

Use groups of 4.
Materials: Newspapers

➡ Suppose that your group is in charge of planning the raffle at your school's annual Spring Jamboree. Last year, the grand prize was a television set; first prize was a portable stereo; second prize was a gift certificate for five CDs; and third prize was a pair of tickets to a major-league baseball game.

Decide what items you want to offer as prizes this year. Looking at newspaper advertisements, determine the value of these items. Determine how many first, second, and third prizes you will offer and how many tickets you will sell altogether. Find the expected value of one ticket for different numbers of prizes offered and total tickets sold. How much will you charge for one ticket? Tell how you decided what to charge and why you think people will pay this amount. How much money will you raise? (Hint: Multiply the difference between the selling price and the expected value by the number of tickets sold.)

Share your work with other groups.

Glencoe Mathematics: Applications and Connections, Course 2

NCTM Standards: 1–7, 9

Lesson Resources
- Study Guide Master 5-9
- Practice Master 5-9
- Enrichment Master 5-9
- Group Activity Card 5-9

 Transparency 5-9 contains the 5-Minute Check and a teaching aid for this lesson.

⏱ 5-Minute Check
(Over Lesson 5-8)

Use the spinner to find each of the following.

1. P(spinning a 0) $\frac{1}{3}$
2. P(spinning a 1) $\frac{1}{3}$
3. P(spinning a 2) $\frac{1}{6}$
4. P(spinning a 4) $\frac{1}{6}$
5. If the numbers on the spinner are dollars, find the expected value of a spin.   about $1.33
6. Would you expect to win, lose, or break even over the long-term if each spin costs $1.50?   lose

---

1 FOCUS

Motivating the Lesson

Situational Problem Ask students how they could use mental math to figure out how much money Ernie earns if he works for $2\frac{1}{4}$ hours at an hourly rate of $8 per hour.

2 TEACH

Using Charts Have students copy the chart from the lesson into their notebooks. Ask them to replace examples in the arithmetic column with examples of their own.

Objective
Use addition, multiplication, and distributive properties to solve problems mentally.

Words to Learn
commutative
associative
identity
inverse
multiplicative
  inverse
reciprocal
distributive

5-9 Properties

Don't ever try to outrun a cheetah. The cheetah is the fastest land animal in the world. Its speed is $2\frac{1}{2}$ times that of the fastest human's speed. If the fastest recorded speed for a human is 28 miles per hour, how fast can the cheetah run? You can use fraction properties of multiplication to compute the speed mentally. *You will solve this problem in Example 1.*

Addition and multiplication of fractions have the same properties you learned for addition and multiplication of whole numbers. These properties are important when you are computing sums and products. The properties are summarized in the chart below.

Property	Arithmetic	Algebra
Commutative	$\frac{1}{5} + \frac{2}{5} = \frac{2}{5} + \frac{1}{5}$	$a + b = b + a$
	$\frac{1}{2} \times \frac{3}{8} = \frac{3}{8} \times \frac{1}{2}$	$a \times b = b \times a$
Associative	$\left(\frac{1}{8} + \frac{3}{8}\right) + \frac{5}{8} = \frac{1}{8} + \left(\frac{3}{8} + \frac{5}{8}\right)$	$(a + b) + c = a + (b + c)$
	$\left(\frac{1}{2} \times \frac{2}{3}\right) \times \frac{1}{4} = \frac{1}{2} \times \left(\frac{2}{3} \times \frac{1}{4}\right)$	$(a \times b) \times c = a \times (b \times c)$
Identity	$\frac{1}{2} + 0 = \frac{1}{2}$	$a + 0 = a$
	$\frac{1}{2} \times 1 = \frac{1}{2}$	$a \times 1 = a$

There is a property that applies to multiplication. It is called the **inverse** property of multiplication. Two numbers whose product is 1 are **multiplicative inverses,** or **reciprocals,** of each other.

Inverse Property of Multiplication	The product of a number and its multiplicative inverse is 1. **Arithmetic:** $\frac{5}{6} \times \frac{6}{5} = 1$ **Algebra:** For all fractions $\frac{a}{b}$, where $a, b \neq 0$, $\frac{a}{b} \times \frac{b}{a} = 1$.

204   Chapter 5 Applications with Fractions

OPTIONS

Reteaching Activity

Using Manipulatives Use base-ten blocks or counters to illustrate the commutative, associative, and distributive properties for whole-number expressions. For example, $5 \times 3 = 3 \times 5$, $3 \times (4 \times 5) = (3 \times 4) \times 5$, and $3 \times (4 + 5) = 3 \times 4 + 3 \times 5$.

Study Guide Masters, p. 47

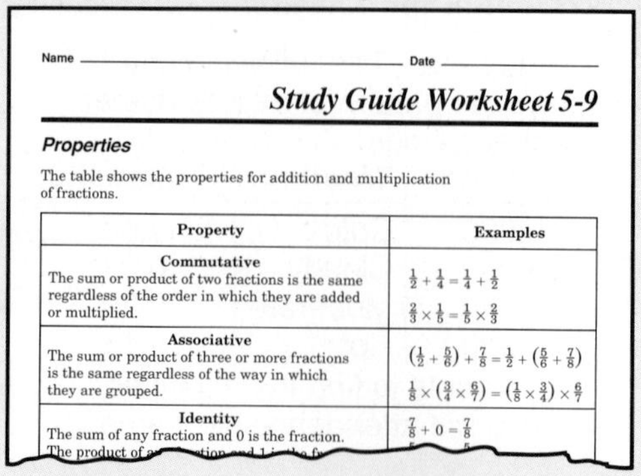

Name _____ Date _____

Study Guide Worksheet 5-9

Properties

The table shows the properties for addition and multiplication of fractions.

Property	Examples
Commutative The sum or product of two fractions is the same regardless of the order in which they are added or multiplied.	$\frac{1}{2} + \frac{1}{4} = \frac{1}{4} + \frac{1}{2}$ $\frac{2}{3} \times \frac{1}{5} = \frac{1}{5} \times \frac{2}{3}$
Associative The sum or product of three or more fractions is the same regardless of the way in which they are grouped.	$\left(\frac{1}{2} + \frac{5}{6}\right) + \frac{7}{8} = \frac{1}{2} + \left(\frac{5}{6} + \frac{7}{8}\right)$ $\frac{1}{6} \times \left(\frac{3}{4} \times \frac{4}{9}\right) = \left(\frac{1}{6} \times \frac{3}{4}\right) \times \frac{4}{9}$
Identity The sum of any fraction and 0 is the fraction. The product of a fraction and 1 is the fraction.	$\frac{7}{8} + 0 = \frac{7}{8}$

The **distributive** property involves two operations.

Distributive Property of Multiplication over Addition	The sum of two addends multiplied by a number is the sum of the product of each addend and the number.
	Arithmetic: $\frac{1}{2} \times \left(\frac{2}{5} + \frac{1}{3}\right) = \frac{1}{2} \times \frac{2}{5} + \frac{1}{2} \times \frac{1}{3}$
	Algebra: $a \times (b + c) = a \times b + a \times c$

Examples

1 Find the speed of a cheetah, using the information given in the lesson opener.

$$2\frac{1}{2} \times 28 = \left(2 + \frac{1}{2}\right) \times 28$$
$$= 2 \cdot 28 + \frac{1}{2} \cdot 28 \qquad \textit{Distributive property}$$
$$= 56 + 14$$
$$= 70$$

The cheetah can run 70 miles per hour.

2 Name the multiplicative inverse of $2\frac{3}{4}$.

$$2\frac{3}{4} = \frac{11}{4} \qquad \textit{Rename the mixed number as an improper fraction.}$$
$$\frac{11}{4} \times \square = 1 \qquad \textit{What number can you mutiply by } \frac{11}{4} \textit{ to get 1?}$$
$$\frac{11}{4} \times \frac{4}{11} = 1$$

The multiplicative inverse of $2\frac{3}{4}$ is $\frac{4}{11}$.

3 Compute $\frac{1}{4} \times 8\frac{4}{5}$ mentally.

$$\frac{1}{4} \times 8\frac{4}{5} = \frac{1}{4}\left(8 + \frac{4}{5}\right)$$
$$= \frac{1}{4} \times 8 + \frac{1}{4} \times \frac{4}{5} \qquad \textit{Think: } \frac{1}{4} \textit{ of 8 is 2.}$$
$$= 2 + \frac{1}{5} \text{ or } 2\frac{1}{5} \qquad \qquad \frac{1}{4} \textit{ of } \frac{4}{5} \textit{ is } \frac{1}{5}.$$

Mental Math Hint
• • • • • • • • • • • • • •
The distributive property allows you to "break apart" one of the factors into a sum. You can then add the two products mentally.

Checking for Understanding

Communicating Mathematics Read and study the lesson to answer each question.

1. **Write** an arithmetic sentence that shows the associative property of addition. $(1 + 2) + 3 = 1 + (2 + 3)$

   Tell how the identity property of addition is similar to the identity property of multiplication. **With both properties, the result is the original number.**

Lesson 5-9 Properties **205**

More Examples

For Example 1
Jill runs for $1\frac{3}{4}$ as long as Eva. Find Jill's running time if Eva runs for 48 minutes.
84 min

For Example 2
Name the multiplicative inverse of $3\frac{1}{4}$. $\frac{4}{13}$

For Example 3
Compute $\frac{1}{3} \times 9\frac{3}{8}$ mentally. $3\frac{1}{8}$

Checking for Understanding

Exercises 1-2 are designed to help you assess students' understanding through reading, writing, speaking, and modeling. You should work through these exercises with your students and then monitor their work on Guided Practice Exercises 3-11.

Practice Masters, p. 47

Name _____ Date _____

Practice Worksheet 5-9

Properties
Name the property shown by each statement.

1. $\frac{3}{8} + 0 = \frac{3}{8}$ **identity**
2. $\frac{3}{4} \times \left(\frac{1}{2} \times \frac{1}{3}\right) = \left(\frac{3}{4} \times \frac{1}{2}\right) \times \frac{1}{3}$ **associative**
3. $\frac{1}{3} \times \left(\frac{1}{4} + \frac{2}{5}\right) = \frac{1}{3} \times \frac{1}{4} + \frac{1}{3} \times \frac{2}{5}$ **distributive**
4. $\frac{3}{9} + \frac{5}{9} = \frac{5}{9} + \frac{3}{9}$ **commutative**
5. $\frac{1}{6} \times \frac{3}{4} = \frac{3}{4} \times \frac{1}{6}$ **commutative**
6. $1\frac{7}{9} \times 1 = 1\frac{7}{9}$ **identity**

State which pairs of numbers are multiplicative inverses. Write yes or no.

7. $8, \frac{1}{8}$ **yes**
8. $5, \frac{2}{5}$ **no**
9. $1\frac{3}{5}, \frac{5}{8}$ **yes**

Compute mentally.

10. $3 \times 1\frac{1}{5}$ $3\frac{3}{5}$
11. $\frac{1}{2} \times 6\frac{2}{7}$ $3\frac{1}{7}$
12. $9\frac{9}{24} \times \frac{1}{3}$ $3\frac{3}{24}$

13. $8\frac{5}{9} \times \frac{1}{4}$ $2\frac{1}{9}$
14. $6 \times \frac{2}{3}$ 4
15. $7\frac{1}{10} \times 8$ $56\frac{4}{5}$

Name the multiplicative inverse of each number.

16. 5 $\frac{1}{5}$
17. $1\frac{3}{4}$ $\frac{4}{7}$
18. $\frac{7}{9}$ $\frac{9}{7}$, or $1\frac{2}{7}$

19. 1 1
20. $2\frac{1}{2}$ $\frac{2}{5}$
21. $\frac{3}{13}$ $\frac{13}{3}$, or $4\frac{1}{3}$

T47
Glencoe Division, Macmillan/McGraw-Hill

205

Watch for students who confuse the commutative property with the associative property.

Prevent by pointing out that the commutative property involves only the *order* of addends or factors, while the associative property involves only the *grouping* of addends or factors.

Close

Have students demonstrate how to use the commutative, associative, and distributive properties to compute fraction exercises mentally.

3 PRACTICE/APPLY

Assignment Guide

Maximum: 12–29

Minimum: 12–23 odd, 24–29

For **Extra Practice,** see p. 584.

Alternate Assessment

Writing Have students show by example that subtraction of fractions is neither commutative nor associative.

Enrichment Masters, p. 47

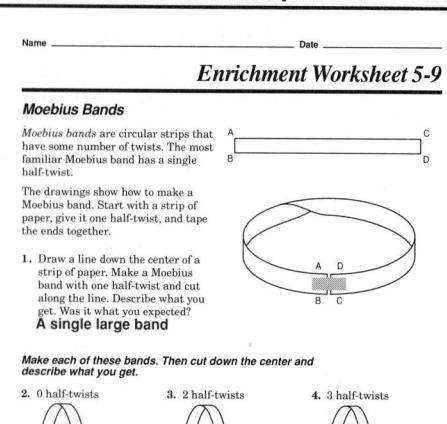

Name _____ Date _____

Enrichment Worksheet 5-9

Moebius Bands

Moebius bands are circular strips that have some number of twists. The most familiar Moebius band has a single half-twist.

The drawings show how to make a Moebius band. Start with a strip of paper, give it one half-twist, and tape the ends together.

1. Draw a line down the center of a strip of paper. Make a Moebius band with one half-twist and cut along the line. Describe what you get. Was it what you expected?
A single large band

Make each of these bands. Then cut down the center and describe what you get.

2. 0 half-twists   3. 2 half-twists   4. 3 half-twists

2 bands   2 bands   1 band

Experiment with bands that have more half-twists. Use your results to complete these conclusions.

5. If a band is cut in half along a line down its middle and 2 bands are created, then the number of half-twists in the original band must be _____ **even**

6. If a band is cut in half along a line down its middle and 1 band is created, then the number of half-twists in the original band must be _____ **odd**

T 47
Glencoe Division, Macmillan/McGraw-Hill

Guided Practice Name the property shown by each statement.

3. $\frac{7}{8} + 0 = \frac{7}{8}$ **Identity of +**

4. $\frac{1}{8} + \frac{3}{4} = \frac{3}{4} + \frac{1}{8}$ **Associative of ×**

State which pairs of numbers are multiplicative inverses. Write *yes* or *no*.

5. $\frac{2}{3}$, 3 **no**

6. $\frac{4}{5}$, $1\frac{1}{4}$ **yes**

7. 7, $\frac{1}{7}$ **yes**

8. $\frac{3}{10}$, $\frac{10}{3}$ **yes**

Compute mentally.

9. $2 \times 1\frac{1}{6}$ **$2\frac{1}{3}$**

10. $\frac{1}{2} \times 4\frac{2}{5}$ **$2\frac{1}{5}$**

11. $8\frac{1}{2} \times \frac{1}{4}$ **$2\frac{1}{8}$**

Exercises

Independent Practice Name the multiplicative inverse of each number.

12. $\frac{9}{10}$ **$\frac{10}{9}$**

13. $\frac{7}{8}$ **$\frac{8}{7}$**

14. $1\frac{2}{3}$ **$\frac{3}{5}$**

15. 3 **$\frac{1}{3}$**

Name the property shown by each statement.

16. **associative of +**

16. $\left(\frac{1}{3} + \frac{1}{2}\right) + 7 = \frac{1}{3} + \left(\frac{1}{2} + 7\right)$

17. $\frac{3}{5} \times 1\frac{2}{3} = 1$ **multiplicative inverse**

18. $\frac{3}{10} \times 1 = \frac{3}{10}$
identity for ×

19. $\frac{2}{3} \times \left(\frac{1}{2} + \frac{3}{4}\right) = \frac{2}{3} \times \frac{1}{2} + \frac{2}{3} \times \frac{3}{4}$
distributive of + over ×

Compute mentally.

20. $4 \times 6\frac{1}{8}$ **$24\frac{1}{2}$**

21. $2 \times 5\frac{1}{2}$ **11**

22. $1\frac{1}{3} \times 6$ **8**

23. $\frac{1}{3} \times 9\frac{1}{2}$ **$3\frac{1}{6}$**

Mixed Review

24. A typist types 1,950 words in 30 minutes. What is her typing rate in words per minute? *(Lesson 1-1)* **65 words/minute**

25. Divide 12.36 by 3.5. Round to the nearest tenth. *(Lesson 2-8)* **3.5**

26. **Probability** There are 36 ways for two dice to land. What is the probability that you will roll an 8? *(Lesson 4-8)* **$\frac{5}{36}$**

Problem Solving and Applications

27. **Critical Thinking** Use the properties of addition and multiplication to compute $50\left(3\frac{3}{8}\right) + 50\left(6\frac{5}{8}\right)$ mentally. **500**

28. **Cooking** The shortcake recipe at the right is for 6 servings. Write the recipe that will make 12 servings.

$2\frac{1}{3}$ cups of biscuit mix	$4\frac{2}{3}$ cups
$\frac{1}{2}$ cup milk	1 cup
3 tablespoons of sugar	6 Tbsp
3 tablespoons of margarine	6 Tbsp

29. **Geometry** Find the area of the rectangle at the right. **$1\frac{1}{6}$ in²**

$2\frac{1}{3}$ in. $\frac{1}{2}$ in.

OPTIONS

Extending the Lesson

Using Number Sense Have students experiment to find out whether multiplication distributes over subtraction as well as addition. It does.

Cooperative Learning Activity

Number of players: 2
Materials: Spinners

Totally Mental 5-9

▮ Label equal sections of one spinner "2," "4," "6," "8," "12," "16." Label equal sections of a second spinner "$8\frac{1}{2}$," "$3\frac{5}{6}$," "$4\frac{1}{4}$," "$1\frac{7}{8}$," "$2\frac{3}{16}$," "$5\frac{5}{12}$."

➡ Both partners spin a spinner at the same time. The first partner to find the product of the resulting two factors *mentally* gets 1 point. Continue in the same manner until one partner has 10 points.

Glencoe Mathematics: Applications and Connections, Course 2

5-10 Dividing Fractions and Mixed Numbers

Objective
Divide fractions and mixed numbers.

Ellen is in charge of buying groceries for her 4-H overnight camping trip. She figures that each person will drink an average of $1\frac{1}{3}$ cups of orange juice for breakfast. If she buys one quart of orange juice for five people, will there be enough juice? *Recall that 1 quart = 4 cups.*

To solve this problem, we need to find how many $1\frac{1}{3}$ cups are in 4 cups. Divide 4 by $1\frac{1}{3}$.

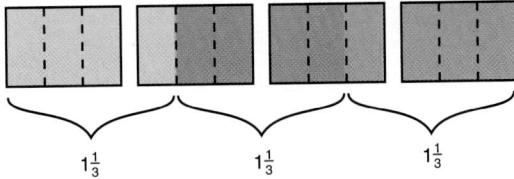

So, $4 \div 1\frac{1}{3} = 3$.

We can also divide by a fraction or mixed number. To do this multiply by its multiplicative inverse.

$$4 \div 1\frac{1}{3} = \frac{4}{1} \div \frac{4}{3} \qquad \textit{Rename 4 as } \frac{4}{1} \textit{ and } 1\frac{1}{3} \textit{ as } \frac{4}{3}.$$

$$= \frac{4}{1} \times \frac{3}{4} \qquad \textit{Dividing by } \frac{4}{3} \textit{ is the same as}$$

$$= \frac{3}{1} \textit{ or } 3 \qquad \textit{multiplying by } \frac{3}{4}.$$

One quart of orange juice will be enough for 3 people, *not* 5 people.

Division of Fractions and Mixed Numbers	To divide by a fraction, multiply by its multiplicative inverse.
	Arithmetic: $\frac{4}{5} \div \frac{2}{3} = \frac{4}{5} \cdot \frac{3}{2}$
	Algebra: $\frac{a}{b} \div \frac{c}{d} = \frac{a}{b} \cdot \frac{d}{c}$, where b, c, and $d \neq 0$.

Lesson 5-10 Dividing Fractions and Mixed Numbers **207**

OPTIONS

Reteaching Activity

Using Manipulatives Have students model division of fractions on a number line, by counting intervals. For example, in the lesson opener they would count off groups of $\frac{1}{3}$ until they reach 4.

Study Guide Masters, p. 48

Name _____ Date _____

Study Guide Worksheet 5-10

Dividing Fractions and Mixed Numbers

To divide fractions and mixed numbers:
1. Write any mixed numbers as improper fractions.
2. Find the reciprocal of the divisor.
3. Multiply the dividend by the reciprocal of the divisor.

Examples

1. $\frac{5}{8} \div \frac{5}{12}$ The reciprocal of $\frac{5}{12}$ is $\frac{12}{5}$.

$\frac{5}{8} \div \frac{5}{12} = \frac{5}{8} \times \frac{12}{5} = \frac{60}{40} = 1\frac{1}{2}$

2. $7 \div 3\frac{1}{2}$ $\frac{7}{1} \div \frac{7}{2}$ The reciprocal of $\frac{7}{2}$ is $\frac{2}{7}$.

$7 \div 3\frac{1}{2} = \frac{7}{1} \times \frac{2}{7} = \frac{14}{7} = 2$

5-10 Lesson Notes

NCTM Standards: 1–7, 13

Lesson Resources
- Study Guide Master 5-10
- Practice Master 5-10
- Enrichment Master 5-10
- Multicultural Activity, p. 5
- Group Activity Card 5-10

Transparency 5-10 contains the 5-Minute Check and a teaching aid for this lesson.

🕐 5-Minute Check
(Over Lesson 5-9)

1. Name the multiplicative inverse of $\frac{4}{5}$. $\frac{5}{4}$

Name the property shown by each statement.

2. $\frac{3}{4} \times \frac{2}{3} = \frac{2}{3} \times \frac{3}{4}$ comm.

3. $\frac{1}{2} \times \left(\frac{2}{3} + \frac{2}{5}\right) = \frac{1}{2} \times \frac{2}{3} + \frac{1}{2} \times \frac{2}{5}$ distr.

Compute mentally.

4. $4 \times 6\frac{1}{2}$ 26

5. $\frac{1}{5} \times 10\frac{1}{2}$ $2\frac{1}{10}$

1 FOCUS

Motivating the Lesson

Questioning Have students read the opening paragraph. Then tell them that Ellen is taking $2\frac{1}{2}$ pounds of trail mix on the camping trip. She wants to put it into 10 bags. How can she put the same amount of trail mix into each bag? Divide $2\frac{1}{2}$ by 10.

2 TEACH

Using Models Have a student model the solution to the lesson opener at the chalkboard by using four fraction circles, each divided into thirds. As this student shows how many groups of $1\frac{1}{3}$ there are in 4, have another student solve the problem by multiplying 4 by the reciprocal of $1\frac{1}{3}$. Repeat the process with other examples.

207

208

Divide. Write each quotient in simplest form.

1 $\frac{1}{2} \div \frac{2}{3}$ *Estimate:* $\frac{1}{2} \div 1 = \frac{1}{2}$

$\frac{1}{2} \div \frac{2}{3} = \frac{1}{2} \times \frac{3}{2}$ *Dividing by $\frac{2}{3}$ is the same as multiplying by $\frac{3}{2}$.*

$= \frac{3}{4}$

2 $\frac{3}{4} \div 4\frac{1}{2}$ *Estimate:* $1 \div 5 = \frac{1}{5}$

$\frac{3}{4} \div 4\frac{1}{2} = \frac{3}{4} \div \frac{9}{2}$ *Rename $4\frac{1}{2}$ as $\frac{9}{2}$.*

$= \frac{\overset{1}{\cancel{3}}}{\underset{2}{\cancel{4}}} \times \frac{\overset{1}{\cancel{2}}}{\underset{3}{\cancel{9}}}$ *Dividing by $\frac{9}{2}$ is the same as multiplying by $\frac{2}{9}$.*

$= \frac{1}{6}$

3 $2\frac{2}{3} \div 1\frac{1}{2}$ *Estimate:* $3 \div 2 = 1\frac{1}{2}$

$2\frac{2}{3} \div 1\frac{1}{2} = \frac{8}{3} \div \frac{3}{2}$ *Rename $2\frac{2}{3}$ as $\frac{8}{3}$ and $1\frac{1}{2}$ as $\frac{3}{2}$.*

$= \frac{8}{3} \times \frac{2}{3}$ *Dividing by $\frac{3}{2}$ is the same as multiplying by $\frac{2}{3}$.*

$= \frac{16}{9}$

$= 1\frac{7}{9}$ *Rename as a mixed number.*

Example 4   *Problem Solving*

Food   Mrs. Lazo had $\frac{2}{3}$ of a pie left for dinner. She divided it into 4 equivalent parts for her family. What part of a pie will each family member get?

$\frac{2}{3} \div 4 = \frac{2}{3} \div \frac{4}{1}$ *Rename 4 as $\frac{4}{1}$.*

$= \frac{\overset{1}{\cancel{2}}}{3} \times \frac{1}{\underset{2}{\cancel{4}}}$ *Dividing by $\frac{4}{1}$ is the same as multiplying by $\frac{1}{4}$.*

$= \frac{1}{6}$ *Each serving is $\frac{1}{6}$ of a pie.*

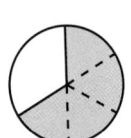

Checking for Understanding

Communicating Mathematics   Read and study the lesson to answer each question.

1. **Draw a model** to show what $4\frac{1}{2} \div \frac{3}{4}$ means. **See Solutions Manual.**

2. **Write** the multiplicative inverse of $2\frac{1}{4}$. $\frac{4}{9}$

208   **Chapter 5** Applications with Fractions

Name the multiplicative inverse of each number.

3. $\frac{3}{5}$ $\frac{5}{3}$ 4. 2 $\frac{1}{2}$ 5. $\frac{1}{3}$ 3 6. $4\frac{1}{2}$ $\frac{2}{9}$

Divide. Write each quotient in simplest form.

7. $\frac{3}{4} \div \frac{1}{2}$ $1\frac{1}{2}$ 8. $3 \div \frac{6}{7}$ $3\frac{1}{2}$ 9. $2\frac{2}{3} \div 4$ $\frac{2}{3}$ 10. $1\frac{1}{4} \div 3\frac{1}{2}$ $\frac{5}{14}$

11. $\frac{1}{8} \div \frac{1}{3}$ $\frac{3}{8}$ 12. $4\frac{2}{3} \div \frac{7}{8}$ $5\frac{1}{3}$ 13. $\frac{9}{10} \div 2\frac{1}{4}$ $\frac{2}{5}$ 14. $\frac{3}{4} \div \frac{1}{2}$ $1\frac{1}{2}$

Exercises

Name the multiplicative inverse of each number.

15. $\frac{5}{6}$ $\frac{6}{5}$ 16. 3 $\frac{1}{3}$ 17. $\frac{4}{5}$ $\frac{5}{4}$ 18. $2\frac{9}{10}$ $\frac{10}{29}$ 19. $3\frac{3}{5}$ $\frac{5}{18}$

Divide. Write each quotient in simplest form.

20. $\frac{2}{3} \div \frac{1}{2}$ $1\frac{1}{3}$ 21. $\frac{3}{5} \div \frac{1}{4}$ $2\frac{2}{5}$ 22. $\frac{5}{6} \div \frac{2}{3}$ $1\frac{1}{4}$ 23. $\frac{1}{6} \div \frac{1}{4}$ $\frac{2}{3}$

24. $6 \div \frac{1}{2}$ 12 25. $\frac{3}{8} \div \frac{6}{7}$ $\frac{7}{16}$ 26. $\frac{4}{9} \div 2$ $\frac{2}{9}$ 27. $\frac{5}{9} \div \frac{5}{6}$ $\frac{2}{3}$

28. $\frac{3}{4} \div \frac{3}{8}$ 2 29. $\frac{2}{3} \div 2\frac{1}{2}$ $\frac{4}{15}$ 30. $5 \div 1\frac{1}{3}$ $3\frac{3}{4}$ 31. $2\frac{1}{4} \div \frac{2}{3}$ $3\frac{3}{8}$

32. $2\frac{2}{3} \div 5\frac{1}{3}$ $\frac{1}{2}$ 33. $1\frac{1}{9} \div 1\frac{2}{3}$ $\frac{2}{3}$ 34. $5\frac{1}{4} \div 3$ $1\frac{3}{4}$ 35. $4\frac{1}{2} \div 6\frac{3}{4}$ $\frac{2}{3}$

36. Find the quotient of $\frac{1}{8}$ and $\frac{1}{9}$. $1\frac{1}{8}$

37. Solve the equation $x = \left(\frac{1}{5} + \frac{1}{12}\right) \div 3\frac{1}{2}$. $\frac{17}{210}$

38. Solve mentally $\frac{t}{5} = 15$. *(Lesson 1-10)* **75**

39. Round 10.2573 to the nearest tenth. *(Lesson 2-2)* **10.3**

40. Add $\frac{1}{3}$ and $\frac{1}{4}$. *(Lesson 5-3)* $\frac{7}{12}$

41. **Health** Tim jogs on a circular track that has a diameter of 77 feet. How far does Tim jog each time he goes around the track? *(Lesson 5-7)* **241.78 feet**

42. Compute mentally $\frac{2}{3} \times 6\frac{3}{7}$. *(Lesson 5-9)* $\frac{30}{7}$ **or** $4\frac{2}{7}$

43. **Housing** A contractor is going to develop land for single-family homes near the Eastland Mall. If she buys 12 acres of land, how many $\frac{3}{4}$-acre lots can she sell? **16 lots**

44. **Portfolio Suggestion** Select your favorite word problem from this chapter. Attach a note explaining why it is your favorite. **See students' work.**

45. **Critical Thinking** Will the quotient $5\frac{1}{8} \div 3\frac{1}{4}$ be a proper fraction or a mixed number? Why? **mixed number, $5\frac{1}{8} > 3\frac{1}{4}$**

Lesson 5-10 Dividing Fractions and Mixed Numbers   **209**

Extending the Lesson

Using Patterns Have students make up number sequences using fractions, mixed numbers, or both. Make the rule for the sequence involve division or multiplication. Ask students to challenge others to discover their rule.

Cooperative Learning Activity

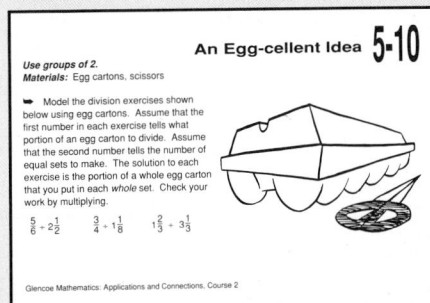

An Egg-cellent Idea **5-10**

Use groups of 2.
Materials: Egg cartons, scissors

➡ Model the division exercises shown below using egg cartons. Assume that the first number in each exercise tells what portion of an egg carton to divide. Assume that the second number tells the number of equal sets to make. The solution to each exercise is the portion of a whole egg carton that you put in each *whole* set. Check your work by multiplying.

$\frac{5}{6} \div 2\frac{1}{2}$ $\frac{3}{4} \cdot 1\frac{1}{8}$ $1\frac{2}{3} \div 3\frac{1}{3}$

Glencoe Mathematics: Applications and Connections, Course 2

Have students explain a procedure for dividing fractions and mixed numbers, as if to a classmate who has missed the lesson.

3 PRACTICE/APPLY

Assignment Guide
Maximum: 15–45
Minimum: 15–37 odd, 38–45

For **Extra Practice,** see p. 584.

Alternate Assessment

Writing Have students write a word problem that can be solved by dividing fractions or mixed numbers. Ask students to exchange problems with classmates.

Enrichment Masters, p. 48

Enrichment Worksheet 5-10

Continued Fractions

The expression at the right is an example of a *continued fraction*. Although continued fractions may look complicated, they are just a combination of addition and division. Here is one way to simplify a continued fraction.

$1 + \cfrac{1}{1 + \cfrac{1}{1 + \frac{1}{9}}}$

$1 + \cfrac{1}{1 + \cfrac{1}{1 + \frac{1}{9}}} = 1 + [1 \div (1 + [1 \div (1 + \frac{1}{9})])]$

$= 1 + [1 \div (1 + [1 \div \frac{10}{9}])]$
$= 1 + [1 \div (1 + \frac{9}{10})]$
$= 1 + [1 \div \frac{19}{10}]$
$= 1 + \frac{10}{19}$
$= \frac{29}{19}$

Write each continued fraction as an improper fraction.

1. $1 + \cfrac{1}{3 + \frac{1}{3}}$ $\frac{13}{10}$ 2. $2 + \cfrac{1}{2 + \frac{1}{2}}$ $\frac{12}{5}$ 3. $1 + \cfrac{2}{3 + \frac{2}{3}}$ $\frac{17}{11}$

4. $1 + \cfrac{3}{3 + \frac{1}{4}}$ $\frac{25}{13}$ 5. $5 + \cfrac{1}{1 + \frac{1}{5}}$ $\frac{35}{6}$ 6. $2 + \cfrac{2}{2 + \frac{2}{5}}$ $\frac{17}{6}$

7. $1 + \cfrac{1}{1 + \cfrac{1}{1 + \frac{1}{2}}}$ $\frac{8}{5}$ 8. $1 + \cfrac{1}{1 + \cfrac{1}{1 + \frac{1}{3}}}$ $\frac{11}{7}$ 9. $1 + \cfrac{1}{1 + \cfrac{1}{1 + \frac{1}{5}}}$ $\frac{17}{11}$

10. $2 + \cfrac{1}{2 + \cfrac{1}{2 + \frac{1}{2}}}$ $\frac{29}{12}$ 11. $3 + \cfrac{1}{3 + \cfrac{1}{1 + \frac{1}{3}}}$ $\frac{29}{9}$ 12. $6 + \cfrac{1}{1 + \cfrac{1}{3 + \frac{1}{3}}}$ $\frac{88}{13}$

Management Tips

For Students Have students work with partners to model the situations and solve the problems in each activity. They can draw and label circles and rectangles to represent the money amounts if play money is unavailable.

For the Overhead Projector
Overhead Manipulative Resources provides appropriate materials for teacher or student demonstration of the activities in this Mathematics Lab.

1 FOCUS

Introducing the Lab

Discuss with students any prior knowledge they may have about unit prices. Ask them to describe the relationship between unit prices and smart shopping.

Cooperative Learning

5-10B Fraction Patterns

A Follow-Up of Lesson 5-10

Objective
Find unit price.

Words to Learn
unit price

Materials
play money
sheets of paper

Anna wants to find the **unit price** for each item she bought at the grocery store. To find the unit price means to find the cost per pound, yard, gallon, square foot, or some other unit of measure.

Grocery Item	Cost
5 pounds of potatoes	$3.75
$3\frac{1}{2}$-ounce box of ground cinnamon	$2.10
half-pound box of turkey stuffing mix	$1.09

Activity One

Help Anna find the unit price of potatoes by using 5 sheets of paper to represent 5 pounds of potatoes. Using the play money, distribute $3.75 evenly on the 5 sheets of paper to find the price of 1 pound.

1 lb　　1 lb　　1 lb　　1 lb　　1 lb

Find $3.75 ÷ 5. What is the price per pound? **75¢**

What do you think?

A can of three tennis balls costs $2.40. What is the cost per tennis ball?
1. How many sheets of paper are needed? **3 sheets**
2. What is the cost per tennis ball? **80¢**
3. Find $2.40 ÷ 3 to check your answer. **See students' work.**

Extension

4. Doughnuts are $1.50 for a half dozen. What is the cost per donut? **25¢**

Activity Two

To help Anna find the unit price of ground cinnamon, use $3\frac{1}{2}$ sheets of paper to represent $3\frac{1}{2}$ ounces. Using the play money, distribute $2.10 so that the half sheet of paper has half the money as each full sheet of paper.

1 oz   **1 oz**   **1 oz**   **½oz**

Find $2.10 ÷ 3½. What is the price per ounce? 60¢

What do you think?

Mrs. Grant paid $3.75 for 2½ yards of dress material. What is the cost per yard?

5. How many sheets of paper are needed? 2½ sheets

6. How much money should a half sheet of paper contain? 75¢

7. What is the cost of dress material per yard? $1.50

8. Find $3.75 ÷ 2½ to check your answer. See students' work.

Extension

9. Mr. O'Grady bought 1½ pounds of nails for 90¢. What was the price per pound? 60¢

Activity Three

To help Anna find the unit price of the turkey stuffing, use a half sheet of paper to represent ½ pound. Put $1.09 on the half sheet of paper. A whole pound would be represented by two half sheets of paper. Put $1.09 on a second half sheet of paper to find the price per pound.

½lb   **½lb**

Find $1.09 ÷ ½. What is the price per pound? $2.18

What do you think?

A ¼-pound box of chocolates sells for 95¢. How much would a pound of chocolates cost?

10. What is the cost of one pound of chocolates? $3.80

11. Find 95¢ ÷ ¼ to check your answer. See students' work.

Extension

12. One-third of an acre of residential property costs $5,000. What is the cost per acre? $15,000

Math Lab 5-10B Fraction Patterns **211**

NCTM Standards: 1–5, 7, 8

Lesson Resources
- Study Guide Master 5-11
- Practice Master 5-11
- Enrichment Master 5-11
- Evaluation Master, Quiz B, p. 43
- Group Activity Card 5-11

 Transparency 5-11 contains the 5-Minute Check and a teaching aid for this lesson.

 5-Minute Check
(Over Lesson 5-10)
Write in simplest form.
1. $r = \frac{1}{2} \div \frac{2}{3}$ $\frac{3}{4}$
2. $t = \frac{2}{5} \div \frac{3}{4}$ $\frac{8}{15}$
3. $\frac{5}{8} \div 1\frac{1}{4} = s$ $\frac{1}{2}$

1 FOCUS

Motivating the Lesson

Questioning   Ask students how many handshakes they think six people can exchange.

Practice Masters, p. 49

Name _____ Date _____

Practice Worksheet 5-11

Problem-Solving Strategy: Eliminate Possibilities

Solve. Use estimation to eliminate the possibilities.

1. Pam bought 3 cans of soup for $0.59 each, a loaf of bread for $1.39, and four candy bars for $0.45 each. Choose the best estimate for the change she should get from $10.
$2 ($5) $6 $7

2. Joanna's quiz scores were 23, 14, 18, 15, 21, and 20. Choose the best estimate of her average quiz score.
15 (18) 20 22

Solve using any strategy.

3. The You-Rent-It Auto Company charges $30 a day or $166 a week to rent a compact car. Choose the best estimate of how much money the weekly rate saves the customer who rents a car for 7 days.
$25 $35 ($45) $55

4. If it takes Tony's mom 15 minutes to make a party favor for Tony's birthday party, how many favors can she make in $2\frac{1}{2}$ hours? **10**

5. A circular stadium has a diameter of 300 feet. What is its circumference?
942 ft

6. Jonathan plans to plant a privacy hedge along the sides and back of his lot, which is 120 feet wide and 120 feet long. How many hedges will he plant if they need to be 3 feet apart?
121

7. Juan bought a midsize car with a $1,000 down payment and a plan to pay $210.89 per month for 48 months. Choose the best estimate of the total cost of the car.
$5,000 $8,000 ($11,000) $14,000

8. Mrs. Maxwell bought $6\frac{1}{2}$ yards of fabric to make two identical costumes. How much fabric is needed for each costume? $3\frac{1}{4}$ **yd**

T49
Glencoe Division, Macmillan/McGraw-Hill

212

5-11 Eliminate Possibilities

Objective
Solve problems by using estimation to eliminate possibilities.

Today the Camera Club had a show of its best work. After the show, the six winners shook hands. Each winner shook hands once with the other five. How many handshakes were there in all? Choose the best estimate from the list below.

$$36 \qquad 30 \qquad 15 \qquad 6$$

Explore   What do you know?
There were six winners. Each winner shook hands one time with the other five winners.

What are you trying to find?
You are trying to find the best estimate of how many handshakes there were.

Plan   Look at the choices of estimates to see which ones are impossible and eliminate those. Then concentrate on the other estimates to choose the best one.

Solve

Handshakes	Interpret	Eliminate?
6 shakes	One person shakes the hands of the other five. Then there is only one shake left. So 6 is too few handshakes.	yes
36 shakes	Six times six means that six persons each shake hands with 6 different people. But no person shakes his own hand, so 36 is too many handshakes.	yes
30 shakes	Six times five means that six persons each shake hands with 5 different people. But once the first person shakes hands with the second person, those two don't shake again. So 30 is too many handshakes.	yes

The best estimate must be 15 shakes.

OPTIONS

Reteaching Activity

Using Applications   Have 6 students act out the handshaking described while a student records the number of handshakes. Before they begin, have students guess how many handshakes there will be. Have them revise their guesses as the activity progresses.

Study Guide Masters, p. 49

Name _____ Date _____

Study Guide Worksheet 5-11

Problem-Solving Strategy: Eliminate Possibilities

Royce wants to buy a bicycle that costs $428. He can pay for it in 12 payments of $39.23 each. How much more will the bicycle cost him if he makes payments than if he pays for it in total when he buys it? Choose the best estimate.

Explore   What do you know?   The bicycle costs $428. It can be paid for in 12 payments of $39.23 each.

What are you trying to find out?   You are trying to find the best estimate of how much more Royce will pay by making payments.

Plan   Eliminate impossible estimates. Then choose the best estimate.

Solve   Estimate
$10
$428 + $10 is about $440. $39.23 is about $40. $40 × 12 = $480. $440 and $480 are not close. So $10 is too little.

Eliminate
Yes

Examine   The first person shakes hands with the other five people. Then the next person only has 4 handshakes left. The third has 3, the fourth has 2, and the final shake is that of the fifth and sixth winners.

$$5 + 4 + 3 + 2 + 1 = 15$$

The total is 15 handshakes.

Checking for Understanding

Communicating Mathematics

Read and study the lesson to answer each question.

1. **Write** a problem with multiple-choice answers. **See students' work.**
2. **Tell** how you use the strategy of eliminating possibilities to solve a problem. **Sample answer: List probabilities, interpret, and determine whether or not to eliminate.**

Guided Practice

Solve by eliminating the possibilities.

3. Jessica's math test scores were 80, 78, 87, 70, and 81. Choose the best average for her test scores.

          75   80   83   86   **80**

4. Jeff bought felt-tipped pens, 3 for $1.39; pencils, 2 for $0.49; and an eraser for $0.29. Choose the best estimate for the amount of change he will get from $5.

    $0.30 $1.80 $2.70 $3.30   **$2.70**

Problem Solving

Practice

Solve using any strategy.

Strategies
••••••••••
Look for a pattern.
Solve a simpler problem.
Act it out.
Guess and check.
Draw a diagram.
Make a chart.
Work backward.

5. A taxi charges $1.15 for the first $\frac{1}{5}$ mile and $0.50 for each additional $\frac{1}{5}$ mile. Choose the best estimate for the cost of a 4-mile taxi ride.

    $13.65 $12.65 $11.65 $10.65   **$10.65**

6. Meagan has 4 less than 3 times as many compact discs as Jason. Meagan has 92 compact discs. How many CDs does Jason have? **32 CDs**

7. Luis bought a VCR for $280. He could have paid for it in 12 monthly installments of $26.50 each. If he paid cash, choose the best estimate for the amount of money he saved.

    $80 $54 $38 $28   **$38**

Lesson 5-11 Problem-Solving Strategy: Eliminate Possibilities   **213**

Extending the Lesson

Soccer Tournament Present the following problem: *Thirty-two teams are playing in a single-elimination soccer tournament. As soon as a team loses, it is eliminated. How many games must be played to determine a champion?* Then ask students to solve the problem using any strategy.

Cooperative Learning Activity

Process of Elimination 5-11

Number of players: 2
Materials: index cards

● Draw a circle on each of ten index cards. Fill in the circle on five cards *only*. Mix the cards thoroughly and divide them evenly.

➡ Using the symbols on your cards, write a pattern such as ●   ●●   on a separate sheet of paper. Do not let your partner see the pattern. Take turns trying to guess each other's pattern. On your turn write a pattern such as the one above on a sheet of paper and show it to your partner. Your partner writes the number of symbols whose position in his or her pattern you guessed and hands the sheet of paper back to you. Try to be the first to guess the pattern. (Hint: The symbols on the cards in your hand should allow you to eliminate some possibilities because you know that there are five cards with the ● symbol and five cards with the   symbol.)

Glencoe Mathematics: Applications and Connections, Course 2

The Chapter Study Guide and Review begins with a section on Communicating Mathematics. This includes questions that review the new terms and concepts that were introduced in the chapter.

Then, the Skills and Concepts presented in the chapter are reviewed using a side-by-side format. Encourage students to refer to the Objectives and Examples on the left as they complete the Review Exercises on the right.

The Chapter Study Guide and Review ends with problems that review Applications and Problem Solving.

Study Guide and Review

Chapter

5 Study Guide and Review

Communicating Mathematics

Choose the letter that best matches each phrase.
1. a fraction that has a numerator that is less than the denominator f
2. the sum of a whole number and a fraction a
3. the least common denominator of $\frac{1}{8}$ and $\frac{1}{6}$ c
4. the distance around a rectangle b
5. the distance across a circle through the center j
6. the property that states $(a + b) + c = a + (b + c)$ k
7. In your own words, explain how the distributive property can be used to compute the product of a mixed number and a whole number. **Answers will vary.**

a. mixed number
b. perimeter
c. 24
d. circumference
e. commutative
f. proper fraction
g. 48
h. radius
i. expected value
j. diameter
k. associative
l. distributive

Self Assessment

Objectives and Examples

Upon completing this chapter, you should be able to:

Review Exercises

Use these exercises to review and prepare for the chapter test.

• change mixed numbers to improper fractions and vice versa *(Lesson 5-1)*

$$3\frac{4}{9} = \frac{(3 \times 9) + 4}{9} = \frac{31}{9}$$

$$\frac{12}{8} \rightarrow 8\overline{)12} \quad \begin{array}{r} 1 \\ -8 \\ \hline 4 \end{array} \rightarrow 1\frac{4}{8} \text{ or } 1\frac{1}{2}$$

Change each mixed number to an improper fraction.

8. $5\frac{2}{5}$ $\frac{27}{5}$ 9. $3\frac{4}{7}$ $\frac{25}{7}$ 10. $2\frac{9}{10}$ $\frac{29}{10}$

Change each improper fraction to a mixed number in simplest form or a whole number.

11. $\frac{63}{4}$ $15\frac{3}{4}$ 12. $\frac{12}{5}$ $2\frac{2}{5}$ 13. $\frac{21}{8}$ $2\frac{5}{8}$

• estimate sums, differences, products, and quotients of fractions and mixed numbers *(Lesson 5-2)*

Estimate $14\frac{5}{9} + 2\frac{1}{6}$.

$15 + 2 = 17$

Estimate.

14. $\frac{2}{3} + \frac{7}{9}$ 2   15. $6\frac{5}{4} + 11\frac{2}{7}$ 18

16. $\frac{1}{3} \times \frac{5}{8}$ $\frac{1}{2}$ 17. $\frac{2}{5} \div \frac{3}{4}$ $\frac{1}{2}$

18. $\frac{14}{15} - \frac{1}{8}$ 1   19. $99\frac{9}{10} - 9\frac{9}{10}$ 90

20. $1\frac{21}{25} \times 16\frac{4}{13}$ 32   21. $6\frac{1}{8} \div 1\frac{5}{6}$ 3

Objectives and Examples

- add and subtract fractions *(Lesson 5-3)*

$$\frac{11}{14} - \frac{1}{6} = \frac{33}{42} - \frac{7}{42}$$
$$= \frac{26}{42} \text{ or } \frac{13}{21}$$

- add and subtract mixed numbers with unlike denominators *(Lesson 5-4)*

$$6\frac{3}{4} + 9\frac{2}{3} = 6\frac{9}{12} + 9\frac{8}{12}$$
$$= 15\frac{17}{12} \text{ or } 16\frac{5}{12}$$

- multiply fractions and mixed numbers *(Lesson 5-5)*

$$\frac{2}{5} \times \frac{1}{3} = \frac{2}{15}$$

$$4\frac{1}{4} \times 2\frac{2}{3} = \frac{17}{\overset{}{4}} \times \frac{\overset{2}{8}}{3}$$
$$= \frac{34}{3} \text{ or } 11\frac{1}{3}$$

- find perimeter using fractional measurements *(Lesson 5-6)*

Find the perimeter of a rectangle $4\frac{3}{4}$ feet long and $2\frac{1}{3}$ feet wide.

$$P = 4\frac{3}{4} + 4\frac{3}{4} + 2\frac{1}{3} + 2\frac{1}{3}$$
$$= 14\frac{2}{12} \text{ or } 14\frac{1}{6} \text{ feet}$$

- find the circumference of circles *(Lesson 5-7)*

If the diameter is $3\frac{1}{2}$ feet, then find the circumference.

$$C = \pi d$$
$$= \frac{22}{7} \times 3\frac{1}{2}$$
$$= \frac{22}{7} \times \frac{7}{2}$$
$$= 11 \quad \text{The circumference is 11 feet.}$$

Review Exercises

Add or subtract. Write each sum or difference in simplest form.

22. $\begin{aligned}&\frac{3}{5}\\+&\frac{2}{7}\end{aligned}$ $\frac{31}{35}$

23. $\begin{aligned}&\frac{3}{4}\\-&\frac{1}{2}\end{aligned}$ $\frac{1}{4}$

24. $\frac{7}{33} + 1\frac{6}{11}$

25. $\frac{5}{8} - \frac{3}{20}$ $\frac{19}{40}$

Add or subtract. Write each sum or difference in simplest form.

26. $9 + 5\frac{4}{9}$ $14\frac{4}{9}$

27. $4\frac{5}{12} + 3\frac{5}{6}$ $8\frac{1}{4}$

28. $2\frac{5}{8} - \frac{1}{6}$ $2\frac{11}{24}$

29. $16\frac{1}{7} - 2\frac{1}{2}$ $13\frac{9}{14}$

Multiply. Write each product in simplest form.

30. $\frac{4}{9} \times \frac{2}{5}$ $\frac{8}{45}$

31. $\frac{21}{5} \times 4\frac{1}{3}$ $18\frac{1}{5}$

32. $5 \times 3\frac{1}{8}$ $15\frac{5}{8}$

33. $6\frac{2}{7} \times 5\frac{1}{2}$ $34\frac{4}{7}$

Find the perimeter of each figure.

34. rectangle: $\ell = 4\frac{1}{2}$ yd $16\frac{1}{2}$ yd
    $w = 3\frac{3}{4}$ yd

35. rectangle: $\ell = 25\frac{1}{7}$ feet $75\frac{13}{21}$ ft
    $w = 12\frac{2}{3}$ feet

Find the circumference of each circle. Use $\pi = \frac{22}{7}$.

36. $d = 6$ in. $18\frac{6}{7}$ in.

37. $r = 3.7$ yd $23\frac{9}{35}$ yd

38. $r = \frac{7}{9}$ ft $4\frac{8}{9}$ ft

39. $d = 6\frac{3}{5}$ ft $20\frac{26}{35}$ ft

You may wish to use a Chapter Test from the Evaluation Masters booklet as an additional chapter review. The two free-response forms are shown below. One of the two multiple-choice forms is shown on the next page.

Study Guide and Review

Evaluation Masters, pp. 41–42

Name _____ Date _____

Form 2A _____ *Chapter 5 Test*

Change each improper fraction to a mixed number or vice versa.
1. $\frac{9}{4}$ 2. $4\frac{6}{7}$ 3. $\frac{28}{6}$

Estimate.
4. $\frac{8}{9} + 2\frac{1}{4}$ 5. $10\frac{7}{8} - 6\frac{1}{5}$ 6. $12\frac{6}{8} \div 1\frac{1}{5}$

Compute mentally.
7. $4 \times 5\frac{1}{2}$ 8. $2\frac{1}{3} \times 9$ 9. $\frac{5}{8} \times 12\frac{3}{5}$

Add, subtract, multiply, or divide. Write each answer in simplest form.
10. $\frac{2}{8} + \frac{5}{8}$ 11. $\frac{11}{13} + \frac{2}{3}$
12. $\frac{4}{5} - \frac{8}{15}$ 13. $\frac{7}{12} \times \frac{3}{14}$
14. $\frac{9}{7} + \frac{5}{14}$ 15. $1\frac{3}{8} + \frac{7}{15}$
16. $4\frac{1}{3} + 2\frac{1}{2}$ 17. $15\frac{2}{7} - \frac{10}{21}$
18. Find the perimeter of a rectangle with $l = 4\frac{1}{4}$ ft and $w = 3\frac{1}{2}$ ft.

Find the circumference for each circle. Use $\pi \approx \frac{22}{7}$.
19. $d = \frac{8}{9}$ mi   20. $r = 2\frac{1}{3}$ yd

21. The spinner at the right tells the number of dollars you win. Over the long run, would you expect to win, lose, or break even if each spin costs $3?

22. Thirty-five slices of chocolate cake were sold at the bake sale. If each piece was a tenth of a cake, how many cakes did they sell?

23. After school, Patsy spends $\frac{1}{2}$ of an hour on the telephone, $\frac{5}{8}$ of an hour exercising, and $\frac{3}{4}$ of an hour studying. What is the total time Patsy spends in these activities?

24. The length of a jogging trail is $5\frac{2}{3}$ miles. If you jog two-thirds of the length of the trail, how far have you jogged?

25. Amy parked in a lot that charges $3.00 for the first hour and $0.75 for each additional hour or part thereof. She parked there from 7:00 A.M. to 2:30 P.M. About how much did she pay?
$24.00 $8.25 $15.00 $6.00

BONUS A tire has a 13-inch radius. About how far will the tire travel in 12 rotations?

1. $2\frac{1}{4}$
2. $\frac{34}{7}$
3. $4\frac{2}{3}$
4. 3
5. 5
6. 6
7. 22
8. 21
9. $10\frac{1}{2}$
10. $1\frac{1}{40}$
11. $1\frac{20}{39}$
12. $\frac{4}{15}$
13. $\frac{1}{8}$
14. $1\frac{1}{5}$
15. $3\frac{7}{9}$
16. $6\frac{5}{6}$
17. $12\frac{17}{21}$
18. $15\frac{1}{2}$ ft
19. $1\frac{5}{28}$ mi
20. $14\frac{2}{3}$ yd
21. win
22. $3\frac{1}{2}$ cakes
23. $1\frac{7}{8}$ hours
24. $3\frac{7}{9}$ mi
25. $8.25

about 980 in.

41
Glencoe Division, Macmillan/McGraw-Hill

Name _____ Date _____

Form 2B _____ *Chapter 5 Test*

Change each improper fraction to a mixed number or vice versa.
1. $\frac{108}{8}$ 2. $3\frac{4}{9}$ 3. $\frac{30}{8}$

Estimate.
4. $3\frac{7}{9} + \frac{6}{7}$ 5. $9\frac{1}{3} - 5\frac{5}{8}$ 6. $10\frac{2}{5} \div 4\frac{1}{4}$

Compute mentally.
7. $5 \times 2\frac{1}{8}$ 8. $3\frac{1}{4} \times 8$ 9. $\frac{4}{3} \times 9\frac{9}{16}$

Add, subtract, multiply, or divide. Write each answer in simplest form.
10. $\frac{3}{4} + \frac{8}{9}$ 11. $\frac{7}{8} + \frac{5}{8}$
12. $\frac{2}{3} - \frac{5}{7}$ 13. $\frac{8}{9} \times \frac{10}{27}$
14. $\frac{9}{16} + \frac{3}{8}$ 15. $2\frac{4}{8} \div \frac{5}{9}$
16. $1\frac{1}{8} + 5\frac{1}{4}$ 17. $20\frac{5}{9} - 3\frac{5}{8}$
18. Find the perimeter of a rectangle with $l = 8\frac{1}{2}$ in. and $w = 5\frac{3}{4}$ in.

Find the circumference for each circle. Use $\pi \approx \frac{22}{7}$.
19. $d = \frac{7}{9}$ yd   20. $r = 1\frac{3}{4}$ ft

21. The spinner at the right tells the number of dollars you win. Over the long-run, would you expect to win, lose, or break even if each spin costs $3?

22. Ella walks $3\frac{1}{2}$ miles a day. How far does she walk in one week if she walks every day?

23. Rolando finds a $\frac{1}{5}$-off sale. About how much did he pay for a $39.50 golf shirt and a $51.25 pair of golf shoes?

24. The combined thickness of the pages of a textbook is $1\frac{1}{16}$ inches. Each cover is $\frac{1}{8}$ of an inch thick. What is the thickness of the textbook?

25. Theresa parked in a lot that charges $4.50 for the first hour and $1.25 for each additional hour or part thereof. She parked there from 7:00 A.M. to 6:30 P.M. About how much did she pay?
$4.50 $15.75 $18.25 $54

BONUS A brick is put on a balance scale. The brick balances exactly with $\frac{3}{4}$ of a brick and a $\frac{3}{4}$-pound weight. How much does the brick weigh?

1. $13\frac{1}{2}$
2. $\frac{31}{9}$
3. $3\frac{3}{4}$
4. 5
5. 3
6. 2
7. 11
8. 26
9. $4\frac{1}{4}$
10. $1\frac{23}{36}$
11. $1\frac{17}{24}$
12. $\frac{2}{3}$
13. $\frac{2}{3}$
14. $1\frac{1}{2}$
15. $3\frac{2}{5}$
16. $6\frac{9}{20}$
17. $16\frac{13}{18}$
18. $28\frac{1}{2}$ in.
19. $2\frac{4}{9}$ yd
20. 11 ft
21. lose
22. $24\frac{1}{2}$ mi
23. about $72
24. $1\frac{3}{16}$ in.
25. $18.25

3 lb

42
Glencoe Division, Macmillan/McGraw-Hill

216

Objectives and Examples

• find expected value of outcomes *(Lesson 5-8)*

Find the expected winnings.

Amount Won	$1	$3	$5
Probability	$\frac{2}{5}$	$\frac{3}{10}$	$\frac{3}{10}$

$1\left(\frac{2}{5}\right) + 3\left(\frac{3}{10}\right) + 5\left(\frac{3}{10}\right) = \$2.80$

• use addition and multiplication properties to solve problems mentally *(Lesson 5-9)*

$$\frac{1}{5} \times 10\frac{3}{4} = \frac{1}{5}\left(10 + \frac{3}{4}\right)$$
$$= 2 + \frac{3}{20} \text{ or } 2\frac{3}{20}$$

• divide fractions and mixed numbers *(Lesson 5-10)*

$$1\frac{2}{5} \div \frac{7}{10} = \overset{1}{\underset{1}{\cancel{\frac{7}{5}}}} \times \overset{2}{\underset{1}{\cancel{\frac{10}{7}}}} = \frac{2}{1} \text{ or } 2$$

Review Exercises

40. Find the expected winnings.

Amount Won	$0	$1	$5	$10
Probability	$\frac{17}{20}$	$\frac{1}{10}$	$\frac{1}{50}$	$\frac{1}{100}$

$0.30

Compute mentally.
41. $6 \times 2\frac{1}{8}$ $12\frac{3}{4}$ 42. $\frac{5}{9} \times 3\frac{1}{5}$ $1\frac{7}{9}$

43. $\frac{2}{3} \times 6\frac{1}{12}$ $4\frac{1}{18}$ 44. $4\frac{1}{6} \times 3$ $12\frac{1}{2}$

Divide. Write each quotient in simplest form.
45. $\frac{3}{5} \div \frac{1}{6}$ $3\frac{3}{5}$ 46. $1\frac{7}{8} \div 2\frac{4}{9}$ $\frac{135}{176}$

Applications and Problem Solving

47. **Cooking** A recipe calls for $2\frac{3}{4}$ cups of flour, $1\frac{3}{8}$ cups of sugar, and $1\frac{1}{3}$ cups of brown sugar. How many cups are in the mixture? *(Lesson 5-4)* $5\frac{11}{24}$ cups

48. Lou parked at a parking lot from 8:30 A.M. until 2:45 P.M. It cost $2.25 for the first hour and $0.90 for each additional hour or part of an hour. How much did Lou pay when he left the lot? *(Lesson 5-11)* **$7.65**

Curriculum Connection Projects

• **Physical Education** Find how far you travel with each complete turn of your bicycle wheel.

• **Science** How would you find the perimeter of one side of the school building without using a ladder? Try it!

Read More About It

Barron, T. A., *Heartlight.*
Sitomer, Mindel and Harry. *Circles.*

Buchman, Dian Dincin, and Seli Groves. *What If? Fifty Discoveries that Changed the World.*

5 Test

Express each improper fraction as a mixed number or vice versa.

1. $\frac{124}{12}$ $10\frac{1}{3}$

2. $6\frac{5}{9}$ $\frac{59}{9}$

3. **Music** Philip's rock band recorded 13 songs during an afternoon recording session. Each song took $\frac{1}{6}$ of a side of a tape to record. How many sides were used during the session? $2\frac{1}{6}$ **sides**

Estimate.

4. $1\frac{1}{3} + \frac{7}{8}$ **2**

5. $11\frac{4}{5} - 6\frac{1}{8}$ **6**

6. $16\frac{1}{8} \div \frac{5}{6}$ **16**

Add, subtract, multiply, or divide. Write each sum, difference, product, or quotient in simplest form.

7. $\frac{3}{5} + \frac{4}{9}$ $1\frac{2}{45}$

8. $\frac{5}{6} - \frac{13}{27}$ $\frac{19}{54}$

9. $\frac{5}{12} \times \frac{3}{10}$ $\frac{1}{8}$

10. $2\frac{5}{12} \div \frac{3}{8}$ $6\frac{4}{9}$

Add or subtract. Write each sum or difference in simplest form.

11. $4\frac{1}{3} + 3\frac{1}{4}$ $7\frac{7}{12}$

12. $16\frac{5}{9} - 3\frac{1}{12}$ $13\frac{17}{36}$

13. $14\frac{2}{3} - 8\frac{7}{8}$ $5\frac{19}{24}$

14. Find the perimeter of a rectangle with a length of $5\frac{3}{4}$ yards and a width of 3 yards. $17\frac{1}{2}$ **yd**

Find the circumference for each circle. Use $\pi = \frac{22}{7}$.

15. $d = 5\frac{3}{4}$ in. $18\frac{1}{14}$ in.

16. $r = \frac{2}{3}$ yd $4\frac{4}{21}$ yd

17. The spinner to the right tells the number of dollars you win. Over the long run, would you expect to win, lose, or break even if each spin costs $2. **win**

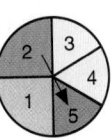

Compute mentally.

18. $6 \times 3\frac{1}{5}$ $19\frac{1}{5}$

19. $\frac{4}{5} \times 1\frac{1}{4}$ **1**

20. Kate found a $\frac{1}{3}$-off sale. About how much did she pay for a $39.95 golf jacket and a set of $18.65 sweats?

$9.07 $14.20 $20.00 $39.07   **$39.07**

Bonus The wheel of a car is $2\frac{6}{11}$ feet in diameter. If the car travels 80 feet, how many times does the wheel rotate? **10 times**

This page may be used as a chapter test or another chapter review.

Evaluation Masters, pp. 37–38

Name _____ Date _____

Form 1A   *Chapter 5 Test*

1. Change $\frac{8}{5}$ to a mixed number.
   A. 2.6   B. $3\frac{1}{5}$ C. $2\frac{3}{5}$ D. $2\frac{3}{5}$
   1. **D**

2. Change $3\frac{4}{5}$ to an improper fraction.
   A. $\frac{19}{5}$ B. $\frac{17}{5}$ C. $\frac{19}{4}$ D. $\frac{19}{3}$
   2. **A**

3. Estimate $\frac{7}{8} + 3\frac{1}{15}$.
   A. 5   B. 2   C. 4   D. 3
   3. **C**

4. Estimate $9\frac{1}{4} - 4\frac{8}{9}$.
   A. 6   B. 4   C. 5   D. 7
   4. **B**

5. Estimate $11\frac{2}{3} \div 1\frac{8}{9}$.
   A. 11   B. 12   C. 10   D. 6
   5. **D**

Add, subtract, multiply, or divide. Write the answer in simplest form.

6. $\frac{2}{8} + \frac{3}{8}$
   A. $\frac{5}{11}$ B. $\frac{5}{24}$ C. $\frac{1}{4}$ D. $1\frac{5}{24}$
   6. **D**

7. $\frac{9}{11} + \frac{1}{2}$
   A. $1\frac{9}{22}$ B. $\frac{10}{13}$ C. $\frac{29}{13}$ D. $\frac{9}{22}$
   7. **A**

8. $\frac{5}{8} - \frac{6}{8}$
   A. $\frac{1}{12}$ B. 1   C. $\frac{1}{24}$ D. $\frac{1}{7}$
   8. **C**

9. $\frac{11}{12} \times \frac{9}{22}$
   A. $\frac{10}{17}$ B. $\frac{3}{8}$ C. $\frac{3}{4}$ D. $\frac{99}{264}$
   9. **B**

10. $\frac{3}{5} + \frac{7}{15}$
    A. $\frac{4}{9}$ B. $\frac{7}{25}$ C. $\frac{1}{2}$ D. $1\frac{1}{7}$
    10. **D**

11. $2\frac{4}{5} \div \frac{4}{5}$
    A. 3   B. $\frac{7}{22}$ C. $3\frac{1}{7}$ D. $\frac{88}{28}$
    11. **C**

12. $\frac{11}{12} - \frac{5}{8}$
    A. $\frac{3}{2}$ B. $\frac{3}{10}$ C. $\frac{7}{24}$ D. $\frac{3}{8}$
    12. **C**

13. $\frac{3}{5} \times \frac{5}{18}$
    A. $\frac{5}{12}$ B. $\frac{2}{9}$ C. $\frac{2}{9}$ D. $\frac{5}{8}$
    13. **A**

37

Name _____ Date _____

Chapter 5 Test Form 1A (continued)

14. Compute $6 \times 2\frac{5}{8}$ mentally.
    A. 13   B. 17   C. 18   D. 14
    14. **B**

15. Compute $\frac{3}{8} \times 8\frac{8}{9}$ mentally.
    A. 8   B. 9   C. $3\frac{1}{3}$ D. 6
    15. **C**

Add or subtract. Write the answer in simplest form.

16. $2\frac{2}{3} + 1\frac{7}{12}$
    A. $3\frac{1}{10}$ B. $3\frac{5}{96}$ C. $3\frac{1}{4}$ D. $3\frac{13}{24}$
    16. **D**

17. $10\frac{1}{4} - 4\frac{3}{14}$
    A. $5\frac{21}{21}$ B. $6\frac{1}{4}$ C. $6\frac{1}{10}$ D. $5\frac{1}{4}$
    17. **A**

18. Find the perimeter of a square with side $3\frac{3}{4}$ feet.
    A. 15 ft   B. 16 ft   C. $15\frac{1}{4}$ ft   D. $16\frac{1}{2}$ ft
    18. **A**

19. Find the circumference of a circle whose diameter is $\frac{6}{5}$ yard.
    A. 2 yd   B. $3\frac{41}{63}$ yd   C. $1\frac{47}{163}$ D. 4 yd
    19. **C**

20. Find the circumference of a circle whose radius is 2.75 feet.
    A. 18.84 ft   B. 17.27 ft   C. 17 ft   D. 18 ft
    20. **B**

21. The spinner at the right tells the number of dollars you win. Find the expected value of a spin.
    A. $2.00   B. $2.25
    C. $3.00   D. $2.75
    21. **A**

22. In Exercise 21, over the long-term, would you expect to win, lose, or break even if each spin cost $2?
    A. win   B. lose   C. break even   D. none
    22. **C**

23. Jaime and three friends bought $\frac{3}{4}$ pound of trail mix. If they split the mix equally, how much will each person get?
    A. $\frac{1}{16}$ lb   B. $\frac{3}{8}$ lb   C. $\frac{3}{16}$ lb   D. $\frac{2}{8}$ lb
    23. **C**

24. A taxi charges $1.20 for the first $\frac{1}{5}$ mile and 50¢ for each additional $\frac{1}{5}$ mile. What is the best estimate for the cost of a 5-mile taxi ride?
    A. $13   B. $11   C. $15   D. $10
    24. **A**

25. Rosa bought a container of peanuts. She gave $\frac{1}{4}$ of it to one sister, $\frac{1}{3}$ to another, $\frac{1}{6}$ to her brother, and kept the rest for herself. How much did she keep?
    A. $\frac{1}{2}$ B. $\frac{1}{8}$ C. $\frac{3}{4}$ D. $\frac{1}{4}$
    25. **D**

BONUS Solve $\frac{1}{4} + \frac{5}{24} = x - \frac{3}{8}$.
    A. $\frac{5}{6}$ B. $\frac{1}{12}$ C. $\frac{5}{12}$ D. $\frac{6}{7}$
    A

38

Test and Review Generator software is provided in Apple, IBM, and Macintosh versions. You may use this software to create your own tests or worksheets, based on the needs of your students.

The **Performance Assessment Booklet** provides an alternate assessment for evaluating student progress. An assessment for this chapter can be found on pages 9–10.

6 An Introduction to Algebra

Previewing the Chapter

This chapter introduces algebra by exploring equations. This is done first by emphasizing the use of inverse operations and of models, such as cups and counters. Only later are the properties of equality introduced. Curriculum connections include geometry and measurement. In particular, equation solving skills are applied to the area formulas for rectangles and parallelograms. The **problem-solving strategy** of using an equation is also applied to a real-estate purchase.

Lesson	Lesson Objectives	NCTM Standards	State/Local Objectives
6-1	Solve equations using inverse operations.	1–7, 9, 10	
6-2A	Solve equations using models.	1–6, 9	
6-2	Solve equations using the addition and subtraction properties of equality.	1–7, 9	
6-3	Solve equations using the multiplication and division properties of equality.	1–7, 9	
6-3B	Solve two-step equations using models.	1–6, 9	
6-4	Write simple algebraic expressions from verbal phrases.	1–5, 9	
6-5	Solve problems by using an equation.	1–7, 9	
6-6	Change units in the customary system.	1–5, 7, 13	
6-7A	Use models to find the area of rectangles and parallelograms.	1–4, 12	
6-7	Find the area of rectangles and parallelograms.	1–5, 7, 9, 12	

Organizing the Chapter

A complete, 1-page lesson for each plan is provided for each lesson in the Lesson Plans Masters Booklet.

LESSON PLANNING GUIDE

Lesson	Materials/ Manipulatives	Extra Practice (Student Edition)	Blackline Masters Booklets									
			Study Guide	Practice	Enrichment	Evaluation	Technology	Lab Manual	Multicultural Activities	Application and Interdisciplinary Activities	Transparencies	Group Activity Cards
6-1		p. 585	p. 50	p. 50	p. 50		p. 20				6-1	6-1
6-2A	cups, counters, mats							p. 51				
6-2	calculator	p. 585	p. 51	p. 51	p. 51		p. 6				6-2	6-2
6-3	calculator	p. 585	p. 52	p. 52	p. 52				p. 6		6-3	6-3
6-3B	cups, counters, mats							p. 52				
6-4		p. 586	p. 53	p. 53	p. 53	Quiz A, p. 52				p. 20	6-4	6-4
6-5			p. 54	p. 54	p. 54						6-5	6-5
6-6		p. 586	p. 55	p. 55	p. 55						6-6	6-6
6-7A	grid paper scissors							p. 53				
6-7	grid paper calculator	p. 586	p. 56	p. 56	p. 56	Quiz B, p. 52				p. 6	6-7	6-7
Study Guide and Review			Multiple Choice Test, Forms 1A and 1B, pp. 46–49 Free Response Test, Forms 2A and 2B, pp. 50–51 Cumulative Review, p. 53 (free response)									
Test			Cumulative Test, p. 54 (multiple choice)									

Pacing Guide: Option I (Chapters 1–12) - 11 days; Option II (Chapters 1–13) - 11 days; Option III (Chapters 1–14) - 10 days
You may wish to refer to the complete **Course Planning Guides** on page T25.

OTHER CHAPTER RESOURCES

Student Edition
Chapter Opener, pp. 218–219
Save Planet Earth, p. 222
Mid-Chapter Review, p. 231
Portfolio Suggestions, pp. 231, 245
Academic Skills Test, pp. 250–251

 Manipulatives
Overhead Manipulative Resources
Middle School Mathematics Manipulative Kit

 Software/Technology
Interactive Mathematics Tools (Macintosh)
Test and Review Generator (IBM, Apple, Macintosh)
Teacher's Guide for Software Resources

Other Supplements
Transparency 6-0
Performance Assessment, pp. 11–12
Glencoe Mathematics Professional Series
Lesson Plans, pp. 61–70

INTERDISCIPLINARY BULLETIN BOARD

Science Connection

Objective Write and solve equations using data about some unique animals.

How To Use It Have students use the data on the bulletin board to formulate problems that can be solved by writing and solving equations. Then have them do research to uncover equally unique information to add to the bulletin board to be used for additional problem solving.

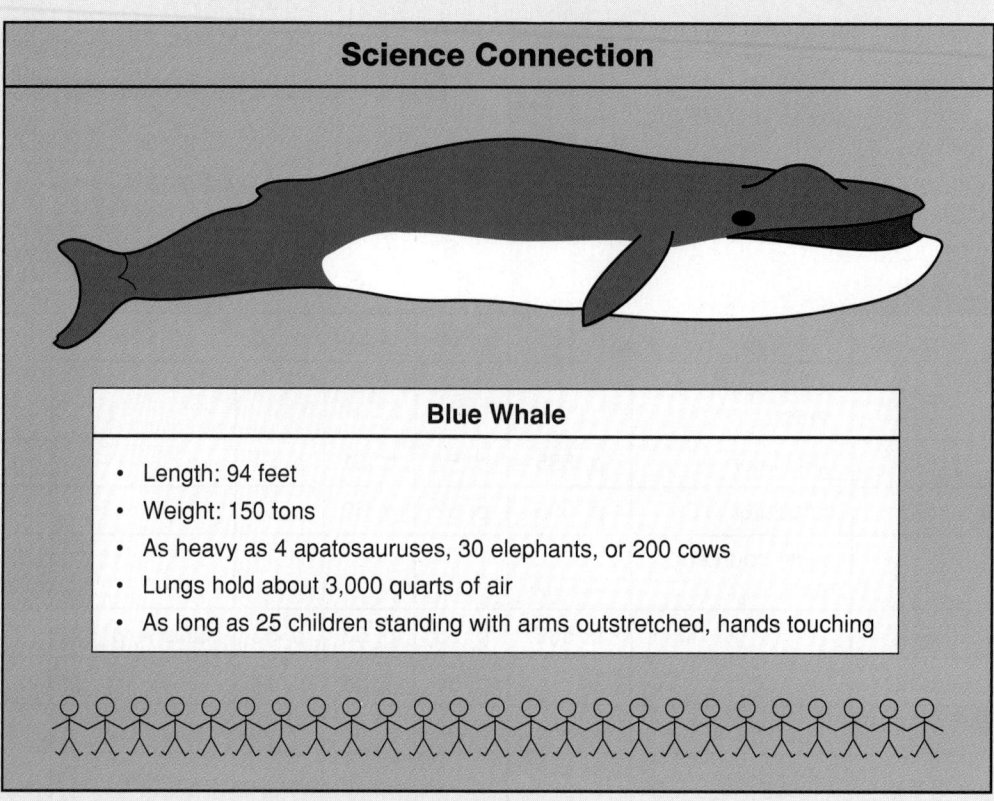

Science Connection

Blue Whale

- Length: 94 feet
- Weight: 150 tons
- As heavy as 4 apatosauruses, 30 elephants, or 200 cows
- Lungs hold about 3,000 quarts of air
- As long as 25 children standing with arms outstretched, hands touching

APPLICATIONS AND CONNECTIONS

Applications	Lesson	Example	Exercise
Sports	6-1		44, 45
Stock Market	6-2		38
Law Enforcement	6-2		39
Marketing	6-3	1	
Earning Money	6-3		30
Engineering	6-3		36
Energy	6-3		37
Computers	6-3		39
Biology	6-4		49
Highway Safety	6-6	1	
Biology	6-6		38
Construction	6-7		25
Connections			
Geometry	6-1		42
Statistics	6-1		43
Statistics	6-4		47

TEAM ACTIVITIES

Multicultural Experiences

Outside Field Trips A trip to a real estate office can be useful to students by showing them how algebraic formulas are used daily in the process of buying and selling property to determine downpayments and mortgage, tax, or maintenance payments.

During a visit to a bank or mortgage company, a mortgage broker can explain briefly to students how banks use formulas to determine how much money homebuyers can safely borrow.

In-Class Speakers Ask a delicatessen owner or worker to visit and show students the many food containers they use that are measured in customary units.

Ask a real estate developer or contractor to give a practical slant to area formulas by discussing sizes of lots and square footage of houses and buildings.

Supplementary Blackline Master Booklets

Some of the blackline masters for enhancing this chapter are shown below.

Application and Interdisciplinary Activity Masters, pp. 6, 20

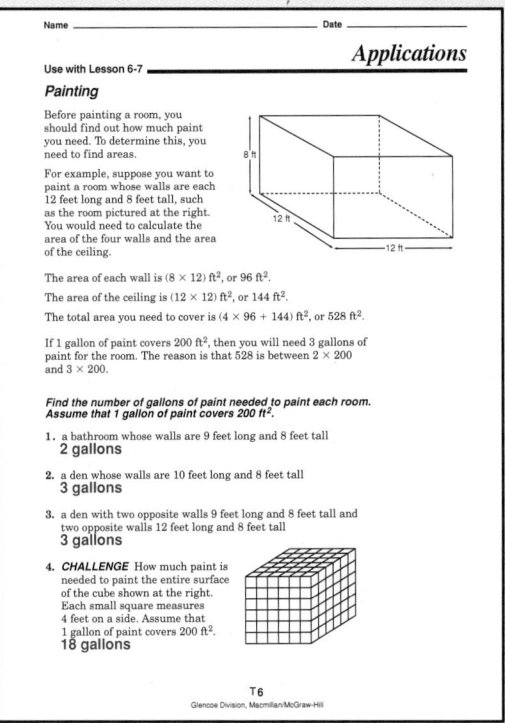

Name _____ Date _____

Applications

Use with Lesson 6-7

Painting

Before painting a room, you should find out how much paint you need. To determine this, you need to find areas.

For example, suppose you want to paint a room whose walls are each 12 feet long and 8 feet tall, such as the room pictured at the right. You would need to calculate the area of the four walls and the area of the ceiling.

The area of each wall is (8×12) ft², or 96 ft².

The area of the ceiling is (12×12) ft², or 144 ft².

The total area you need to cover is $(4 \times 96 + 144)$ ft², or 528 ft².

If 1 gallon of paint covers 200 ft², then you will need 3 gallons of paint for the room. The reason is that 528 is between 2×200 and 3×200.

Find the number of gallons of paint needed to paint each room. Assume that 1 gallon of paint covers 200 ft².

1. a bathroom whose walls are 9 feet long and 8 feet tall
   2 gallons

2. a den whose walls are 10 feet long and 8 feet tall
   3 gallons

3. a den with two opposite walls 9 feet long and 8 feet tall and two opposite walls 12 feet long and 8 feet tall
   3 gallons

4. *CHALLENGE* How much paint is needed to paint the entire surface of the cube shown at the right. Each small square measures 4 feet on a side. Assume that 1 gallon of paint covers 200 ft².
   18 gallons

T6
Glencoe Division, Macmillan/McGraw-Hill

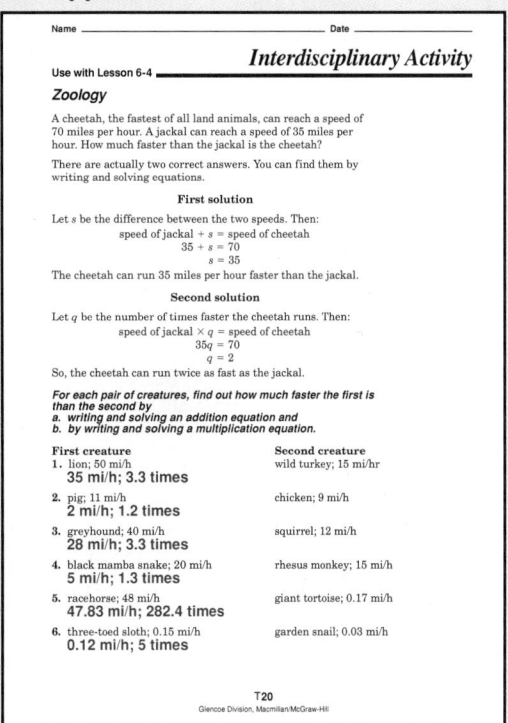

Name _____ Date _____

Interdisciplinary Activity

Use with Lesson 6-4

Zoology

A cheetah, the fastest of all land animals, can reach a speed of 70 miles per hour. A jackal can reach a speed of 35 miles per hour. How much faster than the jackal is the cheetah?

There are actually two correct answers. You can find them by writing and solving equations.

First solution

Let s be the difference between the two speeds. Then:

$$\text{speed of jackal} + s = \text{speed of cheetah}$$
$$35 + s = 70$$
$$s = 35$$

The cheetah can run 35 miles per hour faster than the jackal.

Second solution

Let q be the number of times faster the cheetah runs. Then:

$$\text{speed of jackal} \times q = \text{speed of cheetah}$$
$$35q = 70$$
$$q = 2$$

So, the cheetah can run twice as fast as the jackal.

For each pair of creatures, find out how much faster the first is than the second by
a. writing and solving an addition equation and
b. by writing and solving a multiplication equation.

	First creature	**Second creature**
1.	lion; 50 mi/h	wild turkey; 15 mi/hr
	35 mi/h; 3.3 times	
2.	pig; 11 mi/h	chicken; 9 mi/h
	2 mi/h; 1.2 times	
3.	greyhound; 40 mi/h	squirrel; 12 mi/h
	28 mi/h; 3.3 times	
4.	black mamba snake; 20 mi/h	rhesus monkey; 15 mi/h
	5 mi/h; 1.3 times	
5.	racehorse; 48 mi/h	giant tortoise; 0.17 mi/h
	47.83 mi/h; 282.4 times	
6.	three-toed sloth; 0.15 mi/h	garden snail; 0.03 mi/h
	0.12 mi/h; 5 times	

T20
Glencoe Division, Macmillan/McGraw-Hill

Multicultural Activity Masters, p. 6

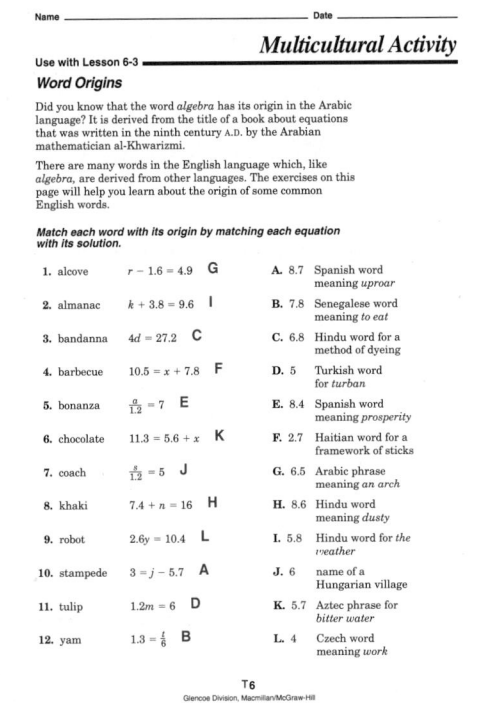

Name _____ Date _____

Multicultural Activity

Use with Lesson 6-3

Word Origins

Did you know that the word *algebra* has its origin in the Arabic language? It is derived from the title of a book about equations that was written in the ninth century A.D. by the Arabian mathematician al-Khwarizmi.

There are many words in the English language which, like *algebra*, are derived from other languages. The exercises on this page will help you learn about the origin of some common English words.

Match each word with its origin by matching each equation with its solution.

1. alcove	$r - 1.6 = 4.9$	**G**	A.	8.7	Spanish word meaning *uproar*
2. almanac	$k + 3.8 = 9.6$	**I**	B.	7.8	Senegalese word meaning *to eat*
3. bandanna	$4d = 27.2$	**C**	C.	6.8	Hindu word for a method of dyeing
4. barbecue	$10.5 = x + 7.8$	**F**	D.	5	Turkish word for *turban*
5. bonanza	$\frac{a}{1.2} = 7$	**E**	E.	8.4	Spanish word meaning *prosperity*
6. chocolate	$11.3 = 5.6 + x$	**K**	F.	2.7	Haitian word for a framework of sticks
7. coach	$\frac{s}{1.2} = 5$	**J**	G.	6.5	Arabic phrase meaning *an arch*
8. khaki	$7.4 + n = 16$	**H**	H.	8.6	Hindu word meaning *dusty*
9. robot	$2.6y = 10.4$	**L**	I.	5.8	Hindu word for *the weather*
10. stampede	$3 = j - 5.7$	**A**	J.	6	name of a Hungarian village
11. tulip	$1.2m = 6$	**D**	K.	5.7	Aztec phrase for *bitter water*
12. yam	$1.3 = \frac{4}{8}$	**B**	L.	4	Czech word meaning *work*

T6
Glencoe Division, Macmillan/McGraw-Hill

Technology Masters, p. 20

Name _____ Date _____

Computer Activity

Use with Lesson 6-1

Mental Math Game

The program below gives you addition, subtraction, or division equations to solve. Use mental math strategies to solve the equation. The program then checks your solution and corrects it. At the end, the computer displays the number of correct answers which you entered.

```
TYPE   NEW
       10   FOR K = 1 TO 10
       20   LET B = INT(RND(1) * 10) + 1
       30   LET C = INT(RND (1) * 20) + 10
       40   LET D = INT(RND(1) *3) + 1
       50   IF D = 1 THEN S$ ="+"
       60   IF D = 2 THEN S$ ="-"
       70   IF D = 3 THEN S$ ="/"
       80   PRINT "WHAT IS THE SOLUTION TO X";S$;B;"=";C;"?"
       90   INPUT P
       100  IF D = 1 THEN A = C - B
       110  IF D = 2 THEN A = C + B
       120  IF D = 3 THEN A = C * B
       130  IF A = P THEN 160
       140  PRINT "SORRY. THE CORRECT ANSWER IS ";A;"."
       150  GOTO 170
       160  J = J + 1: PRINT "GREAT!!"
       170  NEXT K
       180  PRINT "FINISHED. YOUR SCORE IS ";J;"/10.
       190  END
```

Partial Sample Run:

```
WHAT IS THE SOLUTION TO X/7 = 15?
? 105
GREAT!!
WHAT IS THE SOLUTION TO X - 10 = 11?
? 20
SORRY. THE CORRECT ANSWER IS 21.
WHAT IS THE SOLUTION TO X + 8 = 19?
? 11
GREAT!!

FINISHED. YOUR SCORE IS 7/10.
```

T20
Glencoe Division, Macmillan/McGraw-Hill

Recommended Outside Resources

Books/Periodicals

Litwiller, Bonnie and David Duncan, *Activities for the Maintenance of Computational Skills and the Discovery of Patterns,* Reston, VA: NCTM, 1980.

Weiss, Malcolm E., *666 Jelly Beans! All that? An Introduction to Algebra,* New York, NY: Crowell, 1976.

Films/Videotapes/Videodiscs

Equations in Algebra, Chicago, IL: International Film Bureau, Inc., 1963.

Length and Distance, Los Angeles, CA: Oxford Films, 1974.

The Story of Weights and Measures, 2nd ed., Chicago, IL: Coronet Films, 1973.

Software

Algebra Concepts, (Apple II, IBM/ Tandy, Macintosh), Ventura Educational Systems

For addresses of companies handling software, please refer to page T24.

This two-page introduction to the chapter provides a visual, relevant way to engage students in the mathematics of the chapter. Questions are included that help students see the need to learn the mathematics in the chapter. Data in charts and graphs provide statistical information that students can analyze and interpret at this point as well as later in the chapter. The Chapter Project provides an activity that applies the mathematics of the chapter.

MAKING MATHEMATICS RELEVANT

Spotlight on Temperature

Examining temperature provides students with an opportunity to apply some of the mathematics of the chapter, for example using an equation to represent a relationship between two temperatures.

Chapter

6

An Introduction to Algebra

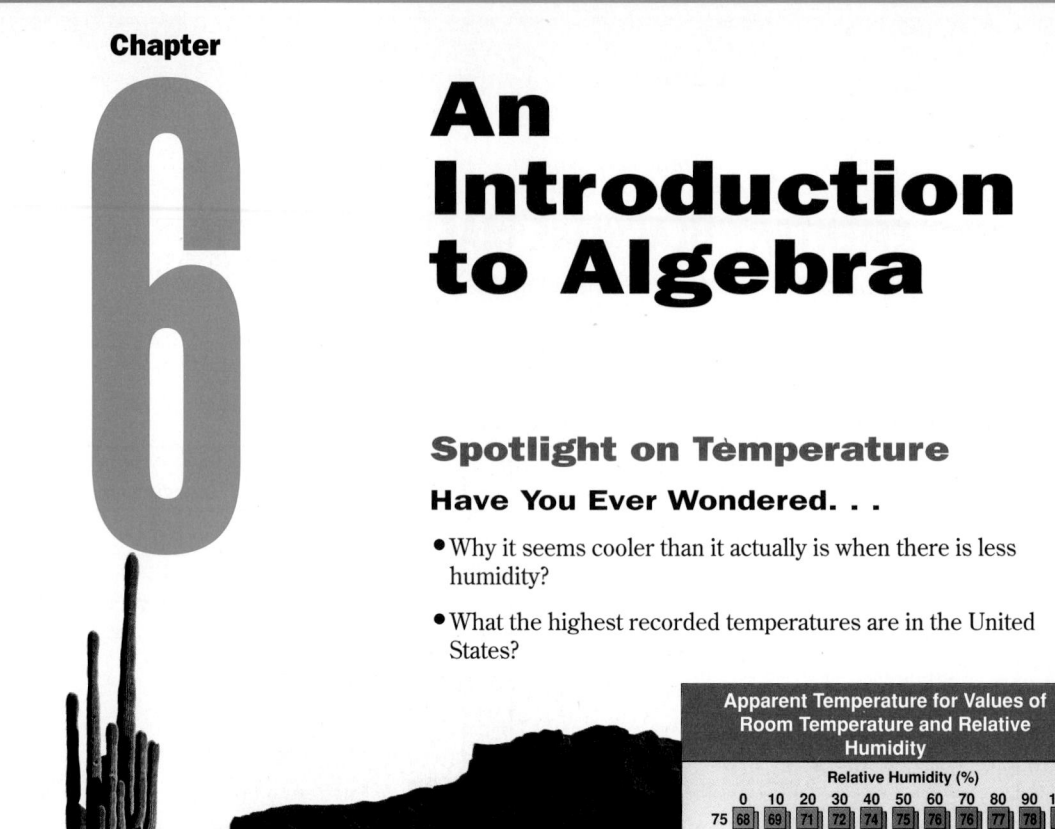

Spotlight on Temperature

Have You Ever Wondered. . .

- Why it seems cooler than it actually is when there is less humidity?

- What the highest recorded temperatures are in the United States?

Apparent Temperature for Values of Room Temperature and Relative Humidity

Room Temperature (°F)	Relative Humidity (%)										
	0	10	20	30	40	50	60	70	80	90	100
75	68	69	71	72	74	75	76	76	77	78	79
74	66	68	69	71	72	73	74	75	76	77	78
73	65	67	68	70	71	72	73	74	75	76	77
72	64	65	67	68	70	71	72	73	74	75	76
71	63	64	66	67	68	70	71	72	73	74	75
70	63	64	65	66	67	68	69	70	71	72	
69	62	63	64	65	66	67	68	69	70	71	72
68	61	62	63	64	65	66	67	68	69	70	71
67	60	61	62	63	64	65	66	67	68	68	69

218

"Have You Ever Wondered?" Answers

- If the air is very dry, perspiration is more readily absorbed by the air, cooling the skin. Thus, the temperature appears to be cooler than it otherwise would.

- The highest recorded temperature is 134° F, in California.

Recorded Highest Temperatures for Selected States

States (top to bottom): Alaska, Arizona, Arkansas, California, Georgia, Mississippi, Missouri, Nevada, New Hampshire, Ohio, Oklahoma, Tennesee, Texas, Virginia, Washingtion

Degrees (°F): 100, 102, 104, 106, 108, 110, 112, 114, 116, 118, 120, 122, 124, 126, 128, 130, 132, 134, 136

Looking Ahead

In this chapter, you will see how mathematics can be used to answer the questions about temperature and humidity. The major objectives of the chapter are to:

- write simple algebraic expressions
- solve equations by using mental math, models, and inverse operations
- solve addition, subtraction, multiplication, and division equations
- find the area of rectangles and parallelograms

Chapter Project

Temperature

Work in a group.

1. Keep a chart of the high temperature in your community each day for one month.

2. Be creative in showing what the temperature was on each day.

3. Show how the temperature on each day of the month varied (higher or lower) from the temperature on the first day of the project. Include any other descriptions about the weather that would help make your presentation clearer.

DATA ANALYSIS

Have students examine the tables. Ask them whether they live in an area that has either high or low humidity compared to other parts of the country. Ask them how altitude, proximity of bodies of water, and other geographic features affect actual temperature. Then have them tell the highest and lowest temperatures they have ever experienced, or to recall the greatest difference in high and low temperatures they remember experiencing in one day.

Data Search

A question related to these data is provided in Lesson 6-6, page 240, Exercise 39.

CHAPTER PROJECT

Suggest that group members take turns gathering and recording the information. If it suits your class schedule, you may consider shortening the project. Encourage students to be creative when making their presentations. Have students use simple equations to show how temperatures vary from the temperature recorded on the first day.

NCTM Standards: 1–7, 9, 10

Lesson Resources
- Study Guide Master 6-1
- Practice Master 6-1
- Enrichment Master 6-1
- Technology Master, p. 20
- Group Activity Card 6-1

 Transparency 6-1 contains the 5-Minute Check and a teaching aid for this lesson.

⏱ 5-Minute Check
(Over Chapter 5)

Solve each equation. Write each solution in simplest form.

1. $\frac{2}{3} + \frac{5}{6} = x$ $1\frac{1}{2}$

2. $t = \frac{3}{4} - \frac{1}{9}$ $\frac{23}{36}$

3. $2\frac{5}{12} + \frac{7}{8} = y$ $3\frac{7}{24}$

4. Find the circumference if $r = \frac{7}{8}$ in. Use $\pi \approx \frac{22}{7}$.
$5\frac{1}{2}$ in.

5. Compute mentally:
$8 \times 3\frac{1}{8}$ 25

---

1 FOCUS

Motivating the Lesson

Situational Problem Present the following problem: *Sal has 8 coins and a balance scale. All the coins look alike, but one is fake, and weighs less than the others. How can Sal find the fake coin using only two weighings on the scale?*

2 TEACH

Using Models Provide students with a balance scale and pennies. Have them place an unequal number of pennies on each pan. Ask students what they can do to get the scale to balance. Have students write equations to express their solutions.

6-1 Solving Equations Using Inverse Operations

Objective
Solve equations using inverse operations.

Words to Learn
inverse operation

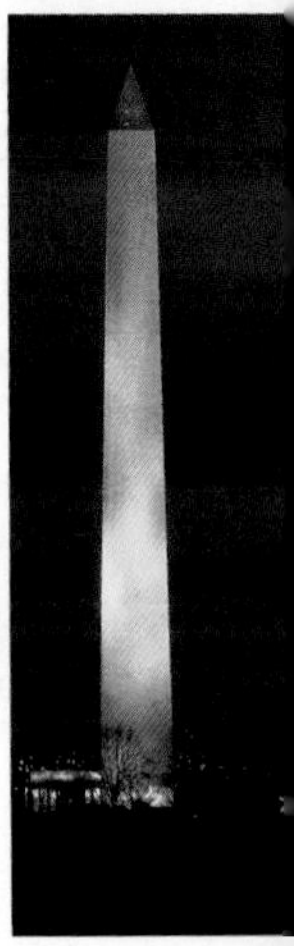

The Washington Monument is located in Washington, D.C., and stands 555 feet tall. The Gateway to the West Arch is located in St. Louis and is our nation's tallest monument. The Washington Monument is 75 feet shorter than the Arch. How tall is the Arch?

Let a be the height of the Arch. Then the equation $555 = a - 75$ can be used to solve the problem.

You could solve this equation by using mental math. But, as the numbers get larger or more difficult for mental math, you need another strategy. One such strategy is described below.

LOOKBACK
You can review variables on page 28.

$$555 = a - 75$$
$$555 + 75 = a \qquad \textit{Undo the subtraction by adding.}$$
$$630 = a \qquad \textit{Check: } 555 = 630 - 75$$

The height of the Arch is 630 feet.

You can undo the operation because addition and subtraction are **inverse operations.** *Related* addition and subtraction sentences are shown below.

$$11 + 4 = 15 \rightarrow 15 - 11 = 4 \qquad 18 + d = 24 \rightarrow 24 - 18 = d$$
$$\rightarrow 15 - 4 = 11 \qquad\qquad\qquad \rightarrow 24 - d = 18$$

Examples

Solve each equation by using inverse operations. This can be shown by writing a related sentence.

1 $\quad t - 5 = 11$
$\quad t = 11 + 5 \qquad \textit{Write a related addition sentence.}$
$\quad t = 16 \qquad\quad \textit{Check: } 16 - 5 = 11$

Estimation Hint
•••••••••••••
In Example 2, think
$b + 4 = 13$.
The solution is
about 9.

2 $\quad b + 3\frac{1}{5} = 12\frac{3}{5}$
$\quad b = 12\frac{3}{5} - 3\frac{1}{5} \qquad \textit{Write a related subtraction sentence.}$
$\quad b = 9\frac{2}{5}$

Similarly, multiplication and division are *inverse operations. Related* multiplication and division sentences are shown below.

$$7 \cdot 8 = 56 \rightarrow 56 \div 7 = 8 \qquad 7m = 35 \rightarrow 35 \div 7 = m$$
$$\rightarrow 56 \div 8 = 7 \qquad\qquad\qquad \rightarrow 35 \div m = 7$$

OPTIONS

Reteaching Activity

Using Modeling Make a simple balance scale using a wire hanger and small sandwich bags taped to each end. Place about 15 marbles in one bag and fewer marbles in the other. Ask students to write a number sentence for the number of marbles they must add to the lighter bag to make the scale balance.

Study Guide Masters, p. 50

Name _____   Date _____

Study Guide Worksheet 6-1

Solving Equations Using Inverse Operations

Addition and subtraction are inverse operations. You can undo addition by subtracting. You can undo subtraction by adding.

Examples $r + 2.4 = 7.8$
$\quad r = 7.8 - 2.4 \qquad$ Write a related subtraction sentence.
$\quad r = 5.4$

$\quad 3.3 = m - 1.9$
$\quad 3.3 + 1.9 = m \qquad$ Write a related addition sentence.
$\quad 5.2 = m$

Multiplication and division are inverse operations. You can undo multiplication by dividing. You can undo division by multiplying.

Examples $\frac{k}{3} = 1.5$
$\quad k = 1.5 \cdot 3 \qquad$ Write a related multiplication sentence.
$\quad k =$

3 $\frac{m}{2} = 7$

$m = 7 \cdot 2$ *Write a related multiplication sentence.*

$m = 14$

4 $2.3n = 75$

$n = 75 \div 2.3$ *Write a related division sentence.*

$75 \boxed{\div} 2.3 \boxed{=} 32.608695$

$n \approx 32.6$ Round to the nearest tenth.   *≈ means "is approximately equal to"*

Teaching Tip In Example 4, suggest that students estimate first so that they know whether their solution is reasonable.

More Examples

Solve each equation by using inverse operations.

For Example 1

$r - 4 = 12$ 16

For Example 2

$a + 2\frac{1}{4} = 13\frac{1}{4}$ 11

For Example 3

$\frac{n}{4} = 3$ 12

For Example 4

$2.5m = 24$ 9.6

Checking for Understanding

Communicating Mathematics

Read and study the lesson to answer each question.

1. **Tell** what the inverse of a temperature increase of three degrees would be.   **a decrease of 3 degrees**

2. **Tell** the operation you would use to undo subtraction.   **addition**

3. **Write** an open sentence using multiplication. Then write two related division sentences.   **See students' work.**

Guided Practice

For each sentence, write a related sentence using the inverse operation.

4. $3 + 5 = 8$ $8 - 5 = 3$
5. $9 - 5 = 4$ $4 + 5 = 9$
6. $m + 7 = 19$ $19 - 7 = m$

7. $n - 12 = 21$ $21 + 12 = n$
8. $6 \cdot 5 = 30$ $30 \div 5 = 6$
9. $\frac{54}{9} = 6$ $6 \cdot 9 = 54$

10. $\frac{a}{2} = 13$ $13 \cdot 2 = a$
11. $c = 3 \cdot 14$ $c \div 3 = 14$
12. $4e = 48$ $48 \div 4 = e$

Checking for Understanding

Exercises 1-3 are designed to help you assess students' understanding through reading, writing, speaking, and modeling. You should work through these exercises with your students and then monitor their work on Guided Practice Exercises 4-12.

Exercises

Independent Practice

Solve each equation by using the inverse operation. Round to the nearest tenth.

13. $f + 7 = 15$ **8**
14. $l + 4 = 13$ **9**
15. $9 + n = 16$ **7**

16. $t - 5 = 17$ **22**
17. $p - 9 = 22$ **31**
18. $63 = r - 8$ **71**

19. $\frac{a}{6} = 19$ **114**
20. $\frac{b}{7} = 25$ **175**
21. $60 = \frac{c}{5}$ **300**

22. $4d = 64$ **16**
23. $9e = 104$ **11.6**
24. $102 = 6g$ **17**

25. $n + 3.8 = 17.2$ **13.4**
26. $m + 14.1 = 26.5$ **12.4**

27. $1\frac{3}{4} = r + \frac{1}{2}$ **$1\frac{1}{4}$**
28. $s - 5.6 = 8.9$ **14.5**

29. $t - 18.8 = 3.2$ **22**
30. $5\frac{3}{8} = d - 1\frac{1}{4}$ **$6\frac{5}{8}$**

31. $\frac{x}{2.3} = 4$ **9.2**
32. $\frac{y}{4.7} = 3.9$ **18.3**

33. $5.6 = \frac{z}{2.4}$ **13.4**
34. $1.8a = 9.72$ **5.4**

35. What is the solution to $2.6b = 2.08$?   **0.8**

36. Solve the equation $0.79 = 0.6c$.   **1.3**

Practice Masters, p. 50

Name _____ Date _____

Practice Worksheet 6-1

Solving Equations Using Inverse Operations

For each sentence, write a related sentence using the inverse operation.

1. $14 + 13 = 27$ $27 - 13 = 14$
2. $\frac{72}{8} = 9$ $9 \cdot 8 = 72$
3. $16 - 12 = 4$ $16 = 4 + 12$

4. $w + 15 = 32$ $w = 32 - 15$
5. $92 = s \cdot 16$ $92 \div 16 = s$
6. $6y = 48$ $y = 48 \div 6$

Solve each equation by using the inverse operation. Round decimal answers to the nearest tenth.

7. $y + 8 = 19$ 11
8. $4 + x = 12$ 8
9. $\frac{w}{?} + 2 = 9$ 7

10. $p - 10 = 15$ 25
11. $z - 13 = 24$ 37
12. $73 = t - 24$ 97

13. $\frac{b}{8} = 32$ 256
14. $\frac{g}{5} = 44$ 220
15. $22 = \frac{d}{7}$ 154

16. $6c = 78$ 13
17. $4h = 108$ 27
18. $78 = 5y$ 15.6

19. $x + 4.1 = 18.6$ 14.5
20. $r - 4.8 = 9.6$ 14.4
21. $6.4a = 7.2$ 1.1

22. $2\frac{3}{4} = y + 1\frac{1}{4}$ $1\frac{1}{4}$
23. $9\frac{7}{9} = m - 2\frac{1}{5}$ $12\frac{7}{45}$
24. $7.9 = \frac{g}{2.3}$ 18.2

T50

Glencoe Division, Macmillan/McGraw-Hill

Bell Ringer

Write the following addition magic square on the chalkboard. Have students fill in the boxes to complete the square. Then challenge them to create one of their own.

8.0	6.4	6.0	2.0
5.2	2.8	10.4	4.0
3.6	4.4	4.8	9.6
5.6	8.8	1.2	6.8

Watch for students who use incorrect related number sentences.

Prevent by emphasizing which operations undo others, and by having these students use smaller numbers initially.

Close

Have students solve the equation $g + 263 = 473$ to find the size of the George Washington Carver National Monument. It is 263 acres smaller than the 473-acre Casa Grande National Monument. **210 acres**

3 PRACTICE/APPLY

Assignment Guide
Maximum: 13–46
Minimum: 13–35 odd, 37–41, 43, 45

For **Extra Practice,** see p. 585.

Alternate Assessment
Writing Have students write an equation with one variable for a partner to solve by writing and solving a related sentence.

Enrichment Masters, p. 50

Name _____ Date _____

Enrichment Worksheet 6-1

A Double-6 Pattern

Twenty-eight dominoes, from 0-0 to 6-6, are used to form the double-6 pattern below.

The dominoes are placed such that adjacent half-tiles must show the same number. Use trial-and-error and logical reasoning to complete the pattern.

Arrange the 28 dominoes in the double-6 set to form this pattern.

T50
Glencoe Division, Macmillan/McGraw-Hill

222

Mixed Review 37. Estimate the quotient $\$4{,}724 \div 6$. *(Lesson 1-3)* **about $800**

38. **Smart Shopping** Pilar bought 3.75 pounds of beef that is priced at $2.29 a pound. Find the total amount she spent on the beef. *(Lesson 2-4)* **$8.59**

39. **Statistics** Construct a stem-and-leaf plot for 12, 7, 23, 9, 10, 20, 0, 4, 19, 13, 5, 7, 2, 13, 18, and 2. *(Lesson 3-6)* **See Solutions Manual.**

40. Write $\frac{18}{24}$ in simplest form. *(Lesson 4-6)* $\frac{3}{4}$

41. Divide $4\frac{2}{5}$ by $\frac{1}{2}$. *(Lesson 5-10)* $8\frac{4}{5}$

Problem Solving and Applications

42. **Geometry** Suppose that the sum of the measures of two angles is 180°. One angle measures 96°. Solve the equation $a + 96 = 180$ to find a, the measure of the second angle. **84°**

43. **Statistics** The range of a set of scores is found by subtracting the lowest score from the highest. The range of a set of scores is 54 and the lowest score is 44. Solve the equation $s - 44 = 54$ to find s, the highest score. **98**

44. 6.25 meters per second

DATA SEARCH

44. **Sports** A skateboarder travels 100 meters in 16 seconds. Solve the equation $100 = 16r$ to find r, the average speed in meters per second.

45. **Data Search** Refer to page 651. If a 12-year old boy weighs 35.9 kg, by how much does his weight differ from the average? **1.8 kg. less**

46. **Critical Thinking** Think about the division sentence $\frac{3}{0} = h$ and its related multiplication sentence, $0 \cdot h = 3$. Use these sentences to explain why division by 0 is not defined. **0 times anything equals 0, thus the equation would read $0 = 3$ which is not possible.**

Save Planet Earth

Plant a Tree The atmosphere that covers the surface of Earth traps the heat of the sun near Earth. Without this *greenhouse effect*, temperatures on Earth would be about 59 degrees lower than they are today. Certain gases, called *greenhouse gases*, warm Earth even more. While the greenhouse gases are necessary, overproduction of these gases and the depletion of oxygen and other gases could cause Earth to become too warm. This could kill valuable small organisms which oxidize the water in the oceans and feed other animals, or it could even eventually melt the polar ice cap.

How You Can Help
One way to help maintain the delicate balance in the atmosphere is to plant a tree. Trees use carbon dioxide, the main greenhouse gas, and produce oxygen. So trees not only make the world a more beautiful place, they make it a more livable place.

OPTIONS

Extending the Lesson

Save Planet Earth Ask students to investigate other benefits of planting trees. Also, explore programs involving tree planting in your community.

Comparative Learning Activity

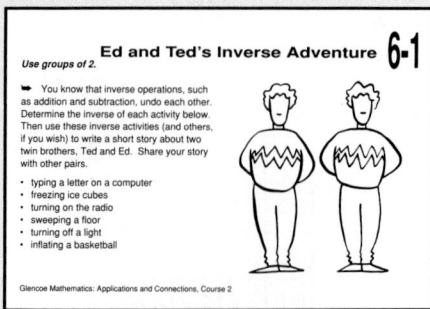

Ed and Ted's Inverse Adventure **6-1**

Use groups of 2.

➡ You know that inverse operations, such as addition and subtraction, undo each other. Determine the inverse of each activity below. Then use these inverse activities (and others, if you wish) to write a short story about two twin brothers, Ted and Ed. Share your story with other pairs.

• typing a letter on a computer
• freezing ice cubes
• turning on the radio
• sweeping a floor
• turning off a light
• inflating a basketball

Glencoe Mathematics: Applications and Connections, Course 2

6-2A Solving Equations Using Models

A Preview of Lesson 6-2

Objective

Solve equations using models.

Materials

cups
counters
mats

In the preceding lesson, you learned to solve an equation by using inverse operations. In this lab, you will use models to discover another method for solving equations.

Activity One

Work with a partner.

In this lab, a counter represents 1 and a cup represents the variable.

- Find the solution to the equation $x + 3 = 5$ by using models.

- On the first mat, place a cup and 3 counters. On the second mat, place 5 counters.

- To find the value of x, remove (subtract) 3 counters from the first mat and 3 counters from the second mat.

- The solution is $x = 2$.

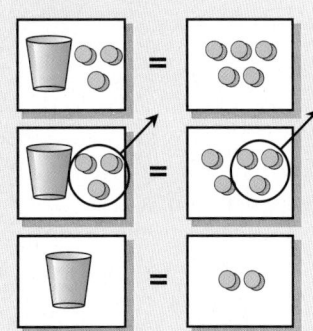

What do you think?

1. Using the models, how could you check your solution? **Substitute 2 counters for x (the cup).**
2. Study the model. In your own words, what did you do to find the solution? **Removed 3 from each side.**

Mathematics Lab 6-2A Solving Equations Using Models **223**

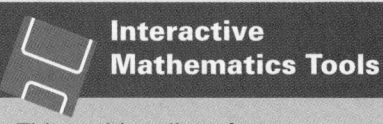

Interactive Mathematics Tools

This multimedia software provides an interactive lesson that is tied directly to Lesson 6-2A. Students will click and drag cups and counters to solve equations.

NCTM Standards: 1–7, 9

Management Tips

For Students Each group of students will need 5 cups and 24 counters. The counters can be anything uniform in size, such as coins, buttons, or peanuts.

For the Overhead Projector
Overhead Manipulative Resources provides appropriate materials for teacher or student demonstration of the activities in this Mathematics Lab.

1 FOCUS

Introducing the Lab

Ask students to recall the meaning of variables. Have them suggest ways to use counters and cups to represent variables and to model the solving of equations.

Using Discussion Discuss with students what a "solution" to an equation means. Have a student or partners in each group model the solution process while other group members watch. Ask students to discuss how removing the same number of counters from each mat provides the solution to the equation.

3 PRACTICE/APPLY

Using Communication Have students use one of the given equations to explain how they can use models to solve equations involving addition. You may wish to ask students to demonstrate how they could use models to solve an equation such as $x - 4 = 8$.

Close

Have students solve an addition or multiplication equation using different models. Ask them to explain what they do to find the solution.

---

3. Repeat Activity 1 for the equations $w + 7 = 12$ and $8 + b = 14$. Explain to your group how you arrived at your solutions. **Answers will vary.**
4. Draw a picture of the steps taken to find the solution to the equation $m + 5 = 11$. **See students' work.**

Activity Two

- Find the solution to the equation $4x = 12$ by using models.

- Place 4 cups on the first mat. On the second mat, place 12 counters.

- Each cup must contain the same number of counters.

What do you think?

5. How would you complete the model shown above to find the value of x? *(Hint: Separate each side into the same number of groups.)* **Divide both sides into 4 equal parts.**
6. What is the solution? **3**

7. How could you check your solution? **multiply**

8. In your own words, what did you do to find the solution? **Split the counters into 4 groups.**
9. Repeat the activity for the equations $5e = 20$ and $2t = 24$. Explain to your group how you arrived at your solutions. **Answers will vary.**

10. Draw a picture of the steps taken to find the solution to the equation $3n = 18$. **See students' work.**

11. Write two equations that are related to $7q = 63$. How are they related to each other? $q = \frac{63}{7}$; $7 = \frac{63}{q}$; q **always equals 9.**

Extension

12. In the equation $x + 9 = 15$, 9 was added to x. To solve it, you subtracted 9. Suppose you were solving the equation $2x - 3 = 13$. What operations would you use with 2 and 3 to find x? **addition, division**

OPTIONS

Lab Manual You may wish to make copies of the blackline master on p. 51 of the *Lab Manual* for students to use as a recording sheet.

Lab Manual, p. 51

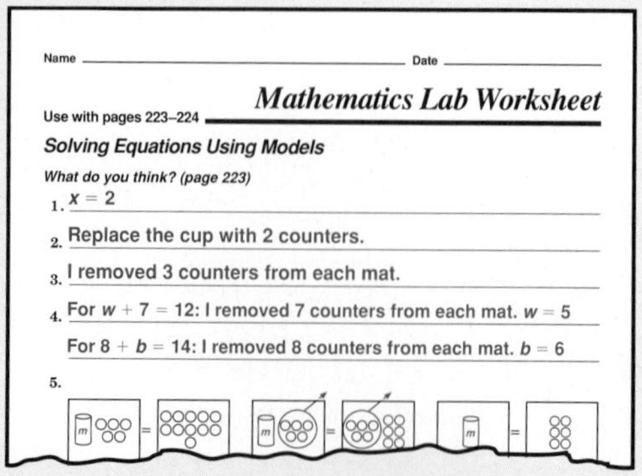

Name _____   Date _____

Mathematics Lab Worksheet

Use with pages 223–224

Solving Equations Using Models

What do you think? (page 223)

1. $x = 2$
2. Replace the cup with 2 counters.
3. I removed 3 counters from each mat.
4. For $w + 7 = 12$: I removed 7 counters from each mat. $w = 5$
   For $8 + b = 14$: I removed 8 counters from each mat. $b = 6$
5.

6-2 Solving Addition and Subtraction Equations

Objective

Solve equations using the addition and subtraction properties of equality.

Words to Learn

equivalent equations
addition property
 of equality
subtraction
 property of equality

Orville and Wilbur Wright repaired bicycles for a living, but dreamed of inventing a flying machine. On December 17, 1903, in Kitty Hawk, North Carolina, they flew their airplane called the *Flyer I* for the first time. Wilbur was the first to fly the plane, but his flight ended up being 244 feet shorter than Orville's. If Wilbur flew a total of 120 feet, how long was Orville's flight?

Let f represent the number of feet Orville flew the plane. Then, use the equation $f - 244 = 120$ to solve the problem.

In the previous Mathematics Lab, you learned that an equation can be solved by keeping the equation balanced. If you add or subtract the same quantity to or from each side of the equation, the result is an equation that has the same solution. Such equations are called **equivalent equations.**

Solve $f - 244 = 120$.

$$f - 244 = 120$$
$$f - 244 + 244 = 120 + 244 \quad \textit{Add 244 to each side.}$$
$$f = 364 \quad \text{The solution is 364. Orville flew 364 feet.}$$

The property that was used to add 244 to both sides of the equation is called the **addition property of equality.**

Addition Property of Equality	In words: If you add the same number to each side of an equation, then the two sides remain equal.
	Arithmetic **Algebra**
	$4 = 4$ $a = b$
	$4 + 3 = 4 + 3$ $a + c = b + c$
	$7 = 7$

There is a similar property when subtraction is used.

Subtraction Property of Equality	In words: If you subtract the same number from each side of an equation, then the two sides remain equal.
	Arithmetic **Algebra**
	$4 = 4$ $a = b$
	$4 - 3 = 4 - 3$ $a - c = b - c$
	$1 = 1$

Lesson 6-2 Solving Addition and Subtraction Equations **225**

Checking for Understanding

Exercises 1–4 are designed to help you assess students' understanding through reading, writing, speaking, and modeling. You should work through these exercises with your students and then monitor their work on Guided Practice Exercises 5–13.

Additional Answer

35. Range: 20; Scale: 20–50; Interval: 5

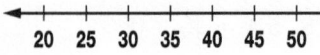

226

Examples

Solve each equation. Check your solution.

1 $x + 3.6 = 12.4$
$x + 3.6 - 3.6 = 12.4 - 3.6$ *Subtract 3.6 from each side.*
$12.4 \boxed{-} 3.6 \boxed{=} 8.8$
$x = 8.8$

Check: $x + 3.6 = 12.4$
$8.8 \boxed{+} 3.6 \boxed{=} 12.4$ *Replace x with 8.8.*
$12.4 = 12.4 \checkmark$ The solution is 8.8.

LOOK BACK

You can review adding and subtracting fractions on page 185.

2 $8\frac{2}{3} + m = 15\frac{1}{6}$
$8\frac{2}{3} - 8\frac{2}{3} + m = 15\frac{1}{6} - 8\frac{2}{3}$ *Subtract $8\frac{2}{3}$ from each side.*
$m = 14\frac{7}{6} - 8\frac{4}{6}$ $15\frac{1}{6} = 14\frac{7}{6}, 8\frac{2}{3} = 8\frac{4}{6}$
$m = 6\frac{3}{6}$ or $6\frac{1}{2}$

Check: $8\frac{2}{3} + m = 15\frac{1}{6}$
$8\frac{2}{3} + 6\frac{1}{2} \stackrel{?}{=} 15\frac{1}{6}$ *Replace m with $6\frac{1}{2}$.*
$8\frac{4}{6} + 6\frac{3}{6} \stackrel{?}{=} 15\frac{1}{6}$ $8\frac{2}{3} = 8\frac{4}{6}, 6\frac{1}{2} = 6\frac{3}{6}$
$14\frac{7}{6} \stackrel{?}{=} 15\frac{1}{6}$
$15\frac{1}{6} = 15\frac{1}{6} \checkmark$ The solution is $6\frac{1}{2}$.

Checking for Understanding

Communicating Mathematics

Read and study the lesson to answer each question. **Substitute the number back in the equation.**

1. **Tell** how to check your solution to an equation. **in the equation.**
2. **Model** the equation $y + 3 = 9$. Use the model to solve the equation. **6**
3. **Tell** whether $m + 5 = 14$ and $m = 9$ are equivalent equations. Explain why or why not. **Yes, $m = 9$ in both equations.**
4. **Write** a sentence or two explaining how to solve $d - 8 = 12$. **Add 8 to both sides; $12 + 8 = 20$, so $d = 20$.**

Guided Practice

Complete the solution of each equation.

6. 14, 22, 14
7. 19, 19, 19

5. $p + 21 = 46$
$p + 21 - 21 = 46 - \underline{?}$ **21**
$p = \underline{?}$ **25**

6. $t - 14 = 22$
$t - 14 + \underline{?} = \underline{?} + \underline{?}$
$t = \underline{?}$ **36**

7. $58 = s + 19$
$58 - \underline{?} = s + \underline{?} - \underline{?}$
$\underline{?} = s$ **39**

Solve each equation. Check your solution.

8. $a + 3 = 12$ **9**
9. $k - 7.2 = 4.5$ **11.7**
10. $m - 8 = 13$ **21**
11. $2\frac{1}{4} + p = 6\frac{1}{2}$ **$4\frac{1}{4}$**
12. $27 = 18 + g$ **9**
13. $b - 4\frac{1}{3} = 3\frac{5}{12}$ **$7\frac{3}{4}$**

226   Chapter 6 An Introduction to Algebra

OPTIONS

Limited English Proficiency

Review the terms *variable*, *balanced*, and *equation* before beginning the lesson. As you introduce the properties of equality, write the terms and examples on the chalkboard. Do the same as you

introduce the concept of equivalent equations. Have the students verbalize these new terms. Repeat their answers.

Exercises

Independent Practice

Solve each equation. Check your solution.

14. $32 + c = 56$ **24**

15. $m + 18 = 34$ **16**

16. $x + 27 = 39$ **12**

17. $y + 43 = 68$ **25**

18. $17\frac{3}{4} + a = 51\frac{1}{8}$ **$33\frac{3}{8}$**

19. $35 + n = 73$ **38**

20. $b - 63 = 14$ **77**

21. $e - 56 = 17$ **73**

22. $h - 13 = 47$ **60**

23. $42\frac{1}{4} = k - 5\frac{1}{6}$ **$47\frac{5}{12}$**

24. $102 = x - 15$ **117**

25. $44 = f - 83$ **127**

26. $a + 3.9 = 5.6$ **1.7**

27. $e + 11.8 = 13.1$ **1.3**

28. $p + 4.7 = 13.2$ **8.5**

29. $s - 5.9 = 4.8$ **10.7**

30. $e - 0.4 = 14.3$ **14.7**

31. $h - 28\frac{2}{5} = 47\frac{2}{3}$ **$76\frac{1}{15}$**

32. Solve the equation $46 + f = 98$. **52**

33. Find the solution to $e - 6.9 = 13.3$. **20.2**

Mixed Review

34. Express 9,800 in scientific notation. *(Lesson 2-6)* **9.8×10^3**

35. **Statistics** Find the range and appropriate scale and interval for 45, 29, 31, 38, and 25. Then draw a number line to show the scale and interval. *(Lesson 3-3)* **See margin.**

36. Find the LCM for 8 and 12. *(Lesson 4-9)* **24**

37. Solve the equation $\frac{r}{12} = 4$. *(Lesson 6-1)* **48**

Problem Solving and Applications

38. **Stock Market** Cho purchased a share of Hershey's stock at $38\frac{1}{4}$. The next month it was selling for $40\frac{3}{8}$.

   a. Solve the equation $38\frac{1}{4} + m = 40\frac{3}{8}$ to find the value of m, the increase in the stock. **$2\frac{1}{8}$**

   b. How much would Cho make if she sold her stock? **$2.13**

39. **Law Enforcement** At the end of each working day, highway police must report the total amount of time spent performing certain types of tasks. During one 8-hour shift, an officer spent 30 minutes aiding vehicles in distress, $1\frac{3}{4}$ hours at the scene of an accident, and 2 hours 30 minutes writing tickets.

   a. How much time did the officer spend doing these tasks? **$4\frac{3}{4}$ hours**

   b. Use the equation $a + \frac{1}{2} + 1\frac{3}{4} + 2\frac{1}{2} = 8$ to find a, the amount of time the officer spent performing other tasks. **$3\frac{1}{4}$ hours**

40. **Critical Thinking** Place one of the digits 1, 2, 4, 5, 6, and 8 in each of the boxes so that a true sentence results. Use each digit exactly once. **A sample answer is shown below.**

   8 5   6 1   2 4

41. **Journal Entry** How do you solve an addition or subtraction equation? How do you know when to add and when to subtract? **See students' work.**

Lesson 6-2 Solving Addition and Subtraction Equations **227**

Extending the Lesson

Using Cooperative Groups Have each student in the group write an equation and read it to the group. Each member must write a word problem that can be solved by solving each of the equations. Have students solve each other's problems.

Cooperative Learning Activity

Number of players: 2
Materials: Index cards

Double Take 6-2

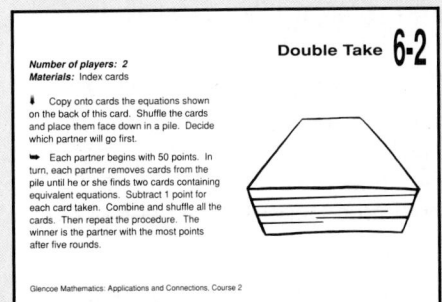

✦ Copy onto cards the equations shown on the back of this card. Shuffle the cards and place them down in a pile. Decide which partner will go first.

✦ Each partner begins with 50 points. In turn, each partner removes cards from the pile until he or she finds two cards containing equivalent equations. Subtract 1 point for each card taken. Combine and shuffle all the cards. Then repeat the procedure. The winner is the partner with the most points after five rounds.

Glencoe Mathematics: Applications and Connections, Course 2

Close

Have students explain and then show by example how solving equations by using properties of equality differs from solving them by using inverse operations.

3 PRACTICE/APPLY

Assignment Guide

Maximum: 14–41

Minimum: 15–33 odd, 34–38, 40

For **Extra Practice,** see p. 585.

Alternate Assessment

Writing Have students write two equations—one that can be solved by using the addition property of equality, and one that can be solved using the subtraction property of equality.

Enrichment Masters, p. 51

Name _____ Date _____

Enrichment Worksheet 6-2

Equation Hexa-maze

This figure is called a *hexa-maze* because each cell has the shape of a hexagon, or six-sided figure.

To solve the maze, start with the number in the center. This number is the solution to the equation in one of the adjacent cells. Move to that cell. The number in the new cell will then be the solution to the equation in the next cell. At each move, you may only move to an adjacent cell. Each cell is used only once.

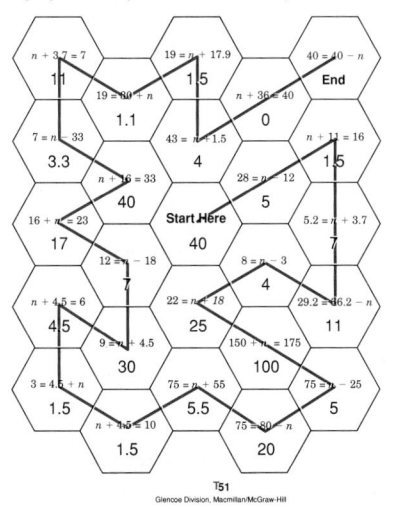

T51
Glencoe Division, Macmillan/McGraw-Hill

NCTM Standards: 1–7, 9

Lesson Resources
- Study Guide Master 6-3
- Practice Master 6-3
- Enrichment Master 6-3
- Multicultural Activity, p. 6
- Group Activity Card 6-3

 Transparency 6-3 contains the 5-Minute Check and a teaching aid for this lesson.

🕐 5-Minute Check
(Over Lesson 6-2)

Solve each equation. Check your solution.
1. $b + 7 = 22$ 15
2. $t - 5.6 = 8.4$ 14
3. $p - 23\frac{4}{5} = 35\frac{7}{10}$ $59\frac{1}{2}$
4. $r + 0.4 = 11.5$ 11.1
5. Wayne bought a share of stock at $29\frac{3}{4}$. A year later, the stock was selling for $42\frac{1}{8}$. How much would Wayne have gained if he had sold his stock then? $12\frac{3}{8}$ dollars, or $12.38

1 FOCUS

Motivating the Lesson

Situational Problem Tell students that in a community with 201 television sets, each household has 3 television sets. This fact can be represented by the equation $3m = 201$. How can this equation be used to find the number of households?

2 TEACH

Using Discussion Discuss with students why multiplication and division are inverse operations. Then review the concept of equivalent equations, pointing out that when multiplying or dividing to "undo" an operation on one side of an equation, students must also perform that operation on the other side of the equation in order to obtain an equivalent equation.

6-3 Solving Multiplication and Division Equations

Objective
Solve equations using the multiplication and division properties of equality.

Words to Learn
division property of equality
multiplication property of equality

How can you tell the difference between fraternal twins and identical twins? Fraternal twins do not necessarily look alike. They are not always the same sex, so you can't always tell they are twins. Identical twins look alike and are of the same sex. In the United States, an average of 434 twin babies are born each day. How many sets of twins are born each day?

You know that twins means two. So two times the number of sets of twins is the number of twin babies. If 434 twin babies are born each day, you can solve the equation $434 = 2s$ to find s, the average number of sets of twins born each day.

Since multiplication and division are inverse operations, equations that involve multiplication can be solved by dividing each side of the equation by the same number. Solve $434 = 2s$ using this method.

$$434 = 2s$$
$$\frac{434}{2} = \frac{2s}{2} \qquad \textit{Divide each side by 2 to undo}$$
$$217 = s \qquad \textit{the multiplication by 2.}$$

Check: $434 = 2s$
$$434 \overset{?}{=} 2 \cdot 217 \qquad \textit{Replace s with 217.}$$
$$434 = 434 \checkmark$$

The solution is 217. On the average, 217 sets of twins are born each day in the United States.

Division Property of Equality	**In words:** If each side of an equation is divided by the same nonzero number, then the two sides remain equal.
	Arithmetic **Algebra**
	$8 = 8$ $a = b$
	$\frac{8}{2} = \frac{8}{2}$ $\frac{a}{c} = \frac{b}{c}, c \neq 0$
	$4 = 4$

OPTIONS

Meeting Needs of Middle School Students

Middle-school students are very receptive to humorous or amazing facts such as those that appear in sources such as the Guinness Book of World Records or a book of sports records. You may wish to use such references when you write problems for the students that can be solved by writing and solving equations.

Equations that involve division can be solved by multiplying each side of the equation by the same number.

Example 1 *Problem Solving*

You can review fractions on page 190.

Marketing Did you know that chewing gum loses its flavor after only about 20 minutes ($\frac{1}{3}$ hour)? However, scientists have recently invented chewing gum that will keep its flavor longer, using synthetically derived polymers. If the newly-developed polymer chewing gum keeps its flavor 30 times as long, use the equation $\frac{1}{3} = \frac{h}{30}$ to find h, the number of hours it keeps its flavor.

$$\frac{1}{3} = \frac{h}{30}$$
$$\frac{1}{3} \cdot 30 = \frac{h}{30} \cdot 30 \qquad \textit{Multiply each side by 30}$$
$$10 = h \qquad\qquad \textit{to undo the division by 30.}$$

Check: $\frac{1}{3} = \frac{h}{30}$

$\frac{1}{3} \overset{?}{=} \frac{10}{30}$ *Replace h with 10.*

$\frac{1}{3} = \frac{1}{3}$ ✓

The solution is 10. The newly-developed polymer chewing gum may keep its flavor up to 10 hours.

Multiplication Property of Equality	**In words:** If each side of an equation is multiplied by the same number, then the two sides remain equal.	
	Arithmetic	**Algebra**
	$4 = 4$	$a = b$
	$4 \cdot 2 = 4 \cdot 2$	$ac = bc$
	$8 = 8$	

Example 2

Estimation Hint

• • • • • • • • • • • • •

In Example 2, think $360 \div 2 = 180$. The solution is about 180.

Solve $368 = 2.3b$. Check your solution.

$368 = 2.3b$

$\frac{368}{2.3} = \frac{2.3b}{2.3}$ *Divide each side by 2.3.*

$368 \;\boxed{\div}\; 2.3 \;\boxed{=}\; 160$

$160 = b$

Check: $368 = 2.3b$

$368 \overset{?}{=} 2.3 \cdot 160$ *Replace b with 160.*

$368 = 368$ ✓

The solution is 160.

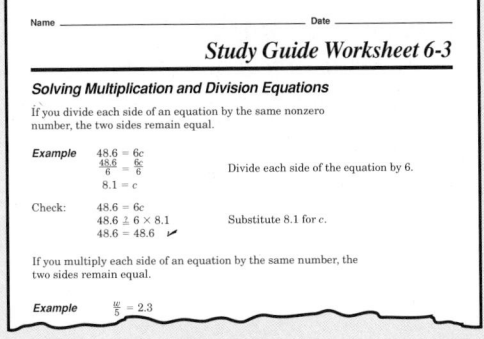

Study Guide Masters, p. 52

Name _____ Date _____

Study Guide Worksheet 6-3

Solving Multiplication and Division Equations

If you divide each side of an equation by the same nonzero number, the two sides remain equal.

Example $48.6 = 6c$
$\frac{48.6}{6} = \frac{6c}{6}$ Divide each side of the equation by 6.
$8.1 = c$

Check: $48.6 = 6c$
$48.6 \overset{?}{=} 6 \times 8.1$ Substitute 8.1 for c.
$48.6 = 48.6$ ✔

If you multiply each side of an equation by the same number, the two sides remain equal.

Example $\frac{w}{5} = 2.3$

Watch for students who neglect to either multiply or divide *both* sides by the same number.

Prevent by reminding students that they must keep the equation in balance by doing to one side what they do to the other.

Close

Have students summarize the lesson by writing two equations—one that can be solved by solving a multiplication equation and one that can be solved by solving a division equation.

3 PRACTICE/APPLY

Assignment Guide
Maximum: 13–39
Minimum: 13–29 odd, 31–38
All: Mid-Chapter Review

For **Extra Practice,** see p. 585.

Practice Masters, p. 52

Name _____ Date _____

Practice Worksheet 6-3

Solving Multiplication and Division Equations

Complete the solution of each equation.

1. $12h = 48$
   $\frac{12h}{12} = \frac{48}{12}$ **12**
   $h = \blacksquare$ **4**

2. $\frac{m}{8} = 7$
   $8 \cdot \frac{m}{8} = 7(\blacksquare)$ **8**
   $m = \blacksquare$ **56**

3. $34 = \frac{r}{3}$
   $34(\blacksquare) = \frac{r}{3} \cdot (\blacksquare)$ **3,3**
   $\blacksquare = r$ **102**

Solve each equation. Check your solution.

4. $4n = 52$
   13

5. $\frac{y}{12} = 18$
   216

6. $49 = \frac{t}{5}$
   245

7. $64 = 2v$
   32

8. $23 = \frac{b}{7}$
   161

9. $\frac{x}{2} = 20$
   40

10. $1.8a = 0.9$
    0.5

11. $\frac{b}{3.5} = 7.3$
    25.55

12. $195 = 15s$
    13

13. $\frac{p}{2.8} = 0.6$
    1.68

14. $121 = 11d$
    11

15. $1.5z = 7.5$
    5

16. $c \div \frac{1}{4} = \frac{1}{2}$
    $\frac{1}{8}$

17. $4.8g = 15.36$
    3.2

18. $h \div 12 = 4.8$
    57.6

T**52**
Glencoe Division, Macmillan/McGraw-Hill

Checking for Understanding

Communicating Mathematics

Read and study the lesson to answer each question.

1. **Write** an equation in the form of $\frac{x}{a} = b$. Then explain why a cannot be 0. Sample: $\frac{3}{a} = 6$; Because $0 \cdot 6 \neq 3$.

2. **Tell** if 3 is a solution of $\frac{y}{3} = 12$. Explain why or why not. No, Because $3 \cdot 12 \neq 3$.

3. **Write** the equation shown by the model at the right. Then find the solution. $3x = 12, 4$

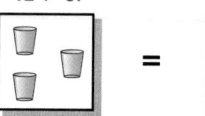

Guided Practice

Complete the solution of each equation.

4. $4m = 20$
   $\frac{4m}{4} = \frac{20}{?}$ **4**
   $m = \underline{\ 5\ }$

5. $\frac{n}{12} = 3$
   $(12)\frac{n}{12} = (?)3$ **12**
   $n = \underline{\ 36\ }$

6. $42 = \frac{r}{7}$
   $42(?) = \frac{r}{7}(?)$ **7, 7**
   $\underline{\ 294\ } = r$

Solve each equation. Check your solution.

7. $7c = 49$ **7**

8. $\frac{a}{3.1} = 7.75$ **24.025**

9. $9e = 54$ **6**

10. $\frac{4}{5} = \frac{1}{2}f$ $1\frac{3}{5}$

11. $72 = \frac{x}{12}$ **864**

12. $\frac{y}{4} = 24$ **96**

Exercises

Independent Practice

Solve each equation. Check your solution.

13. $3c = 21$ **7**

14. $\frac{1}{2}f = \frac{2}{5}$ $\frac{4}{5}$

15. $12x = 156$ **13**

16. $34 = 2g$ **17**

17. $54 = 3p$ **18**

18. $182 = 13s$ **14**

19. $\frac{a}{3} = 17$ **51**

20. $x \div \frac{1}{8} = \frac{1}{2}$ $\frac{1}{16}$

21. $\frac{m}{4} = 11$ **44**

22. $28 = \frac{\ell}{4}$ **112**

23. $96 = \frac{n}{8}$ **768**

24. $13 = \frac{t}{5}$ **65**

25. $\frac{m}{5} = 1.2$ **6**

26. $\frac{p}{3.6} = 0.8$ **2.88**

27. $\frac{t}{2.4} = 13.5$ **32.4**

28. Find the solution of the equation $1.2x = 2.4$. **2**

29. Solve the equation $0.4m = 16$. **40**

30. **Earning Money** If Max Stahler receives 26 paychecks a year and each check is for \$763.50, what is his yearly salary? To solve, use the equation $s \div 26 = 763.50$. **\$19,851**

OPTIONS

Gifted and Talented Needs

Have students write a quiz to test the concepts introduced in this lesson. They should include word problems, some of which might involve data from their science texts.

31. Evaluate b^5 if $b = 3$. *(Lesson 1-9)* **243**

32. mean = 14
median = 14

32. **Statistics.** Zina has seven brothers and sisters. Their ages are 5, 12, 8, 17, 14, 20, and 22. Find the mean age and median age. *(Lesson 3-5)*

33. Write the prime factorization of 24. *(Lesson 4-2)* **2 · 2 · 2 · 3**

34. Subtract $1\frac{1}{3}$ from $4\frac{3}{4}$. *(Lesson 5-4)* **$3\frac{5}{12}$**

35. Solve the equation $p - 25.55 = 74.45$. *(Lesson 6-2)* **100**

Problem Solving and Applications

36. **Engineering** In designing gasoline storage tanks, engineers multiply the government-required minimum thickness by a factor of 2.5 for added safety. Use the equation $2.5m = 1.625$, where m is the minimum thickness.
   a. Solve for m.   **0.65**
   b. What is the required minimum thickness?   **0.65**

37. **Energy** Hydrogen is being considered as a safe alternative fuel. It may also be more economical. Over long distances, the amount of hydrogen equivalent to a kilowatt-hour of electricity can be transported via pipeline for about $\frac{1}{8}$ the cost of sending the electricity through transmission lines. Use the equation $400 = \frac{1}{8}e$ to find the cost of transmitting electricity to a site where it costs only $400 to transmit hydrogen.   **$3,200**

38. You cannot divide a number by 0 because $0 \cdot n \neq m$.

38. **Critical Thinking** What is wrong with the equation $m \div 0 = n$? Explain.

39. **Computers** Computer modems transmit data at different speeds. One type of modem transmits at 9,600 bits per second. This is four times faster than a second modem.
   a. Write an equation that when solved will give the speed of the second modem   **$9,600 = 4m$**
   b. Solve the equation and give the speed of the second modem.   **2,400 bits per second**

40. **Portfolio Suggestion** Select one of the assignments from this chapter that you found particularly challenging. Place it in your portfolio.
   See students' work.

Assessment: Mid-Chapter Review

Solve each equation by using the inverse operation. *(Lesson 6-1)*
1. $23 + p = 71$ **48**
2. $1.8n = 2.16$ **1.2**
3. $68 = g - 89$ **157**

Solve each equation. Check your solution. *(Lessons 6-2, 6-3)*
4. $41 + w = 71$ **30**
5. $s - 33 = 35$ **68**
6. $y + 19 = 24$ **5**
7. $\frac{c}{1.5} = 0.3$ **0.45**
8. $11b = 121$ **11**
9. $\frac{k}{9} = 34$ **306**

Extending the Lesson

Connections Have students summarize the process of solving equations by writing a list of steps that can be used no matter what operations are involved.

Cooperative Learning Activity

Use groups of 4.
Materials: Newspapers, catalogs, calculators

Take Charge 6-3

❧ Read the following.

Harvey-Sloan, a department store, uses the equation $m = \frac{2}{3}$ to determine the minimum amount a new charge-card customer must pay one month after receiving his or her card. In this equation, b stands for the total cost of the items charged during the month.

➡ Using newspapers and/or catalogs, write the prices of five items you would like to buy at a department store—for example, clothes or a television set. Then suppose that you have just received a Harvey-Sloan charge card and that you use it to charge the five items whose prices you found. Trade papers with another group member. Find the total cost of the five items and then, using the equation above, find the minimum payment this person must make. Compare your results. Which group member has the highest minimum payment? Which group member has the lowest minimum payment?

Glencoe Mathematics: Applications and Connections, Course 2

Alternate Assessment

Speaking Have students describe how they would solve multiplication and division equations to a student who has missed the lesson.

Enrichment Masters, p. 52

Name _____   Date _____

Enrichment Worksheet 6-3

Describing Variation

Equations of the form $y = ax$ and $y = x \div a$ can be used to show how one quantity varies with another. Here are two examples.

Driving at a speed of 50 miles per hour, the distance you travel (d) varies directly with the time you are on the road (t). The longer you drive, the farther you get. $d = 50t$

It is also the case that the time (t) varies directly with the distance (d). The farther you drive, the more time it takes. $t = \frac{d}{50}$

Complete the equation for each situation. Then describe the relationship in words.

1. If you go on a diet and lose 2 pounds a month, after a certain number of months (m), you will have lost p pounds. $p = 2m$
   The longer you diet, the more weight you will lose.

2. You and your family are deciding between two different places for your summer vacation. You plan to travel by car and estimate you will average 55 miles per hour. The distance traveled (d) will result in a travel time of t hours. $t = \frac{d}{55}$
   The farther you drive, the more time it will take.

3. You find that you are spending more than you had planned on renting video movies. It costs $2.00 to rent each movie. You can use the total amount spent (a) to find the number of movies you have rented (m). $m = \frac{a}{2}$
   The greater the amount spent, the more movies rented.

4. You spend $30 a month to take the bus to school. After a certain number of months (m), you will have spent a total of d dollars on transportation to school. $d = 30m$
   The longer you ride the bus, the more you will spend.

5. You are saving money for some new athletic equipment and have 12 weeks before the season starts. The amount you need to save each week (s) will depend on the cost (c) of the equipment you want to buy. $s = \frac{c}{12}$
   The more expensive the equipment, the more money must be saved each week.

T52
Glencoe Division, Macmillan/McGraw-Hill

NCTM Standards: 1–6, 9

Management Tips

For Students Have students work in small groups. Provide each group with 5 cups and 20 counters. Students should take turns modeling the solutions to the equations.

For the Overhead Projector *Overhead Manipulative Resources* provides appropriate materials for teacher or student demonstration of the activities in this Mathematics Lab.

1 FOCUS

Introducing the Lab

Ask students to suggest things they do that require two steps, such as inserting the key in a door, then turning the knob to open it. Ask them to suggest situations in which the order of the steps matters and those in which the order does not matter.

2 TEACH

Using Models Write some two-step equations on the chalkboard. Have students model each with cups and counters, describing what must be done in each equation to isolate the cups on one side of the mat. Remind students that each cup contains the same number of counters.

3 PRACTICE/APPLY

Using Critical Thinking Ask students to name the two operations in each equation that they have modeled and to think about the order in which they are "undone." Ask them to compare that order with the order of operations.

Close

Have students write a summary of the method they have been using to solve two-step equations.

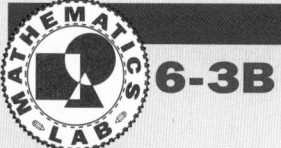

6-3B Solving Two-Step Equations

A Follow-Up of Lesson 6-3

Objective
Solve two-step equations using models.

Materials
cups
counters
mats

In this lab, you will use what you know about solving one-step equations to solve two-step equations like $2x + 3 = 7$.

Try this!

Work with a partner.

- First, let's build the equation $2x + 3 = 7$ using models. On the left side, we need two cups and three counters. On the right side, we need seven counters.

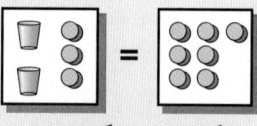

- Remember, the goal is to get the cup(s) by itself on one side of the mat. Remove three counters from each side of the mat. Now the model shows the equation $2x = 4$.

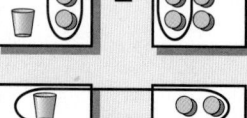

- Each cup must contain the same number of counters. Therefore, $x = 2$.

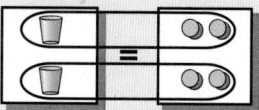

What do you think?

1. You must subtract and then divide.

1. Why is an equation like $2x + 3 = 7$ called a two-step equation?
2. Write the equation that is shown at the right. $3x + 4 = 10$

Application

Make a model of each equation. Solve the equation.

3. $3x + 1 = 7$ 2   4. $2y + 4 = 12$ 4   5. $5x + 1 = 11$ 2
6. $9 = 4m + 1$ 2   7. $3x + 5 = 14$ 3   8. $3 = 2a + 3$ 0

See Solutions Manual for models.

Extension

9. Make a model of the equation $2x + 5 = 10$. See Solutions Manual.
   a. Solve the equation. $2\frac{1}{2}$
   b. Write a paragraph that describes the process you used. In your paragraph, describe any difference between the solution of this equation and the equations you solved previously. See students' work.

OPTIONS

Lab Manual You may wish to make copies of the blackline master on p. 52 of the *Lab Manual* for students to use as a recording sheet.

Lab Manual, p. 52

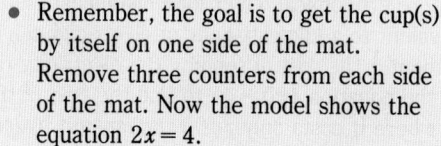

Name _____   Date _____

Mathematics Lab Worksheet

Use with page 232

Solving Two-Step Equations

What do you think?

1. It is solved in two steps. First 3 counters are removed from each mat. Then the counters are divided into 2 equal groups.
2. $3x + 4 = 10$

Application

3. ___2___   4. ___4___   5. ___2___
6. ___2___   7. ___3___   8. ___0___

6-4 Writing Algebraic Expressions

6-4 Lesson Notes

NCTM Standards: 1–5, 9

Lesson Resources
- Study Guide Master 6-4
- Practice Master 6-4
- Enrichment Master 6-4
- Evaluation Master, Quiz A, p. 52
- Interdisciplinary Master, p. 20
- Group Activity Card 6-4

Transparency 6-4 contains the 5-Minute Check and a teaching aid for this lesson.

Objective

Write simple algebraic expressons from verbal phrases.

Suppose you are attending Space Camp in Huntsville, Alabama, and you take a simulated trip to the moon. When you get to the moon, you find that you weigh more on Earth than you do on the moon. In fact, you weigh 6 times more on Earth than you do on the moon. The chart at the right shows weights that are equivalent on the moon and on Earth.

Weight (In Pounds)	
On Moon	**On Earth**
8	$6 \cdot 8$ or 48
20	$6 \cdot 20$ or 120
40	$6 \cdot 40$ or 240
n	$6 \cdot n$

LOOK BACK

You can review variables and expressions on page 28.

In this lesson, you will learn how to translate verbal phrases such as *6 times a number* into an algebraic expression.

Words and phrases often suggest addition, subtraction, multiplication, and division. Here are some examples.

DID YOU KNOW

Although your weight is less on the moon, your mass is exactly the same.

+	−	×	÷
plus	minus	times	divided
sum	difference	product	quotient
more than	less than	multiplied	
increased by	subtract		
total	decreased by		

You can write algebraic expressions to represent verbal phrases.

Examples

Translate each phrase into an algebraic expression.

1 7 more runs scored than the Bruins

Let b represent the number of runs scored by the Bruins. The words *more than* suggest addition.

The algebraic expression is $b + 7$.

2 John's test score decreased by 5

Let s represent John's test score. The words *decreased by* suggest subtraction.

The algebraic expression is $s - 5$.

Lesson 6-4 Writing Algebraic Expressions **233**

 5-Minute Check
(Over Lesson 6-3)

Solve each equation. Check your solution.

1. $4t = 36$ 9
2. $\frac{1}{3}c = \frac{3}{4}$ $2\frac{1}{4}$
3. $\frac{w}{6} = 0.6$ 3.6
4. $24 = \frac{r}{2.5}$ 60
5. Manuel is paid 52 times a year by a check for $450. What is his annual salary? $23,400

1 FOCUS

Motivating the Lesson

Situational Problem Tell students that Linda is trying to improve her vocabulary by learning the same number of new words each week. Today she learned her thousandth word. Ask students to write an expression using variables to state how many words Linda will know 3 weeks from today.

2 TEACH

Using Charts Have students begin a chart that they can use here and in subsequent lessons. The chart will have two columns—one for word phrases and one for the algebraic expressions having the same meaning.

OPTIONS

Reteaching Activity

Using Manipulatives Have students, working with partners, use cups and counters to model the verbal phrases and algebraic expressions presented in the lesson. Help students to see how to use counters to model expressions indicating division.

Study Guide Masters, p. 53

Name _____ Date _____

Study Guide Worksheet 6-4

Writing Algebraic Expressions

The table shows phrases written as mathematical expressions.

Phrase	Expression	Phrase	Expression
9 more than a number the sum of 9 and a number a number plus 9 a number increased by 9 the total of x and 9	$x + 9$	4 subtracted from a number a number minus 4 4 less than a number a number decreased by 4 the difference of h and 4	$h - 4$

Phrase	Expression	Phrase	Expression
6 multiplied by g 6 times a number the product of g and 6	$6g$	a number divided by 5 the quotient of t and 5 divide a number by 5	$\frac{t}{5}$

Translate each phrase into an algebraic expression.

233

3 the number of shirts divided among four teams

Let s represent the number of shirts. The words *divided by* suggest division.

The algebraic expression is $\frac{s}{4}$.

4 Write verbal phrases for the algebraic expression $r - 6$.

Several phrases can represent $r - 6$.
- a number decreased by 6
- subtract 6 from a number
- 6 points less than Ben's score
- a number of trees minus 6

Checking for Understanding

Communicating Mathematics

Read and study the lesson to answer each question.

1. **Tell** which operation the phrase *increased by* suggests. addition
2. **Write** two verbal phrases for the algebraic expression $\frac{x}{3}$.
3. **Tell** what the expression $n - 2$ could represent if n is the number of games the Dodgers won. the number of games another team won
4. **Tell** how the expressions $n - 3$ and $3 - n$ are different. The terms are reversed.

2. the quotient of x and 3, x divided by 3

Guided Practice

Translate each phrase into an algebraic expression.

5. seven more than t $t + 7$
6. the sum of r and 2 $r + 2$
7. eight less than p $p - 8$
8. the difference of g and 4 $g - 4$
9. twelve plus s $12 + s$
10. eighteen minus y $18 - y$
11. c divided by 4 $\frac{c}{4}$
12. three times a $3a$
13. the quotient of b and 2 $\frac{b}{2}$
14. the product of a number and 7 $7a$

Write two verbal phrases for each algebraic expression. See margin.

15. $t - 10$
16. $4 \div d$
17. $10n$
18. $14 + h$

Exercises

Independent Practice

Translate each phrase into an algebraic expression.

19. five more hits than the Yankees $y + 5$
20. ten fewer points than the Bulls $B - 10$
21. twice as many calories as a slice of pizza $2p$
22. five less n $5 - n$
23. your age divided by 3 $\frac{a}{3}$
24. nine increased by x $9 + x$
25. the quotient of a and 6 $\frac{a}{6}$
26. seventeen less than p $p - 17$
27. nineteen less r $19 - r$
28. the product of b and 4 $4b$
29. Jan's salary plus \$1,110 $J + 1,110$
30. five years older than Paul $5 + p$
31. the difference of 8 and d $8 - d$
32. four times as many bees $4b$
33. six divided by k $\frac{6}{k}$
34. l increased by 4 $l + 4$
35. Sue's score decreased by 8 $s - 8$
36. 19 divided into n $\frac{n}{19}$
37. x decreased by 15 $x - 15$

OPTIONS

Team Teaching

Inform the other teachers on your team that your classes are studying how to write algebraic expressions. Suggestions for curriculum integration are:

Science: temperature and cricket chirps

Social Studies: congressional representation

Additional Answers

15. t minus 10; 10 less than t
16. the quotient of 4 and d; 4 divided by d
17. 10 times n; the product of 10 and n
18. 14 plus h; 14 more than h

See students' work.

An airplane is at an altitude of t feet. Write a related situation for each expression.

38. $t - 1,000$ 39. $2t$ 40. $t + 6,500$

Mixed Review

41. Solve $32t = 8$ mentally. *(Lesson 1-10)* $t = \frac{1}{4}$

42. **Measurement** Bill is 5.875 feet tall and Diego is 5.785 feet tall. Who is taller? *(Lesson 2-1)* **Bill**

43. Find the GCF of 36 and 48. *(Lesson 4-5)* **12**

44. Subtract $\frac{24}{25} - \frac{2}{3}$. *(Lesson 5-3)* $\frac{22}{75}$

45. Dr. Green charges \$45.50 for a half-hour office visit. Solve the equation $\frac{d}{3} = 45.50$ to find the charge for an office visit that lasts $1\frac{1}{2}$ hours. *(Lesson 6-3)* **\$136.50**

Problem Solving and Applications

46. **Critical Thinking** If x is an odd number, how would you represent the odd number immediately following it? preceding it? $x + 2$, $x - 2$

47. **Statistics** Use the information in the graph at the right to answer each question.

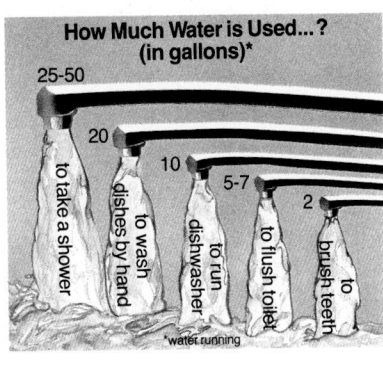

How Much Water is Used...?
(in gallons)*

25-50   to take a shower
20   to wash dishes by hand
10   to run dishwasher
5-7   to flush toilet
2   to brush teeth

*water running

a. Suppose n represents the most water used by the average American to take a shower. Which activity can be expressed by $n - 48$? **brushing teeth**

b. If t represents the amount of water used to wash dishes by hand, write an expression to represent how much water can be saved by running a dishwasher. $\frac{t}{2}$

48. **Answers will vary.**

48. **Collect Data** Find yesterday's high and low temperature. Let t represent the low temperature. Write an expression for the high temperature.

49. **Biology** A blue whale gains an average of 2.3 tons a month for the first year of life. Copy and complete the table below.

Current weight (tons)	15	23.7	38	?	45	53.9	?
Weight in 1 month (tons)	?	?	?	44.1	?	?	63

(answers above/below table) 41.8 ... 60.7 ; 17.3   26   40.3   47.3   56.2

50. **Journal Entry** Write a verbal phrase for the algebraic expression $5 \div n$.
5 divided by n

Lesson 6-4 Writing Algebraic Expressions   **235**

Extending the Lesson

Consumer At Milt's Sporting Goods store, bats cost \$35 each and gloves are \$55 each. Write an algebraic expression for the total cost of x bats and y gloves.
$35x + 55y$ Make up other problems like this one for the classmates to solve.

Cooperative Learning Activity

A Sure Aid for Expressions 6-4

Use groups of 4.
Materials: Index cards

• Copy onto cards the expressions shown on the back of this card, one expression per card. Shuffle the cards and place them face down in a pile.

➡ Work in pairs. Decide which pair will go first. One partner from the first pair selects a card. The first pair acts out each word of the expression while the other pair tries to guess the word. When you and your partner have guessed the entire verbal phrase, write it and then translate it into an algebraic expression. Trade roles and repeat the procedure. Continue in this way until no cards remain.

Glencoe Mathematics: Applications and Connections, Course 2

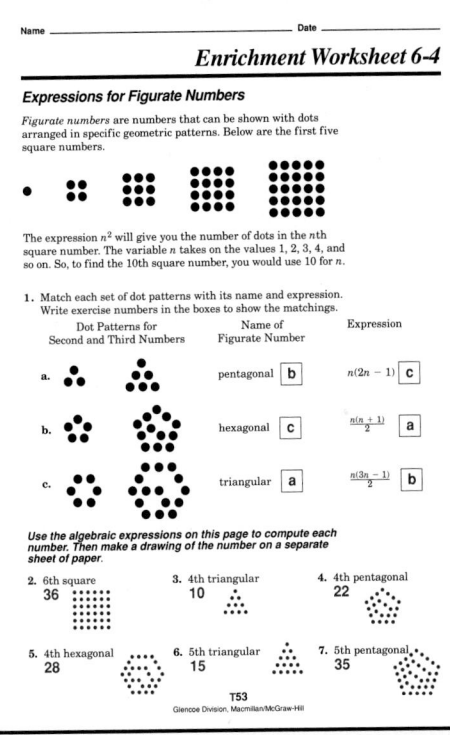
235

6-5 Use an Equation

NCTM Standards: 1–7, 9

Lesson Resources
- Study Guide Master 6-5
- Practice Master 6-5
- Enrichment Master 6-5
- Group Activity Card 6-5

 Transparency 6-5 contains the 5-Minute Check and a teaching aid for this lesson.

🕐 5-Minute Check
(Over Lesson 6-4)

Translate each phrase into an algebraic expression.

1. three fewer runs than the Tigers $t - 3$

2. eight increased by m $8 + m$

3. twelve divided by y $12 \div y$

4. Dan's score decreased by 9 $n - 9$

5. the product of w and 7 $7w$

Objective
Solve problems by using an equation.

When am I ever going to use this?

Real Estate Agent

A real estate agent helps people to buy and sell properties. Being a real estate agent requires patience, a knack for selling, and consumer math skills to compute down payment amounts, interest rates, closing costs, taxes, and insurance. Most agents work on commission.

For more information, contact the Department of Regulatory Agencies, Real Estate Commission, in your state.

 SOLD

The Jacobson's sold their house for $135,000. This price is four times the amount they originally paid for it 15 years ago. How much did they originally pay for the house?

Explore   What do you know?
The Jacobson's sold their house for $135,000. The price is four times the amount they paid for it.

What do you need to find?
You need to find how much they originally paid for the house.

Plan   Choose a variable and decide what unknown number it will represent. Write an equation for the problem. Then solve the equation.

Solve   Let p represent the price they originally paid for the house.

The price is 4 times the amount they paid for it.   *Selling Price*

$$4p = \$135{,}000$$

$$\frac{4p}{4} = \frac{\$135{,}000}{4}$$

$135000 \;\boxed{\div}\; 4 \;\boxed{=}\; 33750$

$$p = \$33{,}750$$

The Jacobson's originally paid $33,750 for their house.

Examine   You can check the answer by replacing the p in $4p = 135{,}000$ with $33{,}750$.

$4 \;\boxed{\times}\; 33750 \;\boxed{=}\; 135000$

Practice Masters, p. 54

Name _____ Date _____

Practice Worksheet 6-5

Problem-Solving Strategy: Use an Equation

Solve by using an equation.

1. The total number of players on a minor league baseball team is seven more than twice the number of players who are playing at a given time. If there are 25 team members, how many team members play at one time?   **9**

2. A number is multiplied by 12. Then 3 is added to the result. If the answer is 51, what is the original number?   **4**

Solve. Use any strategy.

3. A library charges $0.50 for the first day a book is overdue and $0.25 for each day after that. What is the charge for a book that is overdue for 10 days?   **$2.75**

4. There are three yellow, four blue, and five red slips of paper in a hat.
   a. What is the probability of choosing a blue slip of paper from the hat without looking? $\frac{1}{3}$
   b. What is the probability of choosing a red or a blue slip? $\frac{3}{4}$

5. Suppose a bridge has a 5-ton weight limit posted. Should a truck weighing 4,000 pounds which is carrying a load equal to half its weight be allowed to cross the bridge?   **yes**

6. Latasha spent $54 on three compact discs and one cassette tape. How much did each compact disc cost?   **Not enough information.**

7. Jim bought a new car in 1989 for $9,000. If the car lost one-fifth of its original value for each of the next three years, what was the value of the car in 1992?   **$3,600**

8. How many ways are there to cut a square into four pieces with equal area? Circle the answer.   Less than 4   4   ⟨More than 4⟩

9. A scale can hold a maximum of 1 ton. Can objects weighing 400 pounds, 1,200 pounds, and 850 pounds, be placed on the scale at the same time?   **no**

10. Jamie bought a rare coin for $240. Its value increased by one-quarter of its original value each year. What is the value of the coin after 4 years?   **$480**

T54
Glencoe Division, Macmillan/McGraw-Hill

OPTIONS

Reteaching Activity

Using Calculators   Since the focus of the lesson is on writing the correct equation to solve a problem, allow students to compute with calculators to solve the problem more quickly and possibly more accurately.

Study Guide Masters, p. 54

Name _____ Date _____

Study Guide Worksheet 6-5

Problem-Solving Strategy: Use an Equation

The owner of a sporting goods store ordered 3 times as many golf balls as tennis balls. He ordered 288 balls in all. How many golf balls and how many tennis balls did he order?

Explore   What do you know?
You know that the store owner ordered 3 times as many golf balls as tennis balls and that he ordered 288 balls in all.

What do you want to find?
You want to find how many tennis balls and how many golf balls he ordered.

Plan   Write an equation. Choose a variable to represent the number of tennis balls. The number of golf balls is 3 times the number of tennis balls. The sum is 288.

Solve   Let t represent the number of tennis balls.

Checking for Understanding

Communicating Mathematics

Read and study the lesson to answer each question.

1. **Tell** what a variable is. **a letter that stands for a number**

2. **Write** an alternative strategy for solving the problem in the example. **guess and check**

Guided Practice

Solve by using an equation.

3. The number of receivers on a football team is three times the number of quarterbacks. If there are nine receivers on a team, how many quarterbacks are there? **3 quarterbacks**

4. Twelve is subtracted from a number. If the difference is 98, what was the original number? **110**

Problem Solving

Practice

Solve using any strategy.

5. A linen manufacturer sends 250 tablecloths to several discount stores. Each store was sent the same number of tablecloths. How many did each store receive? **not enough information**

6. The greater of two numbers is 25 more than the other number. If the greater number is 82, find the lesser number. **57**

7. There are 10 red, 5 white, and 3 blue marbles in a bag. What is the probability of picking a red marble from the bag without looking? $\frac{5}{9}$

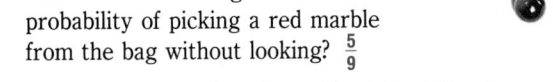

8. **Mathematics and Sociology** Read the following paragraph.

> Although homeless people have become a common sight in many communities, there is very little reliable information available about who they are, and how many of them live in shelters or on the street. The various federal government programs to assist the homeless are grouped under the Stewart B. McKinney Homeless Assistance Act. In 1990, Congress appropriated $1.1 billion for these programs.

A 1988 U.S. Department of Education survey estimated that there were 220,000 homeless school-age children in this country. There are 90,000 more homeless children that go to school than those that do not. How many homeless children go to school and how many do not? **155,000 do and 65,000 don't**

Lesson 6-5 Problem-Solving Strategy: Use An Equation   **237**

Extending the Lesson

Mathematics and Sociology If students have difficulty writing an equation in the exercise about children who don't go to school, have them let *x* represent the number of children who don't go to school. Then *x* + 90,000 represents the number of children who do go to school.

Cooperative Learning Activity

Right from the Start 6-5

Number of players: 2
Materials: Index cards, spinners

▸ Write the numbers 1 through 15 on index cards. Shuffle the cards and place them face down in a pile. Label equal sections of one spinner "× 3," "× 4," "× 5," "× 8." This will be spinner A. Label equal sections of a second spinner "+ 3," "− 1," "+ 12," "− 2." This will be spinner B. Decide who will be player 1 and player 2.

▸ Player 1 selects a card. Player 2 then spins spinner A and player 1 mentally performs the operation shown on the spinner on the number he or she selected. Player 2 then spins spinner B and player 1 mentally performs this operation on the product he or she just found. Player 1 then says the resulting number. Player 2 must guess player 1's original number. Write equations to help you guess numbers. Trade roles and repeat the procedure. Each partner should guess at least three original numbers.

Glencoe Mathematics: Applications and Connections, Course 2

Name _____   Date _____

Enrichment Worksheet 6-5

Pentomino Puzzles

When 2 squares of equal size are joined together, they are called a *domino.* Joining 5 squares gives you a figure called a *pentomino.* There are just 12 possible different pentominoes.

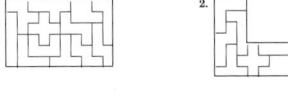

The most common type of pentomino problem is that of covering a given shape with all 12 pieces. Although the pieces cannot overlap, it is okay for you to turn them over.

Show how all 12 pentominoes can be used to cover each shape. There is more than one solution to most of the problems.

1.   2.

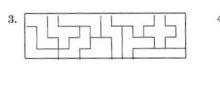 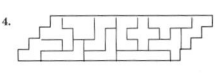

3.   4.

5.   6.

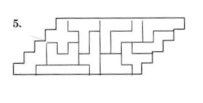 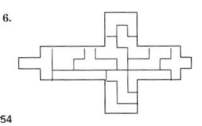

T54
Glencoe Division, Macmillan/McGraw-Hill

Lesson Resources
- Study Guide Master 6-6
- Practice Master 6-6
- Enrichment Master 6-6
- Group Activity Card 6-6

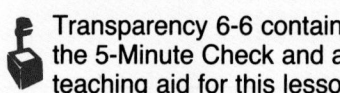 Transparency 6-6 contains the 5-Minute Check and a teaching aid for this lesson.

⏱ 5-Minute Check

(Over Lesson 6-5)

Solve by using an equation.

1. The number of boys on a chess team is 1 more than twice the number of girls. If there are 5 boys on the team, how many girls are there?
$2x + 1 = 5$; 2 girls

2. A number is multiplied by 5 and 6 is subtracted from the result. If the answer is 54, what is the number? $5x - 6 = 54$; 12

---

1 FOCUS

Motivating the Lesson

Situational Problem   Ask students who gets the better gas mileage—Jack, whose motorcycle gets 18 miles per quart, or Tanya, whose car gets 55 miles per gallon?

2 TEACH

Using Applications   Provide newspapers, catalogues, and magazines. Have students read through them to find several examples of customary measurements. Ask them to list the items measured and convert their measurements to either larger or smaller units.

6-6 Changing Units in the Customary System

Objective

Changing units in the customary system

Words to Learn

ounce
pound
ton
cup
pint
quart
gallon

A newborn hooded seal pup weighs about 45 pounds at birth. In the first four days of life, the pup gains about 56 ounces a day. How many pounds will the average pup gain in one day?

Customary units of weight are **ounce, pound,** and **ton.** The following table gives the relationships among these units.

> 1 pound (lb) = 16 ounces (oz)
> 1 ton = 2,000 pounds (lb)

DID YOU KNOW

The hooded seal got its name because of the bright red hood on the male seal's head. When he is angry, he blows air into it and it expands like a balloon. It is used to frighten attackers.

In the seal pup problem above, you need to change 56 ounces to pounds. When you change from a smaller unit to a larger unit, divide.

$$56 \text{ oz} = \underline{\ ?\ } \text{ lb}$$

56 $\boxed{÷}$ 16 $\boxed{=}$ **3.5**   *Since 16 oz = 1 lb, divide by 16.*

The average pup will gain 3.5 pounds in one day.

Sometimes you will need to convert from a larger unit to a smaller unit. In this case, multiply.

Example 1   *Problem Solving*

Highway Safety   Have you ever crossed over a small country bridge? Normally a sign will be posted just before the entrance to the bridge warning drivers of the weight limit. Suppose you cross a small bridge with a $3\frac{1}{2}$ ton weight limit. How many pounds can the bridge hold?

$$3\frac{1}{2} \text{ ton} = \underline{\ ?\ } \text{ lb}$$

$$3\frac{1}{2} \cdot 2,000 = 7,000 \qquad \textit{Since 2,000 lb = 1 ton, multiply by 2,000.}$$

The bridge will hold 7,000 pounds.

OPTIONS

Reteaching Activity

Using Manipulatives   Provide students with opportunities to handle and use some of the measures to get an idea of their size. For example, provide students with a glass quart measuring cup so that they can see the capacity of a quart and how pints and ounces compare in capacity with it and with each other.

Study Guide Masters, p. 55

Name _____ Date _____

Study Guide Worksheet 6-6

Changing Units in the Customary System

Customary Units	
Weight	Liquid Capacity
16 ounces (oz) = 1 pound (lb)	8 fluid ounces (fl oz) = 1 cup (c)
2,000 pounds = 1 ton	2 cups = 1 pint (pt)
	2 pints = 1 quart (qt)
	4 quarts = 1 gallon (gal)

Multiply to change from a larger unit to a smaller unit.

Example $5\frac{1}{2}$ lb = $\underline{\ ?\ }$ oz
$5\frac{1}{2} \cdot 16 = 88$ Since 16 oz = 1 lb, multiply by 16.
There are 88 oz in $5\frac{1}{2}$ lb.

Customary units of liquid capacity are **cup, pint, quart,** and **gallon.** The following table shows the relationships among these units.

> 1 cup (c) = 8 fluid ounces (fl oz)
> 1 pint (pt) = 2 cups (c)
> 1 quart (qt) = 2 pints (pt)
> 1 gallon (gal) = 4 quarts (qt)

Example 2

How many fluid ounces are in 3 cups?

3 c = _?_ fl oz
3 · 8 = 24   *Multiply by 8 since there are 8 fl oz in a cup.*
3 c = 24 fl oz

There are 24 fluid ounces in 3 cups.

Remember that dividing by any number is the same as multiplying by its multiplicative inverse. For example, dividing by 4 is the same as multiplying by $\frac{1}{4}$. You can use this fact when you change from smaller units to larger units.

Example 3

19 qt = _?_ gal

- Method 1: Divide by 4.
  19 ÷ 4 = **4.75**
  19 qt = 4.75 gal

- Method 2: Multiply by $\frac{1}{4}$.
  19 qt = _?_ gal
  $19 \times \frac{1}{4} = 4\frac{3}{4}$
  $19 \text{ qt} = 4\frac{3}{4} \text{ gal}$

There are 4.75 or $4\frac{3}{4}$ gallons in 19 quarts.

Checking for Understanding

Communicating Mathematics

Read and study the lesson to answer each question.

1. **Tell** which operation is needed to convert from pints to gallons. Explain how you know. **Division; gallons are bigger than pints.**

2. **Tell** how to change 8 quarts to gallons. **divide by 4, 4 quarts = 1 gallon**

Guided Practice

Complete.

3. 3 pt = _?_ c **6**   4. 2 tons = _?_ lb **4,000**   5. 5 lb = _?_ oz **80**
6. 2 gal = _?_ qt **8**   7. 6,000 lb = _?_ tons **3**   8. 12 qt = _?_ gal **3**
9. 15 pt = _?_ qt **7.5**   10. 12 c = _?_ pt **6**   11. 128 oz = _?_ lb **8**

Lesson 6-6 Measurement Connection: Converting in the Customary System **239**

More Examples

For Example 1

How many pounds can an elevator safely hold if its sign says that it can carry $1\frac{1}{2}$ tons?   3,000 lb

For Example 2

How many cups are in 2 quarts?   8 cups

For Example 3

23 qt = _?_ gal $5\frac{3}{4}$

Checking for Understanding

Exercises 1-2 are designed to help you assess students' understanding through reading, writing, speaking, and modeling. You should work through these exercises with your students and then monitor their work on Guided Practice Exercises 3-13.

Practice Masters, p. 55

Name _____   Date _____

Practice Worksheet 6-6

Changing Units in the Customary System

Complete.

1. 4 lb = ___ oz **64**
2. 12 qt = ___ gal **3**
3. 10 c = ___ pt **5**
4. 10,000 lb = ___ tons **5**
5. 16 fl oz = ___ c **2**
6. 32 oz = ___ lb **2**
7. 5 c = ___ fl oz **40**
8. 12 gal = ___ qt **48**
9. 12 pt = ___ qt **6**
10. 7 c = ___ pt **3.5**
11. 5 tons = ___ lb **10,000**
12. 6 gal = ___ qt **24**
13. 3 gal = ___ qt **12**
14. 24 pt = ___ c **48**
15. 17 tons = ___ lb **34,000**
16. 24 fl oz = ___ c **3**
17. 9 gal = ___ qt **36**
18. 53 qts = ___ gal **13.25**
19. 9.5 tons = ___ lb **19,000**
20. 15 c = ___ pt **7.5**
21. 3.5 c = ___ fl oz **28**
22. 11 c = ___ pt **5.5**
23. 23 pt = ___ qt **11.5**
24. 0.5 qt = ___ pt **1**

Solve.

25. At liftoff, the space shuttle *Atlantis* weighed 100 tons. How many pounds is this? **200,000 lb**
26. The gasoline tank of a minivan holds 18 gallons. How many quarts is this? **72 qt**
27. The average weight of a baby at birth is 7 pounds. How many ounces is this? **112 oz**
28. Portable telephones can weigh as little as 8 ounces. How many pounds is this? **0.5 lb**
29. Milk is sold in 8 fl oz, 16 fl oz, 32 fl oz, and 64 fl oz cardboard containers. Change these sizes to cups. **1c, 2c, 4c, and 8c**
30. The United States exports over 200 billion pounds of coal. How many tons is this? **100 million**

T55
Glencoe Division, Macmillan/McGraw-Hill

240

Close

Have students, without referring to their texts, make a table showing the relationships among the different customary units of weight and liquid capacity. Then have them name an item that represents each measure.

3 PRACTICE/APPLY

Assignment Guide
Maximum: 14–39
Minimum: 15–31 odd, 32–38

For **Extra Practice,** see p. 586.

Alternate Assessment

Writing Have students make up a cross-number puzzle in which all clues are conversions between customary measures. Have students exchange puzzles and solve those of their classmates.

Enrichment Masters, p. 55

Name _____ Date _____

Enrichment Worksheet 6-6

Changing Measurements with Factors of 1

Multiplying an expression by the number 1 does not change its value. This property of multiplication can be used to change measurements.

Let's say you wanted to change 4.5 hours to seconds. Start by multiplying 4.5 by the number 1 written in the form $\frac{60 \text{ minutes}}{1 \text{ hour}}$. This first step changes 4.5 hours to minutes.

$$4.5 \text{ hours} \times \frac{60 \text{ minutes}}{1 \text{ hour}}$$

Now, multiply by the number 1 again. This time use the fact that $1 = \frac{60 \text{ seconds}}{1 \text{ minute}}$.

$$4.5 \text{ hours} \times \frac{60 \text{ minutes}}{1 \text{ hour}} \times \frac{60 \text{ seconds}}{1 \text{ minute}} = 16{,}200 \text{ seconds}$$

Complete by writing the last factor and the answer. You may need to use a table of measurements to find the factors.

1. Change 5 pints to fluid ounces.

$5 \text{ pints} \times \frac{2 \text{ cups}}{1 \text{ pint}} \times \frac{8 \text{ fluid ounces}}{1 \text{ cup}} = \textbf{80 fluid ounces}$

2. Change 0.8 miles to inches.

$0.8 \text{ mile} \times \frac{5{,}280 \text{ feet}}{1 \text{ mile}} \times \frac{12 \text{ inches}}{1 \text{ foot}} = \textbf{50,688 inches}$

3. Change 4 square yards to square inches.

$4 \text{ yd}^2 \times \frac{9 \text{ ft}^2}{1 \text{ yd}^2} \times \frac{144 \text{ in}^2}{1 \text{ ft}^2} = \textbf{5,184 in}^2$

4. Change 12 bushels to pints.

$12 \text{ bushels} \times \frac{4 \text{ pecks}}{1 \text{ bushel}} \times \frac{8 \text{ quarts}}{1 \text{ peck}} \times \frac{2 \text{ pints}}{1 \text{ quart}} = \textbf{768 pints}$

5. Change one-half of an acre to square inches.

$\frac{1}{2} \text{ acre} \times \frac{4{,}840 \text{ yd}^2}{1 \text{ acre}} \times \frac{9 \text{ ft}^2}{1 \text{ yd}^2} \times \frac{144 \text{ in}^2}{1 \text{ ft}^2} = \textbf{3,136,320 in}^2$

T55
Glencoe Division, Macmillan/McGraw-Hill

---

12. How many tons are in 3,600 pounds? **1.8 tons**

13. A customer orders 1,500 pounds of rock. The supply truck holds $\frac{3}{4}$ ton. Will the truck be able to deliver the order with one load? **yes**

Exercises

Independent Practice   Complete.

14. 3 lb = ? oz **48**   15. 5 tons = ? lb **10,000**   16. 3 c = ? fl oz **24**

17. 5 pt = ? c **10**   18. 4,000 lb = ? tons **2**   19. 48 oz = ? lb **3**

20. 16 qt = ? gal **4**   21. 8 pt = ? qt **4**   22. 2.5 lb = ? oz **40**

23. 2.5 qt = ? pt **5**   24. 0.5 gal = ? qt **2**   25. 4.5 pt = ? c **9**

26. 1 pt = ? qt $\frac{1}{2}$ 27. 2 fl oz = ? c $\frac{1}{4}$ 28. 5 c = ? pt $2\frac{1}{2}$

29. How many pints are in $4\frac{1}{2}$ quarts? **9 pints**

30. Change 11 quarts to gallons. $2\frac{3}{4}$ **gallons**

31. Convert 4 ounces to pounds. $\frac{1}{4}$ **lb**

Mixed Review   32. Evaluate the expression $3 \cdot 0.50 + 4 \cdot 0.75$. *(Lesson 1-7)* **4.5**

33. **Earning Money** Ginny receives a paycheck for 12 days of work in the amount of $732.25. How much did she earn per day? Round to the nearest cent. *(Lesson 2-8)* **$61.02**

34. **Statistics** Construct a line plot for 5, 2, 0, 3, 2, 5, 15, 4, 3, and 0. Circle any outliers. *(Lesson 3-4)* **See Solutions Manual.**

35. Multiply $5\frac{3}{8}$ and $\frac{2}{3}$. *(Lesson 5-5)* $3\frac{7}{12}$

36. Translate the phrase *12 more than d* into an algebraic expression. *(Lesson 6-4)* **12 + d**

Problem Solving and Applications   37. **Critical Thinking** The owner's manual of Car A states that it has a capacity of 13.2 gallons of gasoline. Car B has a capacity of 13 gallons 1 quart.

    a. Which car has the greater gasoline capacity? **Car B**

    b. How many more quarts will it hold? **0.2 quarts**

38. **Biology** About 190 million years ago, a giant lizard-like dinosaur called a brontosaurus was roaming Earth. It weighed about 30 tons. Today the largest living land animal is the African elephant. It weighs about 16,500 pounds. How many more tons did the brontosaurus weigh than today's elephant? **21.75 or $21\frac{3}{4}$ tons**

39. **Data Search** Refer to pages 218 and 219. What is the apparent temperature when the room temperature is 73°F with a relative humidity of 20%? What is the apparent temperature when the room temperature is 73°F, but the relative humidity is 90%? **68°, 76°**

OPTIONS

Extending the Lesson

Measurement Have students work in groups to make a chart showing the customary units of *length*. Under the chart, have them list examples of classroom objects or local distances that are approximately equal in length to each of the measures.

Cooperative Learning Activity

It Really Adds Up 6-6

Use groups of 4 or more.
Materials: Soft-drink bottles and/or cans, cereal boxes

➤ Use the information printed on soft-drink containers and cereal boxes to find the number of fluid ounces of soft drinks and ounces of cereal each group member consumes each week. Multiply each amount by 52 weeks and then find the sum of the four amounts. This is the group's yearly total. Then answer the following questions.

• How many gallons of soft drinks does your group consume in one year?
• How many tons of cereal does your group consume in one year?

Share your findings with other groups.

Glencoe Mathematics: Applications and Connections, Course 2

Cooperative Learning

6-7A Preview of Geometry: Area

A Preview of Lesson 6-7

Objective
Use models to find the area of rectangles and parallelograms.

Words to Learn
area
parallelogram
base
height

Materials
grid paper
scissors
pencil

In this lab, you will investigate the areas of rectangles and parallelograms by using models.

Activity One

- On grid paper, draw a rectangle with a length of 6 units and a width of 4 units as shown at the right.
- The **area** of a geometric figure is the number of square units needed to cover the surface within the figure.

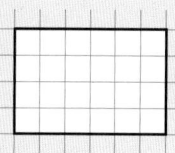

What do you think?

1. How many squares are found within this rectangle? **24 squares**

2. How does the area relate to the length and width of the rectangle?
   $\ell \times w = \text{area}$

A **parallelogram** is a four-sided figure whose opposite sides are parallel. One of its sides may be identified as its **base**. The distance from the base to the opposite side is called the **height**.

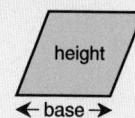
height
← base →

Activity Two

- On grid paper, draw a parallelogram with a base of 6 units and a height of 4 units as shown at the right.
- Draw a line to represent the height as shown.
- Use your scissors to cut out the parallelogram.
- Then cut the parallelogram along the line for the height as shown below.

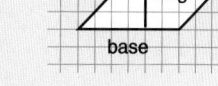
height
base

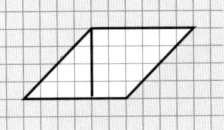 →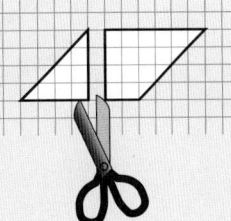

Mathematics Lab 6-7A Preview of Geometry: Area **241**

Mathematics Lab 6-7A

NCTM Standards: 1–4, 12

Management Tips

For Students Have students work with a partner. Provide each group with centimeter grid paper and a pair of scissors.

For the Overhead Projector
Overhead Manipulative Resources provides appropriate materials for teacher or student demonstration of the activities in this Mathematics Lab.

1 FOCUS

Introducing the Lab

Before presenting the lesson, ask questions to assess students' prior knowledge of the relationship between rectangles and parallelograms. Ask them how they could use grid paper to show how one can be reassembled to form the other.

Interactive Mathematics Tools

This multimedia software provides an interactive lesson that is tied directly to Lesson 6–7A. Students will use changeable quadrilaterals to explore the area of parallelograms.

2 TEACH

Using Critical Thinking
Ask students what figure will be formed if they draw a rectangle, cut off a triangle whose height is one side of that rectangle, and then move the triangle to the other side. Have them use grid paper and scissors to find out. **forms a parallelogram**

3 PRACTICE/APPLY

Using models Have students use geoboards and rubber bands to explore how changing the bases and heights affects the areas of rectangles and parallelograms.

Close

Ask students to explain how they know that rectangles and parallelograms with the same base and height will have the same area.

Additional Answers

7. 15 square units
8. 15 square units
9. 8 square units
10. 8 square units

- Move the triangle to the opposite end of the parallelogram to form a rectangle.

Talk About It

3. What is the area of the newly-formed rectangle? **24 square units**
4. How are the area of the original parallelogram and the area of the newly-formed rectangle related? **They are the same.**
5. How does the area of the parallelogram relate to its base and height? $b \times h = $ **area**
6. How does this compare to the number of square units in the rectangle you drew? **The areas are the same.**

Applications For answers to Exercises 7–10, see margin.

Use your grid paper to draw the following figures. Cut them out and find their areas by counting squares.

7. rectangle: ℓ, 5; w, 3   8. parallelogram: b, 5; h, 3
9. rectangle: ℓ, 4; w, 2   10. parallelogram: b, 4; h, 2

11. What is the height of a parallelogram if its area is 36 square units and its base is 9 units long? **4 units**
12. Think about the length of the base and the height of a parallelogram if its area is 16 square units.
    a. Can other parallelograms be made with the same area, but different base and height? **yes**
    b. If so, what is the base and height of your other parallelograms? Draw some examples. **Sample answer; 2 × 8**

Extension

13. If you double the length and width of a rectangle, how does its area change? Explain your reasoning in words and by drawing diagrams. **Area increased 4 times; see students' work.**

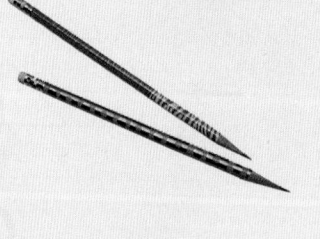

242   Chapter 6 An Introduction to Algebra

OPTIONS

Lab Manual You may wish to make copies of the blackline master on p. 53 of the *Lab Manual* for students to use as a recording sheet.

Lab Manual, p. 53

Name _____ Date _____

Mathematics Lab Worksheet

Use with pages 241–242

A Preview of Geometry: Area

1. __15 squares__
2. __15 squares__
3. __8 squares__
4. __8 squares__
5. __4 units__
6. a. __yes__

6-7 Area

Objective
Find the area of rectangles and parallelograms.

Basketball was invented in 1891 by Dr. James Naismith of Springfield, Massachusetts. He wanted a game that could be played indoors during the winter and in the evening. Dr. Naismith used two wooden peach baskets nailed to the balcony of the school gym.

Today we use net baskets and play on a court shaped like a rectangle. The length of a regulation size court for professional and college basketball is 94 feet and the width is 50 feet. What is the area of the court?

One way to find the area is to count the number of square feet by marking off a grid on the court. This method is not practical, however. In the Mathematics Lab, you discovered that the area of a rectangle can be found as follows.

Area of Rectangles	**In words:** The area of a rectangle equals the product of its length (ℓ) and width (w).
	In symbols: $A = \ell w$

Examples

1 Find the area of a regulation size basketball court with a length of 94 feet and a width of 50 feet.

$A = \ell w$ *Write the formula for area.*
$A = 94 \cdot 50$ *Replace l with 94 and w with 50.*

94 ⊠ 50 ⊟ 4700

$A = 4,700$ The area of a regulation size basketball court is 4,700 square feet (ft²).

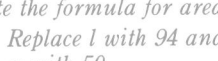
50 ft
94 ft

Problem-Solving Hint
•••••••••••••
For problems like the one in Example 2, it may be helpful to make a drawing.

2 Find the width of a rectangle with an area of 260.4 square inches and a length of 16.8 inches.

$A = \ell w$ *Write the formula for area.*
$260.4 = 16.8w$ *Replace A with 260.4 and l with 16.8.*
$\dfrac{260.4}{16.8} = \dfrac{16.8w}{16.8}$ *Divide each side by 16.8.*

260.4 ⊡ 16.8 ⊟ 15.5

$15.5 = w$

Lesson 6-7 Geometry Connection: Area   **243**

OPTIONS

Reteaching Activity

Using Connections Guide students to see that the formula for the area of parallelograms is derived from the formula for the area of rectangles. Use a geoboard and rubber bands to construct a rectangle. Stretch the rubber band to form a parallelogram of the same base and height as the rectangle.

Study Guide Masters, p. 56

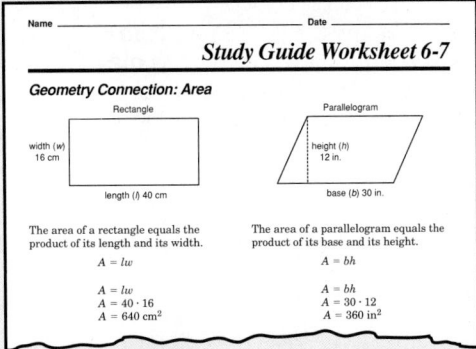

Name _____ Date _____

Study Guide Worksheet 6-7

Geometry Connection: Area

Rectangle

width (w) 16 cm

length (l) 40 cm

Parallelogram

height (h) 12 in.

base (b) 30 in.

The area of a rectangle equals the product of its length and its width.

$A = lw$

$A = lw$
$A = 40 \cdot 16$
$A = 640 \text{ cm}^2$

The area of a parallelogram equals the product of its base and its height.

$A = bh$

$A = bh$
$A = 30 \cdot 12$
$A = 360 \text{ in}^2$

6-7 Lesson Notes

NCTM Standards: 1–5, 7, 9, 12

Lesson Resources
• Study Guide Master 6-7
• Practice Master 6-7
• Enrichment Master 6-7
• Evaluation Master, Quiz B, p. 52
• Application Master, p. 6
• Group Activity Card 6-7

 Transparency 6-7 contains the 5-Minute Check and a teaching aid for this lesson.

🕐 **5-Minute Check**
(Over Lesson 6-6)
Complete.
1. 4 lb = <u>?</u> oz   64
2. 2.5 qt = <u>?</u> pt   5
3. 7 c = <u>?</u> pt   3.5
4. 3,000 lb = <u>?</u> tons   1.5
5. 4 fl oz = <u>?</u> c   0.5

1 FOCUS

Motivating the Lesson

Activity Read the opening two paragraphs with students. Ask them how they think the basketball court in their school compares in size with a regulation court. To check the students' conjectures, have them measure the school's court using a tape measure, yardstick, or trundle wheel.

2 TEACH

Using Applications Have students first estimate the area of their classroom floor and then check their estimate by measuring the dimensions and using the area formula. If the floor is not a rectangle or parallelogram, help students to see that they can break it up into smaller rectangles or parallelograms and combine those shapes to get the total area.

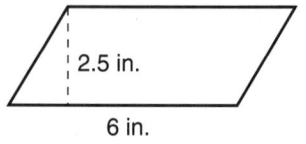
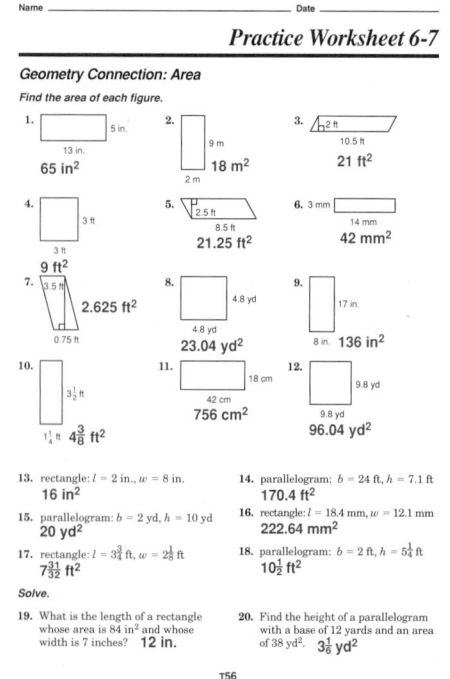
Check: $260.4 = 16.8w$
$260.4 \overset{?}{=} 16.8 \cdot 15.5$ *Replace with 15.5.*
$260.4 = 260.4$ ✓
The width is 15.5 inches.

You also discovered in the Mathematics Lab that the area of a parallelogram is closely related to the area of a rectangle.

Area of Parallelograms	**In words:** The area of a parallelogram equals the product of its base (b) and its height (h).
	In symbols: $A = bh$

Example 3

Find the area of the parallelogram at the right.

$A = bh$ *Write the formula for area.*
$A = 5 \cdot 3\frac{1}{2}$ *Replace b with 5 and w with $3\frac{1}{2}$.*
$A = \frac{5}{1} \cdot \frac{7}{2}$
$A = \frac{35}{2}$ or $17\frac{1}{2}$ The area is $17\frac{1}{2}$ square inches (in²).

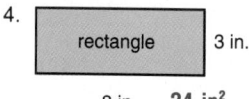
$3\frac{1}{2}$ in.
5 in.

Checking for Understanding

Communicating Mathematics

Read and study the lesson to answer each question.

1. **Model** a parallelogram with a base of 8 units and a height of 5 units using grid paper. What is its area? **40 square units**
2. **Tell** how the formula $A = bh$ is also appropriate for finding the area of a rectangle. **A rectangle is a type of parallelogram.**
3. **Write** two sentences comparing the similarities and differences of rectangles and parallelograms. **Area computed the same, parallelograms do not have to have right angles.**

Guided Practice

Find the area of each figure shown or described below.

4. rectangle 3 in. / 8 in. **24 in²**
5. rectangle 2 m / 7 m **14 m²**
6. 5 ft / 6.5 ft **32.5 ft²**

7. rectangle: ℓ, 1 in.; w, 6 in. **6 in²**
8. rectangle: ℓ, 18 cm; w, 12 cm **216 cm²**

244   Chapter 6 An Introduction to Algebra

Exercises

Find the area of each figure shown or described below.

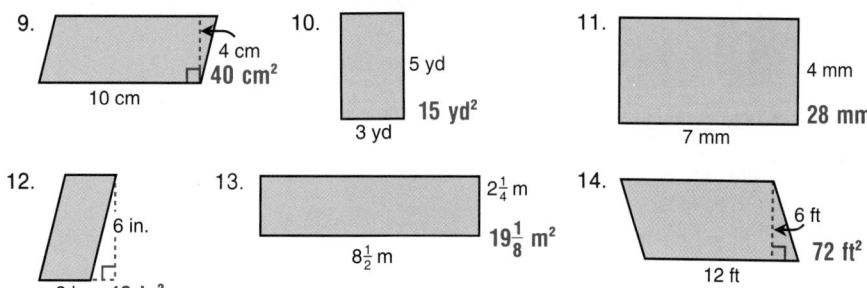

9. 4 cm 40 cm² 10 cm

10. 5 yd 15 yd² 3 yd

11. 4 mm 28 mm² 7 mm

12. 6 in. 3 in. 18 in²

13. 2¼ m 19⅛ m² 8½ m

14. 6 ft 72 ft² 12 ft

15. parallelogram: *b,* 23 ft; *h,* 18 ft **414 ft²**

16. rectangle: *ℓ,* 8.5 mm; *w,* 7.5 mm **63.75 mm²**

17. parallelogram: *b,* 12.6 ft; *h,* 11.3 ft **142.38 ft²**

18. rectangle: *ℓ,* 6⅓ yd; *w,* 5 yd **31⅔ yd²**

19. Find the area of a parallelogram with a base of 4.5 centimeters and a height of 4 centimeters. **18 cm²**

20. What is the length of a rectangle with an area of 31⅔ square yards and a width of 5 yards? **6⅓ yd**

21. Use front-end estimation to find the difference of 365 and 151. *(Lesson 1-2)* **about 210**

22. Multiply 100 and 30. *(Lesson 2-5)* **3,000**

23. How many ½-cup servings of ice cream are there in a gallon of chocolate ice cream? *(Lesson 6-6)* **32 servings**

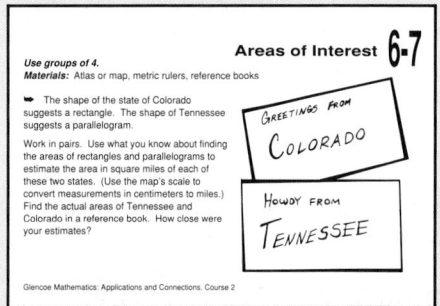

24. **Critical Thinking** If you cut a cardboard tube, you will find that it is a rectangle. How much cardboard is used in a tube if its length is 4½ inches and its circumference is 5 inches? **22½ in²**

25. **Construction** Philip Frazier wants to build a deck with an area of at least 120 square feet. He has space for a length of up to 14 feet, but no more than 9 feet for the width.
   a. Will he be able to build a deck as large as he wants? **yes**
   b. If so, what will be the area of the largest deck possible? **126 ft²**

26. **Journal Entry** Collect data by measuring the playing surface of a court or playing field at your school. Make and label a scale drawing of it. What is its area? **See students' work.**

27. **Portfolio Suggestion** Select an item from this chapter that shows your creativity and place it in your portfolio. **See students' work.**

Lesson 6-7 Geometry: Area **245**

Error Analysis

Watch for students who try to calculate the area of a parallelogram by multiplying its base by the length of one of its sides.

Prevent by stressing that the length of the side of a parallelogram is its height only when the figure is a rectangle.

Close

Have students write a word problem that can be solved by finding the area of a region that is a parallelogram. Ask students to exchange papers and solve each other's problem.

3 PRACTICE/APPLY

Assignment Guide
Maximum: 9–26
Minimum: 9–15 odd, 16–24

For **Extra Practice,** see p. 586.

Alternate Assessment

Speaking Have students explain how the formulas for area of rectangles and parallelograms are related.

Enrichment Masters, p. 56

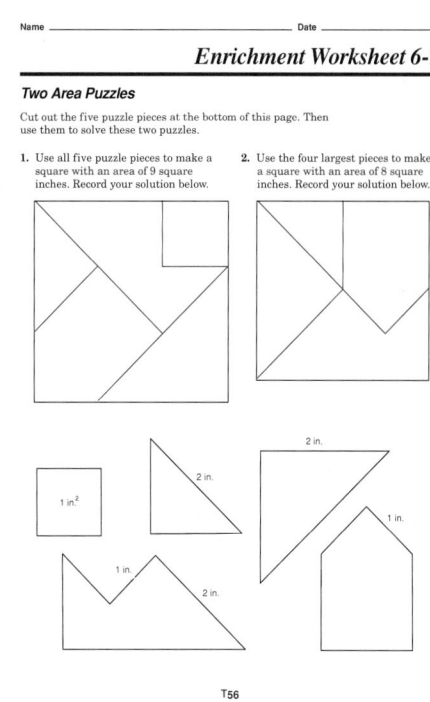

Name _____ Date _____

Enrichment Worksheet 6-7

Two Area Puzzles

Cut out the five puzzle pieces at the bottom of this page. Then use them to solve these two puzzles.

1. Use all five puzzle pieces to make a square with an area of 9 square inches. Record your solution below.

2. Use the four largest pieces to make a square with an area of 8 square inches. Record your solution below.

2 in.
2 in.
1 in²
1 in.
1 in.
2 in.
1 in.
2 in.

T56
Glencoe Division, Macmillan/McGraw-Hill

Extending the Lesson

Using Critical Thinking Tell students to imagine that they had 28 feet of fencing. Ask them to give the whole-number dimensions of a rectangular garden with the greatest area that could be formed with that fencing. Then ask students what they notice when they try the same problem using different lengths of fence. **7 ft × 7 ft; The rectangle with the greatest area is a square.**

Cooperative Learning Activity

Use groups of 4.
Materials: Atlas or map, metric rulers, reference books

Areas of Interest 6-7

➡ The shape of the state of Colorado suggests a rectangle. The shape of Tennessee suggests a parallelogram.

Work in pairs. Use what you know about finding the areas of rectangles and parallelograms to estimate the area in square miles of each of these two states. (Use the map's scale to convert measurements in centimeters to miles.) Find the actual areas of Tennessee and Colorado in a reference book. How close were your estimates?

GREETINGS FROM
COLORADO

HOWDY FROM
TENNESSEE

Glencoe Mathematics: Applications and Connections, Course 2

245

The Chapter Study Guide and Review begins with a section on Communicating Mathematics. This includes questions that review the new terms and concepts that were introduced in the chapter.

Then, the Skills and Concepts presented in the chapter are reviewed using a side-by-side format. Encourage students to refer to the Objectives and Examples on the left as they complete the Review Exercises on the right.

The Chapter Study Guide and Review ends with problems that review Applications and Problem Solving.

Chapter

6 Study Guide and Review

Study Guide and Review

Communicating Mathematics

State whether each sentence is *true* or *false*. If false, replace the underlined word to make a true sentence.

1. Equations that have the same solution are called <u>equivalent</u> equations. **true**
2. The multiplication property of equality states that if you multiply each side of an equation by the same number, the two sides will then be <u>unequal</u>. **false-equal**
3. The words "more than" suggest <u>multiplication</u> in algebraic terms. **false-addition**
4. To change from pounds to tons, the number of pounds should be <u>multiplied</u> by 2,000 since 1 ton equals 2,000 pounds. **false-divided**
5. To change 6 cups to fluid ounces, 6 should be <u>multiplied</u> by 8. **true**
6. The formula for the area of a <u>parallelogram</u> is $A = \ell w$. **false-rectangle**
7. In your own words, explain the addition property of equality. **If you add the same number to both sides of the equation, the two sides will still be equal.**

Self Assessment

Objectives and Examples	Review Exercises
Upon completing this chapter, you should be able to:	*Use these exercises to review and prepare for the chapter test.*

• solve equations using inverse operations *(Lesson 6-1)*

Solve $p + 3 = 5$ *Write the related*
$\quad\quad p = 5 - 3$ *subtraction*
$\quad\quad p = 2$ *sentence.*

Solve each equation by using the inverse equation.

8. $x - 14 = 15$ **29**   9. $m + \frac{7}{2} = 5$ $1\frac{1}{2}$
10. $t - 3.6 = 10.1$ **13.7** 11. $26 + p = 26$ **0**
12. $5q = 6$ **1.2**   13. $\frac{2}{3}y = \frac{1}{4}$ $\frac{3}{8}$
14. $\frac{s}{2} = 13$ **26**   15. $\frac{b}{4.6} = 3.1$ **14.26**

• solve equations using the addition and subtraction properties of equality *(Lesson 6-2)*

Solve $c - 32 = 112$
$\quad c - 32 + 32 = 112 + 32$
$\quad\quad\quad\quad c = 144$

Solve each equation. Check your solution.

16. $w + 13 = 25$ **12**   17. $f - 3\frac{1}{2} = 3$ $6\frac{1}{2}$
18. $10.9 + r = 11$ **0.1** 19. $54 = m - 9$ **63**
20. $3\frac{2}{5} = 1\frac{1}{3} + x$ $2\frac{1}{15}$
21. $s + 3.75 = 5.25$ **1.5**
22. $\frac{100}{9} = \frac{100}{9} + k$ **0**

Objectives and Examples

- solve equations using the multiplication and division property of equality *(Lesson 6-3)*

Solve $33y = 132$

$$\frac{33y}{33} = \frac{132}{33} \quad \textit{Divide each}$$
$$\qquad\qquad\quad \textit{side by 33.}$$
$$y = 4$$

- write algebraic expressions from verbal phrases *(Lesson 6-4)*

Translate "4 times the price" into an algebraic expression.

Let p represent the price. The word *times* suggests multiplication. The algebraic expression is $4p$.

- convert within the customary system *(Lesson 6-6)*

Complete: $12 \text{ lb} = \underline{\ ?\ } \text{ oz}$

Since 1 lb = 16 oz, multiply by 16.
$12 \cdot 16 = 192$
$12 \text{ lb} = 192 \text{ oz}$

- find the area of rectangles and parallelograms *(Lesson 6-7)*

Find the area of a parallelogram with a base of 6 inches and a height of 3 inches.

$A = bh$
$A = 6 \cdot 3 \quad$ *Replace b with 6 and*
$A = 18 \qquad$ *h with 3.*

The area is 18 square inches.

Review Exercises

Solve each equation. Check your solution.

23. $4b = 32$ **8**
24. $\frac{p}{6} = 4.5$ **27**
25. $\frac{3}{2}m = \frac{5}{4}$ $\frac{5}{6}$
26. $5.9r = 0.59$ **0.1**
27. $64 = 16a$ **4**
28. $\frac{g}{15} = \frac{3}{5}$ **9**
29. $\frac{g}{3.6} = 10$ **36**
30. $1.333t = 0$ **0**

Translate each phrase into an algebraic expression.

31. the sum of x and 5 $x + 5$
32. 13 less than s $s - 13$
33. 13 less r $13 - r$
34. e multiplied by 2 $2e$
35. 9 increased by q $9 + q$
36. the quotient of z and 15 $\frac{z}{15}$
37. 23 fewer than b $b - 23$
38. t times 3.6 $3.6t$
39. c divided by 100 $\frac{c}{100}$

Complete.

40. $3 \text{ qt} = \underline{\ ?\ } \text{ pt}$ **6**
41. $5 \text{ gal} = \underline{\ ?\ } \text{ qt}$ **80**
42. $6{,}000 \text{ lb} = \underline{\ ?\ } \text{ tons}$ **3**
43. $54 \text{ oz} = \underline{\ ?\ } \text{ lb}$ $3\frac{3}{8}$
44. $24 \text{ fl oz} = \underline{\ ?\ } \text{ c}$ **3**
45. $5\frac{3}{4} \text{ qt} = \underline{\ ?\ } \text{ pt}$ $11\frac{1}{2}$

Find the area of each figure described below.

46. rectangle: ℓ, 12 in.; w, 4 in. **48 in²**
47. parallelogram: b, 15 yd; h, 3 yd **45 yd²**
48. rectangle: ℓ, $5\frac{1}{2}$ ft; w, $\frac{3}{4}$ ft **4.125 or $4\frac{1}{8}$ ft²**
49. parallelogram: b, 13.6 in.; h, 2.7 in. **36.72 in²**
50. rectangle: ℓ, 12.5 ft; w, 1.6 ft **20 ft²**
51. parallelogram: b, $3\frac{5}{8}$ in.; h, $1\frac{2}{3}$ in. **$6\frac{1}{24}$ in²**

You may wish to use a Chapter Test from the Evaluation Masters booklet as an additional chapter review. The two free-response forms are shown below. One of the two multiple-choice forms is shown on the next page.

Evaluation Masters, pp. 50–51

Applications and Problem Solving

52. **Fund Raiser**   In 1991, Central Junior High School raised $335 more during their annual fund-raising drive than they had during the previous year's drive. Write an algebraic expression for the amount raised in 1991. Let r represent the amount raised in 1990. *(Lesson 6-4)* **$r + 335$**

53. **Highway Safety**   Ben Johnson is driving a semitrailer-tractor truck that weighs in at 13,596 pounds when fully loaded. He approaches a bridge that is marked with a sign stating the maximum weight allowed is 6 tons. If Bob's semitrailer-tractor truck is fully loaded, should he attempt to cross the bridge? *(Lesson 6-6)* **no**

54. Patrick earned $65 in January shoveling snow. The total was 4 times more than his January earnings last winter. How much did he earn last January? *(Lesson 6-5)* **$16.25**

55. Ellen is making invitations for a surprise party to celebrate her mother's birthday. The invitations are designed in the shape of a parallelogram with a base of 5 inches and a height of $2\frac{1}{2}$ inches. How much paper will Ellen need to make 20 invitations? *(Lesson 6-7)* **250 square inches**

Curriculum Connection Projects

- **Health**   Have a friend measure your pulse rate while resting and again after running in place for a short time. Write a formula for finding the difference in the two pulse rates.

- **Art**   List and measure rectangles and parallelograms that you find in patterns on clothing, quilts, wallpaper, wall hangings, carpets, curtains, and so on. Then find the area of each item you have listed.

Read More About It

Manes, Stephen. *Chocolate Covered Ants.*

Angell, Judie. *Leave the Cooking to Me.*

Bjork, Christina and Anderson, Lena. *Elliot's Extraordinary Cookbook.*

Chapter

6 Test

Solve each equation by using the inverse operations.

1. $h + 6 = 19$ 13
2. $3.5d = 14.7$ 4.2
3. $7\frac{3}{8} = x - \frac{15}{2}$ $14\frac{7}{8}$

4. **Chemistry**   During a chemical reaction, 3 mL of the original chemical evaporates, leaving 2.6 mL in the test tube. Solve the equation $a - 3 = 2.6$ to find a, the amount of chemical in the test tube before the reaction occurs.   5.6 mL

Solve each equation. Check your solution.

5. $p + 21 = 35$ 14
6. $\frac{3}{2} + r = \frac{8}{3}$ $1\frac{1}{6}$
7. $12e = 120$ 10
8. $\frac{3}{2}f = 3$ 2
9. $\frac{7}{6} = b - \frac{1}{8}$ $1\frac{7}{24}$
10. $0.01m = 50$ 5,000
11. $s - 5.9 = 12.1$ 18
12. $\frac{y}{3} = 36$ 108
13. $0.997 + t = 1$ 0.003

14. Ann prices a sweater in two stores and finds it is $29 in the first store and $34 in the second. Solve the equation $29 + p = 34$ to find p, the price difference between the two stores. $5

15. **Inflation**   Economists say that, on average, the 1991 price of a gallon of gas was 1.7 times what it was in 1980. The average 1991 price of a gallon of gas was $1.19. Solve the equation $1.7g = 1.19$ to find g, the average price in 1980. $0.70

Translate each phrase into an algebraic expression.

16. 26 less x $26 - x$
17. t increased by 23 $t + 23$
18. 5 divided into w $\frac{w}{5}$

19. Debbie's aunt is 60 years old. Her age is six years more than Debbie's age. How old is Debbie?   54 years old

Complete.

20. 24 qt = _?_ gal   6
21. $3\frac{1}{4}$ lb = _?_ oz   52
22. 4,500 lb = _?_ tons   2.25

23. **Sports**   The attendance at the last football game of the season was 97 fewer than the attendance at the first game. Let y represent the attendance at the first game. Write an expression for the last game's attendance. $y - 97$

24. A typical soft drink can holds 12 fluid ounces. How many cups is this? $1\frac{1}{2}$ cups

25. **Geometry**   Theresa argues that the area of a parallelogram with a base of 6 inches and a height of 3 inches is the same as the area of a rectangle with a length of 10 inches and width of 1.8 inches. Is she correct?   yes

Bonus   Write an expression for the difference of two consecutive even numbers. $(2n + 2) - 2n$

This page may be used as a chapter test or another chapter review.

Evaluation Masters, pp. 46–47

Name _____   Date _____

Form 1A _____   *Chapter 6 Test*

1. Solve $p + 2\frac{1}{2} = 10\frac{3}{4}$ by using the inverse operation.   1. __C__
   A. $13\frac{1}{4}$ B. $8\frac{1}{2}$ C. $8\frac{1}{4}$ D. $7\frac{1}{4}$
2. Solve $7.9 = c - 4.7$ by using the inverse operation.   2. __D__
   A. 2.3   B. 3.2   C. 1.26   D. 12.6
3. Solve $108 = 6c$ by using the inverse operation.   3. __A__
   A. 18   B. 102   C. 114   D. 648
4. What is the solution to $\frac{x}{7} = 11$?   4. __B__
   A. 18   B. 77   C. 4   D. $1\frac{4}{7}$
5. Solve $19 + b = 44$.   5. __D__
   A. 63   B. 24   C. 836   D. 25
6. Solve $81 = 3k$ 6. __A__
   A. 27   B. 243   C. 78   D. 84
7. Solve $\frac{m}{6} = 0.9$.   7. __C__
   A. 6.9   B. 5.1   C. 5.4   D. $6\frac{2}{3}$
8. Solve $f + 12.8 = 14.1$.   8. __A__
   A. 1.3   B. 26.9   C. 2.69   D. 180.48
9. Solve $y - 6 = 102$.   9. __B__
   A. 612   B. 108   C. 17   D. 96
10. Solve $r \div \frac{1}{4} = \frac{1}{2}$.   10. __A__
   A. $\frac{1}{8}$ B. $\frac{1}{4}$ C. $\frac{1}{2}$ D. 2
11. Solve $\frac{l}{0.8} = 1.6$.   11. __C__
   A. 2   B. 0.8   C. 1.28   D. 2.4
12. Translate *fifteen less than w* into an algebraic expression.   12. __B__
   A. $w + 15$ B. $w - 15$ C. $15 - w$ D. $15 + w$
13. Translate *h increased by 9* into an algebraic expression.   13. __D__
   A. $h - 9$ B. $9h$ C. $h \div 9$ D. $h + 9$
14. Translate *the difference of 2 and d* into an algebraic expression.   14. __A__
   A. $2 - d$ B. $2 + d$ C. $2d$ D. $d - 2$

Name _____   Date _____

Form 1A (continued)   Chapter 6 Test

15. Translate *the product of 7 and m* into an algebraic expression.   15. __B__
   A. $7 + m$ B. $7m$ C. $7 \div m$ D. $7 - m$
16. Complete 3.5 tons = ∎ lb.   16. __A__
   A. 7,000   B. 3,000   C. 3,500   D. 6,500
17. Complete ∎ c = 2.5 pt.   17. __C__
   A. 10   B. 7.5   C. 5   D. 1.25
18. How many quarts are in $4\frac{1}{2}$ gallons?   18. __D__
   A. 16   B. 2.25   C. 9   D. 18
19. Change 1.5 pounds to ounces.   19. __B__
   A. 3   B. 24   C. 12   D. 36

Find the area of each figure in Exercises 20 and 21.

20. [rectangle: 0.8 m, 3.2 m]   20. __A__
   A. 2.56 m²   B. 3.0 m²   C. 8.0 m²   D. 4.0 m²
21. [parallelogram: 0.8 cm, 1.4 cm, 2.4 cm]   21. __D__
   A. 2.0 cm²   B. 3.36 cm²   C. 7.6 cm²   D. 1.92 cm²
22. Find the area of the parallelogram with a base of 3.5 meters and a height of 6 meters.   22. __A__
   A. 21.0 m²   B. 19 m²   C. 9.5 m²   D. 3.5 m²
23. What is the length of a rectangle with an area of 23.8 square miles and a width of 3.5 miles?   23. __C__
   A. 8.4 mi   B. 7.5 mi   C. 6.8 mi   D. 4.8 mi
24. Edwin's mother is 57 years old. Her age is three years more than twice Edwin's age. What is Edwin's age?   24. __B__
   A. 30 years   B. 27 years   C. 15 years   D. 37 years
25. A number is divided by 6. Then the quotient is decreased by 1. If the result is 3, what was the original number?   25. __D__
   A. 19   B. 11   C. 12   D. 24

BONUS Solve $\frac{2}{3}x = 3\frac{1}{4}$.   __C__
   A. 0.33   B. 2.1   C. 4.875   D. 2.625

Test and Review Generator software is provided in Apple, IBM, and Macintosh versions. You may use this software to create your own tests or worksheets, based on the needs of your students.

The **Performance Assessment Booklet** provides an alternate assessment for evaluating student progress. An assessment for this chapter can be found on pages 11–12.

The Academic Skills Test may be used to help students prepare for standardized tests. The test items are written in the same style as those in state proficiency tests. The test items cover skills and concepts presented up to this point in the text.

These pages can be used as an overnight assignment. After students have completed the pages, discuss how each problem can be solved, or provide copies of the solutions from the *Solutions Manual*.

Chapter

6 Academic Skills Test

Directions: Choose the best answer. Write A, B, C, or D.

1. Mike is reading a 258-page novel. If he reads 8 pages an hour, *about* how long will it take him to read the entire book?

   D

   A 8 hours   B 16 hours
   C 24 hours   D 30 hours

2. Sandy is knitting scarves for her 3 sisters. She needs to buy 9 skeins of yarn. Each skein costs $2.59, including tax. Which information do you need to find the cost of the yarn?

   D

   A 3 sisters, 9 skeins, $2.59 each
   B 3 sisters, $2.59 each
   C 3 sisters, 9 skeins
   D 9 skeins, $2.59 each

3. What is the value of x^5 if $x = 3$?

   A

   A 243   B 125
   C 15   D 3

4. Which is the best estimate for the total cost?

   C

   | $1.89 |
   | 2.08 |
   | 2.00 |
   | 1.95 |
   | 1.88 |
   | 2.10 |

   A $8.00
   B $10.00
   C $12.00
   D $13.00

5. 2.36×100

   C

   A 0.236   B 2.36
   C 236   D 2,360

6. George earned $18.20 for babysitting 6.5 hours. How much was he paid per hour?

   D

   A $6.50   B $3.80
   C $3.00   D $2.80

7. The frequency table below contains data about students' test scores on a 20-point test.

   C

Score	14	15	16	17	18	19	20
No. of Students	2	1	5	4	6	5	2

   How many students had a score greater than 16?

   A 4   B 5
   C 17   D 22

8. Use the data in Exercise 7. What is the mode of the scores?

   D

   A 6   B 17
   C 17.36   D 18

9. The stem-and-leaf plot shows the Wildcats' basketball scores for this season.

   C

   ```
   1 | 8 9
   2 | 0 2 3 3 6 8 8
   3 | 0 1 4 4 5 6 8 9
   4 | 0 1 2
       1 | 8 = 18 points
   ```

   In how many games did they score at least 30 points?

   A 8   B 9
   C 11   D 20

10. Which number comes next in this pattern?

D

$$0.5, 2, 3.5, 5, \ldots$$

A 8   B 7.5

C 7   D 6.5

11. Which fraction is in simplest form?

A

A $\frac{4}{15}$ B $\frac{6}{21}$

C $\frac{8}{10}$ D $\frac{9}{27}$

12. What is the least common multiple of 25 and 45?

B

A 45   B 225

C 1,125   D none of these

13. Change $3\frac{5}{8}$ to an improper fraction.

D

A $\frac{35}{8}$ B $\frac{20}{8}$

C $\frac{15}{8}$ D $\frac{29}{8}$

14. $\frac{3}{4} + \frac{1}{2}$

D

A $\frac{1}{4}$ B $\frac{3}{8}$

C $\frac{4}{6}$ D $1\frac{1}{4}$

15. $\frac{1}{4} \times 2\frac{1}{2}$

C

A 10   B 1

C $\frac{5}{8}$ D $\frac{3}{8}$

16. To the nearest whole number, what is the circumference of the circle?

B

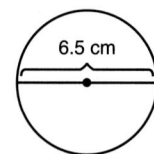
6.5 cm

A 10 cm   B 20 cm

C 32 cm   D 41 cm

17. If $n + 3.9 = 4.2$, what is the value of n?

D

A 1.7   B 3.9

C 8.1   D none of these

18. If $15a = 20$, what is the value of a?

B

A $\frac{3}{4}$ B $1\frac{1}{3}$

C 5   D 100

19. Which expression represents *five more than a number?*

D

A $5 - n$ B $n - 5$

C $5n$ D $n + 5$

20. A coffee can contains 1 pound 10 ounces of coffee. What is this equivalent to?

C

A 18 oz   B 20 oz

C 26 oz   D 42 oz

Chapter 6 Academic Skills Test   **251**

7 Integers

Previewing the Chapter

This chapter explores integers and their many applications. In developing integer concepts, extensive use is made of models such as counters of two colors. Students learn to compare and order integers, graph points on a coordinate plane, and add, subtract, multiply, and divide integers. They solve equations involving integers and interpret and write numbers with negative exponents. The **problem-solving strategy** lesson focuses on the strategy of solving a problem by finding and extending a pattern.

Lesson	Lesson Objectives	NCTM Standards	State/Local Objectives
7-1	Read and write integers. Find the opposite and absolute value of an integer.	1–6	
7-2	Compare and order integers.	1–6	
7-3	Graph points on a coordinate plane.	1–6, 12	
7-4A	Add integers by using models.	1–6	
7-4	Add integers.	1–7, 9	
7-5A	Subtract integers by using models.	1–6	
7-5	Subtract integers.	1–7, 9	
Decision Making	Plan for profit and good nutrition.	1–5, 7	
7-6	Solve problems by finding and extending a pattern.	1–5, 7, 8	
7-7A	Multiply integers by using models.	1–6	
7-7	Multiply integers.	1–9	
7-8	Divide integers.	1–7, 9, 10	
7-9A	Solve equations by using models.	1–7, 9	
7-9	Solve equations with integer solutions.	1–7, 9	
7-10	Use negative exponents.	1–9	

Organizing the Chapter

A complete, 1-page lesson plan is provided for each lesson in the Lesson Plans Masters Booklet.

LESSON PLANNING GUIDE

| Lesson | Materials/ Manipulatives | Extra Practice (Student Edition) | Blackline Masters Booklets | | | | | | | | | | |
			Study Guide	Practice	Enrichment	Evaluation	Technology	Lab Manual	Multicultural Activities	Application and Interdisciplinary Activities	Transparencies	Group Activity Cards
7-1	calculator counters	p. 587	p. 57	p. 57	p. 57						7-1	7-1
7-2		p. 587	p. 58	p. 58	p. 58						7-2	7-2
7-3	graph paper	p. 587	p. 59	p. 59	p. 59						7-3	7-3
7-4A	counters, mat							p. 54				
7-4	counters, graph paper, calculator	p. 588	p. 60	p. 60	p. 60		p. 7				7-4	7-4
7-5A	counters, mat							p. 55				
7-5	graph paper counters	p. 588	p. 61	p. 61	p. 61	Quiz A, p. 61				p. 7	7-5	7-5
7-6			p. 62	p. 62	p. 62						7-6	7-6
7-7A	counters, mat							p. 56				
7-7	counters	p. 588	p. 63	p. 63	p. 63		p. 21				7-7	7-7
7-8		p. 589	p. 64	p. 64	p. 64				p. 7		7-8	7-8
7-9A	counters, cups, mats							p. 57				
7-9	calculator counters	p. 589	p. 65	p. 65	p. 65						7-9	7-9
7-10		p. 589	p. 66	p. 66	p. 66	Quiz B, p. 61				p. 21	7-10	7-10
Study Guide and Review	graph paper, globe, deck of cards		Multiple Choice Test, Forms 1A and 1B, pp. 55–58 Free Response Test, Forms 2A and 2B, pp. 59–60 Cumulative Review, p. 62 (free response) Cumulative Test, p. 63 (multiple choice)									
Test	graph paper											

Pacing Guide: Option I (Chapters 1–12) - 14 days; Option II (Chapters 1–13) - 13 days; Option III (Chapters 1–14) - 13 days
You may wish to refer to the complete **Course Planning Guides** on page T25.

OTHER CHAPTER RESOURCES

Student Edition
Chapter Opener, pp. 252–253
Mid-Chapter Review, p. 271
Cultural Kaleidoscope, p. 276
Portfolio Suggestion, p. 286

 Manipulatives
Overhead Manipulative Resources
Middle School Mathematics Manipulative Kit

 Software/Technology
Interactive Mathematics Tools (Macintosh)
Test and Review Generator (IBM, Apple, Macintosh)
Teacher's Guide for Software Resources

Other Supplements
Transparency 7-0
Performance Assessment, pp. 13–14
Glencoe Mathematics Professional Series
Lesson Plans, pp. 71–84

Enhancing the Chapter

INTERDISCIPLINARY BULLETIN BOARD

Science Connection

Objective Solve equations with integers using information from a trail map.

How To Use It Have students talk about what it would be like to hike a trail that drops 5,000 feet and passes through several distinct habitats. Have them write problems using the information about the Bright Angel Trail that can be solved by writing and solving equations with integers. Then ask students to write to other national parks to obtain trail maps and geological information that can be added to the bulletin board.

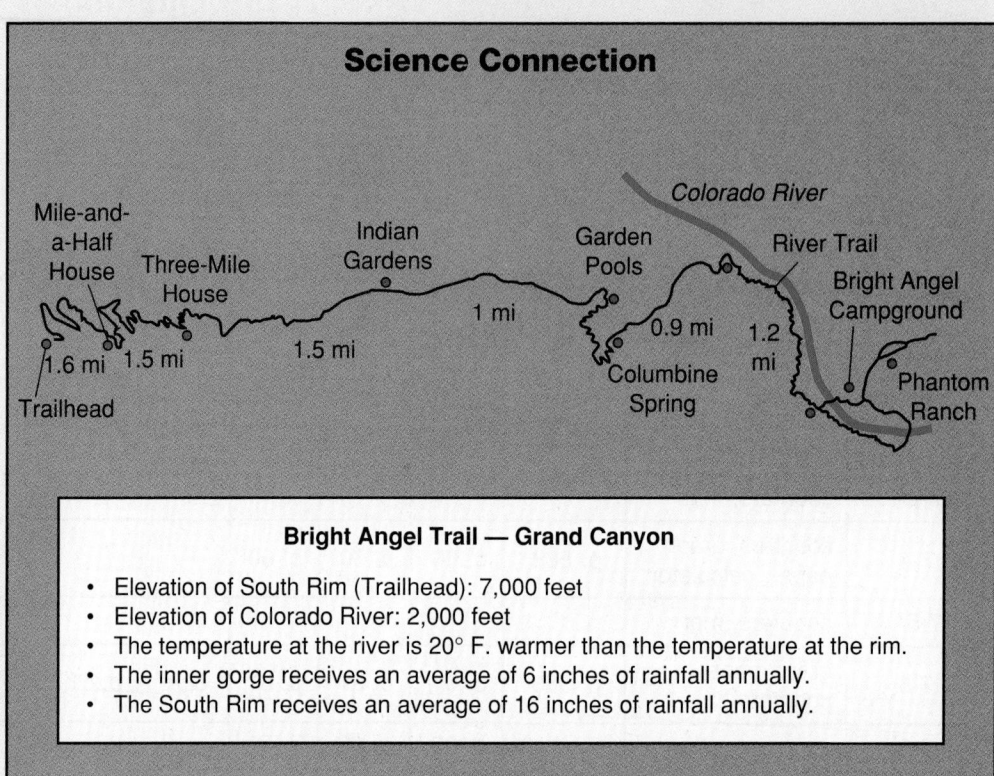

Science Connection

Bright Angel Trail — Grand Canyon

- Elevation of South Rim (Trailhead): 7,000 feet
- Elevation of Colorado River: 2,000 feet
- The temperature at the river is 20° F. warmer than the temperature at the rim.
- The inner gorge receives an average of 6 inches of rainfall annually.
- The South Rim receives an average of 16 inches of rainfall annually.

APPLICATIONS AND CONNECTIONS

Applications	Lesson	Example	Exercise
Weather	7-1		18, 39
Geography	7-1		37
Calculator	7-1		38
Weather	7-2		23
Computer	7-2		25
Geography	7-3		36
Geology	7-4	5	
Personal Finance	7-4		42
Space Travel	7-4		43
Environment	7-5		45
Weather	7-5		47
Earth Science	7-7		45
Engineering	7-8		32
Weather	7-9	2	
Environment	7-9		39
Biology	7-10	2	
Physics	7-10		28
Manufacturing	7-10		29
Connections			
Statistics	7-2	3	
Algebra	7-5	4	
Algebra	7-7	5	
Number Patterns	7-7		47
Statistics	7-8		33
Geometry	7-9		37

TEAM ACTIVITIES

Multicultural Experiences

Outside Field Trips Your students may benefit from a visit to the County Clerk's office to examine changes in population statistics and other data in your area.

A visit to a weather station, or if possible, a lighthouse or Coast Guard station, can provide students with first-hand evidence of how people predict changes in weather conditions.

In-Class Speakers Ask a travel agent to speak to the class about how long-distance travel planning must include consideration of time-zone changes.

Invite a diver to visit the class and talk about how changes in diving depths affect preparation and activity.

SUPPLEMENTARY BLACKLINE MASTER BOOKLETS

Some of the blackline masters for enhancing this chapter are shown below.

Application and Interdisciplinary Activity Masters, pp. 7, 21

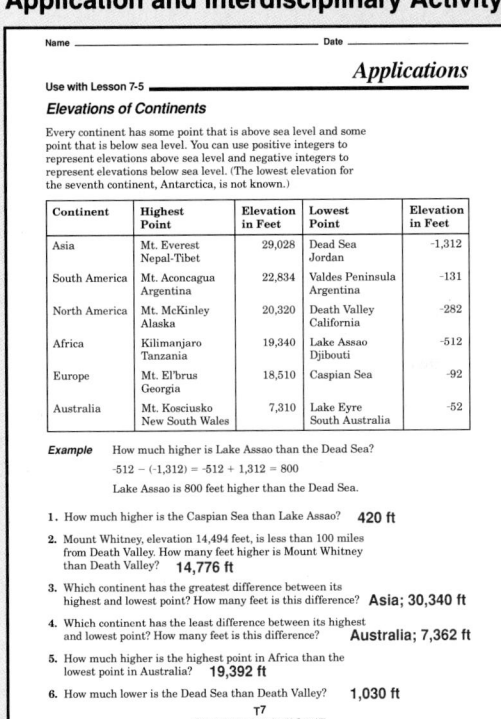

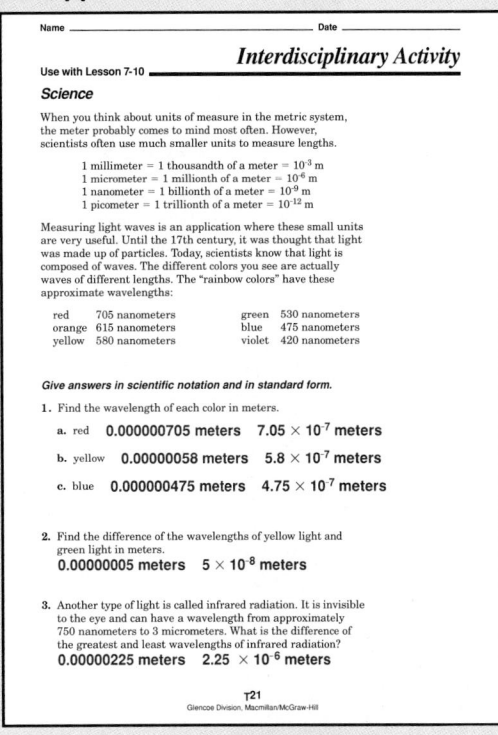

Multicultural Activity Masters, p. 7

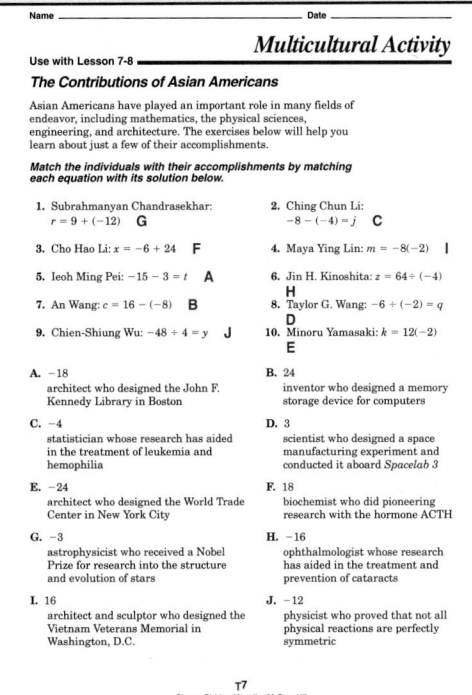

Technology Masters, p. 7

RECOMMENDED OUTSIDE RESOURCES

Books/Periodicals

Cooney, Thomas, ed., *Teaching and Learning Mathematics in the 1990s, 1990 Yearbook,* Reston, VA: NCTM, 1990.

Easterly, Kenneth E., Loren L. Henry, and F. Morgan Simpson, *Activities for Junior High School and Middle School Mathematics,* Reston, VA: NCTM, 1981.

Films/Videotapes/Videodiscs

Equations in Algebra, Chicago, IL: International Film Bureau, Inc., 1963.

Multiplying Options and Subtracting Bias, Reston, VA: NCTM, 1981.

Software

Teasers by Tobbs with Integers, (Apple II), Wings for Learning/ Sunburst

For addresses of companies handling software, please refer to page T24.

This two-page introduction to the chapter provides a visual, relevant way to engage students in the mathematics of the chapter. Questions are included that help students see the need to learn the mathematics in the chapter. Data in charts and graphs provide statistical information that students can analyze and interpret at this point as well as later in the chapter. The Chapter Project provides an activity that applies the mathematics of the chapter.

MAKING MATHEMATICS RELEVANT

Spotlight on Wind Storms

Wind velocities can be either positive or negative, depending upon the direction in which the wind is blowing. The positive and negative integers of this chapter can thus be applied to the behavior of the wind.

Chapter

7 Integers

Spotlight on Wind Storms

Have You Ever Wondered. . .

- How fast wind can actually blow?
- At what time of the year most tropical storms and hurricanes occur?

Beaufort Scale

Sailors commonly use the Beaufort Scale to describe wind strengths. The scale classifies strong winds as storms or hurricanes. When using a number to describe a wind strength, the word force is used. A force 9 means the wind is a strong gale.

Beaufort Number	Type of Wind	Wind Speed	Description and Effect
0	Calm	less than 1 mi/h	still; smoke rises vertically
1	Light Air	1-5 mi/h	wind direction shown by smoke drift; weather vanes inactive
2	Light breeze	6-11 mi/h	wind felt on face; leaves rustle; weather vanes active
3	Gentle breeze	12-19 mi/h	leaves and small twigs move constantly; wind extends lightweight flags
4	Moderate breeze	20-28 mi/h	raises dust and loose paper; moves twigs and thin branches
5	Fresh breeze	29-38 mi/h	small trees in leaf begin to sway
6	Strong breeze	39-49 mi/h	large branches move; telephone wires whistle; umbrella difficult to control
7	Moderate gale	50-61 mi/h	whole trees sway; somewhat difficult to walk
8	Fresh gale	62-74 mi/h	twigs broken off trees; walking against wind very difficult
9	Strong gale	75-88 mi/h	slight damage to buildings, shingles blown off roof
10	Whole gale	89-102 mi/h	trees uprooted; considerable damage to buildings
11	Storm	103-117 mi/h	widespread damage, rarely occurs inland
12-17	Hurricane	greater than 117 mi/h	extreme destruction

252

"Have You Ever Wondered?" Answers

- Wind can attain speeds of at least 117 mi/h.
- during September

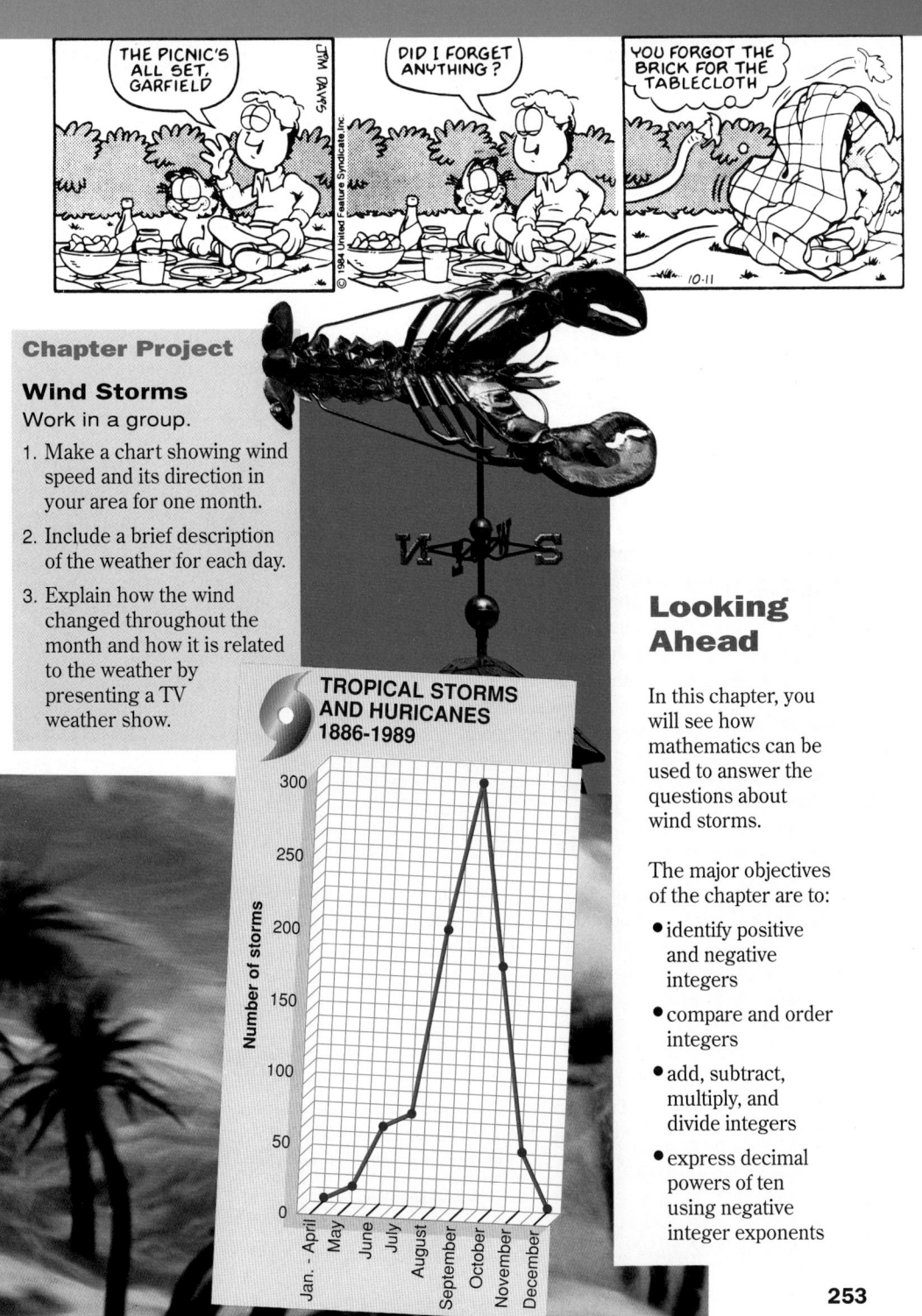

Chapter Project

Wind Storms

Work in a group.

1. Make a chart showing wind speed and its direction in your area for one month.

2. Include a brief description of the weather for each day.

3. Explain how the wind changed throughout the month and how it is related to the weather by presenting a TV weather show.

Looking Ahead

In this chapter, you will see how mathematics can be used to answer the questions about wind storms.

The major objectives of the chapter are to:

- identify positive and negative integers

- compare and order integers

- add, subtract, multiply, and divide integers

- express decimal powers of ten using negative integer exponents

253

TROPICAL STORMS AND HURICANES 1886-1989

(line graph; vertical axis: Number of storms, 0 to 300; horizontal axis: Jan.–April, May, June, July, August, September, October, November, December)

DATA ANALYSIS

Have students examine and discuss the information in the Beaufort Scale table. Ask them questions such as the following in which they interpret the data in the table.

- *What distinguishes one type of wind (and its Beaufort Number) from another?* wind speed

- *Give the difference in wind speed between the strongest moderate breeze and the mildest storm.* 75 mi/h

You may wish to have a student research who the Beaufort Scale was named for. an admiral in the British Navy, who devised his scale at the beginning of the nineteenth century

Data Search

A question related to these data is provided in Lesson 7-5, page 271, Exercise 49.

CHAPTER PROJECT

You may wish to provide students with a key to weather symbols that they can use in their charts. Have them practice adding and subtracting integers by calculating the difference in wind speeds between certain days. If the weather is too stable throughout the duration of the project, you can provide the groups with weather charts obtained in previous months from a local weather station.

Lesson Resources
- Study Guide Master 7-1
- Practice Master 7-1
- Enrichment Master 7-1
- Group Activity Card 7-1

 Transparency 7-1 contains the 5-Minute Check and a teaching aid for this lesson.

⏱ 5-Minute Check
(Over Chapter 6)

Translate each phrase into an algebraic expression.

1. 14 less than y $y - 14$
2. w increased by 7 $w + 7$

Solve each equation.

3. $r + 32 = 45.5$ 13.5
4. $\frac{t}{4} = 6.6$ 26.4

Complete.

5. $2\frac{3}{4}$ lb = _?_ oz   44

---

1 FOCUS

Motivating the Lesson

Situational Problem   Ask students to name the number with the greater absolute value: a rise in the Dow Jones Industrial Average of 31 points, or a loss of 37 points.

2 TEACH

Using Applications   Have students come up with as many real-world applications of integers as they can. Ask them to give an example of each. For each integer they write, ask the class to decide whether the integer that is its opposite is also a reasonable number.

7-1   Integers

Objectives
Read and write integers. Find the opposite and absolute value of an integer.

Words to Learn
integer
positive integer
negative integer
opposite
absolute value

Do you like cold weather? If so, you might want to move to Alaska. The average high temperature in Anchorage, Alaska, for January is 7 degrees below zero. You can express this temperature using the negative number -7. This number is a member of the set of **integers.**

Integers	An integer is any number from the set $\{\ldots, -4, -3, -2, -1, 0, +1, +2, +3, +4, \ldots\}$.

Integers greater than 0 are **positive integers.** Integers less than zero are **negative integers.** Zero itself is neither positive nor negative. Positive integers usually are written without the $+$ sign, so $+4$ and 4 are the same. Use negative and positive counters to represent integers.

> **Calculator Hint**
> • • • • • • • • • • • • •
> To enter a negative integer on a calculator, use the
> [+/-] key. For example, to enter -7, press 7 [+/-].

You can also represent integers as points on a number line. On a horizontal number line, positive integers are represented as points to the right of 0, and negative integers as points to the left of 0. The integers -4 and $+5$ are graphed on the number line below.

Two numbers are **opposites** of one another if they are represented by points that are the same distance from zero, but on opposite sides of zero. The number line below shows that -4 and 4 are opposites.

OPTIONS

Reteaching Activity

Using Applications   Have students think of absolute value as a distance and relate it to a common activity, such as riding in an elevator or playing football. Guide students to see, for example, that the same distance is traveled whether the elevator goes up 3 floors ($+3$) or down 3 floors (-3).

Study Guide Masters, p. 57

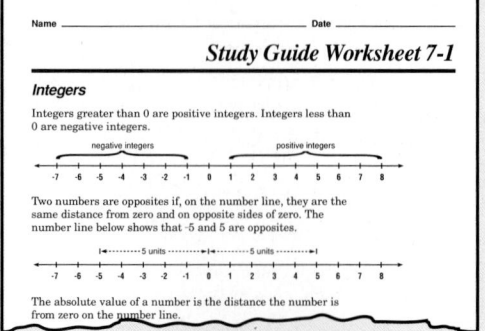

Name _____ Date _____

Study Guide Worksheet 7-1

Integers

Integers greater than 0 are positive integers. Integers less than 0 are negative integers.

Two numbers are opposites if, on the number line, they are the same distance from zero and on opposite sides of zero. The number line below shows that -5 and 5 are opposites.

The absolute value of a number is the distance the number is from zero on the number line.

The **absolute value** of an integer tells how far the point that represents it is from the point for 0.

Absolute Value	The absolute value of a number is the number of units its graph is from the graph of 0 on a number line.

The *absolute value of n* is written as $|n|$. So, $|-4| = 4$ and $|4| = 4$.

Example

Find the opposite and the absolute value of -7.

On the number line, -7 is at the point 7 units to the left of 0. The opposite of -7 would be at the point 7 units to the right of 0.

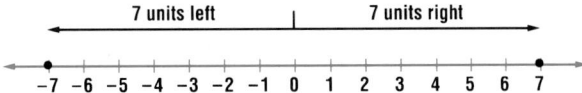

So, the opposite of -7 is 7.

The point that represents -7 is 7 units from 0, so the absolute value of -7 is 7. Write $|-7| = 7$.

Checking for Understanding

Communicating Mathematics

Read and study the lesson to answer each question.

1. **Show** -7 by using counters and also on a number line. **See margin.**
2. **Draw** a number line that shows 5 and its opposite. **See margin.**
3. **Tell** how to find the absolute value of -8. **See margin.**
4. **Write** about an everyday situation in which negative integers are used.
   Sample answer: temperature

Guided Practice

Write an integer for each situation.

5. a profit of $4 **+4**
6. a withdrawal of $5 **−$5**
7. 12 yards gained **+12**
8. a gain of 6 pounds **+6**
9. a loss of 6 points **−6**
10. 10°F above zero **+10**

Write the integer represented by the point for each letter.
Then find its opposite and its absolute value.

11. A **−5, 5, 5**
12. B **−1, 1, 1**
13. C **−8, 8, 8**
14. D **8, −8, 8**
15. E **0, 0, 0**
16. F **3, −3, 3**

17. Name the least positive integer. **1**

18. **Weather** In 12 hours on December 24, 1924, the temperature in Fairfield, Montana, fell from 63°F above zero to 21°F below zero. Write these temperatures as integers. **63°F → −21°F**

Lesson 7-1 Integers   255

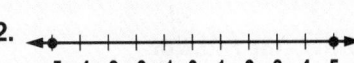

256

Close

Have students use integers to show a withdrawal of $55 from a bank account and a deposit of $44. Ask them to write the absolute value of each.

3 PRACTICE/APPLY

Assignment Guide
Maximum: 19–40
Minimum: 19–31 odd, 33–39

For **Extra Practice,** see p. 587.

Alternate Assessment

Speaking Have students use two integers and the terms "integers," "opposites," and "absolute value" in a sentence that explains the relationship of the three terms.

Additional Answer

34.

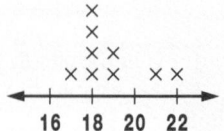

Enrichment Masters, p. 57

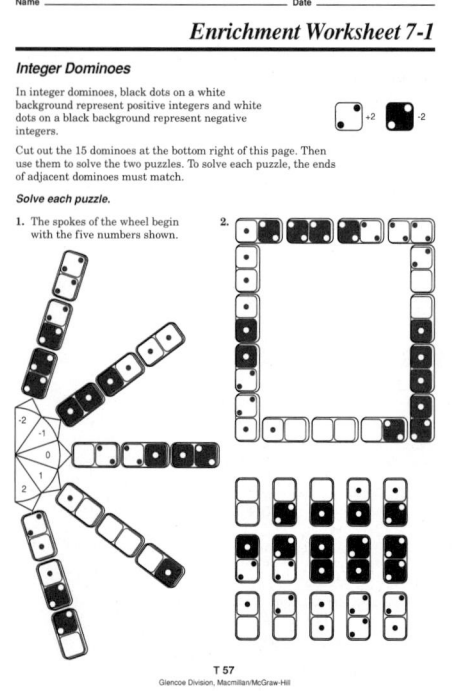

Name _____ Date _____

Enrichment Worksheet 7-1

Integer Dominoes

In integer dominoes, black dots on a white background represent positive integers and white dots on a black background represent negative integers.

Cut out the 15 dominoes at the bottom right of this page. Then use them to solve the two puzzles. To solve each puzzle, the ends of adjacent dominoes must match.

Solve each puzzle.

1. The spokes of the wheel begin with the five numbers shown.
2.

T 57
Glencoe Division, Macmillan/McGraw-Hill

Exercises

Exercises

Independent Practice

Write an integer for each situation.
19. a deposit of $6 +$6
20. a loss of $10 −$10
21. a gain of 2 yards +2
22. 4 seconds before liftoff −4
23. 25 points lost −25
24. 10°F above 0 +10

Write the integer represented by the point for each letter. Then find its opposite and its absolute value.

25. A −6, 6, 6
26. B 0, 0, 0
27. C −9, 9, 9
28. D 5, −5, 5
29. E −1, 1, 1
30. F 7, −7, 7

31. What is the greatest negative integer? −1
32. Find the absolute value of the opposite of −8. 8

Mixed Review

33. Is $196 \div 18 = 18.8$ reasonable? *(Lesson 1–4)* **no**
34. **Statistics** Construct a line plot for the following data: 18, 21, 19, 18, 18, 17, 18, 22, 19. *(Lesson 3–4)* **See margin.**
35. Express $\frac{100}{9}$ as a mixed number. *(Lesson 5–1)* $11\frac{1}{9}$
36. **Real Estate** A house advertised in the real estate section of the newspaper claims to have a rectangular lot with a length of 250 feet and a width of 120 feet. What is the area of the lot? *(Lesson 6–7)* **30,000 square feet**

Problem Solving and Applications

37. **Geography** The highest point in the United States is Mount McKinley, Alaska, which rises 20,320 feet above sea level. The lowest point is Death Valley, California, which is 282 feet below sea level. Write integers to represent these elevations. **20,320; −282**

38. **Calculators** If you press 6 [+/−], you get −6.
   a. What is the result when you press 6 [+/−] [+/−]? **6**
   b. What is the result when you press 6 [+/−] [+/−] [+/−]? **−6**
   c. What can you conclude about the number of times you press [+/−] and the result?
   odd number of times—negative; even number of times—positive
39. **Critical Thinking** Complete each sentence using either the word *positive* or *negative*.
   a. If the absolute value of an integer is equal to the integer itself, then the integer is either __?__ or zero. **positive**
   b. If the absolute value of an integer is equal to the opposite of the integer, then the integer is __?__. **negative**
40. **Journal Entry** Write a sentence about each of three different real-world situations that might be represented by the integer −5. **See students' work.**

OPTIONS

Extending the Lesson

Using an Almanac Have students use an almanac to find the height, in feet, of the tallest mountain on Earth and the depth of the deepest undersea trench. Have them compare the two using integers.
The Mariana Trench (−35,840) has a greater absolute value than Mt. Everest (29,028).

Cooperative Learning Activity

One Step Forward, Two Steps Back **7-1**

Number of players: 2
Materials: Counters, index cards

↓ Copy onto cards the descriptions shown on the back of this card. Shuffle the cards and place them face down in a pile. Then copy onto a large sheet of paper (or several sheets taped together) the game board shown below.

→ Each partner places a counter on the "Start" square. In turn, each partner selects a card. The number on the card tells how many spaces to the right or left to move your counter. If the number is positive, move to the right. If the number is negative, move to the left. Try to be first to reach the last square on the right. If you land on or go past the last square on the left, you automatically lose.

Lose									Start								Win

Glencoe Mathematics: Applications and Connections, Course 2

7-2 Comparing and Ordering Integers

Objective

Compare and order integers.

John and Barry were playing Jeopardy®. In Jeopardy®, a player can end up with negative scores. John's final score was −800, and Barry's final score was −200. Whose score was greater?

You can use a number line to answer this question. On a number line, values increase as you go right and decrease as you go left.

LOOK BACK

You can review inequalities on page 48.

Since Barry's score is to the right of John's score on the number line, Barry's score is greater than John's. You can write −200 > −800 or −800 < −200.

Examples

1 Replace ● with <, >, or = in −5 ● −1 to make a true sentence. Draw the graph of each integer on a number line.

$$-7\ -6\ -5\ -4\ -3\ -2\ -1\ \ 0\ \ 1\ \ 2\ \ 3\ \ 4\ \ 5\ \ 6\ \ 7$$

Since −5 is to the left of −1 on the number line, −5 < −1.

Mental Math Hint
••••••••••••
On a number line, any positive integer is to the right of a negative integer. So, when comparing a positive and negative integer, the positive integer will always be greater.
$1 > -1,000,000$
$-1,000,000 < 1$

2 Order the integers −4, 5, 3, −2, and 0 from least to greatest. Draw the graph of each integer on a number line.

Order the integers by reading from left to right.
$$-4, -2, 0, 3, 5$$

Example 3 Connection

LOOK BACK

You can review median on page 102.

Statistics Find the median of the temperatures in the chart.

Monthly Record Low Temperatures for Juneau, Alaska (°F)

J	F	M	A	M	J	J	A	S	O	N	D
−22	−22	−15	6	25	31	36	27	23	11	−5	−21

List the temperatures in order from least to greatest.
$$-22, -22, -21, -15, -5, \mathbf{6}, \mathbf{11}, 23, 25, 27, 31, 36$$
There are two middle numbers, 6 and 11. So the median is $\frac{6+11}{2}$ or 8.5. The median of the temperatures is 8.5°F.

Lesson 7-2 Comparing and Ordering Integers **257**

NCTM Standards: 1–6

Lesson Resources
• Study Guide Master 7-2
• Practice Master 7-2
• Enrichment Master 7-2
• Group Activity Card 7-2

Transparency 7-2 contains the 5-Minute Check and a teaching aid for this lesson.

🕐 **5-Minute Check**
(Over Lesson 7-1)
Write an integer for each.
1. a loss of $12   − 12
2. 42°F above 0   + 42
3. a gain of 8 yards   + 8

1 FOCUS

Motivating the Lesson

Questioning Ask the increasing order of 12, − 15, 8, and −8.
−15, −8, 8, 12

Practice Masters, p. 58

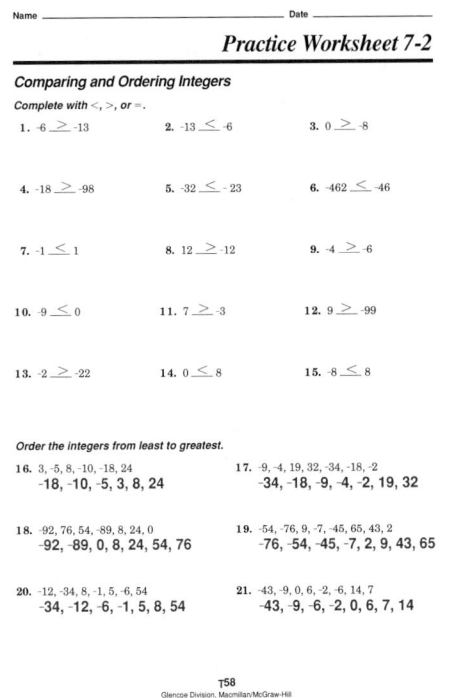

OPTIONS

Reteaching Activity

Using Manipulatives Use a thermometer, as a vertical number line, to help students understand how to compare integers. Guide them to see that a temperature of −8°F is greater than (warmer than) a temperature of −9°F. Provide additional examples.

Study Guide Masters, p. 58

Name _____ Date _____

Study Guide Worksheet 7-2

Comparing and Ordering Integers

To compare or order integers, think of a number line. The number farther to the right on the number line is greater.

$$-7\ -6\ -5\ -4\ -3\ -2\ -1\ \ 0\ \ 1\ \ 2\ \ 3\ \ 4\ \ 5\ \ 6\ \ 7$$

−3 < 2 since 2 is to the right of −3 on the number line.

Example Use >, <, or = to compare the integers.

−3 ____ 3   A negative integer is less than a positive integer.
−3 < 3

−2 ____ −5   −2 is to the right of −5 on the number line.
−2 > −5

Example Order the integers 0, 3, −1, −3, 5 from least to greatest.
−3 is farthest to the left on the number line, so it is least.

2 TEACH

More Examples

For Example 1

Replace ● with <, >, or =
to make a true sentence:
-6 ● -2 **<**

For Example 2

Order from least to greatest:
$-3, 5, -2, 0$ **$-3, -2, 0, 5$**

For Example 3

Find the median: $-1, 8, 6,$
$-7, 0$ **0**

Close

Have students explain whether
-12 is less than, greater than, or
equal to -4.

3 PRACTICE/APPLY

Assignment Guide
Maximum: 10–26
Minimum: 11–19 odd, 20–24

For **Extra Practice,** see p. 587.

Enrichment Masters, p. 58

Checking for Understanding

Communicating Mathematics

Read and study the lesson to answer each question.

1. **Show** that $-3 < 4$ using a number line. **See Solutions Manual.**

2. **Tell** how to determine when one integer is greater than another integer.
The number farthest to the right on a number line is the greater number.

Guided Practice

Replace each ● with <, >, or = to make a true sentence.

3. -9 ● -19 **>**   4. -19 ● -9 **<**   5. -6 ● 0 **<**

6. -12 ● -121 **>**   7. -87 ● -78 **<**   8. 0 ● -5 **>**

9. Order $56, -1, 31, -98, 14,$ and -76 from least to greatest. **$-98, -76,$**
$-1, 14, 31, 56$

Exercises

Independent Practice

Replace each ● with >, <, or = to make a true sentence.

10. 1 ● -9 **>**   11. 5 ● -98 **>**   12. -2 ● -9 **>**

13. -98 ● -987 **>**   14. -1 ● 1 **<**   15. -8 ● -5 **<**

Order the integers from least to greatest.   **$-91, -76, -9, -6, 2, 18, 32$**

16. $3, -4, 0, -9, 29, -76$ **$-76, -9,$**   17. $2, -9, -76, -91, 32, 18, -6$
                              $-4, 0, 3, 29$

18. Which is greater, -11 or 9? **9**   **$-14, -7, -1, 0, 5, 13$**

19. Order $13, 5, -7, 0, -1,$ and -14 from least to greatest.

Mixed Review

20. $2,245$

20. **Income Tax**   A U.S. citizen pays an average of
$\$2,245.48$ in income tax annually. How much is
this to the nearest dollar? *(Lesson 2-2)*

21. Name two numbers that are divisible by both 3
and 8. *(Lesson 4-1)* **Sample answer: 24, 48**

22. Find the opposite and absolute value of -21.
(Lesson 7-1) **21, 21**

Problem Solving and Applications

23. **Weather**   The table below gives the monthly record low temperatures (°F)
in Wilmington, Delaware. Find the median of the temperatures. **21°F**

J	F	M	A	M	J	J	A	S	O	N	D
-14	-6	2	18	30	41	48	43	36	24	14	-7

COMPUTER CONNECTION

24. **Critical Thinking**   Points *A, B, C,* and *D* are different points on a number
line. Using the following clues, order the integers for *A, B, C,* and *D*.
  • *D* is the least of the integers.   • Point *C* is a positive integer.
  • Points *A* and *D* are the same distance from 0.
  • Point *C* is closer to *D* than it is to *B*. **D, C, A, B from least to greatest**

25. **Computer Connection**   In the BASIC computer language, the INT(X)
function finds the greatest integer that is *not* greater than X. For example,
INT(3.5) = 3 because 3 is not greater than 3.5. Find INT(−2.1). **−3**

26. **Journal Entry**   How do you remember which symbol, > or <, represents
"greater than" and which represents "less than"? **See students' work.**

OPTIONS

Extending the Lesson

Using a Game   Challenge students
to make up tic-tac-toe game boards
and play a game in which the object
is to place counters either to cover
integers in order from least to
greatest or cover them from greatest
to least. The boards should include
positive and negative integers and
zero.

Cooperative Learning Activity

Number of players: 2
Materials: Index cards

Captured Integers 7-2

◆ Copy onto cards the integers shown on the back of this card, one integer per card.
Shuffle the cards and place them face down in a pile. Decide which partner will go first.

➤ The first partner selects two cards from the pile and places them face up, with the greater
integer on the right. The second partner then selects two cards and arranges all four cards in
order from least to greatest. Each partner takes the two cards he or she selected unless two
of one partner's cards surround one or both of the other partner's cards. If you can place the
card to the left and to the right of one or both of your partner's cards, you "capture" the card or
cards. Continue in the same way, taking turns drawing the first two cards of each round, until
no card remains in the pile. The partner with more cards wins.

Glencoe Mathematics: Applications and Connections, Course 2

7-3 The Coordinate System

Objective

Graph points on a coordinate plane.

Words to Learn

coordinate
 system
x-axis
y-axis
origin
quadrant
ordered pair
x-coordinate
y-coordinate

DID YOU KNOW

Most volcanoes in the world are in the "Ring of Fire." The "Ring of Fire" is a circle of volcanic activity surrounding the Pacific Ocean.

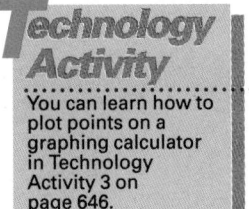

Technology Activity

You can learn how to plot points on a graphing calculator in Technology Activity 3 on page 646.

One way that geologists keep track of volcanic activity is by graphing volcanoes on a world map. The longitudinal (vertical) and latitudinal (horizontal) lines help you to locate specific volcanoes. Mt. St. Helens, for example, is at 122°W longitude and 48°N latitude.

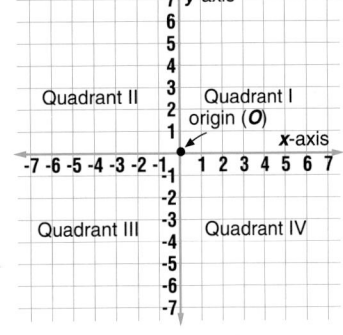

In mathematics, a **coordinate system,** or coordinate plane, is used to graph points in a plane. It is made up of a horizontal number line and a vertical number line that intersect. On the vertical number line, positive integers are represented as points above 0 and negative integers as points below 0.

The horizontal line is called the **x-axis,** and the vertical line is called the **y-axis.** They intersect at their zero points. This is called the **origin.** Together, they make up a coordinate system that separates the plane into four **quadrants.**

Points graphed on a coordinate system are identified using **ordered pairs.** The first number in an ordered pair is the **x-coordinate,** and the second number is the **y-coordinate.**

An ordered pair is written in this form.
  (x-coordinate, y-coordinate)

7-3 Lesson Notes

NCTM Standards: 1–6, 12

Lesson Resources
• Study Guide Master 7-3
• Practice Master 7-3
• Enrichment Master 7-3
• Group Activity Card 7-3

Transparency 7-3 contains the 5-Minute Check and a teaching aid for this lesson.

⏱5-Minute Check
(Over Lesson 7-2)

Replace each ● with >, <, or =.

1. $2 ● -6$ $>$
2. $-78 ● 3$ $<$
3. $-2 ● 2$ $<$

Order the integers from least to greatest.

4. $4, -6, 31, 0, -9$ $-9, -6, 0, 4, 31$
5. $6, -27, -22, 21, 12, -11$ $-27, -22, -11, 6, 12, 21$

1 FOCUS

Motivating the Lesson

Activity Discuss the concepts of latitude and longitude with students. Have them use a globe, an atlas, or an almanac to locate 10 cities around the world according to their coordinates of latitude and longitude.

2 TEACH

Using Applications Use a coordinate system to show locations of places in your city, neighborhood, school grounds, or classroom. Provide groups of students with a coordinate plane. Have them work together to assign coordinates to various points of interest. Alternatively, have group members indicate the location of an unnamed place by graphing its approximate coordinates, and then challenge one another to find what is located at that point.

OPTIONS

Reteaching Activity

Using Communication Focus on the steps students must always follow to locate or graph a point on the coordinate plane: first locate the x-coordinate by starting at (0, 0) and moving units to the *left* or *right* along the x-axis; then locate the y-coordinate by moving units *up* or *down* along the y-axis.

Study Guide Masters, p. 59

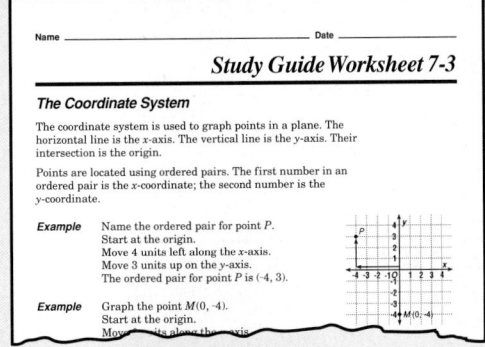

259

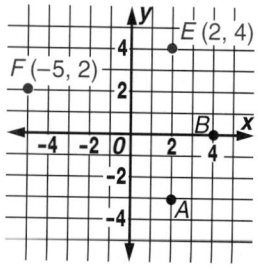
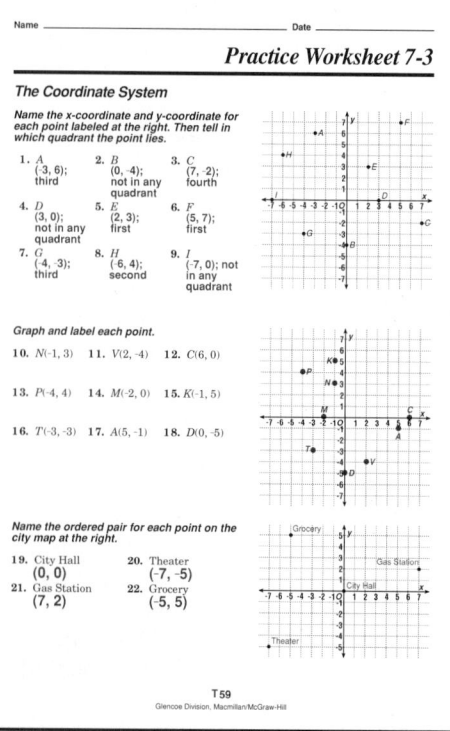
1 Name the ordered pair for point *A* and identify its quadrant.

Start at the origin, *O*. Locate point *A* by moving right 3 units along the *x*-axis. The *x*-coordinate is +3. Now move down 5 units along the *y*-axis. The *y*-coordinate is −5. The ordered pair is $(3, -5)$. Point *A* is in quadrant IV.

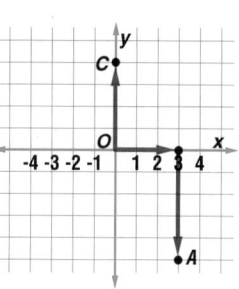

2 Name the ordered pair for point *C* and identify its quadrant.

The ordered pair is $(0, 4)$. Point *C* is not in a quadrant because it is on an axis.

To graph a point in a coordinate system, draw a dot at the location named by its ordered pair.

3 Graph the point $D(3, 5)$.

First draw a coordinate system. Start at the origin, *O*. Move 3 units to the right. Then move 5 units up to locate the point. Draw a dot and label it $D(3, 5)$.

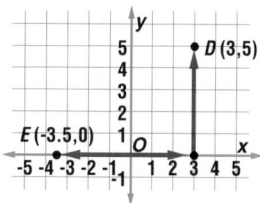

4 Graph the point $E(-3.5, 0)$.

Start at *O*. Move 3.5 units to the left. Do not move up or down. Draw a dot and label it $E(-3.5, 0)$.

Checking for Understanding

Communicating Mathematics

Read and study the lesson to answer each question.

1. **Write** the name of the point where the *x*-axis and the *y*-axis intersect. What is the ordered pair for this point? **origin, (0, 0)**

2. **Show** why the point $(2, 5)$ is different from the point $(5, 2)$. **See Solutions Manual.**

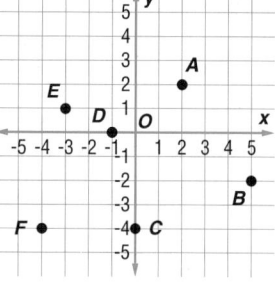

Guided Practice

Name the *x*-coordinate and *y*-coordinate for each point labeled at the right. Then tell in which quadrant the point lies.

3. *A* (2, 2), I
4. *B* (5, −2), IV
5. *C* (0, −4), *y*-axis
6. *D* (−1, 0), *x*-axis
7. *E* (−3, 1), II
8. *F* (−4, −4), III

260 **Chapter 7** Integers

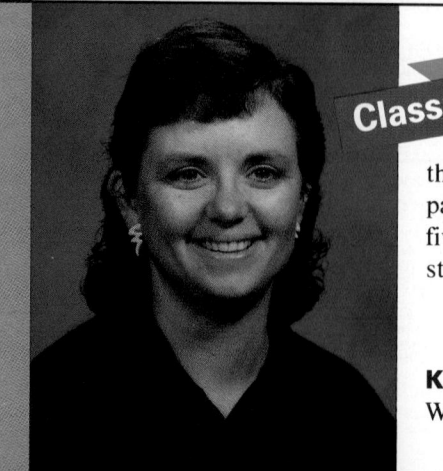

Classroom Vignette

''To reinforce this lesson, students play 'Coordinate System Battleship.' This is played like the commercial game Battleship but with graph paper. Students graph adjacent points to represent five different size ships. When a ship is located, students mark them with an X.''

Karey Killion

Karey Killion, Teacher
Westbridge Middle School, Grand Island, NE

For answers to Exercises 9-14, see Solutions Manual.
On graph paper, draw a coordinate plane. Then graph and label each point.

9. $T(-2, 5)$ 10. $N(3, -4)$ 11. $P(-\frac{1}{2}, -1)$

12. $L(2.5, 7)$ 13. $B(0, -2)$ 14. $W(4, 0)$

Exercises

Independent Practice

Name the ordered pair for each point on the city map at the right.

15. bank   16. library

17. grocery   18. gas station

19. theater   20. city hall

15. (4, 4)
16. (−3, −2)
17. (−5, 5)
18. (1, −5)
19. (2, −1)
20. (0, 0)

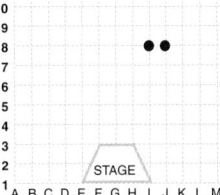

For answers to Exercises 21-29, see Solutions Manual.
On graph paper, draw a coordinate plane. Then graph and label each point.

21. $Q(-2, 7)$ 22. $B(1\frac{1}{2}, 5)$ 23. $M(-1, -3)$

24. $K(-6, 5.5)$ 25. $P(-3, 4)$ 26. $C(4, 0)$

27. $N(0, -3)$ 28. $A(6, -2)$ 29. $E(5, 1)$

Mixed Review

30. Evaluate $6x - 3(x - y)$ if $x = 8$ and $y = 2$. *(Lesson 1-8)* **30**

31. **Statistics** Construct a stem-and-leaf plot for the following data: 95, 83, 66, 81, 92, 85, 62, 90. *(Lesson 3-6)* **See Solutions Manual.**

32. **Geometry** Find the perimeter of a rectangle having a length of 7 cm and a width of $3\frac{1}{2}$ cm. *(Lesson 5-6)* **21 cm**

33. **Sports** During a golf game, Jonathon scored 6 below par and Jose scored 4 below par. Who had the lower score? *(Lesson 7-2)* **Jonathon**

Problem Solving and Applications

34. **Concerts** You and your friend are planning to attend a concert this weekend.

a. What are the coordinates of your seats?

b. What are the coordinates of the corners of the stage? **(E, 1), (I, 1), (H, 3), (F, 3)**

34. a. (I, 8), (J, 8)
36. a. (10°S, 70°W)
b. (70°N, 20°W)
c. (20°N, 160°W)
d. (60°N, 160°W)

35. **Critical Thinking** Suppose for any ordered pair, the x-coordinate is negative and the y-coordinate is positive. Name the quadrant where the point is graphed. **II**

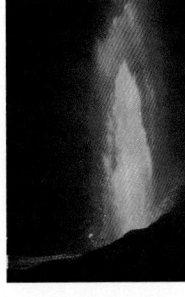

36. **Geography** Refer to the map at the beginning of this lesson. Estimate the latitude and longitude of each volcano listed below to the nearest tens place. Write the location of the volcano as an ordered pair (latitude, longitude).

a. Cotopaxi   b. Hekla

c. Mauna Loa   d. Mount Katmai

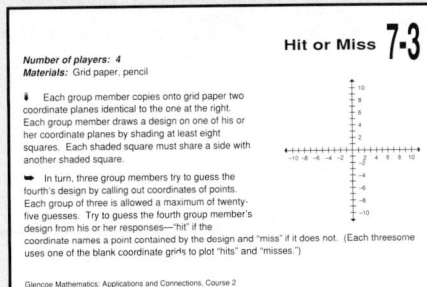

Extending the Lesson

Using Geometry Challenge students to give the coordinates of key points that form a polygon, such as a parallelogram or a pentagon.

Cooperative Learning Activity

Hit or Miss 7-3

Number of players: 4
Materials: Grid paper, pencil

◆ Each group member copies onto grid paper two coordinate planes identical to the one at the right. Each group member draws a design on one of his or her coordinate planes by shading at least eight squares. Each shaded square must share a side with another shaded square.

➥ In turn, three group members try to guess the fourth's design by calling out coordinates of points. Each group of three is allowed a maximum of twenty-five guesses. Try to guess the fourth group member's design from his or her responses—"hit" if the coordinate names a point contained by the design and "miss" if it does not. (Each threesome uses one of the blank coordinate grids to plot "hits" and "misses.")

Glencoe Mathematics: Applications and Connections, Course 2

Error Analysis

Watch for students who reverse the order of the coordinates, incorrectly writing or naming them in the order (y, x).

Prevent by having students use the fact that the x precedes y in the alphabet as a reminder of the order in which to write and locate ordered pairs.

Close

Have students give the ordered pairs that name 4 points, one in each quadrant. Then have them graph and label those points in a coordinate plane.

3 PRACTICE/APPLY

Assignment Guide
Maximum: 15–36
Minimum: 15–29 odd, 30–36

For **Extra Practice,** see p. 587.

Alternate Assessment

Modeling Have students explain why the ordered pair $(4, -3)$ is not the same as $(-3, 4)$. Ask them to graph and label each point.

Enrichment Masters, p. 59

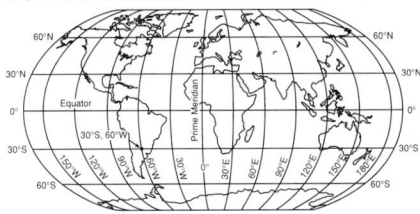

NCTM Standards: 1–6

Management Tips

For Students Have students work with partners using at least seven counters of one color and at least seven counters of a second color. Each counter of one color represents 1, each of the other counters − 1. Have one student in the pair use only positive counters, the other student only negative counters.

For the Overhead Projector
Overhead Manipulative Resources provides appropriate materials for teacher or student demonstration of the activities in this Mathematics Lab.

1 FOCUS

Introducing the Lab

Tell students that they can use the counters to model gains and losses for a runner in a football game. Each of the positive counters can represent 1 yard gained and each of the negative counters can represent a loss of 1 yard. Ask students how they would represent a gain of 5 yards followed by a loss of 3 yards.

2 TEACH

Using Models After the students use the counters to model 5 + 3 and − 5 + 3, have them try to find other combinations that give those same sums.

3 PRACTICE/APPLY

Using Critical Thinking Have students experiment with the counters to determine when sums of two integers will be negative, 0, or positive. Ask each group to write a summary of its findings.

Close

Ask students to use positive and negative counters to show what floor you would be on if you start on the ground floor, go up 7 floors, and then go down 5 floors.

Cooperative Learning

7-4A Adding Integers

A Preview of Lesson 7-4

Objective
Add integers by using models.

Materials
counters of two colors
mat

In this lab, you will use counters to model addition with integers. Let one color of counter represent positive integers and another color represent negative integers.

Try this!

Work with a partner.

- Remember that $5 + 3$ means *combine a set of five items with a set of three items*. In this lab, the addition $5 + 3$ tells you to combine a set of 5 positive counters with a set of 3 positive counters.

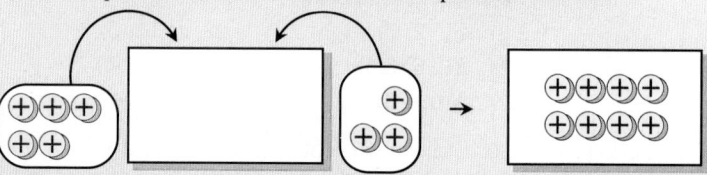

So, $5 + 3 = 8$.

- Place 5 negative counters on the mat. Place 3 more negative counters on the mat. Use your results to complete the addition sentence $-5 + (-3) = \underline{\ ?\ }$. **−8**

- Place 5 positive counters and 3 negative counters on the mat.

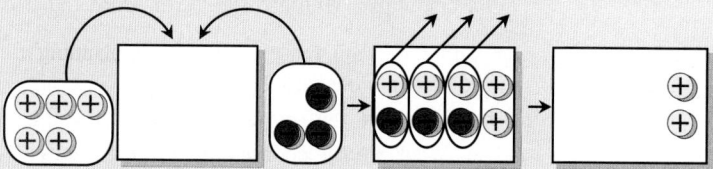

In this case, it is possible to pair a positive counter with a negative counter. This is called a *zero pair*. Remove as many zero pairs as possible. Use your result to complete this addition sentence $5 + (-3) = \underline{\ ?\ }$. **2**

- Use counters to model $-5 + 3$. Then write an addition sentence.

$$-5 + 3 = -2$$

What do you think?

1. negative sum

1. What is the result when you add two negative integers?

2. What is the result when you add a positive and a negative integer?
   The sum has the sign of the integer with the greater absolute value.   **See Solutions Manual.**

Model each addition. Use your result to write an addition sentence.

3. $7 + 2$ 4. $7 + (-2)$ 5. $-7 + 2$ 6. $-7 + (-2)$

Interactive Mathematics Tools

This multimedia software provides an interactive lesson that is tied directly to Lesson 7-4A. Students will click and drag counters to add integers as in the Mathematics Lab.

Lab Manual, p. 54

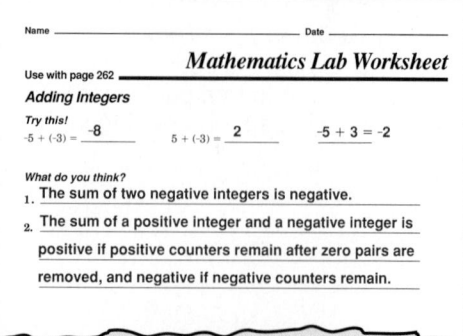

Name _____   Date _____

Mathematics Lab Worksheet

Use with page 262

Adding Integers

Try this!
−5 + (−3) = __−8__   5 + (−3) = __2__   −5 + 3 = −2

What do you think?
1. The sum of two negative integers is negative.

2. The sum of a positive integer and a negative integer is positive if positive counters remain after zero pairs are removed, and negative if negative counters remain.

7-4 Adding Integers

Objective
Add integers.

Words to Learn
additive inverse

DID YOU KNOW

Without the weather to spread the Sun's heat around the world, the tropics would get hotter and the poles would get colder. Nothing would be able to live on Earth.

Did you know that the moon has mountains taller than Mount Everest, but has no rain or snow? In 1966, the United States' spacecraft Surveyor I landed on the moon. Its purpose was to send back to Earth television pictures and moon measurements. Changes in temperature were one such measurement.

At lunar noon, the temperature on the moon's surface was 235°F. By midnight the temperature had dropped 485 degrees. You can write the drop in temperature as −485 degrees. What was the temperature at midnight? *This question will be answered in Example 5.*

To solve the problem like the one about moon temperatures, you can add integers. One way to add integers is by using arrows on a number line. Positive integers are represented by arrows pointing *right*. Negative integers are represented by arrows pointing *left*.

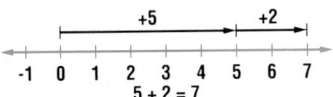
$$5 + 2 = 7$$

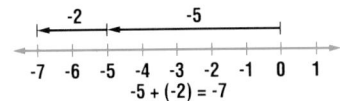
$$-5 + (-2) = -7$$

Adding Integers with the Same Sign	The sum of two positive integers is positive. The sum of two negative integers is negative.

Examples

1 Solve $a = 60 + 15$.
Use a number line.
Start at 60. Since 15 is positive, go 15 units to the right.

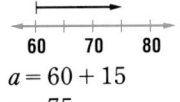

$a = 60 + 15$
$a = 75$

2 Solve $-3 + (-2) = t$.
Use counters. Put in 3 negative counters. Add 2 more negatives.

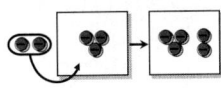

$-3 + (-2) = t$
$-5 = t$

Lesson 7-4 Adding Integers   **263**

OPTIONS

Gifted and Talented Needs

Have students make integer mazes for others to solve. Each maze (a 4 × 4 grid) contains integers from −9 to 9. Start with an integer in the top row and end in a final sum written in a circle below an integer in the bottom row. To complete the maze, move down, left, or right in an addition path from Start to Finish.

(See sample below.) To add interest, specify that none of the integers may be repeated.

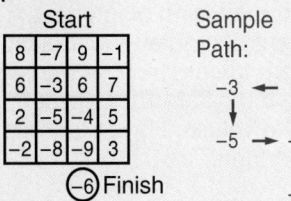

NCTM Standards: 1–7, 9

Lesson Resources
• Study Guide Master 7-4
• Practice Master 7-4
• Enrichment Master 7-4
• Technology Master, p. 7
• Group Activity Card 7-4

Transparency 7-4 contains the 5-Minute Check and a teaching aid for this lesson.

🕐 5-Minute Check
(Over Lesson 7-3)

On graph paper, draw a coordinate plane. Then graph and label each point.

1. $P(-3, 4)$
2. $F(2, 1)$
3. $R(3, -2)$
4. $J(-6, -2.5)$

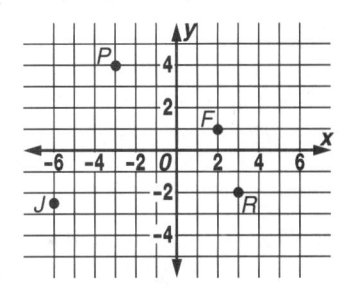

1 FOCUS

Motivating the Lesson

Questioning Ask students why this opening problem would be impractical to solve using counters. Have them suggest other methods for combining the numbers.

2 TEACH

Using Discussion Review the meaning of absolute value with students. Since the method for adding integers with different signs may confuse students, try to provide several examples of how the method works, using real life examples such as stock market gains and losses.

More Examples

For Example 1

Solve $b = 40 + 18$.   58

For Example 2

Solve $-4 + (-3) = r$. -7

For Example 3

Solve $a = 26 + (-14)$.   12

For Example 4

Solve $-43 + 18 = k$. -25

For Example 5

From sea level, a rock climber ascends 523 feet and then drops down 88 feet to a resting place. How high above sea level is the resting place?   435 feet

Checking for Understanding

Exercises 1-4 are designed to help you assess students' understanding through reading, writing, speaking, and modeling. You should work through these exercises with your students and then monitor their work on Guided Practice Exercises 5-19.

Error Analysis

Watch for students who misapply the rule for adding integers by obtaining 25 instead of -25 as the solution to $-43 + 18 = k$.

Prevent by using arrows on a number line (see below) to show why the sum has the same sign as the addend with the greater absolute value.

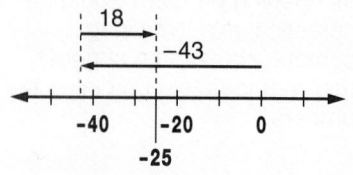

What happens when you add integers with different signs? Let's first look at the sum $5 + (-2)$: $5 + (-2) = 3$.

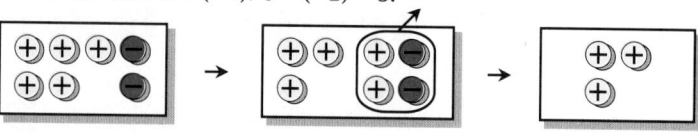

Now, let's look at the sum $-5 + 2$.

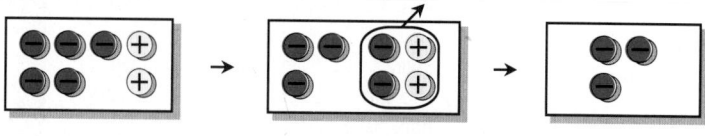

$$-5 + 2 = -3$$

The results above suggest the following rule for adding two integers with different signs.

Adding Integers with Different Signs	To add integers with different signs, subtract their absolute values. The sum is: • positive if the positive integer has the greater absolute value. • negative if the negative integer has the greater absolute value.

Examples

3 Solve $a = 23 + (-18)$.
$|23| > |-18|$, so the sum is positive.
The difference of 23 and 18 is 5.
So, $a = 5$.

4 Solve $-39 + 19 = w$.
$|-39| > |19|$, so the sum is negative.
The difference of 39 and 19 is 20.
So, $w = -20$.

Example 5 *Problem Solving*

Geology Refer to the problem in the lesson introduction. What was the temperature at midnight?

Explore At noon, the temperature was 235°F. By midnight, the temperature dropped 485 degrees. You can write this drop as -485 degrees.

Plan Let $t =$ the temperature at midnight.
Solve the equation $t = 235 + (-485)$.

Solve $|-485| > |235|$, so the sum is negative.
The difference of 485 and 235 is 250. So, $t = -250$.
The temperature at midnight is 250°F below zero.

264   Chapter 7 Integers

OPTIONS

Reteaching Activity

Using Problem Solving As needed, spend more time using either counters or a number line to show the addition of integers. Then use several problems with simple numbers to demonstrate adding by finding the difference between absolute values. Have students work with partners.

Study Guide Masters, p. 60

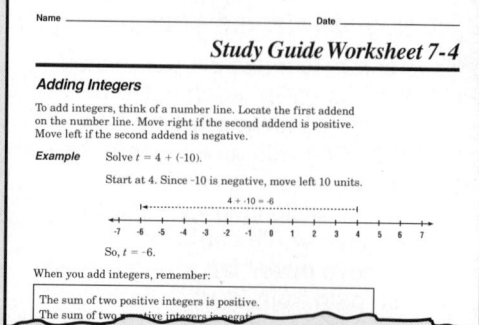

Examine   Use a calculator to check.

$$235 \; \boxed{+} \; 485 \; \boxed{+/-} \; \boxed{=} \; \text{-250} \qquad \text{It checks.}$$

What happens when you add two integers that are opposites, like 2 and -2? In a sense, adding its opposite "undoes" the first integer, and the result is 0. For this reason, two integers that are opposites of each other are called **additive inverses.**

Additive Inverse Property	**In words:** The sum of any number and its additive inverse is zero.
	Arithmetic **Algebra**
	$2 + (-2) = 0$ $a + (-a) = 0$

Checking for Understanding

Communicating Mathematics

Read and study the lesson to answer each question.

1. **Tell** how you know the sign of the result when adding integers with different signs. **sign of the integer with the greater absolute value**

2. **Show** three examples of integers and their additive inverses. **Sample answers: $4 + (-4)$, $-5 + 5$, $6 + (-6)$**

3. **Draw** a model that shows $4 + (-4) = k$. How many zero pairs are there? **4**

4. **Write** the addition sentence shown by each model.

a. 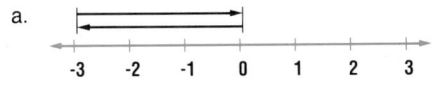 $-3 + 3 = 0$

b. $2 + (-3) = -1$

c. 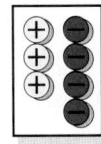   d.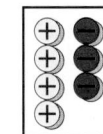

$3 + (-4) = -1$ $4 + (-3) = 1$

Guided Practice   Tell whether the sum is positive, negative, or zero.

5. $6 + (-6)$ **0**   6. $-9 + (-13)$ **—**   7. $-5 + 9$ **+**   8. $-7 + 12$ **+**

9. $7 + (-1)$ **+**   10. $8 + (-11)$ **—**   11. $-12 + (-7)$ **—**   12. $-11 + 18$ **+**

Solve each equation.

13. $y = 4 + (-9)$ **-5**   14. $-9 + (-1) = f$ **-10**   15. $y = -3 + 14$ **11**

16. $-5 + 12 = w$ **7**   17. $-5 + 5 = r$ **0**   18. $h = 17 + (-8)$ **9**

Lesson 7-4 Adding Integers   **265**

---

38. Range: 38; scale: 45–85;
interval: 5 units

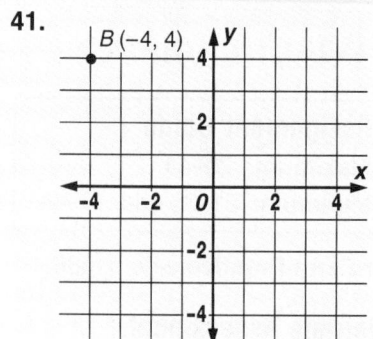

45 50 55 60 65 70 75 80 85

41.

$B(-4, 4)$

---

19. Sports The Bulldogs lost five yards on one play, then gained nine yards on the next play. What was the total number of yards gained or lost? **gained 4 yards**

Exercises

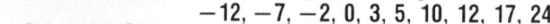

Independent Practice

Solve each equation.

20. $3 + (-8) = u$ **−5** 21. $q = 5 + (-9)$ **−4** 22. $c = -10 + 12$ **2**

23. $-7 + 13 = p$ **6** 24. $-9 + -19 = u$ **−28** 25. $b = 35 + (-10)$ **25**

26. $-3 + 10 = i$ **7** 27. $200 + (-100) = v$ **100** 28. $-57 + 10 = k$ **−47**

Evaluate each expression if $a = -10$, $b = 10$, and $c = -5$.

29. $a + (-3)$ **−13** 30. $-6 + b$ **4** 31. $c + (-1)$ **−6**

32. $0 + a$ **−10** 33. $a + b$ **0** 34. $c + b$ **5**

35. Evaluate $a + 9$ if $a = -23$. **−14**

36. Evaluate $b + a$ if $b = -4$ and $a = 19$. **15**

Mixed Review

37. **Smart Shopping** Angela purchases 3.9 pounds of coffee for $23.75. Estimate the price per pound of the coffee. *(Lesson 2-3)* **$6 per pound**

38. **Statistics** Find the range for the following set of data. Choose an appropriate scale and interval. Then draw a number line to show the scale and interval. *(Lesson 3-3)* **See margin.**
57, 62, 75, 55, 59, 63, 63, 45, 83, 61

39. Find the next three terms in $\frac{1}{2}, \frac{1}{4}, \frac{1}{8}, \dots$ *(Lesson 4-4)* $\frac{1}{16}, \frac{1}{32}, \frac{1}{64}$

40. Solve using the inverse operation $8t = 64$. *(Lesson 6-1)* **8**

41. On graph paper, draw coordinate axes. Then graph the point $B(-4, 4)$. *(Lesson 7-3)* **See margin.**

Problem Solving and Applications

42. **Personal Finance** Rosa opened a checking account with a balance of $150. She wrote a check for $87.
   a. Write an addition sentence to represent this situation.
   b. How much money remained in the account? **$63** $\$150 + (-\$87) = x$

43. **Space Travel** During a space shuttle launch, a maneuver is scheduled to begin at T minus 75 seconds, which is 75 seconds before liftoff. The maneuver lasts 2 minutes. At what time will this maneuver be complete? **T + 45 seconds**

44. **Critical Thinking** Jack made up a game of darts using the target at the right. Each person throws three darts. The score is the sum of the numbers in the regions that the darts hit. If all the darts hit the target, list all possible scores.
−12, −7, −2, 0, 3, 5, 10, 12, 17, 24

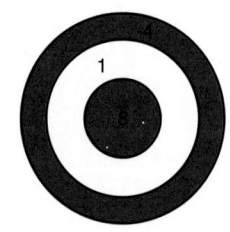

266　Chapter 7 Integers

 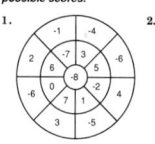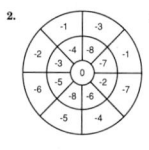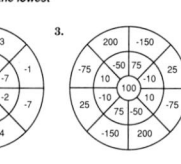
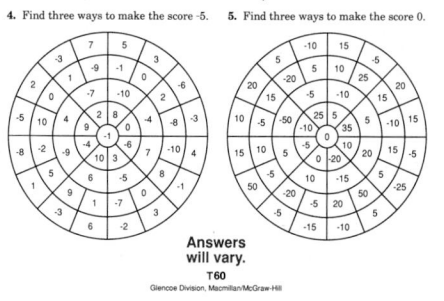

OPTIONS

Extending the Lesson

Number Sense Tell students that *consecutive integers* are 1 apart. For example, 1 and 2 are consecutive integers, as are also -6, -5, and -4. Ask the students to name two consecutive integers whose sum is -27 and then three consecutive integers whose sum is 0. **−13, −14; −1, 0, 1**

Cooperative Learning Activity

Once Around 7-4

Number of players: 4
Materials: Counters, number cube

‣ Copy onto a large sheet of paper (or several smaller sheets taped together) the game board shown at the right. Make sure that a counter will fit in each box.

↠ Each group member places a counter on the "Start" square. In turn, each group member rolls a number cube and moves his or her counter the number of spaces indicated. Write the value of the squares you land on on a separate sheet of paper. Do not toss the number cube after you have passed the "Start" square for a second time. Find the sum of the values of the squares you landed on. The winner is the group member with the greatest sum. Play several rounds.

Glencoe Mathematics: Applications and Connections, Course 2

Start →	2	−3	1	−5	4
−2					−1
−3					3
4					6
−7					−6
1	2	7	5	−4	−2

7-5A Subtracting Integers

A Preview of Lesson 7-5

Objective
Subtract integers by using models.

Materials
counters of two colors
mat

In this lab, you will use counters to model subtraction with integers.

Try this!

Work with a partner.
- Consider $7 - 3$. Place 7 positive counters on the mat and then remove 3.

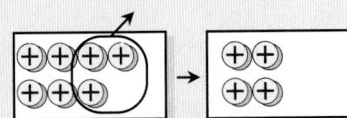

So, $7 - 3 = 4$.

- Consider $-7 - (-3)$. Place 7 negative counters on the mat. Remove 3 of them. Use your result to complete this subtraction sentence $-7 - (-3) = \underline{\ ?\ }$. **−4**

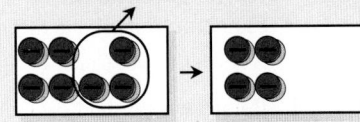

Now consider $7 - (-3)$. This means start with a set of 7 *positive* counters and remove 3 *negative* counters. Add 3 zero pairs to the set. The value of the set does not change. Now you can remove 3 negative counters.

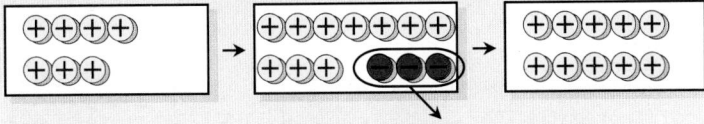

Use the result to complete this sentence $7 - (-3) = \underline{\ ?\ }$. **10**

What do you think?
1. See Solutions Manual.

1. Model $7 - 5$ and $7 + (-5)$. How are they alike? How are they different? Describe any relationship in your own words.

2. If you subtract a positive integer from a lesser positive integer, is the difference positive or negative? **negative**

Model each subtraction. Use your result to write a subtraction sentence. **For models for Exercises 3-10, see Solutions Manual.**

3. $8 - 2$ **6**   4. $-8 - (-2)$ **−6**   5. $8 - (-2)$ **10**   6. $-8 - 2$ **−10**
7. $1 - 4$ **−3**   8. $1 - (-4)$ **5**   9. $-1 - (-4)$ **3**   10. $-1 - 4$ **−5**

Mathematics Lab 7-5A Subtracting Integers   **267**

Interactive Mathematics Tools

This multimedia software provides an interactive lesson that is tied directly to Lesson 7-5A. Students will click and drag counters to subtract integers as in the Mathematics Lab.

Lab Manual, p. 55

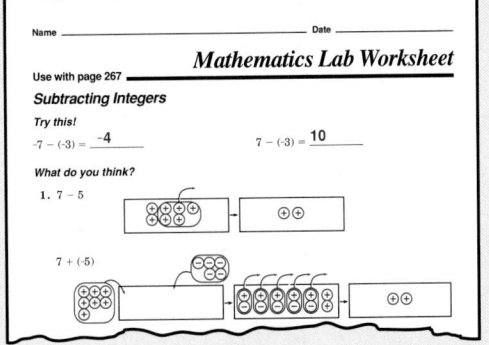

NCTM Standards: 1–6

Management Tips

For Students Have students work with partners to model the subtractions. Each pair will need a set of two-color counters. You may wish to have each student work with either only positive counters or negative ones.

For the Overhead Projector
Overhead Manipulative Resources provides appropriate materials for teacher or student demonstration of the activities in this Mathematics Lab.

1 FOCUS

Introducing the Lab

Remind students of how they used counters to model addition of integers. Have them demonstrate how they think they can use the counters to model subtraction.

2 TEACH

Using Models Ask students to name the property that allows them to use zero pairs in order to subtract negative integers. After working through the three examples, ask students how they would model the subtraction of a positive integer from a negative one.

3 PRACTICE/APPLY

Using Critical Thinking Have students experiment with the counters to determine cases when the difference between two integers is negative, equal to zero, or positive.

Close

Have students work with partners. Each provides integer subtraction exercises for the other to solve by modeling the subtraction with counters. Ask students to verbalize the placing and removing procedure as they work.

267

Lesson Resources
- Study Guide Master 7-5
- Practice Master 7-5
- Enrichment Master 7-5
- Evaluation Master, Quiz A, p. 61
- Interdisciplinary Master, p. 21
- Group Activity Card 7-5

 Transparency 7-5 contains the 5-Minute Check and a teaching aid for this lesson.

🕐 5-Minute Check
(Over Lesson 7-4)

Solve each equation.
1. $4 + (-5) = t$ -1
2. $-6 + 15 = w$ 9
3. $q = 26 + (-16)$ 10

Evaluate each expression if $a = 8$, $b = 12$, and $c = -6$.
4. $-7 + b$ 5
5. $c + a$ 2

1 FOCUS

Motivating the Lesson

Questioning   Have students read the opening paragraph and examine the thermometer. Ask them to suggest a method for subtracting integers that doesn't involve using counters.

2 TEACH

Using Applications   Provide students with a table of reasonable high and low temperatures for 5 states, including some for which the low temperature is below 0°F. Ask them first to estimate the difference between each state's high and low temperature and then to find that difference.

7-5 Subtracting Integers

Objective
Subtract integers.

Global warming, or the greenhouse effect, makes Earth liveable. However, because of atmospheric changes people are causing, scientists fear the greenhouse effect could increase too much.

The greenhouse effect occurs on other planets. The thermometer shows how it affects temperatures on Mars, Earth, and Venus. What is the difference between the actual temperature and the temperature without the greenhouse effect on each planet? *You will answer this question in Exercise 45.*

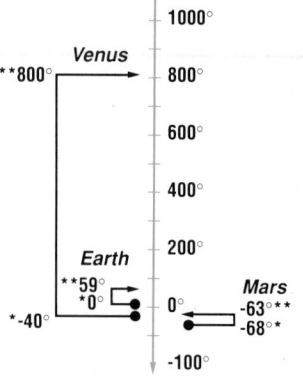

* actual temperature
** temperature with greenhouse effect

> Suppose you are traveling from Seattle to Sydney, Australia. How many hours ahead will you have to set your watch?
>
> Time zones separate the world into 24 sections. The 12th zone east ($+12$) and the 12th zone west (-12) are separated by the International Date Line.
>
> Seattle is in zone -8 and Sydney is in zone $+10$, so you would have to set your watch $-8 + (-10)$ or ahead 18 hours.

Before we can find each difference, let's see how addition and subtraction of integers are related. Let's compare the subtraction $5 - 2$ to the addition $5 + (-2)$.

$5 - 2 = 3$

$5 + (-2) = 3$

The diagrams above show that $5 - 2 = 5 + (-2)$. This example suggests that adding the additive inverse of an integer produces the same result as subtracting it.

Subtracting Integers	**In words:** To subtract an integer, add its additive inverse.
	Arithmetic **Algebra**
	$5 - 2 = 5 + (-2)$ $a - b = a + (-b)$

OPTIONS

Bell Ringer

Present the following problem: *It is 5:00 P.M. in Boston where you live, but you are in Albany, 4 hours from home. You want to get home in time to watch the Red Sox play the Seattle Mariners in a game that starts in Seattle at 7:00 P.M. Will you be home by game time?*   yes

Ask students to solve the problem and then make up others like it for classmates to solve.

Examples

1 Solve $x = -8 - 5$.

$$x = -8 - 5$$
$$= -8 + (-5) \quad \textit{To subtract 5, add } -5.$$
$$= -13$$

2 Solve $-13 - (-6) = w$.

$$-13 - (-6) = w$$
$$-13 + 6 = \quad \textit{To subtract } -6, \textit{ add } 6.$$
$$-7 =$$

3 Solve $t = 54 - (-4)$.

$$t = 54 - (-4)$$
$$= 54 + 4 \quad \textit{To subtract } -4, \textit{ add } 4.$$
$$= 58$$

Example 4 *Connection*

Algebra Evaluate $a - b$ where $a = 3$ and $b = 12$.

$$a - b = 3 - 12 \quad \textit{Replace a with 3 and b with 12.}$$
$$= 3 + (-12) \quad \textit{To subtract 12, add } -12.$$
$$= -9$$

Communicating Mathematics

Read and study the lesson to answer each question.

1. **Tell** how addition and subtraction of integers are related. Subtraction is adding the opposite.

2. **Tell** how to find the additive inverse of an integer. Negate the integer.

3. **Show** how to use the additive inverse to solve $6 - 8 = n$. $6 + (-8) = n$

4. **Write** a subtraction sentence shown by each model.

a.
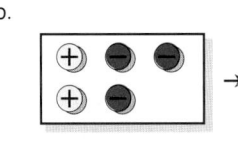 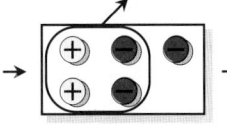 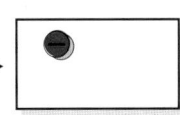 $8 - 5 = 3$

b.
  $2 - 3 = -1$

Guided Practice

Solve each equation.

5. $k = 4 - (-15)$ **19**
6. $-7 - 5 = g$ **−12**
7. $s = 7 - (-20)$ **27**
8. $6 - 13 = y$ **−7**
9. $r = 35 - (-10)$ **45**
10. $1 - 9 = x$ **−8**

Lesson 7-5 Subtracting Integers **269**

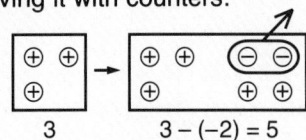

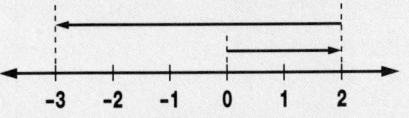
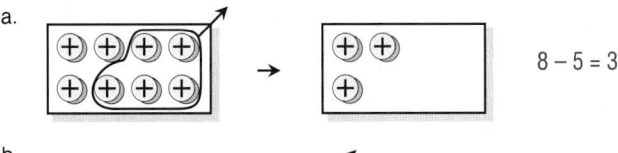
269

Close

Have students summarize the lesson by explaining why the result of subtracting −6 from 6 is not 0.

3 PRACTICE/APPLY

Assignment Guide

Maximum: 11-49

Minimum: 11-39 odd, 40-44, 46-48

All: Mid-Chapter Review

For **Extra Practice,** see p. 588.

Alternate Assessment

Writing Have students explain how they would determine how many years ago Confucious died, in 479 B.C. Subtract −479 from current year.

Practice Masters, p. 61

Name ______ Date ______

Practice Worksheet 7-5

Subtracting Integers

Solve each equation.

1. $j = 6 - (-8)$ 14	2. $-2 - 3 = t$ -5	3. $y = -8 - (-10)$ 2
4. $9 - 14 = k$ -5	5. $s = 36 - (-12)$ 48	6. $5 - 12 = f$ -7
7. $n = 15 - (-8)$ 23	8. $-16 - 6 = v$ -22	9. $m = -4 - 9$ -13
10. $-17 - 13 = h$ -30	11. $g = 12 - (-9)$ 21	12. $b = 14 - (-22)$ 36
13. $x = 5 - (-25)$ 30	14. $-19 - (-50) = a$ 31	15. $12 - (-52) = w$ 64

Evaluate each expression if r = -6, s = 10, and t = -8.

16. $r - 8$ -14	17. $t - s$ -18	18. $-12 - r$ -6
19. $t - r$ -2	20. $s - t$ 18	21. $r - s$ -16

T61

Exercises

Independent Practice

Solve each equation.

11. $9 - 12 = t$ **−3**	12. $54 - (-8) = w$ **62**	13. $-12 - 15 = q$ **−27**
14. $-3 - (-5) = a$ **2**	15. $y = -12 - 56$ **−68**	16. $g = 6 - (-35)$ **41**
17. $10 - (-10) = q$ **20**	18. $17 - (-9) = w$ **26**	19. $-87 - (-87) = k$ **0**
20. $-50 - 45 = f$ **−95**	21. $3 - 86 = h$ **−83**	22. $k = 6 - (-23)$ **29**
23. $-8 - (-8) = q$ **0**	24. $42 - 100 = y$ **−58**	25. $m = -8 - (-19)$ **11**

Evaluate each expression if $t = -2$, $y = 8$, and $e = 4$.

26. $t - 5$ **−7**	27. $y - 7$ **1**	28. $-8 - e$ **−12**	29. $-10 - y$ **−18**
30. $3 - y$ **−5**	31. $t - y$ **−10**	32. $y - e$ **4**	33. $e - y$ **−4**
34. $y - t$ **10**	35. $-e - y$ **−12**	36. $t + e$ **2**	37. $-t - e$ **−2**

38. Evaluate $m - n$ if $m = 5$ and $n = -6$. **11**
39. Evaluate $-p - q$ if $p = -3$ and $q = 9$. **−6**

Mixed Review

40. Estimate 2,367 + 1,248. *(Lesson 1-2)* **3,500**
41. Find the LCM of 14 and 21. *(Lesson 4-9)* **42**
42. **Probability** Gwen buys one ticket for a raffle which has 1 grand prize of $500 and 2 second-place prizes of $100. A total of 500 tickets are sold. Find Gwen's expected winnings. *(Lesson 5-8)* **$1.40**
43. Translate the phrase *65 less than w* into an algebraic expression. *(Lesson 6-4)* **$w - 65$**
44. Solve the equation $d = -3 + (-2)$. *(Lesson 7-4)* **−5**

Problem Solving and Applications

45. **Environment** Refer to the problem in the lesson introduction. Find the difference between the actual temperature and the temperature without the greenhouse effect for Earth, Venus, and Mars. **59°, 840°, 5°**
46. **Critical Thinking** Evaluate $a - b$ if $a = -4$ and $b = 10$. Then evaluate $b - a$ for the same values of the variables. Use your results to make a conjecture about the relationship between $a - b$ and $b - a$. Does your conjecture hold true if $a = 7$ and $b = 9$? **−14; 14; They are opposites; yes.**
47. **Weather** Use the graph at the right to answer each question.
    a. What does the zero point on this graph represent? **normal rainfall**
    b. Write an integer to represent the rainfall for each month shown.
    c. Can you use this graph to decide in which of these months the least rain fell? Explain.
    d. Write a sentence that describes the message this graph is meant to convey. **There was a drought this summer.**

b. −3, −2, −4, 2

c. August; it has the lowest rainfall compared to normal.

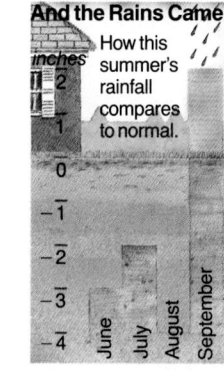

And the Rains Came!
How this summer's rainfall compares to normal.
inches
2
1
0
−1
−2
−3
−4
June
July
August
September

OPTIONS

Multicultural Education

Chinese mathematicians are known to have used negative integers in about 200 B.C. By the 14th century, the Chinese were representing such a number as a black numeral with a slash through it.

48. History Refer to the time line below.

ANCIENT CIVILIZATIONS

a. For how many years was the Olmec civilization in existence? **1,000 years**
b. How many years were there between the beginning of the Mound Builders and Columbus' arrival in America? **about 2,492 years**

49. Data Search Refer to pages 252 and 253. Between the years 1886 and 1989, how many tropical storms occurred during the first five months of the year? How many tropical storms were there during August, September, and October? **17 storms; 633 storms**

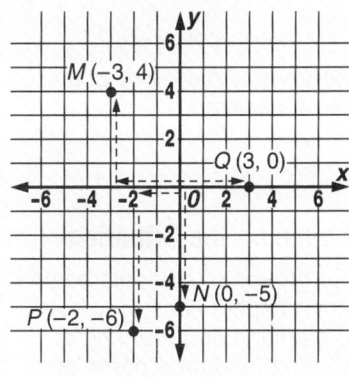

---

7 Assessment: Mid-Chapter Review

Find the opposite and absolute value of each integer. *(Lesson 7-1)*

1. -15 **15, 15**   2. 23 **-23, 23**   3. 0 **0, 0**

4. Order the integers 4, 3, -3, 5, -5, and 6 from least to greatest. *(Lesson 7-2)* **$-5, -3, 3, 4, 5, 6$**

On graph paper, draw coordinate axes. Then graph and label each point. *(Lesson 7-3)* **See margin.**

5. $M(-3, 4)$ 6. $N(0, -5)$ 7. $P(-2, -6)$ 8. $Q(3, 0)$

Solve each equation. *(Lesson 7-4)*

9. $y = -15 + 3$ **-12**   10. $3 + (-5) = t$ **-2**   11. $-2 + (-5) = n$ **-7**

Solve each equation *(Lesson 7-5)*

12. $x = 3 - 15$ **-12**   13. $3 - (-5) = p$ **8**   14. $-2 - (-5) = r$ **3**

Lesson 7-5 Subtracting Integers   **271**

Extending the Lesson

Using Patterns Have students make up number patterns using addition, subtraction, or both addition and subtraction of integers. Classmates are to find the rule and complete the pattern. Provide this sample: $-6, -2, -4, 0, -2, 2,$ $\underline{?}, \underline{?}$ Sample answer: Add 4, add -2, alternately; 0, 4

Cooperative Learning Activity

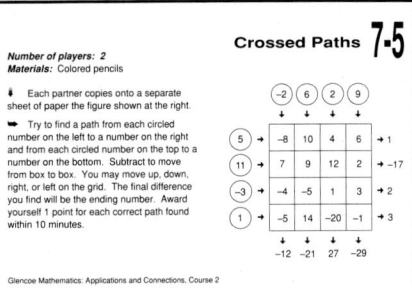

Enrichment Masters, p. 61

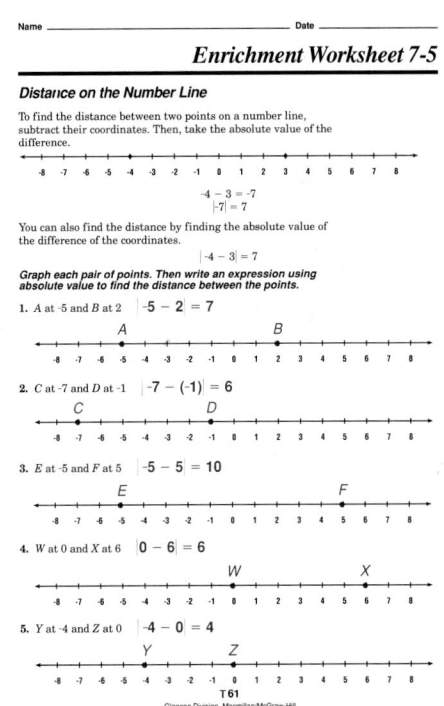

271

DECISION MAKING

Planning for Good Nutrition

Situation

The challenge to your Snack Bar Committee for Sport's Night is to make $1,000 profit and still have a nutritious menu. Jack Bell, the student committee leader, has a menu from the deli at Superior Market and an agreement from the manager to supply all catered food at half price. How many of which items will you choose? How will you price them to make a profit?

Hidden Data

Will the deli furnish the paper and plastic products or is there a charge?
Does the deli have a delivery charge?
Is ice available from the deli?
What should the serving size of a salad be?
Since milk and juices are not on the deli list, will Superior Market give you a price break on these items?

NCTM Standards: 1–5, 7
Objective Analyze data and make a decision.

1 FOCUS

Introducing the Situation

Have groups of students begin by sharing experiences they have had planning and ordering or preparing food for a party, or planning a meal for a large group. Have them discuss costs and other considerations. As they work through the lesson, one group member should record questions students have, as well as their responses to the questions in the activity. Another group member should present the results of their work to the class. The group should work together to come up with a nutritious menu, to answer all questions, and to determine the best way to present their final product.

2 TEACH

Using Applications Suggest that representatives from the groups visit or call a local deli to find out more about the services they offer and how they estimate quantities of food for large groups. Have them share information with the class. The information they gather can help students make better decisions when addressing the questions raised in the Hidden Data section.

Analyzing the Data

Have students formulate questions like these for other members of the group to solve.

The Deli at Superior Market

All sandwiches are spread with low-fat mayonnaise.

New Yorker: Swiss cheese, tomato and lettuce on rye..............$3.50
San Franciscan: Turkey, shredded cabbage on sourdough........$3.90
Chicagoan: Chicken, watercresss on whole wheat....................$3.75
Miamian: Tuna salad, lettuce in a pita...................................$4.10
Bostonian: Roast beef, horseradish on cracked wheat..............$4.00

All salads are mixed with low-fat, low-cholesterol dressings.

Idaho potato salad.........................$6/qt
Indiana coleslaw............................$5/qt
Texas apple salad..........................$8/qt
California orange salad....................$9/qt
National Mix vegetable sticks........$4/qt

All baked goods are made from scratch, no preservatives, no extra sugar frostings.

Seattle Currant honey muffin ....$0.90 each
Oklahoma City Pumpkin bran muffins................$0.85 each
Philadelphia Giant soft pretzels...........................$0.45 each
North-East Blueberry nut bread...........................$2/loaf
South-West Pineapple nut bread..........................$2/loaf
Juices are $5.45/gal, milk is $2.55/gal at Superior Market.
(not available at the deli counter)

272

Analyzing the Data

1. What is the total cost of a New Yorker sandwich and a Bostonian sandwich?

Making a Decision

2. **What is** the cost of 3 quarts of Texas apple salad?
3. **How much** variety is needed?
4. **Can you** feature a favorite as a "Sportsnight Sale" item?
5. **Will you** be able to return leftovers or have a sell-off?
6. **What is** the expected attendance?
7. **Will you** need an alternate place if attendance is low or if sales are low?

Making Decisions in the Real World

8. Investigate the cost of deli products from another grocery store. Ask the deli for a price cut.

273

Teaching Tip You may wish to have students confer with a parent, a school cafeteria worker or nutritionist to find out more about nutrition or about serving sizes.

Checking for Understanding

Have a representative of each group explain how the group has decided to approach the activity. Ask them what tasks they have identified, what plans they have to accomplish the tasks, and what additional questions or issues they have raised.

3 PRACTICE/APPLY

Making a Decision

Have representatives from each group share their final product with the class, including their responses to the questions raised in the activity. Ask them to present their reports verbally, supported by a chart, menu, or any other visual aid.

Making Decisions in the Real World

Invite a representative from a local deli or restaurant to sit in on the group presentations and, after hearing them, to provide helpful suggestions and answer questions students might have. Then have groups repeat the activity using menus and price lists from actual stores in the neighborhood.

Answers

1. $7.50
2. $24
3.–7. Answers will vary

NCTM Standards: 1–5, 7, 8

Lesson Resources
• Study Guide Master 7-6
• Practice Master 7-6
• Enrichment Master 7-6
• Group Activity Card 7-6

 Transparency 7-6 contains the 5-Minute Check and a teaching aid for this lesson.

🕐 5-Minute Check
(Over Lesson 7-5)

Solve each equation.

1. $4 - 11 = r$ -7
2. $32 - (-15) = t$ 47
3. $m = -41 - 26$ -67
4. $-14 - (-14) = k$ 0
5. Evaluate the expression $y - x$, if $y = -8$ and $x = -5$. -3

1 FOCUS

Motivating the Lesson

Questioning Ask groups of students to study the population chart. Have them evaluate the information it displays, summarizing it and looking for any trends or patterns. Ask them to compare their inferences with those of other groups. If possible, have students compare the data shown with data about the population in your area.

2 TEACH

Using Applications Have students discuss the usefulness of examining data to look for patterns. Ask them to suggest jobs, tasks, or situations in which looking for patterns is a necessity. Then have them talk about when the strategy of finding and using patterns can be a reasonable one to use.

7-6 Find a Pattern

Objective
Solve problems finding and extending a pattern.

The United States Bureau of the Census can predict the population of the world and the median age of the people. The partial chart below shows some actual and some predicted data. Use the chart to find a pattern that will help you predict the world's population in the year 2000.

The World's Population					
Year	1980	1985	1990	1995	2000
World's Total Population in millions	4,478	4,889	5,326	5,786	?
per square mile	85	93	102	110	?
Median Age	22.6	23.5	24.3	25.2	?
Industrialized Nations	1,136	1,172	1,204	1,232	?
Non-Industrialized Nations	3,343	3,717	4,122	4,554	?

Explore What do you know?
You know the actual population for 1980 and 1990.
You know the predicted population for 1985 and 1995.

What are you trying to find?
You are trying to find the population for the year 2000.

Plan Study the chart. You can see in the millions line that the world's population is growing. Find the pattern to predict the world's population for the year 2000.

Solve To find how much the population is increasing, subtract each year's population from the population before it. Then subtract the differences.

1985　　1980
4889 ⊟ 4478 🟰 411

1990　　1985
5326 ⊟ 4889 🟰 437

1995　　1990
5786 ⊟ 5326 🟰 460

Since $437 - 411$ is 26, and $460 - 437$ is 23, you can see that the amount of growth is decreasing.

OPTIONS

Reteaching Activity

Using Problem Solving Some students may benefit from additional practice with sequences involving simpler numbers, or from examining patterns containing shapes, colors, or letters.

Study Guide Masters, p. 62

Name _____ Date _____

Study Guide Worksheet 7-6

Problem-Solving Strategy: Find a Pattern

Find the next three numbers in the pattern:
1, 2, 4, 7, 11, 16, 22, . . .

Explore What do you know?
You know the first seven numbers in the pattern.

What are you trying to find?
You are trying to find the next three numbers in the pattern.

Plan Find the difference between consecutive numbers.
Try to find a pattern.

Solve 1 2 4 7 11 16 22
　　　　+1 +2 +3 +4 +5 +6

The amount of growth decreased by 3 million every 5 years. To find the amount of growth from 1995 to 2000, subtract 3 from 23. The result is 20. So, 20 + 460 is 480. This is the amount of increase from 1995 to 2000. To predict the world's population for the year 2000, add.

5,786	*predicted 1995 population*
+ 480	*amount of increase from 1995 to 2000*
6,266	*predicted population for 2000*

In the year 2000, the world's population is predicted to be 6,266,000.

Examine   The answer 6,266,000 seems reasonable because the differences in population increase follow a pattern: 411, 437, 460, and 480. The differences between each of these numbers are 26, 23, and 20.

Example

Complete the pattern: 63, 48, 35, 24, __?__, __?__, __?__.

What do you add to each term to get the succeeding term?

$$48 - 63 = -15 \qquad 35 - 48 = -13 \qquad 24 - 35 = -11$$

To continue the pattern, add 2 less each time; first add -9, then -7, and then -5. So, $24 + (-9) = 15$, $15 + (-7) = 8$, and $8 + (-5) = 3$.

The next three numbers in the sequence are 15, 8, and 3.

Checking for Understanding

Communicating Mathematics

Read and study the lesson to answer each question.

1. **Tell** why the prediction for the median age in the world for the year 2000 is about 26. **The pattern shows that each year 0.9 or 0.8 is added.**

2. **Write** another rule for the pattern in the example above. **Sample answer: using digits 8 to 2, number squared minus one**

Guided Practice

Solve by finding a pattern.

3. State the pattern. Then complete the sequence.
   1, 3, 1, 3, __?__, __?__, __?__ **1 and 3 alternating; 1, 3, 1**

4. State two different rules for the sequence 1, 4, 9, 16, 25, ... **squares of ordered whole numbers; add 3, 5, 7, 9, . . .**

5. Complete the sequence 60, __?__, __?__, 42, 36. **54, 48**

Lesson 7-6 Problem-Solving Strategy: Find a Pattern   **275**

Meeting Needs of Middle School Students

Encourage students to work with parents or other family members to solve the problems on page 276 by looking for patterns or by using other strategies. Have them talk with these family members about the patterns they can discern in all their daily lives, both numerical and otherwise. Ask students to share their findings with classmates.

More Examples

For the Example

Complete the pattern: 60, 54, 46, 36, __?__, __?__, __?__
24, 10, −6

Teaching Tip   After students complete the Example, you may wish to point out that rules for some patterns can involve operations other than addition and subtraction, or can involve more than one operation. Tell them that some sequences can be described by more than one rule.

Checking for Understanding

Exercises 1-2 are designed to help you assess students' understanding through reading, writing, speaking, and modeling. You should work through these exercises with your students and then monitor their work on Guided Practice Exercises 3-5.

Practice Masters, p. 62

Name _____   Date _____

Practice Worksheet 7-6

Problem-Solving Strategy: Find A Pattern

Solve by looking for a pattern.

1. State the pattern. Then complete the sequence.
   12, 17, 22, 27, __?__, __?__, __?__
   Add 5; 32, 37, 42

2. Give two different rules for the sequence 2, 3, 5, 8, . . .
   Add 1, add 2, add 3, and so on. Add the previous two numbers.

3. Complete the pattern.
   400, 200, 100, __?__, 25, __?__
   50, 12.5

4. Find the number of lines determined by the four vertices of a square.   **6**

Solve. Use any strategy.

5. In 11,436 times at bat, Ty Cobb had 4,190 hits. What is a reasonable estimate of his batting average (number of hits divided by number of times at bat)?
   Sample: 0.350

6. Suppose a box of floppy disks costs $19.95, a three-ring notebook costs $2.98, a printer ribbon costs $7.98, and a box of computer paper costs $15.98. Will $50 be enough to buy all of these items (exluding tax)?
   yes

7. Choose three different digits. Use these digits to make all possible two-digit numbers in which the tens digits and the ones digit are different (six different numbers). Add them. Add the three original digits. Divide the first sum by the second. What is the answer? Try three other different numbers less than 10. What is the pattern in the answers?
   22; always 22

8. The NCAA basketball tournament starts with 64 teams. After the first round, there are 32 teams left; after the second round there are 16 teams left, and so on. Complete the pattern until there is only one team left. How many rounds does it take to determine a winner?   **6**

T62
Glencoe Division, Macmillan/McGraw-Hill

Close

Have students write number sequences for others to complete by finding and continuing a pattern. Ask the problem solvers to state the rule used.

3 PRACTICE/APPLY

Assignment Guide
Maximum: 6–12
Minimum: 6–12

Alternate Assessment

Writing Have students use the chart at the opening of the lesson to predict the population in industrialized nations in the year 2000. Ask them to explain their method and to describe the pattern they found.   Increase is 4 million less each time; 1,256 million in 2000

Additional Answer

9.

Enrichment Masters, p. 62

Name _____ Date _____

Enrichment Worksheet 7-6

Patterns in Pascal's Triangle

Many interesting and beautiful patterns can be found in Pascal's triangle. In the figure at the right, the first few numbers divisible by 2 have been shaded.

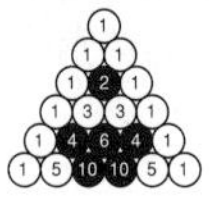

On a separate sheet of paper, extend Pascal's triangle until you have 13 rows. Then use the numbers for these problems.

1. In the figure below, shade the circles representing all numbers divisible by 2. This pattern has been started in the figure above.

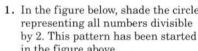
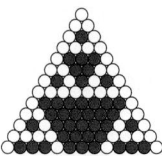

2. In the figure below, shade the circles representing all numbers divisible by 3.

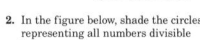
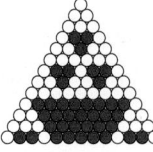

3. In the figure below, shade the circles representing all numbers divisible by 4. Predict the pattern before you start.

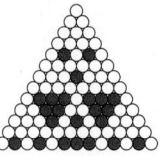

4. In the figure below, shade the circles representing all numbers divisible by 5. Predict the pattern before you start.

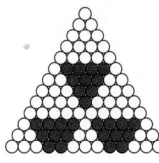

T62
Glencoe Division, Macmillan/McGraw-Hill

276

Problem Solving

Practice   Solve. Use any strategy.

Strategies
●●●●●●●●●
Look for a pattern.
Solve a simpler problem.
Act it out.
Guess and check.
Draw a diagram.
Make a chart.
Work backward.

6. Find the number of line segments determined by six points on a line. **15**

7. Gloria made enough money with her computer graphics to buy a new printer. She told Al and Sue who each let two of their computer network friends know ten minutes later. If the news spread like this every ten minutes, how many people knew by the end of the hour? **255 people**

8. Complete the pattern 100, 98, 94, __?__ , 80, __?__ . **88, 70**

9. You plant 10 hyacinths in exactly 5 rows. There are 4 bulbs in each row. Draw a diagram of your garden. **See margin.**

9. Drawing shows plants are at the vertices and segment crossings of a five-pointed star.

10. This pattern is known as Pascal's Triangle. Find the pattern and complete the 6th and 7th rows.

1st row	1	1 5 10 10 5 1
2nd row	1 1	1 6 15 20 15 6 1
3rd row	1 2 1	
4th row	1 3 3 1	
5th row	1 4 6 4 1	

11. A college student sent home this letter. If each letter stands for one digit 0–9, how much money did he ask for?

$$\begin{array}{r} \text{SEND} \\ + \text{MORE} \\ \hline \text{MONEY} \end{array} \qquad \begin{array}{r} 9{,}567 \\ + 1{,}085 \\ \hline 10{,}652 \end{array}$$

12. Complete the chart on page 274. **6,266; 119; 26; 1,256; 5,009**

13. **Data Search** Refer to page 651. If the actual temperature is 15 degrees Fahrenheit, how much colder does it feel when the wind increases from 5 mph to 10 mph? **15°**

DATA SEARCH

CULTURAL KALEIDOSCOPE

Pat Neblett

If children are our future, Pat Neblett wants to make sure that they know and understand different cultures. With $2,000, the former real estate agent founded Tuesday's Child Books in 1988 from her Randolph, Massachusetts home. She began selling African-American books through direct mail catalogs. Now most of her business comes from sales to schools. The titles have expanded to include children's books about Asians, Hispanics, Native Americans, and minority groups in the United States. Neblett carries more than 300 titles. She reads each book herself to ensure that the content positively reinforces a child's self-worth.

Sales have increased from $7,000 in her first year to a projected $25,000 in 1991. She plans to open her own retail store if her business continues to grow.

276   Chapter 7 Integers

OPTIONS

Extending the Lesson

Cultural Kaleidoscope Ask students to make a list of mathematical skills that are needed to own and operate your own business. Discuss how estimation and making predictions are used to project annual sales.

Cooperative Learning Activity

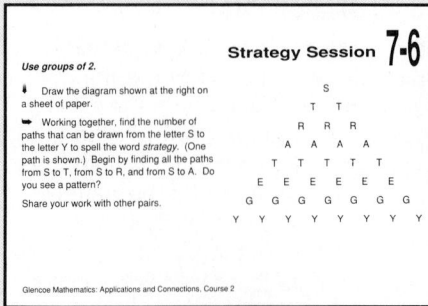

Strategy Session **7-6**

Use groups of 2.

♦ Draw the diagram shown at the right on a sheet of paper.

➡ Working together, find the number of paths that can be drawn from the letter S to the letter Y to spell the word *strategy*. (One path is shown.) Begin by finding all the paths from S to T, from S to R, and from S to A. Do you see a pattern?

➡ Share your work with other pairs.

Glencoe Mathematics: Applications and Connections, Course 2

Cooperative Learning

7-7A Multiplying Integers

A Preview of Lesson 7-7

Objective
Multiply integers by using models.

Materials:
counters of two colors
mat

In this lab, you will use counters to model multiplication of integers.

Try this!

Work with a partner.

- Remember that 2×4 means *two sets of four items*. Using models, 2×4 means to *place* 2 sets of 4 *positive* counters on a mat.

So, $2 \times 4 = 8$.

- Place 2 sets of 4 negative counters on the mat. Use your result to complete: $2 \times (-4) = \underline{\ ?\ }$. -8

- Since -2 is the opposite of 2, -2×4 means to *remove* 2 sets of 4 *positive* counters. How can you remove 2 sets? First, put in as many zero pairs as you need. Then remove 2 sets of 4 positive counters. Use your result to complete: $-2 \times 4 = \underline{\ ?\ }$. -8

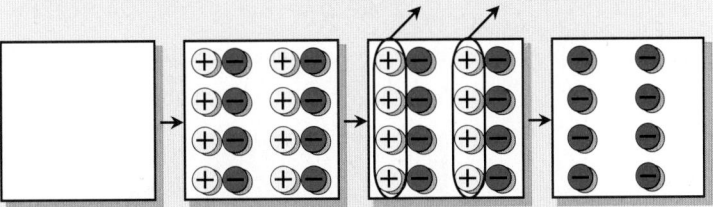

- Use counters to model $-2 \times (-4)$. Use your result to write a multiplication sentence. $-2 \times (-4) = 8$

What do you think?

1. They represent the same product; the commutative property changed their positions.

1. How are -3×7 and $7 \times (-3)$ the same? How are they different?
For answers to Exercises 2–9, see Solutions Manual.
Model each multiplication and write a multiplication sentence.

2. 3×5 3. $3 \times (-5)$ 4. -3×5 5. $-3 \times (-5)$

6. 5×3 7. $5 \times (-3)$ 8. -5×3 9. $-5 \times (-3)$

Mathematics Lab 7-7A Multiplying Integers   **277**

Mathematics Lab 7-7A

NCTM Standards: 1–6

Management Tips

For Students Have students work with partners using two-color counters. You will need to provide at least 30 counters for each group. Encourage groups to assist one another with the modeling. Such cooperation may be particularly useful in the case of modeling multiplication by negative integers.

For the Overhead Projector
Overhead Manipulative Resources provides appropriate materials for teacher or student demonstration of the activities in this Mathematics Lab.

1 FOCUS

Introducing the Lab

Tell students that they can use counters to model multiplication of integers, just as they did with addition and subtraction of integers. Guide students to see how they again can use zero pairs, this time to model multiplication by negative integers.

2 TEACH

Using Models Have students work with partners to model additional examples of each case of integer multiplication. Each student models a multiplication sentence that another student formulates.

3 PRACTICE/APPLY

Using Connections Ask students which property of multiplication assures that the answer to -3×7 is equal to $7 \times (-3)$. commutative

Close

Have students summarize the procedure for using counters to model multiplication of integers. Ask them to explain what it means to multiply by a negative integer, using counters. removing sets

---

OPTIONS

Lab Manual You may wish to make copies of the blackline master on p. 56 of the *Lab Manual* for students to use as a recording sheet.

Lab Manual, p. 56

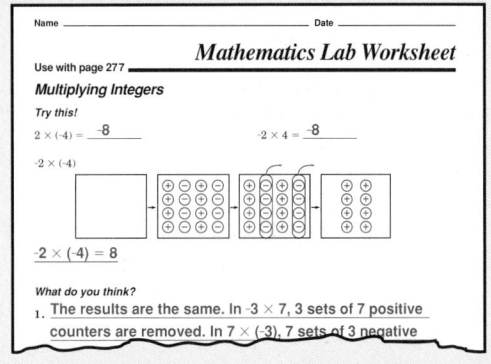

277

NCTM Standards: 1–9

Lesson Resources
• Study Guide Master 7-7
• Practice Master 7-7
• Enrichment Master 7-7
• Technology Master, p. 21
• Group Activity Card 7-7

 Transparency 7-7 contains the 5-Minute Check and a teaching aid for this lesson.

⏱ 5-Minute Check
(Over Lesson 7-6)

Solve using the find-a-pattern strategy.

1. State the pattern; then complete the sequence:
   −2, 1, 3, 6, 8, _?_, _?_, _?_
   Add 3, add 2; 11, 13, 16

2. Complete the sequence:
   20, _?_, _?_, 8, 2, −5   17, 13; subtract 3, 4, 5, · · ·.

3. What is the ones digit in the number 4^{15}?   4; Odd powers end in 4, even powers in 6.

---

1 FOCUS

Motivating the Lesson

Questioning Have students read the two opening paragraphs of the lesson. Ask them whether after 4 years the amount that the beach recedes, a negative number, will continue to be negative, or whether it will become nonnegative (positive or zero).

2 TEACH

Using Connections Review the commutative and associative properties of multiplication as well as the property of multiplication by zero. Then focus on the rules for finding the sign of the product of two numbers: same signs—a positive product; different signs—a negative product.

7-7 Multiplying Integers

Objective
Multiply integers.

When the first two-piece swimsuit was seen at the beach, it was named for the shock it caused. Bikini is the name of an island in the Pacific Ocean where the hydrogen bomb was first tested.

The wearing away of a coastline by the action of water is called wave erosion. Wave erosion can cause a coastline to recede at a rate of a few centimeters each year.

Suppose a beach recedes 2 centimeters each year. In four years, how many centimeters will the beach recede? Let r represent the number of centimeters the beach recedes. Let -2 mean that the beach recedes 2 centimeters.

The equation $r = 4(-2)$ can be used to represent this problem. You can solve this problem by using counters or by observing a pattern.

Using Counters:

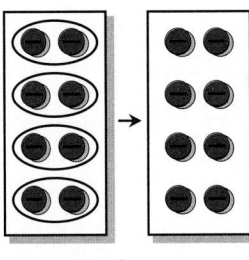

$$4(-2) = -8$$

Observing a pattern:

$$4 \cdot 2 = 8$$
$$4 \cdot 1 = 4 \quad {\scriptstyle -4}$$
$$4 \cdot 0 = 0 \quad {\scriptstyle -4}$$
$$4 \cdot (-1) = -4 \quad {\scriptstyle -4}$$
$$4 \cdot (-2) = -8 \quad {\scriptstyle -4}$$

So, $r = -8$. In four years, the beach will recede 8 centimeters.

The diagram and pattern above illustrate the following rule.

Multiplying Integers with Different Signs	The product of two integers with different signs is negative.

Examples

1 Solve $g = 5(-4)$.
The two integers have different signs. The product will be negative.
$g = 5(-4)$
$g = -20$

2 Solve $-6(5) = h$.
The two integers have different signs. The product will be negative.
$-6(5) = h$
$-30 = h$

278   Chapter 7 Integers

OPTIONS

Reteaching Activity

Using Connections Some students may benefit from visualizing multiplication of integers as repeated addition shown on a number line. For example, show $4 \times (-2)$ as
$-2 + (-2) + (-2) + (-2) = -8$.
Try this before illustrating the rules for multiplication by using patterns.

Study Guide Masters, p. 63

Name _____   Date _____

Study Guide Worksheet 7-7

Multiplying Integers

The product of two positive integers is positive.

Examples Solve $m = 5(8)$.   Solve $n = 4(5)(6)$.   Solve $p = (2)(8)(1)$.
                    $m = 40$ $n = 20(6)$ $p = 16(1)$
                                      $n = 120$ $p = 16$

The product of two negative integers is positive.

Examples Solve $y = (-6)(-9)$.   Solve $x = (-7)^2$.   Solve $z = (-3)(-5)(2)$.
                    $y = 54$ $x = (-7)(-7)$ $z = 15(2)$
                                          $x = 49$ $z = 30$

The product of a positive integer and a negative integer is negative.

How would you solve $-4(-2) = y$? You can use the same methods to multiply two integers with the same sign. When using counters, $-4(-2)$ means that you will remove 4 sets of 2 negative counters.

Using counters:

Observing a pattern:

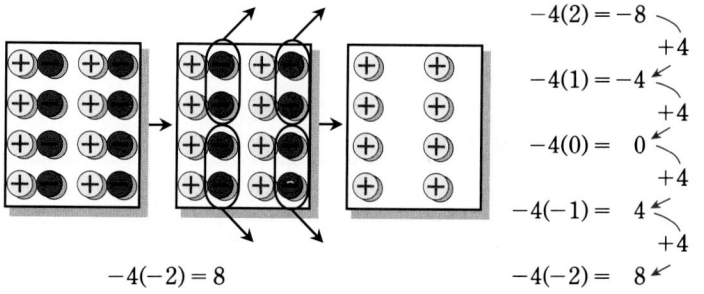

$$-4(2) = -8 \quad \searrow {}_{+4}$$
$$-4(1) = -4 \quad \swarrow {}_{+4}$$
$$-4(0) = \quad 0 \quad \swarrow {}_{+4}$$
$$-4(-1) = \quad 4 \quad \swarrow {}_{+4}$$

$$-4(-2) = 8 \qquad\qquad -4(-2) = \quad 8 \swarrow$$

So, the solution of $-4(-2) = y$ is 8. This suggests the following rule.

Multiplying Integers with the Same Sign	The product of two integers with the same sign is positive.

Examples

3 Solve $a = -5(-4)$.

The two integers have the same sign. The product will be positive.

$$a = -5(-4)$$
$$= 20$$

4 Solve $(-7)^2 = z$.

The exponent says there are two factors of -7. The product will be positive.

$$(-7)^2 = z$$
$$(-7)(-7) =$$
$$49 =$$

Example 5 *Connection*

Algebra Evaluate abc, where $a = -2$, $b = 5$, and $c = 2$.

$$abc = (-2)(5)(2) \qquad \textit{Replace } a \textit{ with } -2, b \textit{ with } 5, \textit{ and } c \textit{ with } 2.$$
$$= [(-2)(5)](2) \qquad \textit{Use the associative property to group the factors.}$$
$$= (-10)(2)$$
$$= -20$$

1. One is positive and one is negative.
Checking for Understanding

Communicating Mathematics

Read and study the lesson to answer each question.

1. **Tell** what you can say about two integers if their product is negative.
2. **Show** a pattern to explain why the solution of $q = 4(-3)$ must be -12. **See margin.**
3. **Draw** a model that shows $-3(-5) = k$. **See margin.**
4. **Show** another way to complete the product in Example 5. **See margin.**

Lesson 7-7 Multiplying Integers **279**

Gifted and Talented Needs

Have students make an integer multiplication magic square (3×3) for classmates to solve.

Additional Answers

2. $4 \cdot 2 = 8$
   $4 \cdot 1 = 4$
   $4 \cdot 0 = 0$
   $4 \cdot (-1) = -4$
   $4 \cdot (-2) = -8$
   $4 \cdot (-3) = -12$

3.

4. $abc = (-2)(5)(2)$
   $ = (-2)[(5)(2)]$
   $ = (-2)(10)$
   $ = -20$

Checking for Understanding

Exercises 1-4 are designed to help you assess students' understanding through reading, writing, speaking, and modeling. You should work through these exercises with your students and then monitor their work on Guided Practice Exercises 5-16.

Practice Masters, p. 63

Name _____ Date _____

Practice Worksheet 7-7

Multiplying Integers

Solve each equation.

1. $m = 2(-8)$
   -16
2. $-3(-4) = t$
   12
3. $x = 8(-4)$
   -32

4. $(-5)(-5) = p$
   25
5. $r = -12(5)$
   -60
6. $(-4)^2 = w$
   16

7. $e = -12(13)$
   -156
8. $14(-3) = v$
   -42
9. $n = -14(-5)$
   70

10. $(-11)^2 = h$
    121
11. $d = -7(-8)$
    56
12. $b = -9(10)$
    -90

Evaluate each expression if $m = -6$, $n = 3$, and $p = -4$.

13. $-4m$
    24
14. np
    -12
15. $2mn$
    -36

16. $-2m^2$
    -72
17. $-5np$
    60
18. $-10mp$
    -240

19. $-12np$
    144
20. mnp
    72
21. p^2
    16

T63
Glencoe Division, Macmillan/McGraw-Hill

279

Error Analysis

Watch for students who assign the wrong sign to the products of one or more negative integers.

Prevent by suggesting to them that they should multiply first, disregarding the signs, and then use the rules provided to affix the correct sign.

Close

Have students tell whether the following products will be positive or negative, and why:
1. $-4 \times (-9)$ **2.** $6 \times (-7)$
1. positive, since both factors are negative; **2.** negative, since the factors have different signs

3 PRACTICE/APPLY

Assignment Guide
Maximum: 17–46
Minimum: 17–39 odd, 40–44

For **Extra Practice,** see p. 588.

Alternate Assessment

Writing Have students write four integer multiplication exercises, two with positive products and two with negative products.

Enrichment Masters, p. 63

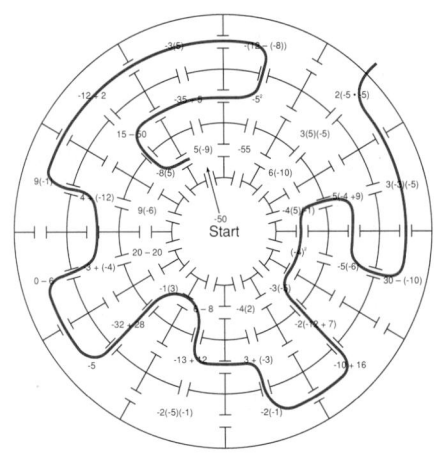
280

Guided Practice Solve each equation.

5. $c = 21(-2)$ -42
6. $-4(-5) = u$ 20
7. $t = 6(-3)$ -18
8. $-9(9) = h$ -81
9. $-15(3) = j$ -45
10. $k = (-3)^2$ 9

Evaluate each expression if $x = -9$, $y = 2$, $z = -3$, and $w = 6$.

11. $-3w$ -18
12. xy -18
13. z^2 9
14. $2xw$ -108
15. $-4x^2$ -324
16. xyz 54

Exercises

Independent Practice Solve each equation.

17. $z = -6(-15)$ 90
18. $(-5)^2 = h$ 25
19. $-11(-11) = g$ 121
20. $h = -9(5)$ -45
21. $(-6)(-6) = p$ 36
22. $f = (-12)^2$ 144
23. $8(-12) = n$ -96
24. $-7(15) = k$ -105
25. $-34(2) = q$ -68
26. Find the product of -8 and -6.   48   27. Multiply -7 and 10. -70

Evaluate each expression if $a = -7$, $b = 3$, $c = -5$, and $d = 7$.

28. $-5d$ -35
29. $7d$ 49
30. $-6bd$ -126
31. $-9ab$ 189
32. $-16c$ 80
33. a^2 49
34. $-2d^2$ -98
35. $-10bc$ 150
36. $-2bd$ -42
37. $-5abc$ -525
38. $-acd$ -245
39. $-3bc$ 45

Mixed Review
40. Divide 2.25 by 1.5. *(Lesson 2-7)*   1.5
41. Write $\frac{3}{8}$ as a decimal. *(Lesson 4-7)*   **0.375**
42. Subtract $\frac{1}{9}$ from $\frac{5}{12}$. *(Lesson 5-3)* $\frac{11}{36}$
43. Solve the equation $\frac{k}{21} = 4$. *(Lesson 6-3)*   84
44. **Hiking** Jay's boy scout troop is hiking on a trail that is 75 feet above sea level. They hike into a canyon that is 12 feet below sea level. How many feet has Jay's troop hiked? *(Lesson 7-5)*   **87 feet**

Problem Solving and Applications

45. **Earth Science** Earth's atmosphere exerts a pressure of 14.7 pounds per square inch at the ocean's surface. The pressure increases by 2.7 pounds per square inch for every 6 feet that you descend. Yung-Mi says that the pressure at -17 feet will be 132.5 pounds per square inch. Is this reasonable? Explain. **No; at -18 feet the pressure dropped 3(2.7), so it is 22.8 pounds per sq in.**

46. **Critical Thinking** Find each product.
a. $(-2)(3)(4)$ -24 b. $(-2)(-3)(4)$ 24
c. What is the sign of the product $(2)(-3)(-4)$? $+$
d. Write a rule for determining the sign of the product of *three* integers. **odd number of neg. signs, neg. answer; even number of neg. signs, pos. answer**

280   **Chapter 7** Integers

OPTIONS

Extending the Lesson

Using Number Sense Have students explore integer multiplication with more than two negative factors. Ask them to look for a pattern to help them figure out a rule for finding the products. **odd number of negative factors: a negative product; even number of negative factors: a positive product**

Cooperative Learning Activity

Plug It In **7-7**

Number of players: 2
Materials: Index cards, spinners

• Copy onto cards the expressions shown on the back of this card, one per card. Shuffle the cards and place them face down in a pile. Label equal sections of one spinner "-5," "-3," "-1," "2," "3," "6." You will replace the variable a in the expressions on the cards with these numbers. Label equal sections of another spinner "-6," "-4," "-2," "1," "4," "5." You will replace the variable b with these numbers.

➔ One partner flips over a card. Try to be the first to evaluate the expression correctly by replacing the variables with the numbers on the spinners. The winner of each round gets 1 point. Continue, taking turns flipping over cards, until no cards remain in the pile. The overall winner is the partner with the most points.

Glencoe Mathematics: Applications and Connections, Course 2

7-8 Dividing Integers

Objective

Divide integers.

The list at the right shows some of the stocks traded on the New York Stock Exchange. Rod and Linda Conley invested money in the Heinz Company. During a 2-day period, Rod and Linda's stock price had a change of -2. What was the average change per day?

Stock	High	Low	Last	Change
Heinz	34	32	32	-2
HeleneC	7 7/8	7 3/4	7 7/8	
Hellrint	21 7/8	19 1/4	21	$+3/4$
HelmrP	71 3/4	67 3/4	71 1/2	$+7/8$
HemCap	4 1/8	4	4 1/8	$+1/8$
Heminc	8 1/4	8	8 1/4	
Herculs	22	20 1/2	21	-1
Hershy	25 1/2	24 3/4	25 1/2	$+1/4$

Let a represent the average change per day. To find a, divide -2 by 2.

$$-2 \div 2 = a$$

Division of integers is related to multiplication. The division sentence $-2 \div 2 = a$ can be written as the multiplication sentence $a \times 2 = -2$. Think: 2 times what number equals -2?

$$2(1) = 2$$
$$2(-1) = -2 \ \checkmark$$

So, $a = -1$. Rod and Linda's stock dropped an average of $1 per day.

Let's see how some other division sentences are related to multiplication sentences.

$$4 \div (-2) = b \quad \rightarrow \quad -2 \times b = 4$$
$$-15 \div (-3) = c \quad \rightarrow \quad -3 \times c = -15$$
$$-63 \div 7 = d \quad \rightarrow \quad 7 \times d = -63$$

Since division is related to multiplication, you can follow the multiplication rules for signs to determine the sign of a quotient.

Dividing Integers	The quotient of two integers with the same sign is positive.
	The quotient of two integers with different signs is negative.

Examples

1 Solve $a = -20 \div (-4)$.

$a = -20 \div (-4)$ *The signs are the same.*
$\quad = 5$ *The quotient is positive.*

2 Solve $-10 \div 2 = x$.

$-10 \div 2 = x$ *The signs are different.*
$\quad -5 = x$ *The quotient is negative.*

Lesson 7-8 Dividing Integers **281**

OPTIONS

Reteaching Activity

Using Connections Use related multiplication and division sentences to help students see how they can apply the same rules for determining the sign of the answer.

7-8 Lesson Notes

NCTM Standards: 1–7, 9, 10

Lesson Resources
- Study Guide Master 7-8
- Practice Master 7-8
- Enrichment Master 7-8
- Multicultural Activity, p. 7
- Group Activity Card 7-8

 Transparency 7-8 contains the 5-Minute Check and a teaching aid for this lesson.

🕐 5-Minute Check
(Over Lesson 7-7)
Solve each equation.
1. $r = -4(-12)$ 48
2. $f = -8(14)$ -112
3. $p = (-11)^2$ 121

1 FOCUS

Motivating the Lesson

Activity Provide students with financial pages from a newspaper. Guide them to understand what the numbers mean in each column.

More Examples

For Example 1

Solve $a = -28 \div (-7)$. 4

For Example 2

Solve $-18 \div 3 = y$. -6

Close

Have students write one division exercise in which the quotient is a negative integer and one in which the quotient is a positive integer.

3 PRACTICE/APPLY

Assignment Guide

Maximum: 12–34

Minimum: 13–27 odd, 29–34

For **Extra Practice,** see p. 589.

Enrichment Masters, p. 64

Name _____ Date _____

Enrichment Worksheet 7-8

Division by Zero?

Some interesting things happen when you try to divide by zero. For example, look at these two equations.

$$\frac{5}{0} = x \qquad \frac{0}{0} = y$$

If you can write the equations above, you can also write the two equations below.

$$0 \cdot x = 5 \qquad 0 \cdot y = 0$$

However, there is no number that will make the left equation true. This equation has no solution. For the right equation, *every* number will make it true. The solutions for this equation are "all numbers."

Because division by zero leads to impossible situations, it is not a "legal" step in solving a problem. People say that division by zero is undefined, or not possible, or simply not allowed.

Describe the solution set for each equation.

1. $4x = 0$ 0
2. $x \cdot 0 = 0$ all numbers
3. $x \cdot 0 = x$ 0

4. $\frac{0}{x} = 0$ all numbers but 0
5. $\frac{0}{x} = x$ no solution
6. $\frac{0}{x} = 5$ no solution

What values for x must be excluded to prevent division by 0?

7. $\frac{1}{x^2}$ 0
8. $\frac{1}{x-1}$ 1
9. $\frac{1}{x+1}$ -1

10. $\frac{0}{2x}$ 0
11. $\frac{1}{2x-2}$ 1
12. $\frac{1}{3x+6}$ -2

Explain what is wrong with this "proof."

13. **Step 1** $0 \cdot 1 = 0$ and $0 \cdot (-1) = 0$.

   Step 2 Therefore, $\frac{0}{0} = 1$ and $\frac{0}{0} = -1$.

   Step 3 Therefore, $1 = -1$.

   Step 2 involves division by zero.

T 64
Glencoe Division, Macmillan/McGraw-Hill

Checking for Understanding

Communicating Mathematics

Read and study the lesson to answer each question.

1. **Write** a division sentence related to the multiplication sentence $6n = -12$. $-12 \div 6 = n$

2. **Tell** why the solution of $x = -50 \div 10$ is equal to the solution of $x = 50 \div (-10)$. **Quotient of integers with different signs is negative no matter which integer has which sign.**

Guided Practice

Solve each equation.

3. $c = 45 \div (-15)$ -3
4. $-250 \div 25 = u$ -10
5. $a = -35 \div -7$ 5
6. $500 \div (-25) = h$ -20
7. $-68 \div (-4) = b$ 17
8. $-84 \div 12 = p$ -7

Evaluate each expression if $v = -12$, $e = 6$, and $q = 4$.

9. $\frac{124}{q}$ 31
10. $\frac{v^2}{e}$ 24
11. $\frac{-96}{v}$ 8

Exercises

Independent Practice

Solve each equation.

12. $c = 56 \div (-2)$ -28
13. $-88 \div (-22) = u$ 4
14. $t = -56 \div 4$ -14
15. $45 \div (-9) = h$ -5
16. $-45 \div 9 = b$ -5
17. $-33 \div 11 = p$ -3
18. $-100 \div (-10) = k$ 10
19. $a = 56 \div (-1)$ -56
20. $m = -120 \div 6$ -20

21. Divide -64 by 8. -8

22. Find the quotient of -28 and -7. 4

Evaluate each expression if $v = -24$, $e = 8$, and $q = 3$.

23. $\frac{v}{q}$ -8
24. $v \div (-e)$ 3
25. $\frac{v}{eq}$ -1
26. $v^2 \div e$ 72
27. $\frac{v^2}{eq}$ 24
28. $\frac{eq}{v}$ -1

Mixed Review

29. Evaluate 4^3. *(Lesson 1-9)* 64

30. **Statistics** A survey concerning the number of hours a junior high student spends doing homework each day produces the following data: 2, 4, 3, 2, 1, 2, 2, 4. Find the mean, median, and mode for the data. *(Lesson 3-5)* 2.5, 2, 2

31. Solve the equation $s = -5(12)$. *(Lesson 7-7)* -60

Problem Solving and Applications

32. **Engineering** The water level in a tank decreased 8 inches in 4 minutes. The tank drains at a steady rate. What is the change in the water level each minute? -2 inches per minute

33. **Statistics** Soya Gilbers recorded the following noon temperatures, in degrees Fahrenheit for one week. What is the mean? $-2°F$

Sun.	Mon.	Tues.	Wed.	Thurs.	Fri.	Sat.
-10	-8	-10	0	4	1	9

34. **Critical Thinking** Find all values of a and b for which $ab = \frac{a}{b} = \frac{b}{a}$.
$a = 1, b = 1; a = -1, b = 1; a = 1, b = -1; a = -1, b = -1$

282   Chapter 7 Integers

OPTIONS

Extending the Lesson

Using a Formula Tell students that the formula $F = C \times 9 \div 5 + 32$ converts Celsius degrees to Fahrenheit degrees. Ask them to give the Fahrenheit temperature for a Celsius temperature of -5 degrees. Then ask what the Celsius temperature is for a Fahrenheit temperature of 32 degrees. 23°; 0°

Cooperative Learning Activity

It's Greek to Me **7-8**

Use groups of 4.

The figure at the right is a type of *Greek square*. A Greek square can be used to create a secret code. In this Greek square, dividends are written above the columns and divisors are written to the left of the rows. Each letter, then, may be replaced by a quotient. For example, the letter A is in the first column and first row. Therefore, it could be replaced in a coded message by $6 \div 1$, or 6. The word *code* would be written 12/-6/-12/-24.

On a sheet of paper, write a secret message using the code in the Greek square. Trade papers with another group member and decipher his or her message.

	6	-6	12	-12	-24
1	A	B	C	D	E
-1	F	G	H	J	K
2	L	M	N	O	P
-2	Q	R	S	T	U
-3	V	W	X	Y	Z

Glencoe Mathematics: Applications and Connections, Course 2

Cooperative Learning

7-9A Solving Equations

A Preview of Lesson 7-9

Objective
Solve equations by using models.

Materials
counters
cups
mats

You have used counters to solve equations in Chapter 6. These can also be used to solve equations that involve integers.

Try this!

Work in groups of three.

- Start with two empty mats. Use counters and a cup to show the equation $x + (-2) = -3$. This equation can be solved by removing 2 negative counters from each mat. So, $x = -1$.

- Start again with two empty mats. Use counters to show the equation $x + (-2) = 3$. In this case, the counters on each side of the equals sign are different. Add 2 positive counters to each side of the equation. Then remove 2 zero pairs from the left side. So, $x = 5$.

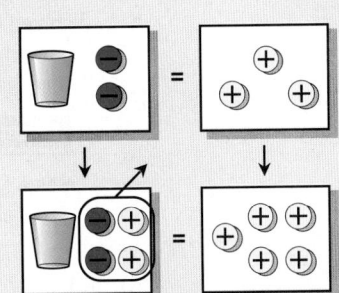

What do you think?

1. Write an equation for the model shown below.
   $x + 4 = -9$

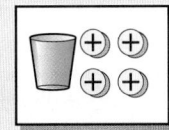 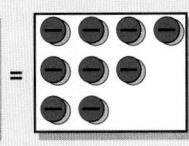

2. The opposite of the counter with x cup; the same number as the amount with the x cup.

2. How do you know what type of counter to add to each side to solve an equation? How many counters need to be added?

Make a model of each equation. Then solve the equation. **See Solutions Manual.**

3. $x + 4 = -6$ −10   4. $c - 5 = 7$ 12   5. $m + 6 = -20$ −26
6. $g - (-4) = 8$ 4   7. $b + (-1) = 0$ 1   8. $a + (-7) = 16$ 23
9. $y - 2 = -1$ 1   10. $p + (-8) = 3$ 11   11. $g + (-4) = -4$ 0

Extension

12. Make a model of $2x = -8$. Then solve the equation. −4

Mathematics Lab 7-9A Solving Equations **283**

Mathematics Lab 7-9A

NCTM Standards: 1–7, 9

Management Tips

For Students Provide groups with sufficient numbers of two-color counters and one cup. Have students take turns doing the modeling, as the others watch and help.

For the Overhead Projector
Overhead Manipulative Resources provides appropriate materials for teacher or student demonstration of the activities in this Mathematics Lab.

1 FOCUS

Introducing the Lab

Ask students to describe how they previously used counters to solve equations. Then ask them how they could use counters to model the solutions to equations involving integers.

2 TEACH

Using Drawings Have one of the students in each group draw pictures of the steps they take to solve each equation.

3 PRACTICE/APPLY

Using Cooperative Groups
Have students in each group make up equations for the others to solve with the counters. Students should explain to the group how they arrive at their solutions. Have students take turns making up and solving the equations.

Close

Have students summarize how to use counters to model the solution to an equation involving integers.

OPTIONS

Lab Manual You may wish to make copies of the blackline master on p. 57 of the *Lab Manual* for students to use as a recording sheet.

Lab Manual, p. 57

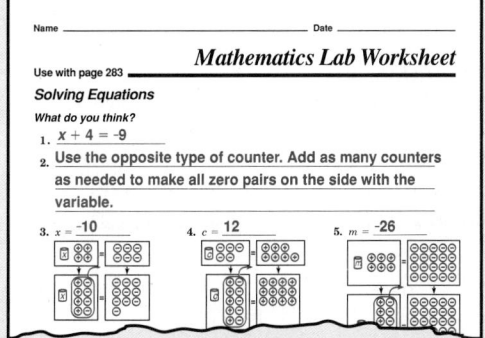

Name _____ Date _____

Mathematics Lab Worksheet
Use with page 283
Solving Equations
What do you think?
1. $x + 4 = -9$ _____
2. Use the opposite type of counter. Add as many counters as needed to make all zero pairs on the side with the variable.
3. $x = $ −10   4. $c = $ 12   5. $m = $ −26

Lesson Resources
• Study Guide Master 7-9
• Practice Master 7-9
• Enrichment Master 7-9
• Group Activity Card 7-9

 Transparency 7-9 contains the 5-Minute Check and a teaching aid for this lesson.

🕐 **5-Minute Check**
(Over Lesson 7-8)

Solve each equation.
1. $d = 54 \div (-6)$ -9
2. $-42 \div (-7) = z$ 6
3. $m = -32 \div 4$ -8

Evaluate each expression if $t = -27$, $u = 9$, and $v = -3$.
4. $\frac{t}{v}$ 9
5. $u^2 \div 9$ 9

---

1 FOCUS

Motivating the Lesson

Questioning Discuss with students the effects wind can have on the temperature or on the way the temperature feels. Ask them what is meant by "wind-chill factor". Wind blows away warm air that ordinarily surrounds the body.

2 TEACH

Using Connections: Algebra
Have students recall how they had previously solved equations with whole numbers. Guide them to see that since all whole numbers are integers, it is reasonable to suppose that rules and properties they used to solve equations with whole numbers can be used to solve equations with integers. Remind students to begin solving each problem by assigning a variable to represent the unknown quantity.

7-9 Solving Equations

Objective
Solve equations with integer solutions.

LOOKBACK

You can review addition and subtraction equations on page 225.

Chinook is an Indian word for a warm dry wind on the east side of the Rocky Mountains that causes a rapid rise in temperature. For example, a chinook once caused the temperature in Rapid City, South Dakota to increase 25°C in 15 minutes. If the final temperature was 15°C, what was the temperature before rising 25°C? *This question will be answered in Example 2.*

You solve equations involving integers in the same way you have solved equations involving whole numbers. Remember that when you perform the same addition or subtraction on each side of an equation, the two sides will remain equal.

Example 1

Solve $-5 + v = 3$.

$$-5 + v = 3$$
$$-5 + v + 5 = 3 + 5 \qquad \textit{Add 5 to each side.}$$
$$v = 8$$

Check: $-5 + v = 3$
$$-5 + 8 \stackrel{?}{=} 3 \qquad \textit{Replace v with 8.}$$
$$3 = 3 \checkmark$$

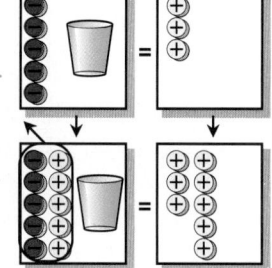

Example 2 *Problem Solving*

Weather Refer to the problem in the lesson introduction. What was the temperature before it rose 25°C?

Let $t =$ the original temperature. Since the wind is increasing the temperature, the equation $t + 25 = 15$ represents the situation. Solve $t + 25 = 15$.

$$t + 25 = 15$$
$$t + 25 - 25 = 15 - 25 \qquad \textit{Subtract 25 from each side.}$$
$$t = -10$$

Check: $t + 25 = 15$
$$-10 + 25 \stackrel{?}{=} 15 \qquad \textit{Replace t with } -10.$$
$$15 = 15 \checkmark \qquad \text{The original temperature was } -10°C.$$

OPTIONS

Reteaching Activity

Using Models Review how to solve equations with whole numbers. Then guide students to see how equations with integers can be done the same way. Next, have students finish partially completed examples, such as:

$$n - 4 = -7$$
$$n - 4 + \underline{4} = -7 + \underline{4}$$
$$n = \underline{-3}$$

Study Guide Masters, p. 65

Name _____ Date _____

Study Guide Worksheet 7-9

Algebra Connection: Solving Equations

Integer equations are solved like whole number equations. For addition or subtraction equations, add or subtract the same number on each side of the equation. The two sides will remain equal.

Examples   Solve $m + (-8) = -15$.   Solve $r - (-10) = 15$.

$$m + (-8) = -15 \qquad\qquad r - (-10) = 15$$
$$m + (-8) + 8 = -15 + 8 \qquad r + 10 = 15$$
$$m = -7 \qquad\qquad r + 10 - 10 = 15 - 10$$
$$r = 5$$

Check   Check
$$-7 + (-8) \stackrel{?}{=} -15 \qquad 5 - (-10) \stackrel{?}{=} 15$$
$$-15 = -15 \checkmark \qquad 5 + 10 \stackrel{?}{=} 15$$
$$15 = 15 \checkmark$$

You can also perform the same multiplication or division on each side of an equation.

LOOK BACK

You can review multiplication and division equations on page 228.

Examples

3 Solve $-196 = 4s$.

$$-196 = 4s$$

$$\frac{-196}{4} = \frac{4s}{4} \qquad \textit{Divide each side by 4.}$$

$$-49 = s$$

Check: Use your calculator. Replace s with -49.

4 ⊠ 49 +/- = -19b ✓

4 Solve $\frac{g}{9} = -81$.

$$\frac{g}{9} = -81 \qquad \textit{$\frac{g}{9}$ means g divided by 9.}$$

$$\left(\frac{g}{9}\right)(9) = (-81)(9) \qquad \textit{Multiply each side by 9.}$$

$$g = -729$$

Check: Use your calculator. Replace g with -729.

729 +/- ÷ 9 = -8L ✓

Checking for Understanding

Communicating Mathematics

Read and study the lesson to answer each question.

1. **Tell** what operation you would use to solve the equation $17 = m + (-9)$. **addition**

2. **Write** the equation shown by each model. Then solve the equation.

   a. 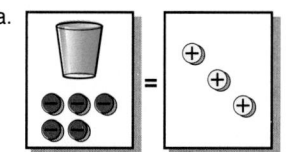 =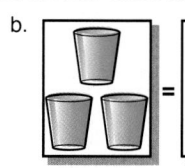

   b.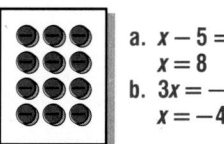

   a. $x - 5 = 3$; $x = 8$
   b. $3x = -12$; $x = -4$

3. **Draw** a model that shows the equation in Example 2. **See margin.**

4. **Tell** how to check your solution to an equation. **Substitute the solution for the variable in the equation.**

Guided Practice

Solve each equation. Check your solution.

5. $m - 5 = -9$ **−4**
6. $5t = -140$ **−28**
7. $35 = -5m$ **−7**
8. $-9 = 3 + r$ **−12**
9. $y + (-7) = 6$ **13**
10. $18 = \frac{r}{-3}$ **−54**
11. $\frac{\ell}{10} = -1{,}010$ **−10,100**
12. $24 = g - 8$ **32**
13. $-60 = \frac{n}{-7}$ **420**

14. When a number w is multiplied by 6, the result is -48. What is the value of w? **−8**

Lesson 7-9 Algebra Connection: Solving Equations **285**

Teaching Tip Have students show all steps in the solution process.

More Examples

For Example 1
Solve $-4 + t = 1$. **5**

For Example 2
Solve $r + 15 = 6$. **−9**

For Example 3
Solve $-156 = 6n$. **−26**

For Example 4
Solve $\frac{p}{7} = -14$. **−98**

Checking for Understanding

Exercises 1-4 are designed to help you assess students' understanding through reading, writing, speaking, and modeling. You should work through these exercises with your students and then monitor their work on Guided Practice Exercises 5-14.

Practice Masters, p. 65

Name _____ Date _____

Practice Worksheet 7-9

Algebra Connection: Solving Equations

Solve each equation. Check your solution.

1. $6n = -42$ **−7**
2. $-12 = 4 + n$ **−16**
3. $s + (-6) = -18$ **−12**
4. $\frac{k}{12} = -3$ **−36**
5. $s - 8 = -36$ **−28**
6. $54 = g - (-12)$ **42**
7. $n - 15 = -8$ **7**
8. $-30 = \frac{v}{5}$ **150**
9. $8p = -88$ **−11**
10. $-870 = 10k$ **−87**
11. $g - (-8) = 19$ **11**
12. $37 = \frac{k}{-2}$ **−74**
13. $-8x = -96$ **12**
14. $-52 = -13a$ **4**
15. $12 + w = -32$ **−44**

Write an equation for each problem and solve.

16. The sum of a number b and 8 is -14. Find b. **−22**

17. When a number y is multiplied by -8, the result is -72. What is the value of y? **9**

T65
Glencoe Division, Macmillan/McGraw-Hill

Gifted and Talented Needs

Have students decide whether each of the following is *always*, *sometimes*, or *never* true.

1. The quotient of two integers is a negative integer. **sometimes**
2. If x is a negative integer, then $40 \div (-x)$ is a negative integer. **never**
3. If x is a positive integer and y is a negative integer, then $\frac{-x}{-y} = \frac{x}{y}$. **always**

Additional Answer

3.
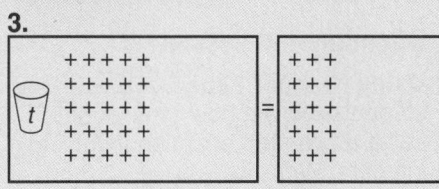

Watch for students who use an incorrect operation when solving equations involving integers.

Prevent by having these students decide what steps they would take if the equation had the same operation signs, but contained only whole numbers. Then have them take those same steps with the integers given.

Close

Have students write a problem that can be solved by solving the equation $m + 5 = -2$. Sample: The temperature rose 5° to -2. What had the temperature been?

3 PRACTICE/APPLY

Assignment Guide

Maximum: 15–40

Minimum: 15–29 odd, 31–37, 40

For **Extra Practice**, see p. 589.

Alternate Assessment

Writing Have students explain how solving equations involving integers is similar to solving equations with whole numbers.

Enrichment Masters, p. 65

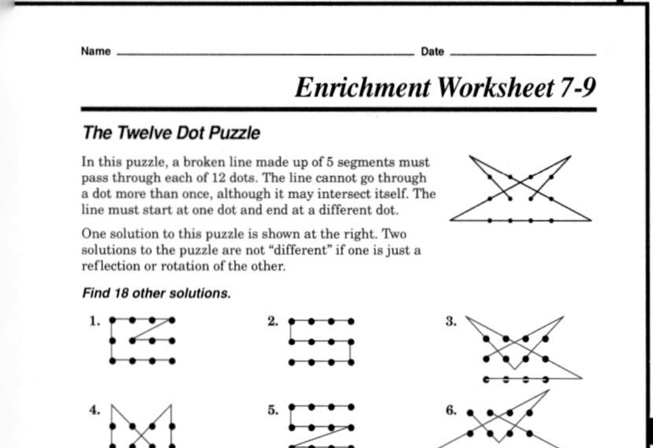

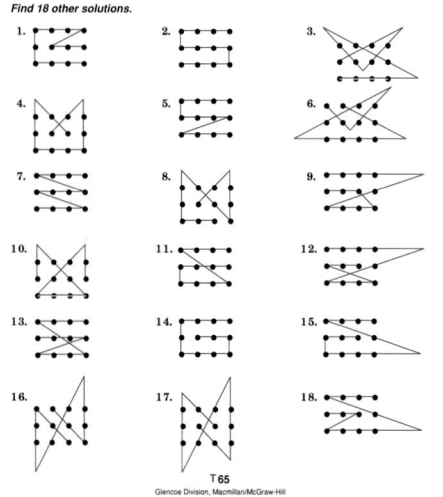

Name _____ Date _____

Enrichment Worksheet 7-9

The Twelve Dot Puzzle

In this puzzle, a broken line made up of 5 segments must pass through each of 12 dots. The line cannot go through a dot more than once, although it may intersect itself. The line must start at one dot and end at a different dot.

One solution to this puzzle is shown at the right. Two solutions to the puzzle are not "different" if one is just a reflection or rotation of the other.

Find 18 other solutions.

T 65
Glencoe Division, Macmillan/McGraw-Hill

Exercises

Independent Practice

Solve each equation. Check your solution.

15. $-168 = 3m$ **-56**
16. $t + 9 = -34$ **-43**
17. $y - 45 = -2$ **43**
18. $-9 + w = 12$ **21**
19. $-345 = t + 56$ **-401**
20. $6 + p = 98$ **92**
21. $-570 = 3t$ **-190**
22. $75 + p = -100$ **-175**
23. $-8y = -368$ **46**
24. $\frac{r}{15} = -90$ **$-1,350$**
25. $56 = \frac{n}{-3}$ **-168**
26. $98 = \frac{a}{-4}$ **-392**

Write an equation for each problem below. Then solve.

27. When a number k is multiplied by -9, the result is 45. Find k. **$-9k = 45$; $k = -5$**

28. The sum of a number v and 7 is -11. Find v. **$v + 7 = -11$; $v = -18$**

29. $d - (-4) =$ 10; $d = 6$ 29. If you decrease a number d by -4, the result is 10. Find d.

30. The quotient when a number r is divided by -6 is 12. Find r. **$\frac{r}{-6} = 12$; $r = -72$**

Mixed Review

31. Complete: 245 mm = ___?___ cm. (*Lesson 2-9*) **24.5 cm**

32. Compute $\frac{5}{8} \times 2\frac{1}{3}$ mentally. (*Lesson 5-9*) **$\frac{35}{24}$**

33. Complete: 40 oz = ___?___ lb. (*Lesson 6-6*) **2.5 lb**

34. **Ballooning** A hot air balloon starts a descent from 1,000 feet above the ground. After 10 minutes, the balloon is at 600 feet above the ground. Find the rate of its descent in feet per minute. (*Lesson 7-8*) **40 ft/min**

Problem Solving and Applications

Write an integer equation to represent each problem in Exercises 35–39. Then solve the problem.

35. **Diving** A diver begins an ascent from 160 feet below sea level. A few minutes later, the diver is 50 feet below sea level. How many feet did the diver ascend? **110 feet; $-160 + x = -50$**

36. **Business** In her new position as manager, Jennifer earns \$250 more than three times the salary she earned as a cashier. If she now earns \$10,300, how much did she earn as a cashier? **$250 + 3x = 10,300$; $x = \$3,350$**

37. $(18 + 23 + 12 + 15) \div 4 = n$; $n = 17$ cm   37. **Geometry** Find the side of a square that has a perimeter equal to the perimeter of a quadrilateral with sides the length of 18 centimeters, 23 centimeters, 12 centimeters, and 15 centimeters.

 38. **Portfolio Suggestion** Review the items in your portfolio. Make a table of contents of the items, noting why each item was chosen. Replace any items that are no longer appropriate. **See students' work.**

39. **Environment** Geologists calculated that a section of coastline is eroding at a steady rate of 4 centimeters per year. How many years will it take for this coastline to erode 96 cm? **$-4y = -96$; 24 years**

40. **Critical Thinking** Describe how you would solve $2x + 5 = 4$. **Subtract 5 from both sides and then divide both sides by 2.**

OPTIONS

Extending the Lesson

Using Number Sense Have students explain how they would solve a two-step equation involving integers. Write $2x + 5 = -13$ on the chalkboard. Ask them to demonstrate their method using this example.

Cooperative Learning Activity

Do You Believe in Magic? **7-9**

Use groups of 2.
Materials: Index cards

▪ Copy onto cards the equations shown on the back of this card, one equation per card. Shuffle the cards and divide them evenly. On a sheet of paper, copy the magic square shown at the right.

➡ Each partner solves the equations on his or her cards. Then, working together, both partners use the solutions they found to complete the magic square. (In a magic square, the sum of the numbers in any row, column, or diagonal is equal to the same number.)

-2		11	
			-9
	10		-5
13			12

Glencoe Mathematics: Applications and Connections, Course 2

7-10 Integers as Exponents

Objective
Use negative exponents.

 LOOK BACK
You can review
positive exponents on
page 32.

Red blood cells are the majority of living cells that make up the blood. Their main purpose is to carry oxygen from the lungs to body tissues and to carry carbon dioxide from the body tissues to the lungs. The diameter of each red blood cell is 0.0003 inch.

You have already seen how large numbers can be written using powers of 10. A number such as 0.0003 can also be written using powers of 10.

Study the pattern in this table.

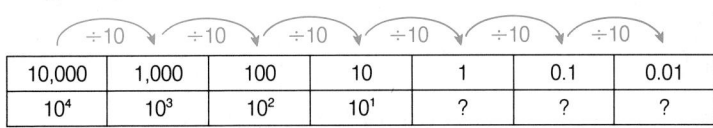

10,000	1,000	100	10	1	0.1	0.01
10^4	10^3	10^2	10^1	?	?	?

The pattern indicates that, when you divide a power of 10 by 10, the exponent decreases by 1. This suggests how to define the power with a zero exponent.

$$10^0 = 1$$

The pattern also suggests how to define powers with negative exponents.

$$10^{-1} = 0.1$$
$$= \tfrac{1}{10} \text{ or } \tfrac{1}{10^1}$$

$$10^{-2} = 0.01$$
$$= \tfrac{1}{100} \text{ or } \tfrac{1}{10^2}$$

$$10^{-3} = 0.001$$
$$= \tfrac{1}{1,000} \text{ or } \tfrac{1}{10^3}$$

Negative Exponents	**Arithmetic**	**Algebra**
	$10^{-2} = \tfrac{1}{10^2}$	$10^{-n} = \tfrac{1}{10^n}$

A number written in scientific notation with a negative exponent can be rewritten in standard form.

Calculator Hint

You enter numbers in scientific notation using the $\boxed{EE}$ or $\boxed{EXP}$ key. When the exponent is negative, press the $\boxed{+/-}$ key after entering the exponent. For example, use this key sequence to enter 2×10^{-9}.

$2 \boxed{EE} 9 \boxed{+/-}$

 LOOK BACK
You can review
scientific notation on
page 67.

Example 1

Write 4×10^{-3} in standard form.

$4 \times 10^{-3} = 4 \times \tfrac{1}{10^3}$

$\quad\quad\quad = 4 \times \tfrac{1}{1,000}$ $10^3 = 1,000$

$\quad\quad\quad = 4 \times 0.001$ *Move decimal point three places to the left.*

$\quad\quad\quad = 0.004$

Lesson 7-10 Integers as Exponents   **287**

OPTIONS

Reteaching Activity

Using Connections Point out to students that the absolute value of the negative exponent in the scientific notation form of a number is equal to the number of places to the right of the decimal point in the leading digit of that number written in standard form. Provide examples.

Study Guide Masters, p. 66

Name _____ Date _____

Study Guide Worksheet 7-10

Integers as Exponents

	Powers of 10		
Exponential Form	**Product Form**	**Standard Form**	
10^3	$10 \times 10 \times 10$	1,000	
10^2	10×10	100	
10^1	10	10	
10^0	1	1	
10^{-1}, or $\tfrac{1}{10^1}$	$\tfrac{1}{10}$	$\tfrac{1}{10}$, or 0.1	
10^{-2}, or $\tfrac{1}{10^2}$	$\tfrac{1}{10} \times \tfrac{1}{10}$	$\tfrac{1}{100}$, or 0.01	
10^{-3}, or $\tfrac{1}{10^3}$	$\tfrac{1}{10} \times \tfrac{1}{10} \times \tfrac{1}{10}$	$\tfrac{1}{1,000}$, or 0.001	

7-10 Lesson Notes

NCTM Standards: 1–9

Lesson Resources
- Study Guide Master 7-10
- Practice Master 7-10
- Enrichment Master 7-10
- Evaluation Master, Quiz B, p. 61
- Interdisciplinary Master, p. 21
- Group Activity Card 7-10

Transparency 7-10 contains the 5-Minute Check and a teaching aid for this lesson.

🕐 5-Minute Check
(Over Lesson 7-9)

Solve each equation. Check your solution.

1. $-144 = 8y$ -18
2. $-14 + k = 4$ 18
3. $72 = \tfrac{b}{-3}$ -216

Write an equation for each problem and solve.

4. The sum of a number w and -22 is -6. Find w.   16
5. When a number t is multiplied by -8, the result is 48. What is the value of t? -6

1 FOCUS

Motivating the Lesson

Questioning Have students read the opening paragraphs. Then have them recall how they used scientific notation to write large numbers. Ask students to speculate how they could use it to express very small numbers.

2 TEACH

Using Connections Guide students to understand that writing a number in scientific notation does not change its value. Then give them practice writing powers of 10 in standard form by extending the chart on the page, beginning with 10^0. Ask students to explain the advantages of writing numbers using scientific notation with integer exponents.

287

Checking for Understanding

Exercises 1-2 are designed to help you assess students' understanding through reading, writing, speaking, and modeling. You should work through these exercises with your students and then monitor their work on Guided Practice Exercises 3-9.

288

Negative exponents can be used to write numbers between 0 and 1 in scientific notation.

Example 2 *Problem Solving*

Biology Refer to the problem in the lesson introduction. How is the diameter of a red blood cell written in scientific notation?

$$0.0003 = 3 \times 0.0001 \quad \text{\textit{Write a 0.0003 as the product of 3}}$$
$$\text{\textit{and a power of ten.}}$$
$$= 3 \times \left(\frac{1}{10,000}\right) \quad \text{\textit{Rename 0.0001 as }} \frac{1}{10,000}.$$
$$= 3 \times \frac{1}{10^4} \quad \text{\textit{10,000}} = 10^4$$
$$= 3 \times 10^{-4} \quad \frac{1}{10^4} = 10^{-4}$$

In scientific notation, the diameter of a red blood cell is 3×10^{-4} inches.

Checking for Understanding

Communicating Mathematics

Read and study the lesson to answer each question.

1. **Tell** how many zeros are to the right of the decimal point when you write 10^{-3} as a decimal. **2**

2. **Tell** the exponent you get when you write 0.0001 as a power of 10. **−4**

Guided Practice

Write each number in standard form.

3. 3×10^{-4} **0.0003**
4. 6×10^{-1} **0.6**
5. 7×10^{-5} **0.00007**

Write each decimal in scientific notation.

6. 0.00002 2×10^{-5}
7. 0.005 5×10^{-3}
8. 0.0000009 9×10^{-7}

9. **Computers** A nanosecond is 1×10^{-9} seconds. Write this number as a decimal. **0.000000001**

Exercises

Independent Practice

Write each number in standard form.

10. 5×10^{-4} **0.0005**
11. 7×10^{-1} **0.7**
12. 2×10^{-3} **0.002**
13. 3×10^{-5} **0.00003**
14. 9×10^{-6} **0.000009**
15. 8×10^{-7} **0.0000008**

Write each decimal in scientific notation.

16. 0.04 4×10^{-2}
17. 0.001 1×10^{-3}
18. 0.00007 7×10^{-5}
19. 0.9 9×10^{-1}
20. 0.0006 6×10^{-4}
21. 0.0000003 3×10^{-7}

22. Write 0.0005 in scientific notation. 5×10^{-4}

23. Write 6×10^{-5} in standard form. **0.00006**

OPTIONS

Bell Ringer

Challenge students to explain how they could find the width of a sheet of notebook paper given only a centimeter ruler. Ask them to use their method to determine whether paper is indeed about 2×10^{-3} cm thick. Sample method: measure the width of 100 sheets and divide by 100.

24. **Data analysis** Refer to the graph at the top of page 114. What appears to be the slowest time of day at this particular McDonald's? *(Lesson 3-7)* **3 P.M.**

25. Use one or more strategies to compare $\frac{1}{4}$ and $\frac{2}{7}$. *(Lesson 4-10)* $\frac{1}{4} < \frac{2}{7}$

26. Compare the fractions $\frac{5}{9}$ and $\frac{3}{4}$. *(Lesson 5-10)* $\frac{5}{9} < \frac{3}{4}$

27. Solve the equation $\frac{g}{-16} = -2$. *(Lesson 7-9)* **32**

Problem Solving

28. **Physics** The diameter of a silver atom is about 0.0000000003 meter. Write this measurement in scientific notation. 3×10^{-10} m

29. **Manufacturing** The thickness of a sheet of paper is about 2×10^{-3} centimeter. Write this measurement as a decimal. **0.002 cm**

30. **Critical Thinking** The average American male is expected to live 72.2 years. In contrast, some white blood cells live only 10 hours or 0.00114 years. Write this measurement in scientific notation. 1.14×10^{-3} years

31. **Food** A Jelly Belly® is a gourmet jelly bean that has 4 calories and weighs 4×10^{-2} ounce. Write this weight as a decimal. **0.04 oz**

32. **Science** The bacterium E. coli has a diameter of 0.001 millimeter. Write this number in scientific notation. 1×10^{-3} mm

33. **Critical Thinking** Copy and complete the table.

2^4	2^3	2^2	2^1	2^0	2^{-1}	2^{-2}
16	?	?	?	?	?	?

8, 4, 2, 1, $\frac{1}{2}$, $\frac{1}{4}$

Write a definition for 2^{-n}, where n is a positive integer. $2^{-n} = \frac{1}{2^n}$

34. **Journal Entry** What concept in this chapter have you found most challenging? What do you think made it more difficult for you? **See students' work.**

35. **Mathematics and Science** Read the following paragraphs.

The air pressing down on Earth is called *air pressure,* or atmospheric pressure. The weight of air pressing down on each 1 square meter of Earth's surface is greater than that of a large elephant. Air pressure is greatest at ground level and decreases the higher up you go.

Barometers are used to measure air pressure. On an aneroid barometer, a needle on the dial moves as the air pressure changes. Pressure can also be measured with a mercury barometer.

A *bar* is a measure of pressure slightly less than Earth's air pressure at sea level under normal conditions, or about 29.92 inches of mercury. Earth's air pressure at sea level is 0.98 bar.

0.000000000000001

a. The atmospheric pressure at the surface of Mercury is 10^{-15} bar. Write this number in standard form.

b. Saturn's atmospheric pressure is 8,000,000 bar. Write this number in scientific notation. 8×10^6

Lesson 7-10 Integers as Exponents **289**

Extending the Lesson

Mathematics and Science Ask students why, although air pressure decreases the higher up you go, it is not difficult to breathe in an airplane.

Cooperative Learning Activity

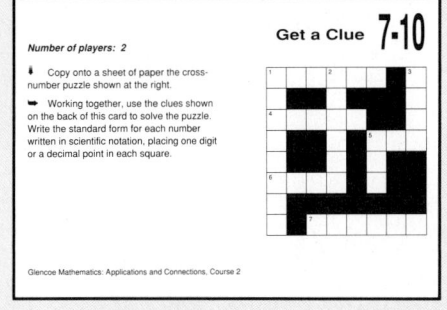

Get a Clue **7-10**

Number of players: 2

Copy onto a sheet of paper the cross-number puzzle shown at the right.

Working together, use the clues shown on the back of this card to solve the puzzle. Write the standard form for each number written in scientific notation, placing one digit or a decimal point in each square.

Glencoe Mathematics: Applications and Connections, Course 2

Close

Have students use their science texts or other sources to find three examples of very small numbers. Ask them to rewrite these in scientific notation.

3 PRACTICE/APPLY

Assignment Guide
Maximum: 10–34
Minimum: 11–23 odd, 24–33

For **Extra Practice,** see p. 589.

Alternate Assessment

Speaking Have students explain how to write the number 0.000007 in scientific notation, and the number 8×10^{-5} in standard form. 7×10^{-6}; 0.00008

Enrichment Masters, p. 66

Name _____ Date _____

Enrichment Worksheet 7-10

An Enterprising Goal

Solve the following puzzle by finding the correct path through the boxes. The solution is part of the mission of the starship *Enterprise.*

Starting with Box 1, draw an arrow to the adjacent box with the expression of the smallest value. (You can use each box only once.) The first arrow has been drawn to get you started.

When you have finished drawing your path through the boxes, write the box numbers in order on the lines below. Then use the chart at the right to convert each box number to a letter.

1	G
2	E
3	H
4	O
5	N
6	R
7	O
8	W
9	O
10	E
11	F
12	E
13	N
14	H
15	S
16	O
17	E
18	E
19	A
20	G
21	E
22	R
23	B
24	N
25	O

1 -5^3	2 10^{-3}	3 $2^8 - 4^4$	4 2^6	5 $2^4 \cdot 3^2$
6 13^{-2}	7 $4^3 - 3^4$	8 $11^2 - 5^3$	9 $2^{-3} + 3^2$	10 6^3
11 $4^4 + 16^2$	12 4^{-3}	13 5^{-2}	14 $4^5 - 9^3$	15 $5^3 + 3^5$
16 $3^6 - 6^3$	17 $8^3 - 1^8$	18 $16^2 + 6^3$	19 $(-19)^2$	20 $2^8 + 11^2$
21 $2^9 + 9^2$	22 $(-23)^2$	23 $3^6 - 3^5$	24 21^2	25 $2^3 \cdot 7^2$

Box Number	1	7	8	3	2	6	12	13	9	4	5	10
Letter	G	O	W	H	E	R	E	N	O	O	N	E

Box Number	14	19	15	20	25	24	18	23	17	11	16	22	21
Letter	H	A	S	G	O	N	E	B	E	F	O	R	E

T66

Glencoe Division, Macmillan/McGraw-Hill

The Chapter Study Guide and Review begins with a section on Communicating Mathematics. This includes questions that review the new terms and concepts that were introduced in the chapter.

Then, the Skills and Concepts presented in the chapter are reviewed using a side-by-side format. Encourage students to refer to the Objectives and Examples on the left as they complete the Review Exercises on the right.

The Chapter Study Guide and Review ends with problems that review Applications and Problem Solving.

Chapter

7 Study Guide and Review

Communicating Mathematics

Choose the correct term or number to complete the sentence.
1. The absolute value of an integer is its (distance, direction) from 0 on a number line. **distance**
2. On a number line, values (decrease, increase) as you move to the right. **increase**
3. In an ordered pair, the second number is the (x-coordinate, y-coordinate). **y-coordinate**
4. Two integers that are opposites of each other are called (additive inverses, similar). **additive inverses**
5. The product of two integers with (same, different) signs is negative. **different**
6. The quotient of two integers with the same sign is (negative, positive). **positive**
7. In your own words, explain how to graph the point $A(-4, 3)$ on a coordinate system. **From (0, 0), move 4 places to the left and then 3 places up from there.**

Self Assessment

Objectives and Examples	Review Exercises
Upon completing this chapter, you should be able to:	*Use these exercises to review and prepare for the chapter test.*
• read and write integers *(Lesson 7-1)* Write 4°F below 0 as an integer. You can write 4°F below 0 as −4°F.	Write an integer for each situation. 8. a loss of $150 −$150 9. a gain of 42 yards +42 10. 5°F below 0 −5° 11. a deposit of $75 +$75 12. 12 points gained +12 13. a loss of 5 pounds −5
• find the opposite and absolute value of an integer *(Lesson 7-1)* Find the opposite and the absolute value of −7. The opposite of −7 would be at the point 7 units to the right of 0. So, the opposite of −7 is 7. The point that represents −7 is 7 units from 0. So $|-7| = 7$.	Write the integer represented by the point for each letter. Then find its opposite and its absolute value. A B C -4 -3 -2 -1 0 1 2 3 4 14. A 15. B 16. C −3, 3, 3, −1, 1, 1 2, −2, 2

Objectives and Examples	Review Exercises

• compare and order integers
(Lesson 7-2)

Replace the ● with $<$, $>$, or $=$.

$$2 \, ● \, -6$$

Since 2 is to the right of -6 on the number line, $2 > -6$.

Replace each ● with $<$, $>$, or $=$ to make a true sentence.

17. $-4 \, ● \, 3$ $<$

18. $-18 \, ● \, -19$ $>$

19. $12 \, ● \, -12$ $>$

20. $-100 \, ● \, -10$ $<$

21. $0 \, ● \, -8$ $>$

22. $8 \, ● \, 0$ $>$

• graph points on a coordinate plane *(Lesson 7-3)*

Find the coordinates of point A and identify its quadrant.

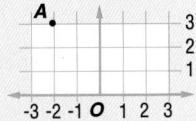

The ordered pair is $(-2, 3)$.
A is in the second quadrant.

On graph paper, draw a coordinate plane. Then graph and label each point. Identify its quadrant. **For answers to 23-28, see margin.**

23. $B(3, 6)$ I

24. $C(3, -5)$ IV

25. $D(-1.5, -4)$ III

26. $E(-5, 1)$ II

27. $F(0, 6)$ *y*-axis

28. $G(-2, 0)$ *x*-axis

• add integers *(Lesson 7-4)*

Solve $p = 4 + (-3)$.

$|4| > |-3|$, so the sum is positive. The difference of 4 and 3 is 1. So, $p = 1$.

Solve each equation.

29. $c = 6 + (-2)$ 4

30. $-10 + 4 = r$ -6

31. $-5 + 12 = m$ 7

32. $b = -1 + (-1)$ -2

33. $s = 25 + (-50)$ -25

34. $-7 + (-6) = t$ -13

• subtract integers *(Lesson 7-5)*

Solve $y = -2 - 4$.

$y = -2 - 4$
$ = -2 + (-4)$ *To subtract 4,*
$ = -6$ *add -4.*

Solve each equation.

35. $k = 5 - 7$ -2

36. $-13 - 4 = q$ -17

37. $z = 6 - (-2)$ 8

38. $-8 - (-10) = m$ 2

39. $a = -2 - 4$ -6

40. $12 - (-12) = p$ 24

• multiply integers *(Lesson 7-7)*

Solve $h = -2(5)$.

The two integers have different signs, so the product will be negative.

$h = -2(5)$
$ = -10$

Solve each equation.

41. $w = 4(-2)$ -8

42. $b = -6(-2)$ 12

43. $c = (-3)^2$ 9

44. $-8(4) = g$ -32

45. $j = -5(5)$ -25

46. $-100(-1) = y$ 100

Chapter 7 Study Guide and Review **291**

Study Guide and Review

Additional Answers
23–28.

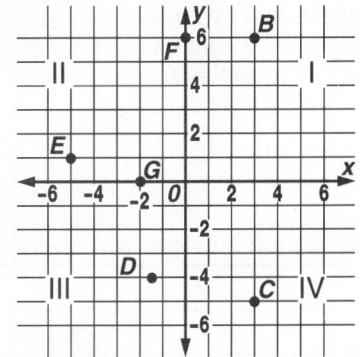

You may wish to use a Chapter Test from the Evaluation Masters booklet as an additional chapter review. The two free-response forms are shown below. One of the two multiple-choice forms is shown on the next page.

Evaluation Masters, pp. 59–60

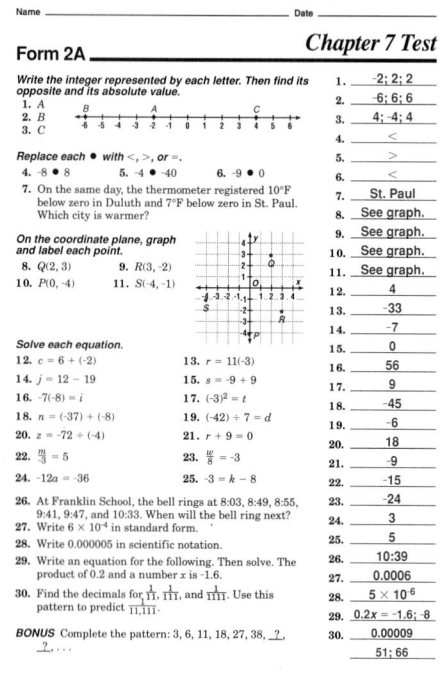

Objectives and Examples	Review Exercises
• divide integers *(Lesson 7-8)*	Solve each equation.
solve $-15 \div (-3) = a$.	47. $v = 45 \div (-9)$ -5
The signs are the same, so the quotient is positive.	48. $s = -10 \div 10$ -1
$-15 \div (-3) = a$	49. $-12 \div (-2) = b$ 6
$5 = a$	

• solve equations with integer solutions *(Lesson 7-9)*	Solve each equation. Check your solution.
Solve $t + 6 = -3$.	50. $m - 8 = -2$ 6 51. $-3 + p = -6$ -3
$t + 6 = -3$	52. $11s = -55$ -5 53. $-25c = 125$ -5
$t + 6 - 6 = -3 - 6$ *Subtract 6 from*	54. $\frac{f}{3} = -5$ -15 55. $240 = \frac{g}{-2}$ -480
$t = -9$ *each side.*	

• use negative exponents *(Lesson 7-10)*	Write each decimal in scientific notation.
$0.004 = \frac{4}{1,000}$	56. 0.06 57. 0.000000005
$= \frac{4}{10^3}$	6×10^{-2} 5×10^{-9}
$= 4 \times 10^{-3}$	Write each number in standard form.
	58. 8×10^{-5} 0.00008 59. 2×10^{-3} 0.002

Applications and Problem Solving

60. Use a pattern to find the sum of the numbers in each set. *(Lesson 7-6)* 55; 20,100
    a. from 1 to 10   b. from 1 to 200   *Hint: Try pairing numbers.*

61. **Sports**   On the first play of the 4th quarter, the Bearcats lost 10 yards. After the second play, their position was 5 yards behind where they had started on the first play. What happened on the second play? *(Lesson 7-9)*
    They gained 5 yards.

Curriculum Connection Projects

• **Geography**   Spin a globe and stop it with your finger. Record the latitude and longitude of the location where your finger points. Then find the number of degrees latitude and longitude of that location from your home state.

• **Recreation**   Shuffle a deck of cards. Consider black cards as positive and red cards as negative. Turn over one card at a time. Record and add each card to the one before it.

Read More About It

Buffie, Margaret. *The Haunting of Frances Rain.*
Miller, Marvin. *You Be the Jury: Courtroom 3.*
Ratner, Marilyn. *Plenty of Patches: An Introduction to Patchwork Quilting and Appliqué.*

7 Test

Write the integer represented by each letter.
Then find its opposite and its absolute value.

A   B   C

-5 -4 -3 -2 -1 0 1 2 3 4

1. A **-2, 2, 2**
2. B **0, 0, 0**
3. C **4, -4, 4**

Replace each ⬤ with $<$, $>$, or $=$ to make a true sentence.

4. -9 ⬤ 6 **<**
5. 0 ⬤ -3 **>**

6. On the same day, the thermometer registered 5° below zero in Cleveland, and 2° below zero in Cincinnati. Which city was colder? **Cleveland**

On graph paper, draw a coordinate plane. Then graph and label each point. **See Solutions Manual.**

7. $P(6, -3)$
8. $B(0, -9)$
9. $T(-5, 1)$

Solve each equation.

10. $g = 5 + (-3)$ **2**
11. $-9 + (-3) = m$ **-12**
12. $r = -4 + 4$ **0**

13. $k = 11 - 15$ **-4**
14. $-7 - (-2) = s$ **-5**
15. $b = -3 - 4$ **-7**

16. $c = -5(-3)$ **15**
17. $h = 12(-2)$ **-24**
18. $(-7)^2 = p$ **49**

19. $q = 90 \div (-3)$ **-30**
20. $(-25) \div 5 = t$ **-5**
21. $m = (-72) \div (-9)$ **8**

22. $8 + x = 0$ **-8**
23. $-5 = r - 3$ **-2**
24. $-16f = 32$ **-2**

25. $\frac{b}{15} = -3$ **-45**
26. $\frac{d}{-16} = 1$ **-16**
27. $-4 \cdot 5 = s$ **-20**

28. Find a pattern in these statements. Then write two true statements using the pattern. **Sample answer: $50 \times 50 - 50 = 49 \times 49 + 49$**

$$4 \times 4 - 4 = 3 \times 3 + 3 \qquad 70 \times 70 - 70 = 69 \times 69 + 69$$

29. **Travel** Patricia left home to drive to a friend's house. She drove 12 miles before realizing that she had gone too far. She retraced her path backward for 3 miles and arrived at her destination.

   a. Write an addition sentence to represent this situation. **$12 - 3 = x$**
   b. How far does Patricia live from her friend's house? **9 miles**

30. **Games** Byron is playing Monopoly® and has $250 left. He lands on Boardwalk and needs $200 more to pay the rent. How much is the rent on Boardwalk? **$450**

31. **Allowance** Ming is supposed to receive an allowance of $25 each month. However, for each day he forgets to take out the garbage, his allowance decreases by $2. Ming forgets to take the garbage out three times during October. Find the amount of his allowance for October. **$19**

32. Write 0.6 using negative exponents. **6×10^{-1}**
33. Write 3×10^{-5} as a decimal. **0.00003**

Bonus Evaluate $(-1)^{1357}$. **-1**

Test and Review Generator software is provided in Apple, IBM, and Macintosh versions. You may use this software to create your own tests or worksheets, based on the needs of your students.

The **Performance Assessment Booklet** provides an alternate assessment for evaluating student progress. An assessment for this chapter can be found on pages 13–14.

8 Investigations in Geometry

Previewing the Chapter

This chapter explores some concepts of geometry, including angles, characteristics of polygons, tessellations, translations, and reflections. Students learn how to construct bisectors of segments and angles, perpendiculars, and regular polygons. Some lessons feature algebra connections. Applications include art, with an emphasis on the work of the Dutch artist, M. C. Escher. In the **problem-solving strategy** lesson, students use logical reasoning to solve problems involving classification.

Lesson	Lesson Objectives	NCTM Standards	State/Local Objectives
8-1A	Measure angles by using a protractor.	1–5, 12, 13	
8-1	Classify angles.	1–5, 9, 12, 13	
8-1B	Construct a line perpendicular to another line.	1–4, 12	
8-2	Identify polygons.	1–4, 12	
8-2B	Discover the sum of the angle measures of any polygon.	1–6, 9, 12	
8-3	Classify triangles and quadrilaterals.	1–4, 12	
8-4A	Construct angle bisectors and segment bisectors.	1–6, 12	
8-4	Identify regular polygons.	1–5, 9, 12	
8-4B	Construct a regular triangle and hexagon.	1–4, 12	
8-5	Solve problems by using logical reasoning.	1–5, 7, 12	
8-6	Determine which regular figures can be used to form a tessellation.	1–5, 7–9, 12	
8-7	Create Escher-like drawings by using translations.	1–4, 8, 12	
8-8	Create Escher-like drawings by using reflections.	1–4, 12	

Organizing the Chapter

A complete, 1-page lesson plan is provided for each lesson in the Lesson Plans Masters Booklet.

LESSON PLANNING GUIDE

Lesson	Materials/ Manipulatives	Extra Practice (Student Edition)	Study Guide	Practice	Enrichment	Evaluation	Technology	Lab Manual	Multicultural Activities	Application and Interdisciplinary Activities	Transparencies	Group Activity Cards
8-1A	protractor							p. 58				
8-1	protractor	p. 590	p. 67	p. 67	p. 67					p. 8	8-1	8-1
8-1B	compass							p. 59				
8-2		p. 590	p. 68	p. 68	p. 68		p. 22				8-2	8-2
8-2B	protractor scissors							p. 60				
8-3		p. 590	p. 69	p. 69	p. 69						8-3	8-3
8-4A	protractor compass							p. 61				
8-4	calculator	p. 591	p. 70	p. 70	p. 70	Quiz A, p. 70	p. 8				8-4	8-4
8-4B	compass protractor							p. 62				
8-5			p. 71	p. 71	p. 71					p. 8	8-5	8-5
8-6	tracing paper calculator		p. 72	p. 72	p. 72						8-6	8-6
8-7			p. 73	p. 73	p. 73						8-7	8-7
8-8			p. 74	p. 74	p. 74	Quiz B, p. 70				p. 22	8-8	8-8
Study Guide and Review	weighted string protractor, street map		Multiple Choice Test, Forms 1A and 1B, pp. 64–67 Free Response Test, Forms 2A and 2B, pp. 68–69 Cumulative Review, p. 71 (free response) Cumulative Test, p. 72 (multiple choice)									
Test												

Pacing Guide: Option I (Chapters 1–12) - 13 days; Option II (Chapters 1–13) - 13 days; Option III (Chapters 1–14) - 12 days
You may wish to refer to the complete **Course Planning Guides** on page T25.

OTHER CHAPTER RESOURCES

Student Edition
Chapter Opener, pp. 294–295
Mid-Chapter Review, p. 316
Portfolio Suggestions, pp. 316, 326

 Manipulatives
Overhead Manipulative Resources
Middle School Mathematics Manipulative Kit

 Software/Technology
Interactive Mathematics Tools (Macintosh)
Test and Review Generator (IBM, Apple, Macintosh)
Teacher's Guide for Software Resources

Other Supplements
Transparency 8–0
Performance Assessment, pp. 15–16
Glencoe Mathematics Professional Series
Lesson Plans, pp. 85–97

INTERDISCIPLINARY BULLETIN BOARD

Music Connection

Objective Recognize geometric shapes and ideas.

How To Use It Have groups make detailed drawings of a guitar or other instrument and attach it to the bulletin board. Ask students to identify as many different shapes as they can in these drawings. Have them pay special attention to familiar geometric shapes.

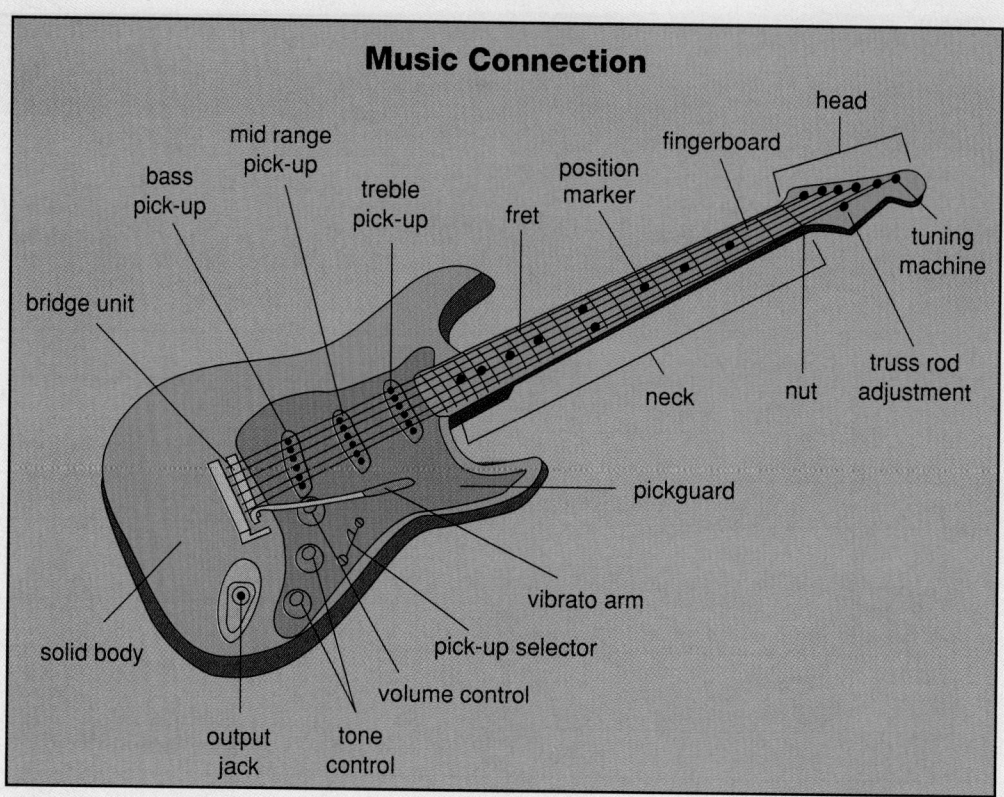

Music Connection

head

mid range pick-up

bass pick-up

treble pick-up

fret

fingerboard

position marker

tuning machine

bridge unit

neck

nut

truss rod adjustment

pickguard

vibrato arm

pick-up selector

solid body

volume control

output jack

tone control

APPLICATIONS AND CONNECTIONS

Applications	Lesson	Example	Exercise
Physical Fitness	8-1		27
Physics	8-1		29
Baseball	8-2		16
Traffic Safety	8-2		17
Make a Model	8-3		28
Art	8-3		29
Carpentry	8-4		20
Computer	8-4		21
Design	8-6	2	
Design	8-7		14
Biology	8-8		15
Connections			
Algebra	8-1	4	23–25
Language Arts	8-2	4	
Algebra	8-4	3	
Algebra	8-6	1	

TEAM ACTIVITIES

Multicultural Experiences

Outside Field Trips A brief walk around the neighborhood may be helpful in having students observe the shapes of traffic signs and other signs around them.

A visit to an art museum may provide students with the opportunity to see art consisting of geometric shapes and patterns, such as mosaics and Escher-like paintings and drawings.

In-Class Speakers Ask a carpenter or builder to visit the class to talk about how angles are used in construction.

Invite an art teacher to present pictures of mosaics to students and to provide more information about them.

SUPPLEMENTARY BLACKLINE MASTER BOOKLETS

Some of the blackline masters for enhancing this chapter are shown below.

Application and Interdisciplinary Activity Masters, pp. 8, 22

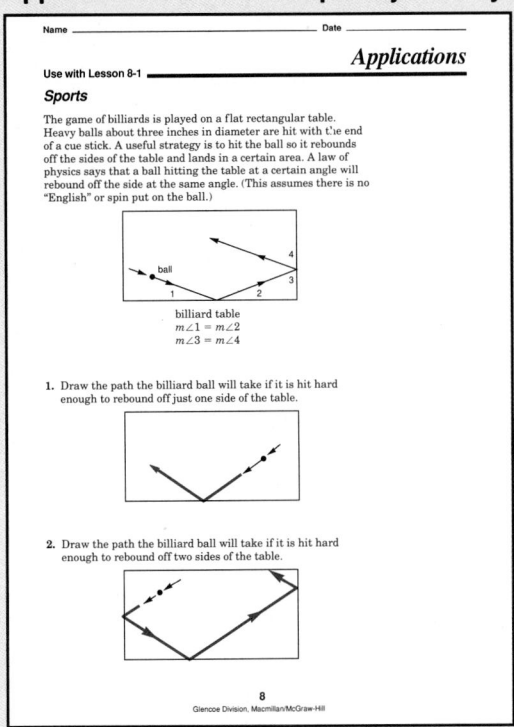

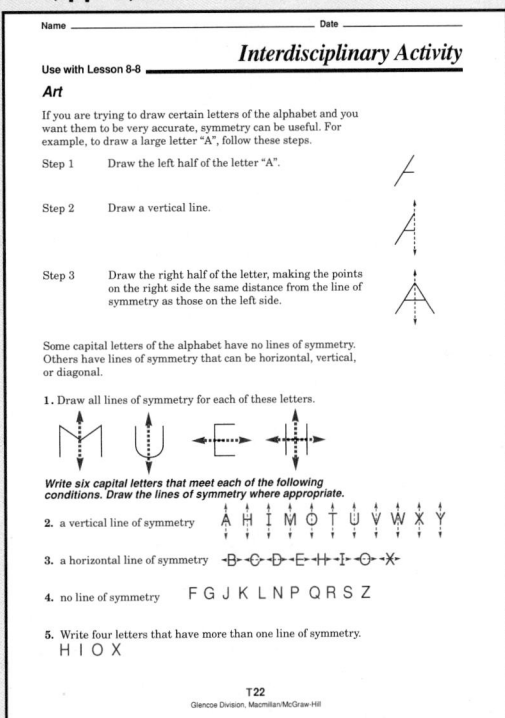

Multicultural Activity Masters, p. 1

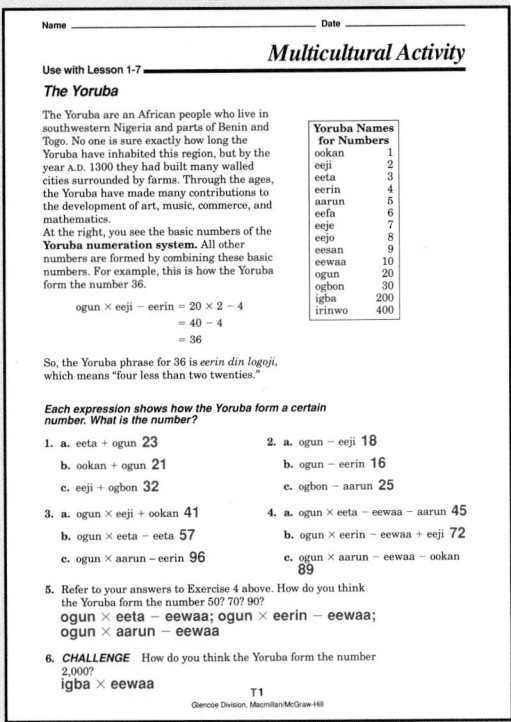

Technology Masters, p. 22

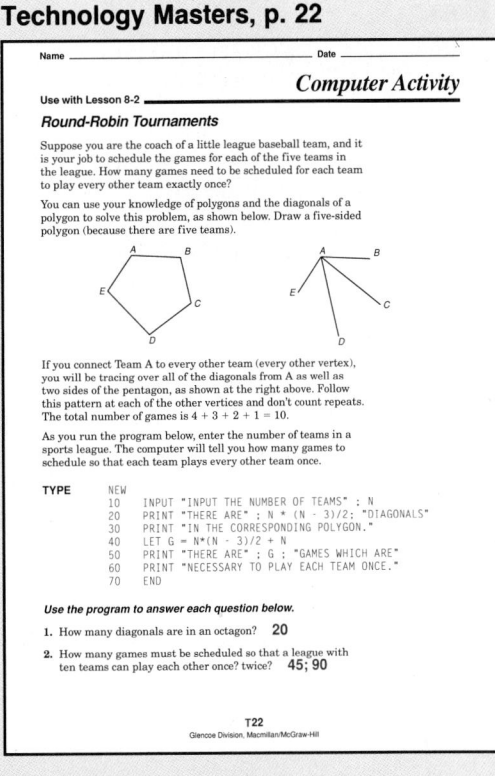

RECOMMENDED OUTSIDE RESOURCES

Books/Periodicals

National Council of Teachers of Mathematics, *Learning and Geometry, K–12, 1987 Yearbook,* Reston, VA: NCTM, 1987.

Phillips, Hubert, *My Best Puzzles in Logic and Reasoning,* New York, NY: Dover Publications, Inc., 1961.

Films/Videotapes/Videodiscs

Classic Antics in Mathematics, Glendale, CA: AIMS Instructional Media, 1976.

Geometry—What's That? San Rafael, CA: Coronet Media, 1975.

Mathematics of the Honeycomb, Whittier, CA: Moody Institute of Science, 1964.

Software

Color and Canvas, (Apple IIGS), Wings for Learning/Sunburst

For addresses of companies handling software, please refer to page T24.

Glencoe's *Interactive Mathematics: Activities and Investigations* consists of 18 units that may be used as alternatives or supplemental material for *Mathematics: Applications and Connections.* The suggested unit for this chapter is Unit 12, *Treasure Island.* See page T18 for more information.

Chapter

8

Investigations in Geometry

Spotlight on Highways and Byways

Have You Ever Wondered. . .

- How many miles there are between various U.S. cities?

- What the lengths are of some of the longest tunnels in the world?

Road Mileage Between Selected U.S. Cities

	Atlanta	Boston	Chicago	Cincinnati	Cleveland	Dallas	Denver	Detroit	Houston
Atlanta, GA	. . .	1,037	674	440	672	795	1,398	699	789
Boston, MA	1,037	. . .	963	840	628	1,748	1,949	695	1,804
Chicago, IL	674	963	. . .	287	335	917	996	266	1,067
Cincinnati, OH	440	840	287	. . .	244	920	1,164	259	1,029
Cleveland, OH	672	628	335	244	. . .	1,159	1,321	170	1,273
Dallas, TX	795	1,748	917	920	1,159	. . .	781	1,143	243
Denver, CO	1,398	1,949	996	1,164	1,321	781	. . .	1,253	1,019
Detroit, MI	699	695	266	259	170	1,143	1,253	. . .	1,265
Houston, TX	789	1,804	1,067	1,029	1,273	243	1019	1,265	. . .

Vehicular Tunnel

Name	Location	Length (miles)
St.Gotthard	Alps, Switzerland	10.2
Mt. Blanc	Alps, France-Italy	7.5
Great St. Bernard	Alps, Switzerland	3.4
Lincoln	Hudson River, New York-New Jersey	2.5
Queensway Road	Mersey River, Liverpool, England	2.2
Brooklyn-Battery	East River, New York City	2.1
Holland	Hudson River, New York-New Jersey	1.7
Fort McHenry	Baltimore, Maryland	1.7
Hampton Roads	Norfolk, Virginia	1.4
Queens-Midtown	East River, New York City	1.3
Liberty Tubes	Pittsburgh, Pennsylvania	1.2
Baltimore Harbor	Baltimore, Maryland	1.2
Allegheny Tunnels	Pennsylvania Turnpike	1.2

294

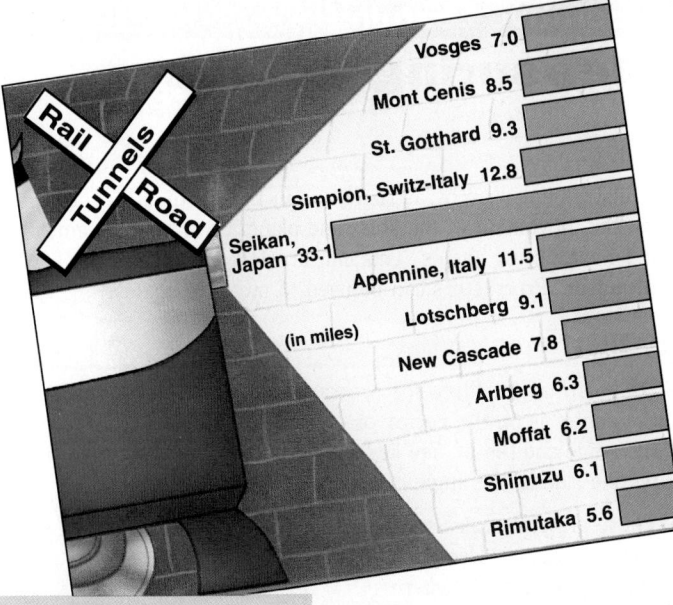

Vosges 7.0
Mont Cenis 8.5
St. Gotthard 9.3
Simpion, Switz-Italy 12.8
Seikan, Japan 33.1
Apennine, Italy 11.5
Lotschberg 9.1
(in miles)
New Cascade 7.8
Arlberg 6.3
Moffat 6.2
Shimuzu 6.1
Rimutaka 5.6

Looking Ahead

In this chapter, you will see how geometry is involved in answering questions about highways and byways.

The major objectives of the chapter are to:

- classify angles by their measure
- classify and construct polygons
- construct perpendiculars
- relate polygon shapes and angle measure to tiling and tessellations

Chapter Project

Highways and Byways

Work in a group.

1. Obtain a detailed street map of a local area.

2. List 20 major street intersections or crossroads.

3. Measure the angles formed by the various streets or the roads.

4. Make a verbal presentation of your results to the class.

DATA ANALYSIS

Have students examine the tables. One student should explain how to read the mileage table, which is the kind found in road atlases. Have students add your city or the nearest one to it to the table, and fill in the row and column for it with the correct distances.

Data Search

A question related to these data is provided in Lesson 8-7, page 326, Exercise 15.

CHAPTER PROJECT

Provide groups with street maps from different areas. Show them a few intersections that form angles. Then show them how to measure angles and to recognize which ones are greater than others. You can extend the project by having groups design their own towns, drawing in all roads and intersections. Encourage them to name the roads and to place traffic lights, buildings, and parks where they want.

Chapter Opener Transparency

Transparency 8-0 is available in the Transparency Package. It provides another full-color, motivating activity that you can use to capture students' interest.

295

Classroom Vignette

"I developed a vocabulary sheet of all the 'Words to Learn' in this chapter. When students learned the meaning of a term, they wrote its definition in their own words. This mini-glossary became a quick-reference guide that students used throughout the chapter."

Lucy Aikerson

Lucy Aikerson, Teacher
Washington Middle School, Aurora, IL

295

NCTM Standards: 1–5, 12, 13

Management Tips

For Students Students should have protractors that are sturdy and semi-circular. Encourage students, working with a partner, to align the protractor with the angle and to read the right measurement on the scale.

For the Overhead Projector *Overhead Manipulative Resources* provides appropriate materials for teacher or student demonstration of the activities in this Mathematics Lab.

1 FOCUS

Introducing the Lab

Ask students to describe what an angle is. Have them suggest ways in which angles are used. Ask them what reasons they can think of for knowing the measures of angles and also for knowing how to measure them.

2 TEACH

Using Manipulatives You may find that you will need to work with some students at their desks, physically demonstrating how to use the protractor to measure an angle. Guide them to place the protractor correctly and how to read the appropriate scale.

3 PRACTICE/APPLY

Using Critical Thinking Guide students to recognize that angles smaller than the corner of a page measure less than 90° and that those that are larger measure more than 90°. If they are able to recognize this distinction, students will know whether they are reading the correct scale.

Close

Have students use the protractor to draw two angles–one that measures 55° and one that measures 115°.

8-1A Measuring Angles

A Preview of Lesson 8-1

Objective
Measure angles by using a protractor.

Materials
protractor
straightedge

You may need to extend the sides of your angle in order to measure it.

The instrument used by astronomers in the thirteenth century to track the movement of the stars and planets contained a semicircular unit for measuring angles. This unit is a forerunner of today's **protractor.** Protractors can be used to measure angles.

Try this!

- Draw any angle. Place the protractor on the angle so that the center is on the vertex of the angle and the 0° line lies on one side of the angle.

- There are two scales on your protractor. Use the one that begins with 0° where the side aligns with the protractor.

- Follow the scale from the 0° point to the point where the other side of the angle meets the scale. This is the angle's measure.

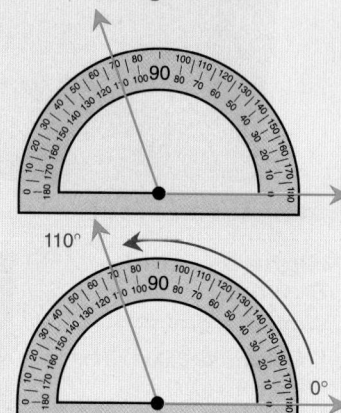

The measure of the angle is 110°

What do you think?

1. How do you know which scale to read? **See Solutions Manual.**
2. What do you need to do if the sides of your angle do not intersect the scale of the protractor? **Extend them.**
3. Sam says the angle above has a measure of 70°. What's wrong? **He read the wrong scale.**

Extension

4. You can use a protractor to draw an angle of a given measure. Suppose you want to draw a 65° angle. **See students' work.**
   a. Draw a line segment.
   b. Align your protractor on the segment with the center on one endpoint of the segment.
   c. Find the scale that starts with 0°. Go along that scale until you find 65°. Put a mark at this point.
   d. Draw a line through the endpoint of the segment and the mark.

OPTIONS

Lab Manual You may wish to make copies of the blackline master on p. 58 of the *Lab Manual* for students to use as a recording sheet.

Lab Manual, p. 58

Name _____ Date _____

Use with page 296   *Mathematics Lab Worksheet*

Measuring Angles

Try this!
Answers will vary.

What do you think?
1. Use the scale that begins with 0° where the side

8-1 Angles

8-1 Lesson Notes

Objective

Classify angles.

Words to Learn

vertex
degrees
right
acute
obtuse
straight
congruent
bisect

Carpenters used many tools to make sure that all the pieces of wood they cut fit together properly. One tool they use is a miter box. The miter box guides the saw so that the correct angle is cut.

When two segments or rays have a common endpoint, they form an angle. The point where they meet is called the **vertex** of the angle. An angle can be named by its vertex. To say *an angle with vertex B,* we write ∠B. Angles can also be named using a point from each side and the vertex, ∠*ABC* or ∠*CBA.* The vertex letter always goes in the middle. Another way to name an angle is to use a number inside the angle, ∠1.

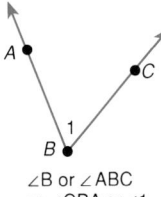

∠B or ∠ABC
or ∠CBA or ∠1

An angle is not measured by the length of its sides, but in units called **degrees.**

The corner of a picture frame is a **right** angle. Its measure is 90°. We often use the ⌐ symbol to indicate a right angle.

Angles that have a measure less than 90° are called **acute** angles. Those that have a measure greater than 90° but less than 180° are called **obtuse** angles. A **straight** angle has a measure of 180°.

There is a Sequoia pine tree that is 250 feet tall and 94 feet around the base. It has been calculated that there would be enough wood in this tree to make 40 five-room houses or 5,000,000,000 matches.

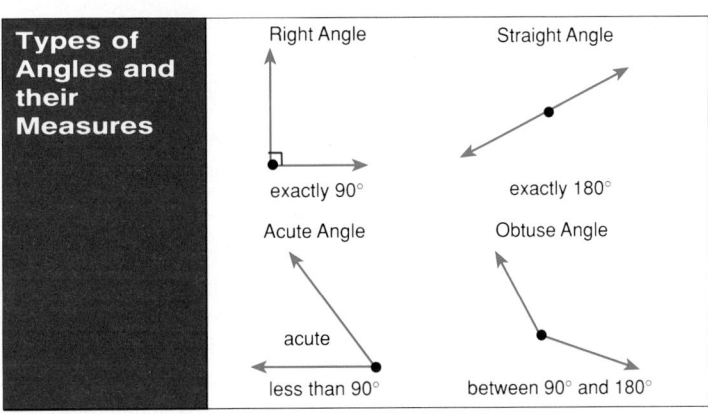

Types of Angles and their Measures

Right Angle — exactly 90°

Straight Angle — exactly 180°

Acute Angle — acute — less than 90°

Obtuse Angle — between 90° and 180°

Lesson 8-1 Angles   **297**

OPTIONS

Team Teaching

Inform the other teachers on your team that your classes are studying geometry. Suggestions for curriculum integration are:

Art: architecture and design, space art, dance choreography

Science: physics (light), machines and work, astronomy, engineering

Physical Fitness: squash and racquetball, gymnastics, baseball

Social Studies: navigation

NCTM Standards: 1–5, 9, 12, 13

Lesson Resources
• Study Guide Master 8-1
• Practice Master 8-1
• Enrichment Master 8-1
• Application Master, p. 8
• Group Activity Card 8-1

 Transparency 8-1 contains the 5-Minute Check and a teaching aid for this lesson.

⏱ 5-Minute Check
(Over Chapter 7)

Replace each ● with <, >, or = to make a true sentence.

1. −5 ● 1   <
2. −14 ● −2   <

Solve each equation.

3. $a = 3 + (-5)$ −2
4. $b = -10 - 4$ −14
5. $c = -7(-3)$ 21

1 FOCUS

Motivating the Lesson

Activity To prepare students for the concepts presented in this lesson, review some of the basic ideas of geometry. Have students look around them to identify examples of planes, points, lines, rays, and line segments. Ask students to sketch each figure and describe or define it.

2 TEACH

Using the Mini-Lab Ask students to do the activity more than once, with angles of different degree measures. Have them label the rays and vertex of the angles formed in order to be able to refer to them. Ask students to describe what the fold in the paper does.   It bisects the angle.

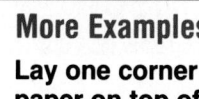

More Examples

Lay one corner of your paper on top of each angle to determine whether each is acute, obtuse, right, or straight.

For Example 1

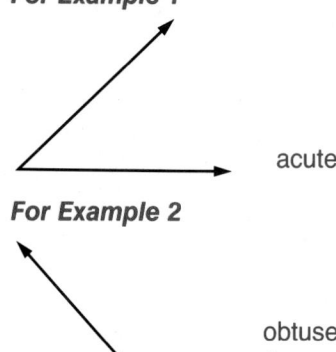

acute

For Example 2

obtuse

For Example 3   straight

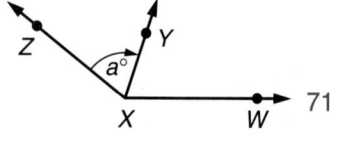

For Example 4

In the figure, $\overrightarrow{XY}$ bisects ∠WXZ. Use an equation to find the value of *a* if the measure of ∠WXZ is 142°.

$$Z \quad \overset{Y}{\underset{a°}{\swarrow}} \quad$$

71

X   W

Checking for Understanding

Exercises 1-3 are designed to help you assess students' understanding through reading, writing, speaking, and modeling. You should work through these exercises with your students and then monitor their work on Guided Practice Exercises 4-11.

Additional Answer

b. The sum of the measures of the smaller angles equals the measure of the larger angle.

298

Lay one corner of your notebook paper on top of each angle to determine whether each angle is acute, obtuse, right, or straight.

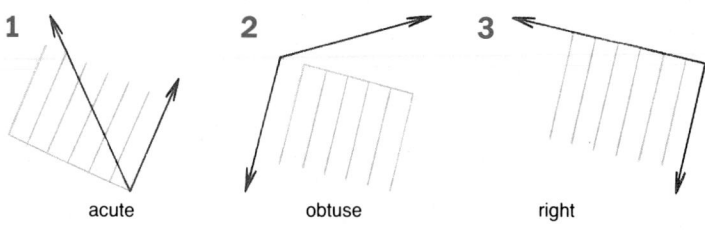

| 1 | 2 | 3 |

acute   obtuse   right

When two angles have the same measure, they are **congruent angles.**

$\cong$ *means is congruent to.*

Congruent angles	**In words:** If ∠A has the same measure as ∠B, then ∠A is congruent to ∠B.
	In symbols: If $m\angle A = m\angle B$, then $\angle A \cong \angle B$.

$\overrightarrow{BE}$ *is read ray BE.*

When you separate an angle into two congruent angles, you **bisect** the angle. In the figure, $\overrightarrow{BE}$ bisect ∠ABC. So, $m\angle 1 = m\angle 2$. This means that $\angle 1 \cong \angle 2$.

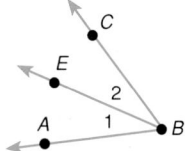

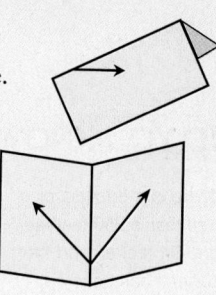

Mini-Lab

Work with a partner.
Materials: straightedge, protractor

• Use your straightedge to draw any angle.

• Fold the paper through the vertex so that the two sides match when you hold the paper up to the light.

• Unfold the paper and use your straightedge to draw a segment on the fold.

Talk About It

a. Use your protractor to measure the original angle. Then measure the two smaller angles. **See students' work.**

b. Write a sentence to relate the measure of the smaller angles to that of the larger one. **See margin.**

OPTIONS

Reteaching Activity

Using Applications In a diagram of a baseball diamond, including the outfield, use homeplate as the vertex. Guide students to see that a right angle is formed by rays going from homeplate toward the foul poles along the left-field and right-field foul lines.

Study Guide Masters, p. 67

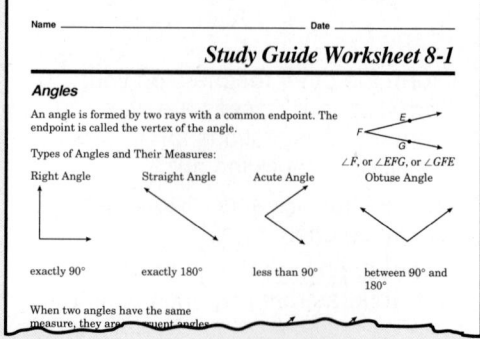

Name _____ Date _____

Study Guide Worksheet 8-1

Angles

An angle is formed by two rays with a common endpoint. The endpoint is called the vertex of the angle.

∠F, or ∠EFG, or ∠GFE

Types of Angles and Their Measures:

Right Angle	Straight Angle	Acute Angle	Obtuse Angle
exactly 90°	exactly 180°	less than 90°	between 90° and 180°

When two angles have the same measure, they are congruent angles.

Example 4 *Connection*

Algebra In the figure, $\overrightarrow{BA}$ bisects $\angle DBC$. Use an equation to find the value of x if the measure of $\angle DBC$ is 136°.

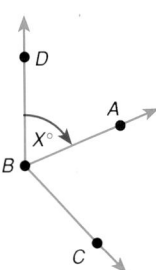

$\overrightarrow{BA}$ bisects $\angle DBC$. So,
$m \angle DBA = m \angle ABC$. Since
$m \angle DBA = x$, it follows that
$m \angle ABC = x$. So, $x + x = 136$.

$$2x = 136$$
$$x = 68 \qquad \text{The value of } x \text{ is 68.}$$

Checking for Understanding

Communicating Mathematics

Read and study the lesson to answer each question.

1. **Show** how you can use the corner of your paper to classify an angle. **See students' work.**

2. **Tell** what it means to bisect an angle. **See margin.**

3. **Show** whether $\overrightarrow{XZ}$ bisects $\angle WXY$ by tracing the figure at the right and folding the paper so that the two sides of the angle match. **See students' work.**

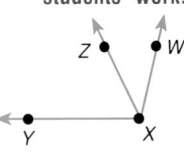

Guided Practice

Classify each angle as acute, obtuse, right, or straight.

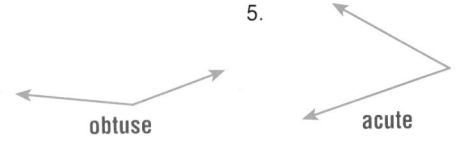

4. obtuse   5. acute   6. right

7. 124° angle — obtuse
8. 90° angle — right
9. 42° angle — acute
10. 180° angle — straight

11. Angle A has a measure of 84°. If it is bisected, which is the measure of each of the two angles formed? **42°**

Exercises

Independent Practice

Classify each angle as acute, obtuse, right, or straight.

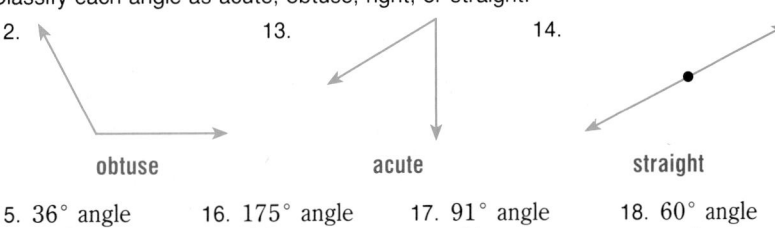

12. obtuse   13. acute   14. straight

15. 36° angle — acute
16. 175° angle — obtuse
17. 91° angle — obtuse
18. 60° angle — acute

Bell Ringer

Provide students with the following drawing in which $\angle AEC$ is congruent to $\angle BED$, and $\overrightarrow{EB}$ and $\overrightarrow{EC}$ are angle bisectors.

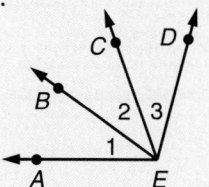

Ask students to name the other congruent angles and to explain their reasoning.

$\angle 1 \cong \angle 3$ Sample reasoning: angles that are halves of congruent angles are congruent.

Close

Have students use a straightedge to draw obtuse angle *DEF* and sketch $\overrightarrow{EG}$, which bisects it. Have them describe the relationship between the two angles formed and between each and $\angle DEF$. The angles are congruent; in each case, angle = $\frac{1}{2}$ m $\angle DEF$.

3 PRACTICE/APPLY

Assignment Guide

Maximum: 12–32
Minimum: 12–24, 26–28, 30–31

For **Extra Practice**, see p. 590.

Alternate Assessment

Writing Have students use a straightedge to draw an acute angle, a right angle, an obtuse angle, and a straight angle. Ask them to sketch a bisector within one of these angles so that two right angles are formed.

Additional Answer

2. Separate into two congruent angles.

Practice Masters, p. 67

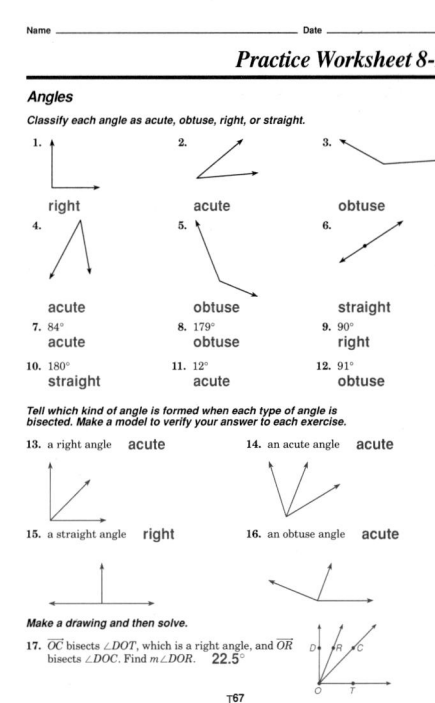

Name _____ Date _____

Practice Worksheet 8-1

Angles

Classify each angle as acute, obtuse, right, or straight.

1. right   2. acute   3. obtuse
4. acute   5. obtuse   6. straight

7. 84° — acute
8. 179° — obtuse
9. 90° — right
10. 180° — straight
11. 12° — acute
12. 91° — obtuse

Tell which kind of angle is formed when each type of angle is bisected. Make a model to verify your answer to each exercise.

13. a right angle   acute
14. an acute angle   acute
15. a straight angle   right
16. an obtuse angle   acute

Make a drawing and then solve.

17. $\overline{OC}$ bisects $\angle DOT$, which is a right angle, and $\overline{OR}$ bisects $\angle DOC$. Find $m \angle DOR$.   22.5°

T67
Glencoe Division, Macmillan/McGraw-Hill

299

Tell which kind of angle is formed when each type of angle is bisected. Make a model to verify your answer to each question.

19. an acute angle **acute**   20. a right angle **acute**

21. an obtuse angle **acute**   22. a straight angle **right**

Make a drawing for each situation. Then solve.

23. **Algebra** Angle B and angle C are congruent. If $m \angle B = 100°$ and $m \angle C = x + 80$, find the value of x. **20**

24. **Algebra** $\overrightarrow{EF}$ bisects $\angle BED$, which is a right angle. Find the value of y, if $m \angle BEF = 5y$. **9**

25. **Algebra** $\overrightarrow{XY}$ bisects $\angle AXE$. Suppose $m \angle AXY = 3z$ and $m \angle EXY = 4w$. If $z = 12$ and $w = 9$, find $m \angle AXE$. **72°**

Mixed Review 26. Find 2.5×0.3. *(Lesson 2-4)* **0.75**

27. **Physical Fitness** Every evening, Alicia walks around a neighborhood block, which is a rectangle of length 0.75 miles and width 0.2 miles. How far does Alicia walk each evening? *(Lesson 5-6)* **1.9 miles**

28. Express 0.00006 using negative exponents. *(Lesson 7-10)* 6×10^{-5}

Problem Solving and Applications

29. **Physics** Light reflects off a mirror at an outgoing angle congruent to the incoming angle. In each figure below, tell which ray is the correct outgoing ray of light.

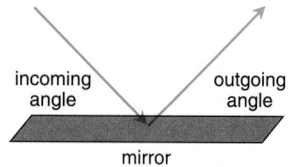

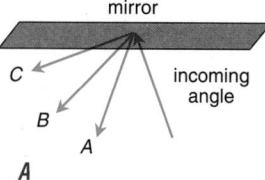
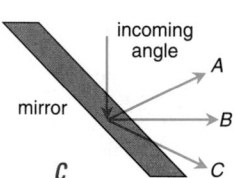

30. **Critical Thinking** Without measuring, match each angle to the appropriate measurement. Write a sentence using symbols to state your answers.

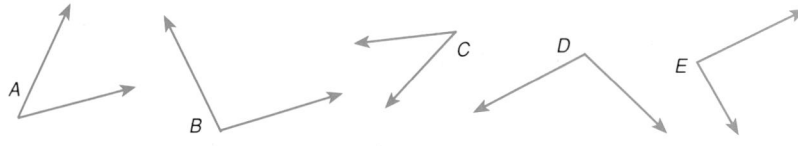

a. 40°   b. 50°   c. 85°   d. 100°   e. 110°
$m \angle C = 40°$ $m \angle A = 50°$ $m \angle E = 85°$ $m \angle B = 100°$ $m \angle D = 110°$

31. **Research** Find the name used for an angle that measures more than 180°.
reflex angle

32. **Journal Entry** Write a sentence telling five places where you see an angle in your classroom. Be sure to include the classification of each angle.
Sample answers: corner, right; top of blackboard, straight

Enrichment Masters, p. 67

Enrichment Worksheet 8-1

Compass Directions

There are 360° in a complete rotation. The directions north, east, south, and west are shown on the compass at the right.

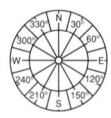
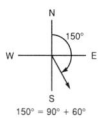

To find the direction a boat or airplane is heading, measure clockwise from north around the compass. The example shows a heading of 150°.

150° = 90° + 60°

Use a protractor. Write the compass heading in degrees for each diagram.

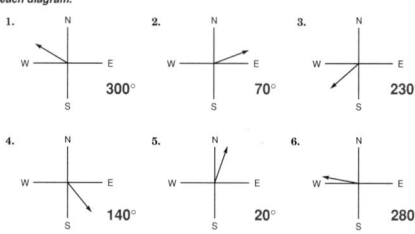

1. **300°**   2. **70°**   3. **230°**

4. **140°**   5. **20°**   6. **280°**

The drawing at the right is called a *compass rose*. Use the compass rose to translate each direction into degrees.

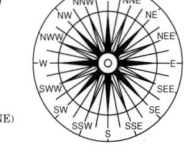

7. East **90°**
8. North **0°, or 360°**
9. Northeast (NE) **45°**
10. Southwest (SW) **225°**
11. South **180°**
12. Southeast (SE) **135°**
13. Northwest (NW) **315°**
14. North northeast (NNE) **22.5°**

300

OPTIONS

Extending the Lesson

Using Applications Have students work in groups to construct a quiz for classmates testing the concepts of this lesson and the Mathematics Lab preceding it. Have them provide solutions to the problems on the quiz.

Cooperative Learning Activity

Turn, Turn, Turn **8-1**

Use groups of 3.
Materials: String, index cards, protractor

● Collect at least seven different objects from the classroom. Place them as shown in the figure on the back of this card. Write the name of each object on an index card. Shuffle the cards and place them face down in a pile. Cut two pieces of string that are about a foot longer than the radius of the circle you made.

➡ One group member selects a card and then stands at the center of the circle. The other two group members stand just outside the circle, beside the point indicated by the X.

The group member in the center of the circle holds one end of both strings. Each of the other group members holds one of the other ends. The group member at the center reads the name of the object on the card, and one of the other group members walks counterclockwise around the circle to stand beside that object. Discuss the angle formed by the string. Is it right, acute, or obtuse? Estimate the measure of the angle formed. Later, use the string and a protractor to check your estimates.

Continue in the same manner, taking turns standing at the center.

8-1B Perpendicular Lines

A Follow-Up of Lesson 8-1

Objective

Construct a line perpendicular to another line.

Materials

compass
straightedge

An arc is part of a circle.

Perpendicular lines are lines in the same plane that form right angles when they intersect. In the figure, line ℓ is perpendicular to line m. This can also be written as $\ell \perp m$. Two ways to construct perpendicular lines are described below.

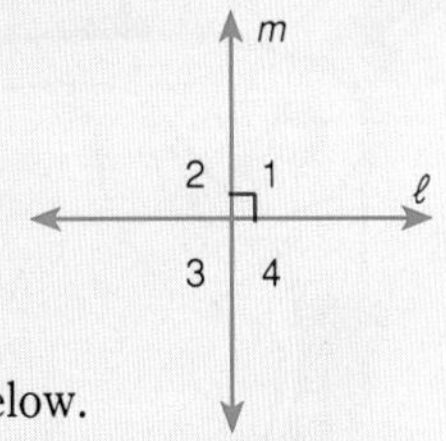

Activity One

Construct a line perpendicular to line m through point P on m.

- Draw a line and label it m. Draw a dot on the line and label it point P.

- Place the compass point on P and draw arcs to intersect line m twice. Label these points Q and R.

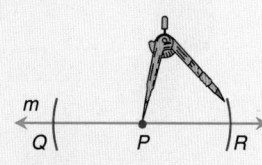

- Open your compass wider. Put the compass at Q and draw an arc above line m.

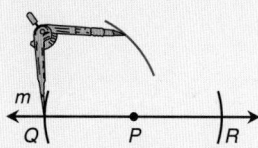

- With the same setting, put the compass at R and draw an arc to intersect the one you just drew. Label this intersection point S.

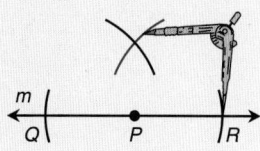

- Use a straightedge to draw a line through S and P.

By construction, $\overleftrightarrow{PS} \perp m$.

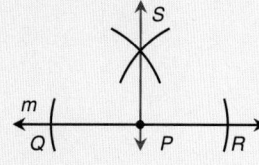

$\overleftrightarrow{PS}$ is read line PS.

Activity Two

Construct a line perpendicular to line m through point P not on m.

- Draw a line and label it m. Draw a dot above m and label it point P.
- Open the compass to a width greater than the distance from P to m. Draw a large arc to intersect m twice. Label these points of intersection Q and R.

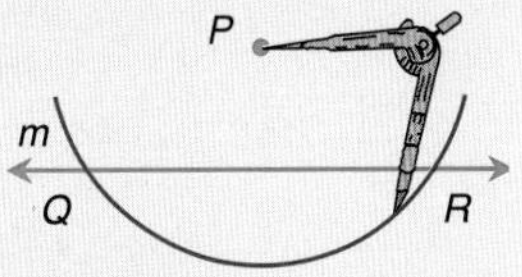

Mathematics Lab 8-1B Constructing Perpendiculars **301**

NCTM Standards: 1–4, 12

Management Tips

For Students Have students work individually. Each will need a compass with a sharpened pencil, a straightedge, and a few sheets of paper. Advise students to keep the compass setting tight to avoid changing the size of the arc.

For the Overhead Projector
Overhead Manipulative Resources provides appropriate materials for teacher or student demonstration of the activities in this Mathematics Lab.

1 FOCUS

Introducing the Lab

Have students experiment with using a compass. Tell them that they can use a compass together with a straightedge to make geometric constructions. Have students practice drawing circles and arcs with their compasses.

302

2 TEACH

Using Manipulatives   Provide opportunities for students to construct several perpendiculars through points that are on, above, or below a line. Ask students to think about which aspects of the constructions are the same.

3 PRACTICE/APPLY

Using Critical Thinking   Ask students what would happen to the line they are constructing if they were to make one of the arcs smaller than the other.   It will not be perpendicular; two acute angles and two obtuse angles will be formed.

Close

Have students list the steps they would follow to construct two lines perpendicular to a line, one from a point on the line, and the other from a point not on the line.

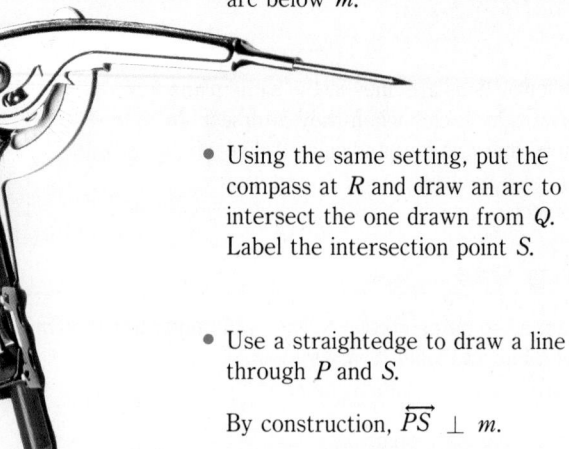

- Put the compass at Q and draw an arc below m.

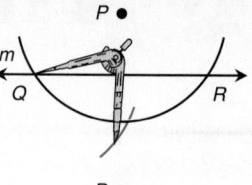

- Using the same setting, put the compass at R and draw an arc to intersect the one drawn from Q. Label the intersection point S.

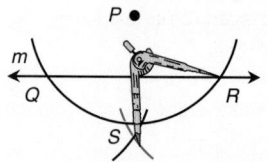

- Use a straightedge to draw a line through P and S.

  By construction, $\overleftrightarrow{PS} \perp m$.

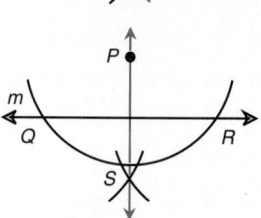

What do you think?

1. What type of angles are formed by perpendicular lines?   **right angles**
2. Measure the angles on your constructions. Explain why these measures may not exactly agree with your answer in Exercise 1.
   Answers will vary.

Extension
   3. Answers will vary.

3. You can construct a square by using perpendiculars.
   a. Draw line ℓ. Draw two dots on ℓ and label them points R and S. Construct a perpendicular through R.
   b. Use the compass to measure the distance from R to S. Using the same setting, place the compass at R and draw an arc on the perpendicular through R. Label this point T.
   c. Using the same setting, place the compass at T and draw an arc to the right of T. Then place the compass at S and draw an arc to intersect the one you just drew. Call this point U.
   d. Use a straightedge to draw $\overline{TU} \ and \ \overline{US}$. Figure $RSUT$ is a square.

a. 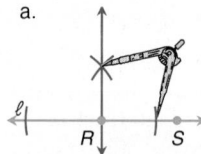   b-c. 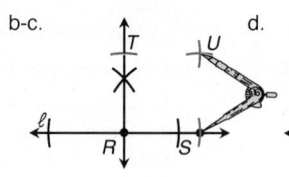   d.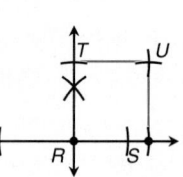

302   **Chapter 8** Investigations in Geometry

OPTIONS

Lab Manual   You may wish to make copies of the blackline master on p. 59 of the *Lab Manual* for students to use as a recording sheet.

Lab Manual, p. 59

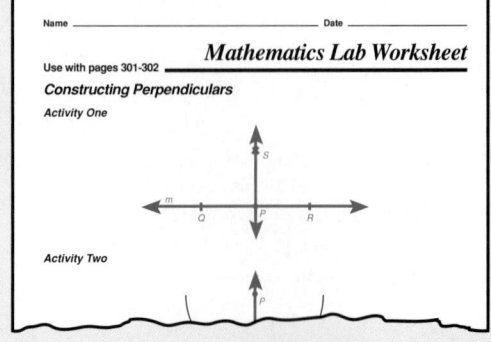

8-2 Polygons

Objective

Identify polygons.

Words to Learn

polygon
triangle
quadrilateral
pentagon
hexagon
heptagon
octagon
nonagon
decagon
undecagon
dodecagon

Vertices is the plural of vertex.

Many words in the English language have their origins in ancient Greek and Latin words. The word **polygon** comes from the prefix *poly-* meaning *many* and the suffix *-gon* meaning *angle*. So, a polygon is a many-angled figure.

Actually, a polygon is a closed figure whose sides are line segments in the same plane. Since the segments meet to form angles and angles have vertices, polygons also have vertices.

Figures A, B, and C are polygons. Figures D, E, and F are *not polygons.*

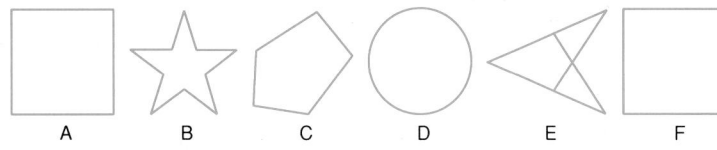

A   B   C   D   E   F

Definition of Polygon	A polygon is a closed figure in a plane that • has at least three sides, all of which are segments, • has sides that meet only at a vertex, and • has exactly two sides meeting at each vertex.

Examples

Determine which figures are polygons. If the figure is not a polygon, explain why.

1

2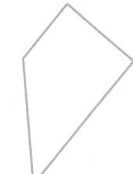

3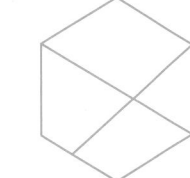

DID YOU KNOW

The languages of French, Italian, Spanish, Portuguese, Romanian, and Latin are part of the family called the Romance languages.

The figure is not a polygon because all sides are not segments.

The figure is a polygon.

The figure is not a polygon because some sides meet at places other than at endpoints.

Lesson 8-2 Polygons   **303**

NCTM Standards: 1–4, 12

Lesson Resources
• Study Guide Master 8-2
• Practice Master 8-2
• Enrichment Master 8-2
• Technology Master, p. 22
• Group Activity Card 8-2

 Transparency 8-2 contains the 5-Minute Check and a teaching aid for this lesson.

⏱ 5-Minute Check
(Over Lesson 8-1)

Classify each angle as acute, obtuse, right, or straight.

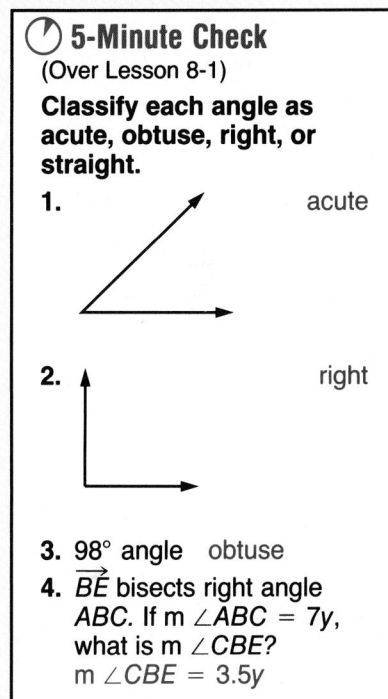

1.   acute

2.   right

3. 98° angle   obtuse

4. $\overrightarrow{BE}$ bisects right angle ABC. If m $\angle ABC = 7y$, what is m $\angle CBE$?
m $\angle CBE = 3.5y$

1 FOCUS

Motivating the Lesson

Activity Show students a large photograph such as a cityscape, in which many different shapes and figures can be found. Ask students to identify as many plane figures as they can.

2 TEACH

Using Logical Reasoning First have students explain why each of the figures in the second set of five figures is not a polygon. Then have them use pencils to copy this set of figures. Ask them to adjust each one by adding or removing line segments, or by erasing parts, so that it becomes a polygon.

OPTIONS

Reteaching Activity

Using Manipulatives Have students use pattern blocks to show and make polygons. Have them discuss the similarities and differences they notice among the figures they create. Ask students to try to build different figures having the same number of sides.

Study Guide Masters, p. 68

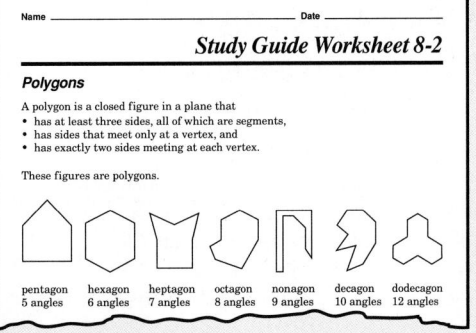

Name _____ Date _____
Study Guide Worksheet 8-2

Polygons

A polygon is a closed figure in a plane that
• has at least three sides, all of which are segments,
• has sides that meet only at a vertex, and
• has exactly two sides meeting at each vertex.

These figures are polygons.

pentagon hexagon heptagon octagon nonagon decagon dodecagon
5 angles 6 angles 7 angles 8 angles 9 angles 10 angles 12 angles

More Examples

For Examples 1-3

Is the figure a polygon? If not, explain why.

1.

no; a portion is curved.

2.

polygon

3.

no; the sides don't meet.

For Example 4

Sketch a nonagon.

Checking for Understanding

Exercises 1-2 are designed to help you assess students' understanding through reading, writing, speaking, and modeling. You should work through these exercises with your students and then monitor their work on Guided Practice Exercises 3-5.

Practice Masters, p. 68

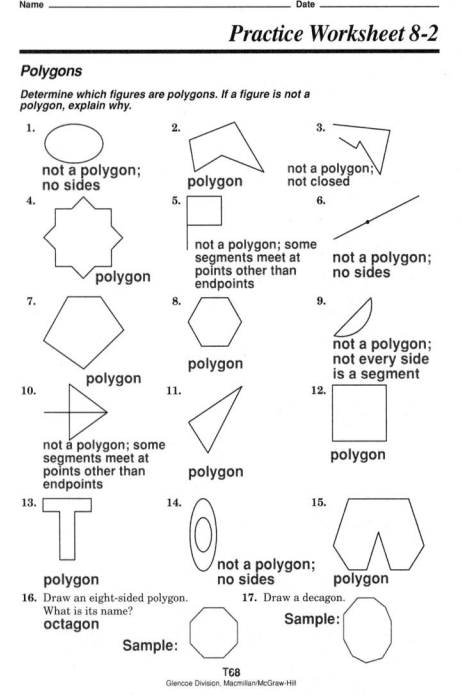

Name _____ Date _____

Practice Worksheet 8-2

Polygons

Determine which figures are polygons. If a figure is not a polygon, explain why.

1. not a polygon; no sides
2. polygon
3. not a polygon; not closed
4. polygon
5. not a polygon; some segments meet at points other than endpoints
6. not a polygon; no sides
7. polygon
8. polygon
9. not a polygon; not every side is a segment
10. not a polygon; some segments meet at points other than endpoints
11. polygon
12. polygon
13. polygon
14. not a polygon; no sides
15. polygon
16. Draw an eight-sided polygon. What is its name? octagon   Sample:
17. Draw a decagon. Sample:

T68
Glencoe Division, Macmillan/McGraw-Hill

Some polygons have special names. Triangles and quadrilaterals are polygons. The word **triangle** means *three angles*. The word **quadrilateral** means *four sides*. The names of other polygons also describe them.

Example 4 *Connection*

Language Arts Use the meaning of each prefix to sketch each polygon.

penta-	5	*nona-*	9
hexa-	6	*deca-*	10
hepta-	7	*undeca-*	11
octa-	8	*dodeca-*	12

Each of these is only one example of the type of figure you might draw.

a. octagon
8 angles

b. pentagon
5 angles

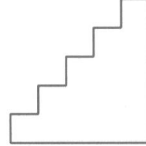

c. dodecagon
12 angles

d. hexagon
6 angles

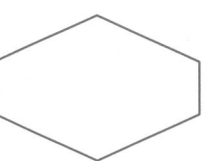

e. decagon
10 angles

f. heptagon
7 angles

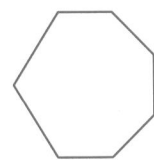

Checking for Understanding

Communicating Mathematics

Read and study the lesson to answer each question. See Solutions Manual.

1. **Tell** what conditions a figure must meet in order to be a polygon.
2. **Write** a sentence that relates the number of angles in a polygon to the number of sides in a polygon.
   The number of angles equals the number of sides.

Guided Practice

Determine which figures are polygons. If a figure is not a polygon, explain why.

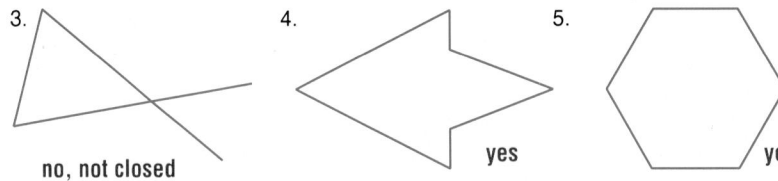

3.

no, not closed

4.

yes

5.

yes

OPTIONS

Limited English Proficiency

Review the new vocabulary with students, focusing on the use of prefixes to identify the polygons according to sides. Have them define words that name the more frequently encountered figures, draw a picture of each figure, and then add the words to a vocabulary list that includes other geometric terms.

Interactive Mathematics Tools

This multimedia software provides an interactive lesson that is tied directly to Lesson 8-2. Students will use changeable polygons to explore the measures of the interior angles of polygons.

Exercises

Independent
Practice

Determine which figures are polygons. If a figure is not a polygon, explain why.

6. 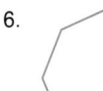 yes

7.

8. 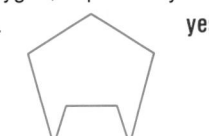 yes

7. No; the sides do not meet at a vertex.

9.  yes

10. 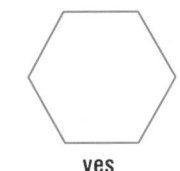 yes

11. 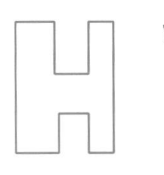 yes

12. Draw a nine-sided polygon. What is its name? **nonagon**

Mixed Review

13. Find the least common multiple of 14 and 35. *(Lesson 4-9)* **70**

14. Classify the angle at the right as acute, obtuse, right, or straight. *(Lesson 8-1)*
    acute

Problem Solving
and
Applications

15. **Critical Thinking** A segment that connects two nonconsecutive vertices of a polygon is called a *diagonal. Nonconsecutive* means not next to each other. For example, a quadrilateral has two diagonals.
    a. Find the total number of diagonals in a pentagon. **5**
    b. Find the total number of diagonals in a hexagon. **9**
    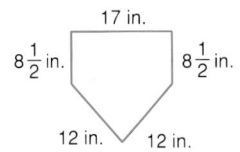

16. **Baseball** Home plate is made of white rubber set into the ground so that it is level with the ground.
    a. What shape is home plate? **pentagon**
    b. The perimeter of home plate is the sum of the lengths of its sides. What is the perimeter of home plate? **58 inches**

    17 in.
    $8\frac{1}{2}$ in. $8\frac{1}{2}$ in.
    12 in.   12 in.

17. **Traffic Safety** There are certain types of traffic signs that always have the same shape. Identify the shape of each sign below and tell what the sign means.

    a.    b.    c. 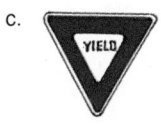   d.

    octagon, stop   square, curve   triangle, yield   rectangle, speed limit 50

18. **Journal Entry** Draw the shape of some other signs or objects you see everyday. Name each shape and identify which type of polygon it is, if any.
    See students' work.

Extending the Lesson

Using Logic Each figure in the top row below is a *tweeb;* in the bottom row, none is. Have students draw a tweeb and a non-tweeb.

tweeb: a figure with 2 curved portions

Cooperative Learning Activity

It's in the Stars 8-2

Use groups of 4 or more.
Materials: Reference books, tracing paper

➡ Read the following passage. Then do the activity.

You probably know that a constellation is a pattern made up of a group of stars. In 1934, the International Astronomical Union recognized and defined the borders of 88 constellations. Prior to that time, various astronomers had identified and named many other constellations.

Find a star map in a reference book. Each group member traces the stars on the map. Each group member then draws line segments connecting the points representing the stars to form constellations in the shape of the following polygons: pentagon, heptagon, octagon, decagon, and undecagon. Name each of the constellations you drew. Write each name beside the constellation and, if possible, label the stars that make up the pattern. Share your work with the other group members.

Glencoe Mathematics: Applications and Connections, Course 2

Close

Ask students to draw a row of figures, some of which are polygons and some which aren't. Have students exchange papers and decide which drawings are not polygons and tell why they aren't.

3 PRACTICE/APPLY

Assignment Guide
Maximum: 6–18
Minimum: 6–17

For **Extra Practice,** see p. 590.

Alternate Assessment

Modeling Provide students with geoboards and rubber bands. Have them build three different polygons and three figures that are not polygons.

Enrichment Masters, p. 68

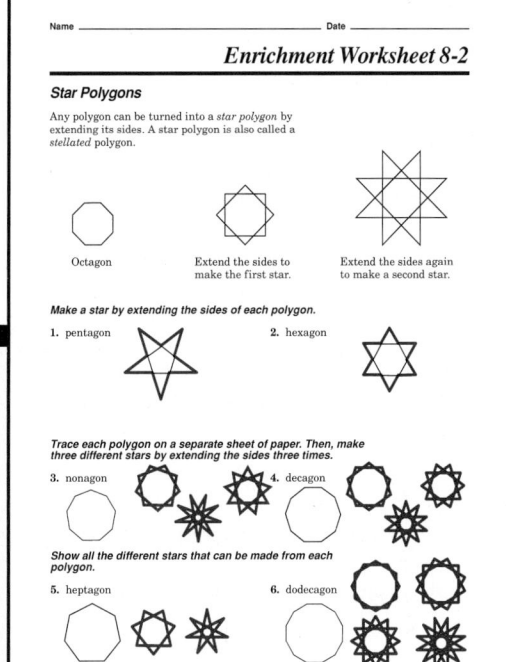

305

NCTM Standards: 1–5, 9, 12

Management Tips

For Students Have students draw their triangles using a straightedge. Each pair of students should experiment with differently shaped triangles to determine whether all have the same sum of angle measures.

For the Overhead Projector
Overhead Manipulative Resources provides appropriate materials for teacher or student demonstration of the activities in this Mathematics Lab.

1 FOCUS

Introducing the Lab

Before students begin the lesson, ask them to suggest ways for finding the sum of the measures of the angles of a polygon without measuring each angle with a protractor.

2 TEACH

Using Manipulatives Ask students to arrange the cut-out pieces of the triangle in as many ways as they can, to see whether the sum of the angle measures changes. Before students do Activity Two, be sure they know what a diagonal is.

3 PRACTICE/APPLY

Using Critical Thinking Ask students to identify the relationship between the number of sides in a polygon and the number of diagonals that can be drawn from any vertex. Ask them to express this relationship as an algebraic expression. 3 less than the number of sides; $n - 3$

Close

Have students use mental math to find the sum of the measures of the angles of a 22-sided figure. 3,600°; Think: 20 × 180

8-2B Sum of the Angles of a Polygon

A Follow-Up of Lesson 8-2

Objective
Discover the sum of the angle measures of any polygon.

Materials
protractor
scissors

A convex polygon is a polygon whose diagonals lie entirely within the polygon. To find the sum of the angle measures in any convex polygon, you could measure each angle and find the sum. This method may not give you an accurate sum because of human error.

Activity One

Work with a partner.
- Draw any triangle on a piece of paper and cut it out.

- Tear off the angles and arrange as shown.

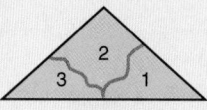

What do you think?

1. What type of angle do the three angles form when put together?
2. What is the measure of this type of angle? 180° straight angle
3. Complete this statement: The sum of the measures of the angles of a triangle is ___?___ °. 180

Activity Two

- Draw a convex hexagon.

- Pick one vertex and draw all the diagonals possible from that vertex.

What do you think?

4. How many triangles were formed when you drew the diagonals? 4
5. How could you find the sum of the measures of the angles in a hexagon? 4 · 180
6. Find the sum of the measures of the angles of each convex polygon by using triangles.
   a. pentagon 540°   b. heptagon 900°   c. octagon 1,080°
   d. **Algebra** If n is the number of sides, write an algebraic expression that tells the sum of the measures of the angles of any polygon. $180(n - 2)$

OPTIONS

Lab Manual You may wish to make copies of the blackline master on p. 60 of the *Lab Manual* for students to use as a recording sheet.

Lab Manual, p. 60

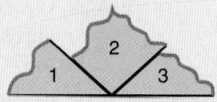

Name _____ Date _____

Mathematics Lab Worksheet

Use with page 306 _____

Sum of the Angles of a Polygon

Activity One

What do you think?

1. The three angles of the triangle form a straight angle .

2. ___180°___

3. The sum of the measures of the angles of a triangle is ___180°___ .

Activity Two

What do you think?

8-3 Triangles and Quadrilaterals

Objective
Classify triangles and quadrilaterals.

Words to Learn
congruent
scalene
isosceles
equilateral
rhombus
trapezoid

Early in the nineteenth century, chemists began to seek ways to classify the elements. Today, these classifications are organized into the periodic table. This table arranges elements in families according to their common characteristics.

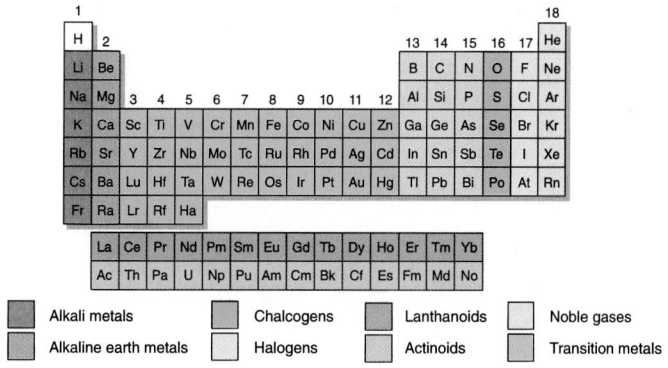

Just as with the elements, each category of polygons can be classified according to their common characteristics.

Triangles can be classified by their angle measures. Each has two acute angles. Classify using the third angle.

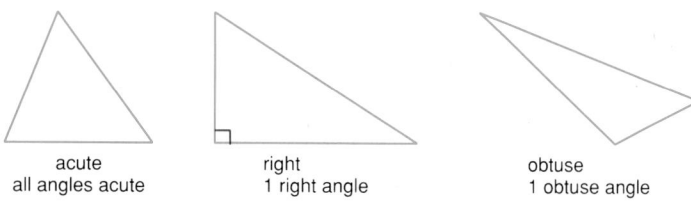

| acute | right | obtuse |
| all angles acute | 1 right angle | 1 obtuse angle |

They can also be classified by the number of congruent sides they have. **Congruent** sides are sides that have the same length.

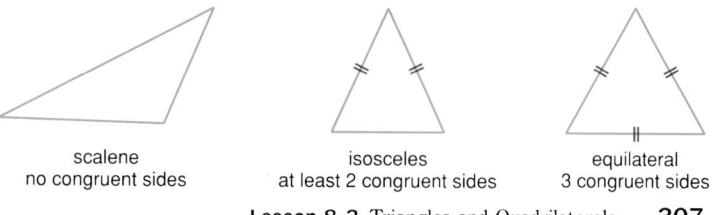

| scalene | isosceles | equilateral |
| no congruent sides | at least 2 congruent sides | 3 congruent sides |

Slashes show which sides are congruent.

Lesson 8-3 Triangles and Quadrilaterals **307**

8-3 Lesson Notes

NCTM Standards: 1–4, 12

Lesson Resources
• Study Guide Master 8-3
• Practice Master 8-3
• Enrichment Master 8-3
• Group Activity Card 8-3

 Transparency 8-3 contains the 5-Minute Check and a teaching aid for this lesson.

5-Minute Check
(Over Lesson 8-2)

Determine which figures are polygons. If a figure is not a polygon, explain why.

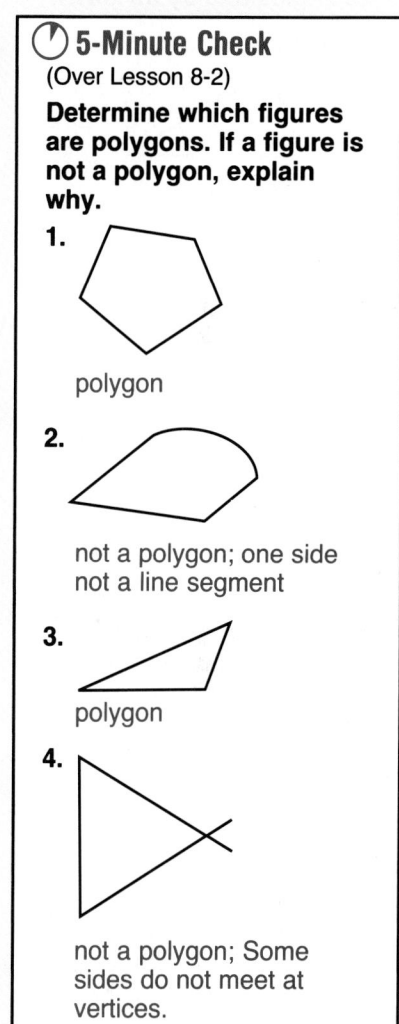

1.

polygon

2.

not a polygon; one side not a line segment

3.

polygon

4.

not a polygon; Some sides do not meet at vertices.

OPTIONS

Gifted and Talented Needs

Have students use centimeter rulers and protractors to determine whether the diagonals of parallelograms are congruent and whether they bisect the angles.

Diagonals of squares are congruent and bisect the angles. Diagonals of rectangles are congruent but do not bisect the angles. Diagonals of parallelograms that are not rectangles are not congruent and do not bisect the angles.

1 FOCUS

Motivating the Lesson

Activity Have students look about the room to find examples of shapes that are triangles or quadrilaterals. Ask them to work with partners to think of ways that these figures could be classified further.

307

2 TEACH

Using Questioning Have students work with partners to formulate questions such as "I am a 3-sided polygon with 3 congruent angles. What figure am I?" Collect students' puzzles and present them to the class.

More Examples

For Examples 1-3

Classify each triangle by its angles and by its sides.

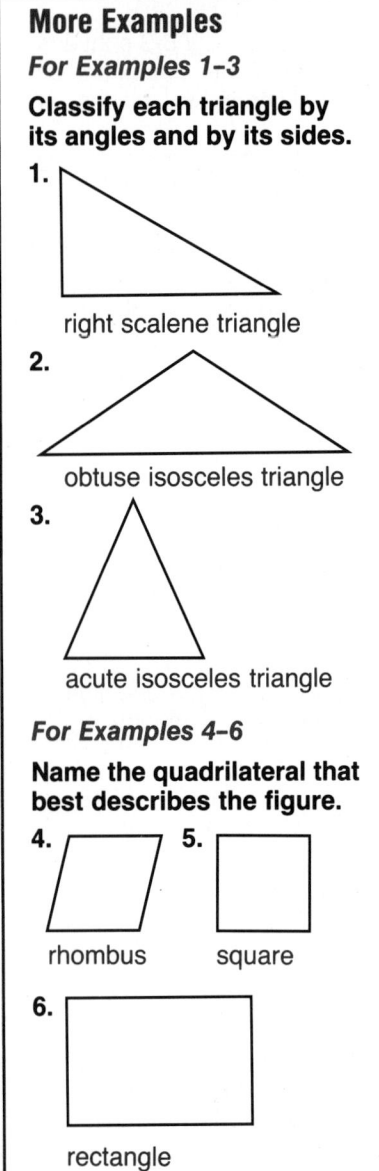

1.

right scalene triangle

2.

obtuse isosceles triangle

3.

acute isosceles triangle

For Examples 4-6

Name the quadrilateral that best describes the figure.

4.

rhombus

5.

square

6.

rectangle

Checking for Understanding

Exercises 1-3 are designed to help you assess students' understanding through reading, writing, speaking, and modeling. You should work through these exercises with your students and then monitor their work on Guided Practice Exercises 4-9.

308

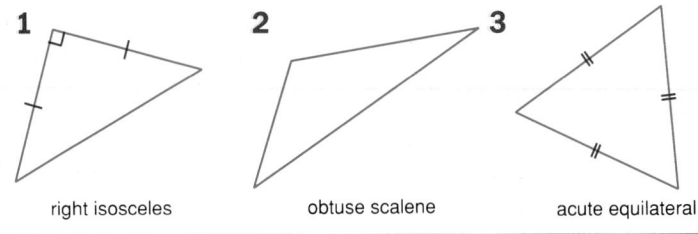

Suppose you are building bleachers at the football field. How will you build them so they will support the weight of all the people who sit on them?

In construction, right triangles are often used to provide extra strength. In bleachers, right triangles would be used in the supports or the frame.

Classify each triangle by its angles and by its sides.

1

right isosceles

2

obtuse scalene

3

acute equilateral

You are already familiar with three types of quadrilaterals. They are squares, rectangles, and parallelograms. Two other types of quadrilaterals are the **rhombus** and the **trapezoid.** The chart below shows how the figures are related and some of their characteristics.

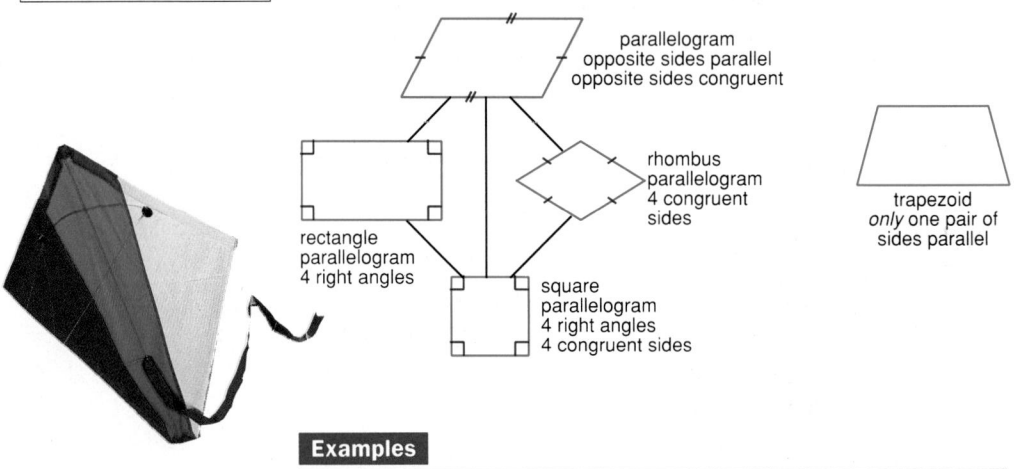

parallelogram
opposite sides parallel
opposite sides congruent

rhombus
parallelogram
4 congruent
sides

trapezoid
only one pair of
sides parallel

rectangle
parallelogram
4 right angles

square
parallelogram
4 right angles
4 congruent sides

Examples

Name every quadrilateral that describes each figure. Then state which name best describes the figure.

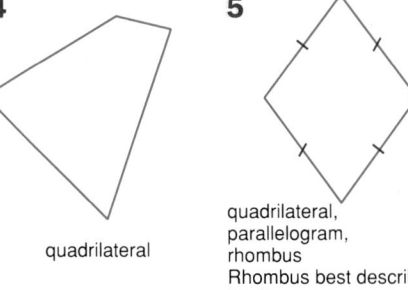

4

quadrilateral

5

quadrilateral,
parallelogram,
rhombus
Rhombus best describes
the figure.

6

quadrilateral,
trapezoid
Trapezoid best describes
the figure.

308   **Chapter 8** Investigations in Geometry

OPTIONS

Reteaching Activity

Using Manipulatives Have students use geoboards to form the polygons introduced and to examine the characteristics by which they are classified. Ask them to make additional examples of each figure and classify each by the measures of its angles and lengths of its sides.

Study Guide Masters, p. 69

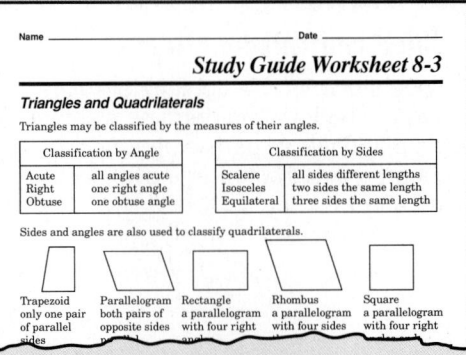

Name _____ Date _____

Study Guide Worksheet 8-3

Triangles and Quadrilaterals

Triangles may be classified by the measures of their angles.

Classification by Angle	
Acute	all angles acute
Right	one right angle
Obtuse	one obtuse angle

Classification by Sides	
Scalene	all sides different lengths
Isosceles	two sides the same length
Equilateral	three sides the same length

Sides and angles are also used to classify quadrilaterals.

| Trapezoid only one pair of parallel sides | Parallelogram both pairs of opposite sides | Rectangle a parallelogram with four right | Rhombus a parallelogram with four sides | Square a parallelogram with four right |

For Exercises 1–3, see Solutions Manual.

Checking for Understanding

Communicating Mathematics

Read and study the lesson to answer each question.

1. **Write** a sentence that tells how a trapezoid is different from a parallelogram.
2. **Tell** why all squares are rectangles but not all rectangles are squares.
3. **Draw** an equilateral parallelogram. Name the figure you drew.

Guided Practice

Classify each triangle by its sides and by its angles.

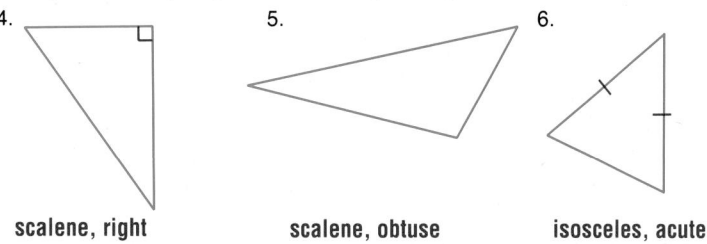

4. scalene, right
5. scalene, obtuse
6. isosceles, acute

Name every quadrilateral that describes each figure. Then underline the name that best describes the figure.

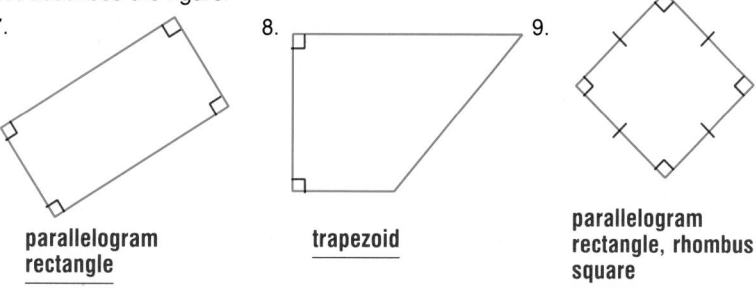

7. parallelogram
   <u>rectangle</u>

8. <u>trapezoid</u>

9. parallelogram
   rectangle, rhombus
   <u>square</u>

Exercises

Independent Practice

Classify each triangle by its sides and by its angles.

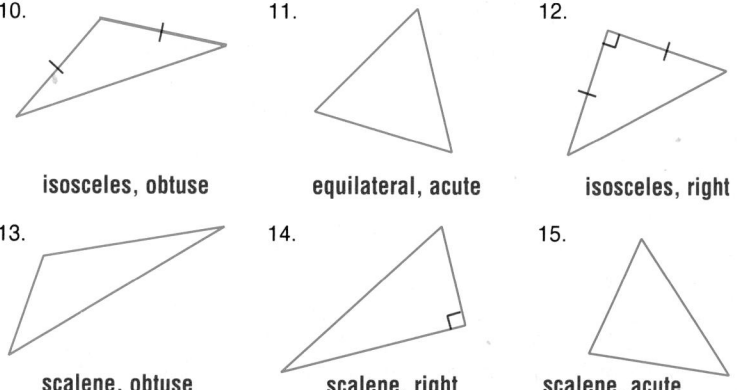

10. isosceles, obtuse
11. equilateral, acute
12. isosceles, right
13. scalene, obtuse
14. scalene, right
15. scalene, acute

Lesson 8-3 Triangles and Quadrilaterals   309

Error Analysis

Watch for students who omit essential information when describing a particular kind of quadrilateral.

Prevent by focusing on how quadrilaterals are related according to the chart on page 308. For example, guide students to see that each particular parallelogram (rectangles, rhombuses, and squares) has every characteristic of a parallelogram as well as special characteristics of its own.

Close

Have students classify triangles and to supply examples. Ask them to explain why a square is a parallelogram and a trapezoid isn't.   square: both pairs of opposite sides are parallel; trapezoid: only one pair of sides is parallel.

3 PRACTICE/APPLY

Assignment Guide
Maximum: 10–29
Minimum: 11–23 odd, 24–29

For **Extra Practice,** see p. 590.

Practice Masters, p. 69

Name _____ Date _____

Practice Worksheet 8-3

Triangles and Quadrilaterals

Classify each triangle by its sides and by its angles.

1. isosceles; obtuse
2. scalene; right
3. scalene; obtuse
4. scalene; obtuse
5. equilateral; acute
6. isosceles; right

Name every quadrilateral that describes each figure. Then state which name best describes the figure.

7. quadrilateral, parallelogram, rhombus, rectangle, square; square
8. quadrilateral
9. quadrilateral, trapezoid; trapezoid
10. quadrilateral, parallelogram, rhombus; rhombus
11. quadrilateral, parallelogram, rectangle; rectangle
12. quadrilateral
13. quadrilateral, parallelogram, rectangle; rectangle
14. quadrilateral, trapezoid; trapezoid
15. quadrilateral, parallelogram; parallelogram
16. Which quadrilaterals have four congruent sides? rhombus and square
17. A figure is a rectangle but not a rhombus. Draw the figure. Sample:

T69
Glencoe Division, Macmillan/McGraw-Hill

Bell Ringer

Tell students to suppose that in a poster, all parallelograms are colored red or green, all triangles are blue, all rectangles are green, and all trapezoids are purple. Ask them what color the squares and rhombuses would be.   squares: green; rhombuses: either red or green

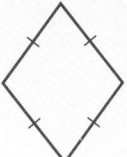
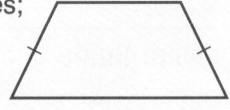
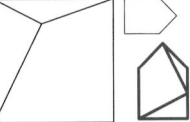
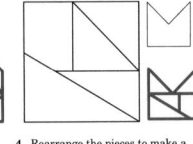
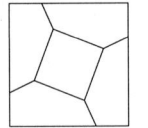
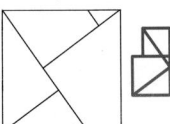
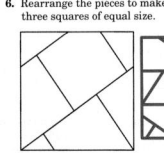
310

Name every quadrilateral that describes each figure. Then underline the name that best describes the figure. **For answers to Exercises 16-21, see margin.**

16.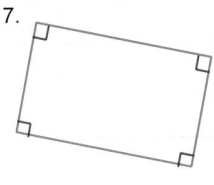
17.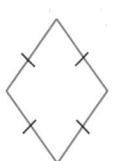
18.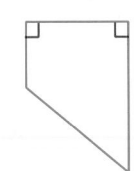

19. 20. 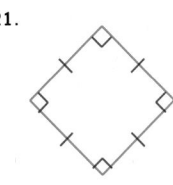 21.

22. Which quadrilaterals can have four right angles? **See margin.**
23. A figure is a rhombus but not a rectangle. Draw the figure. **See margin.**

Mixed Review
24. Evaluate $3(6-2)+2+4$. *(Lesson 1-7)* **18**
25. On his most recent math test, Ricardo scored 84 out of 100 points. Express this fraction in simplest terms. *(Lesson 4-6)* $\frac{21}{25}$
26. Identify the polygon at the right. *(Lesson 8-2)* **octagon**

See margin.

Problem Solving and Applications
27. **Critical Thinking** Can a trapezoid ever have two congruent sides? Draw a figure to verify your answer. What might you call such a trapezoid?

28. **Make a Model** Begin with a large square of paper. **See students' work.**
   a. Fold the paper to make an isosceles right triangle.
   b. Fold the triangle to make a trapezoid.
   c. Fold the triangle to make a rectangle.
   d. Fold the triangle to make a parallelogram.
   e. Fold the triangle to make a square.

29. **Mathematics and Art** Read the following paragraph.

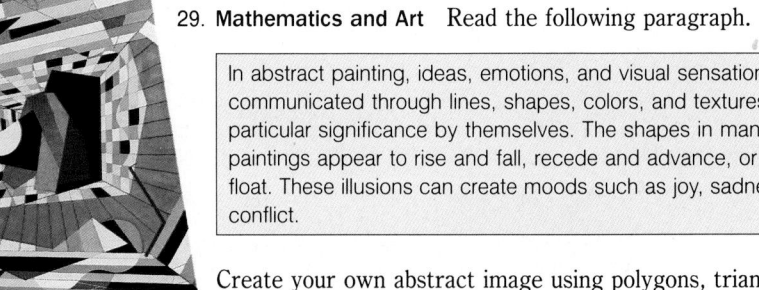

> In abstract painting, ideas, emotions, and visual sensations are communicated through lines, shapes, colors, and textures that have no particular significance by themselves. The shapes in many of these paintings appear to rise and fall, recede and advance, or balance and float. These illusions can create moods such as joy, sadness, peace, and conflict.

Create your own abstract image using polygons, triangles, and quadrilaterals. Share you artwork with the class and discuss what it is trying to communicate. **See students' work.**

310 **Chapter 8** Investigations in Geometry

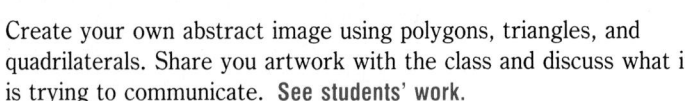

Cooperative Learning

8-4A Bisecting Angles and Segments

A Preview of Lesson 8-4

Objective
Construct angle bisectors and segment bisectors.

Materials
straightedge
compass
protractor

$\overline{XY}$ *is read line segment XY.*

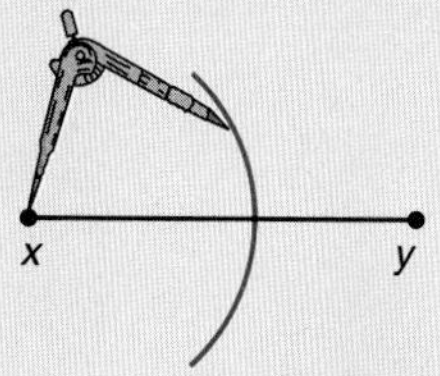

A bicycle has two wheels. A biathlon is an event composed of two sports, cross-country skiing and rifle sharpshooting. A bicolored guinea pig is one that has two colors. The prefix *bi* means two.

To *bisect* an angle or a segment means to separate it into two congruent parts. Bisecting a segment is similar to the constructions you studied in Mathematics Lab 8-1B.

Activity One

Draw a segment and bisect it.

* Use a straightedge to draw a segment. Label the endpoints *X* and *Y*.

* Open your compass to a setting that is longer than half the length of $\overline{XY}$. Place the compass point at *X* and draw a large arc.

* Using the same setting, place the compass point at *Y* and draw a large arc to intersect the first arc twice.

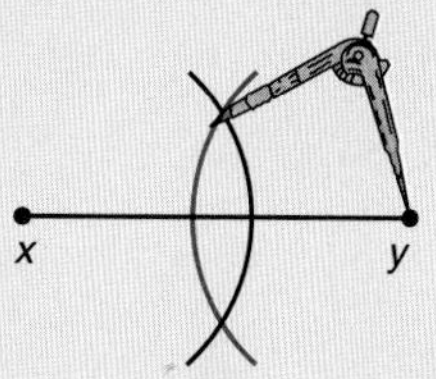

* Use a straightedge to draw a segment connecting the two intersection points. This segment intersects $\overline{XY}$. Label this point *Z*.

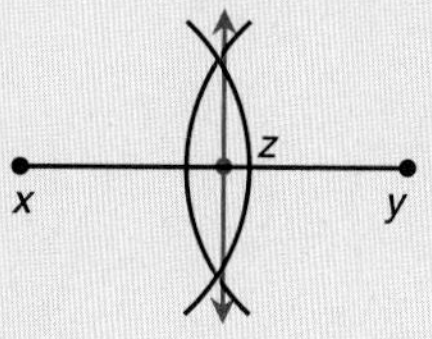

What do you think?

1. Use the compass to measure the distance from *X* to *Z*. Compare this to the distance from *Z* to *Y*. What do you find? **same length**

2. How is $\overline{XZ}$ related to $\overline{ZY}$? $\overline{XZ} \cong \overline{ZY}$

3. How is the segment you drew through *Z* related to $\overline{XY}$? **The segment bisects $\overline{XY}$ at point Z.**

Mathematics Lab 8-4A Bisecting Angles and Segments   **311**

NCTM Standards: 1–4, 12

Management Tips

For Students   Have students work with partners, helping each other interpret directions, and examining each other's constructions.

For the Overhead Projector
Overhead Manipulative Resources provides appropriate materials for teacher or student demonstration of the activities in this Mathematics Lab.

1 FOCUS

Introducing the Lab

Have students review how they used a compass and straightedge previously to make constructions. Challenge them to experiment with these tools to see whether they can figure out a way to use them to bisect angles and segments.

3 PRACTICE/APPLY

Using Critical Thinking Ask students how else they can verify that $\overline{XZ}$ and $\overline{ZY}$ of Activity One are congruent and that m $\angle$ QPW = m $\angle$ WPR. Also, ask them whether the segment they drew through Z is perpendicular to $\overline{XY}$, and if it is, how they know that it is. Use a centimeter ruler; use a protractor; the segment is perpendicular to $\overline{XY}$ because the 2 points where the arcs intersect are equidistant from X and Y.

Close

Ask students to explain how the two methods for bisecting angles and line segments are similar. Sample answer: both use intersecting arcs at the same settings; both create congruent figures half the size of the original figure.

Activity Two

Draw an angle and bisect it.

* Use a straightedge to draw any angle. Label the vertex P. Place the compass at the vertex and draw a large arc to intersect each side. Label the intersection points Q and R.

* Place the compass at Q and draw an arc on the inside of the angle. Using the same setting, place the compass at R and draw an arc to intersect the one you just drew. Label the intersection point W.

* Draw ray PW.

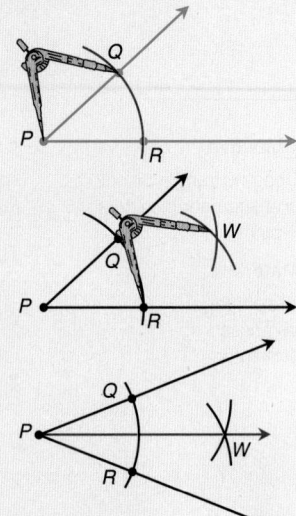

What do you think?

4. Use your protractor to measure $\angle QPW$ and $\angle WPR$. What do you find? **same measure**

5. How is $\angle QPW$ related to $\angle QPR$? $m \angle QPW = \frac{1}{2} m \angle QPR$

Extension 6a–d. See students' work.

6. Suppose you are given an angle and told that its measure is half that of a larger angle. How would you construct the larger angle?

a. Draw any angle and label it $\angle A$.

b. Draw an arc through the sides of the angle into the outside of the angle. Label the intersection points C and T.

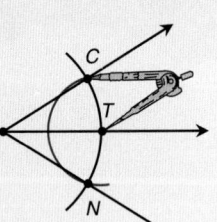

c. Put the compass point at T. Adjust the setting so that it measures the distance from T to C. Without removing your compass, draw an arc to intersect the large arc outside of $\angle A$. Call this point N.

d. Draw $\overrightarrow{AN}$. $\overrightarrow{AT}$ is the bisector of $\angle CAN$.

e. Complete: $m\angle CAT = \underline{\quad?\quad}\ m\angle CAN$. $\frac{1}{2}$

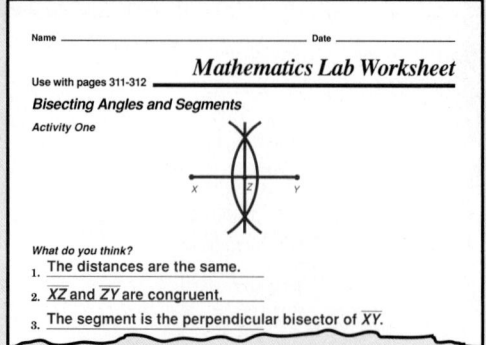

OPTIONS

Lab Manual You may wish to make copies of the blackline master on p. 61 of the *Lab Manual* for students to use as a recording sheet.

Lab Manual, p. 61

Name _____ Date _____

Mathematics Lab Worksheet

Use with pages 311-312

Bisecting Angles and Segments

Activity One

What do you think?

1. The distances are the same.

2. $\overline{XZ}$ and $\overline{ZY}$ are congruent.

3. The segment is the perpendicular bisector of $\overline{XY}$.

8-4 Regular Polygons

Objective
Identify regular polygons.

Words to Learn
regular polygon
equiangular
exterior angle

A colony of honey bees may contain as many as 50,000 to 60,000 bees. The honeycomb, built by the worker bees, is made of cells of wax shaped like hexagons. These cells are used to raise young bees and store the food we know as honey.

These hexagons each have six congruent sides and six congruent angles. Any polygon that has all sides congruent and all angles congruent is called a **regular polygon.** So, the cells in the honeycombs are regular hexagons.

An equilateral triangle is a regular polygon. Its name means *equal sides.* An equilateral triangle can also be called an **equiangular** triangle. This means all its angles have equal measures. These words can be used to define a regular polygon.

Regular Polygon	A polygon that is both equiangular and equilateral is a regular polygon.

Examples

1 Draw a regular pentagon.

2 Draw a regular octagon.

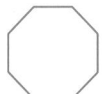

In Mathematics Lab 8-2B, you learned to find the sum of the measures of the angles of a polygon by drawing all the diagonals from one vertex and counting the triangles formed. Then you multiplied that number by 180°. In the figure at the right, there are 3 triangles, so the sum of the measure of the angles of the pentagon is 3 · 180° or 540°.

Lesson 8-4 Regular Polygons **313**

NCTM Standards: 1–5, 9, 12

Lesson Resources
• Study Guide Master 8-4
• Practice Master 8-4
• Enrichment Master 8-4
• Evaluation Master, Quiz A, p. 70
• Technology Master, p. 8
• Group Activity Card 8-4

 Transparency 8-4 contains the 5-Minute Check and a teaching aid for this lesson.

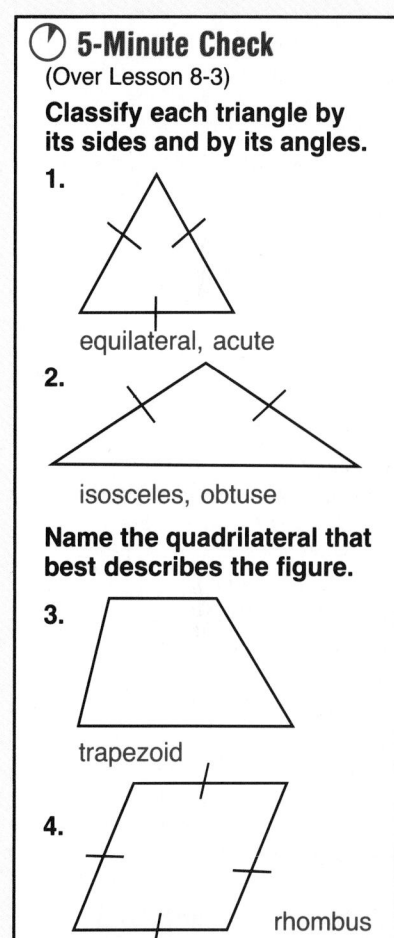

5-Minute Check
(Over Lesson 8-3)
Classify each triangle by its sides and by its angles.
1.
equilateral, acute
2.
isosceles, obtuse
Name the quadrilateral that best describes the figure.
3.
trapezoid
4.
rhombus

1 FOCUS

Motivating the Lesson

Situational Problem Ask students to imagine that they are helping to tile a floor using hexagonal tiles with all congruent sides. Ask them how they could figure out the measure of each angle of a tile.

Classroom Vignette

"Once students have read through Example 2, they can use geoboards to make as many examples of regular polygons as they can. If you have dot paper, have students copy the figures they've made onto dot paper and place them in their journals."

Beatrice Moore-Harris
Author

313

Using the Mini-Lab Have students try both the exterior-angles method and the method that uses triangles to find the measure of each angle of an octagon. Ask them which method they prefer and why.

More Examples

For Example 1

Draw a regular hexagon.

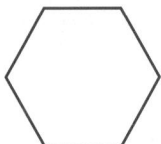

For Example 2

Draw a regular decagon.

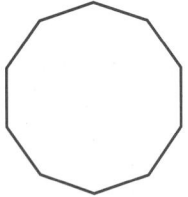

For Example 3

Use an equation to find the measure of each angle of a regular decagon.   144°

Teaching Tip Some students may find it easier to find angle measures of regular polygons by using the method of counting triangles. You may wish to show these students how to multiply by 180 using mental math: multiply by 9, double the answer, then affix a zero to the end.

Checking for Understanding

Exercises 1-4 are designed to help you assess students' understanding through reading, writing, speaking, and modeling. You should work through these exercises with your students and then monitor their work on Guided Practice Exercises 5-8.

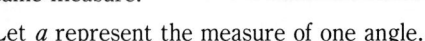

Example 3 *Connection*

Algebra Use an equation to find the measure of each angle of a regular pentagon.

Since the pentagon is regular, all angles have the same measure.

Let *a* represent the measure of one angle.

The sum of the measures of the angles is 540°. So, $5a = 540$.

To solve $5a = 540$, divide each side by 5.

540 ÷ 5 = 108

Each angle of a regular pentagon measures 108°.

If you extend a side of a polygon, a special angle is formed. This angle is called an **exterior angle** of the polygon. If one exterior angle is drawn at each vertex, the sum of the measures of all the exterior angles is always 360°.

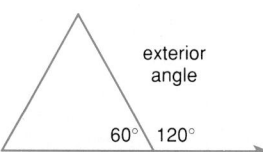

exterior angle

60° 120°

Mini-Lab

Work with a partner.
Materials: straightedge, pencil, paper

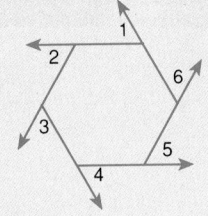

- Sketch a regular hexagon and draw one exterior angle at each vertex.

- Divide 360° by the number of exterior angles you drew. What is the measure of each exterior angle? **60°**

- The exterior angle and the angle of the hexagon form a straight angle. So the sum of the measures of the two angles is 180°. What is the measure of an angle of the regular hexagon? **120°**

Talk About It

a. Draw a regular hexagon and draw the diagonals from one vertex. Use the triangles to figure the measure of each angle of the hexagon. How does this compare with the result in the activity above? **120°; same measure**

b. How would you find the measure of each angle of a regular octagon? **180(n − 2) ÷ n**

OPTIONS

Reteaching Activity

Using Models Make two hexagons—one that is regular and one that isn't. Ask students to examine both figures to note similarities and differences. Have them measure the sides and the angles. Repeat the process with a pentagon. Ask students to form a definition of a regular polygon.

Study Guide Masters, p. 70

Name _____ Date _____

Study Guide Worksheet 8-4

Regular Polygons

A polygon that has all sides the same length and all angles the same measure is called a regular polygon. A regular polygon is equilateral and equiangular. Equilateral means equal sides. Equiangular means equal angles.

If you extend a side of a regular polygon, an exterior angle is formed. The sum of the mesures of the exterior angles is always 360°. You can use exterior angles to find the measures of the angles of a regular polygon.

Example   Sketch a regular pentagon and draw one exterior angle at each vertex.

Divide 360° by the number of exterior angles to find the measure of each exterior angle.
360° ÷ 5 = 72°

Since an exterior angle and an angle of the pentagon form a straight angle, their

exterior angle

For answers to Exercises 1-4, see margin.

Checking for Understanding

Communicating Mathematics

Read and study the lesson to answer each question.

1. **Tell** the difference between equiangular and equilateral.
2. **Draw** a regular quadrilateral.
3. **Draw** a figure that is equilateral, but not equiangular.
4. **Write**, in your own words, how you can use the exterior angles to find the measure of each angle in a regular octagon.

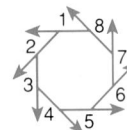

Guided Practice

Tell whether each polygon is a regular polygon. If not, tell why.

5. no, not equiangular

6. yes

7. no, not equilateral or equiangular

8. Find the measure of an angle of a regular quadrilateral. Name this figure. 90°; square

Exercises

Independent Practices

Tell whether each polygon is a regular polygon. If not, tell why.

9. yes

10. no, not equiangular or equilateral

11. yes

14. 30°; 150°

Sketch each figure. Find the measure of an exterior angle. Then find the measure of an angle of the polygon. 12. 51.4°; 128.6° 13. 36°; 144°

12. regular heptagon
13. regular decagon
14. regular dodecagon
15. Which type of quadrilateral is an equilateral quadrilateral, but may not be an equiangular quadrilateral? rhombus
16. An equiangular triangle is also an equilateral triangle. Why doesn't this same relationship always hold true for other polygons? See margin.

Mixed Review

17. **Statistics** The chart at the right shows the number of births per 1,000 people in the United States. Round the birth rate for each year to the nearest whole number. *(Lesson 2-2)*

Year	Birth Rate	
1960	23.7	24
1970	18.4	18
1980	15.9	16
1989	16.2	16

18. **Algebra** Solve $18 = m - 5$. *(Lesson 6-2)* 23

Error Analysis

Watch for students who too quickly assume that angles in a regular hexagon have twice (or half) the measure of angles in an equilateral triangle, and so on.

Prevent by having students faithfully apply one of the two methods presented.

Close

Have students determine the sum of the measures of the angles of a regular 12-sided polygon, and the measure of each angle in the figure. 1,800°; 150°

3 PRACTICE/APPLY

Assignment Guide

Maximum: 9–21

Minimum: 9–20

All: Mid-Chapter Review

For **Extra Practice,** see p. 591.

Alternate Assessment

Speaking Have students define *regular polygon* and explain how to find the degree measure of each of its angles.

Practice Masters, p. 70

Name ______ Date ______

Practice Worksheet 8-4

Regular Polygons

Tell whether each polygon is a regular polygon. If not, tell why.

1. regular
2. not regular: sides not congruent
3. not regular; sides not congruent, angles not congruent
4. not regular: sides not congruent, angles not congruent
5. regular
6. regular

Sketch each figure. Find the measure of an exterior angle. Then find the measure of an angle of the polygon.

7. regular hexagon 60°; 120°
8. regular octagon 45°; 135°
9. regular nonagon 40°; 140°

10. Which type of quadrilateral is an equiangular quadrilateral, but is not an equilateral quadrilateral? rectangle
11. Which type of quadrilateral is regular? square
12. Which type(s) of regular polygon has each exterior angle equal to each interior angle? square
13. Which type(s) of polygon has at least two exterior angles which are obtuse angles? triangle
14. Which type of quadrilateral is equilateral but not equiangular? rhombus

T70

Limited English Proficiency

Introduce the new terms presented in the lesson. Help students distinguish between the everyday meaning of "regular" and its meaning in geometry. Help them differentiate between interior and exterior angles on a diagram.

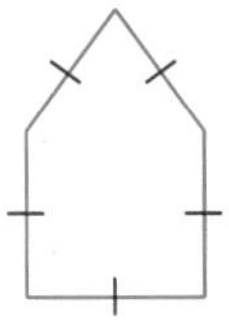

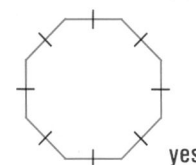

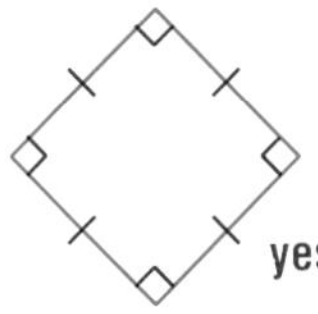

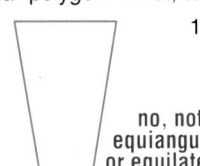

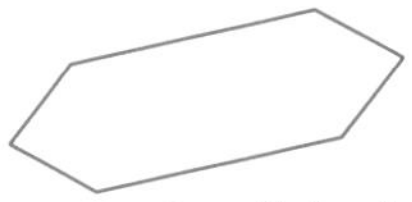

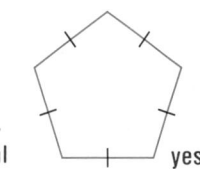

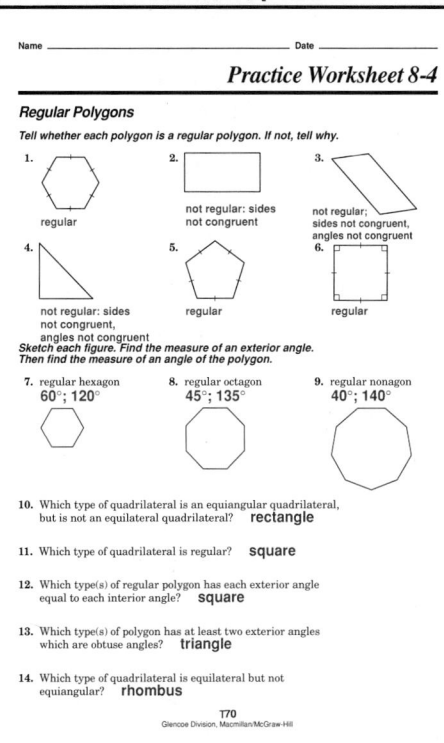

Additional Answers

1. equiangular: All angles have same measure; equilateral: All sides have same measure.
2.
3.
4. Divide 360° by 8 and subtract the result from 180°.
16. Answers will vary.

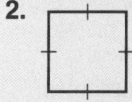

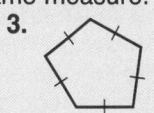

5. Sample answers are given.

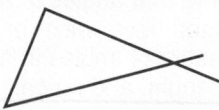

More than two sides meet at a vertex.

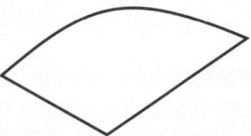

Not all sides are segments.

The figure is not closed.

Enrichment Masters, p. 70

Name _____ Date _____

Enrichment Worksheet 8-4

Compass Creations

The designs on this page can all be constructed using just a compass and straightedge. Follow the steps below to make each design in the right column. Then remove the dotted lines that do not appear in the final constructions. **Check students' constructions**

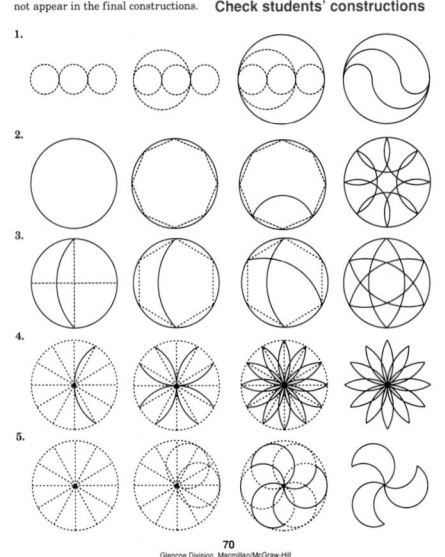

70
Glencoe Division, Macmillan/McGraw-Hill

316

Problem Solving and Applications

19. Critical Thinking Draw a star. **a. decagon** 
a. Which polygon describes the shape of the star?
b. Is the star equilateral? **yes**
c. Is the star equiangular? **no**

20. They could each be a rhombus if boards weren't perpendicular.

20. Carpentry Arturo is taking an industrial technology class. He decides to make a hat rack frame by drilling three holes into six boards and attaching them with bolts. He says that making the rack in this way will form squares. His teacher says, "Not necessarily." What does his teacher mean?

21. Computer Connection You can use Logo software to draw regular polygons. The following program uses the exterior angle to create the regular polygon. In the program, N represents the number of sides in the polygon.

```
TO POLY :N
    REPEAT :N[FD 40 RT 360/:N]
END
```

a. The FD command tells how long each side is. How long are the sides in this program? **40**
b. Use this program to draw four different regular polygons. Then use it to draw a 100-sided polygon. What do you notice? **See students' work; 100-sided polygon looks like a circle.**

22. Portfolio Suggestion Select some of your work from this chapter that shows how you used a calculator or computer. Place it in your portfolio. **See students' work.**

---

8 Assessment: Mid-Chapter Review

Use the figure for Exercises 1–4.

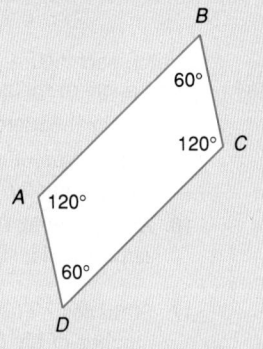

1. Classify ∠A as acute, right, obtuse, or straight. *(Lesson 8-1)* **obtuse**
2. How are ∠A and ∠C related? *(Lesson 8-1)* **congruent**
3. Name every quadrilateral that describes figure *ABCD*. Underline the name that best describes it. *(Lesson 8-3)* **parallelogram**
4. Is quadrilateral *ABCD* a regular quadrilateral? Explain. *(Lesson 8-4)* **no, not equilateral or equiangular**
5. Draw three examples of figures that are not polygons. Tell why they are not. *(Lesson 8-2)* **See margin.**

OPTIONS

Extending the Lesson

Using Logic Have groups of students make up statements to use in an *Always, Sometimes, or Never* quiz. Provide the example "A rhombus is a regular quadrilateral." (Sometimes) Have each group present its quiz to another group.

Cooperative Learning Activity

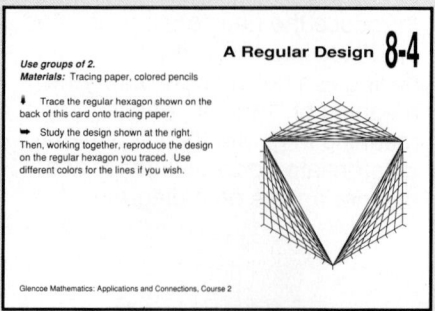

A Regular Design **8-4**

Use groups of 2.
Materials: Tracing paper, colored pencils

Trace the regular hexagon shown on the back of this card onto tracing paper.

Study the design shown at the right. Then, working together, reproduce the design on the regular hexagon you traced. Use different colors for the lines if you wish.

Glencoe Mathematics: Applications and Connections, Course 2

8-4B Constructing Regular Polygons

A Follow-Up of Lesson 8-4

NCTM Standards: 1–4, 12

Objective

Construct a regular triangle and hexagon.

Materials

straightedge
compass
proctractor

In Mathematics Lab 8-1B, you learned to construct a square in the Extension. A square is a regular polygon. Other regular polygons can be constructed using the constructions you already have learned.

Activity One

Construct a regular triangle.

● Draw a line segment and place a point on it. Call this point *P*.

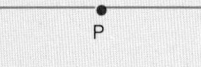

● Put the point of the compass at *P* and draw a large arc to intersect the segment. Label the intersection point *Q*.

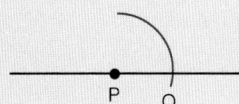

● With the same setting, place the compass at *Q* and draw another arc to intersect the one you just drew. Label this intersection point *R*.

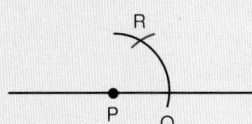

● Draw $\overline{PR}$ and $\overline{QR}$.

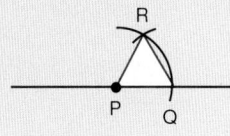

What do you think?

1. Think about the settings you used in this construction. Why do you think *ΔPQR* is regular? **You are using same setting for each side.**

2. Use your protractor to measure the angles in *ΔPQR*. You may have to extend the sides. What do you find? Is the triangle regular?
Each angle measures 60°; yes.

Activity Two

Construct a regular hexagon.
● Use your compass to draw a circle. Put a point on the circle.

Management Tips

For Students Have students work with partners, each helping the other, as necessary, to understand and complete the constructions.

For the Overhead Projector *Overhead Manipulative Resources* provides appropriate materials for teacher or student demonstration of the activities in this Mathematics Lab.

1 FOCUS

Introducing the Lab

Before presenting the lesson, and without providing any new information, ask students to use the constructions and concepts they know to make a regular polygon. Have them share their methods and results.

Mathematics Lab 8-4B Constructing Regular Polygons **317**

318

2 TEACH

Using Connections Ask students to use the constructions they already know to draw a square inside a circle. Sample answer: draw a diameter, bisect it with a perpendicular segment (a diameter), connect the four points in order along the circumference.

3 PRACTICE/APPLY

Using Critical Thinking Ask students why the method for constructing a regular hexagon works. Ask them whether they think the same method could be used to construct a regular pentagon. Sample answer: Draw six radii to the intersection points. Six equilateral triangles are formed. Thus, each side of the regular hexagon is congruent to a radius of the circle.

Close

Have students explain how they would construct a 24-sided regular polygon. Sample answer: use a 12-sided regular polygon, bisect each side, connect the points along the circumference.

- With the same setting, place the compass on that point. Draw a small arc that intersects the circle.

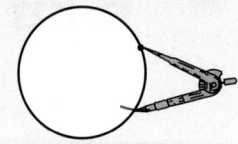

- Place the compass on the point where the arc intersects the circle. Draw another small arc to intersect the circle.

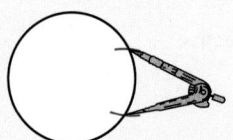

- Continue the process until you come back to the first point. Use the straightedge to connect the intersection points in order as shown.

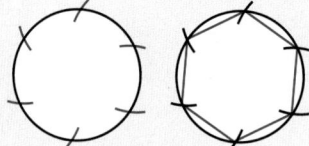

What do you think?

3. When you finished drawing all the arcs, you may have had difficulty meeting the original point. Why do you think that happened? **construction error**
4. Use your protractor to measure the angles of your hexagon. You may have to extend the sides. What do you find? Is the hexagon regular? **Each angle measures 120°; yes.**

Extension

5. You can construct a regular dodecagon by starting with the construction for a regular hexagon.
    a. After drawing the arcs for the hexagon, draw one of the sides and bisect it.
    b. Using the setting you used to draw the circle, place the compass where the bisector meets the circle. Draw six arcs as you did before with the hexagon.
    c. Draw the 12 sides by connecting the intersection points in order.

6. You can also construct a regular octagon using a circle.
    a. Draw a circle and fold it in half.
    b. Without opening, fold it in half again and then once more.
    c. Open the circle up and connect the points where the folds intersect the circle.

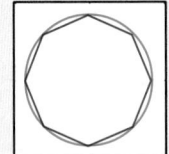

318   **Chapter 8** Investigations in Geometry

OPTIONS

Lab Manual You may wish to make copies of the blackline master on p. 62 of the *Lab Manual* for students to use as a recording sheet.

Lab Manual, p. 62

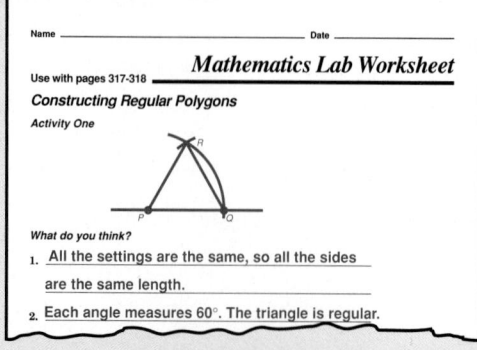

Name _____ Date _____

Mathematics Lab Worksheet

Use with pages 317-318

Constructing Regular Polygons

Activity One

What do you think?

1. All the settings are the same, so all the sides are the same length.

2. Each angle measures 60°. The triangle is regular.

8-5 Use Logical Reasoning

Objective
Solve problems by using logical reasoning.

Jason, Conrad, and Alton play safety, running back, and quarterback on a football team, but not necessarily in that order. Jason and the quarterback drove Alton to practice on Saturday. Jason does not play safety. Who is the safety?

Explore   What do you know?
Jason and the quarterback drove Alton to practice on Saturday. Jason does not play safety.

You need to find out who plays safety.

Plan   Make a chart to organize the information logically. Start with the information you already know. Then reread the problem, searching for clues. Write *no* in the chart when you use a fact to eliminate a possibility.

Solve   Begin by completing the chart with information you already know. You know that Jason does not play safety, so put a *no* in the appropriate column and row.

	Safety	Running Back	Quarterback
Jason	no		
Conrad			
Alton			

Now reread the problem searching for clues. Jason and the quarterback drove Alton to practice on Saturday. This means that neither Jason nor Alton can be the quarterback. So Conrad must be the quarterback.

	Safety	Running Back	Quarterback
Jason	no		
Conrad	no	no	yes
Alton			

Now you know that Alton is the safety.

	Safety	Running Back	Quarterback
Jason	no		
Conrad	no	no	yes
Alton	yes		

Lesson 8-5 Problem-Solving Strategy: Use Logical Reasoning   **319**

OPTIONS

Reteaching Activity

Using Problem Solving   Try a simpler problem first that students can solve by making and completing a chart. Write this one on the chalkboard: *Andy and Carlos entered a race. One of them finished first and the other second. Andy did not finish first. Who did?*   Carlos

Study Guide Masters, p. 71

Name _____   Date _____

Study Guide Worksheet 8-5

Problem-Solving Strategy: Use Logical Reasoning

Pam, Bob, and Chi each have a collection. One collects stamps, one coins, and the other pins. The coin collector showed Bob and Pam his collection last Saturday. Pam does not collect pins. Who collects stamps?

Explore   You know that the coin collector showed Bob and Pam his collection and that Pam does not collect pins. You want to find who collects stamps.

Plan   Make a chart to organize the information logically. Use what you know. Write *yes* when you know what a person collects and *no* when you eliminate a possibility.

Solve   You know the coin collector showed Pam and Bob his collection, so Pam and Bob are not the coin collectors. Write *no* in Pam's row and in Bob's row under the coin column.

You know that Pam does not collect pins,

8-5 Lesson Notes

NCTM Standards: 1–5, 7, 12

Lesson Resources
• Study Guide Master 8-5
• Practice Master 8-5
• Enrichment Master 8-5
• Multicultural Activity, p. 8
• Group Activity Card 8-5

Transparency 8-5 contains the 5-Minute Check and a teaching aid for this lesson.

5-Minute Check
(Over Lesson 8-4)
Draw a regular octagon. Find the measure of one of its exterior angles, and one of its angles.   45°; 135°

1 FOCUS

Motivating the Lesson

Questioning   Ask students why the quarterback cannot be Jason or Alton.

Practice Masters, p. 71

Name _____   Date _____

Practice Worksheet 8-5

Problem-Solving Strategy: Use Logical Reasoning

Solve. Use the logical reasoning strategy.

1. Connie, Kristine, and Roberta are the pitcher, catcher, and shortstop for a softball team, but not necessarily in that order. Kristine is not the catcher. If Kristine and Roberta share a locker with the shortstop, who is the pitcher?   **Kristine**

2. Dan, Nan, and Fran have lockers next to each other. Nan rides the bus with the person whose locker is at the right. Dan's locker is not next to Nan's locker. Who has the locker at the left?   **Nan**

Solve. Use any strategy.

3. Joan used $8\frac{3}{4}$ yards of fabric to make two dresses. One dress required $1\frac{1}{2}$ yards of fabric more than the other dress. How much fabric was used for each dress?   **$3\frac{5}{8}$ yd; $5\frac{1}{8}$ yd**

4. During May, Chris deposited $82.04, $57.56, and $16.00 in his savings account to give him a balance of $524.09. What was the previous balance?   **$368.49**

5. State the pattern in the sequence below.
2,123 2,121 2,118 2,114, ...
Then give the next three terms.   **Subtract 2, subtract 3, subtract 4, ...**
2,109, 2,103, 2,096

6. American football is played on a rectangular field which is 160 feet by 120 yards (including the end zones). What is a reasonable estimate of the area of the playing field in square feet?   **58,000 ft²**

7. Coach Miller's soccer team had the win-lose record shown in the table below.

Year	Wins	Losses	Year	Wins	Losses
1982	15	4	1987	12	7
1883	10	9	1988	8	11
1984	12	7	1989	15	4
1985	10	9	1990	18	1
1986	14	5	1991	10	9

a. What was the average number of wins in a season?
b. What was the median number of wins?   **12.4; 12**
c. What was the mode of the losses?   **9**

T71
Glencoe Division, Macmillan/McGraw-Hill

319

2 TEACH

More Examples

Mrs. Wilson gave each of her three children a chore to do. Each child did as he or she was told. She told one to wash the dishes, one to go to the store, and one to take out the garbage. Jackie did not wash the dishes. Al did not take out the garbage. Corey did not go to the store or take out the garbage. What chore did each child do? **Jackie: garbage; Al: store; Corey: dishes**

Close

Have students write a problem that can be solved by using the strategy of logical reasoning.

3 PRACTICE/APPLY

Assignment Guide
Maximum: 6–8
Minimum: 6–8

Enrichment Masters, p. 71

Name _____ Date _____

Enrichment Worksheet 8-5

The Four-Colored Triangles

A set of 24 different puzzle pieces can be made from the three-part equilateral triangles shown in Exercise 1. Each third of a triangle is colored with one of four different colors.

1. Finish shading the triangles in the second, third, and fourth rows to show all 24 puzzle pieces. The four "colors" used are white, black, striped, and dotted.

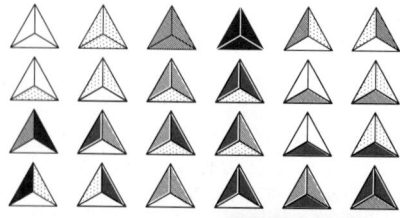

2. Use all 24 pieces to complete this puzzle. When finished, the figure will be a regular hexagon. The colors on adjacent sides of pieces must be the same. And, the border of the design is all black.

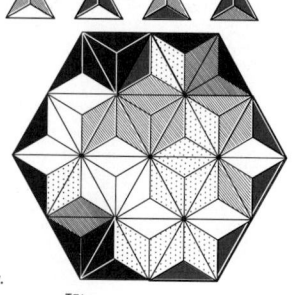

3. There are many different ways to use the 24 pieces to make a regular hexagon. Find two other solutions for this puzzle.
Answers will vary.

T71
Glencoe Division, Macmillan/McGraw-Hill

320

Examine You can also arrive at the answer using this reasoning: Jason and Alton are not the quarterback, so Conrad must be the quarterback. Since Jason is not the safety, then Alton must be the safety.

Checking for Understanding

Communicating Mathematics
1. Tell how you use the logical reasoning strategy to solve problems. **See students' work.**
2. Who is the running back? **Jason**

Guided Practice Solve. Use logical reasoning.

3. Regular polygons *Q, R,* and *S* are a hexagon, a square, and an octagon but not necessarily in that order. Polygon *Q* and *S* have the same number of letters in their names. Each angle of polygon *S* measures less than 135°. Classify the polygons. **Q, octagon; R, square; S, hexagon**

4. Use the pattern to draw the next two figures in the sequence. **See Solutions Manual.**

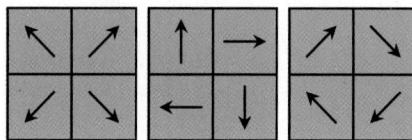

5. Jim Banker, Susan Sales, and Jessica Clerk are a banker, salesperson, and a clerk. Their occupations do not match their last names. Susan Sales is the clerk's cousin. Who is the banker? **Susan Sales**

Exercises

Independent Practice Solve. Use any strategy.

6. Is the average of 85.6, 112.5, 90.3, 101.7, 42.2, and 66.7 about 83 or 8.3? **about 83**

7. During their first possession of the ball, the Bayfield Buffalos gained 12 yards, gained 10 yards, lost 5 yards and then lost 7 yards. Was their net gain about 2 yards or 10 yards? **about 10 yards**

8. Ken, Carly, Francoise, and Kirby each have favorite sports: bowling, basketball, softball, and football. Ken's cousin's favorite sport is basketball. Francoise and Kirby do not like football. Carly's favorite sport is softball. Kirby no longer likes bowling. Which sport is Ken's favorite? **football**

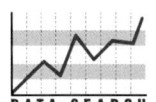
DATA SEARCH

9. **Data Search** Refer to page 650. Draw the first four figures in a series of hexagonal numbers. Name the numbers in the series. Then find the next number in the series. **See students' figures; 1, 6, 15, 28; 45**

Strategies
• • • • • • • • •
Look for a pattern.
Solve a simpler problem.
Act it out.
Guess and check.
Draw a diagram.
Make a chart.
Work backward.

OPTIONS

Extending the Lesson

Using Logic Mr. Wang awoke to find the gerbil loose in the den. He questioned his four children to find out who left the cage open. Ed said that Tom left it open. Tom said Lian did it. Chen said, "I didn't do it." Lian said that Tom was lying. Only one child is telling the truth. Who left the door open? **Chen**

Cooperative Learning Activity

Number of players: 4
Materials: Index cards

Get a Clue 8-5

◆ Copy onto cards the names, locations, and types of clothing shown on the back of this card, one per card. For each category, shuffle the cards and then remove one card. Place these three cards aside, face down. Shuffle the remaining cards together and divide them evenly.

➡ You will use your cards and the answers other group members give to determine what will be on the cover of the next J. Tweedies catalog. The three cards that remain face down tell what *will* be on the cover, so the cards that were selected tell what *won't* be.

One player asks the player to his or her left a question in this form: "Is it (model) on the (location) wearing the (clothing type)?" If the player being asked has a card that will eliminate one of these possibilities, he or she must show it to the player asking the question. Continue in the same way, taking turns asking questions and writing "yes" and "no" in the chart to confirm or eliminate possibilities. If you think you know the cover, you may guess and look at the cards on your turn. If you are wrong, you may not guess again, but you may continue to be asked questions by the other players.

Glencoe Mathematics: Applications and Connections, Course 2

8-6 Tessellations

Objective

Determine which regular figures can be used to form a tessellation.

Words to Learn

tiling
tessellation

Mosaic is the art of covering a surface with small squares, triangles, or other regular shapes, called *tesserae*. In Mexico, one of the most stunning mosaics is the outside structure of the Central Library of the National Autonomous University of Mexico. It was designed by Juan O'Gorman and is composed of over 7.5 million pieces.

Covering a surface with regular figures is called **tiling**. The result of tiling is called a **tessellation**. A tessellation can be made of one kind of polygon or several kinds of polygons.

Mini-Lab

Work with a partner.
Materials: tracing paper

• Trace the equilateral triangle.

• Turn your paper and trace the triangle again so that the two triangles share a common side.

• Continue the process until you notice a pattern.

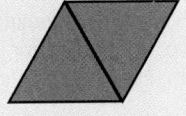 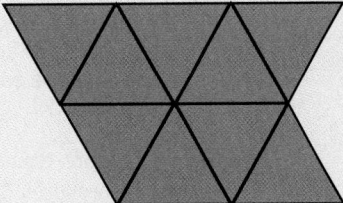

Talk About It

a. Would you be able to completely cover a large surface with equilateral triangles? Explain your answer. **yes**

b. Find a place where the vertex of several triangles meet. What is the sum of the measures of the angles whose vertices are at this point? **360°**

Lesson 8-6 Tessellations   321

NCTM Standards: 1–5, 7–9, 12

Lesson Resources
• Study Guide Master 8-6
• Practice Master 8-6
• Enrichment Master 8-6
• Group Activity Card 8-6

Transparency 8-6 contains the 5-Minute Check and a teaching aid for this lesson.

⏱ 5-Minute Check
(Over Lesson 8-5)

Solve.

1. Juan is shorter than Adam and Denise is taller than Adam. Is Denise taller or shorter than Juan?   taller

2. Alan, Becky, Claudia, and Davis were standing in line to buy tickets. Alan was in front of Becky and neither was first in line. Claudia was second. Davis was not last. In what order were the four students standing in line? Davis, Claudia, Alan, Becky

1 FOCUS

Motivating the Lesson

Activity   Provide students with graph paper. Ask them to choose a shape and to try to completely cover the paper by drawing the shape repeatedly.

2 TEACH

Using the Mini-Lab   Encourage students to experiment to see whether they can tessellate a surface using any triangle or quadrilateral. Ask them what they discover.   All triangles and quadrilaterals tessellate.

OPTIONS

Reteaching Activity

Using Connections   As necessary, review methods for finding the measures of each angle of a regular polygon. When students use a combination of polygons to tessellate a surface, suggest that they color the shapes differently to see the pattern more clearly.

Study Guide Masters, p. 72

Name _____   Date _____

Study Guide Worksheet 8-6

Tessellations

A tessellation, or tiling, is an arrangement of polygons that completely covers a plane surface without leaving gaps or overlapping.

The sum of the angle measures at any vertex of a tessellation is 360°. To determine whether a regular polygon tessellates, divide 360 by the measure of any angle of the polygon. If the quotient is a whole number, the polygon tessellates.

Examples   A hexagon:

The measure of an angle is 120°. 360 ÷ 120 = 3. A hexagon can be used to form a tessellation.

A pentagon:

The measure of an angle is 108°. 360 ÷ 108 = 3.3. A pentagon cannot be used to form a tessellation.

To determine how a combination of regular polygons tessellates,

Checking for Understanding

Exercises 1-2 are designed to help you assess students' understanding through reading, writing, speaking, and modeling. You should work through these exercises with your students and then monitor their work on Guided Practice Exercises 3-5.

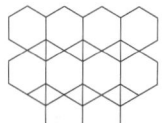 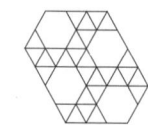
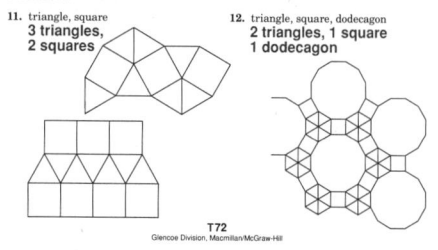
322

In the Mini-Lab, you found that where triangles meet the sum of the angle measures is 360°. The sum of the angle measures at the vertex of any tessellation must be 360°.

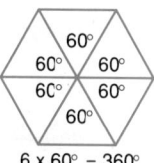
6 x 60° = 360°

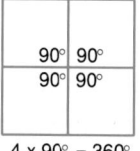
4 x 90° = 360°

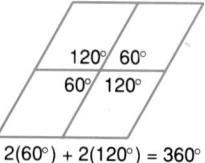
2(60°) + 2(120°) = 360°

Example 1 Connection

Algebra The sum of the measures of the angles of an octagon is 1,080°. Can you tessellate a regular octagon by itself?

Each angle of a regular octagon has a measure of $1,080° ÷ 8$ or 135°. To find out if a regular octagon tessellates, solve $135n = 360$, where n is the number of angles at a vertex.

To solve $135n = 360$, divide each side by 135.

360 $\boxed{÷}$ 135 $\boxed{=}$ 2.6666667

The solution is not a whole number. So we cannot tessellate a regular octagon by itself.

As you saw in Example 1, not all regular polygons can tessellate by themselves. However, when you use a combination of polygons to form a tessellation, there is often more than one pattern possible.

Example 2 Problem Solving

Design Mr. Concepción bought hexagonal stones and triangular stones to arrange in a tessellation for a patio. The sides of the stones have the same length. How many of each stone does he need at each vertex?

More than one answer is possible. Each angle of a regular hexagon measures 120° and each angle of an equilateral triangle measures 60°.

Try 1 hexagon.

total at _ one angle of
vertex   hexagon
360° −   120°   = 240°
240° = ___?___ triangles
240° = 4 triangles

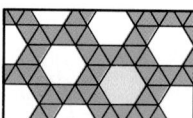
hexagon and 4 triangles at each vertex

322   **Chapter 8** Investigations in Geometry

OPTIONS

Multicultural Education

The word *tessellation* comes from *tesselae*, the Latin word for *tile*. Romans used tessellations to make floor mosaics two thousand years ago. In later centuries, tiled floors became widespread in Arabian cultures, a practice explained by the Islamic religion's prohibition of decorations based on the human form.

Try 2 hexagons.

total at _ two angles
vertex   of hexagon

$360° - 2(120°) = 120°$
$120° = \underline{\quad?\quad}$ triangles
$120° = 2$ triangles

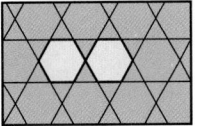
2 hexagons and 2 triangles
at each vertex

Checking for Understanding

Communicating Mathematics

Read and study the lesson to answer each question.

1. **Tell** when a regular polygon can be used by itself to make a tessellation.

2. **Show** how you can make a tessellation out of squares. **See margin.**

Guided Practice

Assume each polygon is regular. Determine if it can be used by itself to make a tessellation.

1. when sum of angle measures at vertex is 360°

3. hexagon **yes**   4. pentagon **no**   5. decagon **no**

Exercises

Independent Practice

Assume each polygon is regular. Determine if it can be used by itself to make a tessellation.

For sketches to Exercises 10-11, see Solutions Manual.

6. heptagon **no**   7. nonagon **no**   8. dodecagon **no**

9. Sketch a tessellation made with equilateral triangles and squares. **See Solutions Manual.**

The following regular polygons tessellate. Determine how many of each you need at each vertex and sketch the tessellation.

10. triangle, dodecagon **1 triangle, 2 dodecagons**

11. square, octagon **1 square, 2 octagons**

12. **Statistics** Look at the graph to answer these questions.
(Lesson 3-1)

a. What is the estimated increase in rollerblade sales from 1989 to 1990? **$110 million**

b. Which year has the greatest increase in sales? **1991**

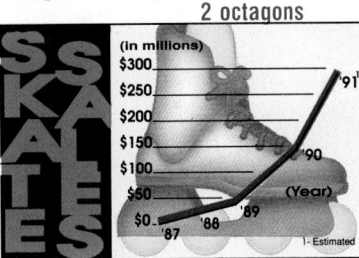

Mixed Review

13. no, not equilateral or equiangular

13. Tell whether the polygon at the right is a regular polygon. If not, tell why.
(Lesson 8-4)

Problem Solving and Applications

14. **Critical Thinking** Can you find a non-regular triangle that tessellates? If so, sketch the tessellation. **See margin.**

15. **Design** Kitchen Boutique has its artists creating tile trivets for their stores. They have square, hexagonal, and dodecagonal tiles. Draw a tessellation they could use in their designs. **One of each; see Solutions Manual for drawing.**

Lesson 8-6 Tessellations   323

Close

Have students explain how to determine whether a regular polygon can be used by itself or in combination with another to tessellate a surface. The sum of the angle measures at the vertex must be 360°.

3 PRACTICE/APPLY

Assignment Guide
Maximum: 6–15
Minimum: 6–15

Alternate Assessment

Modeling Have students create a design using regular polygons to tessellate a designated region.

Additional Answers

2.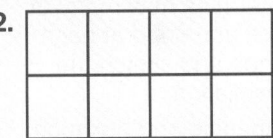

14.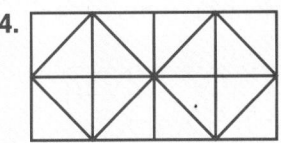

Enrichment Masters, p. 72

Name _____   Date _____

Enrichment Worksheet 8-6

Tessellated Patterns for Solid Shapes

Tessellations made from equilateral triangles can be used to build three-dimensional shapes. In Exercise 1, you should get a shape like the one shown at the right. It is called a pyramid.

Copy each pattern. Crease the pattern along the lines. Then follow the directions for folding the pattern. Use tape to secure the folded parts. When you have finished each model, describe it in words.

1. Fold 5 over 1.
   Repeat, in this order:
   fold 6 over 7,
   fold 2 over 6.
   pyramid with four triangular faces

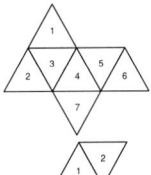

2. Cut between 4 and 5. Then fold 5 over 3.
   Repeat, in this order:
   fold 6 over 5,
   fold 7 over 12, and
   fold 2 over 9.
   double pyramid with six triangular faces

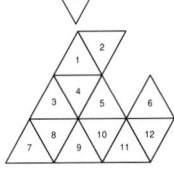

3. Cut between 1 and 2 and between 14 and 15. Then fold 15 over 14.
   Repeat, in this order:
   fold 1 over 2,
   fold 4 over 3,
   fold 11 over 1,
   fold 16 over 5, and
   fold 12 over 13.
   pentagonal shape with ten triangular faces

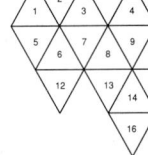

T72
Glencoe Division, Macmillan/McGraw-Hill

Lesson Resources
- Study Guide Master 8-7
- Practice Master 8-7
- Enrichment Master 8-7
- Group Activity Card 8-7

 Transparency 8-7 contains the 5-Minute Check and a teaching aid for this lesson.

⏱ 5-Minute Check
(Over Lesson 8-6)

1. Determine whether a regular hexagon can be used by itself to tessellate.   yes

2. The following regular polygons tessellate. Determine how many of each you need at each vertex and sketch the tessellation.

   triangle and hexagon

   4 triangles, 1 hexagon

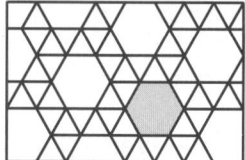

1 FOCUS

Motivating the Lesson

Activity   Prior to introducing the lesson in the text, obtain a book of Escher prints to share with the class. Have students suggest any connections between Escher's work and tessellations. Then have them try their hand at creating Escher-like drawings.

2 TEACH

Using Graph Paper   Have students use graph paper to introduce the concept of translations. Have them practice creating translation images by sliding simple figures, such as triangles, horizontally, vertically, or diagonally into a new position.

8-7 Translations

Objective
Create Escher-like drawings by using translations.

Words to Learn
translation

Maurits Cornelis Escher (1898–1972), a Dutch artist, was impressed by the Moorish mosaics he saw while traveling through southern Spain. He was inspired to create recognizable figures to fill space like the pieces of stone that filled the surface of the mosaic. His figures were often in the shapes of birds, fish, or reptiles.

© M.C. Escher/Cordon Art—Baarn—Holland
Collection Haags Gemeentemuseum—The Hague

Many of Escher's sketches began as tessellations of polygons. You can make Escher-like drawings by making changes in the polygons of the tessellation. One way to do this is by using a **translation.**

A translation is a slide. The square below has the left side changed. To make sure the pieces, or pattern units, will still tessellate, we are going to slide or translate that change to the opposite side and copy it.

 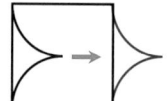 

Now change all the squares in a tessellation the same way. The tessellation takes on Escher-like qualities when you use different colors.

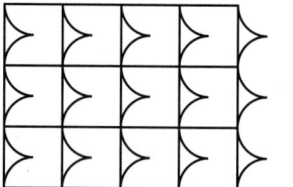 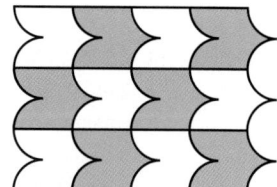

OPTIONS

Reteaching Activity

Using Cooperative Groups   Have students work in groups of four to create an Escher-like design using more than one pattern of figures. Partners within the group are responsible for one pattern and for helping other pairs as necessary. Display the completed designs.

Study Guide Masters, p. 73

Name _____   Date _____

Study Guide Worksheet 8-7

Art Connection: Translations

You can make changes in the polygons that tessellate to create new pattern units that will tessellate. One way to do this is by using a translation, or a slide.

Example   Change the square by sliding a piece from the left to the right to make a new pattern piece.

Then change all the squares in a tessellation the same way.

Teaching Tip   Have students
work with partners, using pencil
and different sizes of graph paper.

Example 1

Draw a tessellation using the
change shown at the right.

First complete the
pattern unit.

*A cardboard pattern unit
can help in creating the
tessellation.*

Translate the change to all squares in the tessellation. Use color to
complete the effect.

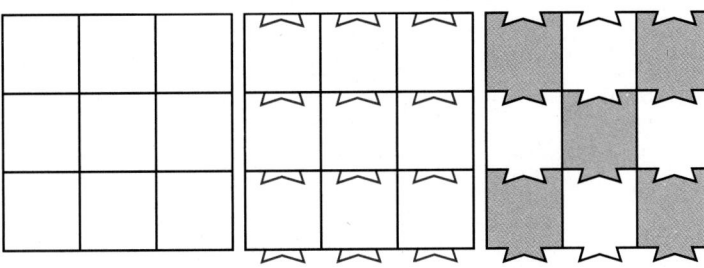

You can make more complex tessellations by doing two translations.

Example 2

Draw a tessellation using both
changes shown at the right.

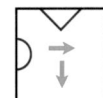

First complete the
pattern unit.

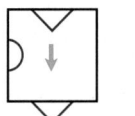 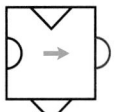 

Then complete the tessellation.

Lesson 8-7 Art Connection: Translations   **325**

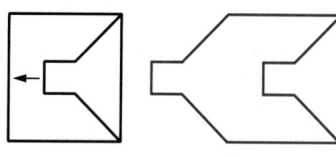
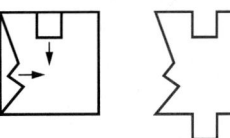
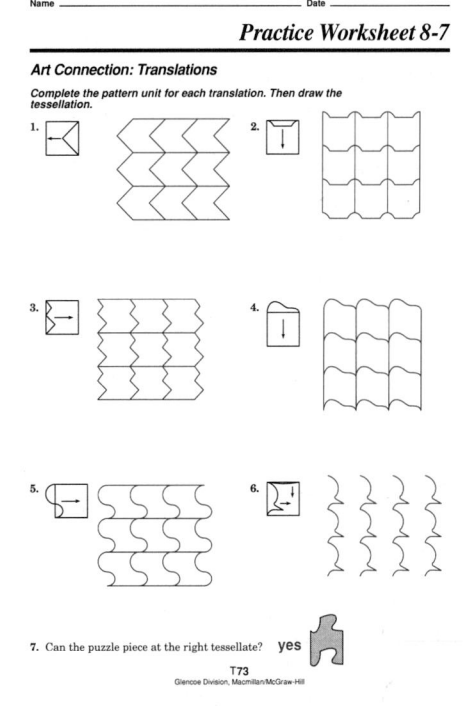
Meeting Needs of Middle School Students

Some students may wonder why
they are learning about tessellations
and translations. Discuss the
historical significance of tessellations
in Native American, Muslim, and
other cultures, showing examples of
artwork if possible. Then guide
students to see how many geometric
concepts are involved with the
tessellation of translated figures.

For answers to Exercises 1–2, see Solutions Manual.
Checking for Understanding

Communicating Mathematics

Read and study the lesson to answer each question.

1. **Tell** how a translation can be used to form an Escher-like drawing.
2. **Write** a definition of translation.

For answers to Exercises 3–5, see Solutions Manual.

Guided Practice

Complete the pattern unit for each translation. Then draw the tessellation.

3. 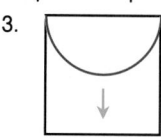 4. 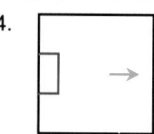 5.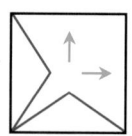

Exercises

For answers to Exercises 6–8, see Solutions Manual.

Independent Practice

Complete the pattern unit for each translation. Then draw the tessellation.

6.  7. 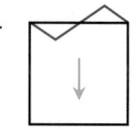 8.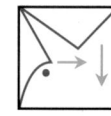

9. Can the puzzle piece at the right tessellate? Explain. **No; the patterns on the top and bottom will not tessellate.**

Mixed Review

10. Divide $4\frac{3}{8}$ by $2\frac{1}{3}$. *(Lesson 5-10)* $1\frac{7}{8}$

11. **Art** Alex wishes to construct a tessellation for a wall-hanging made only from decagons. Is this possible? *(Lesson 8-6)* **no**

Problem Solving and Applications

12. **Critical Thinking** The Escher work below is sometimes called *Pegasus*. It was created from a tessellation of squares. Study the print and locate the changes and the position of the squares. **See students' work.**

13. **Critical Thinking** Is it possible to make a tessellation with translations by using equilateral triangles? Explain your answer and make a drawing. **No; no opposite side; see students' work.**

14. **Design** The Art Club is making designs for wrapping paper. They want to use a tessellation of parallelograms as their basis. Create an Escher-like drawing using tessellated parallelograms. **See students' work.**

15. **Data Search** Refer to pages 294 and 295. How much longer is the Lincoln Tunnel than the Liberty Tubes? **1.3 miles**

16. **Portfolio Suggestion** Select an item from this chapter that shows your creativity and place it in your portfolio. **See students' work.**

© M.C. Escher/Cordon Art—Baarn—Holland
Collection Haags Gemeentemuseum—The Hague

326 **Chapter 8** Investigations in Geometry

8-8 **Reflections**

Objective

Create Escher-like drawings by using reflections.

Words to Learn

line symmetry
line of symmetry
reflection

Have you ever made a valentine heart by folding a piece of paper and cutting half a heart? When you unfolded the paper, there was the heart with both sides evenly matched.

Figures that match exactly when folded in half have **line symmetry.** The figures below have line symmetry. Some figures can be folded in more than one way to show symmetry. Each fold line is called a **line of symmetry.**

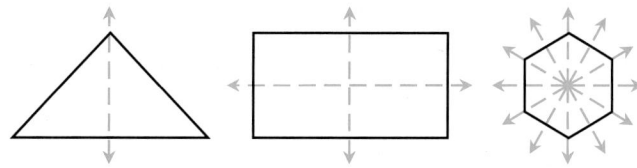

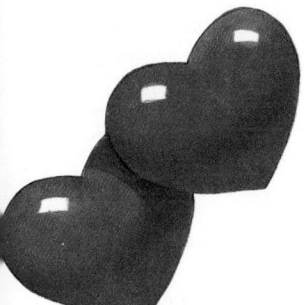

Examples

Determine which figures have line symmetry. Draw all lines of symmetry.

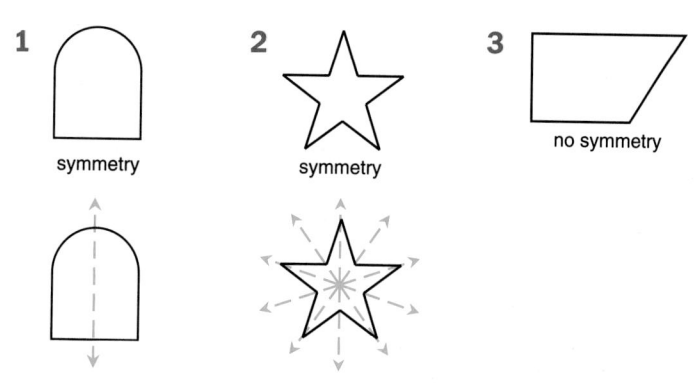

1   symmetry

2   symmetry

3   no symmetry

You can create figures that have line symmetry by using a **reflection.** A reflection is a mirror image of a figure across a line of symmetry.

Lesson 8-8 Art Connection: Reflections   **327**

OPTIONS

Reteaching Activity

Using Manipulatives Have students trace one pattern block onto graph paper. Discuss whether it is symmetrical and if it is, how many lines of symmetry it has. Have students repeat the procedure with other pattern blocks.

Study Guide Masters, p. 74

Name _____   Date _____

Study Guide Worksheet 8-8

Art Connection: Reflections

Figures that match exactly when folded in half have a line of symmetry. Some figures have more than one line of symmetry.

Examples   One line of symmetry   More than one line of symmetry   No line of symmetry

You can create figures that have a line of symmetry by using a reflection. A reflection is a mirror image across a line of symmetry.

Example

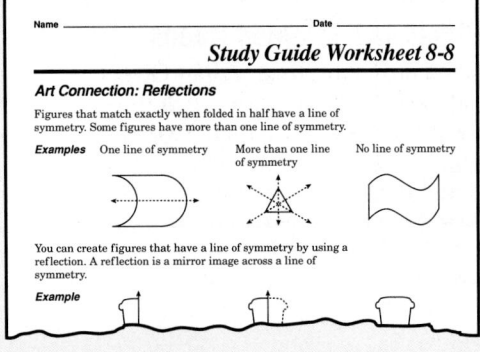

NCTM Standards: 1–4, 12

Lesson Resources

- Study Guide Master 8-8
- Practice Master 8-8
- Enrichment Master 8-8
- Evaluation Master, Quiz B, p. 70
- Interdisciplinary Master, p. 22
- Group Activity Card 8-8

 Transparency 8-8 contains the 5-Minute Check and a teaching aid for this lesson.

🕐 5-Minute Check
(Over Lesson 8-7)

Complete the pattern unit for each translation. Then draw the tessellation.

1.

2.

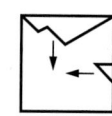 

1 FOCUS

Motivating the Lesson

Activity Have students work with partners. Ask them to write the alphabet using capital letters. Have them decide whether each letter has a horizontal line of symmetry, a vertical line of symmetry, both a horizontal and a vertical line of symmetry, or no line of symmetry. Have groups compare results.

2 TEACH

Using Modeling Have students draw triangles, rectangles, and circles using graph paper or a compass and a straightedge. Have them cut out the figures and try to fold each to create two matching halves.

327

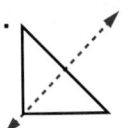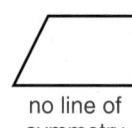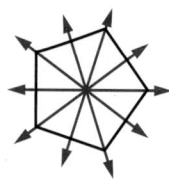
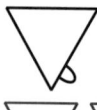
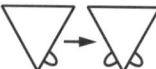 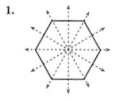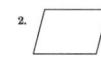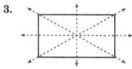
 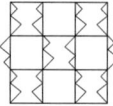

328

Escher also used reflections in some of his works. You can create different types of drawings using reflections. However, in these tessellations, two pattern units are used.

Example 4

Complete an Escher-like drawing using the change shown at the right.

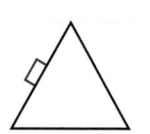

Complete the first pattern unit by drawing the reflection of the design on another side of the triangle.

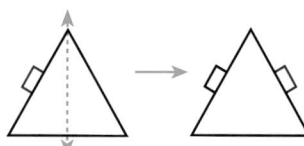

Now look at what happens when there are two triangles. The pattern on the left side of the second triangle is different from the pattern on the first triangle. Reflect the new pattern in the second triangle.

 →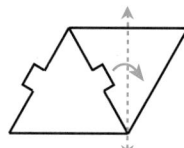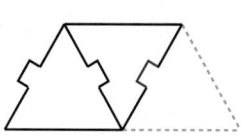

Notice that the pattern on the right side of the second triangle now matches the pattern of the first triangle. Continue this process to complete the tessellation.

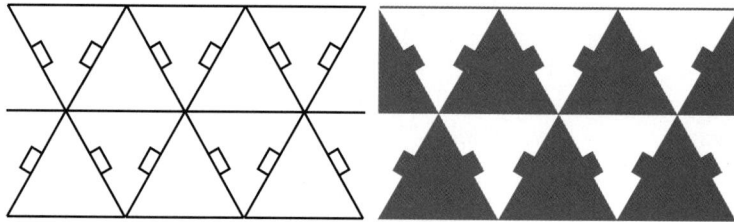

For answers to Exercises 1-2, see students' work.

Checking for Understanding

Communicating Mathematics

Read and study the lesson to answer each question.

1. **Tell** how a reflection is different from a translation.

2. **Write** a brief description of how to do a tessellation by using reflections.

328   **Chapter 8** Investigations in Geometry

OPTIONS

Gifted and Talented Needs

Have students draw regular polygons on their paper. Ask them what conclusions, if any, they can draw about the relationship between a regular polygon and the number of lines of symmetry it has.   A regular polygon has as many lines of symmetry as it has sides.

Guided Practice

3. Copy the figure at the right. Draw all lines of symmetry. **See Solutions Manual.**

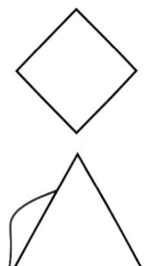

4. Complete both pattern units for the reflection shown at the right. Then draw the tessellation. **See Solutions Manual.**

Exercises

For answers to Exercises 5-7, see Solutions Manual.

Independent Practice

Copy each figure. Draw all lines of symmetry.

5.

6.

7.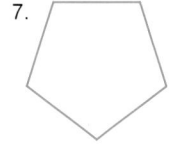

For answers to Exercises 8-10, see Solutions Manual.

Complete both pattern units for each reflection. Then draw the tessellation.

8.

9.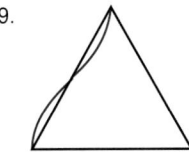

10.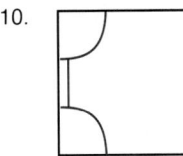

11. Complete the tessellation described by the pattern shown at the right. **See Solutions Manual.**

Mixed Review

12. **Jobs** As part of his summer job, Andrew is responsible for mowing a soccer field that is rectangular in shape. It is 100 yards long and 45 yards wide. Find the total area of the grass Andrew mows. *(Lesson 6-7)* **4,500 square yards**

13. **Art** Complete the pattern unit for the translation at the right. Then draw the tessellation. *(Lesson 8-7)* **See Solutions Manual.**

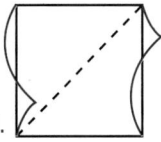

Problem Solving and Applications

14. **Critical Thinking** The double change at the right is reflected over the diagonal of the square instead of to the opposite side. Draw the two unit patterns. **See Solutions Manual.**

15. **Biology** Some insects under the influence of certain substances alter their behavior in unusual ways. Some bees alter the way they build honeycombs. Create a honeycomb that involves a reflection. **See students' work.**

16. **Journal Entry** Write your impressions of Escher's artwork. **See students' work.**

Lesson 8-8 Art Connection: Reflections   **329**

Extending the Lesson

Using Palindromes Discuss what palindromes are. Then have each student draw a line down the center of a sheet of paper. On one side, students write half of a palindrome. Then a classmate completes the palindrome, begins another below it, and passes the paper to a third student, and so on.

Cooperative Learning Activity

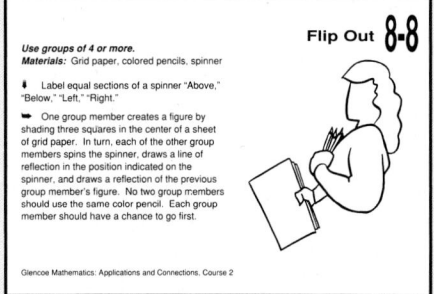

Flip Out 8-8

Use groups of 4 or more.
Materials: Grid paper, colored pencils, spinner

↓ Label equal sections of a spinner "Above," "Below," "Left," "Right."

→ One group member creates a figure by shading three squares in the center of a sheet of grid paper. In turn, each of the other group members spins the spinner, draws a line of reflection in the position indicated on the spinner, and draws a reflection of the previous group member's figure. No two group members should use the same color pencil. Each group member should have a chance to go first.

Glencoe Mathematics: Applications and Connections, Course 2

Checking for Understanding

Exercises 1-2 are designed to help you assess students' understanding through reading, writing, speaking, and modeling. You should work through these exercises with your students and then monitor their work on Guided Practice Exercises 3-4.

Close

Have students describe the relationship between lines of symmetry and reflections. Reflection is a mirror image across a line of symmetry.

3 PRACTICE/APPLY

Assignment Guide
Maximum: 5–16
Minimum: 5–15

Alternate Assessment

Modeling Have students work with partners. Each student draws a figure on graph paper with a design. Then they exchange papers and create a pattern by drawing the reflection of their partner's design.

Enrichment Masters, p. 74

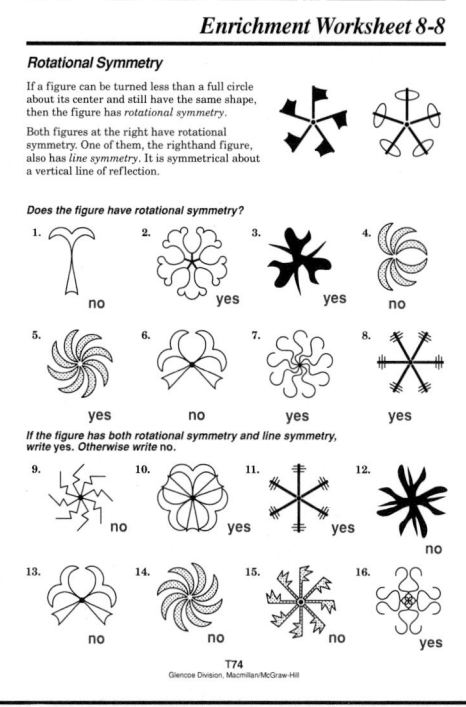

Name _____   Date _____

Enrichment Worksheet 8-8

Rotational Symmetry

If a figure can be turned less than a full circle about its center and still have the same shape, then the figure has *rotational symmetry*.

Both figures at the right have rotational symmetry. One of them, the righthand figure, also has *line symmetry*. It is symmetrical about a vertical line of reflection.

Does the figure have rotational symmetry?

1. no   2. yes   3. yes   4. no

5. yes   6. no   7. yes   8. yes

If the figure has both rotational symmetry and line symmetry, write yes. Otherwise write no.

9. no   10. yes   11. yes   12. no

13. no   14. no   15. no   16. yes

T74
Glencoe Division, Macmillan/McGraw-Hill

329

The Chapter Study Guide and Review begins with a section on Communicating Mathematics. This includes questions that review the new terms and concepts that were introduced in the chapter.

Then, the Skills and Concepts presented in the chapter are reviewed using a side-by-side format. Encourage students to refer to the Objectives and Examples on the left as they complete the Review Exercises on the right.

The Chapter Study Guide and Review ends with problems that review Applications and Problem Solving.

Chapter

Study Guide and Review

Communicating Mathematics

State whether each sentence is true or false. If false, replace the underlined word to make the sentence true.

1. Angles that have a measure <u>greater</u> than 90° are called acute angles. **F, less**
2. A decagon is a polygon having <u>10</u> sides. **T**
3. A <u>scalene</u> triangle has 3 congruent sides. **F, equilateral**
4. A parallelogram which has 4 congruent sides is called a <u>trapezoid</u>. **F, rhombus**
5. A polygon that is both <u>equiangular</u> and equilateral is a regular polygon. **T**
6. The sum of the angle measures at the vertex of any tessellation is <u>180°</u>. **F, 360°**
7. A <u>reflection</u> is a mirror image of a figure across a given line. **T**
8. In your own words, explain how a translation can be used in constructing a tessellation.
   A translation is a slide of the same pattern over and over.

Self Assessment

Objectives and Examples	Review Exercises
Upon completing this chapter, you should be able to:	*Use these exercises to review and prepare for the chapter test.*

• classify angles *(Lesson 8-1)*

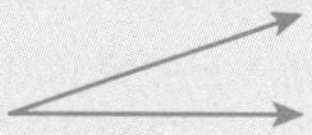

The angle above is an acute angle because its measure is less than 90°.

Classify each angle as acute, obtuse, right, or straight.

9. 49° angle **acute**   10. 90° angle **right**

11. 180° angle **straight**   12. 113° angle **obtuse**

13. 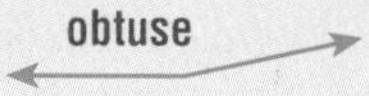   **straight** 14.

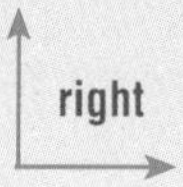

obtuse   **right**

• identify polygons *(Lesson 8-2)*

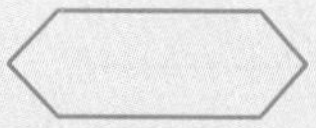

16. **No; more than 2 sides meet at vertex.**

The figure above is a six-sided polygon. It is called a hexagon.

Determine which figures are polygons. If a figure is not a polygon, explain why.

15. 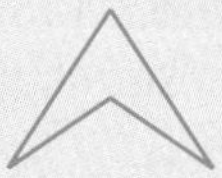   **yes**   16.

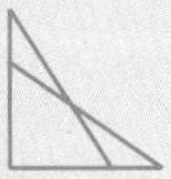

17. 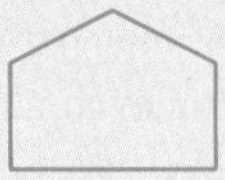   **yes**   18. 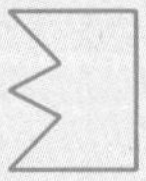   **yes**

Review Exercises

- classify triangles and quadrilaterals
  (Lesson 8-3)

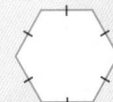

The figure above has 3 congruent sides and all of its angles are acute. It is an acute equilateral triangle.

Classify each triangle by its sides and by its angles.

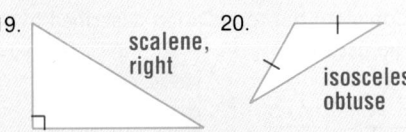

19. scalene, right

20. isosceles, obtuse

Name every quadrilateral that describes each figure. Then underline the name that best describes the figure.

21. parallelogram
    rhombus

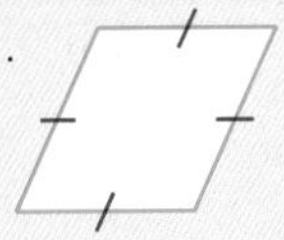

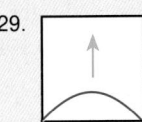

22. 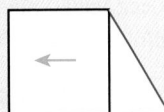 trapezoid

- identify regular polygons *(Lesson 8-4)*

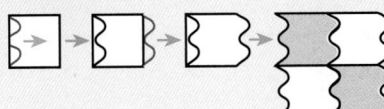

The figure above has 6 congruent sides and all of its angles are of equal measure. It is a regular hexagon.

Tell whether each polygon is a regular polygon. If not, tell why.

23. no, not equilateral
    or equiangular

24. yes

25. no, not equilateral
    or equiangular

26. yes

- determine which regular figures can be used to form a tessellation *(Lesson 8-6)*

A tessellation cannot be made out of regular pentagons alone because each angle of a pentagon measures 108° and there is no whole number n such that $108n = 360$.

If each polygon is regular, determine if it can be used by itself to make a tessellation.

27. hexagon yes

28. decagon no

- create Escher-like drawings by using translations *(Lesson 8-7)*

Complete the pattern unit and then the tessellation.

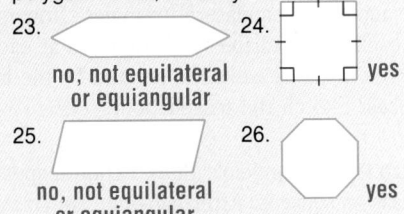

Complete the pattern unit for each translation. Then draw the tessellation.

29.

30.

For answers to Exercises 29–30, see Solutions Manual.

Study Guide and Review

You may wish to use a Chapter Test from the Evaluation Masters booklet as an additional chapter review. The two free-response forms are shown below. One of the two multiple-choice forms is shown on the next page.

Evaluation Masters, pp. 68–69

332

Objectives and Examples

• create Escher-like drawings by using reflections *(Lesson 8-8)*

Complete the tessellation described by the pattern.

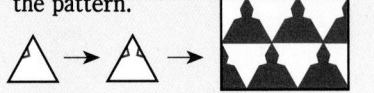

Review Exercises

Complete both pattern units for each reflection. Then draw the tessellation.

31.   32.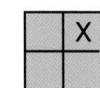

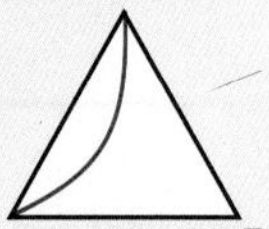

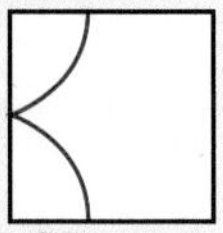

For answers to Exercises 31–32, see Solutions Manual.

Applications and Problem Solving

33. **Logic** Use the pattern at the right to draw the next two figures in the sequence. *(Lesson 8-5)* **See margin.**

34. **Arts and Crafts** Edwyna is piecing together a quilt from fabric pieces in the shapes of hexagons and equilateral triangles. How many of each of the shapes will she need at each vertex in the tessellation created by the fabric pieces? Sketch the tessellation. *(Lesson 8-6)*

35. **Pizza Parlor** Angelo's Pizza Parlor shapes its pizzas as squares. After cooking, the pizzas are cut along the diagonal into two triangles. Describe completely the triangles that result. *(Lesson 8-3)* **isosceles right**

34. 1 hexagon, 4 triangles; 2 hexagons, 2 triangles

Curriculum Connection Projects

• **Science** Attach a weighted string to the midpoint of the straight edge of a protractor. With the straight edge of the protractor up, look down the edge at several objects in the room. Have another student record the angle measure where the string crosses the protractor. Subtract your measure from 90 degrees.

• **Geography** Find acute, obtuse, and right angles on a street map. Use a protractor to measure and record each angle and location.

Read More About It

Cumming, Robert. *Just Look. . . . A Book About Paintings.*
Taylor, Barbara. *Bouncing and Bending Light.*
Spinelli, Jerry. *Space Station Seventh Grade.*

332   **Chapter 8** Study Guide and Review

Additional Answer

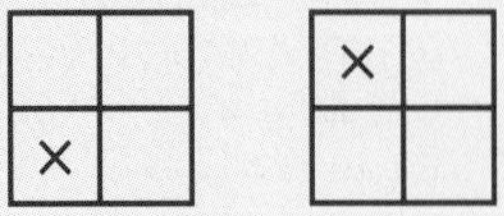

33.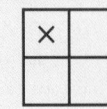

Chapter

8 Test

Classify each angle as acute, obtuse, right, or straight.

1. **acute**

2. $135°$ angle **obtuse**

3. **straight**

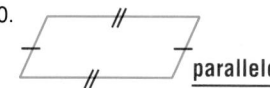

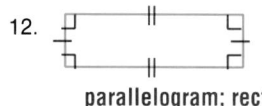

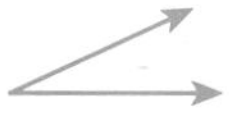

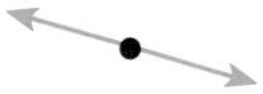

4. **Architecture** Classify the angle made by a wall and the ceiling of your classroom. **$90°$, right angle**

Determine which figures are polygons. If a figure is not a polygon, explain why.

5. **yes**

6. **yes**

7. **no, more than two sides meet at a vertex**

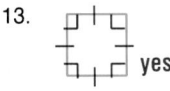

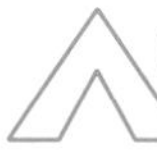

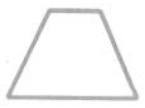

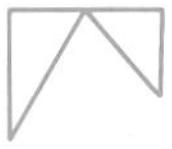

Classify each triangle by its sides and by its angles.

8. **isosceles, right**

9. **scalene, obtuse**

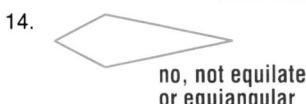

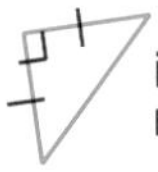

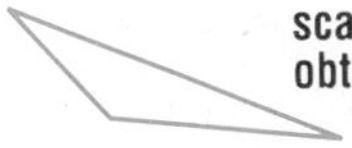

Name every quadrilateral that describes each figure. Then underline the name that best describes the figure.

10. **parallelogram**

11. **trapezoid**

12. **parallelogram; rectangle**

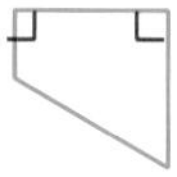

Tell whether each polygon is a regular polygon. If not, tell why.

13. **yes**

14. **no, not equilateral or equiangular**

15. **Logic** Nancy, Marti, Jessica, and Paul are studying music, journalism, physical education, and home economics. None of them is studying a subject that begins with the same letter of his or her first name. Jessica is practicing scales. Nancy has never taken physical education. Paul is reading about headlines. What subject is each student most likely studying? **Nancy, home economics; Marti, physical education; Jessica, music; Paul, journalism**

16. If an octagon is regular, determine if it can be used by itself to make a tessellation. **no**

Complete the pattern unit for each translation. Then draw the tessellation. **For answers to Exercises 17–18, see Solutions Manual.**

17.

18.

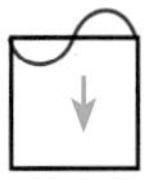

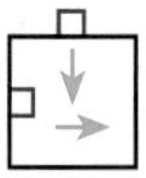

Complete both pattern units for each reflection. Then draw the tessellation. **For answers to Exercises 19–20, see Solutions Manual.**

19.

20.

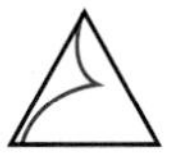

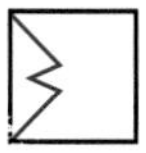

Bonus A square is separated into four triangles by drawing the diagonals. Are the resulting triangles equilateral? Explain your reasoning. **No, the triangles are isosceles.**

Chapter Test

Using the Chapter Test

This page may be used as a chapter test or another chapter review.

Evaluation Masters, pp. 64–65

Name ________ Date ________

Form 1A *Chapter 8 Test*

1. The measure of an angle is 45°. Classify the angle. A. acute B. straight C. obtuse D. right — 1. A
2. The measure of an angle is 180°. Classify the angle. A. acute B. straight C. obtuse D. right — 2. B
3. The measure of an angle is 135°. Classify the angle. A. acute B. straight C. obtuse D. right — 3. C
4. Which figure is a polygon? A. B. C. D. — 4. A
5. Which figure is *not* a polygon? A. B. C. D. — 5. D
6. Classify a polygon having eight sides. A. hexagon B. heptagon C. octagon D. decagon — 6. C
7. Classify triangle *X* by its sides and by its angles. A. scalene, obtuse B. scalene, right C. isosceles, right D. scalene, acute — 7. B
8. Classify triangle *Y* by its sides and by its angles. A. equilateral, acute B. isosceles, obtuse C. equilateral, right D. equilateral, obtuse — 8. A
9. Classify triangle *Z* by its sides and by its angles. A. isosceles, right B. isosceles, obtuse C. isosceles, acute D. equilateral, acute — 9. C

Use quadrilaterals J and K below for Exercises 10 and 11. Let P = parallelogram, R = rectangle, S = square, RH = rhombus, and T = trapezoid. Which letters describe each quadrilateral?

10. Quadrilateral *J* A. P B. P, RH C. R D. S, RH — 10. A
11. Quadrilateral *K* A. S, P B. S, RH C. S, R D. P, R, S, RH — 11. D
12. Which quadrilateral does *not* have two pairs of parallel sides? A. trapezoid B. rectangle C. rhombus D. square — 12. A

64
Glencoe Division, Macmillan/McGraw-Hill

Name ________ Date ________

Chapter 8 Test Form 1A (continued)

13. Which figure is a regular polygon? A. B. C. D. — 13. D
14. Which figure is *not* a regular polygon? A. B. C. D. — 14. B
15. Which regular polygon can be used by itself to make a tessellation? A. octagon B. pentagon C. square D. decagon — 15. C
16. Which regular polygon *cannot* be used by itself to make a tessellation? A. heptagon B. hexagon C. square D. equilateral triangle — 16. A
17. At the right is a pattern unit *x* for a translation. Identify the tessellation. A. B. C. D. — 17. B
18. At the right is a pattern unit *y* for a translation. Identify the tessellation. A. B. C. D. — 18. D
19. At the right is a pattern unit *z* for a reflection. Identify the tessellation. A. B. C. D. — 19. A
20. Mindy, Sam, Nathan, and Jodi attend different schools. The names of the schools are Jefferson, Saltonstall, Newton, and Medfield. Mindy goes to the Saltonstall School. None goes to the school whose name begins with the same letter as his or her name. Neither Nathan or Jodi has ever been to the Medfield School. Which school does Sam attend? A. Jefferson B. Saltonstall C. Newton D. Medfield — 20. D

BONUS Suppose the perimeter, in millimeters, of an equilateral triangle is the same as the sum of the measures of the angles of a pentagon. Find the length of one side of the triangle. A. 540 mm B. 108 mm C. 180 mm D. 500 mm — C

65
Glencoe Division, Macmillan/McGraw-Hill

Test and Review Generator software is provided in Apple, IBM, and Macintosh versions. You may use this software to create your own tests or worksheets, based on the needs of your students.

The **Performance Assessment Booklet** provides an alternate assessment for evaluating student progress. An assessment for this chapter can be found on pages 15–16.

9 Area

Previewing the Chapter

In this chapter, students find and estimate square roots by relating the area of a square to the length of its side. Then they explore the relationship among the sides of a right triangle and apply the Pythagorean Theorem. The Pythagorean Theorem is then used to solve problems. In the **problem-solving strategy** lesson, students solve problems by guessing and checking. The area concept is extended to irregular figures, triangles, trapezoids, and circles. Probability is also studied using area models.

Lesson	Lesson Objectives	NCTM Standards	State/Local Objectives
9-1	Solve problems by using guess and check.	1–5, 7	
9-2	Find square roots of perfect squares.	1–7, 12	
9-3	Estimate square roots.	1–7, 12	
9-4A	Find the relationship among the sides of a right triangle.	1–6, 12	
9-4	Find the length of a side of a right triangle using the Pythagorean Theorem.	1–7, 12	
9-5	Solve problems using the Pythagorean Theorem.	1–7, 12	
9-6	Estimate the area of irregular figures.	1–5, 7, 12	
9-7A	Find the area of a trapezoid.	1–5, 12	
9-7	Find the area of triangles and trapezoids.	1–5, 7, 12	
9-8	Find the area of circles.	1–7, 12	
9-9A	Estimate the area of a figure using probability.	1–5, 7, 11, 12	
9-9	Find the probability using area models.	1–5, 7, 11, 12	

Organizing the Chapter

A complete, 1-page lesson plan is provided for each lesson in the Lesson Plans Masters Booklet.

LESSON PLANNING GUIDE

Lesson	Materials/ Manipulatives	Extra Practice (Student Edition)	Study Guide	Practice	Enrichment	Evaluation	Technology	Lab Manual	Multicultural Activities	Application and Interdisciplinary Activities	Transparencies	Group Activity Cards
9-1			p. 75	p. 75	p. 75						9-1	9.1
9-2	base ten blocks, calculator	p. 591	p. 76	p. 76	p. 76		p. 9				9-2	9-2
9-3	base ten blocks calculator	p. 591	p. 77	p. 77	p. 77						9-3	9-3
9-4A	grid paper scissors							p. 63				
9-4	calculator, grid paper	p. 592	p. 78	p. 78	p. 78		p. 23				9-4	9-4
9-5			p. 79	p. 79	p. 79	Quiz A, p. 79			p. 9	p. 23	9-5	9-5
9-6	grid paper	p. 592	p. 80	p. 80	p. 80						9-6	9-6
9-7A	graph paper, scissors, tape							p. 64				
9-7	scissors calculator	p. 592	p. 81	p. 81	p. 81						9-7	9-7
9-8	scissors compass calculator	p. 593	p. 82	p. 82	p. 82					p. 9	9-8	9-8
9-9A	inch grid paper ruler, counters							p. 65				
9-9	grid paper		p. 83	p. 83	p. 83	Quiz B, p. 79					9-9	9-9
Study Guide and Review			Multiple Choice Test, Forms 1A and 1B, pp. 73–76 Free Response Test, Forms 2A and 2B, pp. 77–78 Cumulative Review, p. 80 (free response) Cumulative Test, p. 81 (multiple choice)									
Test												

Pacing Guide: Option I (Chapters 1–12) - 14 days; Option II (Chapters 1–13) - 12 days; Option III (Chapters 1–14) - 12 days
You may wish to refer to the complete **Course Planning Guides** on page T25.

OTHER CHAPTER RESOURCES

Student Edition
Chapter Opener, pp. 334–335
Mid-Chapter Review, p. 350
Portfolio Suggestion, p. 342
Academic Skills Test, pp. 372–373

Manipulatives
Overhead Manipulative Resources
Middle School Mathematics Manipulative Kit

Software/Technology
Interactive Mathematics Tools (Macintosh)
Test and Review Generator (IBM, Apple, Macintosh)
Teacher's Guide for Software Resources

Other Supplements
Transparency 9–0
Performance Assessment, pp. 17–18
Glencoe Mathematics Professional Series Lesson Plans, pp. 98–109

INTERDISCIPLINARY BULLETIN BOARD

Physical Fitness Connection

Objective   Find the area of regular and irregular regions.

How To Use It   Have groups of students find the dimensions of all the regions of a sports court such as a basketball court, handball court, or tennis court. Ask them to draw the court and then compute the area of all its regions. Students may need to use school facilities or even visit a local park to measure to obtain the data.

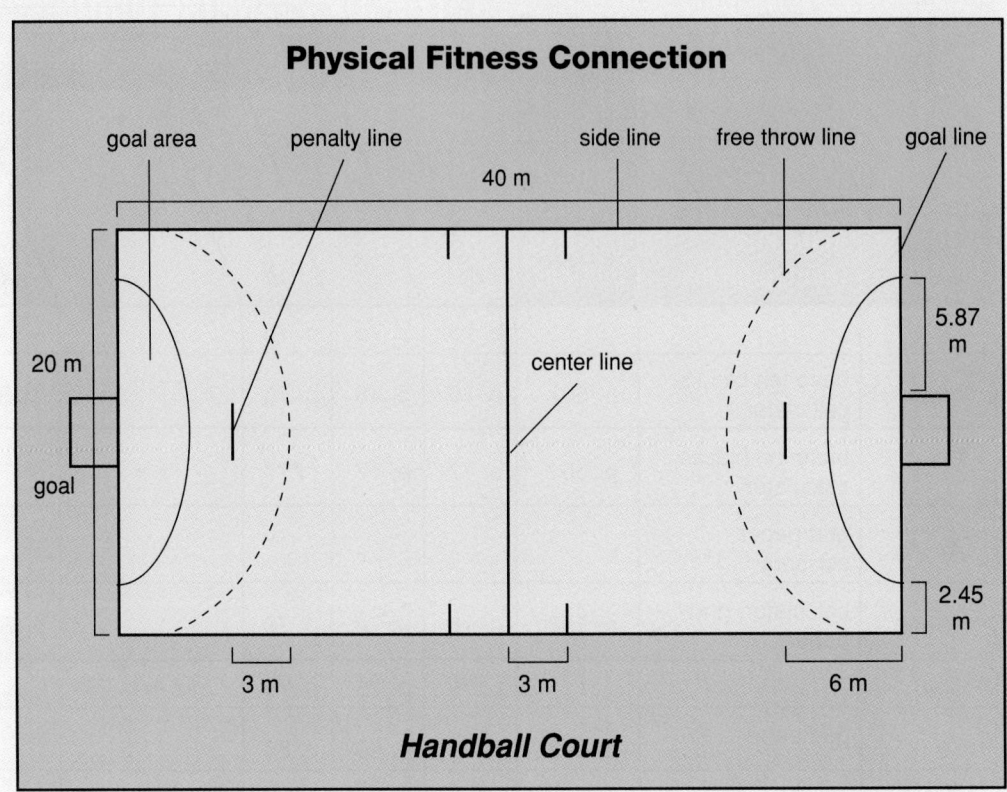

Physical Fitness Connection

goal area   penalty line   side line   free throw line   goal line

40 m

20 m

center line

5.87 m

goal

2.45 m

3 m   3 m   6 m

Handball Court

APPLICATIONS AND CONNECTIONS

Applications	Lesson	Example	Exercise
Board Games	9-2		45
Sports	9-2		46
Sightseeing	9-3		28
Construction	9-3		29
Building Maintenance	9-4		44
Sales	9-5	1	
Computer	9-5		11
Construction	9-5		12
Geography	9-6		19
Cooking	9-6		21
Construction	9-7		26
Sports	9-8	1	
History	9-8		37
Food	9-8		38
Sports	9-9	2	16
Geology	9-9		15
Connections			
Geometry	9-2	5	
Geometry	9-5	2	
Geometry	9-7	2	

TEAM ACTIVITIES

Multicultural Experiences

Outside Field Trips   On a trip to a local park, students can measure the area of parts of playing fields, such as the key on a basketball court, the infield of a baseball diamond, or the backcourt of a tennis court.

A visit to a pizza parlor can be helpful in showing students the different dimensions of pizzas in different shapes. Students can use the information to find the best buys in pizzas.

In-Class Speakers   Ask a landscape architect to visit the class and talk about what he or she does, with particular attention to areas of both regular and irregular shapes.

Invite a carpet installer to visit and talk about how to carpet regions with irregular shapes.

SUPPLEMENTARY BLACKLINE MASTER BOOKLETS

Some of the blackline masters for enhancing this chapter are shown below.

Application and Interdisciplinary Activity Masters, pp. 9, 23

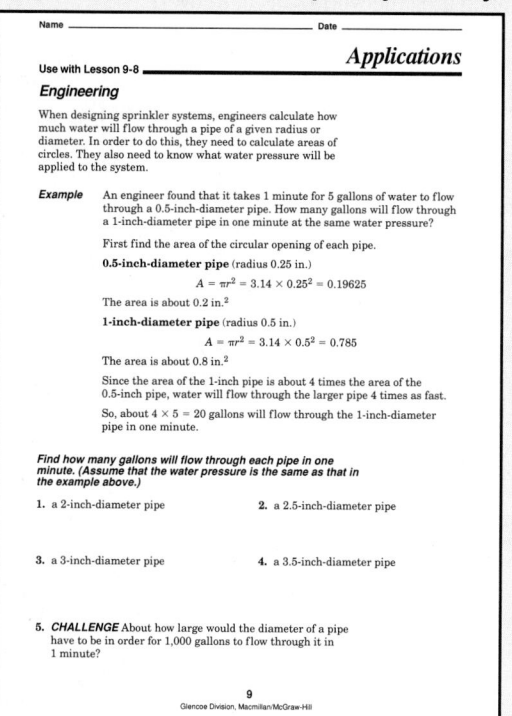

Name _____ Date _____

Applications

Use with Lesson 9-8 _____

Engineering

When designing sprinkler systems, engineers calculate how much water will flow through a pipe of a given radius or diameter. In order to do this, they need to calculate areas of circles. They also need to know what water pressure will be applied to the system.

Example An engineer found that it takes 1 minute for 5 gallons of water to flow through a 0.5-inch-diameter pipe. How many gallons will flow through a 1-inch-diameter pipe in one minute at the same water pressure?

First find the area of the circular opening of each pipe.

0.5-inch-diameter pipe (radius 0.25 in.)
$$A = \pi r^2 = 3.14 \times 0.25^2 = 0.19625$$
The area is about 0.2 in.^{2}

1-inch-diameter pipe (radius 0.5 in.)
$$A = \pi r^2 = 3.14 \times 0.5^2 = 0.785$$
The area is about 0.8 in.^{2}

Since the area of the 1-inch pipe is about 4 times the area of the 0.5-inch pipe, water will flow through the larger pipe 4 times as fast.

So, about $4 \times 5 = 20$ gallons will flow through the 1-inch-diameter pipe in one minute.

Find how many gallons will flow through each pipe in one minute. (Assume that the water pressure is the same as that in the example above.)

1. a 2-inch-diameter pipe   2. a 2.5-inch-diameter pipe

3. a 3-inch-diameter pipe   4. a 3.5-inch-diameter pipe

5. **CHALLENGE** About how large would the diameter of a pipe have to be in order for 1,000 gallons to flow through it in 1 minute?

9
Glencoe Division, Macmillan/McGraw-Hill

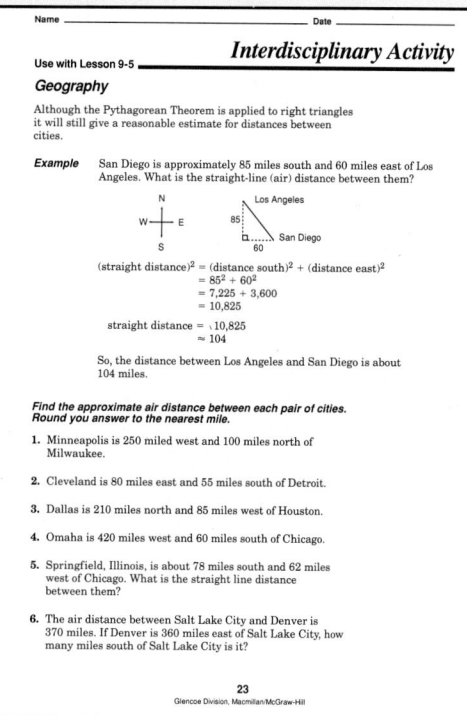

Name _____ Date _____

Interdisciplinary Activity

Use with Lesson 9-5 _____

Geography

Although the Pythagorean Theorem is applied to right triangles it will still give a reasonable estimate for distances between cities.

Example San Diego is approximately 85 miles south and 60 miles east of Los Angeles. What is the straight-line (air) distance between them?

(straight distance)^2 = (distance south)^2 + (distance east)^2
$$= 85^2 + 60^2$$
$$= 7,225 + 3,600$$
$$= 10,825$$

straight distance = $\sqrt{10,825}$
$$\approx 104$$

So, the distance between Los Angeles and San Diego is about 104 miles.

Find the approximate air distance between each pair of cities. Round you answer to the nearest mile.

1. Minneapolis is 250 miled west and 100 miles north of Milwaukee.

2. Cleveland is 80 miles east and 55 miles south of Detroit.

3. Dallas is 210 miles north and 85 miles west of Houston.

4. Omaha is 420 miles west and 60 miles south of Chicago.

5. Springfield, Illinois, is about 78 miles south and 62 miles west of Chicago. What is the straight line distance between them?

6. The air distance between Salt Lake City and Denver is 370 miles. If Denver is 360 miles east of Salt Lake City, how many miles south of Salt Lake City is it?

23
Glencoe Division, Macmillan/McGraw-Hill

Multicultural Activity Masters, p. 9

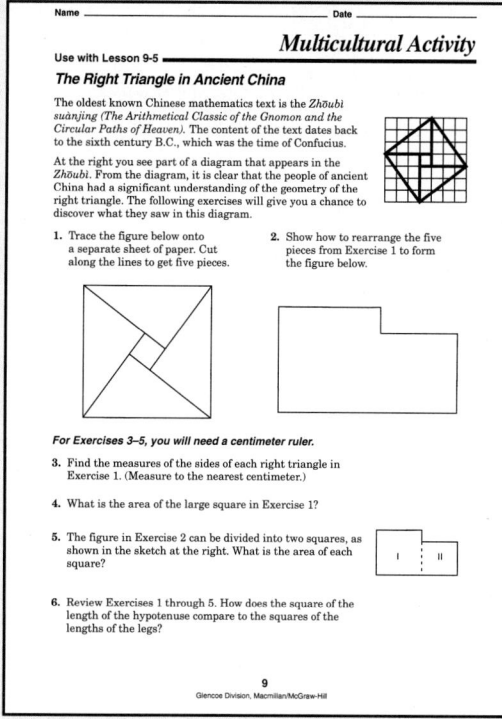

Name _____ Date _____

Multicultural Activity

Use with Lesson 9-5 _____

The Right Triangle in Ancient China

The oldest known Chinese mathematics text is the *Zhōubì suànjīng* (The Arithmetical Classic of the Gnomon and the Circular Paths of Heaven). The content of the text dates back to the sixth century B.C., which was the time of Confucius.

At the right you see part of a diagram that appears in the *Zhōubì*. From the diagram, it is clear that the people of ancient China had a significant understanding of the geometry of the right triangle. The following exercises will give you a chance to discover what they saw in this diagram.

1. Trace the figure below onto a separate sheet of paper. Cut along the lines to get five pieces.

2. Show how to rearrange the five pieces from Exercise 1 to form the figure below.

For Exercises 3–5, you will need a centimeter ruler.

3. Find the measures of the sides of each right triangle in Exercise 1. (Measure to the nearest centimeter.)

4. What is the area of the large square in Exercise 1?

5. The figure in Exercise 2 can be divided into two squares, as shown in the sketch at the right. What is the area of each square?

6. Review Exercises 1 through 5. How does the square of the length of the hypotenuse compare to the squares of the lengths of the legs?

9
Glencoe Division, Macmillan/McGraw-Hill

Technology Masters, p. 9

Name _____ Date _____

Calculator Activity

Use with Lesson 9-2 _____

The Square and Square Root Keys

Most calculators have a key to find the square root of a number. Usually the key is labeled ⎷. Many calculators also have a key to square a number. The key is usually labeled x².

Example Find $\sqrt{2,025}$.

2025 ⎷

$\sqrt{2,025} = 45$

Example Find the square of 84.

84 x²

$84^2 = 7,056$

Find each square root.

1. $\sqrt{900}$ 2. $\sqrt{289}$ 3. $\sqrt{5,184}$

4. $\sqrt{1,681}$ 5. $\sqrt{5,476}$ 6. $\sqrt{576}$

7. $\sqrt{1,024}$ 8. $\sqrt{676}$ 9. $\sqrt{2,704}$

Find the square of each number.

10. 38   11. 51   12. 77

13. 101   14. 28.8   15. 15.5

16. 18.7   17. 9.9   18. 39

19. 1   20. 8.2   21. 222

9
Glencoe Division, Macmillan/McGraw-Hill

RECOMMENDED OUTSIDE RESOURCES

Books/Periodicals

Schulte, Albert P., ed., *Teaching Statistics and Probability*, 1981 Yearbook, NCTM, 1981.

Stenmark, J.K., *Assessment Alternatives in Mathematics*, Berkeley, CA: EQUALS, Lawrence Hall of Science, 1989.

Films/Videotapes/Videodiscs

Probability, Wilmette, IL: Films Inc., 1970.

The Theory of Pythagoras, NCTM, 1988.

Software

Perimeter, Area, & Volume, (Apple II, IBM/Tandy), Gamco Industries

For addresses of companies handling software, please refer to page T24.

INTER·ACTIVE Mathematics

Glencoe's *Interactive Mathematics: Activities and Investigations* consists of 18 units that may be used as alternatives or supplemental material for *Mathematics: Applications and Connections*. The suggested unit for this chapter is Unit 9, *Don't Fence Me In*. See page T18 for more information.

Chapter

9

Area

Spotlight on Oceans and Islands

Have You Ever Wondered. . .

- How large some of the world's islands are?
- How much area the world's oceans cover?

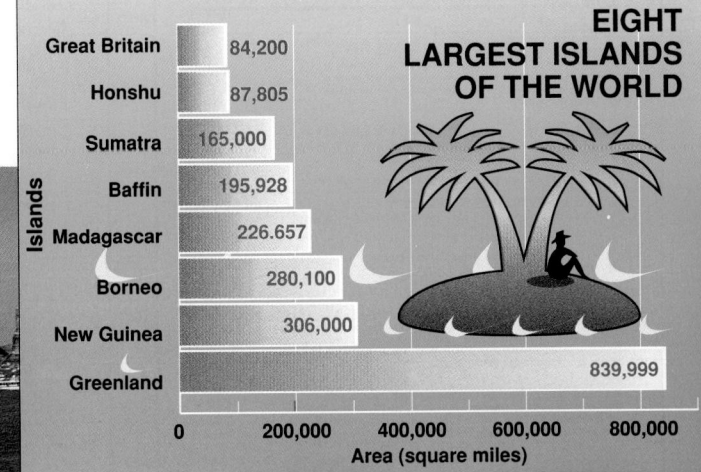

EIGHT LARGEST ISLANDS OF THE WORLD

Islands / Area (square miles)

Island	Area
Great Britain	84,200
Honshu	87,805
Sumatra	165,000
Baffin	195,928
Madagascar	226.657
Borneo	280,100
New Guinea	306,000
Greenland	839,999

Oceans and Seas

Name	Area (Sq mi)	Average Depth (Feet)
Pacific Ocean	64,186,300	12,925
Atlantic Ocean	33,420,000	11,730
Indian Ocean	28,350,500	12,598
Arctic Ocean	5,105,700	3,407
South China Sea	1,148,500	4,802
Caribbean Sea	971,400	8,448
Mediterranean Sea	969,100	4,926
Bering Sea	873,000	4,893
Gulf of Mexico	582,100	5,297
Sea of Okhotsk	537,500	3,192
Sea of Japan	391,100	5,468

334

Chapter Project

Oceans and Islands
Work in a group.

1. Copy a simple world map.

2. Color in the oceans and indicate the approximate size of each.

3. Color in any islands that you see and indicate the approximate size of each.

4. Indicate where you live on the map. Find out how large your state is (in square miles). Add this information to your map.

Looking Ahead

In this chapter, you will see how mathematics can be used to answer questions about the area of the world's oceans and islands.

The major objectives of the chapter are to:

- find square roots

- use the Pythagorean Theorem

- estimate the area of irregular figures

- find the area of triangles, trapezoids, and circles

335

DATA ANALYSIS

Have students examine the data presented. Ask questions to assess their understanding, such as *Which two bodies of water are closest in maximum depth?* Mediterranean and Bering Seas Then ask students to think about bodies of water and islands that are nearest to your area. Have them find the depth and area of the water and the area of the land. Have students work together to estimate the area of these familiar places using strategies they learn in the chapter for estimating area of irregular figures. Students can compare the actual areas with their estimates.

Data Search

A question related to these data is provided in Lesson 9-9, page 367, Exercise 17.

CHAPTER PROJECT

Distribute complete and blank world maps to groups. Suggest to students that they color-code the oceans and islands according to size or location. Encourage students to include additional islands with which they are familiar.

Chapter Opener Transparency

Transparency 9-0 is available in the Transparency Package. It provides another full-color, motivating activity that you can use to capture students' interest.

9-1 Guess and Check

NCTM Standards: 1–5, 7

Lesson Resources
- Study Guide Master 9-1
- Practice Master 9-1
- Enrichment Master 9-1
- Group Activity Card 9-1

 Transparency 9-1 contains the 5-Minute Check and a teaching aid for this lesson.

🕐 5-Minute Check
(Over Chapter 8)

1. Classify the angle as acute, obtuse, right, or straight. 
   acute

2. If the figure is not a polygon, explain why. 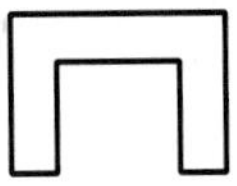
   polygon

3. Classify the triangle by its sides and angles. 
   obtuse isosceles triangle

Practice Masters, p. 75

Name _____ Date _____

Practice Worksheet 9-1

Problem-Solving Strategy: Guess and Check

Solve. Use the guess-and-check strategy.

1. Sam is thinking of two even numbers. When he adds them, he gets 208. When he subtracts the lesser number from the greater number, he gets 24. What are his numbers?
   92, 116

2. Andy has $2.80 worth of quarters and dimes in his pocket. If the number of quarters equals the number of dimes, how many quarters does he have? **8**

Solve. Use any strategy.

3. Barb estimates that $100 will be enough to buy a sweatshirt for $20.99, a pair of walking shoes for $48, and a blouse for $19.50. Is her estimate a good one? Why or why not?
   Yes.
   A reasonable estimate is $20 + $50 + $20 = $90

4. If it takes 20 seconds to inflate a balloon with helium from a tank, how many balloons can be inflated in 6 minutes?
   18

5. Find the length of the side of a square with area 196 cm².
   14 cm

6. The product of a number and 12 is 216. What is the number?
   18

7. The width of a rectangle is 10 in. less than the length. What are the length and width if the area is 144 in²?
   length: 18 in.; width: 8 in.

8. Use the bar graph below to predict which age group will be increasing in numbers in the next century.
   65 and over

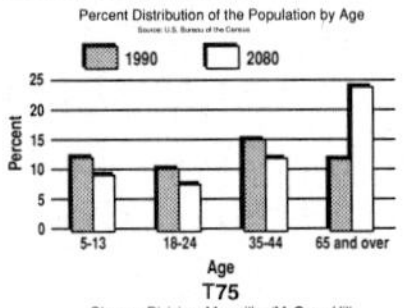

Percent Distribution of the Population by Age
Source: U.S. Bureau of the Census

☐ 1990   ☐ 2080

Age
T75
Glencoe Division, Macmillan/McGraw-Hill

Objective
Solve problems by using guess and check.

Mr. Andrews tells his math class that when two consecutive even numbers are multiplied, the product is 2,808. What are the two numbers?

Explore
What do you know?
The product of two consecutive even numbers is 2,808. Consecutive even numbers are pairs of numbers like 10 and 12 or 28 and 30.

What do you need to find?
You need to find the two numbers.

Plan
Multiply each multiple of 10 by the next consecutive even number to find a reasonable range for the number. Then guess numbers within that range.

Solve
$40 \times 42 = 1,680$
$50 \times 52 = 2,600$ ← 2,808
$60 \times 62 = 3,720$

The two consecutive even numbers are between 50 and 60. Since 2,808 is closer to 2,500 than to 3,600, try two consecutive even numbers close to 50.

Try 52 and 54.   52 ⊠ 54 ⊟ 2808

The consecutive even numbers are 52 and 54.

Examine
Since $52 \times 54 = 2,808$, the two numbers are 52 and 54.

Checking for Understanding

Communicating Mathematics

1. **Tell** why, in the problem above, it is best to first find a range in which to guess numbers rather than just randomly choosing numbers. **too time consuming otherwise**

OPTIONS

Reteaching Activity

Using Problem Solving   Provide students with problems to solve using the guess-and-check strategy that have smaller numbers. For example, present problems such as these: *Which two consecutive odd numbers have a product of 195?*

13, 15

Study Guide Masters, p. 75

Name _____ Date _____

Study Guide Worksheet 9-1

Problem-Solving Strategy: Guess and Check

The product of two consecutive prime numbers is 2,021. What are the two numbers?

Explore   What do you know?
The product of two consecutive prime numbers is 2,021.
What do you want to find?
what the two numbers are

Plan   Use the guess-and-check strategy.
Multiply multiples of 10 to find a reasonable range for the numbers. Then guess consecutive prime numbers within the range.

Solve $30 \times 30 = 900$
$40 \times 40 = 1,600$ } 2,021 is between 1,600 and 2,500.
$50 \times 50 = 2,500$

Guided Practice Solve. Use the guess-and-check strategy.

2. Julie arranged square tables, each seating 4 people, into one long rectangular table so that her 16 dinner guests could eat together. How many tables did she use? **7 tables**

3. Masao is thinking of two whole numbers. When he adds them together, the sum is 107. When he subtracts the lesser number from the greater number, their difference is 17. What are the numbers? **45, 62**

4. Seth is the oldest of four children. Each of his sisters is 3 years older than the next oldest sibling. The combined age of Seth and his three sisters is 46. None of the children are over the age of 20. How old is Seth? **16 years old**

Problem Solving

Practice Solve. Use any strategy.

5. The Pike's Peak souvenir shop sells standard size postcards in packages of 5 and large size postcards in packages of 3. Bonnie bought 16 postcards. How many packages of each did she buy? **2 packages of each**

Strategies
• • • • • • • • •

Look for a pattern.

Solve a simpler problem.

Act it out.

Guess and check.

Draw a diagram.

Make a chart.

Work backwards.

6. See students' work; girls average weight increases earlier, but boys catch up at age 14

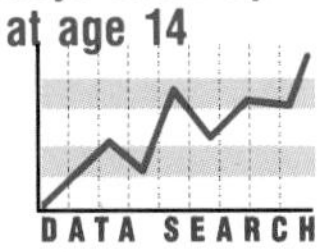

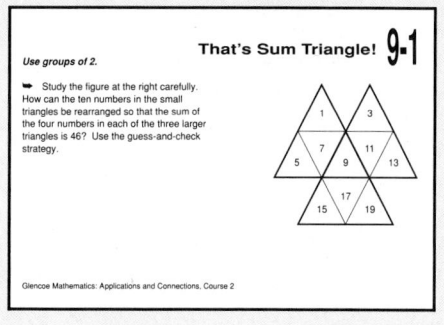
DATA SEARCH

8. The length is 14 in., the width is 6 in.

6. **Data Search** Refer to page 651. Construct a double-line graph showing the data on average weight. What does the graph show?

7. How many different ways can you arrange the numbers 1, 2, 3, and 4 as the last four digits in a telephone number? **24 ways**

8. The length of a rectangle is 8 inches longer than its width. What are the length and width if the area of the rectangle is 84 square inches?

9. Anne used her calculator to divide 4,567,325 by 326.4. She should expect the result to be about: **b**
   a. 150   b. 15,000   c. 150,000

10. The product of a number and 47 is 1,081. Find the number. **23**

Extending the Lesson

Using Money Present the following problem for students to solve by guessing and checking: *Louise has quarters, dimes, and nickels. She has the same number of quarters as dimes and the same number of dimes as nickels. In all, she has $4 in change. How many nickels does she have?* **10 nickels**

Cooperative Learning Activity

Use groups of 2.

That's Sum Triangle! 9-1

➡ Study the figure at the right carefully. How can the ten numbers in the small triangles be rearranged so that the sum of the four numbers in each of the three larger triangles is 46? Use the guess-and-check strategy.

1, 3, 7, 11, 5, 9, 13, 17, 15, 19

Glencoe Mathematics: Applications and Connections, Course 2

Situational Problem Tell students that together, Ray and Kate have $1.10. Kate has a dollar more than Ray. Ask them to determine how much money each has.

2 TEACH

More Examples
A mother is 28 years older than her son. Their ages total 70 years. How old is each? **49; 21**

Close
Have students write a problem for others to solve by using the guess-and-check strategy.

3 PRACTICE/APPLY

Assignment Guide
Maximum: 5–10
Minimum: 5–10

Enrichment Masters, p. 75

Name _____   Date _____

Enrichment Worksheet 9-1

Circular Tangrams

Two circles can be cut into the seven puzzle pieces shown at the right. The pieces are called *circular tangrams*.

Trace the circles and make a set of circular tangrams. Then use all seven tangrams to make each shape. Record your answers.

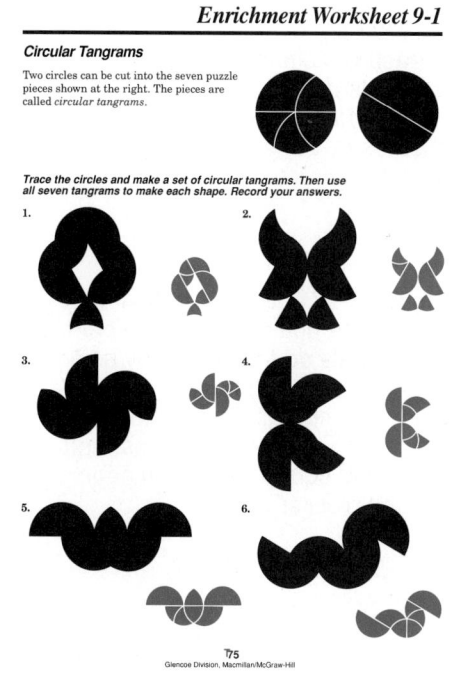

75
Glencoe Division, Macmillan/McGraw-Hill

Lesson Resources
- Study Guide Master 9-2
- Practice Master 9-2
- Enrichment Master 9-2
- Technology Master, p. 9
- Group Activity Card 9-2

Transparency 9-2 contains the 5-Minute Check and a teaching aid for this lesson.

5-Minute Check
(Over Lesson 9-1)

Solve. Use the guess-and-check strategy.

1. Two consecutive odd numbers have a sum of 1,800. What are the numbers? **899, 901**

2. Over a 3-day period Noemi did 105 sit-ups. She did 10 more each day than she did on the day before. How many sit-ups did Noemi do on the third day? **45 sit-ups**

1 FOCUS

Motivating the Lesson

Activity Point out to students that the 5-cm square shown in the lesson opener does not actually measure 5 cm by 5 cm. Have students draw what they think is a 5-cm square using graph paper, then use a centimeter ruler to check their estimates.

2 TEACH

Using the Mini-Lab If base-ten blocks are unavailable, have pairs of students do the activity by using graph paper to form squares. They can cut out and manipulate 10 × 10 squares, tens strips, and individual squares of graph paper as unit blocks.

Additional Answer

b. Sample answers: 144, 12; 169, 13; 196, 14

9-2 Squares and Square Roots

Objective
Find square roots of perfect squares.

Words to Learn
square
perfect square
square root
radical sign

LOOKBACK

You can review exponents on page 32.

DID YOU KNOW

The first world championship in skydiving was held in Yugoslavia in 1951. Later world championships followed at two-year intervals with as many as 40 national teams competing.

Skydivers leap from an airplane at heights of up to 15,000 feet and fall freely at speeds of more than 100 miles an hour. In accuracy skydiving competitions, participants try to land on a square target that may measure only 5 centimeters across. The area of the target is 5×5 or 25 square centimeters.

Remember that an *exponent* tells how many times a number, called the *base*, is used as a *factor*. In the expression 5×5, 5 is used as a factor twice. When you compute 5×5 or 5^2, you are finding the **square** of 5.

$$5^2 = 5 \times 5$$
$$= 25 \qquad \text{The square of 5 is 25.}$$

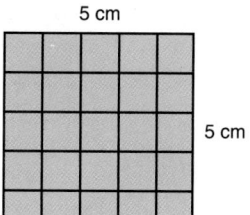

5 cm

5 cm

Examples

1 Evaluate 8^2.
$8 \times 8 = 64$

2 Evaluate 27^2.
$27 \boxed{y^x} 2 = $ **729**

Numbers such as 25, 64, and 729 are called **perfect squares** because they are squares of whole numbers.

Mini-Lab

Work in pairs.
Materials: base-ten blocks

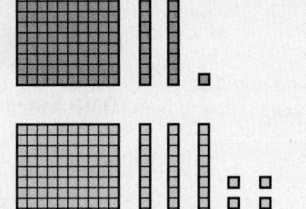

- Try to form a square with 121 unit blocks.

- Now try to form a square with 136 unit blocks.

Talk About It

a. Which number of unit blocks is a perfect square? What is the length of the side of its square? **121; 11**

b. Form three other perfect squares for numbers greater than 100. What is the length of each side? **See margin.**

OPTIONS

Reteaching Activity

Using Models Have students use graph paper to draw squares. Guide students to see that these represent perfect squares and that a side of a perfect square represents the square root of the square. Have them tell how many small squares each large square contains and give the whole number square root.

Study Guide Masters, p. 76

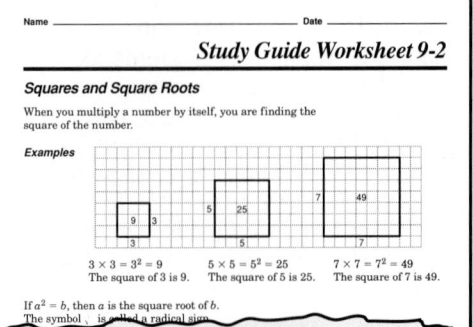

Name _____ Date _____

Study Guide Worksheet 9-2

Squares and Square Roots

When you multiply a number by itself, you are finding the square of the number.

Examples

$3 \times 3 = 3^2 = 9$
The square of 3 is 9.

$5 \times 5 = 5^2 = 25$
The square of 5 is 25.

$7 \times 7 = 7^2 = 49$
The square of 7 is 49.

If $a^2 = b$, then a is the square root of b.
The symbol is called a radical sign.

Let's return to the skydiving problem at the beginning of this lesson. The target region has an area of 25 square centimeters. You can find the length of a side by arranging 25 base-ten blocks into a square as in the Mini-Lab, *or* you can find the **square root** of 25.

Square Root	If $a^2 = b$, then a is the square root of b.

Since $5^2 = 25$, one square root of 25 is 5. It is also true that $(-5)^2 = 25$, so another square root of 25 is -5. Since the length of a side of the target region must be a whole number, the answer is 5 centimeters.

The symbol used to represent a nonnegative square root is $\sqrt{\ }$. It is called a **radical sign.**

$\sqrt{25} = 5$ *The square root of 25 is 5.*

Examples

3 Find $\sqrt{49}$.

Since $7^2 = 49$, $\sqrt{49} = 7$.

4 Find $\sqrt{961}$.

961 [$\sqrt{x}$] ∃1

So, $\sqrt{961} = 31$.

Example 5 *Connection*

Geometry The area of a square is 16 square feet. Find the length of a side using the definition of square root.

Since $4^2 = 16$, $\sqrt{16} = 4$. The side of the square is 4 feet long.

Communicating Mathematics

Checking for Understanding

Read and study the lesson to answer each question.

1. **Tell** what it means to square a number. **See margin.**
2. **Draw** a picture that shows $\sqrt{196} = 14$. **See Solutions Manual.**
3. **Tell** how finding the square root of a number is like finding the length of the side of a square given its area. $A = s^2$, therefore $\sqrt{A}$ is length of side of square.

Guided Practice Find the square of each number.

4. 2 **4**   5. 3 **9**   6. 7 **49**

7. 10 **100**   8. 11 **121**   9. 12 **144**

Find each square root.

10. $\sqrt{4}$ **2**   11. $\sqrt{36}$ **6**   12. $\sqrt{81}$ **9**   13. $\sqrt{100}$ **10**

Lesson 9-2 Squares and Square Roots   **339**

Interactive Mathematics Tools

Checking for Understanding

Exercises 1-3 are designed to help you assess students' understanding through reading, writing, speaking, and modeling. You should work through these exercises with your students and then monitor their work on Guided Practice Exercises 4-13.

Additional Answer

1. to multiply a number by itself

Watch for students who confuse the terms square and square root.

Prevent by suggesting to students that they express and record the meaning of each term *in their own words* to help them remember the difference between the terms.

Close

Have students write a problem using real-life data that can be solved by finding the square root of a number. Ask students to exchange papers and solve the problems. Have them explain their methods.

3 PRACTICE/APPLY

Assignment Guide
Maximum: 14–48
Minimum: 15–39 odd, 40–47

For **Extra Practice,** see p. 591.

Alternate Assessment

Modeling Have students use graph paper to show that the square root of 225 is 15.

Enrichment Masters, p. 76

Name _____ Date _____

Enrichment Worksheet 9-2

The Geometric Mean

The square root of the product of two numbers is called their *geometric mean*.

The geometric mean of 12 and 48 is $\sqrt{12 \cdot 48} = \sqrt{576} = 24$.

Find the geometric mean for each pair of numbers.

1. 2 and 8
   4
2. 4 and 9
   6
3. 9 and 16
   12

4. 16 and 4
   8
5. 16 and 36
   24
6. 12 and 3
   6

7. 18 and 8
   12
8. 2 and 18
   6
9. 27 and 12
   18

Recall the definition of a *geometric sequence*. Each term is found by multiplying the previous term by the same number. A missing term in a geometric sequence equals the geometric mean of the two terms on either side.

Find the missing term in each geometric sequence.

10. 4, 12, $\boxed{?}$, 108, 324
    36
11. 10, $\boxed{?}$, 62.5, 156.25, 390.625
    25

12. 1, 0.4, $\boxed{?}$, 0.064, 0.0256
    0.16
13. 700, 70, 7, 0.7, $\boxed{?}$, 0.007
    0.07

14. 6, $\boxed{?}$, 24
    12
15. 18, $\boxed{?}$, 32
    24

T76
Glencoe Division, Macmillan/McGraw-Hill

340

Exercises

Independent Practice

Find the square of each number.

14. 1 **1**
15. 5 **25**
16. 13 **169**
17. 14 **196**
18. 16 **256**
19. 20 **400**
20. 25 **625**
21. 30 **900**
22. 32 **1,024**

Find each square root.

23. $\sqrt{64}$ **8**
24. $\sqrt{121}$ **11**
25. $\sqrt{144}$ **12**
26. $\sqrt{225}$ **15**
27. $\sqrt{400}$ **20**
28. $\sqrt{625}$ **25**
29. $\sqrt{1,600}$ **40**
30. $\sqrt{256}$ **16**
31. $\sqrt{441}$ **21**

32. **Geometry** Find the length of a side of a square whose area is 784 square feet. **28 feet**

33. **Geometry** Find the area of a square whose side is 15 meters. **225 m²**

Determine whether each number is a perfect square. Write *yes* or *no*.

34. 36 **yes**
35. 49 **yes**
36. 136 **no**
37. 289 **yes**
38. 645 **no**
39. 961 **yes**

about $1,500

Mixed Review

40. **Finances** Alexander had $2,345 in his checking account at the beginning of the month. During the month, he wrote checks in the amounts of $595, $75, and $123. Estimate his balance at the end of the month. *(Lesson 1-2)*

41. **Statistics** During a typical work week, Samantha records the number of minutes it takes her to drive to work each day. Find the mean and median for the following times: 12, 23, 10, 14, and 11. *(Lesson 3-5)* **14, 12**

42. Find the least common multiple of 35 and 49. *(Lesson 4-9)* **245**

43. Solve $t - 3.6 = 4$. *(Lesson 6-2)* **7.6**

44. **Geometry** Complete the pattern unit for the reflection. Then draw the tesselation. *(Lesson 8-8)* **See Solutions Manual.**

Problem-Solving and Applications

45. **Board Games** A checkerboard has 8 squares on each side. How many small squares are there on the board? **64 squares**

46. **Sports** The backboard on a basketball hoop is a square with an area of 16 square feet. What is the length of a side? **4 feet**

47. **Critical Thinking** Numbers like 1, 8, and 27 are called perfect cubes because $1^3 = 1$, $2^3 = 8$, and $3^3 = 27$. Find two numbers that are both perfect squares and perfect cubes. **Sample answers: 1, 64, 729**

48. **Journal Entry** Make up a real-life problem where you need to find the square root of a number. **See students' work.**

OPTIONS

Extending the Lesson

Decorating Tell students that Marcia's quilt is a large square made from 100 small squares. The entire border of the quilt is blue. Ask students how many blue squares are in the border. **36 blue squares**

Cooperative Learning Activity

Use groups of 2.
Materials: Dot paper, scissors

Square (Not) **9-2**

Certain numbers can be represented with a picture. For instance, 3 and 6 are called *triangular numbers* because you can make a triangle with 3 and 6 points. Similarly, because you can make a square with 4 or 9 points, these numbers are called square numbers. *Square numbers are perfect squares.*

Every square number is the sum of two consecutive triangular numbers. In the figure on the back of this card, 16 is shown to be the sum of 6 and 10.

➡ Working together, model the square numbers 64, 169, 324, and 400 by cutting out sections of dot paper. Then draw a diagonal line to show that each of these numbers is the sum of two consecutive triangular numbers.

Triangular numbers   Square numbers

Glencoe Mathematics: Applications and Connections, Course 2

9-3 Estimating Square Roots

Objective
Estimate square roots.

Most professional baseball diamonds are covered with a square tarp to protect them when it rains. Suppose the tarp has an area of 1,000 square meters. What is the length of the side?

To find the answer, you need to find $\sqrt{1,000}$. Use your calculator.

1000 $\boxed{\sqrt{x}}$ **31.622777**

The length of a side is about 31.6 meters.

You know that the square root of a perfect square is a whole number. What happens when you try to find the square root of a number that is *not* a perfect square? Estimating the square root is often helpful.

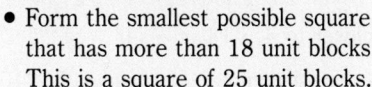

Mini-Lab

Work in pairs.
Materials: base-ten blocks

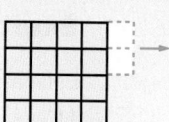

* Form the largest possible square using 18 unit blocks. This is a square of 16 unit blocks.

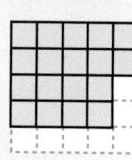

* Form the smallest possible square that has more than 18 unit blocks. This is a square of 25 unit blocks.

d. $6 < \sqrt{41} < 7$;
$12 < \sqrt{150} < 13$

You can review $>$ and $<$ on page 48.

How does this method of estimating square roots compare to the one in the Mini-Lab?

Talk About It
a. What is the area of each square? **16 square units, 25 square units**
b. What is the length of the side of each square? **4 units, 5 units**
c. Estimate $\sqrt{18}$. **4 < $\sqrt{18}$ < 5**
d. Use base-ten blocks to estimate $\sqrt{41}$ and $\sqrt{150}$.

Since 18 is not a perfect square, estimate $\sqrt{18}$ by finding the two perfect squares closest to 18.

$$16 < 18 < 25$$
$$\sqrt{16} < \sqrt{18} < \sqrt{25} \qquad \textit{Take the square root of each number.}$$
$$4 < \sqrt{18} < 5 \qquad \textit{Simplify, if possible.}$$

So, $\sqrt{18}$ is between 4 and 5. Since 18 is closer to 16 than 25, $\sqrt{18}$ is closer to 4 than to 5. The best whole number estimate for $\sqrt{18}$ is 4.

Lesson 9-3 Estimating Square Roots **341**

9-3 Lesson Notes

NCTM Standards: 1–7, 12

Lesson Resources
* Study Guide Master 9-3
* Practice Master 9-3
* Enrichment Master 9-3
* Group Activity Card 9-3

 Transparency 9-3 contains the 5-Minute Check and a teaching aid for this lesson.

⏱ 5-Minute Check
(Over Lesson 9-2)

Find the square of each number.
1. 12   144   **2.** 27   729

Find each square root.
3. $\sqrt{256}$ 16
4. $\sqrt{1,156}$ 34

5. Find the area of a square whose side is 18 meters. 324 square meters

---

Practice Masters, p. 77

Name _____ Date _____

Practice Worksheet 9-3

Estimating Square Roots

Estimate.

1. $\sqrt{13}$ 4	2. $\sqrt{27}$ 5	3. $\sqrt{60}$ 8
4. $\sqrt{84}$ 9	5. $\sqrt{101}$ 10	6. $\sqrt{72}$ 8
7. $\sqrt{97}$ 10	8. $\sqrt{132}$ 11	9. $\sqrt{1,000}$ 32
10. $\sqrt{160}$ 13	11. $\sqrt{600}$ 24	12. $\sqrt{260}$ 16
13. $\sqrt{800}$ 28	14. $\sqrt{189}$ 14	15. $\sqrt{850}$ 29
16. $\sqrt{123}$ 11	17. $\sqrt{50}$ 7	18. $\sqrt{369}$ 19
19. $\sqrt{450}$ 21	20. $\sqrt{399}$ 20	21. $\sqrt{150}$ 12
22. $\sqrt{220}$ 15	23. $\sqrt{1,200}$ 35	24. $\sqrt{37}$ 6
25. $\sqrt{1,869}$ 43	26. $\sqrt{24}$ 5	27. $\sqrt{196}$ 14

177

Glencoe Division, Macmillan/McGraw-Hill

OPTIONS

Reteaching Activity

Using Connections Guide students to see that except for perfect squares, all square roots contain non-repeating decimals and are therefore best expressed as estimates. Use a calculator to demonstrate this by finding square roots for numbers such as 5, 6, 8, and 10.

Study Guide Masters, p. 77

Name _____ Date _____

Study Guide Worksheet 9-3

Estimating Square Roots

Estimate to find the square root of a number that is not a perfect square.

Example   Estimate $\sqrt{95}$.

$81 < 95 < 100$	Find the last perfect square less than 95 and the first perfect square greater than 95.
$\sqrt{81} < \sqrt{95} < \sqrt{100}$	Take the square root of each number. The square root of 95 is between the square root of 81 and the square root of 100.
$9 < \sqrt{95} < 10$	Find the square roots. The square root of 95 is between 9 and 10.

342

1 FOCUS

Motivating the Lesson

Situational Problem Have students suppose that they had to paint a giant checkerboard in the school yard to cover an area of 150 square meters. Ask them to explain how they would determine the length of each side.

2 TEACH

More Examples

For the Example

Estimate $\sqrt{62}$.   about 8

Close

Have students explain how to estimate the square root of 70.

3 PRACTICE/APPLY

Assignment Guide

Maximum: 11–29

Minimum: 11–23 odd, 24–29

For **Extra Practice**, see p. 591.

Enrichment Masters, p. 77

Name _____ Date _____

Enrichment Worksheet 9-3

World Series Records

Each problem gives the name of a famous baseball player. To find who set each record, graph the points on the number line.

1. **pitched 23 strikeouts in one World Series**
U at 3, X at 3.3, K at 0.75, O at $\frac{3}{4}$, F at 6, A at $2\frac{7}{8}$

K   O   U   F   A   X
+---+---+---+---+---+
0   1   2   3   4

2. **71 base hits in his appearances in World Series**
B at 5, R at 12, A at 3.75, G at $\frac{16}{13}$, E at $\frac{9}{2}$, Y at 0.375, R at $\frac{13}{4}$, I at 1.6, and O at $0.77\overline{7}$

Y   O   G   I   B E   R R   A
+---+---+---+---+
0   1   2   3   4

3. **10 runs in a single World Series**
N at 60, K at 30, A at 4.3, S at 6.2, C at $\frac{46}{9}$, O at 45, and J at 17

J A   C   K   S   O   N
+---+---+---+---+
4   5   6   7   8

4. **Batting average of 0.625 in a single World Series**
E at 32, U at $6\frac{5}{8}$, A at $\frac{14}{3}$, T at 55, B at 5.3, R at 40, H at 7.75, B at $\frac{21}{5}$

B   A   B   E   R   U   T   H
+---+---+---+---+
4   5   6   7   8

5. **42 World Series runs in his career**
E at 140, Y at 9.6, I at 8.6, E at 90, A at $\frac{21}{2}$, M at 70, C at $8\frac{6}{8}$, M at 100, N at 10.7, K at $9\frac{3}{11}$, T at 120, L at 11.4

M   I C K   E Y   M   A N T   L   E
+---+---+---+---+
8   9   10   11   12

T77
Glencoe Division, Macmillan/McGraw-Hill

342

Example

Estimate $\sqrt{52}$.

Find the two perfect squares closest to 52.

$$49 < 52 < 64$$
$$\sqrt{49} < \sqrt{52} < \sqrt{64}$$
$$7 < \sqrt{52} < 8$$

Since 52 is closer to 49 than to 64, the best whole number estimate is 7.

Checking for Understanding

Communicating Mathematics

Read and study the lesson to answer each question.

1. **Tell** how the drawing at the right can help you estimate $\sqrt{10}$. $3 < \sqrt{10} < 4$

2. **Tell**, in your own words, why 4 is the best whole number estimate for $\sqrt{18}$. $4^2 = 16$ and $5^2 = 25$ and since 18 is closer to 16, then $\sqrt{18} \approx 4$.

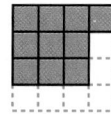

Guided Practice

Estimate. **Approximations are given.**

3. $\sqrt{11}$ 3
4. $\sqrt{23}$ 5
5. $\sqrt{27}$ 5
6. $\sqrt{34}$ 6
7. $\sqrt{59}$ 8
8. $\sqrt{70}$ 8
9. $\sqrt{99}$ 10
10. $\sqrt{105}$ 10

Exercises

Independent Practice

Estimate. **Approximations are given.**

11. $\sqrt{12}$ 3
12. $\sqrt{21}$ 5
13. $\sqrt{56}$ 7
14. $\sqrt{85}$ 9
15. $\sqrt{91}$ 10
16. $\sqrt{116}$ 11
17. $\sqrt{145}$ 12
18. $\sqrt{215}$ 15
19. $\sqrt{350}$ 19
20. $\sqrt{500}$ 22
21. $\sqrt{721}$ 27
22. $\sqrt{1,050}$ 32

23. Which is closer to 4, $\sqrt{14}$ or $\sqrt{24}$? $\sqrt{14}$

Mixed Review

24. Find the greatest common factor of 125, 240, and 375. *(Lesson 4-5)* **5**

25. Find the difference of $1\frac{3}{4}$ and $\frac{4}{5}$. *(Lesson 5-4)* $\frac{19}{20}$

26. Find the square root of 196. *(Lesson 9-2)* **14**

Problem-Solving and Applications

27. **Critical Thinking** Tell what happens when you use a calculator to find $\sqrt{-25}$. Is it possible to take the square root of a negative number? Explain. **E; no; No number squared equals a negative number.**

28. **Sightseeing** The distance you can see to the horizon in clear weather is given by the formula $d = 1.22\sqrt{h}$. In this formula, d represents the distance in miles and h represents the height in feet your eyes are from the ground. Estimate how far you can see if you are at the top of the Sears Tower in Chicago, 1,454 feet above the ground. **about 47 miles**

29. **Portfolio Suggestion** Select your favorite word problem from this chapter and place your solution to it in your portfolio. Attach a note explaining why it is your favorite. **See students' work.**

OPTIONS

Extending the Lesson

Using Estimation Ask students to explain how they would find the square root of a number to the nearest tenth or hundredth. Have them demonstrate their method.

Cooperative Learning Activity

Good, Better, Best 9-3

Number of players: 3
Materials: Index cards, spinner

♦ Copy onto cards the square roots shown on the back of this card, one per card. Shuffle the cards and divide them evenly. Label equal sections of a spinner "4," "5," "6," "7," "8," "9."

➥ One group member spins the spinner. If possible, each group member then removes from his or her hand one card for which the number on the spinner is the best estimate. Group members must decide whether cards that have been discarded show best whole number estimates. Continue in this way, taking turns at the spinner, until one group member has no cards left.

Glencoe Mathematics: Applications and Connections, Course 2

Objective
Find the relationship among the sides of a right triangle.

Materials
grid paper
straightedge
scissors

In this Lab, you will investigate the relationship that exists among the sides of a right triangle.

Try this!

Work in groups of three.

- Each member of your group should draw a segment that is 3 units long on a piece of grid paper.

- At one end of this segment, draw a perpendicular segment that is 4 units long.

- Draw a third segment to form a triangle. Cut out the triangle.

- Measure the length of the longest side in terms of units on the grid paper.

- Cut out three squares: one with 3 units on a side, one with 4 units on a side, and one with 5 units on a side.

- Place the edges of the squares against the corresponding sides of the right triangle.

- Find the area of each square.

What do you think?

1. Sum of area of two smaller squares equals area of largest square.
2. yes; 289 sq units; 100 sq units; 169 sq units
3. Sum of squares of two legs of right triangle equals square of side opposite right angle.

1. What relationship exists among the areas of the three squares?
2. Do you think the relationship you described in Exercise 1 is true for *any* right triangle? Repeat the activity for three other right triangles whose perpendicular sides are 8 units, 15 units; 6 units, 8 units; and 5 units, 12 units.
3. Write one or more sentences that summarize your findings.

Extension

4. Do you think your findings are true in other kinds of triangles? To test your theory, draw five different, non-right triangles on grid paper. Repeat the activity. Write one or more sentences to summarize your findings. No; see students' work.

Lesson 9-4A Mathematics Lab: Pythagorean Theorem   **343**

OPTIONS

Lab Manual   You may wish to make copies of the blackline master on p. 63 of the *Lab Manual* for students to use as a recording sheet.

Lab Manual, p. 63

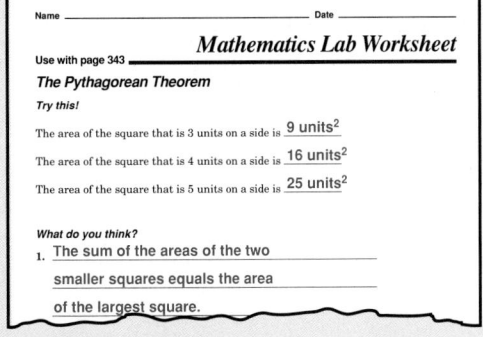

Name _____ Date _____

Mathematics Lab Worksheet
Use with page 343

The Pythagorean Theorem
Try this!

The area of the square that is 3 units on a side is 9 units²

The area of the square that is 4 units on a side is 16 units²

The area of the square that is 5 units on a side is 25 units²

What do you think?
1. The sum of the areas of the two
   smaller squares equals the area
   of the largest square.

NCTM Standards: 1–6, 12

Management Tips

For Students   Have one student in each group, with the help of others, draw and cut out the initial triangle and the squares. Students can use clear tape to attach the squares to the triangle.

For the Overhead Projector
Overhead Manipulative Resources provides appropriate materials for teacher or student demonstration of the activities in this Mathematics Lab.

1 FOCUS

Introducing the Lab

Tell students that they are going to be exploring the Pythagorean Theorem. Ask them to describe what they think a theorem is. Then have a student look up the meaning in a glossary or dictionary and read it to the class.   a statement that can be proved to be true

2 TEACH

Using Connections   Ask students to describe the relationship between the length of a side of the triangle and the area of the square formed along that segment.   The area is the square of the length of the segment.

3 PRACTICE/APPLY

Using Models   Have students use graph paper, geoboards or dot paper to model several other right triangles. Have them first guess, then measure, to find the length of the third side of each triangle once they have drawn or modeled the first two sides. Ask them to summarize their findings.

Close

Have students describe the relationship among the three squares formed using the sides of a right triangle.

343

NCTM Standards: 1-7, 12

Lesson Resources

- Study Guide Master 9-4
- Practice Master 9-4
- Enrichment Master 9-4
- Technology Master, p. 23
- Group Activity Card 9-4

Transparency 9-4 contains the 5-Minute Check and a teaching aid for this lesson.

5-Minute Check

(Over Lesson 9-3)

Estimate.

1. $\sqrt{14}$ about 4
2. $\sqrt{35}$ about 6
3. $\sqrt{118}$ about 11
4. $\sqrt{395}$ about 20
5. Which is closer to 5, $\sqrt{23}$ or $\sqrt{32}$? $\sqrt{23}$

1 FOCUS

Motivating the Lesson

Situational Problem Tell students that a scrap metal dealer has a storage bay that is 4 feet high. From the top of the bay, a 10-foot ramp goes to the floor. Ask them how the scrap dealer can figure out how far from the bay the ramp reaches along the floor.

2 TEACH

Using Connections Have students use what they know about equations to rewrite the formula for finding the square of the hypotenuse so that it can be used to find the square of either leg. They can use $c^2 - b^2 = a^2$ or $c^2 - a^2 = b^2$.

9-4 The Pythagorean Theorem

Objective

Find the length of a side of a right triangle using the Pythagorean Theorem.

Words to Learn

hypotenuse
leg
Pythagorean Theorem

The ancient Egyptians used mathematics to lay out their fields with square corners. About 2000 B.C. they discovered a 3-4-5 right triangle. They took a piece of rope and knotted it into 12 equal spaces. Taking three stakes, they stretched the rope around the stakes to form a right triangle. The sides of the triangle had lengths of 3, 4, and 5 units.

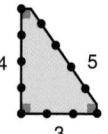

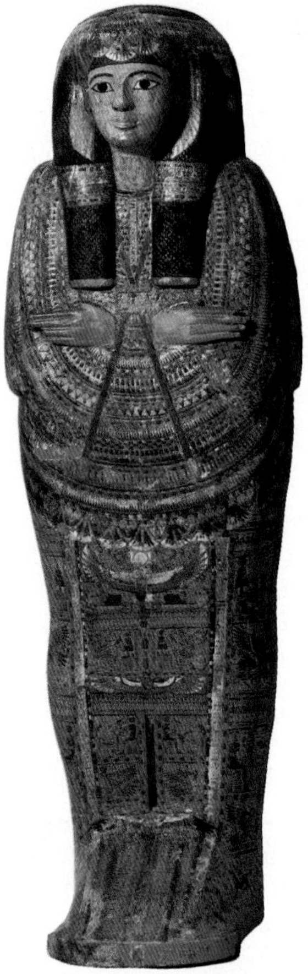

The longest side of a right triangle is called the **hypotenuse,** and is opposite the right angle. The other two sides, called **legs,** form the right angle.

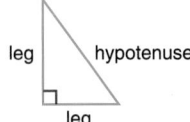

Several hundred years later, a Greek mathematician, Pythagoras, formalized a relationship between the sides of any right triangle. It became known as the **Pythagorean Theorem.**

In this theorem, a and b are the lengths of the legs and c is the length of the hypotenuse.

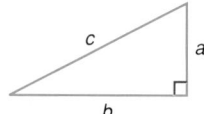

Pythagorean Theorem

In words: In a right triangle, the square of the measure of the hypotenuse is equal to the sum of the squares of the measures of the legs.

Arithmetic	**Algebra**
$3^2 + 4^2 = 5^2$	$a^2 + b^2 = c^2$

Given the lengths of the two legs of a right triangle, you can use the Pythagorean Theorem to find the length of the hypotenuse.

OPTIONS

Gifted and Talented Needs

Have students try a number of examples to find out whether they can obtain a perfect square by adding 1 to the product of any 4 consecutive whole numbers. Ask them if this strategy will work for consecutive odd or even numbers. It works only for consecutive whole numbers.

1 Find the length of the hypotenuse of the triangle at the right.

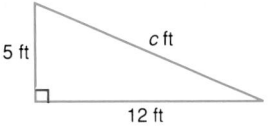

5 ft c ft

12 ft

$$a^2 + b^2 = c^2 \quad \textit{Pythagorean Theorem}$$
$$5^2 + 12^2 = c^2 \quad \textit{Replace a with 5 and b with 12.}$$
$$25 + 144 = c^2$$
$$169 = c^2$$
$$\sqrt{169} = c \quad \textit{Definition of square root}$$
$$13 = c \quad \text{The hypotenuse is 13 feet long.}$$

2 Find the length of the hypotenuse of a right triangle whose legs are 7 meters and 9 meters.

$$a^2 + b^2 = c^2 \quad \textit{Pythagorean Theorem}$$
$$7^2 + 9^2 = c^2 \quad \textit{Replace a with 7 and b with 9.}$$
$$49 + 81 = c^2$$
$$130 = c^2$$
$$\sqrt{130} = c \quad \textit{Definition of square root}$$

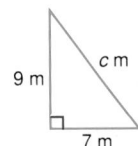

9 m c m

7 m

Estimation Hint
••••••••••••••
$121 < 130 < 144$
$11 < \sqrt{130} < 12$

130 $\boxed{\sqrt{x}}$ 11.401754

The hypotenuse is about 11.4 meters long.

You can use the Pythagorean Theorem to find the length of a leg of a right triangle if you are given the lengths of the other leg and the hypotenuse.

Example 3

Find the length of the leg in the triangle at the right.

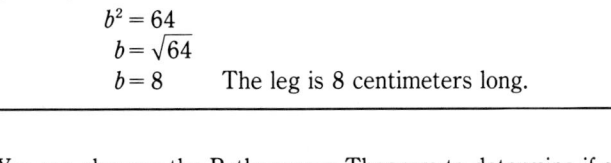

6 cm b cm

10 cm

$$a^2 + b^2 = c^2$$
$$6^2 + b^2 = 10^2$$
$$36 + b^2 = 100$$
$$36 - 36 + b^2 = 100 - 36$$
$$b^2 = 64$$
$$b = \sqrt{64}$$
$$b = 8 \qquad \text{The leg is 8 centimeters long.}$$

You can also use the Pythagorean Theorem to determine if a triangle is a right triangle. The examples on the following page illustrate this.

Lesson 9-4 The Pythagorean Theorem   **345**

Teaching Tip Have students write the Pythagorean Theorem first when solving any problem. Allow them to compute with calculators.

More Examples

For Example 1

Find the length of the hypotenuse of the triangle below.   17 ft

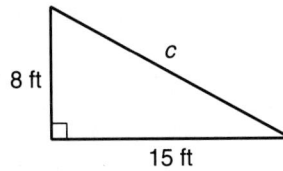

8 ft c

15 ft

For Example 2

Find the length of the hypotenuse of a right triangle whose legs are 6 meters and 10 meters.
$\sqrt{136}$, or about 11.7 meters

For Example 3

Find the length of the leg of the triangle below.
$b = 24$ meters

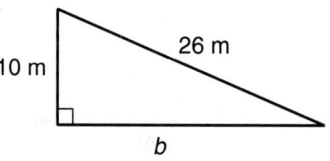

10 m   26 m

b

For Examples 4–5

Given the following lengths, determine whether each triangle is a right triangle.
6 feet, 8 feet, 12 feet   no
9 feet, 12 feet, 15 feet   yes

Checking for Understanding

Exercises 1-3 are designed to help you assess students' understanding through reading, writing, speaking, and modeling. You should work through these exercises with your students and then monitor their work on Guided Practice Exercises 4-17.

Reteaching Activity

Using Models Have students use graph paper or dot paper to draw some right triangles. Guide them to use the Pythagorean Theorem to find the length of each hypotenuse. Then have students measure each hypotenuse to confirm their calculations.

Study Guide Masters, p. 78

Name _____ Date _____

Study Guide Worksheet 9-4

The Pythagorean Theorem

The longest side of a right triangle is the hypotenuse. The hypotenuse is the side opposite the right angle. The other two sides of the triangle are the legs.

hypotenuse a c legs b

The Pythagorean Theorem relates the lengths of the sides of a right triangle. The theorem states:

For any right triangle, the square of the length of the hypotenuse is equal to the sum of the squares of the length of the legs.

You can use the Pythagorean Theorem to find the length of a side of a right triangle if the lengths of the other two sides are known.

$c^2 = a^2 + b^2$

Example Find the length of the leg.
$$c^2 = a^2 + b^2$$
$$10^2 = 5^2 + b^2$$
$$100 = 25 + b^2$$

Error Analysis

Watch for students who neglect to find the square root of the length of the leg or hypotenuse.

Prevent by encouraging students to estimate the answer first and to compare their answers with the estimate.

Close

Have students explain how to determine whether a 9-inch, 40-inch, 41-inch triangle is a right triangle. $9^2 + 40^2 = 41^2$; yes

3 PRACTICE/APPLY

Assignment Guide
Maximum: 18–45
Minimum: 19–37 odd, 39–45

For **Extra Practice,** see p. 592.

Alternate Assessment

Writing Have students draw a right triangle and label two of its sides with dimensions. Ask students to exchange drawings and use the Pythagorean Theorem to find the length of the third side.

Practice Masters, p. 78

Given the following lengths, determine whether each triangle is a right triangle.

Remember the hypotenuse is always the longest side.

4 7 inches, 24 inches, 25 inches

$$a^2 + b^2 = c^2$$
$$7^2 + 24^2 \stackrel{?}{=} 25^2$$
$$49 + 576 \stackrel{?}{=} 625$$
$$625 = 625$$

It is a right triangle.

5 8 inches, 13 inches, 16 inches

$$a^2 + b^2 = c^2$$
$$8^2 + 13^2 \stackrel{?}{=} 16^2$$
$$64 + 169 \stackrel{?}{=} 256$$
$$233 \neq 256$$

It is not a right triangle.

Checking for Understanding

Communicating Mathematics

Read and study the lesson to answer each question.

1. **Write** an equation that describes the relationship among the three large squares in the figure at the right. $4^2 + 3^2 = 5^2$

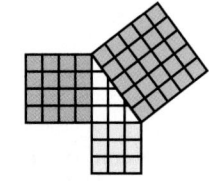

2. See margin.

2. **Draw** and label a right triangle with a hypotenuse of 17 units and legs of 8 units and 15 units.

3. **Write** the Pythagorean Theorem in your own words. **See students' work.**

Guided Practice

State the lengths of the legs and hypotenuse of each triangle.

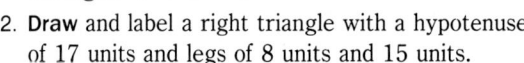

4. 4 ft, 5 ft, 3 ft **3, 4; 5**

5. 5 m, 13 m, 12 m **5, 12; 13**

6. 25 in., 24 in., 7 in. **7, 24; 25**

For answers to Exercises 7–10, see margin.

State the equation you would use to find the length of the hypotenuse of each right triangle. Then solve. Round answers to the nearest tenth.

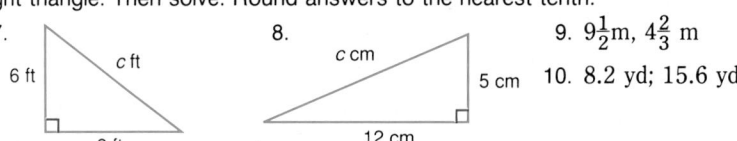

7. 6 ft, c ft, 8 ft

8. c cm, 5 cm, 12 cm

9. $9\frac{1}{2}$ m, $4\frac{2}{3}$ m

10. 8.2 yd; 15.6 yd

State the equation you would use to find the length of the leg of each right triangle. Then solve. **For answers to Exercises 11–14, see margin.**

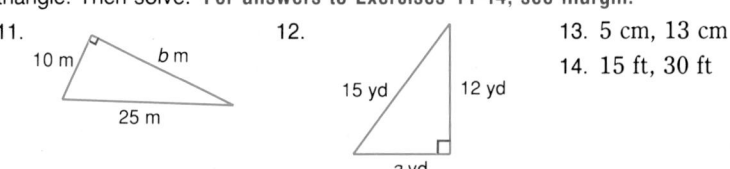

11. 10 m, b m, 25 m

12. 15 yd, 12 yd, a yd

13. 5 cm, 13 cm

14. 15 ft, 30 ft

OPTIONS

Limited English Proficiency

Have students draw or describe what a right triangle is. Then introduce the terms *legs,* and *hypotenuse.* Have students add the terms to their glossaries, along with a sketch of a right triangle showing the sides labeled a, b, and c, as appropriate.

Given the following lengths, determine whether each triangle is a right triangle. Write *yes* or *no*.

15. 2 m, 3 m, 4 m
no

16. 3 in., 4 in., 5 in.
yes

17. 5 ft, 7 ft, 9 ft
no

Exercises

Independent Practice

Use the Pythagorean Theorem to find the length of each hypotenuse given the lengths of the legs. Round answers to the nearest tenth.

18. 2 ft, 5 ft **5.4 ft**

19. 3 in., 7 in. **7.6 in.**

20. 9 cm, 40 cm **41 cm**

21. 14 ft, 8 ft **16.1 ft**

22. 13 mm, 9 mm **15.8 mm**

23. 11 yd, 17 yd **20.2 yd**

24. Draw a right triangle with legs of 4 centimeters and 7 centimeters. Find the length of the hypotenuse to the nearest tenth. **8.1 cm**

Find the missing lengths. Round decimal answers to the nearest tenth.

25.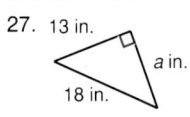
7 ft, 18 ft, *b* ft
b = **16.6 ft**

26.
23 cm, *b* cm, 6 cm
b = **22.2 cm**

27. 13 in., *a* in., 18 in.
a = **12.4 in.**

28. *b:* 9 yd; *c:* 15 yd
a = **12 yd**

29. *a:* 13 cm; *c:* 27 cm
b = **23.7 cm**

30. *b:* 24 m; *c:* 25 m
a = **7 m**

Given the following lengths, determine whether each triangle is a right triangle. Write *yes* or *no*.

31. 5 m, 12 m, 19 m **no**

32. 7 ft, 24 ft, 25 ft **yes**

33. 8 cm, 11 cm, 19 cm **no**

34. 9 in., 12 in., 15 in. **yes**

35. 20 ft, 25 ft, 30 ft **no**

36. 30 yd, 40 yd, 50 yd **yes**

37. 19 m, 20 m, 21 m **no**

38. 9 cm, 40 cm, 41 cm **yes**

Mixed Review

39. **Birthdays** Lisa's birthday is December 12. Julie's birthday is 19 days later. Solve mentally to find the date of Julie's birthday. *(Lesson 1-10)* **Dec. 31**

40. Use a factor tree to find the prime factorization of 720. *(Lesson 4-2)* $2^4 \times 3^2 \times 5$

41. Use inverse operations to solve $\frac{n}{15} = 5$. *(Lesson 6-1)* **75**

42. Solve the equation $m = 6 - (-12)$. *(Lesson 7-5)* **18**

43. **Real Estate** Ms. Snyder owns a square plot of land that has an area of 8 square miles. Estimate to the nearest whole mile the length of a side of her plot of land. *(Lesson 9-3)* **about 3 miles**

Problem Solving and Applications

44. **Building Maintenance** A 15-foot ladder is propped against a wall. The base of the ladder is 3 feet from the base of the wall. How far up the wall does the ladder reach? Use a calculator and round to the nearest tenth. **about 14.7 feet**

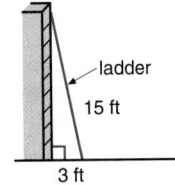
ladder
15 ft
3 ft

45. **Critical Thinking** On grid paper, draw a right triangle whose hypotenuse is 10 units long. **See margin.**

Additional Answers

2.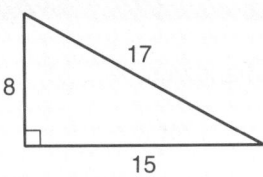
17, 8, 15

7. $6^2 + 8^2 = c^2; c = 10$ ft

8. $5^2 + 12^2 = c^2; c = 13$ cm

9. $(9\frac{1}{2})^2 + (4\frac{2}{3})^2 = c^2;$
   $c = 10.6$ m

10. $(8.2)^2 + (15.6)^2 = c^2;$
    $c = 17.6$ yd

11. $10^2 + b^2 = 25^2; b \approx 23$ m

12. $12^2 + a^2 = 15^2; a = 9$ yd

13. $5^2 + b^2 = 13^2; b = 12$ cm

14. $15^2 + b^2 = 30^2; b \approx 26$ ft

45.

10 units

Enrichment Masters, p. 78

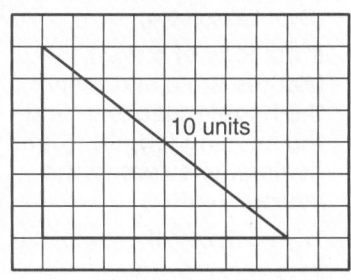

Lesson Resources
• Study Guide Master 9-5
• Practice Master 9-5
• Enrichment Master 9-5
• Evaluation Master, Quiz A, p. 79
• Multicultural Activity, p. 9
• Interdisciplinary Master, p. 23
• Group Activity Card 9-5

 Transparency 9-5 contains the 5-Minute Check and a teaching aid for this lesson.

🕐 **5-Minute Check**
(Over Lesson 9-4)

If the legs of a right triangle are *a* and *b* and the hypotenuse is *c*, find the missing length. Round decimal answers to the nearest tenth.

1. *a*: 3 ft; *b*: 7 ft   7.6 ft

2. *a*: 8 cm; *b*: 10 cm   12.8 cm

3. *b*: 5 yd; *c*: 8 yd   6.2 yd

4. *a*: 12 m; *c*: 20 m   16 m

5. Given the following lengths, find whether the triangle is a right triangle. Write *yes* or *no*.
   3 m, 8 m, 10 m   no

---

1 FOCUS

Motivating the Lesson

Questioning Ask students to explain why they can use the Pythagorean Theorem to solve the problem. Ask them to describe any other methods they might use to figure out how far Matt would be sitting from the speakers.

2 TEACH

Using Problem Solving When students use the Pythagorean Theorem to determine distances, encourage them to draw diagrams of the triangles, labeling the sides *a*, *b*, and *c*, and indicating on the sketch all the information they know.

348

9-5 Using the Pythagorean Theorem

Objective
Solve problems using the Pythagorean Theorem.

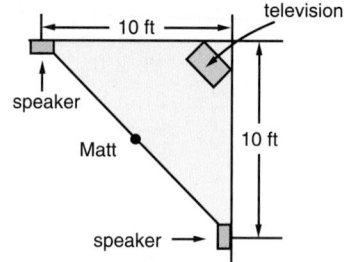

In order to get that "in concert" feeling while watching a singing group on TV, Matt positions the television in a corner, puts the speakers along the wall 10 feet from the corner, and sits midway between the speakers. About how far is he from each speaker?

The two speakers and the television form a right triangle. To find the distance between the two speakers, use the Pythagorean Theorem.

$$a^2 + b^2 = c^2$$
$$10^2 + 10^2 = c^2 \quad \textit{Replace a and b with 10.}$$
$$100 + 100 = c^2$$
$$200 = c^2$$
$$\sqrt{200} = c$$

200 $\boxed{\sqrt{x}}$ **14.142136**

The speakers are about 14 feet apart. If Matt is sitting halfway between the speakers, he is about 7 feet from each speaker.

Example 1 *Problem Solving*

Sales When a TV is advertised as a 40-inch TV, the 40-inch label refers to the length of the diagonal of the screen. Find the length of a side of a 40-inch big-screen TV if the screen is square.

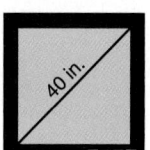

Since the screen is square, the sides will have the same length.

$$a^2 + a^2 = 40^2$$
$$2a^2 = 1{,}600 \qquad a^2 + a^2 = 2a^2$$
$$\frac{2a^2}{2} = \frac{1{,}600}{2} \qquad \textit{Divide each side by 2.}$$
$$a^2 = 800$$
$$a = \sqrt{800}$$

800 $\boxed{\sqrt{x}}$ **28.284271**

The sides of the television screen are about 28 inches.

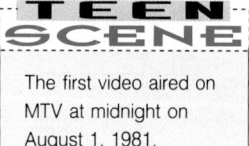
TEEN SCENE
The first video aired on MTV at midnight on August 1, 1981.

OPTIONS

Reteaching Activity

Using Models Have students use centimeter graph paper to draw one of the problems in the Guided Practice. Have them work through the equation, step by step, with a partner, and then check their results by actually measuring with a centimeter ruler.

Study Guide Masters, p. 79

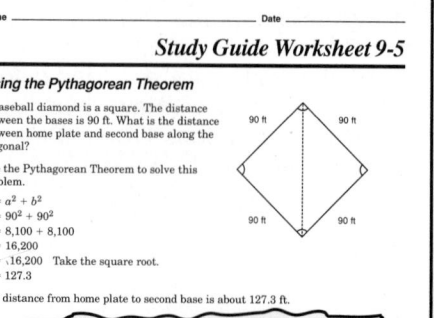

Name _____ Date _____
Study Guide Worksheet 9-5

Using the Pythagorean Theorem

A baseball diamond is a square. The distance between the bases is 90 ft. What is the distance between home plate and second base along the diagonal?

Use the Pythagorean Theorem to solve this problem.

$$c^2 = a^2 + b^2$$
$$c^2 = 90^2 + 90^2$$
$$c^2 = 8{,}100 + 8{,}100$$
$$c^2 = 16{,}200$$
$$c = \sqrt{16{,}200} \quad \text{Take the square root.}$$
$$c \approx 127.3$$

The distance from home plate to second base is about 127.3 ft.

Example 2 *Connection*

Geometry Find the perimeter of the triangle at the right.

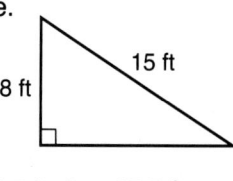

First, find *b*.

$$a^2 + b^2 = c^2$$
$$9^2 + b^2 = 17^2 \quad \textit{Replace a with 9 and c with 17.}$$
$$81 + b^2 = 289$$
$$81 - 81 + b^2 = 289 - 81 \quad \textit{Subtract 81 from each side.}$$
$$b^2 = 208$$
$$b = \sqrt{208}$$

208 $\boxed{\sqrt{x}}$ **14.422205**   So, $b \approx 14.4$

To find the perimeter, add the lengths of the three sides.
$$P \approx 9 + 17 + 14.4$$
$$\approx 40.4$$
The perimeter of the triangle is about 40.4 feet.

Checking for Understanding

Communicating Mathematics

Read and study the lesson to answer each question.

1. **Draw** and label a right triangle that shows Bob and Mary sitting 5 feet apart. If Bob sits along the wall 3 feet from the corner of the room, how far from the corner of the room is Mary if she sits along the wall? **See margin.**

2. **Tell** if the hypotenuse of a right triangle is used to find the height. Explain. **No; the hypotenuse is not vertical.**   **For answers to Exercises 3-5, see margin.**

Guided Practice

Write the equation you would use to find the value of x in each triangle. Then solve. Round decimal answers to the nearest tenth.

3.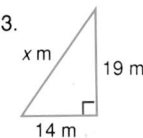

4.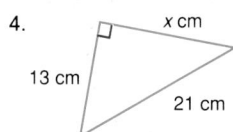

5.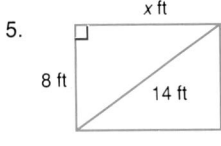

6. Lidia walks 8 miles north and 5 miles east. How far is she from her starting point? Find the straight-line distance. **about 9.4 miles**

Exercises

Independent Practice

Solve. Round decimal answers to the nearest tenth.

7. Rob is flying a kite. Ellen is standing directly underneath the kite. If Rob and Ellen are 40 feet apart and Rob has let out 110 feet of string, how high is the kite? **about 102.5 feet**

8. Bo wants to put a diagonal brace across a gate that is 3 feet wide and 6 feet high. He has a board that is 8 feet long. About how much will he have left over after he cuts the board to make the brace? **about 1.3 feet**

More Examples

For Example 1

Find the length of a side of a square picture frame if the diagonal measures 32 inches.   **22.627416 in., or about 23 in.**

For Example 2

Find the perimeter of the triangle.

$b \approx 12.7$ ft; $P \approx 35.7$ ft

Checking for Understanding

Exercises 1-2 are designed to help you assess students' understanding through reading, writing, speaking, and modeling. You should work through these exercises with your students and then monitor their work on Guided Practice Exercises 3-6.

Practice Masters, p. 79

Gifted and Talented Needs

Have students explain how they would figure out the length of a catcher's throw to second base in a baseball diamond and in a softball diamond.
baseball: $90^2 + 90^2 = c^2$
softball: $60^2 + 60^2 = c^2$

Additional Answers

1.

4 ft (or 8 ft, if she sits along the *same* wall as Bob)

3. $x^2 = 14^2 + 19^2$; $x \approx 23.6$ m
4. $21^2 = 13^2 + x^2$; $x \approx 16.5$ cm
5. $14^2 = 8^2 + x^2$; $x \approx 11.5$ ft

Have students explain how to use the Pythagorean theorem to solve problems. Ask them what information they would need.

3 PRACTICE/APPLY

Assignment Guide
Maximum: 7–13
Minimum: 7–11, 13
All: Mid-Chapter Review

Alternate Assessment

Writing Have students write a problem about a ladder leaning against a wall that can be solved by using the Pythagorean Theorem. Have students exchange papers and solve the problems.

Enrichment Masters, p. 79

Name _____ Date _____

Enrichment Worksheet 9-5

Two Star Puzzles

1. Cut apart these puzzle pieces. Reassemble them to make a six-pointed star.

2. Cut apart these puzzle pieces. Reassemble them to make three identical twelve-pointed stars.

T 79
Glencoe Division, Macmillan/McGraw-Hill

350

Mixed Review 9. **Smart Shopping** At the deli, 2.5 pounds of roast beef cost $7.50. What is the price per pound? *(Lesson 2-7)* **$3 per pound**

10. Is a triangle having sides of lengths 5 inches, 8 inches, and 10 inches a right triangle? *(Lesson 9-4)* **no**

Problem Solving and Applications

COMPUTER CONNECTION

11. **Computer Connection** The numbers 3, 4, and 5 are called *Pythagorean triples* because they are whole numbers that satisfy the Pythagorean Theorem. The computer program at the right will print all Pythagorean triples less than 21. Run the program and list the Pythagorean triples.

```
10 FOR A = 1 TO 21
20 FOR B = A TO 21
30 FOR C = B TO 21
40 IF A * A + B * B = C *
   C THEN PRINT A, B, C:
   GOTO 70
50 NEXT C
60 NEXT B
70 NEXT A
```

11. (3, 4, 5),
(5, 12, 13),
(6, 8, 10),
(8, 15, 17),
(9, 12, 15),
(12, 16, 20)

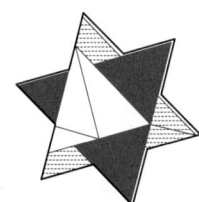

12. **Construction** A construction company is installing a roof on a new house. The width of the house is 26 feet. If the sides of the roof are to form a right angle and to be the same length, how long should each supporting board be, to the nearest tenth?
18.4 feet

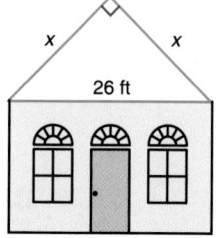

13. **Critical Thinking** Explain how to draw a right triangle with a hypotenuse of $\sqrt{10}$ units. If $a = 1$ unit and $b = 3$ units, then c will be $\sqrt{10}$ units.

9 Assessment: Mid-Chapter Review

1. The product of a number and itself is 1,296. What is the number? *(Lesson 9-1)* **36**

Find the square of each number. *(Lesson 9-2)*

2. 9 **81**   3. 22 **484**   4. 31 **961**

Find each square root. If it is not a perfect square, estimate. *(Lessons 9-2, 9-3)*

5. $\sqrt{13} \approx 4$ 6. $\sqrt{64}$ **8**   7. $\sqrt{138} \approx 12$

If the measures of the legs of a right triangle are a and b and the measures of the hypotenuse is c, find the missing length. Round decimal answers to the nearest tenth. *(Lesson 9-4)*

8. a: 9 feet; c: 41 feet **$b = 40$ ft**   9. a: 11 inches; b: 15 inches **$c \approx 18.6$ inches**

10. A helicopter rises vertically 800 feet and then travels west 1,200 feet. How far is it from its starting point? Round your answer to the nearest whole number. *(Lesson 9-5)* **1,442 feet**

OPTIONS

Extending the Lesson

Problem Solving The top of Miguel's worktable is a 7.5 ft by 7.5 ft square. Determine whether he can fit the table through a doorway that is 2.5 feet wide and 7 feet high. Why or why not? He can't; the longest distance of the doorway is a diagonal, which measures $\sqrt{55.25}$, or about 7.4 feet.

Cooperative Learning Activity

Bring the String 9-5

Use groups of 3.
Materials: String, scissors, metersticks

• Find the lengths of five large objects in the classroom using string. Cut off the string to indicate each length.

➡ In a corner of the classroom, two group members hold the string against the two adjoining walls so that there is no slack. (See the figure on the back of this card.) The other group member measures the distance in meters between the corner and the point at which each of the other two group members is holding one end of the string.

Use the Pythagorean Theorem to find the length in meters of the object whose string measurement you found.

Repeat the procedure for the other objects.

Glencoe Mathematics: Applications and Connections, Course 2

9-6 Area of Irregular Figures

Objective

Estimate the area of irregular figures.

Words to Learn

irregular figure

Paul Melendez entered the "Design a Skateboard" contest sponsored by the Broadsports Supply Company. The only limitation was that the area of the board could not exceed 250 square inches. Will Paul's entry be accepted?

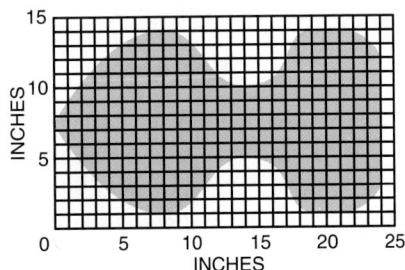

Paul's skateboard drawing is an **irregular figure.** Irregular figures do not necessarily have straight sides and square corners. One way to estimate the area of an irregular figure is to find the mean of the inner measure and outer measure. The inner measure is the number of whole squares within the figure. The outer measure is the number of squares inside of and touching the figure anywhere.

Example

Estimate the area of the skateboard.

inner measure: 187 in^2
outer measure: 230 in^2
mean: $\frac{(187 + 230)}{2} = 208.5$

An estimate of the area of Paul's skateboard is 208.5 square inches. Since the area is less than the limit of 250 square inches, Paul's entry will be accepted.

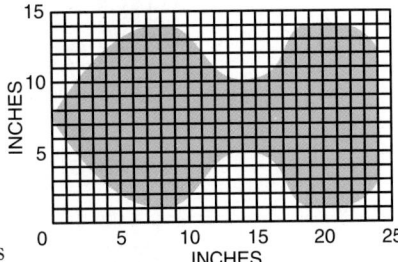

Mini-Lab

Work with a partner.
Materials: centimeter grid paper

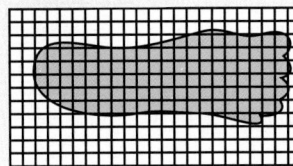

- Draw an outline of your foot on a piece of grid paper.

Talk About It

a. Find the inner measure and outer measure of the outline of your foot. **See students' work.**

Lesson 9-6 Area of Irregular Figures   **351**

OPTIONS

Reteaching Activity

Using Connections   Another way to estimate the area of an irregular figure is to separate it into a number of rectangles of various sizes and combine their areas. Guide students to see that the estimate improves as the number of rectangles into which a figure is separated increases.

Study Guide Masters, p. 80

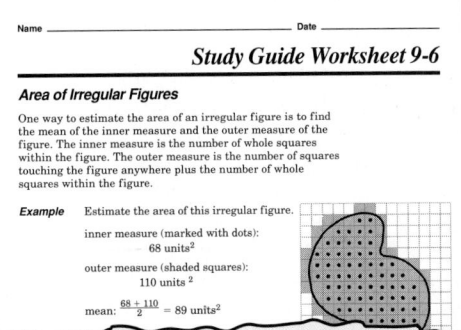

Name _____ Date _____

Study Guide Worksheet 9-6

Area of Irregular Figures

One way to estimate the area of an irregular figure is to find the mean of the inner measure and the outer measure of the figure. The inner measure is the number of whole squares within the figure. The outer measure is the number of squares touching the figure anywhere plus the number of whole squares within the figure.

Example   Estimate the area of this irregular figure.

inner measure (marked with dots): 68 units^2

outer measure (shaded squares): 110 units^2

mean: $\frac{68 + 110}{2} = 89$ units^2

NCTM Standards: 1–5, 7, 12

Lesson Resources
- Study Guide Master 9-6
- Practice Master 9-6
- Enrichment Master 9-6
- Group Activity Card 9-6

 Transparency 9-6 contains the 5-Minute Check and a teaching aid for this lesson.

⏱ 5-Minute Check

(Over Lesson 9-5)

Solve.

1. Two wires extend from the top of a tall pole and brace it by attaching it to the ground. If each wire is 25 feet long and is attached to a point on the ground 10 feet from the pole, how tall is the pole? about 23 feet tall

2. A 12-foot ladder reaches a point 9 feet up a wall. How far from the wall is the base of the ladder? about 8 feet

1 FOCUS

Motivating the Lesson

Activity   Draw a curved figure on the chalkboard. Ask students to work in small groups to come up with ways to estimate the area of the figure. Have the class discuss the methods they have chosen. Ask students to suggest uses for knowing how to measure the area of irregular shapes.

2 TEACH

Using the Mini-Lab   Have students tell why they think the averaging method for estimating area of irregular figures works. Encourage them to explore different methods or combinations of methods for making closer estimates.

351

Checking for Understanding

Exercises 1–2 are designed to help you assess students' understanding through reading, writing, speaking, and modeling. You should work through these exercises with your students and then monitor their work on Guided Practice Exercises 3–8.

Practice Masters, p. 80

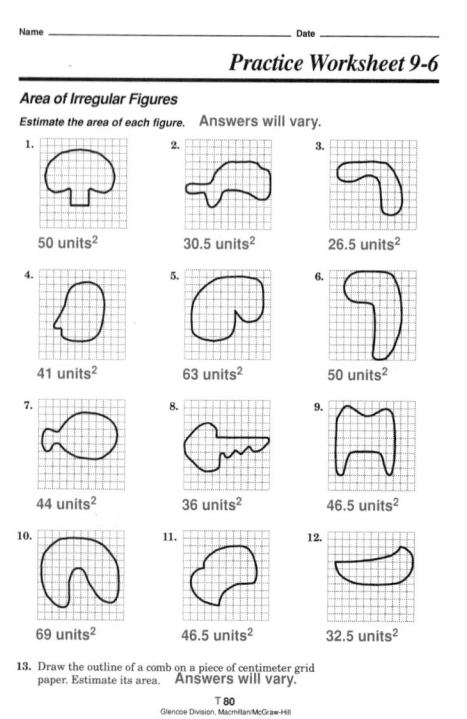

Name _____ Date _____

Practice Worksheet 9-6

Area of Irregular Figures

Estimate the area of each figure. Answers will vary.

1. 50 units² 2. 30.5 units² 3. 26.5 units²
4. 41 units² 5. 63 units² 6. 50 units²
7. 44 units² 8. 36 units² 9. 46.5 units²
10. 69 units² 11. 46.5 units² 12. 32.5 units²

13. Draw the outline of a comb on a piece of centimeter grid paper. Estimate its area. Answers will vary.

T 80
Glencoe Division, Macmillan/McGraw-Hill

352

---

b. Estimate the area by finding the mean. **See students' work.**

c. Find another way you can estimate the area of the outline of your foot. **See students' work.**

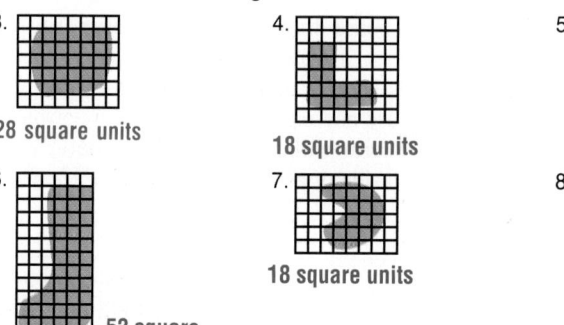

Checking for Understanding

Communicating Mathematics

Read and study the lesson to answer each question.

1. **Draw** an outline of your hand on a piece of centimeter grid paper. Estimate the area. **See students' work.**

2. **Describe** an irregular shape that you have seen and estimate its area.

Answers will vary.

Guided Practice

Estimate the area of each figure.

3.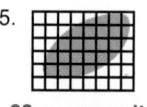
28 square units

4.
18 square units

5.
22 square units

6.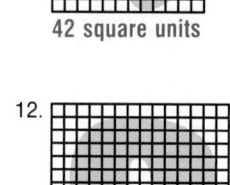
52 square units

7.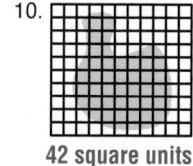
18 square units

8.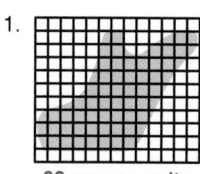
56 square units

Exercises

Independent Practice

Estimate the area of each figure.

9.
42 square units

10.
42 square units

11.
63 square units

12.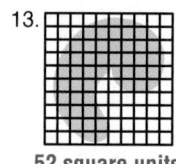
59 square units

13.
52 square units

14.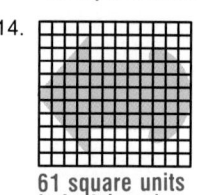
61 square units
See students' work.

15. Draw a spoon on a piece of centimeter grid paper. Estimate its area.

16. Draw a hammer on a piece of centimeter grid paper. Estimate its area. **See students' work.**

OPTIONS

Bell Ringer

Have students examine an outline map of the United States. Ask them why they think some state borders are straight lines and others are curved. Straight lines reflect artificial borders; jagged or curved lines reflect natural borders such as rivers or mountain ranges.

Interactive Mathematics Tools

This multimedia software provides an interactive lesson that is tied directly to Lesson 9–6. Students will use grids to explore irregular areas as in the introductory example.

17. Classify the triangle at the right by sides and by angles. *(Lesson 8-3)*
scalene, right

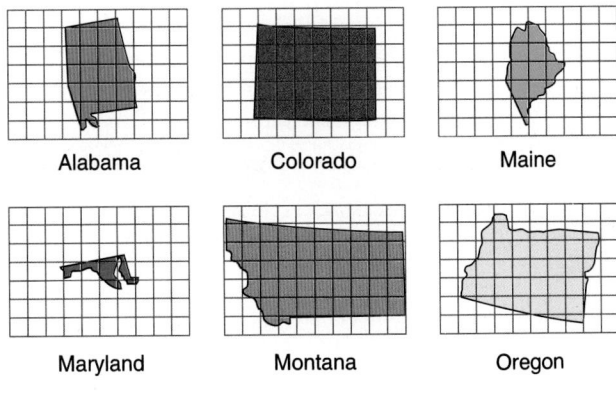

18. **Sailing** The main sail of a sailboat is in the shape of a right triangle. The hypotenuse of the sail is 32 feet long and the leg parallel to the water is 12 feet long. How tall is the sail? Round your answer to the nearest tenth. *(Lesson 9-5)* ≈ **29.7 feet**

a. **Alabama, Colorado, Montana, Oregon**

19. **Geography** Refer to the maps of the states shown below.
    a. Which states most closely resemble a rectangle?
    b. Which states most closely resemble a triangle? **Maryland, Maine**
    c. Use estimation to order the areas of the states below from largest to smallest. **Montana, Colorado, Oregon, Alabama, Maine, Maryland**

Alabama   Colorado   Maine

Maryland   Montana   Oregon

☐ = 50 square miles

20. **Critical Thinking** Estimate the area of your state in square miles. Explain the process you used. **See students' work.**

21. **Cooking** Mrs. Rosales bakes cakes for special events. She has an order for a large sheet cake in the shape of Cookie Monster® for a child's birthday party. To figure out how much icing she needs to make, she estimates the area of the top of the cake. What is a good estimate of this area?

21. **48 square units**

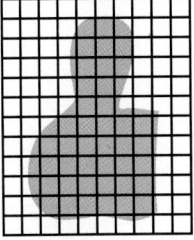

22. **Journal Entry** Make a drawing of a skateboard that you would like to enter in a contest. Estimate its area. Is it less than 250 square inches? **See students' work.**

Lesson 9-6 Area of Irregular Figures   **353**

Extending the Lesson

Using a Theorem Introduce students to Pick's Theorem for finding the area of an irregular-shaped polygon: $A = \frac{1}{2}b + (i - 1)$, where b = the number of points on the boundary of the figure, and i = the number of points within the interior of the figure. Have students explore this theorem using dot paper.

Cooperative Learning Activity

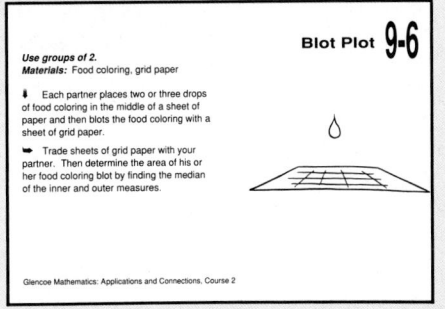

Blot Plot **9-6**

Use groups of 2.
Materials: Food coloring, grid paper

■ Each partner places two or three drops of food coloring in the middle of a sheet of paper and then blots the food coloring with a sheet of grid paper.

➡ Trade sheets of grid paper with your partner. Then determine the area of his or her food coloring blot by finding the median of the inner and outer measures.

Glencoe Mathematics: Applications and Connections, Course 2

Close

Have students draw an irregular shape on centimeter grid paper and exchange papers with a classmate. Each student must estimate the area of the figure, showing all work.

3 PRACTICE/APPLY

Assignment Guide
Maximum: 9–22
Minimum: 9–15 odd, 17–21

For **Extra Practice,** see p. 592.

Alternate Assessment

Speaking Have students explain how they would estimate the area of the figure formed by a rubber band dropped on a sheet of centimeter grid paper.

Enrichment Masters, p. 80

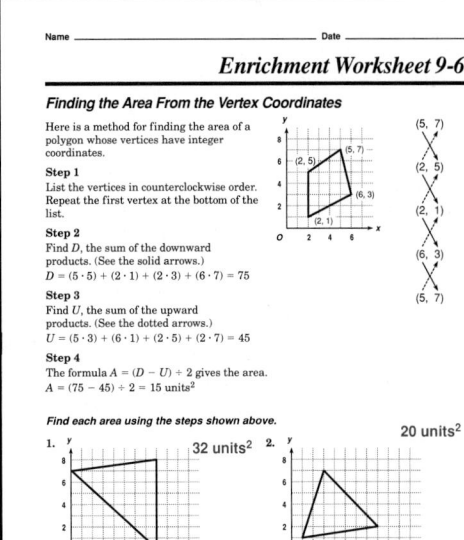

Name _____   Date _____

Enrichment Worksheet 9-6

Finding the Area From the Vertex Coordinates

Here is a method for finding the area of a polygon whose vertices have integer coordinates.

Step 1
List the vertices in counterclockwise order. Repeat the first vertex at the bottom of the list.

Step 2
Find D, the sum of the downward products. (See the solid arrows.)
$D = (5 \cdot 5) + (2 \cdot 1) + (2 \cdot 3) + (6 \cdot 7) = 75$

Step 3
Find U, the sum of the upward products. (See the dotted arrows.)
$U = (5 \cdot 3) + (6 \cdot 1) + (2 \cdot 5) + (2 \cdot 7) = 45$

Step 4
The formula $A = (D - U) \div 2$ gives the area.
$A = (75 - 45) \div 2 = 15 \text{ units}^2$

Find each area using the steps shown above.

1.   **14 units²**
2.   **20 units²**   **32 units²**
3.
4.   **36.5 units²**

T 80
Glencoe Division, Macmillan/McGraw-Hill

353

NCTM Standards: 1–5, 12

Management Tips

For Students Suggest to students that they use centimeter grid paper and a straightedge. They should draw their trapezoids large enough for them to be folded easily, cut, and rearranged.

For the Overhead Projector *Overhead Manipulative Resources* provides appropriate materials for teacher or student demonstration of the activities in this Mathematics Lab.

1 FOCUS

Introducing the Lab

Remind students that in an earlier chapter they explored the concept of area by rearranging a parallelogram to form another quadrilateral (a rectangle). Tell them that in this Lab activity they are going to reshape a trapezoid in order to find its area.

2 TEACH

Using Connections Ask students to describe the characteristics a trapezoid and a parallelogram have in common and to explain the ways in which the two figures differ. Have students justify their answers.

3 PRACTICE/APPLY

Using Critical Thinking Have students try out their equations for finding the area of trapezoids using other trapezoids. Groups should share their equations and explain how they arrived at their decision. Have students use what they know about solving equations to identify those that are equivalent.

Close

Have students explain how they were able to use prior knowledge to formulate an equation for finding the area of a trapezoid.

Cooperative Learning

9-7A Finding the Area of a Trapezoid

A Preview of Lesson 9-7

Objective
Find the area of a trapezoid.

In Lesson 8-3, you learned that a trapezoid is a quadrilateral with exactly one pair of parallel sides. In this lab, you will find the area of a trapezoid.

Materials
graph paper
scissors
tape

Try this!

Work in groups of three.

• Each student should draw a trapezoid on a piece of graph paper. Your trapezoid can be of any size or shape.

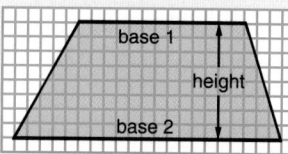

• Cut out your trapezoid. Label the bases and height as shown.

• Measure the length of base 1 and base 2. Measure the height. Record the measurements in a chart.

• Fold base 1 onto base 2. Unfold.

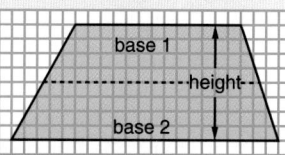

• Cut each trapezoid on the fold line. Then form a parallelogram.

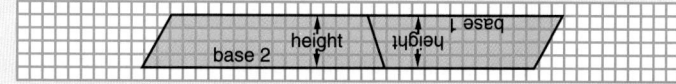

What do you think?

1. Find the length of the base of your parallelogram. How does it compare with the bases of your trapezoid? **See Solutions Manual.**
2. Measure the height of your parallelogram. How does this height compare with the height of your trapezoid? **See Solutions Manual.**
3. Find the area of your parallelogram. **See students' work.**
4. What is the area of your trapezoid? **See students' work.**
5. What conclusions can you make about the areas of all trapezoids?
6. Discuss in your group how to find the area of a trapezoid, given the lengths of base 1, base 2, and the height. Write a formula.

$$A = \frac{1}{2}h(b_1 + b_2)$$

5. See Solutions Manual.

LOOKBACK

You can review area of parallelograms on page 244.

354 Chapter 9 Measuring Area

OPTIONS

Lab Manual You may wish to make copies of the blackline master on p. 64 of the *Lab Manual* for students to use as a recording sheet.

Lab Manual, p. 64

Name _____ Date _____

Mathematics Lab Worksheet
Use with page 354

Finding the Area of a Trapezoid
Try this!
base 1 Answers will vary.
base 2 Answers will vary.
height Answers will vary.

What do you think?
1. The base of the parallelogram equals the sum of the bases of the trapezoid.

9-7 Area of Triangles and Trapezoids

Objective
Find the area of triangles and trapezoids.

Words to Learn
trapezoid

Delaware is nicknamed the Diamond State, but its shape looks more like a triangle. A triangle is a polygon that has three sides.

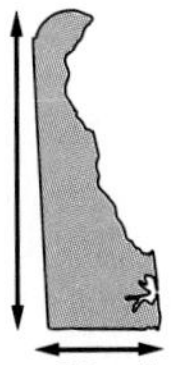

In this Mini-Lab, you will find the area of a triangle.

96 mi

39 mi

Mini-Lab

Work with a partner.
Materials: graph paper, scissors

- Draw a parallelogram of any shape or size on a piece of graph paper.
- Draw a diagonal in the parallelogram.
- Cut along the diagonal.

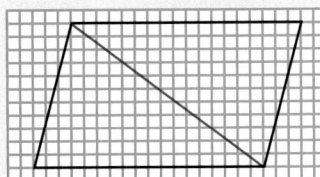

Talk About It
a. What two shapes are formed? triangles
b. How do the two shapes compare? They are congruent.
c. What is the area of the original parallelogram? See students' work.
d. What is the area of each triangle? $\frac{1}{2}$ area of parallelogram

Area of a Triangle	**In words:** The area of a triangle is equal to half the product of the length of its base and height. **In symbols:** If a triangle has a base of b units and a height of h units, then the area, A square units, is $$A = \frac{1}{2}bh.$$

Lesson 9-7 Area of Triangles and Trapezoids **355**

9-7 Lesson Notes

NCTM Standards: 1–5, 7, 12

Lesson Resources
- Study Guide Master 9-7
- Practice Master 9-7
- Enrichment Master 9-7
- Group Activity Card 9-7

Transparency 9-7 contains the 5-Minute Check and a teaching aid for this lesson.

5-Minute Check
(Over Lesson 9-6)
Estimate the area of the figure. 20

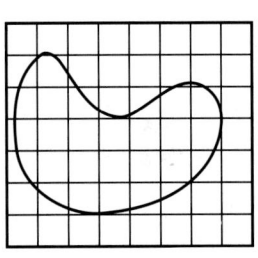

1 FOCUS

Motivating the Lesson

Activity Ask students to list as many real-world applications as they can for the area of a triangle or a trapezoid. Then have them identify something in the classroom that has the shape of either polygon and estimate its area just by looking at it. After students complete the lesson, ask them to calculate the area and compare the result with their estimate.

2 TEACH

Using the Mini-Lab Ask students whether they think the relationship that exists between the areas of the triangles and the area of the parallelogram will be the same every time any parallelogram is cut along its diagonal. Have them investigate other parallelograms.

More Examples

For Example 1

Find the area of the triangle.

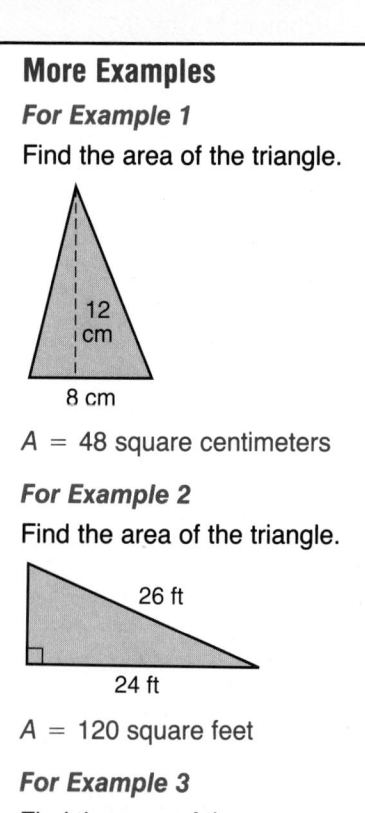

8 cm

$A = 48$ square centimeters

For Example 2

Find the area of the triangle.

26 ft

24 ft

$A = 120$ square feet

For Example 3

Find the area of the trapezoid.

25 m

14 m

38 m

$A = 441$ square meters

Checking for Understanding

Exercises 1-3 are designed to help you assess students' understanding through reading, writing, speaking, and modeling. You should work through these exercises with your students and then monitor their work on Guided Practice Exercises 4-11.

356

Mental Math Hint

• • • • • • • • • • • • •

If the base measure of a triangle is an odd number, it is easier to multipy the base measure and height first rather than multiplying the base by $\frac{1}{2}$ and getting a mixed number.

Example 1

Find the area of the triangle at the right.

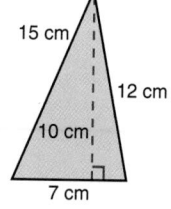

First identify the base and height.
base: 7 centimeters
height: 10 centimeters

$$A = \frac{1}{2}bh$$
$$= \frac{1}{2} \times 7 \times 10 \qquad \textit{Replace b with 7 and h with 10.}$$
$$= \frac{1}{2} \times 70 \qquad \textit{Associative property}$$
$$= 35$$

The area of the triangle is 35 square centimeters.

Example 2 *Connection*

Geometry Find the area of the triangle at the right.

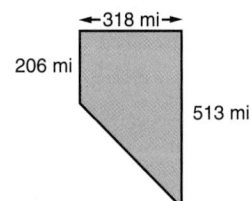

In a right triangle, one leg is the base and the other leg is the height.

Find the height by finding the length of the missing side.

$$a^2 + b^2 = c^2 \qquad \textit{Pythagorean Theorem}$$
$$8^2 + b^2 = 10^2 \qquad \textit{Replace a with 8 and c with 10.}$$
$$64 + b^2 = 100$$
$$64 - 64 + b^2 = 100 - 64 \qquad \textit{Subtract 64 from each side.}$$
$$b^2 = 36$$
$$b = \sqrt{36} \qquad \textit{Definition of square root}$$
$$b = 6$$

Now find the area. The base is 8 feet and the height is 6 feet.

$$A = \frac{1}{2}bh$$
$$= \frac{1}{2} \times 8 \times 6 \qquad \textit{Replace b with 8 and h with 6.}$$
$$= 4 \times 6$$
$$= 24 \qquad \text{The area of the triangle is 24 square feet.}$$

The state of Nevada has a shape that looks like a **trapezoid.** A trapezoid is a quadrilateral with exactly one pair of parallel sides.

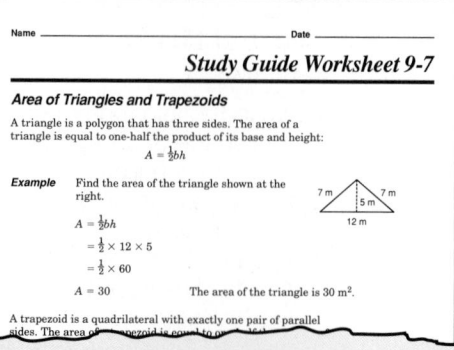

OPTIONS

Reteaching Activity

Using Models Have students use geoboards to form triangles and trapezoids from parallelograms. They can compare areas by counting enclosed squares.

Study Guide Masters, p. 81

Name _____ Date _____

Study Guide Worksheet 9-7

Area of Triangles and Trapezoids

A triangle is a polygon that has three sides. The area of a triangle is equal to one-half the product of its base and height:

$$A = \tfrac{1}{2}bh$$

Example Find the area of the triangle shown at the right.

7 m   5 m   7 m

12 m

$$A = \tfrac{1}{2}bh$$
$$= \tfrac{1}{2} \times 12 \times 5$$
$$= \tfrac{1}{2} \times 60$$
$$A = 30 \qquad \text{The area of the triangle is 30 m}^2.$$

A trapezoid is a quadrilateral with exactly one pair of parallel sides. The area of a ~~trapezoid is equal to on~~

In Mathematics Lab 9-7A you found the area of a trapezoid by folding base a onto base b. Cut the trapezoid along this fold line and form a parallelogram.

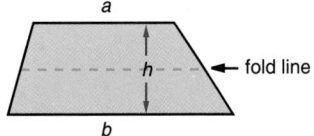

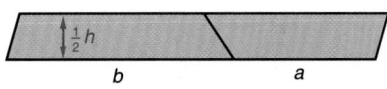

LOOK BACK

You can review the commutative property on page 204.

$A = \text{base} \times \text{height}$ *Area of a parallelogram*

$A = (a + b) \times \frac{1}{2}h$ *Substitute $a + b$ for the base and $\frac{1}{2}h$ for the height.*

$A = \frac{1}{2}h(a + b)$ *Commutative property*

Area of a Trapezoid	**In words:** The area of a trapezoid is equal to half the product of the height and the sum of the bases. **In symbols:** If a trapezoid has bases of a and b units and a height of h units, the area, A square units, is $$A = \frac{1}{2}h(a + b).$$

Example 3

Find the area of the trapezoid.

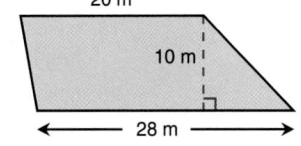

bases: 20 meters, 28 meters
height: 10 meters

$A = \frac{1}{2}h(a + b)$

$= \frac{1}{2}(10)(20 + 28)$ *Replace h with 10, a with 20, and b with 28.*

1 $\div$ 2 $\times$ 10 $\times$ (20 $+$ 28) $=$ **240**

The area of the trapezoid is 240 square meters.

For answers to Exercises 1-2, see margin.

Checking for Understanding

Communicating Mathematics

Read and study the lesson to answer each question.

1. **Describe** the relationship between the area of a parallelogram and the area of a triangle with the same height and base. Explain.

2. **Draw** a trapezoid with at least one right angle.

3. **Draw** a trapezoid with bases of 6 centimeters and 12 centimeters and a height of 7 centimeters.
   a. Cut the trapezoid like you did on page 354 and form a parallelogram. Find the area of the parallelogram. **63 sq cm**
   b. Find the area of the trapezoid using the formula. Check by comparing it to the area of the parallelogram. **63 sq cm**

Lesson 9-7 Area of Triangles and Trapezoids **357**

Gifted and Talented Needs

Have students use a geoboard to explore what happens to the area of a triangle if its shape changes, but its base and height do not. Area remains the same.

Additional Answers

1. The area of a triangle is half the area of a parallelogram with the same base and height.

2.

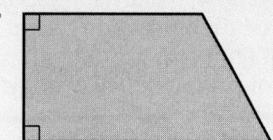

Error Analysis

Watch for students who use a side of either a triangle or a trapezoid for the height of the figure when finding its area.

Prevent by stressing that the height of a triangle or trapezoid is perpendicular to its base.

Close

Have students draw both a triangle and a trapezoid. Ask them to write an equation they can use to find the area of each figure. Then have them measure the needed parts of the figure and apply the equation.

3 PRACTICE/APPLY

Assignment Guide
Maximum: 12–28
Minimum: 13–21 odd, 23–27

For **Extra Practice,** see p. 592.

Alternate Assessment

Writing Have students write a problem that can be solved by finding the area of either a triangle or a trapezoid. Students must be sure to include all necessary data.

Practice Masters, p. 81

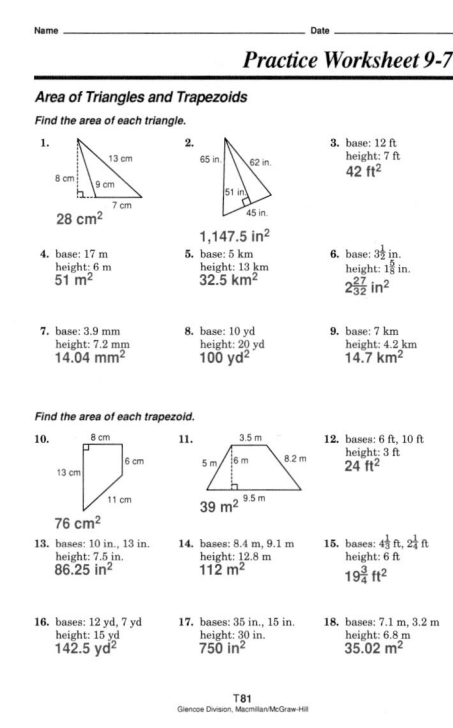

357

Additional Answer

27. $A = \frac{1}{2}h(a + b)$

$= \frac{1}{2}h(0 + b)$

$= \frac{1}{2}bh$

See diagram below.

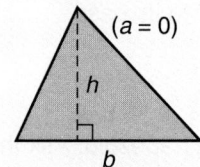

$(a = 0)$

h

b

Enrichment Masters, p. 81

Name _____ Date _____

Enrichment Worksheet 9-7

Heron's Formula

A formula named after Heron of Alexandria, Egypt, can be used to find the area of a triangle given the lengths of its sides.

Heron's formula states that the area A of a triangle whose sides measure a, b, and c is given by

$$A = \sqrt{s(s - a)(s - b)(s - c)},$$

where s is the semiperimeter:

$$s = \frac{a + b + c}{2}$$

Estimate the area of each triangle by finding the mean of the inner and outer measures. Then use Heron's Formula to compute a more exact area. Give each answer to the nearest tenth of a square unit.

Estimates will vary.

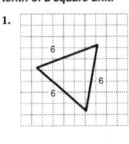 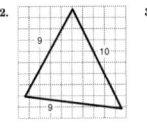 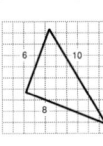

1. Estimated area: 15 — Computed area: 15.6
2. Estimated area: 38 — Computed area: 37.4
3. Estimated area: 25 — Computed area: 24.0

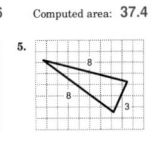 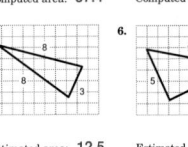

4. Estimated area: 20.5 — Computed area: 21.2
5. Estimated area: 12.5 — Computed area: 11.8
6. Estimated area: 18 — Computed area: 17.4

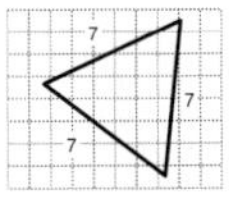

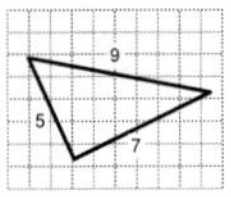

T81
Glencoe Division, Macmillan/McGraw-Hill

358

Guided Practice

Find the area of each triangle.

4.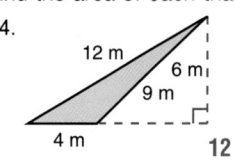
12 m, 6 m, 9 m, 4 m — **12 m²**

5.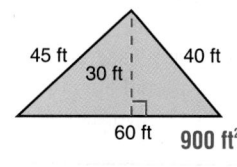
45 ft, 30 ft, 40 ft, 60 ft — **900 ft²**

6. base: 9 in. height: 6 in. **27 in²**

7. base: 5 ft height: 12 ft **30 ft²**

Find the area of each trapezoid.

8. 10 in., 14 in., 18 in., 16 in., 24 in. — **238 in²**

9. 14 m, 21.7 m, 27 m, 10.2 m — **248.37 m²**

10. bases: 5 cm, 14 cm height: 6 cm **57 cm²**

11. bases: 4 yd, 12 yd height: 10 yd **80 yd²**

Exercises

Independent Practice

Find the area of each triangle.

12. base: 16 m height: 12 m **96 m²**

13. base: 4 km height: 28 km **56 km²**

14. base: 7 ft height: 12 ft **42 ft²**

15. base: 1.4 in. height: 1.1 in. **0.77 in²**

16. base: 8 cm height: 19 cm **76 cm²**

17. base: $2\frac{1}{3}$ yd height: $1\frac{5}{6}$ yd **$2\frac{5}{36}$ yd²**

Find the area of each trapezoid.

18. bases: 4 in., 8 in. height: 6 in. **36 in²**

19. bases: 12 yd, 18 yd height: 10 yd **150 yd²**

20. bases: 7.3 cm, 9.5 cm height: 8.8 cm **73.92 cm²**

21. bases: $6\frac{1}{2}$ ft, $11\frac{2}{3}$ ft height: 14 ft **$127\frac{1}{6}$ ft²**

22. Find the area of a trapezoid that has bases of 11 yards and 19 yards and a height of $7\frac{1}{2}$ yards. **$112\frac{1}{2}$ yd²**

Mixed Review

23. **Statistics** Find the range for the following data. Then find an appropriate scale and interval. 25, 34, 16, 9, 22, 19, 31 *(Lesson 3-5)* **25; scale: 5 to 35; intervals of 5**

24. Find $4\frac{5}{8} \times 1\frac{2}{3}$. *(Lesson 5-5)* **$7\frac{17}{24}$**

25. Estimate the area of the irregular figure at the right. *(Lesson 9-6)* **about 32 sq units**

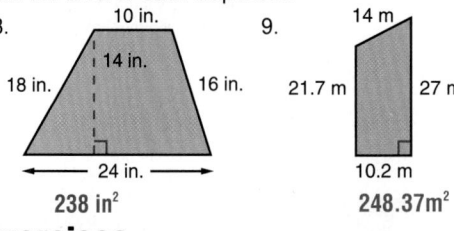
12 ft, 5 ft, 10 ft, 6 ft, 5 ft

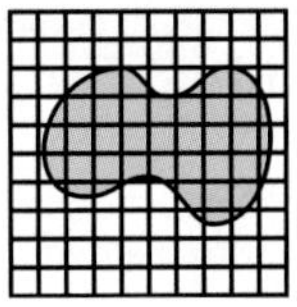

Problem Solving and Applications

26. **Construction** The Deck and Porch Company has several designs for decks. One of them is shown at the right. Find the area of the deck. **82.5 ft²**

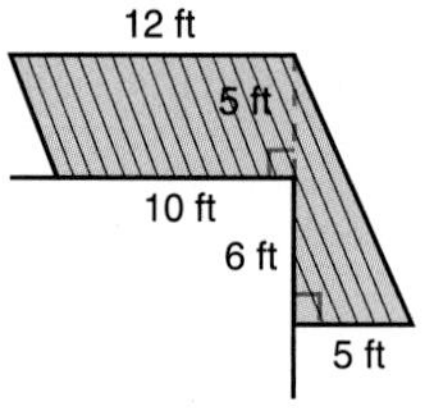

27. **Critical Thinking** Show how the area of a triangle could be found using the trapezoid formula. **See margin.**

28. **Journal Entry** Give at least three examples where you would need to be able to find the area of a triangle or trapezoid. **See students' work.**

358 **Chapter 9** Measuring Area

OPTIONS

Extending the Lesson

Using Number Sense Ask students to predict what will happen to the area of a triangle if its height or base (but not both) is doubled. Ask them how the area will change if *both* the height and base are halved. Have them investigate to check their predictions. **It doubles; it is multiplied by $\frac{1}{4}$.**

Cooperative Learning Activity

Strange Arranging 9-7

Use groups of 2.
Materials: Centimeter grid paper, metric ruler, scissors

➤ Cut out an 8 x 8 grid from centimeter grid paper. What is the area of the square?

Draw lines to make triangles A and B and trapezoids C and D, as shown in Figure A on the back of this card. Find the area of each figure in square centimeters. (The sum of these areas should equal the area you found above.)

Cut out the triangles and trapezoids and arrange them as shown in Figure B on the back of this card. The area of Figure B is 65 square centimeters. Is this the area you found for Figure A? If not, how do you explain the difference? Discuss your results with other pairs.

Glencoe Mathematics: Applications and Connections, Course 2

9-8 Area of Circles

Objective
Find the area of circles.

Could the Houston Astrodome fit inside the Louisiana Superdome? The highest point of the Superdome is 273 feet and the Astrodome is only 208 feet tall. The distance across the Astrodome is about 214 yards, and the floor area of the Superdome is 41,000 square yards. Since both structures are in the shape of circles, you will need to find the area of the circular floor of the Astrodome to answer the question in Example 1. To find the area of a circle, we will need to use the formula for the area of a parallelogram.

Mini-Lab

Work in pairs.
Materials: paper, compass, straightedge, scissors, pencil

- Draw a circle and several radii that separate the circle into equal-sized sections.

  Let r units represent the length of the radius of the circle and let C units represent its circumference.

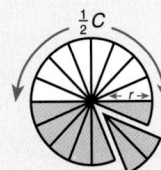

- Cut out each section of the circle.

- Reassemble the sections in the form of a parallelogram.

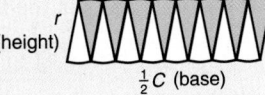

Talk About It

a. What is the height of this "parallelogram"? the length of the base? r; $\frac{1}{2}c$

b. What is the formula for the area of a parallelogram? $A = b \cdot h$

c. How could you use this formula to find the area of a circle? $A = (\frac{1}{2}C)r$ by substitution and then simplify to $A = \pi r^2$

Lesson 9-8 Area of Circles   **359**

9-8 Lesson Notes

NCTM Standards: 1–7, 12

Lesson Resources
- Study Guide Master 9-8
- Practice Master 9-8
- Enrichment Master 9-8
- Application Master, p. 9
- Group Activity Card 9-8

Transparency 9-8 contains the 5-Minute Check and a teaching aid for this lesson.

🕐 5-Minute Check
(Over Lesson 9-7)

Find the area of each triangle.

1. base: 14 m, height: 9 m
   A = 63 square meters

2. base: 2.6 cm, height: 1.7 cm A = 2.21 square centimeters

Find the area of each trapezoid.

3. bases: 4 in., 7 in. height: 5 in. A = 27.5 square inches

4. bases: $3\frac{1}{2}$ ft, 8 ft height: 6 ft A = $34\frac{1}{2}$ square feet

1 FOCUS

Motivating the Lesson

Situational Problem Ask students how they could determine which is larger, the center circle of a soccer field or the center circle of a basketball court.

OPTIONS

Multicultural Education

The great Mexican-American golfer, Lee Trevino, has won many important golfing championships during his distinguished career. Among these are the United States Open in 1968 and 1971, the British Open in 1971 and 1972, and the Professional Golfers Association Championship in 1974 and 1984.

Using the Mini-Lab Have students use a compass to make their circle. Discuss with them how to divide the circle into equal-sized sections (or *sectors,* which is the conventional term for pie-slice shapes). One method is to draw a diameter, bisect it, and then repeatedly bisect the angles formed. Point out that although the figure formed by reassembling the sections resembles a parallelogram, the resemblance is only approximate.

More Examples

For Example 1

Find the floor area of a ring in a circus if the diameter is 12 yards. $A \approx 113$ square yards, to the nearest whole number

For Example 2

Find the radius of a circle if its area is 176 square inches. $r \approx 7.5$ in.

Checking for Understanding

Exercises 1-3 are designed to help you assess students' understanding through reading, writing, speaking, and modeling. You should work through these exercises with your students and then monitor their work on Guided Practice Exercises 4-11.

LOOKBACK

You can review circumference on pages 197 and 198.

The base of the parallelogram shown on the previous page is equal to one half of the circumference of the circle ($\frac{1}{2}C$). The height of the parallelogram is the measure of the radius of the circle (r). Substitute this information into the formula for the area of a parallelogram.

$A = bh$ *Formula for area of a parallelogram*

$\quad = (\frac{1}{2}C)r$ *Substitute $\frac{1}{2}C$ for b and substitute r for h.*

$\quad = (\frac{1}{2} \times 2\pi r)r$ *Substitute $2\pi r$ for C.*

$\quad = \pi r^2$ *Simplify: $\frac{1}{2} \times 2 = 1$, $r \times r = r^2$.*

Area of a Circle	**In words:** The area of a circle is equal to pi times the square of the radius. **In symbols:** If a circle has a radius of r units, then $A = \pi r^2$.

Example 1 *Problem Solving*

Sports Find the floor area of the Astrodome if its diameter is 214 yards.

$r = \frac{1}{2}d$ *The radius is one half of the diameter.*

$\quad = \frac{1}{2} \times 214$ *Replace d with 214.*

$\quad = 107$

LOOKBACK

You can review π, pi, on page 198.

Use the measure to find the area.

$A = \pi r^2$

$\quad = \pi \times 107^2$ *Replace r with 107.*

$\quad = 3.14 \times 11,449$ *Replace π with 3.14.*

$\boxed{\pi}\ \boxed{\times}\ 11{,}449\ \boxed{=}\ 35968.094$

To the nearest whole number, the floor area of the Astrodome is 35,950 square yards. Could the Astrodome fit inside the Superdome?

DID YOU KNOW

The Houston Astrodome was completed in 1965. It was the first baseball and football stadium to be completely enclosed by a roof. The Louisiana Superdome was completed in 1977. It is the world's largest indoor arena.

You can also use the formula for the area of a circle to find the length of the radius when the area is known.

Example 2

Find the length of the radius of a circle if its area is 79 square inches.

$A = \pi r^2$

$79 \approx 3.14 \times r^2$ *Replace A with 79 and π with 3.14.*

$\dfrac{79}{3.14} \approx \dfrac{3.14 \times r^2}{3.14}$ *Divide each side by 3.14.*

$25.16 \approx r^2$

$\sqrt{25.16} \approx r$ *Definition of square root*

$5.02 \approx r$ The radius of the circle is about 5 inches long.

OPTIONS

Reteaching Activity

Using Applications Have students choose circular objects from within the classroom or draw them with a compass. Have them measure the radius or diameter of each, and use their measurement to find the area. Encourage students to compute with calculators.

Study Guide Masters, p. 82

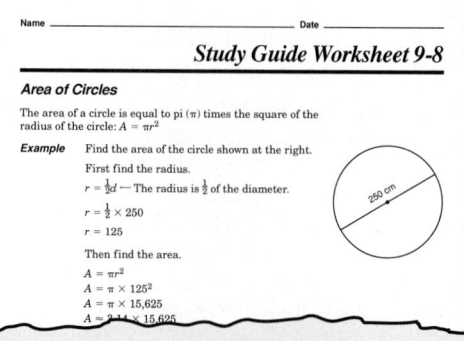

Name _____ Date _____

Study Guide Worksheet 9-8

Area of Circles

The area of a circle is equal to pi (π) times the square of the radius of the circle: $A = \pi r^2$

Example Find the area of the circle shown at the right.
First find the radius.
$r = \frac{1}{2}d$ — The radius is $\frac{1}{2}$ of the diameter.
$r = \frac{1}{2} \times 250$
$r = 125$

Then find the area.
$A = \pi r^2$
$A = \pi \times 125^2$
$A = \pi \times 15{,}625$
$A = 3.14 \times 15{,}625$

(250 cm)

Checking for Understanding

Communicating Mathematics

Read and study the lesson to answer each question.

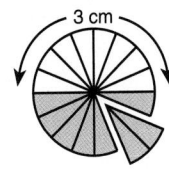

1. **Tell** how you can find the area of a circle given the length of the diameter of the circle. **See margin.**

2. **Draw** a circle with radius of 1 inch. Find its area.

3. **Tell** the base measures and the height of a parallelogram formed from the circle at the right. Find the area. $3; r; A = 3r$

1. $r = \frac{1}{2}d$; find r and then use area formula.

Guided Practice

Find the area of each circle given the following information. Round answers to the nearest tenth.

4. 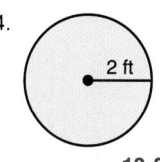 2 ft

12.6 ft²

5. 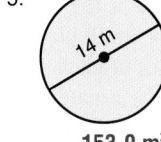 14 m

153.9 m²

6. radius, 5 in.   78.5 in²

7. diameter, 1.4 cm   1.5 cm²

Find the radius of each circle given the following areas. Round answers to the nearest tenth.

8. 12 cm²   9. 27 ft²   10. 75 m²   11. 112 in²
  2.0 cm   2.9 ft   4.9 m   6.0 in.

Exercises

Independent Practice

Find the area of each circle shown or described below. Round answers to the nearest tenth.

12. 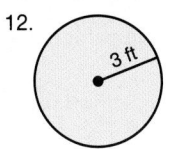 3 ft

28.3 ft²

13. 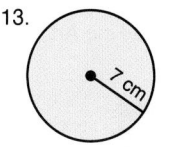 7 cm

153.9 cm²

14. 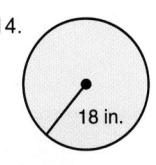 18 in.

1,017.4 in²

15. 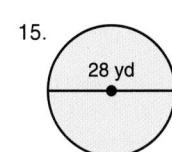 28 yd

615.4 yd²

16. 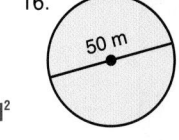 50 m

1,962.5 m²

17. 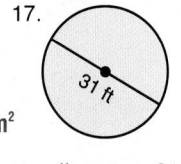 31 ft

754.4 ft²

18. 153.9 in²
19. 113.0 cm²
20. 346.2 km²
21. 1,962.5 ft²
22. 40.7 yd²
23. 1,194.0 m²
24. 4.1 ft
25. 5.0 m
26. 6.0 in.
27. 0.6 km
28. 5.1 cm
29. 1.8 yd
30. 9.0 ft
31. 5.3 m

18. radius, 7 in.   19. diameter, 12 cm   20. diameter, 21 km
21. radius, 25 ft   22. diameter, 7.2 yd   23. radius, 19.5 m

Find the length of the radius of each circle given the following areas. Round answers to the nearest tenth.

24. 53 ft²   25. 79.4 m²   26. 112 in²   27. 1.05 km²
28. 82 cm²   29. 10.64 yd²   30. 254 ft²   31. 88.2 m²

32. Find the length of the diameter of a circle whose area is 134 square meters. $d \approx 13$ **meters**

Classroom Vignette

"After students have completed Exercise 13, I have them draw a circle with a radius of 7 centimeters, using a compass, on centimeter grid paper. Then they count the number of squares and compare that number to their computed answer."

Ron Pelfrey

Ronald S. Pelfrey
Author

Close

Have students explain how they would find the area of a circular rug with a diameter of 6 feet. Divide the diameter by 2, then square the result and multiply by 3.14.

3 PRACTICE/APPLY

Assignment Guide
Maximum: 12–40
Minimum: 13–31 odd, 33–39

For **Extra Practice,** see p. 593.

Alternate Assessment

Writing Have students explain why a circular room with an area of about 700 square feet could not have a diameter of about 20 feet. Sample answer: If $d = 20$, then $r = 10$, and $A \approx 314$ square feet.

Additional Answer

2.

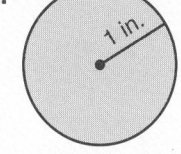 1 in.

$A = \pi \times 1^2$
≈ 3.14 square inches

Practice Masters, p. 82

 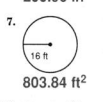

33. **Recycling** Kimi collects 5.6 pounds of aluminum cans. The recycling center will pay her $0.42 per pound. How much will Kimi receive when she turns in the cans? *(Lesson 2-4)* **$2.36**

−8, −4, −3, 0, 1, 4, 6

34. Order 6, −3, 0, 4, −8, 1, −4 from least to greatest. *(Lesson 7-2)*

35. Which quadrilaterals have four congruent sides? *(Lesson 8-3)* **square, rhombus**

36. Find the area of a trapezoid whose bases are 8 inches and 12 inches long and whose height is 6 inches. *(Lesson 9-7)* **60 in²**

37. **History** Stonehenge, an ancient monument in England, may have been used as a calendar. The stones are arranged in a circle 30 meters in diameter. Find the area of the circle. **A ≈ 706.5 m²**

38. **Food** The table at the right gives the diameter of three pizza sizes.
    a. Find the area of each size.
    b. Which has the greatest area: 1 large pizza or 2 medium pizzas? **2 medium pizzas**

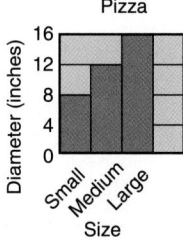

Pizza

39. **Critical Thinking** The floor of the Superdome can be set up as a track for track and field events. Find the area inside the track. **A ≈ 4,486.5 yd²**

a. small—50.24 in²
   med—113.04 in²
   large—200.96 in²

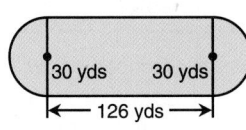

Hint: The track is formed by a rectangle and two semicircles.

40. **Mathematics and Fine Art** Read the following paragraphs.

A fresco is a special kind of wall painting that is made when the wall is plastered. Paints are mixed with the wet plaster as it is applied to the wall. The colors show up brightly when the plaster dries.

Diego Rivera was a Mexican painter whose bold murals stimulated a revival of fresco painting in Latin America and the United States. During the Great Depression, he was commissioned to paint a massive fresco honoring American auto workers. It fills an entire room in the Detroit Institute of Arts. His largest and most ambitious mural was an epic of the history of Mexico for the National Palace in Mexico City. It was unfinished when he died in 1957.

An artist wants to paint the sun in his fresco. He wants it to have an area of 40 square feet. What would be the diameter of this sun? **d ≈ 7.14 feet**

362   **Chapter 9** Measuring Area

Enrichment Masters, p. 82

Name _____ Date _____

Enrichment Worksheet 9-8

Extending the Pythagorean Theorem

The Pythagorean Theorem says that the sum of the areas of the two smaller squares is equal to the area of the largest square. Show that the Pythagorean Theorem can be extended to include other shapes on the sides of a triangle. To do so, find the areas of the two smaller shapes. Then, check that their sum equals the area of the largest shape.

1. area of smallest shape: **3.5 in²**
   area of middle shape: **6.3 in²**
   area of largest shape: **9.8 in²**

2. area of smallest shape: **2.25 in²**
   area of middle shape: **4 in²**
   area of largest shape: **6.25 in²**

3. area of smallest shape: **4.5 in²**
   area of middle shape: **8 in²**
   area of largest shape: **12.5 in²**

4. area of smallest shape: **3.9 in²**
   area of middle shape: **6.9 in²**
   area of largest shape: **10.8 in**

(*Hint:* For an equilateral triangle, A = $\frac{s^2}{4}\sqrt{3}$.)

T82
Glencoe Division, Macmillan/McGraw-Hill

OPTIONS

Extending the Lesson

Mathematics and Fine Art Ask students to describe the role mathematics plays in a painter's work. What is the importance of calculating the area of canvasses or walls? Discuss what might happen if such planning is not done before the artist begins to paint.

Cooperative Learning Activity

Number of players: 2
Materials: Hole punch, construction paper, scissors, spinner

Hole Punch of Fun **9-8**

On construction paper draw the figures shown on the back of this card. Then cut the figures out. Label equal sections of a spinner "1," "5," "10," and "20."

Each partner selects a figure and spins the spinner. Each partner then punches out of the figure the number of holes indicated on the spinner. Working together, find the area of each figure that remains. (Hint: The area of each figure is reduced by the area of the circle made by the hole punch each time you punch a hole.) The partner with the greater remaining area wins the round. Trade roles and play again.

9-9A Probability and Area Models

A Preview of Lesson 9-9

Objective
Estimate the area of a figure using probability.

Materials
inch grid paper
ruler
small counters

In this activity, you will investigate the relationship between area and probability.

Try this!

Work in groups of three.

- Draw a square that has sides 8 inches long on your grid paper. Inside the square, draw a triangle with one side 6 inches long and the other side 5 inches long.

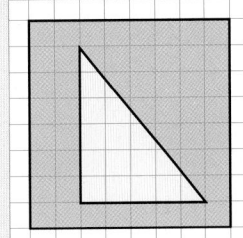

- Hold 20 counters about 5 inches above the paper and drop them onto the paper.

- Count the number of counters that landed completely within the square. (This includes those that landed within the triangle.) Count the number that landed completely inside the triangle. Do not count those that landed on a side of the triangle. These two numbers make up the first sample.

- Repeat the activity nine more times.

- Add the results of your ten samples to find the total number of counters that fell within the square and the total number that fell within the triangle.

You can review probability on page 157.

- The probability that a counter will land inside the triangle is expressed by the fraction:

$$\frac{\text{total counters within the triangle}}{\text{total counters within the square}} = \text{probability}$$

Calculate this experimental probability based on your findings.

Lesson 9-9A Mathematics Lab: Probability and Area Models   **363**

Mathematics Lab 9-9A

NCTM Standards: 1–5, 7, 11, 12

Management Tips

For Students Have students take turns dropping the counters. One student should draw the square and triangle. Another should record the results. A third should use a calculator to find the experimental probability and calculate the areas.

For the Overhead Projector
Overhead Manipulative Resources provides appropriate materials for teacher or student demonstration of the activities in this Mathematics Lab.

1 FOCUS

Introducing the Lab

Discuss the difference between experimental and theoretical probability. Use simple experiments to demonstrate the distinction, such as flipping a coin or spinning a spinner. Ask students whether it is possible to flip 10 heads in a row. Ask them to explain how doing many trials of an experiment affects the relationship between experimental and theoretical probability.   The greater the number of trials, the closer the two probabilities are likely to become.

Using Connections You may need to explore or review the concept of proportions with students so they will understand the step in which they cross multiply to find the area of the triangle.

3 PRACTICE/APPLY

Using Critical Thinking Ask students whether the results of the experiment would change if they were to place the triangle in the corner of the square, or if they were to drop the counters ten additional times or drop them from a greater or lesser height.

Close

Ask students to summarize the results of their experiment. Have them explain how they are able to use probability to estimate the area of a figure within another figure whose area is known.

• You can compute the following probability to estimate the area of the triangle.

$$\text{probability} = \frac{\text{area of triangle}}{\text{area of square}}$$

Substitute the probability into the left side of the equation. Calculate the area of the square and substitute it in the denominator of the right side. Then solve to find the area of the triangle.

What do you think?

1. Count the number of grid squares inside your triangle to get an estimate of the area. Since not all the squares are complete squares, you will sometimes need to combine two or three partial squares to get an estimate of the number of complete squares. How does this estimate of the area compare with the experimental probability estimate you found above? **See students' work.**

2. Measure the base and height of the triangle. Find the area using the formula $A = \frac{1}{2}bh$. How does it compare with your experimental probability estimate? $A = 15$ in²; **See students' work.**

Extension   For answers to Exercises 3 and 4, see students' work.

3. Repeat this activity with a circle inside your square.
4. Repeat this activity with an irregular figure inside your square.

OPTIONS

Lab Manual You may wish to make copies of the blackline master on p. 65 of the *Lab Manual* for students to use as a recording sheet.

Lab Manual, p. 65

Name _____ Date _____

Mathematics Lab Worksheet

Use with pages 363-364

Probability and Area Models

Try this!   Answers will vary.

Sample	1	2	3	4	5	6	7	8	9	10	Sum
Counters in the square											
Counters in the triangle											

Experimental probability = _____   Area of the triangle = _____

What do you think?

1. The area of the triangle is 15 in². Answers will vary.

9-9 Area Models and Probability

Objective
Find the probability using area models.

Alberto Davilla designed the archery target shown at the right as part of a cooperative project for his art and physical education classes. An arrow is shot and hits the target. What is the probability that the arrow landed in the yellow region if it is equally likely to hit any square?

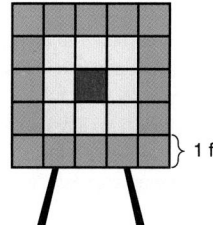

1 ft

In order to solve this problem, we need to know the area of the entire target and the area of the yellow region. Since the target is in the shape of a square, we can find the area of the target by either counting the small squares or by using the area formula.

$$A = s^2$$
$$= 5^2 \quad \textit{Substitute 5 for s.}$$
$$= 25$$

The target has an area of 25 square feet.

Next we need to find the area of the yellow region. We can count the yellow squares and find the area to be 8 square feet.

Now we can find the probability of an arrow landing in the yellow region. Remember the definition of probability.

$$\text{probability} = \frac{\text{number of ways an event can occur}}{\text{number of possible outcomes}}$$

In our target problem, the *event* is hitting the yellow region. This would be the area of the yellow region, 8 square feet. *All possible outcomes* would be hitting anywhere on the target. This would be the total area of the target, 25 square feet.

$$\text{probability} = \frac{\text{number of ways an event can occur}}{\text{number of possible outcomes}}$$
$$= \frac{8}{25}$$

The probability of hitting the yellow region is $\frac{8}{25}$ or 0.32.

Lesson 9-9 Area Models **365**

Study Guide Masters, p. 83

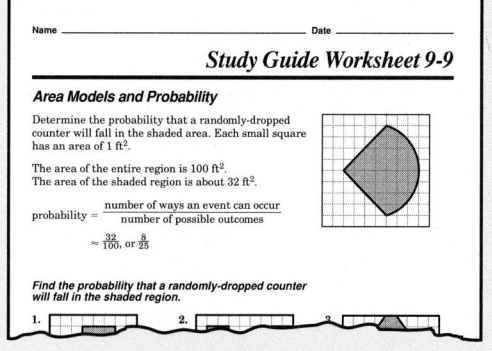

Name _____ Date _____

Study Guide Worksheet 9-9

Area Models and Probability

Determine the probability that a randomly-dropped counter will fall in the shaded area. Each small square has an area of 1 ft².

The area of the entire region is 100 ft².
The area of the shaded region is about 32 ft².

$$\text{probability} = \frac{\text{number of ways an event can occur}}{\text{number of possible outcomes}}$$
$$\approx \frac{32}{100}, \text{ or } \frac{8}{25}$$

Find the probability that a randomly-dropped counter will fall in the shaded region.

1. ___ 2. ___

9-9 Lesson Notes

NCTM Standards: 1–5, 7, 11, 12

Lesson Resources
• Study Guide Master 9-9
• Practice Master 9-9
• Enrichment Master 9-9
• Evaluation Master, Quiz B, p. 79
• Group Activity Card 9-9

Transparency 9-9 contains the 5-Minute Check and a teaching aid for this lesson.

5-Minute Check
(Over Lesson 9-8)

Find the area of each circle shown or described.

1.
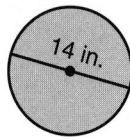

14 in.

$A \approx 153.86$ square inches

2. radius, 3.4 m $A \approx 36.3$ square meters

3. diameter, 22 km $A \approx 379.9$ square kilometers

4. Find, to the nearest hundredth, the radius of a circle whose area is 62 square feet. $r \approx 4.44$ ft

1 FOCUS

Motivating the Lesson

Situational Problem Ask students to describe how they could theoretically figure out the probability of a dart landing on any region of a dartboard. Ask them to discuss how probability can be used to design dartboards and develop a scoring system.

2 TEACH

Using Discussion As you work through the opening situation and examples with students, ask them to identify the information they would need in order to be able to predict the number of times a counter will drop on a particular shaded region.

365

More Examples

For Examples 1 and 2

Determine the probability that a randomly dropped counter will fall in the shaded area.

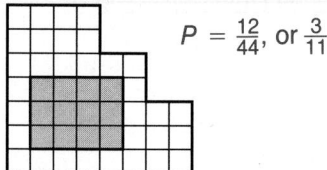

$$P = \frac{12}{44}, \text{ or } \frac{3}{11}$$

Find the probability that a golf ball will land in the region shown.

$$P = \frac{1,600}{9,600}, \text{ or } \frac{1}{6}$$

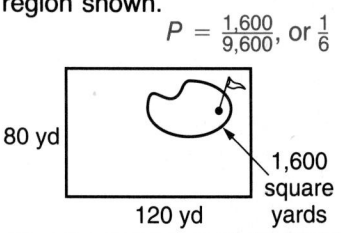

80 yd

1,600 square yards

120 yd

Checking for Understanding

Exercises 1-2 are designed to help you assess students' understanding through reading, writing, speaking, and modeling. You should work through these exercises with your students and then monitor their work on Guided Practice Exercises 3-5.

Practice Masters, p. 83

Name _____ Date _____

Practice Worksheet 9-9

Area Models and Probability

Find the probability that a randomly-dropped counter will fall in the shaded region.

1. $\frac{1}{25}$ 2. $\frac{2}{7}$ 3. $\frac{3}{20}$

4. $\frac{1}{4}$ 5. $\frac{1}{6}$ 6. $\frac{1}{2}$

7. $\frac{4}{13}$ 8. $\frac{5}{27}$ 9. $\frac{2}{5}$

10. $\frac{7}{22}$ 11. $\frac{5}{21}$ 12. $\frac{1}{2}$

13. Draw a square 4 units on a side on a piece of grid paper. Shade in 12 squares. What is the probability that a randomly-dropped counter will fall in the shaded area? $\frac{3}{4}$

14. Draw a square 6 units on a side on a piece of grid paper. Shade in 14 squares. What is the probability that a randomly-dropped counter will fall in the shaded area? $\frac{7}{18}$

T83
Glencoe Division, Macmillan/McGraw-Hill

366

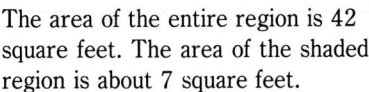 **When am I ever going to use this?**

Suppose you are going to carpet and tile different sections of your L-shaped kitchen floor. The carpeted area will lead into the living room. You want the probability of any food or drink spilling on the carpeted area kept to a minimum. Where and how large will the carpeted area be?

Example 1

Determine the probability that a randomly-dropped counter will fall in the shaded area. Each unit square is 1 square foot.

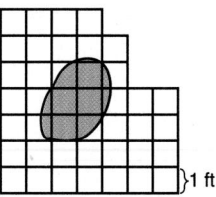

}1 ft

The area of the entire region is 42 square feet. The area of the shaded region is about 7 square feet.

$$\text{probability} = \frac{\text{number of ways an event can occur}}{\text{number of possible outcomes}}$$

$$= \frac{7}{42} \text{ or } \frac{1}{6}$$

Example 2   *Problem Solving*

Sports   A golfer tees off and the ball lands in the rectangular region at the right. What is the probability that the ball lands on the green?

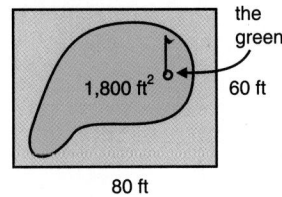

the green

1,800 ft²   60 ft

80 ft

The area of the rectangular region is 80×60 or 4,800 square feet. The area of the green is 1,800 square feet.

$$\text{probability} = \frac{\text{number of ways an event can occur}}{\text{number of possible outcomes}} = \frac{1,800}{4,800} \text{ or } \frac{3}{8} \text{ or } 0.375$$

Checking for Understanding

Communicating Mathematics

Read and study the lesson to answer each question.

1. **Tell** how you would find the probability of an arrow landing in the red region of the target on page 365. **See margin.**

2. **Write** the equation you would use to estimate the area of the trapezoid at the right if 8 out of 20 counters landed in the trapezoid. $\frac{8}{20} = \frac{A}{84}$

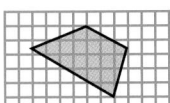

Guided Practice

Find the probability that a randomly-dropped counter will fall in the shaded region.

3. 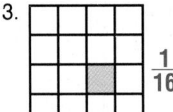 $\frac{1}{16}$

4. 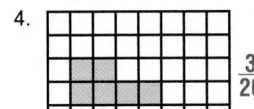 $\frac{3}{20}$

5. 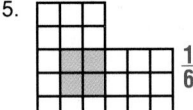 $\frac{1}{6}$

OPTIONS

Bell Ringer

Have students obtain a map of your state. Ask them to imagine that scientists have predicted that a meteor is going to land somewhere in the state, but they have no idea exactly where. Have students determine the probability that the meteor will land in your county or in any other identifiable region.

Additional Answer

1. Find the area of the entire target and the area of the red region. Then write the probability as a fraction:

$$\frac{\text{area of red squares}}{\text{area of target}}$$

Exercises

Independent Practice

Find the probability that a randomly-dropped counter will fall in the shaded region.

6. 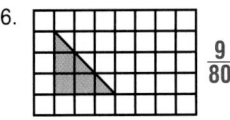 $\frac{9}{80}$

7. 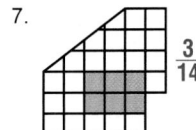 $\frac{3}{14}$

8. 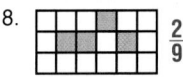 $\frac{2}{9}$

9. 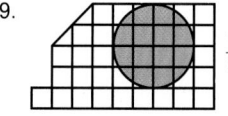 $\frac{1}{3}$

10. 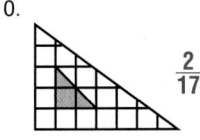 $\frac{2}{17}$

11. 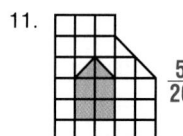 $\frac{5}{26}$

12. Draw a square on a piece of grid paper that is 6 units on a side. Shade in 4 squares. What is the probability that a randomly-dropped counter will fall in the shaded area? $\frac{1}{9}$

Mixed Review

13. Classify the angle at the right as acute, obtuse, right, or straight. *(Lesson 8-1)* **obtuse**

14. ≈ **2.83 cm²**
≈ **3.46 cm²**
≈ **2.54 cm²**
≈ **4.52 cm²**

14. **Coin Collection** The diameters of some United States coins are listed at the right. Find the area of each. *(Lesson 9-8)*

Coin	Diameter (cm)
penny	1.9
nickel	2.1
dime	1.8
quarter	2.4

Problem Solving and Applications

15. **Geology** Sam Tex owns an 18,000-acre ranch. A geologist told him that he can expect to find oil under 400 acres of his property. If Sam Tex randomly starts drilling, what is the probability of striking oil? $\frac{1}{45}$

16. **Sports** A skydiver parachutes onto a square field that contains a pond. The field is 150 feet on a side and the pond has an area of 750 square feet. If there is an equal chance of landing at any point in the field, what is the probability that the diver has a dry landing? $\frac{29}{30}$

17. **Data Search** The island of Greenland is larger than some seas. Use the information on page 335 to figure out which seas it is larger than. **Gulf of Mexico, Sea of Okhotsk, Sea of Japan**

18. **Critical Thinking** What is the probability that a randomly-dropped counter will land on the green, yellow, or blue region? $\frac{28}{120}$ or $\frac{7}{30}$

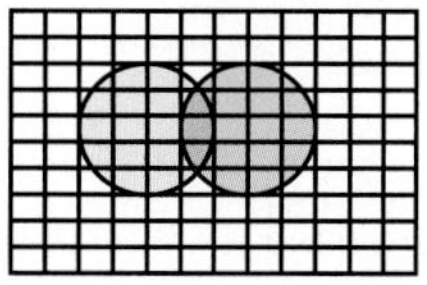

Lesson 9-9 Area Models **367**

 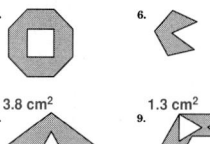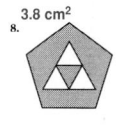

Extending the Lesson

Using Critical Thinking Draw a target on grid paper with three regions; the probability of landing in the shaded region is greater than in the starred region, but half that of the dotted region. Sample answer: target with fewer than 36 squares, 18-square region has dots, 9-square region is shaded, fewer-than-9-square region has stars.

Cooperative Learning Activity

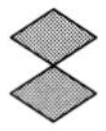

Game Makers 9-9

Use groups of 2.
Materials: Centimeter grid paper, spinners, colored pencils

➊ Copy the figure shown on the back of this card onto centimeter grid paper. Label equal sections of one spinner with the letters A through J. Label equal sections of a second spinner with the numbers 1 through 10.

➋ Using the figure you drew on grid paper, design a game with the following probabilities for scoring points: 0.2 for 0 points; 0.6 for 1 point; 0.15 for 2 points; and 0.05 for 5 points. Use colored pencils to shade squares showing different point values.

Play the game you created. In turn, each player spins both spinners, locates the square identified by the coordinates shown, and writes the value of that square. Find the sum of your points after ten spins. Who won? Could the game board be changed to make the game more interesting?

Glencoe Mathematics: Applications and Connections, Course 2

367

The Chapter Study Guide and Review begins with a section on Communicating Mathematics. This includes questions that review the new terms and concepts that were introduced in the chapter.

Then, the Skills and Concepts presented in the chapter are reviewed using a side-by-side format. Encourage students to refer to the Objectives and Examples on the left as they complete the Review Exercises on the right.

The Chapter Study Guide and Review ends with problems that review Applications and Problem Solving.

Chapter

9 Study Guide and Review

Communicating Mathematics

Choose the correct term to complete each sentence.

1. The number (49, 1,000) is a perfect square. **49**
2. In a right triangle, the square of the measure of the hypotenuse is (equal to, greater than) the sum of the squares of the measures of the legs. **equal to**
3. A trapezoid is a quadrilateral with exactly (one, two) pair(s) of parallel sides. **one**
4. $A = \frac{1}{2}bh$ is the formula for the area of a (trapezoid, triangle). **triangle**
5. The formula for the area of a circle includes the (height, radius). **radius**
6. Probability can be expressed as a (mixed number, fraction). **fraction**
7. In your own words, explain how you would estimate the square root of 55.
   $7^2 = 49$ and $8^2 = 64$; since 49 is closer to 55 than 64, $\sqrt{55}$ is about 7.

Self Assessment

Objectives and Examples	*Review Exercises*
Upon completing this chapter, you should be able to:	*Use these exercises to review and prepare for the chapter test.*

* find the square roots of perfect squares *(Lesson 9-2)*

  Evaluate $\sqrt{225}$.

  Since $15^2 = 225$, $\sqrt{225} = 15$.

Find each square root.

8. $\sqrt{9}$ **3**   9. $\sqrt{1}$ **1**
10. $\sqrt{100}$ **10**   11. $\sqrt{169}$ **13**
12. $\sqrt{900}$ **30**   13. $\sqrt{10,000}$ **100**

* estimate square roots *(Lesson 9-3)*

  Estimate $\sqrt{75}$.

  $64 < 75 < 81$ Since 75 is closer
  $\sqrt{64} < \sqrt{75} < \sqrt{81}$ to 81 than to 64,
  $8 < \sqrt{75} < 9$ $\sqrt{75}$ is closer to 9.

Estimate.

14. $\sqrt{5}$ **2**   15. $\sqrt{35}$ **6**
16. $\sqrt{116}$ **11**   17. $\sqrt{40}$ **6**
18. $\sqrt{435}$ **21**   19. $\sqrt{399}$ **20**

* find the length of a side of a right triangle using the Pythagorean Theorem *(Lesson 9-4)*

  Find the missing length.

  5 in. ◣ c in.
  12 in.

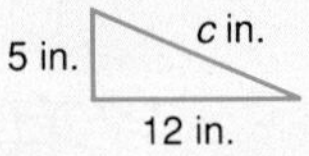

  $a^2 + b^2 = c^2$
  $5^2 + 12^2 = c^2$
  $169 = c^2$
  $13 = c$

  The hypotenuse is 13 inches long.

If the measures of the legs of a right triangle are a and b and the hypotenuse is c, find the missing length. Round decimal answers to the nearest tenth.

20. a: 5 ft; b: 7 ft $c \approx 8.6$ ft
21. b: 10 yd; c: 15 yd $a \approx 11.2$ yd
22. a: 12 in.; b: 3 in. $c \approx 12.4$ in.
23. c: 18 m; a: 6 m $b \approx 17.0$ m

Objectives and Examples

- solve problems using the Pythagorean Theorem *(Lesson 9-5)*

Judy leans a 6-foot mirror against a wall by placing the bottom 2 feet from the base of the wall. How far up the wall is the top of the mirror?

$$2^2 + b^2 = 6^2$$
$$4 + b^2 = 36$$
$$b^2 = 32$$
$$b = \sqrt{32}$$
$$b \approx 5.7 \text{ ft}$$

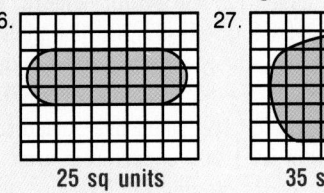

The mirror is about 5.7 feet up the wall.

- estimate the area of irregular figures *(Lesson 9-6)*

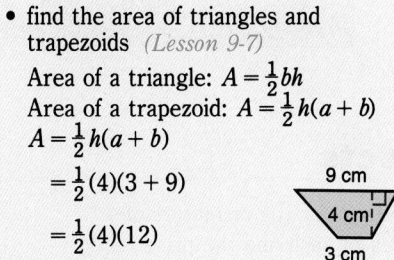
369b

inner measure: 4
outer measure: 15
mean: 9.5
A good estimate is 9.5 square units.

- find the area of triangles and trapezoids *(Lesson 9-7)*

Area of a triangle: $A = \frac{1}{2}bh$
Area of a trapezoid: $A = \frac{1}{2}h(a+b)$

$$A = \frac{1}{2}h(a+b)$$
$$= \frac{1}{2}(4)(3+9)$$
$$= \frac{1}{2}(4)(12)$$
$$= 2(12)$$
$$= 24 \text{ cm}^2 \quad \text{The area is 24 cm}^2.$$

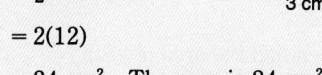

- find the area of circles *(Lesson 9-8)*

Area of a circle: $A = \pi r^2$

The area of a circle with a radius of 6 inches is:
$$A = \pi r^2$$
$$\approx (3.14)(6^2)$$
$$\approx (3.14)(36)$$
$$\approx 113.04 \text{ in}^2$$

The area is about 113 square inches.

Review Exercises

Solve. Round answers to the nearest tenth.

24. Pete builds a swimming pool in the shape of a right triangle with legs that are 50 feet and 75 feet long. How far would a person walk if they walked the perimeter of Pete's pool?
≈ 215.1 feet

25. While hiking in the woods, Angela walks 3 miles south and 5 miles west. How far is she from her starting point? Find the straight-line distance. ≈ 5.8 mi

Estimate the area of each figure.

26.

27.

25 sq units   35 sq units

Find the area of each triangle or trapezoid.

28. bases: 6 m, 9 m; height: 5 m
29. base: 15 yd; height: 8 yd
30. bases: 4 in., 8 in.; height: 5 in.
31. base: 5 ft; height: 12 ft
28. $A = 37.5$ m²   29. $A = 60$ yd²
30. $A = 30$ in²   31. $A = 30$ ft²

Find the area of each circle. Round answers to the nearest hundredth. Use 3.14 for π.

32. r, 7 ft $A \approx 153.86$ ft²
33. d, 18 mm $A \approx 254.34$ mm²
34. r, 25 in. $A \approx 1,962.50$ in²
35. d, 11 yd $A \approx 94.99$ yd²

Chapter 9 Study Guide and Review   **369**

You may wish to use a Chapter Test from the Evaluation Masters booklet as an additional chapter review. The two free-response forms are shown below. One of the two multiple-choice forms is shown on the next page.

Objectives and Examples

• find the probability using area models *(Lesson 9-9)*

probability of hitting a green square

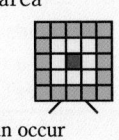

$$= \frac{\text{number of ways an event can occur}}{\text{number of possible outcomes}}$$

$$= \frac{16}{25}$$

Review Exercises

Find the probability that a randomly-dropped counter will fall in the shaded region.

36.  $\frac{19}{36}$　　37. $\frac{1}{3}$

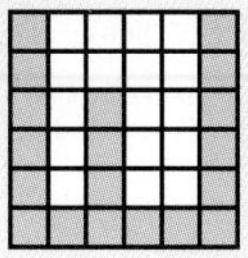

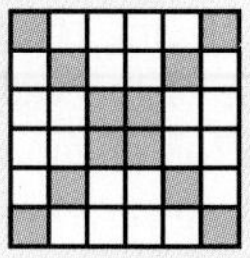

Evaluation Masters, pp. 77–78

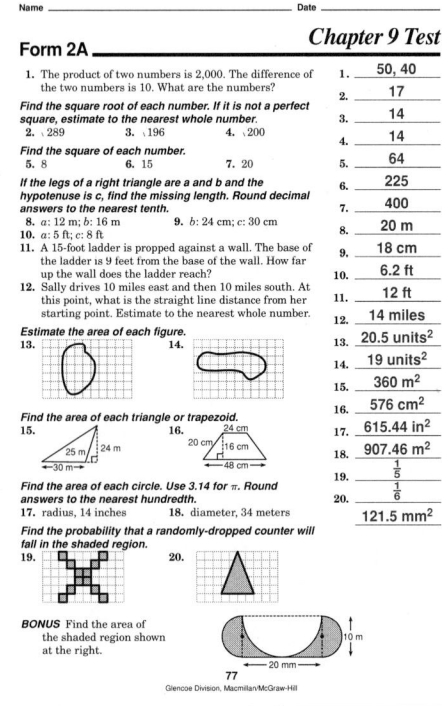

Name _____ Date _____

Form 2A _____ *Chapter 9 Test*

1. The product of two numbers is 2,000. The difference of the two numbers is 10. What are the numbers?

Find the square root of each number. If it is not a perfect square, estimate to the nearest whole number.
2. √289　　3. √196　　4. √200

Find the square of each number.
5. 8　　6. 15　　7. 20

If the legs of a right triangle are a and b and the hypotenuse is c, find the missing length. Round decimal answers to the nearest tenth.
8. a: 12 m; b: 16 m　　9. b: 24 cm; c: 30 cm
10. a: 5 ft; c: 8 ft
11. A 15-foot ladder is propped against a wall. The base of the ladder is 9 feet from the base of the wall. How far up the wall does the ladder reach?
12. Sally drives 10 miles east and then 10 miles south. At this point, what is the straight line distance from her starting point. Estimate to the nearest whole number.

Estimate the area of each figure.
13.　　14.

Find the area of each triangle or trapezoid.
15.　　16.

Find the area of each circle. Use 3.14 for π. Round answers to the nearest hundredth.
17. radius, 14 inches　　18. diameter, 34 meters

Find the probability that a randomly-dropped counter will fall in the shaded region.
19.　　20.

BONUS Find the area of the shaded region shown at the right.
10 m ↕
←—— 20 mm ——→

1.	50, 40
2.	17
3.	14
4.	14
5.	64
6.	225
7.	400
8.	20 m
9.	18 cm
10.	6.2 ft
11.	12 ft
12.	14 miles
13.	20.5 units²
14.	19 units²
15.	360 m²
16.	576 cm²
17.	615.44 in²
18.	907.46 m²
19.	$\frac{1}{5}$
20.	$\frac{1}{6}$
	121.5 mm²

77
Glencoe Division, Macmillan/McGraw-Hill

Name _____ Date _____

Form 2B _____ *Chapter 9 Test*

1. The product of two consecutive even numbers is 960. What are the two numbers?

Find the square root of each number. If it is not a perfect square, estimate to the nearest whole number.
2. √256　　3. √441　　4. √120

Find the square of each number.
5. 12　　6. 7　　7. 40

If the legs of a right triangle are a and b and the hypotenuse is c, find the missing length. Round decimal answers to the nearest tenth.
8. a: 15 m; b: 20 m　　9. a: 30 cm; c: 50 cm
10. b: 7 ft; c: 11 ft
11. A rectangular field is 80 meters long by 60 meters wide. What is the diagonal distance across the field?
12. A 25-foot cable is used to brace a ship mast. The cable is anchored 7 feet from the foot of the mast. How tall is the mast?

Estimate the area of each figure.
13. 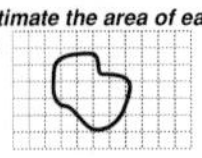　　14.

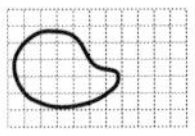

Find the area of each triangle or trapezoid.
15. 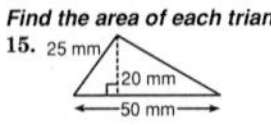　　16.

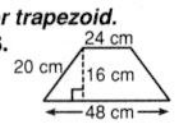

Find the area of each circle. Use 3.14 for π.
17. radius, 18 cm　　18. diameter, 42 inches

Find the probability that a randomly-dropped counter will fall in the shaded region.
19. 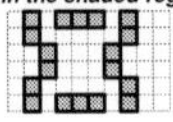　　20.

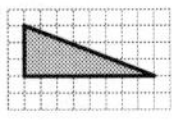

BONUS Find the area of the shaded region at the right.
4 cm ↕ 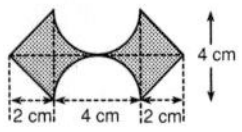
|2 cm| 4 cm |2 cm|

1.	30, 32
2.	16
3.	21
4.	11
5.	144
6.	49
7.	1,600
8.	25 m
9.	40 cm
10.	8.5 ft
11.	100 m
12.	24 ft
13.	16.5 units²
14.	20 units²
15.	500 mm²
16.	720 m²
17.	1,017.36 cm²
18.	1,384.74 in²
19.	$\frac{3}{10}$
20.	$\frac{1}{5}$
	11.44 cm²

78
Glencoe Division, Macmillan/McGraw-Hill

---

38. Admission to the zoo is $5 for adults, $3.50 for children under 12, and $3 for seniors. Ten people paid a total of $37.50. If 3 adults attended, how many children and seniors were in the group? *(Lesson 9-1)* **3 children, 4 seniors**

39. **Treasure Island** An island has buried treasure under 50 of its 1,000 square feet area. If Amber randomly starts digging for treasure, what is the probability that she will find something? *(Lesson 9-9)* $\frac{1}{20}$

Curriculum Connection Projects

• **Home Economics** Call your favorite pizza shop and ask for the diameters of their small, medium, and large pizzas. Find the area of each and the price per square inch.

• **History** Find the dimensions of an Aztec pyramid. Then find the area of each of its trapezoidal faces.

Read More About It

Wilcox, Charlotte. *A Skyscraper Story.*
Froman, Robert. *Rubber Bands, Baseballs, and Doughnuts: A Book About Topology.*
Paulson, Gary. *The Hatchet.*
Michener, James. *Journey.*

370 Chapter 9 Study Guide and Review

9 Test

1. What is the fewest number of square tables, each seating 4 people, that can be used to seat 20 people if the tables are arranged in one long rectangle? **9 tables**

Find each square root.

2. $\sqrt{49}$ **7**

3. $\sqrt{625}$ **25**

4. $\sqrt{22,500}$ **150**

5. **Physical Fitness** Every morning, Ichiko jogs around a group of blocks that make up a square having an area of 4 square miles. How far does Ichiko jog each morning? **8 miles**

Estimate.

6. $\sqrt{18}$ **≈4**

7. $\sqrt{90}$ **≈9**

8. $\sqrt{490}$ **≈22**

If the measures of the legs of a right triangle are *a* and *b* and the measure of the hypotenuse is *c*, find the missing length. Round decimal answers to the nearest tenth.

9. *a*: 5 m,; *b*: 3 m
$c \approx 5.8$ m

10. *b*: 12 in.; *c*: 25 in.
$a \approx 21.9$ in.

11. *a*: 4 yd; *c*: 8 yd
$b \approx 6.9$ yd

12. **Road Trip** Sam gets lost while driving to a new vacation spot. After looking at a map, he sees that he is 18 miles too far east and 10 miles too far north. How far is Sam's drive to his intended target if he is able to drive a straight path? **about 20.6 miles**

Estimate the area of each figure.

13.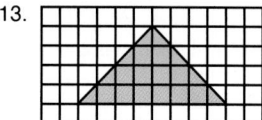

14.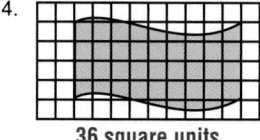

16 square units

36 square units

Find the area of each triangle or trapezoid.

15. triangle: base: 12 ft; height: 6 ft $A = 36$ ft²

16. trapezoid: bases: 5 km, 11 km; height: 4 km $A = 32$ km²

Find the area of each circle.

17. *r*, 11 cm $A \approx 379.94$ cm²

18. *d*, 23 in. $A \approx 415.265$ in²

$d \approx 50.5$ feet

19. **Amusement** The merry-go-round at an amusement park covers an area of 2,000 square feet. Find the length of its diameter. Round to the tenths place.

20. **Carnival Game** A carnival game requires that a blindfolded contestant throw a dart at a wall partially covered with balloons. If a balloon is popped, the contestant wins. The wall has an area of 16 square feet. Six square feet are covered with balloons. What is the probability that a contestant wins? $\frac{3}{8}$

Bonus What is the formula for the area of a semi-circle? $A = \frac{1}{2}\pi r^2$

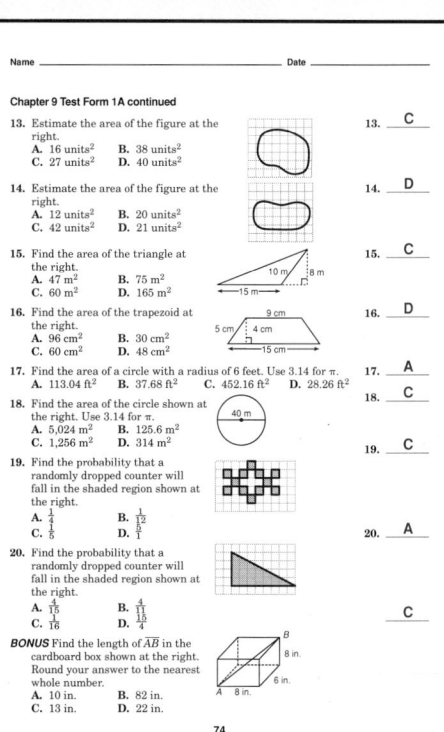

Test and Review Generator software is provided in Apple, IBM, and Macintosh versions. You may use this software to create your own tests or worksheets, based on the needs of your students.

The **Performance Assessment Booklet** provides an alternate assessment for evaluating student progress. An assessment for this chapter can be found on pages 17–18.

The Academic Skills Test may be
used to help students prepare for
standardized tests. The test items
are written in the same style as
those in state proficiency tests.
The test items cover skills and
concepts covered up to this point
in the text.

These pages can be used as an
overnight assignment. After
students have completed the
pages, discuss how each problem
can be solved, or provide copies
of the solutions from the *Solutions
Manual*.

Academic Skills Test

Chapter

9 Academic Skills Test

Directions: Choose the best answer. Write A, B, C, or D.

1. What is the value of $3b + 4a$ if $a = 2$
B and $b = 6$?

   A 30   B 26

   C 17   D 12

2. Joyce is writing a book report. One
D page contains 175 words. If her
   report is 5 pages long and each page
   is about the same length, about how
   many words are in her report?

   A 40 words   B 175 words

   C 500 words   D 850 words

3. Kenny is saving to buy a computer
C that will cost about $1,200. He
   already has saved $500. If he can save
   $75 a month, it is reasonable to
   expect that he can buy the computer in

   A 3 months?   B 7 months?

   C 10 months?   D 16 months?

4.
A

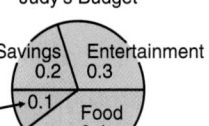
Judy's Budget

Savings 0.2   Entertainment 0.3

Misc. → 0.1   Food 0.4

   If Judy has $50 for the week, about
   how much can she spend on food?

   A $20   B $30

   C $40   D $50

5. What is the prime factorization of 60?
D
   A $1 \cdot 60$ B $2 \cdot 3 \cdot 3 \cdot 5$

   C $2 \cdot 3 \cdot 10$ D $2 \cdot 2 \cdot 3 \cdot 5$

6. Rolito wants to find $\frac{3}{5}$ of $65 using a
C calculator. What decimal can he enter
   for $\frac{3}{5}$?

   A 0.3   B 0.5

   C 0.6   D 0.65

7. Which sentence is true?
C
   A $\frac{5}{8} < 0.6$ B $\frac{5}{8} = 0.6$

   C $\frac{5}{8} > 0.6$ D none of these

8. A person's weight on the moon is
A about $\frac{1}{6}$ of their weight on Earth.
   About how much would a person
   weigh on the moon if their weight on
   Earth is 125 pounds?

   A 20 lb   B 60 lb

   C 200 lb   D 600 lb

9. What is the reciprocal of $3\frac{3}{4}$?
D
   A $\frac{4}{3}$ B $\frac{4}{33}$

   C $\frac{15}{4}$ D $\frac{4}{15}$

10. Claire worked 20 hours last week. She
C earned $5.00 per hour. Which
    equation can be used to find her total
    earnings?

    A $x = 20 \div 5$ B $5x = 20$

    C $20 \times 5 = x$ D $20x = 5.00$

11. How much carpeting is needed to
C   cover the floor of a 10 foot by 12 foot
    room?

    A 22 ft^2 B 44 ft^2
    C 120 ft^2 D 480 ft^2

12. $|24| =$
D
    A -24 B 0
    C 1 D 24

13. $-12 + 30 =$
A
    A 18 B 8
    C -18 D -42

14. $0.001 =$
D
    A 10^1 B 10^{-1}
    C 10^{-2} D 10^{-3}

15. Which polygon is *not* regular?
B
    A    B

    C    D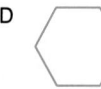

16. Which type of quadrilateral is an
D   equilateral quadrilateral and an
    equiangular quadrilateral?

    A rectangle   B parallelogram
    C rhombus   D square

17.
A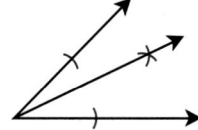

    This drawing shows how to

    A construct an angle bisector.
    B construct an angle congruent to a
      given angle.
    C construct perpendicular lines.
    D construct a segment bisector.

18. Which is a perfect square?
D
    A 88 B 125
    C 181 D 625

19. What is the length of the hypotenuse of
C   this triangle?

    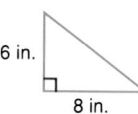
    6 in.
    8 in.

    A 6 in.   B 8 in.
    C 10 in.   D 14 in.

20. Jay walks 5 kilometers east and 5
C   kilometers south. To the nearest
    kilometer, how far is he from his
    starting point?

    A 25 km   B 10 km
    C 7 km   D 5 km

10 Surface Area and Volume

Previewing the Chapter

This chapter considers surface area and volume of solid, or 3-dimensional figures. Students first explore 3-dimensional figures by building and drawing the figures. Later, they learn how to calculate the surface area and volumes of some of these figures, with particular attention paid to prisms and cylinders. There are two **problem-solving strategy** lessons. In the first, students solve problems by making models. In the second, they apply formulas to solve problems.

Lesson	Lesson Objectives	NCTM Standards	State/Local Objectives
10-1A	Build and draw three-dimensional figures given the front, side, and top views.	1–4, 12	
10-1	Draw three-dimensional figures.	1–4, 12	
10-2	Solve problems by making a model.	1–5, 7, 12	
10-3	Find the surface area of rectangular prisms.	1–5, 7, 9, 12	
10-4A	Develop the formula for surface area of a cylinder by constructing a cylinder.	1–5, 7, 12	
10-4	Find the surface area of cylinders.	1–5, 7, 12	
Decision Making	Choose a scholarship prize fund.	1–5, 7	
10-5	Find the volume of rectangular prisms.	1–5, 7, 9, 12	
10-6	Find the volume of cylinders.	1–5, 7, 12, 13	
10-6B	Estimate and compare volume of cylinders of various sizes.	1–5, 7, 12, 13	
10-7	Solve problems by using a formula.	1–5, 7, 9, 12	

A complete, 1-page lesson plan is provided for each lesson in the Lesson Plans Masters Booklet.

LESSON PLANNING GUIDE

Lesson	Materials/ Manipulatives	Extra Practice (Student Edition)	Study Guide	Practice	Enrichment	Evaluation	Technology	Lab Manual	Multicultural Activities	Application and Interdisciplinary Activities	Transparencies	Group Activity Cards
10-1A	cubes							p. 66				
10-1			p. 84	p. 84	p. 84						10-1	10-1
10-2			p. 85	p. 85	p. 85						10-2	10-2
10-3	graph paper calculator gift box	p. 593	p. 86	p. 86	p. 86		p. 24				10-3	10-3
10-4A	centimeter grid paper, compass, scissors, tape							p. 67				
10-4	calculator	p. 593	p. 87	p. 87	p. 87	Quiz A, p. 88	p. 10			p. 24	10-4	10-4
10-5	20 × 20 grid paper, scissors, tape, calculator	p. 594	p. 88	p. 88	p. 88						10-5	10-5
10-6	calculator	p. 594	p. 89	p. 89	p. 89					p. 10	10-6	10-6
10-6B	cylinder-shaped objects, rulers, calculator							p. 68				
10-7			p. 90	p. 90	p. 90	Quiz B, p. 88			p. 10		10-7	10-7
Study Guide and Review			Multiple Choice Test, Forms 1A and 1B, pp. 82–85 Free Response Test, Forms 2A and 2B, pp. 86–87 Cumulative Review, p. 89 (free response)									
Test			Cumulative Test, p. 90 (multiple choice)									

Pacing Guide: Option I (Chapters 1–12) - 11 days; Option II (Chapters 1–13) - 11 days; Option III (Chapters 1–14) - 10 days
You may wish to refer to the complete **Course Planning Guides** on page T25.

OTHER CHAPTER RESOURCES

Student Edition
Chapter Opener, pp. 374–375
Cultural Kaleidoscope, p. 386
Mid-Chapter Review, p. 391
Portfolio Suggestions, pp. 386, 400

 Manipulatives
Overhead Manipulative Resources
Middle School Mathematics Manipulative Kit

 Software/Technology
Interactive Mathematics Tools (Macintosh)
Test and Review Generator (IBM, Apple, Macintosh)
Teacher's Guide for Software Resources

Other Supplements
Transparency 10-0
Performance Assessment, pp. 19–20
Glencoe Mathematics Professional Series
Lesson Plans, pp. 110–119

INTERDISCIPLINARY BULLETIN BOARD
Consumer Connection

Objective   Use concepts of surface area and volume to design a package.

How To Use It   Have students imagine that they are package designers assigned the task of designing a package to enclose a new toy or game. Ask them to choose a toy as a model, and then create a pattern for a box to hold it. When students work together to create this box, they should try to make one that holds the toy without excessive surface area or use of material. Have groups draw, decorate, and label the box their pattern is for, and display both the patterns and the drawings on the bulletin board.

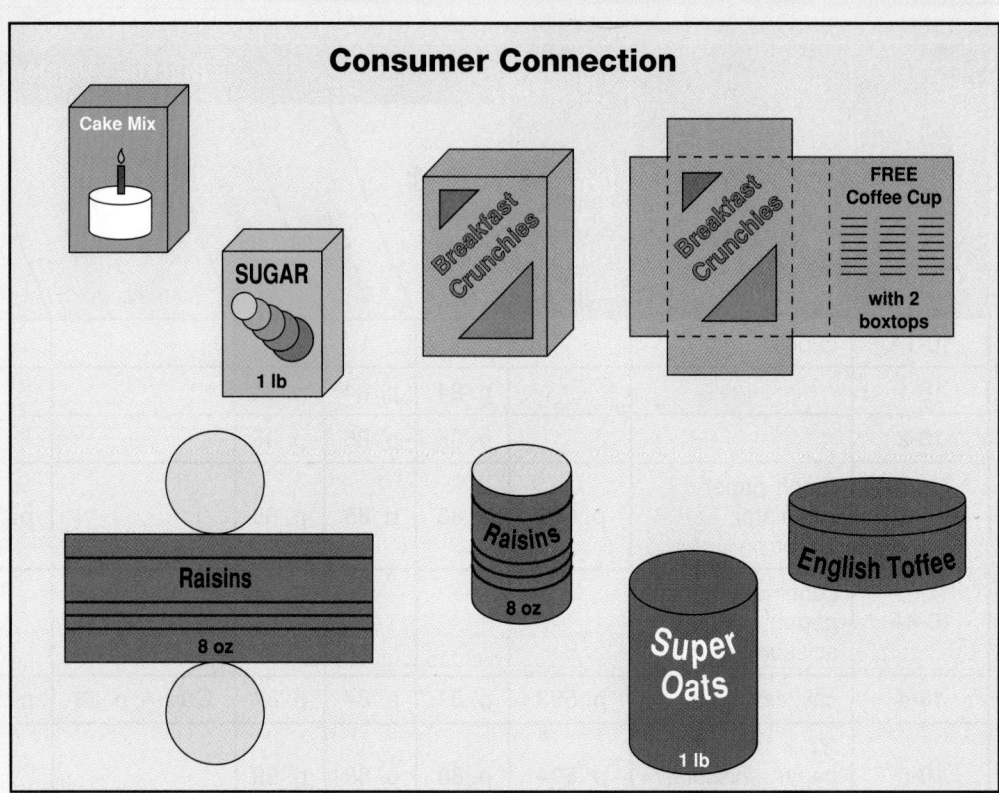

Consumer Connection

APPLICATIONS AND CONNECTIONS

Applications	Lesson	Example	Exercise
Construction	10-1		21
Architecture	10-1		22
Manufacturing	10-3		24
Gifts	10-3		25
Marketing	10-4		26
Agriculture	10-4		27
Exercise	10-5		24
Manufacturing	10-6	2	
Computer	10-7		10
Connections			
Algebra	10-3	1	
Geometry	10-3		26
Algebra	10-5		23
Measurement	10-6		24–25

TEAM ACTIVITIES
Multicultural Experiences

Outside Field Trips   Students would benefit from a trip to the gift-wrapping section of a department store to see how the gift wrappers use surface area and estimation.

A trip to an architect's office can provide students with the opportunity to see that architects draw diagrams of a three-dimensional building from different perspectives.

In-Class Speakers   Ask a package designer to visit the class to talk about the part surface area and volume plays in the designing of packaging.

Invite a set designer to visit the class and discuss the importance of perspective and of envisioning different views in the process of designing, constructing, painting, and arranging objects on a stage.

SUPPLEMENTARY BLACKLINE MASTER BOOKLETS

Some of the blackline masters for enhancing this chapter are shown below.

Application and Interdisciplinary Activity Masters, pp. 10, 24

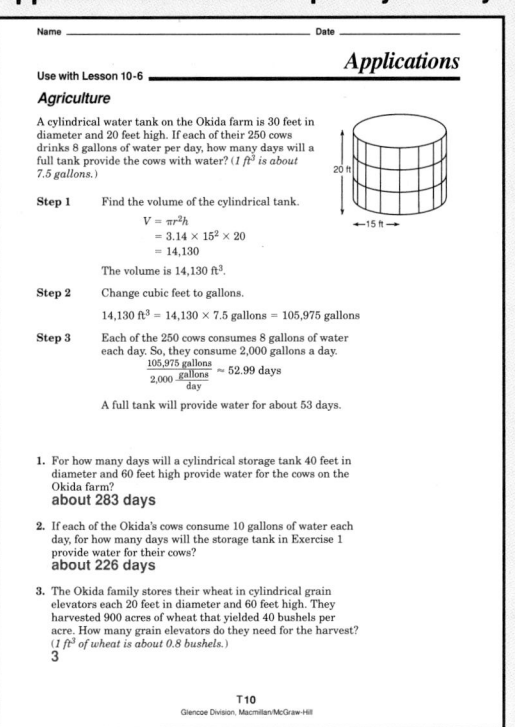

Name _____ Date _____

Applications

Use with Lesson 10-6

Agriculture

A cylindrical water tank on the Okida farm is 30 feet in diameter and 20 feet high. If each of their 250 cows drinks 8 gallons of water per day, how many days will a full tank provide the cows with water? (*1 ft³ is about 7.5 gallons.*)

Step 1 Find the volume of the cylindrical tank.

$$V = \pi r^2 h$$
$$= 3.14 \times 15^2 \times 20$$
$$= 14{,}130$$

The volume is 14,130 ft³.

Step 2 Change cubic feet to gallons.

14,130 ft³ = 14,130 × 7.5 gallons = 105,975 gallons

Step 3 Each of the 250 cows consumes 8 gallons of water each day. So, they consume 2,000 gallons a day.

$$\frac{105{,}975 \text{ gallons}}{2{,}000 \frac{\text{gallons}}{\text{day}}} \approx 52.99 \text{ days}$$

A full tank will provide water for about 53 days.

1. For how many days will a cylindrical storage tank 40 feet in diameter and 60 feet high provide water for the cows on the Okida farm?
   about 283 days

2. If each of the Okida's cows consume 10 gallons of water each day, for how many days will the storage tank in Exercise 1 provide water for their cows?
   about 226 days

3. The Okida family stores their wheat in cylindrical grain elevators each 20 feet in diameter and 60 feet high. They harvested 900 acres of wheat that yielded 40 bushels per acre. How many grain elevators do they need for the harvest? (*1 ft³ of wheat is about 0.8 bushels.*)
   3

T10
Glencoe Division, Macmillan/McGraw-Hill

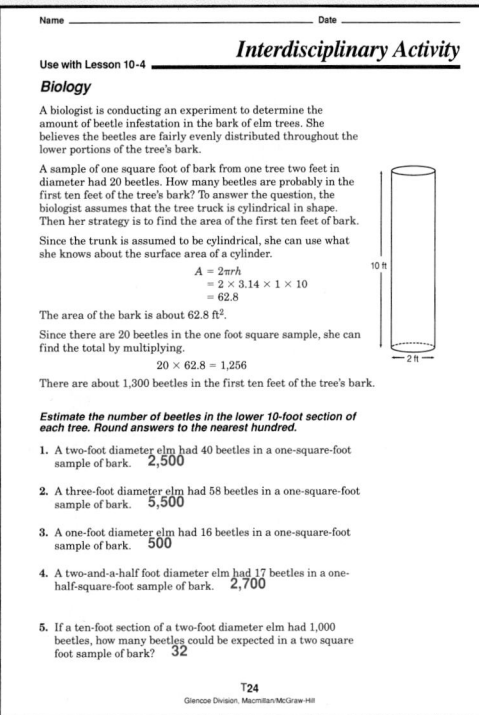

Name _____ Date _____

Interdisciplinary Activity

Use with Lesson 10-4

Biology

A biologist is conducting an experiment to determine the amount of beetle infestation in the bark of elm trees. She believes the beetles are fairly evenly distributed throughout the lower portions of the tree's bark.

A sample of one square foot of bark from one tree two feet in diameter had 20 beetles. How many beetles are probably in the first ten feet of the tree's bark? To answer the question, the biologist assumes that the tree trunk is cylindrical in shape. Then her strategy is to find the area of the first ten feet of bark.

Since the trunk is assumed to be cylindrical, she can use what she knows about the surface area of a cylinder.

$$A = 2\pi rh$$
$$= 2 \times 3.14 \times 1 \times 10$$
$$= 62.8$$

The area of the bark is about 62.8 ft².

Since there are 20 beetles in the one foot square sample, she can find the total by multiplying.

20 × 62.8 = 1,256

There are about 1,300 beetles in the first ten feet of the tree's bark.

Estimate the number of beetles in the lower 10-foot section of each tree. Round answers to the nearest hundred.

1. A two-foot diameter elm had 40 beetles in a one-square-foot sample of bark. **2,500**

2. A three-foot diameter elm had 58 beetles in a one-square-foot sample of bark. **5,500**

3. A one-foot diameter elm had 16 beetles in a one-square-foot sample of bark. **500**

4. A two-and-a-half foot diameter elm had 17 beetles in a one-half-square-foot sample of bark. **2,700**

5. If a ten-foot section of a two-foot diameter elm had 1,000 beetles, how many beetles could be expected in a two square foot sample of bark? **32**

T24
Glencoe Division, Macmillan/McGraw-Hill

Multicultural Activity Masters, p. 10

Name _____ Date _____

Multicultural Activity

Use with Lesson 10-7

Antonia Novello

Antonia Novello (1944–) was born in Fajardo, Puerto Rico. In 1990, she became the first woman Surgeon General of the United States. In her position, Dr. Novello coordinates the work of more than 6,500 employees of the Public Health Service. She plays a major role in shaping national policy on issues related to health.

Doctors and other health care professionals use many formulas in their work. For example, the following formula can be used to determine the dose of a medicine that a child should receive.

$$C = \frac{a}{a+12} \times D$$

In this formula, C is the child's dose, a is the child's age in years, and D is the adult dose. The formula is used for children up to 12 years of age. For children who are older than 12 years, the adult dose is usually prescribed.

Use the information above to complete the chart.

	Child's Age	Adult Dose	Child's Dose
1.	4 years	600 milligrams	**150 milligrams**
2.	12 years	10 milliliters	**5 milliliters**
3.	36 months	500 milligrams	**100 milligrams**
4.	18 months	450 milligrams	**50 milligrams**
5.	13 years	500 milligrams	**500 milligrams**

6. An alternative formula for determining the amount of a child's dose of a medicine is $C = \frac{b}{1.7} \times D$. In this formula, C is the child's dose, b is the surface area of the child's body in square meters, and D is the adult dose. Determine the appropriate dose of a medicine for a child whose body surface area is 0.34 square meters, if the adult dose is 400 milligrams. **80 milligrams**

T10
Glencoe Division, Macmillan/McGraw-Hill

Technology Masters, p. 24

Name _____ Date _____

Computer Activity

Use with Lesson 10-3

Surface Area of a Rectangular Prism

You can find the surface area A of a rectangular prism whose dimensions are L, W, and H by using the formula
$$A = 2(LH + LW + WH).$$

Use the BASIC program below to find the surface area of a rectangular prism.

```
TYPE   NEW
       10  PRINT "THIS PROGRAM CALCULATES THE SURFACE"
       20  PRINT "AREA OF A RECTANGULAR PRISM"
       30  PRINT "INPUT SIDES L, W, AND H IN ORDER"
       40  INPUT L, W, H
       50  PRINT "INPUT THE UNITS"
       60  INPUT U$
       70  S = 2*(L * H + L * W + W * H)
       80  PRINT "THE SURFACE AREA IS " ; S ; U$; "^2"
       90  END
```

Use the computer program above to find the surface area of each rectangular prism.

1. 16 in., 8 in., 12 in.
   832 in²

2. 2.5 cm, 6.4 cm, 7.1 cm
   158.38 cm²

3. 10 ft, 11 ft, 22 ft
   1,144 ft²

4. 9.2 m, 17 m, 21.5 m
   1,439.4 m²

5. 40 in., 50 in., 65 in.
   15,700 in²

6. 8.4 mm, 8.4 mm, 8.4 mm
   423.3599 mm²

7. 6.23 cm, 12.4 cm, 9.5 cm
   508.474 cm²

8. 26 in., 27 in., 24 in.
   3,948 in²

T24
Glencoe Division, Macmillan/McGraw-Hill

RECOMMENDED OUTSIDE RESOURCES

Books/Periodicals

Corcoran, Thomas, Lisa Walker, and J. Lynn White, *Working in Urban Schools,* Washington, DC: Institute for Educational Leadership, 1988.

Fuys, David, Dorothy Geddes, and Rosamond Tischler, *The van Heile Model of Thinking in Geometry Among Adolescents,* Reston, VA: NCTM, 1988.

Films/Videotapes/Videodiscs

Geometry—What's That? San Rafael, CA: Coronet Media, 1975.

Volume and Capacity, Oxford Films, 1974.

Software

Perimeter, Area, & Volume, (Apple II, IBM/Tandy), Gamco Industries

For addresses of companies handling software, please refer to page T24.

Glencoe's *Interactive Mathematics: Activities and Investigations* consists of 18 units that may be used as alternatives or supplemental material for *Mathematics: Applications and Connections.* The suggested units for this chapter are Unit 14, *Run For Cover,* and Unit 4, *Through the Looking Glass.* See page T18 for more information.

This two-page introduction to the chapter provides a visual, relevant way to engage students in the mathematics of the chapter. Questions are included that help students see the need to learn the mathematics in the chapter. Data in charts and graphs provide statistical information that students can analyze and interpret at this point as well as later in the chapter. The Chapter Project provides an activity that applies the mathematics of the chapter.

MAKING MATHEMATICS RELEVANT

Spotlight on Volcanoes

Studying volcanoes provides opportunities for students to solve problems by making a model and to measure surface area and volume. These are among the mathematics concepts explored in this chapter.

Using the Timeline

Have students research the dates of other major eruptions of volcanoes or earthquakes that occurred in the twentieth century and add this information to the timeline.

Chapter

10

Surface Area and Volume

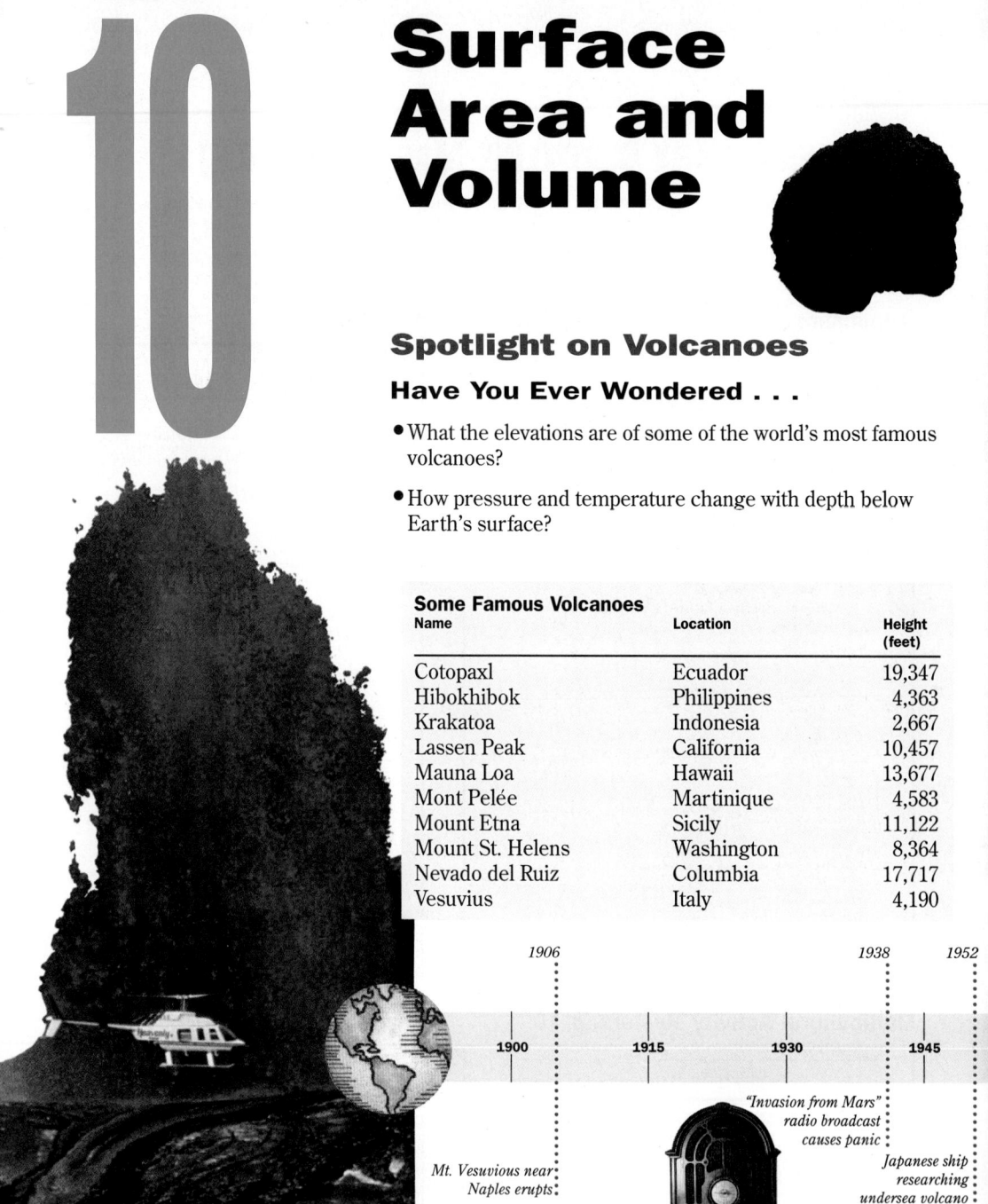

Spotlight on Volcanoes

Have You Ever Wondered . . .

• What the elevations are of some of the world's most famous volcanoes?

• How pressure and temperature change with depth below Earth's surface?

Some Famous Volcanoes

Name	Location	Height (feet)
Cotopaxl	Ecuador	19,347
Hibokhibok	Philippines	4,363
Krakatoa	Indonesia	2,667
Lassen Peak	California	10,457
Mauna Loa	Hawaii	13,677
Mont Pelée	Martinique	4,583
Mount Etna	Sicily	11,122
Mount St. Helens	Washington	8,364
Nevado del Ruiz	Columbia	17,717
Vesuvius	Italy	4,190

1906   *1938*   *1952*

1900   **1915**   **1930**   **1945**

"Invasion from Mars" radio broadcast causes panic

Mt. Vesuvious near Naples erupts

Japanese ship researching undersea volcano is destroyed by eruption

374

"Have You Ever Wondered?" Answers

• The elevations are as high as 19,347 ft, in Ecuador.

• Temperature and pressure increase with depth. A volcanic eruption is a release of hot lava containing built-up energy that was created by high pressure and temperature.

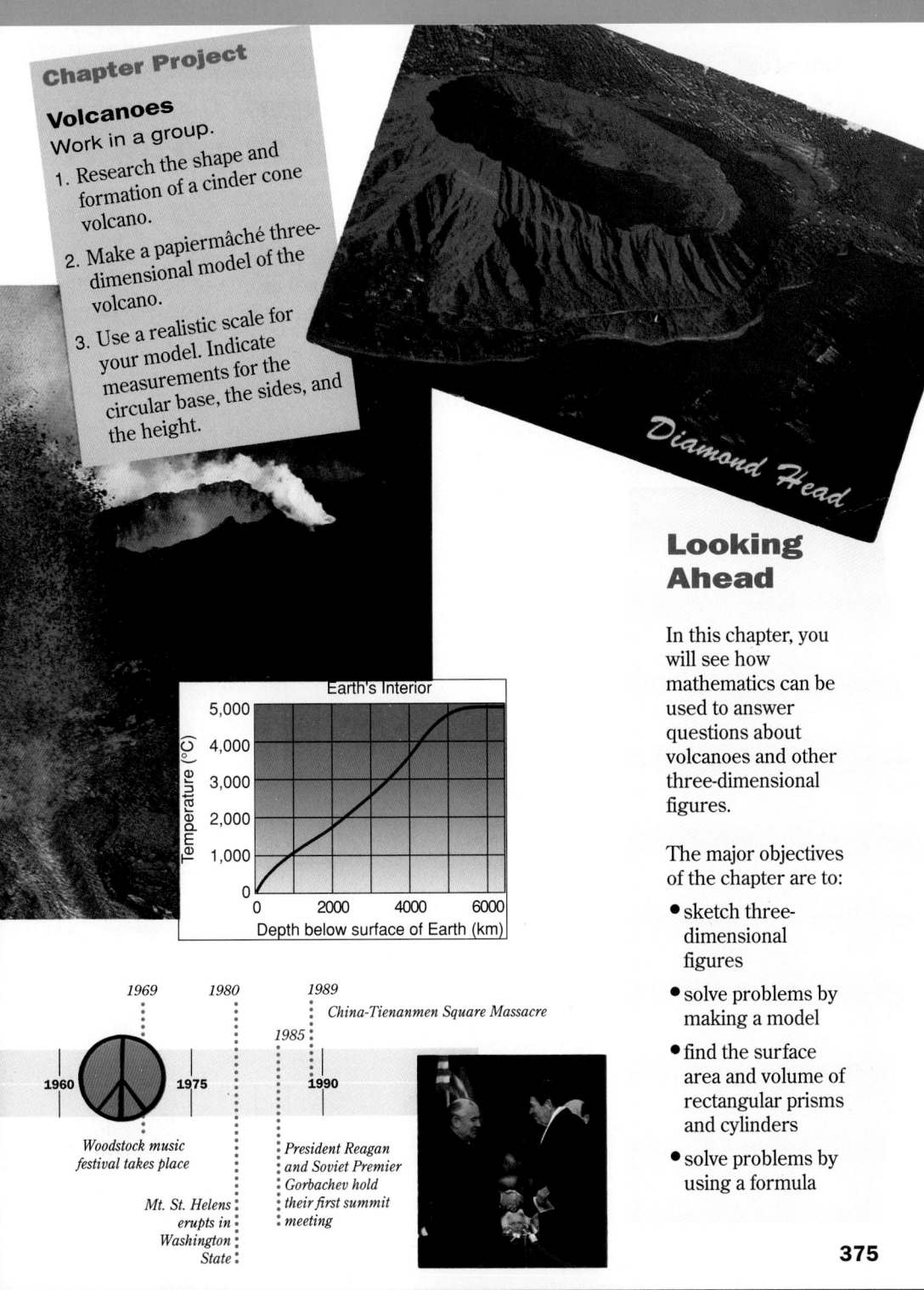

Chapter Project

Volcanoes

Work in a group.

1. Research the shape and formation of a cinder cone volcano.

2. Make a papiermâché three-dimensional model of the volcano.

3. Use a realistic scale for your model. Indicate measurements for the circular base, the sides, and the height.

Diamond Head

Earth's Interior

Graph showing Temperature (°C) on the vertical axis from 0 to 5,000, and Depth below surface of Earth (km) on the horizontal axis from 0 to 6000.

1969
1980
1989
China-Tienanmen Square Massacre
1985

1960 ☮ **1975** **1990**

Woodstock music festival takes place

Mt. St. Helens erupts in Washington State

President Reagan and Soviet Premier Gorbachev hold their first summit meeting

Looking Ahead

In this chapter, you will see how mathematics can be used to answer questions about volcanoes and other three-dimensional figures.

The major objectives of the chapter are to:

- sketch three-dimensional figures
- solve problems by making a model
- find the surface area and volume of rectangular prisms and cylinders
- solve problems by using a formula

375

DATA ANALYSIS

Provide small groups of students with outline maps of the world. Have them plot on these maps the locations of the volcanoes listed here together with other volcanoes. Ask them to examine their completed maps to see whether the geographic location of volcanoes form a discernible pattern. Perhaps a trip to the school or public library will yield an answer to this question.

Data Search

A question related to these data is provided in Lesson 10-5, page 397, Exercise 26.

CHAPTER PROJECT

Point out to students that a cinder volcano forms when the explosive eruption throws out mostly cinders and other rock particles. Tell them that these cinders and rocks pile up around the vent, producing a shape that is an almost perfect cone. You can extend the project by having students draw the cones they have built. By finding the volume of their shape, they will see how changing the size of the base affects the volume of the cone.

Chapter Opener Transparency

Transparency 10-0 is available in the Transparency Package. It provides another full-color, motivating activity that you can use to capture students' interest.

NCTM Standards: 1–4, 12

Management Tips

For Students Provide each group with 30 blocks. Suggest that students take turns building each view to complete the figure.

For the Overhead Projector
Overhead Manipulative Resources provides appropriate materials for teacher or student demonstration of the activities in this Mathematics Lab.

1 FOCUS

Introducing the Lab

Display a three-dimensional object so that all students can see it. Ask students to draw it as it would appear if viewed from the front, the side, or from directly above.

A Preview of Lesson 10-1

Objective
Build and draw three-dimensional figures given the front, side, and top view.

Materials
cubes
pencil
paper

The cubes you will be using in this lab are examples of three-dimensional figures. A three-dimensional figure has length, width, and depth. A two-dimensional figure has no depth, so it appears as a flat object.

Activity One

Work with a partner.

- Use the cubes to build the three-dimensional model of the shape that is described by each drawing below. The front view, a side view, and the top view of each shape are given. **For answers to Exercises a–c, see margin.**

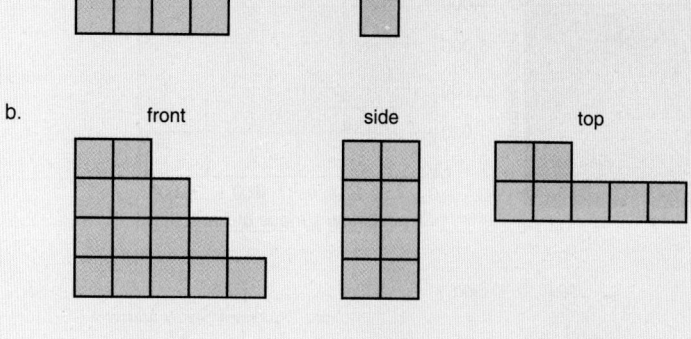

Additional Answers

a.

b.

c.

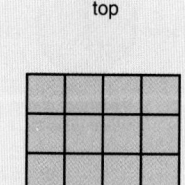

Note: In parts b and c, if certain cubes are removed, the front, side, and top views will not change. For example, the views will not change if the three top cubes are removed from the left rear column in part b.

What do you think?

1. See students' work.

1. Share with other groups how you began building the figures.

2. Do you think you could have built the figures without one of the views? Explain. **Model a: yes; you don't need the side view. Models b and c: no, all views are necessary.**

3. Is there only one way to build the figures from the drawings given? If no, build another model. If yes, explain. **Model a: yes; you can build the figures using one of the other sides as the top. Models b and c: no, even with given side, there are other arrangements.**

Activity Two

- After you have built each figure and both partners have agreed that it is correct, draw a three-dimensional figure that shows depth as well as length and width.

What do you think?

4. Compare your models and drawings with other groups. Are they the same? Tell how they are different. **See margin.**

5. Describe a real-life situation where it might be necessary for you to draw a three-dimensional figure. **Answers will vary.**

Extension

By using one-point perspective, you can create the illusion of depth. Study the example of one-point perspective below. The following characteristics give the illusion of depth.

- The front of the building is drawn like a rectangle.
- The sides of the building are drawn along lines to the vanishing point.

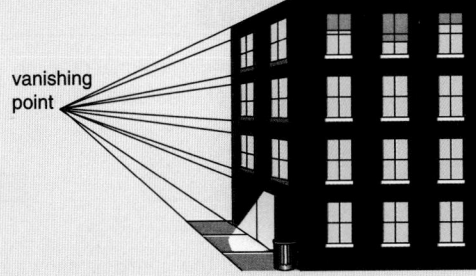

vanishing point

6. **Art** Make a drawing of your own using one-point perspective.
See students' work.

Mathematics Lab 10-1A Building Three-Dimensional Figures **377**

377

---

2 TEACH

Using Models Ask students to describe the views of the figures they are modeling according to the shapes. For example, you might ask which figures look like rectangles when viewed from the side   (a and b), or which figure appears to take up the most space when viewed only from above   (c)

3 PRACTICE/APPLY

Using Visual Reasoning Ask students to draw some of the real-life three-dimensional figures they named. Have them discuss the results and suggest ways to make some drawings appear more accurate.

Close

Ask students to use the blocks to show how providing a description of only two views of a three-dimensional figure may give an inaccurate description of what the figure actually looks like.

Additional Answer

4. Except for Model a, models may be different.

OPTIONS

Lab Manual You may wish to make copies of the blackline master on p. 66 of the *Lab Manual* for students to use as a recording sheet.

Lab Manual, p. 66

Name _____ Date _____

Mathematics Lab Worksheet

Use with pages 376-377

Building Three-Dimensional Figures

What do you think?

1. Answers will vary. Students need to begin by building the bottom layer.

2. No. The front, side, and top views are needed to build a three-dimensional model.

3. Yes. The figures need to be built layer by layer.

Try this!

Draw your own figure in

NCTM Standards: 1–4, 12

Lesson Resources
- Study Guide Master 10-1
- Practice Master 10-1
- Enrichment Master 10-1
- Group Activity Card 10-1

 Transparency 10-1 contains the 5-Minute Check and a teaching aid for this lesson.

5-Minute Check
(Over Chapter 9)
1. Find $\sqrt{169}$.   13
2. Estimate $\sqrt{80}$.   about 9
3. If the legs of a right triangle are a and b, and the hypotenuse is c, find the length of side b if $a = 6$ m and $c = 12$ m. Round your answer to the nearest tenth.   10.4 m
4. Find the area of a trapezoid with bases of 12 cm and 4.5 cm, and a height of 8 cm.
   66 square centimeters
5. Find the area of a circular wading pool with a diameter of 18 feet.
   about 254.34 square feet

1 FOCUS

Motivating the Lesson

Activity Ask students to make a pencil drawing of their house or apartment. Ask them what shapes they would see if they were to view the building from the front, side, or top.

2 TEACH

Using Applications Have students name common objects that are examples of the solid figures. Ask which might look alike when viewed from above, the front, or the side.   Sample answers: from above: cones, cylinders; from the side: triangular and rectangular prisms; from the front: cylinder, rectangular prism

---

10-1 Drawing Three-Dimensional Figures

Objective
Draw three-dimensional figures.

DID YOU KNOW

A totem is a symbol for a family or tribe. Native American tribes of the Northwest coast carved their totem, often a bird or animal, on a pole to mark land ownership and as a record of important events.

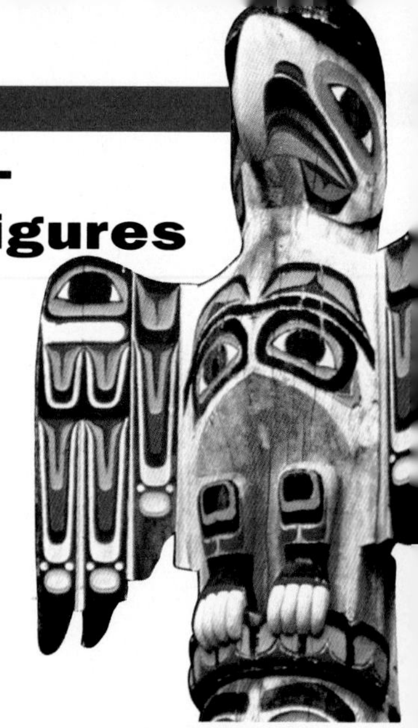

The photograph at the right has two dimensions, width and height. Yet when you look at it, you can visualize what the real totem pole must look like in three dimensions.

As in Mathematics Lab 10-1A, we often need to make a two-dimensional drawing of a three-dimensional object. How you go about that may depend on which view is the most important. For example, photographing the back or top of the totem pole would have eliminated many of the important features of the pole.

Think about drawing a two-dimensional cylinder.
- If you simply look down from directly above, you would see a *circle*. Drawing a circle would not indicate that the figure has three dimensions.
- Looking at the cylinder directly from the side, you can see a *rectangle*. Again this does not give any indication that this is a view of a cylinder.
- However, if you make a drawing that is somewhere between a top and side view, you are able to see that the figure has three dimensions.

Example 1

Make a two-dimensional drawing of a figure by using the top, front, and side views of the figure below.

   front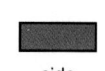

top   side

By drawing the figure as shown, you are able to see how all three views are correct.

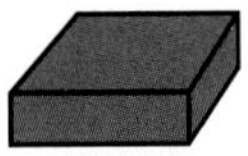

OPTIONS

Reteaching Activity

Using Models Provide models of each solid figure shown. Have students manipulate the models in order to see the three views of each. Have them use the models to help them draw the views.

Study Guide Masters, p. 84

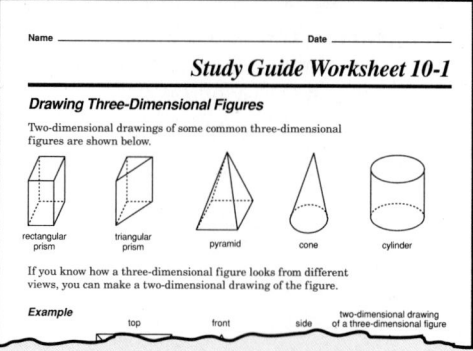

Name _____ Date _____

Study Guide Worksheet 10-1

Drawing Three-Dimensional Figures

Two-dimensional drawings of some common three-dimensional figures are shown below.

rectangular prism   triangular prism   pyramid   cone   cylinder

If you know how a three-dimensional figure looks from different views, you can make a two-dimensional drawing of the figure.

Example
   top   front   side   two-dimensional drawing of a three-dimensional figure

In geometry, we study three-dimensional figures called *solids*. Some common solids are shown below.

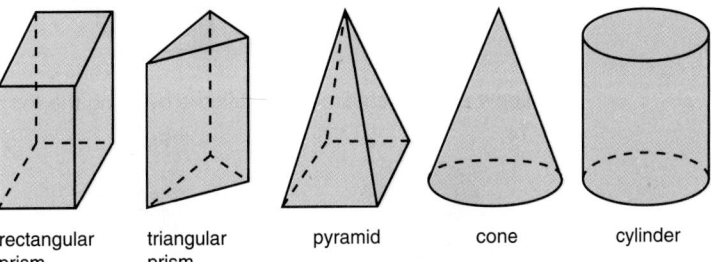

rectangular prism   triangular prism   pyramid   cone   cylinder

Checking for Understanding

Communicating Mathematics

Read and study the lesson to answer each question.

1. **Tell** why there can be more than one two-dimensional drawing of a three-dimensional object. **See margin.**

2. **Make a model** of a solid figure that would have the same view from the top and the bottom. **See students' work; sample answer: cylinder.**

3. **Write** the names of two solids that would have a different view from the top and bottom. **Sample answer: cone and pyramid**

Guided Practice

Draw a top, front, and side view of each figure.

4. 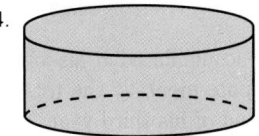 5. 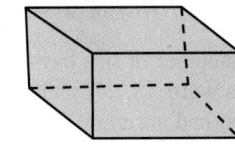 6.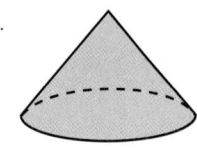

For answers to Exercises 4–6, see Solutions Manual.

Draw a three-dimensional figure given the top, front, and side views shown below.
See margin.

7.   Top   Front   Side

 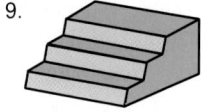 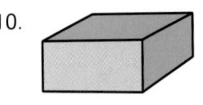

Exercises

For answers to Exercises 8–13, see Solutions Manual.

Independent Practice

Draw top, front, and side views of each figure.

8.   9.   10.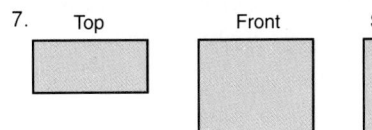

Lesson 10-1 Drawing Three-Dimensional Figures   **379**

Team Teaching

Inform the other teachers on your team that your classes are studying surface area and volume of three-dimensional figures. Suggestions for curriculum integration are:

Science: crystalography

Art: architecture, sculpture

Additional Answers

1. The drawing depends upon which parts of the object are used for the top, the front, and the side.

7.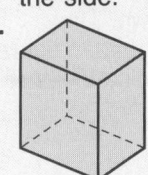

More Examples

For the Example

Make a two-dimensional drawing of a figure by using the top, front, and side views of the figure.

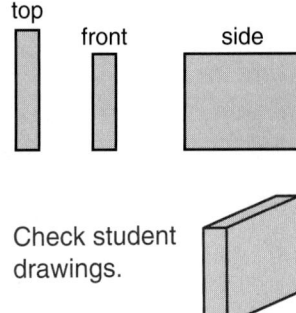

top   front   side

Check student drawings.

Checking for Understanding

Exercises 1-3 are designed to help you assess students' understanding through reading, writing, speaking, and modeling. You should work through these exercises with your students and then monitor their work on Guided Practice Exercises 4-7.

Practice Masters, p. 84

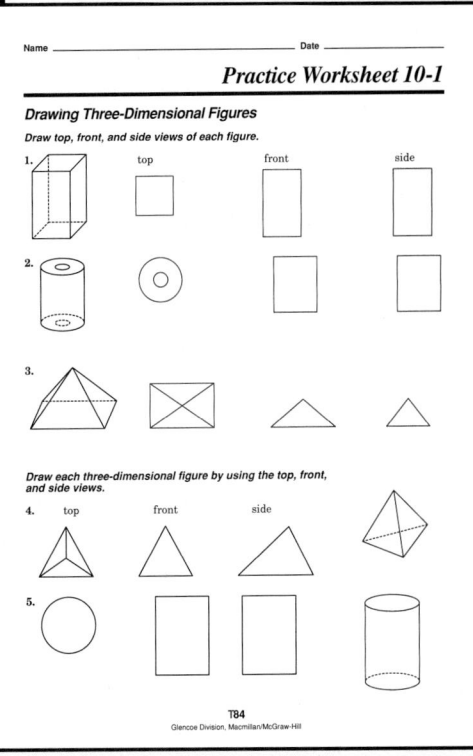

Name _____ Date _____

Practice Worksheet 10-1

Drawing Three-Dimensional Figures

Draw top, front, and side views of each figure.

1.   top   front   side

2.

3.

Draw each three-dimensional figure by using the top, front, and side views.

4.   top   front   side

5.

T84
Glencoe Division, Macmillan/McGraw-Hill

379

Close

Have students draw three different views of a rectangular prism and three different views of a cone.

3 PRACTICE/APPLY

Assignment Guide

Maximum: 8–24
Minimum: 9–17 odd, 18–23

Alternate Assessment

Writing Draw the top, front, and side view of a figure on the chalkboard. Have students draw the figure given these views.

Additional Answers

Sample answers:

14.   15.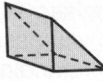

16.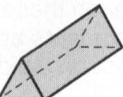

Enrichment Masters, p. 84

 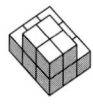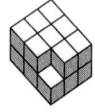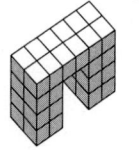
11. 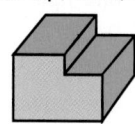   12. 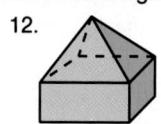   13.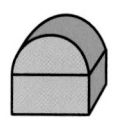

For answers to Exercises 14–16, see margin.

Draw each three-dimensional figure by using the top, front, and side views.

14. Top    Front 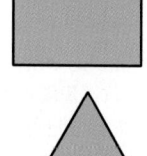   Side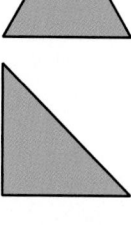

15.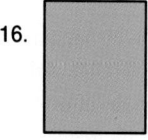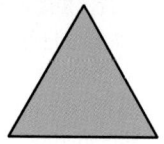

16.

17. In Exercise 7, would you expect your drawings to be the same as others in your class? Why or why not? **Yes, everyone is using the same figures. There is only one top, front, and side.**

Mixed Review 18. The number of sick days Aaron accumulated at his job during the first three years were 23, 17, and 9. Compute mentally the total number of sick days Aaron had accumulated at the end of his third year. *(Lesson 1-4)* **49 sick days**

19. **Geometry** Find the area of a parallelogram having a base of 2.3 centimeters and a height of 1.6 centimeters. *(Lesson 6-7)* **3.68 cm²**

20. **Probability** Find the probability of a counter that is randomly dropped falling in the shaded region. *(Lesson 9-9)* $\frac{34}{100} = \frac{17}{50}$

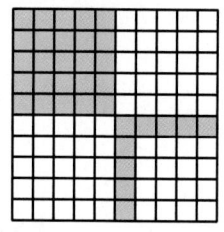

21. Side views; so he can see the windows.

Problem Solving and Applications

21. **Construction** Mr. Sims installs windows in homes. Which views of a house would be most helpful to Mr. Sims? Why?

22. **Architecture** Why would it be necessary for an architect to draw several different views of a building before starting construction? **See Solutions Manual.**

23. **Critical Thinking** Explain what two-dimensional and three-dimensional means. What do you think the fourth dimension might be? **See Solutions Manual.**

24. **Journal Entry** Write about some real objects that will help you remember what a cone, a cube, and a pyramid look like. **See students' work.**

380   **Chapter 10** Surface Area and Volume

OPTIONS

Extending the Lesson

Using Models Have students design paper models for at least two of the solid figures shown. They should make a sketch of each figure, using dotted lines to indicate where the figure should be folded.

Cooperative Learning Activity

10-2 Make a Model

Objective
Solve problems by making a model.

Materials
sugar cubes

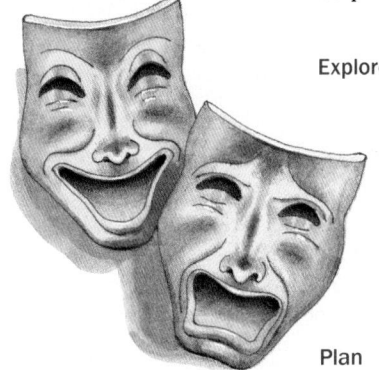

Concheta Lopez is building props for an upcoming school play. She is making a large display stand made from 20 boxes that are cubes that will be placed up against a wall during Scene I of the play. To save time and money, she wants to paint only the sides of each box that the audience will see. How many sides will be painted?

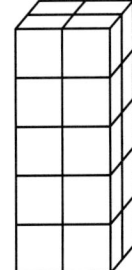

Explore   What do you know?
You know that the display is made from 20 boxes that are cubes. Concheta will paint only the sides of the boxes that the audience will see.

What are you trying to find?
You are trying to find the number of sides on the boxes that Concheta will paint.

Plan   Use sugar cubes to make a model of the display stand shown above. Count the sides of each box that could be visible to the audience.

Solve

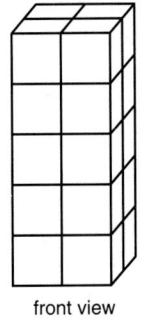
front view

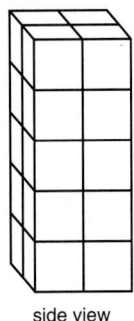
side view

The display stand will have 34 sides painted.

Examine   The stack has 5 layers with 2 cubes in each layer. There are 3 sides visible to the audience plus the 4 sides on the top of the display stand.
$3 \times (5 \times 2) + 4 = 34$

Lesson 10-2 Problem-Solving Strategy: Make a Model   **381**

10-2 Lesson Notes

NCTM Standards: 1–5, 7, 12

Lesson Resources
• Study Guide Master 10-2
• Practice Master 10-2
• Enrichment Master 10-2
• Group Activity Card 10-2

 Transparency 10-2 contains the 5-Minute Check and a teaching aid for this lesson.

🕐 5-Minute Check
(Over Lesson 10-1)
Draw the three-dimensional figure by using the top, front, and side views.

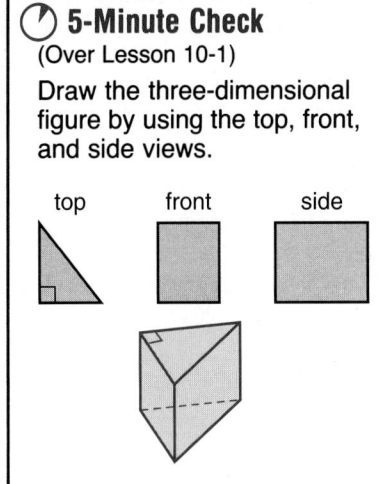

top   front   side

Practice Masters, p. 85

Name _____   Date _____

Practice Worksheet 10-2

Problem-Solving Strategy: *Make a Model*

Solve by making a model.

1. Toothbrushes are boxed and shipped in cartons each containing packages of 36. If each toothbrush box is 15 mm by 182 mm by 24 mm, what are the dimensions of the carton?
Sample: 182 mm by 90 mm by 144 mm

2. Ronnie used blocks to build a "fort". The blocks were cubes and were stacked five high. The top, front, and side views were all squares. How many blocks did Ronnie need to build the fort? **80**

Solve. Use any strategy.

3. What is a reasonable estimate of how long it will take an airplane to land if it starts its descent at 36,000 feet and descends at a rate of 900 feet per minute?
40 min

4. How many different shapes of rectangular prism can be formed using exactly 24 cubes?
six

5. Find the number of lines determined by the vertices of a pentagon.
10

6. Anisha bought blank videotapes for $3.99 each and labels for $0.49 per package. He spent $12.46. How many of each did he buy?
3 videotapes and one package of labels

7. Suppose a $599 television set is being offered at a discount of $109 along with an additional $50 discount off the sale price. What is the final selling price?
$440

8. Twelve one-inch-tall square snack cakes are packed in a box. No two cakes are stacked on top of one another. What are some possible dimensions of the box if the top view of each cake is a 2 in. by 2 in. square?
Samples: 24 in. by 2 in. by 1 in.; 12 in. by 4 in. by 1 in.

T85
Glencoe Division, Macmillan/McGraw-Hill

OPTIONS

Reteaching Activity

Using Problem Solving Guide students to see the advantages of making models to solve a wide variety of problems. Have students work in groups to list real-world applications of making models to solve problems. Ask them to discuss why a set designer would want to make models.

Study Guide Masters, p. 85

Name _____   Date _____

Study Guide Worksheet 10-2

Problem-Solving Strategy: *Make a Model*

Mark wants to make a pyramid-shaped display of basketballs for his sports shop. Each basketball comes in a 10-inch cubic box. Mark starts with a base six boxes wide and six boxes long. He decreases each dimension by one box for each layer, how many basketballs will he need for his display?

Explore   What do you know?
Mark wants to make a pyramid-shaped display. He starts with a six-box by six-box base. Each layer is one box shorter in each dimension.

You want to find out how many basketballs he needs.

Plan   Use cubes to make a model.
Count the number of cubes.

Solve   The display will require

1 FOCUS

Motivating the Lesson

Questioning Ask students how to use models to rearrange furniture in a room.

2 TEACH

More Examples

For the Example

Use models to show how to design a 20-ft by 30-ft rectangular space to include a sofa, TV-stand, table, and chairs. Answers will vary.

Close

Have students design a new office building so that as much of it as possible receives early morning sun.

3 PRACTICE/APPLY

Assignment Guide
Maximum: 5–10
Minimum: 5–10

Enrichment Masters, p. 85

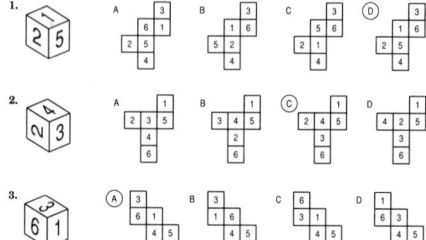

Checking for Understanding

Read and study the lesson to answer each question.

1. **Tell** what the advantages are of using a model instead of a drawing in the example on page 381. **See Solutions Manual.**

2. **Write** a sentence that explains how to use the make-a-model strategy. **See Solutions Manual.**

Solve by making a model.   20 in. × 8 in. × 8 in.

3. A publisher packages six small books for a children's collection in a decorated 4-inch cube. They are shipped to bookstores in cartons. Twenty cubes fit in a carton. What are the dimensions of the carton?

4. During a special on repair work, eight customers lined up outside Brian's Bicycle Shop with either a bicycle or a tricycle that needed repair. When Brian looked out the window, he counted 21 wheels outside the shop. How many tricycles and bicycles are outside the shop? **5 tricycles and 3 bicycles**

Problem Solving

Solve. Use any strategy.

Strategies
• • • • • • • • •
Look for a pattern.
Solve a simpler problem.
Act it out.
Guess and check.
Draw a diagram.
Make a chart.
Work backward.

DATA SEARCH

5. José is building a triangular-shaped display of facial tissues in the supermarket. Each box of facial tissue is in the shape of a cube. There are 10 boxes of tissue in the 10th and bottom row of the display. If there is one less box in each of the rows above, how many boxes does José use to make the display? **55 boxes**   Fred—Spanish, Sarah—German, Greg—French

6. Fred, Sarah, and Greg take French, Spanish, and German. No person's language class begins with the same letter of their first name. Sarah's best friend takes French. Which language does each person take?

7. How many different-shaped rectangular prisms can be formed using exactly 16 cubes? **4 prisms**

8. Jenna spent 3 hours addressing 50 graduation announcements. At this rate, how long will it take her to address 125 announcements? $7\frac{1}{2}$ **hours**

9. **Data Search** Refer to page 652. What was the number of cable subscribers and the average monthly rate in 1980? By how much had each increased by 1990? **20 million, $8; 30 million, $10**

10. Al bought $5\frac{1}{4}$-inch floppy diskettes for $1.19 each and labels for $0.59 per package. He spent $15.44. How many of each did he buy? **10 diskettes and 6 packages of labels**

OPTIONS

Extending the Lesson

Using Community Resources
Have groups of students interview people in your community who make models in order to solve work-related problems. Have them report their findings to the class, including pictures of the models, if possible.

Cooperative Learning Activity

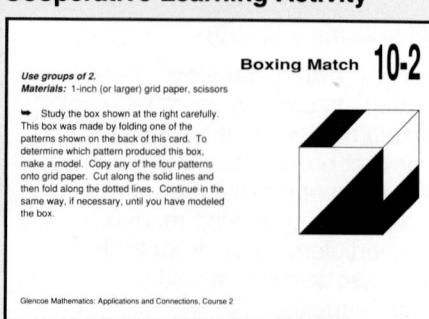

Use groups of 2.
Materials: 1-inch (or larger) grid paper, scissors

Boxing Match 10-2

➤ Study the box shown at the right carefully. This box was made by folding one of the patterns shown on the back of this card. To determine which pattern produced this box, make a model. Copy any of the four patterns onto grid paper. Cut along the solid lines and then fold along the dotted lines. Continue in the same way, if necessary, until you have modeled the box.

Glencoe Mathematics: Applications and Connections, Course 2

10-3 Surface Area of Prisms

Objective
Find the surface area of rectangular prisms.

Words to Learn
surface area
face
rectangular prism
base

Many department stores offer gift-wrapping services. If you don't have time to wrap the gift yourself, or if you're all thumbs when you try, you can pay an employee to do it for you.

Suppose your gift is in a box that is 2 feet by 1 foot by 3 feet. If you know the surface area of the box, you can find out how much paper it would take to cover the box.

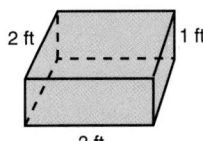

The **surface area** is the sum of the areas of all of the surfaces or **faces** of the box. Boxes such as the one we want to wrap are called **rectangular prisms** since all of the faces are in the shape of a rectangle. The faces on the top and the bottom are called the **bases**.

You can find the surface area of a prism by finding the area of each face. The sum of the six areas will be the surface area of the box.

Mini-Lab

Work with a partner.
Materials: gift box, graph paper, pencil.

Unfold or cut apart the gift box. It should resemble the frame at the right.

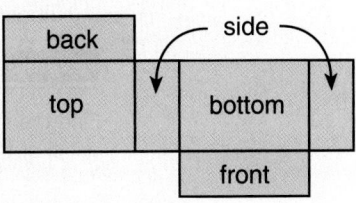

- Trace each side of the box onto your graph paper to make a figure like the one at the right.
- Label the dimensions of each rectangle on the graph paper.
a. See margin.

Talk About It

a. What is the area of each base and the other four faces? To help you, copy and complete the following chart.

b. What is the total surface area of the gift box? **22 ft²**

	Dimensions	Area
front		
back		
top		
bottom		
left side		
right side		
	Total:	

OPTIONS

Gifted and Talented Needs

Tell students that a cube is a rectangular prism with 6 congruent faces. Ask them how the surface area of a cube would change if its length were doubled. Ask what would happen if its length were tripled.   Surface area would be 4 times as great; it would be 9 times as great.

Additional Answer

a.

	Dimensions (ft × ft)	Area (ft²)
front	3 × 1	3
back	3 × 1	3
top	2 × 3	6
bottom	2 × 3	6
left	1 × 2	2
right	1 × 2	2

Total surface area: 22 ft²

10-3 Lesson Notes

NCTM Standards: 1–5, 7, 9, 12

Lesson Resources
- Study Guide Master 10-3
- Practice Master 10-3
- Enrichment Master 10-3
- Technology Master, p. 24
- Group Activity Card 10-3

Transparency 10-3 contains the 5-Minute Check and a teaching aid for this lesson.

5-Minute Check
(Over Lesson 10-2)

Solve using the make-a-model strategy.

1. Elise counted 18 wheels go by as she looked up from her book in the park. If eight children rode by, how many were on bicycles and how many on tricycles?   bicycles: 6, tricycles: 2

2. A display that is shaped like a rectangular prism is made of 24 1-foot cubes. It is 4 feet high, 3 feet wide, and 2 feet deep. The outside of the display is red. How many cubes have exactly 1 red face? 4

1 FOCUS

Motivating the Lesson

Activity   Display a closed box you have in the classroom. Ask students how they would figure out the exact amount of paper needed to cover the box.

2 TEACH

Using the Mini-Lab   Have students examine the model and design another model that could be folded into the same rectangular prism. Ask students whether another design would change the surface area of the package.

383

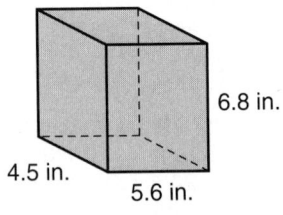
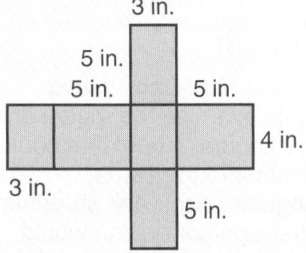
You can see that the length and height were multiplied to find the areas of the front and back. You multiplied length and width to find the areas of the top and bottom, and you multiplied width and height to find the areas of the sides.

You can write this as a formula.

$$A = \ell h + \ell h + \ell w + \ell w + wh + wh$$

Since there are two of each face that are exactly the same, you can write the formula a shorter way.

$$A = 2\ell h + 2\ell w + 2wh$$
$$A = 2(\ell h + \ell w + wh) \qquad \textit{Distributive property}$$

Example 1 *Connection*

Algebra Use the formula, $A = 2(\ell h + \ell w + wh)$ to find the surface area of a rectangular prism that is 3 inches by 4 inches by 5 inches.

$$
\begin{aligned}
A &= 2(\ell h + \ell w + wh) \\
&= 2\,(3 \times 4 + 3 \times 5 + 5 \times 4) \qquad \textit{Replace } \ell \textit{ with 3, h with 4,} \\
&= 2\,(12 + 15 + 20) \qquad\qquad \textit{and w with 5.} \\
&= 2(47) \qquad \textit{Add first. Then multiply.} \\
&= 94 \text{ in}^2 \qquad \textit{The area of a 2-dimensional figure uses the} \\
&\qquad\qquad\qquad \textit{exponent 2 with the unit of measure.}
\end{aligned}
$$

L◯◯K **BACK**

You can review order of operations on page 24.

The surface area is 94 square inches.

You can use a calculator to compute surface area. Remember to enter a multiplication sign in front of the parentheses.

Example 2

Find the surface area of the rectangular prism at the right by using a calculator.

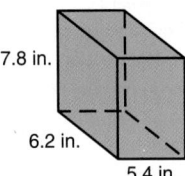

7.8 in.

6.2 in.

5.4 in.

$$
\begin{aligned}
A &= 2(\ell h + \ell w + wh) \\
&= 2(5.4 \times 6.2 + 5.4 \times 7.8 + 6.2 \times 7.8)
\end{aligned}
$$

2 [×] [(] 5.4 [×] 6.2 [+] 5.4 [×] 7.8 [+] 6.2 [×] 7.8 [)] [=] 247.92

The surface area of the rectangular prism is about 248 square inches.

Checking for Understanding

Communicating Mathematics

Read and study the lesson to answer each question.

1. **Draw** a rectangular prism that is unfolded with the dimensions of 3 inches, 4 inches, and 5 inches. **See margin.**

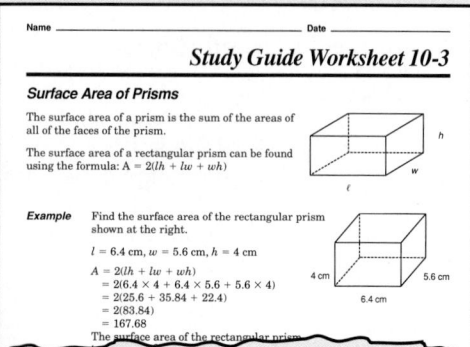

2. **Tell** which property allows you to state $\ell h + \ell h + \ell w + \ell w + wh + wh$ as $2(\ell h + \ell w + wh)$. **Distributive**

3. **Write** a sentence explaining why it is important to know how to find surface area when you paint the walls in a room. **You need to know the surface area to decide how much paint to buy.**

Guided Practice Explain how you would find the surface area of each rectangular prism. Then find the surface area. **Use the formula $2(\ell h + \ell w + wh)$.**

4.
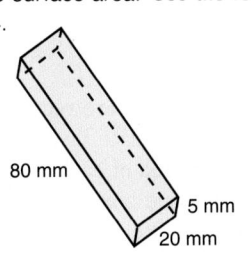
80 mm
5 mm
20 mm
4,200 mm²

5.
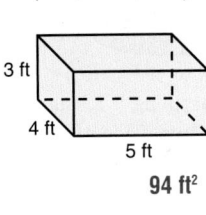
3 ft
4 ft
5 ft
94 ft²

6.
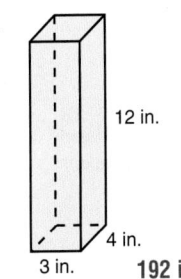
12 in.
4 in.
3 in.
192 in²

7. length, 2 yd
   width, 4 yd
   height, 6 yd
   88 yd²

8. length, 4.5 m
   width, 5.4 m
   height, 6 m
   167.4 m²

9. length, 5 cm
   width, 10 cm
   height, 7 cm
   310 cm²

Exercises

Independent Practice Find the surface area of each rectangular prism. Round answers to the nearest tenth.

10.
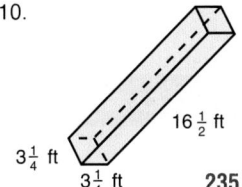
$16\frac{1}{2}$ ft
$3\frac{1}{4}$ ft
$3\frac{1}{4}$ ft
$235\frac{5}{8}$ ft²

11.
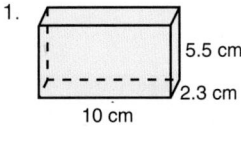
5.5 cm
2.3 cm
10 cm
181.3 cm²

12.
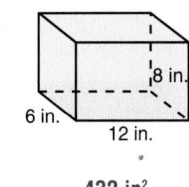
8 in.
6 in.
12 in.
432 in²

13. length, $7\frac{1}{2}$ ft
    width, $5\frac{1}{4}$ ft
    height, 9 ft **$308\frac{1}{4}$ ft²**

14. length, 6 in.
    width, 4 in.
    height, 15 in.
    348 in²

15. length, 16 cm
    width, 11 cm
    height, 8 cm
    784 cm²

16. length, $8\frac{2}{3}$ in.
    width, $4\frac{1}{2}$ in.
    height, $10\frac{1}{4}$ in **$347\frac{11}{12}$ in²**

17. length, 35 m
    width, 18 m
    height, 24 m
    3,804 m²

18. length, 14 yd
    width, 27 yd
    height, 32.5 yd
    3,421 yd²

19. Each face of a cube has an area of 8 square inches. What is the surface area of the cube? **48 in²**

20. A cube has a surface area of 42 square feet. What is the area of one face? **7 ft²**

3 PRACTICE/APPLY

Practice Masters, p. 86

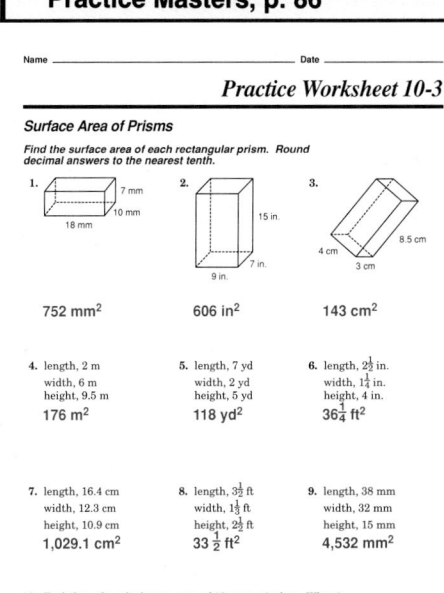

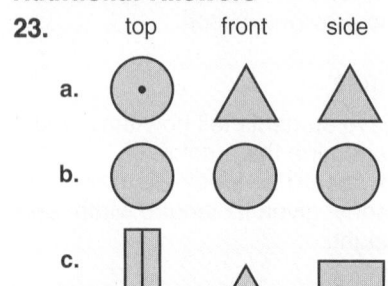
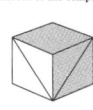
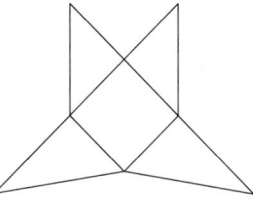
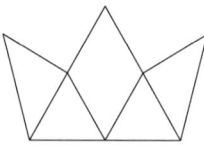
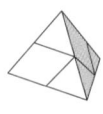
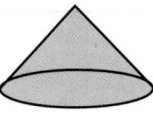

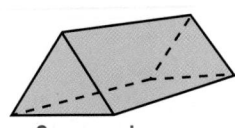

CULTURAL KALEIDOSCOPE

Maya Lin

In 1981, at the age of 22, Chinese-American Maya Lin won the national design competition for the Vietnam Veterans Memorial in Washington, D.C. The memorial is a symbol of United States honor and recognition of the men and women who served in the armed forces in the Vietnam War. It is inscribed with the names of the more than 58,000 persons who gave their lives for their country and those that are still missing.

Ms. Lin is the daughter of Taiwanese immigrants who make their home in Ohio. She viewed herself as just an American student until criticism of her design and heated opposition to the memorial changed her life and her attitudes. She believed that some of the criticism stemmed from prejudice toward her as a person of Chinese descent. The competition was anonymous but Maya often wonders what would have happened if names were allowed on the entries. She said, "Until that time, I hope I am an example for people who are young and who have a chance to say something when they should."

386 Chapter 10 Surface Area and Volume

10-4A Introduction to Surface Area of a Cylinder

A Preview of Lesson 10-4

Objective
Develop the formula for surface area of a cylinder by constructing a cylinder.

Materials
centimeter grid paper
compass
scissors
tape

In this lab, you will be constructing a cylinder that will help you to develop the formula for surface area of a cylinder.

Try this!

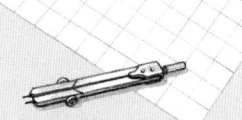

● On centimeter grid paper, draw a circle whose radius is 5 centimeters.

● Cut out the circle.

● Repeat the process so that you have two circles of exactly the same size.

● Cut out a rectangle that is 12 centimeters wide and 33 centimeters long.

● Roll the rectangle into a cylinder so that each circle fits into the end. You should have enough to be able to overlap the rectangle. Tape it so that the grid side of the paper is showing.

● Tape the circles onto each end, forming a cylinder. Make sure that the grid side of the paper is showing.

Let's investigate how we might find the surface area of the cylinder we have constructed.

What do you think?

LOOKBACK

You can review area of a circle on page 359.

4. 533.8 cm²; Add area of curved surface to area of bases.

5. *S.A.* = $2\pi r^2 + 2\pi rh$

1. What is the shape of each end of the cylinder? **a circle**
2. Find the area of each end. **78.5 cm²**
3. Now find the area of the curved surface. Before you rolled it into a cylinder, what was its shape? **376.8 cm²; rectangle**
4. What is the total surface area? How did you find it?
5. Write a formula for the surface area of a cylinder.
6. Will a cylinder *always* be made up of the same three shapes? Explain. **Yes; see margin.**

Mathematics Lab 10-4A Introduction to Surface Area of a Cylinder   **387**

OPTIONS

Lab Manual   You may wish to make copies of the blackline master on p. 67 of the *Lab Manual* for students to use as a recording sheet.

Additional Answer

6. top and bottom: always circles; curved surface: always a rectangle, when flattened out

Lab Manual, p. 67

Name _____ Date _____

Mathematics Lab Worksheet

Use with page 387 _____

Introduction to Surface Area of a Cylinder

What do you think?

1. Each end of the cylinder is shaped like a __circle__ .

2. The area of each end = __78.5 cm²__

3. The area of the curved surface = __396 cm²__

   The curved surface was a __rectangle that was 12 cm wide and 33 cm long.__

NCTM Standards: 1–5, 7, 12

Management Tips

For Students   If centimeter grid paper is not available, students can use a compass set at a radius of 5 centimeters to make the bases of the cylinder, and a centimeter ruler to measure the rectangle that is the curved surface.

For the Overhead Projector
Overhead Manipulative Resources provides appropriate materials for teacher or student demonstration of the activities in this Mathematics Lab.

1 FOCUS

Introducing the Lab

Discuss with students what a cylinder is, perhaps comparing its characteristics to those of a rectangular prism by focusing on its two congruent bases. Ask students to suggest examples of cylindrical objects.

2 TEACH

Using Models   You may wish to have students take apart their cylinders and lay them out to visualize the two circles and the rectangle.

3 PRACTICE/APPLY

Using Connections   Guide students to see the relationship between the length of the rectangle and the circumference of the base. Ask them how their formulas would change if they were to find the surface area of a can of tuna with the top off.

Close

Ask students to describe a way to find the surface area of a can of frozen orange juice.

NCTM Standards: 1–5, 7, 12

Lesson Resources
- Study Guide Master 10-4
- Practice Master 10-4
- Enrichment Master 10-4
- Evaluation Master, Quiz A, p. 88
- Technology Master, p. 10
- Interdisciplinary Master, p. 24
- Group Activity Card 10-4

 Transparency 10-4 contains the 5-Minute Check and a teaching aid for this lesson.

🕐 5-Minute Check
(Over Lesson 10-3)

Find the surface area of each prism.

1.

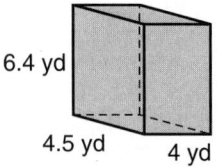

6.4 yd

4.5 yd   4 yd

144.8 square yards

2. length, 18 in.; width, 14 in.; height, 21 in.
1,848 square inches

3. A sculpture is shaped like a cube with a surface area of 294 square yards. What is the length of one edge?   7 yd

1 FOCUS

Motivating the Lesson

Questioning   Ask students to distinguish between a cylinder and a rectangular prism, and between a cylinder and a cone. Ask them why they think so many kinds of food are packaged in containers that are cylinders.

10-4   Surface Area of Cylinders

Objective
Find the surface area of cylinders.

Words to Learn
cylinder

If you live in New Jersey, you probably say "soda." If you live in Ohio, you probably say "pop." What are we talking about? Carbonated beverages, or soft drinks.

Carbonated beverages have become very popular in the past three decades, mostly because of modern bottling methods. Today, most carbonated beverages are "bottled" in aluminum cans.

Aluminum cans are in the shape of **cylinders.** You can find the surface area of a cylinder by finding the area of all of the surfaces.

You can see that the top and the bottom of a cylinder are in the shape of a circle. If you take the remainder of the can and unfold it, you see the curved surface is in the shape of a rectangle. By finding the area of these three surfaces, you can calculate the surface area.

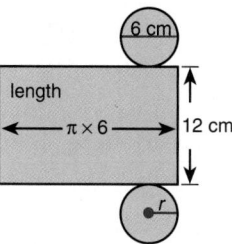

The length equals the circumference of the circle.

Example 1   *Problem Solving*

Find the surface area of a soft drink can.

The height of a soft drink can is about 12 centimeters, and the diameter is about 6 centimeters.

- First, find the area of the top and bottom. Use the formula for the area of a circle.

$$A = \pi r^2$$

Since the diameter is 6 centimeters, the radius is 3 centimeters.

 28.274334

The area of one circle is about 28.3 square centimeters.

The area of the two circles is about 28.3×2 or 56.6 square centimeters or 56.6 cm².

Calculator Hint
• • • • • • • • • • • • •
You can use the π key when you need to find area or circumference of a circle.

OPTIONS

Meeting Needs of Middle School Students

Discuss the usefulness of knowing about surface area. For example, point out how package designers and advertisers, who often use all surfaces of a box or can, need to know the space they have to use. Ask students to suggest other applications.

- Now calculate the area of the curved surface. When unfolded, the curved surface has the shape of a rectangle. The width of the rectangle is the height of the can, and the length is the circumference of the base.

$A = \ell w$
$\quad = 2\pi r \times w$ *Replace ℓ with $2\pi r$, the circumference.*
$\quad = 2\pi r \times h$ *Replace w with h.*
$\quad = 2 \times \pi \times 3 \times 12$ *Replace r with 3 and h with 12.*

2 ⊠ π ⊠ 3 ⊠ 12 ⊟ **226.19467**

To the nearest tenth, the area of the curved surface is 226.2 square centimeters.

- Then add the area of the curved surface to the area of the two circles.

226.2 ⊞ 56.6 ⊟ **282.8**

The surface area of a soft drink can is about 282.8 square centimeters.

You can combine the steps to find the surface area of a cylinder.

Example 2

Find the surface area of the cylinder at the right.

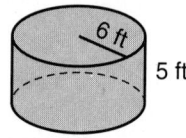

$A = $ *areas of* $+$ *area of*
     bases   *curved surface*
$A = (2\pi r^2) + \quad (2\pi rh)$
$A = (2 \cdot \pi \cdot 4^2) + (2 \cdot \pi \cdot 4 \cdot 7)$ *Replace r with 4 and h with 7.*

(2 ⊠ π ⊠ 4 x²) ⊞ (2 ⊠ π ⊠ 4 ⊠ 7)
⊟ **276.46015**

To the nearest tenth, the surface area is 276.5 square feet.

Checking for Understanding

Communicating Mathematics

Read and study the lesson to answer each question.

1. **Tell** which two measurements must be known to find the surface area of a cylinder. **radius and height**
2. **Draw** a model of an unfolded cylinder. **See margin.**
3. **Write** one sentence explaining why we use the formula for the area of a rectangle in finding the surface area of a cylinder. **The curved surface of a cylinder is a rectangle when it is flattened out.**

Lesson 10-4 Surface Area of Cylinders   **389**

Reteaching Activity

Using Models   To further demonstrate that the curved surface of a cylinder is a rectangle whose length is equal to the circumference of the base, have students tear off the paper label that covers a can of soup, lay it out flat on a table, and then measure it and the circumference of the can.

Study Guide Masters, p. 87

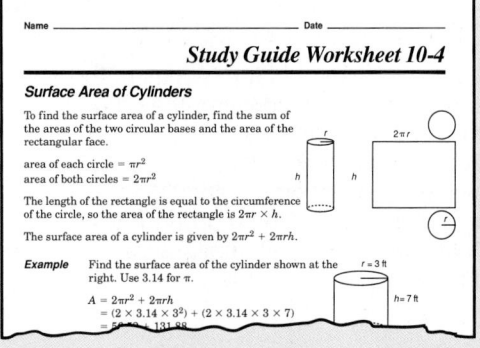

Name _____ Date _____

Study Guide Worksheet 10-4

Surface Area of Cylinders

To find the surface area of a cylinder, find the sum of the areas of the two circular bases and the area of the rectangular face.

area of each circle = πr^2
area of both circles = $2\pi r^2$

The length of the rectangle is equal to the circumference of the circle, so the area of the rectangle is $2\pi r \times h$.

The surface area of a cylinder is given by $2\pi r^2 + 2\pi rh$.

Example   Find the surface area of the cylinder shown at the right. Use 3.14 for π. $r = 3$ ft

$A = 2\pi r^2 + 2\pi rh$
$\quad = (2 \times 3.14 \times 3^2) + (2 \times 3.14 \times 3 \times 7)$ $h = 7$ ft
$\quad = $ ... 131.88

Error Analysis

Watch for students who confuse area with circumference when using the formula to find surface area of a cylinder.

Prevent by pointing out that the circumference of the base is equal to the length of the rectangle obtained by "unrolling" the cylinder.

Close

Have students explain how they use the formulas for area of a circle and for circumference of a circle in order to find the surface area of a cylinder.

3 PRACTICE/APPLY

Assignment Guide

Maximum: 8–27
Minimum: 9–21 odd, 22–27
All: Mid-Chapter Review

For **Extra Practice,** see p. 593.

Alternate Assessment

Writing Have students find the surface area of a cylindrical object found in the classroom.

Practice Masters, p. 87

Name _____ Date _____

Practice Worksheet 10-4

Surface Area of Cylinders

Find the surface area of each cylinder with the given height and radius. Use 3.14 for π. Round answers to the nearest tenth.

1. 602.9 mm²   2. 604.45 ft²   3. 355.7 yd²

4. 1,761.5 in²   5. 1,406.7 cm²   6. 107.3 ft²

Find the surface area of each cylinder. Use 22/7 for π.

7. height, 12 cm, radius, 9 cm   1,188 cm²
8. height, 3.2 ft, radius, 4.5 ft   217.8 ft²
9. height, 7 mm, radius, 8 mm   754 2/7 mm²

10. height, 18 ft, radius, 20 ft   4,777 1/7 ft²
11. height, 6 in, radius, 9 in.   848 4/7 in²
12. height, 10 1/2 yd, radius, 9 1/4 yd   1,148 9/28 yd²

13. Find the surface area of a cylinder whose height is 18 inches and whose base has a diameter of 19 inches.   1,640.65 in²

T87
Glencoe Division, Macmillan/McGraw-Hill

390

Guided Practice

4. a. Find the area of each base of the cylinder. **12.56 cm²**

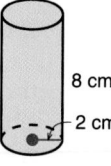

8 cm
2 cm

   b. Find the area of the curved surface in the cylinder. Record your answer. **100.48 cm²**

   c. What is the surface area of the cylinder above? **125.6 cm²**

Find the surface area of each cylinder. Use 3.14 for π.

5. height, 2.5 m
   radius, 3.4 m
   125.9768 m²

6. height, 4 ft
   radius, 5 ft
   282.6 ft²

7. height, 5 cm
   diameter, 20 cm
   942 cm²

Exercises

Independent Practice Find the surface area of each cylinder. Use 3.14 for π. Round answers to the nearest tenth.

8.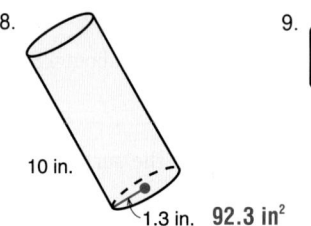
   10 in.
   1.3 in. **92.3 in²**

9.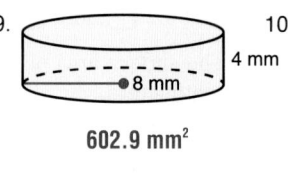
   4 mm
   8 mm
   602.9 mm²

10.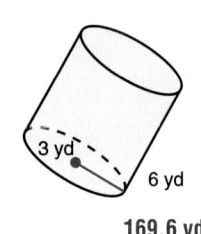
   3 yd
   6 yd
   169.6 yd²

11. 12 2/3 ft
   3 1/4 ft
   324.9 ft²

12.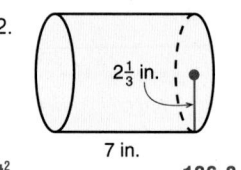
   2 1/3 in.
   7 in.
   136.8 in²

13.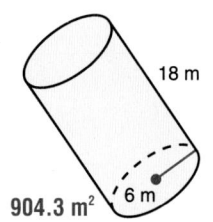
   18 m
   6 m
   904.3 m²

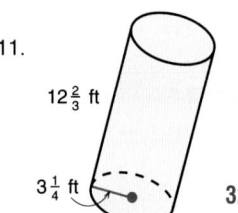

Find the surface area of each cylinder. Use 22/7 for π.

14. height, 5 in.
    radius, 11 in. **1,106 2/7 in²**

15. height, 4.2 cm
    diameter, 12.6 cm **415.8 cm²**

16. height, 8 mm
    radius, 9 mm **961 5/7 mm²**

17. height, 7 m
    radius, 16 m **2,313 1/7 m²**

18. height, 10 ft
    diameter, 24 ft **1,659 3/7 ft²**

19. height, 12 1/2 yd
    radius, 8 3/4 yd
    1,168 3/4 yd²

20. Find the surface area of a cylinder whose height is 14 inches and whose base has a diameter of 16 inches. **1,106 2/7 in²**

21. Find the surface area of a cylinder whose height is 12 inches and whose base has a circumference of 37.68 inches. Use 3.14 for π. **678.24 in²**

OPTIONS

Limited English Proficiency

Have students add the names of the three-dimensional figures they are studying to their vocabulary lists. A picture should accompany each written description, as should an example of a common object having that shape. Have students work together.

22. **Statistics** Construct a line plot for the following set of data: 65, 72, 83, 81, 65, 71, 72, 70, 81. *(Lesson 3-4)* **See Solutions Manual.**

23. **Geometry** Describe the quadrilateral at the right. *(Lesson 8-3)*

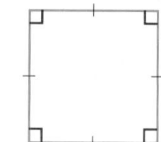

quadrilateral
parallelogram
rectangle
square

24. Nicole has a cushion of an old chair that she would like to cover with a new fabric. The cushion is in the shape of a rectangular prism with a length of 1.5 feet, a width of 1.5 feet, and a height of 0.25 feet. How much fabric will she need to cover the cushion? *(Lesson 10-3)* **6 ft²**

25. **Critical Thinking** If you double the height of a cylinder, will its surface area double? Explain. **See margin.**

26. 62.8 in² 26. **Marketing** A can of vegetables is 5 inches high, and its base has a radius of 2 inches. How much paper is needed to make the label on the can?

27. **Agriculture** A cylindrical gasoline storage tank on Mr. Baker's farm needs to be painted. The tank is 8 feet long and has a diameter of 4 feet. If one gallon of paint covers 350 square feet, how many cans of paint will Mr. Baker need? **1 can**

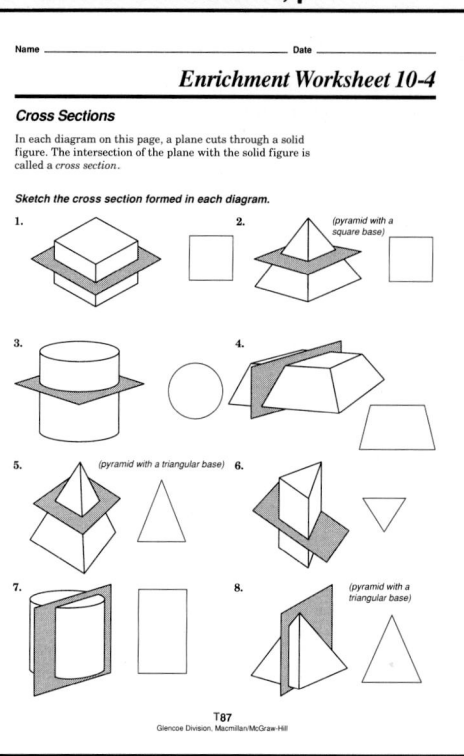

10 Assessment: Mid-Chapter Review

1. **Draw** three different views of a cylinder and a rectangular prism. *(Lesson 10-1)* **See students' work.**

2. During the Pee-Wee race, Jonah saw 4 cyclists cross the finish line. Jessie counted 11 wheels go by. How many bicycles and tricycles did they see cross the finish line? *(Lesson 10-2)* **1 bicycle, 3 tricycles**

Find the surface area of each rectangular prism. *(Lesson 10-3)*

3. length, 6 cm
width, 4 cm
height, 2 cm
88 cm²

4. **136 m²**

8 m
4 m
3 m

Find the surface area of each cylinder. *(Lesson 10-4)*

5. height, 3 ft
radius, 2.2 ft
71.8432 ft²

6.

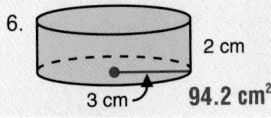

2 cm
3 cm   **94.2 cm²**

Lesson 10-4 Surface Area of Cylinders   **391**

Additional Answer
25. No. The area of the curved surface will double but not the entire surface area.

Enrichment Masters, p. 87

Name _____ Date _____

Enrichment Worksheet 10-4

Cross Sections

In each diagram on this page, a plane cuts through a solid figure. The intersection of the plane with the solid figure is called a *cross section*.

Sketch the cross section formed in each diagram.

1.   2. (pyramid with a square base)

3.   4.

5. (pyramid with a triangular base) 6.

7.   8. (pyramid with a triangular base)

T87
Glencoe Division, Macmillan/McGraw-Hill

Extending the Lesson

Using Number Sense Have students first guess and then investigate to determine the effect on the surface area of a cylinder if its height and the radius of its base were both doubled or tripled. **The surface area would be, respectively, 4 times as great and 9 times as great.**

Cooperative Learning Activity

Number of players: 2
Materials: Spinners

Master Cylinders **10-4**

• Label equal sections of two spinners "2," "3," "4," "5," "6," "7." Decide which spinner you want to stand for the height of a cylinder and which spinner you want to stand for the radius of a cylinder's base. (You and your partner must choose differently.)

• Each partner spins a spinner. Then both partners compute the surface area for a cylinder with the resulting height and radius of a base. The partner with the greater surface area wins the round. Play five rounds, comparing your results each time.

Suppose the spinner were labeled with different numbers. Is there a way to determine the winner of the round without actually calculating surface areas?

Glencoe Mathematics: Applications and Connections, Course 2

DECISION MAKING

1 FOCUS

NCTM Standards: 1–5, 7

Objective Analyze data and make a decision.

Introducing the Situation

Have students begin by sharing experiences they have had either performing in or organizing tournaments. Ask for an explanation of what a *single-elimination tournament* is and for some real examples. Guide groups to see that a great deal of discussion will take place during the activity. Suggest that groups share the large recording task.

2 TEACH

Using Discussion Groups may experience difficulty coming to a consensus on the decisions they need to make. Guide students to see that in the real world, the existence of a large number of reasonable choices often makes it difficult to reach a decision. Stress that groups should consider points of view of all members, and then come up with a way to choose a plan.

Analyzing the Data

Tell students that the data to be analyzed should answer questions about the relative advantages of the plans. What are some of these questions? Sample answers: Which plan distributes the most money? Which plan benefits the largest number of students? (Plan C, in both cases)

Choosing a Scholarship Prize

Situation

A bowling association is holding a two-day single elimination scholarship tournament for middle school students. The winners receive scholarships to a college of their choice. As secretary of the bowling association, you must decide which of the scholarship funds shown below to select for the tournament.

Hidden Data

How much, if anything, will each participant have to pay for an entry fee?
How much of the entry fee will go towards the scholarship fund?
Will the scholarship be awarded at the end of the tournament or upon registering for college?
How many students will participate?

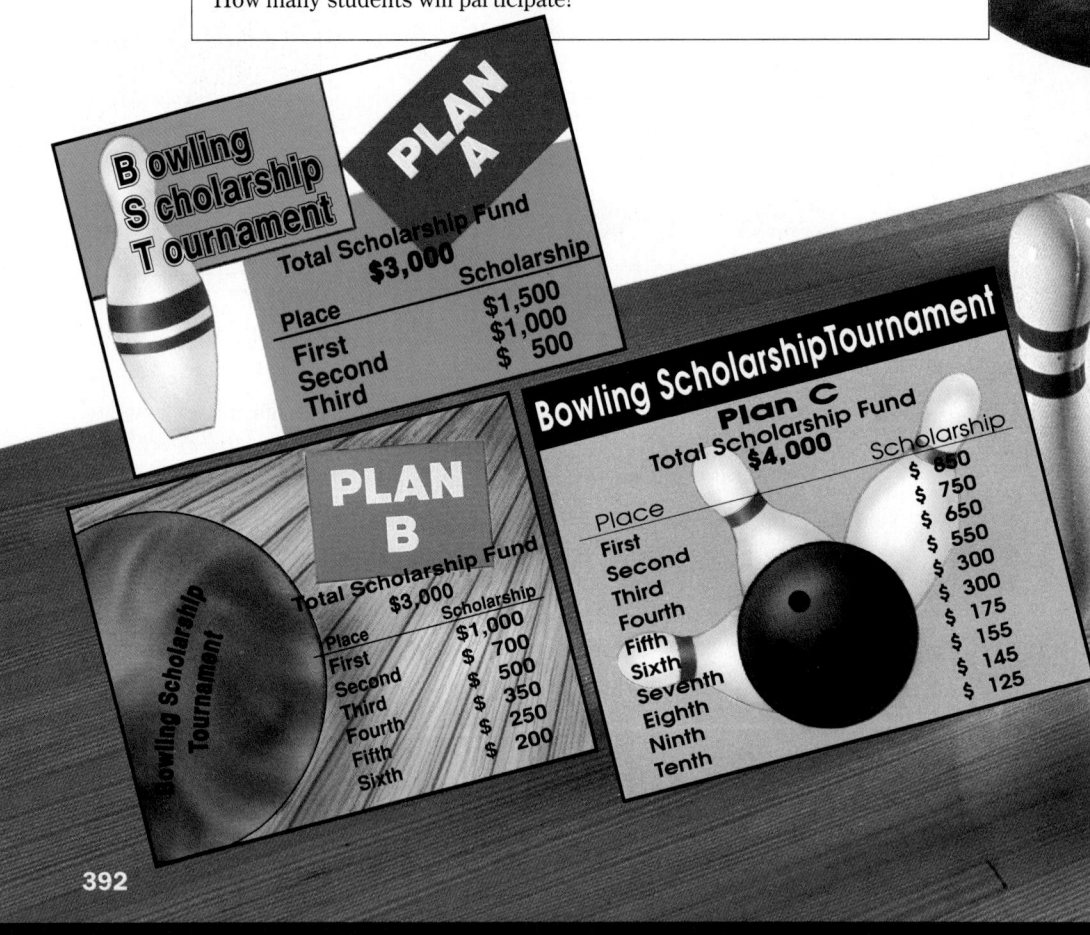

Bowling Scholarship Tournament

PLAN A

Total Scholarship Fund **$3,000**

Place	Scholarship
First	$1,500
Second	$1,000
Third	$ 500

PLAN B

Total Scholarship Fund $3,000

Place	Scholarship
First	$1,000
Second	$ 700
Third	$ 500
Fourth	$ 350
Fifth	$ 250
Sixth	$ 200

Bowling Scholarship Tournament

Plan C

Total Scholarship Fund **$4,000**

Place	Scholarship
First	$ 850
Second	$ 750
Third	$ 650
Fourth	$ 550
Fifth	$ 300
Sixth	$ 300
Seventh	$ 175
Eighth	$ 155
Ninth	$ 145
Tenth	$ 125

392

Classroom Vignette

"When my students begin working on the Decision Making features, they think that the decision-making process will be a simple one. But as they begin to discuss the facts and things to be considered, they uncover layers that make their decisions more difficult. This is a good activity for them."

Barbara D. Smith

Barbara Smith
Author

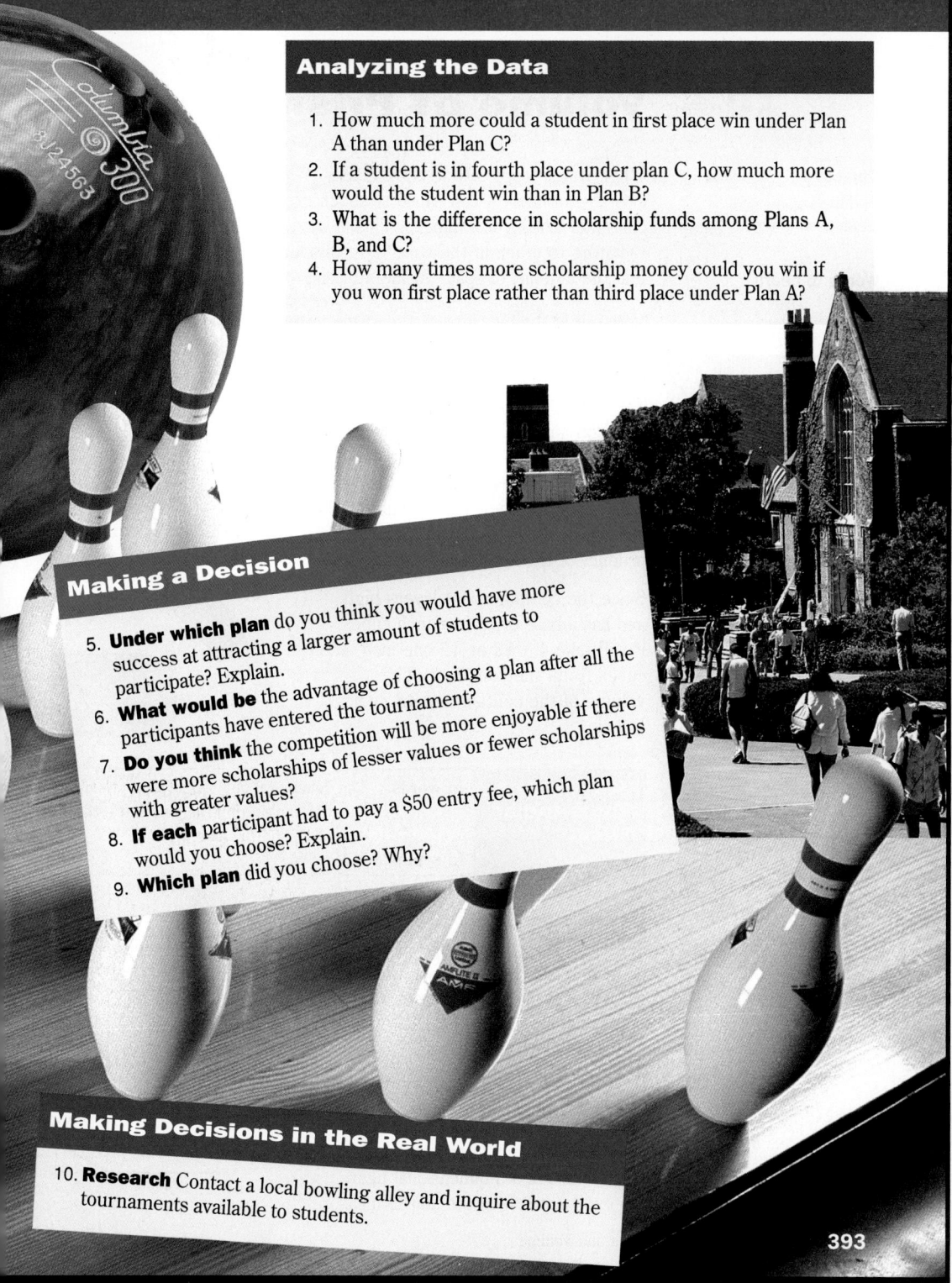

Analyzing the Data

1. How much more could a student in first place win under Plan A than under Plan C?
2. If a student is in fourth place under plan C, how much more would the student win than in Plan B?
3. What is the difference in scholarship funds among Plans A, B, and C?
4. How many times more scholarship money could you win if you won first place rather than third place under Plan A?

Making a Decision

5. **Under which plan** do you think you would have more success at attracting a larger amount of students to participate? Explain.
6. **What would be** the advantage of choosing a plan after all the participants have entered the tournament?
7. **Do you think** the competition will be more enjoyable if there were more scholarships of lesser values or fewer scholarships with greater values?
8. **If each** participant had to pay a $50 entry fee, which plan would you choose? Explain.
9. **Which plan** did you choose? Why?

Making Decisions in the Real World

10. **Research** Contact a local bowling alley and inquire about the tournaments available to students.

393

Checking for Understanding

Ask questions to ascertain that students understand the task at hand and the differences among the plans. Lead them to see, for example, that while Plan A has the largest first-place scholarship, Plan C has a larger total amount of money and benefits more students.

3 PRACTICE/APPLY

Teaching Tip Have a member of each group share its decisions with the class. Have students discuss some of the issues that arose during the decision-making process, and how they eventually chose a plan.

Making a Decision

Have each group get together again after hearing the choices and issues raised by other groups. Ask the groups to examine their original decisions and choice of plan, and to reaffirm or revise their thinking in light of the new information.

Making Decisions in the Real World

Tell students to visit more than one bowling alley, and to find out more about their tournaments. Have them report on what these tournaments have in common and how they differ. If the bowling alleys do not have tournaments or do not raise money for causes, have students investigate where in their community tournaments are held that do so, and find out more about these places or organizations.

Answers

1. $650
2. $200
3. Plans A and B: $0;
   Plans B and C: $1,000;
   Plans A and C: $1,000
4. three times more
5–10. See students' work.

Lesson Resources
- Study Guide Master 10-5
- Practice Master 10-5
- Enrichment Master 10-5
- Group Activity Card 10-5

 Transparency 10-5 contains the 5-Minute Check and a teaching aid for this lesson.

🕐 5-Minute Check
(Over Lesson 10-4)

Find the surface area of each cylinder. Use 3.14 for π.

1.

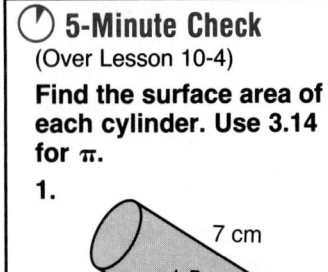

about 80.07 square centimeters

2.

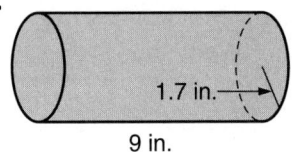

about 114.23 square inches

3. Find the surface area of the cylinder. Use $\frac{22}{7}$ for π.

   height, $8\frac{3}{4}$ m

   radius, $1\frac{3}{4}$ m

   about $115\frac{1}{2}$ square meters

---

1 FOCUS

Motivating the Lesson

Situational Problem Ask students how they would go about figuring out the amount of space within the classroom.

10-5 Volume of Prisms

Objective
Find the volume of rectangular prisms.

Words to Learn
volume

When water turns into ice, it expands. When it expands inside a closed container, it can cause so much pressure to build up that the container cracks or explodes. This is what causes water pipes and car radiators to crack in the winter. In this lesson, you will learn how to find the amount of space inside a prism.

Volume is the measure of the space occupied by a solid figure. It is measured in cubic units. You can use cubes to make models of solid figures.

The container at the right has a length of 6 inches, a width of 2 inches, and a height of 4 inches. The model is made of 4 layers. Each layer has 12 cubes. The area of the base is 12 square inches, the product of the length and width.

Since the container is 4 layers high and has a base of 12 one-inch cubes, it will take 4 · 12 or 48 one-inch cubes to fill the container. The volume of the container is 48 cubic inches.

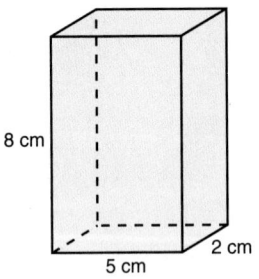

Volume of a Rectangular Prism	**In words:** The volume (v) of a rectangular prism is found by multiplying the length (ℓ), the width (w), and the height (h).
	In symbols: $V = \ell w h$

Example 1

Draw and label a rectangular prism whose length is 5 centimeters, width is 2 centimeters, and height is 8 centimeters. Find its volume.

$V = \ell w h$
$\quad = 5 \cdot 2 \cdot 8$ *Replace ℓ with 5, w*
$\quad = 80$ *with 2, and h with 8.*

The prism has a volume of 80 cm³.
The volume of a 3-dimensional figure uses the exponent 3 with the unit of measure.

OPTIONS

Gifted and Talented Needs

Have students work cooperatively in a group to find the approximate volume of classroom space occupied by air. Students should consider the volume of all classroom objects that take up space, such as tables, fishtanks, and books (but not one another).

Example 2

Find the volume of the rectangular prism at the right.

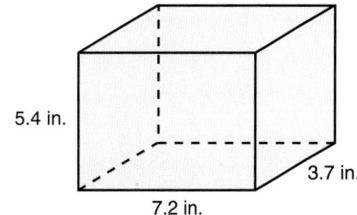
5.4 in.
3.7 in.
7.2 in.

$V = \ell w h$

$\quad = 7.2 \cdot 3.7 \cdot 5.4$

$7.2 \boxed{\times} 3.7 \boxed{\times} 5.4 \boxed{=} \text{143.856}$

The prism has a volume of 146.52 cubic inches.

Mini-Lab

Work with a partner.
Materials: 20 × 20 grid paper, scissors, tape

- Cut off square corner sections from each corner of the 20 × 20 grid paper to make an open box that is 14 × 14 × 3.

- Fold the paper to make the box. Then tape the corners together.

- Find the volume of the box.

- Continue making boxes by cutting off square corners from 20 × 20 grids until you have found a box that has the greatest volume. How do you know when you have found the box with the greatest volume?

- Once you have found a box with the greatest volume, convince another group that yours has the greatest volume.

Checking for Understanding

Communicating Mathematics

Read and study the lesson to answer each question.

1. **Tell** the difference between volume and surface area. **See margin.**

2. **Write** an example to show that you can find the volume of a rectangular prism by multiplying the height, width, and length. **See margin.**

Lesson 10-5 Volume of Prisms   **395**

Reteaching Activity

Using Models Have students investigate the concept of volume by using centimeter cubes to fill boxes of different sizes. Guide them to recognize shortcuts to counting all cubes in order to find volume. For example, have them count one layer of cubes and multiply the result by the number of layers to fill the box. This leads to the use of *V = lwh*.

Study Guide Masters, p. 88

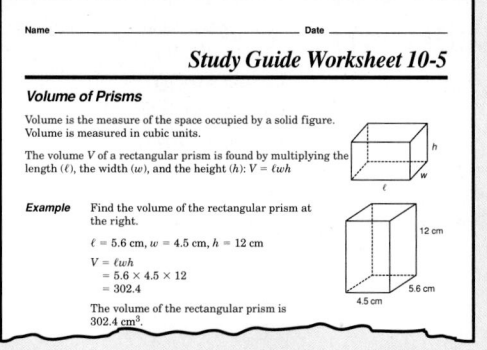

Name _____ Date _____

Study Guide Worksheet 10-5

Volume of Prisms

Volume is the measure of the space occupied by a solid figure. Volume is measured in cubic units.

The volume V of a rectangular prism is found by multiplying the length (ℓ), the width (w), and the height (h): $V = \ell w h$

Example   Find the volume of the rectangular prism at the right.

$\ell = 5.6$ cm, $w = 4.5$ cm, $h = 12$ cm

$V = \ell w h$
$\quad = 5.6 \times 4.5 \times 12$
$\quad = 302.4$

The volume of the rectangular prism is 302.4 cm³.

12 cm
4.5 cm
5.6 cm

---

2 TEACH

Using the Mini-Lab Suggest to students that they make a chart to record the different shapes they make and the volume of each. Have students think about ways to prove that their box has the greatest volume without using the formula *V = lwh*.

More Examples

For Example 1

Draw and label a rectangular prism whose length is 6 centimeters, width is 4 centimeters, and height is 10 centimeters. Find its volume.   Check students' drawings; 240 cubic centimeters

For Example 2

Find the volume of the rectangular prism.

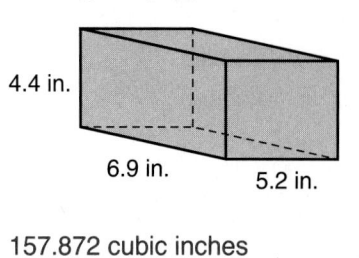

4.4 in.
6.9 in.
5.2 in.

157.872 cubic inches

Checking for Understanding

Exercises 1-2 are designed to help you assess students' understanding through reading, writing, speaking, and modeling. You should work through these exercises with your students and then monitor their work on Guided Practice Exercises 3-8.

Additional Answers

1. Volume is the measure of the space occupied by a solid. Surface area is the sum of the areas of all of its surfaces.

2. A rectangular prism is 9 cm long, 10 cm wide, and 8 cm high. Its volume is 9 × (10 × 8), or 9 × 80, or 720 cm³.

395

Close

Have students explain how they would find the volume of an aquarium in the shape of a rectangular prism.

3 PRACTICE/APPLY

Assignment Guide
Maximum: 9–27
Minimum: 9–19 odd, 20–25, 27

For **Extra Practice,** see p. 594.

Alternate Assessment

Writing Have students write a problem for classmates that can be solved by finding the volume of a rectangular prism. Students should be sure to include all essential data.

Practice Masters, p. 88

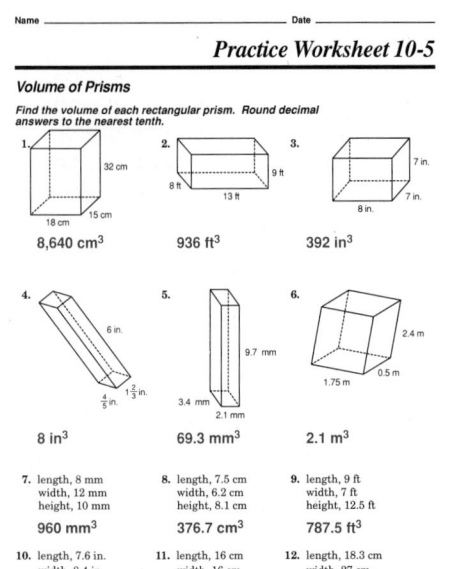

Guided Practice   Find the volume of each rectangular prism.

3.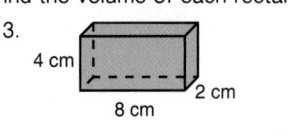

4 cm, 8 cm, 2 cm

64 cm³

4.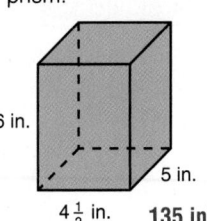

6 in., 5 in., $4\frac{1}{2}$ in.

135 in³

5.

10 mm, 3 mm, 4 mm

120 mm³

6. length, 2.2 cm
width, 4.4 cm
height, 5.5 cm
53.24 cm³

7. length, 5 in.
width, 3 in.
height, 10 in.
150 in³

8. length, 4 cm
width, 6 cm
height, 1 cm
24 cm³

Exercises

Independent Practice   Find the volume of each rectangular prism.

9.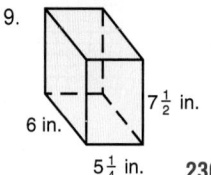

$7\frac{1}{2}$ in., 6 in., $5\frac{1}{4}$ in.   **$236\frac{1}{4}$ in³**

10.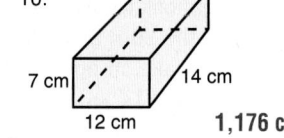

7 cm, 14 cm, 12 cm   **1,176 cm³**

11.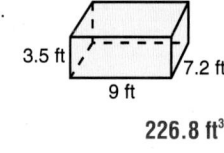

3.5 ft, 7.2 ft, 9 ft   **226.8 ft³**

12.

3 cm, 1.5 cm, 4.4 cm

19.8 cm³

13.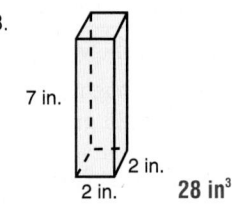

7 in., 2 in., 2 in.

28 in³

14.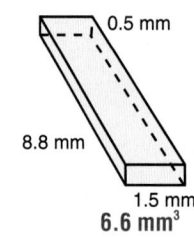

0.5 mm, 8.8 mm, 1.5 mm

6.6 mm³

15. length, 5 mm
width, 7 mm
height, 10 mm   **350 mm³**

16. length, 12 in.
width, 9 in.
height, 7 in.   **756 in³**

17. length, 12.1 cm
width, 8.2 cm
height, 10.6 cm
1,051.732 cm³

18. Find a volume of a rectangular prism whose length is 14 centimeters, width is 7 centimeters, and height is 12 centimeters.   **1,176 cm³**

19. A cube has sides that are 7 inches long.
a. What is the volume of the cube?   **343 in³**
b. Write a formula for finding the volume of a cube. $V = s^3$

396   Chapter 10   Surface Area and Volume

OPTIONS

Bell Ringer

Have students investigate to determine what general shape of prism seems to have the least surface area for a given volume.
a cube

Mixed Review

20. Use divisibility rules to determine whether 4,500 is divisible by 2, 3, 4, 5, 6, 9, or 10. *(Lesson 4-1)* **2, 3, 4, 5, 6, 9, 10**

21. Find the best whole number estimate for $\sqrt{167}$. *(Lesson 9-3)* **about 13**

22. **Construction** The Blue Mountain Oil Company stores the heating oil it produces in tanks that are in the shape of cylinders with heights of 10 meters, and radii of 2.5 meters. How much steel is needed to construct each tank? *(Lesson 10-4)* **196.25 m²**

Problem Solving and Applications

23. **Algebra** Write a formula for the volume of a cube that has sides x units long. $V = x^3$

24. **Exercise** A swimming pool is 75 feet long, 45 feet wide, and 8 feet deep. It is filled to a depth of 5 feet.

a. How much water is in the pool? **16,875 ft³**

b. Water weighs about 62 pounds per cubic foot. What is the weight of the water in the swimming pool? **1,046,250 pounds**

c. In the winter, the water in the pool freezes and the volume expands to 20,250 cubic feet without the pool breaking. How much does the volume increase? **3,375 ft³**

25. **Critical Thinking** Refer to Exercise 24c.

a. What would be the dimensions of the frozen water? **75 ft × 45 ft × 6 ft**

b. Which dimension changed? Explain. **Depth; see margin.**

26. **Data Search** Refer to pages 374 and 375. Find the height of the tallest volcano in the chart and the height of the shortest volcano in the chart. What is the difference in their heights? **16,680 feet**

DATA SEARCH

27. **Mathematics and History** Read the following paragraph.

> Ever since he was a boy, Frederick McKinley Jones (1892–1961) enjoyed taking machines apart and putting them together again. In 1935, he began working on an invention that made him famous. After listening to farmers complain about losing truckloads of crops because they spoiled during shipping, Mr. Jones began putting odds and ends of machinery together. When he finished building his machine, he attached it to a truck and created the first mechanically-refrigerated truck. Food was shipped longer distances across the country without spoiling. Soon his mechanical refrigerating system was placed in ships and railway cars.

Find the volume of a refrigerated compartment 12 meters by 5 meters by 8 meters. **480 cubic meters**

Lesson 10-5 Volume of Prisms **397**

Extending the Lesson

Mathematics and History
Students may wish to draw a diagram of the figure before finding the volume. Discuss with the class the importance of such an invention both to the economy in general and the farming industry in particular.

Cooperative Learning Activity

Pump Up the Volume 10-5

Number of players: 3
Materials: Index cards

▪ Copy onto cards the lengths, widths, and heights shown on the back of this card, one per card. Shuffle the cards and divide them evenly.

➡ Each group member places face up cards showing the length, width, and height of a rectangular prism. The group member whose cards show the prism with the greatest volume wins the round and collects all of the cards that were placed face up. Place the nine cards you win in a round aside. At the beginning of any round, you may ask another group member to trade between one and three cards with you if you cannot form a rectangular prism with the cards in your hand.

Continue in this way until all of the cards have been played. The overall winner is the group member who has won the most cards.

Glencoe Mathematics: Applications and Connections, Course 2

Additional Answer

25b. When freezing water expands, it fills whatever space is available.

Enrichment Masters, p. 88

Name _____ Date _____

Enrichment Worksheet 10-5

Volumes of Pyramids

A pyramid and a prism with the same base and height are shown below.

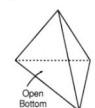 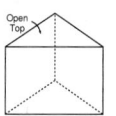

The exercises on this page will help you discover how their volumes are related.

Make copies of the two patterns below to make the open pyramid and the open prism shown above. (Each equilateral triangle measures 8 centimeters on a side.)

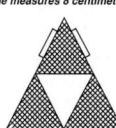 

1. Describe the bases of the two solids.
   equilateral triangles

2. How do the heights of the solids compare?
   They are the same.

3. Fill the open pyramid with sand or sugar. Pour the contents into the open prism. How many times must you do this to fill the open prism?
   three times

4. Describe how you would find the volume of the pyramid shown at the right.
   Divide the volume of a prism with the same base and height by 3.

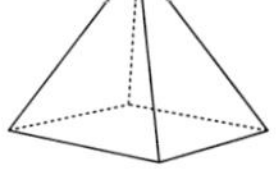

5. Generalize: State a formula for the volume of a pyramid.
   The volume is $\frac{1}{3}$ × area of the base × height

T88
Glencoe Division, Macmillan/McGraw-Hill

397

NCTM Standards: 1–5, 7, 12, 13

Lesson Resources
• Study Guide Master 10-6
• Practice Master 10-6
• Enrichment Master 10-6
• Application Master, p. 10
• Group Activity Card 10-6

 Transparency 10-6 contains the 5-Minute Check and a teaching aid for this lesson.

⏱ 5-Minute Check
(Over Lesson 10-5)

Find the volume of each rectangular prism.

1.

5 mm
6 mm
11 mm
330 cubic millimeters

2.

3.8 in.
6.5 in.
4.7 in.
116.09 cubic inches

3. length, $4\frac{1}{3}$ ft
width, $3\frac{3}{4}$ ft
height, 5 ft
$81\frac{1}{4}$ cubic feet

1 FOCUS

Motivating the Lesson

Situational Problem Have students imagine that they have some grain in a sack and want to place some of it into a jar. Ask them how they can know how much of the grain will fill the jar.

2 TEACH

Using Connections Ask students why they can use what they know about rectangular prisms to find the volume of a cylinder. Sample answer: The two figures both have two parallel congruent bases.

10-6 Volume of Cylinders

Objective
Find the volume of cylinders.

Ms. Eng makes candles and sells them at arts and crafts festivals. She is planning to make one that is 8 inches high and 4 inches in diameter. The candle wax comes in 72 cubic-inch blocks. Will one block of wax be enough to make the candle?

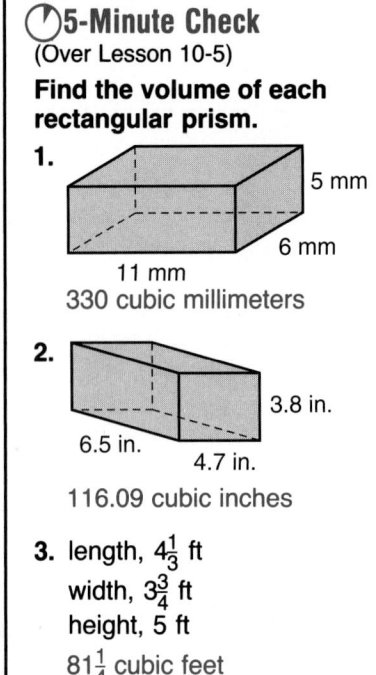

base
4 in.
h   8 in.
base
3 in.   6 in.
4 in.

In Lesson 10-5, you found the volume of a rectangular prism by using the formula $V = \ell wh$. Remember that ℓw square units is equal to the area of the base.

To find the volume of a cylinder, such as the candle, multiply the area of the base by the height. The area of the base of a cylinder is the area of a circle, πr^2. So, the volume of a cylinder is $(\pi r^2)h$ or $\pi r^2 h$.

$$V = \pi r^2 h$$
$$= \pi \cdot 2^2 \cdot 8 \quad \textit{Since the diameter is 4 inches,}$$
$$= \pi \cdot 4 \cdot 8 \quad \textit{the radius is 2 inches.}$$

$\boxed{\pi}\,\boxed{\times}\,4\,\boxed{\times}\,8\,\boxed{=}\,\text{100.53096}$ *Round to the nearest whole number.*

$$V \approx 101$$

The candle has a volume of *about* 101 cubic inches. Since the block of wax is only 72 cubic inches, one block will not be enough.

Estimation Hint
• • • • • • • • • • • • •
You can estimate the volume of a cylinder by squaring the radius and multiplying by 3 ($\approx \pi$) and the height. In Example 1, the volume of the cylinder is about $3 \times 3 \times 3 \times 5$ or 135 cubic inches.

| **Volume of a Cylinder** | **In words:** The volume of a cylinder is found by multiplying the area of the base (πr^2) times the height (h). |
| | **In symbols:** $V = \pi r^2 h$ |

Example 1

Find the volume of a cylinder with a radius of 3 inches and a height of 5 inches.

$$V = \pi r^2 h$$
$$\approx 3.14 \cdot 3^2 \cdot 5 \quad \textit{Replace r with 3 and h with 5. Use 3.14 for } \pi.$$
$$\approx 3.14 \cdot 9 \cdot 5$$
$$\approx 141.3 \quad \text{The cylinder has a volume of } about \text{ 141.3 cubic inches.}$$

OPTIONS

Reteaching Activity

Using Models Remind students of how they used centimeter cubes to model the volume of a prism. Have them use checkers to model the volume of a cylinder, using one checker to represent the area of the base, just as they used a layer of cubes to model the area of the base of the prism.

Study Guide Masters, p. 89

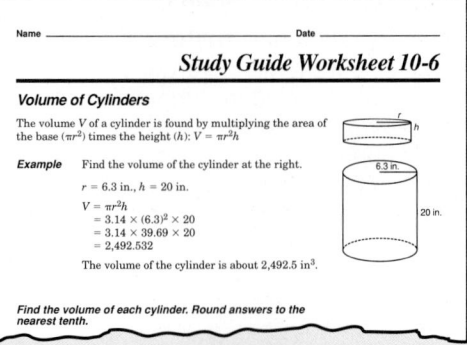

Name _____ Date _____

Study Guide Worksheet 10-6

Volume of Cylinders

The volume V of a cylinder is found by multiplying the area of the base (πr^2) times the height (h): $V = \pi r^2 h$

Example   Find the volume of the cylinder at the right.

$r = 6.3$ in., $h = 20$ in.

$$V = \pi r^2 h$$
$$= 3.14 \times (6.3)^2 \times 20$$
$$= 3.14 \times 39.69 \times 20$$
$$= 2,492.532$$

The volume of the cylinder is about 2,492.5 in³.

6.3 in.
20 in.

Find the volume of each cylinder. Round answers to the nearest tenth.

Example 2 *Problem Solving*

Manufacturing Suppose you are designing a glass that has a radius of 3.5 centimeters and a height of 15 centimeters. If one cubic centimeter can contain one milliliter of liquid, how many milliliters of liquid will it hold?

Find the volume of the glass.

$$V = \pi r^2 h$$
$$= \pi \cdot 3.5^2 \cdot 15 \qquad \textit{Replace r with 3.5 and h with 15.}$$

$\boxed{\pi}$ $\boxed{\times}$ 3.5 $\boxed{x^2}$ $\boxed{\times}$ 15 $\boxed{=}$ $\boxed{577.26765}$

The glass has a volume of *about* 577.3 cubic centimeters. So it will hold about 577.3 milliliters of liquid.

Checking for Understanding

Communicating Mathematics

Read and study the lesson to answer each question.

1. **Tell** how the formula for the volume of a cylinder is similar to the formula for the volume of a prism. **See margin.**

2. **Write** a sentence explaining why you express the volume of a cylinder in cubic units. **See margin.**

3. **Tell** why the volume of a cylinder is an approximation. **See margin.**

4. **Tell** how many blocks of wax are needed to make 4 of the candles described on the previous page. **6 blocks of wax**

Guided Practice

Find the volume of each cylinder. Round answers to the nearest tenth.

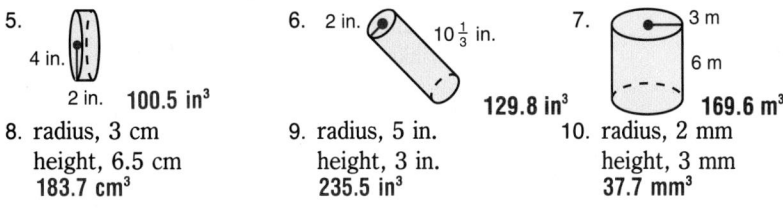

5. 4 in. / 2 in. **100.5 in³**

6. 2 in. / 10⅓ in. **129.8 in³**

7. 3 m / 6 m **169.6 m³**

8. radius, 3 cm
   height, 6.5 cm
   183.7 cm³

9. radius, 5 in.
   height, 3 in.
   235.5 in³

10. radius, 2 mm
    height, 3 mm
    37.7 mm³

Exercises

Independent Practice

Find the volume of each cylinder. Round answers to the nearest tenth. **401.9 cm³**

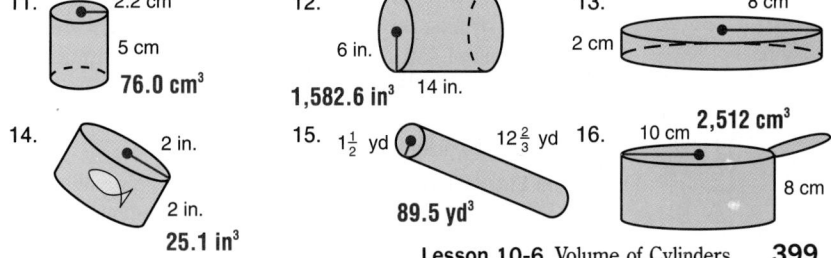

11. 2.2 cm / 5 cm **76.0 cm³**

12. 6 in. / 14 in. **1,582.6 in³**

13. 8 cm / 2 cm

14. 2 in. / 2 in. **25.1 in³**

15. 1½ yd / 12⅔ yd **89.5 yd³**

16. 10 cm / 8 cm **2,512 cm³**

Lesson 10-6 Volume of Cylinders **399**

Additional Answers

1. In each case, you multiply the area of the base by the height.
2. Sample answer: Square units (area of the base) times units (measure of the height) is (units × units) × units, or cubic units.
3. because the value of π is approximated

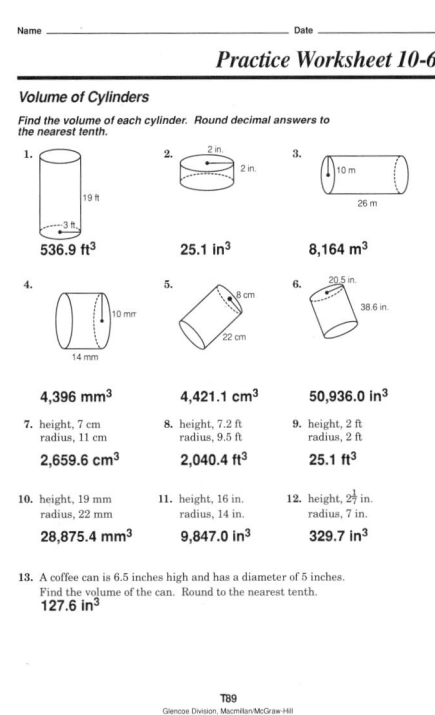

Name _____ Date _____

Practice Worksheet 10-6

Volume of Cylinders

Find the volume of each cylinder. Round decimal answers to the nearest tenth.

1. 19 ft / 3 ft **536.9 ft³**
2. 2 in. / 2 in. **25.1 in³**
3. 10 m / 26 m **8,164 m³**
4. 10 mm / 14 mm **4,396 mm³**
5. 8 cm / 22 cm **4,421.1 cm³**
6. 20.5 in. / 38.6 in. **50,936.0 in³**

7. height, 7 cm
   radius, 11 cm
   2,659.6 cm³
8. height, 7.2 ft
   radius, 9.5 ft
   2,040.4 ft³
9. height, 2 ft
   radius, 2 ft
   25.1 ft³
10. height, 19 mm
    radius, 22 mm
    28,875.4 mm³
11. height, 16 in.
    radius, 14 in.
    9,847.0 in³
12. height, 2⅔ in.
    radius, 7 in.
    329.7 in³

13. A coffee can is 6.5 inches high and has a diameter of 5 inches. Find the volume of the can. Round to the nearest tenth.
    127.6 in³

Error Analysis

Watch for students who multiply the height of a cylinder by the circumference rather than by the area of the base.

Prevent by guiding students to see that volume is not about finding distance around a figure, but rather the measure of space the figure occupies.

Close

Have students explain what else they need to know to find the volume of a cylindrical gas tank with a height of 8 feet.   the radius

3 PRACTICE/APPLY

Assignment Guide
Maximum: 11–30
Minimum: 11–19 odd, 21–29

For **Extra Practice,** see p. 594.

Alternate Assessment

Speaking Tell students that a cylindrical container has radius of 4 inches and a volume of about 400 cubic inches. Ask them to estimate its height.   about 8 inches

Enrichment Masters, p. 89

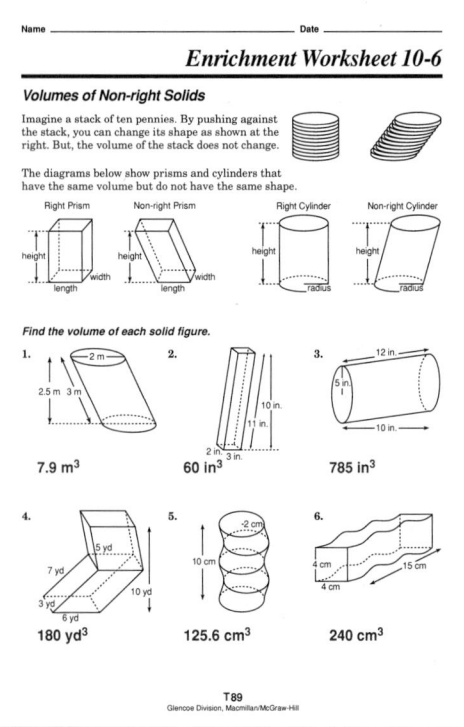

Find the volume of each cylinder. Round answers to the nearest tenth.

17. radius, 3 in.
    height, 10 in.
    282.6 in³

18. radius, 6 mm
    height, 6.8 mm
    768.7 mm³

19. radius, $2\frac{1}{2}$ ft
    height, $8\frac{1}{4}$ ft **161.9 ft³**

20. A can of potato chips is 8 inches high and has a radius of 1.5 inches. Find the volume of the can. **56.52 in³**

Mixed Review

21. Typing paper measures $8\frac{1}{2}$ inches wide and 11 inches long. Find the perimeter of typing paper. *(Lesson 5-6)* **39 inches**

22. Solve $z = 360 \div (-6)$. *(Lesson 7-8)* **−60**
    152.88 cm³

23. Find the volume of a rectangular prism having a length of 6 centimeters, a width of 4.9 centimeters, and a height of 5.2 centimeters. *(Lesson 10-5)*

Problem Solving and Applications

24. **Measurement** If a 12-ounce soft drink can is *about* $4\frac{3}{4}$ inches tall and has a diameter of *about* $2\frac{1}{2}$ inches, to the nearest whole number, how many cubic inches of a soft drink fill a can? **about 23 in³**

25. **Portfolio Suggestion** Review the items in your portfolio. Make a table of contents of the items, noting why each item was chosen. Replace any items that are no longer appropriate. **See students' work.**

Use the graph to answer Exercises 26–28.

26. In which country does each person consume the most soft drinks? the least? **USA; France**

27. How many more 8-ounce soft drinks does a person in Belgium consume than a person in France? **132 soft drinks**

28. If the numbers on the graph represent 8-ounce soft drinks, how many gallons of soft drinks does each American drink in a year? *(1 gallon = 128 fluid ounces)* **18.125 gallons**

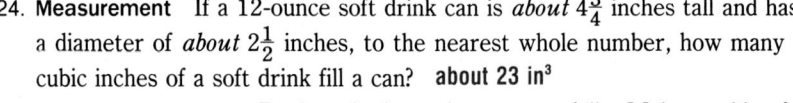

Soft Drink Consumption
Average number of 8-ounce soft drinks consumed by each person in one year.
France 48
Belgium 180
Germany 150
USA 290

29. **Critical Thinking** If you double the height of a cylinder, how does that affect its volume? Explain. **It doubles the volume.**

30. **Journal Entry** Draw and label a cylinder to help you write an explanation of how to find the volume of a cylinder. **See students' work.**

OPTIONS

Extending the Lesson

Using Connections Have students write a problem for classmates to solve that involves finding the volume of a rectangular prism with a large hole drilled all the way through it in the shape of a cylinder. Have them provide a solution to the problem.

Cooperative Learning Activity

Package Deal 10-6

Use groups of 2.
Materials: Tennis ball

➡ Suppose you and your partner work for a company that makes tennis balls. Your company has decided to start selling tennis balls in packages of four, rather than the usual three.

Now suppose that each partner has been asked to design two packages. One partner's packages are to be cylinders, while the other partner's packages are to be rectangular prisms.

After you have determined the dimensions of your two packages, write a brief statement telling the advantages and disadvantages of each one.

Glencoe Mathematics: Applications and Connections, Course 2

400

10-6B Volume of Cylinders

A Follow-Up of Lesson 10-6

Objective
Estimate and compare volumes of cylinders of various sizes.

Materials
cylinder-shaped
 objects
rulers
paper
pencil
calculator

Cylinder-shaped objects come in many sizes and shapes. Companies often do research to determine which shape is best for their product.

Try this!

Work in small groups.

- Place all of the cylinders so that everyone can see them. Number each item so that it can be identified easily.
- Rank the cylinders according to their volume from smallest to largest using estimation.
- Display your rankings and compare with other groups in the class.
- Measure the height and the radius of the base of each cylinder to the nearest tenth of a centimeter.
- Calculate the volume of each cylinder.
- Rank the cylinders according to their volume from smallest to largest based on your calculations.
- Display your rankings. Compare your estimated rankings with your calculated rankings.

What do you think?   For Exercises 1–3, answers will vary.

1. How close were your estimates to your actual calculations?
2. Was it more difficult to estimate when the cylinders had different relative shapes (such as short and fat compared to tall and thin)?
3. Which shape of the cylinders was the most misleading as far as what you expected the volume to be?

Extension

4. Without measuring, determine which is greater, the circumference of a tennis ball or the height of the tennis ball can. Explain how you arrived at your answer. See margin.

Mathematics Lab 10-6B Volume of Cylinders   **401**

NCTM Standards: 1–5, 7, 12, 13

Management Tips

For Students Provide each group with at least 5 cylinders. Have students estimate the volume of each cylinder. Have a group member record the volume in a chart with room also for the actual measurements.

For the Overhead Projector
Overhead Manipulative Resources provides appropriate materials for teacher or student demonstration of the activities in this Mathematics Lab.

1 FOCUS

Introducing the Lab

Have students discuss situations in which they have had to make a visual estimate of a volume, such as deciding which container would be best for holding dinner leftovers.

2 TEACH

Using Critical Thinking You may wish to have students both estimate and measure the volume of all but two of the cylinders. They can use their experiences with the first group of cylinders to obtain better estimates of the volumes of the remaining cylinders.

3 PRACTICE/APPLY

Using Applications Have students imagine that they are soft drink manufacturers who are considering container shapes for a new line of soft drink. Have them use what they have learned about the relationship between shape, surface area, and volume of cylinders to make their choice.

Close

Have each student use rolled paper, scissors, and tape to make a cylinder. Have them first estimate and then measure to determine the volume.

OPTIONS

Lab Manual You may wish to make copies of the blackline master on p. 68 of the *Lab Manual* for students to use as a recording sheet.

Additional Answer

4. diameter of ball and can: d; circumference: πd; can's height: $3d$; $3.14 > 3$, so $\pi d > 3d$; Circumference of ball is greater.

Lab Manual, p. 68

Name _____ Date _____

Mathematics Lab Worksheet

Use with page 401 _____

Volume of Cylinders

Try this! **Answers will vary.**

Estimates of volumes of cylinders from smallest to largest:

_____

Cylinder	1	2	3	4	5	6	7	8	9	10
Height										
Radius of base										
Volume										

NCTM Standards: 1–5, 7, 9, 12

Lesson Resources
- Study Guide Master 10-7
- Practice Master 10-7
- Enrichment Master 10-7
- Evaluation Master, Quiz B, p. 88
- Multicultural Activity, p. 10
- Group Activity Card 10-7

 Transparency 10-7 contains the 5-Minute Check and a teaching aid for this lesson.

⏱ **5-Minute Check**
(Over Lesson 10-6)

Find the volume of each cylinder.

1.

2 in.
6.5 in.

about 81.64 cubic inches

2. radius, 5 m
   height, 9.6 m
   about 753.6 cubic meters

Practice Masters, p. 90

Name _____ Date _____

Practice Worksheet 10-7

Problem-Solving Strategy: Use a Formula

Solve by using a formula.

1. One day in January, 6 inches of snow fell. If Mr. Garcia's driveway is 48 feet by 24 feet, what volume of snow was on the driveway?
   576 ft³

2. Janice bought 100 feet of fence to make a rectangular dog run. She made the pen the same width as a shed which was 10 feet wide. What were the dimensions of the dog run?
   10 ft by 40 ft

Solve. Use any strategy.

3. In 1990, the U.S. population was about 63 times what it was in 1790. If the population in 1790 was 3,929,214, what was the approximate population in 1990, 24,800,000 or 248,000,000?
   248,000,000

4. A number is tripled and then 14 is added. The result is five times the original number. What is the number? **7**

5. Lisa wants to make a box out of a 1-square-foot sheet of cardboard. Does she have enough to make a cubical box which is 6 inches on a side?
   no

6. Martin spent 22 minutes on the telephone talking long-distance to his cousin. If the rate was $0.20 for each of the first 3 minutes and $0.15 for each minute after that, how much did the call cost? **$3.45**

7. There are eight green marbles, three red marbles, and four white marbles in a carton. What is the probability of choosing a red marble without looking?
   1/5

8. Fair Fashions is selling sweaters for $22.95. Juanita thinks she can buy three sweaters for under $60.00. Can she?
   No. Since 3 × 20 = 60 and each sweater is over $20, 3 sweaters will cost more than $60.

T90
Glencoe Division, Macmillan/McGraw-Hill

402

10-7 Use a Formula

Objective
Solve problems by using a formula.

The Eppersteins decided to landscape a rectangular part of their front lawn with rocks. First they covered the 40-foot by 12-foot section with heavy plastic to prevent weeds from growing through the cracks. Then they spread rocks on top of the plastic. If they ordered 120 cubic feet of rocks, how deep will the rocks be?

Explore   What do you know?
You know the space to be covered with rocks is in the shape of a rectangle. It is 40 feet long and 12 feet wide. The volume is 120 ft³.

What do you need to find?
You need to find the depth of the rectangular space.

Plan   Use a formula for the volume of a rectangular prism, $V = \ell wh$. Substitute the given measure into the formula. Then divide to find the value of h.

Solve   To find the depth, use the formula $V = \ell wh$.
$$V = \ell wh$$
$$120 = 40 \times 12 \times h$$
$$120 = 480h$$
$$\frac{120}{480} = \frac{480h}{480}$$
$$\frac{1}{4} = h$$

Examine   The rocks will be $\frac{1}{4}$ foot or 3 inches deep. Check your answer by replacing the variables in the formula, $V = \ell wh$.
$$V = \ell wh$$
$$120 = 40 \times 12 \times \frac{1}{4}$$
$$120 = 120 \checkmark$$

Checking for Understanding

Communicating Mathematics

Read and study the lesson to answer each question.   **See students' work.**

1. **Draw** a labeled diagram of the rectangular prism in the example.
2. Suppose the Eppersteins wanted the rocks to be 4 inches in depth. How many cubic feet of rocks would they need to order? **160 ft³**

402   Chapter 10 Surface Area and Volume

OPTIONS

Reteaching Activity

Using Problem Solving   Some students may find it useful to rewrite the formula so that the width, the unknown, is on one side of the equals sign: $w = \frac{V}{lh}$. Other students may benefit by drawing a sketch first.

Study Guide Masters, p. 90

Name _____ Date _____

Study Guide Worksheet 10-7

Problem-Solving Strategy: Use a Formula

Gloria has a piece of glass that is 20 inches wide and 24 inches long. Does she have enough glass to build the terrarium shown at the right?

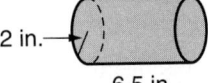
10 in.
10 in.
12 in.

Explore   What do you know?
Gloria has a 20 inches × 24 inches piece of glass. She wants to build a terrarium that is 12 inches long, 10 inches wide, and 10 inches high.

You want to find out if Gloria has enough glass.

Plan   Use the formula for the surface area of a prism, $A = 2(lh + lw + lh)$. Find the amount of glass needed to make the terrarium.

Solve $A = 2(lh + lw + lh)$

Solve by using a formula.

3. Chris is covering all sides of a cylinder-shaped can with contact paper. The radius of the can is 4 centimeters, and its height is 10 centimeters. How much contact paper does he need? **351.68 cm²**

4. Donna Mendez's new office is 20 feet long, 15 feet wide, and 12 feet high. If it costs 9 cents per year to air condition one cubic foot of space, how much does it cost to air condition her office for one month? **$27**

Problem Solving

Practice Solve. Use any strategy.

5. A number is doubled and then 10 is added. The result is −8. What is the number? **−9**

6. What are the next two numbers in this sequence: 5, 9, 7, 11, 9, . . . ? **13, 11**

7. A gardener is digging a rectangular space for a new flower bed that is 6 feet by 6 feet by $1\frac{1}{2}$ feet. How many cubic yards of topsoil does he need to fill this space? **2 yd³**

8. Kayla spent 3 hours calling 25 potential magazine subscribers. At this rate, how many hours will it take her to call 100 people? **12 hours**

9. Ralph has 5,000 cm² of wrapping paper. Does he have enough to wrap a present in a box that measures 30 cm long by 40 cm wide by 20 cm high? **No; The box has a surface area of 5,200 cm².**

COMPUTER CONNECTION

10. **Computer Connection** Suppose a gardener has 80 feet of fencing with which to enclose a vegetable garden. What is the greatest area she can enclose?

The BASIC computer program at the right will test all possible integer values for the length and width, and compute each area.

```
10 INPUT P
20 FOR W = 1 TO P/2
30 L = (P - 2 * W)/2
40 A = W * L
50 PRINT W, L, A
60 NEXT W
```

a. Run the program.
b. What is the greatest area? **400 ft²**
c. What is the shape of the garden? **square**
d. Run the program again for a perimeter of 120 feet.
e. What is the greatest area? **3,600 ft²**
f. What is the shape of the garden? **square**

Lesson 10-7 Problem-Solving Strategy: Use a Formula **403**

Extending the Lesson

Consumer Connection A can of Dog Yummies is 13 cm high and has a radius of 5.5 cm. A can of Pooch Pellets is the same height, with a diameter of 7 cm. Pooch Pellets sells for $1.50, Dog Yummies for $0.75. Ask students which is the better buy.
Dog Yummies

Cooperative Learning Activity

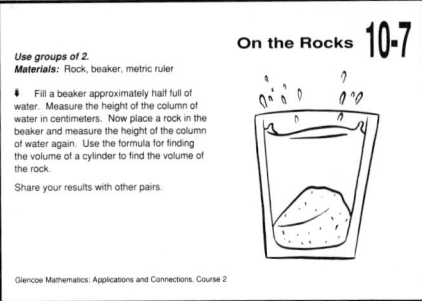

On the Rocks 10-7

Use groups of 2.
Materials: Rock, beaker, metric ruler

● Fill a beaker approximately half full of water. Measure the height of the column of water in centimeters. Now place a rock in the beaker and measure the height of the column of water again. Use the formula for finding the volume of a cylinder to find the volume of the rock.

Share your results with other pairs.

Glencoe Mathematics: Applications and Connections, Course 2

Name _____ Date _____

Enrichment Worksheet 10-7

Two Truncated Solids

To create a truncated solid, you could start with an ordinary solid and then cut off the corners. Another way to make such a shape is to use the patterns on this page.

The Truncated Octahedron

1. Two copies of the pattern at the right can be used to make a truncated octahedron, a solid with 6 square faces and 8 regular hexagonal faces.

   Each pattern makes half of the truncated octahedron. Attach adjacent faces using glue or tape to make a cup-shaped figure.

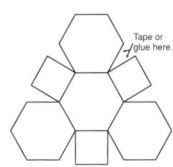

Tape or glue here.

The Truncated Tetrahedron

2. The pattern below will make a truncated tetrahedron, a solid with 8 polygonal faces: 4 hexagons and 4 equilateral triangles.

Now solve these problems.

3. Find the surface area of the truncated octahedron if each polygon in the pattern has sides of 3 inches. **241.1 in²**

4. Find the surface area of the truncated tetrahedron if each polygon in the pattern has sides of 3 inches. **109.1 in²**

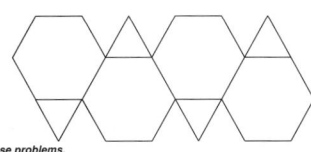

Area Formulas for Regular Polygons	
(s is the length of one side)	
triangle	$A = \frac{s^2}{4}\sqrt{3}$
hexagon	$A = \frac{3s^2}{2}\sqrt{3}$
octagon	$A = 2s^2(\sqrt{2} + 1)$

The Chapter Study Guide and Review begins with a section on Communicating Mathematics. This includes questions that review the new terms and concepts that were introduced in the chapter.

Then, the Skills and Concepts presented in the chapter are reviewed using a side-by-side format. Encourage students to refer to the Objectives and Examples on the left as they complete the Review Exercises on the right.

The Chapter Study Guide and Review ends with problems that review Applications and Problem Solving.

Chapter

10 Study Guide and Review

Communicating Mathematics

Choose the correct term or expression to complete each sentence.

1. Another name for a box is a(n) ___?___. **cube or rectangular prism**

2. The formula for the surface area of a rectangular prism is ___?___. **2 ($\ell h + \ell w + wh$)**

3. The surface area of a(n) ___?___ can be found by finding the area of both a circle and a rectangle. **cylinder**

4. ___?___ is the measure of the space occupied by a solid figure. **volume**

5. The formula for the volume of a cylinder is ___?___. **$\pi r^2 h$**

6. In your own words, explain the relationship between the area of a square and the surface area of a cube. **The surface area of a cube is 6 times the area of one side.**

area
cube
$\pi r^2 h$
rectangular prism
$\ell w h$
$2(\ell h + \ell w + wh)$
cylinder
volume
$2\pi r$
square
πr^2

Self Assessment

Objectives and Examples	Review Exercises
Upon completing this chapter, you should be able to:	*Use these exercises to review and prepare for the chapter test.*

- draw three-dimensional figures (*Lesson 10-1*)

  Draw a three-dimensional figure by using the top, front, and side views.

  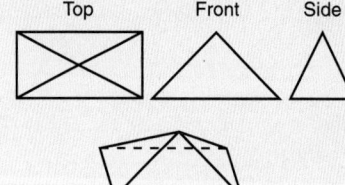

  Top   Front   Side

Draw each three-dimensional figure by using the top, front, and side views.

7.   Top   Front   Side
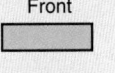

8.

9.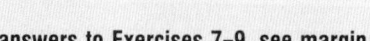

For answers to Exercises 7–9, see margin.

Additional Answers

7.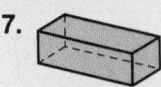

8.

9.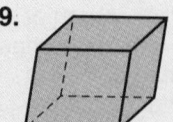

Objectives and Examples

Review Exercises

- find the surface area of rectangular prisms *(Lesson 10-3)*

  Find the surface area of a prism having a length of 3 centimeters, a width of 8 centimeters, and a height of 2 centimeters.

  $A = 2(\ell h + \ell w + wh)$
  $= 2(3 \times 2 + 3 \times 8 + 8 \times 2)$
  $= 2(46)$
  $= 92$

  The surface area is 92 cm².

Find the surface area of each prism. Round answers to the nearest tenth.

10. length, $4\frac{1}{3}$ in.
    width, $2\frac{1}{4}$ in. **98 $\frac{1}{2}$ in²**
    height, 6 in.

11. length, 2.6 yd
    width, 2.6 yd **23.9 yd²**
    height, 1 yd

12.

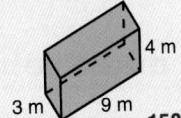

    4 m
    3 m   9 m
    150 m²

- find the surface area of cylinders *(Lesson 10-4)*

  Find the surface area of a cylinder with a height of 6 millimeters and a radius of 2 millimeters.

  $A = 2\pi r^2 + 2\pi rh$
  $\approx 2 \times 3.14 \times 4 + 2 \times 3.14 \times 2 \times 6$
  ≈ 100.48 square millimeters

  The surface area is about 100.5 mm².

Find the surface area of each cylinder. Use 3.14 for π. Round answers to the nearest tenth.

13. height, $5\frac{3}{8}$ in.
    radius, $3\frac{1}{2}$ in. **195.1 in²**

14. height, 6 ft
    radius, 0.5 ft **20.4 ft²**

15.

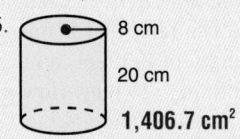

    8 cm
    20 cm
    1,406.7 cm²

- find the volume of rectangular prisms *(Lesson 10-5)*

  Find the volume of a rectangular prism having a length of 5 inches, a width of 3 inches, and a height of 2 inches.

  $V = \ell wh$
  $= 5 \times 3 \times 2$
  $= 30$

  The volume is 30 in³.

Find the volume of each rectangular prism.

16. length, 6.3 mm
    width, 2.5 mm **18.9 mm³**
    height, 1.2 mm

17. length, $4\frac{1}{2}$ ft
    width, $6\frac{1}{4}$ ft **168 $\frac{3}{4}$ ft³**
    height, 6 ft

18.

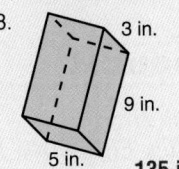

    3 in.
    9 in.
    5 in.
    135 in³

Chapter 10 Study Guide and Review   **405**

You may wish to use a Chapter Test from the Evaluation Masters booklet as an additional chapter review. The two free-response forms are shown below. One of the two multiple-choice forms is shown on the next page.

Evaluation Masters, pp. 86–87

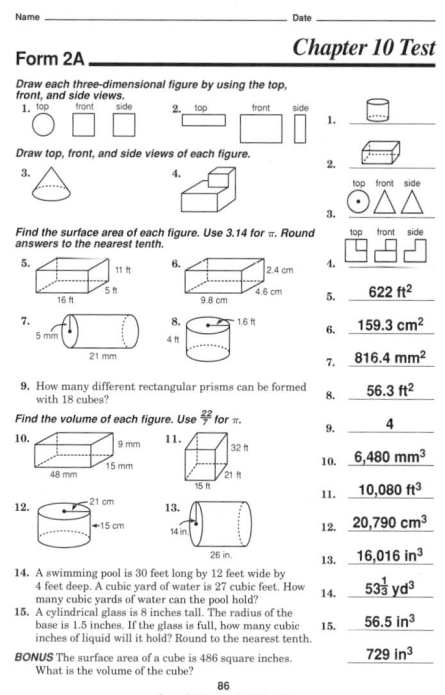

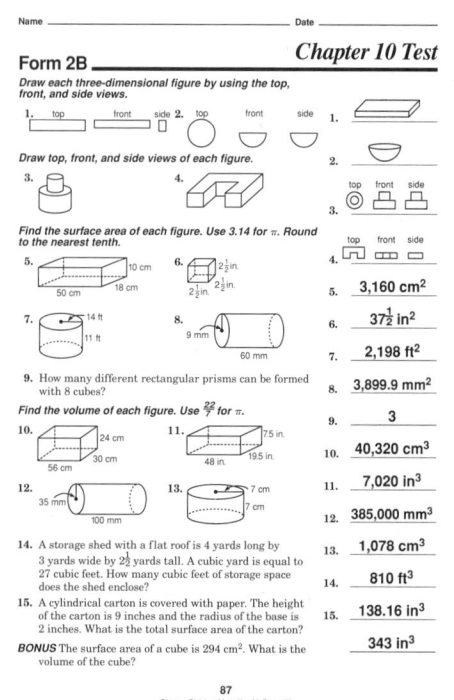

406

Study Guide and Review

Objectives and Examples

• find the volume of cylinders
(*Lesson 10-6*)

Find the volume of a cylinder with a radius of 4 centimeters and a height of 8 centimeters.

$V = \pi r^2 h$
$\approx 3.14 \times 4^2 \times 8$
≈ 401.92

The volume is about 402 cm³.

Review Exercises

Find the volume of each cylinder. Round answers to the nearest tenth.

19. radius, 1 ft
height, 3 ft **9.4 ft³**

20. radius, $3\frac{2}{3}$ yd
height, $6\frac{4}{5}$ yd **287.1 yd³**

21.

1.7 in.
5.2 in. **47.2 in³**

Applications and Problem Solving

22. **Design** A large cube is made up of 27 small cubes. The outside of the cube is painted blue. If the large cube is taken apart, how many small cubes would have none of their sides painted? (*Lesson 10-2*) **1 cube**

23. **Manufacturing** A cereal box has a length of 11 inches, a height of 14 inches, and a depth of 1.5 inches. (*Lesson 10-7*)
a. What is the volume of the box? **231 in³**
b. If each cubic inch holds about 0.08 ounce of cereal, about how many ounces of cereal can one box hold? **about 18 ounces**

24. **Pet Supplies** The Pets Are Us Company wants to make a fish tank that is open on the top and has a length of 2.5 feet, a height of 1 foot, and a width of 1.25 feet. How much glass is needed to make this tank? (*Lesson 10-3*) **10.625 ft²**

25. **Pottery** In her art class, Andrea made a vase in the shape of a cylinder. The diameter is 5 inches, and the height is 10 inches. Find the maximum volume of water the vase can hold. (*Lesson 10-6*) **196.25 in³**

Curriculum Connection Projects

• **Automotive** Find the approximate surface area and volume of your family's car or a friend's car.
• **Art** Construct a three-dimensional drawing of your home from at least two different views.

Read More About It

Rinaldi, Ann. *The Last Silk Dress.*
Johnson, Neil. *Fire and Silk: Flying in a Hot Air Balloon.*
McCauley, David. *Pyramid.*

406   Chapter 10 Study Guide and Review

Chapter

10 Test

Draw each three-dimensional figure by using the top, front, and side views. **See Solutions Manual.**

1. Top 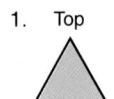   Front   Side

2. Top   Front   Side

Find the surface area of each rectangular prism. Round answers to the nearest tenth.

3. length, $2\frac{2}{3}$ ft

   width, $1\frac{3}{4}$ ft

   height, $4\frac{1}{2}$ ft **$49\frac{1}{12}$ ft²**

4. length, 3.6 cm
   width, 2.1 cm
   height, 8 cm **106.3 cm²**

5. 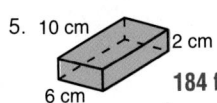 10 cm, 2 cm, 6 cm **184 ft²**

Find the surface area of each cylinder. Round answers to the nearest tenth.

6. height, 3.7 yd
   radius, 0.4 yd **10.3 yd²**

7. height, $\frac{1}{3}$ yd
   diameter, 14 yd **322.4 yd²**

8. **274.8 in²**
   15 in.
   $2\frac{1}{2}$ in.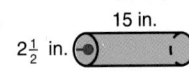

9. The Andersons' backyard pool is in need of a paint job. The pool is 30 feet long, 18 feet wide, and 6 feet deep. One gallon of pool paint will cover 12 square feet. How many gallons of paint are needed? *Remember, a pool does not have a top.* **93 gallons**

Find the volume of each rectangular prism.

10. length, 3 mm
    width, 2 mm
    height, 1 mm **6 mm³**

11. length, 10.4 ft
    width, 2.5 ft
    height, 3 ft **78 ft³**

Find the volume of each cylinder. Round answers to the nearest tenth.

12. radius, 6.3 cm
    height, 3.1 cm **386.3 cm³**

13. radius, 2 yd
    height, $1\frac{1}{2}$ yd **18.8 yd³**

14. A rectangular prism is formed using exactly 20 cubes. How many different prisms can be formed? **4 prisms**

15. The standard-size drinking straw has a radius of $\frac{1}{8}$ inch and a height of $7\frac{3}{4}$ inches. What is the maximum volume of liquid that can be contained in the straw at any given time? **0.38 in³**

Bonus If one view of a figure is △ and another view of the same figure is □, what is the third view of the same figure? □

Chapter 10 Test **407**

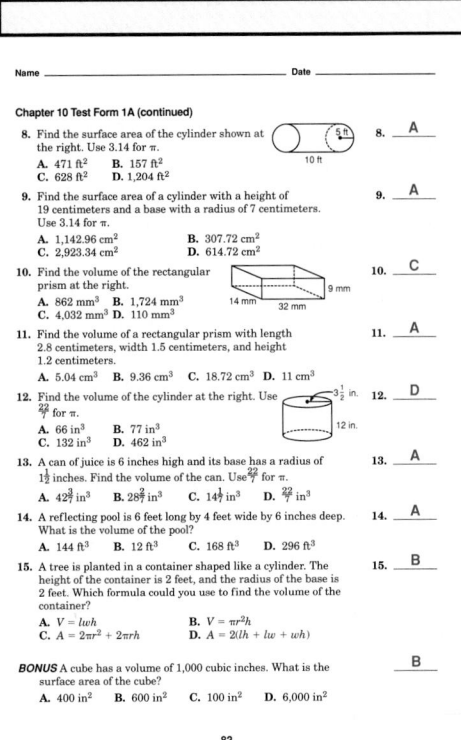

Using the Chapter Test

This page may be used as a chapter test or another chapter review.

Evaluation Masters, pp. 82–83

Test and Review Generator software is provided in Apple, IBM, and Macintosh versions. You may use this software to create your own tests or worksheets, based on the needs of your students.

The **Performance Assessment Booklet** provides an alternate assessment for evaluating student progress. An assessment for this chapter can be found on pages 19–20.

407

11 Ratio, Proportion, and Percent

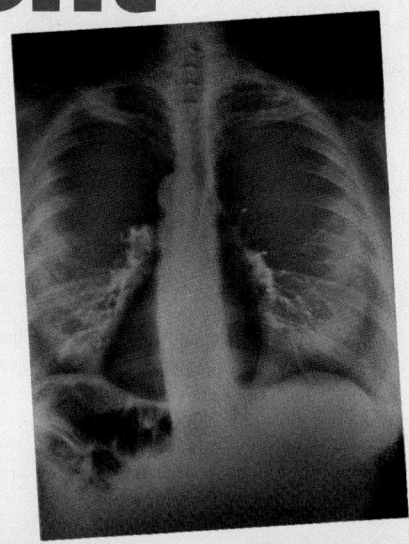

Previewing the Chapter

This chapter explores ratio, proportion, and percent. Students learn to relate fractions, decimals, and percent to one another. After a careful survey of ratios, rates, and proportions, students apply the concept of *proportion* to similar figures and scale drawings. Percents are introduced as a special kind of ratio and various percent problems are solved, including problems involving percents greater than 100% and percents less than 1%. In the **problem-solving strategy** lesson, students draw diagrams to solve problems.

Lesson	Lesson Objectives	NCTM Standards	State/Local Objectives
11-1A	Explore the meaning of ratio and proportion.	1–6	
11-1	Express ratios as fractions and determine whether two ratios are equivalent.	1–7, 9, 11, 12	
11-2	Determine unit rates.	1–7	
11-3	Solve proportions.	1–7, 9, 13	
11-3B	Use the capture-recapture technique to estimate.	1–7	
11-4	Identify corresponding parts of similar polygons. Find missing measures by using lengths of corresponding sides.	1–7, 9, 12, 13	
11-5	Solve problems involving scale drawings.	1–7, 9	
11-6	Solve problems by drawing a diagram.	1–5, 7	
11-7	Illustrate the meaning of percent using models or symbols.	1–5, 12	
11-8	Express fractions as percents and vice versa.	1–5, 7, 10	
11-9	Express decimals as percents and vice versa.	1–7	
11-10	Express percents greater than 100% and percents less than 1% as fractions and as decimals, and vice versa.	1–5, 7, 10	

Organizing the Chapter

A complete, 1-page lesson plan is provided for each lesson in the Lesson Plans Masters Booklet.

LESSON PLANNING GUIDE

Lesson	Materials/ Manipulatives	Extra Practice (Student Edition)	Study Guide	Practice	Enrichment	Evaluation	Technology	Lab Manual	Multicultural Activities	Application and Interdisciplinary Activities	Transparencies	Group Activity Cards
							Blackline Masters Booklets					
11-1A	dried beans or squares of paper							p. 69				
11-1	calculator	p. 594	p. 91	p. 91	p. 91					p. 11	11-1	11-1
11-2	calculator	p. 595	p. 92	p. 92	p. 92						11-2	11-2
11-3	calculator	p. 595	p. 93	p. 93	p. 93						11-3	11-3
11-3B	bowl, lima beans, marker							p. 70				
11-4	calculator	p. 595	p. 94	p. 94	p. 94						11-4	11-4
11-5	calculator, ruler, measuring tape, ¼ inch graph paper	p. 596	p. 95	p. 95	p. 95	Quiz A, p. 97		p. 71	p. 11		11-5	11-5
11-6			p. 96	p. 96	p. 96						11-6	11-6
11-7	grid paper, markers	p. 596	p. 97	p. 97	p. 97						11-7	11-7
11-8			p. 596	p. 98	p. 98	p. 98	p.11				11-8	11-8
11-9	calculator, tape measure, yardstick	p. 597	p. 99	p. 99	p. 99		p. 25				11-9	11-9
11-10	grid paper, markers, calculator	p. 597	p. 100	p. 100	p. 100	Quiz B, p. 97				p. 25	11-10	11-10
Study Guide and Review	5 different boxes of cereal		Multiple Choice Test, Forms 1A and 1B, pp. 91–94 Free Response Test, Forms 2A and 2B, pp. 95–96 Cumulative Review, p. 98 (free response)									
Test			Cumulative Test, p. 99 (multiple choice)									

Pacing Guide: Option I (Chapters 1–12) - 15 days; Option II (Chapters 1–13) - 14 days; Option III (Chapters 1–14) - 13 days
You may wish to refer to the complete **Course Planning Guides** on page T25.

OTHER CHAPTER RESOURCES

Student Edition
Chapter Opener,
 pp. 408–409
Mid-Chapter Review,
 p. 429
Save Planet Earth, p. 443
Portfolio Suggestion, p. 443

Manipulatives
Overhead Manipulative
 Resources
Middle School Mathematics
 Manipulative Kit

Software/Technology
Interactive Mathematics
 Tools (Macintosh)
Test and Review Generator
 (IBM, Apple, Macintosh)
Teacher's Guide for
 Software Resources

Other Supplements
Transparency 11–0
Performance Assessment,
 pp. 21–22
Glencoe Mathematics
 Professional Series
Lesson Plans, pp. 120–131

INTERDISCIPLINARY BULLETIN BOARD

Science Connection

Objective   Find ratios and percents with real-world facts.

How To Use It   Tell students that there is a rainforest in North America that extends 2,000 miles down the Pacific coast from Alaska to California. Have them find out about life in this temperate rainforest and to display statistics related to their discoveries. Have them use ratios and percents to compare what they discover with data from other forests.

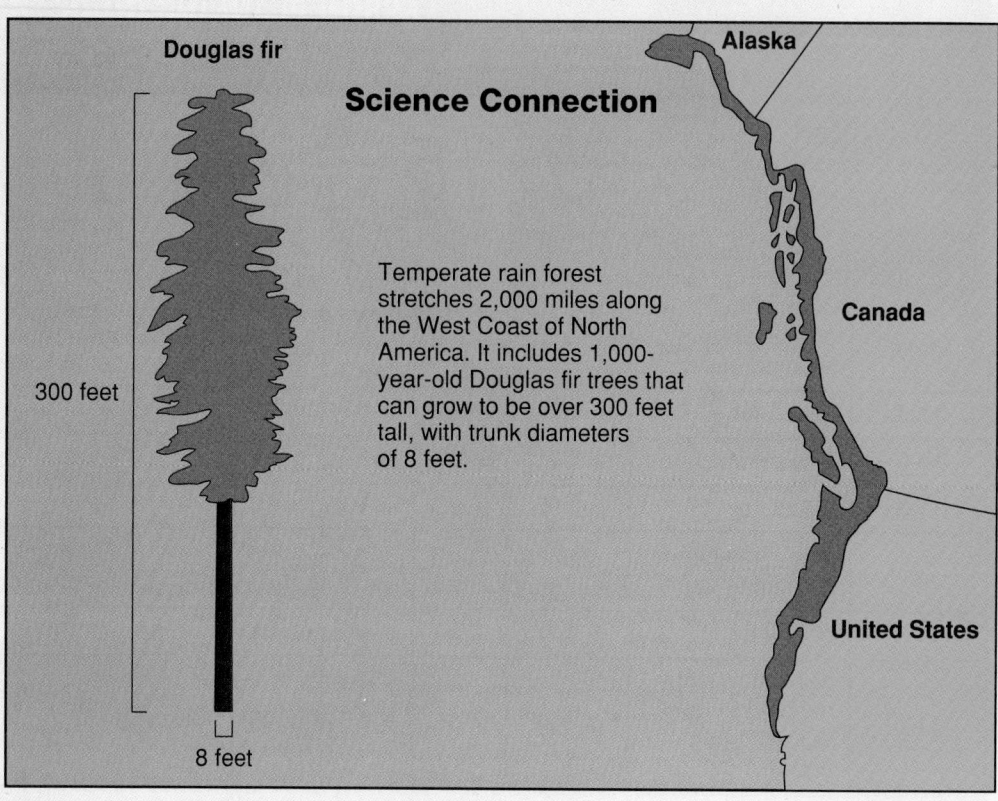

Douglas fir

Alaska

Science Connection

Canada

300 feet

Temperate rain forest stretches 2,000 miles along the West Coast of North America. It includes 1,000-year-old Douglas fir trees that can grow to be over 300 feet tall, with trunk diameters of 8 feet.

United States

8 feet

APPLICATIONS AND CONNECTIONS

Applications	Lesson	Example	Exercise
Real Estate	11-1	1	
Family	11-1		12
Nutrition	11-2	1	
Social Studies	11-2	3	
Population	11-2		25
Entertainment	11-2		30
Sports	11-3	2	
Finance	11-3		12
Nutrition	11-3		32
Geography	11-5	1	
Structural Engineering	11-5		10
Horticulture	11-5		27
Entertainment	11-8		13
Animals	11-8		52–55
Navigation	11-9	2	
Sports	11-9		53
Consumer Math	11-9		54
Connections			
Geometry	11-1		35
Probability	11-1		36
Algebra	11-3	1	
Measurement	11-3		31
Measurement	11-4		22
Statistics	11-7		31
Statistics	11-8		56
Statistics	11-10	1,4	23, 67

TEAM ACTIVITIES

Multicultural Experiences

Outside Field Trips   A visit to a natural history museum can be useful in helping students to see another application of ratio and proportion. There they can talk with a staff member to find out how proportions are used to construct models and dioramas.

A brief trip to a local restaurant can be helpful in showing students how managers use proportions to help them determine how much food to order.

In-Class Speakers   Ask a real estate agent or management agent to give examples of how ratios and proportions are used to make floor plans of houses and apartments.

Invite a bus driver or pilot to describe how he or she uses proportion and percent to read maps and charts and to estimate travel times.

SUPPLEMENTARY BLACKLINE MASTER BOOKLETS

Some of the blackline masters for enhancing this chapter are shown below.

Application and Interdisciplinary Activity Masters, pp. 11, 25

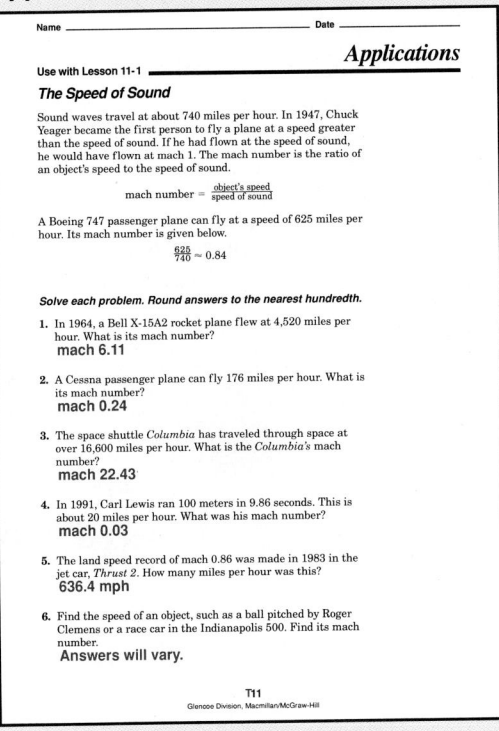

Name _____ Date _____

Applications

Use with Lesson 11-1

The Speed of Sound

Sound waves travel at about 740 miles per hour. In 1947, Chuck Yeager became the first person to fly a plane at a speed greater than the speed of sound. If he had flown at the speed of sound, he would have flown at mach 1. The mach number is the ratio of an object's speed to the speed of sound.

$$\text{mach number} = \frac{\text{object's speed}}{\text{speed of sound}}$$

A Boeing 747 passenger plane can fly at a speed of 625 miles per hour. Its mach number is given below.

$$\frac{625}{740} \approx 0.84$$

Solve each problem. Round answers to the nearest hundredth.

1. In 1964, a Bell X-15A2 rocket plane flew at 4,520 miles per hour. What is its mach number?
   mach 6.11

2. A Cessna passenger plane can fly 176 miles per hour. What is its mach number?
   mach 0.24

3. The space shuttle *Columbia* has traveled through space at over 16,600 miles per hour. What is the *Columbia's* mach number?
   mach 22.43

4. In 1991, Carl Lewis ran 100 meters in 9.86 seconds. This is about 20 miles per hour. What was his mach number?
   mach 0.03

5. The land speed record of mach 0.86 was made in 1983 in the jet car, *Thrust 2*. How many miles per hour was this?
   636.4 mph

6. Find the speed of an object, such as a ball pitched by Roger Clemens or a race car in the Indianapolis 500. Find its mach number.
   Answers will vary.

T11
Glencoe Division, Macmillan/McGraw-Hill

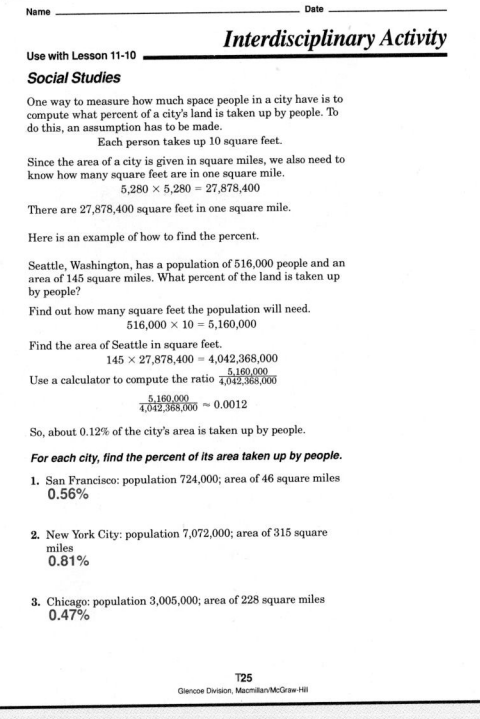

Name _____ Date _____

Interdisciplinary Activity

Use with Lesson 11-10

Social Studies

One way to measure how much space people in a city have is to compute what percent of a city's land is taken up by people. To do this, an assumption has to be made.

Each person takes up 10 square feet.

Since the area of a city is given in square miles, we also need to know how many square feet are in one square mile.

$$5,280 \times 5,280 = 27,878,400$$

There are 27,878,400 square feet in one square mile.

Here is an example of how to find the percent.

Seattle, Washington, has a population of 516,000 people and an area of 145 square miles. What percent of the land is taken up by people?

Find out how many square feet the population will need.
$$516,000 \times 10 = 5,160,000$$

Find the area of Seattle in square feet.
$$145 \times 27,878,400 = 4,042,368,000$$
Use a calculator to compute the ratio $\frac{5,160,000}{4,042,368,000}$

$$\frac{5,160,000}{4,042,368,000} \approx 0.0012$$

So, about 0.12% of the city's area is taken up by people.

For each city, find the percent of its area taken up by people.

1. San Francisco: population 724,000; area of 46 square miles
   0.56%

2. New York City: population 7,072,000; area of 315 square miles
   0.81%

3. Chicago: population 3,005,000; area of 228 square miles
   0.47%

T25
Glencoe Division, Macmillan/McGraw-Hill

Multicultural Activity Masters, p. 11

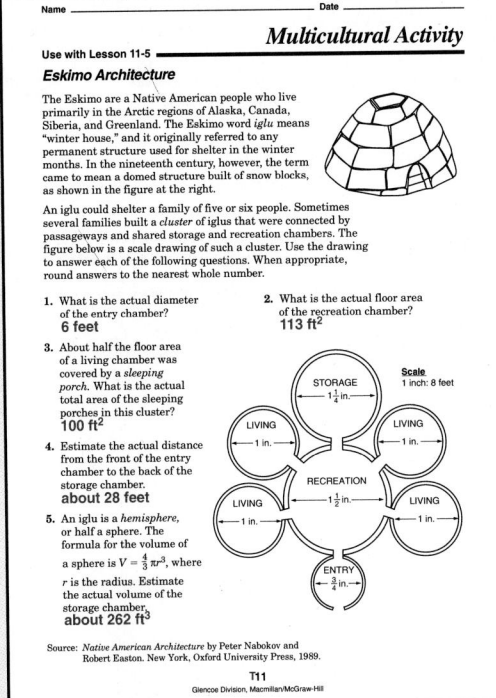

Name _____ Date _____

Multicultural Activity

Use with Lesson 11-5

Eskimo Architecture

The Eskimo are a Native American people who live primarily in the Arctic regions of Alaska, Canada, Siberia, and Greenland. The Eskimo word *iglu* means "winter house," and it originally referred to any permanent structure used for shelter in the winter months. In the nineteenth century, however, the term came to mean a domed structure built of snow blocks, as shown in the figure at the right.

An iglu could shelter a family of five or six people. Sometimes several families built a *cluster* of iglus that were connected by passageways and shared storage and recreation chambers. The figure below is a scale drawing of such a cluster. Use the drawing to answer each of the following questions. When appropriate, round answers to the nearest whole number.

1. What is the actual diameter of the entry chamber?
   6 feet

2. What is the actual floor area of the recreation chamber?
   113 ft²

3. About half the floor area of a living chamber was covered by a *sleeping porch*. What is the actual total area of the sleeping porches in this cluster?
   100 ft²

4. Estimate the actual distance from the front of the entry chamber to the back of the storage chamber.
   about 28 feet

5. An iglu is a *hemisphere*, or half a sphere. The formula for the volume of a sphere is $V = \frac{4}{3}\pi r^3$, where r is the radius. Estimate the actual volume of the storage chamber.
   about 262 ft³

Source: *Native American Architecture* by Peter Nabokov and Robert Easton. New York, Oxford University Press, 1989.

T11
Glencoe Division, Macmillan/McGraw-Hill

Technology Masters, p. 11

Name _____ Date _____

Calculator Activity

Use with Lesson 11-8

The Percent Key

The percent key % on a calculator may be used to express a fraction as a percent.

Example Express $\frac{3}{8}$ as a percent.

3 ÷ 8 % = 37.5

$\frac{3}{8} = 37.5\%$

Example Express $\frac{2}{3}$ as a percent.

2 ÷ 3 % = 66.666667

Round to the nearest hundredth.

$\frac{2}{3} \approx 66.67\%$

Express each fraction as a percent. Round to the nearest hundredth if necessary.

1. $\frac{3}{4}$ **75%**
2. $\frac{5}{8}$ **62.5%**
3. $\frac{16}{20}$ **80%**
4. $\frac{7}{16}$ **43.75%**
5. $\frac{1}{3}$ **33.33%**
6. $\frac{9}{12}$ **75%**
7. $\frac{7}{200}$ **3.5%**
8. $\frac{15}{325}$ **4.62%**
9. $\frac{62}{137}$ **45.26%**
10. $\frac{13}{91}$ **14.29%**
11. $\frac{127}{357}$ **35.57%**
12. $\frac{89}{342}$ **26.02%**
13. $\frac{759}{1,000}$ **75.9%**
14. $\frac{89}{90}$ **98.89%**
15. $\frac{67}{101}$ **66.34%**
16. $\frac{875}{2,000}$ **43.75%**
17. $\frac{346}{400}$ **86.5%**
18. $\frac{329}{658}$ **50%**

T11
Glencoe Division, Macmillan/McGraw-Hill

408d

This two-page introduction to the chapter provides a visual, relevant way to engage students in the mathematics of the chapter. Questions are included that help students see the need to learn the mathematics in the chapter. Data in charts and graphs provide statistical information that students can analyze and interpret at this point as well as later in the chapter. The Chapter Project provides an activity that applies the mathematics of the chapter.

MAKING MATHEMATICS RELEVANT

Spotlight on Health and Safety

Health and safety are topics that are readily explored through the application of ratio, proportion, and percent. The latter concept is illustrated in the graph on drunk driving and the table on smoking.

Using the Timeline

Have students add three events to the timeline that occurred in American history between the time that Alcoholics Anonymous was formed and Ronald Reagan was elected President.

Chapter

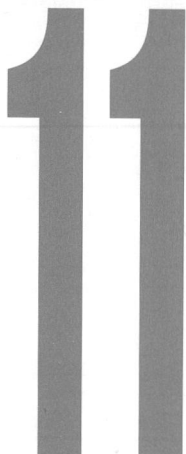

Ratio, Proportion, and Percent

Spotlight on Health and Safety

Have You Ever Wondered. . .

- If fewer people are drinking and driving now than in the past?

- What percent of high school students smoke?

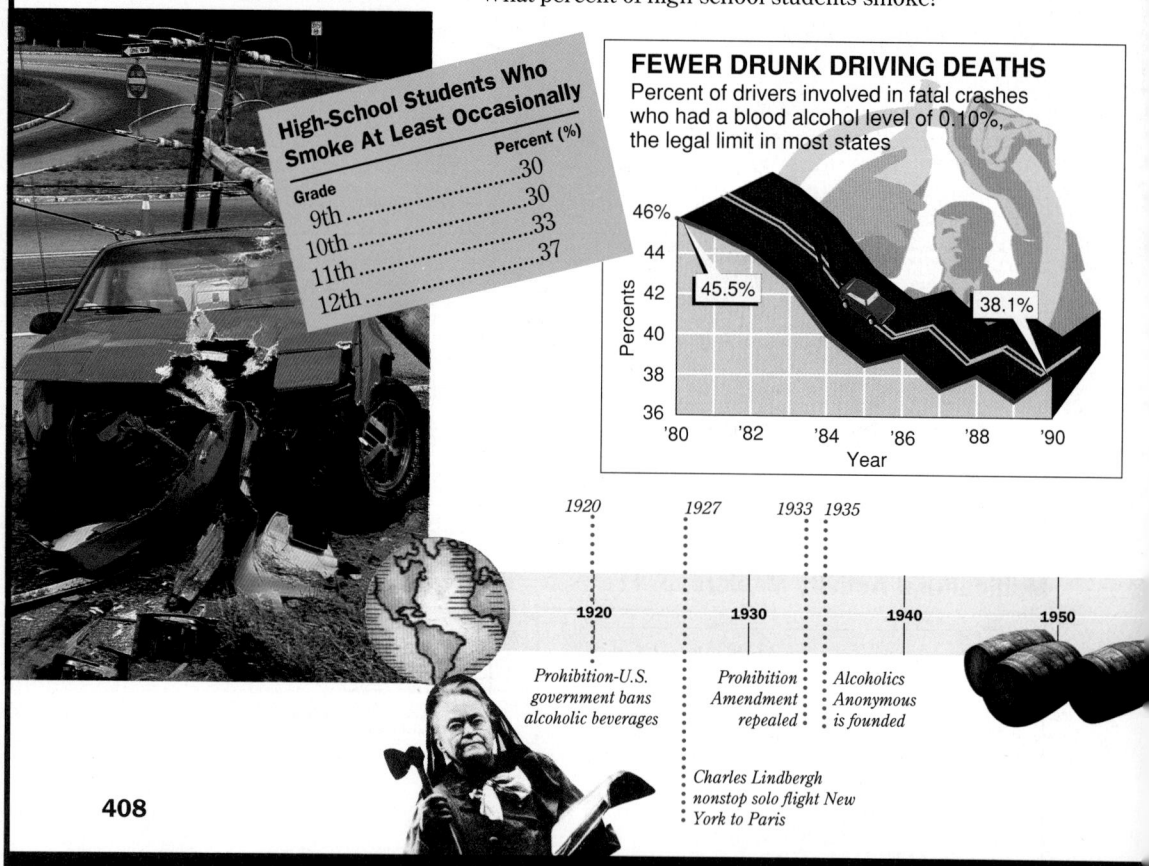

High-School Students Who Smoke At Least Occasionally	
Grade	Percent (%)
9th	30
10th	30
11th	33
12th	37

FEWER DRUNK DRIVING DEATHS
Percent of drivers involved in fatal crashes who had a blood alcohol level of 0.10%, the legal limit in most states

45.5%

38.1%

1920   1927   1933   1935

1920   1930   1940   1950

Prohibition-U.S. government bans alcoholic beverages

Prohibition Amendment repealed

Alcoholics Anonymous is founded

Charles Lindbergh nonstop solo flight New York to Paris

408

"Have You Ever Wondered?" Answers

- The number of deaths due to drunk driving have been decreasing.
- Between 30 and 37 percent of high-school students smoke.

Chapter Project

Health and Safety
Work in a group.

1. Conduct a poll about smoking. Interview at least 10 people who used to smoke cigarettes but have quit.

2. Find out why these people started smoking, at what age, and how long they smoked. Also ask them why and how they quit.

3. Make an oral presentation of your findings.

Looking Ahead

In this chapter, you will see how mathematics can be used to answer the questions about health and safety.

The major objectives of the chapter are to:

- express ratios as fractions
- solve proportions
- solve problems involving scale drawings and diagrams
- express percents as fractions and decimals

| 1964 | 1966 | 1971 | 1979 | 1991 |

1960 1970 1980 1990

Surgeon General warns of dangers of cigarette smoking

Cigarette advertising is banned from radio and television

Iraqi soldiers dump oil in Persian Gulf

Nuclear accident at Three Mile Island

409

DATA ANALYSIS
Have a group of students survey at least 5 high school students each to find out whether they smoke cigarettes. Students can combine results to see how they compare with information in the table on page 408. Guide students to word their questions so that they will find out the information they are seeking.

Data Search
A question related to these data is provided in Lesson 11-8, page 439, Exercise 58.

CHAPTER PROJECT
Suggest that students work together to prepare a list of their questions before they begin interviewing. You may choose to have students combine the results of the polls so that the final presentation contains a larger number of people. Encourage them to be creative in their presentations.

Chapter Opener Transparency
Transparency 11-0 is available in the Transparency Package. It provides another full-color, motivating activity that you can use to capture students' interest.

NCTM Standards: 1–6

Management Tips

For Students Have each group use a full sheet of paper to draw each table. They do not have to fill in all the spaces simultaneously. Each group will need to have about 120 beans or slips of paper. The group should record its solutions.

For the Overhead Projector *Overhead Manipulative Resources* provides appropriate materials for teacher or student demonstration of the activities in this Mathematics Lab.

1 FOCUS

Introducing the Lab

Have students share what they already know about ratio. Ask them to use the term in a sentence that makes sense or that explains its meaning. Have them give examples of how ratio is used in daily life.

2 TEACH

Using Applications You may wish to have some groups use the beans to form additional ratios. One student makes the first ratio and one pile of the next. The next student completes the equal ratio by making another pile for the third student, and so on.

3 PRACTICE/APPLY

Using Communication Have students compare answers and describe to the class their strategy for forming equal ratios.

Close

Have students use beans or slips of paper to form three ratios equal to the ratio 3 to 1.

Additional Answer

1. Make equivalent fractions.
$$\frac{2}{6} = \frac{6}{16} = \frac{3}{9} = \frac{18}{54}$$

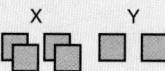

11-1A Equal Ratios

A Preview of Lesson 11-1

Objective
Explore the meaning of ratio and proportion.

Words to Learn
ratio

Materials
dried beans or squares of paper

A **ratio** is the comparison of two numbers. Often ratios are used to show how large one quantity is compared to another. For example, for every two squares in pile X there is one square in pile Y. We say that piles X and Y have the ratio 2 to 1.

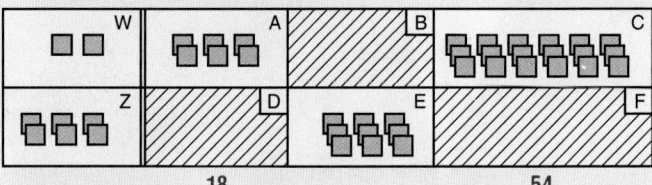

Try this!

Work in groups of two.

● Use dried beans or small squares of paper to make the arrangements shown below.

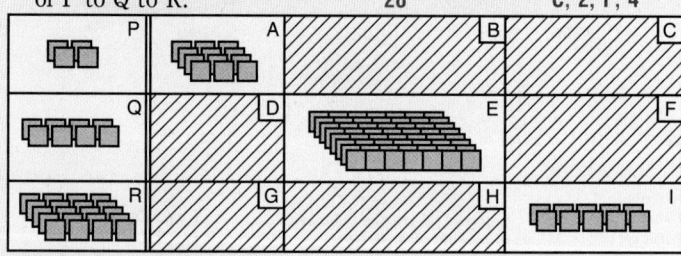

● Work together to place piles of squares in spaces B, D, and F. The ratio of the piles in each column should be equal to the ratio of piles W and Z.

What do you think?

1. See margin.

2. 33 squares

1. How did you decide how many squares to put in space D? B? F?

2. If space D has 99 squares, how many squares will be in space A?

3. Copy the table shown below. Place squares in spaces B, C, D, F, G, and H so that the ratios in each column are equal to the ratio of P to Q to R.

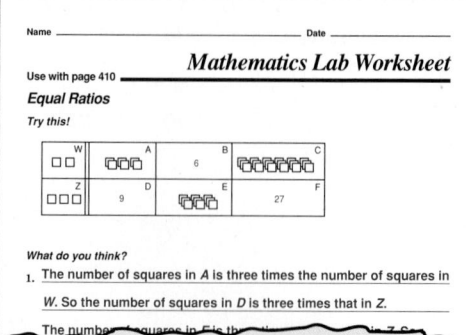

4. Did you use multiplication or division to decide on your answers? **both**

OPTIONS

Lab Manual You may wish to make copies of the blackline master on p. 69 of the *Lab Manual* for students to use as a recording sheet.

Lab Manual, p. 69

Name _____ Date _____

Mathematics Lab Worksheet

Use with page 410
Equal Ratios
Try this!

What do you think?

1. The number of squares in *A* is three times the number of squares in *W*. So the number of squares in *D* is three times that in *Z*.

11-1 Ratios

Objective
Express ratios as fractions and determine whether two ratios are equivalent.

Words to Learn
ratio

Where did people move in 1991? The ratio of people moving in to people moving out is greatest in Spokane, Washington.

Where People Moved in '91
1. Spokane, WA
2. Springfield, MO
3. Greenville-Washington, NC
4. Nashville, TN
5. Las Vegas, NV
6. San Antonio, TX
7. Fresno-Visalla, CA
8. Richmond, VA
9. Albuquerque, NM
10. Raleigh-Durham, NC

During the first six months of 1991, for every 100 families who moved out of Nashville, 137 families moved in. The **ratio** of the number of families who moved out of Nashville to the number of families who moved in was 100 to 137.

Ratio	In words:	A ratio is a comparison of two numbers by division.		
		Arithmetic		**Algebra**
	100 to 137	100:137	$\frac{100}{137}$	a to b $a:b$ $\frac{a}{b}$

Since a ratio can be written as a fraction, ratios are often written in simplest form.

Example 1 *Problem Solving*

Real Estate   Mr. McLevy, a real estate agent, knew that last year 480 families had moved out of Broome County and 560 families had moved in. Write the ratio of the number of families moving out to the number of families moving in.

Write the ratio in simplest form.

families moving out → $\frac{480}{560} = \frac{480 \div 80}{560 \div 80}$ *The GCF of 480*
families moving in → $\phantom{\frac{480}{560}}\quad and\ 560\ is\ 80.$
$$= \frac{6}{7}$$

The ratio in simplest form is $\frac{6}{7}$, or 6 to 7, or 6:7.

Ratios can also be expressed as decimals. The ratio in Example 1 can be expressed as a decimal in the following way.

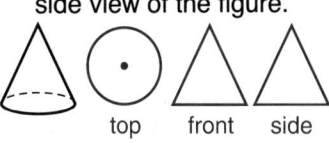

480 ⌹ 560 ⊟ 0.857143

To simplify a ratio that compares measurements, you must be sure that the measurements have the same unit of measure.

OPTIONS

Reteaching Activity

Using Manipulatives   Have students group differently colored counters or centimeter cubes. Ask them to write ratios in simplest form to compare the groups. Give students simple ratios for them to model using the counters.

Study Guide Masters, p. 91

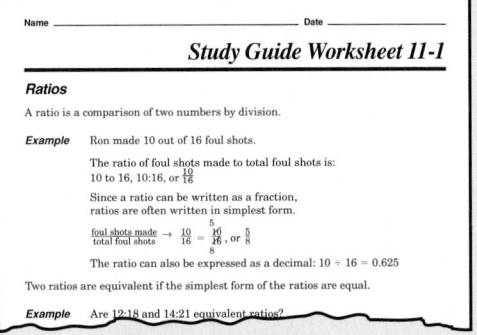

Name _____ Date _____

Study Guide Worksheet 11-1

Ratios

A ratio is a comparison of two numbers by division.

Example   Ron made 10 out of 16 foul shots.

The ratio of foul shots made to total foul shots is:
10 to 16, 10:16, or $\frac{10}{16}$

Since a ratio can be written as a fraction, ratios are often written in simplest form.

$\frac{\text{foul shots made}}{\text{total foul shots}} \rightarrow \frac{10}{16} = \frac{10}{16}$, or $\frac{5}{8}$

The ratio can also be expressed as a decimal: $10 \div 16 = 0.625$

Two ratios are equivalent if the simplest form of the ratios are equal.

Example   Are 12:18 and 14:21 equivalent ratios?

NCTM Standards: 1–7, 9, 11, 12

Lesson Resources
• Study Guide Master 11-1
• Practice Master 11-1
• Enrichment Master 11-1
• Application Master, p. 11
• Group Activity Card 11-1

Transparency 11-1 contains the 5-Minute Check and a teaching aid for this lesson.

5-Minute Check
(Over Chapter 10)
1. Draw a top, front, and side view of the figure.

top   front   side

2. Find the surface area of a rectangular prism that is 4 feet long, 3 feet wide, and 2.75 feet high.
62.5 square feet

3. What is the volume of a cube with an edge of 4.5 meters?
91.125 cubic meters

1 FOCUS

Motivating the Lesson

Activity   Ask students to write a ratio that compares the number of hours they spend on homework each week with the number of hours they spend in school. Have students compare their ratios.

2 TEACH

Using Application   Have students work together to write ratios in simplest form that compare the number of boys to girls in the class, the number of girls to students in the class, as well as other comparisons using data that students generate.

More Examples

For Example 1

A story sold 360 newspapers last week and 440 this week. Write a ratio in simplest form comparing last week's sales to this week's. $\frac{9}{11}$, 9 to 11,

For Example 2

Write the ratio 6 inches : 3 feet in simplest form. $\frac{1}{6}$ or 1 : 6

For Example 3

Are 10 : 12 and 24 : 30 equivalent ratios? no; $\frac{5}{6} \neq \frac{4}{5}$

Checking for Understanding

Exercises 1-3 are designed to help you assess students' understanding through reading, writing, speaking, and modeling. You should work through these exercises with your students and then monitor their work on Guided Practice Exercises 4-12.

412

Example 2

Write the ratio 4 inches:2 feet in simplest form.

$$\frac{4 \text{ inches}}{2 \text{ feet}} = \frac{\overset{1}{\cancel{4}} \text{ inches}}{\underset{6}{24} \text{ inches}} \qquad 2 \text{ feet} = 24 \text{ inches}$$

$$= \frac{1}{6} \qquad \text{The GCF of 4 and 24 is 4.}$$

The ratio in simplest form is $\frac{1}{6}$, or 1:6.

Two ratios are equivalent if they have the same value.

Example 3

Are 12:16 and 21:28 equivalent ratios?

Express each ratio as a fraction in simplest form.

$$\frac{12}{16} = \frac{12 \div 4}{16 \div 4} \qquad\qquad \frac{21}{28} = \frac{21 \div 7}{28 \div 7}$$

$$= \frac{3}{4} \qquad\qquad\qquad = \frac{3}{4}$$

Since the ratios in simplest form are equal, 12:16 and 21:28 are equivalent ratios.

Checking for Understanding

Communicating Mathematics

Read and study the lesson to answer each question.

1. **Draw** the chart at the right and draw squares in space D such that A : B and C : D are equivalent.
   3:4 and 6:8

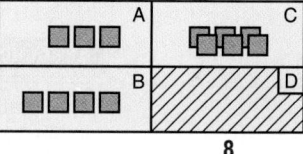

2. 19 to 24; 19:24; $\frac{19}{24}$

2. **Write** the ratio *19 students out of 24 students* in three different ways.

3. **Tell** how to simplify a ratio written as a fraction. **Divide numerator and denominator by their GCF.**

Guided Practice

Express each ratio as a fraction in simplest form.

4. $\frac{9}{12}$ $\frac{3}{4}$

5. 6 to 12 $\frac{1}{2}$

6. 24:4 $\frac{6}{1}$

7. 45 minutes out of 1 hour $\frac{3}{4}$

8. 2 pounds:24 ounces $\frac{4}{3}$

Tell whether the ratios in each pair are equivalent. Show your answer by simplifying.

9. No; $\frac{65}{100} = \frac{13}{20}$.

10. Yes; $\frac{36}{81} = \frac{4}{9}$.

11. No; $\frac{12}{9} = \frac{4}{3}$ and $\frac{15}{12} = \frac{5}{4}$.

9. $\frac{65}{100}$ and $\frac{5}{8}$

10. $\frac{4}{9}$ and $\frac{36}{81}$

11. $\frac{12}{9}$ and $\frac{15}{12}$

12. **Family** Alma is 12 years old. Her brother Javier is 4 years old and their mother is 36 years old. Is the ratio of Javier's age to Alma's age equivalent to the ratio of Alma's age to their mother's age? Show your answer by simplifying ratios. **Yes; $\frac{4}{12} = \frac{1}{3}$ and $\frac{12}{36} = \frac{1}{3}$.**

412   **Chapter 11** Ratio, Proportion, and Percent

OPTIONS

Team Teaching

Inform the other teachers on your team that your classes are studying ratio, proportion, and percent. Suggestions for curriculum integration are:

Science: mixing chemicals, gear ratios, nutrition

Social Studies: surveys, population changes and demographics

Additional Answers

35a. $\frac{8}{6}, \frac{12}{9}, \frac{40}{30}$

b. $\frac{8}{6} = \frac{4}{3}, \frac{12}{9} = \frac{4}{3}, \frac{40}{30} = \frac{4}{3}$

c. $\frac{96}{54} = \frac{16}{9}, \frac{16}{9} = \left(\frac{4}{3}\right)^2$

Exercises

Independent Practice

Express each ratio as a fraction in simplest form.

13. 27 to 15 $\frac{9}{5}$

14. 21:45 $\frac{7}{15}$

15. 49:14 $\frac{7}{2}$

16. 125 to 25 $\frac{5}{1}$

17. 11 weeks out of 33 weeks $\frac{1}{3}$

18. 64 inches to 18 inches $\frac{32}{9}$

19. 2 feet to 6 yards $\frac{1}{9}$

20. 5 pounds to 10 ounces $\frac{8}{1}$

21. 36 to 27 $\frac{4}{3}$

22. 21 minutes:66 minutes $\frac{7}{22}$

23. 48 hours:21 hours $\frac{16}{7}$

24. 625 to 25 $\frac{25}{1}$

Tell whether the ratios in each pair are equivalent. Show your answer by simplifying.

25. 2 pounds:24 ounces and 6 pounds:72 ounces **Yes; 32:24 = 4:3 and 96:72 = 4:3.**

26. 13 to 39 and 26 to 78 **Yes; 13 to 39 = 1 to 3 and 26 to 78 = 1 to 3.**

27. 4 hours to 3 days and 12 hours to 9 days **Yes; 4 to 72 = 1 to 18 and 12 to 216 = 1 to 18.**

28. 150 to 15 and 3 to 1 **No; 150 to 15 = 10 to 1.**

29. 6 to 39 and 3 to 13 **No; 6 to 39 = 2 to 13.**

30. $\frac{65}{5}$ and $\frac{1}{13}$ **No; $\frac{65}{5} = \frac{13}{1}$.**

Mixed Review

31. **Algebra** Evaluate $6m - 2(m - n) + mn$ if $m = 10$ and $n = 5$. *(Lesson 1-8)* **100**

32. Describe the pattern in the sequence 4, 12, 36, 108, ... Then find the next three terms. *(Lesson 4-3)* **Multiply by 3; 324, 972, 2,916.**

33. Order the integers 5, −1, 3, and −5 from least to greatest. *(Lesson 7-2)* **−5, −1, 3, 5**

34. **Packaging** Production specialists suggest that a good way to package flour is in containers shaped as cylinders. The package they suggest has a radius of 2.5 inches and a height of 6 inches. Find the volume of this package. *(Lesson 10-6)* **117.75 in³**

For answers to Exercises 35a–c, see margin.

Problem Solving and Applications

35. **Geometry** Complete the following for the rectangles shown at the right.

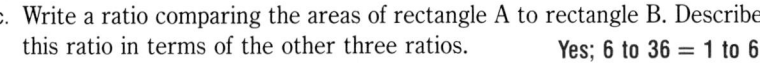
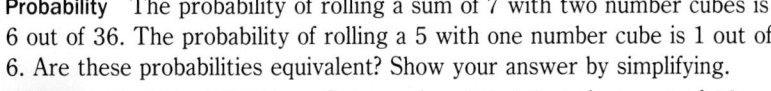

a. Write ratios comparing the widths, the lengths, and the perimeters of rectangle A to rectangle B.

b. Show whether or not these ratios are equivalent.

c. Write a ratio comparing the areas of rectangle A to rectangle B. Describe this ratio in terms of the other three ratios. **Yes; 6 to 36 = 1 to 6.**

36. **Probability** The probability of rolling a sum of 7 with two number cubes is 6 out of 36. The probability of rolling a 5 with one number cube is 1 out of 6. Are these probabilities equivalent? Show your answer by simplifying.

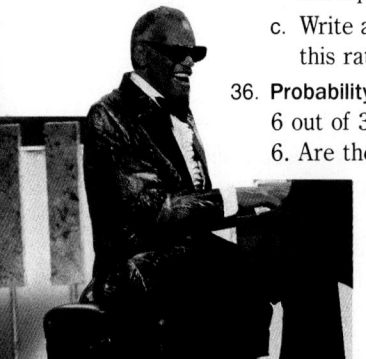

37. **Critical Thinking** Susanne found that 6 students out of 18 students she surveyed liked rock music. Sam found that 9 students out of 24 students he surveyed liked rock music. Which result shows a greater preference for rock music? **Sam's survey**

Lesson 11-1 Ratios **413**

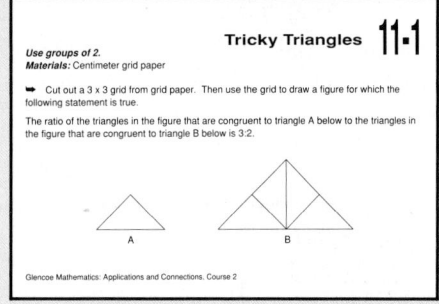

413

NCTM Standards: 1–7

Lesson Resources
- Study Guide Master 11-2
- Practice Master 11-2
- Enrichment Master 11-2
- Group Activity Card 11-2

 Transparency 11-2 contains the 5-Minute Check and a teaching aid for this lesson.

⏱ 5-Minute Check
(Over Lesson 11-1)

Express each ratio as a fraction in simplest form.

1. 30 to 12 $\frac{5}{2}$

2. 15 : 50 $\frac{3}{10}$

3. 2 feet : 6 yards $\frac{1}{9}$

Tell whether the ratios in each pair are equivalent. Show your answer by simplifying.

4. $\frac{4}{15}$ and $\frac{12}{45}$ $\frac{4}{15} = \frac{4}{15}$; yes

5. 6 hours to 4 days and 8 hours to 6 days.
$\frac{1}{16} \neq \frac{1}{18}$; no

---

1 FOCUS

Motivating the Lesson

Situational Problem   A driver can go from the south rim of the Grand Canyon to Durango, Colorado, 318 miles away, in 6 hours. Ask students to describe the average rate of speed for the trip.

2 TEACH

Using Applications   Provide a price list from a supermarket. Have students identify the unit prices of several items, and then find the unit prices for some comparable items in order to find the best buys.

414

11-2   Rates

Objective
Determine unit rates.

Words to Learn
rate
unit rate
unit price
population
 density

George is in charge of buying paper plates, napkins, and cups for the middle school dance. Fourth Street Market sells 100 plates for $1.39. Ben's Supermarket sells the same plates at 50 for $0.74. Which store has the better buy?   *This problem will be solved in Example 2.*

Often you must compare quantities with different units. For example, the ratio $1.39 for 100 plates compares a number of dollars to a number of plates. This type of ratio is called a **rate**.

Rate	A rate is a ratio of two measurements with different units.

Example 1   *Problem Solving*

Nutrition   There are 264 calories in an 8-ounce serving of soup. How many calories are there in one ounce of soup?

$$\frac{calories}{ounces} \rightarrow\atop\rightarrow \frac{264}{8} = \frac{264 \div 8}{8 \div 8} = \frac{33}{1}$$

There are 33 calories in one ounce of soup, or 33 calories *per ounce*.

A rate such as *33 calories per ounce* is an example of a **unit rate**.

Unit Rate	A unit rate is a rate in which the denominator is 1 unit.

Some other common unit rates are given at the right.

miles per gallon	mi/gal (or mpg)
miles per hour	mi/h (or mph)
price per pound	dollars/lb
meters per second	m/s

In some grocery stores, the labels on the shelves give the cost of the item and its unit rate, which is called the **unit price.** This information helps consumers to make good buying decisions.

Example 2   *Problem Solving*

Smart Shopping   Refer to the problem in the lesson introduction. Which store, Fourth Street Market or Ben's Supermarket, has the better buy on paper plates?

Explore   To determine which store has the better buy, George needs to find the unit price for the plates at each store.

OPTIONS

Reteaching Activity

Using Applications   Have students record the rate at which they do regular activities, such as the number of pages of a reading assignment per hour and the number of miles of jogging in a week.

Study Guide Masters, p. 92

Name _____   Date _____

Study Guide Worksheet 11-2

Rates

A rate is a ratio of two measurements with different units.

Example   Six bottles of mineral water cost $2.59.
The ratio 6 bottles for $2.59 is a rate.

A rate in which the denominator is 1 is a unit rate.

Example   Express 6 bottles for $2.59 as a unit rate.

$$\frac{\$2.59}{6} = \frac{\$2.59 \div 6}{6 \div 6}$$
$$\frac{\$0.4317}{1}$$

The unit rate is about $0.43 per bottle.

Plan   Find the unit price for plates at each store and compare.

Solve   **Fourth Street:** $\frac{\$1.39}{100 \text{ plates}}$

1.39 ⌷÷⌷ 100 ⌷=⌷ **0.0139**

Ben's Supermarket: $\frac{\$0.74}{50 \text{ plates}}$

0.74 ⌷÷⌷ 50 ⌷=⌷ **0.0148**

The price per plate, or unit price, at Fourth Street Market is $0.0139. The unit price at Ben's Supermarket is $0.0148. Since 0.0139 < 0.0148, the Fourth Street Market has the better buy on plates.

Examine   To check your answer, multiply. One hundred plates at $0.0139 per plate cost $1.39. One hundred plates at $0.0148 per plate cost $1.48. So the Fourth Street Market has the better buy.

Community planners use a unit rate called **population density**, which is the population per square mile.

Example 3 *Problem Solving*

Social Studies   In 1991, New York State had a population of 17,950,000 people and an area of 49,108 square miles. What was the population density of New York State in 1991?

$\frac{17,950,000 \text{ people}}{49,108 \text{ square miles}}$ → 17,950,000 ⌷÷⌷ 49,108 ⌷=⌷ **365.520893**

In 1991, New York State had a population density of about 366 people per square mile.

2. A ratio compares two of the same units while a rate compares two different units.

Checking for Understanding

Communicating Mathematics

Read and study the lesson to answer each question.

1. **Tell** whether the rate is a unit rate.
   a. 240 km in 5 hours **no**   b. $3.20 per pound **yes**   c. 8 miles per hour **yes**
2. **Write**, in your own words, the difference between a ratio and rate.
3. **Tell** why unit rates are more helpful than rates that are not unit rates.
   It is easier to compare 1 to another number.

Guided Practice   Express each rate as a unit rate.

4. $2.37 for 3 pounds **$0.79 per pound**   5. 200 miles in 5 hours **40 mph**
6. 6 cups for 3 pounds **2 cups per pound**   7. $11.90 for 10 disks **$1.19 per disk**
8. $350 for 5 days **$70 per day**   9. 12 people in 3 cars **4 people per car**
10. 12 pounds in 3 weeks **4 pounds per week**   11. 150 tickets in 5 days **30 tickets per day**

Lesson 11-2 Rates   **415**

Have students describe how to determine which of two products is the better buy. Find and compare unit prices.

3 PRACTICE/APPLY

Assignment Guide
Maximum: 12–32
Minimum: 13–19 odd, 21–31

For **Extra Practice,** see p. 595.

Alternate Assessment

Writing Tell students that 4 buses are taking 180 people to the concert. Have them express this bus capacity information as a unit rate. **45 people per bus**

Additional Answers

12. 5 people per row
13. 80 miles per day
14. $1.24 per pound
15. $1.45 per disk
16. 150 tickets per day
17. 0.5 cup per pound
20a. napkins: $0.00763, $0.035; cups: $0.00745, $0.0356

Enrichment Masters, p. 92

416

Exercises

Independent Practice Express each rate as a unit rate. **For answers to Exercises 12–17, see margin.**

12. 20 people in 4 rows
13. 480 miles in 6 days
14. $6.20 for 5 pounds
15. $29.00 for 20 disks
16. 1,200 tickets in 8 days
17. 12 cups for 24 pounds
18. $960 for 16 days **$60 per day**
19. 24 people in 8 cars **3 people per car**

20. The Fourth Street Market sells napkins at $2.29 for 300 and cups at $1.75 per 50. At Ben's Supermarket, the same napkins cost $1.49 for 200, and cups are $0.89 for 25.
   a. Find the unit price for each item at each store. **See margin.**
   b. Which store has the better buy for napkins and for cups? **napkins, Ben's Supermarket; cups, Fourth Street Market**

Mixed Review 21. **Chemistry** Bob is performing a chemistry experiment that requires that 3 milligrams of potassium be added to the solution. How many grams of potassium chloride will Bob add? *(Lesson 2-9)* **0.003 g**

22. Express $\frac{35}{4}$ as a mixed number. *(Lesson 5-1)* **$8\frac{3}{4}$**

23. **Geometry** What is the name of a polygon having 6 sides? *(Lesson 8-2)* **hexagon**

24. Write the ratio 45:81 in simplest form. *(Lesson 11-1)* **5:9**

Problem Solving and Applications **Population** Find the population density, to the nearest person, for each country.

	Country	Population	Square Miles	
25.	Brazil	153,771,000	3,286,470	**47 people per mile²**
26.	Canada	26,527,000	3,558,096	**7 people per mile²**
27.	China	1,130,065,000	3,705,390	**305 people per mile²**
28.	Egypt	54,139,000	386,650	**140 people per mile²**
29.	Hong Kong	5,693,000	409	**13,919 people per mile²**

30. **Entertainment** The chorus has 5 days to sell 195 tickets to ensure a sell-out at their spring concert. At what rate must they sell the tickets?

31. **Critical Thinking** The heart beat of an average adult human is 72 beats per minute. The average number of heart beats for an elephant is 35 beats per minute.
   a. Whose heart will beat more in an hour? **adult human**
   b. About how many days will it take for a human's heart to beat 1,000,000 times? **about 10 days**
   c. About how many days will it take an elephant's heart to beat 1,000,000 times? **about 20 days**

32. **Journal Entry** Suppose the Fourth Street Market and Ben's Supermarket are on opposite sides of a large town. Should George go to each store and purchase the items that gave him the better buy or should he go to one store to purchase everything? Explain.

30. 39 tickets per day
32. He should purchase everything at one store. The difference in price is not enough to offset the cost of gas and the time it would take him to cross town.

416 Chapter 11 Ratio, Proportion, and Percent

OPTIONS

Extending the Lesson

Consumer Connection Have students in each group guess the unit price for five foods they like to eat. Then have them find the prices for these items, and identify or figure out the actual unit prices to compare with their estimates.

Cooperative Learning Activity

Stuff It **11-2**

Use groups of 2.
Materials: Typing paper, legal-size envelopes, watch or clock with second hand

▲ In this activity you will determine the rate at which each partner can stuff and address envelopes. (This is an important job in many organizations, including political campaigns.)

➡ One partner follows the procedure described below. The other partner states when 5 minutes have passed and records the number of completed envelopes. Then partners trade roles and repeat the activity. Finally, partners compare their hourly rates for stuffing and addressing envelopes.

INSTRUCTIONS
Fold the bottom third of each sheet of paper up and then fold the top third down over it. Place the folded sheet of paper in the envelope, seal the envelope, and write the address shown below on the front.

Ms. Jane Q. Public
1234 Main Street
City, State 12345

Glencoe Mathematics: Applications and Connections, Course 2

11-3 Proportions

Objective
Solve proportions.

Words to Learn
proportion
cross products

The first jumbo jet was the Boeing 747. It began airline service in 1970. Because of its long, wide body, it can seat nearly 500 passengers. The length of the Boeing 747 is 70.5 meters, or 7,050 centimeters. The wingspan is about 60 meters, or 6,000 centimeters.

A model of this plane has a wingspan of 80 centimeters and a length of 94 centimeters.

You can find the ratios of the wingspan to the length for the plane and then for the model. How do they compare?

plane: $\dfrac{wingspan}{length} \rightarrow \dfrac{6,000}{7,050} = \dfrac{6,000 \div 150}{7,050 \div 150} = \dfrac{40}{47}$

model: $\dfrac{wingspan}{length} \rightarrow \dfrac{80}{94} = \dfrac{80 \div 2}{94 \div 2} = \dfrac{40}{47}$

The ratios $\dfrac{6,000}{7,050}$ and $\dfrac{80}{94}$ are equivalent. So, you can write $\dfrac{6,000}{7,050} = \dfrac{80}{94}$. This equation is an example of a **proportion**.

The fastest jet is the U.S. Lockheed SR-71. It can reach a speed of 2,200 miles per hour.

Proportion	**In words:** A proportion is an equation that shows that two ratios are equivalent.
	Arithmetic $\qquad\qquad$ **Algebra**
	$\dfrac{3}{4} = \dfrac{9}{12}$ $\qquad\qquad$ $\dfrac{a}{b} = \dfrac{c}{d},\ b \neq 0,\ d \neq 0$

In a proportion, the two **cross products** are equal. The cross products in the proportion below are 4×9 and 3×12.

$\dfrac{3}{4} = \dfrac{9}{12}$ $\qquad\qquad$ $4 \times 9 = 36$
$\qquad\qquad\qquad\qquad\qquad$ $3 \times 12 = 36$

Property of Proportion	**In words:** The cross products of a proportion are equal.
	In symbols: If $\dfrac{a}{b} = \dfrac{c}{d}$, then $ad = bc$.

In a proportion like $\dfrac{2}{5} = \dfrac{3}{n}$, if one of the terms is not known, you can use cross products to find the unknown, n. This is known as *solving the proportion.*

Lesson 11-3 Proportions $\quad$ **417**

NCTM Standards: 1–7, 9, 13

Lesson Resources
- Study Guide Master 11-3
- Practice Master 11-3
- Enrichment Master 11-3
- Group Activity Card 11-3

Transparency 11-3 contains the 5-Minute Check and a teaching aid for this lesson.

5-Minute Check
(Over Lesson 11-2)

Express each rate as a unit rate.

1. 315 miles in 7 hours
   45 miles per hour

2. $42.00 for 6 tapes
   $7.00 per tape

3. 1,500 tickets in 6 days
   250 tickets per day

4. Mike's Market sells Kittie Treats at $2.00 for 5 boxes. At Donna's Deli, a 6-pack of the same product sells for $2.30. Which store has the better buy? Donna's Deli

1 FOCUS

Motivating the Lesson

Activity Ask students how they can find the size of a real object given a model of it, or determine the actual distance between two places on a map, using a map scale.

OPTIONS

Bell Ringer

Tell students that a picture frame is 35 inches wide and 24 inches high. Ask them to list the ways in which the dimensions of a picture can be chosen so that the ratio of the length of the shorter side of the picture to the length of the longer side is 2 to 3, and so that neither side is less than 14 inches long.

Possible lengths for sides, in inches:
$\dfrac{33}{22}, \dfrac{30}{20}, \dfrac{27}{18}, \dfrac{24}{16},$ and $\dfrac{21}{14}$

2 TEACH

Using Critical Thinking Guide students to see that proportions can be solved in more than one way. Encourage them to use any of the solution methods and to use mental math whenever possible. For example, guide them to compare numerators or compare denominators of two ratios to see whether they are multiples of one another.

Teaching Tip Encourage students to simplify one of the ratios, if possible, prior to solving the proportion.

More Examples

For Example 1

Solve $\frac{3}{5} = \frac{2}{n}$. $3\frac{1}{3}$

For Example 2

Jenny got 3 hits in her first 8 at-bats this season. How many hits must she get in her next 200 at-bats to maintain this ratio? 75 hits

---

Checking for Understanding

Exercises 1-3 are designed to help you assess students' understanding through reading, writing, speaking, and modeling. You should work through these exercises with your students and then monitor their work on Guided Practice Exercises 4-12.

418

Mental Math Hint
• • • • • • • • • • • •
Sometimes you can solve a proportion mentally by using equivalent fractions.

$$\frac{5}{9} = \frac{20}{m}$$

$$\underset{\times 4}{\frac{5}{9}} = \underset{\times 4}{\frac{20}{36}}$$

So, $m = 36$.

Problem Solving Hint
• • • • • • • • • • • •
Often there is more than one way to solve a problem that involves proportions. Just be sure that each side of the proportion compares the quantities in the same order. For instance, here is another way to write a proportion for the problem in Example 2.

$$\begin{array}{c} wins\ \ games \\ 1st\ week \to \dfrac{6}{n} = \dfrac{8}{164} \leftarrow 1st\ week \\ season \to \qquad\qquad \leftarrow season \end{array}$$

Example 1 Connection

Algebra Solve $\frac{2}{5} = \frac{3}{n}$.

$$\frac{2}{5} = \frac{3}{n}$$

$2 \times n = 5 \times 3$ *Find the cross products.*

$2n = 15$

$\dfrac{2n}{2} = \dfrac{15}{2}$ *Divide each side by 2.*

$n = 7\frac{1}{2}$ The solution is $7\frac{1}{2}$.

Example 2 Problem Solving

Sports During the first week of baseball season, the Minnesota Twins won 6 games out of 8 games. How many of the 162 regular season games must they win to maintain this ratio?

Explore In the first week, they won 6 games out of 8 games. The regular season has 162 games.

Plan Let n represent the number of games they must win. Write a proportion.

$$\begin{array}{ccccc} & & \text{first week} & & \text{season} \\ wins & \to & \dfrac{6}{8} & = & \dfrac{n}{162} & \to & wins \\ games & \to & & & & \to & games \end{array}$$

Find the cross products. Then solve the proportion.

Solve

$$\frac{6}{8} = \frac{n}{162}$$

$6 \times 162 = 8n$ *Find the cross products.*

$6 \; \boxed{\times} \; 162 \; \boxed{\div} \; 8 \; \boxed{=} \; \mathtt{121.5}$

$n = 121.5$

Since the number of games must be expressed as a whole number, the Minnesota Twins must win 122 games to maintain the ratio of 6 to 8.

Examine Express each ratio as a decimal and compare.

$\dfrac{6}{8}$: $6 \; \boxed{\div} \; 8 \; \boxed{=} \; \mathtt{0.75}$

$\dfrac{121.5}{162}$: $121.5 \; \boxed{\div} \; 162 \; \boxed{=} \; \mathtt{0.75}$

Since the decimals are equal, the ratios are equivalent. So, 121.5 is correct.

OPTIONS

Reteaching Activity

Using Connections Focus on the concept of proportions as equal ratios. Write a number of pairs of ratios on the chalkboard. Have students work in groups to find those pairs that are equal ratios and those that are not. Ask them to explain their answers and methods.

Study Guide Masters, p. 93

Name _____ Date _____

Study Guide Worksheet 11-3

Proportions

A proportion is an equation that shows that two ratios are equivalent. The cross products of a proportion are equal.

Example Find the cross products. $\frac{2}{3} = \frac{12}{18}$
$3 \times 12 = 36$
$2 \times 18 = 36$
So, $\frac{2}{3} = \frac{12}{18}$ is a proportion.

If one term of a proportion is not known, you can use cross products to find the term. This is called solving the proportion.

Example Solve $\frac{r}{24} = \frac{7}{8}$.

$$\frac{r}{24} = \frac{7}{8}$$

Checking for Understanding

Communicating Mathematics

Read and study the lesson to answer each question.

1. **Tell** how you can determine whether two ratios are equivalent. **See margin.**

2. **Write** the cross products for $\frac{1}{3} = \frac{5}{n}$ $1 \times n = 3 \times 5$

3. **Tell** how to solve $\frac{n}{4} = \frac{9}{17}$ with a calculator. **Multiply 4 times 9, then divide the answer by 17.**

Guided Practice

Solve each proportion.

4. $\frac{3}{4} = \frac{n}{8}$ **6**
5. $\frac{6}{9} = \frac{4}{m}$ **6**
6. $\frac{5}{t} = \frac{2}{6}$ **15**
7. $\frac{x}{3} = \frac{18}{27}$ **2**

8. $\frac{x}{36} = \frac{15}{24}$ **22.5**
9. $\frac{r}{3} = \frac{5}{9}$ **$1\frac{2}{3}$**
10. $\frac{6}{5} = \frac{k}{4}$ **4.8**
11. $\frac{2.5}{4} = \frac{10}{y}$ **16**

12. **Finance** Paul saves 10 cents of every dollar of his allowance. Paul's allowance is $2.50 a week. How much does he save each week? **$0.25**

Exercises

Independent Practice

Solve each proportion.

13. $\frac{3}{4} = \frac{9}{n}$ **12**
14. $\frac{8}{12} = \frac{a}{3}$ **2**
15. $\frac{10}{t} = \frac{15}{9}$ **6**
16. $\frac{5}{n} = \frac{6}{3}$ **2.5**

17. $\frac{n}{7} = \frac{18}{42}$ **3**
18. $\frac{2.6}{13} = \frac{8}{h}$ **40**
19. $\frac{8}{20} = \frac{30}{n}$ **75**
20. $\frac{12}{4} = \frac{y}{12}$ **36**

25. No; $7 \times 15 = 105$ and $8 \times 13 = 104$.

21. $\frac{5}{9} = \frac{n}{5.4}$ **3**
22. $\frac{21}{m} = \frac{10}{20}$ **42**
23. $\frac{1,200}{s} = \frac{6}{1}$ **200**
24. $\frac{0.1}{x} = \frac{3}{10}$ **$\frac{1}{3}$**

25. Do $\frac{7}{8}$ and $\frac{13}{15}$ form a proportion? Explain why or why not.

Mixed Review

26. Express 2,000,000 in scientific notation. *(Lesson 2-6)* **2.0×10^6**

27. **Statistics** The number of days that it rains each month in Cincinnati, Ohio, is recorded for a complete year with the following results: 12, 17, 9, 21, 15, 7, 14, 7, 15, 22, 14, 19. Construct a stem-and-leaf plot for this data. *(Lesson 3-6)* **See Solutions Manual.**

28. Solve $5t = 125$. *(Lesson 6-3)* **25**

29. **Consumer Math** Find the unit price for cheese that is sold in 12-ounce packages priced at $3.72. *(Lesson 11-2)* **$0.31 per ounce**

Problem Solving and Applications

30. **School Planning** Smallwood Middle School has 1,000 students, 40 teachers, and 5 administrators. If the school grows to 1,200 students and the ratios are maintained, find the number of teachers and administrators that will be needed. **48 teachers and 6 administrators**

Meeting Needs of Middle School Students

Have students and a family member choose a recipe that they cook at home. Have them list all the ingredients and then adjust the amounts so that the recipe will serve the entire class. Students can use this opportunity to work together with their parents to review customary units of measure such as teaspoons, tablespoons, cups, and ounces.

Additional Answer

1. Sample answer: They are equivalent if their cross products are equal.

Error Analysis

Watch for students who do not divide once they cross multiply to solve a proportion.

Prevent by reminding students that a proportion, being an equation, is not solved until the variable is alone on one side of the equals sign.

Close

Have students write and solve a proportion to find the number of people who voted for Ms. Gomez in a mayoral election, given that two-thirds of the 375 voters voted for her. **250**

3 PRACTICE/APPLY

Assignment Guide

Maximum: 13–34
Minimum: 13–25 odd, 26–33

For **Extra Practice**, see p. 595.

Alternate Assessment

Writing Have students write a problem for a classmate to solve that involves writing and solving a proportion.

Practice Masters, p. 93

Name _____ Date _____

Practice Worksheet 11-3

Proportions

Solve each proportion.

1. $\frac{9}{8} = \frac{12}{16}$ **6**
2. $\frac{3}{k} = \frac{5}{15}$ **9**
3. $\frac{18}{30} = \frac{r}{4}$ **2.4**

4. $\frac{2.8}{4} = \frac{7}{x}$ **10**
5. $\frac{r}{5} = \frac{65}{75}$ **$4\frac{1}{3}$**
6. $\frac{18}{m} = \frac{3}{36}$ **216**

7. $\frac{24}{13} = \frac{b}{26}$ **48**
8. $\frac{300}{24} = \frac{18}{j}$ **1.44**
9. $\frac{w}{5} = \frac{25}{1,000}$ **0.125**

10. $\frac{0.24}{a} = \frac{3}{9.6}$ **0.768**
11. $\frac{17}{8.5} = \frac{z}{0.01}$ **0.02**
12. $\frac{8}{45} = \frac{80}{q}$ **450**

13. $\frac{0.1}{8.2} = \frac{1.8}{a}$ **147.6**
14. $\frac{4.2}{b} = \frac{8}{5}$ **2.625**
15. $\frac{c}{5} = \frac{650}{6.5}$ **500**

16. Josh spends 40 cents out of every dollar on snacks, 14 cents out of every dollar on school supplies, and saves the rest. If Josh earns $32.00 per week cutting lawns, how much does he save per week? **$14.72**

31. Measurement Elmer uses an old spring scale to weigh his fish. The markings have rusted off the scale, but Elmer knows that a 3-pound fish pulls the spring down $1\frac{7}{8}$ inches. Today his fish pulled the spring down $3\frac{1}{2}$ inches. How much does his fish weigh? **5.6 pounds**

32. Nutrition For her health class Noelle must record what she eats for breakfast and compute the total number of calories consumed. Write and solve the proportions that you can use to find the number of calories in Noelle's breakfast. **See margin.**

Noelle's Breakfast
$\frac{1}{2}$ banana
6 oz orange juice
$\frac{3}{4}$ cup corn flakes
$\frac{1}{2}$ cup milk

Calories:

1 medium banana	100
8 oz orange juice	100
1 cup corn flakes	112
$\frac{3}{4}$ cup milk	126

33. Sample answer:

$\frac{2}{3} = \frac{6}{9}, \frac{4}{1} = \frac{8}{2},$

$\frac{1}{3} = \frac{2}{6}, \frac{1}{4} = \frac{2}{8}$

33. Critical Thinking Use the digits 1 through 9 to write as many proportions as possible. Each digit may be used only once in a proportion. The numbers that make up the proportion can consist of only one digit. For example, one proportion could be $\frac{1}{2} = \frac{3}{6}$.

34. Mathematics and Design Read the following paragraph.

> Throughout the ages, designers and architects have attempted to establish ideal proportions. The most famous of all principles about proportion was the **golden section** established by the ancient Greeks. According to this principle, a line segment can be separated into two parts so that the ratio of the shorter section to the longer section is equal to the ratio of the longer section to the whole line. This proportion is believed to be pleasing to the eye and has been used in the design of many buildings, both old and new, as well as sculptures and paintings.

Show the golden section by separating a line segment into two sections so that the ratio of the shorter section to the longer section is equal to the ratio of the longer section to the whole line. Label the line segment and write the proportion. **See students' work. The ratios should be about 2:3.**

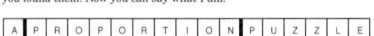
420

OPTIONS

Extending the Lesson

Mathematics and Design Ask students to explain why proportion is essential to both architecture and design. Have them imagine a room with furniture in it that is not in proportion to the rest of the room or house.

Cooperative Learning Activity

Left from the Start 11-3

Number of players: 2
Materials: Spinners, counters

- Copy onto a large sheet of paper (or several smaller sheets taped together) the game board shown on the back of this card. Make sure that a counter will fit inside each square. Label equal sections of a spinner "10," "12," "15," "20," "24," "30," "40," "60."

- Each partner places a counter on the "Start" square. One partner spins the spinner and substitutes the number on the spinner for x in the proportion $\frac{x}{15} = \frac{6}{y}$. Then the other partner spins the spinner and substitutes the number on the spinner for y in the proportion. Each partner solves the proportion and moves his or her spinner the number of spaces given by the missing value. The first partner to reach the "End" square wins the round.

Play several rounds.

Glencoe Mathematics: Applications and Connections, Course 2

11-3B Capture and Recapture

A Follow-Up of Lesson 11-3

Objective
Use the capture-recapture technique to estimate.

Materials
bowl
lima beans
marker

One method of estimating a population is the **capture-recapture** technique. Naturalists often use this method to monitor the population of animals and fish. In this lab, you will model this technique. Lima beans will represent deer and the bowl will represent the forest.

Try this!

Work in small groups.

- Fill a small bowl with dried lima beans.
- Grab a small handful of the beans. Count the number of beans selected. These represent the captured deer. Mark each bean selected with an X on both sides.
- Return the beans to the bowl and mix them in well with the rest.
- Grab another handful of beans from the bowl. Count the number of beans selected. This represents the number of deer recaptured. Count the number of beans marked with an X. This represents the number of tagged deer recaptured.
- Use the proportion shown below to estimate the total number of beans in the bowl.

$$\frac{\text{original number captured}}{\text{total population } (P)} = \frac{\text{tagged in sample}}{\text{recaptured}}$$

Record the value of *P*.
- Return the beans to the bowl.
- Repeat this process nine more times.

4. The sample needs to be a random

What do you think? handful of the total number of beans.

1. Do you think that a good estimate for the population *P* is the average of your ten estimates for *P*? **yes**
2. Do you think the population could be greater than any of your estimates? **yes**
3. Count the number of beans in the bowl. How does the actual count compare with your estimates? **Answers will vary.**
4. Why is it important to return the beans to the bowl and mix each time you repeat the experiment?
5. Why is it a good idea to base an estimate on several samples rather than just one sample? **Several samples will give more accurate estimates.**
6. What would happen to your estimate if some of the Xs wore off? How could something like this happen with deer? **decrease; lose tag; die**

Mathematics Lab 11-3B Capture and Recapture **421**

NCTM Standards: 1–7

Management Tips

For Students Have students take turns doing the different tasks: filling the bowl and removing, marking, and returning the beans; taking the remaining handfuls and counting marked beans; writing and solving each proportion; counting all the beans; and recording all results.

For the Overhead Projector
Overhead Manipulative Resources provides appropriate materials for teacher or student demonstration of the activities in this Mathematics Lab.

1 FOCUS

Introducing the Lab

Have students discuss what they know about the tagging of animals in the wild. Ask them what naturalists can hope to learn about the animals and how what they learn might be beneficial to both animals and people. Ask them how the capture-recapture process can give an estimate of the size of an animal population.

2 TEACH

Using Charts Have groups record their data in a chart, which can include a double-bar graph showing the difference between "tagged" beans and beans in each sample. Have each group present its findings to the class.

3 PRACTICE/APPLY

Using Critical Thinking Ask students what effect increasing the number of trials would have on the estimates. You may wish to have one group repeat the process 50 times to find out.

Close

Have students write a summary about how the activity simulates the capture-recapture process used by scientists.

OPTIONS

Lab Manual You may wish to make copies of the blackline master on p. 70 of the *Lab Manual* for students to use as a recording sheet.

Lab Manual, p. 70

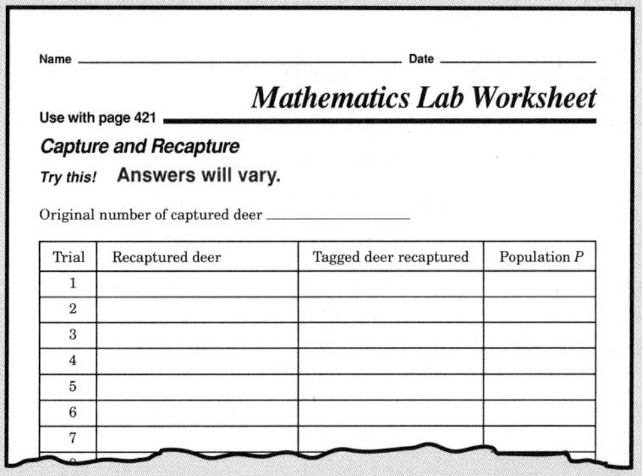

Name _____ Date _____

Mathematics Lab Worksheet

Use with page 421

Capture and Recapture

Try this! Answers will vary.

Original number of captured deer _____

Trial	Recaptured deer	Tagged deer recaptured	Population P
1			
2			
3			
4			
5			
6			
7			

11-4 **Similar Polygons**

NCTM Standards: 1–7, 9, 12, 13

Lesson Resources
- Study Guide Master 11-4
- Practice Master 11-4
- Enrichment Master 11-4
- Group Activity Card 11-4

 Transparency 11-4 contains the 5-Minute Check and a teaching aid for this lesson.

⏱ 5-Minute Check
(Over Lesson 11-3)

Solve each proportion.

1. $\frac{4}{9} = \frac{6}{n}$ $13\frac{1}{2}$

2. $\frac{n}{39} = \frac{2}{3}$ 26

3. $\frac{900}{600} = \frac{21}{n}$ 14

4. $\frac{12.5}{40} = \frac{2.5}{n}$ 8

5. Elena saves 15 cents on every dollar of her weekly allowance. She gets $5.00. How much does she save each week?
   $0.75

---

1 FOCUS

Motivating the Lesson

Situational Problem   Ask students how they would figure out how wide an enlargement of a photo is, if the original is 5 inches wide and 7 inches long and the enlargement is 21 inches long.

2 TEACH

Using Models   Students can use graph paper, rulers, and protractors to examine the properties of similar figures. Have them draw two right triangles, one with legs that measure 3 units and 4 units, and the other with legs that measure legs 9 units and 12 units. First have students measure all angles. Then ask them to measure each hypotenuse. Ask students what they can say about the measures of the corresponding angles and the ratio of the lengths of the two hypotenuses.

422

Objectives

Identify corresponding parts of similar polygons. Find missing measures by using lengths of corresponding sides.

Words to Learn

similar polygons

Jamie sizes and positions photos for the Menden Junior High Yearbook. She enlarges a photo that is 3 inches wide and 5 inches long. The enlargement is 6 inches wide and 10 inches long.

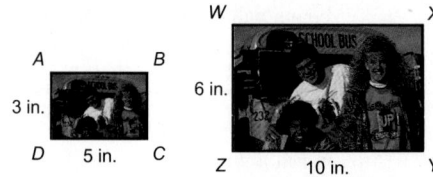

When you compare the dimensions of the photos, you get a proportion.

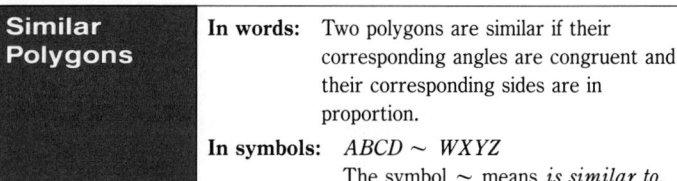

$$\frac{photo\ width}{enlargement\ width} \rightarrow \frac{3}{6} = \frac{5}{10} \leftarrow \frac{photo\ length}{enlargement\ length}$$

The photo and its enlargement are said to be **similar polygons.** Similar polygons have the same shape but may not have the same size.

Similar Polygons	**In words:** Two polygons are similar if their corresponding angles are congruent and their corresponding sides are in proportion.
	In symbols: $ABCD \sim WXYZ$ The symbol $\sim$ means *is similar to.*

Proportions are useful in finding the missing length of a side in any pair of similar polygons.

Example 1

If $\triangle ABC \sim \triangle DEF$, find the length of $\overline{DE}$.

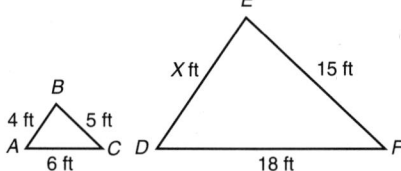

$\overline{AB}$ and $\overline{DE}$ are corresponding sides. $\overline{AC}$ and $\overline{DF}$ are corresponding sides. You can write a proportion using the measures of corresponding sides.

OPTIONS

Limited English Proficiency

Help students understand the distinction between "similar" as a mathematical term, and "similar" as it is commonly used in everyday speech. Have them add the term to their vocabulary list, along with a labeled example of two similar figures. You may also wish to have students help one another understand the meaning of corresponding parts by pointing to them in the similar figures.

$$\frac{\overline{AB}}{\overline{DE}} \to \frac{4}{x} = \frac{6}{18} \leftarrow \frac{\overline{AC}}{\overline{DF}}$$

$$4 \times 18 = 6x \qquad \textit{Find the cross products.}$$

4 ⊠ 18 ⊡ 6 ⊟ 12

$$x = 12 \qquad \text{The length of } \overline{DE} \text{ is 12 feet.}$$

Example 2

Rectangles A and B are similar. The ratio of rectangle B's width to rectangle A's width is 3:2. Rectangle A has a length of 24 inches and a width of 16 inches. What is the perimeter of rectangle B?

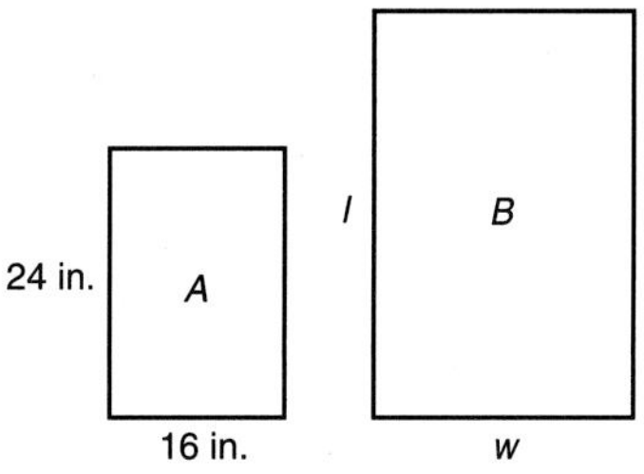

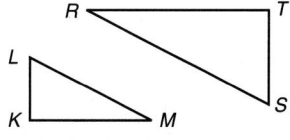

First use proportions to find the length ℓ and width w of rectangle B.

$$\begin{array}{l} \textit{length of B} \\ \textit{length of A} \end{array} \to \quad \frac{\ell}{24} = \frac{3}{2}$$

$$2\ell = 3 \times 24$$
$$2\ell = 72$$
$$\frac{2\ell}{2} = \frac{72}{2}$$
$$\ell = 36$$

$$\begin{array}{l} \textit{width of B} \\ \textit{width of A} \end{array} \to \quad \frac{w}{16} = \frac{3}{2}$$

$$2w = 3 \times 16$$
$$2w = 48$$
$$\frac{2w}{2} = \frac{48}{2}$$
$$w = 24$$

Now use the formula for the perimeter of a rectangle.

$$\begin{aligned} P &= 2\ell + 2w \\ &= 2(36) + 2(24) \qquad \textit{Substitute 36 for } \ell \textit{ and 24 for w.} \\ &= 72 + 48 \\ &= 120 \end{aligned}$$

The perimeter of rectangle B is 120 inches.

Checking for Understanding

Communicating Mathematics

Read and study the lesson to answer each question.

1. **Draw** two rectangles whose corresponding sides have measures in the ratio 3 to 1. **See students' work.**

2. **Write** the pairs of sides that correspond in similar triangles *KLM* and *TSR* shown at the right. $\overline{LK}$ and $\overline{ST}$, $\overline{KM}$ and $\overline{TR}$, $\overline{ML}$ and $\overline{RS}$

3. **Tell** the difference between similar polygons and congruent polygons. **See margin.**

Lesson 11-4 Geometry Connection: Similar Polygons **423**

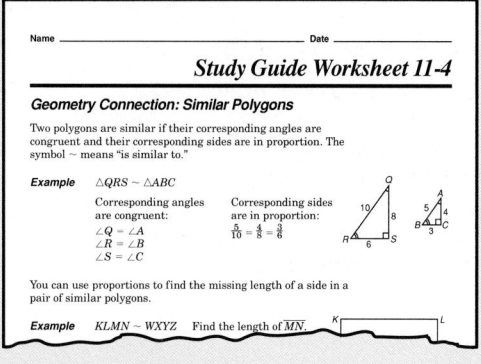

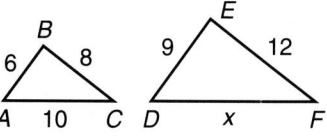
423

Error Analysis

Watch for students who incorrectly identify corresponding sides of the figures, and thus write a wrong proportion.

Prevent by having students develop a consistent way, such as using hash marks, to label corresponding sides according to which lengths are known.

Close

Have students draw and label the lengths of the sides of a pair of similar figures providing all but one length. Students should exchange papers and find the missing length.

3 PRACTICE/APPLY

Assignment Guide
Maximum: 9–23
Minimum: 9–17 odd, 18–23

For **Extra Practice,** see p. 595.

Alternate Assessment

Speaking Have students explain the concept of similar figures, identifying the relationship between corresponding parts.

Practice Masters, p. 94

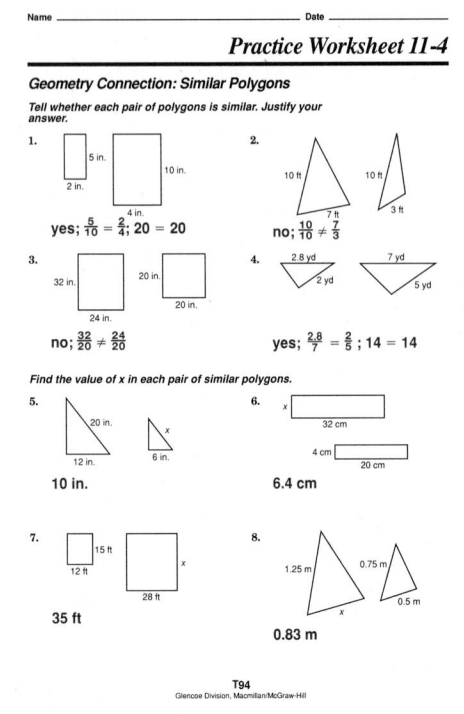

Guided Practice Tell whether each pair of polygons is similar. Justify your answer.

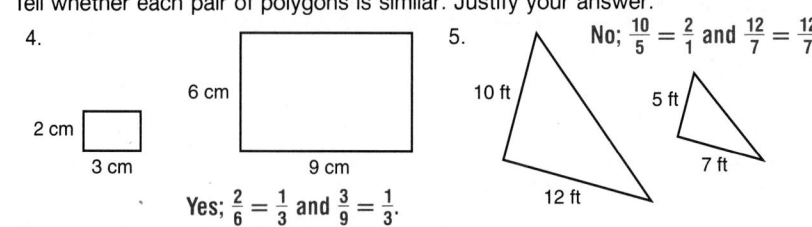

4.   6 cm / 2 cm / 3 cm / 9 cm

5.   10 ft / 5 ft / 12 ft / 7 ft   No; $\frac{10}{5} = \frac{2}{1}$ and $\frac{12}{7} = \frac{12}{7}$.

Yes; $\frac{2}{6} = \frac{1}{3}$ and $\frac{3}{9} = \frac{1}{3}$.

Find the value of x in each pair of similar polygons.

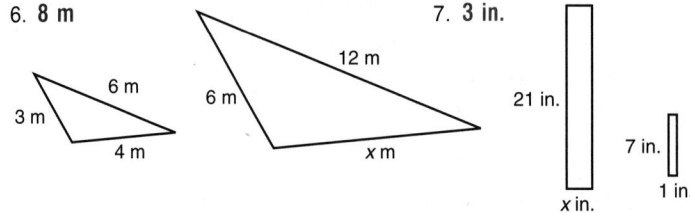

6. **8 m** / 6 m / 3 m / 4 m / 12 m / 6 m / x m

7. **3 in.** / 21 in. / 7 in. / 1 in. / x in.

8. Triangles A and B are similar. The ratio of a side of triangle B to a corresponding side of triangle A is 5:3. The sides of triangle A measure 18 feet, 27 feet, and 30 feet. Find the perimeter of triangle B. **125 feet**

Exercises

Independent Practice Tell whether each pair of polygons is similar. Justify your answer.

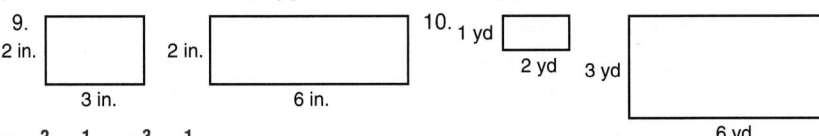

9.   2 in. / 2 in. / 3 in. / 6 in.

No; $\frac{2}{2} = \frac{1}{1}$ and $\frac{3}{6} = \frac{1}{2}$.

10. 1 yd / 2 yd / 3 yd / 6 yd

Yes; $\frac{1}{3}$ and $\frac{2}{6} = \frac{1}{3}$.

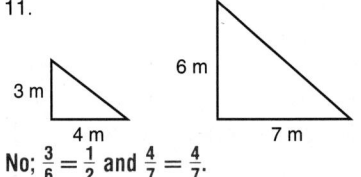

11.   3 m / 4 m / 6 m / 7 m

No; $\frac{3}{6} = \frac{1}{2}$ and $\frac{4}{7} = \frac{4}{7}$.

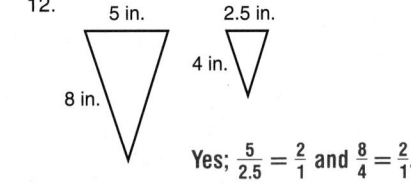

12.   5 in. / 2.5 in. / 4 in. / 8 in.

Yes; $\frac{5}{2.5} = \frac{2}{1}$ and $\frac{8}{4} = \frac{2}{1}$.

Find the value of x in each pair of similar polygons.

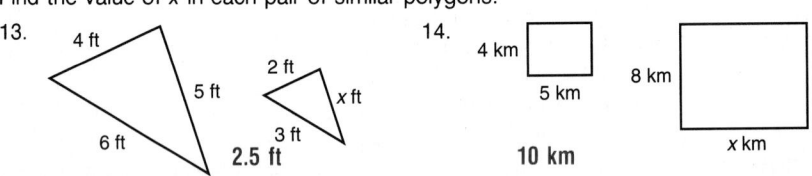

13.   4 ft / 5 ft / 6 ft / 2.5 ft / 2 ft / x ft / 3 ft

14.   4 km / 5 km / 10 km / 8 km / x km

Name _____   Date _____

Practice Worksheet 11-4

Geometry Connection: Similar Polygons

Tell whether each pair of polygons is similar. Justify your answer.

1.   5 in. / 2 in. / 10 in. / 4 in.
yes; $\frac{5}{10} = \frac{2}{4}$; 20 = 20

2.   10 ft / 10 ft / 7 ft / 3 ft
no; $\frac{10}{10} \neq \frac{7}{3}$

3.   32 in. / 20 in. / 24 in. / 20 in.
no; $\frac{32}{20} \neq \frac{24}{20}$

4.   2.8 yd / 2 yd / 7 yd / 5 yd
yes; $\frac{2.8}{7} = \frac{2}{5}$; 14 = 14

Find the value of x in each pair of similar polygons.

5.   20 in. / 12 in. / x / 6 in.
10 in.

6. x / 32 cm / 4 cm / 20 cm
6.4 cm

7.   15 ft / 12 ft / x / 28 ft
35 ft

8.   1.25 m / 0.75 m / 0.5 m / x
0.83 m

T94
Glencoe Division, Macmillan/McGraw-Hill

OPTIONS

Bell Ringer

There are three seventh grade classes. Class A has 12 boys and 15 girls, class B has 33 students, of which 18 are girls, and class C has 22 students, with two more girls than boys. Ask students which two classes have identical boy-girl ratios.   classes B and C

15.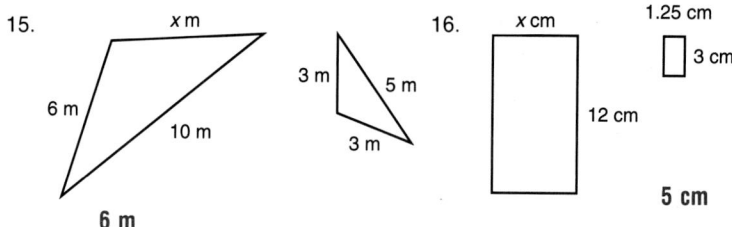

16.

17. Rectangles F and G are similar. The ratio of rectangle F's width to rectangle G's width is 2:3. The length of rectangle F is 15 inches and its width is 10 inches. Find the perimeter of rectangle G. **75 inches**

Mixed Review 18. **Physical Fitness** Heather does 47 sit-ups in 98 seconds. Estimate the number of seconds it takes her to do one sit-up. *(Lesson 1-3)*
about 2 seconds

19. **Statistics** Takeo surveyed 50 of his classmates to find out their favorite winter sport. Which sport was the most popular? *(Lesson 3-1)* **skiing**

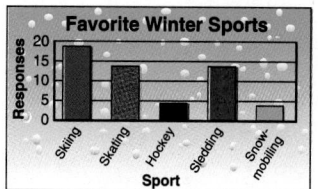

20. Solve $\frac{15}{32} = \frac{5}{p}$. *(Lesson 11-3)* $10\frac{2}{3}$

Problem Solving and Applications 21. **Photography** Juana wants to have an enlargement made of a photo she took at the Grand Canyon. The negative is 1.5 centimeters by 2.2 centimeters. What will be the perimeter of the enlargement if its width is 22 centimeters? Solve mentally. **74 cm**

22. **Measurement** Sara's shadow is 60 inches long. A nearby bush casts a shadow 40 inches long. If Sara is 48 inches tall, what is the height of the bush? **32 inches**

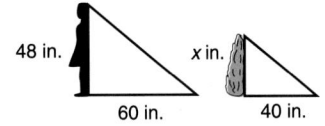

23. **Critical Thinking**
    a. Copy and complete this table.

	Length	Width	Perimeter	Area
Rectangle I	5	3	?	?
Rectangle II	20	12	?	?

16 units   15 units²
64 units   240 units²

   b. Compute $\frac{\text{length I}}{\text{length II}}$, $\frac{\text{perimeter I}}{\text{perimeter II}}$, and $\frac{\text{area I}}{\text{area II}}$. $\frac{1}{4}, \frac{1}{4}, \frac{1}{16}$

   c. What pattern do you see? **ratio of length × ratio of perimeter = ratio of area**

   d. Does your pattern apply to the rectangles in Example 2? Explain.
   Yes; see margin.

Lesson 11-4 Geometry Connection: Similar Polygons **425**

Additional Answer

23d. $\frac{\text{length A}}{\text{length B}} = \frac{24}{36} = \frac{2}{3}$;

$\frac{\text{perimeter A}}{\text{perimeter B}} = \frac{80}{120} = \frac{2}{3}$;

$\frac{\text{area A}}{\text{area B}} = \frac{384}{864} = \frac{4}{9} = \left(\frac{2}{3}\right)^2$

Extending the Lesson

Art Have students work with partners. Each draws a polygon on graph paper. The figure can have any shape and any number of sides. The partner must draw a figure similar to it.

Cooperative Learning Activity

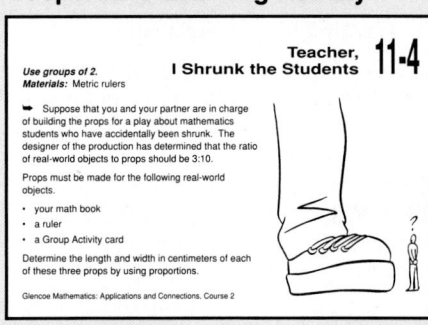

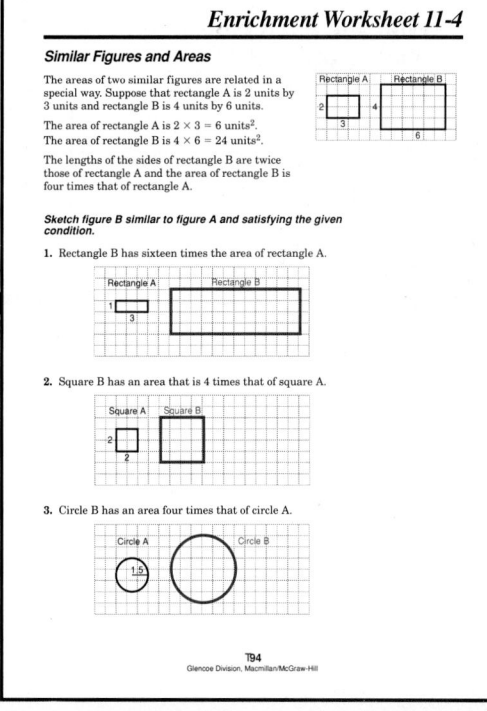

Use groups of 2.
Materials: Metric rulers

Teacher, **I Shrunk the Students** **11-4**

➤ Suppose that you and your partner are in charge of building the props for a play about mathematics students who have accidentally been shrunk. The designer of the production has determined that the ratio of real-world objects to props should be 3:10.

Props must be made for the following real-world objects.

• your math book
• a ruler
• a Group Activity card

Determine the length and width in centimeters of each of these three props by using proportions.

Glencoe Mathematics: Applications and Connections, Course 2

🕐 5-Minute Check
(Over Lesson 11-4)

Tell whether each pair of polygons is similar. Justify your answer.

1.

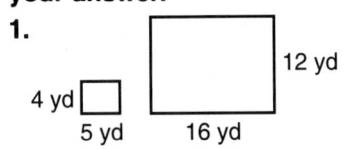

12 yd

4 yd

5 yd   16 yd

no; $\frac{4}{12} = \frac{1}{3}$ and $\frac{5}{16} \neq \frac{1}{3}$

2. In the triangles below, the corresponding angles are congruent.

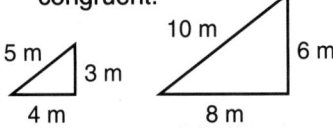

10 m

5 m   3 m   6 m

4 m   8 m

yes; Corresponding sides are proportional.

Find x in each pair of similar polygons.

3.

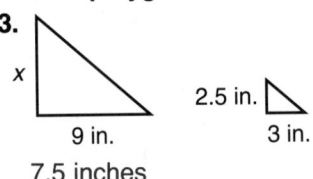

x

2.5 in.

9 in.   3 in.

7.5 inches

4.

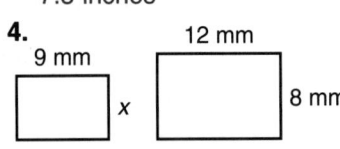

9 mm   12 mm

x   8 mm

6 millimeters

426

11-5 Scale Drawings

Objective

Solve problems involving scale drawings.

Words to Learn

scale drawing

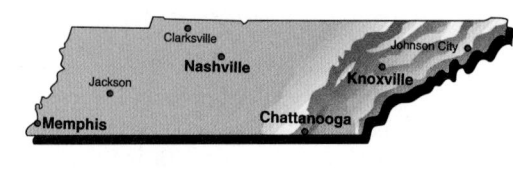

Jack and Jessie Anderson are planning a trip from Knoxville to Memphis to attend a family reunion. A map of Tennessee is shown below. The scale of the map is 1 inch:152 miles. The distance between Knoxville and Memphis on the map is $2\frac{1}{4}$ inches. What is the actual distance between Knoxville and Memphis?

1 inch = 152 miles

A map is an example of a scale drawing. A **scale drawing** is used to present something that is too large or too small to be conveniently drawn to actual size.

The scale on a map is the ratio of the distance on the map of the actual distance. When you know the scale of a map, you can find actual distances by writing and solving proportions.

Example 1 *Problem Solving*

Geography   Refer to the problem in the lesson introduction. Find the actual distance between Knoxville and Memphis.

Let n represent the actual distance between the cities. Write and solve a proportion.

$$\begin{array}{l} map\ distance \\ actual\ distance \end{array} \rightarrow \frac{1\ inch}{152\ miles} = \frac{2\frac{1}{4}\ inches}{n} \leftarrow \begin{array}{l} map\ distance \\ actual\ distance \end{array}$$

$$1 \times n = 2\frac{1}{4} \times 152$$

$$n = 342$$

The actual distance between Knoxville and Memphis is 342 miles.

“When am I ever going to use this?”

If your family is planning to travel this summer, you will probably use a map to help you get to your destination. You can find out how many miles you will be traveling by using the scale on the map and writing a proportion.

OPTIONS

Multicultural Education

Evelyn Boyd Granville and Marjorie Lee Browne were the first African-American women to earn doctorates in mathematics. Both received their Ph.D. degrees in 1949, Granville from Yale University, and Browne from Howard University.

Example 2 *Problem Solving*

Decorating   A building is 275 feet long. On a scale drawing, 1 inch represents 25 feet. What is the length of the building in the scale drawing?

Let ℓ represent the length of the building in the scale drawing.

$$\begin{array}{ccc} \frac{scale}{actual} & \to & \dfrac{1 \text{ in.}}{25 \text{ ft}} = \dfrac{\ell \text{ in.}}{275 \text{ ft}} \quad \leftarrow \quad \frac{scale}{actual} \end{array}$$

$$1 \times 275 = 25\,\ell \qquad \textit{Find the cross products.}$$

$$275 \;[\div]\; 25 \;[=]\; \boxed{11}$$

$$11 = \ell$$

On the scale drawing, the building will be 11 inches long.

Mini-Lab

Work with a partner.

Materials: measuring tape, $\frac{1}{4}$-inch graph paper, ruler

- Use the measuring tape to find the length of each wall, door, window, and chalkboard in your classroom.

- Round each length to the nearest inch. Record the lengths.

- On a sheet of grid paper, make a scale drawing of your classroom like the one above. Use $\frac{1}{4}$ inch:12 inches as the scale.

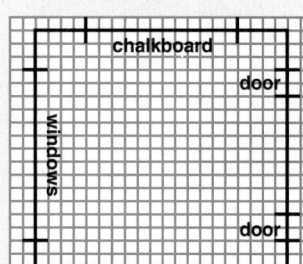

Talk About It

a. What proportion did you use to find the length of the chalkboard on your scale drawing?   **Answers will vary.**

b. Describe how a scale drawing with $\frac{1}{4}$ inch:24 inch would differ from your scale drawing with $\frac{1}{4}$ inch:12 inch.

b. The first scale drawing would be half as large.

Lesson 11-5 Application: Scale Drawings   **427**

427

Error Analysis

Watch for students who do not set up proportions correctly.

Prevent by having the students label the units to make sure that the numerators and denominators of both ratios have their dimensions in the same relative positions.

Close

Have students explain how they can use proportions to find missing lengths of similar figures.

3 PRACTICE/APPLY

Assignment Guide
Maximum: 11–28
Minimum: 11–23 odd, 24–28
All: Mid-Chapter Review

For **Extra Practice,** see p. 596.

Alternate Assessment

Writing Have students use a road atlas and its map scale to write a proportion problem. It should involve finding either a map distance or the actual distance.

Practice Masters, p. 95

Name _____ Date _____

Practice Worksheet 11-5

Application: Scale Drawings

On a map, the scale is 1 inch:150 miles. For each map distance, find the actual distance.

1. 3 inches
450 miles

2. 8 inches
1,200 miles

3. $\frac{3}{4}$ inch
112.5 miles

4. $1\frac{5}{8}$ inches
$243\frac{3}{4}$ miles

5. $3\frac{1}{2}$ inches
525 miles

6. $\frac{1}{4}$ inch
$37\frac{1}{2}$ miles

On a scale drawing, the scale is $\frac{1}{4}$ inch:1 foot. Find the dimensions of each room in the scale drawing.

7. 15 feet by 25 feet
$3\frac{3}{4}$ in. by $6\frac{1}{4}$ in.

8. 20 feet by 12 feet
5 in. by 3 in.

9. 10 feet by 9 feet
$2\frac{1}{2}$ in. by $2\frac{1}{4}$ in.

10. 14 feet by 14 feet
$3\frac{1}{2}$ in. by $3\frac{1}{2}$ in.

11. 8 feet by 14 feet
2 in. by $3\frac{1}{2}$ in.

12. 28 feet by 18 feet
7 in. by $4\frac{1}{2}$ in.

13. On a scale drawing, 1 centimeter represents 4 meters. What length on the drawing would be used to represent 6.5 meters?
1.625 centimeters

14. On a scale drawing, 1 inch represents 8 feet. What are the dimensions on the scale drawing that represent a 32 feet by 24 feet room? **4 in. by 3 in.**

T95
Glencoe Division, Macmillan/McGraw-Hill

428

Checking for Understanding

Communicating Mathematics

Read and study the lesson to answer each question.

1. **Tell,** in your own words, what a scale drawing is. **See margin.**

2. **Draw** a scale drawing of your bedroom on $\frac{1}{4}$-inch graph paper. Use $\frac{1}{4}$ inch:12 inches as the scale. Include the closet(s), the window(s), and the door(s) in your drawing. **See students' work.**

3. **Tell** what important information must be given on a scale drawing in order to use it. **the scale**

Guided Practice

Find the actual distance between each pair of cities, given the map distance. Use the scale 1 inch:152 miles.

4. Chattanooga and Memphis, $1\frac{3}{4}$ inches **266 miles**

5. Knoxville and Chattanooga, $\frac{3}{4}$ inch **114 miles**

6. **Geography** Choose two cities in Tennessee, using the map on page 426. Find the actual distance between them. **See students' work.**

Find the length of each object on a drawing with the given scale.

7. a room whose length is 50 feet; 1 inch:2 feet **25 inches**

8. a window whose height is 30 inches; $\frac{1}{2}$ inch:6 inches **$2\frac{1}{2}$ inches**

9. a car that is 135 inches long; $\frac{1}{4}$ inch:2 feet **$1\frac{13}{32}$ inches**

10. **Structural Engineering** The longest suspension bridge in the United States is the Verrazano-Narrows Bridge connecting Staten Island and Brooklyn, New York. Its length is 4,260 feet. On a scale drawing, 1 inch represents 60 feet. Find the length of the bridge in the scale drawing. **71 inches**

Exercises

Independent Practice

On a map, the scale is 1 inch:120 miles. For each map distance, find the actual distance.

11. 4 inches **480 mi**
12. $2\frac{1}{2}$ inches **300 mi**
13. $\frac{7}{8}$ inch **105 mi**
14. $4\frac{3}{8}$ inches **525 mi**

15. $3\frac{1}{4}$ inches **390 mi**
16. $\frac{1}{2}$ inch **60 mi**
17. $\frac{1}{4}$ inch **30 mi**
18. $5\frac{3}{4}$ inches **690 mi**

19. On a scale drawing, 1 centimeter represents 2 meters. What length on the drawing would be used to represent 3.2 meters? **1.6 cm**

On a scale drawing, the scale is $\frac{1}{2}$ inch:1 foot. Find the dimensions of each room in the scale drawing.

20. 30 feet by 20 feet **15 in. by 10 in.**
21. 18 feet by 12 feet **9 in. by 6 in.**

22. 15 feet by 7 feet **$7\frac{1}{2}$ in. by $3\frac{1}{2}$ in.**
23. 10 feet by 11 feet **5 in. by $5\frac{1}{2}$ in.**

428 Chapter 11 Ratio, Proportion, and Percent

OPTIONS

Gifted and Talented Needs

Provide small groups of students with a road map of your state. Have them play a game in which one student chooses two towns on the map that the others have to find given certain clues. These should include either the map distance or actual distance between the towns.

Additional Answer

1. Sample answer: It is a small drawing that is in the same proportion as a larger drawing or object.

24. Express $\frac{144}{180}$ in simplest form. *(Lesson 4-6)* $\frac{4}{5}$

25. **Stock Market** A particular stock on the New York Stock Exchange lost a total of 6 points over a period of 2 days. What was the change in points per day? *(Lesson 7-8)* **3 points per day**

26. **Geometry** Tell whether the polygons at the right are similar. *(Lesson 11-4)* **no**

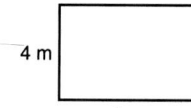
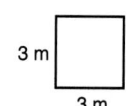

27. **Horticulture** Ms. Lee wants to plant some flowers and bushes in her front yard. The width of her yard is 40 feet, and the length is 35 feet.

    a. Draw a scale drawing of her yard using a scale of $\frac{1}{2}$ inch:5 feet.

    b. Assuming she has nothing in her front yard right now, use your scale drawing and your creativity to come up with a design for her front yard.

27a-b. See students' work.

28. **Critical Thinking** A computer chip measures $\frac{1}{2}$ inch by $\frac{3}{8}$ inch. A scale drawing of the chip measures 6 inches by $4\frac{1}{2}$ inches. What is the scale of the drawing? **1 foot : 1 inch**

---

11 Assessment: Mid-Chapter Review

Write each ratio as a fraction in simplest form. *(Lesson 11-1)*

1. 12:60 $\frac{1}{5}$ 2. 36 to 4 $\frac{9}{1}$ 3. 120:35 $\frac{24}{7}$ 4. $\frac{72}{64}$ $\frac{9}{8}$

Express each rate as a unit rate. *(Lesson 11-2)*

5. $2.38 for 2 pounds **$1.19 per pound**   6. 640 miles in 5 hours **128 mph**

7. 18 inches over 3 days **6 inches per day**   8. $350 in 5 days **$70 per day**

Solve each proportion. *(Lesson 11-3)*

9. $\frac{x}{9} = \frac{48}{36}$ **12**   10. $\frac{15}{n} = \frac{3}{1}$ **5**   11. $\frac{15}{5} = \frac{x}{20}$ **60**

Find the value of x in each pair of similar polygons. *(Lesson 11-4)*

12.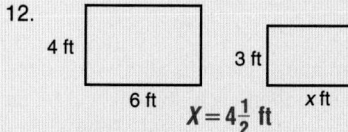

    $X = 4\frac{1}{2}$ ft

13.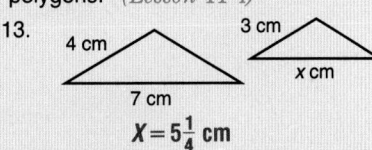

    $X = 5\frac{1}{4}$ cm

On a scale drawing, the scale is 1 inch:4 feet. Find the length of each object on the scale drawing. *(Lesson 11-5)*

14. a desk 60 inches long $1\frac{1}{4}$ inches   15. a car 10 feet long $2\frac{1}{2}$ inches

Lesson 11-5 Application: Scale Drawings   **429**

Extending the Lesson

At Home Have students measure the size of a room in their home, including the major pieces of furniture in it. Have them choose a reasonable scale and make a scale drawing of the room on grid paper.

Cooperative Learning Activity

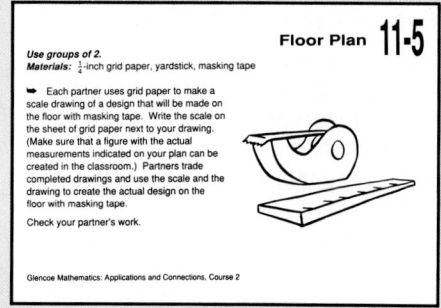

Floor Plan **11-5**

Use groups of 2.
Materials: $\frac{1}{4}$-inch grid paper, yardstick, masking tape

➤ Each partner uses grid paper to make a scale drawing of a design that will be made on the floor with masking tape. Write the scale on the sheet of grid paper next to your drawing. (Make sure that a figure with the actual measurements indicated on your plan can be created in the classroom.) Partners trade completed drawings and use the scale and the drawing to create the actual design on the floor with masking tape.

Check your partner's work.

Glencoe Mathematics: Applications and Connections, Course 2

Enrichment Masters, p. 95

Name _____   Date _____

Enrichment Worksheet 11-5

Scale Drawings

Use the scale drawings of two different apartments to answer the questions.

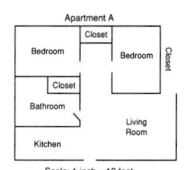
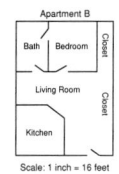

1. Which apartment has the greater area? **Apartment B**

2. What is the difference in square feet between Apartment A and Apartment B? **48 ft²**

3. How much more closet space is offered by Apartment B than Apartment A? **40 ft²**

4. How much more bathroom space is offered by Apartment B than Apartment A? **6 ft²**

5. A one-year lease for Apartment A costs $450 per month. A one-year lease for Apartment B costs $525 per month. Which apartment offers the greatest value in terms of the cost per square foot? **Apartment A**

T95
Glencoe Division, Macmillan/McGraw-Hill

11-6 Draw a Diagram

NCTM Standards: 1–5, 7

Lesson Resources
- Study Guide Master 11-6
- Practice Master 11-6
- Enrichment Master 11-6
- Group Activity Card 11-6

 Transparency 11-6 contains the 5-Minute Check and a teaching aid for this lesson.

🕐 5-Minute Check
(Over Lesson 11-5)

On a map, the scale is 1 inch : 150 miles. For each map distance, find the actual distance.

1. 5 inches   750 miles
2. $3\frac{1}{2}$ inches   525 miles
3. $2\frac{3}{4}$ inches   412.5 miles

On a scale drawing, the scale is $\frac{1}{4}$ inch : 1 foot. Find the dimensions of each room in the scale drawing.

4. 20 feet by 25 feet
   5 inches by $6\frac{1}{4}$ inches
5. 16 feet by 12 feet
   4 inches by 3 inches

---

1 FOCUS

Motivating the Lesson

Situational Problem Tell students to suppose that there is going to be a single-elimination chess tournament with 32 entrants. Ask them to figure out how many matches must be played to determine a winner.

2 TEACH

Using Problem Solving
Discuss how drawing diagrams can be an effective strategy for solving problems. Ask students to suggest the sorts of people who might use this strategy to do their jobs. Ask them to describe situations in which they or other family members have drawn diagrams to solve problems that have come up in their daily lives.

430

Objective

Solve problems by drawing a diagram.

The Science Club at Crestview Middle School is planning an end-of-year picnic at Whetstone Park. If it looks like it will rain, the picnic will be rescheduled for the following weekend. The club president decides to set up a "telephone tree" so that everyone in the club will be notified quickly in the event that the picnic has to be rescheduled. The club president plans to call three members and have each of them call three other members and so on. If each phone call takes 1 minute, how long will it take to notify all 40 members of the club?

Explore   What do you know?
Each person will call 3 people and each phone call will take 1 minute. There are 40 members in the club. A hidden assumption is that there will be no busy signals.

What do you need to find?
You need to find how long it will take to notify all 40 members.

Plan   Make a diagram of the phone calls.
Count the number of minutes.

Solve   Use an "o" to stand for each person who is called.

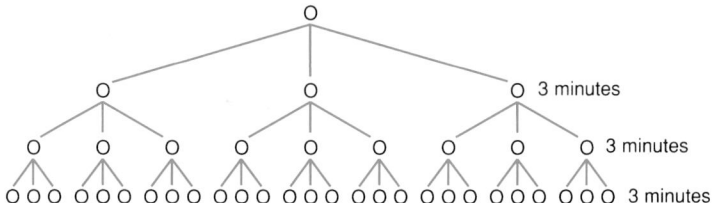

The diagram above includes all 40 members. If each call takes 1 minute, then each student will be on the phone 3×1, or 3 minutes. Each level of the diagram, then, represents 3 minutes. All the students can be notified in $3 + 3 + 3$, or 9 minutes.

Examine $3 \times 3 = 9$ ✓   The answer checks.

OPTIONS

Reteaching Activity

Using Problem Solving Provide problems that can be solved with simple diagrams and that involve relatively small numbers. If necessary, help students choose and begin their diagrams.

Study Guide Masters, p. 96

Name _____ Date _____

Study Guide Worksheet 11-6

Problem-Solving Strategy: Draw a Diagram

A group of six people assemble for a meeting. Each person shakes hands with each other person at the meeting. How many handshakes are there in all?

Explore   What do you know?
There are 6 people in the group. Each person shakes hands with each other person.

What do you need to find?
You need to find the total number of handshakes.

Plan   Make a diagram. Draw a dot for each person and then use lines to show each handshake.

Solve   There are 15 lines. The total number of handshakes in a group of 6 people is 15.

Examine   If one person shakes hands with each of the other...

Juan and Diego are brothers sharing the same bedroom. Juan's alarm is set for 6:30 A.M., and it has a snooze alarm that goes off every 9 minutes. Diego's alarm is set for 6:50 A.M., and its snooze alarm goes off every 5 minutes. If both Juan and Diego hit the snooze alarm several times in one morning, at what time would both alarms go off at the same time?

Explore What do you know?
Juan's alarm is set for 6:30 A.M. and has a snooze alarm that goes off every 9 minutes. Diego's alarm is set for 6:50 A.M. and has a snooze alarm that goes off every 5 minutes.

What do you need to find?
You need to find when the two alarms will go off at the same time.

Plan Draw a diagram that includes the times that the alarms go off. The solution will be the time when both alarms go off at the same time.

Solve

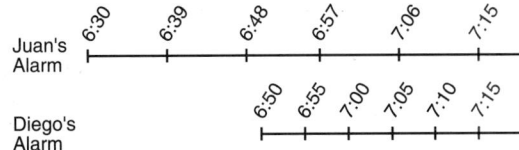

Both alarms will go off at 7:15 A.M.

Examine The number of minutes from 6:30 to 7:15 is 45. 45 is a multiple of 9.

The number of minutes from 6:50 to 7:15 is 25. 25 is a multiple of 5.

Checking for Understanding

Communicating Mathematics

1. **Tell** at what time Juan's and Diego's alarm clocks will go off together if Diego's snooze alarm went off every 4 minutes. **7:06 A.M.**

2. **Write** one or two sentences explaining why a diagram can be a useful strategy in solving problems. **See margin.**

Lesson 11-6 Problem-Solving Strategy: Draw a Diagram   **431**

Bell Ringer

Zack and Inez are building rectangular rabbit cages. Each has 24 feet of fencing in 1-foot segments. Zack wants to build a cage to enclose the largest possible area and Inez wants her cage to enclose the least amount of space that is at least 2 feet wide. Ask students what the difference will be in the areas of their cages.   16 square feet

Additional Answer

2. Answers will vary. Sample answer: It is often easier to solve a problem by drawing a diagram than by writing an equation or solving mentally.

More Examples

For the Example

From Al's campsite, Spruce Trail goes north 3 miles to Beaver Creek, then east 1.5 miles to Lone Rock. Next, it winds north 2 miles to Wilson Falls, then southeast 4.25 miles to Bain's Bridge. Then it ends 2.75 miles southwest. Al walked 7 miles. Which landmark was he closest to?   Wilson Falls

Teaching Tip Guide students to see that different kinds of diagrams can be used to solve problems. Encourage them to use their imagination when choosing a diagram.

Checking for Understanding

Exercises 1–2 are designed to help you assess students' understanding through reading, writing, speaking, and modeling. You should work through these exercises with your students and then monitor their work on Guided Practice Exercises 3–4.

Practice Masters, p. 96

Name _____ Date _____

Practice Worksheet 11-6

Problem-Solving Strategy: Draw a Diagram

Solve by drawing a diagram.

1. Coach Williams wants to schedule a round-robin tournament (every student plays every other student) for his chess club. If there are seven club members, how many games should the coach schedule?   **21**

2. After a little-league baseball game, each player must shake hands with every player on the opposing team. If each team has 12 members, how many handshakes are there?   **144**

Solve. Use any strategy.

3. Larue's parents loaned him money to buy a video game entertainment system for $129 along with three games for $39 each. Larue paid them back monthly by mowing lawns. If it took him one year to pay them back, how much did he pay each month?   **$20.50**

4. Ms. Bosco's class started a six-day problem-solving contest. Each day only students who solve the previous day's problem correctly are allowed to participate. There are 32 students in the class. If only half the students get a problem right on any day, how many students can participate on the fourth day?   **4**

5. State the pattern. Then complete the sequence. 324, 329, 325, 330, 326, ___, ___, ___
    Add five, subtract four, add five, subtract 4, etc. 331, 327, 332

6. The product of two consecutive positive numbers is 2,652. What are the numbers?   **51, 52**

7. Carolyn, Linda, Cameron, and Shelli went to see a movie. Cameron did not sit next to Linda and Shelli sat on the right. If Linda sat to the left of Carolyn, who sat to the left of Shelli?   **Cameron**

8. A train leaves Union Station every 20 minutes. How many trains left the station after four hours?   **13**

Have students write a problem that classmates can solve by drawing a simple diagram, such as a map.

3 PRACTICE/APPLY

Assignment Guide
Maximum: 5–12
Minimum: 5–12

Alternate Assessment

Writing   Have students prepare the diagram for the following problem. *Jack's house, the post office, the bank, and the library are on the same road. Jack lives 3.5 miles from the library, which is 2.25 miles further from his house than the bank. The post office is between the bank and the library and 0.75 miles from the bank. How far is it from Jack's house to the post office?*

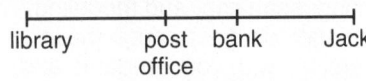

library   post   bank   Jack
             office

2 miles

Enrichment Masters, p. 96

Name _____ Date _____

Enrichment Worksheet 11-6

Making Diagrams

Diagrams are useful tools. For example, if three people in a room shake hands with each other, how many handshakes occur?

The diagram at the right shows that *A* shakes hands with *B* and *C*, and *B* shakes hands with *C*. All other handshakes are duplicates. There are three handshakes in all.

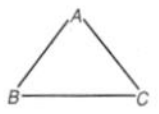

Solve each problem. Draw a diagram as needed.

1. There are four people in a room. If each person shakes hands with each other, how many handshakes occur?
   6

2. There are five people in a room. If each person shakes hands with each other, how many handshakes occur?
   10

3. There are six people in a room. If each person shakes hands with each other, how many handshakes occur?
   15

4. There are twenty people in a room. If each person shakes hands with each other, how many handshakes occur? (Hint: Find a pattern by using your answers above.)
   190

5. After ten people were seated for dinner at a round table, each person shook hands with the person immediately to the left and to the right. After dinner, each person shook hands with everyone except the people with whom they shook hands previously. How many handshakes occurred after dinner?
   35

T96
Glencoe Division, Macmillan/McGraw-Hill

Guided Practice   Solve by drawing a diagram.

3. A shuttle bus at Cedar Point Amusement Park holds 30 passengers. It starts out empty and picks up 1 passenger at the first stop, 2 passengers at the second stop, 3 at the third stop, and so on. After how many stops will the bus be full? **after 7 stops; For diagram, see students' work.**

4. After a student council meeting, each of the five members shook hands with each other. How many handshakes were there in all? **10 handshakes; For diagram, see students' work.**

Exercises

Practice   Solve. Use any strategy.

5. Marie buys T-shirts for $12.95 and gym shorts for $6.99. She spends a total of $72.77. How many of each did she buy? **4 T-shirts and 3 gym shorts**

Strategies
● ● ● ● ● ● ● ● ●
Look for a pattern.
Solve a simpler problem.
Act it out.
Guess and check.
Draw a diagram.
Make a chart.
Work backward.

6. An airplane flew 6,000 miles in 12 hours. What was its rate? **b**
   a. 72,000 mph   b. 500 mph   c. 6,262 mph

7. Estrella mails a recipe to four of her friends. Each of the four friends mails the recipe to four of their friends and so on. How many recipes are in the fifth mailing? **1,024 recipes**

8. Sixteen softball teams are participating in a single-elimination contest; that is, only the winners of each game go on to play the next game. How many games will the winning team have played? **4 games**

9. Chairs are to be set up in a meeting room so that each row has 1 more chair than the previous row. This way, none of the chairs will be directly behind another.

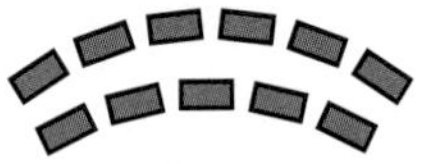

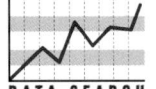

If there are 5 chairs in the first row, how many chairs will be in the sixth row? **10 chairs**

10. Some people are involved in more than one type.

DATA SEARCH

10. **Data Search**   Refer to page 652. Why do the percentages of population involved in each type of gardening in 1990 not add to 100%?

11. Marla has a total of 44 compact discs and cassette tapes. If she has three times as many compact discs as tapes, how many of each does she have?

11. 11 tapes and 33 compact discs

12. A ball is dropped from 10 feet above ground. It hits the ground and bounces up half as high as it fell.

   a. What is the height of the ball after the fourth bounce? $\frac{5}{8}$ **ft**

   b. What is the total up and down distance the ball has traveled when it hits the ground the fifth time? $28\frac{3}{4}$ **feet or 345 inches**

OPTIONS

Extending the Lesson

Provide partners with a street map of a neighborhood. Have them imagine that a treasure is buried on one of the street corners. Have the pair choose a location for the treasure and write clues for finding it. Others must make a diagram and use the clues to find the treasure.

Cooperative Learning Activity

Use groups of 2.   Pit Stop **11-6**

➡ Work together to solve the following problem. (Hint: Draw a diagram.)

An adventurer is staring at a huge pile of gold in an ancient treasure chamber. There is just one problem: A portion of the floor has been dug out all the way around the square portion of the floor on which the treasure is sitting. The distance across the pit on each side of the center square is 13 feet. The pit is very deep and is filled with poisonous snakes. The adventurer has no rope, and the only objects in the treasure chamber are two 12-foot-long boards. How can the adventurer use these boards to get to the treasure?

Glencoe Mathematics: Applications and Connections, Course 2

11-7 Percent

Objective
Illustrate the meaning of percent using models or symbols.

Words to Learn
percent

Does it seem like you're always buying pens or pencils? In the United States, people buy about $1.9 billion worth of pens and pencils each year. Of all these pens and pencils, 33 of every 100 are ballpoint pens. The shaded area in the grid at the right shows the ratio 33 out of 100. Another name for this ratio is 33 **percent**.

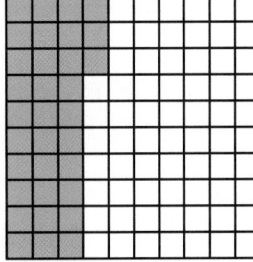

Percent	**In words:**	A percent is a ratio that compares a number to 100.
	In symbols:	$\frac{n}{100} = n\%$
		The symbol % means *percent*.

Examples

Express each ratio as a percent.

1 $\frac{33}{100} = 33\%$ **2** 62.5 out of 100 = 62.5%   **3** $8\frac{1}{2}$ per 100 = $8\frac{1}{2}\%$

Example 4

Write a percent to represent the number of shaded squares.

The grid has one hundred squares in all. Count the number that are shaded.

$(3 \times 8) + (3 \times 4) + (5 \times 1) = 41$

There are 41 squares shaded. So, 41% represents the shaded area.

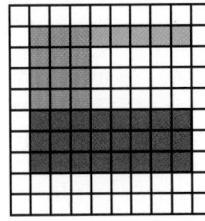

 Mini-Lab

Work with a partner.
Materials: grid paper, markers

- Draw nine 10×10 squares on your grid paper.
- For each percent below, shade three different 10×10 grids, each in a different way.

  a. 80%   b. 35%   c. $41\frac{1}{2}\%$

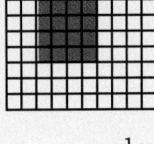

For answers to Exercises a–c, see Solutions Manual.

Lesson 11-7 Percent **433**

OPTIONS

Reteaching Activity

Using Applications Provide real-life examples of how percent is used, such as in describing tax rates or test scores. Have students use the 10 × 10 grid to show a sales rate of 8% or a test score when 77 out of 100 questions are answered correctly.

Study Guide Masters, p. 97

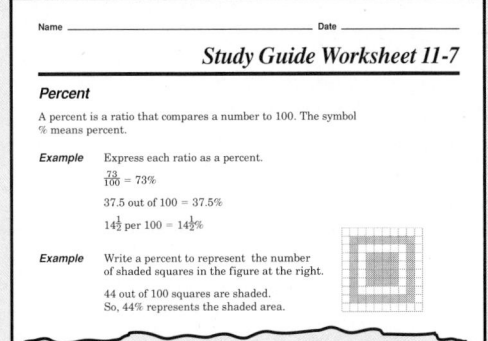

NCTM Standards: 1–5, 12

Lesson Resources
- Study Guide Master 11-7
- Practice Master 11-7
- Enrichment Master 11-7
- Group Activity Card 11-7

 Transparency 11-7 contains the 5-Minute Check and a teaching aid for this lesson.

5-Minute Check
(Over Lesson 11-6)

1. There are 6 members of a committee. If each shakes hands with every other member once, how many handshakes will there be?   15

2. A club president set up a telephone tree in which every member calls 4 people and each call takes 30 seconds. It takes 4 minutes for all the calls. How many members does the club have?   21

1 FOCUS

Motivating the Lesson

Activity Have students list as many uses of percent as they can. Ask them what is meant by 100% effort. Ask them what is incorrect about claiming to give 110% effort.

2 TEACH

Using the Mini-Lab Ask students what percent each unshaded region represents.
20%, 65%, $58\frac{1}{2}\%$
Ask them what each small square represents.   1%
Challenge them to give the number of ways 99% can be shown on the grid.   100

433

More Examples

For Examples 1–3

Express each ratio as a percent.

1. $\frac{37}{100}$ 37%

2. 37.5 out of 100 37.5%

3. $9\frac{1}{2}$ per 100 $9\frac{1}{2}$%

For Example 4

Write a percent to represent the number of shaded squares. 32%

Checking for Understanding

Exercises 1–4 are designed to help you assess students' understanding through reading, writing, speaking, and modeling. You should work through these exercises with your students and then monitor their work on Guided Practice Exercises 5–16.

Practice Masters, p. 97

Name ______ Date ______

Practice Worksheet 11-7

Percent

Express each ratio as a percent.

1. $\frac{68}{100}$ 68%	2. $\frac{47}{100}$ 47%	3. 17 hundredths 17%
4. 19.4 out of 100 19.4%	5. $16\frac{1}{2}$:100 $16\frac{1}{2}$%	6. 74.3 to 100 74.3%
7. 82 per 100 82%	8. \$22 per \$100 22%	9. 6 rows out of 100 rows 6%

Write a percent to represent the shaded area.

10. 45% 11. 38% 12. $38\frac{1}{2}$%

13. 35% 14. 44% 15. 40%

16. $59\frac{1}{2}$% 17. 57% 18. 66%

T97

Glencoe Division, Macmillan/McGraw-Hill

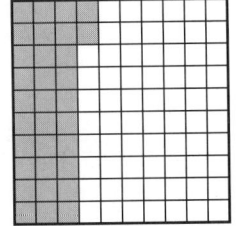

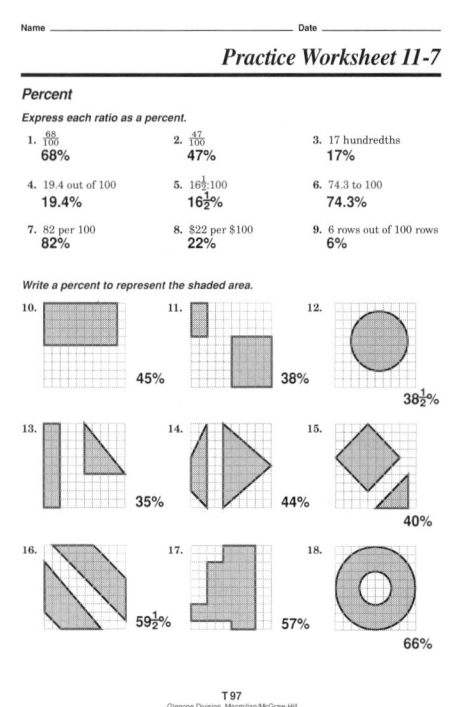

Talk About It

d. Compare your shaded areas with others in your class. Do the shaded areas need to be the same shape in order to represent the same percent? Explain why or why not. **No; the same number of squares must be shaded.**

e. How many different ways can you shade a 10×10 grid in order to represent 100%? **1 way**

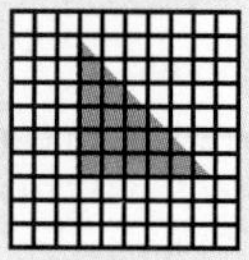

f. How can you find the percent represented by the shaded area at the right if you don't count squares?

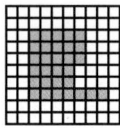

Find the area of the triangle. Then divide by 100.

LOOKBACK

You can review area of triangles on page 355.

Checking for Understanding

For answers to Exercises 1–2, see margin.

Communicating Mathematics

Read and study the lesson to answer each question.

1. **Tell**, in your own words, what percent means.
2. **Draw** a diagram to show 30%.
3. **Write** a percent that means 3 out of 100. **3%**
4. **Write** a percent to show the ratio of the number of squares shaded to the total number of squares in the figure at the right. **30%**

Guided Practice

Express each ratio as a percent.

5. $\frac{45}{100}$ **45%**
6. 37 out of 100 **37%**
7. 13 hundredths **13%**
8. 18.5 out of 100 **18.5%**
9. $12\frac{1}{2}$:100 **$12\frac{1}{2}$%**
10. 98.5 to 100 **98.5%**

Write a percent to represent the shaded area. If necessary, round answers to the nearest percent.

11. **42%**

12. **30%**

13. **50%**

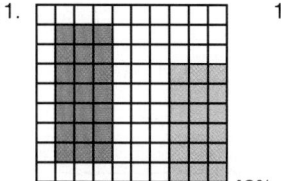

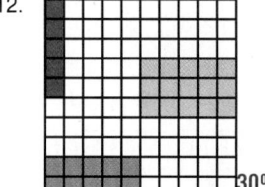

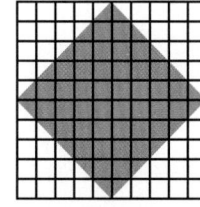

14. **28%**

15. **60%**

16. **79%**

OPTIONS

Gifted and Talented Needs

Challenge students to describe how to use percents to represent fractions with denominators of 10 and of 1,000. Sample answers: Multiply numerator by 10 and affix a % symbol; divide numerator by 10 and affix a % symbol.

Additional Answers

1. Sample answer: a ratio that compares a number to 100
2.

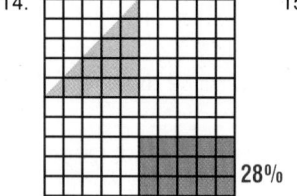

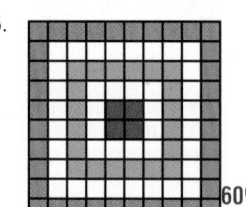

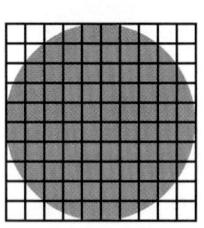

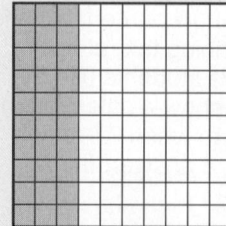

Exercises

Express each ratio as a percent.

17. 22 people out of 100 **22%**

18. 1 clown out of 100 **1%**

19. 98:100 **98%**

20. 60 of 100 flowers **60%**

21. $11 per $100 **11%**

22. 9 rows out of 100 rows **9%**

Write a percent to represent the shaded area. If necessary, round answers to the nearest percent.

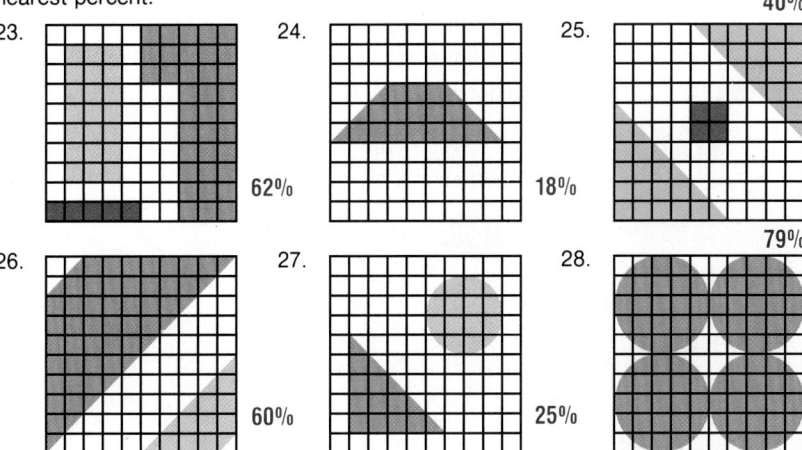

23.

24. **62%**

25. **40%**

26. **79%**

27. **18%**

28. **25%**

60%

29. **Geometry** Square *A* measures 10 units on a side. Square *B* measures 6 units on a side. Write a percent for the ratio of the area of square *B* to the area of square *A*. **36%**

30. Round 125.0765 to the underlined place-value position. *(Lesson 2-2)* **125.1**

31. Multiply 4 and $4\frac{3}{8}$. *(Lesson 5-5)* **$17\frac{1}{2}$**

32. **Geometry** Complete the pattern unit for the translation at the right. Then draw the tessellation. *(Lesson 8-7)* **See Solutions Manual.**

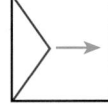

33. **Critical Thinking** Copy and complete each diagram so that it shows 60%.

a.

b.

c.

d.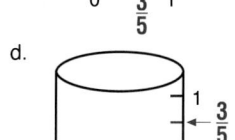

e.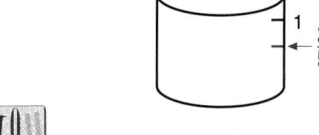

34. **Journal Entry** Find an advertisement that uses percents. Draw a diagram to illustrate the percent. What does the percent mean? **See students' work.**

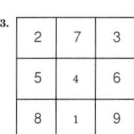
435

Lesson Resources
- Study Guide Master 11-8
- Practice Master 11-8
- Enrichment Master 11-8
- Technology Master, p. 11
- Group Activity Card 11-8

 Transparency 11-8 contains the 5-Minute Check and a teaching aid for this lesson.

🕐 5-Minute Check
(Over Lesson 11-7)

Write a percent to represent the shaded area.

1.

32%

2.

66%

Express each ratio as a percent.

3. 46 people out of 100
46%

4. 87 : 100   87%

1 FOCUS

Motivating the Lesson

Situational Problem Tell students that in one basketball game, Tina made 7 of her 8 free throw attempts. Ask them to express her free-throw shooting as a percent.

Objective
Express fractions as percents, and vice versa.

11-8 Percents and Fractions

Did you know that bananas do not grow on trees? They grow on plants that can be as tall as 30 feet. A banana is $\frac{3}{4}$ water. What percent of a banana is water?

You can express any fraction as a percent. One way to change the fraction $\frac{3}{4}$ to a percent is to find an equivalent fraction with a denominator of 100.

$$\frac{3}{4} = \frac{3 \times 25}{4 \times 25} = \frac{75}{100} = 75\%$$ So, 75% of the banana is water.

Another way to express a fraction as a percent is to use a proportion.

Examples

Express each fraction as a percent.

1 $\frac{3}{8}$

$\frac{3}{8} = \frac{n}{100}$ *Find the cross products.*

$300 = 8n$

$\frac{300}{8} = \frac{8n}{8}$ *Divide each side by 8.*

$37.5 = n$

So, $\frac{3}{8} = 37.5\%$.

2 $\frac{5}{24}$

$\frac{5}{24} = \frac{n}{100}$ *Find the cross products.*

$5 \times 100 = 24n$

5 ⊠ 100 ÷ 24 =
20.833333

So, $\frac{5}{24}$ is about 20.8%.

To write a percent as a fraction, write a fraction with a denominator of 100. Then write the fraction in simplest form.

Examples

Express each percent as a fraction.

3 65%

$65\% = \frac{65}{100}$

$= \frac{65 \div 5}{100 \div 5}$ *The GCF is 5.*

$= \frac{13}{20}$

So, $65\% = \frac{13}{20}$.

4 $16\frac{2}{3}\%$

$16\frac{2}{3}\% = \frac{16\frac{2}{3}}{100}$

$= 16\frac{2}{3} \div 100$

$= \frac{50}{3} \div 100$

$= \frac{50}{3} \times \frac{1}{100}$ *To divide by 100, multiply by $\frac{1}{100}$.*

$= \frac{50}{300}$ or $\frac{1}{6}$

So, $16\frac{2}{3}\% = \frac{1}{6}$.

OPTIONS

Gifted and Talented Needs

Ask students to guess which vowel is the one most commonly used in the English language. Then have them choose a paragraph from a book and record the percent that each vowel is of the total number of vowels or letters. Have students share their findings.   The most common letter is e.

 **Interactive Mathematics Tools**

This multimedia software provides an interactive lesson that is tied directly to Lesson 11–8. Students will use decimal grids to explore fractions and percents.

Estimation Hint
••••••••••••
Sometimes you only need to find a fraction that is reasonably close to a given percent. When this happens, try to work with one of the common percents from the table.

38.9% is close to 40%. So, 38.9% is about $\frac{2}{5}$.

In everyday situations, some percents are used much more frequently than others. For this reason, you probably will find it helpful to memorize the equivalent percents and fractions listed in the table below.

$20\% = \frac{1}{5}$	$25\% = \frac{1}{4}$	$12\frac{1}{2}\% = \frac{1}{8}$	$16\frac{2}{3}\% = \frac{1}{6}$
$40\% = \frac{2}{5}$	$50\% = \frac{1}{2}$	$37\frac{1}{2}\% = \frac{3}{8}$	$33\frac{1}{3}\% = \frac{1}{3}$
$60\% = \frac{3}{5}$	$75\% = \frac{3}{4}$	$62\frac{1}{2}\% = \frac{5}{8}$	$66\frac{2}{3}\% = \frac{2}{3}$
$80\% = \frac{4}{5}$		$87\frac{1}{2}\% = \frac{7}{8}$	$83\frac{1}{3}\% = \frac{5}{6}$

$100\% = 1$

Mini-Lab

Work with a partner.
Materials: paper and pencil

What percent of the students in your class do you think are in each category? Estimate by using one of the choices listed at the right. **For answers to Exercises a–e, see students' work.**

a. left-handed
b. male
c. wear glasses or contact lenses
d. less than 2 years old
e. at school today

0%
less than 10%
about 25%
about 50%
at least 75%
100%

Talk About It

g. Sample answer: survey the class and find actual percents.

f. How does your group's estimate for each category compare with the estimates of the other groups in your class? **Answers will vary.**

g. How can you tell if your estimates are reasonable?

Checking for Understanding

Communicating Mathematics

Read and study the lesson to answer each question.

1. **Show** one way to express $\frac{7}{20}$ as a percent. **35%**

2. **Tell** what percent of the students in your classroom are wearing something that has blue in it: less than 50%, about 50%, more than 50%. **Answers will vary.**

Guided Practice

Express each fraction as a percent.

3. $\frac{9}{10}$ **90%** 4. $\frac{9}{20}$ **45%** 5. $\frac{1}{3}$ **$33\frac{1}{3}\%$** 6. $\frac{7}{8}$ **$87\frac{1}{2}\%$** 7. $\frac{5}{16}$ **$31\frac{1}{4}\%$**

Lesson 11-8 Percents and Fractions   437

Using the Mini-Lab Have students explain some of their answers when there are large differences among estimates. Encourage groups to list other things that can be estimated using percents.

More Examples

Express each fraction as a percent.

For Example 1
$\frac{5}{8}$ 62.5%

For Example 2
$\frac{3}{40}$ 7.5%

Express each percent as a fraction.

For Example 3
45% $\frac{9}{20}$

For Example 4
$83\frac{1}{3}\%$ $\frac{5}{6}$

Teaching Tip To reinforce students' understanding of the relationship between fractions and percents, ask questions about the table on page 437, such as *Why aren't $\frac{2}{4}$, $\frac{2}{8}$, $\frac{6}{8}$, $\frac{2}{6}$, $\frac{3}{6}$, and $\frac{4}{6}$ listed in the table?*

Checking for Understanding

Exercises 1-2 are designed to help you assess students' understanding through reading, writing, speaking, and modeling. You should work through these exercises with your students and then monitor their work on Guided Practice Exercises 3-13.

Reteaching Activity

Using Calculators Another way to express a fraction as a percent is to use a calculator to rename the fraction as a decimal first (by dividing the numerator by the denominator) and then renaming the decimal as a percent by mentally moving the decimal point 2 places to the right (multiplying by 100) and affixing a % symbol.

Study Guide Masters, p. 98

Name _____   Date _____

Study Guide Worksheet 11-8

Percents and Fractions

To write a fraction as a percent, use a proportion.

Examples   Express $\frac{5}{8}$ as a percent.   Express $\frac{15}{16}$ as a percent.

$\frac{5}{8} = \frac{x}{100}$ $\frac{15}{16} = \frac{m}{100}$

$500 = 8x$ $1,500 = 16m$
$\frac{500}{8} = \frac{8x}{8}$ $\frac{1,500}{16} = \frac{16m}{m}$
$62.5 = x$ $93.75 = m$
$\frac{5}{8}$ is 62.5% $\frac{15}{16}$ is 93.75%.

To write a percent as a fraction, write a fraction with a denominator of 100. Then write the fraction in simplest form.

437

Error Analysis

Watch for students who affix a percent sign to a fraction when "changing it to a percent," as when expressing $\frac{7}{8}$ as $\frac{7}{8}\%$.

Prevent by reminding the students that the percent symbol takes the place of the denominator 100. Point out that $\frac{7}{8}\%$ means $\frac{7}{8} \div 100$ or 0.00875, while $\frac{7}{8} = 0.875$.

Close

Have students express as a percent the fraction of the total number of students in the class who are 13 years old or older.

3 PRACTICE/APPLY

Assignment Guide
Maximum: 14–59
Minimum: 15–45 odd, 46–57

For **Extra Practice,** see p. 596.

Alternate Assessment

Speaking Have students describe how to express a fraction as a percent and a percent as a fraction.

Practice Masters, p. 98

Name _____ Date _____

Practice Worksheet 11-8

Percents and Fractions

Express each fraction as a percent.

1. $\frac{7}{10}$ **70%** 2. $\frac{3}{4}$ **75%** 3. $\frac{17}{20}$ **85%**

4. $\frac{5}{8}$ **62$\frac{1}{2}$%** 5. $\frac{5}{5}$ **100%** 6. $\frac{23}{25}$ **92%**

7. $\frac{11}{12}$ **91$\frac{2}{3}$%** 8. $\frac{13}{16}$ **81$\frac{1}{4}$%** 9. $\frac{64}{125}$ **51$\frac{1}{5}$%**

10. $\frac{37}{50}$ **74%** 11. $\frac{1}{3}$ **33$\frac{1}{3}$%** 12. $\frac{9}{16}$ **56$\frac{1}{4}$%**

Express each percent as a fraction in simplest form.

13. 75% $\frac{3}{4}$ 14. 84% $\frac{21}{25}$ 15. 90% $\frac{9}{10}$

16. 18$\frac{1}{2}$% $\frac{37}{200}$ 17. 38% $\frac{19}{50}$ 18. 87$\frac{1}{2}$% $\frac{7}{8}$

19. 32% $\frac{8}{25}$ 20. 8$\frac{2}{3}$% $\frac{13}{150}$ 21. 68% $\frac{17}{25}$

22. 14% $\frac{7}{50}$ 23. 6$\frac{1}{4}$% $\frac{1}{16}$ 24. 48% $\frac{12}{25}$

25. 56% $\frac{14}{25}$ 26. 30% $\frac{3}{10}$ 27. 2$\frac{1}{2}$% $\frac{1}{40}$

T98
Glencoe Division, Macmillan/McGraw-Hill

438

Express each percent as a fraction in simplest form.

10. $\frac{9}{20}$

8. 30% $\frac{3}{10}$ 9. 1% $\frac{1}{100}$ 10. 45%

11. 23% $\frac{23}{100}$ 12. 22$\frac{1}{2}$% $\frac{9}{40}$

13. **Entertainment** Three-fifths of the students at the dance were seventh graders.
   a. What percent were seventh graders? **60%**
   b. What percent were *not* seventh graders? **40%**

Exercises

Independent Practice

Express each fraction as a percent.

14. $\frac{24}{25}$ **96%** 15. $\frac{43}{50}$ **86%** 16. $\frac{18}{25}$ **72%** 17. $\frac{2}{5}$ **40%** 18. $\frac{11}{20}$ **55%**

19. $\frac{3}{10}$ **30%** 20. $\frac{19}{20}$ **95%** 21. $\frac{1}{4}$ **25%** 22. $\frac{2}{3}$ **66$\frac{2}{3}$%** 23. $\frac{1}{8}$ **12$\frac{1}{2}$%**

24. $\frac{5}{6}$ **83$\frac{1}{3}$%** 25. $\frac{7}{16}$ **43$\frac{3}{4}$%** 26. $\frac{10}{12}$ **83$\frac{1}{3}$%** 27. $\frac{40}{125}$ **32%** 28. $\frac{3}{3}$ **100%**

Express each percent as a fraction in simplest form.

29. 25% $\frac{1}{4}$ 30. 15% $\frac{3}{20}$ 31. 72% $\frac{18}{25}$ 32. 10% $\frac{1}{10}$ 33. 70% $\frac{7}{10}$

34. 50% $\frac{1}{2}$ 35. 80% $\frac{4}{5}$ 36. 34% $\frac{17}{50}$ 37. 12$\frac{1}{2}$% $\frac{1}{8}$ 38. 11$\frac{1}{2}$% $\frac{23}{200}$

39. 66$\frac{2}{3}$% $\frac{2}{3}$ 40. 62$\frac{1}{2}$% $\frac{5}{8}$ 41. 17$\frac{1}{2}$% $\frac{7}{40}$ 42. 3$\frac{1}{3}$% $\frac{1}{30}$ 43. 6$\frac{1}{4}$% $\frac{1}{16}$

44. Express $\frac{9}{24}$ as a percent. **37$\frac{1}{2}$%**

45. Express *fifty-four percent* as a fraction in simplest form. $\frac{27}{50}$

Mixed Review

46. Compare the fractions $\frac{15}{24}$ and $\frac{17}{32}$ using the least common denominator. *(Lesson 4-10)* $\frac{15}{24} > \frac{17}{32}$

47. Write 0.00005 in scientific notation. *(Lesson 7-10)* 5×10^{-5}

48. **Geometry** Classify the triangle at the right by its sides and by its angles. *(Lesson 8-3)*
    isosceles triangle; obtuse triangle

49. Alfonso places a 10-foot ladder 6 feet from his house and leans the ladder against the house. How high off the ground does the ladder reach on the side of the house? *(Lesson 9-4)* **8 feet**

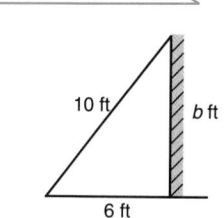

10 ft b ft

6 ft

438 **Chapter 11** Ratio, Proportion, and Percent

Classroom Vignette

"My students practice illustrating fractions or percents by using two different color plastic plates with a radius cut in each plate. Aligning the cuts, students turn the top plate so that it goes through the cut and under the bottom plate to reveal a pie-shaped section of the bottom plate."

Linda D. Woolwine

Linda Woolwine, Teacher
Toano Middle School, Toano, VA

50. **Geometry** Find the volume of a rectangular prism having a length of 5 centimeters, a width of 3 centimeters, and a height of 8 centimeters. *(Lesson 10-5)* **120 cm³**

51. Express *34 hits out of 100* as a percent. *(Lesson 11-7)* **34%**

Problem Solving and Applications

Animals Use the circle graph at the right for Exercises 52–55.

52. What fraction of people surveyed get their pets from animal shelters? $\frac{7}{50}$

53. What fraction of people surveyed get their pets from either breeders or friends? $\frac{11}{20}$

54. What fraction of people surveyed get their pets from places other than pet stores? $\frac{19}{20}$

55. **Answers will vary.**

55. Where do you think is the best place to get a pet? Explain your reasons.

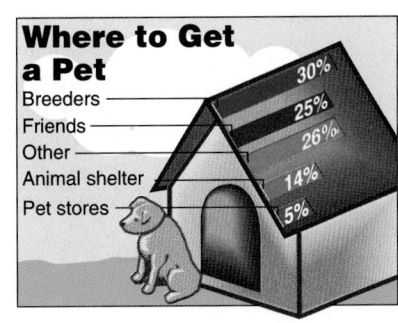

Where to Get a Pet
Breeders — 30%
Friends — 25%
Other — 26%
Animal shelter — 14%
Pet stores — 5%

56. **Statistics** Gail, Jil, and Michael are practicing free throws on the basketball court. Ned kept a tally of their shooting. What percent of shots attempted did each person make?

	Attempts	Made	
Gail	𝍏 𝍏 II	𝍏 II	$58\frac{1}{3}\%$
Michael	𝍏 𝍏 IIII	𝍏 II	50%
Jil	𝍏 𝍏 𝍏	𝍏 III	$53\frac{1}{3}\%$

57. **Critical Thinking** The best player on the girls' basketball team made 12 out of 20 free throws. The best player on the boys' basketball team has made 14 out of 25 free throws. Who is the better free throw shooter? Explain your answer. **See margin.**

DATA SEARCH

58. **Data Search** Refer to pages 408 and 409. Express the number of students that smoke at each grade level as a fraction. $\frac{3}{10}, \frac{3}{10}, \frac{33}{100}, \frac{37}{100}$

59. **Journal Entry** Describe an everyday situation where it may be more convenient to use a fraction and another situation where it may be more convenient to use a percent. Explain your reasoning for each choice. **See students' work.**

Lesson 11-8 Percents and Fractions **439**

Extending the Lesson

Using Logic Provide students with an 8 × 8 array of dots in which you have drawn a triangle and a square that intersect. Ask students to write a percent that expresses the fraction of dots inside both the triangle and the square. Have students make up similar problems for classmates to solve.

Cooperative Learning Activity

Give It a Shot 11-8

Number of players: 4
Materials: Spinners

■ Label equal sections of one spinner "Score" and "No Score." Label equal sections of a second spinner "2," "3," "4," "5," "6," "7."

➡ Work in pairs. This activity simulates a two-on-two basketball game. Each group member spins the 2 through 7 spinner to determine how many two-point field goals he or she will attempt in the "game." To "shoot," each group member spins the "Score/No Score" spinner. If you spin "Score," your team gets 2 points. If you spin "No Score," your team gets 0 points. Whenever possible, teams should alternate shots and partners should take turns shooting. When the game is over, calculate the percent of attempted field goals each player and each team made.

Glencoe Mathematics: Applications and Connections, Course 2

 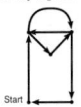
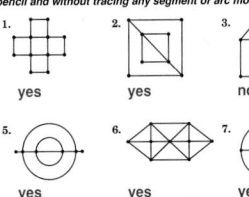 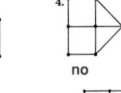 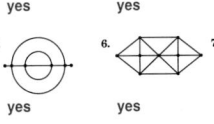
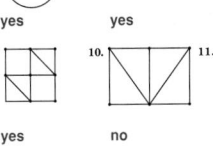 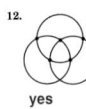

Lesson Resources
- Study Guide Master 11-9
- Practice Master 11-9
- Enrichment Master 11-9
- Technology Master, p. 25
- Group Activity Card 11-9

 Transparency 11-9 contains the 5-Minute Check and a teaching aid for this lesson.

🕐 5-Minute Check
(Over Lesson 11-8)

Express each fraction as a percent.

1. $\frac{21}{25}$ 84%

2. $\frac{7}{10}$ 70%

Express each percent as a fraction in simplest form.

3. 35% $\frac{7}{20}$

4. $16\frac{2}{3}\%$ $\frac{1}{6}$

5. Express *twenty-eight percent* as a fraction in simplest form. $\frac{7}{25}$

1 FOCUS

Motivating the Lesson

Questioning   Tell students that the highest Major League batting average since 1900 occurred in 1924 when Rogers Hornsby hit 0.424. Ask them to give the percent of hits Hornsby got per times at bat.   42.4%

2 TEACH

Using the Mini-Lab   Read through the instructions in the Mini-Lab with students. Have partners first estimate their *r* to *h* ratios. Then ask them whether they think all students will have the same *r* to *h* ratio. Ask them to predict whether the *r* to *h* ratios for adults and for small children will be similar to theirs.

11-9   Percents and Decimals

Objective
Express decimals as percents, and vice versa.

An iceberg is a huge mass of ice that comes from a glacier. Icebergs are made of fresh water even though they float in salt water. If a ship's crew runs out of fresh water, they can get it from an iceberg. The captain must be careful in approaching an iceberg because only about 0.125 of it is above water. What percent of the iceberg is above water?

LOOKBACK
You can review changing decimals to fractions on page 155.

In Chapter 4, you learned that any decimal can be expressed as a fraction. You can use that fact to express any decimal as a percent.

Example 1

Express 0.07 as a percent.

$0.07 = \frac{7}{100}$ *First, express the decimal as a fraction.*

$\quad\quad = 7\%$ *Then, express the fraction as a percent.*

So, $0.07 = 7\%$.

Example 2   *Problem Solving*

Navigation   Refer to the problem in the lesson introduction. What percent of the iceberg is above water?

$0.125 = \frac{125}{1{,}000}$ *First, express 0.125 as a fraction.*

$\quad\quad = \frac{125 \div 10}{1{,}000 \div 10}$ *Divide the numerator and the denominator by 10 to get a denominator of 100.*

$\quad\quad = \frac{12.5}{100}$

$\quad\quad = 12.5\%$

So, 12.5% of the iceberg is above water.

To express a percent as a decimal, express the percent as a fraction with a denominator of 100. Then express the fraction as a decimal.

OPTIONS

Meeting Needs of Middle School Students

Percents are frequently used to express statistics in sports. Using student suggestions, list some of these statistics on the chalkboard. Help students to see that they can use their prior knowledge of these statistics to help them understand the relationship among percents, decimals, and fractions.

Express each percent as a decimal.

3 72%

$$72\% = \frac{72}{100}$$
$$= 0.72$$
So, $72\% = 0.72$.

4 83.5%

$$83.5\% = \frac{83.5}{100}$$
$$= \frac{83.5 \times 10}{100 \times 10}$$
$$= \frac{835}{1{,}000}$$
$$= 0.835$$

Multiply the numerator and denominator by 10 so that the numerator is a whole number.

So, $83.5\% = 0.835$.

5 $37\frac{1}{2}\%$

$$37\frac{1}{2}\% = \frac{37\frac{1}{2}}{100}$$
$$= \frac{37.5}{100}$$

Rewrite $37\frac{1}{2}$ as 37.5.

$$37.5 \div 100 = 0.375$$
$$= 0.375$$ So, $37\frac{1}{2}\% = 0.375$.

b. Yes, armspan is about equal to height.

Mini-Lab

Work with a partner.

Materials: tape measure, yardstick, or meterstick

- Measure your partner's height (h) in inches.
- With your partner's arms outstretched, measure the distance from fingertip to fingertip (r) in inches.
- Compute the ratio r to h for your partner.
- Write the ratio as a percent.
- Repeat these steps as your partner measures you.

Talk About It

a. What does the percent represent? armspan to height ratio

b. If you know the distance from fingertip to fingertip of a person, do you think you could predict that person's height? Explain.

Checking for Understanding

Exercises 1-2 are designed to help you assess students' understanding through reading, writing, speaking, and modeling. You should work through these exercises with your students and then monitor their work on Guided Practice Exercises 3-11.

Reteaching Activity

Using Connections   Use the concept that coins are percents of a dollar to reinforce the relationship among decimals, fractions, and percents. Have students use combinations of coins to make different money amounts. Help students write these amounts in dollar-and-cents notation, as fractions of a dollar and as percents of a dollar.

Study Guide Masters, p. 99

Name _____ Date _____

Study Guide Worksheet 11-9

Percents and Decimals

To write a decimal as a percent, first express the decimal as a fraction. Then rewrite the fraction with a denominator of 100.

Examples   Express 0.77 as a percent.

$$0.77 = \frac{77}{100}$$
$$= 77\%$$

Express 0.323 as a percent.

$$0.323 = \frac{323}{1{,}000}$$
$$= \frac{323 \div 10}{1{,}000 \div 10}$$
$$= \frac{32.3}{100}$$
$$= 32.3\%$$

To write a percent as a decimal, express the percent as a fraction with a denominator of 100. Then express the fraction as a decimal.

Examples   Express 51% as a decimal.   Express 90.2% as a decimal.

Close

Have students explain how to express a percent as a decimal and a decimal as a percent.

3 PRACTICE/APPLY

Assignment Guide
Maximum: 12–55
Minimum: 13–45 odd, 47–55

For **Extra Practice,** see p. 597.

Alternate Assessment

Writing Have students write each of the following as a decimal and as a percent.
a. the odd numbers in the numbers 1 to 10   0.5; 50%
b. the numbers divisible by 4 in the numbers 1 to 24.   0.25; 25%

Practice Masters, p. 99

Name _____ Date _____

Practice Worksheet 11-9

Percents and Decimals

Express each decimal as a percent.

1. 0.52	2. 0.9	3. 0.12
52%	90%	12%
4. 0.825	**5.** 0.06	**6.** 0.066
82.5%	6%	6.6%
7. 0.537	**8.** 0.22	**9.** 0.3
53.7%	22%	30%

Write each percent as a decimal.

10. 82%	11. 61.5%	12. 8.9%
0.82	0.615	0.089
13. 48½%	**14.** 70%	**15.** 27¼%
0.485	0.7	0.2725
16. 3%	**17.** 18%	**18.** 19.6%
0.03	0.18	0.196

Complete with <, >, or =.

19. 19% $\leq$ 1.9	20. 31.2 $\geq$ 31.2%	21. 0.74 $=$ 74%
22. 62.8% $=$ 0.628	**23.** 0.4 $\geq$ 4%	**24.** 0.02 $\leq$ 20%
25. 37% $\geq$ 0.307	**26.** 0.028 $\geq$ 2⅛%	**27.** 0.08 $\geq$ 1%
28. 1% $\leq$ 1	**29.** 1.4 $\geq$ 1.4%	**30.** 0.2 $\geq$ 2%

T99
Glencoe Division, Macmillan/McGraw-Hill

442

Checking for Understanding

Communicating Mathematics

Read and study the lesson to answer each question.
1. **Write** the steps you would use to express a percent as a decimal. **See margin.**
2. **Tell** how the diagram illustrates that any number can be expressed in three ways. **See margin.**

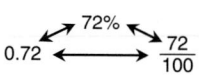
$$0.72 \longleftrightarrow 72\% \longleftrightarrow \frac{72}{100}$$

Guided Practice

Express each decimal as a percent.
3. 0.46 **46%**   4. 0.05 **5%**   5. 0.6 **60%**   6. 0.565 **56.5%**

Express each percent as a decimal.
7. 39% **0.39**   8. 4% **0.04**   9. 70% **0.7**   10. 23¼% **0.2325**

11. Which is greater: 17% or 1.7? **1.7**

Exercises

Independent Practice

Express each decimal as a percent.
12. 0.39 **39%**   13. 0.75 **75%**   14. 0.875 **87.5%**   15. 0.325 **32.5%**
16. 0.4 **40%**   17. 0.03 **3%**   18. 0.07 **7%**   19. 0.01 **1%**
20. 0.075 **7.5%**   21. 0.999 **99.9%**   22. 0.099 **9.9%**   23. 1 **100%**

Express each percent as a decimal.
24. 43% **0.43**   25. 89% **0.89**   26. 7% **0.07**   27. 2% **0.02**
28. 17% **0.17**   29. 90% **0.9**   30. 34.5% **0.345**   31. 13.4% **0.134**
32. 6.2% **0.062**   33. 62½% **0.625**   34. 33¼% **0.3325**   35. 100% **1**

Replace each ⬤ with <, >, or =.
36. 35% ⬤ 3.5 **<**   37. 7.8 ⬤ 78% **>**   38. 0.05 ⬤ 50% **<**
39. 100% ⬤ 1.1 **<**   40. 57.8% ⬤ 0.0578 **>**   41. 0.3 ⬤ 30% **=**
42. 0.09 ⬤ 1% **>**   43. 2.4% ⬤ 0.0204 **>**   44. 1¾% ⬤ 0.175 **<**

45. Which is greater: 0.63 or 6.3%? **0.63**
46. *True* or *false:* 0.425 = 42.5% **true**

Mixed Review

47. Evaluate 5^3. *(Lesson 1-9)* **125**
48. Change 56 ounces to pounds. *(Lesson 6-6)* **3½ pounds**
49. Find the absolute value of −21. *(Lesson 7-1)* **21**
50. Find $\sqrt{144}$. *(Lesson 9-2)* **12**

442   Chapter 11 Ratio, Proportion, and Percent

OPTIONS

Limited English Proficiency

Have students add *percent* to their vocabulary lists. Point out that percents can be used to name the same numbers expressed by decimals and fractions. Present other words with *cent* in them, such as cent (penny), century, centennial, and bicentennial. Guide students to see what meaning these terms share.

Additional Answers

1. Express the percent as a fraction with a denominator of 100. Then express the fraction as a decimal.
2. Sample answer: A number can be expressed as a fraction, decimal, or percent.

51. Andrea must wrap a package shaped as a rectangular prism having length 12 inches, width 8 inches, and height 4 inches. How much paper will Andrea need? *(Lesson 10-3)* **352 in²**

52. Express 35% as a fraction in simplest form. *(Lesson 11-8)* **$\frac{7}{20}$**

Problem Solving and Applications

53. **Sports** Tadashi has a batting average of 0.344.
    a. Write this number as a percent. **34.4%**
    b. About how many hits could he expect to have out of his next 100 times at bat? **about 34 hits**

54. **Consumer Math** The standard rate for tipping in a restaurant is 15% of your total bill.
    a. Write this percent as a decimal. **0.15**
    b. A family of six has a bill of $100 at a restaurant. What should their tip be? **$15**
    c. What is the total amount they should expect to pay at the restaurant? **$115**

55. **Critical Thinking** Write 5.4×10^{-2} as a percent. **5.4%**

56. **Portfolio Suggestion** Select your favorite word problem from this chapter and place it in your portfolio. Attach a note explaining why it is your favorite. **See students' work.**

Save Planet Earth

Up in Smoke Over 467,000 tons of tobacco are burned each year. Smoking is the largest cause of indoor air pollution. It affects not only the smoker, but also those that live and work around smokers. Those that inhale the smoke of other smokers are called "passive smokers."

Because smoking is a health hazard for everyone involved, people and businesses are beginning to take steps to reduce the amount of smoke in the workplace and home.

How You Can Help
- Don't smoke and discourage smoking in your home.
- Encourage smokers to go outdoors to smoke.
- If someone is smoking indoors, make sure the room is ventilated.

Lesson 11-9 Percents and Decimals **443**

Extending the Lesson

Save Planet Earth Discuss with your students some other illnesses that are attributable to smoking. Ask your students how they might approach someone who is smoking in the student's home about putting out his or her cigarette.

Cooperative Learning Activity

Pair Off 11-9

Number of players: 3
Materials: Index cards

Make one set of cards containing the percents shown on the back of this card. Shuffle the cards and divide them evenly. Make a second set of cards containing the decimals shown on the back of this card. Shuffle the cards and place them face down in a pile.

One group member flips over the top card from the pile. The group member with the card showing the same number expressed as a decimal takes the percent card and places both cards aside. Try to be the first to play all of the percent cards in your hand.

Glencoe Mathematics: Applications and Connections, Course 2

Enrichment Masters, p. 99

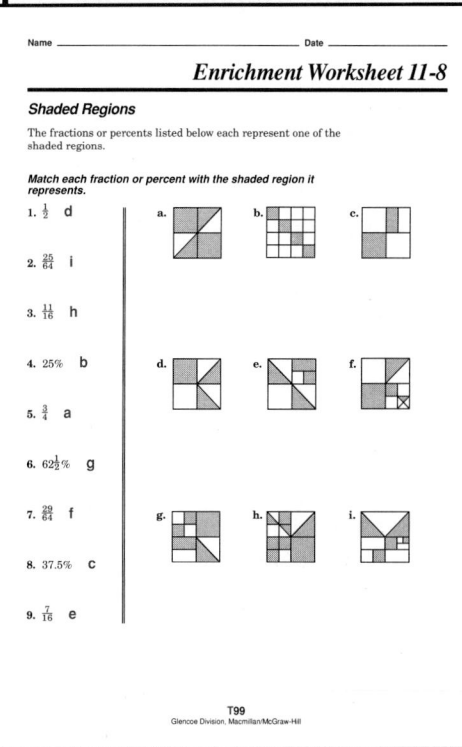

443

NCTM Standards: 1–5, 7, 10

Lesson Resources
• Study Guide Master 11-10
• Practice Master 11-10
• Enrichment Master 11-10
• Evaluation Master, Quiz B, p. 97
• Interdisciplinary Master, p. 25
• Group Activity Card 11-10

 Transparency 11-10 contains the 5-Minute Check and a teaching aid for this lesson.

⏱ 5-Minute Check
(Over Lesson 11-9)

Express each decimal as a percent.

1. 0.52   52%

2. 0.835   83.5%

Express each percent as a decimal.

3. 8%   0.08

4. $32\frac{1}{4}$%   0.3225

Replace the ● with <, >, or =.

5. 45% ● 4.5   <

1 FOCUS

Motivating the Lesson

Situational Problem Ask students to write two statements, one that is reasonable and one that is not, using the number 125%. Have students share and justify their choices. Repeat the process with the number 0.25%.

2 TEACH

Using the Mini-Lab Have students explain how they know that one drawing represents a percent greater than 100% and the other represents a percent less than 1%. Ask students how they would use models to express percents greater than 200%

444

11-10 Percents Greater Than 100% and Less Than 1%

Objectives

Express percents greater than 100% and percents less than 1% as fractions and as decimals, and vice versa.

In 1990, the world's population was 5,292,177,000. Experts estimate that the population will increase to 8,466,516,000 by the year 2025, which is about 160% of the 1990 population. How many times greater than the 1990 population will the 2025 population be? *This question will be answered in Example 1.*

People who analyze and interpret data often use percents greater than 100%. These percents represent numbers that are greater than 1. You can also use percents less than 1%. These precents represent numbers that are less than 0.01 or $\frac{1}{100}$.

🔬 Mini-Lab

Work with a partner.
Materials: grid paper, markers

• Draw two 10×10 squares on your grid paper. Each large square represents 100%, and each small square represents 1%. Shade 160 squares.

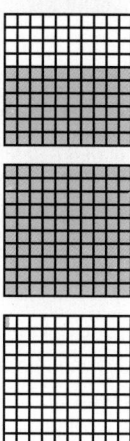

• Draw another 10×10 square. Shade four tenths of one square.

Talk About It

a. Which drawing represents a percent greater than 100%? What is the percent? **first drawing; 160%**

b. Which drawing represents a percent less than 1%. What is the percent? **second drawing; 0.4%**

OPTIONS

Bell Ringer

Have students explain what it means to meet 100% of a goal, 150% of a goal, 200% of a goal, and 300% of a goal. Ask them how much homework they would have in a week if teachers were to give them assignments requiring 150%, 200%, or 300% of the time they ordinarily take to complete their work.

Example 1 Connection

Statistics Refer to the problem in the lesson introduction. Express 160% as a decimal to find out how many times greater the population will be in 2025.

$$160\% = \frac{160}{100}$$
$$= 1.6 \quad \text{So, in the year 2025, the world population will be about}$$
$$\text{1.6 times the 1990 population.}$$

Examples

Express each decimal as a percent.

2 1.25

$$1.25 = 1\frac{25}{100}$$
$$= \frac{125}{100}$$
$$= 125\%$$

So, $1.25 = 125\%$.

3 6.3

$$6.3 = 6\frac{3}{10}$$
$$= \frac{63}{10} \quad \textit{Multiply}$$
$$\textit{numerator and}$$
$$= \frac{630}{100} \quad \textit{denominator}$$
$$\textit{by 10.}$$
$$= 630\%$$

So, $6.3 = 630\%$.

Example 4 Connection

Statistics Recently, it was estimated Nissan and Mitsubishi together had 0.9% of the mini-van market. What is this percent as a fraction and as a decimal?

$$0.9\% = \frac{0.9}{100}$$
$$= \frac{0.9 \times 10}{100 \times 10} \quad \textit{Multiply numerator and}$$
$$\textit{denominator by 10.}$$
$$= \frac{9}{1,000}$$
$$= 0.009 \quad \text{Nissan and Mitsubishi together had about } \frac{9}{1,000}, \text{ or}$$
$$\text{0.009, of the market.}$$

Examples

Express each fraction as a percent.

5 $\frac{3}{400}$

$$\frac{3}{400} = \frac{3 \div 4}{400 \div 4}$$
$$= \frac{0.75}{100} \quad \textit{3 ÷ 4 = 0.75}$$
$$= 0.75\%$$

So, $\frac{3}{400} = 0.75\%$.

6 $\frac{12}{2,000}$

$$\frac{12}{2,000} = \frac{12 \div 20}{2,000 \div 20}$$
$$12 \boxed{÷} 2000 \boxed{=} \text{ 0.006}$$
$$0.006 = 0.6\%$$

So, $\frac{12}{2,000} = 0.6\%$.

In Example 5, explain why the numerator and denominator of $\frac{3}{400}$ are divided by 4.

TEEN SCENE

Saab and Volvo are Swedish-made cars. They made up 40% of all Swedish goods imported to the United States in 1987.

Lesson 11-10 Percents Greater Than 100% and Less Than 1%   **445**

More Examples

For Example 1

Express 180% as a decimal.
1.8

For Example 2

Express 1.45 as a percent.
145%

For Example 3

Express 5.7 as a percent.
570%

For Example 4

Express 0.8% as a decimal.
0.008

Express each fraction as a percent.

For Example 5

$\frac{4}{500}$ 0.8%

For Example 6

$\frac{14}{4,000}$ 0.35%

Checking for Understanding

Exercises 1–4 are designed to help you assess students' understanding through reading, writing, speaking, and modeling. You should work through these exercises with your students and then monitor their work on Guided Practice Exercises 5–23.

Reteaching Activity

Using Connections Use money as in the previous lesson. Guide students to see that if a penny is 1% of a dollar, then it is less than 1% of any amount greater than a dollar. Use coins to help them see that any amount greater than a coin is more than 100% of that coin.

Study Guide Masters, p. 100

Name _____ Date _____

Study Guide Worksheet 11-10

Percents Greater than 100% and Percents Less than 1%

You can express a percent greater than 100% or less than 1% as a decimal.

Examples   Express 725% as a decimal.   Express 0.015% as a decimal.

$725\% = \frac{725}{100}$ $0.015\% = \frac{0.015}{100}$
$= 7.25$ $= \frac{0.015 \times 1,000}{100 \times 1,000}$
$= \frac{15}{100,000}$
$= 0.00015$

You can use percents to represent numbers that are greater than 1.

Examples   Express 5.75 as a percent.   Express $8\frac{9}{10}$ as a percent.

$5.75 = 5\frac{75}{100}$ $8\frac{9}{10} = 8\frac{9 \times 10}{10 \times 10}$
$= \frac{575}{100}$ $= \frac{90}{...}$

Close

Have students write two percents—one that is less than the decimal 0.01 and one that is greater than the decimal 1.00. Then have them use each number in a sentence that makes sense.

3 PRACTICE/APPLY

Assignment Guide
Maximum: 24–68
Minimum: 25–59 odd, 60–68

For **Extra Practice,** see p. 597.

Alternate Assessment

Modeling Have students use 10 × 10 grids to model a percent greater than 100% and one less than 1%. Ask students to label each drawing with the percent it represents.

Practice Masters, p. 100

Name _____ Date _____

Practice Worksheet 11-10

Percents Greater Than 100% and Percents Less Than 1%
Express each percent as a decimal.

1. 520%   2. 140%   3. 235%
   5.2   1.4   2.35

4. 0.32%   5. 0.015%   6. $\frac{1}{4}$%
   0.0032   0.00015   0.0025

7. $\frac{2}{5}$%   8. 1,000%   9. 0.125%
   0.004   10   0.00125

Express each number as a percent.

10. 3.4   11. 0.0026   12. $3\frac{1}{5}$
    340%   0.26%   320%

13. 1.9   14. 8   15. 0.0002
    190%   800%   0.02%

16. 0.00112   17. 63   18. $5\frac{3}{4}$
    0.112%   6,300%   575%

Complete with <, >, or =.

19. 2.4 $=$ 240%   20. 550% $<$ 550   21. 82 $>$ 820%

22. 100% $<$ 10   23. 1.95 $=$ 195%   24. 3,500% $=$ 35

25. 15 × $\frac{1}{4}$ $=$ 15 × 25%   26. 23 × 1$\frac{1}{2}$% $<$ 23 × 10$\frac{1}{2}$

27. 0.0005 $<$ 5%   28. 24 × $\frac{1}{8}$ $=$ 24 × 12.5%

T100
Glencoe Division, Macmillan/McGraw-Hill

446

Checking for Understanding

Communicating Mathematics

Read and study the lesson to answer each question.

1. **Tell** why 175% of 80 must be greater than 80. **175% is greater than 100%.**

2. **Tell** how you know if a decimal or fraction will be a percent greater than 100%. **The decimal or fraction is greater than 1.**

3. **Tell** the percent represented by each diagram below.   **240%**

   a. 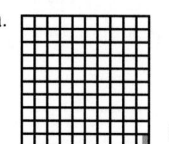   b.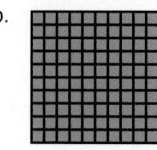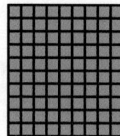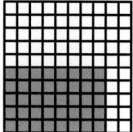

   0.5%

4. a. **Draw** a diagram to represent 130%.

   b. **Draw** a diagram to represent $\frac{1}{2}$%.
      For answers to Exercises 4a-b, see students' work.

Guided Practice

Express each percent as a decimal.

5. 400% **4**   6. 180% **1.8**   7. 130% **1.3**   8. 145% **1.45**

9. 0.75% **0.0075**   10. 0.24% **0.0024**   11. $\frac{1}{5}$% **0.002**   12. $\frac{1}{8}$% **0.00125**

Express each number as a percent.   20. **0.116%**

13. 1.8 **180%**   14. 1.1 **110%**   15. 0.005 **0.5%**   16. 0.0035 **0.35%**

17. $9\frac{1}{4}$ **925%**   18. $7\frac{1}{2}$ **750%**   19. 0.0092 **0.92%**   20. 0.00116

For answers to Exercises 21–22, see margin.

Tell whether each of the following is reasonable. Explain your answer.

21. The 1990 population of California is 115% of its 1980 population.

22. Wayne Gretzky makes 125% of his shots on goal.

23. **Statistics** The population of Mexico in 1990 was 88,597,000. Experts estimate that by the year 2025, the population will be 150,061,000. Use a calculator to find the ratio of the 2025 population to the 1990 population as a percent. Round your answer to the nearest whole percent. **169%**

Exercises

Independent Practice

Express each percent as a decimal.   25. **0.00068**

24. 100% **1**   25. 0.068%   26. 325% **3.25**   27. 200% **2**

28. 0.0025%   29. 0.012%   30. 240% **2.4**   31. 0.032%
    0.000025   **0.00012**   **0.00032**

Express each number as a percent.

32. $3\frac{1}{2}$ **350%**   33. 5 **500%**   34. $4\frac{3}{4}$ **475%**   35. $5\frac{1}{4}$ **525%**

36. $3\frac{2}{5}$ **340%**   37. $1\frac{9}{10}$ **190%**   38. 80 **8,000%**   39. 285 **28,500%**

40. 1.7 **170%**   41. 0.001 **0.1%**   42. 2.25 **225%**   43. 0.009 **0.9%**

44. 18 **1,800%**   45. 3.1 **310%**   46. 0.0025 **0.25%**   47. 4 **400%**

446   Chapter 11 Ratio, Proportion, and Percent

OPTIONS

Gifted and Talented Needs

Tell students that a professional sports team has 12 players and a payroll that is about 300% of what it was the previous year. Ask them to make up two sensible numbers, one for this year's payroll, and one for last year's.   Sample answer:
36 million; 12 million

Additional Answers

21. yes; The ratio of the 1990 population to the 1980 population will be greater than 1 if the population increased. The number 115% is a ratio greater than one.

22. no; He cannot score more shots than he attempted.

Replace each ● with <, >, or =.

48. 1.5 ● 150% =

49. 1.25 ● 125% =

50. 14,000% ● 14 >

51. 560 ● 5,600% >

52. $12 \times \frac{1}{4}$ ● $12 \times 25\%$ =

53. $15 \times 1\frac{1}{3}$ ● $133\frac{1}{3}\% \times 15$ =

For answers to Exercises 54–59, see margin.

Tell whether each of the following is reasonable. Explain your answer.

54. 140% of the M&M® candies in a one-pound bag are brown.

55. An antique toy car is now worth 2,300% of its original price.

56. Nina makes 105% of her free throws.

57. John gave away 130% of his coin collection.

58. The school's enrollment is 118% of last year's enrollment.

59. A pine tree grows to 150% of its present height within two years.

Mixed Review

60. **Statistics** Construct a line plot for the following set of data: 14, 18, 15, 14, 17, 16, 17, 14, 15. *(Lesson 3-4)* **See Solutions Manual.**

61. Find the prime factorization of 140. *(Lesson 4-2)* $2^2 \cdot 5 \cdot 7$

62. **Geometry** Find the area of a rectangle having a length of 8.5 inches and a width of 4 inches. *(Lesson 6-7)* **34 in²**

63. See Solutions Manual.

63. **Geometry** Complete the pattern unit for the reflection at the right. Then draw the tessellation. *(Lesson 8-8)*

64. **Geometry** Find the area of a triangle having a base of 12 centimeters and a height of 7 centimeters. *(Lesson 9-7)* **42 cm²**

65. **Geometry** Find the surface area of the cylinder at the right. *(Lesson 10-4)* **207.24 in²**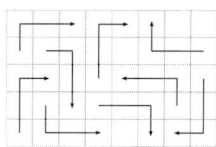

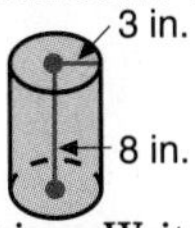

66. **Personal Finance** Wendy spends 45% of her earnings on clothing. Write this percent as a decimal. *(Lesson 11-9)* **0.45**

Problem Solving and Applications

67. **Statistics** The population of Kenya in 1990 was 25,129,000. Experts estimate that by the year 2025 the population will be 77,615,000. Use a calculator to express the ratio of the 2025 population to the 1990 population as a percent. Round your answer to the nearest whole percent. **309%**

68. **Critical Thinking** In 1990, the population of Hong Kong was 5,840,000. Experts estimate that by the year 2025 the population will be 119% of the 1990 population. What is the estimated population of Hong Kong in the year 2025? **about 6,949,600 people**

Lesson 11-10 Percents Greater Than 100% and Less Than 1% **447**

Extending the Lesson

Using Critical Thinking Refer students to Exercises 54–59 on page 447. Challenge them to rewrite the reasonable statements so that they no longer make sense, and to rewrite those that are unreasonable so that they do make sense.

Cooperative Learning Activity

Comparing Countries **11-10**

Use groups of 4 or more.
Materials: Reference books

● Together, find the land areas of the seven continents. Then each group member finds the land area of a different country.

➡ Answer the following questions.

1. What percent of the land area of the country you selected is the land area selected by each of the other group members?
2. What percent of the land area of the country you selected is the continent on which it is located?
3. What percent of the total land area on Earth is the land area of the country you selected?

Each group member shares his or her findings with the group.

Glencoe Mathematics: Applications and Connections, Course 2

Enrichment Masters, p. 100

Name _____ Date _____

Enrichment Worksheet 11-10

Knight Moves

In the game of chess, a knight can move several different ways. It can move two spaces vertically or horizontally, then one space at a 90° angle. It can also move one space vertically or horizontally, then two spaces at a 90° angle. Several examples of a knight's moves are indicated on the grid at the right.

1. Use the diagram at the right. Place a knight or other piece in the square marked 1. Move the knight so that it lands on each of the remaining white squares only once. Mark each square in which the knight lands with 2, then 3, and so on. **Sample answer given. Other answers are possible.**

1	6	3
4		8
7	2	5

2. Use the diagram below. Place a knight or other piece in the square marked 1. Move the knight so that it lands on each of the remaining squares only once. Mark each square in which the knight lands with 2, then 3, and so on.

29	20	25	10	5	14
26	9	28	13	24	11
19	30	21	6	15	4
8	27	2	17	12	23
1	18	7	22	3	16

Sample answer given. Other answers are possible.

T100
Glencoe Division, Macmillan/McGraw-Hill

Using the Chapter Study Guide and Review

The Chapter Study Guide and Review begins with a section on Communicating Mathematics. This includes questions that review the new terms and concepts that were introduced in the chapter.

Then, the Skills and Concepts presented in the chapter are reviewed using a side-by-side format. Encourage students to refer to the Objectives and Examples on the left as they complete the Review Exercises on the right.

The Chapter Study Guide and Review ends with problems that review Applications and Problem Solving.

Additional Answer

6. Sample answer: When you know the scale of a map, you can find actual distances by measuring the map distances with a ruler and writing and solving proportions.

11 Study Guide and Review

Communicating Mathematics

Choose the letter that best matches each phrase.

1. a comparison of two numbers by division **d**

2. a ratio of two measurements with different units **j**

3. an equation that shows that two ratios are equivalent **i**

4. a ratio that compares a number to 100 **a**

5. $\frac{3}{5}$ written as a percent **b**

6. In your words, explain how the scale on a map and a ruler can be used to find the actual distance between two cities. **See margin.**

a. percent
b. 60%
c. decimal
d. ratio
e. equation
f. 30%
g. unit rate
h. fraction
i. proportion
j. rate

Self Assessment

Objectives and Examples	Review Exercises
Upon completing this chapter, you should be able to:	*Use these exercises to review and prepare for the chapter test.*

- express ratios as fractions and determine whether two ratios are equivalent *(Lesson 11-1)*

  Express the ratio 6:18 as a fraction in simplest form.

  $$\frac{6}{18} = \frac{6 \div 6}{18 \div 6} = \frac{1}{3}$$

  The simplest form is $\frac{1}{3}$.

Express each ratio as a fraction in simplest form.

7. 25 to 10 $\frac{5}{2}$ 8. 14:70 $\frac{1}{5}$
9. 11:66 $\frac{1}{6}$ 10. 12 to 64 $\frac{3}{16}$
11. 90 to 33 $\frac{30}{11}$ 12. 50:100 $\frac{1}{2}$
13. 63:9 $\frac{7}{1}$ 14. 5 to 10 $\frac{1}{2}$

- determine unit rates *(Lesson 11-2)*

  Find the unit price for a 16-ounce box of pasta on sale for 96 cents.

  $$\frac{cents}{ounces} \rightarrow \frac{96}{16} = \frac{96 \div 16}{16 \div 16} = \frac{6}{1}$$

  The unit price is 6 cents per ounce.

Express each rate as a unit rate.

15. 16 cups for 4 people **4 cups per person**
16. 150 people for 5 classes **30 people per class**
17. $23.75 for 5 pounds **$4.75 per pound**
18. 810 miles in 9 days **90 miles per day**
19. $38 in 4 hours **$9.50 per hour**
20. 24 gerbils in 3 cages **8 gerbils per cage**

Objectives and Examples

- solve proportions *(Lesson 11-3)*

Solve $\frac{6}{9} = \frac{x}{12}$.

$$\frac{6}{9} = \frac{x}{12}$$
$$6 \times 12 = 9x$$

6 ⊠ 12 ⊟ 9 ⊟ 🔳

$8 = x$ The solution is 8.

- identify corresponding parts of similar polygons *(Lesson 11-4)*

1 cm ▭
3 cm

2 cm ▭
6 cm

The polygons above are similar because corresponding angles are congruent and corresponding lengths are in proportion: $\frac{1}{2} = \frac{3}{6}$.

- solve problems involving scale drawings *(Lesson 11-5)*

On a map, the scale is 1 inch:80 miles. Find the actual distance for a map distance of $3\frac{1}{4}$ inches.

$$\frac{map}{actual} \rightarrow \frac{1}{80} = \frac{3\frac{1}{4}}{n} \leftarrow \frac{map}{actual}$$

$n = 80 \times 3\frac{1}{4}$ or 260 miles

- illustrate the meaning of percent *(Lesson 11-7)*

Express 47:100 as a percent.

$$\frac{47}{100} = 47\%$$

- express fractions as percents, and vice versa *(Lesson 11-8)*

Express $\frac{18}{20}$ as a percent.

$$\frac{18}{20} = \frac{x}{100} \rightarrow 1{,}800 = 20x$$
$$90 = x$$

So, $\frac{18}{20} = 90\%$.

Review Exercises

Solve each proportion.

21. $\frac{13}{25} = \frac{39}{m}$ **75**

22. $\frac{w}{6} = \frac{12}{8}$ **9**

23. $\frac{350}{p} = \frac{2}{10}$ **1,750**

24. $\frac{45}{5} = \frac{x}{7}$ **63**

Tell whether each pair of polygons is similar. Justify your answer.

25. 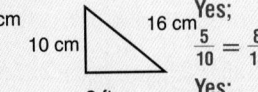 **Yes;** $\frac{5}{10} = \frac{8}{16}$.

26. 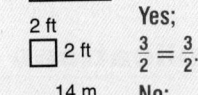 **Yes;** $\frac{3}{2} = \frac{3}{2}$.

27. 4 m / 7 m   6 m / 14 m   **No;** $\frac{4}{6} \neq \frac{7}{14}$.

On a map, the scale is 1 cm:36 km. For each map distance, find the actual distance.

28. 6 cm **216 km**
29. 4 cm **144 km**
30. 45 cm **1,620 km**
31. 10 cm **360 km**
32. 2 cm **72 km**
33. 12 cm **432 km**
34. 3 cm **108 km**
35. 100 cm **3,600 km**

Express each ratio as a percent.

36. 12 out of 100 **12%**
37. 63 out of 100 days **63%**
38. 99 out of 100 students **99%**

Express each fraction as a percent, or vice versa. Express fractions in simplest form.

39. $\frac{3}{5}$ **60%**

40. 65% $\frac{13}{20}$

41. $13\frac{1}{2}\%$ $\frac{27}{200}$

42. $\frac{150}{200}$ **75%**

43. $\frac{5}{8}$ **62.5%**

44. $33\frac{1}{3}\%$ $\frac{1}{3}$

Chapter 11 Study Guide and Review   **449**

You may wish to use a Chapter Test from the Evaluation Masters booklet as an additional chapter review. The two free-response forms are shown below. One of the two multiple-choice forms is shown on the next page.

Evaluation Masters, pp. 95–96

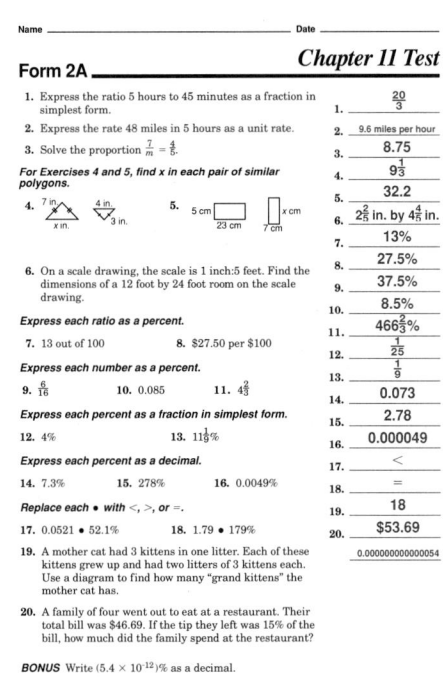

Objectives and Examples

- express decimals as percents, and vice versa *(Lesson 11-9)*

  Express 27% as a decimal.

  $$27\% = \frac{27}{100} = 0.27$$

- express percents greater than 100% and percents less than 1% as fractions and as decimals, and vice versa *(Lesson 11-10)*

  Write 2.35 as a percent.

  $$2.35 = 2\frac{35}{100} = \frac{235}{100} = 235\%$$

Review Exercises

Express each decimal as a percent, or vice versa.

45. 0.47 **47%** 46. 43.5% **0.435**
47. 75% **0.75** 48. 0.375 **37.5%**
49. 0.995 **99.5%** 50. $22\frac{1}{2}$% **0.225**

Express each percent as a decimal, or vice versa.

51. 125% **1.25** 52. 0.25% **0.0025**
53. 0.002 **0.2%** 54. 0.05% **0.0005**
55. 4.75 **475%** 56. 0.0095 **0.95%**

Applications and Problem Solving

57. **Population Density** In 1988, Memphis, Tennessee had a population of 645,190 people and an area of 264 square miles. To the nearest whole number, how many people per square mile are there in Memphis? *(Lesson 11-2)* **2,444 people per square mile**

58. The advisor for the Spanish Club tells three students about a club meeting. It takes 1 minute for her to tell three students and 1 minute for each of those three students to tell three other students, and so on. How many students will know about the meeting in three minutes? *(Lesson 11-6)* **39 students**

Curriculum Connection Projects

- **Sports** Find the fastest times for at least three Olympic running events. Write a ratio for each, comparing the length of the race (in meters) to the running time (in seconds). Find equivalent ratios, comparing kilometers to seconds and centimeters to seconds.

- **Consumer Awareness** Find the unit price of the different-sized boxes of several kinds of cereal. Make comparisons and write out your conclusions about how to be a smart shopper.

Read More About It

Du Bois, William Penn. *Giant.*
Phillips, Louis. *Brain Busters: Just How Smart Are You Anyway?*
Renner, A.G. *How to Build a Better Mousetrap, Car, and Other Experiments.*

450 **Chapter 11** Study Guide and Review

11 Test

Express each ratio as a fraction in simplest form.

1. 35:15 $\frac{7}{3}$

2. 42 out of 60 days $\frac{7}{10}$

Express each ratio as a unit rate.

3. 24 cards for $4.80 **$0.20 per card**

4. 330 miles on 15 gallons of gas **22 mpg**

5. In 1988, Richmond, Virginia had a population of 213,300 people and an area of 60 square miles. How many people per square mile were there in Richmond in 1988?
3,555 people per square mile

Solve each proportion.

6. $\frac{2}{3} = \frac{x}{42}$ **28**

7. $\frac{9}{m} = \frac{12}{36}$ **27**

8. **Physical Fitness** Alissa swims 3 laps in 12 minutes. At this same rate, how many laps will she swim in $10\frac{1}{2}$ minutes? $2\frac{5}{8}$ **laps**

Tell whether each pair of polygons is similar. Justify your answer.

9.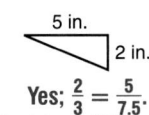
7.5 in.   5 in.
3 in.   2 in.
Yes; $\frac{2}{3} = \frac{5}{7.5}$.

10.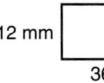
6 mm   12 mm
18 mm   36 mm
Yes; $\frac{6}{12} = \frac{18}{36}$.

On a map, the scale is 1 inch:150 miles. For each map distance, find the actual distance.

11. 5 inches **750 miles**

12. $3\frac{5}{6}$ inches **575 miles**

13. The express bus arrives at the Maple Street bus stop every 25 minutes, beginning at 5:40 A.M. The local bus arrives at this same bus stop every 15 minutes, beginning at 6:00 A.M. What is the first time during the day that the buses will arrive at the same time? **6:30 A.M.**

Express each ratio as a percent.

14. 15:100 **15%**

15. 95 points out of 100 **95%**

Express each fraction as a percent, or vice versa.

16. $\frac{3}{8}$ **37.5%**

17. $24\frac{1}{2}$% $\frac{49}{200}$

Express each decimal as a percent, or vice versa.

18. 0.65 **65%**

19. $\frac{1}{4}$% **0.0025**

20. **Economics** Analysts predict that the minimum wage in the year 2000 will be 130% of the 1991 minimum wage, which was $4.25. What is the predicted minimum wage for the year 2000? Round to the nearest cent. **$5.53**

Bonus Express $\frac{1}{25}$% in scientific notation. 4×10^{-4}

This page may be used as a chapter test or another chapter review.

Evaluation Masters, pp. 91–92

Name _____ Date _____

Chapter 11 Test

Form 1A

1. Express the ratio 12 yards to 8 feet as a fraction in simplest form.   1. **D**
   A. $\frac{12}{8}$ B. $\frac{3}{2}$ C. $\frac{1}{2}$ D. $\frac{9}{2}$

2. Express the rate of $1.35 for 45 pieces of paper as a unit rate.   2. **C**
   A. 30¢ per piece   B. 0.03¢ per piece
   C. 3¢ per piece   D. 9¢ per piece

3. Solve the proportion $\frac{30}{42} = \frac{55}{d}$.   3. **B**
   A. 39.3   B. 77   C. 67   D. 23

For Exercises 4 and 5, find the value of x in each pair of similar polygons.

4. A. 7 in.   B. 6.5 in.   4. **B**
   C. 26 in.   D. 13 in.

5. A. 1 ft   B. 3 ft   5. **C**
   C. $\frac{3}{4}$ ft   D. $\frac{2}{3}$ ft

6. On a map, the scale is 1 inch:125 miles. What is the actual distance if the map distance is $4\frac{1}{5}$ inches?   6. **B**
   A. 525 miles   B. $562\frac{1}{2}$ miles   C. $281\frac{1}{4}$ miles   D. 505 miles

7. On a scale drawing, the scale is $\frac{1}{4}$ inch:1 foot. What are the dimensions in the scale drawing for a room that is 15 feet by 24 feet?   7. **A**
   A. $3\frac{3}{4}$ inches by 6 inches   B. $7\frac{1}{2}$ inches by 12 inches
   C. $1\frac{1}{4}$ inches by 2 inches   D. $1\frac{1}{16}$ inch by 1 inch

8. Express the ratio 3 people out of 100 as a percent.   8. **C**
   A. 300%   B. 0.03%   C. 3%   D. 30%

9. Write a percent to represent the shaded area.   9. **D**
   A. 9%   B. 16%
   C. 38%   D. 31%

Name _____ Date _____

Chapter 11 Test, Form 1A (continued)

10. Express the fraction $\frac{7}{16}$ as a percent.   10. **D**
    A. 0.4375%   B. 437.5%   C. 4.375%   D. 43.75%

11. Express 12% as a fraction in simplest form.   11. **C**
    A. $\frac{12}{1}$ B. $\frac{12}{100}$ C. $\frac{3}{25}$ D. $\frac{6}{50}$

12. Express $6\frac{1}{4}$% as a fraction in simplest form.   12. **A**
    A. $\frac{1}{16}$ B. $\frac{25}{400}$ C. $\frac{1}{4}$ D. $\frac{5}{80}$

13. Express 0.047 as a percent.   13. **B**
    A. 47%   B. 4.7%   C. 0.47%   D. 0.047%

14. Express 3% as a decimal.   14. **A**
    A. 0.03   B. 3.0   C. 0.3   D. 30.0

15. Express 0.89% as a decimal.   15. **A**
    A. 0.0089   B. 89.0   C. 8.9   D. 0.089

16. Express 560% as a decimal.   16. **C**
    A. 56.0   B. 0.56   C. 5.6   D. 560.0

17. Express $1\frac{3}{5}$ as a percent.   17. **C**
    A. 13.5%   B. 135%   C. 160%   D. 16%

18. Replace ● with the correct symbol in $17 \times \frac{5}{8}$ ● $17 \times 83\frac{1}{3}$% to make a true statement.   18. **C**
    A. <   B. >   C. =   D. cannot be determined

19. The Fabulous Flower Shop sells roses at $25.99 for a dozen. Alice's Flower Shop sells roses at $12.99 for a half dozen. At Danitra's, roses sell for $2.25 each, and at Just Flowers, they sell for $8.65 for 4 roses. Which shop has the best buy for roses?   19. **D**
    A. Fab. Flowers   B. Alice's
    C. Danitra's   D. Just Flowers

20. Alexander folds a piece of paper in half and tears the paper along the fold. He then takes one of the pieces, folds it in half and tears it along the fold. How many pieces of paper will Alexander have if he folds and tears 13 times?   20. **C**
    A. 20   B. 13   C. 14   D. 26

BONUS A building actually stands 336 feet high. A scale model of the building stands 4 feet high. What is the scale factor of the model?   **B**
    A. 1 inch:84 feet   B. 1 inch:7 feet
    C. 1 inch:28 feet   D. 84 feet:1 inch

Test and Review Generator software is provided in Apple, IBM, and Macintosh versions. You may use this software to create your own tests or worksheets, based on the needs of your students.

The **Performance Assessment Booklet** provides an alternate assessment for evaluating student progress. An assessment for this chapter can be found on pages 21–22.

12 Applications with Percent

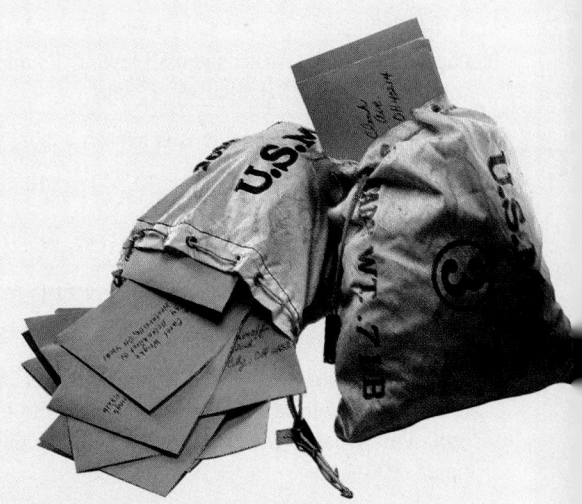

Previewing the Chapter

This chapter explores applications of percents, including interpreting and making circle graphs, calculating percent of change, estimating with percent, and working with discount, simple interest, and sales tax. Math connections include geometry, measurement, and statistics. Especially valuable are the connections of percent to proportion and to algebra. These connections allow students to solve any percent problem without the need to decide which of three special cases is the correct one in a particular instance. In the **problem-solving strategy** lesson, students solve problems by first solving a simpler problem.

Lesson	Lesson Objectives	NCTM Standards	State/Local Objectives
12-1	Find the percent of a number.	1–5, 7, 9	
12-2	Solve problems by solving a simpler problem.	1–5, 7	
12-3	Estimate by using fractions, decimals, and percents interchangeably.	1–5, 7	
12-4	Solve problems using the percent proportion.	1–5, 7	
12-5	Solve problems using the percent equation.	1–5, 7, 9	
12-6A	Make a circle graph.	1–5, 7, 10	
12-6	Construct circle graphs.	1–5, 7, 10	
12-7A	Use dot paper to show percent increase or percent decrease.	1–5	
12-7	Find the percent of increase or decrease.	1–5, 7, 9, 12	
12-8	Solve problems involving sales tax and discount.	1–5, 7, 9	
12-9	Solve problems involving simple interest.	1–5, 7, 9	

Organizing the Chapter

A complete, 1-page lesson plan is provided for each lesson in the Lesson Plans Masters Booklet.

LESSON PLANNING GUIDE

Lesson	Materials/ Manipulatives	Extra Practice (Student Edition)	Study Guide	Practice	Enrichment	Evaluation	Technology	Lab Manual	Multicultural Activities	Application and Interdisciplinary Activities	Transparencies	Group Activity Cards
						Blackline Masters Booklets						
12-1		p. 597	p. 101	p. 101	p. 101				p. 12		12-1	12-1
12-2			p. 102	p. 102	p. 102						12-2	12-2
12-3	calculator, grid paper, marker	p. 598	p. 103	p. 103	p. 103			p. 72			12-3	12-3
12-4	calculator	p. 598	p. 104	p. 104	p. 104						12-4	12-4
12-5	calculator	p. 598	p. 105	p. 105	p. 105	Quiz A, p. 106					12-5	12-5
12-6A	jelly beans, needles, thread, compass, ruler							p. 73				
12-6	compass, protractor	p. 599	p. 106	p. 106	p. 106						12-6	12-6
12-7A	dot paper							p. 74				
12-7	ruler, dot paper, calculator	p. 599	p. 107	p. 107	p. 107					p. 26	12-7	12-7
12-8	calculator	p. 599	p. 108	p. 108	p. 108		p.12			p. 12	12-8	12-8
12-9	calculator	p. 600	p. 109	p. 109	p. 109	Quiz B, p. 106	p. 26				12-9	12-9
Study Guide and Review	newspapers		Multiple Choice Test, Forms 1A and 1B, pp. 100–103 Free Response Test, Forms 2A and 2B, pp. 104–105 Cumulative Review, p. 107 (free response)									
Test			Cumulative Test, p. 108 (multiple choice)									

Pacing Guide: Option I (Chapters 1–12) - 13 days; Option II (Chapters 1–13) - 12 days; Option III (Chapters 1–14) - 11 days
You may wish to refer to the complete **Course Planning Guides** on page T25.

OTHER CHAPTER RESOURCES

Student Edition
Chapter Opener, pp. 452–453
Cultural Kaleidoscope, p. 458
Mid-Chapter Review, p. 468
Portfolio Suggestions, pp. 468, 481
Academic Skills Test, pp. 448–449

Manipulatives
Overhead Manipulative Resources
Middle School Mathematics Manipulative Kit

Software/Technology
Interactive Mathematics Tools (Macintosh)
Test and Review Generator (IBM, Apple, Macintosh)
Teacher's Guide for Software Resources

Other Supplements
Transparency 12–0
Performance Assessment, pp. 23–24
Glencoe Mathematics Professional Series
Lesson Plans, pp. 132–142

INTERDISCIPLINARY BULLETIN BOARD

Language Arts Connection

Objective Use a word list to solve problems involving percent.

How To Use It Have students examine the list of the winning spelling words from the last 20 Scripps Howard National Spelling Bees. (You may wish to give them the test first, preparing them by telling them that these are the last correctly spelled words in the contest each year.) Then ask students to analyze the list to determine what percent of the words they are familiar with, what percent are verbs, nouns, adjectives, or adverbs, and what percent are derived from various languages. Encourage students to come up with other ways to analyze the list using percents.

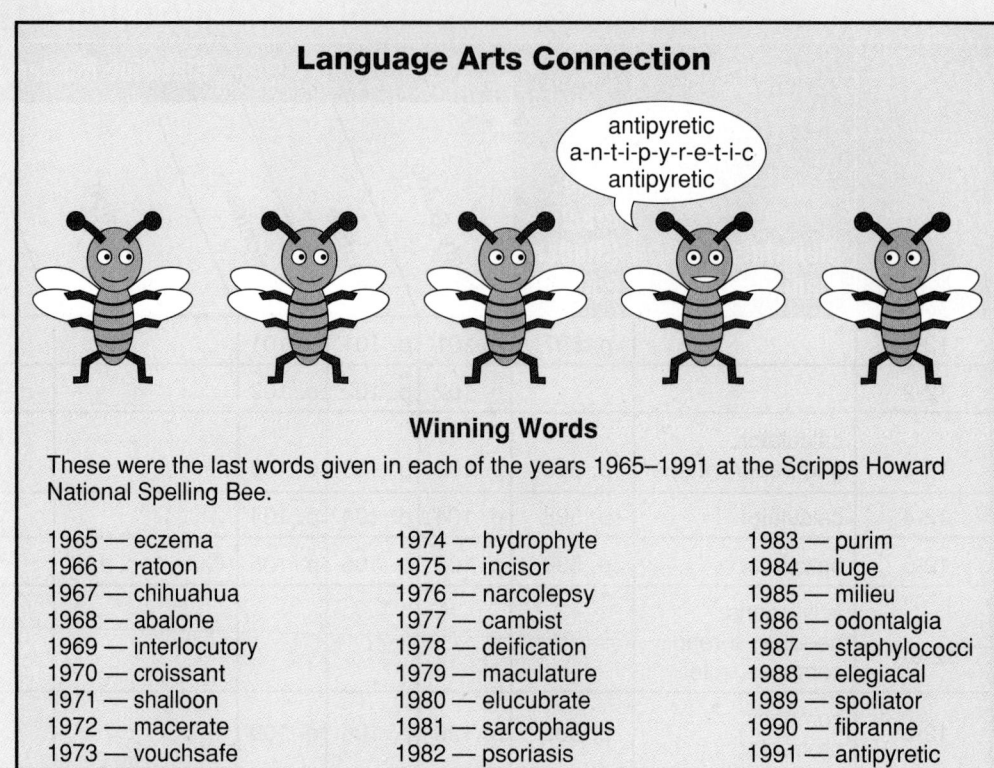

Language Arts Connection

antipyretic
a-n-t-i-p-y-r-e-t-i-c
antipyretic

Winning Words

These were the last words given in each of the years 1965–1991 at the Scripps Howard National Spelling Bee.

1965 — eczema	1974 — hydrophyte	1983 — purim
1966 — ratoon	1975 — incisor	1984 — luge
1967 — chihuahua	1976 — narcolepsy	1985 — milieu
1968 — abalone	1977 — cambist	1986 — odontalgia
1969 — interlocutory	1978 — deification	1987 — staphylococci
1970 — croissant	1979 — maculature	1988 — elegiacal
1971 — shalloon	1980 — elucubrate	1989 — spoliator
1972 — macerate	1981 — sarcophagus	1990 — fibranne
1973 — vouchsafe	1982 — psoriasis	1991 — antipyretic

APPLICATIONS AND CONNECTIONS

Applications	Lesson	Example	Exercise
Music	12-1	X	
Education	12-1		24
Ecology	12-1		25
Immigration	12-1		27
Smart Shopping	12-3	2	
Consumer Math	12-3		40
Animals	12-3		42
Smart Shopping	12-4	2	
Defense	12-4		39
Olympics	12-4		40
Photocopying	12-5		42, 44
Sports	12-5		43
Sales	12-6	1	
Business	12-6		24
Energy	12-6		26
Health	12-7	1	
Retail Sales	12-7	2	
History	12-7		24
Smart Shopping	12-8	1–2	32, 34
Consumer Math	12-8		31, 33
Saving Money	12-9	X	
Consumer Math	12-9		24
Computer	12-9		25
Connections			
Statistics	12-4	1	
Geometry	12-7		29

TEAM ACTIVITIES

Multicultural Experiences

Outside Field Trips Through a trip to a bank and a discussion with a banker there, students can learn more about how banks calculate interest rates for savings and other accounts, as well as for lending money.

Students can visit an office, perhaps one in which a parent works, to find out how percents are used when a copier enlarges or reduces the size of an image.

In-Class Speakers Ask a salesperson to visit and talk with students about how commission works.

Invite a representative from a credit card company to introduce students to some of the various services the company provides and to explain how using a credit card works, including how interest is calculated.

SUPPLEMENTARY BLACKLINE MASTER BOOKLETS

Some of the blackline masters for enhancing this chapter are shown below.

Application and Interdisciplinary Activity Masters, pp. 12, 26

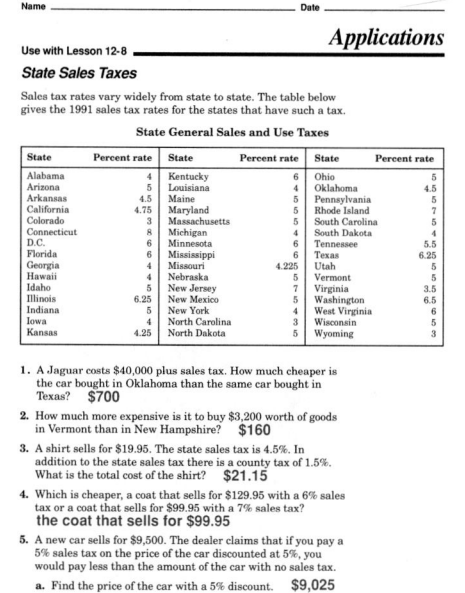

Name _____ Date _____

Applications

Use with Lesson 12-8

State Sales Taxes

Sales tax rates vary widely from state to state. The table below gives the 1991 sales tax rates for the states that have such a tax.

State General Sales and Use Taxes

State	Percent rate	State	Percent rate	State	Percent rate
Alabama	4	Kentucky	6	Ohio	5
Arizona	5	Louisiana	4	Oklahoma	4.5
Arkansas	4.5	Maine	5	Pennsylvania	5
California	4.75	Maryland	5	Rhode Island	7
Colorado	3	Massachusetts	5	South Carolina	5
Connecticut	8	Michigan	4	South Dakota	4
D.C.	6	Minnesota	6	Tennessee	5.5
Florida	6	Mississippi	6	Texas	6.25
Georgia	4	Missouri	4.225	Utah	5
Hawaii	4	Nebraska	5	Vermont	5
Idaho	5	New Jersey	7	Virginia	3.5
Illinois	6.25	New Mexico	5	Washington	6.5
Indiana	5	New York	4	West Virginia	6
Iowa	4	North Carolina	3	Wisconsin	5
Kansas	4.25	North Dakota	5	Wyoming	3

1. A Jaguar costs $40,000 plus sales tax. How much cheaper is the car bought in Oklahoma than the same car bought in Texas? **$700**

2. How much more expensive is it to buy $3,200 worth of goods in Vermont than in New Hampshire? **$160**

3. A shirt sells for $19.95. The state sales tax is 4.5%. In addition to the state sales tax there is a county tax of 1.5%. What is the total cost of the shirt? **$21.15**

4. Which is cheaper, a coat that sells for $129.95 with a 6% sales tax or a coat that sells for $99.95 with a 7% sales tax? **the coat that sells for $99.95**

5. A new car sells for $9,500. The dealer claims that if you pay a 5% sales tax on the price of the car discounted at 5%, you would pay less than the amount of the car with no sales tax.

   a. Find the price of the car with a 5% discount. **$9,025**

   b. Find the total cost of the car based on your answer to part **a**. **$9,476.25**

   c. Use your answer from part **b** to decide if the dealer's claim is true. **The claim is true.**

T12
Glencoe Division, Macmillan/McGraw-Hill

Name _____ Date _____

Interdisciplinary Activity

Use with Lesson 12-7

Social Studies

An immigrant is a person who leaves one country to take up permanent residence in another country. The table below shows comparative statistics for immigration to the United States. Numbers are given in thousands.

Country/Continent	1971-1980	1981-1990
Hong Kong	113.5	98.2
Africa	80.8	176.8
Israel	37.7	44.2
Mexico	640.3	1,655.7
Switzerland	8.2	57.6
France	25.1	92.1
Denmark	4.4	2.8
Argentina	29.9	27.3

Find the percent of increase or decrease for each place over the two decades in the table above. Round answers to the nearest hundredth of a percent.

1. Israel **17.24%**
2. Argentina **8.70%**
3. Denmark **36.36%**
4. France **266.93%**
5. Mexico **158.58%**
6. Switzerland **602.44%**
7. Hong Kong **13.48%**
8. Africa **118.81%**

9. Of the places in the table, which had the greatest percent of increase? **Switzerland**

10. Of the places in the table, which had the greatest percent of decrease? **Denmark**

11. Of the places in the table which had the least change? **Argentina**

T26
Glencoe Division, Macmillan/McGraw-Hill

Multicultural Activity Masters, p. 12

Name _____ Date _____

Multicultural Activity

Use with Lesson 12-1

Charles Richard Drew

Dr. Charles Drew (1904–1950) was an African-American surgeon and scientist who did pioneering research in methods of storing blood plasma. In 1940, at the request of the British government, he organized the world's first blood plasma bank. His blood bank became the model for the system of blood banks opened by the American Red Cross in 1941.

Why was Dr. Drew's work so significant? A doctor who gives a blood transfusion must be sure that the **blood type** of the donor is a safe match to the patient's blood type. If it is not, the patient could become seriously ill or even die. Organized blood banks make a large supply of blood available to doctors in emergency situations, when a safe match is needed at a moment's notice.

There are several different systems of classifying blood. The charts at the right give information about the widely used *ABO system*. Use these charts to answer the following questions.

Blood Types Among the United States Population	
Type	Percent of Population
O	42%
A	44%
B	10%
AB	4%

Safe Blood Matches	
Donor	Patient
AB →	AB
A →	AB or A
B →	AB or B
O →	AB, A, B, or O

All other matches are unsafe.

1. According to the 1990 census, the population of the United States is about 250,000,000. About how many people in the United States have each blood type?

   a. type O **105,000,000**   b. type A **110,000,000**

   c. type B **25,000,000**   d. type AB **10,000,000**

2. What percent of the population can safely donate blood to a type B patient? **52%**

3. What percent of the population can safely receive blood from a type O donor? **100%**

4. One fifth of all type B persons are classified as *B negative*. What percent of the entire population is this? **2%**

5. Seven eighths of all type AB persons are classified as *AB negative*. What percent of the entire population is this? **$3\frac{1}{2}$%**

T12
Glencoe Division, Macmillan/McGraw-Hill

Technology Masters, p. 26

Name _____ Date _____

Computer Activity

Use with Lesson 12-9

Compound Interest

When a bank pays interest on both the deposit and the interest gained, the bank is said to *compound* the interest. An account that earns compound interest will grow faster than an account that earns simple interest.

The BASIC program below will compute the amount in an account that receives compound interest. The program will also compute the total interest gained.

To use the program, you enter the amount of the deposit, the annual interest rate as a decimal, the number of years the amount will be allowed to grow, and the number of times interest will be given in a year. (For example, if interest is given every four months, enter 3 for N.)

```
TYPE    NEW
        10  PRINT "COMPOUND INTEREST"
        20  INPUT "PRINCIPAL AMOUNT" ; P
        30  INPUT "RATE (AS A DECIMAL)" ; R
        40  INPUT "NUMBER OF YEARS" ; T
        50  INPUT "NUMBER OF COMPOUNDING PERIODS PER YEAR" ; N
        60  A = P * ((1 + R/N) ^ (N * T))
        70  A = INT(A * 100 + .5) / 100
        80  I = INT((A - P) * 100 + .5) / 100
        90  PRINT "THE ACCOUNT EARNED $" ; I ;" INTEREST."
        100 PRINT "THE ACCOUNT BALANCE IS $" ; A ; "."
        110 END
```

Use the program above to find each amount and interest earned.

1. $1,000, 6.5%, 2 years, paid every 4 months
   interest, $137.25; balance, $1,137.25

2. $650, 5%, 1.5 years paid every 3 months
   interest, $50.30; balance, $700.30

3. $2,120, 8.4%, 3 years, paid every month
   interest, $605.19; balance, $2,725.19

4. $4,000, 9%, 2.5 years, paid every six months
   interest, $984.73; balance, $4,984.73

5. $500, 4.5%, 1 year paid every 3 months
   interest, $22.88; balance, $522.88

6. $6,200, 9.2%, 3.5 years paid every 4 months
   interest, $2,313.99; balance, $8,513.99

T26
Glencoe Division, Macmillan/McGraw-Hill

RECOMMENDED OUTSIDE RESOURCES

Books/Periodicals

Curcio, Frances, *Developing Graph Comprehension: Elementary and Middle School Activities,* Reston, VA: NCTM, 1989.

Schulte, Albert P., ed., *Teaching Statistics and Probability, 1981 Yearbook,* NCTM, 1981.

Films/Videotapes/Videodiscs

Problem Solving in Mathematics, Mount Kisco, NY: Pathescope Educational Media, 1983.

Teaching Mathematics Effectively, Alexandria, VA: ASCD, 1982.

Software

Elastic Lines: The Electronic Geoboard, (Apple II and IBM/Tandy), Wings for Learning/Sunburst

For addresses of companies handling software, please refer to page T24.

INTER·ACTIVE Mathematics

Glencoe's *Interactive Mathematics: Activities and Investigations* consists of 18 units that may be used as alternatives or supplemental material for *Mathematics: Applications and Connections.* The suggested unit for this chapter is Unit 16, *Growing Pains.* See page T18 for more information.

This two-page introduction to the chapter provides a visual, relevant way to engage students in the mathematics of the chapter. Questions are included that help students see the need to learn the mathematics in the chapter. Data in charts and graphs provide statistical information that students can analyze and interpret at this point as well as later in the chapter. The Chapter Project provides an activity that applies the mathematics of the chapter.

MAKING MATHEMATICS RELEVANT

Spotlight on Mail

Point out that the prices given for stamps are for first class stamps. Ask students to find out other postal rates, such as rates per ounce for mail that weighs more than 1 ounce, or prices for postcards and other classes of mail. A visit to the post office may help. Students can find out how these other prices have changed over the years, too.

There are many opportunities for students to use applications of percents to examine the mail. For example, you may wish to have students figure out the percents of price increases.

Using the Timeline

Have students research the history of price changes for postcard rates. Ask them to indicate where these dates fit on the timeline. Students can talk with older family members to get information as well as visiting the post office.

Chapter

12

Applications with Percent

Spotlight on Mail

Have You Ever Wondered. . .

- What percent of the mail is delivered early or late?
- How the cost of a postage stamp has changed over the years?

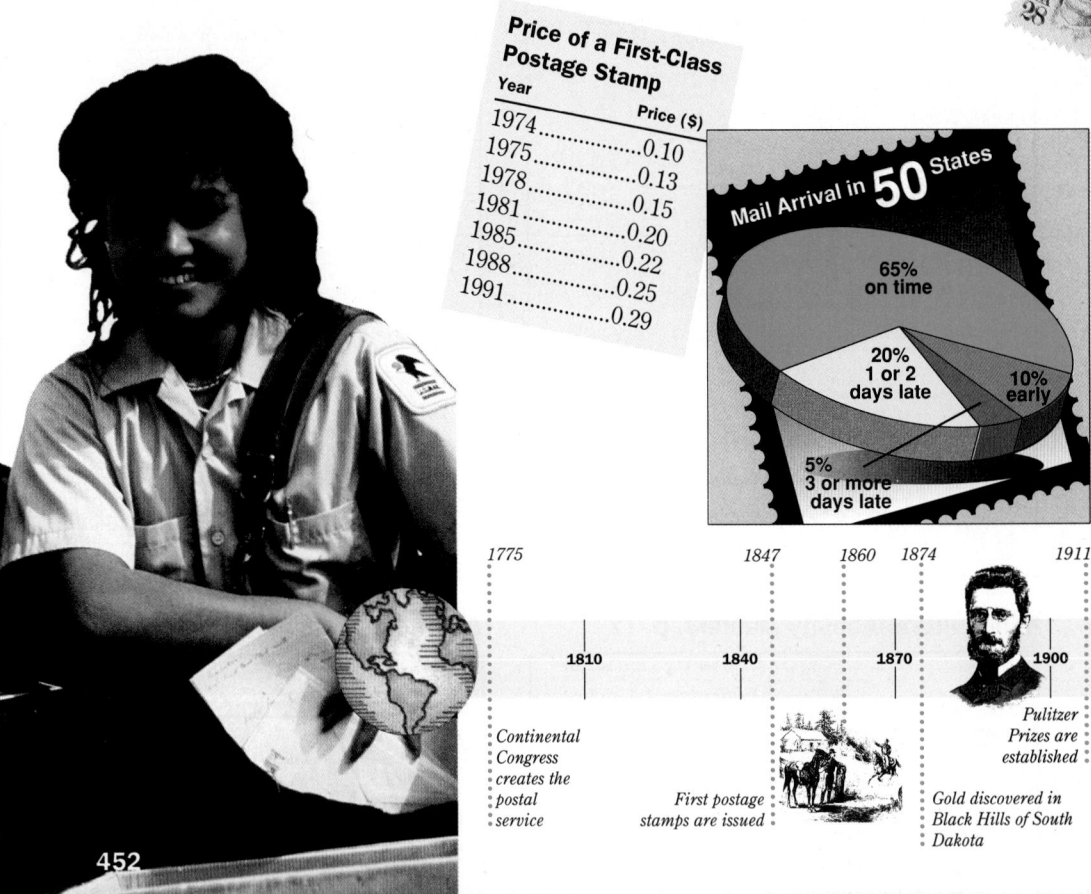

Price of a First-Class Postage Stamp

Year	Price ($)
1974	0.10
1975	0.13
1978	0.15
1981	0.20
1985	0.22
1988	0.25
1991	0.29

Mail Arrival in **50** States

65% on time

20% 1 or 2 days late

10% early

5% 3 or more days late

1775 — Continental Congress creates the postal service

1810

1840

1847 — First postage stamps are issued

1860

1870

1874 — Gold discovered in Black Hills of South Dakota

1900

1911 — Pulitzer Prizes are established

452

"Have You Ever Wondered?" Answers

- Students can see from the circle graph that 10% of the mail is delivered early and 25% of it is delivered late.
- It has almost tripled.

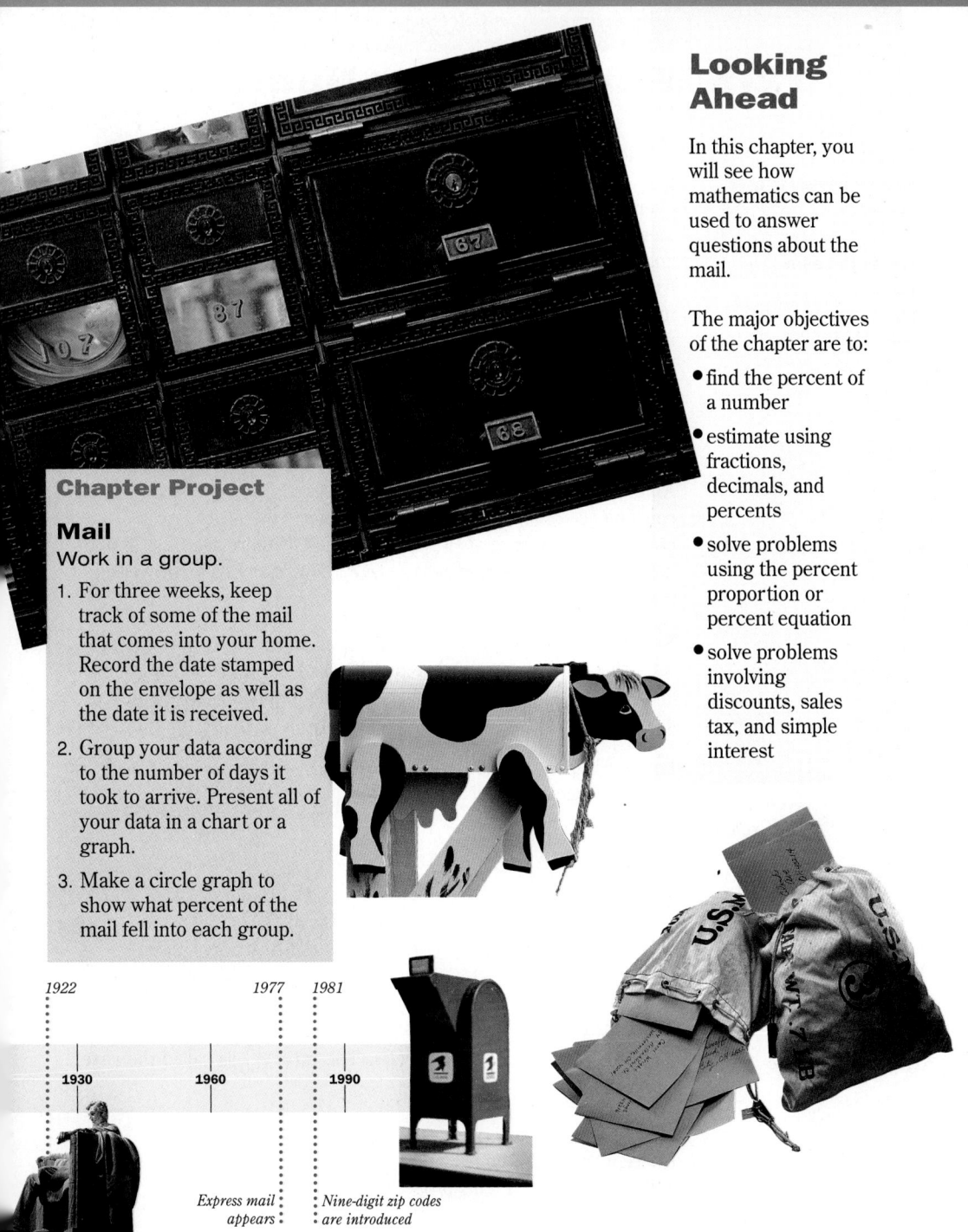

Looking Ahead

In this chapter, you will see how mathematics can be used to answer questions about the mail.

The major objectives of the chapter are to:

- find the percent of a number
- estimate using fractions, decimals, and percents
- solve problems using the percent proportion or percent equation
- solve problems involving discounts, sales tax, and simple interest

Chapter Project

Mail
Work in a group.

1. For three weeks, keep track of some of the mail that comes into your home. Record the date stamped on the envelope as well as the date it is received.

2. Group your data according to the number of days it took to arrive. Present all of your data in a chart or a graph.

3. Make a circle graph to show what percent of the mail fell into each group.

1922   1977 1981

1930   1960   1990

Express mail   Nine-digit zip codes
appears   are introduced

453

DATA ANALYSIS

Have groups of students prepare a list of items other than stamps that people purchase frequently, such as newspapers and magazines, cans of soda, cups of coffee, and subway or bus tokens. Have them do research to make tables showing price increases over the years.

Data Search

A question related to these data is provided in Lesson 12-7, page 478, Exercise 26.

CHAPTER PROJECT

This project is designed to give students an opportunity to record data and express data as percents. Remind students that they do not need to alter the mail in any way; they simply need to record the difference between the date stamped on the envelope and the date received. Combining the data of several students within a group will allow them to calculate the results for a larger test group.

Lesson Resources
- Study Guide Master 12-1
- Practice Master 12-1
- Enrichment Master 12-1
- Multicultural Activity, p. 12
- Group Activity Card 12-1

 Transparency 12-1 contains the 5-Minute Check and a teaching aid for this lesson.

🕐 5-Minute Check
(Over Chapter 11)

1. Find the unit price for 15 cards on sale for $0.75. $0.05 per card
2. Solve $\frac{3}{4} = \frac{x}{24}$.   18
3. On a map, the scale is 1 inch : 120 miles. Find the actual distance for a map distance of $3\frac{1}{2}$ inches.   420 miles
4. Express $\frac{7}{8}$ as a percent. $87\frac{1}{2}\%$
5. Express $\frac{1}{5}\%$ as a decimal. 0.002

1 FOCUS

Motivating the Lesson

Situational Problem Ask students how they would figure out the savings on a car stereo system that is selling for 15% off the regular price of $300.

2 TEACH

Using Applications Survey class members to find out how many of their homes have telephone-answering machines. Use the data to write a ratio and a percent proportion. Then have students use a newspaper to identify the price of an answering machine. Guide students to find out what the reduction in price of the machine would be if it were on sale for 20% off.

12-1 Percent of a Number

Objective
Find the percent of a number.

Words to Learn
percent
percentage
base
rate
percent proportion

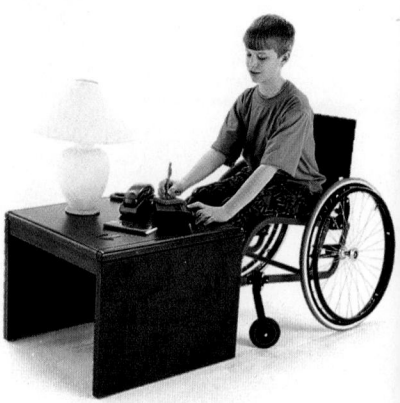

"Hello, we can't come to the phone right now. . . ." Have you ever called a friend and gotten a message like this on their answering machine? It can be frustrating to get the answering machine rather than the person. And yet these devices can also be helpful. Rather than calling someone over and over, you can just leave a message for them to call you back.

Americans are realizing the convenience of answering machines. *About* 40% of American households now have answering machines. If there are 92,800,000 households in the United States, *about* how many have answering machines?

Results of surveys are often reported as percents. A **percent** is a ratio that compares a number to 100. So 40% stated in the problem above means that 40 out of every 100 households have answering machines.

Let x represent the number of households with answering machines. Write a proportion.

LOOKBACK

You can review proportions on page 414.

$$\frac{x}{92,800,000} = \frac{40}{100}$$
$$x \cdot 100 = 92,800,000 \cdot 40$$
$$x = \frac{3,712,000,000}{100} \qquad \textit{Divide each side by 100.}$$
$$x = 37,120,000$$

In the United States, 37,120,000 households have answering machines.

In the proportion above, x is called the **percentage (P).** The number 92,800,000 is called the **base (B).** The ratio $\frac{40}{100}$ is called the **rate.**

$$\frac{40}{100} \quad \rightarrow \quad \frac{Percentage}{Base} = Rate$$

If r represents the number per hundred, the proportion can be written as $\frac{P}{B} = \frac{r}{100}$. This proportion is called the **percent proportion.**

OPTIONS

Reteaching Activity

Using Models Students can model a percent of a number by shading rows of boxes on grid paper.

Study Guide Masters, p. 101

Name _____ Date _____

Study Guide Worksheet 12-1

Percent of a Number

A percent is a ratio that compares a number to 100.

Example   3 out of 4 is what percent?

$$\frac{3}{4} = \frac{r}{100}$$
$$3 \times 100 = 4r \qquad \text{Find cross products.}$$
$$\frac{300}{4} = \frac{4r}{4} \qquad \text{Divide each side by 4.}$$
$$75 = r$$

3 out of 4 is 75%.

You can use the proportion below to solve percent problems.

$$\frac{P}{B} = \frac{r}{100} \qquad P = \text{percentage} \quad B = \text{base} \quad \frac{r}{100} = \text{rate}$$

Music Compact disc players are on sale for 20% off. If the regular price is $200, what is the discount?

You can draw a diagram to show 20% of 200.

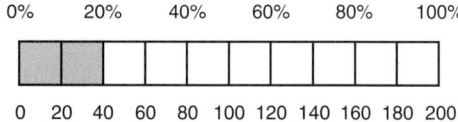

You can also use the percent proportion to find 20% of 200.

$$\frac{P}{B} = \frac{r}{100}$$

$$\frac{P}{200} = \frac{20}{100}$$ *Replace B with 200 and r with 20.*

$$P \cdot 100 = 200 \cdot 20$$ *Write the cross products.*

$$\frac{P \cdot 100}{100} = \frac{4{,}000}{100}$$ *Divide each side by 100.*

$$P = 40$$

The discount is $40.

Checking for Understanding

For answers to Exercises 1–4, see margin.

Communicating Mathematics

Read and study the lesson to answer each question.

1. **Tell** what is meant by the rate.

2. **Write** a proportion that can be used to find 42% of 386.

3. **Write** a percent proportion that represents the diagram at the right.

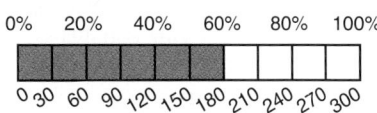

4. **Show** how you would express a fraction as a percent.

Guided Practice

Complete each proportion or write a proportion for each problem. Then solve. Round answers to the nearest tenth.

5. Find 93% of 215.
$$\frac{P}{B} = \frac{r}{100}$$
$$\frac{P}{215} = \frac{?}{?} \quad \frac{93}{100}; P = 200.0$$

6. Find 64% of 88.
$$\frac{P}{B} = \frac{r}{100}$$
$$\frac{?}{?} = \frac{64}{100} \quad \frac{P}{88}; P = 56.3$$

7. What number is 40% of 220?
$$\frac{P}{220} = \frac{40}{100}; \quad 88$$

8. 12% of 16.5 is what number?
$$\frac{P}{16.5} = \frac{12}{100}; \quad 2.0$$

Exercises

Independent Practice

Use a proportion to solve each problem. Round answers to the nearest tenth.

9. What number is 25% of 560? **140**

10. Find $37\frac{1}{2}$% of 64. **24**

11. 50% of 128 is what number? **64**

12. What number is 25% of 36? **9**

13. Find 80% of $90\frac{1}{2}$. **72.4**

14. What number is 75% of 92? **69**

Lesson 12-1 Percent of a Number   455

Additional Answers

1. the ratio $\frac{r}{100}$

2. $\frac{P}{386} = \frac{42}{100}$

3. $\frac{P}{300} = \frac{60}{100}$

4. Sample answer: $\frac{3}{5} = \frac{r}{100}$; $5r = 300$; $r = 60$; $\frac{3}{5} = \frac{60}{100}$, or 60%

More Examples

For the Example

Use the percent proportion to find 30% of 300.   **90**

Teaching Tip Encourage students to look for common-fraction equivalents of the percents in the problems. If the base is a multiple of the denominator of that fraction, another way to solve the problem is to multiply the fraction by the base. Thus, 30% of 300 is $\frac{30}{100} \times 300$, or 30×3.

Checking for Understanding

Exercises 1–4 are designed to help you assess students' understanding through reading, writing, speaking, and modeling. You should work through these exercises with your students and then monitor their work on Guided Practice Exercises 5–8.

Practice Masters, p. 101

Name _____   Date _____

Practice Worksheet 12-1

Percent of a Number

Express each ratio as a percent.

1. $\frac{7}{10}$
70%

2. $\frac{6}{25}$
24%

3. $\frac{16}{50}$
32%

Express each fraction as a percent.

4. $\frac{3}{5}$
60%

5. $\frac{19}{5}$
380%

6. $\frac{15}{40}$
37.5%

Use a proportion to solve each problem. Round answers to the nearest tenth.

7. What number is 18% of 450?
81

8. Find 92% of 120.
110.4

9. $37\frac{1}{2}$ is 30% of what number?
125

10. 45% of 156 is what number?
70.2

11. 96 is 30% of what number?
320

12. Forty percent of 80 is what number?
32

13. What number is 58% of 200?
116

14. $33\frac{1}{3}$% of 249 is what number?
83

15. What number is 12% of one-hundred fifty?
18

16. Find $82\frac{1}{2}$% of 400.
330

T101
Glencoe Division, Macmillan/McGraw-Hill

Have students explain what happens to a percent of a number as the percent increases. Ask them what happens when it decreases.

3 PRACTICE/APPLY

Assignment Guide
Maximum: 9–30
Minimum: 9–19 odd, 20–30

For **Extra Practice,** see p. 597.

Alternate Assessment

Writing Have students give an example of how to find the percent of a number using a percent proportion.

Enrichment Masters, p. 101

Name _____ Date _____

Enrichment Worksheet 12-1

Model Behavior

When a block is painted and then separated into small cubes, some of the faces of the cubes will have paint on them and some will not.

For each set of blocks determine the percent of cubes that are painted on the given number of faces.

1. 0 faces   0
2. 1 face   0
3. 2 faces   64
4. 3 faces   32
5. 4 faces   4
6. 5 faces   0
7. 6 faces   0

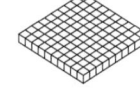

8. 0 faces   0
9. 1 face   0
10. 2 faces   0
11. 3 faces   0
12. 4 faces   90
13. 5 faces   10
14. 6 faces   0

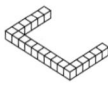

15. 0 faces   0
16. 1 face   0
17. 2 faces   0
18. 3 faces   0
19. 4 faces   100
20. 5 faces   0
21. 6 faces   0

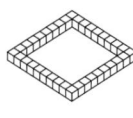

T 101
Glencoe Division, Macmillan/McGraw-Hill

456

---

15. 30% of 96 is what number? **28.8**
16. 28% of 14 is what number? **3.9**
17. Twenty-five percent of 32 is what number? **8**
18. What number is 20% of twenty? **4**
19. The purchase price of an answering machine is $140. The state tax rate is 6.5% of the purchase price.
    a. How much state tax is charged? **$9.10**
    b. What is the total cost? **$149.10**

Mixed Review
20. Find 2.6×0.3. *(Lesson 2-4)* **0.78**
21. Find $12 - (-4)$. *(Lesson 7-5)* **16**
22. **Measurement** A can of mixed vegetables is in the shape of a cylinder with a radius of 1.5 inches and a height of 6 inches. Find the amount of paper necessary to make a label for the can. Remember, the label on a can does not cover the ends. *(Lesson 10-4)* **56.52 in²**
23. Express 0.00065 as a percent. *(Lesson 11-9)* **0.065%**

Problem Solving and Applications
24. **Education** In the United States, approximately 30% of the students entering ninth grade do not graduate from high school. Of the 345 people entering the ninth grade class at Jefferson High, how many of these students are likely to graduate from high school? **about 242 students**
25. **Ecology** On an average day, approximately 93.3 million aluminum cans are produced. Of these, *about* 50% are recycled. **about 47 million**
    a. To the nearest million, how many aluminum cans are recycled each day?
    b. If an aluminum can weighs *about* 0.5 ounce, how many pounds of aluminum are recycled on an average day? **about 1,468,750 pounds**
26. **Critical Thinking** Ngan paid $224 for a remote-control, color television. Tim paid 110% of this amount for the same television at another store. How much more did Tim pay for the same television? **$22.40**

27. **676 immigrants**

27. **Immigration** On an average day 1,648 persons immigrate to the United States. Nearly 41% of these will become naturalized American citizens. On an average day, how many of the immigrants are likely to become citizens?

DATA SEARCH

28. **Data Search** Refer to page 649. About how much popped popcorn do Americans consume at home? **12.6 billion quarts or 49.7 gallons per person**

29. **Consumer Math** Sam Davis bought a couch that cost $899. The store required a 25% down payment to hold the couch. How much was the down payment? **$224.75**

30. **Travel** The travel club is going to the Grand Canyon. There are 44 members. If 75% of the members sign up for the trip, how many members are going to the Grand Canyon? **33 members**

OPTIONS

Extending the Lesson

Using Percents Have students write a quiz for classmates consisting of 5 problems to solve by finding the percent of a number. If possible, students should use actual information from a newspaper, magazine, or catalogue to formulate their problems.

Cooperative Learning Activity

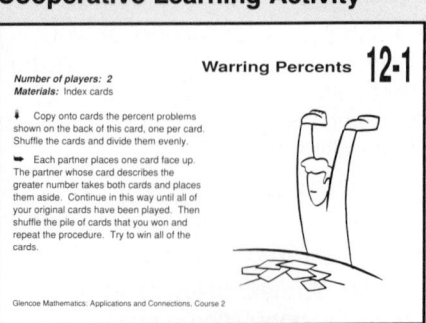

Number of players: 2   **Warring Percents** **12-1**
Materials: Index cards

♣ Copy onto cards the percent problems shown on the back of this card, one per card. Shuffle the cards and divide them evenly.

♣ Each partner places one card face up. The partner whose card describes the greater number takes both cards and places them aside. Continue in this way until all of your original cards have been played. Then shuffle the pile of cards that you won and repeat the procedure. Try to win all of the cards.

Glencoe Mathematics: Applications and Connections, Course 2

12-2 Solve a Simpler Problem

Objective

Solve problems by solving a simpler problem.

A 1989 survey of 58,000 households found that 11 states west of the Mississippi River had the highest percent of high school graduates, while the Washington, D.C. area had the highest percent with college degrees.

Suppose the number of people over the age of 25 in a certain county is 14,757,899. If 78.6% of the people over 25 have high school diplomas, *about* how many people have diplomas?

Explore   What do you know?
You know that the county's population is 14,757,899 and that the percent of people over 25 who graduated from high school is 78.6%.

What are you trying to find?
You are trying to find *about* how many people over the age of 25 in this county have high school diplomas.

Plan   Round the numbers to make a simpler problem. Then use patterns to find the product.

Solve   Round each number to its greatest place value.

$$14{,}757{,}889 \rightarrow 10{,}000{,}000$$
$$78.6\% \rightarrow 80\%$$

Think: 80% of 10 = 8
80% of 100 = 80
80% of 1,000 = 800
80% of 10,000 = 8,000
80% of 100,000 = 80,000
80% of 1,000,000 = 800,000
80% of 10,000,000 = 8,000,000

About 8,000,000 people have diplomas.

Examine   You could also solve the problem by changing 80% to a fraction and multiply mentally to find $\frac{4}{5}$ of 10,000,000.

$$\frac{4}{5} \times 10{,}000{,}000 = 8{,}000{,}000 \checkmark$$

Lesson 12-2 Problem-Solving Strategy: Solve a Simpler Problem   **457**

OPTIONS

Reteaching Activity

Using Problem Solving   Rather than rounding the numbers in the opening situation, you may wish to have students work through a similar, but simpler problem. For example, use 24 rather than 23,667,764, and 75% rather than 78.6%. Think: Find 75% of 24.

Practice Masters, p. 102

Name _____   Date _____

Practice Worksheet 12-2

Problem-Solving Strategy: Solve a Simpler Problem
Solve by solving a simpler problem.

1. How many diagonals does a 20-sided polygon have?   **170**

2. Lisa sent a recipe to five of her friends. Each friend then sent a recipe to five of their friends, who then sent a recipe to five of their friends. How many recipes were sent in all?   **155**

Solve. Use any strategy.

3. Lindsay built a 3-sided rectangular dog run up against the side of a shed. The length is twice the width. If Lindsay used 100 feet of fence, what is the area of the dog run?   **1,250 ft² or 800 ft²**

4. Thirty-three percent of the persons who voted in the 1988 presidential election lived in the South. If there were 102,000,000 voters, how many lived in the South?   **33,660,000**

5. Brian types word processing documents at a speed of thirty words per minute. If Travis types 20% faster than Brian, what is Travis' typing speed?   **36 words per minute**

6. A number is tripled and then six is added to it. The result is sixty. What is the number?   **18**

7. Rosemarie ordered pizza, a chocolate shake, a salad, and breadsticks for dinner. The salad was $1.00 more than the breadsticks, and the shake cost the same as the salad. The pizza cost eight times as much as the shake. The total cost of dinner was $12.00. How much did the pizza cost?   **$8**

8. Shnea earned $1,985.72 in 1991. If 14% of the money was paid in federal and state taxes, what was her average weekly salary after taxes were taken out?   **$32.84**

T102
Glencoe Division, Macmillan/McGraw-Hill

Study Guide Masters, p. 102

Name _____   Date _____

Study Guide Worksheet 12-2

Problem-Solving Strategy: Solve a Simpler Problem

The Oakland Coliseum has a capacity of 48,621 people. For one afternoon baseball game, 38,824 tickets were sold. About what percent of the stadium was full?

Examine   What do you know?
You know that the Oakland Coliseum has a capacity of 48,621 people and that 38,824 tickets were sold for a game.

What are you trying to find?
You are trying to find about what percent of the stadium was full.

Plan   Round the numbers to make a simpler problem. Then find the percent.

Solve   Round each number to its greatest place value.

Questioning Ask students what other applications of this problem-solving strategy they might have used, such as games won in a tournament.

2 TEACH

More Examples

Twenty-four percent of the 26,488 voters voted for Kane. About how many people voted for Kane?
about 6,000 people

Close

Have students explain how to use the strategy of solving a simpler problem.

3 PRACTICE/APPLY

Assignment Guide
Maximum: 4–7
Minimum: 4–7

Enrichment Masters, p. 102

Name _____ Date _____

Enrichment Worksheet 12-2

Working With Percents

Percent problems can be solved by using the percent proportion. Solve each equation at the bottom of the page by using the percent proportion. Then from the table below, choose the correct symbol for each answer.

⊠ = 15%	▭ = 8	△ = 64	○ = 40%
⟋ = 450	▢ = 60%	▭ = 75%	⊕ = 2
⊖ = 2.56	⊠ = 62.5%	△ = 37.5%	⊞ = 84

1. 12.5% of 16 = ⊕

2. ▭ = 80% of 10

3. ▭ of 180 = 135

4. 21 = 25% of ⊞

5. 0.18 = ⊠ of 1.2

6. 8% of 32 = ⊖

7. 50 = ○ of 125

8. ⊠ of 64 = 40

9. ⟋ = 75% of 600

10. 13.5 = △ of 36

11. 28% of △ = 17.92

12. ▢ of 120 = 72

T102
Glencoe Division, Macmillan/McGraw-Hill

458

Checking for Understanding

Communicating Mathematics

Read and study the lesson to answer each question.

1. **Tell** how you would use a calculator to find the exact number of people in California who have high school diplomas. Enter 78.6 [%] [×] the population of California [=]

Guided Practice

Solve by solving a simpler problem.

2. Rochelle sent out 24 invitations to her party and asked each guest to RSVP by Saturday. Twenty-five percent of the guests could not attend. How many people were at her party? **18 people**

3. Michael made a 30% down payment on a $12,000 car. How much was his down payment? **$3,600**

Problem Solving

Practice

Solve. Use any strategy.

Strategies
•••••••••
Look for a pattern.
Solve a simpler problem.
Act it out.
Guess and check.
Draw a diagram.
Make a chart.
Work backwards.

4. Two thirds of the student body voted in the Student Council election. If there are 600 students, how many people voted? **400 people**

5. There are 16 dancers trying out for a musical. Twenty-five percent of them will receive a part. How many parts are there for dancers? **4 parts**

6. There are 24,624 high school seniors applying to a certain college for enrollment. If the college only accepts 2 out of every 9 applicants, how many of the seniors will be accepted? **5,472 seniors**

7. A number is doubled and −9 is added to it. The result is −1. What is the number? **4**

CULTURAL KALEIDOSCOPE

Henry Cisneros

Henry Cisneros was aware of his Mexican-American heritage and keenly interested in helping poorer citizens. His doctorate in public administration took him to San Antonio State University in Texas, where he began his teaching and political careers.

At 27 he became the youngest councilman in San Antonio history (1975–1981). During his term, he became involved with the Mexican-American community action group called Communities Organized for Public Service

(COPS). He gained national attention as a leading Hispanic politician and was appointed by President Reagan to serve on the National Bi-Partisan Commission on Central America. In 1981, he was elected Mayor of San Antonio and retired from office in 1989. During his administration, San Antonio benefitted from his vision and desire for improvement in the lives of all citizens. He brought revenue, jobs, and revitalization to San Antonio.

OPTIONS

Extending the Lesson

Cultural Kaleidoscope Discuss with your students the importance of mathematics in the economic development of a city. Ask them what elements they might use to develop a budget for a city the size of San Antonio.

Cooperative Learning Activity

Reading Is Fundamental **12-2**

Use groups of 4.
Materials: Reference books

Read the following.

A country's literacy rate tells the percent of the country's people who can read. In richer countries, such as the United States and Japan, the literacy rate is more than 90%. In poorer countries, such as Ethiopia or India, the literacy rate is much lower than 50%.

The literacy rates of ten countries are given below. Working in pairs, find the populations of these countries. Try to be the first to list the countries in order from greatest number of people who *cannot* read to least number of people who cannot read.

Colombia	88%	Egypt	45%
Denmark	99%	Kenya	59%
Malta	82%	Morocco	28%
Nepal	20%	Pakistan	26%
Madagascar	68%	Kuwait	71%

Glencoe Mathematics: Applications and Connections, Course 2

12-3 Percent and Estimation

Objective
Estimate by using fractions, decimals, and percents interchangeably.

Suppose that ElectroWorld is having a 25% off sale on all CD players in February. You decide to buy one that regularly costs $239. *About how much money could you save during this sale?*

You can estimate the savings by rounding $239 to $240 and using one of the methods below.

Fraction Method	1% Method	Meaning of Percent Method
25% is the same as $\frac{1}{4}$. $\frac{1}{4}$ of $240 is $60.	1% means $\frac{1}{100}$. 1% of 240 is $\frac{1}{100}$(240) or 2.40. $2.40 rounds to $2. Now find 25% or 25(1%). $25 \times \$2 = \$50$	25% means $25 for every $100 and $2.50 for every $10. $240 = 2(\$100) + 2(\$20)$ $25(2) + \$2.50(4) = \$60$
Estimate: $60	**Estimate: $50**	**Estimate: $60**

Calculator Hint
• • • • • • • • • • • •
You can use the $\boxed{\%}$ key on your calculator to compute with percents. The percent key replaces the percent with its decimal equivalent.

You can use a calculator to find the exact savings. $25 \boxed{\%} \boxed{\times} 239 \boxed{=} 59.75$

The exact savings would be $59.75. Compare this to the estimates to see if the answer is reasonable.

The following Mini-Lab will help you relate area and percent.

Mini-Lab

Work with a partner.
Materials: grid paper, marker

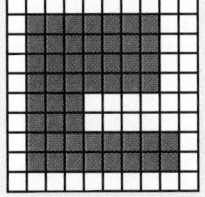 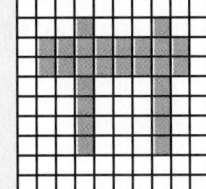 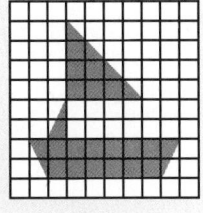

Sample answers:
50%, 20%, 25%;
50%, 26%, 23%;
See students' work.

They are not exact.

- Estimate the percent of the shaded portion of each figure.
- Then count grid squares to find the percent shaded.
- Draw a design on a 10×10 grid and shade it. Estimate the percent shaded. Then count to find the exact percent.

Talk About It
How do the estimates compare with the actual percents?

Lesson 12-3 Percent and Estimation **459**

OPTIONS

Reteaching Activity

Using Number Sense Encourage students to use any of the methods shown and to round numbers and percents prior to computing the estimates. Suggest that they look for compatible numbers.

Study Guide Masters, p. 103

Name _____ Date _____

Study Guide Worksheet 12-3

Percent and Estimation

You can use these three methods to estimate with percents.

Example   Estimate 77% of 800. Use the fraction method.

77% is about 75%, which is $\frac{3}{4}$.
$\frac{3}{4}$ of 800 = $\frac{3}{4} \times 800 = 600$
So, 77% of 800 is about 600.

Example   Estimate 122% of 42. Use the meaning of percent method.

122% is about 120%   120% = 100% + 20%
42(100% + 20%) = 42 + 2(4.2)   20% means 2 × 10%.
               = 42 + 8.4
               = 50.4
So, 122% of 42 is about 50.4.

459

Checking for Understanding

Exercises 1-2 are designed to help you assess students' understanding through reading, writing, speaking, and modeling. You should work through these exercises with your students and then monitor their work on Guided Practice Exercises 3-8.

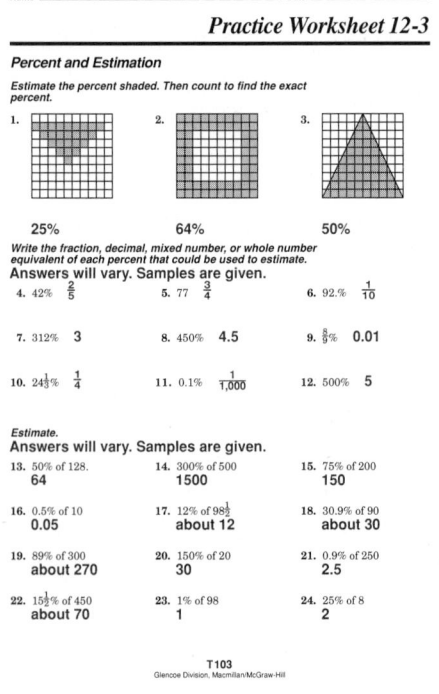
460

Example 1

Estimate 38% of 500.

38% is about 40% or $\frac{2}{5}$.

$\frac{1}{5}$ of 500 is 100.

$\frac{2}{5}$ of 500 is 200.

So, 38% of 500 is *about* 200.

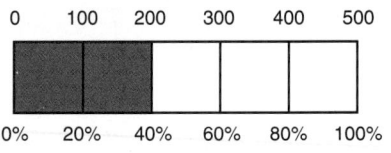

Example 2 *Problem Solving*

Smart Shopping   Estimate the savings on a $349 item with 30% off.

10% of $349 is $34.90

$34.90 rounds to $35.00.

3 times $35.00 is $105.00   The savings is *about* $105.00.

You can also estimate percents of numbers when the percent is less than 1 or the percent is greater than 100.

Examples

3   Estimate 112% of $36.

112% is more than 100%, so 112% of 36 is greater than 36.

112% is *about* 110%.

110% = 100% + 10%

36(100% + 10%) = 36 + 3.6
                = 39.6

112% of 36 is *about* 39.6.

4   Estimate 0.5% of 521.

0.5% is half of 1%.

521 is about 500.

1% means $\frac{1}{100}$.

$\frac{1}{100} \cdot 500 = 5$

$\frac{1}{2}$ of 5 is 2.5.

0.5% of 521 is *about* 2.5.

Checking for Understanding

Communicating Mathematics

Read and study the lesson to answer each question.

1. **Draw** a figure or design on a 10×10 grid. Shade $\frac{2}{10}$ of the figure or design. What percent is shaded? **20%**

2. **Show** how you would find a percent of a number using a calculator. See students' work.

Estimate the percent shaded. Then count to find the exact percent.

3. about 30%; 36%
4. about 60%; 52%
5. about 30%; 30%

3. 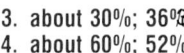   4. 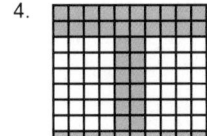   5.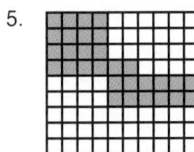

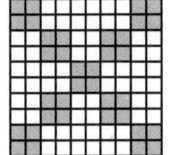

OPTIONS

Gifted and Talented Needs

Have students estimate percents of distances that others have marked off on the classroom floor. For example, a pair of students measures a distance of 20 feet, marking only the beginning and end points, and then challenges another pair to mark a spot that is 75% of that distance.

Interactive Mathematics Tools

This multimedia software provides an interactive lesson that is tied directly to Lesson 12-3. Students will use grids to estimate areas as in the Mini Lab.

Estimate. **For Exercises 6-8, sample answers are given.**

6. 25% of 408 **100**   7. 0.3% of 425 **1.2**   8. 121% of $56 **$68**

Exercises

Independent Practice

Write the fraction, decimal, mixed number, or whole number equivalent of each percent that could be used to estimate. **For Exercises 9-20, sample answers given.**

9. 37% **0.4**   10. 25% $\frac{1}{4}$ 11. 200% **2**   12. 87% **0.9**

13. 13% **0.1**   14. $4\frac{1}{2}$% **0.05**   15. 0.8% **0.01**   16. 43.5% **0.4**

17. $\frac{7}{8}$% **0.01**   18. 16.97% **0.2**   19. $12\frac{2}{5}$% $\frac{1}{8}$ 20. 350% **3.5**

Estimate. **For Exercises 21-32, sample answers given.**

21. 40% of 62 **24**   22. 25% of 18 **4**   23. 16% of 32.6 **6**

24. 1% of 89 **0.9**   25. $6\frac{1}{2}$% of 236 **10**   26. 30.5% of 50 **15**

27. 0.6% of 220 **1.1**   28. 150% of 52 **78**   29. 75% of 125 **90**

30. 8% of $12\frac{3}{4}$ **1.2**   31. 0.3% of 35 **0.1**   32. 200% of 540 **1,000**

33. What number is 20% of $16.21? Estimate. **about $3**

34. Estimate 50% of 89. **about 45**

Mixed Review

35. **Statistics** Find an appropriate scale and interval for the following data. Then construct a number line using the scale and interval. 25, 39, 15, 48, 33, 27, 14. *(Lesson 3-3)* **See Solutions Manual.**

36. Solve $p - 14 = 27$. *(Lesson 6-2)* **41**

37. **Geometry** Classify the angle at right as acute, obtuse, right, or straight. *(Lesson 8-1)* **acute**

38. **Travel** On his summer vacation, Matthew drove 350 miles in 5 hours on the first day. He continued driving at the same rate the second day and drove for 8 hours. How many miles did Matthew drive the second day of his vacation? *(Lesson 11-2)* **560 miles**

39. Find 45% of 1,600. *(Lesson 12-1)* **720**

Problem Solving and Applications

40. **Consumer Math** When the McGraw family went out for pizza, their bill was $21.97. They wanted to leave a tip of approximately 15%. What is a reasonable estimate of the tip? **about $3**

41. **Horoscope** On an average day, more than 105 million Americans read a newspaper. Of these, 26% of the people read their horoscope. Estimate the number of newspaper readers who read their horoscope.

42. **Animals** A flying squirrel ranges from 20 to 37 inches in length. Its tail is 40% of the squirrel's total length. Estimate the length of the tail of a flying squirrel.   **about 8 to 16 inches**

43. **Journal Entry** When do you think it will be useful to be able to estimate using percents, fractions, or decimals? Can you think of a time where you heard or read estimates in these forms? **See students' work.**

41. **about 25 million Americans**

Lesson 12-3 Percent and Estimation   **461**

Error Analysis

Watch for students who do not recognize cases for which applying the fraction method makes the most sense.

Prevent by having students review their lists of commonly used percents and fractional equivalents.

Close

Have students distinguish among the three methods for estimating percents and provide examples of each method.

3 PRACTICE/APPLY

Assignment Guide
Maximum: 9-43
Minimum: 9-33 odd, 35-42

For **Extra Practice,** see p. 598.

Alternate Assessment

Writing Have students write a problem that involves estimating the percent of a number. Have them exchange papers and solve the problems.

Enrichment Masters, p. 103

Name _____ Date _____

Enrichment Worksheet 12-3

Mapping A Strategy

1. The distance between each pair of intersections in the diagram below is 250 feet. A mail carrier must walk each path, and would like to choose a route through the diagram that is the shortest route. If the carrier must begin at intersection 1 and end at intersection 2, what is the length of the shortest route? Show that route.

Answers may vary. A sample is given.

3,500 feet

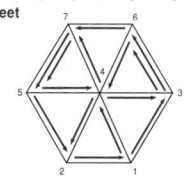

2. A newspaper carrier must bicycle each path on the diagram below and would like to choose a route through the diagram that is the shortest. If the carrier can begin at any location on the diagram, what is the length of the shortest route? Show that route.

6,700 feet

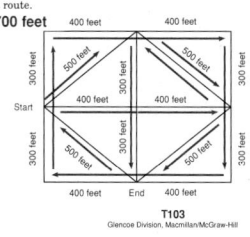

T103
Glencoe Division, Macmillan/McGraw-Hill

Extending the Lesson

Consumer Math Have students obtain advertisements for products in newspapers, fliers, or catalogues. Ask them to choose a budget, such as $200, and select 3 or 4 items they estimate they can afford within that budget. Students should include estimates of the sales tax when choosing the items. They should check their estimates with a calculator.

Cooperative Learning Activity

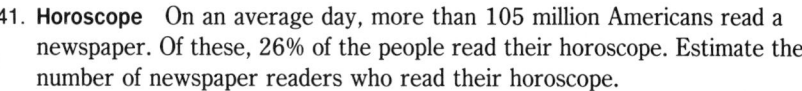

Use groups of 3.
Materials: Newspapers

Supermarket Markup **12-3**

♦ Read the following.

When a supermarket owner buys the items that fill the shelves in his or her store, he or she pays less for them than you do. Charging you more than he or she has to pay allows the supermarket owner to pay for and maintain a building that is located near you. It also allows the owner to hire people to serve you and to make a living for himself or herself. The price a supermarket owner pays for most items is usually 85% of the price he or she charges you for the same items.

➡ Each group member finds the prices of five items you could buy at a supermarket and estimates the price the supermarket owner had to pay for each item.

Glencoe Mathematics: Applications and Connections, Course 2

NCTM Standards: 1–5, 7

Lesson Resources
• Study Guide Master 12-4
• Practice Master 12-4
• Enrichment Master 12-4
• Group Activity Card 12-4

 Transparency 12-4 contains the 5-Minute Check and a teaching aid for this lesson.

🕐 5-Minute Check
(Over Lesson 12-3)

Write the fraction, decimal, mixed number, or whole number equivalent of each percent that could be used to estimate. All answers are sample answers.

1. 89% $\frac{9}{10}$

2. 13% $\frac{1}{8}$

Estimate.

3. 60% of 31   18

4. 300% of 78   240

5. 75% of 410   300

1 FOCUS

Motivating the Lesson

Activity Have students use an almanac or other source to compare changes in results of women's Olympic track and field events to changes in results of men's track and field events. Ask them to describe what they find and try to explain the differences.

2 TEACH

Using Connections In this lesson students will be using proportions to solve three different kinds of problems involving percent. First they find a percent of a number, then what percent one number is of another, and finally they find a number given a percent of it. You may wish to distinguish among these three kinds of percent problems.

12-4 The Percent Proportion

Objective
Solve problems using the percent proportion.

DID YOU KNOW

Betsy King is a golfer; Steffi Graf is a tennis player; Ingrid Kristiansen is a runner.

What do Betsy King, Steffi Graf, and Ingrid Kristiansen have in common? They are all women athletes.

Women are competing in more and more sporting events these days. And yet women's sporting events only get 5% of the total television air time. If there are a total of 140 hours of air time in an average week, how many of these hours are in women's sporting events? Use the percent proportion to solve this problem.

$$\frac{P}{B} = \frac{r}{100}$$

$$\frac{P}{140} = \frac{5}{100} \qquad B = 140, \ r = 5$$

$$P \cdot 100 = 140 \cdot 5 \qquad \textit{Find the cross products.}$$

$$\frac{P \cdot 100}{100} = \frac{700}{100} \qquad \textit{Divide each side by 100.}$$

$$P = 7 \quad \text{Women's sporting events are aired 7 hours per week.}$$

There are many competitors for each position in professional and amateur sports. Competition for the Olympics is very fierce. The graph shows an estimated number of athletes who competed for Olympic teams and the number of athletes who were selected to attend the games.

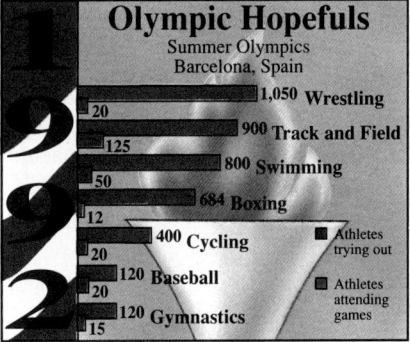

Olympic Hopefuls
Summer Olympics
Barcelona, Spain

1,050 Wrestling — 20
900 Track and Field — 125
800 Swimming — 50
684 Boxing — 12
400 Cycling — 20
120 Baseball — 20
120 Gymnastics — 15

■ Athletes trying out
■ Athletes attending games

Example 1   *Connection*

Statistics What percent of the athletes trying out for boxing in the 1992 Olympics actually got to attend the games?

$$\frac{P}{B} = \frac{r}{100}$$

$$\frac{12}{684} = \frac{r}{100} \qquad \textit{Replace B with 684 and P with 12.}$$

$$12 \cdot 100 = 684 \cdot r \quad \textit{Find the cross products.}$$

$$1,200 = 684r$$

$$1200 \ \boxed{\div} \ 684 \ \boxed{=} \ \mathbf{1.754386} \qquad \textit{Divide each side by 684.}$$

$$1.754386 \approx r$$

OPTIONS

Reteaching Activity

Using Discussion Carefully work through the problems with students, focusing on what the problem asks and what information is given, in terms of the percent, base (*B*), and percentage (*P*). Guide them to understand that $\frac{r}{100}$ always represents the percent.

Study Guide Masters, p. 104

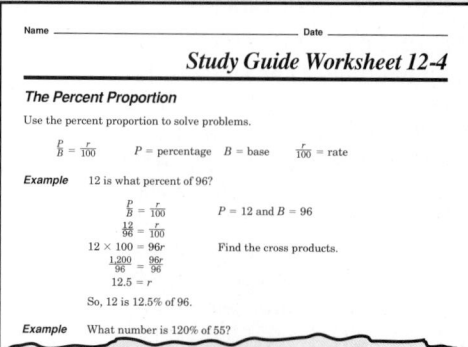

Name _____ Date _____

Study Guide Worksheet 12-4

The Percent Proportion

Use the percent proportion to solve problems.

$$\frac{P}{B} = \frac{r}{100} \qquad P = \text{percentage} \quad B = \text{base} \quad \frac{r}{100} = \text{rate}$$

Example   12 is what percent of 96?

$$\frac{P}{B} = \frac{r}{100} \qquad P = 12 \text{ and } B = 96$$

$$\frac{12}{96} = \frac{r}{100}$$

$$12 \times 100 = 96r \qquad \text{Find the cross products.}$$

$$\frac{1,200}{96} = \frac{96r}{96}$$

$$12.5 = r$$

So, 12 is 12.5% of 96.

Example   What number is 120% of 55?

To the nearest tenth of a percent, *about* 1.8% of the athletes who tried out for the 1992 Olympic boxing team got to attend the games.

You can also use the percent proportion to find the base when the percentage and rate are known.

Example 2 *Problem Solving*

Smart Shopping A combination speakerphone/answering machine is on sale for $140. This is 70% of the regular price. What is the regular price?

$$\frac{P}{B} = \frac{r}{100}$$

$$\frac{140}{B} = \frac{70}{100} \qquad P = 140, \ r = 70$$

$$140 \cdot 100 = B \cdot 70 \qquad \text{Find the cross products.}$$

$$\frac{14{,}000}{70} = \frac{B \cdot 70}{70}$$

$$200 = B$$

The regular selling price is $200. *You can check by finding 70% of $200.*

Checking for Understanding

For answers to Exercises 1–3, see Solutions Manual.

Communicating Mathematics

Read and study the lesson to answer each question.

1. **Tell** what P, B, and r represent in the percent proportion.

2. **Tell** why the percent proportion is helpful.

3. **Show** how you would use the percent proportion to find the rate if the percentage is 18 and the base is 54.

Guided Practice

Match each rate with its corresponding proportion.

4. 48 is 75% of what number? **b**   a. $\frac{P}{48} = \frac{75}{100}$

5. 48 is what percent of 75? **c**   b. $\frac{48}{B} = \frac{75}{100}$

6. What number is 75% of 48? **a**   c. $\frac{48}{75} = \frac{r}{100}$

Write a proportion for each problem. Then solve. Round answers to the nearest tenth.

7. What number is 45% of 60? **27**   8. 3 is what percent of 40? **7.5%**

9. 80 is 75% of what number? **106.7**   10. What percent of 24 is 12? **50%**

11. Find 42.5% of 48. **20.4**   12. 20% of what number is 25? **125**

13. The class picture included 95% of the students. Seven students were missing from the picture. How many students were in the class?
140 students

Classroom Vignette

"Students can act as servers with menus from local restaurants. Students switch from the role of server, (where they total the bills and calculate the tax), to the role of customer, (where they check the total and determine the tip). This is a practical use of percents that everyone needs to practice."

Virginia P. Healy

Virginia P. Healy, Teacher
Thomas Harrison Middle School,
Harrisonburg, VA

More Examples

For Example 1

What percent of the athletes who tried out for the baseball team in the Olympics actually attended the games? $16\frac{2}{3}\%$

For Example 2

A printer is on sale for $400. This is 80% of the regular price. What is the regular price? $500

Checking for Understanding

Exercises 1-3 are designed to help you assess students' understanding through reading, writing, speaking, and modeling. You should work through these exercises with your students and then monitor their work on Guided Practice Exercises 4-13.

Error Analysis

Watch for students who, by confusing the terms, set up their proportions incorrectly.

Prevent by having students first estimate a reasonable answer and then write the proportion accordingly.

Practice Masters, p. 104

Name _____   Date _____

Practice Worksheet 12-4

The Percent Proportion

Name the percentage, base, or rate.

1. 12 is what percent of 30?
   percentage: 12, base: 30

2. 40% of what number is 82?
   percentage: 82, rate: 40%

3. What percent of 49 is 7?
   percentage: 7, base: 49

4. 6.25% of 190 is what number?
   base: 190, rate: 6.25%

5. 64.2% of 84 is what number?
   base: 84, rate: 64.2%

6. What percent of 76 is 14?
   percentage: 14, base: 76

Write a proportion for each problem. Then solve. Round answers to the nearest tenth.

7. What number is 32% of 1,000?
   $\frac{P}{1{,}000} = \frac{32}{100}$, 320

8. What is 84% of 180?
   $\frac{P}{180} = \frac{84}{100}$, 151.2

9. $12\frac{1}{2}$ is 25% of what number?
   $\frac{12\frac{1}{2}}{B} = \frac{25}{100}$, 50

10. 85% of 190 is what number?
    $\frac{P}{190} = \frac{85}{100}$, 161.5

11. What percent of 128 is 24?
    $\frac{24}{128} = \frac{R}{100}$, 18.8%

12. 25 is what percent of 365?
    $\frac{25}{365} = \frac{R}{100}$, 6.8%

13. What number is 20% of 625?
    $\frac{P}{625} = \frac{20}{100}$, 125

14. $33\frac{1}{3}\%$ of 900 is what number?
    $\frac{P}{900} = \frac{33\frac{1}{3}}{100}$, 300

T104
Glencoe Division, Macmillan/McGraw-Hill

463

Have students explain how to use the percent proportion to solve problems.

3 PRACTICE/APPLY

Assignment Guide
Maximum: 14–42
Minimum: 15–31 odd, 33–42

For **Extra Practice,** see p. 598.

Alternate Assessment

Writing Have students use real Olympics data to write a problem for classmates to solve by using the percent proportion.

Enrichment Masters, p. 104

Exercises

Independent Practice

Name the percentage, base, or rate. **For answers to Exercises 14–17, see Solutions Manual**

14. 8 is what percent of 16?
15. 20% of what number is 18?
16. 58.2% of 50 is what number?
17. What number is 105% of 36?
18. 5% of what number is $6\frac{1}{2}$? **rate = 5% percentage = $6\frac{1}{2}$**
19. What percent of 30 is 15? **base = 30 percentage = 15**

Write a proportion for each problem. Then solve. Round answers to the nearest tenth. **For proportions in Exercises 20–31, see Solutions Manual.**

20. What number is 38% of 70? **26.6**
21. 14 is what percent of 49? **28.6%**
22. 61 is 35% of what number? **174.3**
23. 7.5% of 48 is what number? **3.6**
24. What percent of 180 is 30? **16.7%**
25. $12\frac{1}{2}$% of what number is 24? **192**
26. 63 is what percent of 42? **150%**
27. 50% of what number is 15.8? **31.6**
28. $6\frac{1}{4}$% of 235 is what number? **14.7**
29. What percent of 250 is 25? **10%**
30. What number is 40% of 86? **34.4**
31. 20% of what number is 12? **60**

32. Use the graph on page 462 to find the percent of the 1992 Olympic hopefuls in track and field that actually got to attend the games. **13.9%**

Mixed Review

33. **Finances** The Andrews' savings account has a balance of $8,750. Mrs. Andrews deposits a check in the amount of $2,175. Estimate the new balance. *(Lesson 1-2)* **about $10,800**

34. Use divisibility rules to determine whether 2,350 is divisible by 2, 3, 4, 5, 6, 9, or 10. *(Lesson 4-1)* **2, 5, 10**

35. Find $\frac{9}{12} - \frac{3}{8}$. *(Lesson 5-3)* $\frac{3}{8}$

36. **Geometry** Find the value of X for the right triangle. *(Lesson 9-5)* **4**

37. Estimate 28% of 160. *(Lesson 12-3)* **about 48**

Problem Solving and Applications

38. **Critical Thinking** Use the graph on page 462. The teams of wrestling, baseball, and cycling have the same number of Olympic competitors. Order the sports from highest to lowest percent of hopefuls who made the cut. Explain how you can determine the order without determining the actual percents. **See Solutions Manual.**

about 12.2%

39. **Defense** On an average day, 715 men and 99 women enlist in the armed forces. What percent of the enlistees are women?

40. **Olympics** Use the graph on page 462 to determine what percent of the Olympic hopefuls attended the Olympics in each sport.
    a. swimming **6.25%**
    b. cycling **5%**
    c. wrestling **1.9%**

41. **Library** About 32% of the 1,290 library books have been checked out during the past month. How many library books were checked out? **about 413 books**

42. **School** Twenty-six of the 168 students in Mrs. Johnson's math classes received As on the last test. *About* what percent of the class earned As? **about 15%**

OPTIONS

Extending the Lesson

Consumer Math Challenge students to explain how they would go about finding the percent of a percent of a number, such as 25% of 25% of 24. Ask students to write a problem of this kind for classmates to solve.

Cooperative Learning Activity

Personal Percents 12-4

Use groups of 4.

➡ Each group member copies the table shown at the right. Then each group member writes the number of minutes he or she spends doing each activity in a typical school day. Find the total number of minutes in a school day and then find the percent of each day you spend doing each activity.

Share your work with the other group members.

Activity	Time (in minutes)
Learning math	
Daydreaming	
Eating	
Walking to and from class	
Talking	
Playing sports	
Other	

Glencoe Mathematics: Applications and Connections, Course 2

12-5 The Percent Equation

Objective

Solve problems using the percent equation.

Retail Sales

An interest in working with people and an outgoing personality are an asset to any salesperson in retail sales.

Mathematical knowledge and skills are essential in retail. Calculating sales tax, price reductions, commissions, and making change are all in a day's work.

For additional information, contact:
Professional Salespersons of America
3801 Monaco NE
Albuquerque, NM 87111

Salespeople often work on commission. Mr. O'Donnell sells sports equipment on commission. He sold $14,207 of equipment last month. If he earns 12% commission, how much did he earn that month?

To find out how much commission Mr. O'Donnell earns, find 12% of $14,207.

You can write an equation to solve this problem.

Commission is 12% of $14,207.

$$c = 0.12 \cdot \$14,207 \qquad 12\% = \frac{12}{100} \text{ or } 0.12$$
$$c = 0.12 \cdot 14,207$$

$$.12 \;\boxed{\times}\; 14207 \;\boxed{=}\; \boxed{1704.84}$$

$$c = 1,704.84$$

Mr. O'Donnell earned $1,704.84 in commission.

Compared to the estimate, is the answer reasonable?

The percent proportion could also have been used to solve this problem.

Steps	Arithmetic	Algebra
Use the percent proportion.	$\frac{P}{14,000} = \frac{12}{100}$	$\frac{P}{B} = \frac{r}{100}$
Multiply each side by the base.	$\frac{P}{14,000} \cdot 14,000 = \frac{12}{100} \cdot 14,000$	$\frac{P}{B} \cdot B = \frac{r}{100} \cdot B$
Simplify.	$P = \frac{12}{100} \cdot 14,000$	$P = \frac{r}{100} \cdot B$

Lesson 12-5 Algebra Connection: The Percent Equation   465

NCTM Standards: 1–5, 7, 9

Lesson Resources
- Study Guide Master 12-5
- Practice Master 12-5
- Enrichment Master 12-5
- Evaluation Master, Quiz A, p. 106
- Group Activity Card 12-5

Transparency 12-5 contains the 5-Minute Check and a teaching aid for this lesson.

5-Minute Check
(Over Lesson 12-4)

Name the percentage, base, or rate.

1. 6 is what percent of 40?
   15%
2. What number is 35% of 35? 12.25

Write a proportion for each problem. Then solve. Round answers to the nearest tenth.

3. What number is 42% of 80?   33.6
4. 44 is what percent of 26?
   169.2%
5. $12\frac{1}{2}$% of what number is 32?   256.0

1 FOCUS

Motivating the Lesson

Questioning Have students read the opening paragraph. Ask them how they can find approximately the commissions percent that sales people generally earn selling items, such as cars, CD players, apartments, and furniture. Have some students investigate this, and report back to the class.

OPTIONS

Bell Ringer

Tell students that at Gene's Jeans, pants are priced as follows: list price when they arrive in the store, 25% off after one week on the shelf, 20% off the reduced price after two weeks on the shelf, and then 50% off the second reduced price after three weeks. Ask them what a customer would pay for a pair of jeans that originally listed for $40 but have been in the store for a month. $12

Using Calculators Encourage students to estimate the answer first, then write the percent equation. Finally, have them use a calculator to solve the problem. You may wish to point out that they can multiply to find P, and divide to find either R or B.

More Examples

For Example 1

What number is 73% of 640?   467.2

For Example 2

36 is what percent of 64?
$56\frac{1}{4}\%$

For Example 3

42 is 60% of what number?
70

Checking for Understanding

Exercises 1-3 are designed to help you assess students' understanding through reading, writing, speaking, and modeling. You should work through these exercises with your students and then monitor their work on Guided Practice Exercises 4-15.

Additional Answers

2. If P and R are given or P and B are given, $P = R \cdot B$ must be solved for B or R. Using the percent proportion may be easier.

3. Percent is *defined* as the ratio of a number compared to 100.

Remember that $\frac{r}{100}$ is called the *rate*. Let R represent $\frac{r}{100}$.

$$P = R \cdot B, \text{ where } R = \frac{r}{100}$$

Percentage = rate · base

> **Mental Math Hint**
> • • • • • • • • • • • • •
> When solving a percent problem where the base and rate are given, using the equation $P = R \cdot B$ is very convenient.

Examples

1 What number is 32% of 870?   *Estimate:* $\frac{1}{3} \cdot 900 = 300$
$P = R \cdot B$
$P = 0.32 \cdot 870$ *Replace R with 0.32 and B with 870.*
$P = 278.4$

32% of 870 is 278.4.   Compare to the estimate.

2 28 is what percent of 86?   *Estimate:* $\frac{28}{86} = \frac{30}{90}$
$\qquad\qquad\qquad\qquad\qquad\qquad\qquad = \frac{1}{3} \text{ or } 33\frac{1}{3}\%$

$P = R \cdot B$
$28 = R \cdot 86$ *Replace P with 28 and B with 86.*

$28 \boxed{\div} 86 \boxed{=} 0.3255813$ *Divide each side by 86.*

$0.33 \approx R$ *Round to the nearest hundredth.*

28 is about 33% of 86. Compare to the estimate.

3 44 is 55% of what number?   *Estimate: 44 is 50% or $\frac{1}{2}$ of 88.*
$P = R \cdot B$
$44 = 0.55 \cdot B$ *Replace P with 44 and R with 0.55.*

$44 \boxed{\div} 0.55 \boxed{=} 80$ *Divide each side by 0.55.*

$80 = B$

44 is 55% of 80.

Compared to the estimate, 55% is close to 50% or $\frac{1}{2}$.

Checking for Understanding

For answers to Exercises 2–3, see margin.

Communicating Mathematics

Read and study the lesson to answer each question.

1. **Tell** if the percentage is greater than or less than the base if the rate is less than 100%. **less**

2. **Write** a sentence explaining why the percent proportion is sometimes easier to use than $P = R \cdot B$.

3. **Tell** why percent is equal to the ratio of a number compared to 100.

OPTIONS

Reteaching Activity

Using Models Have students shade 10 × 10 grids to model finding a percent of a number, finding what percent one number is of another, and finding a total when given a number and a percent.

Study Guide Masters, p. 105

Name _____ Date _____

Study Guide Worksheet 12-5

Algebra Connection: The Percent Equation

In the percent proportion, $\frac{r}{100}$ is the rate. Let $R = \frac{r}{100}$.

Then $\frac{P}{B} = \frac{r}{100}$ becomes $\frac{P}{B} = R$.

Rewrite the equation at the right above to make it easier to solve equations when the rate and base are given.
$$P = R \times B$$

Example   What number is 35% of 480?

$P = R \times B$
$P = 0.35 \times 480$ $R = 35\%$, or 0.35, and $B = 480$
$P = 168$
So, 35% of 480 is 168.

Example   56 is what percent of 224?

Write each equation in $P = R \cdot B$ form. Then solve. Round answers to the nearest tenth. **For equations in Exercises 4-9, see Solutions Manual.**

4. $24 = 60\%$ of   **40**
5. $22 =$ % of 50 **44%**
6. 16% of $32 =$ **5.1**
7. $17 =$ % of 68 **25%**
8. 30% of $= 27$ **90**
9. $= 28\%$ of 32 **9.0**

Write an equation for each problem. Then solve. Round answers to the nearest tenth. **For equations in Exercises 10-15, see Solutions Manual.**

10. Find 26% of 119. **30.9**
11. 29 is what percent of 61? **47.5%**
12. 17 is 40% of what number? **42.5**
13. What percent of 87 is 57? **65.5%**
14. 26% of 48 is what number? **12.5**
15. 75 is 78% of what number? **96.2**

Exercises

Write an equation for each problem. Then solve. Round answers to the nearest tenth. **For equations in Exercises 16-33, see Solutions Manual.**

16. 15% of what number is 21? **140**
17. 45 is what percent of 36? **125%**
18. Find 8% of 38. **3.0**
19. 55% of what number is 1.265? **2.3**
20. 70% of what number is 42? **60**
21. Find 20% of 68. **13.6**   **64**
22. 24 is what percent of 25? **96%**
23. 18.5% of what number is 11.84?
24. 33% of 72 is what number? **23.8**
25. 75% of what number is 93? **124**
26. 25 is what percent of 75? **33.3%**
27. 6% of what number is 30? **500**
28. Find 36% of 228. **82.1**
29. 42.5% of what number is 36? **84.7**
30. 44 is what percent of 62? **71.0%**
31. $12\frac{3}{4}\%$ of 54 is what number? **6.9**
32. What is 15% of $9.00? **$1.35**
33. 30 is what percent of 45? **66.7%**

34. A class picnic was attended by 85% of the students. Nine students did not attend. How many students were in the class? **60 students**

35. If you copy a picture on the photocopying machine at 85%, are you enlarging or reducing the picture? Explain. **See margin.**

38. It is not a closed figure and is not made up of straight lines.

39. 326.56 cm³

36. Find the greatest common factor of 24 and 42. *(Lesson 4-5)* **6**
37. Multiply -13 and -4. *(Lesson 7-6)* **52**
38. **Geometry** Explain why the figure at the right is not a polygon. *(Lesson 8-2)*
39. **Geometry** Find the volume of a cylinder having a radius of 4 centimeters and a height of 6.5 centimeters. *(Lesson 10-6)*

40. 76.67%

40. Alex answered 23 of the 30 questions on his French test correctly. Find the percent of the questions that Alex answered correctly. *(Lesson 12-4)*

41. **Critical Thinking** Is a 20% discount on a $35 item the same as a 35% discount on a $20 item? Explain. **See margin.**

Meeting Needs of Middle School Students

Discuss with students how understanding operations with percents is fundamental to functioning in the world as a consumer and citizen. Have small groups of students peruse the sections of a daily newspaper to record the different ways in which percents are used.

Additional Answers

35. reducing; If the picture's dimensions are 5 in. by 10 in., then an 85% reproduction will measure 4.25 in. by 8.5 in.
41. yes; $0.20 \times \$35 = \$7.00$ and $0.35 \times \$20 = \$7.00$

Close

Have students write an equation they could use to figure the amount of commission a salesperson would earn on sales of $5,500, if her rate of commission is 3%.
$c = 0.03 \times 5,500$

3 PRACTICE/APPLY

Assignment Guide
Maximum: 16-44
Minimum: 17-35 odd, 36-44
All: Mid-Chapter Review

For **Extra Practice**, see p. 598.

Alternate Assessment

Writing Have students write a problem that involves finding the amount of a sale, given the commission rate and the commission. Students should provide the solutions to their problems.

Practice Masters, p. 105

Name _____ Date _____

Practice Worksheet 12-5

Algebra Connection: The Percent Equation

Write each equation in $P = R \cdot B$ form. Then solve.

1. $18 = 24\%$ of ■
   $18 = 0.24 \cdot B$; 75
2. $36 = $ ■% of 80.
   $35 = R \times 80$; 45%
3. 25% of $176 = $ ■
   $P = 0.25 \cdot 176$; 44

Write an equation for each problem. Then solve.

5. 45% of what number is 121.5?
   $121.5 = 0.45 \times B$; 270
6. 80% of what number is 94?
   $94 = 0.80 \times B$; 117.5
7. 32.5% of 256 is what number?
   $P = 0.325 \times 256$; 83.2
8. What percent of 125 is 25?
   $25 = R \times 125$; 20%
9. $18\frac{3}{4}$ is 25% of what number?
   $18\frac{3}{4} = 0.25 \times B$; 75
10. 15% of 290 is what number?
   $P = 0.15 \times 290$; 43.5
11. What percent of 224 is 28?
   $28 = R \times 224$; 12.5%
12. 344.8 is what percent of 862?
   $344.8 = R \times 862$; 40%
13. What number is 60% of 605?
   $P = 0.60 \times 605$; 363
14. 32% of 250 is what number?
   $P = 0.32 \times 250$; 80

T105
Glencoe Division, Macmillan/McGraw-Hill

**42. 2.4 in.
by 3.6 in.**

**43. 16 free
throws**

**44. 6.88 in.
by 3.44 in.**

42. **Photocopying** Suppose you enlarge a drawing to 120% of its original size on the photocopy machine. If the drawing is 2 inches long and 3 inches wide, what are the dimensions of the copy?

43. **Sports** If a pro basketball player makes free throws 92% of the time, how many free throws would you expect him to make if he attempted 18?

44. **Photocopying** Suppose you copy a newspaper ad at 86% on the photocopy machine. If the ad measures 8 inches long and 4 inches wide, what are the dimensions of the copy?

45. **Portfolio Suggestion** Select an item from this chapter that shows your creativity and place it in your portfolio. **See students' work.**

12 Assessment: Mid-Chapter Review

Use a proportion to solve each problem. Round answers to the nearest tenth. *(Lesson 12-1)*

1. What number is 25% of $40? **$10**
2. Find 33% of 18. **5.9**
3. 20% of 30 is what number? **6**
4. 42.5% of 60 is what number? **25.5**

Solve. *(Lesson 12-2)*

5. **Sports** Of the 57,545 fans at Yankee Stadium for Bat Day, about 40% of them were children 14 and under and received a free bat. About how many children received free bats? **about 23,018 children**

Estimate. *(Lesson 12-3)* **For Exercises 6–8, sample answers given.**

6. 22% of 19 **4**
7. $8\frac{1}{2}$% of 32 **3**
8. 175% of 370 **640**

Write a proportion for each problem. Then solve. **For proportions in Exercises 9–12, see Solutions Manual.** Round answers to the nearest tenth. *(Lesson 12-4)*

9. What number is 27% of 29? **7.8**
10. 22 is what percent of 88? **25%**
11. 40 is 50% of what number? **80**
12. What percent of 220 is 100? **45.5%**

Write an equation for each problem. Then solve. **For equations in Exercises 13–16, see Solutions Manual.** Round answers to the nearest tenth. *(Lesson 12-5)*

13. 10% of what number is $12\frac{1}{2}$? **125**
14. Find 61% of 83. **50.6**
15. 35 is what percent of 105? **33.3%**
16. 200% of what number is 720? **360**

OPTIONS

Extending the Lesson

Using Number Sense On a trip, George took 25 photos and Karin took 30. George says that he took $16\frac{2}{3}$% fewer pictures than Karin, who claims that she took 20% more pictures than he. Ask students who is right. Both are.

Cooperative Learning Activity

Number of players: 2
Materials: Index cards

Percent Puzzle 12-5

▪ Each partner makes a set of cards containing the expressions shown on the back of this card and arranges them as shown.

▪ The object of this game is to form equations in the bottom row by moving the cards up, down, right, or left within the five rows and three columns. (For example, at the beginning of the game, you could move the first card in the fourth row down or the last card in the second column to the left.) Write each equation you form. Try to find more correct equations than your partner in 10 minutes.

Glencoe Mathematics: Applications and Connections, Course 2

Cooperative Learning

12-6A Jelly Bean Statistics

A Preview of Lesson 12-6

Objective
Make a circle graph.

Materials
jelly beans
needles
thread
compass
straightedge

You can review frequency tables on page 93.

What is your favorite flavor of jelly bean? Almost everyone has a favorite.

Try this!

Work with a partner.

- Take a survey of the people in your class. Tally responses by flavor in a frequency table.

- Sort the jelly beans to reflect the results of the survey. For example, if there are 3 people whose favorite flavor is licorice (black), you would select 3 black jelly beans, and so on.

- String the jelly beans with like flavors together.

- Arrange the jelly beans in a circle. Use a compass to draw a circle the same size.

- On the circle, mark sections to indicate the separation by flavor.

- Draw a radius from each mark on the circle to the center.

- Identify each section by flavor.

For answers to Exercises 1–5, see students' work.

What do you think?

1. Write a short paragraph describing the circle graph. Include a description of the sizes of the sections in relation to each other.

2. Is there a relationship between the number of tally marks and the size of a section by flavor? If so, write a sentence to describe that relationship.

3. Explain how you can use the percent proportion to find the percent represented by each flavor.

4. Find the percent represented by each flavor. Label each section by flavor and by the percentage it represents.

5. The circle graph represents the same information as the frequency table. Discuss the advantages and disadvantages of each.

Mathematics Lab 12-6A Jelly Bean Statistics   **469**

NCTM Standards: 1–5, 7, 10

Management Tips

For Students Each pair of students will need at least as many jellybeans as there are students in the class. You may find it most efficient to take *one* class survey, and write the results on the chalkboard.

For the Overhead Projector
Overhead Manipulative Resources provides appropriate materials for teacher or student demonstration of the activities in this Mathematics Lab.

1 FOCUS

Introducing the Lab

Ask students to describe graphs they could use to effectively display the results of surveys about foods, flavors, or other preferences.

2 TEACH

Using Manipulatives If it is not feasible for your students to string the jellybeans, suggest that they use a compass to make a large circle. Then have them place the jellybeans, grouped by flavor, around the entire circumference of the circle so that there is approximately the same distance between each jellybean.

3 PRACTICE/APPLY

Using Connections Ask students to explain how the function of a circle graph differs from the function of a line graph and a bar graph. Ask them to describe the kind of data that is best shown with a circle graph. Sample answer: Circle graph shows how parts are related to a whole, such as parts of a budget.

Close

Have students determine the size, in degrees, of the sector of a jellybean circle graph showing that a fourth of a class prefers red jellybeans.   90°

OPTIONS

Lab Manual You may wish to make copies of the blackline master on p. 73 of the *Lab Manual* for students to use as a recording sheet.

Lab Manual, p. 73

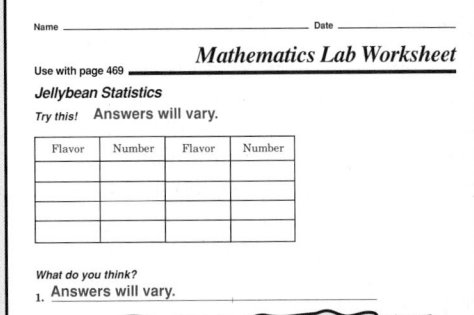

Name _____ Date _____
Mathematics Lab Worksheet
Use with page 469
Jellybean Statistics
Try this! Answers will vary.

Flavor	Number	Flavor	Number

What do you think?
1. Answers will vary.

NCTM Standards: 1–5, 7, 10

Lesson Resources
- Study Guide Master 12-6
- Practice Master 12-6
- Enrichment Master 12-6
- Group Activity Card 12-6

Transparency 12-6 contains the 5-Minute Check and a teaching aid for this lesson.

5-Minute Check
(Over Lesson 12-5)

Write an equation for each problem. Then solve.

1. 20% of what number is 16? 80
2. Find 34% of 330 112.2
3. What is 45% of $75.80? $34.11
4. 8.4 is what percent of 67.2? 12.5%
5. 30% of what number is 300? 1,000

1 FOCUS

Motivating the Lesson

Activity Have students conduct a class survey to find out students' favorite movies of the current year. Write the results on the chalkboard. Ask students to sketch a circle graph to display the data.

2 TEACH

Using Critical Thinking Point out to students that a circle graph provides a quick view of how a whole is divided into its parts. Ask students what information a circle graph *does not* provide that a bar graph does. the size of the whole

---

Statistics Connection

 **Circle Graphs**

Objective
Construct circle graphs.

Words to Learn
circle graph

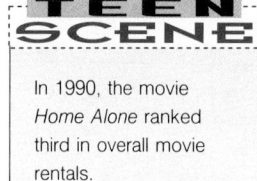

In 1990, the movie *Home Alone* ranked third in overall movie rentals.

In *The Wizard of Oz,* Dorothy discovers that "there's no place like home." Most people today would agree with that. Whether you live in an apartment, a mobile home, or a house, there is something special about being home.

American households, or homes, can be broken down into the categories shown in the chart at the right.

American Households 1990	
House	71%
Apartment	15%
Mobile Home	6%
Condominium	3%
Other	5%

You can draw a circle graph to show this information. A **circle graph** is used to compare parts of a whole.

Make a circle graph as follows.

a. Find the number of degrees for each section of the graph. There are 360° in a circle.

House	$71\% \times 360° = 0.71 \times 360° = 255.6°$
Apartment	$15\% \times 360° = 0.15 \times 360° = 54°$
Mobile Home	$6\% \times 360° = 0.06 \times 360° = 21.6°$
Condominium	$3\% \times 360° = 0.03 \times 360° = 10.8°$
Other	$5\% \times 360° = 0.05 \times 360° = 18°$

b. Use a compass to draw a circle. Then draw a radius as shown.

c. You can start with the least number of degrees, in this case, 10.8°. Use your protractor to draw an angle of 10.8°.

d. Repeat for the remaining sections. Label each section of the graph with the category and percent. Give the graph a title.

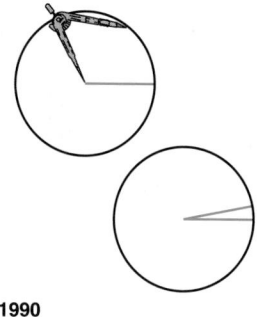

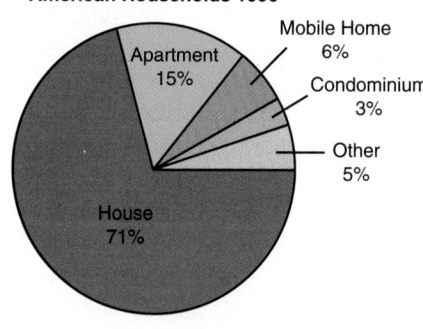

American Households 1990

Apartment 15% · Mobile Home 6% · Condominium 3% · Other 5% · House 71%

OPTIONS

Gifted and Talented Needs

Have students think about how a cat, dog, or other pet might spend its day, considering such activities as sleeping, eating, waiting to eat, chewing on toys, and so on. Encourage students to use their senses of humor to compile the pertinent data and then make a circle graph to show it.

 **Interactive Mathematics Tools**

This multimedia software provides an interactive lesson that is tied directly to Lesson 12–6. Students will explore the relationship between the angles in a circle graph.

Sales Bicycles sold in your local bike shop may be made in the United States or imported from another country. Make a circle graph to represent the types of bicycles sold in 1989 in the U.S that were made in the U.S.

Type of bicycle	U.S. Made 1980	U.S. Made 1989	Foreign Made 1980	Foreign Made 1989
Twenty-inch wheels	3.7	2.3	0	1.5
Lightweight	3.2	1.1	1.7	2.3
Other	0.1	1.9	0.3	1.5

U.S. Bicycle Sales (in millions)

- Find the total number of U.S. made bicycles sold in 1989.

  Twenty-inch wheels: 2.3 million
  Lightweight: 1.1 million
  Other: 1.9 million
  Total sold: 5.3 million

- Find the ratio that compares the number sold of each type with the total number sold. Round to the nearest hundredth.

  Twenty-inch wheels: $\frac{2.3}{5.3} = 0.43$

  Lightweight: $\frac{1.1}{5.3} = 0.21$

  Other: $\frac{1.9}{5.3} = 0.36$

- Find the number of degrees for each section of the graph.

  Twenty-inch wheels: $0.43 \times 360° = 155°$ *Note that the sum of the*
  Lightweight: $0.21 \times 360° = 76°$ *degrees is not 360° due*
  Other: $0.36 \times 360° = 130°$ *to rounding.*

- Make the circle graph.

U.S. Sales of Bicycles Made in U.S., 1989

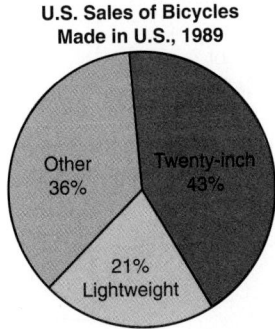

More Examples

For the Example

The table shows the results of a survey in which seventh graders named their favorite sport.

Sport	Number of Votes
Baseball	10
Basketball	12
Football	6
Hockey	3
Soccer	8
Tennis	2
Swimming	5
Track	2

Make a circle graph to show this information.

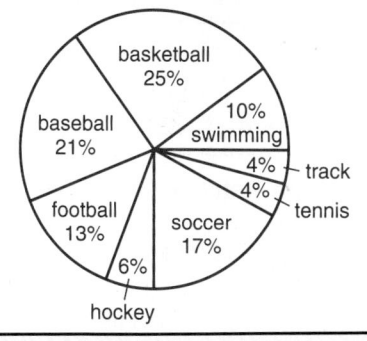

Teaching Tip Have students make their graphs large enough to display on a bulletin board.

Checking for Understanding

Exercises 1-2 are designed to help you assess students' understanding through reading, writing, speaking, and modeling. You should work through these exercises with your students and then monitor their work on Guided Practice Exercises 3-15.

Reteaching Activity

Using Cooperative Groups Have students work together to make a circle graph to show the favorite ice cream flavors of 12 classmates. Have them discuss how to calculate the percents and the degree measures of the angles for circle sections.

Study Guide Masters, p. 106

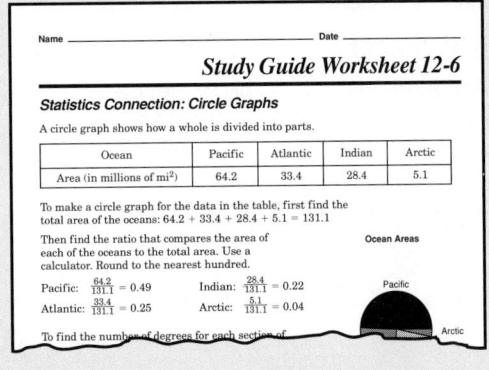

Name _____ Date _____

Study Guide Worksheet 12-6

Statistics Connection: Circle Graphs

A circle graph shows how a whole is divided into parts.

Ocean	Pacific	Atlantic	Indian	Arctic
Area (in millions of mi²)	64.2	33.4	28.4	5.1

To make a circle graph for the data in the table, first find the total area of the oceans: 64.2 + 33.4 + 28.4 + 5.1 = 131.1

Then find the ratio that compares the area of each of the oceans to the total area. Use a calculator. Round to the nearest hundred.

Ocean Areas

Pacific: $\frac{64.2}{131.1} = 0.49$ Indian: $\frac{28.4}{131.1} = 0.22$

Atlantic: $\frac{33.4}{131.1} = 0.25$ Arctic: $\frac{5.1}{131.1} = 0.04$

To find the number of degrees for each section of

471

Error Analysis

Watch for students whose percents do not add to 100% when they gather the data for their graphs.

Prevent by stressing that since a circle graph represents one whole, which is 100% of the data being considered, they must be sure to account for exactly 100% of the data.

Close

Have students list the steps in the process of constructing a circle graph, given a table of data.

3 PRACTICE/APPLY

Assignment Guide
Maximum: 16–26
Minimum: 16–24

For **Extra Practice,** see p. 599.

Alternate Assessment

Modeling Survey the class to find out students' favorite TV comedy programs. Have the class make circle graphs to show the results.

Practice Masters, p. 106

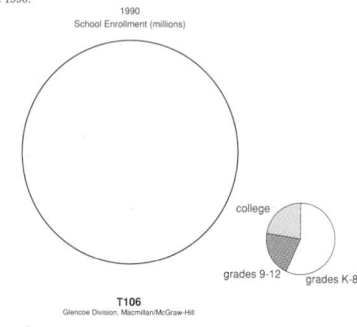

Name _____ Date _____

Practice Worksheet 12-6

Statistics Connection: Circle Graphs

Write a ratio that compares the number of students enrolled in each category of school to the total number of students in school.

	1990 School Enrollment by Grade (millions)
Grades K-8	33.6
Grades 9-12	12.2
College	13.2
TOTAL	59.0

1. grades K-8 $\frac{336}{590}$
2. grades 9-12 $\frac{122}{590}$
3. college $\frac{132}{590}$

Use the ratios from exercises 1–3 to find the number of degrees in each category that would be on a circle graph.

4. grades K-8 **205°**
5. grades 9-12 **74°**
6. college **81°**

7. Make a circle graph that shows the composition of the school population in 1990.

1990 School Enrollment (millions)

T106
Glencoe Division, Macmillan/McGraw-Hill

Checking for Understanding For answers to Exercises 1–2, see margin.

Communicating Mathematics

Read and study the lesson to answer each question.

1. **Tell** how to make a circle graph when you know the percent represented by different parts of the whole.

2. **Write** a sentence explaining why it would not be appropriate to make a circle graph called "U.S. Bicycle Sales 1980–1989" using the information in the chart on page 471.

Guided Practice

Write a ratio that compares the number of students who chose each type of pizza to the total number of students surveyed. Use the graph.

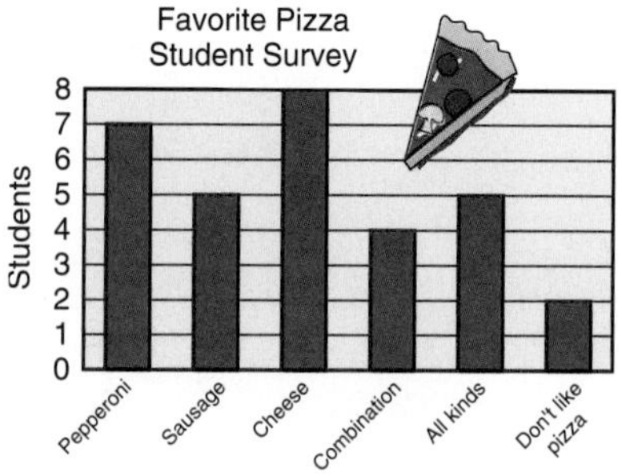

Favorite Pizza Student Survey

3. pepperoni $\frac{7}{31}$
4. sausage $\frac{5}{31}$
5. cheese $\frac{8}{31}$
6. combination $\frac{4}{31}$
7. all kinds $\frac{5}{31}$
8. don't like pizza $\frac{2}{31}$

Use the ratios from Exercises 3-8 to find the number of degrees each choice of pizza would be on a circle graph.

9. pepperoni **83°**
10. sausage **58°**
11. cheese **94°**
12. combination **47°**
13. all kinds **58°**
14. don't like pizza **22°**

15. Make a circle graph that shows the results of the pizza survey. **See Solutions Manual.**

Exercises

Independent Practice

16. Use the chart on page 471 to make a circle graph that shows the types of bicycles sold in 1989 that were foreign made. **See Solutions Manual.**

17. See Solutions Manual.

17. Use the information from the chart at the right to make a circle graph of the colors of bicycles sold in 1989.

18. Suppose you are a domestic manufacturer of bicycles. Explain how the information in Exercise 17 would affect the color of bicycles you produce. **See margin.**

Bicycle Sales by Color for 1989	
Color	Percent
Blue	24
Black	23
Red	22
White	8
Silver	5
Yellow	2
All others	16

Mixed Review

19. **Smart Shopping** Philip purchases 0.70 pounds of cheese priced at $3.15 per pound. What is the cost of his purchase? Round to the nearest cent. *(Lesson 2-4)* **$2.21**

20. **Geometry** Determine whether the polygon at the right is a regular polygon. *(Lesson 8-4)* **no**

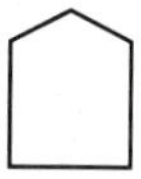

OPTIONS

Bell Ringer

Ask students to use the graph below to make a circle graph using the data shown.

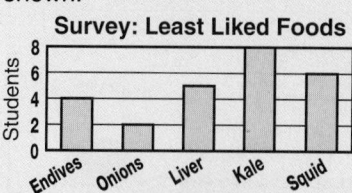

Survey: Least Liked Foods

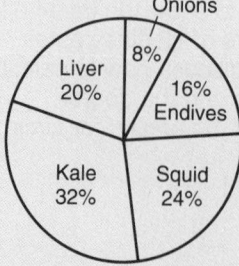

Least Liked Foods

Onions

Liver 20%

8%

16% Endives

Kale 32%

Squid 24%

21. Find the number that is 35% of 20 using the percent equation. *(Lesson 12-5)* **7**

22. **Critical Thinking** Using the chart for bicycles sales in 1980 and 1989 on page 471, explain how this information would be useful to you as the owner of a bicycle shop.

23. **Collect Data** Make a circle graph that represents the colors of your classmates' eyes. **See students' work.**

24. **Business** Use the chart on page 471. **For graphs to Exercises a-b, see Solutions Manual.**
   a. Make a circle graph that compares the U.S. made bicycle sales and foreign-made bicycle sales for 1989.
   b. Make a circle graph that compares the U.S. made bicycle sales and foreign-made bicycle sales for 1980.
   c. What similarities or differences do you notice between the graphs for 1980 and 1989? **See margin.**

25. **Journal Entry** Write a sentence explaining how to construct a circle graph for a given set of data. **See margin.**

26. **Mathematics and Energy** Read the following paragraphs.

> Energy is usually measured in millions (or even larger quantities) of British thermal units (Btus). One Btu is approximately the energy released in burning a wooden match. An automobile engine burning eight gallons of gasoline releases one million Btus.
>
> Historically, three fossil fuels (coal, crude oil, natural gas) have accounted for most of the U.S. energy production, which totaled 66 quadrillion Btus in 1989. Transportation, residential, and commercial use accounted for the increase in energy usage during 1949–1989. Following the decline in energy prices in 1986 and 1988, residential and commercial consumption grew to a record 29.6 quadrillion Btus.

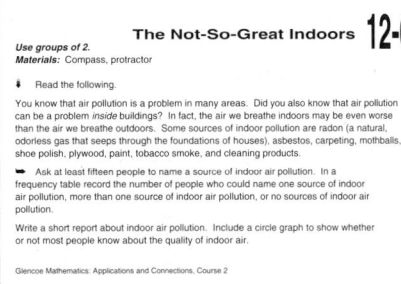

U.S. Energy Production
66 quadrillion Btu

Natural Gas 24%
Petroleum Products 42%
Coal 23%
Hydroelectric 4%
Nuclear Power 7%

Using the circle graph above, what percent of the energy production comes from sources other than the three fossil fuels? **11%**

Additional Answers

1. Change percents to decimal form. Multiply by 360° to obtain the number of degrees in the sections of the circle graph.
2. The two totals involved, 1980 and 1989, cannot be compared in one graph.
18. It would help to decide how many bicycles of each color to make.
22. It would help decide how many bicycles of each type to buy.
24c. Sample answer: Sales of U.S. made bicycles were greater than sales of foreign made bicycles in 1980 but not in 1989.
25. Divide each data item by the sum of the data and write as a decimal. Multiply each decimal by 360° to get the number of degrees for each item. Separate a circle into sections with these degree measures. Label the graph.

Enrichment Masters, p. 106

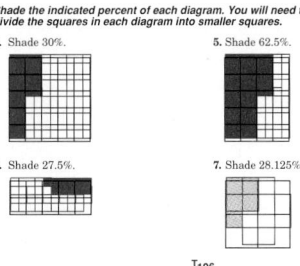

Name _____ Date _____

Enrichment Worksheet 12-6

Made in the Shade

To shade 25% of the figure at the right below, ask yourself how many of the eight squares need to be shaded. Then use the percent proportion to find the answer.

$$\frac{x}{8} = \frac{25}{100}$$
$$100x = 8 \times 25$$
$$\frac{100x}{100} = \frac{200}{100}$$
$$x = 2$$

If you shade two squares, you have shaded 25% of the figure.

Shade the indicated percent of each diagram.
1. Shade 40%.   2. Shade 37.5%.   3. Shade $16\frac{2}{3}$%.

Shade the indicated percent of each diagram. You will need to divide the squares in each diagram into smaller squares.
4. Shade 30%.   5. Shade 62.5%.
6. Shade 27.5%.   7. Shade 28.125%.

T-106
Glencoe Division, Macmillan/McGraw-Hill

Extending the Lesson

Mathematics and Energy Ask students how many Btus of energy were represented in 1989 by hydroelectric and nuclear power.   **about 7.3 quadrillion Btus**

Cooperative Learning Activity

Use groups of 2.
Materials: Compass, protractor

The Not-So-Great Indoors **12-6**

Read the following.

You know that air pollution is a problem in many areas. Did you also know that air pollution can be a problem *inside* buildings? In fact, the air we breathe indoors may be even worse than the air we breathe outdoors. Some sources of indoor pollution are radon (a natural, odorless gas that seeps through the foundations of houses), asbestos, carpeting, mothballs, shoe polish, plywood, paint, tobacco smoke, and cleaning products.

Ask at least fifteen people to name a source of indoor air pollution. In a frequency table record the number of people who could name one source of indoor air pollution, more than one source of indoor air pollution, or no sources of indoor air pollution.

Write a short report about indoor air pollution. Include a circle graph to show whether or not most people know about the quality of indoor air.

Glencoe Mathematics: Applications and Connections, Course 2

Management Tips

For Students Provide groups with several sheets of dot or graph paper. Suggest that within the groups, students should work both together and individually, discussing each other's work and results.

For the Overhead Projector
Overhead Manipulative Resources provides appropriate materials for teacher or student demonstration of the activities in this Mathematics Lab.

1 FOCUS

Introducing the Lab

Ask students what it means when the price of an item in a store is increased by 20% or decreased by 20%. Ask them whether the price change is an increase of $33\frac{1}{3}\%$ or 25% when a shirt that once sold for $30 now sells for $40.   increase of $33\frac{1}{3}\%$

Additional Answer

2. Separate the square into four equal squares and remove one.

12-7A Dot Paper and Percent
A Preview of Lesson 12-7

Objective
Use dot paper to show percent increase or percent decrease.

Materials
dot paper or graph paper
pencil

You can use dot paper or graph paper to help you understand the meaning of percent increase or percent decrease.

Try this!

Work in groups of three.

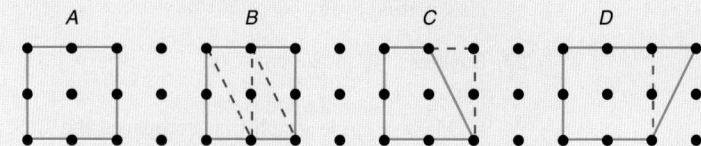

- Make a 2×2 square like the one shown in Figure A.

- Suppose you want to decrease the area of square A by 25%. Think: $25\% = \frac{1}{4}$. Separate the square into 4 equal parts as in Figure B.

- Remove 25% or $\frac{1}{4}$ from the original figure to show a decrease of 25%. See Figure C.

- Figure D shows an increase of 25% from the original figure.

What do you think?

1. Once you showed a 25% decrease in Figure A, what percent remains? 75%

2. Describe other ways you could show a 25% decrease in the area of Figure A. See margin.

3. Explain how an increase of 25% was shown in Figure D. **25% of the original figure was added to it.**

4. Use Figures E, F, and G below. Explain how you can determine by what percent the original figure was increased or decreased. **See margin.**

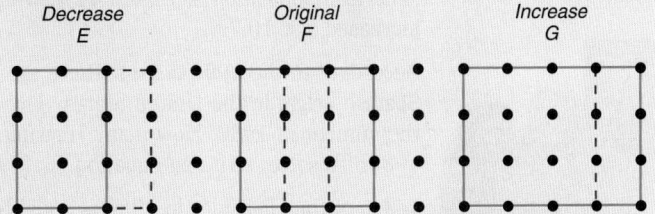

Decrease
E

Original
F

Increase
G

5. Use Figure H to draw figures that show an increase of $16\frac{2}{3}\%$ and a decrease of $16\frac{2}{3}\%$. *(Hint: What fraction is equal to $16\frac{2}{3}\%$?)* **See Solutions Manual.**

H

I

6. For Figure I, draw figures to indicate an increase of 50% and a decrease of 50%. **See Solutions Manual.**

7. **See Solutions Manual.**

7. Copy and complete the chart for Figures A, E, H, and I.

Decreased area (units²)	% of original area	Original area (units²)	Increased area (units²)	% of original area

8. When finding the increase or decrease, explain what number is used as your base. **original area**

Extension For answers to Exercises 9–10, see students' work.

9. Construct or draw a 3×3 square. Remove $33\frac{1}{3}\%$ from the figure to show a decrease of $33\frac{1}{3}\%$.

10. Construct or draw a 5×5 square. Add or draw an area to the original figure to show an increase of 20%.

Mathematics Lab 12-7A Dot Paper and Percent   **475**

OPTIONS

Lab Manual You may wish to make copies of the blackline master on p. 74 of the *Lab Manual* for students to use as a recording sheet.

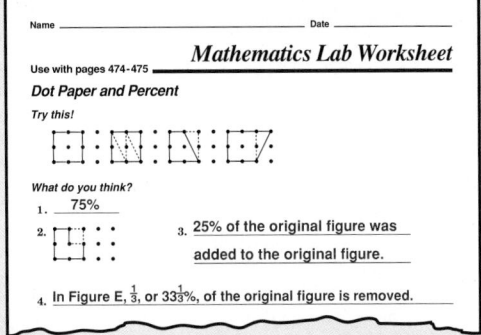
2 TEACH

Using Models Some students may find that using scissors to cut and reassemble the figures facilitates their understanding of percents of increase and decrease.

3 PRACTICE/APPLY

Using Applications Have students formulate other problems about percent increase and percent decrease for group members to solve by using dot paper or graph paper.

Close

Have students construct a 4 × 4 square and show a percent decrease of 75% by removing part of the figure.

Additional Answer

4. E : 1 of F's 3 sections was removed, so the decrease is 1 out of 3, or $33\frac{1}{3}\%$.
   G : F's 3 sections were expanded by 1 section, so the increase is 1 out of 3, or $33\frac{1}{3}\%$.

NCTM Standards: 1–5, 7, 9, 12

Lesson Resources
- Study Guide Master 12-7
- Practice Master 12-7
- Enrichment Master 12-7
- Interdisciplinary Master, p. 26
- Group Activity Card 12-7

 Transparency 12-7 contains the 5-Minute Check and a teaching aid for this lesson.

⏱ 5-Minute Check
(Over Lesson 12-6)

The table shows the results of a poll in which seventh graders were asked to name their favorite of 5 music groups. Use the data to make a circle graph.

Music Group	Percent Chosen
Nails	43%
The Muffins	15%
Mole Food	20%
For Profit	8%
Old Kids	14%

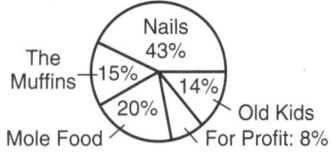

1 FOCUS

Motivating the Lesson

Activity Have students use an almanac to determine how the population change in your state in the 1980s compares with that of the entire country.

2 TEACH

Using the Mini-Lab Have students continue the activity by estimating distances 25%, 50%, and 100% longer than distances drawn or identified by their partners.

476

12-7 Percent of Change

Objective
Find the percent of increase or decrease.

In the past few decades, the United States has become increasingly multicultural. For example, between 1980 and 1990, the Hispanic-American population increased 44%, while the entire population increased just 10.2%.

According to the 1990 census, there are 21,032,471 people of Spanish origin in the United States. This is equal to *about* 144% of the number in 1980. How many Hispanic-Americans were there in 1980? To solve, write an equation.

$\underbrace{144\%}$ of $\underbrace{\text{the Hispanics in 1980}}$ is equal to $\underbrace{21{,}032{,}471}$.

$1.44 \cdot h = 21{,}032{,}471$

$\dfrac{1.44 \cdot h}{1.44} = \dfrac{21{,}032{,}471}{1.44}$ *Divide each side by 1.44.*

$21{,}032{,}471 \div 1.44 = 14605883$

$h = 14{,}605{,}883$

There were *about* 14,605,883 Hispanic-Americans living in the United States in 1980.

Mini-Lab

Work with a partner.
Materials: ruler, paper, pencil

- Draw a segment that you estimate to be 25% longer than $\overline{MN}$.

  ●————————————●
  M   N

- Measure the length of $\overline{MN}$. Use this number as the base, B.
- Measure the length of your segment. Use this as the percentage, P.

Talk About It

a. Will 50% of the length of $\overline{MN}$ be greater or less than its length? **less**

b. Will 100% of the length of $\overline{MN}$ be greater or less than its length? **equal**

c. Do you think the length of your segment is greater or less than 100% of the length of $\overline{MN}$? **greater**

d. Write a proportion or equation to find the percent the length of $\overline{MN}$ is of the length of your segment. Solve. **Answers will vary.**

e. The segment you drew is actually what percent longer than $\overline{MN}$? **Answers will vary.**

OPTIONS

Reteaching Activity

Using Connections Focus on the similarities between percent increase and percent decrease. Point out that in both cases one finds the difference between two amounts and then solves a proportion to find what percent of the original amount the difference is.

Study Guide Masters, p. 107

Name _____ Date _____

Study Guide Worksheet 12-7

Percent of Change

To find the percent of change, first find the amount of increase or decrease. Then find the ratio of that amount to the original amount and express the ratio as a percent.

Example Last year, 2,376 people attended the rodeo. This year, attendance was 2,954. What was the percent of increase in rodeo attendance?

$2{,}954 - 2{,}376 = 578$ Find the amount of the increase.

$\frac{578}{2{,}376} \approx 0.24$ Compare the amount of increase to the original amount.

Rodeo attendance increased by about 24%.

Example John _____ on the first math

When using the percent proportion to find the percent of increase or decrease, compare the amount of the increase to the original amount.

Example 1 *Problem Solving*

Health   When Lisa started using the exercise machine, she could only work out for 8 minutes. Now she can work out on it for 15 minutes. Find the percent of increase.

$15 - 8 = 7$ *Find the amount of increase.*

$\frac{7}{8} = \frac{r}{100}$ *Write the percent proportion.*

$7 \cdot 100 = 8r$ *The original time was 8 minutes.*

$\frac{700}{8} = \frac{8r}{8}$ *Find the cross products.*

$87.5 = r$ *Divide each side by 8.*

The percent of increase is 87.5%.

You can find the percent of decrease in a similar way.

Example 2 *Problem Solving*

Retail Sales   In 1970, a desktop calculator sold for *about* $100. Today the same type of calculator sells for as little as $25. What was the percent of decrease in the cost of desktop calculators?

$100 - 25 = 75$ *Find the amount of decrease.*

$\frac{75}{100} = \frac{r}{100}$ *The original cost was $100.*

$75 \cdot 100 = 100r$ *Find the cross products.*

$\frac{7,500}{100} = \frac{100r}{100}$ *Divide each side by 100.*

$75 = r$

The percent of decrease was 75%.

Checking for Understanding

Communicating Mathematics

Read and study the lesson to answer each question.   **See students' work.**

1. **Draw** a picture on dot paper to show an increase in area of 75%.

2. **Tell** what amount is used as a base in the percent proportion when finding the percent of change. **original amount**

3. **Write** a sentence explaining the first step in finding the percent of increase or decrease. **Subtract to find the amount of increase or decrease.**

Guided Practice

Estimate the percent of increase or decrease.

4. old: $4
   new: $6   **50%**

5. old: $30
   new: $24   **20%**

6. old: $0.36
   new: $0.18   **50%**

Lesson 12-7   Percent of Change   **477**

Bell Ringer

A basketball team played three games. In the first game it scored *n* points. In the second game it scored 10% more points than in the first game. In the third game, the score was a decrease of 10% from the second game. Ask students how the team's score in the third game compared with its score in the first game.   It was lower.

Close

Have students explain how to find the percent of increase or decrease from one number to another.

3 PRACTICE/APPLY

Assignment Guide
Maximum: 11–26
Minimum: 11–19 odd, 21–25

For **Extra Practice,** see p. 599.

Alternate Assessment

Speaking The population of Town A dropped by 2,000 from 12,000 while that of Town B rose by 2,000 from 7,000. Ask students which town had the greater percent of change and explain why. **B; 2,000 is a larger percent of 7,000 than of 12,000.**

Additional Answers

20.
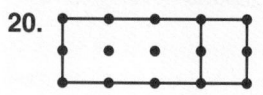

25. no; $24 + discount = original price, but the discount is 25% of the original price, not of $24.

Enrichment Masters, p. 107

Name _____ Date _____

Enrichment Worksheet 12-7

A Taxing Exercise

People who earn income are required by law to pay taxes. The amount of tax a person owes is computed by first subtracting the amount of all *exemptions* and *deductions* from the amount of income, then using a tax table like this.

Schedule X—Use if your filing status is **Single**

If the amount on Form 1040, line 37, is: Over—	But not over—	Enter on Form 1040, line 38	of the amount over—
$0	$20,350	------------15%	$0
20,350	49,300	$3,052.50 + 28%	20,350
49,300	----------	11,158.50 + 31%	49,300

Compute each person's income. Subtract $5,550 for each person's exemption and deduction. Then use the tax rate schedule to compute the amount of federal tax owed.

1. A cashier works 40 hours each week, earns $7.50 per hour, and works 50 weeks each year. **$1,417.50**

2. A newspaper carrier works each day, delivers 154 papers daily, and earns $0.12 delivering each paper. **$179.28**

3. A babysitter earns $3.50 per hour per child. During a year, the babysitter works with two children every Saturday for 8 hours and with three children every other Sunday for 6 hours. **$0.00**

4. While home from college for the summer, a painter earns $17.00 per hour, working 45 hours each week for 15 weeks. **$888.75**

5. Working before and after school in the school bookstore, an employee works 2.5 hours each day for 170 days and earns $4.60 per hour. **$0.00**

6. After graduating from college, a computer programmer accepts a position earning $2,450 monthly. **$4,032.50**

T107
Glencoe Division, Macmillan/McGraw-Hill

Find the percent of change. Round to the nearest whole percent.

7. old: $60
   new: $38 **37%**

8. old: $456
   new: $500 **10%**

9. old: 0.76
   new: 0.9 **18%**

10. Use the figure at the right.
    a. Draw a figure 25% larger.
    b. Draw a figure decreased in size by $66\frac{2}{3}$%.
    See Solutions Manual.

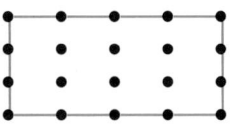

Exercises

Independent Practice

Find the percent of change. Round to the nearest whole percent.

11. old: $85
    new: $68 **20%**

12. old: $126
    new: $150 **19%**

13. old: 1.6
    new: 0.95 **41%**

14. old: 20.5
    new: 35.5 **73%**

15. old: $62
    new: $50 **19%**

16. old: 275
    new: 150 **45%**

17. old: 40
    new: 80 **100%**

18. old: 35
    new: 45 **29%**

19. old: 87.5
    new: 36 **59%**

20. If the figure at the right represents 75% of something, draw a diagram to represent 100%. **See margin.**

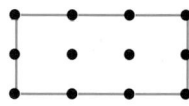

Mixed Review

21. **Probability** A fair die is rolled. Find the probability that the result is an even number. *(Lesson 4-8)* **50%**

22. **Algebra** Write an algebraic expression for the phrase *6 less than w*. *(Lesson 6-4)* **w − 6**

23. **Geometry** Find the surface area of a prism that has a length of 8 centimeters, a width of 6.5 centimeters, and a height of 10.4 centimeters. *(Lesson 10-3)* **405.6 cm²**

Problem Solving and Applications

24. a. state of Georgia; about 24%
b. state of Georgia; about 119%

24. **History** In 1991, the country of Georgia declared independence from the Soviet Union. The population was given as 5.5 million. The area of the country of Georgia was 26,910 square miles.
    The area of the state of Georgia in the United States is 58,910 square miles. The population is 6.8 million.
    a. Which Georgia has the greater population? By what percent is it higher?
    b. Which Georgia has the greater area? By what percent is it higher?

25. **Critical Thinking** A book is on sale for $24. This is 25% off the original price. Can you find the original price by adding 25% of $24 to the sale price? Explain. **See margin.**

26. **Data Search** Refer to pages 452 and 453. What was the percent of increase in the price of postage stamps between the years 1974 and 1975? Between 1981 and 1991? **30%; 45%**

478 Chapter 12 Applications with Percent

OPTIONS

Extending the Lesson

Using Connections Have students determine the percent of increase in their classroom space if the math class were suddenly to be transferred from its present location to the school gymnasium.

Cooperative Learning Activity

Time for a Change **12-7**

Number of players: 4
Materials: Index cards, spinners

◆ Copy onto cards the numbers 11, 28, 45, 62, 84, 98, one number per card. Shuffle the cards and place them face down in a pile. Label equal sections of two spinners with the digits 0 through 9. Decide which spinner will stand for digits in tens place and which spinner will stand for digits in ones place.

➡ One group member selects the top card from the pile. Then, in turn, each group member spins both spinners, records the resulting two-digit number, and computes the percent of change from the number on the card. The group member with the largest percent of increase (or smallest percent of decrease if all of the numbers decreased) wins the round. Continue in this way, taking turns selecting a card, until no cards remain in the pile.

Glencoe Mathematics: Applications and Connections, Course 2

12-8 Discount and Sales Tax

Objective
Solve problems involving sales tax and discount.

Words to Learn
sales tax

Do you know the sales tax rate in your community? **Sales tax** is the main way we pay for many state and city services.

Shalonda goes to the check-out counter with a pair of in-line skates that cost $85. If the sales tax in her city is 6%, find the total cost of her purchase.

You can use two methods to find the total cost. You get the same result using either method.

Method One
First find the amount of the tax.
6% of $85 = t

0.06 ⊠ 85 ▭ **5.1**
The sales tax is $5.10.

Then add to find the total cost.
$85.00 + $5.10 = $90.10

Method Two
First add the percent of tax to 100%.
Since 100% + 6% = 106%, Shalonda will pay 106% of the market price of the skates.

Then multiply to find the total cost including tax.
1.06 ⊠ 85 ▭ **90.1**

The total cost of the in-line skates will be $90.10.

Percents are often used to show discounts during store sales.

Estimation Hint
• • • • • • • • • • • • •
0.06 of 90 is 5.4.
The sales tax is *about* $5.40. The total cost is $85.00 + $5.40 or $90.40.

Example 1   *Problem Solving*

Smart Shopping   Saki plans to buy a pair of jeans that are on sale for 25% off. If the regular price is $27, how much will she have to pay?
What is 25% of $27?

0.25 ⊠ 27 ▭ **6.75**

The discount is $6.75.

Then subtract to find the discount price.

27 ▭ 6.75 ▭ **20.25**

Saki will have to pay $20.25 for the jeans.

Lesson 12-8 Discount and Sales Tax   **479**

NCTM Standards: 1–5, 7, 9

Lesson Resources
• Study Guide Master 12-8
• Practice Master 12-8
• Enrichment Master 12-8
• Technology Master, p. 12
• Application Master, p. 12
• Group Activity Card 12-8

Transparency 12-8 contains the 5-Minute Check and a teaching aid for this lesson.

⏱ 5-Minute Check
(Over Lesson 12-7)
Find the percent of change. Round to the nearest whole percent.
1. old: $75; new: $85   13%
2. old: 60; new: 45   25%
3. old: 360; new: 200   44%
4. old: 40; new: 86   115%

1 FOCUS

Motivating the Lesson

Activity   Ask students whether they think rates of sales tax are the same everywhere, or are the same only within a city, county, state, or other regional unit. Have students share what they know, and investigate to find out more.

2 TEACH

Using Applications   Provide students with newspaper ads for clothing sales. Have them use the information in the ads to identify discount rates, find discount prices, and determine total prices, including the sales tax.

OPTIONS

Reteaching Activity

Using Discussion   Focus on *discount price, discount,* and *rate of discount.* Guide students to see that the discount rate is a percent, the discount is a money amount, a reduction in price. The discount price is the difference between the regular price and the discount.

Study Guide Masters, p. 108

Name _____   Date _____

Study Guide Worksheet 12-8

Discount and Sales Tax
Sales tax is a percent of the purchase price.

Example   Find the total price of a $17.75 soccer ball if the sales tax is 6%.

Method 1
Find the amount of tax.
6% of $17.75 = t
0.06 × $17.75 = 1.07
The sales tax is $1.07.
Add to find the total cost.
$17.75 + $1.07 = $18.82

Method 2
Add the percent of tax to 100%.
100% + 6% = 106%
The total price will be 106% of the price of the soccer ball.
Multiply to find the total cost.
$17.75 × 1.06 = $18.82

The total cost of the soccer ball is $18.82.

Discount is the _____ the sales price is

479

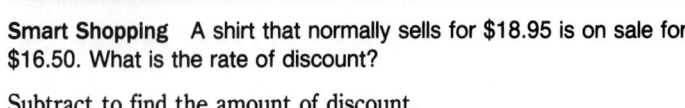

Example 2 *Problem Solving*

Smart Shopping A shirt that normally sells for $18.95 is on sale for $16.50. What is the rate of discount?

Subtract to find the amount of discount.
$$\$18.95 - \$16.50 = \$2.45$$

Then find what percent $2.45 is of $18.95.

$$\frac{2.45}{18.95} = \frac{r}{100}$$ *Use the percent proportion.*
$P = 2.45; B = 18.95$

$2.45 \cdot 100 = 18.95r$ *Find the cross products.*
$245 = 18.95r$ *Divide each side by 18.95.*
$12.928759 = r$ *Round 12.928759 to 13.*

The rate of discount is *about* 13%.

Checking for Understanding

For answers to Exercises 1–2, see Solutions Manual.

Communicating Mathematics

Read and study the lesson to answer each question.

1. **Tell** how you would use a different method in Example 1 to find the sale price.
2. **Show** two different ways that you could find the total purchase price including tax on a sweater selling for $45 if the tax rate is 5%.

Guided Practice

Find the sales tax or discount to the nearest cent.

3. $28 shoes; 5% tax $1.40
4. $17.42 book; 5½% tax $0.96
5. $38.50 sweater; 15% off $5.78
6. $25 watch; 30% discount $7.50

Find the total cost or sale price to the nearest cent.

7. $135.59 speakers; 33% off $90.85
8. $175.95 suit; 6% tax $186.51
9. $9.95 cassette; 6½% tax $10.60
10. $2.50 socks; 25% off $1.87

Find the rate of discount to the nearest percent.

11. regular price, $24
    sale price, $20 17%
12. regular price, $224
    sale price, $180 20%

Exercises

Independent Practice

Find the sales tax or discount to the nearest cent.

13. $37 radio; 6% tax $2.22
14. $16.58 gloves; 6½% tax $1.08
15. $49.50 drill; 35% off $17.33
16. $145 chair; 22% discount $31.90

Find the total cost or sale price to the nearest cent.

17. $15.99 T-shirt; 20% off $12.79
18. $32 coat; 5½% tax $33.76
19. $3.99 toy; 7% tax $4.27
20. $40 video; 20% off $32

480   Chapter 12 Applications with Percent

Classroom Vignette

"I challenge students to write real-world problems that involve percents. An example follows. Jim purchased 9 packages of baseball cards. Each package costs $1.09. The sales tax in his state is 6%. If he handed the cashier a $20 bill, how much change should he receive?"

Alvin E. Hampton

Alvin Hampton, Teacher
Stafford Middle School, Stafford, VA

Find the rate of discount to the nearest percent.

21. regular price, $35   **14%**
    sale price, $30

22. regular price, $44   **23%**
    sale price, $34

23. regular price, $18.99   **30%**
    sale price, $13.29

24. regular price, $70   **25%**
    sale price, $52.50

25. Find the total purchase price to the nearest cent if a $65 dress is on sale
    for 20% off and the sales tax is 6%. **$55.12**

Mixed Review

26. Evaluate $12(5) - 16 \div 8 + 5$. *(Lesson 1-7)* **63**

27. **Geometry** Find the circumference of a circle
    having a diameter of 5 inches. Use 3.14 for π.
    Round to the nearest tenth of an inch.
    (Lesson 5-7) **15.7 inches**

28. Solve $\frac{t}{16} = 8$. *(Lesson 6-1)* **12.8%**

29. **Health** Before beginning his new diet, Peter
    weighed 195 pounds. After dieting for 12 weeks,
    Peter's new weight was 170 pounds. Find the
    percent of decrease in Peter's weight.
    (Lesson 12-7) **12.8%**

Problem Solving and Applications

30. **Critical Thinking** A shirt regularly sells for $22.50. It is on sale at a 15%
    discount. The sales tax is $5\frac{1}{2}\%$. **See Solutions Manual.**
    a. Does it matter in which order the discount and the sales tax are applied?
       Explain.
    b. Would the result change if the sales tax were added before the discount
       was subtracted? Explain.

31. **Consumer Math** The Wilsons went out for hamburgers and salad. The bill
    was $17.70 before tax and tip were added.
    a. What is the total including 5% tax? **$18.59**
    b. If a 15% tip is left on the bill including tax, how much is the tip? **$2.79**

32. **Portfolio Suggestion** Select one of the assignments from this chapter that
    you found particularly challenging. Place it in your portfolio.

32. See students' work.

33. **Consumer Math** James Weaver bought a car for $7,800. He had to pay
    sales tax on the car.
    a. If the sales tax is $6\frac{1}{2}\%$, how much sales tax did he pay? **$507**
    b. What was the cost of the car including sales tax? **$8,307**

34. **Smart Shopping** Ms. Collins bought a new suit that originally cost $175.
    She bought it on sale for 45% off.
    a. What was her discount? **$78.75**
    b. How much did she pay for the suit on sale? **$96.25**

35. **Journal Entry** Make up a problem involving the discount rate where the
    regular price and the sale price are given. Show how to use the percent
    equation to solve the problem. **See students' work.**

Lesson 12-8 Discount and Sales Tax   **481**

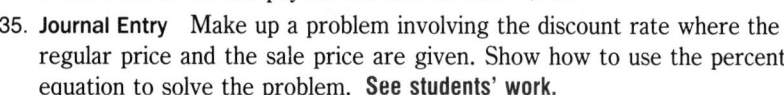

Lesson Resources

- Study Guide Master 12-9
- Practice Master 12-9
- Enrichment Master 12-9
- Evaluation Master, Quiz B, p. 106
- Technology Master, p. 26
- Group Activity Card 12-9

 Transparency 12-9 contains the 5-Minute Check and a teaching aid for this lesson.

⏱ 5-Minute Check

(Over Lesson 12-8)

Find each to the nearest cent.

1. $48 jacket; 5% tax; tax: ? $2.40
2. $70 speaker; 18% off; discount: ? $12.60
3. $12 scarf; 15% off; sale price: ? $10.20
4. $6.79 tape; 8.25% tax; total cost: ? $7.35
5. Find the rate of discount to the nearest percent: regular price, $54; sale price, $45.95   15%

Practice Masters, p. 109

12-9 Simple Interest

Objective

Solve problems involving simple interest.

Words to Learn

interest
principal
rate
time

Credit cards are a convenient way to pay for purchases. But you need to be careful not to buy more than you can afford. Also you will be charged interest if you do not pay the bill off when it is due.

Suppose your parents have a credit card and their monthly balance is $800. If they are charged 18% interest, how much interest will they pay in a year?

Simple **interest** (I) is calculated by finding the product of the **principal** (p), which is the amount borrowed, the **rate** (r), which is a rate of interest as a percent, and the **time** (t), which is given in years. This is expressed by the formula $I = prt$.

Technology Activity

You can learn how to use a spreadsheet to calculate simple interest in Technology Activity 4 on page 647.

$$I = prt$$
$$I = 800 \cdot 0.18 \cdot 1 \quad p = \$800, r = 18\%, t = 1 \text{ year}$$
$$I = 144 \qquad \text{The interest is equal to \$144 in a year.}$$

The formula, $I = prt$, can also be used to find the simple interest when you deposit money in a savings account. In this case, the principal is the amount in your savings account.

Example *Problem Solving*

Saving Money   Ms. Sung deposited $600 in her savings account. Her account earns $6\frac{3}{4}\%$ interest annually. If she does not deposit or withdraw any money, how much will be in her account after 6 months?

$$I = prt$$
$$I = 600 \cdot 0.0675 \cdot 0.5 \quad p = \$600, r = 6\frac{3}{4}\%, t = 6 \text{ months or } 0.5 \text{ year}$$
$$600 \boxed{\times} 6.75 \boxed{\%} \boxed{\times} 0.5 \boxed{=} \boxed{20.25}$$
$$I = 20.25$$

The interest earned on $600 in 6 months was $20.25. So, Ms. Sung will have $600 + $20.25 or $620.25 in her account.

Checking for Understanding

For answers to Exercises 1–2, see margin.

Communicating Mathematics

Read and study the lesson to answer each question.

1. **Explain** how to find the interest on $550 at 8% for one year.
2. **Tell** how to write time in terms of years when it is given in months.

OPTIONS

Reteaching Activity

Using Estimation   Encourage students to round interest rates to determine a reasonable range for answers. Then they may use their calculators and apply the interest formula.

Study Guide Masters, p. 109

Guided Practice

Find the interest to the nearest cent for each principal, interest rate, and time.

3. $200, 6%, 2 years **$24**

4. $340.10, 12%, 1.5 years **$61.22**

5. $121, 16%, 2 months **$3.23**

6. $4,200, $9\frac{1}{4}$%, 3 years **$1,165.50**

Find the interest to the nearest cent on credit cards for each credit card balance, interest rate, and time.

7. $325, 18.5%, 1 year **$60.13**

8. $1,200, 19%, 9 months **$171**

Exercises

Independent Practice

Find the interest to the nearest cent for each principal, interest rate, and time.

9. $2,250, 7%, 3 years **$472.50**

10. $175.80, 12%, 1.25 years **$26.37**

11. $875, 15%, 4 months **$43.75**

12. $98.50, $6\frac{1}{2}$%, 16 months **$8.54**

13. $3,186, 10%, 2 years **$637.20**

14. $514, 8.75%, 6 months **$22.49**

Find the interest to the nearest cent on credit cards for each credit card balance, interest rate, and time.

15. $1,000, $20\frac{1}{2}$%, 1 year **$205**

16. $5,096, 17%, 2 years **$1,732.64**

17. $400, 19%, 6 months **$38**

18. $839, 21%, 1 year **$176.19**
$28.80

19. Find the interest on $443 in a savings account at 6.5% interest for 1 year.

Mixed Review

20. **Statistics** Find the mean, median, and mode for 5, 2, 3, 6, 4, 3, 3, 4, 2, and 8. *(Lesson 3-5)* **4, 3.5, 3**

21. **Geometry** Find the area of a circle having a radius of 6 inches. Use 3.14 for π. *(Lesson 9-8)* **113 in²**

22. **Smart Shopping** At a sale, Barb finds a $125 sweater marked down to $87.50. What percent of decrease is this? *(Lesson 12-8)* **30%**

Problem Solving and Applications

23. **Critical Thinking** Find the amount of simple interest earned on $1,000 at the end of 4 years at 8% per year, if the interest is added to the principal at the end of each year. **$360.49**

24. **Consumer Math** Mitch Lowe bought a watch for $95. He used his credit card, which charges 21% annual interest from the moment of purchase. If he does not make any payments or any additional charges, how much would he owe at the end of the first month? **$96.66**

COMPUTER
CONNECTION

25. **Computer Connection** A spreadsheet can be used to generate a simple interest table for various account balances. Change cell B2 to 6 in the table below. What is the new balance for a principal of $1,000? **$1,120**

	A	B	C	D	E
1	PRINCIPAL	RATE	TIME	INTEREST	NEW BALANCE
2		5	2		
3	500	0.05	2	50	550
4	1000	0.05	2	100	1100

Lesson 12-9 Simple Interest **483**

1 FOCUS

Motivating the Lesson

Questioning Ask students how interest is like rent. a periodic payment for the use of a good

2 TEACH

More Examples

For the Example

Mr. Reilly deposited $800 in a savings account at $5\frac{1}{2}$% annual interest. How much will be in the account after 9 months? **$833**

Close

Have students find the interest earned in 3 months on $500 at 6% annual interest. **$7.50**

3 PRACTICE/APPLY

Assignment Guide

Maximum: 9–25

Minimum: 9–19 odd, 21–24

For **Extra Practice,** see p. 600.

Enrichment Masters, p. 109

Name _____ Date _____

Enrichment Worksheet 12-9

Taking an Interest

When interest is paid on both the amount of the deposit and any interest already earned, interest is said to be compounded. You can use the formula below to find out how much money is in an account for which interest is compounded.

$$A = P(1 + r)^n$$

In the formula, r represents the rate applied each time interest is paid, n represents the number of times interest is given, and A represents the amount in the account.

Example A customer deposited $1,500 in an account that earns 8% per year. If interest is compounded and earned semiannually, how much is in the account after 1 year?

Use the formula $A = P(1 + r)^n$.
Since interest is earned semiannually, $r = 4\%$ and $n = 2$.
$A = 1,500(1 + 0.04)^2$ Use a calculator.
  $= 1,622.40$

After 1 year, there is $1,622.40 in the account.

Use the compound interest formula and a calculator to find the value of each of these investments. Round each answer to the nearest cent.

1. $2,500 invested for 1 year at 6% interest compounded semiannually — **$2,652.25**

2. $3,600 invested for 2 years at 7% interest compounded semiannually — **$4,131.08**

3. $1,000 invested for 5 years at 8% interest compounded annually — **$1,469.33**

4. $2,000 invested for 6 years at 12% interest compounded quarterly — **$4,065.59**

5. $4,800 invested for 10 years at 9% interest compounded annually — **$11,363.35**

6. $10,000 invested for 15 years at 7.5% interest compounded semiannually — **$30,174.71**

T109
Glencoe Division, Macmillan/McGraw-Hill

Extending the Lesson

Managing Money Have students find some current interest rates paid by local banks for savings accounts and certificates of deposit.

Additional Answers

1. Interest equals $550 times 0.08 times 1.

2. Divide the number of months by 12.

Cooperative Learning Activity

Risky Business 12-9

Number of players: 4
Materials: Spinner, index cards

• Label equal sections of a spinner "2%," "3%," "4%," "5%," "6%," "10%."

➡ Suppose that each group member has $100 to invest in a different mutual fund over a period of two years. (A mutual fund is an organization that accepts money from individual investors and invests the combined amount in things like stocks and bonds.)

Each group member writes a period of time in months between 1 month and 24 months on one index card and an amount between $1 and $100 on a second card. One group member then spins the spinner. Each group member computes the amount his or her investment is worth at this rate or interest.

Each group member can continue to "invest" until he or she "runs out" of time. (In other words, the sum of the amounts of time you write must equal 24 months.)

Determine which group member has made the most money after 24 months.

Glencoe Mathematics: Applications and Connections, Course 2

The Chapter Study Guide and Review begins with a section on Communicating Mathematics. This includes questions that review the new terms and concepts that were introduced in the chapter.

Then, the Skills and Concepts presented in the chapter are reviewed using a side-by-side format. Encourage students to refer to the Objectives and Examples on the left as they complete the Review Exercises on the right.

The Chapter Study Guide and Review ends with problems that review Applications and Problem Solving.

Chapter

12 Study Guide and Review

Communicating Mathematics

State whether each sentence is *true* or *false*. If false, replace the underlined word or number to make a true sentence.

1. A percent is a ratio that compares a number to $\underline{100}$. **true**
2. In the proportion $\frac{1}{4} = \frac{25}{100}$, $\frac{25}{100}$ is called the $\underline{\text{percentage}}$. **false; rate**
3. A circle graph is used to $\underline{\text{compare}}$ parts of a whole. **true**
4. There are $\underline{300°}$ in a circle. **false; 360°**
5. When finding a percent of increase, compare the amount of the increase to the $\underline{\text{new}}$ amount. **false; old**
6. The formula for simple interest is $\underline{I = prt}$. **true**
7. In your own words, explain each of the three methods for estimating percents.

See students' work.

Self Assessment

Objectives and Examples	Review Exercises
Upon completing this chapter, you should be able to:	*Use these exercises to review and prepare for the chapter test.*

• find the percent of a number *(Lesson 12-1)*

Find 60% of 300.

$$\frac{P}{B} = \frac{r}{100}$$

$$\frac{P}{300} = \frac{60}{100}$$

$100P = 18,000$ *Find the cross-products.*

$P = 180$

Use a proportion to solve each problem. Round answers to the nearest tenth.

8. What number is 30% of 250? **75**
9. Find 42% of 850. **357**
10. $12\frac{1}{2}$% of 145 is what number? **18.1**
11. Seventy percent of 504 is what number? **352.8**

• estimate by using fractions, decimals, and percents interchangeably *(Lesson 12-3)*

Estimate 57% of 483.
57% is about 60% or $\frac{3}{5}$.
$\frac{3}{5}$ of 500 is 300.
So, 57% of 483 is *about* 300.

Estimate.

12. 12% of 75 **7.5**   13. 89% of 500 **450**
14. $8\frac{3}{4}$% of 15 **1.5**   15. 148% of 20 **30**
16. 0.95% of 800 **8**   17. 65% of 1,000 **650**
18. 99% of 1 **0.99**   19. 14.6% of 78 **12**
For Exercises 12–19, sample answers given.

Objectives and Examples

- solve problems using the percent proportion *(Lesson 12-4)*

  What percent of 80 is 12?

  $$\frac{P}{B} = \frac{r}{100}$$

  $$\frac{12}{80} = \frac{r}{100}$$

  $1,200 = 80r$ *Find the*
  $15 = r$ *cross products.*
  15% of 80 is 12.

- solve problems using the percent equation *(Lesson 12-5)*

  What number is 18% of 120?

  $P = R \cdot B$

  $P = 0.18 \cdot 120$

  $P = 21.6$ 18% of 120 is 21.6.

- construct circle graphs *(Lesson 12-6)*

  Favorite Season:
  Spring, 35%,
  126°; Summer,
  29%, 104.4%;
  Fall, 24%, 86.4°;
  Winter, 12%,
  43.2°

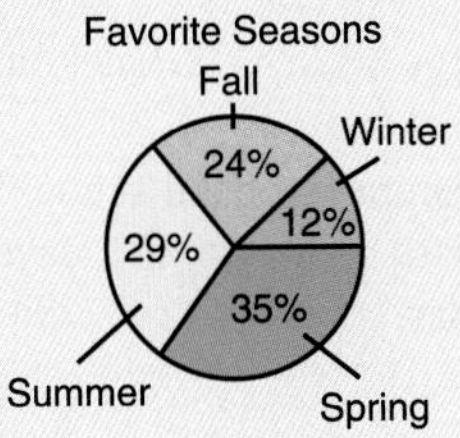

  Favorite Seasons

- find the percent of increase or decrease *(Lesson 12-7)*

  old: $2.95   new: $3.45

  $3.45 − $2.95 = $0.50

  $$\frac{0.50}{2.95} = \frac{r}{100}$$

  $50 = 2.95r$ *Find the*
             cross products.

  $$\frac{50}{2.95} = \frac{2.95r}{2.95}$$ *Divide each*
             side by 2.95

  $16.95 = r$ The percent of increase
             to the nearest whole
             percent is 17%.

Review Exercises

Write a proportion for each problem. Then solve. Round answers to the nearest tenth.

20. Find 36.5% of 150. **54.8**
21. What percent of 95 is 5? **5.3%**
22. 105 is $33\frac{1}{3}$% of what number? **315**

For proportions in Exercises 20–22, see Solutions Manual.

Write an equation for each problem. Then solve. **For equations, see Solutions Manual.**

23. 42 is what percent of 80? **52.5%**
24. 65% of what number is 91? **140**
25. Find 62% of 350. **217**
26. 58% of 450 is what number? **261**
27. 12.5% of what number is 93.75? **750**

Use the information from the chart below to construct a circle graph. **See Solutions Manual.**

28.

Favorite Soft Drink	
Soft Drink	**Percent**
cola	38%
diet cola	26%
lemon-lime	18%
root beer	8%
other	10%

Find the percent of change. Round to the nearest whole percent.

29. old: 42   **55%**
    new: 65
30. old: $23,500 **12%**
    new: $26,400
31. old: $212 **15%**
    new: $180
32. old: 299 **28%**
    new: 216

Chapter 12 Study Guide and Review   **485**

You may wish to use a Chapter Test from the Evaluation Masters booklet as an additional chapter review. The two free-response forms are shown below. One of the two multiple-choice forms is shown on the next page.

Evaluation Masters, pp. 104–105

Name _____ Date _____

Form 2A _____ *Chapter 12 Test*

1. Use a proportion to find $55\frac{1}{2}\%$ of 66. Round your answer to the nearest tenth.   **1.** 36.6
2. Use a proportion to find what number is 78% of 78. Round your answer to the nearest tenth.   **2.** 60.8
3. Estimate 0.25% of 814.   **3.** 2
4. Write a proportion and solve to find what number is 97% of 16. Round your answer to the nearest tenth.   **4.** 15.5
5. Write an equation and find 19% of what number is 31. Round your answer to the nearest tenth.   **5.** 163.2
6. Write an equation and find what percent of 49 is 40. Round your answer to the nearest whole percent.   **6.** 82%
7. The graph at the right displays the results of a survey of 163 seventh-grade pet owners at JFK Middle School. Use the graph to find which pet can be described by $\frac{20}{163}$.   **7.** Fish
   Students who own pets — Fish 12%, Cat 24%, Dog 47%, Other 9%, Bird 8%
8. Find the percent of change if the old price is $65.99 and the new price is $72.99. Round your answer to the nearest whole percent.   **8.** 11%
9. Find the percent of change from 7 to 3. Round your answer to the nearest whole percent.   **9.** 57%
10. Find the sale price of a $57 pair of shoes on sale for 20% off.   **10.** $45.60
11. Find the interest for a principal of $2,500, an interest rate of 8.75%, and a time period of 24 months.   **11.** $437.50
12. Find the interest on a credit card with a principal of $855, an interest rate of 19%, and a time period of 4 months.   **12.** $54.15
13. DaShawna baby-sits for $3 an hour. She wants to buy a shirt that is selling for $15.95 and a pair of pants that are selling for $21.99. About how many hours will she need to baby-sit before she will have enough money to buy both the shirt and pants?   **13.** 13 hours
14. At Oakwood Middle School, Ms. Addams and Mr. Kleckner are the seventh-grade math teachers. Ms. Addams teaches 84 students, and Mr. Kleckner teaches 53 students. What percent of the students does Ms. Addams teach? Round your answer to the nearest whole percent.   **14.** 61%
15. Find the total purchase price to the nearest cent if a $95 radio is on sale for 25% off and the sales tax is 5.75%.   **15.** $75.35

BONUS To the nearest whole percent, 44% of the seventh-graders at King Middle School are girls. There are 428 seventh-graders. What are all the possibilities for the number of girls in the seventh grade?   187, 188, 189, or 190

104
Glencoe Division, Macmillan/McGraw-Hill

Name _____ Date _____

Form 2B _____ *Chapter 12 Test*

1. Use a proportion to find $19\frac{1}{4}\%$ of 45. Round your answer to the nearest tenth.   **1.** 8.7
2. Use a proportion to find what number is 7% of 588. Round your answer to the nearest tenth.   **2.** 41.2
3. Estimate 309% of 26.   **3.** 75
4. Write a proportion and solve to find 63% of what number is 9. Round your answer to the nearest tenth.   **4.** 14.3
5. Write an equation and find what number is 19% of 46. Round your answer to the nearest tenth.   **5.** 8.7
6. Write an equation and find what percent of 32 is 69. Round your answer to the nearest whole percent.   **6.** 216%
7. The circle graph at the right displays the percent of 142 seventh-graders at Lincoln Middle School with each hair color. Use the graph to find which hair color is represented by the ratio $\frac{55}{142}$.   **7.** Black
   Hair Color — Blonde 10%, Black 39%, Brown 43%, Red 5%, Other 3%
8. Find the percent of change if the old price is $36 and the new price is $26. Round your answer to the nearest whole percent.   **8.** 28%
9. Find the percent of change from 44 to 49. Round your answer to the nearest whole percent.   **9.** 11%
10. Find the discount on a $79 jacket that is 30% off.   **10.** $23.70
11. Find the total purchase price to the nearest cent of a $5.99 toy with 6.5% tax.   **11.** $6.38
12. Find the interest to the nearest cent for a principal of $1,900, an interest rate of 13.25%, and a time of 32 months.   **12.** $671.33
13. Eric mows lawns at a rate of $5/lawn. He wants to start saving to buy a bike that costs $95 and a bike helmet that costs $24.50. About how many lawns will he need to mow before he can buy both the bike and the helmet?   **13.** 25 lawns
14. There are 24 boy scouts and 31 girls scouts at East Middle School. To the nearest whole percent, what percent of the scouts are boys?   **14.** 44%
15. Fred went shopping for school clothes. He used the same credit card to buy 2 pairs of pants for $30.98 and 3 shirts for $41.74. His credit card company charges 19.5% annual interest from the moment of purchase. If he does not make any additional charges or payments, how much would he owe at the end of the first month?   **15.** $73.90

BONUS Fifty percent of what amount would be the same as twenty-five percent of thirty-five dollars? $17.50

105
Glencoe Division, Macmillan/McGraw-Hill

486

Objectives and Examples

- solve problems involving sales tax and discount *(Lesson 12-8)*

  Find the sales tax on a $35 pair of shoes at 5% tax. Let t represent the sales tax.
  $$5\% \times \$35 = t$$
  $$0.05 \times 35 = t$$
  $$\$1.75 = t$$

- solve problems involving simple interest *(Lesson 12-9)*

  The interest on $500 at 8% for 5 years is:
  $$I = prt$$
  $$I = 500 \times 0.08 \times 5$$
  $$I = \$200$$

Review Exercises

Find the sales tax or discount to the nearest cent.

33. $175 bicycle; 25% off **$43.75**
34. $7,500 car; 7% tax **$525**
35. $50 sweater; $\frac{1}{3}$ off **$16.67**

Find the interest to the nearest cent for each principal, interest rate, and time given.

36. $6,000, 9%, 2 years **$1,080**
37. $75, $7\frac{1}{2}\%$, 8 months **$3.75**
38. $2,450, 12%, $4\frac{1}{2}$ years **$1,323**
39. $675, 18%, 32 months **$324**

Applications and Problem Solving

40. **Consumer Math** Debbie bought a ski outfit for $325. The sales tax rate was 5%. How much sales tax did she pay? *(Lesson 12-8)* **$16.25**

41. **School** During the 1990–91 school year, Juanita attended school 90% of the days school was in session. She was in class a total of 171 days. Find the total number of days in the school calendar. *(Lesson 12-5)* **190 days**

Curriculum Connection Projects

- **Transportation** Find the percent of your classmates that ride the school bus. Use that percent to find the number of students in the entire school that ride the bus.
- **Economics** Use newspapers from the past week to find the number of points the Dow Jones Averages went up or down each day. Find the percent of change for each day.

Read More About It

Byers, Patricia, and Julia Preston, and Patricia Johnson. *The Kid's Money Book: Great Money Making Ideas.*
Adler, David A. *Banks.*
Bethancourt, T. Ernesto. *The Me Inside of Me.*

12 Test

Use a proportion to solve. Round answers to the nearest tenth.

1. Find 25% of 145. **36.3**

2. 96 is 40% of what number? **240**

3. **College Tuition** State University presently charges $6,500 per year for tuition. Tuition will be going up 6% for the coming academic year. Find the amount of increase. **$390**

4. **Health** Experts recommend that at most 30% of your total calorie intake should come from fat. If you eat 1,600 calories per day, what is the maximum number of calories that should be from fat? **480 calories**

Estimate. **For Exercises 5–7, sample answers given.**

5. 19% of 248 **50**

6. 149% of 79 **120**

7. **Smart Shopping** Grace finds a pair of jeans originally priced $39.95 on a rack labeled 33% off. Estimate the sale price. **about $27**

For proportions, see Solutions Manual.

Write a proportion for each problem. Then solve. Round answers to the nearest tenth.

8. 50% of what number is 334.8? **669.6**

9. What percent of 48 is 7? **14.6%**

Write an equation for each problem. Then solve. **For equations, see Solutions Manual.**

10. Find 12% of 75. **9**

11. 150 is what percent of 120? **125%**

12. Use the information in the bar graph at the right to make a circle graph.
See Solutions Manual.

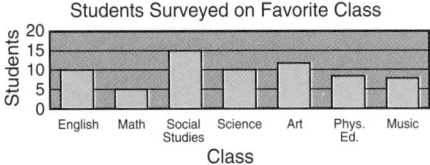

Students Surveyed on Favorite Class

Find the percent of change. Round to the nearest whole percent.

13. old: $59, new: $42 **29%**

14. old: 145, new: 183 **26%**

Find the sales tax or discount to the nearest cent.

15. $29.99 book, 15% off **$4.50**

16. $16.99 CD, $6\frac{1}{2}$% tax **$1.10**

17. Find the total purchase price to the nearest cent if an $85 pair of boots is on sale for 20% off and the sales tax is 7%. **$72.76**

Find the interest to the nearest cent for each principal, interest rate, and time given.

18. $1,350, 12%, 2 years **$324**

19. $2,400, $11\frac{3}{4}$%, 9 months **$211.50**

20. **Finances** Jorge borrows $3,500 to buy a new motorcycle. The loan is for 3 years at an annual interest rate of 9.5%. Find the total amount Jorge will pay over the 3 year life of the loan. **$4,497.50**

Bonus Find 1,000% of 100. **1,000**

Using the Chapter Test

This page may be used as a chapter test or another chapter review.

Evaluation Masters, pp. 100–101

Name _____ Date _____

Form 1A _____ **Chapter 12 Test**

1. Use a proportion to find $70\frac{1}{2}$% of 59. Round your answer to the nearest tenth.
   A. 44.3   B. 41.6   C. 44.2   D. 4.4   1. **B**

2. Use a proportion to find what number is 34% of 34. Round your answer to the nearest tenth.
   A. 100   B. 1,156   C. 11.6   D. 1   2. **C**

3. Estimate 49% of $15\frac{7}{8}$.
   A. 2   B. 7.5   C. 1   D. 4.5   3. **B**

4. Estimate 0.75% of 387.
   A. 300   B. 30   C. 0.3   D. 3   4. **D**

5. Write a proportion and solve to find what number is 48% of 55.
   A. 24.0   B. 26.4   C. 87.3   D. 114.6   5. **B**

6. Write a proportion and solve to find what percent of 184 is 23.
   A. 0.125%   B. 8.0%   C. 12.5%   D. 80%   6. **C**

7. Write an equation and find what number is 74% of 58.
   A. 42.92   B. 69.2   C. 1.4   D. 77.3   7. **A**

8. Write an equation and find what percent of 73 is 99. Round your answer to the nearest whole percent.
   A. 72.27%   B. 73%   C. 1.36%   D. 136%   8. **D**

Use the chart below for Exercises 9–10. The chart displays the results of a survey on the favorite color of all seventh graders at Jones Middle School.

9. Find the ratio that compares the number of students whose favorite color is black with the total number of students. Round your answer to the nearest hundredth.
   A. 0.09   B. 0.13   C. 0.37   D. 0.32   9. **B**

7th Grade Favorite Colors	
Color	Students
red	132
blue	114
black	46
green	32
other	32

10. Find the angle measure, to the nearest degree, that would be used to make the section of a circle graph displaying the percent of students whose favorite color is blue.
    A. 133°   B. 115°   C. 47°   D. 32°   10. **B**

100

Name _____ Date _____

Chapter 12 Test, Form 1A (continued)

11. Find the percent of change if the old price is $34.50 and the new price is $24. Round your answer to the nearest whole percent.
    A. 30%   B. 11%   C. 70%   D. 10%   11. **A**

12. Find the percent of change from 4 to 9.
    A. 125%   B. 44%   C. 56%   D. 80%   12. **A**

13. Find the sales tax to the nearest cent on a $25 pair of shoes with 5.75% tax.
    A. $1.44   B. $1.43   C. $5.75   D. $1.77   13. **A**

14. Find the rate of discount if the regular price is $26 and the sale price is $20.80.
    A. 80%   B. 2%   C. 20%   D. 8%   14. **C**

15. Find the interest for a principal of $500, an interest rate of 8%, and a time period of 4 years.
    A. $250   B. $1,600   C. $660   D. $160   15. **D**

16. Find the interest to the nearest cent for a principal of $4,329, an interest rate of 9.25%, and a time period of 18 months.
    A. $4,929.94   B. $7,207.79   C. $4,356.25   D. $600.65   16. **D**

17. Find the interest to the nearest cent on a credit card with a principal of $205, an interest rate of 21%, and a time period of 6 months.
    A. $55.35   B. $25.83   C. $21.53   D. $27.00   17. **C**

18. Angie wants to put a winter coat in layaway at a store. To do so, she must pay the store 20% of the cost of the coat so they will hold it. If the coat costs $48.99, about how much of a deposit does Angie need to pay the store?
    A. $2.50   B. $10   C. $15   D. $5   18. **B**

19. In Juan's math class, there are 16 boys and 9 girls. What percent of Juan's class is girls?
    A. 36%   B. 56.25%   C. 64%   D. 43.75%   19. **A**

20. Albert Groe bought a suit for $295. He used his credit card which charges 19% annual interest from the moment of purchase. If he does not make any payments or any additional charges, how much would he owe at the end of the first month?
    A. $301.73   B. $56.05   C. $351.05   D. $299.67   20. **D**

BONUS In January, Jenny used her credit card to purchase a pair of shoes for $36 and a pair of gloves for $10. She paid half of her bill at the end of the month. In February, she used her same credit card to buy a pair of pants for $22. If her credit card company charges 18.25% annual interest from the moment of purchase, what will Jenny's bill be at the end of February?
A. $46.04   B. $70.07   C. $46.36   D. $45.69   **A**

101

Test and Review Generator software is provided in Apple, IBM, and Macintosh versions. You may use this software to create your own tests or worksheets, based on the needs of your students.

The **Performance Assessment Booklet** provides an alternate assessment for evaluating student progress. An assessment for this chapter can be found on pages 23–24.

The Academic Skills Test may be used to help students prepare for standardized tests. The test items are written in the same style as those in state proficiency tests. The test items cover skills and concepts covered up to this point in the text.

These pages can be used as an overnight assignment. After students have completed the pages, discuss how each problem can be solved, or provide copies of the solutions from the *Solutions Manual*.

Academic Skills Test

Chapter

12 Academic Skills Test

Directions: Choose the best answer. Write A, B, C, or D.

B 1. What is the value of $8 + x^2$ if $x = 12$?

    A 32   B 152

    C 400   D none of these

C 2. How could you calculate the perimeter of an $8\frac{1}{2}$ by 11 inch piece of paper?

    A Add $8\frac{1}{2}$ and 11.

    B Multiply 2 times $8\frac{1}{2}$ and add 11.

    C Add $8\frac{1}{2}$ and 11 and multiply by 2.

    D Multiply $8\frac{1}{2}$ and 11.

A 3. Which is an equivalent equation, using the inverse operation, for $x - 3.2 = 1.7$?

    A $x = 1.7 + 3.2$ B $x + 3.2 = 1.7$

    C $x - 1.7 = 3.2$ D $x = 3.2 - 1.7$

C 4. What is the probability that a randomly-dropped counter will fall in the shaded region?

    A $\frac{1}{8}$ B $\frac{1}{4}$

    C $\frac{1}{3}$ D $\frac{1}{2}$

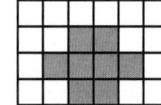

A 5. The top, front, and side views of a figure are given below. What is the figure?

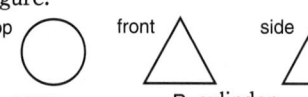

top   front   side

    A cone   B cylinder
    C rectangular   D sphere
       prism

C 6. Jessie has a paper cup that is shaped like a cylinder with a radius of 1.5 in. and a height of 5 in. To the nearest cubic inch, what is the volume of the cup?

    A 7.5 in^3 B 30 in^3

    C 35 in^3 D 45 in^3

D 7. In the proportion $\frac{2}{3} = \frac{x}{8}$, what is the value of x?

    A 12   B 7

    C $6\frac{1}{2}$ D $5\frac{1}{3}$

D 8. $\triangle LMN$ is similar to $\triangle PQR$. What is the length of side PQ?

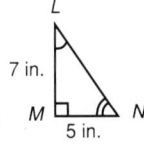 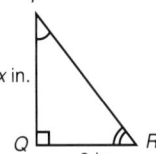

    A $4\frac{3}{8}$ inches

    B 7 inches

    C 10 inches

    D 11.2 inches

A 9. 30% of a number is 24. What is the number?

    A 80   B 72

    C 8   D 7.2

D 10. Colleen wants to buy a pair of shoes that cost $54.98. She must also pay 6% sales tax. To the nearest cent, what is the total cost of the shoes?

    A $3.30   B $51.68

    C $55.31   D $58.28

The questions on this page involve comparing two quantities, one in Column A and one in Column B. In some questions, information related to one or both quantities is centered above them.

Directions: Write A if the quantity in Column A is greater. Write B if the quantity in Column B is greater. Write C if the quantities are equal. Write D if there is not enough information to decide.

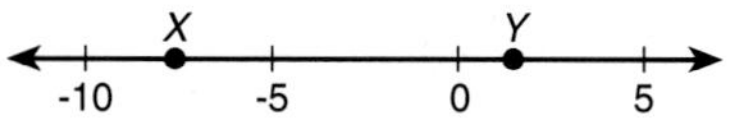

Column A	Column B
11. $0.3 + 0.8 + 1.2$ **A**	0.23
12. $1\frac{1}{4} + 2\frac{2}{3}$ **A**	$1\frac{1}{8} + 2\frac{1}{2}$

13. **B**

the number represented by point X	the number represented by point Y

14. the sum of any three negative integers **D**	the product of any three negative integers

15. **C**

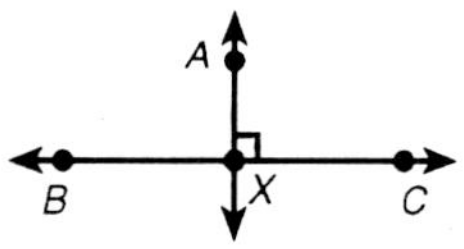

measure of $\angle AXB$	measure of $\angle AXC$

16. $\sqrt{16} + \sqrt{16}$ **A**	$\sqrt{32}$

Column A	Column B

17. **D**

8 ft

surface area of top and bottom	surface area of curved surface

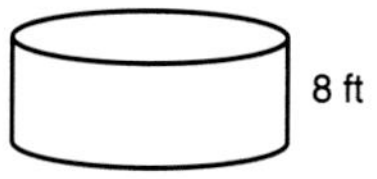

18. ratio of 54 to 45 **C**	ratio of 84 to 70
19. 20% **C**	$\frac{1}{5}$
20. 5% simple interest on $100 for 2 years **A**	8% simple interest on $100 for 1 year

13 Discrete Math and Probability

Previewing the Chapter

This chapter explores discrete math and probability. It includes lessons in which students use tree diagrams and the fundamental counting principle to count outcomes. Students also find and use experimental and theoretical probability, use statistics to make predictions, distinguish betweeen independent and dependent events, and find the probability of two events. Finally, they first explore permutations and combinations and then calculate them. In the **problem-solving strategy** lesson, students solve problems by acting them out.

Lesson	Lesson Objectives	NCTM Standards	State/Local Objectives
13-1	Use tree diagrams to count outcomes.	1–4	
13-2A	Count outcomes to determine whether a game is fair or unfair.	1–5, 11	
13-2	Use multiplication to count outcomes.	1–5, 7, 9	
13-3	Find and compare experimental and theoretical probabilities.	1–5, 7, 11	
13-4	Solve problems by acting them out.	1–5, 7, 11	
13-5	Predict actions of a larger group by using a sample.	1–7, 10	
13-6	Find the probability of independent and dependent events.	1–5, 7, 11	
Decision Making	Choose a camcorder.	1–5, 7	
13-7A	Explore permutations.	1–5	
13-7	Find the number of permutations of a set of objects.	1–5, 7, 11	
13-8A	Explore combinations.	1–5	
13-8	Find the number of combinations of a set of objects.	1–5, 7, 11	

Organizing the Chapter

A complete, 1-page lesson plan is provided for each lesson in the Lesson Plans Masters Booklet.

LESSON PLANNING GUIDE

Lesson	Materials/ Manipulatives	Extra Practice (Student Edition)	Study Guide	Practice	Enrichment	Evaluation	Technology	Lab Manual	Multicultural Activities	Application and Interdisciplinary Activities	Transparencies	Group Activity Cards
13-1	3 plain chips marker	p. 600	p. 110	p. 110	p. 110						13-1	13-1
13-1B	spinners ruler							p. 75				
13-2	calculator	p. 600	p. 111	p. 111	p. 111						13-2	13-2
13-3	dice		p. 112	p. 112	p. 112						13-3	13-3
13-4	spinner divided into 6 sections, index cards, books, paper bag		p. 113	p. 113	p. 113	Quiz A, p. 115					13-4	13-4
13-5	calculator	p. 601	p. 114	p. 114	p. 114					p. 13	13-5	13-5
13-6		p. 601	p. 115	p. 115	p. 115				p. 13		13-6	13-6
13-7A	4 index cards marker							p. 76				
13-7	calculator	p. 601	p. 116	p. 116	p. 116		p. 13				13-7	13-7
13-8A	index cards marker							p. 77				
13-8		p. 602	p. 117	p. 117	p. 117	Quiz B, p. 115	p. 27			p. 27	13-8	13-8
Study Guide and Review			Multiple Choice Test, Forms 1A and 1B, pp. 109–112 Free Response Test, Forms 2A and 2B, pp. 113–114 Cumulative Review, p. 116 (free response)									
Test			Cumulative Test, p. 117 (multiple choice)									

Pacing Guide: Option II (Chapters 1–13) - 12 days; Option III (Chapters 1–14) - 12 days
You may wish to refer to the complete **Course Planning Guides** on page T25.

OTHER CHAPTER RESOURCES

Student Edition
Chapter Opener, pp. 490–491
Mid-Chapter Review, p. 505
Save Planet Earth, p. 520
Portfolio Suggestion, p. 520

Manipulatives
Overhead Manipulative Resources
Middle School Mathematics Manipulative Kit

Software/Technology
Interactive Mathematics Tools (Macintosh)
Test and Review Generator (IBM, Apple, Macintosh)
Teacher's Guide for Software Resources

Other Supplements
Transparency 13-0
Performance Assessment, pp. 25–26
Glencoe Mathematics Professional Series
Lesson Plans, pp. 143–153

INTERDISCIPLINARY BULLETIN BOARD

Social Studies Connection

Objective Play a board game involving the use of logic.

How To Use It Have students make the playing board and play the Egyptian game of Seega. Then have them research other board games around the world that involve the use of logic. Ask students to teach the rules to classmates, and then try to play.

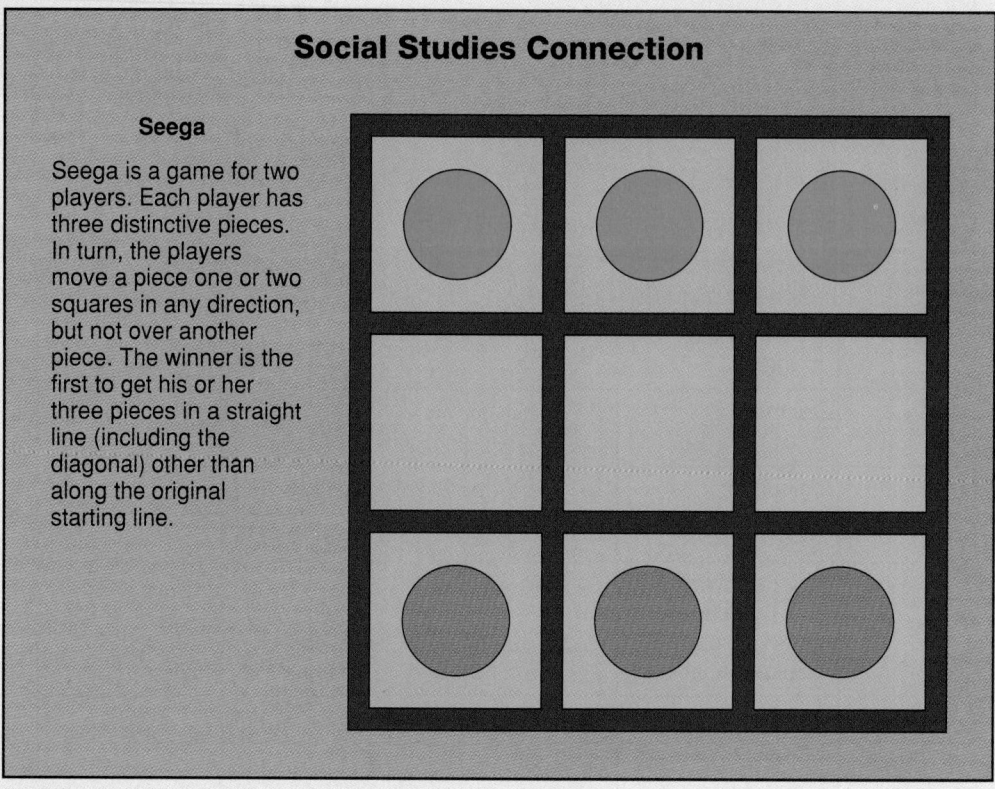

Social Studies Connection

Seega

Seega is a game for two players. Each player has three distinctive pieces. In turn, the players move a piece one or two squares in any direction, but not over another piece. The winner is the first to get his or her three pieces in a straight line (including the diagonal) other than along the original starting line.

APPLICATIONS AND CONNECTIONS

Applications	Lesson	Example	Exercise
Food Service	13-1	X	
Telephones	13-1		15
Food Service	13-2	1	12
Highways	13-2	2	
Games	13-3		12
Coin Toss	13-3		13
Computer	13-3		16
Marketing	13-5	2	
Social Studies	13-5		5–7, 11–15
School	13-5		8–10
Population	13-5		19
Consumer Math	13-5		20
Weather	13-5		23
Traffic Lights	13-6		19
Clothing	13-6		20
Geography	13-7	2	
Vacations	13-7	3	
Celebrations	13-7		23
Architecture	13-7		24
Sports	13-8	1	
Law	13-8	2	
Sales	13-8		24
Food Service	13-8		25
Connections			
Algebra	13-2		13
Probability	13-7		25
Probability	13-8	3	

TEAM ACTIVITIES

Multicultural Experiences

Outside Field Trips On a trip to a delicatessen, students can list the number of different sandwiches that are possible considering the choices for breads, meats, cheeses, and toppings.

Students can visit a pizza restaurant to determine the choices for pizzas given the different sizes and toppings to choose from.

In-Class Speakers Ask a representative from a local TV or radio station to visit the class and talk about the kinds of decisions the station makes based on results from viewer or listener surveys.

Ask a worker from a local greenhouse or garden center to come in and discuss how they use samples to prescribe lawn care.

SUPPLEMENTARY BLACKLINE MASTER BOOKLETS

Some of the blackline masters for enhancing this chapter are shown below.

Application and Interdisciplinary Activity Masters, pp. 13, 27

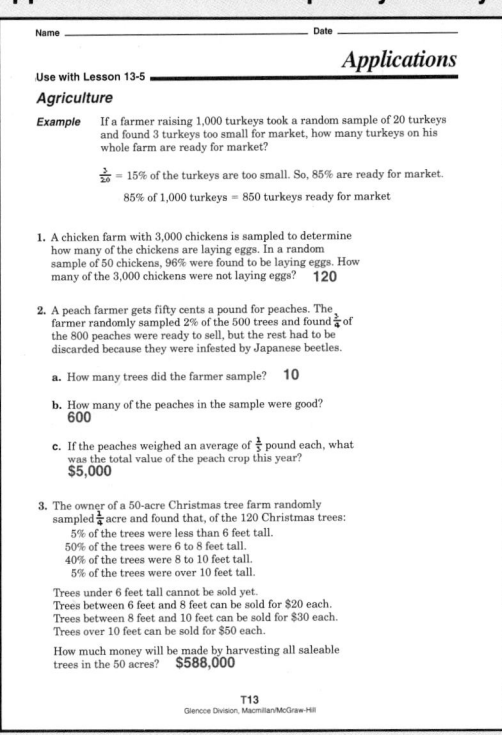

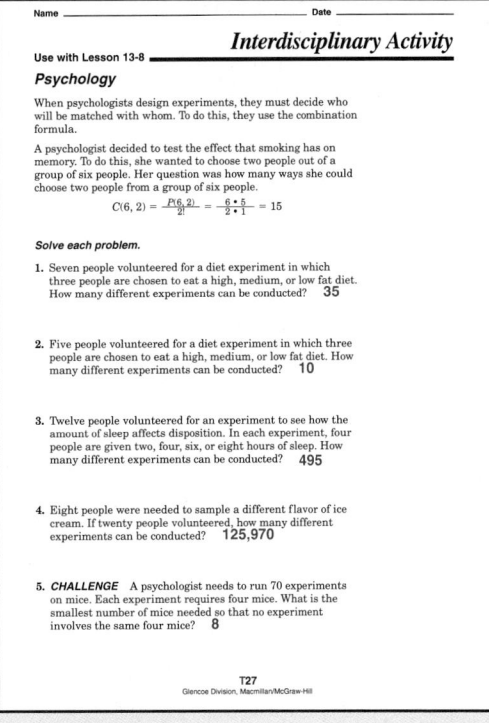

Multicultural Activity Masters, p. 13

Technology Masters, p. 13

RECOMMENDED OUTSIDE RESOURCES

Books/Periodicals

Ecker, Michael W., *Getting Started in Problem Solving and Math Contests,* New York, NY: Franklin Watts, 1987.

Linn, Charles F., *Probability,* New York, NY: Thomas Y. Crowell Co., 1972.

Films/Videotapes/Videodiscs

Probability, Wilmette, IL: Films Incorporated, 1970.

Situational Math, Level II, Niles, IL: United Learning, 1974.

Software

Probability Lab, (Apple II), MECC

For addresses of companies handling software, please refer to page T24.

INTER·ACTIVE Mathematics

Glencoe's *Interactive Mathematics: Activities and Investigations* consists of 18 units that may be used as alternatives or supplemental material for *Mathematics: Applications and Connections.* The suggested units for this chapter are Unit 6, *The Road Not Taken,* and Unit 10, *Against the Odds.* See page T18 for more information.

Chapter

13 Discrete Math and Probability

Spotlight on Earthquakes

Have You Ever Wondered. . .

- What it means when an earthquake measures 6.5 on the Richter scale?

- How much energy is released during an earthquake?

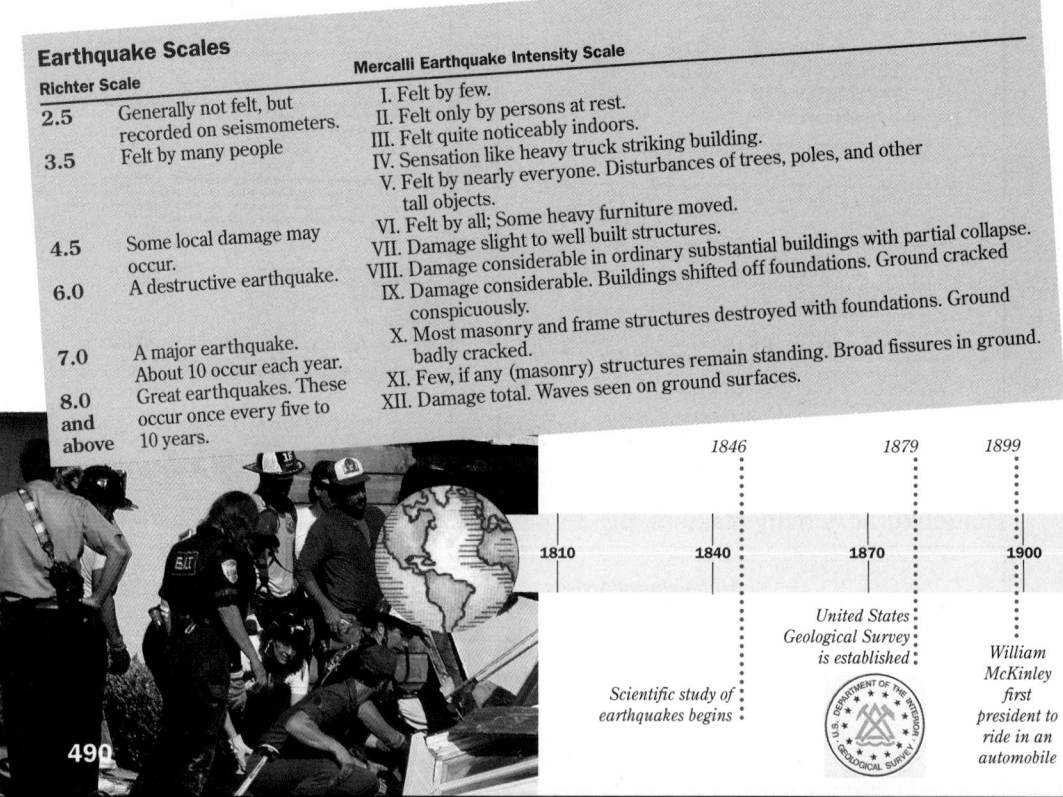

Earthquake Scales

Richter Scale		Mercalli Earthquake Intensity Scale
2.5	Generally not felt, but recorded on seismometers.	I. Felt by few.
3.5	Felt by many people	II. Felt only by persons at rest.
		III. Felt quite noticeably indoors.
		IV. Sensation like heavy truck striking building.
		V. Felt by nearly everyone. Disturbances of trees, poles, and other tall objects.
4.5	Some local damage may occur.	VI. Felt by all; Some heavy furniture moved.
6.0	A destructive earthquake.	VII. Damage slight to well built structures.
		VIII. Damage considerable in ordinary substantial buildings with partial collapse.
		IX. Damage considerable. Buildings shifted off foundations. Ground cracked conspicuously.
7.0	A major earthquake. About 10 occur each year.	X. Most masonry and frame structures destroyed with foundations. Ground badly cracked.
8.0 and above	Great earthquakes. These occur once every five to 10 years.	XI. Few, if any (masonry) structures remain standing. Broad fissures in ground.
		XII. Damage total. Waves seen on ground surfaces.

	1846		1879	1899
1810	1840		1870	1900

Scientific study of earthquakes begins

United States Geological Survey is established

William McKinley first president to ride in an automobile

490

Chapter Project

Earthquakes
Work in a group.

1. During the next two months, collect newspaper clippings dealing with events that change Earth's surfaces—earthquakes, floods, volcanoes.

2. On a map of the world, indicate the site of each event. Include a key with your map.

3. Indicate how each event altered Earth's surface.

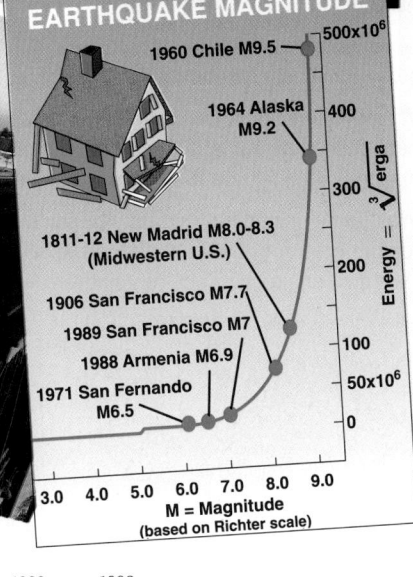

EARTHQUAKE MAGNITUDE

1960 Chile M9.5 — 500x10⁶

1964 Alaska M9.2 — 400

Energy = ∛erga

300

1811-12 New Madrid M8.0-8.3 (Midwestern U.S.) — 200

1906 San Francisco M7.7

1989 San Francisco M7 — 100

1988 Armenia M6.9

1971 San Fernando M6.5 — 50x10⁶

0

3.0 4.0 5.0 6.0 7.0 8.0 9.0
M = Magnitude
(based on Richter scale)

Looking Ahead

In this chapter, you will see how mathematics can be used to answer questions about earthquakes.

The major objectives of the chapter are to:

- find and compare experimental and theoretical probabilities

- predict the actions of a larger group using a sample

- count outcomes using a tree diagram or the Fundamental Principle of Counting

- find the probability of independent events

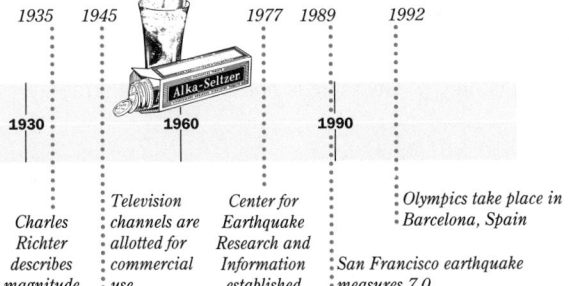

1935   1945   1977 1989   1992

1930   1960   1990

Charles Richter describes magnitude scale for earthquakes

Television channels are allotted for commercial use

Center for Earthquake Research and Information established

Olympics take place in Barcelona, Spain

San Francisco earthquake measures 7.0

491

DATA ANALYSIS

Have students examine the chart and graph. Then have them find out the magnitude of recent earthquakes. Ask them to determine where on the Richter scale most of these earthquakes fall. Ask them how they would feel living in a region that scientists have identified as a likely location for a future earthquake.

Data Search

A question related to these data is provided in Lesson 13-8, page 525, Exercise 27.

CHAPTER PROJECT

The geology department of a university would be a good source of information about earthquakes. You may want to assign a group of students the responsibility of obtaining such information from experts. Other students can use the library's resources. Extend the project by having some students look into the field of earthquake prediction, finding out about the difficulties involved in predicting an occurrence of such a natural event.

Chapter Opener Transparency

Transparency 13-0 is available in the Transparency Package. It provides another full-color, motivating activity that you can use to capture students' interest.

Lesson Resources

- Study Guide Master 13-1
- Practice Master 13-1
- Enrichment Master 13-1
- Group Activity Card 13-1

 Transparency 13-1 contains the 5-Minute Check and a teaching aid for this lesson.

🕐 5-Minute Check
(Over Chapter 12)

1. 57 is 60% of what number? 95

2. To the nearest whole percent, what percent of 48 is 38? 79%

3. Find the percent of change. Round to the nearest whole percent. old: $85, new: $66 22%

4. Find the sales tax to the nearest cent. $42 book, 7.25% tax $3.05

5. Find the interest to the nearest cent. $1,200, 6.5%, 6 months $39.00

1 FOCUS

Motivating the Lesson

Situational Problem Tell students that Elmore is writing a mystery, and that he plans to have as his amateur sleuth, a dentist, a cook, or a bus driver. He plans to have the crime take place in a park, a bowling alley, or a fish market. Ask students how many detective/crime scene choices Elmore has.

2 TEACH

Using the Mini-Lab Ask students to give the probability of having two chips show the same letter and of having three chips show three different letters. $\frac{3}{4}$, $\frac{1}{4}$

13-1 Tree Diagrams

Objective
Use tree diagrams to count outcomes.

Words to Learn
outcomes
sample space
tree diagram

Do you dread surprise quizzes? Most students don't like them. But if you do your homework, you'll be more likely to answer the questions correctly and get a good grade.

Imagine that you walk into science class one day and your teacher hands you a pop quiz with three true-false questions on it. You're not prepared this time, so you guess on the answers and then hand in the quiz.

Is guessing a good strategy? To find out, figure how many possible sets of answers, or **outcomes,** there would be by guessing.

When you guess at the answers to a test, there are several possible outcomes. The set of all possible outcomes is called the **sample space.** Often a **tree diagram** is used to picture a sample space.

What is the sample space for the science quiz? You can guess T or F for the first question, T or F for the second question, and T or F for the third question. The tree diagram below shows the sample space.

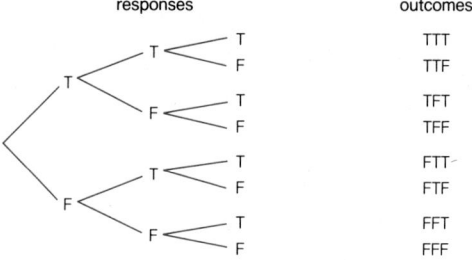

LOOK BACK

You can review probability on page 157.

There are eight different sets of guesses, but only one is the correct set of guesses. The probability that you will get all three answers correct by guessing is only $\frac{1}{8}$. Guessing is not a very good strategy.

Example *Problem Solving*

Food Service A concession stand sells hot dogs, hamburgers, and ham barbecues. They also sell cola, diet cola, and lemon-lime drinks. How many different sandwich/drink choices are sold at the stand?

OPTIONS

Reteaching Activity

Using Models To help students figure out how many possible outcomes there are for a situation, have them use differently colored pattern blocks to represent the choices.

Study Guide Masters, p. 110

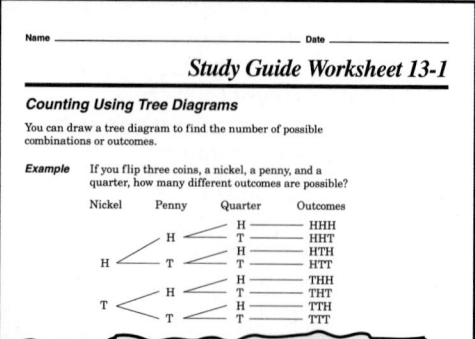

Make a tree diagram. List the kinds of sandwiches. For each kind of sandwich, list the three kinds of drinks. Altogether there are nine different choices of sandwiches and drinks.

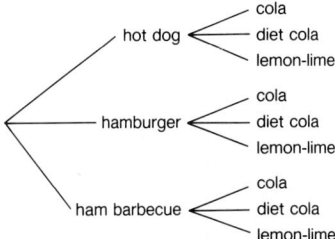

Mini-Lab

Work with a partner.

Materials: three plain chips and a marker

- Mark one side of a chip A. Mark the other side B. Mark one side of another chip A. Mark the other side C. Mark one side of the last chip B. Mark the other side C.
- Decide which student will be Player 1 and which student will be Player 2.
- Player 1 tosses the chips. If two chips show the same letter, Player 1 wins. Otherwise, Player 2 wins. Who won? Record the result.
- Repeat the chip toss experiment 20 more times. Record who won each time.

Talk About It   Yes; sample answer: Player 1 won more times.
a. Is there a pattern to the results? What is it?

b. See students' work.

c. Player 1; because you win more often.

b. Compare the results with those of other pairs of students.

c. Would you rather be Player 1 or Player 2? Why?

d. Make a tree diagram to show all the possible outcomes for the toss of the chips. In how many branches does a letter occur twice? Does this explain your results?   **6; yes**

Checking for Understanding

Communicating Mathematics

Read and study the lesson to answer each question.

1. **Tell** what an outcome and a sample space are.   **See margin.**

2. **Tell** whether guessing TTF on a three-question true-false quiz is the same as guessing TFT. Explain.   **See margin.**

3. **Write** a problem that can be solved by using the tree diagram at the right. **See Solutions Manual.**

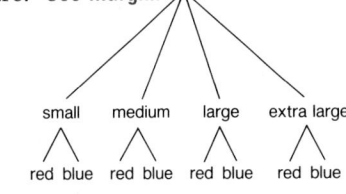

Lesson 13-1 Tree Diagrams   **493**

Team Teaching

Inform the other teachers on your team that your classes are studying statistics and probability. Suggestions for curriculum integration are:

Social Studies: making predictions; traffic patterns/urban planning

Science: meteorology and forecasts; success rates with medicines

Additional Answers

1. An outcome is the result of an event. A sample space is the set of all possible outcomes.

2. No. For example, if TTF happens to be correct, TFT will be incorrect. However, TTF and TFT have the same probability of being correct.

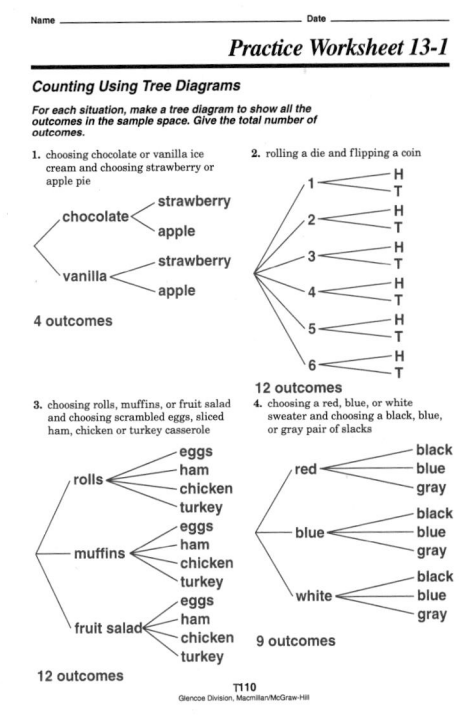

Close

Have students make a tree diagram to show all possible outcomes for choosing Spanish, French, or Latin as a language to study, and cooking, guitar, or photography as an elective course.   **9 outcomes: SC, SG, SP, FC, FG, FP, LC, LG, LP**

3 PRACTICE/APPLY

Assignment Guide
Maximum: 8–16
Minimum: 8–16

For **Extra Practice,** see p. 600.

Alternate Assessment

Writing   Ask students to write a problem about finding outcomes from among different choices of clothing, that can be solved by using a tree-diagram. Their problems should have classmates listing outfit possibilities from among pants, shirts, and sweaters.

Enrichment Masters, p. 110

494

Guided Practice   For each situation, make a tree diagram to show all the outcomes in the sample space. List the outcomes. Then give the total number of outcomes.

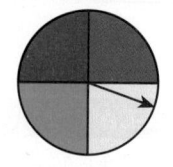

4. choosing one blouse from a red blouse and a white blouse and one skirt from a blue skirt and a black skirt **4 outcomes**

5. flipping a coin and rolling a number cube **12 outcomes**

6. spinning the spinner below and choosing a card **16 outcomes**

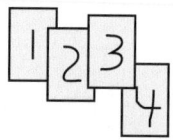

7. Diana is planning a dinner party. She plans to offer three kinds of salad: potato salad, tossed salad, and cole slaw. There will be three kinds of meat: ham, beef, and turkey. For dessert, she plans to offer ice cream, pie, and cake. How many salad/meat/dessert selections are there? **27 outcomes**

Exercises

Independent Practice   Make a tree diagram to show all the outcomes in the sample space. Then give the total number of outcomes.

8. flipping a penny and flipping a dime **4 outcomes**

9. choosing a letter from among the letters A, B, and C and a number from among the numbers 1, 2, and 3 **9 outcomes**

10. choosing cereal, French toast, or pancakes and choosing orange, tomato, or grapefruit juice **9 outcomes**

11. choosing a bicycle having one speed, three speeds, or ten speeds and either red, blue, green, or white in color **12 outcomes**

12. rolling a number cube, flipping a coin, and choosing a card from among cards marked W, X, Y, and Z **48 outcomes**

Mixed Review   13. **Statistics**   Find the mean, median, and mode for the following set of data: 42, 35, 52, 63, 41, 38, and 44. *(Lesson 3-5)* **45, 42, no mode**

14. **Finance**   Margie borrowed $3,500 to help pay for her college tuition. The loan was made at 12% interest for 18 months. Find the amount of interest Margie will pay on the loan. *(Lesson 12-9)* **$630**

Problem Solving and Applications   15. **Telephones**   In a certain area, a telephone number begins with a three-digit number consisting of 2, 3, and 4, where a digit may be used more than once. How many three-digit numbers are possible? **27 numbers**

16. **Critical Thinking**   Without drawing a tree diagram, tell how many sets of guesses there are for a four-question true/false quiz. Use a tree diagram to check. **16 outcomes**

OPTIONS

Extending the Lesson

Using Critical Thinking   Ask students to explain the advantages of using a tree diagram over listing outcomes in no particular order.

Cooperative Learning Activity

Use groups of 2.

Proper Identification **13-1**

➡ Suppose that you and your partner have been chosen to create a new system for identifying students at your school. Each student will be assigned an identification number using the system you create.

Anyone looking at the number should be able to tell at a glance what grade the student is in. You can use letters, digits, or a combination of letters and digits. The system should be as simple as possible, but there must be enough identification numbers so that each student can be assigned a different number. (In other words, the sample space must be larger than the enrollment of your school.)

Share your work with other pairs.

13-1B Fair and Unfair Games

A Follow-Up of Lesson 13-1

Objective

Count outcomes to determine whether a game is fair or unfair.

Materials

spinners
paper
pencil
ruler

Many people enjoy playing games like board games. One of the reasons they enjoy playing games is because players of equal skill have the same chance of winning. That is, each player has a fifty-fifty chance. Such games are called fair games. In an unfair game, players having equal skill do not have an equal chance of winning.

In this mathematics lab, you will play several games to determine whether or not they are fair games.

Activity One

Game 1

Play with a partner.

- Use the spinner shown at the right.
- Spin the spinner twice. Player 1 scores 1 point if the spinner lands on the same letter twice. Player 2 scores 1 point if the spinner lands on different letters.
- Play 50 rounds. The winner is the player with more points.
- Play the game three or four times.

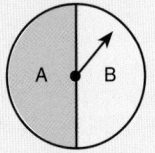

Game 2

- Follow the same rules as Game 1, except use the spinner shown at the right.

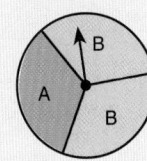

What do you think?

1. Based on your data, is Game 1 a fair game? yes
2. Based on your data, is Game 2 a fair game? no

One way to explain the results of your games is to make a drawing.

Activity Two

Game 1

For the first spin, there is an equal chance of landing in A or B. We can represent this by a square that is divided in half. For the second spin, you can further divide the square in half.

Mathematics Lab 13-1B Fair and Unfair Games   **495**

NCTM Standards: 1–5, 11

Management Tips

For Students Have students make the spinners using cardboard. Students should be sure to use a compass and a protractor to make equal sectors in the second spinner.

For the Overhead Projector
Overhead Manipulative Resources provides appropriate materials for teacher or student demonstration of the activities in this Mathematics Lab.

1 FOCUS

Introducing the Lab

Have students talk about the board games they play, focusing on which ones they think are fair games and which aren't.

Classroom Vignette

"It was easy for my students to make the analogy between spinning the spinner in Game 1 and flipping a coin. However, when I asked them to come up with an example that was like spinning the spinner in Game 2, it took some time before a student suggested rolling a cube labeled 1, 1, 2, 2, 3, 3."

Jack M. Ott

Jack Ott
Author

Using Connections Ask students whether they can immediately tell by looking at the board for Game 1 that the game is fair or unfair. Accept answers students can justify.

3 PRACTICE/APPLY

Using Applications Ask students to draw a game board in which a player has an equal chance of spinning either an A, B, or C.

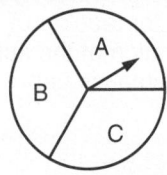

Close

Have students make up and describe a fair game that is played with a spinner or number cube. If a spinner is used, students should include a drawing of it; if a cube is used, they should provide the numbers on its faces.

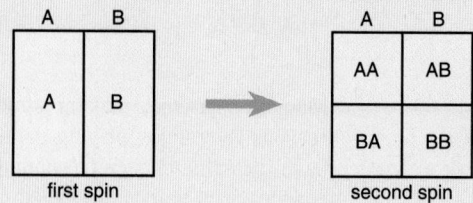

Now you can see four outcomes, AA, AB, BA, and BB. For two of these four outcomes, the letter matches. Therefore, the probability of the spinner landing on the same letter twice is $\frac{2}{4}$ or $\frac{1}{2}$. The game is fair.

Game 2

For the first spin, there are three outcomes: A, B, and B. Divide a square into three sections, as shown at the right.

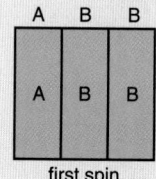

What do you think?

3. How would you show the results of the second spin on the square?

3. Divide the square into thirds again.

4. List all the outcomes for this game. AA, AB, AB, BA, BB, BB, BA, BB, BB

5. What is the probability that the spinner lands on the letter A twice? letter B twice? $\frac{1}{9}, \frac{4}{9}$

Extension

Suppose your teacher has two tickets to a local concert. She devises a game to award the tickets.

- You have five marbles: two red, two green, and one yellow, and two small brown paper bags.
- You can place the marbles any way you want into the bags.
- Your partner then chooses two marbles from one bag. If your partner chooses two red marbles, you and your partner win the tickets.

6. First list all of the possible ways you can distribute the marbles in the bags. **See Solutions Manual.**

7. Use drawings like the ones shown above to devise a "winning" strategy. **See students' work.**

8. Write a paragraph explaining how you would distribute the marbles and why you believe your method is the best strategy. **See students' work.**

496   Chapter 13 Discrete Math and Probability

OPTIONS

Lab Manual You may wish to make copies of the blackline master on p. 75 of the *Lab Manual* for students to use as a recording sheet.

Lab Manual, p. 75

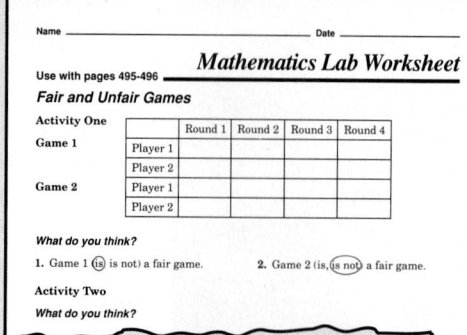

13-2 Counting Using Multiplication

Objective
Use multiplication to count outcomes.

Words to learn
Fundamental Counting Principle

Have you ever wondered why boys' shirts button on the right side and girls' shirts button on the left side? In the 1400s, only wealthy people wore buttons. Women usually had maids to dress them, and the maids buttoned from right to left, but they were facing the shirt, not looking down at it. Men usually didn't have maids, so they buttoned their own shirts.

You may remember when the United States aided Kuwait in the war against Iraq in January 1991. This war was referred to as "Desert Storm" because it was fought in the deserts of the Middle East. Special camouflage clothing was made to blend in with the desert environment. It has been calculated that there were a total of 483 different combinations of tops and bottoms!

Suppose there are 2 choices for tops: small and large. And there are 3 choices for bottoms: short, average, and tall. Draw a tree diagram to determine the number of possible outcomes.

tops	bottoms	outcomes
small	short	(small, short)
	average	(small, average)
	tall	(small, tall)
large	short	(large, short)
	average	(large, average)
	tall	(large, tall)

The total number of possible outcomes is 2×3 or 6. The **Fundamental Counting Principle** gives a way of counting all outcomes by using multiplication instead of a tree diagram.

Fundamental Counting Principle	If there are m ways of selecting an item from set A and n ways of selecting an item from set B, then there are $m \times n$ ways of selecting an item from set A and an item from set B.

Example 1 *Problem Solving*

Food Service The Bowl 'N' Ladle Restaurant advertises that you can have a different lunch every day of the year. They offer 13 different kinds of soups and 24 different kinds of sandwiches. If the restaurant is open every day of the year, is their claim valid? Explain.

$$\binom{number\ of\ choices}{for\ sandwiches} \times \binom{number\ of\ choices}{for\ soup} = \binom{number\ of\ choices}{for\ lunch}$$

$$24 \quad \boxed{\times} \quad 13 \quad \boxed{=} \quad 312$$

Their claim isn't valid, because the number of selections is 312, and $312 < 365$.

13-2 Lesson Notes

NCTM Standards: 1–5, 7, 9

Lesson Resources
- Study Guide Master 13-2
- Practice Master 13-2
- Enrichment Master 13-2
- Group Activity Card 13-2

 Transparency 13-2 contains the 5-Minute Check and a teaching aid for this lesson.

⏱ 5-Minute Check
(Over Lesson 13-1)

Make a tree diagram to show all the outcomes in the sample space. Give the total number of outcomes.

1. flipping a quarter and a nickel   HH, HT, TH, TT; 4

2. choosing a letter from D, E, F, and a number from 1 and 2   D1, D2, E1, E2, F1, F2; 6

3. choosing tuna, ham, or egg sandwiches, and chips, fries, or salad   TC, TF, TS, HC, HF, HS, EC, EF, ES; 9

1 FOCUS

Motivating the Lesson

Situational Problem In a restaurant, there are 3 kinds of appetizers, 6 main courses and 4 choices of dessert. Ask students to find the number of possible complete meals.

2 TEACH

Using Applications Provide a price list from a clothing catalogue. Have students investigate outcomes involving the selection of 3 items, 1 each from 3 clothing categories. Have them apply the Fundamental Counting Principle.

OPTIONS

Reteaching Activity

Using Discussion Guide students to see how multiplication is a time-saving method for finding the number of possible outcomes. Provide additional opportunities for students to apply the Fundamental Counting Principle to solve problems, some with simple numbers.

Study Guide Masters, p. 111

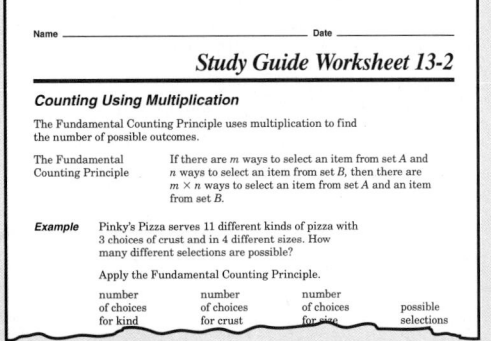

Name _____ Date _____

Study Guide Worksheet 13-2

Counting Using Multiplication

The Fundamental Counting Principle uses multiplication to find the number of possible outcomes.

The Fundamental Counting Principle	If there are m ways to select an item from set A and n ways to select an item from set B, then there are $m \times n$ ways to select an item from set A and an item from set B.

Example Pinky's Pizza serves 11 different kinds of pizza with 3 choices of crust and in 4 different sizes. How many different selections are possible?

Apply the Fundamental Counting Principle.

number of choices for kind	number of choices for crust	number of choices for size	possible selections

497

More Examples

For Example 1

The Cheese 'n Crackers store offers 28 different kinds of cheese and 20 kinds of crackers. They claim that one could shop there once a week and buy a different cheese and cracker combination each time for 10 years. Is their claim valid? yes; $28 \times 20 = 560 > 520$

For Example 2

Kim is choosing from among 3 brands of racquets, 2 kinds of tennis balls, and 2 kinds of headbands. In how many different ways can she buy a racquet, tennis balls, and a headband? **12 ways**

Checking for Understanding

Exercises 1-3 are designed to help you assess students' understanding through reading, writing, speaking, and modeling. You should work through these exercises with your students and then monitor their work on Guided Practice Exercises 4-6.

Practice Masters, p. 111

498

Example 2 *Problem Solving*

Highways   There are three highways connecting Tomville and Greeburg. There are two roads connecting Greeburg and Morristown. There is one superhighway from Morristown to Hodge. How many ways are there to drive from Tomville to Hodge?

Explore	3 highways from Tomville to Greeburg 2 roads from Greeburg to Morristown 1 superhighway from Morristown to Hodge
Plan	Draw a diagram showing the highway system.

Tomville —— Greeburg   Morristown —— Hodge

Solve	Apply the Fundamental Counting Principle. $$3 \times 2 \times 1 = 6$$ There are six ways to drive from Tomville to Hodge.
Examine	Count all the different routes from Tomville to Hodge on the drawing. Did you count six?

Checking for Understanding

Communicating Mathematics

Read and study the lesson to answer each question.

1. **Tell** how to use the Fundamental Counting Principle to find the number of ways of selecting 1 shirt from among 3 different shirts and 1 tie from among 6 different ties. **Find the product of 3 and 6.**

2. **Tell** when the Fundamental Counting Principle is more useful than a tree diagram to count outcomes. **when the number of choices is very large**

3. **Draw** a diagram to show the three roads connecting Tumba City and Birdville and the four roads connecting Birdville and Meclaville. **See margin.**

Guided Practice

Use multiplication to find the total number of outcomes in each situation.

4. choosing an exterior color and an interior color for a new car if there are 5 choices for exterior color and 6 choices for interior color **30 outcomes**

OPTIONS

Bell Ringer

Ask students to use the Fundamental Counting Principle to help them figure out the probability of getting a 10 when tossing a pair of dice. 6×6 or 36 possible outcomes, 3 ways to make 10, so $P(10) = \frac{3}{36}$ or $\frac{1}{12}$

Additional Answers

3.
Tumba City ⊂⊃ Birdville ⊂⊃ Meclaville

5. making a sandwich with raisin bread, whole wheat bread, white bread, or an English muffin and choosing a filling from among peanut butter, jelly, or cream cheese **12 outcomes**

6. choosing the first two letters/digits for a license plate if the license plate begins with a letter of the alphabet and is followed by a digit **260 outcomes**

Exercises

Independent Practice

Find the total number of outcomes in each situation.

7. tossing a penny, a nickel, a dime, and a quarter **16 outcomes**

8. spinning the spinners shown at the right **48 outcomes**

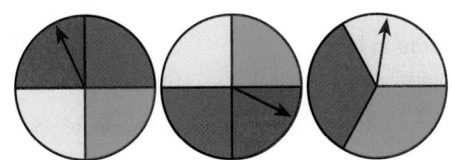

9. choosing a way to drive from Milton to Harper's Township if there are three roads that lead from Milton to Westwood, three highways that connect Westwood to Morgantown, and two streets that join Morgantown to Harper's Township **18 outcomes**

Mixed Review

10. Solve $6p = 72$. *(Lesson 6-3)* **12**

11. **School** Jen must take a science class, a math class, and an English class next semester. She can choose from two science classes, three math classes, and two English classes. Make a tree diagram to show all of the possible schedules she can arrange. *(Lesson 13-1)* **See Solutions Manual.**

Problem Solving and Applications

12. **No; there are only 360 outcomes.**

12. **Food Service** The Soup 'N' Salad Restaurant advertises that you can have a different soup-and-salad lunch every day of the year. They sell 20 different kinds of soup and 18 different kinds of salad. Is their claim valid? Explain.

13. **Algebra** In literature class, each student must read a short story, a poem, and a newspaper article. If there are g short stories, h poems, and n newspaper articles, how many different selections can be made? **ghn selections**

14. **Critical Thinking** How many outcomes are there if you toss
a. one coin? **2** b. two coins? **4** c. three coins? **8** d. n coins? 2^n

15. **Journal Entry** Write about the strong points and weak points of using tree diagrams and using the Fundamental Counting Principle. **See students' work.**

Lesson 13-2 Counting Using Multiplication   **499**

Extending the Lesson

Using Critical Thinking Ask students to describe a circumstance under which they would need to use a tree diagram rather than the Fundamental Counting Principle to find all possible outcomes. **Sample answer: when every outcome has to be identified**

Cooperative Learning Activity

Use groups of 2.

A Not-So-Secret Code 13-2

◆ Read the following.

ZIP (zone improvement plan) codes have been around since 1963. Letters with ZIP codes can be sorted and delivered by the United States Postal Service much more quickly than letters without ZIP codes.

The standard ZIP code is a five-digit number. The first digit identifies a region of the United States. The next two digits, together with the first digit, identify a section (often a large city). The last two digits identify key post offices within the section. Sometimes you see nine-digit ZIP codes (ZIP + 4). The four additional digits identify individual postal routes at the key post offices.

➡ Answer the questions shown on the back of this card. Assume that there are no restrictions on the use of digits.

Glencoe Mathematics: Applications and Connections, Course 2

Name _____   Date _____

Enrichment Worksheet 13-2

Probabilities and Regions

The spinner at the right can be used to indicate that the probability of landing in either of two regions is $\frac{1}{2}$.

$P(A) = \frac{1}{2}$ $P(B) = \frac{1}{2}$

Read the description of each spinner. Using a protractor and ruler, divide each spinner into regions that show the indicated probability.

1. Two regions A and B; the probability of landing in region A is $\frac{3}{4}$. What is the probability of landing in region B?

$P(B) = \frac{1}{4}$

2. Three regions A, B, and C; the probability of landing in region A is $\frac{1}{2}$ and the probability of landing in region B is $\frac{1}{4}$. What is the probability of landing in region C?

 $P(C) = \frac{1}{4}$

3. Three regions A, B, and C; the probability of landing in region A is $\frac{3}{8}$ and the probability of landing in region B is $\frac{1}{8}$. What is the probability of landing in region C?

 $P(C) = \frac{1}{2}$

4. Four regions A, B, C, and D; the probability of landing in region A is $\frac{1}{16}$, the probability of landing in region B is $\frac{1}{8}$, and the probability of landing in region C is $\frac{1}{4}$. What is the probability of landing in region D?

 $P(D) = \frac{9}{16}$

5. The spinner at the right is an equilateral triangle, divided into regions by line segments that divide the sides in half. Is the spinner divided into regions of equal probability?
yes

T111
Glencoe Division, Macmillan/McGraw-Hill

NCTM Standards: 1–5, 7, 11

Lesson Resources

- Study Guide Master 13-3
- Practice Master 13-3
- Enrichment Master 13-3
- Group Activity Card 13-3

 Transparency 13-3 contains the 5-Minute Check and a teaching aid for this lesson.

🕐 5-Minute Check
(Over Lesson 13-2)

Find the total number of outcomes in each situation.

1. choosing the first three letters/digits of a license plate if it begins with Y or M, followed by either A, B, C, or D, and a digit from 1 to 5   **40 outcomes**

2. making a lunch of either a ham, bologna, turkey, or chicken sandwich, with either coleslaw or salad, and either milk, juice, or soda   **24 outcomes**

3. choosing a car in one of 6 colors, either with or without racing stripes, with either a radio or a cassette player, with or without air conditioning, and with either a standard or automatic transmission   **96 outcomes**

---

1 FOCUS

Motivating the Lesson

Activity   Challenge small groups of students to design an experiment to determine the probability of getting a sum of 7 when tossing a pair of dice.

500

13-3 Theoretical and Experimental Probability

Objective

Find and compare experimental and theoretical probabilities.

Words to Learn

theoretical probability
experimental probability

Backgammon is a game played with a board, counters, and dice. It is one of the most ancient games, dating back to 3000 B.C. The game is played by two players, who take turns rolling the dice and moving their counters. Rolling doubles is highly desirable in this game. If a player rolls doubles, that player gets to double the value of the roll. That is, if double 4s are rolled, the value of the roll is four 4s, rather than two 4s.

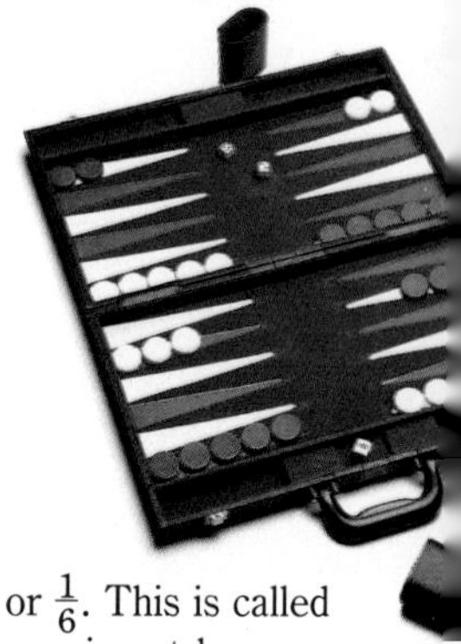

The sample space, or all the possible outcomes, for a roll of two dice is shown below.

1, 1	1, 2	1, 3	1, 4	1, 5	1, 6
2, 1	2, 2	2, 3	2, 4	2, 5	2, 6
3, 1	3, 2	3, 3	3, 4	3, 5	3, 6
4, 1	4, 2	4, 3	4, 4	4, 5	4, 6
5, 1	5, 2	5, 3	5, 4	5, 5	5, 6
6, 1	6, 2	6, 3	6, 4	6, 5	6, 6

The probability of rolling doubles at any time is $\frac{6}{36}$ or $\frac{1}{6}$. This is called the **theoretical probability.** You can also do an experiment by rolling two dice 100 times and recording the number of times you roll doubles. The ratio $\frac{\text{number of doubles}}{100}$ is called the **experimental probability.**

Suppose you are a basketball player. You have made 88 out of your last 100 free throws. You are ready to shoot a free throw that will determine the outcome of a game. Based on your past record, the probability you will make the shot is 0.88. What other factors would you want to take into consideration?

🔵 Mini-Lab

Work with a partner.
Materials: two dice

- Roll two dice 36 times. Record each time doubles occur.
- Compute the ratio $\frac{\text{number of times doubles occur}}{36}$.

Talk About It   **Answers will vary.**

a. How does your ratio compare to the ratio of others?

b. How does your ratio compare to $\frac{1}{6}$? If it is different, why do you think it is different?

c. Combine the results of all your classmates. Find the ratio of the total number of doubles to the total number of rolls. How does it compare to $\frac{1}{6}$? **Answers will vary.**

500   **Chapter 13** Discrete Math and Probability

b. Answers will vary. Sample answer: The dice are not balanced.

OPTIONS

Reteaching Activity

Using Models   Ask students to place different numbers of differently colored cubes in a bag. Have them withdraw a cube, record its color, and put it back. Repeat the process many times. Compare the experimental probability of choosing each color with the theoretical probability.

Study Guide Masters, p. 112

Name _____ Date _____

Study Guide Worksheet 13-3

Theoretical and Experimental Probability

Theoretical probabilities are determined by finding the ratio of the number of ways an event can occur to the number of possible outcomes. Experimental probabilities are determined by conducting an experiment.

Example   Julio tossed two coins and tallied the results. He repeated the experiment 20 times. The chart shows the results.

	2 heads	1 head, 1 tail	2 tails
Tally	ЖЖ I	ЖЖ ЖЖ I	|||
Total	6	11	3

Julio's experimental probability of tossing 1 head and 1 tail is $\frac{11}{20}$.

Find the theoretical probability of getting heads if you toss a coin.

$P(H)$ represents the probability of getting heads.

$$P(H) = \frac{1}{2} \quad \leftarrow \quad \textit{number of ways to toss heads} \\ \leftarrow \quad \textit{number of possible outcomes}$$

Checking for Understanding

Communicating Mathematics

Read and study the lesson to answer each question.

1. **Tell** the difference between experimental probability and theoretical probability. **See Solutions Manual.**

2. a. **Tell** whether the experimental probability of an event is always the same. **no**

   b. **Tell** whether the theoretical probability of an event is always the same. **yes**

   c. **Show** examples to support your answers to parts a and b. **See students' work.**

Guided Practice

3. Find the theoretical probability of choosing a boy's name from 20 boy's names and 10 girl's names. $\frac{2}{3}$

4. Find the theoretical probability of rolling a sum greater than 7 on two dice. $\frac{15}{36}$ or $\frac{5}{12}$

5. Larry tosses a coin 30 times. It lands on heads 16 times.
   a. What is his experimental probability of getting heads? $\frac{16}{30}$ or $\frac{8}{15}$
   b. How does the experimental probability compare to the theoretical probability of getting heads? **The experimental probability is slightly greater.**

Exercises

Independent Practice

6. A soft drink machine contains cola, ginger ale, root beer, orange, and diet cola. Without looking, choose a soft drink.
   a. Find P(cola or diet cola). $\frac{2}{5}$
   b. Write C, G, R, O, and D on slips of paper to represent each type of soft drink. Without looking, choose a slip of paper. Record the letter. Replace the slip. Repeat this 9 times. Compute $\frac{\text{number of Cs or Ds}}{10}$. How does the ratio compare to your answer in part a? **Answers will vary.**

Two dice are rolled. Find each theoretical probability.

7. a sum of 2 $\frac{1}{36}$ 8. a sum less than 4 $\frac{3}{36}$ or $\frac{1}{12}$ 9. a sum of 1 **0**

Lesson 13-3 Theoretical and Experimental Probability   **501**

Meeting Needs of Middle School Students

Discuss with students how coaches of professional sports teams use probability to make strategy decisions. For example, a baseball manager may use experimental probability to decide the kind of pitch to be thrown to a batter.

Interactive Mathematics Tools

This multimedia software provides an interactive lesson that is tied directly to Lesson 13-3. Students will generate data and explore probabilities.

---

2 TEACH

Using the Mini-Lab Ask students how the number of trials of an experiment affects the relationship between theoretical and experimental probabilities. As the number of trials increases, they approach one another.

More Examples

For the Example

Find the theoretical probability of getting an even number when tossing a pair of dice. $\frac{1}{2}$

Checking for Understanding

Exercises 1-2 are designed to help you assess students' understanding through reading, writing, speaking, and modeling. You should work through these exercises with your students and then monitor their work on Guided Practice Exercises 3-5.

Practice Masters, p. 112

Name _____ Date _____

Practice Worksheet 13-3

Theoretical and Experimental Probability

1. Find the theoretical probability of rolling an even number with a die. $\frac{1}{2}$

2. Find the theoretical probability that a family of four children will be all girls. $\frac{1}{16}$

3. Find the theoretical probability of choosing a winning three-digit number in a lottery. $\frac{1}{1,000}$

4. Jessica tosses two coins four times. Twice both coins came up heads.
   a. What is the experimental probability of getting two heads? $\frac{1}{2}$
   b. What is the theoretical probability of getting two heads? $\frac{1}{4}$
   c. What is the theoretical probability of getting two tails? $\frac{1}{4}$
   d. What is the theoretical probability of getting a head and a tail? $\frac{1}{2}$

5. Suppose you have a child's play cube with one of the following letters on each face: A, B, C, D, E, or F. You toss the cube.
   a. What is the theoretical probability of turning up an A, B, or C? $\frac{1}{2}$
   b. If you toss two identical cubes, what is the theoretical probability of turning up an A, A? $\frac{1}{36}$

6. Suppose you have a bag containing two red marbles, two blue marbles, and two white marbles. You choose a marble without looking.
   a. What is the theoretical probability that you will choose a white or a blue marble? $\frac{4}{9}$
   b. What is the theoretical probability that you will choose a red marble or a white marble? $\frac{4}{9}$

Two dice are rolled. Find each theoretical probability.

7. a sum of 8 $\frac{5}{36}$ 8. a sum less than 5 $\frac{1}{6}$ 9. a sum of 12 $\frac{1}{36}$

T112
Glencoe Division, Macmillan/McGraw-Hill

Watch for students who confuse theoretical and experimental probability.

Prevent by guiding them to see that theoretical probability is found by applying a formula, experimental probability by collecting data.

Close

Have students explain how they would find both the experimental and theoretical probability of getting tails when tossing a coin.

3 PRACTICE/APPLY

Assignment Guide
Maximum: 6–16
Minimum: 6–15

Alternate Assessment

Modeling Have students explain how they could find the probability of spinning a sum of 5 using two spinners each separated into 6 equal parts.

Enrichment Masters, p. 112

Name _____ Date _____

Enrichment Worksheet 13-3

Impossible to Certain Events

A probability is often expressed as a fraction. As you know, an event that is impossible is given a probability of 0 and an event that is certain is given a probability of 1. Events that are neither impossible nor certain are given a probability somewhere between 0 and 1. The probability line below shows relative probabilities.

impossible	not so likely	equally likely	pretty likely	certain
0	$\frac{1}{4}$	$\frac{1}{2}$	$\frac{3}{4}$	1

Determine the probability of an event by considering its place on the diagram above. **Accept logical responses.**

1. Medical research will find a cure for all diseases.

2. There will be a personal computer in each home by the year 2000.

3. One day, people will live in space or under the sea.

4. Wildlife will disappear as Earth's human population increases.

5. There will be a fifty-first state in the United States.

6. The sun will rise tomorrow morning.

7. Most electricity will be generated by nuclear power by the year 2000.

8. The fuel efficiency of automobiles will increase as the supply of gasoline decreases.

9. Astronauts will land on Mars.

10. The percent of high school students who graduate and enter college will increase.

11. Global warming problems will be solved.

12. All people in the United States will exercise regularly within the near future.

T112
Glencoe Division, Macmillan/McGraw-Hill

Mixed Review 10. Estimate $\sqrt{236}$. *(Lesson 9-3)* **about 15**

11. **Probability** On a television game show, a contestant selects one of three doors. A great prize is behind only one of the doors. What percent chance does the contestant have of selecting the right door? *(Lesson 12-3)* **about 33%**

Problem Solving and Applications

12. **Games** In a game of backgammon, Lorena rolls doubles 8 times.
    a. If she rolls the dice a total of 56 times during the game, what is her experimental probability of rolling doubles? $\frac{8}{56}$ or $\frac{1}{7}$
    b. How does her experimental probability compare to the theoretical probability of rolling doubles? **The experimental probability is slightly less.**

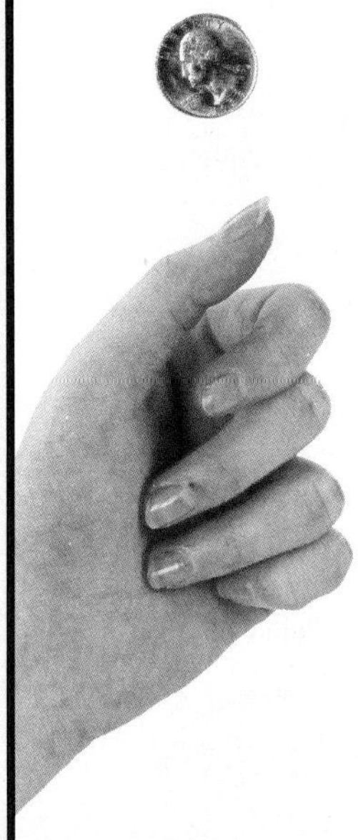

13. **Coin Toss** Ten students in Ms. Imhoff's class believe that a coin is not fair. That is, they believe there is not a fifty-fifty chance that it will land on heads if it is tossed. To find out, each student tosses the coin 10 times and records the results as shown in the table below.

Student	1	2	3	4	5	6	7	8	9	10	Total
Number of heads	4	6	2	3	4	4	7	2	3	3	38
Number of tails	6	4	8	7	6	6	3	8	7	7	62

    a. Find the experimental probability of tossing heads for the total number of tosses. $\frac{19}{50}$ or 0.38
    b. Based on your answer to part a, does the coin appear to be fair? **no**

14. **Critical Thinking** Is the experimental probability of an event ever equal to the theoretical probability? Explain. **Sample answer: Yes; especially if many trials are used.**

15. **Make up a problem** similar to the one in Exercise 6. **See students' work.**
    a. Determine the theoretical probability.
    b. Perform an experiment and determine the experimental probability.
    c. Write a report about the experiment and the results.

16. **Computer Connection** The BASIC program at the right similates tossing a fair coin. A sample output for 10 trials is shown below.

```
HOW MANY TIMES? 10
THHTTTHTHT
YOU TOSSED 4 HEADS
AND 6 TAILS.
```

```
10 INPUT "HOW MANY TRIALS?";N
20 FOR I = 1 TO N
30 C = INT(RND(I)*2)
40 IF C = 0 THEN PRINT "H";;
   H = H + 1
50 IF C = 1 THEN PRINT "T";;
   T = T + 1
70 NEXT I
80 PRINT;PRINT "YOU TOSSED";
   H; " HEADS AND";T;"TAILS."
```

    a. Use the program to simulate tossing a coin for 50 trials and for 100 trials.
    b. For which number of trials is the probability of tossing tails closest to $\frac{1}{2}$? **100 trials**

OPTIONS

Extending the Lesson

Using Applications Mention that experimental probability may be used to estimate the deer population of a region. This is done by counting the tagged and untagged deer in a sample and applying the ratio tagged deer : total deer to the entire population.

Cooperative Learning Activity

Flavorful Probabilities 13-4

Use groups of 2.

♣ A random number table contains the digits 0 through 9 in random order. In the random number table on the back of this card, the digits are arranged in groups of three.

➥ Work together to solve the following problem.

A company makes Fruiterrific fruit snacks in the following flavors: cherry, grape, orange, lemon, lime, pineapple, banana, strawberry, watermelon, and peach. For the company's trial-size packages three fruit snacks are selected at random. What is the probability that a trial-size package will contain at least two of the same flavor?

You could use cards and items that represent each flavor to find the experimental probability. However, using the random number table would be much easier. If you assign a different digit from 0 through 9 to each flavor, the groups of three numbers in the table are like packages of three snacks. Use the random number table to find the experimental probability of getting a package that contains at least two of the same flavor.

Glencoe Mathematics: Applications and Connections, Course 2

13-4 Act It Out

Objective

Solve problems by acting them out.

A baseball card manufacturer is holding a contest. Each package of baseball cards in a limited edition series contains a puzzle piece. If you collect all 6 different pieces, you win two tickets to any home game of your choice. There is an equally likely chance of getting a different puzzle piece each time. How many packages of cards would you need to buy to win the contest?

Explore   What do you know?
If you collect all 6 different puzzle pieces, you will win the contest. There is an equally likely chance of getting a different piece each time.

What do you need to find?
You need to find how many packages of cards you would need to buy to win the contest.

Plan   Act out the problem. Work with a partner.

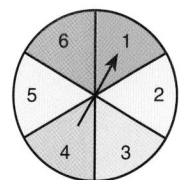

Use a spinner divided into 6 sections to simulate the problem. Each section represents one of the pieces. Spin the spinner until you have one of each number.

Record the data in a frequency table like the one below.

Outcome	Tally	Frequency
1	I	1
2	III	3
3	ﬀ	5
4	I	1
5	II	2
6	I	1

Solve   Find the sum of the frequencies of spinning each number.

$$1 + 3 + 5 + 1 + 2 + 1 = 13$$

According to this simulation, you would have to buy at least 13 packages of cards to collect all 6 puzzle pieces.

Lesson 13-4 Problem-Solving Strategy: Act It Out   **503**

OPTIONS

Reteaching Activity

Using Problem Solving   Have students solve a simpler problem by acting it out, such as finding the probability of choosing a pair of black socks from a drawer that also contains a pair of blue socks and a pair of green socks.

Study Guide Masters, p. 113

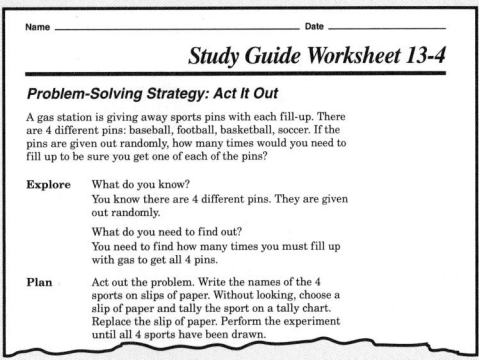

Name _____   Date _____

Study Guide Worksheet 13-4

Problem-Solving Strategy: Act It Out

A gas station is giving away sports pins with each fill-up. There are 4 different pins: baseball, football, basketball, soccer. If the pins are given out randomly, how many times would you need to fill up to be sure you get one of each of the pins?

Explore   What do you know?
You know there are 4 different pins. They are given out randomly.

What do you need to find out?
You need to find how many times you must fill up with gas to get all 4 pins.

Plan   Act out the problem. Write the names of the 4 sports on slips of paper. Without looking, choose a slip of paper and tally the sport on a tally chart. Replace the slip of paper. Perform the experiment until all 4 sports have been drawn.

13-4 Lesson Notes

NCTM Standards: 1–5, 7, 11

Lesson Resources
- Study Guide Master 13-4
- Practice Master 13-4
- Enrichment Master 13-4
- Evaluation Master, Quiz A, p. 115
- Group Activity Card 13-4

Transparency 13-4 contains the 5-Minute Check and a teaching aid for this lesson.

5-Minute Check
(Over Lesson 13-3)

Two dice are rolled. Find each theoretical probability.

1. a sum of 3 $\frac{1}{18}$
2. a sum less than 10 $\frac{5}{6}$
3. a sum greater than 10 $\frac{1}{12}$
4. a sum greater than 12   0

1 FOCUS

Motivating the Lesson

Activity   Tell students that a cereal company packs one toy in each box of cereal, and that there are 8 different toys. Have students design an experiment to find the number of boxes of cereal they would need to buy, on average, in order to be sure to get all 8 toys.

2 TEACH

Using an Experiment   Discuss with students the fact that a simulation is a representation of an experiment. Guide them to see the difficulty in trying to solve the opening problem using theoretical probability. Make sure students understand that in the baseball card simulation they should stop spinning the spinner immediately after they have obtained each outcome at least once.

More Examples

For the Example

Kevin has 8 pockets in his jacket. He is not sure which pocket holds his keys. What is the probability that he reaches into a pocket and finds the keys? Work in a group to act out this problem using index cards.

Checking for Understanding

Exercises 1-2 are designed to help you assess students' understanding through reading, writing, speaking, and modeling. You should work through these exercises with your students and then monitor their work on Guided Practice Exercises 3-5.

Close

Have students explain how they would use the acting-out strategy to determine the number of handshakes that take place when a committee of 5 meets and everybody shakes everybody else's hand.   Strategies will vary; 10 handshakes

Practice Masters, p. 113

504

Example

During a fire drill, Ryan, Debbie, Miguel, and Carianne each left one book in the school library. When they returned to their classroom, their homeroom teacher randomly handed out the four books to the students. What is the probability that Carianne receives the same book she was reading in the library?

You can act out this problem using index cards and books. Work in groups of five.

Write each student's name on two separate index cards. Let one set of cards represent the books. Place the book cards face down on a flat surface and mix them up. Place the other set of index cards in a brown paper bag.

To act out the situation, draw a card out of the bag and choose a book card. Was it the correct book for the first person? the second person? Make a chart like the one below and record this information on the chart.

Trial	Ryan	Debbie	Miguel	Carianne
1	no	no	yes	no
2				
3				

Continue until each book card has been paired with a student. Repeat this activity 20 times.

To solve the problem, find the experimental probability that Carianne receives the correct book.

$$\text{Experimental Probability} = \frac{\text{number of times she received correct book}}{20 \text{ trials}}$$

If Carianne received the correct book 4 times out of 20, the experimental probability is $\frac{4}{20}$, or 0.2.

OPTIONS

Bell Ringer

A pouch of a golf bag has three different brands of golf balls. Ask students to tell the least number of golf balls they must take out in order to be sure of getting at least 3 of one brand.   7 golf balls

Interactive Mathematics Tools

This multimedia software provides an interactive lesson that is tied directly to Lesson 13-4. Students will explore how to simulate situations to solve problems.

Checking for Understanding

Read and study the lesson to answer each question.

1. **Tell** how you can find the answer to the problem in the Example without acting it out. **Sample answer: Use the Fundamental Counting Principle.**

2. **Tell** one advantage of finding the answer by acting it out. **Sample answer: This strategy can be used to predict what will happen in the actual situation.**

Guided Practice Solve by acting it out.

3. Charo has 3 different-colored winter hats. What is the probability that she wears the same hat more than once in a 5-day school week? **1**

4. Suppose the puzzle in the baseball card contest on page 503 had 8 puzzle pieces. How many packages of cards would you need to buy to win the contest? **at least 8 packages**

5. How many times do you need to roll a die to get all 6 numbers? **at least 6 times**

Practice

Problem Solving

<table>
<tr><td>

Strategies
••••••••••
Look for a pattern.
Solve a simpler problem.
Act it out.
Guess and check.
Draw a diagram.
Make a chart.
Work backward.

</td></tr>
</table>

Solve. Use any strategy.

6. A number is multiplied by 4 and 12 is added. The result is 20. What is the number? **2**

7. Yolanda has 8 different-colored pens in a pencil cup. If she chooses 6 times, each time replacing the pen before choosing the next one, what is the probability that she chooses a different color each time without looking? $\frac{3}{4}$

8. Becky buys birthday wrapping paper and cards at the store. Wrapping paper costs $1.75 per package, and cards cost $1.25 each. She spends $12.75. How many of each did she buy? **3 packages of paper, 6 cards**

13 Assessment: Mid-Chapter Review

1. Jeremy has a choice of two juices (orange or apple) and three cereals (wheat, rice, or corn) for breakfast. Make a tree diagram to show all the possible outcomes. *(Lesson 13-1)* **See margin.**

2. Find the total number of outcomes if you toss a penny and spin the spinner at the right. *(Lesson 13-2)* **10 outcomes**

3. Out of 30 rolls of a die, Allison rolls a 4 three times. What is the experimental probability? *(Lesson 13-3)* $\frac{1}{10}$

Answers will vary.

4. Five students forgot to write their names on their test papers. Before the end of the period, the teacher randomly hands back the test papers to these students. What is the probability that each of these five students receives his or her own test? Solve by acting it out. *(Lesson 13-4)*

Extending the Lesson

Using Cooperative Groups Have groups design and carry out a simulation to solve the following problem: *An equipment manager for the high school team mixed up the hats of 6 players, and then handed them out to the players at random. Find the probability that at least one player gets her own cap.*

Cooperative Learning Activity

Flavorful Probabilities **13-4**

Use groups of 2.

♦ A random number table contains the digits 0 through 9 in random order. In the random number table on the back of this card, the digits are arranged in groups of three.

➡ Work together to solve the following problem.

A company makes Fruiterrific fruit snacks in the following flavors: cherry, grape, orange, lemon, lime, pineapple, banana, strawberry, watermelon, and peach. For the company's trial-size packages three fruit snacks are selected at random. What is the probability that a trial-size package will contain at least two of the same flavor?

You could use cards and items that represent each flavor to find the experimental probability. However, using the random number table would be much easier. If you assign a different digit from 0 through 9 to each flavor, the groups of three numbers in the table are like packages of three snacks. Use the random number table to find the experimental probability of getting a package that contains at least two of the same flavor.

Glencoe Mathematics: Applications and Connections, Course 2

---

3 PRACTICE/APPLY

Assignment Guide
Maximum: 6–8
Minimum: 6–8
All: Mid-Chapter Review

Alternate Assessment

Speaking Ask students how they would use a spinner to simulate finding out the number of boxes of cereal they would need to buy, on average, to collect all 5 cards in a series, if the cards are equal in number and randomly placed in boxes, one card to a box.

Additional Answer
(Mid-Chapter Review)

1.

responses		outcomes
orange ⟨ wheat		orange, wheat
rice		orange, rice
corn		orange, corn
apple ⟨ wheat		apple, wheat
rice		apple, rice
corn		apple, corn

Enrichment Masters, p. 113

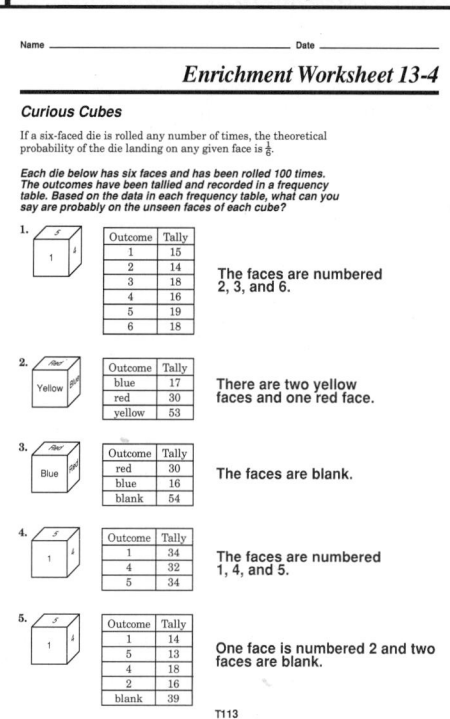

Name _____ Date _____

Enrichment Worksheet 13-4

Curious Cubes

If a six-faced die is rolled any number of times, the theoretical probability of the die landing on any given face is $\frac{1}{6}$.

Each die below has six faces and has been rolled 100 times. The outcomes have been tallied and recorded in a frequency table. Based on the data in each frequency table, what can you say are probably on the unseen faces of each cube?

1.
Outcome	Tally
1	15
2	14
3	18
4	16
5	19
6	18

The faces are numbered 2, 3, and 6.

2.
Outcome	Tally
blue	17
red	30
yellow	53

There are two yellow faces and one red face.

3.
Outcome	Tally
red	30
blue	16
blank	54

The faces are blank.

4.
Outcome	Tally
1	34
4	32
5	34

The faces are numbered 1, 4, and 5.

5.
Outcome	Tally
1	14
5	13
4	18
2	16
blank	39

One face is numbered 2 and two faces are blank.

T113

Glencoe Division, Macmillan/McGraw-Hill

NCTM Standards: 1–7, 10

Lesson Resources
- Study Guide Master 13-5
- Practice Master 13-5
- Enrichment Master 13-5
- Multicultural Activity, p. 13
- Application Master, p. 13
- Group Activity Card 13-5

 Transparency 13-5 contains the 5-Minute Check and a teaching aid for this lesson.

⏲ 5-Minute Check
(Over Lesson 13-4)

Solve by acting out.

Lenore has 4 different scarves. There is an equally likely chance that she will choose any scarf each time she wears one. On average, how many times must she choose a scarf to wear each one at least once?   Sample answer: Using a 1-4 spinner, count the sum of the frequencies of spinning each number.

---

1 FOCUS

Motivating the Lesson

Questioning   Tell students that predicting from samples is a frequently used strategy for making decisions. Ask students to try to explain what it means to use samples to make predictions, and to give examples of when and how this can be done.

13-5 Using Statistics to Predict

Objective
Predict actions of a larger group by using a sample.

Words to Learn
population
sample
random

DID YOU KNOW

In A.D. 1185 an astronomer, Johannes of Toledo (Toledo, a city in Spain both then and now), predicted that a terrible wind would bring famine and destruction to Europe in the following year. People were so scared that they built underground homes to protect themselves. However, the prediction never came true.

Calculator Hint
● ● ● ● ● ● ● ● ● ● ● ● ●
To find 15% of 7,500 on a calculator, enter:

15 `%` `×` 7500 `=`.

The result is 1,125.

Have you ever received a phone call from someone taking a survey? More than likely your phone number was randomly selected out of a list of thousands, or possibly millions, of phone numbers. The reason the surveyors don't call everyone is because it would be too time-consuming and too expensive.

Actually, it is not necessary to call everyone. You can predict the responses of an entire **population** by surveying a representative **sample** of that population. A sample is called **random** if the members of the sample are selected purely on the basis of chance.

Example 1

Members of the student council wanted to know if there was enough time between classes. They asked fifty students leaving gym class what they thought. Forty students responded that there was not enough time. Is this sample random? Explain.

This sample is not random because it does not represent the total student population. Also, no teachers or administrators were surveyed.

If you survey a random sample of the population, you can use the results to make predictions about the actions of the entire population.

Example 2   *Problem Solving*

Marketing   One hundred people chosen at random in a town of 7,500 people were asked what TV station they watched for the morning news. If 15 out of 100 people surveyed responded that they watch Channel 4, how many people in the town can be expected to watch Channel 4?

This ratio, 15 out of 100, is 15%. Find 15% of 7,500.

$$15\% \text{ of } 7{,}500 = 0.15 \times 7{,}500$$
$$= 1{,}125$$

You can predict that about 1,125 people in the town watch Channel 4 for the morning news.

OPTIONS

Gifted and Talented Needs

Ask students to explain exactly what is meant by a "40% chance of rain today."   Sample answer: In the past, when conditions were similar to what they are today, it rained 40% of the time.

Checking for Understanding

Communicating Mathematics

Read and study the lesson to answer each question.

1. **Tell** about a situation in which you might be part of a sample.
2. **Tell** about a situation in which you might be part of a population.
3. **Tell** whether a prediction can ever be exact. **No, it is an estimate.**
4. **Show** an example of a sample that is not random. Explain why the sample is not random. **See students' work.**

1. Sample answer: survey of favorite radio station
2. Sample answer: survey on favorite sport of 7th grade students

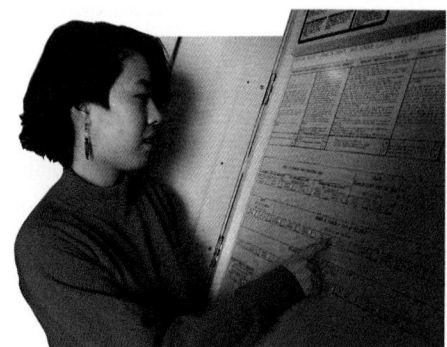

Guided Practice

Social Studies Of 42,000 registered voters, the voting preferences of a sample of 1,200 are listed in the table below.

Candidate	Number of Votes
Jenkins	640
Caldarolla	460
Undecided	100
Total	**1,200**

5. How many voters out of the 42,000 might you expect to vote for Jenkins? **about 22,260 voters**
6. How many voters out of the 42,000 might you expect to be undecided at election time? **about 3,360 voters**
7. If the undecided voters choose Caldarolla, how many votes might Caldarolla expect to receive? **about 19,740 votes**

Exercises

Independent Practice

School Student council members surveyed seniors to find out what they would be willing to pay for a copy of the school yearbook. The results are shown at the right.

Price Range	Number of Students
not more than $18	7
not more than $20	11
not more than $22	33
not more than $24	19

8. 70 students

8. What was the sample size?
9. To the nearest percent, what percent of students responded that they would buy the yearbook if the cost was not more than $20? **16%**
10. If there are 250 seniors at the school, about how many can be expected to buy the yearbook at $19.95? **about 225 seniors**

2 TEACH

Using Discussion Talk about the meaning of the term *random sample* with students. List examples of random samples and samples that are not random. Ask students to suggest a way to get a random sample of your school or community population.

More Examples

For Example 1

To find out about community support for a new sports stadium, a newspaper interviewed the 20 members of the school baseball team. Is this sample random? no

For Example 2

In a community of 35,000 people, 45 out of 100 randomly selected people responded that they prefer vanilla ice cream to chocolate. How many people in the community can be expected to prefer vanilla? about 15,750 people

Teaching Tip Guide students to see that to make a prediction based on a sample, they need to write a ratio to express the results of surveying the sample, and then multiply that ratio by the total population.

Checking for Understanding

Exercises 1-4 are designed to help you assess students' understanding through reading, writing, speaking, and modeling. You should work through these exercises with your students and then monitor their work on Guided Practice Exercises 5-7.

Reteaching Activity

Using Applications Have students survey a small group of classmates to predict the number of class members who are left-handed. Have the students work together to choose the representative sample and to figure out how to use the responses.

Study Guide Masters, p. 114

Name ______ Date ______

Study Guide Worksheet 13-5

Statistics Connection: Using Statistics to Predict

Data gathered by surveying a random sample of the population may be used to make predictions about the entire population.

Example 200 people from a town of 28,000 people were chosen at random and asked if they thought the town needed more bicycle paths. 78 out of the 200 people responded Yes. 84 responded No. Of those surveyed, 38 were undecided. Predict how many of the 28,000 people in the town think more bicycle paths are needed.

78 out of 200 is 39%.
39% of 28,000 = 0.39 × 28,000, or 10,920

You can predict that about 10,920 people think more bicycle paths are needed.

Members of a seventh grade class were surveyed to find out how much they would be willing to pay to go on a class trip.

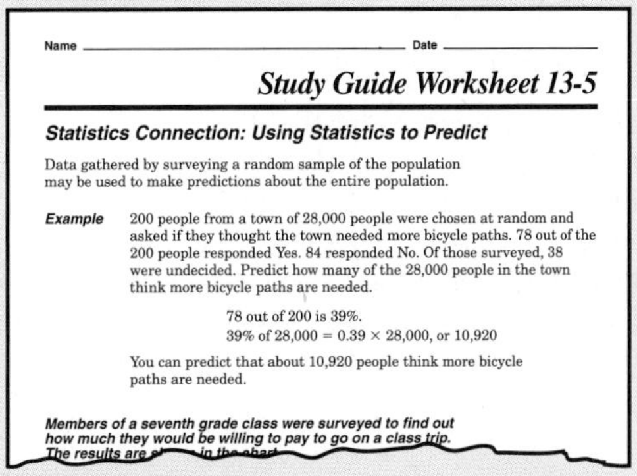

Close

Have students explain how to use samples to make predictions about the actions of a larger population.

3 PRACTICE/APPLY

Assignment Guide

Maximum: 8–23
Minimum: 9–15 odd, 16–21

For **Extra Practice,** see p. 601.

Alternate Assessment

Writing Have students describe how they would go about determining whether seventh graders in the school prefer pizza to hamburgers without actually asking all students.

Practice Masters, p. 114

Name _____ Date _____

Practice Worksheet 13-5

Statistics Connection: Using Statistics to Predict

Sports Of the TV households surveyed by the Nielsen Media Research Company, the top sports shows of 1990-1991 are listed in the table at the right.

Top Sports Shows, 1990-91	
Show	% of TV households
1. Super Bowl XXV	41.9
2. NFC Championship	28.5
3. AFC Playoff Bengals vs. Raiders	24.7
4. NFC Playoff Saints vs. Bears	24.2

1. How many households in a town with 40,000 households might you expect to have watched Super Bowl XXV? **16,760**

2. How many households in a town with 80,000 households might you expect to have watched the fourth top show? **19,360**

3. How many households in a town with 100,000 households might you expect to have watched a program *other* than the NFC Championship game? **71,500**

School Mrs. Romano surveyed her 7th grade class about their favorite foods. The results are shown in the table at the right.

Mrs. Romano's Class	
Favorite Food	Number of Students
spaghetti	10
pizza	9
hamburgers	4
tacos	4
fried chicken	3

4. What was the sample size? **30**

5. What percent of students liked pizza best? **30%**

6. Mr. Peters' class has 24 students in it but otherwise is about the same as Mrs. Romano's class. How many students would you expect to like spaghetti the best? **8**

7. How many students in Mr. Peters' class would you expect to not like tacos the best? **about 21**

8. For the entire 7th grade class of 250 students, how many would you expect to like fried chicken the best? **25**

T114
Glencoe Division, Macmillan/McGraw-Hill

Social Studies Of 32,500 registered voters, 740 were surveyed. Their voting preferences are listed at the right.

Candidate	Number of Votes Received
Memphez	117
Jeniac	276
Steinmetz	235
Undecided	112
Total	**740**

11. To the nearest percent, what percent of the registered voters can be expected to vote for Steinmetz? **32%**

12. To the nearest percent, what percent of the registered voters can be expected to vote for Jeniac or Memphez? **53%**

13. If the undecided choose to vote for Memphez, *about* how many can be expected to vote for Memphez? **about 11,000 voters**

14. If the undecided give their votes to Memphez, who is expected to win the election? **Jeniac**

15. On the evening before the election, a pollster called 500 people whose names were selected at random from the telephone book. Is the sample a random sample? **Sample answer: No, because those called may not be registered voters.**

Mixed Review

16. Multiply 0.0004 and 10^6. *(Lesson 2-5)* **400**

17. **Geometry** Classify the triangle at the right by its sides and by its angles. *(Lesson 8-3)* **scalene, obtuse**

18. Find the probability of observing one head and one tail when two fair coins are tossed. *(Lesson 13-3)* $\frac{1}{2}$

Problem Solving and Applications

19. **Population** In 1989, the total number of unemployed in the United States was about 3,499,000 people. The circle graph below shows the breakdowns by percent.

Unemployment in the United States, 1989

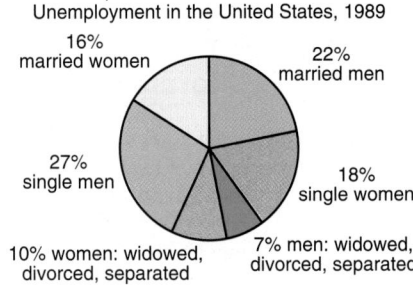

16% married women
22% married men
27% single men
18% single women
10% women: widowed, divorced, separated
7% men: widowed, divorced, separated

Estimate each number of unemployed. **For Exercises a–c, sample answers given.**

a. married women **about 600,000**

b. single men **about 900,000**

c. married women or married men **about 1,200,000**

508   **Chapter 13** Discrete Math and Probability

OPTIONS

Multicultural Education

Many games all over the world require players to make predictions. In the Pakistani game of *Dittar Pradesh,* participants try to guess how many of 16 tossed cowrie shells (rounded on one side, flat on the other) will land mouth-up.

20. **Consumer Math** The chart shows the ownership of video equipment in U.S. households.

Year	1985	1988
Video Cassette Recorders (VCRs)	21%	67%
Video Camera/Camcorders	2%	7%

a. In 1985, there were 87 million households. About how many of them owned a VCR?
Sample answer: about 18 million households

b. In 1988, there were 91 million households. About how many of them owned a video camera or camcorder? **Sample answer: about 6,300,000 households**

c. **Sample answer: Not necessarily; the increase could have been in 1986 or 1987.**

c. Do the data suggest that more VCRs were sold in 1988 than in 1985? Explain.

d. Suppose that you visited a friend in 1985. What is the probability that there was a video camera or a camcorder in your friend's household? $\frac{1}{50}$

21. **Sample answer: about 10,000 people**

21. **Critical Thinking** In a recent survey of radio listeners, a researcher concludes that about 18% of the audience enjoy talk shows. The researcher concludes that this is 1,825 people. Estimate the population of the city.

22. **Journal Entry** Write a paragraph about different ways that people can make sure that a sample is random. **See students' work.**

23. **Mathematics and Weather Forecasting** Read the following paragraphs.

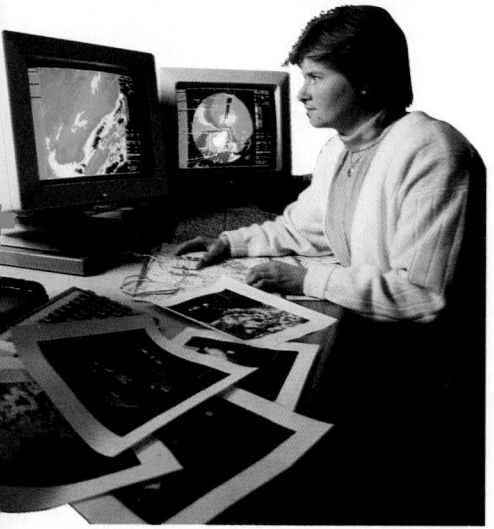

The United States Weather Service makes about 2 million weather forecasts each year. It claims that more than 75% of their one-day forecasts are accurate.

Forecasts are used every day to help people decide what to wear and where to go. In addition, they are vital to pilots, sailors, and farmers who need to know exactly what kind of weather to expect in order to carry out their jobs effectively.

A forecaster is like a detective gathering information and clues. Detailed information about the weather at a certain time of day is collected and plotted on a map called a synoptic chart. Using a computer, the forecasters can predict what the next day's weather will be like.

Mount Wai-'ale-'ale in Hawaii gets more rain than any other place in the world. It rains 92% of the year. To the nearest day, how many days of rain can it expect to get every year? **336 days**

Lesson 13-5 Statistics Connection: Using Statistics to Predict **509**

Extending the Lesson

Mathematics and Weather Forecasting Ask students to conduct a weather forecasting experiment of their own. Have them keep track of the weather conditions for 7 days and have them use the information to predict what the weather will be like on the eighth day.

Cooperative Learning Activity

X-cellent Predictions 13-5

Use groups of 2.
Materials: Index cards, scissors, paper bags

▸ Cut each of fifty index cards into three equal pieces. Divide the pieces evenly. (Each partner gets seventy-five pieces.) Without letting your partner see, make an X on some of the pieces. Then place all of your pieces in a paper bag.

▸ In turn, each partner selects ten pieces from the other partner's bag. Use the number of pieces that are marked with an X out of ten pieces to predict the total number of pieces that your partner marked. How close was your prediction?

Glencoe Mathematics: Applications and Connections, Course 2

Lesson Resources
• Study Guide Master 13-6
• Practice Master 13-6
• Enrichment Master 13-6
• Group Activity Card 13-6

 Transparency 13-6 contains the 5-Minute Check and a teaching aid for this lesson.

⏱ 5-Minute Check
(Over Lesson 13-5)

Students at Pascal School were surveyed to find out how much time they spend on homework each week. These are the results:

Homework Time (hours)	Students
Less than 3	6
Between 3 and 5	12
Between 5 and 7	19
More than 7	18

1. What was the sample size? 55

2. What percent of students spends more than 5 hours on homework each week? about 67%

3. If there are 300 students in the school, how many can be expected to spend more than 7 hours on homework each week? about 98 students

---

1 FOCUS

Motivating the Lesson

Situational Problem Have students guess the probability of getting both an even number and a heads if they were to toss a die and flip a coin simultaneously.

13-6 Probability of Two Events

Objective
Find the probability of independent and dependent events.

Words to Learn
independent events
dependent events

At the Creolia County Fair, there is a booth that has two spinning wheels like the ones shown below.

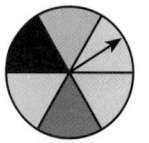   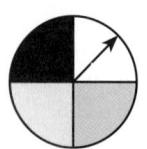   

Wheel 1   Wheel 2

The winner gets a big stuffed animal if Wheel 1 shows black and Wheel 2 shows white. What is the probability of winning?

When the outcome of one event does *not* influence the outcome of a second event, the events are called **independent events.** The results of spinning Wheel 1 and Wheel 2 are independent of one another.

To find the total number of outcomes, you can use the Fundamental Counting Principle. Of the 6×4, or 24, outcomes, there is 1 winning pair (black, white). Compute the probability.

$$P(\text{black, white}) = \frac{\text{favorable}}{\text{total}} = \frac{1}{24}$$

Note that $P(\text{black})$ on Wheel 1 is $\frac{1}{6}$ and $P(\text{white})$ on Wheel 2 is $\frac{1}{4}$. Also notice the following.

$$P(\text{black, white}) = \frac{1}{24}$$
$$= \frac{1}{6} \cdot \frac{1}{4}$$
$$= P(\text{black on 1}) \cdot P(\text{white on 2})$$

This suggests that the probability of two independent events can be found by multiplying.

Probability of Two Independent Events	**In words:** The probability of two independent events can be found by multiplying the probability of one event by the probability of the second event.
	In symbols: If A and B are independent events, then $P(A \text{ and } B) = P(A) \cdot P(B)$.

OPTIONS

Gifted and Talented Needs

Ask students to explain how the probability of two independent events occurring can be the same as the probability of one or both of the events occurring. when one of the probabilities is 0 or 1; when both probabilities are 0 or 1

Example 1

A green die and a red die are rolled. Find the probability that an odd number is rolled on the green die and a multiple of 3 is rolled on the red die.

There are three odd numbers: 1, 3, and 5.
So, $P(\text{odd number}) = \frac{3}{6}$ or $\frac{1}{2}$.

There are two multiples of 3: 3 and 6.
So, $P(\text{multiple of 3}) = \frac{2}{6}$ or $\frac{1}{3}$.

The two rolls are independent of each other.
So $P(\text{odd and multiple of 3}) = \frac{1}{2} \cdot \frac{1}{3}$ or $\frac{1}{6}$.

The probability that an odd number is rolled on the green die and a multiple of 3 is rolled on the red die is $\frac{1}{6}$.

If the result of one event affects the result of a second event, the events are called **dependent events**.

Example 2

A bag contains 5 white, 4 blue, and 3 red marbles. Two marbles are drawn, but the first marble drawn is not replaced. Find $P(\text{blue, then red})$.

$P(\text{blue}) = \frac{4}{12}$ ← *There are 4 blue marbles.*
                 ← *There are a total of 12 marbles.*

The result of the first draw affected the probability of the second draw.

$P(\text{red after blue}) = \frac{3}{11}$ ← *There are 3 red marbles left.*
                      ← *There are a total of 11 marbles left.*

$$P(\text{blue, then red}) = P(\text{blue}) \cdot P(\text{red after blue})$$

$$= \frac{4}{12} \cdot \frac{3}{11}$$

$$= \frac{\overset{1}{\cancel{4}}}{\underset{1}{\cancel{12}}_{3}} \cdot \frac{\overset{1}{\cancel{3}}}{11}$$

$$= \frac{1}{11}$$

The probability of drawing a blue marble and then a red marble is $\frac{1}{11}$.

2 TEACH

Using Critical Thinking
Ask students to explain why the events in Example 1 are independent events and why those in Example 2 are dependent events. Have them suggest additional examples of independent and dependent events.

More Examples

For Example 1

A green die and a red die are rolled. Find the probability that a number less than 3 is rolled on the red die and an even number is rolled on the green die.
$\frac{1}{3} \times \frac{1}{2} = \frac{1}{6}$

For Example 2

A bag contains 5 red cubes, 4 blue cubes, and 6 white cubes. Two cubes are drawn but the first one is not replaced.
Find $P(\text{red, then white})$. $\frac{1}{7}$

Checking for Understanding

Exercises 1-3 are designed to help you assess students' understanding through reading, writing, speaking, and modeling. You should work through these exercises with your students and then monitor their work on Guided Practice Exercises 4-8.

Reteaching Activity

Using Discussion   Guide students to see that, for dependent events, the results of the first event affects the probability of the second because the sample space for the second event has been changed. Provide additional examples of the distinction between independent and dependent probability.

Study Guide Masters, p. 115

Name _____ Date _____

Study Guide Worksheet 13-6

Probability of Two Events

When the outcome of one event does not influence the outcome of a second event, the two events are independent. The probability of two independent events can be found by multiplying the probability of the first event by the probability of the second event.

$$P(A \text{ and } B) = P(A) \cdot P(B)$$

Example   If you draw a card from a deck numbered 1 through 8 and toss a die, what is the probability of getting a 4 and an even number?

$P(4) = \frac{1}{8}$ $P(\text{even}) = \frac{3}{6}$, or $\frac{1}{2}$

$P(4, \text{even}) = \frac{1}{8} \cdot \frac{1}{2} = \frac{1}{16}$

The probability of a 4 and an even number is $\frac{1}{16}$.

Error Analysis

Watch for students who add rather than multiply to find probabilities of multiple events occurring.

Prevent by reminding students that they multiply to find the probability of *both* events occurring: $P(A \text{ and } B) = P(A) \times P(B)$.

Close

Have students summarize the lesson by describing the difference between the probabilities of independent and dependent events.

3 PRACTICE/APPLY

Assignment Guide
Maximum: 9–22
Minimum: 9–13 odd, 14–21

For **Extra Practice,** see p. 601.

Practice Masters, p. 115

Name _____ Date _____

Practice Worksheet 13-6

Probability of Two Events

Tell whether the events are independent or dependent. Explain.

1. rolling a die and then rolling a second die
   Independent; the second die doesn't depend on the first.
2. choosing two cards from a deck so that they make a "pair" (the number value is the same)
   Dependent; the first card is not replaced
3. selecting a compact disc from a storage case and then selecting a second disc without replacing the first
   Dependent; the second disc can't be the same as the first so there are less choices the second time.

Find each probability.

4. Two dice are rolled. Find the probability that an even number is rolled on one die and an odd number is rolled on the second die. $\frac{1}{4}$
5. Two coins are tossed in order. What is the probability of getting a head on the first coin and then getting a tail on the second coin? $\frac{1}{4}$
6. Suppose you have a bag containing two red marbles, two blue marbles, and two white marbles. You choose two marbles without looking.
   a. What is the probability that you will choose a red marble and then a blue marble without replacing the red one? $\frac{2}{15}$
   b. What is the probability that you will choose two red marbles in a row without replacing the first one? $\frac{1}{15}$
7. A coin purse contains 10 pennies, 5 nickels, 3 dimes, and 2 quarters. Two coins are selected without the first one being replaced. Find P(quarter, then nickel). $\frac{1}{38}$
8. A coin purse contains 10 pennies, 5 nickels, 3 dimes, and 2 quarters. Two coins are selected without the first one being replaced. Find P(nickel, then nickel). $\frac{1}{19}$
9. Two dice are rolled. Find the probability that a multiple of three is rolled on one die and an even number is rolled on the second die. $\frac{1}{6}$

T115
Glencoe Division, Macmillan/McGraw-Hill

512

---

3. Multiply the probability of one event by the probability of the second event.

Checking for Understanding

Communicating Mathematics

Read and study the lesson to answer each question. **2. See students' work.**

1. **Tell** when two events are independent. **See margin.**
2. **Write** a paragraph describing two dependent events.
3. **Tell** how to find the probability of an outcome of two independent events.

Guided Practice

Tell whether the events are independent or dependent. Explain.   **dependent**

For explanations to Exercises 4–5, see Solutions Manual.

4. choosing a card from a hat and then choosing a second card without replacing the first one
5. selecting a name from the Chicago telephone book and a name from the Houston telephone book
   independent

Find each probability.

6. A blue die and a yellow die are rolled. Find the probability that an odd number is rolled on the blue die and a multiple of 6 is rolled on the yellow die. $\frac{1}{12}$

7. $\frac{7}{69}$

7. A bag contains 10 white, 8 blue, and 6 red marbles. Two marbles are drawn, but the first marble drawn is not replaced. Find P(blue, then blue).

8. A coin is tossed and a die is rolled. Find the probability of getting heads and a multiple of 2. $\frac{1}{4}$

Exercises

Independent Practice

Tell whether the events are independent or dependent.

9. tossing a coin twice **independent**
10. selecting a computer disk from a file box and choosing a second disk without replacing the first one **dependent**

Find each probability.

11. A wallet contains five $5 bills, three $10 bills, and two $20 bills. Two bills are selected without the first selection being replaced. Find P($10, then $10). $\frac{1}{15}$
12. A wallet contains five $5 bills, three $10 bills, and two $20 bills. Two bills are selected without the first selection being replaced. Find P($5, then $20). $\frac{1}{9}$
13. A blue die and a green die are rolled. Find the probability that a multiple of 2 is rolled on the blue die and a multiple of 3 is rolled on the green die. $\frac{1}{6}$

OPTIONS

Bell Ringer

Anna has bought none of the 1,000 raffle tickets sold thus far. However, only Anna will buy any of the remaining tickets. Ask students what is the fewest number of tickets she must buy in order for the probability of her winning to be $\frac{1}{5}$. **250 tickets**

Boxes A and B contain pecans, cashews, and peanuts. The table shows how many of each are in Boxes A and B.

Box	Pecans	Cashews	Peanuts
A	12	20	24
B	30	18	50

Find the probability of each choice.

14. a peanut from Box A and a peanut from Box B $\frac{75}{343}$

15. a peanut from Box A and a pecan from Box B $\frac{45}{343}$

Mixed Review 16. Add $\frac{3}{15}$ and $\frac{5}{8}$. *(Lesson 5-3)* $\frac{33}{40}$

17. **Geometry** Sketch a three-dimensional figure given the front, side, and top view. *(Lesson 10-1)* **See students' work.**

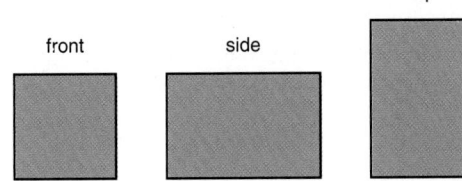

front   side   top

18. **Sports** It is predicted that the Wilson Junior High baseball team will win 65% of their games this season. If they are scheduled to play 60 games, how many games would you expect them to win? *(Lesson 13-5)* **39 games**

Problem Solving and Applications

19. **Traffic Lights** One traffic light is red 60% of the time. The next traffic light is red 50% of the time. If the lights operate independently of one another, find P(red, then red). **0.3**

20. **Clothing** In one drawer, Kwag has 2 pairs of brown socks, 3 pairs of black socks, and 4 pairs of blue socks. In another drawer, he has 3 red sweaters, 2 brown sweaters, and 2 blue sweaters. Suppose Kwag makes a selection from each drawer without looking. What is the probability that he will have brown socks and a brown sweater? $\frac{4}{63}$

21. Subtract the probability that A or B will happen from 1.

21. **Critical Thinking** Suppose that events A and B are independent. How would you find the probability that neither A nor B will happen?

22. **Journal Entry** List the things you do to get ready in the morning, such as take a shower, eat breakfast, and so on. Name which events are dependent and which are independent. The dependent events are the ones that can't be done until you have done an earlier event. **See students' work.**

Lesson 13-6 Probability of Two Events   **513**

Extending the Lesson

Using Models Have students prepare sample spaces to determine the number of times they must toss a die for the probability of every toss getting an even number to be $\frac{1}{32}$.
5 times Then ask them to create problems like this one for classmates to solve.

Cooperative Learning Activity

Prepositional Probabilities 13-6

Use groups of 2.
Materials: Index cards, paper bag

▸ Write the letters "a," "i," "o," "n," and "t" on cards, one per card. Place the cards in a paper bag.

➥ Suppose that you select one card from the bag, replace the card, and then draw another card. What is the theoretical probability that the letters on the cards you selected could be combined in the order in which you drew them to form one of the following prepositions: in, on, at, to?

Suppose that you select one card from the bag and then select a second card without replacing the first. What is the theoretical probability that the letters on the two cards you selected could be combined in the order in which you drew them to form a preposition?

Perform each experiment described above fifty times. Are your experimental probabilities close to your theoretical probabilities?

Glencoe Mathematics: Applications and Connections, Course 2

Objective Analyze data and make a decision.

1 FOCUS

Introducing the Situation

Discuss with students in what ways a school could use a camcorder other than for the Drama Club. Have students begin by sharing any experiences their families have had purchasing a camcorder and other video equipment. Guide them to discuss important considerations, other than cost, that are involved in the purchase.

2 TEACH

Using Discussion

Examine the catalogue page together with the students. Have them look both for features the camcorders have in common, and features that distinguish one brand from another. Guide students to think about how they would actually use the camcorder in school. Ask them how doing so helps them to narrow down their choices.

Analyzing the Data

Have students examine the camcorder page from the catalogue to discover the features and capabilities that distinguish the most expensive camcorders from those that are less expensive.

DECISION MAKING

Choosing a Camcorder

Situation

The Drama Club earned $1,000 in a fundraiser. They plan to purchase a compact camcorder to videotape rehearsals and actual performances of their theater productions. You have been chosen to be on the committee that will make a recommendation to club members and faculty advisors on which kind of camcorder to buy.

Hidden Data

How many hours of use do you get with the battery that is included in the price of the camcorder? How much will it cost to buy a rechargeable battery?

What kind of warranty comes with the camera?

Does the price of the extended service protection plan vary depending on the selling price of an item? If so, which one can you afford?

Is a storage case included in the purchase price or must it be purchased separately?

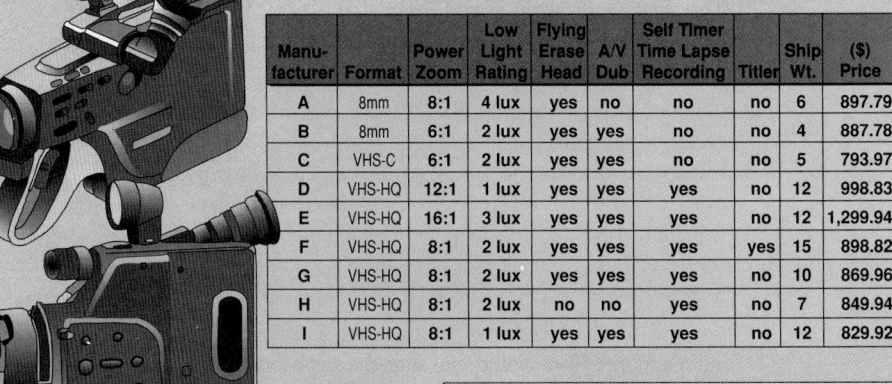

CAMCORDERS *FROM YOUR* *ELECTRONICS* **STORE**

Manu-facturer	Format	Power Zoom	Low Light Rating	Flying Erase Head	A/V Dub	Self Timer Time Lapse Recording	Titler	Ship Wt.	($) Price
A	8mm	8:1	4 lux	yes	no	no	no	6	897.79
B	8mm	6:1	2 lux	yes	yes	no	no	4	887.78
C	VHS-C	6:1	2 lux	yes	yes	no	no	5	793.97
D	VHS-HQ	12:1	1 lux	yes	yes	yes	no	12	998.83
E	VHS-HQ	16:1	3 lux	yes	yes	yes	no	12	1,299.94
F	VHS-HQ	8:1	2 lux	yes	yes	yes	yes	15	898.82
G	VHS-HQ	8:1	2 lux	yes	yes	yes	no	10	869.96
H	VHS-HQ	8:1	2 lux	no	no	yes	no	7	849.94
I	VHS-HQ	8:1	1 lux	yes	yes	yes	no	12	829.92

Extended Service Protection Plan
Cost varies depending on the selling price of the item.

Protect IT

Selling Price of Item	1 Yr Plan Price	2 Yr Plan Price
Up to $99.99	9.99	N/A
$100 - 199.99	19.99	36.99
$200 - 299.99	29.99	49.99
$300 - 999.99	39.99	69.99
$1,000 - 2,000	59.99	99.99

514

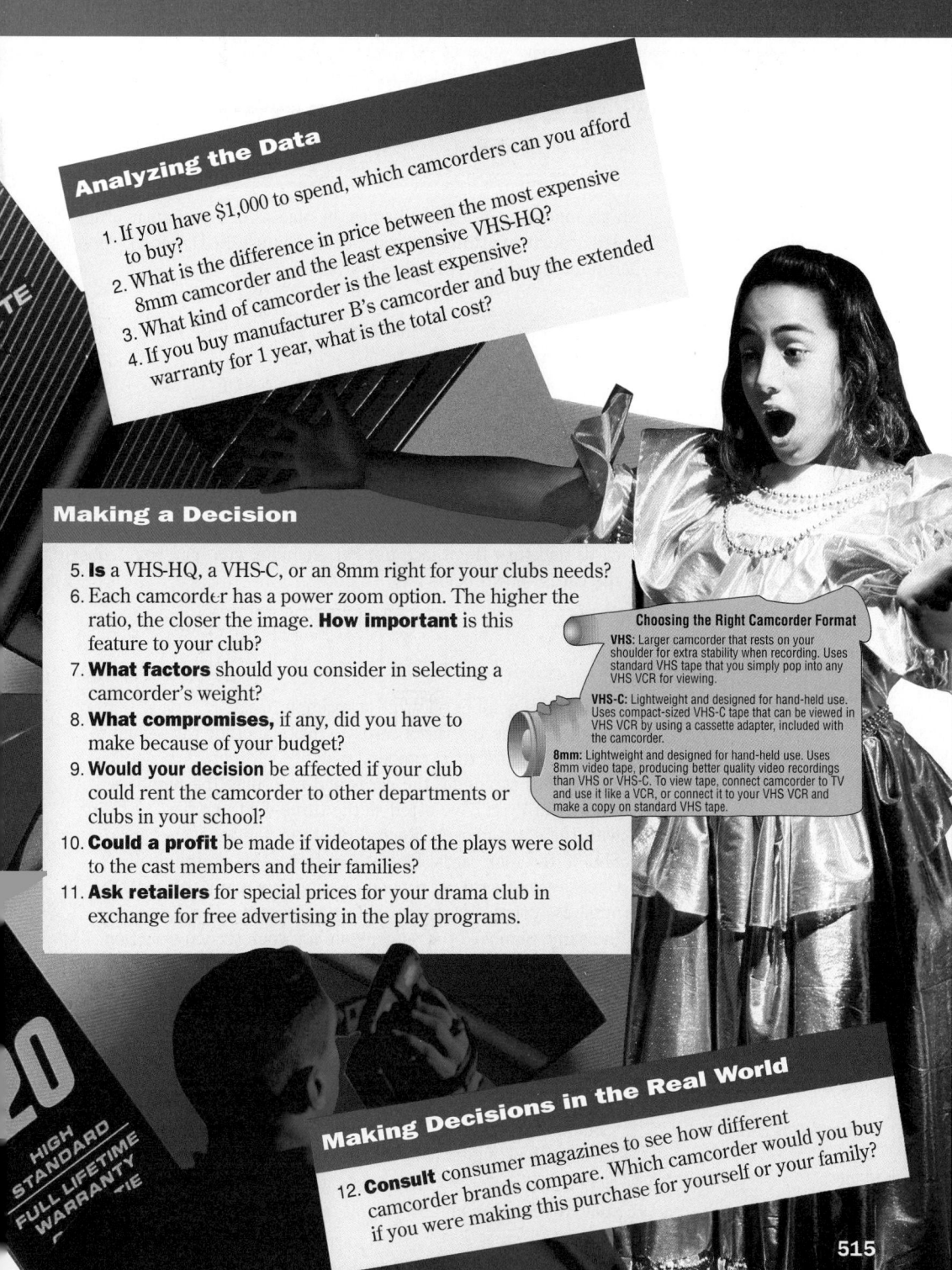

Analyzing the Data

1. If you have $1,000 to spend, which camcorders can you afford to buy?
2. What is the difference in price between the most expensive 8mm camcorder and the least expensive VHS-HQ?
3. What kind of camcorder is the least expensive?
4. If you buy manufacturer B's camcorder and buy the extended warranty for 1 year, what is the total cost?

Making a Decision

5. **Is** a VHS-HQ, a VHS-C, or an 8mm right for your clubs needs?
6. Each camcorder has a power zoom option. The higher the ratio, the closer the image. **How important** is this feature to your club?
7. **What factors** should you consider in selecting a camcorder's weight?
8. **What compromises,** if any, did you have to make because of your budget?
9. **Would your decision** be affected if your club could rent the camcorder to other departments or clubs in your school?
10. **Could a profit** be made if videotapes of the plays were sold to the cast members and their families?
11. **Ask retailers** for special prices for your drama club in exchange for free advertising in the play programs.

Choosing the Right Camcorder Format

VHS: Larger camcorder that rests on your shoulder for extra stability when recording. Uses standard VHS tape that you simply pop into any VHS VCR for viewing.

VHS-C: Lightweight and designed for hand-held use. Uses compact-sized VHS-C tape that can be viewed in VHS VCR by using a cassette adapter, included with the camcorder.

8mm: Lightweight and designed for hand-held use. Uses 8mm video tape, producing better quality video recordings than VHS or VHS-C. To view tape, connect camcorder to TV and use it like a VCR, or connect it to your VHS VCR and make a copy on standard VHS tape.

Making Decisions in the Real World

12. **Consult** consumer magazines to see how different camcorder brands compare. Which camcorder would you buy if you were making this purchase for yourself or your family?

515

Management Tips

For Students Encourage students to arrange and record the cards in an organized manner, so that they include all possible arrangements.

For the Overhead Projector
Overhead Manipulative Resources provides appropriate materials for teacher or student demonstration of the activities in this Mathematics Lab.

1 FOCUS

Introducing the Lab

Ask students to determine the number of seating arrangements in one row that would be possible if four classmates were to go to the movies together.
24 arrangements

2 TEACH

Using Number Sense After discussing the permutation of 3 objects with the class, ask groups to compile all possible arrangements of *four* cards. Then have them predict whether there will be the same number of permutations as for 3 objects, fewer permutations, or more permutations.

3 PRACTICE/APPLY

Using Applications Have students make a tree diagram to see whether it is useful, both for the four-card and five-card permutations.

Close

Have students list all the three-letter permutations of the letters A, B, D, and E.
ABD, ADB, ABE, AEB, ADE, AED,
BAD, BDA, BAE, BEA, BDE, BED,
DAB, DBA, DAE, DEA, DBE, DEB,
EAB, EBA, EAD, EDA, EBD, EDB.

Objective
Explore permutations.

Words to Learn
permutation

Materials
four index cards
marker

An arrangement of letters, names, or objects in a particular order is called a **permutation**. For instance, if you use E, D, and N, three permutations result in English words.

DEN	END	NED

There are three more permutations of these letters, but they are not English words.

DNE	EDN	NDE

Try this!

Work with a partner.

- Place the digits 1, 4, 7, and 9 on four cards, one digit on each card. Shuffle the cards and place them face down. Choose three of the cards and turn them face up. For example, you may have chosen the cards shown below.

- Record the number shown; for example, 719.
- Now rearrange the three cards to make another three-digit number. Record that number.
- Continue rearranging the cards and recording the numbers shown until you have listed all the three-digit numbers you can with the cards chosen. Record the total number. **6**
- Shuffle the four cards. Place them face down on the desk. Choose three cards at random. Count how many three-digit numbers you got from that selection of cards. Did you get the same number of arrangements for your second selection of cards as you did for the first selection? **yes**
- Now use all four cards. Arrange the cards to form all the four-digit numbers that you can. How many arrangements are there? **24 arrangements**

What do you think?

1. No; A tree diagram uses digits more than once.

1. Could a tree diagram be helpful in listing all the permutations of three or four digits? Why or why not?
2. Suppose that you had five cards with five different digits. How many five-digit numbers do you think can be formed? **120 numbers**

516   Chapter 13 Discrete Math and Probability

13-7 Permutations

Objective

Find the number of permutations of a set of objects.

Words to Learn

permutation
factorial

The flag of Mali, Africa, has three vertical stripes. The stripes are green, yellow, and red. The flag of Italy is very similar. It has three vertical stripes that are green, white, and red.

 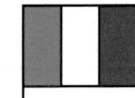

How many different flags can be made from the colors green, yellow, white, and red if each flag has three vertical stripes? *This question will be answered in Example 2.*

A **permutation** is an arrangement, or listing, of objects in which order is important. For example, suppose that the high school band has three seats for their three trumpeters. In how many different ways can they be seated?

> **Problem Solving Hint**
> ••••••••••••
> Make a list.

There are three different choices for the first seat, then two choices for the next seat, and only one choice for the third seat. So, the number of permutations is $3 \cdot 2 \cdot 1 = 6$.

In this example, the symbol $P(3, 3)$ represents the number of permutations of 3 things taken 3 at a time.

$$P(3, 3) = 3 \cdot 2 \cdot 1$$

In general, $P(n, r)$ means the number of permutations of n things taken r at a time.

Example 1

In how many ways can 5 people be seated in a row of 5 chairs?

Find $P(5, 5)$, the number of permutations of 5 things taken 5 at a time. There are 5 choices for the first seat. After that seat is taken, there are 4 choices for the second seat, and so on.

$$P(5, 5) = 5 \cdot 4 \cdot 3 \cdot 2 \cdot 1$$
$$= 120$$

Five people can be seated in 120 ways.

Lesson 13-7 Permutations **517**

OPTIONS

Bell Ringer

Ask students to determine the probability of getting at least two tails in a row if they were to toss a penny four times. $\frac{1}{2}$

13-7 Lesson Notes

NCTM Standards: 1–5, 7, 11

Lesson Resources
- Study Guide Master 13-7
- Practice Master 13-7
- Enrichment Master 13-7
- Technology Master, p. 13
- Group Activity Card 13-7

 Transparency 13-7 contains the 5-Minute Check and a teaching aid for this lesson.

🕐 5-Minute Check
(Over Lesson 13-6)

Find each probability.

1. A green die and a red die are rolled. Find the probability that a multiple of 2 is rolled on the green die and an odd number on the red die. $\frac{1}{4}$

2. A wallet contains six $5 bills, four $10 bills, and two $20 bills. Two bills are selected without the first selection being replaced.
Find $P(\$10, \text{then } \$5)$ $\frac{2}{11}$

1 FOCUS

Motivating the Lesson

Situational Problem Ask students how they would calculate the number of different ways in which 10 people can stand in line for tickets.

2 TEACH

Using Applications Have students choose 3 classmates who will serve as class officers. Tell them that one will be president, one will be treasurer, and one will be secretary. Have students determine the different ways the offices can be filled by using lists, models, and factorials.

517

For Example 1

In how many ways can 6 people be seated at a counter that has 6 stools in a row?   720 ways

For Example 2

How many different flags consisting of 4 vertical stripes can be made from blue, green, red, black, and white?   120 flags

For Example 3

A shelf has a history book, a novel, a biography, a dictionary, a cookbook, and a home-repair book. In how many ways can 3 of these books be rearranged on another shelf?   in 120 different ways

Checking for Understanding

Exercises 1-3 are designed to help you assess students' understanding through reading, writing, speaking, and modeling. You should work through these exercises with your students and then monitor their work on Guided Practice Exercises 4-10.

Calculator Hint

● ● ● ● ● ● ● ● ● ● ● ●

If your calculator has an $\boxed{n!}$ key, you can use it to compute $n!$.

The expression $5 \cdot 4 \cdot 3 \cdot 2 \cdot 1$ can be written as 5!, which is read "five **factorial**." In general, $n!$ is the product of all the counting numbers beginning with n and counting backwards to 1. We define 0! to be 1. For example, this is how to compute 4!.

$$4! = 4 \cdot 3 \cdot 2 \cdot 1$$
$$= 24$$

Some arrangements involve only part of a group.

Example 2   *Problem Solving*
_____

Geography   Refer to the problem in the lesson introduction. How many different flags consisting of three vertical stripes can be made from green, yellow, white, and red?

Find $P(4, 3)$, the number of permutations of four colors taken three at a time.

For the first vertical stripe, there are 4 possible choices. After that stripe is chosen, there are 3 possible choices. Finally, there are 2 possible choices for the third stripe.

$$4 \cdot 3 \cdot 2 = 24$$

There are 24 different flags with three vertical stripes that can be made from green, yellow, white, and red. *To check your answer, use colored pencils and actually draw each possible flag.*

Example 3   *Problem Solving*
_____

Vacations   The DiGrazzias want to visit Arizona, Florida, San Francisco, Chicago, and Boston on their next five vacations. In how many ways can they visit three of these places over the next three years?

Find $P(5, 3)$, the number of permutations of 5 things taken 3 at a time.

For the first vacation, there are 5 possible choices. After they take that vacation, there are 4 possible choices. Then for the third vacation, there are 3 possible choices.

$5 \cdot 4 \cdot 3 = 60$ There are 60 ways to visit three of these places.

DID YOU KNOW?

The total number of ways of arranging a standard deck of 52 playing cards is about 80,660,000,000, 000,000,000,000, 000,000,000,000, 000,000,000,000, 000,000,000,000, 000,000,000.

OPTIONS

Reteaching Activity

Using Connections   Have students solve the opening problem about flags by counting outcomes. Then guide them to use multiplication to obtain the answer. Have students compare the two methods to choose the one that is more efficient. If necessary, repeat with Example 2.

Study Guide Masters, p. 116

Name _____   Date _____

Study Guide Worksheet 13-7

Permutations

An arrangement or listing in which order is important is called a permutation.

Example   There are 6 sailboats in a race. How many arrangements of first, second and third place are possible?

There are 6 choices for first place, then 5 choices for second place, then 4 choices for third place.
$$6 \times 5 \times 4 = 120$$
The number of permutations is 120.

For the example above, the permutation of 6 sailboats taken 3 at a time may be written $P(6, 3)$.
$$P(6, 3) = 6 \times 5 \times 4 = 120$$
Some arrangements involve all of the members of a group.

Checking for Understanding

Communicating Mathematics

Read and study the lesson to answer each question.

Multiply 5 · 4 · 3 · 2 · 1.

1. **Tell** how to find the number of permutations of 5 colors taken 5 at a time.

2. **Tell** how to find the number of permutations of 5 colors taken 2 at a time.

Multiply 5 · 4.

3. **Tell** whether the following list is a list of permutations. Explain.

123, 132, 213, 231, 312, 321

Yes, it is a list of all the ways the digits 1, 2, and 3 can make a 3-digit number.

Guided Practice Find the value of each expression.

4. 3! **6**　　　　5. 0! **1**　　　　6. *P*(4, 1) **4**　　　　7. *P*(5, 2) **20**

8. At a pet show, first, second, and third prizes will be awarded to Eau, Tabbie, and Luv. In how many ways can the prizes be awarded? **6 ways**

9. A license plate begins with three letters. If the possible letters are A, B, C, D, E, and F, how many different permutations of these letters can be made if no letter is used more than once? **120 permutations**

10. A flag consists of three horizontal stripes. If the colors can be chosen from among white, black, green, red, and blue, how many flags can be made? **60 flags**

Exercises

Independent Practice Find the value of each expression.

11. 1! **1**　　　12. 5! **120**　　　13. *P*(6, 4) **360**　　　14. *P*(5, 1) **5**

15. How many different five-letter "words" can be formed from the letters A, B, C, D, and E if no letter may be used more than once? **120 words**
"Words" means any arrangement of letters, not just English words.

16. How many different five-letter "words" can be formed from all the letters of the alphabet if no letter may be used more than once? **7,893,600 words**

17. In how many ways can seven different books be arranged on a shelf? **5,040 ways**

18. In how many ways can a president, a treasurer, and a secretary be chosen from among 8 candidates? **336 ways**

19. A zip code contains 5 digits. How many different zip codes can be made with the digits 0–9 if no digit is used more than once and the first digit is not 0? **27,216 zip codes**

Mixed Review 20. Find the least common multiple of 12 and 27. *(Lesson 4-9)* **108**

21. Solve $6 = \frac{w}{-3}$. *(Lesson 7-9)* **−18**

22. **Medicine** The effect of a drug used to control epilepsy is independent from patient to patient. The probability that the drug is successful is 0.88. What is the probability that the drug is a success with two randomly selected patients? *(Lesson 13-6)* **0.7744**

Lesson 13-7 Permutations　　**519**

Gifted and Talented Needs

Challenge students to simplify $\frac{100!}{99!}$

by first investigating the answers to $\frac{5!}{4!}$, $\frac{4!}{3!}$, and $\frac{3!}{2!}$.　**100**

Error Analysis

Watch for students who multiply the terms to find permutations instead of using factorials.

Prevent by having students list permutations and compare the results with the results of using factorials.

Close

Have students write problems for classmates to solve in which they determine how many orders are possible for making a number of phone calls.

3 PRACTICE/APPLY

Assignment Guide
Maximum: 11–26
Minimum: 11–19 odd, 20–26

For **Extra Practice**, see p. 601.

Alternate Assessment

Writing Ask students to determine the number of ways 4 prizes could be awarded to 4 students from a final group of 10 students.　**5,040 different ways**

Practice Masters, p. 116

Name _____　　Date _____

Practice Worksheet 13-7

Permutations

Find the value of each expression.

1. 6!　　　2. 9!　　　3. *P*(6, 3)
　 720　　　 **362,880**　　 **120**

4. *P*(9, 8)　　5. *P*(10, 1)　　6. *P*(8, 8)
　 362,880　　 **10**　　　 **40,320**

7. How many different ways can seven people be seated in one row of seven people?　**5,040**

8. Suppose that eight students out of ten qualify for the cheerleading squad. In how many ways can you choose the squad?　**1,814,400**

9. In how many ways can a president, vice-president, secretary, and treasurer be chosen from a club with 12 members?　**11,880**

10. In how many ways can five books be arranged on a shelf?　**120**

11. In how many ways can a phone number be created if there are ten ways that the first three digits can be arranged and then each of the remaining four digits can be any digit from 0-9 as long as no digit is repeated in the group of four.　**50,400**

12. How many different four-letter words can be made from the alphabet if the first two letters come from the first half of the alphabet and the second two letters come from the second half of the alphabet?　**24,336**

T116
Glencoe Division, Macmillan/McGraw-Hill

520

Problem Solving
and
Applications

DATA SEARCH

Portfolio

23. **Celebrations** Parade organizers want to place a fire engine, a police car, and an ambulance after the grand marshal's car. In how many ways can the fire engine, the police car, and the ambulance be arranged? **6 ways**

24. **Data Search** Refer to page 652. About what fraction of the population is involved in each type of lawn and plant activity? About what fraction of the population would you expect to be involved in each activity in 1995?

25. **Portfolio Suggestion** Select an item from this chapter that you feel shows your best work and place it in your portfolio. Explain why you selected it.

24. See margin.
25. See students' work.

26. **Critical Thinking** In a certain area, a license plate consists of three letters followed by three digits. No letter may be used twice, no digit may be used twice, and the letters I and O are not used. How many different license plates are possible? **8,743,680 license plates**

Save Planet Earth

Lawn Care

One of the most popular activities of American homeowners is maintaining and beautifying their lawns. Many homeowners put a lot of effort into having the perfect green lawn. This "perfect green lawn," however, comes with a price tag—$6 billion annually.

In addition, lawn care can often lead to problems in the environment. Each American uses about 3 to 10 pounds of chemical products on their lawns each year. Many of these products are intended to kill insects that can damage a lawn. However, the chemicals in these products can also have a hazardous effect on birds, amphibians, and fish (when the chemicals get into the ground water). Humans have also been known to react to the chemicals. Some people have experienced dizziness, rashes, headaches, respiratory illness, and other problems from these chemicals.

How You Can Help

• Take a sample of your grass to a local garden center. Find out the type of grass and how to care for it. Is your family's current lawn care program correct? Are there organic pesticides available that you could use instead of chemicals?

• Eliminate harmful pesticides.

• Water your lawn either in the morning or evening to save water loss through evaporation.

520 **Chapter 13** Discrete Math and Probability

OPTIONS

Extending the Lesson

Save Planet Earth Discuss alternate ways to reduce the use of harmful chemicals on lawns. You may wish to discuss xeriscaping and the advantages this form of landscaping has for the environment.

Cooperative Learning Activity

Puzzling Permutations 13-7

Use groups of 4.
Materials: Dictionaries

A popular puzzle found in many newspapers contains words whose letters have been scrambled. Sometimes you can unscramble the words in your head. Another strategy, especially for words you do not know, is to list all of the permutations of the letters. One of the permutations will be the unscrambled word.

➡ Working in pairs, unscramble each of the words below. Since these words are not common, you may want to list all the permutations and then look up the possibilities. Try to be the first pair to unscramble all three words.

$$^o{}_r{}^d{}^m_k{}^a_{g}{}_s$$

douk   erty   wappa

Glencoe Mathematics: Applications and Connections, Course 2

Cooperative Learning

13-8A Exploring Combinations

A Preview of Lesson 13-8

Objective
Explore combinations.

Materials
index cards
marker

The student council at Arlington Junior High School is planning to have a pizza sale. They plan to offer eight different kinds of pizza.

extra cheese	mushroom
pepperoni	sausage
meatball	onion
pepper	anchovy

The price of a pizza depends on the *combination* of toppings chosen.

Try this!

Work in groups of two or three.

- Write the names of the eight toppings on eight index cards.
- To make a pizza, select any pair of cards. Make a list of all the different combinations that are possible. Note that the order is not important. **See Solutions Manual.**

$$\boxed{\text{extra cheese}} \quad \text{and} \quad \boxed{\text{mushroom}}$$

is considered the same as

$$\boxed{\text{mushroom}} \quad \text{and} \quad \boxed{\text{extra cheese}}$$

- Suppose that the student council decides to offer a deluxe pizza with three toppings on it. Make a list of all the different toppings that are possible if three of the eight toppings are used. How many different combinations did you list? **56 combinations**
- Suppose that the student council decides to offer a small pizza with one topping on it. Make a list of all the different toppings that are possible if one of the eight toppings is used. **See Solutions Manual.**

What do you think?

1. In a permutation, order is important.

1. What is the difference between a combination (like a combination of toppings) and a permutation?
2. Would a tree diagram be a good method for listing all the combinations of two toppings? Why or why not? **No; A tree diagram uses toppings more than once.**

Mathematics Lab 13-8A Exploring Combinations **521**

OPTIONS

Lab Manual You may wish to make copies of the blackline master on p. 77 of the *Lab Manual* for students to use as a recording sheet.

Lab Manual, p. 77

Name _____ Date _____

Mathematics Lab Worksheet

Use with page 521

Exploring Combinations

Try this!

List the different possible combinations for two toppings:

extra cheese and pepperoni	extra cheese and meatball
extra cheese and pepper	extra cheese and mushroom
extra cheese and sausage	extra cheese and onion
extra cheese and anchovy	pepperoni and meatball
pepperoni and pepper	pepperoni and mushroom
pepperoni and sausage	pepperoni and onion
pepperoni and anchovy	meatball and pepper
meatball and mushroom	meatball and sausage
meatball and onion	meatball and anchovy
pepper and mushroom	pepper and sausage
pepper and onion	pepper and anchovy
mushroom and sausage	mushroom and onion
mushroom and anchovy	sausage and onion
sausage and anchovy	

NCTM Standards: 1–5

Management Tips

For Students Provide each group with 8 index cards. Although they should work together to choose the pizzas, one student can name the toppings and then be the combinations recorder.

For the Overhead Projector *Overhead Manipulative Resources* provides appropriate materials for teacher or student demonstration of the activities in this Mathematics Lab.

1 FOCUS

Introducing the Lab

Have students tell how they ordinarily choose toppings for pizza when they order one as a group. Ask them whether they think that they can determine the number of different possible toppings just by using permutations.

2 TEACH

Using Models Have students compare how they used cards in the permutations Mathematics Lab (p. 516) and how they are using cards in this Lab. Ask why the order of the toppings does not matter this time.

3 PRACTICE/APPLY

Using Critical Thinking Ask students to predict the number of combinations of two-topping pizzas possible from a choice of nine toppings and then ten toppings. Have them use the cards to find out. **36 and 45 combinations**

Close

Ask students to explain how a combination differs from a permutation.

Lesson Resources
- Study Guide Master 13-8
- Practice Master 13-8
- Enrichment Master 13-8
- Evaluation Master, Quiz B, p. 115
- Technology Master, p. 27
- Interdisciplinary Master, p. 27
- Group Activity Card 13-8

 Transparency 13-8 contains the 5-Minute Check and a teaching aid for this lesson.

🕐 5-Minute Check
(Over Lesson 13-7)

Find the value of each expression.

1. 7! 5,040
2. $P(4, 2)$ 12
3. $P(8, 3)$ 336
4. $P(7, 1)$ 7
5. In how many ways can 6 different books be arranged on a shelf?
   720

---

1 FOCUS

Motivating the Lesson

Activity Tell students that the following situation represents a permutation. Ask them to rewrite it so that it represents a combination. *In how many ways can 3 books from a set of 5 books be arranged?* Sample answer: How many selections of 3 books can be made from a set of 5 books?

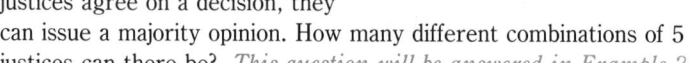

13-8 Combinations

Objective
Find the number of combinations of a set of objects.

Words to Learn
combination

In October 1991, Clarence Thomas was confirmed as a member of the United States Supreme Court. He replaced Justice Thurgood Marshall who announced his retirement in July of the same year.

There are 9 Supreme Court justices in all. If at least 5 of the 9 justices agree on a decision, they can issue a majority opinion. How many different combinations of 5 justices can there be? *This question will be answered in Example 2.*

An arrangement of objects in which order is unimportant is called a **combination.** Since order is not important, the number of combinations of a set of objects is less than the number of permutations of those objects. For example, suppose you are arranging the letters R, E, and D. In a permutation, the arrangements RED and DER are different. But in a combination, the arrangements RED and DER are the same because order is not important.

Example 1 *Problem Solving*

Sports   In how many ways can a basketball coach choose two starting guards from among four capable players?

Call the players A, B, C, and D.
List *all* arrangements of A, B, C, and D.

AB	AC	AD	BC	BD	CD
BA	CA	DA	CB	DB	DC

Count all the *different* arrangements. Arrangements AB and BA are not different here. Altogether, there are six different arrangements.

AB	AC	AD	BC	BD	CD

> **Problem Solving Hint**
> •••••••••••••
> Make a list.

The number of combinations of n things taken r at a time is written as $C(n, r)$. In Example 1, you saw how to find the number of combinations by listing. List all the permutations of a set of objects, then eliminate the arrangements that are the same except for order. Use a formula to find the number of combinations.

OPTIONS

Limited English Proficiency

Have students add *permutation* and *combination* to their vocabulary list, along with the formula for finding each. Use the concept of filling plates in a cafeteria line or at a salad bar to show different combinations of foods. Guide students to see that if a person puts tomatoes and then tuna on a plate, it's the same combination as the plate of a person who chose the tuna first and then the tomato.

In general, $C(n, r)$ means the number of combinations of n things taken r at a time.

$$C(n, r) = \frac{P(n, r)}{r!}$$

Example 2 *Problem Solving*

Law   Refer to the problem in the lesson introduction. In how many ways can five of the nine justices of the Supreme Court agree?

Use the formula to find the number of combinations of nine things taken five at a time.

$$C(9, 5) = \frac{P(9, 5)}{5!}$$

$$= \frac{9 \cdot 8 \cdot 7 \cdot 6 \cdot 5}{5 \cdot 4 \cdot 3 \cdot 2 \cdot 1}$$

$$= \frac{\overset{3}{\cancel{9}} \cdot \overset{2}{\cancel{8}} \cdot 7 \cdot \overset{3}{\cancel{6}} \cdot \overset{1}{\cancel{5}}}{\underset{1}{\cancel{5}} \cdot \underset{1}{\cancel{4}} \cdot \underset{1}{\cancel{3}} \cdot \underset{1}{\cancel{2}} \cdot 1}$$

$$= 126$$

Five of the nine justices can agree in 126 ways.

Example 3 *Connection*

Probability   At Sanchez Taco Restaurant, customers may choose three fillings for their tacos from a list of five fillings. The fillings are beef, chicken, cheese, lettuce, and tomato. If it is equally likely that a customer will choose any combination of three fillings, find the probability that a customer will choose beef, cheese, and lettuce.

Explore   There are five fillings and customers may choose three fillings from among them.

Plan   Use the formula to find the number of combinations of five fillings taken three at a time.

Solve $C(5, 3) = \dfrac{P(5, 3)}{3!}$

$$= \frac{5 \cdot 4 \cdot 3}{3 \cdot 2 \cdot 1}$$

$$= \frac{5 \cdot \overset{2}{\cancel{4}} \cdot \overset{1}{\cancel{3}}}{\underset{1}{\cancel{3}} \cdot \underset{1}{\cancel{2}} \cdot 1}$$

$$= 10$$

(continued on next page)

Lesson 13-8 Combinations   **523**

Reteaching Activity

Using Models   Use outcomes of tossing a red die and a green die to distinguish between permutations and combinations. Guide students to see that every pair of related outcomes such as (red 3, green 1) and (red 1, green 3) represents only one combination.

Study Guide Masters, p. 117

Name _____   Date _____

Study Guide Worksheet 13-8

Combinations

Arrangements or listings in which order is not important are called combinations.

$C(n, r)$ stands for the number of combinations of n things taken r at a time.

$$C(n, r) = \frac{P(n, r)}{r!}$$

Example   In how many ways can 3 toppings for a pizza be chosen from a list of 10 toppings?

$$C(10, 3) = \frac{P(10, 3)}{3!}$$

$$= \frac{10 \times 9 \times 8}{3 \times 2 \times 1}$$ Find $P(10, 3)$.

2 TEACH

Using Formulas   Guide students to see the advantage of using a formula to find combinations. To make sure they understand the formula for finding combinations, and to see that they recognize the relationship between permutations and combinations, have them express in their own words the meaning of the numerator and denominator in the formula. Sample answer: numerator— number of permutations; denominator—factorial of the number of things taken at a time

---

More Examples

For Example 1

In how many ways can a baseball coach choose 3 pitchers from a group of 5 capable pitchers?   10

For Example 2

In how many ways can 6 of the 10 members of a group agree on a plan?   210

For Example 3

At the Burrito Brothers Grill, customers choose from 6 toppings with which to fill their burritos. They can have cheese, onion, pepper, salsa, tomato, and beans. If Gary asks the server to choose any two of the fillings, what is the probability he'll get a bean and salsa burrito? $\frac{1}{15}$

Teaching Tip   Point out to students that $C(n, r)$ is often written $_nC_r$. Similarly, $P(n, r)$ is often expressed as $_nP_r$.

Checking for Understanding

Exercises 1-4 are designed to help you assess students' understanding through reading, writing, speaking, and modeling. You should work through these exercises with your students and then monitor their work on Guided Practice Exercises 5-11.

Have students explain why there are fewer combinations of a set of objects taken 2 at a time than there are permutations of the objects taken 2 at a time.   Order doesn't matter; Divide the number of permutations by 2! to find the number of combinations.

3 PRACTICE/APPLY

Assignment Guide
Maximum: 12–27
Minimum: 13–19 odd, 21–26

For **Extra Practice,** see p. 602.

Alternate Assessment

Writing Ask students to make up a problem for classmates to solve, the solution to which can be found by using C(6, 4).   Sample answer: In how many ways can a conductor choose 4 violinists from a group of 6 violinists of equal talent?

Practice Masters, p. 117

524

Of the 10 combinations, one of them is beef, cheese, and lettuce.

So, P(beef, cheese, lettuce) $= \frac{1}{10}$ or 0.1.

Actually list all the possible combinations of the fillings to check your answer.

Checking for Understanding

Communicating Mathematics

Read and study the lesson to answer each question.   Divide P(3, 2) by 2!.

1. **Write** how to find the number of combinations of 3 letters taken 2 at a time.

2. **Tell** whether the following is a list of permutations or a list of combinations. Explain. **Permutations, because the letters are the same, but the order is different.**   ABC, ACB, BAC, BCA, CAB, CBA

3. **Tell** whether there are more permutations of a set of objects taken 3 at a time or more combinations of the objects taken 3 at a time. **permutations**

4. **Write** a paragraph about why a combination lock really should be called a permutation lock. **See students' work.**

Guided Practice

Find the value of each expression.

5. $\frac{5!}{2!}$ **60**   6. $\frac{8!}{6!}$ **56**   7. C(6, 2) **15**   8. C(4, 3) **4**

RST, RSU, RSV, RTU, RTV, RUV, STU, STV, SUV, TUV

9. List all combinations of the letters R, S, T, U, and V taken 3 at a time.

10. List all combinations of Bob, Debbie, Julio, Terese, and Yoki taken 2 at a time. **See margin.**

11. At Mario's Pizza Parlor, customers may choose 2 pizza toppings from the following: cheese, pepper, onion, pepperoni, salami, meatball, mushroom, or sausage. If it is equally likely that a customer will choose any combinations of 2 toppings, find the probability that a customer will choose cheese/pepperoni or sausage/mushroom. $\frac{1}{14}$

Exercises

Independent Practice

Find the value of each expression.

12. $\frac{7!}{1!}$ **5,040**   13. $\frac{8!}{4!}$ **1,680**   14. C(7, 4) **35**   15. C(8, 6) **28**

462 ways

16. An 11-member city council makes its decisions by simple majority vote. That is, if 6 out of the 11 members vote for an issue, the issue is passed. In how many ways can a simple majority of the council decide on an issue?

17. In a lottery, each ticket has 5 one-digit numbers 0–9 on it. You win if your ticket has the digits *in any order*. What are your chances of winning? $\frac{1}{252}$

OPTIONS

Bell Ringer

Have students investigate the values of C(5, 3) and C(5, 2), and C(4, 1) and C(4, 3), to predict the relationship between the values of C(12, 5) and C(12, 7).   The values will be the same.

Additional Answer

10. Bob, Debbie; Bob, Julio; Bob, Terese; Bob, Yoki; Debbie, Julio; Debbie, Terese; Debbie, Yoki; Julio, Terese; Julio, Yoki; Terese, Yoki

Tell whether each problem involves a permutation or a combination.
Then solve the problem.

18. In how many ways can three swimmers for a team be chosen from six swimmers? **combination; 20 ways**

19. In how many ways can four cars line up for a race? **permutation; 24 ways**

20. In how many ways can seven people make a decision by a simple majority? **combination; 35 ways**

Mixed Review 21. The two graphs below show that the number of farms in the United States is decreasing, but the average size of each farm is increasing. What do you predict the number of farms will be in the year 2000, and what will be the average size of each farm in the year 2000? *(Lesson 3-7)*
Sample answers: 1.9 million farms, 500 acres

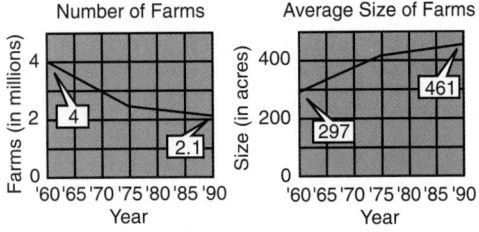

22. Solve $\frac{3}{x} = \frac{25}{15}$. *(Lesson 11-3)* **1.8**

23. **Sailing** When Bob purchased his sailboat, it came with 6 different-colored flags to be used for sending signals. The specific signal depended on the order of the flags. How many different 3-flag signals can Bob send? *(Lesson 13-7)* **120 signals**

Problem Solving and Applications 24. **Sales** In how many ways can 30 different books be displayed 5 at a time if the order of the arrangement is not important? **142,506 ways**

25. **Food Service** At the Grill and Skillet Restaurant, customers may choose 3 toppings for their hamburgers from a list of 6 toppings. The toppings are lettuce, tomato, onion, cheese, pickle, and mushroom. Find the probability that a customer will choose onion, pickle, and cheese. $\frac{1}{20}$

26. **Critical Thinking**
   a. How many combinations of A, B, C, and D are there taken 1 at a time? 2 at a time? 3 at a time? 4 at a time? **4; 6; 4; 1**
   b. What is the sum of the answers to part a? **15**
   c. How is your answer related to 2^4? **It is 1 less.**

27. **Data Search** Refer to pages 490 and 491. Look at the Mercalli Earthquake Intensity Scale.
   a. When an earthquake registers 8.0 and above, what kind of damage occurs? **Damage is total; ground becomes wavy.**
   b. How often does this kind of earthquake occur? **once every 5 to 10 years**

Lesson 13-8 Combinations   **525**

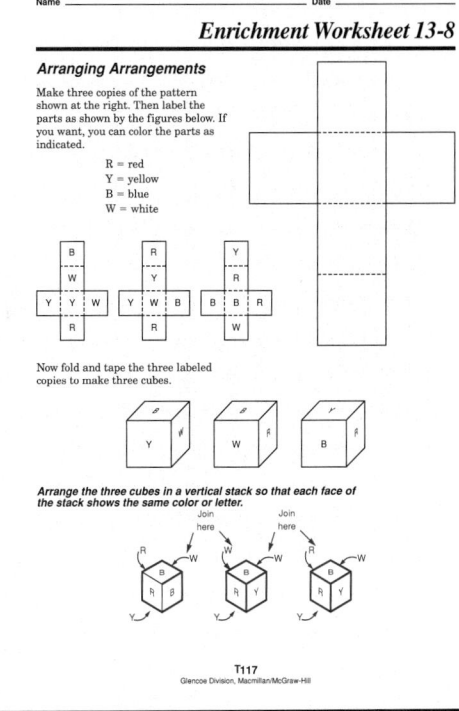

The Chapter Study Guide and Review begins with a section on Communicating Mathematics. This includes questions that review the new terms and concepts that were introduced in the chapter.

Then, the Skills and Concepts presented in the chapter are reviewed using a side-by-side format. Encourage students to refer to the Objectives and Examples on the left as they complete the Review Exercises on the right.

The Chapter Study Guide and Review ends with problems that review Applications and Problem Solving.

Study Guide and Review

Chapter

13 Study Guide and Review

Communicating Mathematics

Choose the correct term to complete the sentence.

1. The set of all possible outcomes for an experiment is called the (sample space, combination). **sample space**
2. The Fundamental Counting Principle counts the number of possible outcomes using the operation of (addition, multiplication). **multiplication**
3. The ratio of the number of times an event occurs to the number of trials done is called the (theoretical, experimental) probability. **experimental**
4. When the outcome of one event influences the outcome of a second event, the events are called (independent, dependent). **dependent**
5. A (permutation, combination) is an arrangement of objects in which order is important. **permutation**
6. In your own words, explain the relationship between a sample and a population. **Sample answer: A sample is a small part of a population.**

Self Assessment

Objectives and Examples	Review Exercises
Upon completing this chapter, you should be able to:	*Use these exercises to review and prepare for the chapter test.*

• use tree diagrams to count outcomes *(Lesson 13-1)*

When a coin is tossed twice,

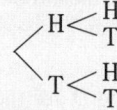

there are 4 possible outcomes.

Make a tree diagram and then give the total number of outcomes. **For tree diagrams to Exercises 7–8, see margin.**

7. choosing a red, black, or white car with either black or gray interior **6 outcomes**
8. tossing a coin and rolling a die **12 outcomes**

• use multiplication to count outcomes *(Lesson 13-2)*

There are 2 possible outcomes each time a coin is tossed. If a coin is tossed 2 times, there are $2 \times 2 = 4$ outcomes.

Use multiplication to find the total number of outcomes in each situation.

9. rolling 3 dice **216 outcomes**
10. selecting a house from 3 styles, 2 locations, and 2 exterior colors **12 outcomes**

526 **Chapter 13** Study Guide and Review

Additional Answers

7.

responses		outcomes
red	black	red, black
	gray	red, gray
black	black	black, black
	gray	black, gray
white	black	white, black
	gray	white, gray

8.

responses		outcomes
heads	1	heads, 1
	2	heads, 2
	3	heads, 3
	4	heads, 4
	5	heads, 5
	6	heads, 6
tails	1	tails, 1
	2	tails, 2
	3	tails, 3
	4	tails, 4
	5	tails, 5
	6	tails, 6

Objectives and Examples

- find and compare experimental and theoretical probabilities *(Lesson 13-3)*

  If 1 marble is drawn from a bag containing 6 red and 4 black marbles, the theoretical probability that it is red is $\frac{6}{10}$ or $\frac{3}{5}$.

Review Exercises

A bowl contains the names of 30 middle school students. Nine are 6th graders, 14 are 7th graders and 7 are 8th graders. One name is randomly selected. Find the probability that the student selected is:

11. a 6th grader $\frac{9}{30}$ or $\frac{3}{10}$

12. not an 8th grader $\frac{23}{30}$

13. at least a 7th grader $\frac{21}{30}$ or $\frac{7}{10}$

- predict actions of a larger group by using a sample *(Lesson 13-5)*

  If 5% of a random sample of 100 students at Roosevelt Junior High have after-school jobs, then we could predict how many out of all 500 students have after-school jobs.

  5% of $500 = 0.05 \times 500$
  $= 25$ students

Of 25,000 registered voters, the preferences of 1,000 are listed in the table below.

Candidate	Number of Votes Received
Chung	240
Brown	380
Armas	300
Undecided	80

14. How many of the 25,000 voters might you expect to vote for Brown? **9,500 voters**

15. How many of the 25,000 voters might you expect to be undecided at election time? **2,000 voters**

- find the probability of independent and dependent events *(Lesson 13-6)*

  If A and B are independent events, then $P(A \text{ and } B) = P(A) \cdot P(B)$.

A bag contains 8 blue, 6 white, and 4 red marbles. Two marbles are randomly drawn. Find P(white, white) if

16. the first marble drawn is replaced $\frac{1}{9}$

17. the first marble drawn is not replaced $\frac{5}{51}$

- find the number of permutations of objects *(Lesson 13-7)*

  $P(4, 2) = 4 \cdot 3$
  $= 12$

Find the value of each expression.

18. 5! **120**   19. 0! **1**

20. $P(8, 3)$ **336**   21. $P(6, 6)$ **720**

Chapter 13 Study Guide and Review   **527**

You may wish to use a Chapter Test from the Evaluation Masters booklet as an additional chapter review. The two free-response forms are shown below. One of the two multiple-choice forms is shown on the next page.

Evaluation Masters, pp. 113–114

Objectives and Examples	Review Exercises

- find the number of combinations of a set of objects *(Lesson 13-8)*

$$C(5, 3) = \frac{P(5, 3)}{3!}$$
$$= \frac{5 \cdot \cancel{4} \cdot \cancel{3}}{\cancel{3} \cdot \cancel{2} \cdot 1}$$
$$= 10$$

Find the value of each expression.
22. $\frac{4!}{3!}$ 4
23. $\frac{7!}{7!}$ 1
24. $C(3, 3)$ 1
25. $C(8, 4)$ 70

Applications and Problem Solving

26. How many times do you need to spin this spinner to spin all seven numbers? Solve by acting it out. *(Lesson 13-4)* at least 7 times

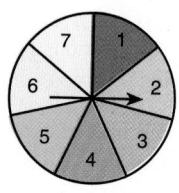

27. **Raffle** In how many ways can the grand-prize ticket, second-prize ticket, and third-prize ticket be selected from the 20 raffle tickets sold? *(Lesson 13-7)* **6,840 ways**

28. **Games** Hoshi has 12 different games that she keeps in her bedroom. She is allowed to bring 2 of these games into the family room for the evening. In how many ways can Hoshi select the 2 games? *(Lesson 13-8)* **66 ways**

Curriculum Connection Projects

- **Home Economics** Make a list of different flavors of potato chips and survey your classmates to find out how many people prefer each flavor. Predict how many students in the school would prefer each flavor.

- **Sports** List the catchers and pitchers on your favorite baseball team. Find how many different catcher-pitcher combinations are possible.

Read More About It

Rubinstein, Gillian. *Beyond the Labyrinth.*
Riedel, Manfred. *Odds and Chances for Kids: A Look at Probability.*
Phillips, Jo. *Exploring Triangles: Paper Folding Geometry.*

13 Test

1. Ben is making a sandwich. He has 2 kinds of bread and 3 kinds of meat. If he only uses one kind of each, how many different sandwiches can Ben make? **6 sandwiches**

2. A couple has 3 children. Make a tree diagram to show all of the possible orders of children if each child is listed as a boy or a girl. **See Solutions Manual.**

3. How many different local telephone numbers (XXX-XXXX) are possible? **10,000,000**

The spinner at the right has an equal chance of landing on each number. Find the probability that the spinner lands on:

4. an even number. $\frac{1}{2}$ 5. a 3 or a 5. $\frac{1}{4}$ 6. a number greater than 6. $\frac{1}{4}$

7. Ryan works at The Eggroll House. He has 6 different kinds of shirts to wear with his uniform. What is the probability that he wears the same shirt more than once in a 3-day work week? $\frac{1}{2}$

The opinions of 1,000 voters on an upcoming school levy are listed at the right. The entire city has 25,000 registered voters.

Opinion	Number of Votes
Oppose	280
Neutral	200
Favor	520

8. How many of the 25,000 voters might you expect to oppose the levy? **about 7,000 voters**

9. How many of the 25,000 voters might you expect to be neutral? **about 5,000 voters**

10. Would you expect the levy to pass? **yes**

Tell whether the events are independent or dependent.

11. rolling a pair of dice and getting a 6 on the first die and a sum of 9 for both dice **dependent**

12. having brown hair and owning a brown car **independent**

13. The two fire engines in a small town operate independently. The probability that each engine is available when needed is 0.96. Find the probability that both engines are available at one time. **0.9216**

Find the value of each expression.

14. 6! **720**   15. $P(7, 3)$ **210**   16. $\frac{5!}{3!}$ **20**   17. 0! **1**   18. $C(9, 2)$ **36**

19. **Sports** Six runners are racing in a 100-meter sprint. In how many ways can the gold, silver, and bronze medals be awarded? **120 ways**

20. **School Government** From a student council consisting of 12 students, 3 are selected to represent the student body at a school board meeting. In how many ways can these students be selected? **220 ways**

Bonus Evaluate $C(n, n)$ for any positive integer n. **1**

This page may be used as a chapter test or another chapter review.

Evaluation Masters, pp. 109–110

Name _____   Date _____

Form 1A _____   *Chapter 13 Test*

1. Justine is taking a test with four true/false questions on it. Use a tree diagram to find how many possible ways the four answers could appear on the test.
   A. 4   B. 8   C. 16   D. 32   1. **C**

2. Use multiplication to find the number of outcomes that are possible if you toss a penny, a nickel, and a quarter.
   A. 8   B. 3   C. 2   D. 10   2. **A**

Cory has two tickets to a baseball game. He can take one of his friends with him, but five of his friends would like to go. They are Jane, Meg, Mike, Tony, and Amy. To decide, Cory writes each of his friends' names on a separate piece of paper and selects one. Use this information to answer Exercises 3–5.

3. What is the probability that Cory picks a girl?
   A. $\frac{1}{5}$ B. $\frac{2}{5}$ C. $\frac{2}{3}$ D. $\frac{3}{5}$ 3. **D**

4. What is the probability that Cory picks someone whose name does not begin with the letter M?
   A. $\frac{2}{5}$ B. $\frac{3}{5}$ C. $\frac{1}{2}$ D. $\frac{1}{5}$ 4. **B**

5. If Cory draws a name 20 times and Amy's name is picked twice, what is the experimental probability that Amy will go to the game?
   A. $\frac{1}{5}$ B. $\frac{2}{5}$ C. $\frac{1}{10}$ D. $\frac{1}{6}$ 5. **C**

The spinner at the right has an equal chance of landing on each number. Use the spinner for Exercises 6 and 7.

6. Find P(an odd number, then an even number).
   A. $\frac{7}{7}$ B. $\frac{12}{49}$ C. $\frac{7}{49}$ D. $\frac{2}{49}$ 6. **B**

7. Find P(3, then 6).
   A. $\frac{1}{2}$ B. $\frac{1}{7}$ C. $\frac{2}{49}$ D. $\frac{1}{49}$ 7. **D**

8. Alex draws a card from a standard deck of 52 cards. Without replacing the first card, he draws a second one. What is P(club, then club)?
   A. $\frac{1}{169}$ B. $\frac{1}{17}$ C. $\frac{1}{26}$ D. $\frac{1}{16}$ 8. **B**

9. Benji has 3 pairs of pants to wear to school. What is the probability that he will wear the same pair of pants more than once in a 5-day school week?
   A. $\frac{3}{5}$ B. $\frac{2}{5}$ C. 1   D. $\frac{5}{3}$ 9. **C**

109
Glencoe Division, Macmillan/McGraw-Hill

Name _____   Date _____

Chapter 13 Test Form 1A continued

Of 350,000 registered voters, 800 were surveyed. Their voting preferences are listed in the chart at the right. Use the chart for Exercises 10–12.

Candidate	Votes
Carroll	154
Ledo	268
Sanchez	218
Undecided	160

10. What percent of the registered voters are undecided?
    A. 20%   B. 80%   C. 0.04%   D. 25%   10. **A**

11. How many registered voters can be expected to vote for Sanchez?
    A. 1,606   B. 174,400   C. 218   D. 95,375   11. **D**

12. If one half of the undecided voters vote for Sanchez and the other half vote for Carroll, who can be expected to win?
    A. Sanchez   B. Ledo   C. Carroll   D. no winner   12. **A**

13. Evaluate 6!.
    A. 21   B. 120   C. 1   D. 720   13. **D**

14. Evaluate $P(4, 4)$.
    A. 24   B. 0   C. 2   D. 10   14. **A**

15. Evaluate $P(8, 3)$.
    A. 6,561   B. 512   C. 336   D. 6,720   15. **C**

16. Evaluate $\frac{1}{5!}$.
    A. $\frac{1}{120}$ B. 0   C. $\frac{1}{5}$ D. undefined   16. **A**

17. Evaluate $\frac{9!}{5!}$.
    A. 3,024   B. 24   C. 6,561   D. 59,049   17. **A**

18. Evaluate $C(7, 4)$.
    A. 210   B. 840   C. 35   D. 9   18. **C**

19. There are 10 different food items in the salad bar. If Phillip made three trips to the salad bar and chose only one different food item each time, in how many ways could he have selected his food?
    A. 1,000   B. 604,800   C. 30   D. 720   19. **D**

20. Carol is in the 7th grade at North Middle School and is making out her 8th grade schedule. She can select two of the 9 courses she will take from the following options: French, Spanish, home economics, industrial technology, art and music. What is the probability that Carol will select industrial technology and music?
    A. $\frac{3}{4}$ B. $\frac{9}{15}$ C. $\frac{2}{9}$ D. $\frac{1}{30}$ 20. **B**

BONUS A deli uses six kinds of meat to make their sandwiches. Their menu lists one fourth of the possible sandwiches that can be made with three kinds of meat and one fifth of the possible sandwiches that can be made with two kinds of meat. How many sandwiches are listed on the menu?
    A. 12   B. 15   C. 7   D. 8   **D**

110
Glencoe Division, Macmillan/McGraw-Hill

Test and Review Generator

software is provided in Apple, IBM, and Macintosh versions. You may use this software to create your own tests or worksheets, based on the needs of your students.

The **Performance Assessment Booklet** provides an alternate assessment for evaluating student progress. An assessment for this chapter can be found on pages 25–26.

14 Functions and Graphs

Previewing the Chapter

This chapter explores two-step equations, equations with two variables, functions, graphing equations in two variables, graphing functions, and graphing transformations and dilations. In the **problem-solving strategy** lesson, students solve problems by working backward.

Lesson	Lesson Objectives	NCTM Standards	State/Local Objectives
14-1	Solve problems by working backward.	1–5, 7	
14-2A	Solve two-step equations with integers using models.	1–5, 9	
14-2	Solve two-step equations.	1–5, 7, 9, 12	
14-3	Solve equations with two variables.	1–5, 7, 9	
14-4	Graph equations by plotting points.	1–5, 7, 9, 12	
14-5A	Use a function rule to find the output of a function.	1–5, 7, 9, 10	
14-5	Complete function tables. Graph functions.	1–5, 7, 8, 12	
14-6	Graph transformations on a coordinate plane.	1–5, 7, 8, 12	
14-6B	Change the size of a figure on a coordinate plane.	1–4, 12	

Organizing the Chapter

A complete, 1-page lesson plan is provided for each lesson in the Lesson Plans Masters Booklet.

LESSON PLANNING GUIDE

| Lesson | Materials/ Manipulatives | Extra Practice (Student Edition) | Blackline Masters Booklets | | | | | | | | | |
			Study Guide	Practice	Enrichment	Evaluation	Technology	Lab Manual	Multicultural Activities	Application and Interdisciplinary Activities	Transparencies	Group Activity Cards
14-1			p. 118	p. 118	p. 118						14-1	14-1
14-2A	cups, counters, mats							p. 78				
14-2		p. 602	p. 119	p. 119	p. 119		p. 28		p. 14		14-2	14-2
14-3		p. 602	p. 120	p. 120	p. 120	Quiz A, p. 124					14-3	14-3
14-4		p. 603	p. 121	p. 121	p. 121					p. 14	14-4	14-4
14-5A	clock with seconds hand, graph paper							p. 79				
14-5		p. 603	p. 122	p. 122	p. 122		p. 14			p. 28	14-5	14-5
14-6		p. 603	p. 123	p. 123	p. 123	Quiz B, p. 124					14-6	14-6
14-6B	picture or cartoon graph paper straightedge colored pencil							p. 80				
Study Guide and Review			Multiple Choice Test, Forms 1A and 1B, pp. 118–121 Free Response Test, Forms 2A and 2B, pp. 122–123 Cumulative Review, p. 125 (free response) Cumulative Test, p. 126 (multiple choice)									
Test												

Pacing Guide: Option III (Chapters 1–14) - 9 days

You may wish to refer to the complete **Course Planning Guides** on page T25.

OTHER CHAPTER RESOURCES

Student Edition
Chapter Opener, pp. 530–531
Cultural Kaleidoscope, p. 534
Mid-Chapter Review, p. 545
Portfolio Suggestion, p. 554
Academic Skills Test, pp. 560–561

 Manipulatives
Overhead Manipulative Resources
Middle School Mathematics Manipulative Kit

 Software/Technology
Interactive Mathematics Tools (Macintosh)
Test and Review Generator (IBM, Apple, Macintosh)
Teacher's Guide for Software Resources

Other Supplements
Transparency 14–0
Performance Assessment, pp. 27–28
Glencoe Mathematics Professional Series Lesson Plans, pp. 154–162

INTERDISCIPLINARY BULLETIN BOARD

Health Connection

Objective   Examine how burning calories is a function of the time, speed, and body weight.

How To Use It   Have students examine the chart and add to it by finding data in health magazines for activities that they participate in. Have them use the data to analyze how the length of time doing an activity, the speed at which the activity is done, and the weight of the person doing the activity are related to the number of calories generated. Ask students to apply these data to activities they engage in.

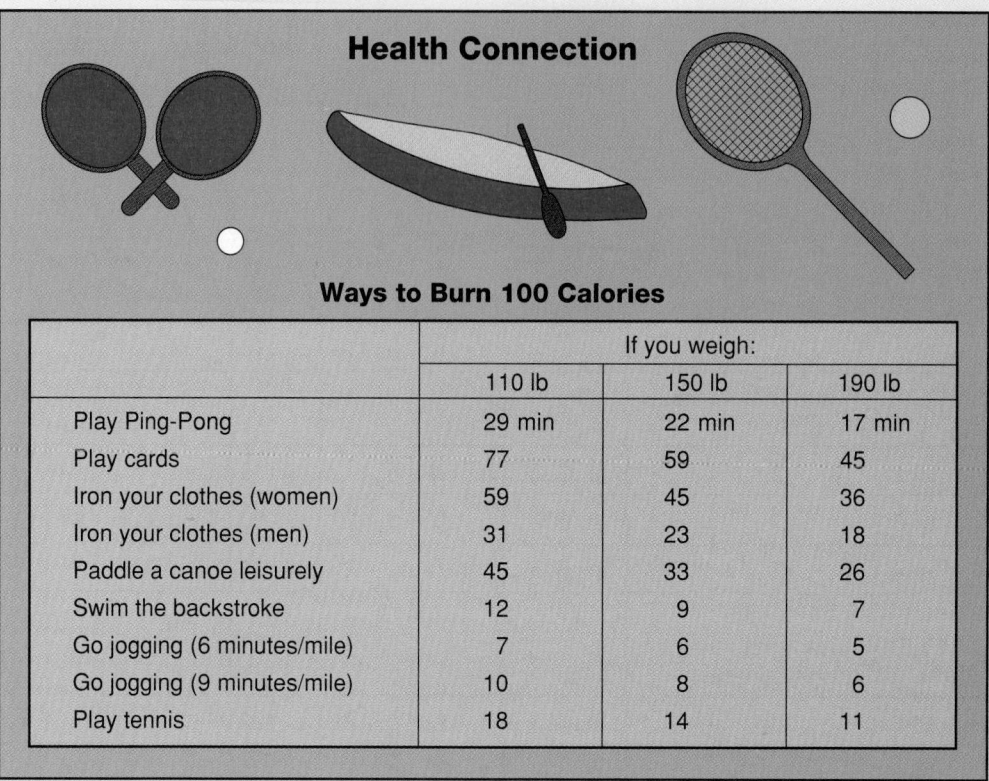

Health Connection

Ways to Burn 100 Calories

	If you weigh:		
	110 lb	150 lb	190 lb
Play Ping-Pong	29 min	22 min	17 min
Play cards	77	59	45
Iron your clothes (women)	59	45	36
Iron your clothes (men)	31	23	18
Paddle a canoe leisurely	45	33	26
Swim the backstroke	12	9	7
Go jogging (6 minutes/mile)	7	6	5
Go jogging (9 minutes/mile)	10	8	6
Play tennis	18	14	11

APPLICATIONS AND CONNECTIONS

Applications	Lesson	Example	Exercise
Smart Shopping	14-1	X	
Weather	14-2	3	44
Business	14-2		42
Transportation	14-2		43
Weather	14-2		44
Conservation	14-3	2	
Sports	14-3		25
Consumer Awareness	14-3		26
Employment	14-4		25
Computer	14-5		26
Art	14-6		15
Games	14-6		17
Crafts	14-6		19
Connections			
Geometry	14-2		32–33
Geometry	14-5		27
Geometry	14-6		16
Geometry	14-6B		3

TEAM ACTIVITIES

Multicultural Experiences

Outside Field Trips   A visit to a local manufacturer can provide students with an opportunity to see examples of the function concept in the relationships between products made, time, and costs.

Visit a bowling alley or golf course to have the professional there explain how handicaps are determined and then used.

In-Class Speakers   Ask an accountant to explain how he or she inputs data into formulas for analysis when doing income tax returns.

Invite a person who works on a salary-plus-commission basis, such as a waiter or salesperson, to talk with the class about how this payment system works.

SUPPLEMENTARY BLACKLINE MASTER BOOKLETS

Some of the blackline masters for enhancing this chapter are shown below.

Application and Interdisciplinary Activity Masters, pp. 14, 28

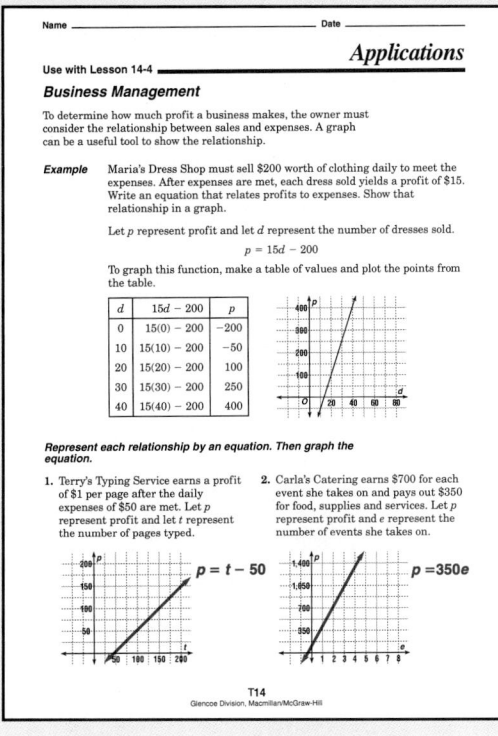

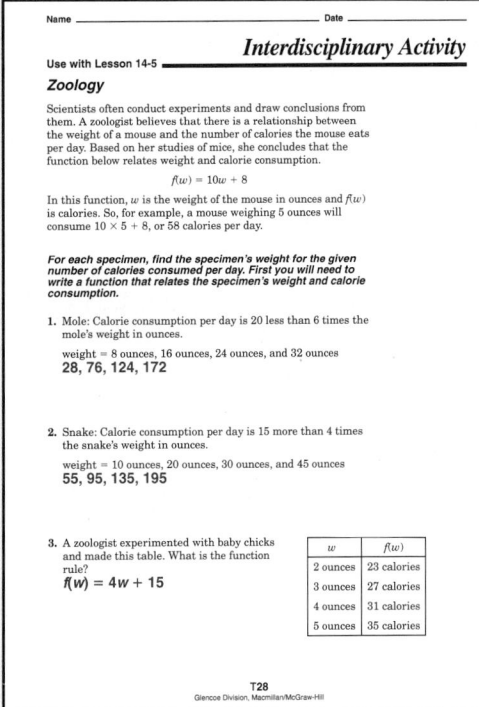

Multicultural Activity Masters, p. 14

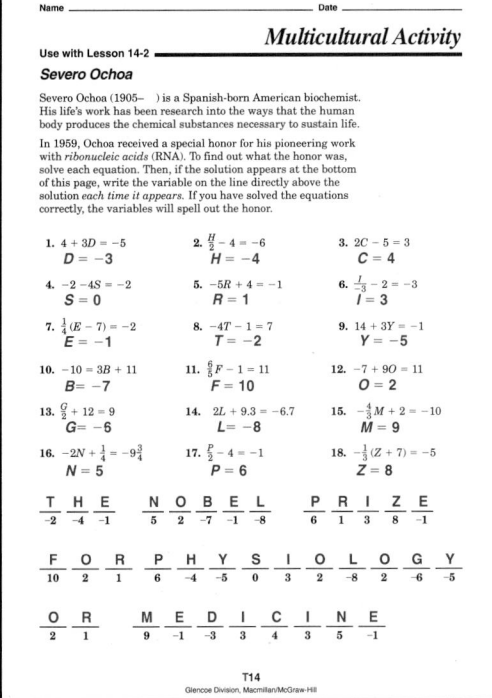

Technology Masters, p. 28

RECOMMENDED OUTSIDE RESOURCES

Books/Periodicals

National Council of Teachers of Mathematics, *Historical Topics for the Mathematical Classroom,* Reston, VA: NCTM, 1989.

Swienciki, Lawrence W., *Adventures in Pre-Algebra,* San Jose, CA. A.R. Davis, 1976.

Films/Videotapes/Videodiscs

Education in Algebra, Chicago, IL: International Film Bureau, Inc., 1963.

Software

Data Insights, (Apple II, IBM/ Tandy), Wings for Learning/ Sunburst

For addresses of companies handling software, please refer to page T24.

Glencoe's *Interactive Mathematics: Activities and Investigations* consists of 18 units that may be used as alternatives or supplemental material for *Mathematics: Applications and Connections.* The suggested unit for this chapter is Unit 16, *Growing Pains.* See page T18 for more information.

This two-page introduction to the chapter provides a visual, relevant way to engage students in the mathematics of the chapter. Questions are included that help students see the need to learn the mathematics in the chapter. Data in charts and graphs provide statistical information that students can analyze and interpret at this point as well as later in the chapter. The Chapter Project provides an activity that applies the mathematics of the chapter.

MAKING MATHEMATICS RELEVANT

Spotlight on Animals

The linear-graphing skills of this chapter contribute to the knowledge needed to construct nonlinear graphs. The population of an endangered species as a function of time is more likely to be nonlinear than linear.

Ask students to name as many endangered animals as they can and also identify those that already have become extinct. Assign a group of students to do research to find out about organizations and government efforts to protect endangered species. Have them present the class with their findings, including addresses to which the class can write for more information.

Using the Timeline

Have students find out the opening dates of several zoos other than those shown, particularly those nearest to your area. Ask them to indicate where these dates fit in the timeline. Also, have them find out when other national parks opened.

Chapter

14

Functions and Graphs

Spotlight on Animals

Have You Ever Wondered. . .

- During what time of the year the most sea creatures are stranded on beaches?

- How many species of animals are threatened or endangered?

BEACHED SEA CREATURES

number of whales, dolphins, and porpoises beached in 1990

THREATENED AND ENDANGERED WILDLIFE

Item	Mammals	Birds	Reptiles	Fishes
Endangered species, total	290	221	74	58
U.S. only	31	61	8	45
U.S. and foreign	19	15	7	2
Foreign only	240	145	59	11
Threatened species, total	30	10	32	30
U.S. only	5	7	14	24
U.S. and foreign	2	3	4	6
Foreign only	23	0	14	0

1859	1872	1889	1896
1864			
1840	1865	1890	1915

Philadelphia Zoological Society marks beginning of American zoos

Central Park Zoo opens in New York City

Yellowstone National Park opens

First American motion pictures appear in theaters

National Zoological Park opens in Washington, DC

"Have You Ever Wondered?" Answers

- Students can see from the graph that January–March is when the largest number of creatures become beached.

- The chart gives an approximate breakdown of threatened and endangered wildlife by major category. In absolute numbers, mammals are the most endangered, fish the least. In relative terms, the table cannot be used to find which class or order is the most endangered.

Have students work with partners to research the status of some endangered species whose habitat is near where they live. They can investigate what is going on locally to protect such animals. Have students display their findings in a chart.

Data Search

A question related to these data is provided in Lesson 14-4, page 545, Exercise 24.

CHAPTER PROJECT

The point of this project is to employ students' powers of observation and to organize the results of their observations as plotted points on a graph. The results will depend on your location and on the time of year in which the project is undertaken. Encourage students to look beyond cats and dogs when making their observations.

Chapter Project

Animals

Work in a group.

1. Several times each month, for the next several months, observe the animals you see each day.

2. Make a list of the animals you see.

3. Make a bar graph showing how many of each animal you see. Indicate how the number of animals you see changes with the time of the year, if it does. Indicate if the number changes with the weather. Explain why.

Looking Ahead

In this chapter, you will see how mathematics can be used to answer the questions about animals.

The major objectives of the chapter are to:

- solve problems by working backward
- solve two-step equations
- graph ordered pairs and transformations on a coordinate plane
- graph linear equations and functions by plotting points

1938

1940

First children's zoo opens in Philadelphia

1958

1965

Congress creates NASA

NASA

1989

1990

Hungary begins taking down its barbed wired border

1993

President Clinton takes office

531

Chapter Opener Transparency

Transparency 14-0 is available in the Transparency Package. It provides another full-color, motivating activity that you can use to capture students' interest.

NCTM Standards: 1–5, 7

Lesson Resources
- Study Guide Master 14-1
- Practice Master 14-1
- Enrichment Master 14-1
- Group Activity Card 14-1

 Transparency 14-1 contains the 5-Minute Check and a teaching aid for this lesson.

⏱ 5-Minute Check
(Over Chapter 13)

1. How many different meat sandwiches can Isabel make using either ham or turkey, and either whole wheat, rye, or white bread?   6 sandwiches

2. What is the probability of spinning a number less than 3 on a spinner having six regions of equal size labeled 1–6?
$\frac{1}{3}$

3. Imagine that you roll a pair of dice. Are getting a 4 on one die and an even number on the other independent or dependent events?
independent

Find the value of each expression.

4. 5!   120   5. $P(8, 3)$ 336

---

1 FOCUS

Motivating the Lesson

Situational Problem   James arrived for piano practice at 4:45 P.M. On the way from school, he stopped in at the video store for 15 minutes and also made a call from a booth for 10 minutes. It usually takes 25 minutes to get from the school to the piano teacher's house. Ask students at what time James left school.

14-1 Work Backward

Objective
Solve problems by working backward.

Sherry and her sister, Ann, each own an equal number of shares of Glaxon stock. Sherry sells one third of her shares for $2,700. What was the total value of Sherry's and Ann's stock just before the sale?

Explore   What do you know?
Each sister owns an equal number of shares of stock. Sherry sells one third of her half for $2,700.

What do you need to find?
The total value of Sherry's and Ann's stock before the sale.

Plan   Multiply to find the value of Sherry's stock. Then double the amount to find the total value of Sherry's and Ann's stock.

Solve   One third of Sherry's half is $2,700. So, Sherry's shares are worth $3 \times 2{,}700$ or $8,100. Ann has the same number of shares as Sherry. The value of their stock is the same. The total value is $2 \times 8{,}100$ or $16,200.

The value of Sherry's and Ann's stock before the sale was $16,200.

Examine   Assume Sherry's and Ann's stock was worth $16,200. The value of Sherry's stock was half of $16,200, or $8,100. She sold one third of her stock: $8,100 ÷ 3 or $2,700. Since $2,700 matches the information given, the answer is correct.

Example

Smart Shopping   Sam is planning a luncheon. He goes to the grocery store and buys a ham for $24.98 and a vegetable tray for $17.49. There is no tax on food. He gives the cashier one bill and receives less than $10 in change. What was the denomination of the bill Sam gave the cashier?

OPTIONS

Reteaching Activity

Using Problem Solving   Often a working-backward solution to a problem means using inverse operations. Guide students to see that if Sheldon sold $\frac{1}{3}$ of his shares (divided his shares by 3), then they can multiply $2,700 by 3 to find out the value of the shares he originally owned.

Study Guide Masters, p. 118

Name _____ Date _____

Study Guide Worksheet 14-1

Problem-Solving Strategy: Work Backward

At a baseball card show, Andy bought twice as many cards as Becky. Becky bought 4 fewer baseball cards than Orestes. Orestes bought 7 more baseball cards than Yoko. Yoko bought 6 baseball cards. How many baseball cards did each person buy?

Explore   What do you know?
Andy bought twice as many as Becky. Becky bought 4 fewer than Orestes. Orestes bought 7 more than Yoko. Yoko bought 6.

What do you want to find?
You want to find the number of baseball cards each person bought.

Plan   Begin with what you know, that Yoko bought 6 cards.
Work backward to solve the problem.

Solve   Start with 6.   Yoko bought 6 baseball cards.
Add 7. $6 + 7 = 13$ Orestes bought 13 baseball cards.

You can estimate the denomination of the bill by working backward. His total purchase was about $25 + $20 or $45. His change was less than $10. Estimate by adding $10 to $45. $55 is an overestimate. The denomination of the bill must be between $45 and $55. So, Sam gave the cashier a $50 bill.

Checking for Understanding

Communicating Mathematics

Read and study the lesson to answer the question.

1. **Tell** how at least two problem-solving strategies are used to solve the problem in the example. **working backward, estimation**

Guided Practice

Solve by working backward.

2. A can of evaporated milk weighs 15 ounces. Mrs. Foster uses half of the milk to make pumpkin pudding. The can and the milk that is left weigh 9 ounces. How much does the can weigh? **3 ounces**

3. Jim rented 3 times as many videotapes as Phyllis last month. Phyllis rented 4 fewer videotapes than Ed, but 4 more than Matsu. Ed rented 10 videotapes. How many videotapes did each person rent?
Jim, 18; Phyllis, 6; Ed, 10; Matsu, 2

Problem Solving

Practice

Solve. Use any strategy.

Strategies
••••••••••
Look for a pattern.
Solve a simpler problem.
Act it out.
Guess and check.
Draw a diagram.
Make a chart.
Work backward.

4. Copy and complete the table.

	4		5		0, 7
	12		13	15	Add 8, 8
Subtract 5		3	8		7, 10
Multiply by 2			16	20	14, 6

5. Ms. Lia orders an oil delivery since her oil tank reads $\frac{1}{5}$ full. After the tank is filled, it reads $\frac{9}{10}$ full. Ms. Lia receives a receipt for a delivery of 105 gallons of oil. How much oil was in the tank before the delivery? **30 gallons**

6. Suppose your locker number has three digits. The digits appear in ascending order. If the product of the digits is 216 and the sum is 19, what is your locker number? **469**

7. Carla is playing a game with her brother. She says that she has some quarters, dimes, and nickels in her pocket. She has two more dimes than quarters and three fewer nickels than dimes. How much money does she have if she has three quarters? **$1.35**

8. Sandy, Toi, and Jessie have careers as a teacher, a doctor, and an actor. If Toi doesn't want to act, and Sandy likes to grade papers, what career does each person have? **Sandy, teacher; Toi, doctor; Jessie, actor**

9. Draw as many different patterns to make a cube as you can. Cut out your patterns to make the cubes. How many different patterns did you make? **See students' work.**

Lesson 14-1 Problem-Solving Strategy: Work Backward **533**

Team Teaching

Inform the other teachers on your team that your classes are studying algebraic functions and graphs. Suggestions for curriculum integration are:

Social Studies: consumer math, economics

Science: Fahrenheit and Celsius temperatures, medicine

Art: architecture and design

Physical Education: fitness, running, swimming, skating, and skiing speeds

2 TEACH

Using Connections Ask students to suggest situations for which the working backward strategy is a reasonable method. Ask them what kinds of jobs require people to use this strategy frequently.

More Examples

For the Example

Lou bought two items of clothing, one for $15.95 and one for $21.95. He paid with four bills of the same denomination. His change was less than $5. With what bills did Lou pay the cashier? **four $10 bills**

Checking for Understanding

Exercise 1 is designed to help you assess students' understanding through reading, writing, speaking, and modeling. You should work through this exercise with your students and then monitor their work on Guided Practice Exercises 2-3.

Practice Masters, p. 118

Name _____ Date _____

Practice Worksheet 14-1

Problem-Solving Strategy: Work Backward

Solve by working backward.

1. A fence is put around a dog run 10 feet wide and 20 feet long. Enough fencing is left over to also fence a square garden with an area of 64 ft. What was the minimum length of fencing used? **92 ft**

2. A fence is put around a square dog run whose area 400 ft. Enough is left over to fence a square garden whose area 25 ft². What is the minimum amount of fencing used? **100 ft**

Solve. Use any strategy.

3. A sailboat has a triangular sail which is 14 feet by 12 feet by 8 feet. What is a reasonable estimate of the area of the sail? 500 square feet (50 square feet)

4. The sale price of a sweater was $19 after an additional $5 was taken off the sweater which was already marked "50% off." What was the original price of the sweater? **$48**

5. Describe the pattern. 30, 42, 56, 72, ... Give the next two numbers in the pattern. **The numbers are the products 5 × 6, 6 × 7, 7 × 8, and so on; 90, 110**

6. Organize the information below into a frequency table.

Favorite Colors of 7th Graders

blue	green	blue	red	red
white	green	red	blue	blue
blue	blue	red	pink	black
yellow	pink	blue	white	red

Color	Tally	Frequency
blue	卌 ||	7
green	||	2
red	卌	5
white	||	2
pink	||	2
black			1
yellow			1

T118
Glencoe Division, Macmillan/McGraw-Hill

Have students write a problem for a classmate to solve by working backward.

3 PRACTICE/APPLY

Assignment Guide
Maximum: 4–14
Minimum: 4–14

Alternate Assessment

Writing Have students work backward to find the time a trip began that ended at 8:30 A.M. and had two parts, one that took $1\frac{1}{2}$ hours and one that took 45 minutes.   6:15 A.M.

Enrichment Masters, p. 118

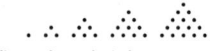
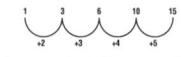

Name _____ Date _____

Enrichment Worksheet 14-1

Number Patterns

The dot diagram below illustrates a number pattern.

You can discover what number in the pattern comes next by drawing the next figure in the dot pattern. You can also use thinking with numbers. Try to see how two consecutive numbers in the pattern are related.

It looks like the next number in the pattern is obtained by adding 6 to 15. The next number in the pattern is 21. You can check this by drawing the next figure in the dot pattern.

Write the next two numbers in the number pattern for each dot diagram.

1. 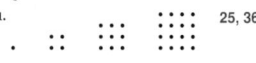   25, 36

2. 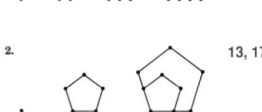    13, 17

3. A staircase is being built from cubes. How many cubes will it take to make a staircase 25 cubes high?   325

T118
Glencoe Division, Macmillan/McGraw-Hill

534

---

10. Look at the models of the triangular numbers below. How many dots would be in a triangle that has 10 dots on a side?   **55 dots**

$$1 \qquad 3 \qquad 6 \qquad 10$$

11. Mr. Rogers is delivering cartons of breakfast cereal to supermarkets. At the first supermarket, he drops off half of the cartons he has in the truck. At each of the other markets, he drops off half of the cartons he has left in the truck. At the eleventh market, he drops off 1 carton, which is the last one. How many cartons were originally in the truck?   **2,048 cartons**

12. Antonio sends letters and postcards to his friends while he is on vacation. He spends $2.48 on postage. If a stamp for a letter costs 29¢ and postcards require 19¢ postage, how many letters and how many postcards did Antonio send?   **2 letters, 10 postcards**

13. A car's gas tank contains 0.0454 m³. The capacity of the *Pierre Guillaumat*, the world's largest oil tanker, is 687,000 m³. How many times could the car fill up its tank from the fully-loaded tanker? Round your answer to the nearest tenth.   **15,132,158.6 times**

14. The rectangular solid shown is painted blue and then cut along the lines to make 1-inch cubes. How many cubes will have exactly two blue faces?   **4 cubes**

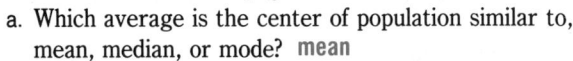
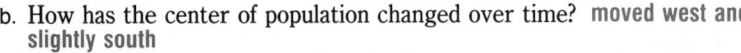

15. **Data Search**   Refer to page 652.
    a. Which average is the center of population similar to, mean, median, or mode?   **mean**
    b. How has the center of population changed over time?   **moved west and slightly south**

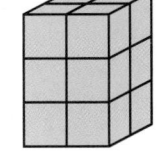

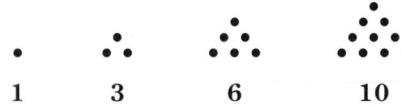

CULTURAL KALEIDOSCOPE

César Chavez

In 1988, César Chavez, protested the use of pesticides, which he said were dangerous to consumers, farm workers, and to the environment.

Mr. Chavez has devoted much of his life to helping migrant farm workers gain rights. Mr. Chavez, a farm laborer himself, began organizing farm workers in 1962 when he created the National Farm Workers Association (NFWA). In 1965, he led California grapepickers on a month-long strike that attracted liberal support throughout the country. The NFWA later merged with other organizations and in 1972 became the United Farm Workers of America (UFW). As UFW president, Mr. Chavez was involved with overall planning and strategy, training local leaders, and forming helpful political alliances. He also tried to increase public understanding of issues of concern to the UFW.

OPTIONS

Extending the Lesson

Cultural Kaleidoscope Explain to students that a union is an organization of workers who engage in collective bargaining with employers for higher wages, better working conditions, and increased benefits. Ask students to explain how they could use the working-backward strategy in collective bargaining.

Cooperative Learning Activity

Use groups of 2.
Materials: Grid paper

You've Got It Backward 14-1

• Copy onto cards the directions shown on the back of this card. Shuffle the cards and divide them into two equal piles. Write "1" on the back of each card in one pile and "2" on the back of each card in the other pile. Shade a 4 x 4 area in the center of a sheet of grid paper.

➡ Each partner selects a shaded square. (Don't forget which square you chose!) Each partner then selects one card from each pile. Follow the directions on card 1 for the square you chose and then follow the directions on card 2. (If you cannot move as indicated on the card, return the card to the bottom of the pile and draw again.) Shade the square that the two sets of directions led you to. Trade papers and cards with your partner. Work backward from the directions on the cards to find each other's starting point. The first partner to find the other partner's starting point wins the round. Play several rounds.

Glencoe Mathematics: Applications and Connections, Course 2

14-2A Two-Step Equations

A Preview of Lesson 14-2

Objective
Solve two-step equations with integers using models.

Materials
cups
counters
mats

Remember how you used cups and counters to solve two-step equations such as $3x + 1 = 7$? You can also use models to solve two-step equations with integers.

Let's start with the equation $2x + (-3) = 1$. You want to find the value of x that makes this equation true.

Try this!

Work in groups of three.

- Make a model of the equation using cups and counters. Remember, a cup represents x.

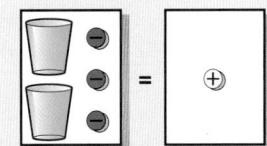

> **LOOKBACK**
>
> You can review solving two-step equations on page 232 and solving one-step equations with integers on page 284.

- Next add 3 positive counters to each side of the equation to create zero pairs on the left side. Remove the zero pairs, since their value is 0. The new equation is $2x = 4$.

- Now pair up an equal number of counters with each cup. Since each cup can be paired with 2 counters, the solution is 2.

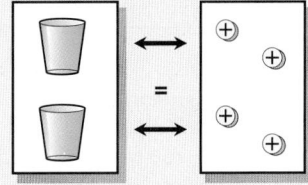

What do you think?

1. Counters need to be paired equally with cups.

1. Why is it important to get the cups on one side by themselves?

2. Why do you need to pair up an equal number of counters with each cup? Each cup must represent same number of counters.

Mathematics Lab 14-2A Two-Step Equations **535**

Interactive Mathematics Tools

This multimedia software provides an interactive lesson that is tied directly to Lesson 14-2A. Students will click and drag counters to solve two-step equations.

Lab Manual, p. 78

Name _____ Date _____

Mathematics Lab Worksheet
Use with page 535

Two-Step Equations
What do you think?

1. It is important to get the cups on one side by themselves so that the cups can be paired up with the counters.

2. An equal number of counters needs to be paired up with each cup because each cup has the same value.

Mathematics Lab 14-2A

NCTM Standards: 1–5, 9

Management Tips

For Students Provide groups with several positive and negative counters. Students should take turns modeling the solutions to the equations.

For the Overhead Projector *Overhead Manipulative Resources* provides appropriate materials for teacher or student demonstration of the activities in this Mathematics Lab.

Lab Manual You may wish to make copies of the blackline master on p. 78 of the *Lab Manual* for students to use as a recording sheet.

1 FOCUS

Introducing the Lab

Remind students of how they used cups and counters to model the solution to two-step equations in an earlier Lab. Ask them how they think solving two-step equations with integers will be different.

2 TEACH

Using Models Ask questions to make sure students understand what is meant by "zero pairs." Have students write several equations for others in the group to solve by using cups and forming zero pairs with counters.

3 PRACTICE/APPLY

Using Models Ask students to tell the number of groups that the counters must be separated into in the last step if there are 4 cups on one side instead of 2.
4 groups

Close

Have students tell, step by step, how they would model the equation $3x + (-4) = 8$. Have them tell the solution also.

535

NCTM Standards: 1–5, 7, 9, 12

Lesson Resources
- Study Guide Master 14-2
- Practice Master 14-2
- Enrichment Master 14-2
- Technology Master, p. 28
- Multicultural Activity, p. 14
- Group Activity Card 14-2

 Transparency 14-2 contains the 5-Minute Check and a teaching aid for this lesson.

🕐 5-Minute Check
(Over Lesson 14-1)

Solve by working backward.

1. Tony rented twice as many video tapes as Li, who rented 3 more video tapes than Erin. If Erin rented 4 fewer video tapes than Karl, and he rented 5 video tapes, how many video tapes did each person rent?
Tony: 8, Li: 4, Erin: 1, Karl: 5

2. Dave has 12 cards left after trading. That is one third as many as he had yesterday, which was 8 less than the day before. How many cards did Dave have on the day before yesterday?
44 cards

1 FOCUS

Motivating the Lesson

Situational Problem Tell students that Aardvark Taxis charge $1.50 for the first half mile and then $0.25 for each additional $\frac{1}{4}$ mile. Ask them to determine the cost of a 2-mile trip.

14-2 Solving Two-Step Equations

Objective

Solve two-step equations.

Have you ever ordered anything from a mail-order catalog? It can save you time and energy as well as money. But you need to make sure you always include the shipping cost in the total price.

Suppose you want to purchase two tie-dyed T-shirts from a catalog. The total price including shipping is $17. If the total shipping cost is $1, how much does each T-shirt cost?

Problem-Solving Hint
• • • • • • • • • • • • •
Work backward.

TEEN SCENE

In the 1909 Sears Roebuck and Company catalog, a boy's cotton shirt cost 35¢. Today, it can cost as much as $35—100 times as much!

LOOK BACK

You can review order of operations on page 24.

First write an equation using the information given. Let t represent the cost of each T-shirt.

Two times the cost of a T-shirt plus shipping cost is $17.

$$2 \quad \times \quad t \quad + \quad 1 \quad = \quad 17$$

The equation is $2t + 1 = 17$. This is a two-step equation because it involves two different operations, multiplication and addition. To solve this equation, we need to "undo" the operations, or work backward. In the equation $2t + 1 = 17$, the order of operation is: multiplication, then addition. To undo these operations in reverse order, we need to subtract first and then divide.

Here is how you solve the equation.

$$2t + 1 = 17$$
$$2t + 1 - 1 = 17 - 1 \quad \textit{Subtract 1 from each side.}$$

$$2t = 16$$
$$\frac{2t}{2} = \frac{16}{2} \quad \textit{Divide each side by 2.}$$
$$t = 8$$

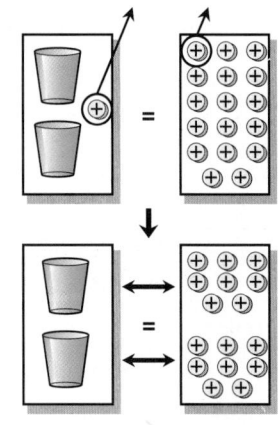

The cost of each T-shirt is $8.

OPTIONS

Gifted and Talented Needs

Write the equation $-3t + 9 = 12$ on the chalkboard. Ask students to solve it. Then ask them to solve it by *dividing* as the first step. (Point out that they must divide into *both* terms of $-3t + 9$.) Ask them if they get the same solution both times. Have them repeat the process with another two-step equation chosen from the Independent Practice exercises. Then ask them to explain when it is reasonable to use the "multiplying or dividing first" method, and to give an example to support their answer.   Sample answer: when all terms have a common divisor

You can graph the solution of the T-shirt problem by drawing a number line and marking a dot on 8.

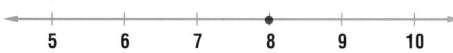

Examples

1 Solve $-2r + 8 = -4$. Graph the solution.

$$-2r + 8 = -4$$
$$-2r + 8 - 8 = -4 - 8 \qquad \textit{Subtract 8 from each side.}$$
$$-2r = -12$$
$$\frac{-2r}{-2} = \frac{-12}{-2} \qquad \textit{Divide each side by } -2$$
$$r = 6$$

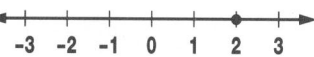

2 Solve $\frac{1}{5}(k - 8) = -3$. Graph the solution.

$$\frac{1}{5}(k - 8) = -3$$
$$5 \times \frac{1}{5}(k - 8) = 5 \times (-3) \qquad \textit{Multiply each side by 5.}$$
$$k - 8 = -15$$
$$k - 8 + 8 = -15 + 8 \qquad \textit{Add 8 to each side.}$$
$$k = -7$$

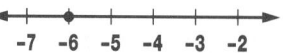

Example 3 *Problem Solving*

Weather On a January day in Buffalo, New York, the temperature dropped to $-5°$F. Find this temperature in degrees Celsius by using the formula $F = \frac{9}{5}C + 32$.

$$F = \frac{9}{5}C + 32$$
$$-5 = \frac{9}{5}C + 32 \qquad \textit{Replace F with } -5.$$
$$-5 - 32 = \frac{9}{5}C + 32 - 32 \qquad \textit{Subtract 32 from each side.}$$
$$-37 = \frac{9}{5}C$$
$$\frac{5}{9} \times (-37) = \frac{5}{9} \times \frac{9}{5}C \qquad \textit{Multiply each side by } \frac{5}{9}.$$
$$\frac{5}{9} \times (-37) = C$$

5 [÷] 9 [×] 37 [+/-] [=] -20.555556

The temperature is about $-20.6°$C.

Lesson 14-2 Solving Two-Step Equations   **537**

---

2 TEACH

Using Discussion Ask students for what purpose they "undo" operations to solve equations. Undo operations to isolate the variable on one side of the equals sign.

More Examples

For Example 1

Solve $-3t + 9 = 3$. Graph the solution.   2

For Example 2

Solve $\frac{1}{4}(r - 2) = -2$. Graph the solution. -6

For Example 3

On a July day in Detroit, Michigan, the temperature rose to $80°$ F. Find this temperature in degrees Celsius.   about $26.7°$ C

Teaching Tip Have students work in pairs, checking each others' solutions to the examples.

Checking for Understanding

Exercises 1-4 are designed to help you assess students' understanding through reading, writing, speaking, and modeling. You should work through these exercises with your students and then monitor their work on Guided Practice Exercises 5-16.

Reteaching Activity

Using Connections Guide students to undo operations in reverse order of the order of operations. Point out how this is done in each of the examples. If necessary, reinforce this concept by providing additional opportunities for students to model solutions using cups and counters.

Study Guide Masters, p. 119

Name _____ Date _____

Study Guide Worksheet 14-2

Solving Two-Step Equations

To solve two-step equations, you need to add or subtract first. You also need to multiply or divide.

Example Solve $7v - 3 = 25$.

$$7v - 3 = 25$$
$$7v - 3 + 3 = 25 + 3 \qquad \text{Add 3 to each side of the equation.}$$
$$7v = 28$$
$$\frac{7v}{7} = \frac{28}{7} \qquad \text{Divide each side of the equation by 7.}$$
$$v = 4$$

Example Solve $\frac{1}{6}(r - 3) = -5$.

$$\frac{1}{6}(r - 3) = -5$$
$$6 \times \frac{1}{6}(r - 3) = 6 \times (-5) \qquad \text{Multiply each side by 6.}$$

537

Watch for students who neglect to multiply or divide by the coefficient of the variable.

Prevent by having students always check their solutions.

Close

Have students write and solve an equation for the sentence *three times a number plus negative five is negative eleven.*
$3n + (-5) = -11; -2$

3 PRACTICE/APPLY

Assignment Guide
Maximum: 17–45
Minimum: 17–35 odd, 37–45

For **Extra Practice,** see p. 602.

Alternate Assessment

Speaking Have students explain how they would solve the equation $2x - 3 = -5$.

Practice Masters, p. 119

Name _____ Date _____

Practice Worksheet 14-2

Solving Two-Step Equations

Name the first step in solving each equation. Then solve the equation and graph the solution.

1. $6n - 2 = 22$
   Add 2 to each side; 4

2. $\frac{1}{2}(y - 3) = 12$
   Multiply each side by 2; 27

Solve each equation and graph the solution.

3. $4x - 5 = 15$

4. $\frac{w}{-3} + 14 = 5$

5. $\frac{3}{2}s - 8 = 19$

6. $24 = 17 - 2c$

7. $6 - 3b = -9$

8. $-5h - 6 = 24$

Translate each sentence into an equation. Then solve the equation and graph the solution.

9. Six less than a number divided by three is 12.
   $\frac{n}{3} - 6 = 12; 54$

10. The sum of a number and four, times 3, is negative twelve.
    $3(n + 4) = -12; -8$

T119
Glencoe Division, Macmillan/McGraw-Hill

Checking for Understanding

Communicating Mathematics

Read and study the lesson to answer each question.

1. **Show** how you would solve the equation represented by the model below.
   See Solutions Manual.

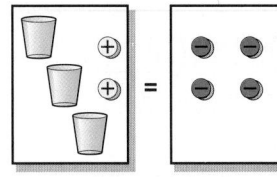

2. **Write** the inverse operation of each of the following.
   a. addition **subtraction**
   b. subtraction **addition**
   c. multiplication **division**
   d. division **multiplication**
   See students'

3. **Write** the inverse of each of five things you do to get ready for school. **work.**

4. **Draw** the graph of the temperature $-4°F$ on a number line. **See margin.**

Guided Practice

Name the first step in solving each equation. Then solve the equation and graph the solution. **For graphs for Exercises 5–13, see Solutions Manual.**

5. $3n - 5 = 16$ **7**
6. $2t - 5 = -1$ **2**
7. $\frac{p}{3} + 6 = -2$ **−24**
8. $-1 - 4y = 7$ **−2**
9. $9 - 3c = 12$ **−1**
10. $\frac{r}{5} + 3 = -5.5$ **−42.5**
11. $-2r + 3.1 = 1.7$ **0.7**
12. $\frac{1}{4}(k - 8) = -3$ **−4**
13. $\frac{t}{3} + \frac{2}{3} = 1\frac{5}{6}$ **$3\frac{1}{2}$**

Translate each sentence into an equation. Then solve the equation and graph the solution. **For graphs for Exercises 14–16, see Solutions Manual.**

14. Four times a number less five is fifteen. $4n - 5 = 15; 5$

15. Three more than a number divided by two is eleven. $3 + \frac{n}{2} = 11; 16$

16. The sum of a number and six, divided by eight, is negative two.
    $\frac{n + 6}{8} = -2; -22$

Exercises
For graphs for Exercises 17–31, see Solutions Manual.

Independent Practice

Solve each equation and graph the solution.

17. $2x + 5 = -13$ **−9**
18. $-3x - 4 = 8$ **−4**
19. $\frac{w}{-2} + 5 = 11$ **−12**
20. $\frac{m}{3} - 5 = -9$ **−12**
21. $-\frac{1}{5}(y + 1) = 4$ **−21**
22. $-12 + 8m = 36$ **6**
23. $-4m + 7.2 = -6.8$ **3.5**
24. $7 - 2m = -3$ **5**
25. $\frac{b}{-7} + 3 = -5$ **56**
26. $13 - 5n = -1.5$ **2.9**
27. $\frac{4}{3}x + 7 = -1$ **−6**
28. $\frac{1}{6}(r - 3) = -5$ **−27**
29. $-3m - 5 = -18$ **$4\frac{1}{3}$**
30. $16 = 35n - 4$ **$\frac{4}{7}$**
31. $-\frac{7}{5}s - 3 = 11$ **−10**

32. **Geometry** Solve $C = \pi d$ for d if $\pi \approx 3.14$ and $C = 100$. **≈ 31.85**

33. **Geometry** Solve $P = 2\ell + 2w$ for ℓ if $w = 4$ and $P = 40$. **16**

OPTIONS

Bell Ringer

Have students solve the following problem: *Maggie is 1 year less than 5 times as old as her cousin Mary. Together their ages total 17 years. How old is each?* Maggie is 14, her cousin is 3. Challenge students to create problems similar to this one for classmates to solve.

Additional Answer

4.
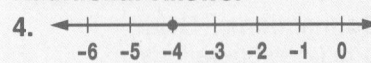

Translate each sentence into an equation. Then solve the equation and graph the solution. **For graphs for Exercises 34–36, see Solutions Manual.**

34. Seven plus the quotient of a number and four is two. $7 + \frac{n}{4} = 2$; -20

35. Three more than the product of a number and five is negative seven.
$3 + 5n = -7$; -2

36. Ten less than twice a number is sixteen.
$2n - 10 = 16$; 13

Mixed Review
37. Is $237 + 412 = 649$ reasonable? *(Lesson 1-4)* **yes**

38. Solve $r = -24 \div 8$ *(Lesson 7-8)* -3

39. **Smart Shopping** Jeanne finds a $52 sweater marked down $13. Express this price reduction as a percent. *(Lesson 11-8)* **25%**

40. **Diets** Elaine Mann weighed 142 pounds when she began her diet. After several months on the diet, she weighed 125 pounds. Find the percent of decrease for Mrs. Mann's body weight. *(Lesson 12-7)* $\approx$ **12% decrease**

41. Evaluate $C(6, 2)$. *(Lesson 13-8)* **15**

Problem Solving and Applications
42. **Business** Dave and three of his friends started a lawn mowing business during the summer. At the end of the summer, they divided the profits equally. With his share of the profits, plus a $50 gift certificate from his parents, Dave had just enough money to buy the new bike he wanted. The bike cost $210.
$160
   a. How much did each of the boys earn in their lawn mowing business?
   b. Graph the solution. **See Solutions Manual.**

43. **Transportation** Ms. Jackson takes a taxi from the airport to her home. The cost of a taxi is $3, plus 60¢ for each mile traveled.
   a. If she is charged $15.60 at the end of the trip, how many miles did she travel? **21 miles**
   b. Graph the solution. **See Solutions Manual.**

44. **Weather** The graph at the right shows the low temperatures for a week in January in Muskegon, Michigan.
   a. Use the formula $C = \frac{5}{9} \times (F - 32)$ to convert the low temperature on January 21 to degrees Celsius. **0°C**
   b. Convert the low temperature on January 24 to degrees Celsius. **$-26.1°$C**
   c. Graph both of these temperatures on a number line. **See Solutions Manual.**

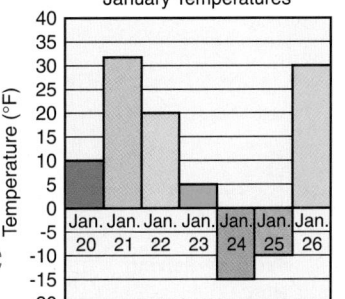
January Temperatures

45. **Critical Thinking** Solve the equation $-3x - 4 = x + 2$. Graph the solution.
$x = -1\frac{1}{2}$; **See Solutions Manual for graph.**

Lesson 14-2 Solving Two-Step Equations **539**

Extending the Lesson

Using Applications Have students write a quiz assessing understanding of two-step equations including integers and integer solutions. The quiz should contain word problems as well as exercises.

Cooperative Learning Activity

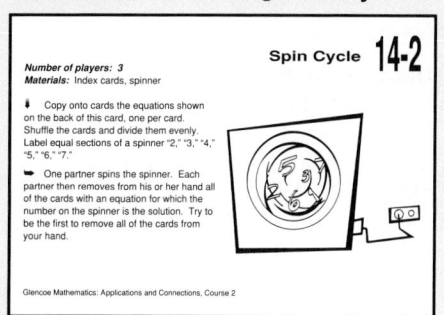

Spin Cycle **14-2**

Number of players: 3
Materials: Index cards, spinner

↓ Copy onto cards the equations shown on the back of this card, one per card. Shuffle the cards and divide them evenly. Label equal sections of a spinner "2," "3," "4," "5," "6," "7."

➥ One partner spins the spinner. Each partner then removes from his or her hand all of the cards with an equation for which the number on the spinner is the solution. Try to be the first to remove all of the cards from your hand.

Glencoe Mathematics: Applications and Connections, Course 2

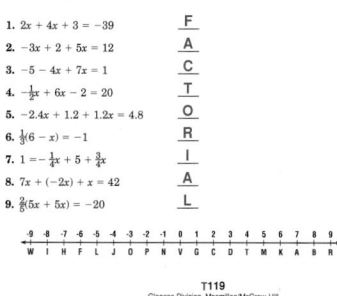
539

NCTM Standards: 1–5, 7–9

Lesson Resources
- Study Guide Master 14-3
- Practice Master 14-3
- Enrichment Master 14-3
- Evaluation Master, Quiz A, p. 124
- Group Activity Card 14-3

 Transparency 14-3 contains the 5-Minute Check and a teaching aid for this lesson.

🕐 5-Minute Check
(Over Lesson 14-2)

1. Solve the equation and graph the solution:
$-3t + 5 = -10$ 5

```
|---|---|---|---|---|---|--->
0   1   2   3   4   5   6
```

2. Translate the sentence into an equation. Then solve the equation and graph the solution: Five less than four times a number is negative one.
$4n - 5 = -1$; 1

```
<---|---|---|---|---|---|---|--->
   -3  -2  -1   0   1   2   3
```

---

1 FOCUS

Motivating the Lesson

Activity The following recipe for strawberry sherbet serves four people.
2 cups of strawberries
$\frac{1}{2}$ cup of sugar
1 cup of plain yogurt
1 tablespoon of lemon juice
Challenge students to write an equation with two variables to apply the recipe to the whole class.

2 TEACH

Using Discussion Encourage students to choose integers close to zero, including negative integers, when selecting values for a variable.

14-3 Equations with Two Variables

Objective
Solve equations with two variables.

Words to Learn
Ordered pair

Bob Learn, Jr., has scored more "300 games" in bowling than any other bowler. A "300 game" means all strikes, or a perfect score. Since average bowlers are not that good, they are given a "handicap" in order to compete with skilled bowlers like Mr. Learn. A handicap is an advantage given to a player in the form of extra points.

Suppose you are given a handicap of 8 points. Your final score would be $x + 8$, where x is your actual score. The table below shows how you can find the final scores given three actual scores.

DID YOU KNOW

The earliest known reference to bowling in the United States is in Washington Irving's short story "Rip Van Winkle," which was written in 1819–1820.

Actual Score	Add the Handicap	Final Score
x	$x + 8$	y
102	$102 + 8$	110
120	$120 + 8$	128
127	$127 + 8$	135

The relationship between the actual score and the final score can be written as an equation with two variables. Let x represent your actual score and y represent your final score, as shown in the table. The equation, then, is $y = x + 8$.

Recall that solving an equation means to replace the variable so that you have a true sentence. A solution of an equation with two variables consists of two numbers, one for each variable. When you replace the variables with the numbers, the result is a true sentence.

A solution of an equation with two variables is usually written as an **ordered pair,** (x, y). Based on the table above, we know that three solutions to the equation $y = x + 8$ are (102, 110), (120, 128), and (127, 135).

Problem-Solving Hint
• • • • • • • • • •
Use a table.

Example 1

Find four solutions for $y = 2x - 3$. Write the solutions as ordered pairs.

Select any four values for x. We chose 2, 1, 0, and -1. Substitute these values for x to find y and complete the table on the next page.

OPTIONS

Reteaching Activity

Using Brainstorming Provide groups of students with an ordered pair. Have them list several equations the ordered pair will satisfy. Repeat with other ordered pairs.

Study Guide Masters, p. 120

Name _____ Date _____

Study Guide Worksheet 14-3

Equations with Two Variables

An ordered pair that makes an equation true is a solution for the equation.

Example   Find four solutions for the equation $y = \frac{1}{2}x - 1$.

Choose values for x.	Calculate y values.	Write ordered pairs.
Let $x = -4$.	$y = \frac{1}{2}(-4) - 1 = -3$	$(-4, -3)$
Let $x = -2$.	$y = \frac{1}{2}(-2) - 1 = -2$	$(-2, -2)$
Let $x = 0$.	$y = \frac{1}{2}(0) - 1 = -1$	$(0, -1)$
Let $x = 2$.	$y = \frac{1}{2}(2) - 1 = 0$	$(2, 0)$

Four solutions are $(-4, -3), (-2, -2), (0, -1), (2, 0)$.

x	2x − 3	y	(x, y)
2	2(2) − 3	1	(2, 1)
1	2(1) − 3	−1	(1, −1)
0	2(0) − 3	−3	(0, −3)
−1	2(−1) − 3	−5	(−1, −5)

Four solutions are (2, 1), (1, −1), (0, −3), and (−1, −5).

Example 2 *Problem Solving*

Conservation In order to conserve America's forests, lumber companies are often required to replace the trees they cut down. About half of the new trees planted are expected to survive and become full-grown trees. Find out how many pine trees are expected to survive if 154 pine trees are planted.

Let x represent the number of new trees planted. Let y represent the number of full-grown trees.

Write an equation.

$$\left(\begin{array}{c}\text{Number of new trees}\\\text{expected to survive}\end{array}\right) = \frac{1}{2} \times \left(\begin{array}{c}\text{Number of new}\\\text{trees planted}\end{array}\right)$$
$$y \qquad\qquad = \frac{1}{2} \times \qquad x$$

The equation is $y = \frac{1}{2}x$.

Now find the number of pine trees expected to survive.

$y = \frac{1}{2}x$
$\quad = \frac{1}{2}(154)$ *Replace x with 154.*
$\quad = 77$

About 77 pine trees are expected to survive.

Checking for Understanding

Communicating Mathematics

Read and study the lesson to answer each question.

1. **Tell** why (1, −1) is a solution of $y = 3x − 4$. $-1 = 3(1) − 4$

2. **Write** two solutions of $y = x − 2$. Sample answers: (1, −1), (−2, −4)

3. **Show** whether (6, 12) is a solution to the equation in Example 2.
$\frac{1}{2}x = \frac{1}{2} \cdot 6 = 3; y = 12; 3 \neq 12$, therefore it is not a solution.

Guided Practice

Copy and complete the table for each equation. Then use the results to write four solutions for each equation. Write the solutions as ordered pairs.

4. $y = 2x + 1$

x	2x + 1	y
1	2(1) + 1	3, (1, 3)
2	2(2) + 1	5, (2, 5)
3	2(3) + 1	7, (3, 7)
4	2(4) + 1	9, (4, 9)

5. $y = 3x$

x	3x	y
−1	3(−1)	−3, (−1, −3)
0	3( )	0, 0, (0, 0)
1	3( )	1, 3, (1, 3)
2	3( )	2, 6, (2, 6)

Lesson 14-3 Equations with Two Variables   **541**

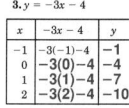

Bell Ringer

Ask students to write an equation with two variables that they could use to express the time it takes in minutes (m) to print a number of pages (p), if it takes 20 seconds to set up the printer and each page takes 10 seconds to print.
$m = \frac{1}{6}p + \frac{1}{3}$

 **Interactive Mathematics Tools**

This multimedia software provides an interactive lesson that is tied directly to Lesson 14-3. Students will explore linear functions and graphs.

542

---

6. $y = -2x + 3$

x	$-2x + 3$	*y*	
−1	−2( )+3		−1, 5, (−1, 5)
0	−2( )+3		0, 3, (0, 3)
1	−2( )+3		1, 1, (1, 1)
2			−2 (2) + 3, −1, (2, −1)

7. $y = 1.5x$

x	1.5x	*y*	
1			1.5(1), 1.5, (1, 1.5)
2			1.5(2), 3, (2, 3)
3			1.5(3), 4.5, (3, 4.5)
4			1.5(4), 6, (4, 6)

Exercises   For sample answers for Exercises 8–19, see Solutions Manual.

Independent Practice

Find four solutions for each equation. Write your solutions as ordered pairs.

8. $y = 2x + 3$ 9. $y = x - 2$ 10. $y = 3x - 1$

11. $y = 5x$ 12. $y = 4x - 1$ 13. $y = -2x$

14. $y = -x - 2$ 15. $y = -2x + 2$ 16. $y = \frac{1}{4}x$

17. $y = \frac{1}{4}x + 1$ 18. $y = \frac{1}{2}x - 1$ 19. $y = -2$

Translate each of the following into an equation. Then find four solutions for each equation. **For answers to Exercises 20–21, see Solutions Manual.**

20. Luis makes $5 per hour. How much does he make in *x* hours?

21. A plumber charges an initial fee of $25, plus $35 for each hour he works. How much does he charge for *x* hours?

Mixed Review

22. $3,000,000 is the winning prize in the Ohio lottery. Express this amount in scientific notation. *(Lesson 2-6)* 3.0×10^6

23. Express $\frac{5}{8}$ as a decimal. *(Lesson 4-7)* **0.625**

24. Solve $2q + 6 = -20$. *(Lesson 14-2)* **−13**

25c. (104, 86), (98, 80), (102, 84), (108, 90), (original score, handicap score)

Problem Solving and Applications

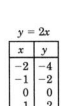

25. **Sports** Like bowling, golf is a game in which players can be given a handicap in order to compete with more skillful players. Since the goal in golf is to get the *lowest* possible score, the handicap is *subtracted* from the actual score.

a. If a golfer is given a handicap of 18 strokes, write an equation for the final score given the actual score. $f = g - 18$

b. If the golfer's actual scores are 104, 98, 102, and 108, what are her final scores? **86, 80, 84, 90**

c. Write the solutions as ordered pairs. Explain what the numbers in the ordered pairs mean.

26. **Consumer Awareness** To rent videos from The Video Store, you must pay a one-time $5 membership fee and then a $2 daily fee for each tape rented.

27. **Sample answers:** (1, 2), (2, 3), (3, 4), (0, 1)

a. Write an equation for the cost of renting tapes on your first visit to The Video Store. $y = 5 + 2x$

b. How much would you have to pay if you rented three videos? **$11**

27. **Critical Thinking** Find four solutions for the equation $y - x = 1$.

28. **Journal Entry** What do you think is the most important concept you have learned in this chapter? Explain why you think it is important. **See students' work.**

542   Chapter 14 Functions and Graphs

14-4 Graphing Equations with Two Variables

Objective
Graph equations by plotting points.

Words to Learn
linear equation

"Don't use up all the hot water!" Have you ever heard this when you were taking a shower? A shower uses about 5 gallons of water per minute. If you want to estimate how much water you are using in the shower, you can use the equation $y = 5x$, where x is the number of minutes you are in the shower, and y is the number of gallons of water.

This equation can be graphed on a coordinate system.

Step 1
Make a table to find at least four solutions to the equation.

x	5x	y	(x, y)
0	5(0)	0	(0, 0)
1	5(1)	5	(1, 5)
2	5(2)	10	(2, 10)
3	5(3)	15	(3, 15)

LOOK BACK
You can review the coordinate system on page 259.

Step 2
Graph the solutions on a coordinate system.

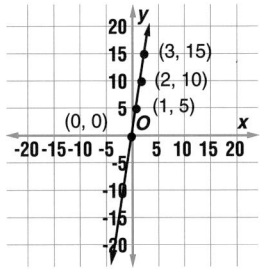

Estimation Hint
• • • • • • • • • • • •
Graphs are useful for approximating answers to equations. For example, by looking at the graph at the right, you can estimate how many gallons of water are used in $2\frac{1}{2}$ minutes.

Step 3
Draw a line passing through the points.

The line is the graph of *all* solutions for $y = 5x$.

An equation like $y = 5x$ is called a **linear equation** because its graph is a straight line. Only two points are needed to graph the line. However, graph more points as a check for accuracy.

Lesson 14-4 Graphing Equations with Two Variables **543**

NCTM Standards: 1–5, 7, 9, 12

Lesson Resources
• Study Guide Master 14-4
• Practice Master 14-4
• Enrichment Master 14-4
• Application Master, p. 14
• Group Activity Card 14-4

 Transparency 14-4 contains the 5-Minute Check and a teaching aid for this lesson.

5-Minute Check
(Over Lesson 14-3)
Find four solutions to each equation. Write your solutions as ordered pairs.
Answers will vary; samples are given.

1. $y = x - 3$ $(-1, -4)$, $(0, -3)$, $(1, -2)$, $(2, -1)$
2. $y = -4x$ $(-1, 4)$, $(0, 0)$, $(1, -4)$, $(2, -8)$
3. $y = -3x + 2$ $(-1, 5)$, $(0, 2)$, $(1, -1)$, $(2, -4)$
4. Translate the following into an equation. Then find four solutions for it. *An electrician charges an initial fee of $40, plus $45 for every hour she works. How much does she charge for x hours?* $y = 45x + 40$; $(1, 85)$, $(2, 130)$, $(3, 175)$, $(4, 220)$

1 FOCUS

Motivating the Lesson

Activity Tell students that some joggers burn 2 calories for every 3 minutes they jog. Ask students to try to make a graph to show this relationship.

2 TEACH

Using Applications Have each group of students write an equation in two variables. Then have them make a table with at least four solutions to their equation and graph the equation on a coordinate system.

OPTIONS

Reteaching Activity

Using Number Sense Guide students to choose *x*-values of 0, 1, and 2 when making a table in order to graph a linear equation.

Study Guide Masters, p. 121

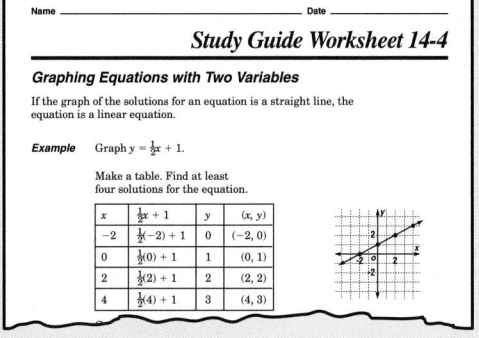

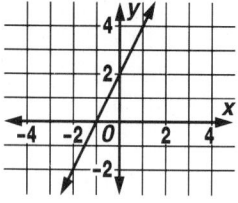
Checking for Understanding

Exercises 1-3 are designed to help you assess students' understanding through reading, writing, speaking, and modeling. You should work through these exercises with your students and then monitor their work on Guided Practice Exercises 4-7.

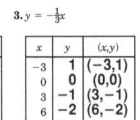
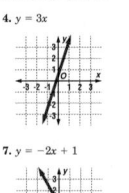 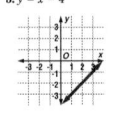 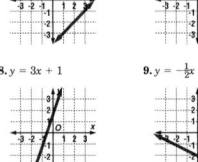
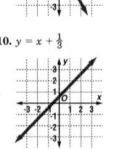 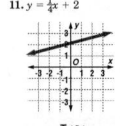 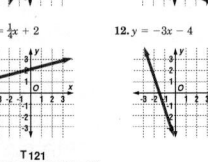
544

Graph the equation $y = 2x - 1$.

Step 1
Make a table to find several solutions.

x	2x − 1	y	(x, y)
2	2(2) − 1	3	(2, 3)
1	2(1) − 1	1	(1, 1)
0	2(0) − 1	−1	(0, −1)
−1	2(−1) − 1	−3	(−1, −3)

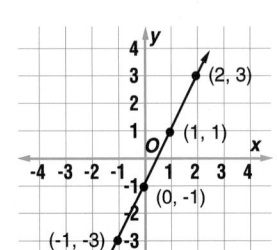

Technology Activity

You can learn how to graph lines on a graphing calculator in Technology Activity 5 on page 648.

Step 2
Graph the solutions on a coordinate system.

Step 3
Draw a line through the points.

Checking for Understanding

Read and study the lesson to answer each question. **See Solutions Manual.**

Communicating Mathematics

2. *x* must be positive; negative minutes don't make sense.

1. **Write**, in your own words, the three steps you take to graph an equation.

2. **Tell** why only those solutions graphed in the first quadrant for the equation $y = 5x$ on page 543 make sense when related to the use of hot water.

3. **Tell** why the equation in the example is a linear equation. **Its graph is a straight line.** **For graphs for Exercises 4–7, see Solutions Manual.**

Guided Practice

Copy and complete each table. Then graph the equation.

4. $y = 3x$

x	y	(x, y)
2		
1		
0		
−1		

6, (2, 6)
3, (1, 3)
0, (0, 0)
−3, (−1, −3)

5. $y = 2x + 2$

x	y	(x, y)
1		
0		
−1		
−2		

4, (1, 4)
2, (0, 2)
0, (−1, 0)
−2, (−2, −2)

6. Graph $y = 2x - 5$.

7. Graph $y = -\frac{1}{2}x$.

Exercises

Independent Practice

Graph each equation. **For answers to Exercises 8–16, see Solutions Manual.**

8. $y = 4x$ 9. $y = x - 3$ 10. $y = -2x + 2$

11. $y = -x + 2$ 12. $y = -3x - 1$ 13. $y = 4x - 3$

14. $y = \frac{1}{2}x + 1$ 15. $y = x + \frac{1}{2}$ 16. $y = \frac{1}{4}x + 2$

OPTIONS

Meeting Needs of Middle School Students

Discuss how graphs in two variables are used frequently to show trends and make predictions. Talk with students about careers in which making or interpreting these kinds of graphs is part of the job.

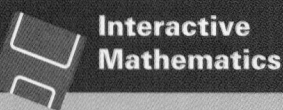

Interactive Mathematics Tools

This multimedia software provides an interactive lesson that is tied directly to Lesson 14-4. Students will use changeable graphs to explore linear and quadratic functions.

For graphs for Exercises 17–19, see Solutions Manual.
Translate each of the following into an equation. Then graph.

17. The first number is three more than the second. $x = y + 3$

18. The first number is two times the second number less five. $x = 2y - 5$

19. The first number is four more than negative three times the second number. $x = -3y + 4$

Mixed Review 20. Complete: 36 oz = __?__ lb *(Lesson 6-6)* $2\frac{1}{4}$

25. Substitute the x and y values back into the equation to see if it is true.

21. **Geometry** Find the missing length in the triangle at the right. *(Lesson 9-4)* **8 m**

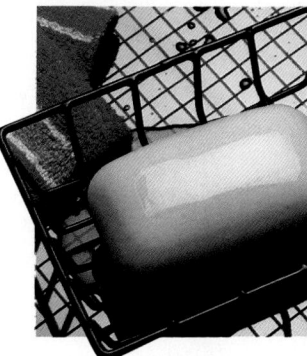

10 m
6 m
x m

22. Find four solutions of $y = -3x + 7$. Write the solutions as ordered pairs. *(Lesson 14-3)* **Sample answers: (−1, 10), (0, 7), (1, 4), (2, 1)**

Problem Solving and Applications

24. See Solutions Manual.

23. **Employment** Angel gets paid $6 per hour for her job at a fast-food restaurant. $y = 6x$
   a. Write an equation that tells how much money Angel makes in x hours.
   b. Graph the equation. Use the graph to estimate how much she will make if she works 7.5 hours. **See Solutions Manual for graph; about $45**

DATA SEARCH

24. **Data Search** Refer to pages 530 and 531. Make a graph showing the total number of endangered species according to classification and location.

25. **Critical Thinking** How can you tell whether a point that appears to lie on a line on a coordinate grid is really on the line?

26. **Journal Entry** How many minutes do you spend in the shower? Use the graph on page 543 to estimate how much water you use in the shower. Then use the equation $y = 5x$ to find out how much water you use. **See students' work.**

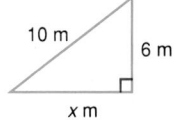

Close

Have students name all the steps involved in graphing a linear equation. Find at least two solutions to the equation, graph the ordered pairs on a coordinate system, then draw a line to connect the points.

3 PRACTICE/APPLY

Assignment Guide
Maximum: 8–26
Minimum: 9–19 odd, 20–23, 25
All: Mid-Chapter Review

For **Extra Practice**, see p. 603.

Alternate Assessment

Writing Have students explain how a graph of a linear equation shows solutions to that equation. Sample answer: It is a line connecting all points indicated by the ordered pairs that are solutions to the equation.

Assessment: Mid-Chapter Review

1. Two whole numbers have a sum of 15 and a product of 54. What are the numbers? *(Lesson 14-1)* **6 and 9**

For graphs for Exercises 2–4, see Solutions Manual.
Solve each equation and graph the solution. *(Lesson 14-2)*

2. $4x + 1 = -15$ **−4**

3. $-\frac{1}{3}(n + 7) = 5$ **−22**

4. $9 - 5x = -6$ **3**

For answers to Exercises 5–7, see Solutions Manual.
Find four solutions for each equation. Write the solutions as ordered pairs. Then graph each equation. *(Lessons 14-3, 14-4)*

5. $y = -x + 3$

6. $y = \frac{1}{2}x + 3$

7. $y = 5x - 2$

Lesson 14-4 Graphing Equations with Two Variables **545**

Extending the Lesson

Using Critical Thinking Tell students that the y-intercept is the y-value at the point where the graph crosses the y-axis. Challenge them to find the y-intercept without graphing the equation. Use $x = 0$ for the x-coordinate of the ordered pair.

Cooperative Learning Activity

It's a Hit 14-4

Number of players: 2
Materials: Grid paper

• Copy onto cards the equations shown on the back of this card, one per card. Shuffle the cards and place them face down in a pile. Write the equations on a sheet of paper.

▶ Each partner selects a card and graphs the equation shown. (Remember, to graph an equation, make a table to find solutions.) Then partners take turns trying to guess which equation the other partner graphed by calling out ordered pairs. If the ordered pair names a point on the line you graphed, say "Hit." If the ordered pair does not name a point on the line you graphed, say "Miss." Try to be the first to guess which of the ten equations your partner graphed. (Hint: You should be able to guess the equation after you have guessed any two points on the line.)

Glencoe Mathematics: Applications and Connections, Course 2

Enrichment Masters, p. 121

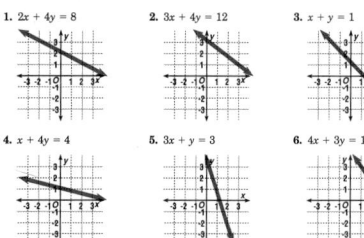

Name _____ Date _____

Enrichment Worksheet 14-4

X-Intercept and Y-Intercept

One way to graph an equation such as $2x + 3y = 6$ is to make a table of values first. However, there is an easier way. Find the coordinates of the points where the graph crosses the axes.

The x-coordinate of the point where the graph crosses the x-axis is called the x-intercept of the graph. The y-coordinate of the point where the graph crosses the y-axis is called the y-intercept.

Here is how you can graph $2x + 3y = 6$.

Let $x = 0$.
$$2(0) + 3y = 6$$
$$3y = 6$$
$$y = 2$$
So, $(0, 2)$ is on the graph of $2x + 3y = 6$.

Let $y = 0$.
$$2x + 3(0) = 6$$
$$2x = 6$$
$$x = 3$$
So, $(3, 0)$ is on the graph of $2x + 3y = 6$.
Now draw a line through the points $(3, 0)$ and $(0, 2)$.

Use x-intercepts and y-intercepts to graph each equation.

1. $2x + 4y = 8$
2. $3x + 4y = 12$
3. $x + y = 1$

4. $x + 4y = 4$
5. $3x + y = 3$
6. $4x + 3y = 12$

T121
Glencoe Division, Macmillan/McGraw-Hill

NCTM Standards: 1–5, 7, 9, 10

Management Tips

For Students If the classroom does not have a clock, use a wrist watch and be the minute timer, or have students work with partners and take turns timing one another.

For the Overhead Projector *Overhead Manipulative Resources* provides appropriate materials for teacher or student demonstration of the activities in this Mathematics Lab.

1 FOCUS

Introducing the Lab

Ask students to guess how many breaths they take in a minute, and to record their guesses.

2 TEACH

Using Number Sense You can save time, or increase the number of trials by having students time their breathing for only 15 or 30 seconds and then multiply to find breaths per minute.

3 PRACTICE/APPLY

Using Applications Ask students to name other functions of time. Suggest that students guess how often they blink in a minute, and then work with partners to time themselves.

Close

Have students name something else that is a function of time, and then name something that is a function of distance. Sample answers: time: distance travelled; distance: rate and time

---

Objective
Use a function rule to find the output of a function.

Materials
clock with second hand
graph paper

Do you ever have to remind yourself to breathe? Probably not. Breathing is something we do naturally, without even thinking about it.

In this lab, you will learn how breathing is a *function* of time. That is, the number of times you breathe is related to time.

Try this!

- Sit quietly at your desk facing the clock. Count the number of times you breathe *out* in one minute. Record your result. Repeat four more times and record each result.

- Find the mean of the five results. This is the average number of times you breathe per minute. Copy the table below and use this average to complete it.

LOOKBACK
You can review mean on page 104.

Minutes	Minutes × Average Breaths per Minute	Total Breaths
1	1× __?__	
2	2× __?__	
3	3× __?__	
4	4× __?__	
5	5× __?__	
6	6× __?__	

DID YOU KNOW

Hiccups are usually caused by improper digestion of food. When you hiccup, the large muscle that controls your breathing, called the diaphragm, jerks quickly. It causes you to take a sudden sharp breath of air—a hiccup!

In this table, the minutes are called *input* values and the total breaths are called *output* values. The middle column contains the *function rule*. When you input a value into the function rule, you get an output value. Since the output depends on the input, we call this a function. We can say that the number of breaths is a function of time.

What do you think?

1. Graph the ordered pair (minutes, breaths). **See students' work.**
2. How can you use the graphs to estimate the number of breaths you take in 12 minutes? **Extend the graph.**

Extension

3. Repeat this lab using heartbeats per minute. **See students' work.**

OPTIONS

Lab Manual You may wish to make copies of the blackline master on p. 79 of the *Lab Manual* for students to use as a recording sheet.

Lab Manual, p. 79

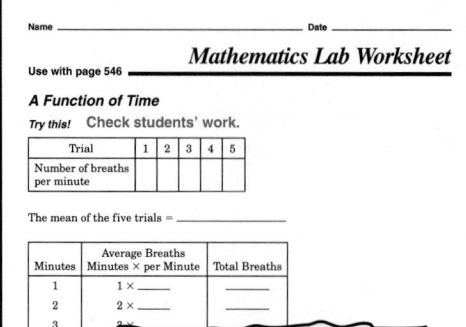

14-5 Functions

Objectives

Complete function tables.
Graph functions.

Words to Learn

function

Modern banking began in the thirteenth century in Italy. The early Italian bankers carried out their business on benches in the street. These benches were called "bancos," which is where we get our word for "bank."

Banking has come a long way since then. Today, we don't even have to talk to another human being to withdraw money from the bank! Automatic teller machines (ATMs) can do that for us. We *input* the amount we need, and the machine *outputs* our money. This relationship is an example of a **function**.

In mathematics, we input a number into a function and compute to find the output. The output produced depends on the *function rule* used. When you use an ATM, the amount of money you ask for determines the amount of money you withdraw. When you use math functions, the output also depends on the input. In mathematics, we say that the output *is a function of* the input.

Example 1

Find the output, given the input and the function rule.

Input: 11, 12, 13

Function rule: The output is double the input.

We can write the function rule as:
$$2 \times input = output.$$

Now make a function table to organize the information.

Input	Function Rule 2 × Input	Output
11	2 × 11	22
12	2 × 12	24
13	2 × 13	26

Place each input number into the function rule. Then compute.

The output is 22, 24, and 26.

Lesson 14-5 Functions **547**

Classroom Vignette

"Up to this point, most students have used functions only in formulas like those for perimeter, area, and volume. I have my students describe the role functions play in developing those formulas."

Jack Price
Author

14-5 Lesson Notes

NCTM Standards: 1–5, 7, 8, 12

Lesson Resources
- Study Guide Master 14-5
- Practice Master 14-5
- Enrichment Master 14-5
- Technology Master, p. 14
- Interdisciplinary Master, p. 28
- Group Activity Card 14-5

Transparency 14-5 contains the 5-Minute Check and a teaching aid for this lesson.

⏱ 5-Minute Check
(Over Lesson 14-4)

Graph each equation.

1. $y = -\frac{1}{2}x$

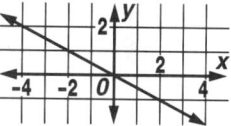

2. $y = x + 1.5$

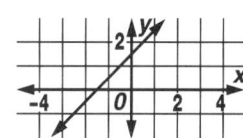

3. $y = x - 2$

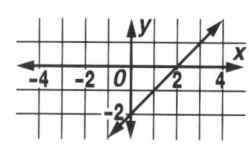

1 FOCUS

Motivating the Lesson

Questioning Have students read the opening paragraphs. Ask them to name the function rule used by the ATM to output money. Then ask them to name other examples of functions found in everyday life.

Using Graphing Ask students what they can say about the input to an ATM and its output of cash. What equation expresses the relationship? What graph can be drawn?   Sample answer: $y = x$
Graph:

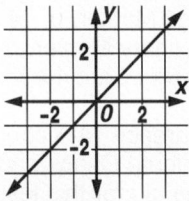

More Examples

For Example 1

Find the output, given the input and the function rule.
Input: 8, 9, 10
Function rule: the output is triple the input   24, 27, 30

For Example 2

Find the output for the function $f(x) = 2x - 4$, given $x = -1, 1, 2,$ and 3.
$-6, -2, 0,$ and 2

For Example 3

Graph $f(x) = -3x + 1.$

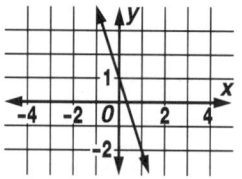

Checking for Understanding

Exercises 1-3 are designed to help you assess students' understanding through reading, writing, speaking, and modeling. You should work through these exercises with your students and then monitor their work on Guided Practice Exercises 4-7.

548

We can write functions using algebraic notation. Let x represent the input numbers. The function rule in Example 1 can be written as $2 \times x$, or $2x$.

The output is usually represented by the notation $f(x)$. This is read *f of x*, which means *function of x*. So, the function in Example 1 can be written as $f(x) = 2x$.

Example 2

Find the output for the function $f(x) = 3x + 5$, given $x = -1, 1, 2,$ and 3.

Make a function table.

The output, $f(x)$, is 2, 8, 11, and 14.

Input	Function Rule	Output
x	**3x + 5**	**f(x)**
−1	3(−1) + 5	2
1	3(1) + 5	8
2	3(2) + 5	11
3	3(3) + 5	14

The solutions for a function are usually written as ordered pairs, $(x, f(x))$. Four solutions for the function in Example 2 are $(-1, 2)$, $(1, 8)$, $(2, 11)$, and $(3, 14)$.

In Example 3, you will use the solutions of a function to graph the function.

Example 3

Graph $f(x) = -2x + 1.$

First make a function table. List at least three values for x.

x	−2x + 1	f(x)	(x, f(x))
1	−2(1) + 1	−1	(1, −1)
0	−2(0) + 1	1	(0, 1)
−1	−2(−1) + 1	3	(−1, 3)

Graph the ordered pairs. Draw a line passing through the points.

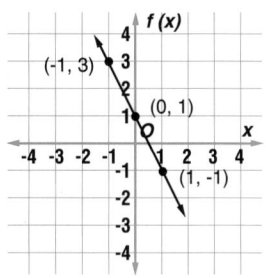

---

66 When am I ever going to use this? 99

Accountants keep track of how money is spent and received. They use functions to help them analyze data. Sometimes, they graph functions so they can get a better picture of what is happening with the budget. These graphs are helpful for people in management who need to make decisions on the budget.

For more information on accounting, contact: American Institute of Certified Public Accountants 1211 Ave. of the Americas New York, NY 10036.

OPTIONS

Reteaching Activity

Using Tables Have students work with partners to complete partially filled-in function tables in which some of the input or output numbers are missing.

Checking for Understanding

Communicating Mathematics

Read and study the lesson to answer each question.

1. **Tell,** in your own words, what $f(x)$ means. **output value**

2. $f(x) = 2x - 5$
2. **Write** the function rule for *the output is 5 less than twice the input.*

3. **Tell** how you would label the axes for the graph of the function $f(x) = -2x + 3$. **The x-axis is x; y-axis is f(x).**

For graphs for Exercises 4–7, see Solutions Manual.

Guided Practice Copy and complete each function table. Then graph the function.

4.

x	x + 3	f(x)
−5		−5 + 3, −2
−1		−1 + 3, 2
0		0 + 3, 3
3		3 + 3, 6

5.

x	3x	f(x)
−2		3(−2), −6
1		3(1), 3
3		3(3), 9
5		3(5), 15

6.

x	−x + 3	f(x)
−2		−(−2) + 3, 5
−1		−(−1) + 3, 4
2		−2 + 3, 1
4		−4 + 3, −1

7. −2(−3) − 3, 3
−2(−1) − 3, −1
−2(1) − 3, −5
−2(3) − 3, −9

7.

x	−2x − 3	f(x)
−3		
−1		
1		
3		

Exercises

Independent Practice

Find the output for each function, given the input and the function rule.

8. $f(x) = 3x - 1$
   $x = -3, -1, 2, 3$

9. $f(x) = 6x$
   $x = -1, 0, \frac{3}{2}, 2$

10. $f(x) = -3x + 4$
    $x = -1, 0, \frac{1}{3}, 1$

11. $f(x) = \frac{1}{2}x + 5$
    $x = -3, -2, -1, 0$

12. $f(x) = x - 1.5$
    $x = 0.5, 1, 1.5, 2$

13. $f(x) = -2x - 4$
    $x = -4.5, -3, -1.5, 0$

8. −10, −4, 5, 8
9. −6, 0, 9, 12
10. 7, 4, 3, 1
11. $3\frac{1}{2}$, 4, $4\frac{1}{2}$, 5
12. −1, −0.5, 0, 0.5
13. 5, 2, −1, −4

14. Find four solutions for the function $f(x) = -4x + 7$. Write the solutions as ordered pairs. **Sample answers: (−1, 11), (0, 7), (1, 3), (2, −1)**

15. Find four solutions for the function $f(x) = \frac{1}{4}x - 2$. Write the solutions as ordered pairs. **Sample answers: (−4, −3), (0, −2), (4, −1), (8, 0)**

Graph each function. **For answers to Exercises 16–21, see Solutions Manual.**

16. $f(x) = 2x - 3$
17. $f(x) = -3x$
18. $f(x) = -x + 6$
19. $f(x) = 5x + 1$
20. $f(x) = \frac{1}{2}x + 4$
21. $f(x) = 1.5x - 2$

Mixed Review

22. **Physical Fitness** Every morning, Juan walks a rectangular route that has a length of 0.5 mile and a width of 0.25 mile. How far does Juan walk each morning? *(Lesson 5-6)* $1\frac{1}{2}$ miles

23. **Geometry** Classify the triangle at the right by its sides and by its angles. *(Lesson 8-3)*
    isosceles, right

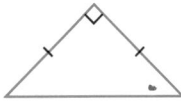

Lesson 14-5 Functions **549**

Close

Have students make a function table for the function $f(x) = 2x - 1$ and then graph the function.

x	2x − 1	f(x)
−1	2(−1) − 1	−3
0	2(0) − 1	−1
1	2(1) − 1	1

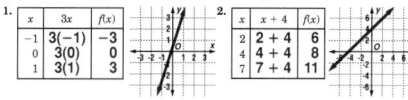

3 PRACTICE/APPLY

Assignment Guide
Maximum: 8–30
Minimum: 9–25 odd, 27–29

For **Extra Practice,** see p. 603.

Alternate Assessment

Writing Have students use the terms *input, output, function,* and *function rule* in a sentence. Sample answer: An output of 6 is a function of an input of 2 according to the function rule *output is three times input.*

Practice Masters, p. 122

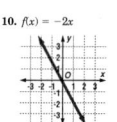
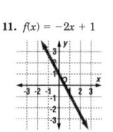
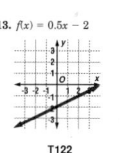
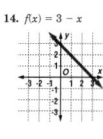

24. Mr. McDaniel is on a business trip in Dallas, Texas. He has 3 different restaurants to choose from for breakfast, 6 different restaurants to choose from for lunch, and 2 different restaurants to choose from for dinner. How many different ways can Mr. McDaniel eat all three meals given the choices? *(Lesson 13-2)* **36 ways**

25. Graph the equation $y = -2x$. *(Lesson 14-4)* **See Solutions Manual.**

Problem Solving and Applications

COMPUTER CONNECTION

26. **Computer Connection** The first step in writing a computer program is often drawing a flow chart. The flow chart below was written to determine solutions for a function.

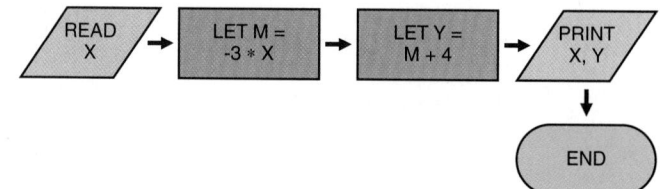

READ X → LET M = -3 * X → LET Y = M + 4 → PRINT X, Y → END

a. Study the flow chart and determine the function it represents.
b. Find the output, given an input of 2. $f(2) = -2$ $f(x) = -3x + 4$
c. Graph the function. **See Solutions Manual.**

27. **Geometry** The circumference (C) of a circle is a function of its diameter (d). The function can be written $C(d) = 3.14d$. *Note: This is the same as $f(x) = 3.14x$.*   **no negative diameters**
a. Why would negative numbers not make sense as input?
b. Make a function table. Find the circumference (output) for four different diameters (input). **See Solutions Manual.**
c. Draw the graph. Tell how you can use the graph to estimate d given C. **See Solutions Manual.**

28. **Sports** In the 1992 Olympics, Bonnie Blair of the United States won the gold medal in the women's 500-meter speed skating competition. Her average speed was about 12.4 meters per second. **See Solutions**
a. Graph the function $d(t) = 12.4t$. **Manual.**
b. How many seconds, t, did it take her to complete the 500-meter race? **40.32 seconds**

29. **Critical Thinking** Find a function rule for the input and output numbers below. $f(x) = x + 4$

x	−1	0	1	2	3
f(x)	3	4	5	6	7

30. **Journal Entry** Explain how a function is like an automatic teller machine. **See students' work.**

550   **Chapter 14** Functions and Graphs

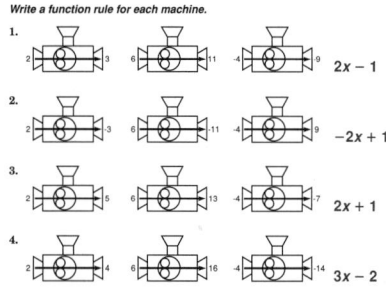

OPTIONS

Extending the Lesson

Using Functions Have students choose 10 money amounts and make a function table to show the correct tax on each, to the nearest cent, using the sales tax in your area.

Cooperative Learning Activity

The Price Is Right 14-5

Number of players: 2
Materials: Grid paper

• Copy the section of a coordinate plane shown on the back of this card.

↪ You may have heard someone say that one thing is a function of another thing. This means that there is a function rule that describes the relationship between the two things.

The number of cups of hot chocolate you will buy may be a function of the weather outside, but *definitely* is a function of the price of one cup. Suppose the function rule that describes the relationship between the number of cups a person will buy and any given price is $n = 5 - 2p$. Graph this function.

Suppose that you decide to open a hot-chocolate stand. You can use the graph you made to decide how much to charge to make the most money. Choose any point on the line. Find the ordered pair that names this point. Then find the product of the ordered pairs. This tells you the amount of money for y cups purchased at a price of x dollars. Find the ordered pair with the greatest product. How much will you charge for a cup? How many cups will the average person buy at this price?

Glencoe Mathematics: Applications and Connections, Course 2

14-6 Graphing Transformations

Objective
Graph transformations on a coordinate plane.

Words to Learn
reflection
translation
transformation

Quillwork is an art that was perfected by Native Americans. The quills of a porcupine were "embroidered" in patterns on tobacco bags, moccasins, and belts. Although this artform is rarely practiced today, the designs have been imitated and used in other forms of art.

Many of these designs consist of a variety of geometric transformations. That is, one geometric shape is used in many different positions to form a pattern or design.

LOOKBACK

You can review reflections on page 327 and translations on page 324.

There are many ways to move a geometric shape on a coordinate plane. A figure can be flipped, turned, slid, stretched, or shrunk. When a figure is flipped, it is called a **reflection**. When it is slid, it is called a **translation**. Each of these kinds of **transformations** can be described using ordered pairs and then graphed.

Example 1

Triangle ABC has vertices $A(1, 1)$, $B(2, 4)$, and $C(5, 2)$. Graph its reflection over the x-axis.

Graph $\triangle ABC$ by graphing each ordered pair and connecting the points to form $\triangle ABC$. Label each vertex.

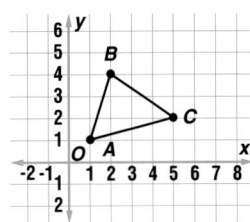

*A′ is read "A prime,"
B′ as "B prime," and
C′ as "C prime."*

Multiply the y-coordinate of each ordered pair by -1. Write the new ordered pair.

Vertex of $\triangle ABC$	Multiply the y-coordinate by -1	New ordered pairs
$A(1, 1)$	$(1, 1(-1))$	$A'(1, -1)$
$B(2, 4)$	$(2, 4(-1))$	$B'(2, -4)$
$C(5, 2)$	$(5, 2(-1))$	$C'(5, -2)$

Lesson 14-6 Geometry Connection: Graphing Transformations **551**

14-6 Lesson Notes

NCTM Standards: 1–5, 7, 8, 12

Lesson Resources
- Study Guide Master 14-6
- Practice Master 14-6
- Enrichment Master 14-6
- Evaluation Master, Quiz B, p. 124
- Group Activity Card 14-6

Transparency 14-6 contains the 5-Minute Check and a teaching aid for this lesson.

5-Minute Check
(Over Lesson 14-5)

Find the output for each function, given the input and the function rule.

1. $f(x) = 2x + 3$;
   $x = -2, -1, 1, 2$
   $-1, 1, 5, 7$
2. $f(x) = 0.5x + 3$;
   $x = 0.5, 1, 1.5, 2$
   $3.25, 3.5, 3.75, 4$
3. Find four solutions for the function $f(x) = -3x + 5$. Write the solutions as ordered pairs. $(-1, 8)$, $(0, 5)$, $(1, 2)$, $(2, -1)$

1 FOCUS

Motivating the Lesson

Questioning Have students read the opening paragraphs. Ask students where else, other than in Native American embroidery, they have seen designs consisting of translations and reflections.

2 TEACH

Using Critical Thinking Ask students how they can determine the coordinates of a reflection without graphing the transformation on a coordinate plane.

OPTIONS

Multicultural Education

The Navajo of northern Arizona are well known for their weaving skills. One style of blanket that was popularized in the late 19th century contains colorful geometric designs consisting mainly of rhombuses and triangles. Originally woven as clothing, these blankets became trade items with the establishment of trading posts in the region.

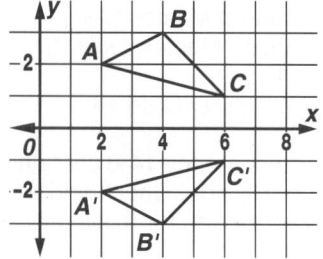
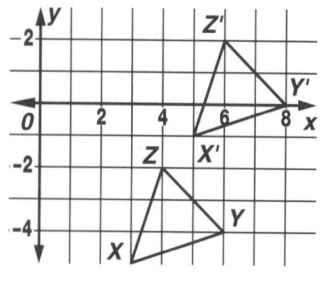
Checking for Understanding

Exercises 1-3 are designed to help you assess students' understanding through reading, writing, speaking, and modeling. You should work through these exercises with your students and then monitor their work on Guided Practice Exercises 4-7.

Graph the new ordered pairs and label each point. Connect these points to form △*A′B′C′*.

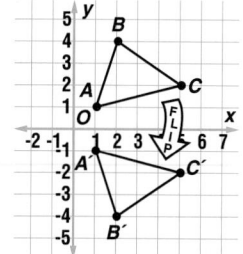

The two triangles are congruent. Triangle *A′B′C′* is the result of flipping △*ABC* over the *x*-axis.

The transformation in Example 1 is a reflection over the *x*-axis. You can also do a reflection over the *y*-axis by multiplying the *x*-coordinate by −1. *You will reflect △ABC over the y-axis in Exercise 2.*

Another transformation is a *translation*. Remember a translation slides the figure from one location to the next without changing its orientation.

Example 2

Graph △*KLM* with vertices *K*(−9, −5), *L*(−7, −1), and *M*(−1, −6). Graph its translation △*K′L′M′* with vertices *K′*(−2, −1), *L′*(0, 3), and *M′*(6, −2). Describe the movement from △*KLM* to △*K′L′M′*.

Graph each triangle. Notice that the two triangles are congruent.

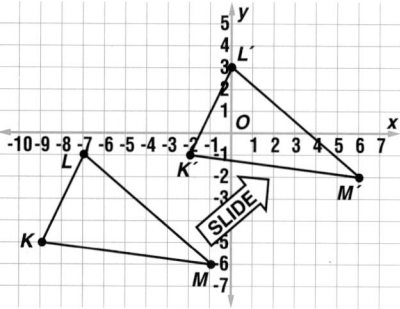

Problem-Solving Hint

•••••••••••••

Look for a pattern in the change of the *x*-coordinates. Then look for a pattern in the *y*-coordinates.

To describe the movement from △*KLM* to △*K′L′M′*, look for a pattern in the ordered pairs.

	x	*y*
K → *K′*	−9 → −2	−5 → − 1
L → *L′*	−7 → 0	−1 → 3
M → *M′*	−1 → 6	−6 → −2
	+7	+4

Each *x*-coordinate was moved 7 units to the right and each *y*-coordinate was moved 4 units up. The movement of each vertex can be described by (7, 4). The new ordered pairs can be written as follows: $(x, y) + (7, 4) = (x + 7, y + 4)$.

OPTIONS

Reteaching Activity

Using Problem Solving Provide students with opportunities to graph transformations that are easier to visualize, such as reflections of triangles or rectangles that have bases parallel to an axis or translations parallel to either axis.

Study Guide Masters, p. 123

Name _____ Date _____

Study Guide Worksheet 14-6

Geometry Connection: Graphing Transformations

One kind of transformation is a reflection. A reflection is a flip.
Multiply the *x*-coordinate by −1 to reflect over the *y*-axis.
Multiply the *y*-coordinate by −1 to reflect over the *x*-axis.

Example △*ABC* has vertices *A*(1, 2), *B*(4, 3) and *C*(3, −1). Graph its reflection over the *y*-axis.

Multiply each *x*-coordinate by −1.

A(1, 2)	*A′*(−1, 2)
B(4, 3)	*B′*(−4, 3)
C(3, −1)	*C′*(−3, −1)

Another type of transformation is a translation. A translation is a slide.

Checking for Understanding

Communicating Mathematics

Read and study the lesson to answer each question.

1. **Tell** what a reflection and a translation mean. **See margin.**

2. See Solutions Manual.

2. **Draw** the result of reflecting $\triangle ABC$ from Example 1 over the y-axis.

3. **Tell** what type of transformation is shown by the table at the right. **translation**

$\triangle RST$	$\triangle R'S'T'$
$R(3, 2)$	$R'(4, 4)$
$S(1, 5)$	$S'(2, 7)$
$T(-1, 2)$	$T'(0, 4)$

Guided Practice

Classify each graph as a reflection or a translation.

4. translation
5. translation
6. reflection

4. 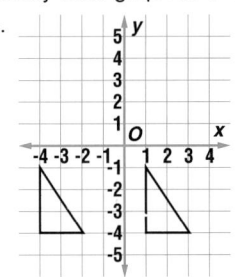 5. 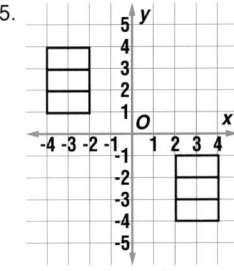 6.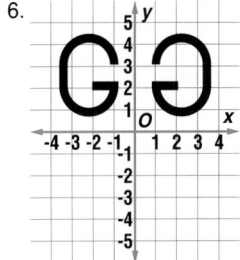

7. a. Graph $\triangle XYZ$, with vertices $X(2, 1)$, $Y(-4, 1)$, and $Z(-1, 5)$.
   b. Reflect $\triangle XYZ$ over the x-axis.
   c. Reflect $\triangle XYZ$ over the y-axis.
   d. Translate $\triangle XYZ$ 4 units down and 3 units left.
   e. Translate $\triangle XYZ$ 3 units up and 2 units right.
   For answers to Exercise 7, see Solutions Manual.

Exercises For graphs for Exercises 8–12, see Solutions Manual.

Independent Practice

Graph each triangle and its transformation. Write the ordered pairs for the vertices of the new triangle.

8. $\triangle ABC$ with vertices $A(-2, 4)$, $B(2, 1)$, and $C(1, 6)$ translated 5 units right and 3 units up **$A'(3, 7)$, $B'(7, 4)$, $C'(6, 9)$**

9. $D'(1, -3)$, $E'(5, -1)$, $F'(5, -8)$

9. $\triangle DEF$ with vertices $D(1, 3)$, $E(5, 1)$, and $F(5, 8)$ reflected over the x-axis

10. $\triangle GHI$ with vertices $G(-3, -1)$, $H(-5, -6)$, and $I(-1, -6)$ translated 2 units down and 4 units right **$G'(1, -3)$, $H'(-1, -8)$, $I'(3, -8)$**

11. $\triangle JKL$ with vertices $J(-5, 7)$, $K(-2, 5)$, and $L(-7, 1)$ reflected over the y-axis **$J'(5, 7)$, $K'(2, 5)$, $L'(7, 1)$**

12. rectangle $PQRS$ with vertices $P(-4, 0)$, $Q(-4, -3)$, $R(-2, -3)$, and $S(-2, 0)$ translated 2 units down and 5 units right **$P'(1, -2)$, $Q'(1, -5)$, $R'(3, -5)$, $S'(3, -2)$**

Mixed Review

13. **Geometry** Find the volume of a rectangular prism having a length of 6 meters, a width of 4 meters, and a height of 1.5 meters. *(Lesson 10-5)* **36 cubic meters**

14. Find the output for the function $f(x) = 4x + 6$, given $x = -3, 2,$ and 20. *(Lesson 14-5)* **$-6, 14, 86$**

Limited English Proficiency

Review the meanings of the terms *reflection* (flip; mirror image) and *translation* (slide). Have students add the terms, along with sketches, to their vocabulary lists. Have students work with a partner throughout the lesson.

Additional Answer

1. A reflection is a flip. A translation is a slide.

Close

Have students work with partners. Each student draws a triangle and his or her partner graphs its reflection over one axis. Then each student draws a figure that the other must translate on the coordinate plane using the movement (8, 5). Students should check each other's transformations.

3 PRACTICE/APPLY

Assignment Guide
Maximum: 8–19
Minimum: 9–11 odd, 13–19

For **Extra Practice**, see p. 603.

Alternate Assessment

Speaking Have students explain how to graph the reflection of a figure over the x-axis. Additionally, ask them to explain the transformation of a figure described by the movement $(5, -4)$.

Practice Masters, p. 123

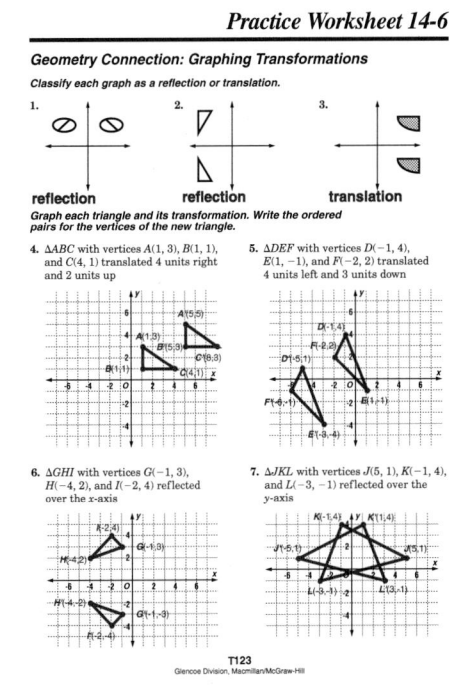

Problem Solving and Applications

15. **Art** Describe the transformations that were used to create the quilled pattern on page 551. **See Solutions Manual.**

16. **Geometry See Solutions Manual for graph.**
    a. Reflect the triangle at the right over the *y*-axis. Name the new figure formed by both triangles. **isosceles triangle**
    b. Reflect the new figure over the *x*-axis. Name this new figure. **rhombus**

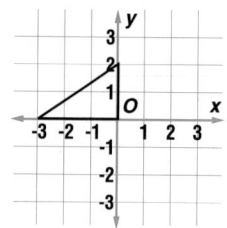

18. See students' work.

17. **Games** In the game of chess, game pieces are slid up or down, left or right, or diagonally.
    a. What type of transformation is used in this game? **translation**
    b. Write the movement of the game piece at the right as an ordered pair. **(2, 4)**

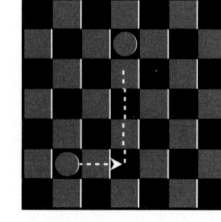

18. **Portfolio Suggestion** Review the items in your portfolio. Make a table of contents of the items, noting why each item was chosen. Replace any items that are no longer appropriate. **See students' work.**

19. **Critical Thinking**
    a. Graph the image of $\triangle XYZ$ if both the *x*- and *y*-coordinates are multiplied by -1.
    b. Describe this transformation.
    double reflection

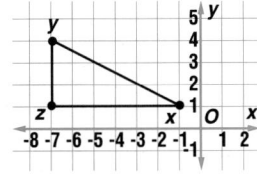

20. **Mathematics and Crafts** Read the following paragraph.

Quilts made in the United States during the 18th and 19th centuries are an important type of American folk art. These quilts were often made of colorful geometric forms that were either pieced together or appliqued onto a large piece of cloth. Sometimes the design on the quilt tells a story, commemorates an important historical event, or describes an important family occasion.

Use graph paper and design a quilt pattern that describes an important occasion in your family. Use reflections and translations to make your pattern. **See students' work.**

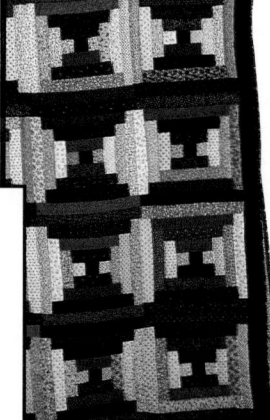

554   Chapter 14 Functions and Graphs

554

OPTIONS

Extending the Lesson

Mathematics and Crafts
Encourage students to make a pattern with coordinates prior to actually drawing on the graph paper. Have students exchange papers and see whether their classmates can tell what their symbols mean.

Cooperative Learning Activity

Use groups of 3.   **Triangle Demolition Derby 14-6**
Materials: Index cards, spinners, grid paper, colored pencils

● Copy onto cards the vertices of triangles shown on the back of this card. Shuffle the cards and place them face down in a pile. Label equal sections of two spinners "–4," "–3," "–2," "–1," "1," "2," "3," "4." Decide which spinner names *x*-coordinates and which spinner names *y*-coordinates.

● Each group member selects a card from the pile and graphs the triangle described on the same coordinate plane using a different colored pencil. Then, in turn, each group member spins both spinners and uses the resulting ordered pair to translate his or her original figure. (The *x*-coordinate of the ordered pair tells how many units left (–) or right (+) to move each *x*-coordinate of the vertices. The *y*-coordinate of the ordered pair tells how many units down (–) or up (+) to move each *y*-coordinate of the vertices.) If your translation touches or overlaps with another group member's translation, award yourself 1 point.

Repeat the procedure several times, reshuffling the cards when necessary. The group member with the most points wins.

Glencoe Mathematics: Applications and Connections, Course 2

Cooperative Learning

14-6B Dilations

A Follow-Up of Lesson 14-6

Objective
Change the size of a figure on a coordinate plane.

Materials
picture or cartoon
graph paper
straightedge
colored pencil

Words to Learn
dilation

Some copy machines can reduce and enlarge images. In mathematics, the process of reducing and enlarging a figure is a transformation called a **dilation.**

Try this!

Work with a partner.

* Place a piece of graph paper over a cartoon or picture you want to enlarge. Trace the picture. *It may help to put the paper against a window pane to see the image more clearly.*

* On another piece of graph paper, use a colored pencil to draw horizontal lines every 2 squares. Then draw vertical lines every 2 squares.

* Now sketch the parts of the figure contained in each small square of your original picture onto each large square of the grid you created.

What do you think?

1. Has the figure been enlarged or reduced? By how much? **enlarged; double**

2. smaller squares
2. What type of grid would you use to *reduce* a picture?

3. **Geometry** Are your two pictures congruent or similar? Explain your answer. **Similar; if they were congruent, they would be the same size.**

Mathematics Lab 14-6B: Dilations **555**

OPTIONS

Lab Manual You may wish to make copies of the blackline master on p. 80 of the *Lab Manual* for students to use as a recording sheet.

Lab Manual, p. 80

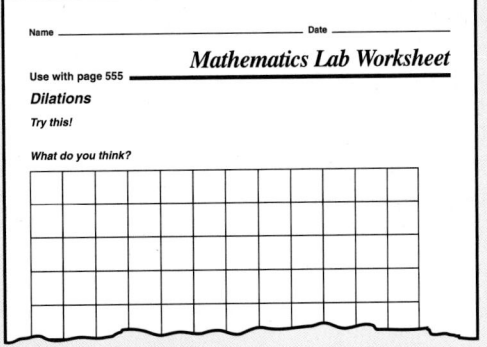

NCTM Standards: 1–4, 12

Management Tips

For Students Suggest that students choose a simple cartoon to begin with since it is likely that they will need to erase and revise their sketches frequently.

For the Overhead Projector
Overhead Manipulative Resources provides appropriate materials for teacher or student demonstration of the activities in this Mathematics Lab.

1 FOCUS

Introducing the Lab

Talk about the concept of dilation with students. Ask them to suggest uses for this process in everyday life. Ask them to think about how they might need to use dilation.

2 TEACH

Using Applications Tell students to expect some inaccuracy when sketching the drawings onto larger or smaller squares.

3 PRACTICE/APPLY

Using Connections Have students draw a simple shape or sketch a cartoon figure on regular paper. Have them exchange pictures with partners, who then are to trace the pictures onto graph paper and then either reduce or enlarge them using another piece of graph paper.

Close

Have students sketch a simple shape or cartoon figure. Ask them to enlarge the figure so that it is three times its original size.

555

The Chapter Study Guide and Review begins with a section on Communicating Mathematics. This includes questions that review the new terms and concepts that were introduced in the chapter.

Then, the Skills and Concepts presented in the chapter are reviewed using a side-by-side format. Encourage students to refer to the Objectives and Examples on the left as they complete the Review Exercises on the right.

The Chapter Study Guide and Review ends with problems that review Applications and Problem Solving.

Chapter

14

Study Guide and Review

Communicating Mathematics

Choose the letter that best matches each of the following.

1. Four times x less six is 14. **c**
2. a solution to $y = -3x + 5$ **e**
3. a term that describes $y = -2x + 6$ **h**
4. a rule that assigns an output to each input **a**
5. a mirror image over a given line **d**

6. In your own words, explain the steps required to graph a linear equation. **Solve the equation; graph solutions as points on a coordinate system; connect the points with a line.**

a. function
b. $(-3, 4)$
c. $4x - 6 = 14$
d. reflection
e. $(1, 2)$
f. translation
g. $6 - 4x = 14$
h. linear equation

Self Assessment

Objectives and Examples

Upon completing this chapter, you should be able to:

• solve two-step equations *(Lesson 14-2)*

$$-6t - 5 = 19$$
$$-6t - 5 + 5 = 19 + 5$$
$$-6t = 24$$
$$\frac{-6t}{-6} = \frac{24}{-6}$$
$$t = -4$$

• solve equations with two variables *(Lesson 14-3)*

Find four solutions for $y = 3x + 2$.

x	3x + 2	y	(x, y)
−1	3(−1) + 2	−1	(−1, −1)
0	3(0) + 2	2	(0, 2)
2	3(2) + 2	8	(2, 8)
3	3(3) + 2	11	(3, 11)

Four solutions are $(-1, -1)$, $(0, 2)$, $(2, 8)$, and $(3, 11)$.

Review Exercises

Use these exercises to review and prepare for the chapter test.

Solve each equation and graph the solution.

7. $3p - 4 = 8$ **4**
8. $\frac{x}{2} + 5 = 3$ **−4**
9. $8 - 6w = 50$ **−7**
10. $5m + 6 = -4$ **−2**
11. $\frac{1}{3}(y - 4) = 5$ **19**
12. $-1.5b + 1 = 7$ **−4**

For graphs for Exercises 7–12, see Solutions Manual.

Find four solutions for each equation. Write your solutions as ordered pairs.

13. $y = 4x - 9$
14. $y = \frac{1}{3}x$
15. $y = -2 - 3x$
16. $y = -6x + 1$
17. $y = x + 5$
18. $y = 3x + 4$
19. $y = 0$
20. $y = -x$

For answers to Exercises 13–20, see Solutions Manual.

556   Chapter 14 Study Guide and Review

Objectives and Examples	*Review Exercises*

- graph equations by plotting points *(Lesson 14-4)*

Graph $y = x + 3$.

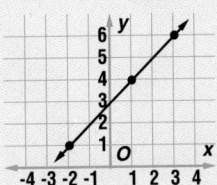

x	x + 3	y	(x, y)
−2	−2 + 3	1	(−2, 1)
1	1 + 3	4	(1, 4)
3	3 + 3	6	(3, 6)

Graph each equation.

21. $y = 2x$
22. $y = -\frac{1}{3}x$
23. $y = 5x + 2$
24. $y = x$

For graphs for Exercises 21–24, see Solutions Manual.

- complete function tables; graph functions *(Lesson 14-5)*

Find the output for the function $f(x) = 2x + 6$, given $x = -3$, 0, 2, and 5.

Input	Function Rule	Output
x	2x + 6	f(x)
−3	2(−3) + 6	0
0	2(0) + 6	6
2	2(2) + 6	10
5	2(5) + 6	16

Find the output for each function, given the input and the function rule.

25. $f(x) = \frac{1}{2}x + 3$
   $x = 4, 0, -2, -4$ **5, 3, 2, 1**
26. $f(x) = -4x$
   $x = -3, -1, 0, 2$ **12, 4, 0, −8**
27. $f(x) = 1.5x - 4$
   $x = -4, -2, 0, 2$ **−10, −7, −4, −1**
28. $f(x) = -6x + 3$
   $x = -\frac{1}{2}, 0, \frac{1}{2}, 1$ **6, 3, 0, −3**

- graph transformations *(Lesson 14-6)*

Graph $\triangle QRS$ with vertices $Q(-3, 4)$, $R(-3, 1)$, and $S(4, 1)$. Then translate $\triangle QRS$ 2 units left and 3 units down.

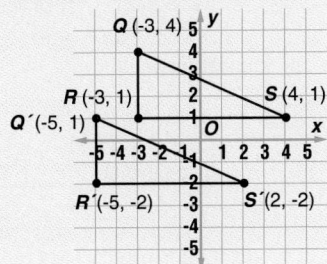

Graph each triangle and its transformation. Write the ordered pairs for the vertices of the new triangle.

29. $\triangle ABC$ with $A(4, -2)$, $B(-2, -3)$, and $C(-1, 6)$ translated 3 units right and 4 units up
30. Reflect $\triangle ABC$ over the x-axis. Name the new figure formed by both triangles. **rhombus**

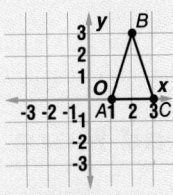

For answers to Exercises 29–30, see Solutions Manual.

Study Guide and Review

557

Evaluation Masters, pp. 122–123

Name _____ Date _____

Form 2A _____ *Chapter 14 Test*

1. A carton of one dozen eggs weighs 16 ounces. Leslie uses 4 of the eggs to make cookies. The carton and remaining eggs weigh 11 ounces. How much does the carton weigh?
   1. __1 ounce__

Solve each equation.
2. $-35 = -6b + 1$ 3. $5.3 - 6m = -1.3$ 4. $\frac{3}{4}(p + 2) = 9$
   2. __6__
   3. __1.1__

Find four solutions for each equation. Write your solutions as ordered pairs.
5. $y = -3x + 2$ 6. $y = 4x - 3$
   4. __10__
7. At a carnival, it costs $3 for admission plus $0.50 for each ride. Write an equation for the cost of rides and admission.
   5. (−1, 5); (0, 2); (1, −1); (2, −4)

Graph each equation.
8. $y = 2x - 2$ 9. $y = -x + 3$
   6. (−1, −7); (0, −3); (1, 1); (2, 5)

10. Translate the sentence *the first number is 7 less than three times the second number* into an equation.
    7. $y = 0.50x + 3$

Find the output for each function, given the input and the function rule.
11. $f(x) = 4x; x = -3, 1, 2, 3.$
    8. See graph.
12. $f(x) = -3x + 4; x = -4, -2, 0, 2$
    9. See graph.
13. Graph the function $f(x) = 0.5x - 2$.
    10. $y = 3x - 7$

Graph each triangle with its transformation. Label all vertices.
14. $\triangle ABC$ with vertices $A(1, 1)$, $B(3, 1)$, and $C(2, 4)$ translated 4 units down and 3 units left.
15. $\triangle MNO$ with vertices $M(-4, 2)$, $N(-2, 1)$, and $O(-1, -4)$ reflected over the y-axis.
    11. −12, 4, 8, 12
    12. 16, 10, 4, −2
    13. See graph.
    14. See graph.
    15. See graph.

BONUS Solve $6x = -3y + 12$ for y. $y = 4 - 2x$

Name _____ Date _____

Form 2B _____ *Chapter 14 Test*

1. Harold, Eugene, and Grace all own an equal number of shares of Anson Stock. Harold sells one fourth of his shares for $3 per share, or a total of $2,100. How many shares of stock did the three own before the sale?
   1. __8,400 shares__

Solve each equation.
2. $-8x + 3 = -29$ 3. $-2.5v - 5 = 4.5$ 4. $\frac{1}{8}(q - 3) = -4$
   2. __4__
   3. __−3.8__

Find four solutions for each equation. Write your solutions as ordered pairs.
5. $y = 5x - 2$ 6. $y = \frac{1}{2}x + 3$
   4. __−21__
7. To attract more customers, an office supply store is giving 50 free bonus points to start out, and then one bonus point for every dollar you spend in the store. Write an equation for the number of bonus points you can earn.
   5. (−1, −7), (0, −2), (1, 3), (2, 8)

Graph each equation.
8. $y = -x + 4$ 9. $y = \frac{1}{2}x - 1$
   6. (−2, 0), (0, −1), (2, −2), (4, −3)

10. Translate the sentence *the first number is five times the second number plus two* into an equation.
    7. $y = 50 + x$

Find the output for each function, given the input and the function rule.
11. $f(x) = 5x; x = -2, 0, 2, 4$
    8. See graph.
12. $f(x) = \frac{1}{4}x - 3; x = -4, -2, 2, 4$
    9. See graph.
13. Graph the function $f(x) = 0.5x + 0.5$.
    10. $y = 5x + 2$

Graph each triangle with its transformation. Label all vertices.
14. $\triangle DEF$ with vertices $D(1, 3)$, $E(4, 1)$, and $F(0, 0)$ translated 3 units left and 1 unit up.
15. $\triangle JKL$ with vertices $J(0, -2)$, $K(2, -1)$, and $L(1, -4)$ reflected over the x-axis.
    11. −10, 0, 10, 20
    12. −4, −3.5, −2.5, −2
    13. See graph.
    14. See graph.
    15. See graph.

BONUS Solve $21x = 3y + 51$ for y. $y = 7x - 17$

Applications and Problem Solving

31. **Stamp Collecting**   Four friends collect stamps. They are comparing how many Mexican stamps they each have. Jeff has 3 times as many as Fina. Mario has 4 fewer stamps than Danielle, but 3 more than Fina. Fina has 9 stamps. How many stamps does each friend have? Jeff, 27; Fina, 9; Mario, 12; Danielle, 16

32. **Consumer Math**   A parking garage in New York City charges $3 for the first two hours and then $0.75 for each additional hour. Walter parks his car in the garage at 9:00 A.M. and when he returns must pay a $5.25 parking fee. What time did Walter return? *(Lesson 14-2)* 2:00 P.M.

33. **Catering**   Christina's Catering Service charges $12.50 per person for a sit-down dinner.
    a. Write a function that represents the cost for x people. $f(x) = 12.50x$
    b. What is the cost for 40 people? $500

Curriculum Connection Projects

- **Travel**   Call two rental car companies and ask them for their rates for a medium-sized car. Write equations for the cost of renting a car from each company. Decide which company you would rent from if you were going to use the car for two days and travel about 150 miles.

- **Art**   Design a quillwork pattern for a belt using reflections, translations, and dilations of triangles.

Read More About It

McCauley, David. *City.*
O'Dell, Scott. *The Captive.*
Burns, Marilyn. *The I Hate Mathematics Book.*

558   **Chapter 14** Study Guide and Review

14 Test

1. **Baking** Ming baked a batch of oatmeal cookies. He kept half of them for himself and donated the other half to a charity bake sale. He packed the bake-sale cookies in 4 boxes, a dozen in each box. How many cookies did Ming bake? **96 cookies**

Solve each equation and graph the solution.

2. $6x - 4 = 3$ $\frac{7}{6}$ 3. $\frac{w}{-3} - 5 = 10$ **−45** 4. $11 = \frac{1}{4}(p - 1)$ **45**

For graphs for Exercises 2–4, see Solutions Manual.

5. **School** Detentions at Morris Junior High are assigned to students who are late in the following manner: 20 minutes of detention for anyone who is up to 15 minutes late and an additional 5 minutes for every minute late beyond 15. Derrick received a 35-minute detention. How late was he? **18 minutes**

Find four solutions for each equation. Write your solutions as ordered pairs. **For answers to Exercises 6–8, see Solutions Manual.**

6. $y = -x + 4$ 7. $y = 3x - 2$ 8. $y = -\frac{1}{2}x$

9. **Sales** Ms. White takes a job at a local computer store at a salary of $200 per week plus a $50 commission on every computer she sells.

$y = 200 + 50x$

a. Write an equation for Ms. White's weekly salary if she sells x computers.

b. What will she earn for a week in which she sells 5 computers? **$450**

Graph each equation. **For graphs for Exercises 10–12, see Solutions Manual.**

10. $y = -3x$ 11. $y = \frac{1}{3}x - 3$ 12. $y = 2x + 5$

13. Margie charges $5 per page for report typing. Translate this information into an equation showing the cost for a report that has x pages. Graph the equation. $y = 5x$; **See Solutions Manual for graph.**

Find the output for each function, given the input and the function rule.

14. $f(x) = -2x - 1$; $x = -1, 2, 5, 100$ 15. $f(x) = \frac{x}{10}$; $x = 20, 5, 0, -10$ **2, $\frac{1}{2}$, 0,**
1, −5, −11, −201 **−1**

Graph each function. **For graphs for Exercises 16–17, see Solutions Manual.**

16. $f(x) = 2x - 5$ 17. $f(x) = 3.5x + 1$

19. $X'(2, -5)$, $Y'(2, 1)$, $Z'(5, 1)$

Graph each triangle and its transformation. Label all vertices. **see Solutions Manual.** **For graphs for Exercises 18–20,**

18. $\triangle ABC$ with vertices $A(-4, 2)$, $B(3, 4)$, and $C(-1, 6)$ translated 2 units right and 4 units down $A'(-2, -2)$, $B'(5, 0)$, $C'(1, 2)$

19. $\triangle XYZ$ with vertices $X(2, 5)$, $Y(2, -1)$, and $Z(5, -1)$ reflected over the x-axis

20. $\triangle QRS$ with vertices $Q(6, 4)$, $R(-1, 2)$, and $S(2, -3)$ translated 1 unit up and 5 units right $Q'(11, 5)$, $R'(4, 3)$, $S'(7, -2)$

Bonus Graph the equation $y = x^2$. **See Solutions Manual.**

Chapter 14 Test 559

Test and Review Generator software is provided in Apple, IBM, and Macintosh versions. You may use this software to create your own tests or worksheets, based on the needs of your students.

The **Performance Assessment Booklet** provides an alternate assessment for evaluating student progress. An assessment for this chapter can be found on pages 27–28.

Name _____ Date _____

Form 1A _____ *Chapter 14 Test*

1. A can of corn weighs 12 ounces. Jimmy eats half of the corn in the can for dinner. The can and the corn that is left weigh 7.25 ounces. How much does the can weigh? 1. **B**
   A. 1.66 oz B. 2.5 oz C. 4.75 oz D. 0.6 oz

2. Solve $3x + 1 = -11$. 2. **C**
   A. 4 B. −3.3 C. −4 D. 3

3. Solve $22 - 4n = 3.6$. 3. **C**
   A. −6.4 B. −4.6 C. 4.6 D. 6.4

4. Solve $\frac{2}{3}(s - 3) = 1.2$. 4. **D**
   A. −1.2 B. −0.53 C. 2.13 D. 4.8

5. Find three solutions of the equation $y = x - 3$. 5. **B**
   A. (−1, −2); (0, 3); (1, 2) B. (−1, −4); (0, −3); (1, −2)
   C. (−1, 3); (0, 0); (1, 3) D. (−1, 4); (0, 3); (1, 4)

6. Find three solutions of the equation $y = -2x + 1$. 6. **C**
   A. (−1, −3); (0, −1); (1, −2) B. (−1, −1); (0, 1); (1, −1)
   C. (−1, 3); (0, 1); (1, −1) D. (−1, −2); (0, −1); (1, 0)

7. Find three solutions of the equation $y = \frac{1}{2}x - 1$. 7. **B**
   A. (−1, −6); (0, −1; (1, 4) B. (−1, −1.5); (0, −1); (1, −0.5)
   C. (−1, −0.5); (0, −1); (1, 0.5) D. (0, −1); (1, −0.5); (2, −0.75)

The phone company charges $1.25 to connect a long-distance telephone call. It also charges $0.25 for each minute you talk. Use this information for Exercises 8 and 9.

8. Write an equation for the cost of making a long-distance telephone call. 8. **C**
   A. $y = 1.5x + 0.25$ B. $y = 1.25x + 0.25$
   C. $y = 0.25x + 1.25$ D. $y = 1.5x + 1.25$

9. How much will a 5-minute long-distance telephone call cost. 9. **D**
   A. $3.00 B. $7.75 C. $6.50 D. $2.50

10. Translate the sentence *the first number is 6 less than two times the second* into an equation. 10. **A**
    A. $y = 2x - 6$ B. $y = 6 - 2x$ C. $y = 6 + 2x$ D. $y = -2x - 6$

11. Translate the sentence *the first number is 1 less than twice the second* into an equation. 11. **C**
    A. $y = 2 - x$ B. $y = 2 + x$ C. $y = 2x - 1$ D. $y = -x - 2$

118
Glencoe Division, Macmillan/McGraw-Hill

Name _____ Date _____

Chapter 14 Test, Form 1A continued

12. Inga baked a batch of bran cookies. She kept one third of them for herself and donated the rest to the school fair. She packed the cookies for the fair in 8 boxes, a dozen in each box. How many cookies did she bake? 12. **D**
    A. 96 B. 343 C. 729 D. 144

Use the graph for Exercises 13 and 14.

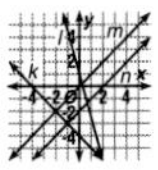

13. Which line is the graph of $y = x - 2$? 13. **D**
    A. line k
    B. line l
    C. line m
    D. line n

14. Which is the graph of $y = -3x - 1$? 14. **B**
    A. line k B. line l C. line m D. line n

15. Find the output for the function $f(x) = 3x$ given the input $x = -2, 0, 1, 2$. 15. **D**
    A. 6, 0, 3, 6 B. 1, 3, 4, 5 C. −5, 0, 3, 5 D. −6, 0, 3, 6

16. Find the output for the function $f(x) = -2x - 1.5$ given the input $x = -2, -1, 1, 2$. 16. **A**
    A. 2.5, 0.5, −3.5, −5.5 B. −2.5, −0.5, −3.5, −5.5
    C. −5.5, −3.5, 0.5, 3.5 D. −5.5, −3.5, −3.5, −5.5

17. Find the output for the function $f(x) = 0.25x - 2$ given the input $x = -4, 0, 4, 8$. 17. **C**
    A. −1, 0, 1, 2 B. 3, 2, 1, 0 C. −3, −2, −1, 0 D. −4, −2, 0, 2

18. Using the graph at the right, which line is the graph of the function $f(x) = -x + 1.5$? 18. **A**
    A. line r
    B. line s
    C. line t
    D. function is not on graph

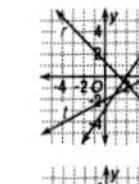

19. Use the graph at the right to describe the movement from $\triangle ABC$ to $\triangle A'B'C'$. 19. **D**
    A. (−5, −7)
    B. (5, 7)
    C. (−7, −5)
    D. (7, 5)

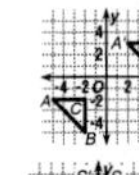

20. Use the graph at the right to describe the movement from $\triangle STU$ to $\triangle S'T'U'$. 20. **B**
    A. translation
    B. reflection over the y-axis
    C. reflection over the x-axis
    D. no movement

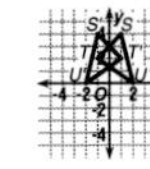

BONUS Which ordered pair describes a reflection over the x-axis and the y-axis? D
    A. (−x, y) B. (x, −y) C. (x, y) D. (−x, −y)

119
Glencoe Division, Macmillan/McGraw-Hill

The Academic Skills Test may be used to help students prepare for standardized tests. The test items are written in the same style as those in state proficiency tests. The test items cover skills and concepts covered up to this point in the text.

These pages can be used as an overnight assignment. After students have completed the pages, discuss how each problem can be solved, or provide copies of the solutions from the *Solutions Manual*.

Academic Skills Test

Chapter

14 Academic Skills Test

Directions: Choose the best answer. Write A, B, C, or D.

1. Which numbers are factors of 1,215?
C
  A 2, 3, 4, and 5
  B 3, 4, and 5
  C 3, 5, and 9
  D 5, 6, and 9

2. If the number on the spinner tells the number of dollars you win, what is the expected value of a spin?
B
  A $1.00
  B $1.75
  C $2.00
  D $2.50

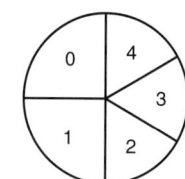

3. $-12 - 10 =$
A
  A -22 B -2
  C 2   D 22

4. The grading scale for a test is shown below. What score would be given for missing six problems?
A

-1	-2	-3	-4
98	95	93	90

  A 85   B 86
  C 87   D 88

5. Which regular polygon can be used by itself to make a tessellation?
B
  A pentagon   B hexagon
  C heptagon   D nonagon

6. What is the area of the trapezoid?
B

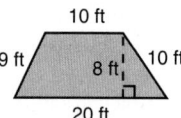

  A 80 ft²   B 120 ft²
  C 160 ft²   D 180 ft²

7. A cube has a surface area of 144 cm². How can you find the surface area of one face?
B
  A Divide 144 by 4.
  B Divide 144 by 6.
  C Divide 144 by 8.
  D None of these

8. How much water is in the pool when filled to a depth of 5 ft?
C
  A 800 ft³
  B 864 ft³
  C 1,200 ft³
  D 1,440 ft³

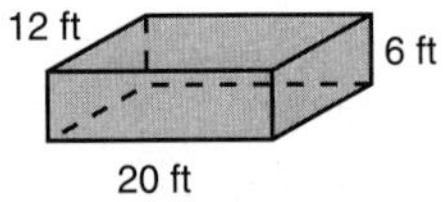

9. What is the unit price per ounce if a 14-oz can of peaches costs $1.19?
B
  A 1.2¢   B 8.5¢
  C 11.8¢   D 16.7¢

10. To find $12\frac{1}{2}\%$ of a number using a calculator, you can enter what decimal for $12\frac{1}{2}$?
A
  A 12.5   B 12.2
  C 0.125   D 0.122

11. 0.5% of $2,405 is about
A
  A $12   B $100
  C $120   D $1,200

12. If $592 was made in sales of
A sweatshirts, what was the total
   amount of sales (to the nearest
   dollar)?

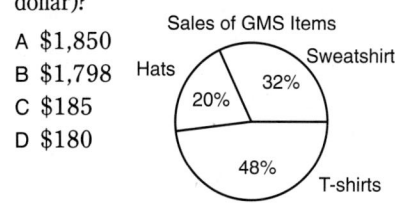

Sales of GMS Items

   A $1,850
   B $1,798
   C $185
   D $180

13. 72 out of 120 students usually buy a
C plate lunch. If there are 500 students
   in the school, about how many plate
   lunches should be prepared?

   A 80   B 210   C 300   D 400

14. There are 4 flavors of yogurt, 6 kinds
D of toppings, and 4 kinds of syrup.
   How many different combinations of
   yogurt, topping, and syrup (one of
   each) can be ordered?

   A 14   B 24   C 48   D 96

15. Suppose you flip a coin twice. Which
D outcome has the greater probability?

   A 2 heads
   B 2 tails
   C 1 head and 1 tail
   D They are all the same.

16. In how many ways can three people
B be arranged in a row?

   A 9   B 6   C 4   D 3

17. The cost of a taxi is $3, plus 75¢ for
C each mile traveled. If the total fare is
   $12, how many miles are traveled?

   A 3.75   B 7.5   C 12   D 16

18. What is the function rule
D for the input and output?

   A $f(x) = x - 3$
   B $f(x) = x + 3$
   C $f(x) = 2x - 1$
   D $f(x) = 3x + 1$

x	$f(x)$
-2	-5
-1	-2
0	1
1	4
2	7

19. Which is an equation
A for the line
   graphed?

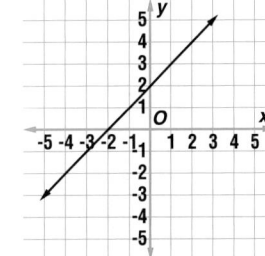

   A $y = x + 2$ B $y = x - 2$
   C $y = 2x$ D $y = 2x + 2$

20. What are the
C vertices of $\triangle EFG$
   reflected over
   the y-axis?

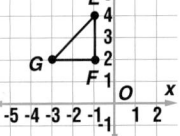

   A $(-1, -4), (-1, -2),$
     $(-3, -2)$
   B $(-1, -4), (-1, 2),$
     $(1, 2)$
   C $(1, 4), (1, 2), (3, 2)$
   D none of these

EXTENDED PROJECTS HANDBOOK

PURPOSE

The projects students will undertake are similar to those people may face in the real world in the course of doing their jobs or in dealing with issues in their lives. The projects involve gathering, organizing, interpreting, and presenting data. They require students to use questioning techniques, and debate real-life issues.

In working through these projects, students will work in groups. Knowing how to work cooperatively with others is an important life-long skill. As part of the problem-solving process, students must learn how to communicate effectively with others, which includes working on their abilities to listen, share, and be supportive.

The projects take place over time and may include out-of-class as well as in-class time. You will need to set aside some class time for groups to share and discuss the results of their work.

In the course of completing the projects, students will need to do research. This research may involve using library resources or it may involve designing and conducting a survey or an experiment to find out what their classmates are thinking.

The goals of these long-term projects are for students to become better at working together to gather, interpret, and use information. They are learning about a real-world process, not merely short answers to short-answer questions. These are not meant to be short-term projects.

In each project, students will need to organize the information they gather in order to use it. One group member can be responsible for this task, but all group members can make suggestions and contributions.

To The Student

One of the goals of *Mathematics: Applications and Connections* is to give you the opportunity to work with the mathematics that you will likely encounter outside the classroom. This includes the mathematics demanded by many of the courses you will take in high school and by most jobs as well as the mathematics that will be required of a good citizen of the United States.

Equally important, the authors want you to approach the mathematics you will encounter in your life with curiosity, enjoyment, and confidence.

Hopefully, the **Extended Projects Handbook** reflects these goals.

Three of the most important "big" ideas you are working with throughout *Mathematics: Applications and Connections* are the following. The **Extended Projects** include "big" ideas.

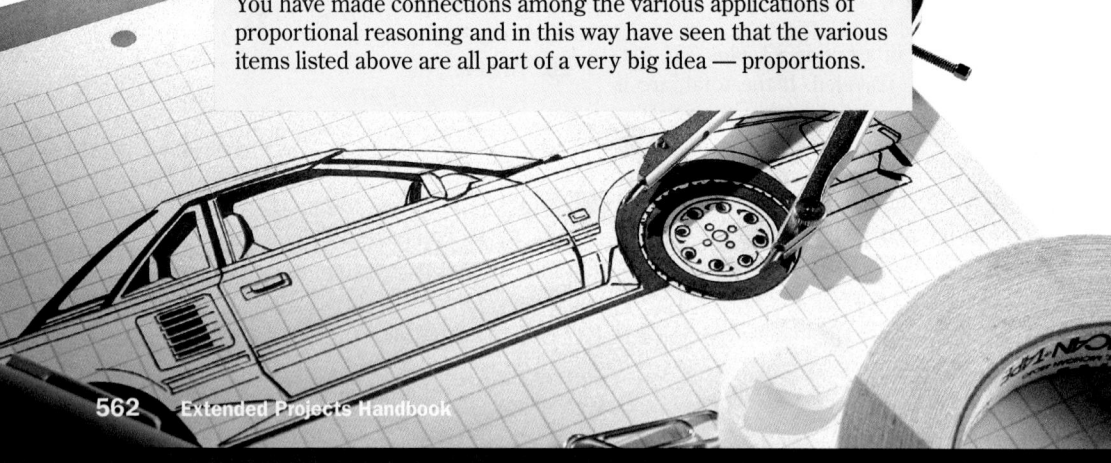

1. Proportional Reasoning

You probably have a great deal of experience with proportional reasoning. One example is a straight line in which the "rise" is proportional to the "run" and their ratio is the slope of the line. Other topics include ratio, rate, percent, similarity, scale drawings, and probability.

You have made connections among the various applications of proportional reasoning and in this way have seen that the various items listed above are all part of a very big idea — proportions.

562 Extended Projects Handbook

2. Multiple Representations

Mathematics provides you with many ways to present information and relationships. These include sketches, perspective drawings, tables, charts, graphs, physical models, verbalizing, and writing. You can use a computer to make graphs, data bases, spreadsheets, and simulations.

You have represented information and relationships in many different ways to completely describe various kinds of situations using mathematics.

3. Patterns and Generalizations

Mathematics has been called the science of patterns. You have experience recognizing and describing simple number and geometric patterns. You will be asked to make, test, and then use generalizations about given information in order to help you solve problems.

You may have used an algebraic expression to generalize a number pattern or the idea of similarity to make a scale drawing.

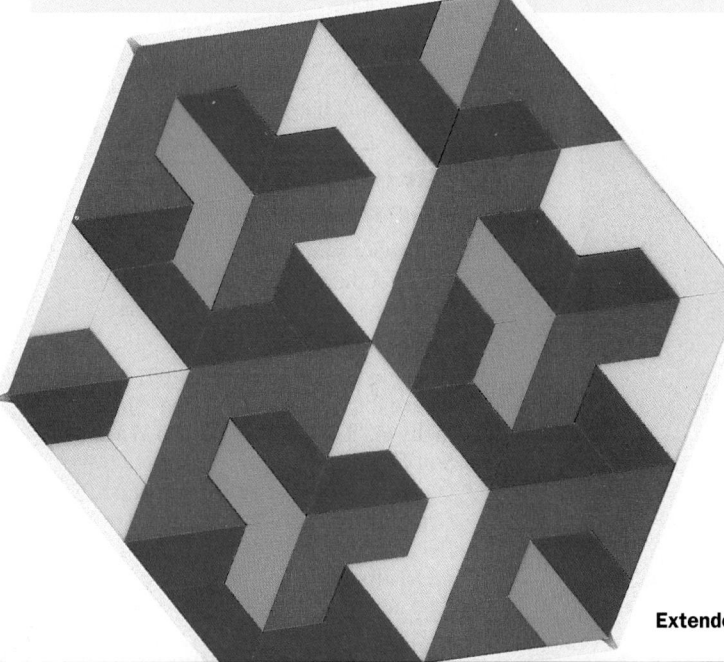

Extended Projects Handbook **563**

In each project, students will need to work together to formulate a plan to attack a problem. It is important that the groups spend enough time on this step in the problem-solving process to develop an effective strategy. Students may find it necessary to revise their plan as they gather new information. Encourage groups to look back at their plan and talk about what worked well, what didn't work as well, and how they would do it differently the next time.

MANAGING COOPERATIVE GROUPS

For successful cooperative learning experiences, research (Johnson and Johnson) indicates that the teacher's responsibilities include:

1. Deciding on the size of the groups.
2. Assigning students to the groups.
3. Arranging the room.
4. Describing the objectives.
5. Planning teaching materials.
6. Assigning roles to students.
7. Explaining the tasks involved.
8. Describing group responsibilities.
9. Establishing individual accountability.
10. Explaining the criteria for success.
11. Specifying desired student behaviors.
12. Monitoring students' behavior.
13. Providing task assistance.
14. Intervening to teach cooperative learning skills.
15. Providing closure to the lesson.
16. Evaluating the quality of learning.
17. Assessing group function.

(See general information about cooperative learning in the Teacher's Handbook, pp. T4–T5.)

OVERVIEW

Objective Design a questionnaire and use it to conduct a survey, then interpret the responses.

Summary

In this project, students will pretend they are hosting a show that salutes outstanding achievements in the music video field, as chosen by the public. To determine the winners, they will identify a "public", design a questionnaire and conduct a survey. Then they will evaluate the procedures they used.

Suggested Group Size

4 students

Time Required

If used as a complete unit:
5 days
If interspersed with other lessons:
2 weeks

Materials Needed

chart paper
ruler or straightedge
markers

Key Terms

opinion poll
survey
questionnaire

Project

1 AND THE WINNER IS...

The first rock video, "Video Killed the Radio Star," performed by the Bugles was aired on MTV at midnight, August 1, 1981. Since that time, music videos have been an important part of music performers' careers as well as the music industry in general.

Each year MTV Networks recognizes outstanding achievement in the field of video music with the MTV Video Music Awards. Since their beginning in 1984, the number of awards has grown to 21. The categories include Best Male Video, Best Female Video, and Best Group Video as well as special categories for rap, heavy metal, and dance videos. The network also recognizes technical achievement, direction, and cinematography.

564   Project 1

Who would be this year's winners if your group were hosting the show? Make up a questionnaire to find out.

Design a questionnaire that will identify the sample of people interviewed.

1. Talk about the importance of including questions on the questionnaire about the people you will be interviewing.

Categorizing your subjects

These questions will give you background information about your sample.
   Examples:
   • Male or female?
   • Age range?
   • How often do you watch MTV?
   • How often do you listen to the radio?
   • Do you buy cassettes and CDs of your favorite music performers regularly?
   • Do you watch award shows on TV?

Awareness responses

These questions inform you of the general awareness of the people you are interviewing about past music winners.
Examples:
   • Do you know who won the 1991 MTV Award for Best Female Video? (Janet Jackson, "Love Will Never Do Without You.")
   • Do you know what 1950s star won a Grammy for Best Male Vocal Performance in 1990? (Roy Orbison, *Oh Pretty Woman*)

- Do you know the month the People's Choice Awards are usually televised? (March)
2. Discuss the types of questions you want to cover in your questionnaire. Your survey can include songs or videos or both. Remember, not all of the people questioned may watch videos.

This opinion poll can include the following kinds of questions.

- Who do you think should win for Best Female Video this year?
- What is your favorite song that was released this year?
- Who would you say is the best all-time group?
- What do you like most about music videos?

3. Conduct your survey with people of many age groups. Record their responses on a worksheet. When the interviewing is complete, transfer your data to a frequency table.
4. Discuss ways to interpret the information you have gathered.
   - Was there one performer or song that was an obvious favorite?
   - Did males prefer different entertainers than females?
   - Were the people who listened to the radio more informed than those who did not?
5. After conducting your interviews, evaluate your procedures.
   - Were there any questions that you wished you had included on the questionnaire? What were they?
   - Was there enough information to draw reasonable conclusions?
   - How many people did your group interview?
   - How can you make your topic more interesting?
6. Present the data you collected and your conclusions to the class in a creative way(s).

EXTENSION: Can Your Vote Be Counted?

In February of each year, nominees for the People's Choice Awards are announced. The awards are presented in March. As the name implies, the winners are chosen by the public, not peers in the industry. Other award shows such as the Soap Opera Digest Awards, created by the magazine *Soap Opera Digest,* surveys its subscribers who choose the winners after the editors select the nominees. Have you ever wondered what it would be like to participate in the voting process and see if your favorite performers are winners?

Research an award show where the American public chooses the winners. You can begin by writing to networks, contacting *TV Guide,* or a production company such as Dick Clark Productions. Discuss other ways you could obtain the information.

Write a story for your school newspaper detailing the steps you took to find out how award shows such as People's Choice Awards determine the winners.

Project 1   565

Observe how the groups work together to interpret their task and how they design their questionnaires. Check to see that all members are participating.

Guide students to realize that the questions provided are samples. For this reason, they should feel free to revise the questions if they think they can improve upon them.

Insist that the groups themselves solve all problems that arise. Step in only when no one has an answer to a question that the group as a whole seems to be concerned about.

EXTENSIONS

Have each group contact a different source for its information. Since the information will not arrive simultaneously, groups might wish to share the data as it becomes available. Have groups compare their questionnaires with those devised by professional opinion-poll takers.

OVERVIEW

Objective Write trivia questions using data from reference sources and from personal interviews.

Summary

In this project, students will do research to write trivia questions about a wide variety of subjects. Each member of the group will have a different task. However, all will work together in the data-gathering phase.

Suggested Group Size

4 students

Time Required

If used as a complete unit:
10 days
If interspersed with other lessons:
4 weeks

Materials Needed

library reference sources

Key Terms

trivia

Project 2

The Question Is . . .

In the late 1980s and early 1990s, trivia was very popular in this country. Trivia is knowledge of unimportant facts. Trivia Bowls were held on college campuses and game shows. Board games focused on the tidbits of knowledge that are stored in our minds. Have you ever wondered who wrote these questions and how they knew the answers?

In this project, your group will act as creative consultants and write trivia questions based on averages. Work in groups of 4.

Each person in your group should be assigned a task based on the following roles. You may wish to change roles after one week.

The Organizer

This person will ensure that the group's information is organized neatly in a file folder. All worksheets, charts, and other information for the group should be contained in one place.

The Investigator

This person will divide the work among group members and try to assist in helping to locate difficult-to-find information.

The Recorder

This person writes a report of the group's progress, decides how often this report is needed, and gives it to the Organizer.

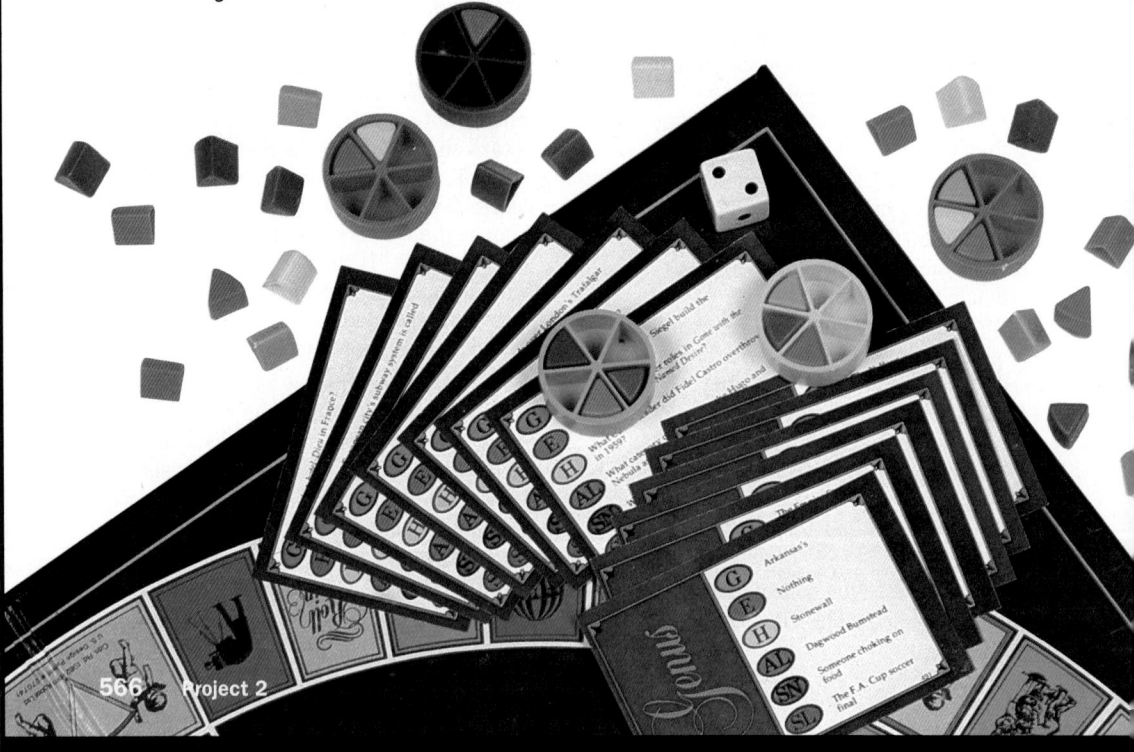

The Question and Answer Person

This person will record all of the facts collected and put it in a question and answer format that can be distributed to the teacher.

All group members will gather facts and data.

One possible way to write each question is to begin with:

Each day in the United States about. . .

Make a list of trivia or fact questions that follow this format. You can group questions by theme if you wish, or write on a variety of topics.

Examples:

1. . . . how many gallons of water do people use in the home?
2. . . . how many times does a 7th grader blink?
3. . . . how many couples get married?
4. . . how many times does a 7th grader's heart beat?
5. . . . how many people immigrate to the United States from other nations?
6. . . . how many magazines are sold?
7. . . . how many disposable diapers make it to landfills?
8. . . . . how many gallons of soft drinks are consumed?

9. . . . how many children go to school?
10. . . . how many ounces of wood do 40,000 termites eat?
11. . . . how many hours of television does a 7th grader watch?
12. . . . how many compact discs are purchased?
13. . . . how many people go to the movies?
14. . . . how many people attend a high school sporting event?
15. . . . how much money do teenagers spend on clothes?

After you have developed your list of questions, be sure to keep a record of your sources and how you arrived at your answers. You can use almanacs and other library resources. Some of your questions may require personal interviews with other students or people in the community. To find answers to some questions, you may need to get results from several people and average them.

When your group is finished, discuss your findings with the class. How did you use what you know about averages to find your answers? Were you surprised by any of your answers?

Project 2   567

OVERVIEW

Objective Design and construct a map that shows facts about countries and oceans of the world and animals that inhabit them.

Summary

In this project, students will work in groups to plan and construct a map of the world that will display various facts of interest. The groups will use principles of proportion to ensure accuracy in their drawings. Then the groups will display their maps and challenge others with questions that can be answered by studying the data that their map presents.

Suggested Group Size

3–5 students

Time Required

If used as a complete unit:
10 days
If interspersed with other lessons:
5 weeks

Materials Needed

chart paper
rulers
stickers or push pins
crayons or markers

Key Terms

legend
map

Project

3 Where In The World?

The National Geographic Society defines geography as "a field of knowledge that deals with the Earth and all the life on it." Geography encompasses many areas of physical, cultural, political, economic, historical, and environmental facts.

In this project, you will make a map of the world and label it with facts about different countries, oceans, and animals found around the world.

Work in a group. Decide how large your map should be. What information do you want to include on it? Will it be something you want to display on a bulletin board when you are finished? How can you use proportions to make your map as accurate as possible?

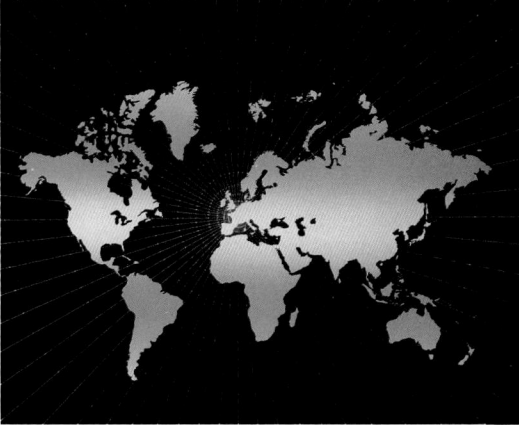

Look at an atlas before you begin drawing. Be as creative as possible. For example, you may want to draw penguins on Antarctica or maple leafs on Canada. You can include a legend to show mountains or bodies of water. You can use color to distinguish countries from each other. Discuss these and other issues with your group to develop a plan on how you will start the project.

Interesting But True

Assign group members different countries to research. Remember, you want to make your map as unique and interesting as possible. So, you will want to find out factual information about different countries that other classmates might not know.

Examples:

Someone told you that the person you are trying to find is in Seattle, Denver, or Houston. Then you receive an anonymous tip that he is in the city with the highest elevation. Where should you look?

Your missing person decides to head toward the most populated country in the world. Where should you look?

Your missing person was spotted in a country that has the largest movie industry in the world. Where should you look?

Take turns solving each question. You could use push pins or stickers to mark the places once each mystery is solved. Some clues may take longer to solve than others so you may want to assign the questions ahead of time and give the detectives time to make an educated guess.

EXTENSION: Where Did It Come From?

You may want to extend this project by examining things you use at home or school to find out in which country they were made. Make a chart of your findings. You can include food, clothing, appliances, games, or electronics on your list. Then locate these countries on your map.

Examples:

More than 40% of the world's oil imports come from the Middle East, where nearly two-thirds of the world's known oil resources are found.

Zambia is a country located in Africa. There are more than 73 ethnic groups speaking more than 80 languages in Zambia.

Share the facts you found with your group members. Choose the most interesting facts and decide how you will label these on your map. If you are not skilled at drawing, you can cut pictures out of magazines and position them on your map.

Once your map is complete, you are now ready to challenge other groups with questions about the world. Have your classmates assume the role of a detective who is trying to locate a missing person.

Your group should make up questions to assist the detectives in finding your missing person.

Project 3 569

Project 4

This Little Piggy

OVERVIEW

Objective Gather data, analyze statistics, and design a way to display the results about a human genetic characteristic.

Summary

In this project, students will collect data on foot length, and then find the mean, median, mode, and range for foot length in different age groupings for males and females. The class will then display and discuss these statistics.

Because this is a characteristic controlled by more than one gene, students should arrive at a bell-shaped curve on a graph. Through collection of large amounts of data, students will experience more accurate results than with a small sample.

Suggested Group Size

4–5 students

Time Required

If used as a complete unit:
5 days
If interspersed with other lessons:
2 weeks

Materials Needed

ruler or flexible paper ruler
chart paper
markers

Key Terms

genetics

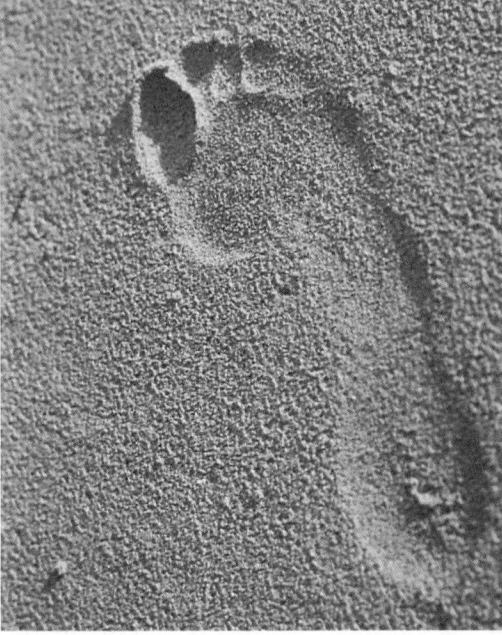

Genetics influences the way you look, the way you act, and your health. Some characteristics like hair color, eye color, and height are very noticeable. Other genetically influenced characteristics are not as obvious. Do you have attached or free earlobes? Do you have a "hitchhiker's thumb"? Can you roll your tongue? Since it is hard to study a number of genetic traits all at once, this project focuses on gathering data on only one characteristic—the length of feet.

The length of the human foot is influenced by multiple genetic factors. To find out about this unique trait in the population, you will gather data, analyze it, and design a method to display the results.

Getting Started

Work in a group. You will collect data about foot length from a variety of people. Include many different ages and both males and females. Record your data in a chart. Each group should measure the feet of *at least* 20 people. You should make your measurements from the tip of the big toe to the bottom of the heel.

HINT: You can make a flexible paper ruler by placing a strip of paper over a plastic ruler with raised markings. Rub over the ruler with your pencil, and the markings will be transferred to your paper ruler.

570 Project 4

Decide how you are going to separate your data into age groups.

- Are you going to make three-year groupings (ages 0–2, 3–5, and so on), five-year groupings (0–4, 5–9 and so on), or some other grouping?
- Are you going to make smaller groupings for young children and increase the age increments to 10 years for adults, or will you use the same groupings for all ages?

Analyze the data in each grouping. You may want to make the following calculations for males and females.

- mean
- median
- mode
- range

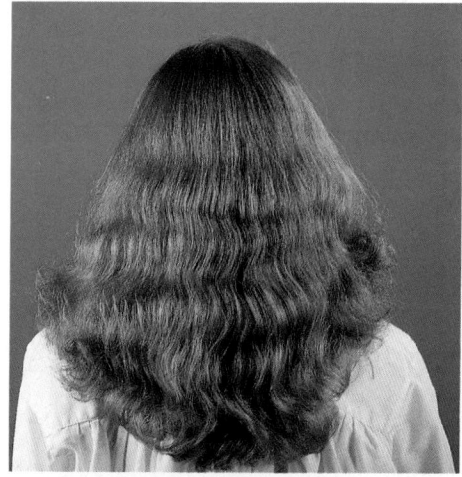

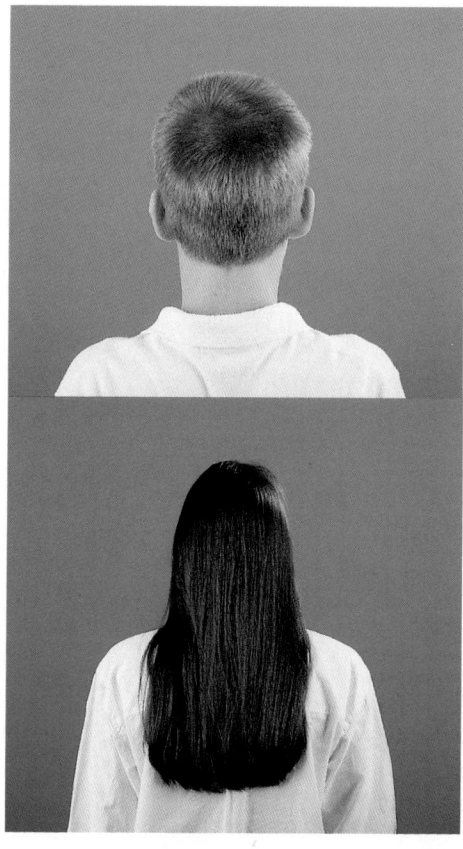

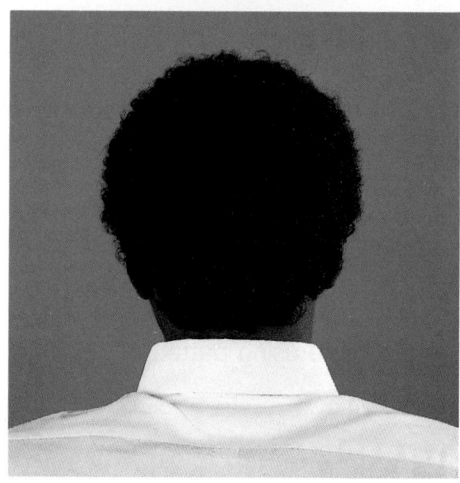

Decide how to display the data you have analyzed so that the differences between males and females and among different age groupings can be easily seen.

Extension

Ask a local podiatrist for charts that list the average foot size for various age groups. See how close your results come to these published averages. Check with several local shoe stores to find out what sizes sell the most.

TEACHING NOTES

This project examines a characteristic governed by multiple genetic factors–the length of feet. Students should make their measurements from the top of the big toe to the heel.

Before dividing into groups, discuss how large amounts of data make the outcome of an investigation more reliable.

After all of the data has been gathered, you may want to assign one particular age grouping to each cooperative group.

Encourage students to be creative with their displays. One suggestion is to make construction paper feet to display the statistics.

EXTENSION

You may wish to have students investigate the variation in foot size within age groupings.

Extra Practice

Lesson 1-2 Estimate using rounding.

1. $216 + 492$ **700**
2. $1,235 + 5,645$ **7,000**
3. $6,478 - 2,345$ **4,000**
4. $1,510 + 523$ **2,000**
5. $298 + 109$ **400**
6. $8,710 - 610$ **8,100**
7. $15,269 + 14,795$ **30,000**
8. $958,752 - 125,568$ **830,000**
9. $145 + 256 + 872$ **1,300**
10. $23,456 + 758,567$ **782,000**
11. $6,915 - 3,854$ **3,000**
12. $7,785 + 563 + 1,973$ **10,400**
13. $1,085,365 - 523,894$ **600,000**
14. $1,616 + 5,897 + 2,439$ **10,000**
15. $\$665 + \$900 + \$213$ **$1,800**
16. $45,648 - 44,896$ **1,000**

Lesson 1-3 Estimate using patterns.

1. $601 \div 6$ **100**
2. 364×6 **2,400**
3. $699 \div 9$ **80**
4. 658×8 **5,600**
5. 821×90 **72,000**
6. $786 \div 80$ **10**
7. 398×13 **4,000**
8. 243×6 **1,200**
9. 269×20 **6,000**
10. $1,423 \times 7$ **9,800**
11. $1,499 \div 50$ **30**
12. $735 \div 8$ **90**
13. $1,602 \times 2$ **3,200**
14. $672 \div 65$ **1,800**
15. 198×9 **20**
16. $410 \div 7$ **60**
17. $8,620 \div 5$ **1,700**
18. $1,410 \div 7$ **200**
19. 41×6 **240**
20. 149×5 **750**

Lesson 1-4 Determine whether the answers shown are reasonable.

1. $44 + 56 = 100$ **yes**
2. $11 \times 36 = 480$ **no**
3. $\$44.59 \div 2 = \$2.35$ **no**
4. $45 + 25 = 70$ **yes**
5. $39 - 27 = -11$ **no**
6. $18 \times 21 = 378$ **yes**
7. $108 + 204 = 389$ **no**
8. $\$0.69 \times 3 = \$2.07$ **yes**
9. $1,620 - 768 = 852$ **yes**
10. $2,569 + 4,298 = 6,867$ **yes**
11. $99 \div 11 = 0.9$ **no**
12. $\$456 + \$1,324 = \$1,780$ **yes**
13. $5,235 - 4,945 = 29$ **no**
14. $633 \div 11 = 6.63$ **no**
15. $108 + 204 = 312$ **yes**

Lesson 1-7   Evaluate each expression.

1. $14 - 5 + 7$ **16**
2. $12 + 10 - 5 - 6$ **11**
3. $50 - 6 + 12 + 4$ **60**
4. $12 - 2 \times 3$ **6**
5. $16 + 4 \times 5$ **36**
6. $5 + 3 \times 4 - 7$ **10**
7. $2 \times 3 + 9 \times 2$ **24**
8. $6 \times 8 + 4 \div 2$ **50**
9. $7 \times 6 - 14$ **28**
10. $8 + 12 \times 4 \div 8$ **14**
11. $13 - 6 \times 2 + 1$ **2**
12. $80 \div 10 \times 8$ **64**
13. $1 + 2 + 3 + 4$ **10**
14. $1 \times 2 \times 3 \times 4$ **24**
15. $6 + 6 \times 6$ **42**
16. $14 - 2 \times 7 + 0$ **0**
17. $156 - 6 \times 0$ **156**
18. $30 - 14 \times 2 + 8$ **10**

Lesson 1-8   Evaluate each expression if $a = 3$, $b = 4$, and $c = 12$.

1. $a + b$ **7**
2. $c - a$ **9**
3. $a + b + c$ **19**
4. $b - a$ **1**
5. $c - a \times b$ **0**
6. $a + 2 \times b$ **11**
7. $b + c \div 2$ **10**
8. ab **12**
9. $a + 3b$ **15**
10. $a + c \div 6$ **5**
11. $25 + c \div b$ **28**
12. abc **144**
13. $2(a + b) \div 7$ **2**
14. $2c \div b$ **6**
15. $144 - abc$ **0**
16. $2ab$ **24**
17. $c \div a + 10$ **14**
18. $9b \div 3$ **12**
19. $2b - a$ **5**
20. ac **36**

Lesson 1-9   Write each product using exponents.

1. $2 \cdot 2 \cdot 2 \cdot 2 \cdot 2$ **2^5**
2. $6 \cdot 6 \cdot 6 \cdot 7 \cdot 7$ **$6^3 \cdot 7^2$**
3. $9 \cdot 9 \cdot 9 \cdot 9 \cdot 9 \cdot 9 \cdot 10$ **$9^6 \cdot 10$**
4. $k \cdot k \cdot k \cdot \ell \cdot \ell \cdot \ell$ **$k^3 \cdot \ell^3$**
5. $14 \cdot 14 \cdot 6$ **$14^2 \cdot 6$**
6. $3 \cdot 3 \cdot 3 \cdot 3 \cdot y \cdot y$ **$3^4 \cdot y^2$**

Write each power as a product.

7. 13^4 **$13 \cdot 13 \cdot 13 \cdot 13$**
8. 9^6 **$9 \cdot 9 \cdot 9 \cdot 9 \cdot 9 \cdot 9$**
9. $2^3 \cdot 3^2$ **$2 \cdot 2 \cdot 2 \cdot 3 \cdot 3$**
10. x^5 **$x \cdot x \cdot x \cdot x \cdot x$**
11. 169^3 **$169 \cdot 169 \cdot 169$**
12. $13{,}410^2$ **$13{,}410 \cdot 13{,}410$**

Evaluate each expression.

13. 5^6 **15,625**
14. 17^3 **4,913**
15. 2^{12} **4,096**
16. $3^5 \cdot 2^3$ **1,944**
17. $6^4 \cdot 3$ **3,888**
18. $2^2 \cdot 3^2 \cdot 4^2$ **576**
19. 176^2 **30,976**
20. $6 \cdot 4^3$ **384**
21. five squared **25**
22. 2 to the fifth power **32**
23. 4 cubed **64**

Lesson 1-10   Solve each equation.

1. $b + 7 = 12$ **5**
2. $a + 3 = 15$ **12**
3. $s + 10 = 23$ **13**
4. $9 + n = 13$ **4**

5. $20 = 24 - n$ **4**
6. $4x = 36$ **9**
7. $2y = 10$ **5**
8. $15 = 5h$ **3**

9. $j \div 3 = 2$ **6**
10. $14 = w - 4$ **18**
11. $24 \div k = 6$ **4**
12. $b - 3 = 12$ **15**

13. $c \div 10 = 8$ **80**
14. $y \div 2 = 8$ **16**
15. $6 = t \div 5$ **30**
16. $42 = 6n$ **7**

17. $14 + m = 24$ **10**
18. $g - 3 = 10$ **13**
19. $7 + a = 10$ **3**
20. $3y = 39$ **13**

21. $\frac{f}{2} = 12$ **24**
22. $16 = 4v$ **4**
23. $81 = 80 + a$ **1**
24. $9 = \frac{72}{x}$ **8**

Lesson 2-1   Replace each ● with <, >, or = .

1. 0.36 ● 0.63 $<$
2. 1.74 ● 1.7 $>$
3. 4.03 ● 4.003 $>$

4. 0.06 ● 0.066 $<$
5. 10.5 ● 10.05 $>$
6. 3.0 ● 3 $=$

7. 5.632 ● 5.623 $>$
8. 0.423 ● 0.5 $<$
9. 2.020 ● 2.202 $<$

10. 0.93 ● 0.9 $>$
11. 0.205 ● 0.025 $>$
12. 0.46 ● 0.49 $<$

13. 13.100 ● 13.1 $=$
14. 6.25 ● 6.20 $>$
15. 9.99 ● 9.099 $>$

16. 0.030 ● 0.03 $=$
17. 0.062 ● 0.62 $<$
18. 1.14 ● 1.09 $>$

19. 10.1 ● 100.0 $<$
20. 0.02 ● 0.002 $>$
21. 2.101 ● 2.11 $<$

Lesson 2-2   Round each number to the underlined place-value position.

1. $5.\underline{6}4$ **5.6**
2. $0.2\underline{6}25$ **0.26**
3. $0.45\underline{6}95$ **0.457**
4. $6.\underline{2}49$ **6.2**

5. $15.\underline{2}98$ **15.3**
6. $0.002\underline{6}325$ **0.0026**
7. $758.9\underline{9}9$ **759.00**
8. $\underline{4}.25$ **4**

9. $32.65\underline{8}2$ **32.658**
10. $\underline{0}.025$ **0**
11. $1.00\underline{4}9$ **1.005**
12. $9.\underline{2}5$ **9.3**

13. $67.4\underline{9}2$ **67.49**
14. $25.\underline{1}9$ **25.2**
15. $26.\underline{9}6$ **27.0**
16. $4.0\underline{0}65$ **4.01**

17. $26.96\underline{6}6$ **26.967**
18. $1.\underline{2}499999$ **1.2**
19. $2.0\underline{1}2$ **2.01**
20. $1\underline{6}.569$ **17**

Lesson 2-3

Estimate. Use an appropriate strategy. Sample answers given.

1. $\begin{array}{r} 0.245 \\ + 0.256 \\ \hline \mathbf{0.51} \end{array}$

2. $\begin{array}{r} 2.45698 \\ - 1.26589 \\ \hline \mathbf{1.2} \end{array}$

3. $\begin{array}{r} 0.5962 \\ + 1.2598 \\ \hline \mathbf{1.9} \end{array}$

4. $\begin{array}{r} 17.985 \\ - 9.001 \\ \hline \mathbf{9} \end{array}$

5. $\begin{array}{r} 12.6589 \\ - 6.3874 \\ \hline \mathbf{6.3} \end{array}$

6. $\begin{array}{r} 0.005698 \\ + 0.015963 \\ \hline \mathbf{0.020} \end{array}$

7. $\begin{array}{r} 1.26589 \\ + 0.76589 \\ \hline \mathbf{2.1} \end{array}$

8. $\begin{array}{r} 15.986325 \\ - 12.965236 \\ \hline \mathbf{3.02} \end{array}$

9. $\begin{array}{r} 8.5 \\ \times 9.1 \\ \hline \mathbf{81} \end{array}$

10. $\begin{array}{r} 12.9568 \\ \times 6.1563 \\ \hline \mathbf{78} \end{array}$

11. $\begin{array}{r} 9.652 \\ \times 6.2 \\ \hline \mathbf{60} \end{array}$

12. $\begin{array}{r} 25.49862 \\ \times 4.2136 \\ \hline \mathbf{100} \end{array}$

13. $1.12 + 0.9865 + 1.023 + 0.89 + 0.99 + 1.03569$ **6**

14. $3\overline{)11.75}$ **4**

15. $82.1 + 79.3 + 81.5 + 79 + 80 + 81.256$ **480**

16. $4.1\overline{)16.123}$ **4**

Lesson 2-4   Multiply.

1. 9.6×10.5 **100.8**

2. 3.2×0.1 **0.32**

3. 10.5×9.6 **100.8**

4. 5.42×0.21 **1.1382**

5. 7.42×0.2 **1.484**

6. 0.001×0.02 **0.00002**

7. 0.6×542 **325.2**

8. 6.7×5.8 **38.86**

9. 3.24×6.7 **21.708**

10. 9.8×4.62 **45.276**

11. 7.32×9.7 **71.004**

12. 0.008×0.007 **0.000056**

13. 0.0001×56 **0.0056**

14. 4.5×0.2 **0.9**

15. 9.6×2.3 **22.08**

16. 5.63×8.1 **45.603**

17. 10.35×9.1 **94.185**

18. 28.2×3.9 **109.98**

19. 102.13×1.221 **124.70073**

20. 2.02×1.25 **2.525**

21. 8.37×89.6 **749.952**

Lesson 2-5   Multiply mentally.

1. 1.2×10 **12**

2. 0.23×100 **23**

3. $1.235 \times 1,000$ **1,235**

4. 1.2×10^3 **1,200**

5. 0.002×100 **0.2**

6. 3.56×10^2 **356**

7. 0.000012×10^{10} **120,000**

8. 95.23×10^1 **952.3**

9. 76.425×10^4 **764,250**

10. $1.0056 \times 10,000$ **10,056**

11. 4.7×1 **4.7**

12. 9.6×10^0 **9.6**

Lesson 2-6

Write each number in scientific notation.

1. 720 7.2×10^2 2. 7,560 3. 892 8.92×10^2 4. 1,400 1.4×10^3 5. 91,256
7.56×10^3 9.1256×10^4

6. 51,000 5.1×10^4 7. 145,600 1.456×10^5 8. 90,100 9.01×10^4 9. 123,580,000,000
1.2358×10^{11}

Write each number in standard form.

10. 4.5×10^3 **4,500** 11. 2×10^4 **20,000** 12. 1.725896×10^6
1,725,896

13. 9.61×10^2 **961** 14. 1×10^7 **10,000,000** 15. 8.256×10^8
825,600,000

16. 5.26×10^4 **52,600** 17. 3.25×10^2 **325** 18. 6.79×10^5 **679,000**

Lesson 2-7   Divide.

1. $9)\overline{0.036}$ **0.004** 2. $13)\overline{39.39}$ **3.03** 3. $45)\overline{0.585}$ **0.013** 4. $8)\overline{0.024}$ **0.003**

5. $6)\overline{0.312}$ **0.052** 6. $7)\overline{0.161}$ **0.023** 7. $7)\overline{7.21}$ **1.03** 8. $3)\overline{9.18}$ **3.06**

9. $0.72 \div 12$ **$0.06** 10. $0.36 \div 9$ **0.04** 11. $0.56 \div 14$ **0.04**

12. $32.2 \div 8$ **4.025** 13. $0.3869 \div 5.3$ **0.073** 14. $0.39 \div 7.8$ **0.05**

15. $0.0426 \div 7.1$ **0.006** 16. $0.1185 \div 7.9$ **0.015** 17. $0.84 \div 12$ **$0.07**

18. $4.544 \div 64$ **0.071** 19. $0.384 \div 9.6$ **0.04** 20. $0.2262 \div 8.7$ **0.026**

Lesson 2-8   Divide. Round to the nearest tenth.

1. $26.5 \div 4$ **6.6** 2. $46.25 \div 8$ **5.8** 3. $19.38 \div 9$ **2.2**

4. $8.5 \div 2$ **4.3** 5. $90.88 \div 14$ **6.5** 6. $23.1 \div 4$ **5.8**

7. $19.5 \div 27$ **0.7** 8. $26.5 \div 19$ **1.4** 9. $46.23 \div 25$ **1.8**

10. $46.25 \div 25$ **1.9** 11. $4.26 \div 9$ **0.5** 12. $18.74 \div 19$ **1.0**

Divide. Round to the nearest hundredth.

13. $17.9 \div 21$ **0.85** 14. $57.9 \div 14$ **4.14** 15. $21.555 \div 6$ **3.59**

16. $6.435 \div 7$ **0.92** 17. $15.23 \div 8$ **1.90** 18. $1.2356 \div 3$ **0.41**

19. $156.8 \div 25$ **6.27** 20. $19.563 \div 6$ **3.26** 21. $0.125 \div 1$ **0.13**

Lesson 2-9   Complete.

1. 400 mm = ___ cm **40**

2. 4 km = ___ m **4,000**

3. 660 cm = ___ m
   6.6

4. 0.3 km = ___ m **300**

5. 30 mm = ___ cm **3**

6. 84.5 m = ___ km
   0.0845

7. ___ m = 54 cm **0.54**

8. 18 km = ___ cm **1,800,000**

9. ___ mm = 45 cm
   450

10. 4 kg = ___ g **4,000**

11. 632 mg = ___ g **0.632**

12. 4,497 g = ___ kg
    4.497

13. ___ mg = 21 g **21,000**

14. 61.2 mg = ___ g **0.0612**

15. 61 g = ___ mg
    61,000

16. ___ mg = 0.51 kg **510,000**

17. 0.63 kg = ___ g **630**

18. ___ kg = 563 g
    0.563

Lesson 3-3   Find the range for each set of data. Choose an appropriate scale and intervals. Draw a number line to show the scale and intervals.

For number lines, see Solutions Manual.

1. 25, 26, 27, 25, 28, 27, 26, 28, 25 **3**

2. 110, 210, 156, 174, 135, 198, 127, 160 **100**

3. 85, 76, 91, 81, 97, 74, 77, 82, 93 **23**

4. 0.5, 0.6, 0.1, 0.4, 0.8, 0.6, 0.3, 0.55 **0.7**

5. 3, 4, 5, 1, 8, 5, 2, 3, 6, 4, 7, 8, 2, 1 **7**

4.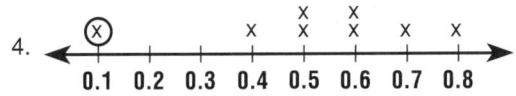

5.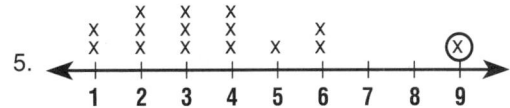

Lesson 3-4   Make a line plot for each set of data. Circle any outliers on the line plot.

1. 25, 26, 27, 25, 28, 27, 21, 26, 28, 25

2. 110, 210, 156, 174, 125, 198, 165, 185

3. 600, 650, 700, 600, 625, 675, 450, 650

4. 0.5, 0.6, 0.1, 0.4, 0.8, 0.6, 0.7, 0.5

5. 3, 4, 5, 2, 6, 1, 2, 4, 3, 6, 9, 1, 2, 3

1.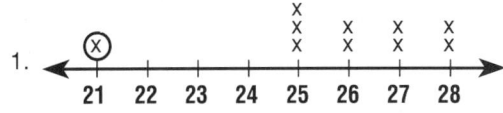

2.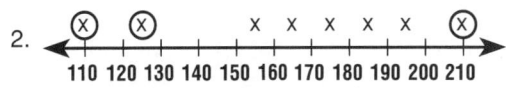

3.

Lesson 3-5 Find the mode(s), median, and mean for each set of data. Round answers to the nearest tenth.

1. 1, 5, 9, 1, 2, 5, 8, 2 **1, 2, and 5; 3.5; 4.1**

2. 2, 5, 8, 9, 7, 6, 3, 5 **5, 5.5, 5.6**

3. 1, 2, 1, 2, 2, 1, 2 **2, 2, 1.6**

4. 12, 13, 15, 12, 12, 11 **12, 12, 12.5**

5. 256, 265, 247, 256 **256, 256, 256**

6. 957, 562, 462, 847, 721 **no mode, 721, 709.8**

7. 46, 54, 66, 54, 46, 66
46, 54 and 66; 54; 55.3

8. 81, 82, 83, 84, 85, 86, 87 **no mode, 84, 84**

Lesson 3-6 Make a stem-and-leaf plot for each set of data.

1. 23, 15, 39, 68, 57, 42, 51, 52, 41, 18, 29

2. 5, 14, 39, 28, 14, 6, 7, 18, 13, 28, 9, 14

3. 189, 182, 196, 184, 197, 183, 196, 194, 184

4. 71, 82, 84, 95, 76, 92, 83, 74, 81, 75, 96

```
1. 1 | 58        2. 0 | 5679
   2 | 39           1 | 34448
   3 | 9            2 | 88
   4 | 12           3 | 9      0|5 = 5
   5 | 127
   6 | 8         3. 18 | 23449
     1|5 = 15      19 | 4667
                     18|9 = 189
```

```
4. 7 | 1456
   8 | 1234
   9 | 256    7|1 = 71
```

Lesson 3-7

1. Darlene's quiz scores in science have been steadily going up since her parents hired a tutor for her. Based on the graph at the right, predict what Darlene's score will be on the next quiz. **7**

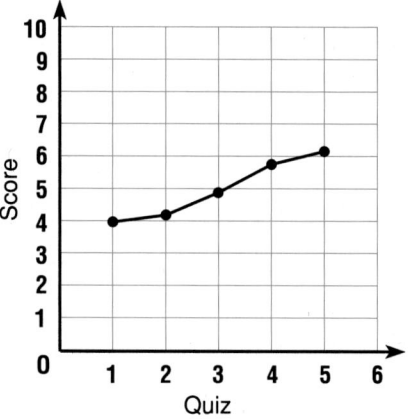

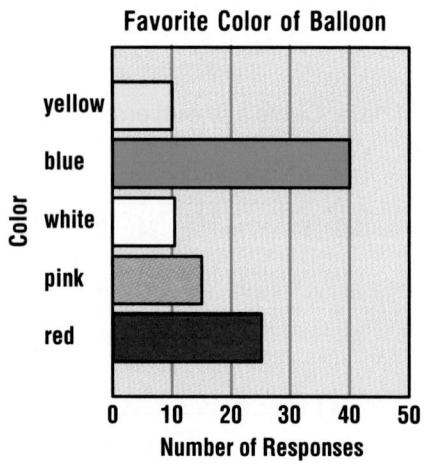

Favorite Color of Balloon

2. A balloon maker asked 100 kids what their favorite color of balloon is. The graph at the left shows their responses. What color of balloon should he make the most of? **blue**

Lesson 4-1
Determine whether the first number is divisible by the second number.

1. 279; 3 **yes**
2. 1,240; 6 **no**
3. 3,250; 5 **yes**
4. 835; 4 **no**
5. 5,550; 10 **yes**
6. 315; 9 **yes**
7. 777; 6 **no**
8. 4,214; 3 **no**
9. 3,012; 2 **yes**
10. 244; 4 **yes**
11. 984; 6 **yes**
12. 1,000; 5 **yes**

Determine whether each number is divisible by 2, 3, 4, 5, 6, 9, or 10.

13. 453 **3**
14. 2,225 **5**
15. 504 **2, 3, 4, 6, 9**
16. 4,300 **2, 4, 5, 10**
17. 672 **2, 3, 4, 6**
18. 8,240 **2, 4, 5, 10**
19. 111 **3**
20. 6,232 **2, 4**
21. 999 **3, 9**
22. 5,200 **2, 4, 5, 10**
23. 3,217 **none**
24. 804 **2, 3, 4, 6**

Lesson 4-2
Determine whether each number is composite or prime.

1. 32 **composite**
2. 417 **composite**
3. 5,212 **composite**
4. 2,111 **prime**
5. 71 **prime**
6. 1,005 **composite**
7. 239 **prime**
8. 3,215 **composite**

Write the prime factorization of each number.

9. 81 3^4
10. 525 $3 \times 5^2 \times 7$
11. 245 5×7^2
12. 1,120 $2^5 \times 5 \times 7$
13. 750 $2 \times 3 \times 5^3$
14. 2,400 $2^5 \times 3 \times 5^2$
15. 914 2×457
16. 975 $3 \times 5^2 \times 13$

Use your calculator to find the prime factors of each number. Then write the prime factorization of each number.

17. 423 $3^2 \times 47$
18. 972 $2^2 \times 3^5$
19. 144 $2^4 \times 3^2$
20. 72 $2^3 \times 3^2$

8. geometric; 1,250; 6,250; 31,250
9. geometric; 648; 1,944; 5,832   17. geometric; 10,000; 100,000; 1,000,000

Lesson 4-3
Identify each sequence as arithmetic, geometric, or neither. Then find the next three terms in each sequence.

1. 5, 9, 13, 17, … **arithmetic; 21, 25, 29**
2. 3, 6, 12, 24, … **geometric; 48, 96, 192**
3. 10, 15, 25, 40, … **neither; 60, 85, 115**
4. 4.5, 5.4, 6.3, 7.2, … **arithmetic; 8.:, 9.0, 9.9**
5. 90, 100, 91, 99, 92, … **neither; 98, 93, 97**
6. 0.5, 0.4, 0.3, … **arithmetic; 0.2, 0.1, 0.0**
7. 64, 16, 4, 1, … **geometric; $\frac{1}{4}$, $\frac{1}{16}$, $\frac{1}{64}$**
8. 10, 50, 250, …
9. 8, 24, 72, 216, …
10. 16, 8, 4, 2, … **geometric; 1, $\frac{1}{2}$, $\frac{1}{4}$**
11. 49, 7, 1, $\frac{1}{7}$, … **geometric; $\frac{1}{49}$, $\frac{1}{343}$, $\frac{1}{2,401}$**
12. 500, 400, 300, … **arithmetic; 200, 100, 0**
13. 40, 42, 46, 52, 60, … **neither; 70, 82, 96**
14. 75, 15, 3, $\frac{3}{5}$, … **geometric; $\frac{3}{25}$, $\frac{3}{125}$, $\frac{3}{625}$**
15. 27, 9, 3, 1, … **geometric; $\frac{1}{3}$, $\frac{1}{9}$, $\frac{1}{27}$**
16. 1, 2, 4, 7, 11, … **neither; 16, 22, 29**
17. 10, 100, 1,000, …
18. 1, 10, 19, 28, 37, … **arithmetic; 46, 55, 64**
19. 225, 250, 275, … **arithmetic; 300, 325, 350**
20. 2.5, 3.0, 3.5, 4.0, … **arithmetic; 4.5, 5.0, 5.5**

Lesson 4-5 Find the GCF of each set of numbers.

1. 12, 16 **4**
2. 63, 81 **9**
3. 225, 500 **25**
4. 37, 100 **1**

5. 240, 32 **16**
6. 640, 412 **4**
7. 36, 81 **9**
8. 350, 140 **70**

9. 72, 170 **2**
10. 255, 51 **51**
11. 48, 72 **24**

12. 86, 200 **2**
13. 24, 56, 120 **8**
14. 48, 60, 84 **12**

15. 32, 80, 96 **16**
16. 49, 14, 70 **7**
17. 6, 8, 12 **2**

18. 33, 55, 77 **11**
19. 27, 15, 300 **3**
20. 45, 150, 225 **15**

Lesson 4-6 Express each fraction in simplest form.

1. $\frac{14}{28}$ **$\frac{1}{2}$**
2. $\frac{15}{25}$ **$\frac{3}{5}$**
3. $\frac{100}{300}$ **$\frac{1}{3}$**
4. $\frac{14}{35}$ **$\frac{2}{5}$**

5. $\frac{9}{51}$ **$\frac{3}{17}$**
6. $\frac{54}{56}$ **$\frac{27}{28}$**
7. $\frac{75}{90}$ **$\frac{5}{6}$**
8. $\frac{24}{40}$ **$\frac{3}{5}$**

9. $\frac{180}{270}$ **$\frac{2}{3}$**
10. $\frac{312}{390}$ **$\frac{4}{5}$**
11. $\frac{240}{448}$ **$\frac{15}{28}$**
12. $\frac{71}{82}$ **$\frac{71}{82}$**

13. $\frac{333}{900}$ **$\frac{37}{100}$**
14. $\frac{85}{255}$ **$\frac{1}{3}$**
15. $\frac{84}{128}$ **$\frac{21}{32}$**
16. $\frac{640}{960}$ **$\frac{2}{3}$**

Lesson 4-7 Express each fraction as a decimal. Use bar notation if necessary.

1. $\frac{16}{20}$ **0.8**
2. $\frac{25}{100}$ **0.25**
3. $\frac{7}{8}$ **0.875**
4. $\frac{48}{60}$ **0.8**

5. $\frac{11}{40}$ **0.275**
6. $\frac{13}{50}$ **0.26**
7. $\frac{55}{300}$ **0.18$\overline{3}$**
8. $\frac{18}{12}$ **1.5**

Express each decimal as a fraction in simplest form.

9. 0.38 **$\frac{19}{50}$**
10. 2.05 **$2\frac{1}{20}$**
11. 0.075 **$\frac{3}{40}$**
12. 0.18 **$\frac{9}{50}$**

13. 0.675 **$\frac{27}{40}$**
14. 15.33 **$15\frac{33}{100}$**
15. 0.64 **$\frac{16}{25}$**
16. 6.04 **$6\frac{1}{25}$**

Lesson 4-8

The spinner shown at the right is equally likely to stop on each of the regions numbered 1 to 8. Find the probability that the spinner will stop on each of the following.

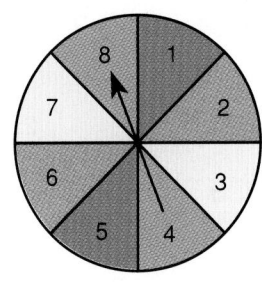

1. an even number $\frac{1}{2}$
2. a prime number $\frac{1}{2}$
3. a factor of 12 $\frac{5}{8}$
4. a composite number $\frac{3}{8}$
5. a number less than 5 $\frac{1}{2}$
6. a factor of 36 $\frac{5}{8}$

A package of balloons contains 5 green, 3 yellow, 4 red, and 8 pink balloons. If you reach in the package and choose one balloon at random, what is the probability that you will select each of the following? Express each ratio as both a fraction and a decimal.

7. a red balloon $\frac{1}{5}$, 0.2
8. a green balloon $\frac{1}{4}$, 0.25
9. a pink balloon $\frac{2}{5}$, 0.4
10. a yellow balloon $\frac{3}{20}$, 0.15
11. a red or yellow balloon $\frac{7}{20}$, 0.35

Lesson 4-9

Find the LCM of each set of numbers.

1. 4, 9 **36**
2. 6, 16 **48**
3. 3, 8, 14 **168**
4. 24, 36 **72**
5. 48, 84 **336**
6. 12, 18, 28 **252**
7. 8, 9 **72**
8. 49, 56 **392**
9. 42, 66 **462**
10. 15, 39 **195**
11. 32, 80, 96 **480**
12. 56, 64 **448**
13. 24, 42 **168**
14. 250, 80 **2,000**
15. 26, 169 **338**
16. 5, 18, 45 **90**
17. 11, 22, 33 **66**
18. 56, 14, 70 **280**
19. 16, 24 **48**
20. 13, 14 **182**

Lesson 4-10

Find the LCD for each pair of fractions.

1. $\frac{3}{8}, \frac{2}{3}$ **24**
2. $\frac{5}{9}, \frac{7}{12}$ **36**
3. $\frac{4}{9}, \frac{8}{15}$ **45**
4. $\frac{11}{24}, \frac{17}{42}$ **168**
5. $\frac{12}{36}, \frac{15}{42}$ **252**
6. $\frac{25}{27}, \frac{43}{81}$ **81**
7. $\frac{32}{64}, \frac{15}{48}$ **192**
8. $\frac{2}{6}, \frac{14}{15}$ **30**

Replace each ● with <, >, or = to make a true statement.

9. $\frac{7}{9}$ ● $\frac{3}{5}$ **>**
10. $\frac{14}{25}$ ● $\frac{3}{4}$ **<**
11. $\frac{8}{24}$ ● $\frac{20}{60}$ **=**
12. $\frac{5}{12}$ ● $\frac{4}{9}$ **<**
13. $\frac{18}{24}$ ● $\frac{10}{18}$ **>**
14. $\frac{4}{6}$ ● $\frac{5}{9}$ **>**
15. $\frac{11}{49}$ ● $\frac{12}{42}$ **<**
16. $\frac{5}{14}$ ● $\frac{2}{6}$ **>**

Lesson 5-1
Change each improper fraction to a mixed number in simplest form or a whole number.

1. $\frac{5}{4}$ $1\frac{1}{4}$ 2. $\frac{10}{7}$ $1\frac{3}{7}$ 3. $\frac{6}{3}$ 2 4. $\frac{9}{4}$ $2\frac{1}{4}$ 5. $\frac{3}{2}$ $1\frac{1}{2}$ 6. $\frac{9}{3}$ 3

7. $\frac{16}{10}$ $1\frac{3}{5}$ 8. $\frac{7}{3}$ $2\frac{1}{3}$ 9. $\frac{3}{1}$ 3 10. $\frac{8}{6}$ $1\frac{1}{3}$ 11. $\frac{21}{20}$ $1\frac{1}{20}$ 12. $\frac{21}{7}$ 3

13. $\frac{12}{4}$ 3 14. $\frac{5}{2}$ $2\frac{1}{2}$ 15. $\frac{7}{4}$ $1\frac{3}{4}$ 16. $\frac{20}{6}$ $3\frac{1}{3}$ 17. $\frac{10}{3}$ $3\frac{1}{3}$ 18. $\frac{26}{5}$ $5\frac{1}{5}$

Lesson 5-2
Round each fraction to 0, $\frac{1}{2}$, or 1.

1. $\frac{3}{8}$ $\frac{1}{2}$ 2. $\frac{1}{9}$ 0 3. $\frac{6}{7}$ 1 4. $\frac{7}{12}$ $\frac{1}{2}$ 5. $\frac{1}{6}$ 0 6. $\frac{10}{12}$ 1

Round to the nearest whole number.

7. $5\frac{7}{8}$ 6 8. $3\frac{7}{12}$ 4 9. $7\frac{1}{10}$ 7 10. $2\frac{5}{12}$ 2 11. $2\frac{4}{9}$ 2 12. $8\frac{3}{4}$ 9

Estimate. **Sample answers given.**

13. $\frac{3}{7}+\frac{6}{8}$ $1\frac{1}{2}$ 14. $\frac{3}{10}+\frac{4}{7}$ 1 15. $\frac{3}{9}+\frac{7}{8}$ $1\frac{1}{2}$ 16. $\frac{1}{8}+\frac{8}{9}$ 1

17. $1\frac{1}{2}+2\frac{1}{4}$ 4 18. $3\frac{1}{8}+7\frac{6}{7}$ 11 19. $4\frac{2}{3}+6\frac{7}{8}$ 12 20. $3\frac{2}{3}\times2\frac{1}{3}$ 8

21. $\frac{4}{5}\times3$ 3 22. $9\frac{7}{8}-6\frac{2}{3}$ 3 23. $\frac{3}{7}-\frac{1}{15}$ $\frac{1}{2}$ 24. $\frac{26}{17}\times\frac{37}{38}$ 1

Lesson 5-3
Add or subtract. Write each sum or difference in simplest form.

1. $\frac{5}{11}+\frac{9}{11}$ $1\frac{3}{11}$ 2. $\frac{5}{8}-\frac{1}{8}$ $\frac{1}{2}$ 3. $\frac{7}{10}+\frac{7}{10}$ $1\frac{2}{5}$ 4. $\frac{9}{12}-\frac{5}{12}$ $\frac{1}{3}$

5. $\frac{2}{9}+\frac{1}{3}$ $\frac{5}{9}$ 6. $\frac{1}{2}+\frac{3}{4}$ $1\frac{1}{4}$ 7. $\frac{1}{4}-\frac{3}{12}$ 0 8. $\frac{3}{7}+\frac{6}{14}$ $\frac{6}{7}$

9. $\frac{1}{4}+\frac{3}{5}$ $\frac{17}{20}$ 10. $\frac{4}{9}+\frac{1}{2}$ $\frac{17}{18}$ 11. $\frac{5}{7}+\frac{4}{6}$ $1\frac{8}{21}$ 12. $\frac{3}{4}-\frac{1}{6}$ $\frac{7}{12}$

13. $\frac{3}{5}+\frac{3}{4}$ $1\frac{7}{20}$ 14. $\frac{2}{3}-\frac{1}{8}$ $\frac{13}{24}$ 15. $\frac{9}{10}+\frac{1}{3}$ $1\frac{7}{30}$ 16. $\frac{8}{15}+\frac{2}{9}$ $\frac{34}{45}$

17. $\frac{6}{7}+\frac{6}{9}$ $1\frac{11}{21}$ 18. $\frac{3}{7}+\frac{3}{4}$ $1\frac{5}{28}$ 19. $\frac{5}{7}+\frac{5}{9}$ $1\frac{17}{63}$ 20. $\frac{7}{8}+\frac{5}{6}$ $1\frac{17}{24}$

Lesson 5-4   Add or subtract. Write each sum or difference in simplest form.

1. $2\frac{1}{3} + 1\frac{1}{3}$ **$3\frac{2}{3}$**   2. $5\frac{2}{7} - 2\frac{3}{7}$ **$2\frac{6}{7}$**   3. $6\frac{3}{8} + 7\frac{1}{8}$ **$13\frac{1}{2}$**   4. $2\frac{3}{4} - 1\frac{1}{4}$ **$1\frac{1}{2}$**

5. $5\frac{1}{2} - 3\frac{1}{4}$ **$2\frac{1}{4}$**   6. $2\frac{2}{3} + 4\frac{1}{9}$ **$6\frac{7}{9}$**   7. $7\frac{4}{5} + 9\frac{3}{10}$ **$17\frac{1}{10}$**   8. $3\frac{3}{4} + 5\frac{5}{8}$ **$9\frac{3}{8}$**

9. $10\frac{2}{3} + 5\frac{6}{7}$ **$16\frac{11}{21}$**   10. $17\frac{2}{9} - 12\frac{1}{3}$ **$4\frac{8}{9}$**   11. $6\frac{5}{12} + 12\frac{5}{12}$ **$18\frac{5}{6}$**   12. $7\frac{1}{4} + 15\frac{5}{6}$ **$23\frac{1}{12}$**

13. $6\frac{1}{8} + 4\frac{2}{3}$ **$10\frac{19}{24}$**   14. $7 - 6\frac{4}{9}$ **$\frac{5}{9}$**   15. $8\frac{1}{12} + 12\frac{6}{11}$ 16. $7\frac{2}{3} + 8\frac{1}{4}$ **$15\frac{11}{12}$**

17. $12\frac{3}{11} + 14\frac{3}{13}$ 18. $21\frac{1}{3} + 15\frac{3}{8}$ **$36\frac{17}{24}$**   19. $19\frac{1}{7} + 6\frac{1}{4}$ **$25\frac{11}{28}$**   20. $9\frac{2}{5} - 8\frac{1}{3}$ **$1\frac{1}{15}$**

    $26\frac{72}{143}$ 15. **$20\frac{83}{132}$**

Lesson 5-5   Multiply. Write each product in simplest form.

1. $\frac{2}{3} \times \frac{3}{5}$ **$\frac{2}{5}$**   2. $\frac{1}{6} \times \frac{2}{5}$ **$\frac{1}{15}$**   3. $\frac{4}{9} \times \frac{3}{7}$ **$\frac{4}{21}$**   4. $\frac{5}{12} \times \frac{6}{11}$ **$\frac{5}{22}$**

5. $\frac{3}{8} \times \frac{8}{9}$ **$\frac{1}{3}$**   6. $\frac{3}{5} \times \frac{1}{12}$ **$\frac{1}{20}$**   7. $\frac{2}{5} \times \frac{5}{8}$ **$\frac{1}{4}$**   8. $\frac{7}{15} \times \frac{3}{21}$ **$\frac{1}{15}$**

9. $\frac{5}{6} \times \frac{15}{16}$ **$\frac{25}{32}$**   10. $\frac{6}{14} \times \frac{12}{18}$ **$\frac{2}{7}$**   11. $\frac{2}{3} \times \frac{3}{13}$ **$\frac{2}{13}$**   12. $\frac{4}{9} \times \frac{1}{6}$ **$\frac{2}{27}$**

13. $3 \times \frac{1}{9}$ **$\frac{1}{3}$**   14. $5 \times \frac{6}{7}$ **$4\frac{2}{7}$**   15. $\frac{3}{5} \times 15$ **9**   16. $3\frac{1}{2} \times 4\frac{1}{3}$ **$15\frac{1}{6}$**

17. $3\frac{5}{8} \times 4\frac{1}{2}$ **$16\frac{5}{16}$**   18. $\frac{4}{5} \times 2\frac{3}{4}$ **$2\frac{1}{5}$**   19. $6\frac{1}{8} \times 5\frac{1}{7}$ **$31\frac{1}{2}$**   20. $2\frac{2}{3} \times 2\frac{1}{4}$ **6**

Lesson 5-6   Find the perimeter of each figure shown below.

1.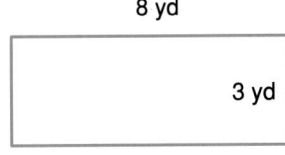

      8 yd   3 yd

22 yd

2.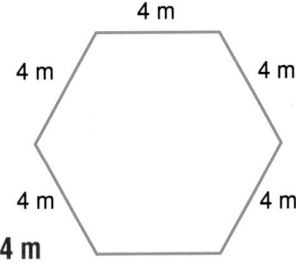

    4 m   4 m   4 m   4 m   4 m

24 m

3.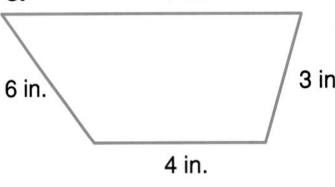

    7 in.   6 in.   3 in.   4 in.

20 in.

4.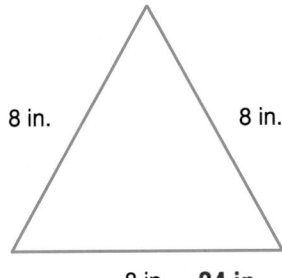

    8 in.   8 in.   8 in.   **24 in.**

5.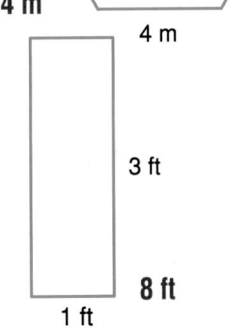

    4 m   3 ft   8 ft   1 ft

6.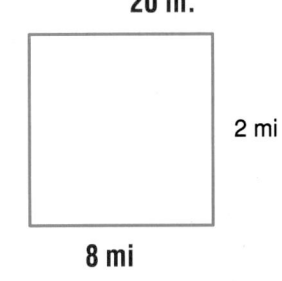

    2 mi   8 mi

Lesson 5-7

Find the circumference of each circle.

1.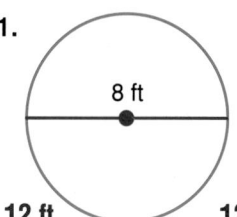

8 ft

25.12 ft

2.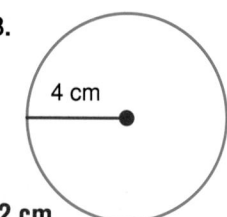

2 in.

12.56 in.

3.

4 cm

25.12 cm

4.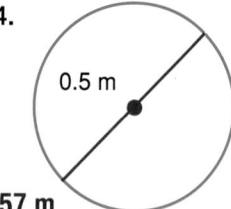

0.5 m

1.57 m

5. $r = 1.5$ in. **9.42 in.**

6. $d = \frac{2}{3}$ cm **2.093 cm**

7. $r = 4$ yd **25.12 yd**

8. $d = 1$ m **3.14 m**

9. $r = 6$ cm **37.68 cm**

10. $r = 1$ m **6.28 m**

11. $d = 1.5$ in. **4.71 in.**

12. $d = 2$ yd **6.28 yd**

13. $r = 0.5$ cm **3.14 cm**

Lesson 5-9

Name the property shown by each statement.

1. $\frac{4}{5} \times \frac{2}{3} = \frac{2}{3} \times \frac{4}{5}$
commutative property of multiplication

2. $\frac{3}{10} \times 3\frac{1}{3} = 1$
inverse property of multiplication

3. $\frac{24}{27} \times 1 = \frac{24}{27}$
multiplicative identity

4. $\left[\frac{1}{2} + \frac{3}{4}\right] + \frac{5}{6} = \frac{1}{2} + \left[\frac{3}{4} + \frac{5}{6}\right]$
associative property of addition

5. $\frac{2}{3} \times \left[\frac{1}{2} + \frac{5}{6}\right] = \frac{2}{3} \times \frac{1}{2} + \frac{2}{3} \times \frac{5}{6}$
distributive property of addition over multiplication

6. $\frac{2}{3} \times \frac{3}{2} = 1$
inverse property of multiplication

Compute mentally.

7. $5 \times 5\frac{1}{5}$ **26**

8. $3 \times 1\frac{2}{5}$ **$4\frac{1}{5}$**

9. $3\frac{2}{7} \times 7$ **23**

10. $\frac{1}{2} \times 2\frac{1}{2}$ **$1\frac{1}{4}$**

11. $3\frac{3}{4} \times \frac{1}{2}$ **$1\frac{7}{8}$**

12. $2\frac{1}{3} \times 6$ **14**

13. $\frac{1}{5} \times 10$ **2**

14. $\frac{1}{3} \times 3\frac{2}{5}$ **$1\frac{2}{15}$**

Lesson 5-10

Divide. Write each quotient in simplest form.

1. $\frac{2}{3} \div \frac{3}{2}$ **$\frac{4}{9}$**

2. $\frac{3}{5} \div \frac{2}{5}$ **$1\frac{1}{2}$**

3. $\frac{7}{10} \div \frac{3}{8}$ **$1\frac{13}{15}$**

4. $\frac{5}{9} \div \frac{2}{5}$ **$1\frac{7}{18}$**

5. $4 \div \frac{2}{3}$ **6**

6. $8 \div \frac{4}{5}$ **10**

7. $9 \div \frac{5}{9}$ **$16\frac{1}{5}$**

8. $\frac{2}{7} \div 2$ **$\frac{1}{7}$**

9. $\frac{1}{14} \div 7$ **$\frac{1}{98}$**

10. $\frac{2}{13} \div \frac{5}{26}$ **$\frac{4}{5}$**

11. $\frac{4}{7} \div \frac{6}{7}$ **$\frac{2}{3}$**

12. $\frac{7}{8} \div \frac{1}{3}$ **$2\frac{5}{8}$**

13. $15 \div \frac{3}{5}$ **25**

14. $\frac{9}{14} \div \frac{3}{4}$ **$\frac{6}{7}$**

15. $\frac{8}{9} \div \frac{5}{6}$ **$1\frac{1}{15}$**

16. $\frac{4}{9} \div 36$ **$\frac{1}{81}$**

17. $\frac{3}{5} \div \frac{2}{3}$ **$\frac{9}{10}$**

18. $\frac{8}{9} \div \frac{4}{5}$ **$1\frac{1}{9}$**

19. $\frac{3}{4} \div \frac{15}{16}$ **$\frac{4}{5}$**

20. $6 \div \frac{1}{5}$ **30**

Lesson 6-1

Solve each equation by using the inverse operation. Round to the nearest tenth.

1. $q - 7 = 7$ **14**
2. $g - 3 = 10$ **13**
3. $b + 7 = 12$ **5**
4. $a + 3 = 15$ **12**
5. $4x = 36$ **9**
6. $39 = 3y$ **13**
7. $4z = 16$ **4**
8. $54 = 9w$ **6**
9. $0.011 + h = 5.0$ **5.0**
10. $63 + f = 71$ **8**
11. $7 = 91 - g$ **84**
12. $9 = 19 - j$ **10**
13. $\frac{x}{6} = 6$ **36**
14. $\frac{x}{7} = 8$ **56**
15. $8 = \frac{c}{10}$ **80**
16. $4 = \frac{x}{2}$ **8**
17. $z + 0.34 = 3.1$ **2.8**
18. $23 = n - 0.09$ **23.1**
19. $2g = 0.6$ **0.3**
20. $r - 3 = 4$ **7**
21. $\frac{t}{3} = 1.2$ **3.6**

Lesson 6-2

Solve each equation. Check your solution.

1. $r - 3 = 14$ **17**
2. $t + 3 = 21$ **18**
3. $s + 10 = 23$ **13**
4. $7 + a = 10$ **3**
5. $14 + m = 24$ **10**
6. $9 + n = 13$ **4**
7. $s - 0.4 = 6$ **6.4**
8. $x - 1.3 = 12$ **13.3**
9. $y + 3.4 = 18$ **14.6**
10. $0.013 + h = 4.0$ **3.987**
11. $6 + f = 71$ **65**
12. $7.2 + g = 9.1$ **1.9**
13. $z - 12.1 = 14$ **26.1**
14. $w - 0.1 = 0.32$ **0.42**
15. $v - 18 = 13.7$ **31.7**
16. $s + 1.3 = 18$ **16.7**
17. $t + 3.43 = 7.4$ **3.97**
18. $x + 7.4 = 23.5$ **16.1**
19. $p + 3.1 = 18$ **14.9**
20. $q - 2.17 = 21$ **23.17**
21. $w - 3.7 = 4.63$ **8.33**

Lesson 6-3

Solve each equation. Check your solution.

1. $2m = 18$ **9**
2. $42 = 6n$ **7**
3. $72 = 8k$ **9**
4. $20r = 20$ **1**
5. $420 = 5s$ **84**
6. $325 = 25t$ **13**
7. $14 = 2p$ **7**
8. $18q = 36$ **2**
9. $40 = 10a$ **4**
10. $100 = 20b$ **5**
11. $416 = 4c$ **104**
12. $45 = 9d$ **5**
13. $\frac{m}{7} = 5$ **35**
14. $\frac{n}{3} = 6$ **18**
15. $4 = \frac{p}{4}$ **16**
16. $4 = \frac{x}{2}$ **8**
17. $\frac{s}{9} = 8$ **72**
18. $6 = \frac{t}{5}$ **30**
19. $\frac{w}{7} = 8$ **56**
20. $\frac{c}{8} = 2$ **16**

Lesson 6-4 Translate each phrase into an algebraic expression.

1. six less than p **$p - 6$**

2. twenty more than c **$20 + c$**

3. the quotient of a and b **$\frac{a}{b}$**

4. Ann's age plus 6 **$a + 6$**

5. x increased by twelve **$x + 12$**

6. $1,000 divided by z **$\frac{\$1,000}{z}$**

7. 3 divided into y **$\frac{y}{3}$**

8. the product of 7 and m **$7m$**

9. the difference of f and 9 **$f - 9$**

10. twenty-six less q **$26 - q$**

11. 19 decreased by z **$19 - z$**

12. two less than x **$x - 2$**

Lesson 6-6 Complete.

1. 4,000 lb = __**2**__ tons

2. 5 tons = ____ lb **10,000**

3. 2 lb = __**32**__ oz

4. 12,000 lb = __**6**__ tons

5. $\frac{1}{4}$ lb = __**4**__ oz

6. 6 lb 2 oz = __**98**__ oz

7. 3 gal = __**24**__ pt

8. 24 fl oz = __**3**__ c

9. 8 pt = __**16**__ c

10. 10 pt = __**5**__ qt

11. $2\frac{1}{4}$ c = __**18**__ fl oz

12. 12 pt = __**24**__ c

13. 4 gal = __**16**__ qt

14. 4 qt = __**128**__ fl oz

15. 4 pt = __**8**__ c

16. 9 lb = __**144**__ oz

17. 15 qt = __**$3\frac{3}{4}$**__ gal

18. 6 lb = __**96**__ oz

19. 2 gal = __**256**__ fl oz

20. 3 tons = ____ lb **6,000**

21. 18 qt = __**36**__ pt

Lesson 6-7 Find the area of each figure shown or described below.

1. 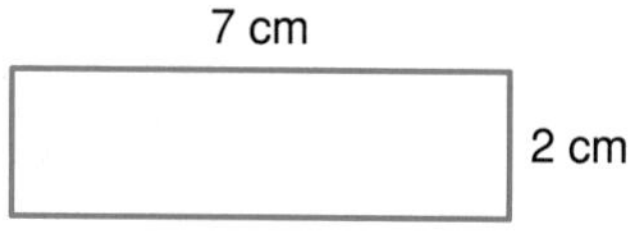
7 cm
2 cm
14 cm²

2. 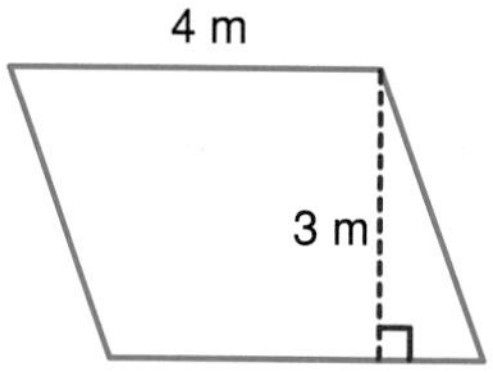
4 m
3 m
12 cm²

3.
2 in.
5 in.
10 in²

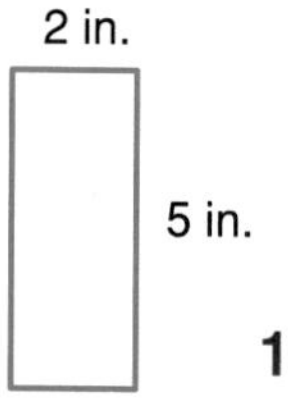

4.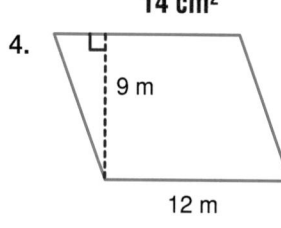
9 m
12 m
108 m²

5. 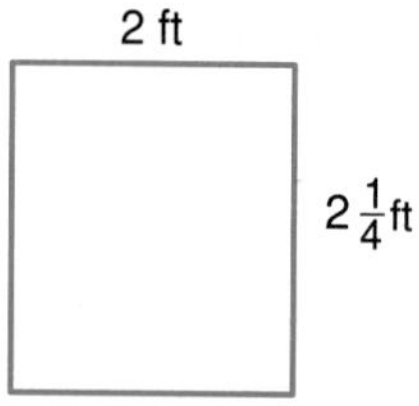
2 ft
$2\frac{1}{4}$ ft
$4\frac{1}{2}$ ft²

6. 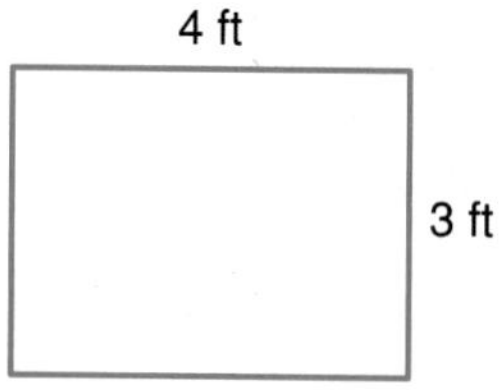
4 ft
3 ft
12 ft²

7. rectangle: $\ell = 19$ m, $w = 6$ m **114m²**

8. parallelogram: $b = 0.2$ m, $h = 0.3$ m **0.06m²**

9. rectangle: $\ell = 0.2$ m, $w = 0.3$ m **0.06m²**

Lesson 7-1 Write an integer for each situation.

1. a gain of 14 points **+14**
2. a $25 withdrawal **-25**
3. six degrees below zero **-6**
4. a loss of 3 pounds **-3**
5. a loss of 20 yards **-20**
6. a profit of $16 **+16**

Write the integer represented by the point for each letter. Then find its opposite and its absolute value.

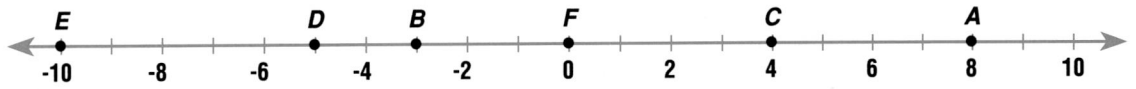

7. A **8, -8, 8**
8. B **-3, 3, 3**
9. C **4, -4, 4**
10. D **-5, 5, 5**
11. E **-10, 10, 10**
12. F **0, 0, 0**

Lesson 7-2 Replace each ● with $<$, $>$, or $=$ to make a true sentence.

1. 7 ● -7 $>$
2. -8 ● 4 $<$
3. -4 ● -9 $>$
4. -3 ● 0 $<$
5. 8 ● 10 $<$
6. -5 ● -4 $<$
7. 6 ● -7 $>$
8. -12 ● -13 $>$

Order the integers from least to greatest.

9. $-2, -8, 4, 10, -6, -12$
-12, -8, -6, -2, 4, 10
10. $19, -19, -21, 32, -14, 18$
-21, -19, -14, 18, 19, 32
11. $18, 23, 95, -95, -18, -23, 2$
-95, -23, -18, 2, 18, 23, 95
12. $46, -48, -47, -52, -18, 12$
-52, -48, -47, -18, 12, 46

Lesson 7-3 Name the *x*-coordinate and *y*-coordinate for each point labeled at the right. Then tell in which quadrant the point lies.

1. A **(3, -1), IV**
2. B **(-2, 2), II**
3. C **(0, -1), none**
4. D **(3, 2), I**
5. E **(-2, -1), III**
6. F **(1, -2), IV**
7. G **(1, 1), I**
8. H **(-3, 1), II**
9. I **(-1, 0), none**

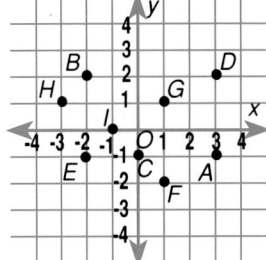

On graph paper, draw a coordinate plane. Then graph and label each point. **See Solutions Manual.**

10. N (-4, 3)
11. K (2, 5)
12. W (-6, -2)
13. X (5, 0)
14. Y (4, -4)
15. M (0, -3)
16. Z (-2, 0.5)
17. S (-1, -3)

Lesson 7-4 Solve each equation.

1. $a = -4 + 8$ **4**
2. $14 + 16 = b$ **30**
3. $-7 + (-7) = h$ **-14**

4. $g = -9 + (-6)$ **-15**
5. $-18 + 11 = d$ **-7**
6. $k = -36 + 40$ **4**

7. $42 + (-18) = f$ **24**
8. $-42 + 29 = r$ **-13**
9. $m = 18 + (-32)$ **-14**

10. $-33 + (-12) = w$ **-45**
11. $h = -13 + (-11)$ **-24**
12. $47 + 12 = y$ **59**

13. $-96 + (-18) = g$ **-114**
14. $x = 95 + (-5)$ **90**
15. $y = -69 + (-32)$ **-101**

16. $-100 + 98 = a$ **-2**
17. $-120 + 2 = b$ **-118**
18. $-120 + (-2) = c$ **-122**

19. $5 + (-7) = y$ **-2**
20. $w = 25 + (-25)$ **0**
21. $x = -56 + (-4)$ **-60**

Lesson 7-5 Solve each equation.

1. $3 - 7 = y$ **-4**
2. $-5 - 4 = w$ **-9**
3. $a = -6 - 2$ **-8**

4. $r = 8 - 13$ **-5**
5. $6 - (-4) = b$ **10**
6. $12 - 9 = x$ **3**

7. $-2 - 23 = c$ **-25**
8. $z = 63 - 78$ **-15**
9. $a = 0 - (-14)$ **14**

10. $-20 - 0 = d$ **-20**
11. $-5 - (-9) = h$ **4**
12. $a = 58 - (-10)$ **68**

13. $55 - 33 = k$ **22**
14. $m = 72 - (-19)$ **91**
15. $n = -41 - 15$ **-56**

16. $84 - (-61) = a$ **145**
17. $-51 - 47 = x$ **-98**
18. $c = -81 - 21$ **-102**

19. $z = -4 - (-4)$ **0**
20. $-99 - 1 = p$ **-100**
21. $26 - (-14) = y$ **40**

Lesson 7-7 Solve each equation.

1. $5(-2) = d$ **-10**
2. $a = 6(-4)$ **-24**
3. $4(21) = y$ **84**

4. $-11(-5) = c$ **55**
5. $x = -6(5)$ **-30**
6. $a = -50(0)$ **0**

7. $-5(-5) = z$ **25**
8. $-4(8) = q$ **-32**
9. $b = 3(-13)$ **-39**

10. $x = -12(5)$ **-60**
11. $3(-16) = y$ **-48**
12. $a = 2(2)$ **4**

13. $b = 2(-2)$ **-4**
14. $c = -2(2)$ **-4**
15. $d = -2(-2)$ **4**

16. $-3(2)(-4) = j$ **24**
17. $6(3)(-2) = k$ **-36**
18. $x = 5(-12)$ **-60**

19. $a = (-4)(-4)$ **16**
20. $y = -3(12)$ **-36**
21. $2(2)(-2) = b$ **-8**

Lesson 7-8   Solve each equation.

1. $a = 4 \div (-2)$ **-2**
2. $16 \div (-8) = x$ **-2**
3. $-14 \div (-2) = c$ **7**
4. $d = 32 \div 8$ **4**
5. $g = 18 \div (-3)$ **-6**
6. $h = -18 \div 3$ **-6**
7. $8 \div (-8) = y$ **-1**
8. $t = 0 \div (-1)$ **0**
9. $-25 \div 5 = k$ **-5**
10. $c = -14 \div (-7)$ **2**
11. $-32 \div 8 = m$ **-4**
12. $n = -56 \div (-8)$ **7**
13. $-81 \div 9 = y$ **-9**
14. $81 \div (-9) = w$ **-9**
15. $x = 81 \div 9$ **9**
16. $q = -81 \div (-9)$ **9**
17. $18 \div (-2) = a$ **-9**
18. $-55 \div 11 = c$ **-5**
19. $25 \div (-5) = r$ **-5**
20. $x = -21 \div 3$ **-7**
21. $-42 \div (-7) = y$ **6**

Lesson 7-9   Solve each equation. Check your solution.

1. $-4 + b = 12$ **16**
2. $z - 10 = -8$ **2**
3. $-7 = x + 12$ **-19**
4. $m + (-2) = 6$ **8**
5. $r - (-8) = 14$ **6**
6. $a + 6 = -9$ **-15**
7. $3m = -15$ **-5**
8. $0 = 6r$ **0**
9. $r \div 7 = -8$ **-56**
10. $\frac{c}{-4} = 10$ **-40**
11. $\frac{y}{12} = -6$ **-72**
12. $-2a = -8$ **4**

Write an equation for each problem below. Then solve.

13. The sum of 5 and a number g is 12. Find g. **$5 + g = 12$, 7**
14. The quotient when 16 is divided by a number x is -4. Find x. **$\frac{16}{x} = -4$, -4**
15. When -6 is multiplied by a number f, the product is -36. Find f. **$-6f = -36$, 6**

Lesson 7-10   Write each number in standard form.

1. 3×10^{-5} **0.00003**
2. 8×10^{-2} **0.08**
3. 6×10^{-6} **0.000006**
4. 4×10^{-3} **0.004**
5. 7×10^{-1} **0.7**
6. 5×10^{-4} **0.0005**

Write each decimal in scientific notation.

7. 0.002 **2×10^{-3}**
8. 0.00008 **8×10^{-5}**
9. 0.00000005 **5×10^{-8}**
10. 0.06 **6×10^{-2}**
11. 0.00000000009 **9×10^{-11}**
12. 0.7 **7×10^{-1}**

Lesson 8-1

Classify each angle as acute, obtuse, right, or straight.

1. 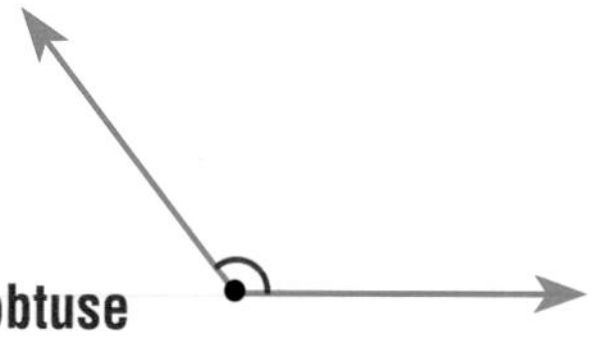 obtuse

2. 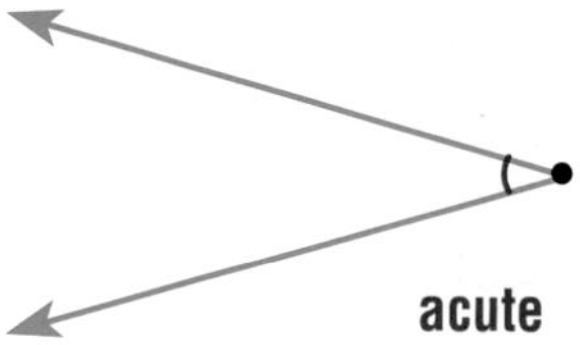 acute

3. 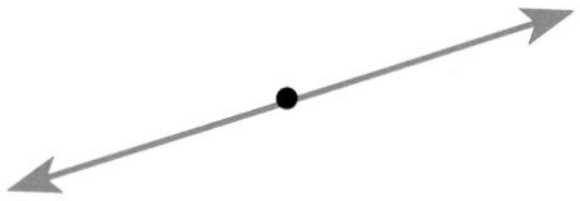 straight

4. 65° angle acute
5. 24° angle acute
6. 110° angle obtuse
7. 112° angle obtuse
8. 90° angle right
9. 97° angle obtuse

Lesson 8-2

Determine which figures are polygons. If a figure is not a polygon, explain why.

1.  yes

2. 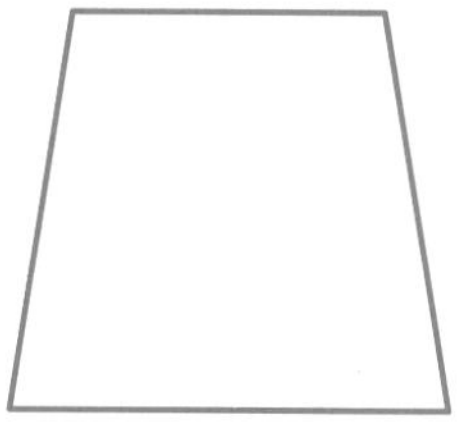 yes

3. 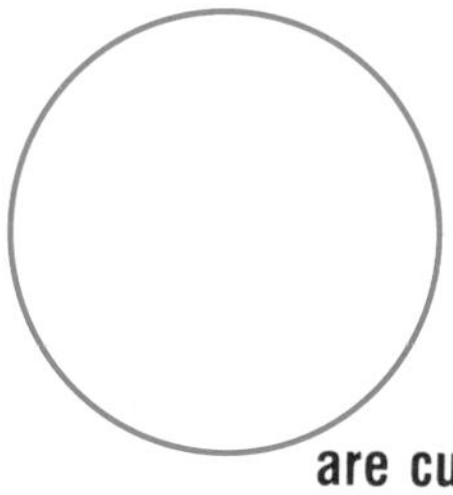 No; sides are curved.

4. 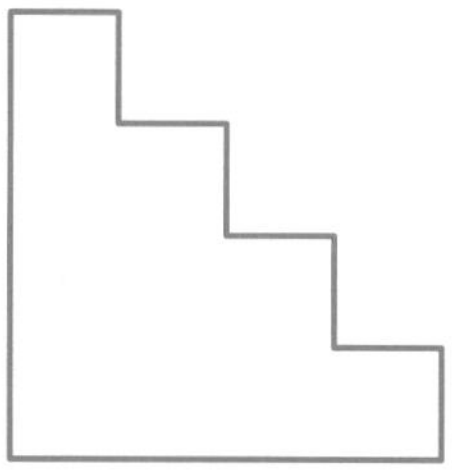 yes

5. 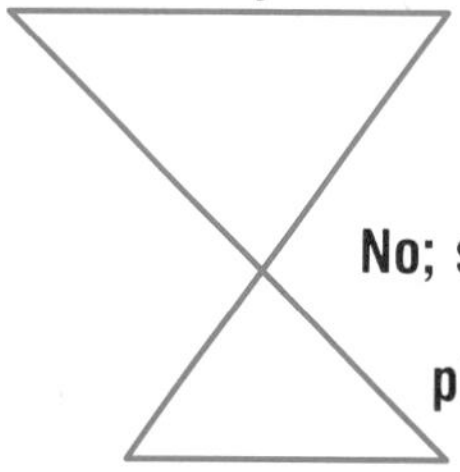 No; some sides meet at places other than endpoints.

6. 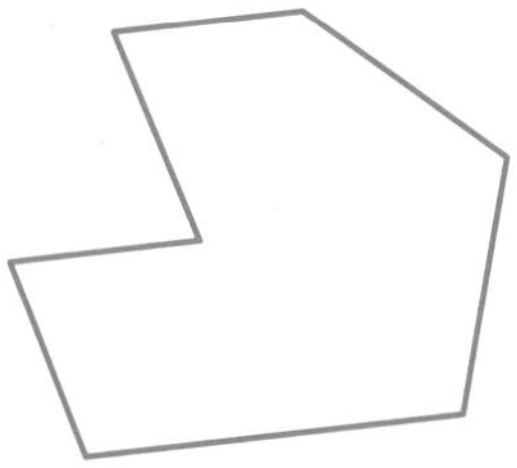 yes

Lesson 8-3

Classify each triangle by its sides and by its angles.

1. 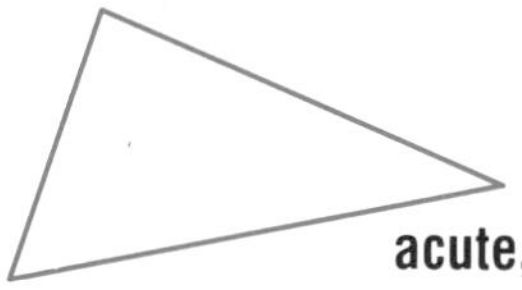 acute, scalene

2.  right, scalene

3. 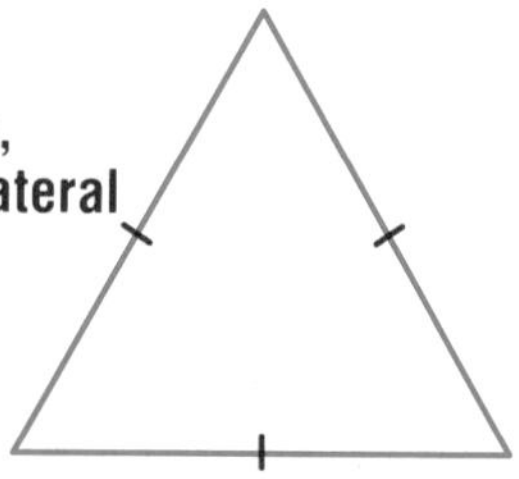 acute, equilateral

Name every quadrilateral that describes each figure. Then underline the name that best describes the figure.

4. 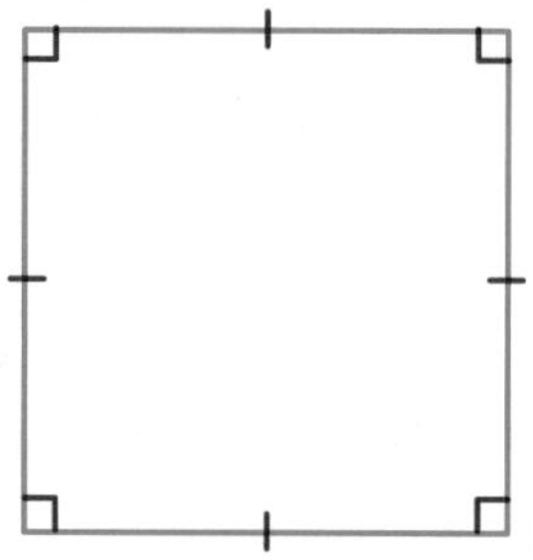 quadrilateral
parallelogram
rectangle
rhombus
<u>square</u>

5. 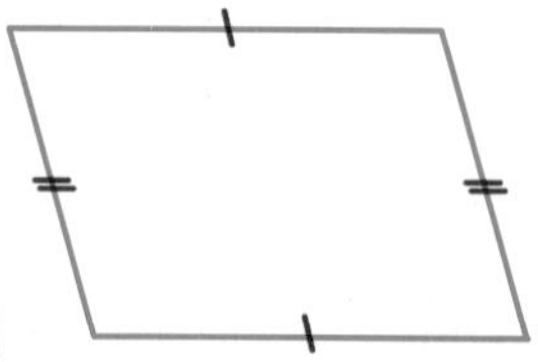 quadrilateral
<u>parallelogram</u>

6. 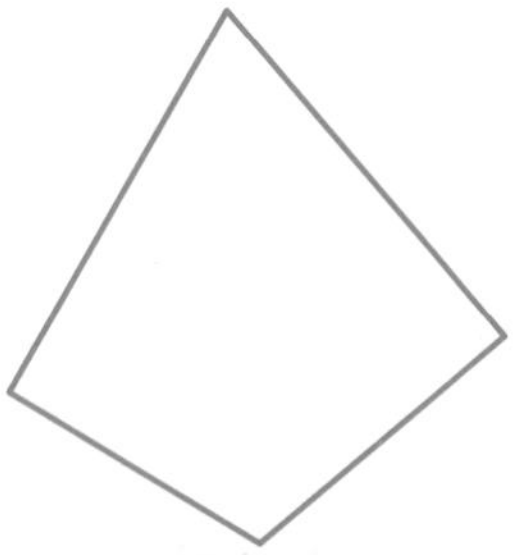 <u>quadrilateral</u>

Lesson 8-4   Tell whether each polygon is a regular polygon. If not, tell why.

1.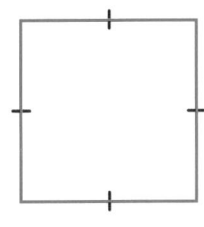

   yes

2.

   No, edges are curved.

3.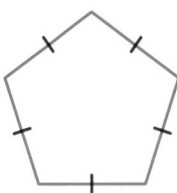

   yes

4.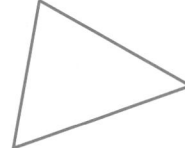

   No, all sides are not equal.

5.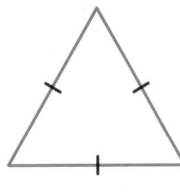

   yes

6.

   No, all angles are not equal.

Lesson 9-2   Find the square of each number.

1. 6 **36**
2. 12 **144**
3. 7 **49**
4. 15 **225**

5. 20 **400**
6. 14 **196**
7. 24 **576**
8. 1 **1**

9. 11 **121**
10. 40 **1,600**
11. 25 **625**
12. 9 **81**

Find each square root.

13. $\sqrt{49}$ **7**
14. $\sqrt{64}$ **8**
15. $\sqrt{169}$ **13**
16. $\sqrt{324}$ **18**

17. $\sqrt{900}$ **30**
18. $\sqrt{225}$ **15**
19. $\sqrt{2,500}$ **50**
20. $\sqrt{81}$ **9**

21. $\sqrt{289}$ **17**
22. $\sqrt{576}$ **24**
23. $\sqrt{8,100}$ **90**
24. $\sqrt{676}$ **26**

Lesson 9-3   Estimate.

1. $\sqrt{15}$ **4**
2. $\sqrt{35}$ **6**
3. $\sqrt{112}$ **11**
4. $\sqrt{75}$ **9**

5. $\sqrt{27}$ **5**
6. $\sqrt{249}$ **16**
7. $\sqrt{88}$ **9**
8. $\sqrt{1,500}$ **39**

9. $\sqrt{612}$ **25**
10. $\sqrt{340}$ **18**
11. $\sqrt{495}$ **22**
12. $\sqrt{264}$ **16**

13. $\sqrt{350}$ **19**
14. $\sqrt{834}$ **29**
15. $\sqrt{3,700}$ **61**
16. $\sqrt{298}$ **17**

17. $\sqrt{101}$ **10**
18. $\sqrt{800}$ **28**
19. $\sqrt{58}$ **8**
20. $\sqrt{750}$ **27**

21. $\sqrt{1,200}$ **35**
22. $\sqrt{1,000}$ **32**
23. $\sqrt{5,900}$ **77**
24. $\sqrt{999}$ **32**

25. $\sqrt{374}$ **19**
26. $\sqrt{512}$ **23**
27. $\sqrt{3,750}$ **61**
28. $\sqrt{255}$ **16**

29. $\sqrt{83}$ **9**
30. $\sqrt{845}$ **29**
31. $\sqrt{200}$ **14**
32. $\sqrt{10,001}$ **100**

Lesson 9-4

Use the Pythagorean Theorem to find the length of each hypotenuse given the lengths of the legs. Round answers to the nearest tenth.

1. 4 ft, 6 ft
7.2 ft

2. 12 cm, 25 cm
27.7 cm

3. 15 yd, 24 yd
28.3 yd

4. 8 mm, 11 mm
13.6 mm

Find the missing lengths. Round decimal answers to the nearest tenth.

5. *a*: 14 cm; *c*: 18 cm **11.3 cm**

6. *b*: 15 ft; *c*: 24 ft **18.7 ft**

7. *a*: 5 yd; *b*: 8 yd **9.4 yd**

Given the following lengths, determine whether each triangle is a right triangle. Write *yes* or *no*.

8. 6 mm, 8 mm, 10 mm **yes**

9. 12 ft, 15 ft, 20 ft **no**

10. 300 m, 400 m, 500 m **yes**

Lesson 9-6

Estimate the area of each figure.

1.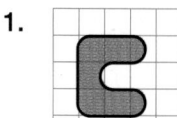
6 square units

2.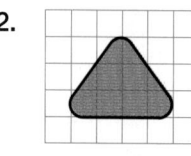
7 square units

3.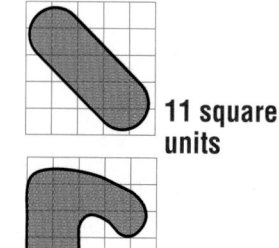
11 square units

4.
7 square units

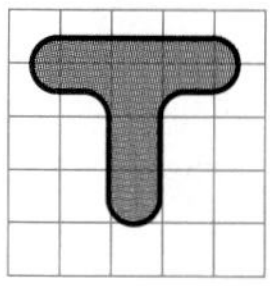

5. 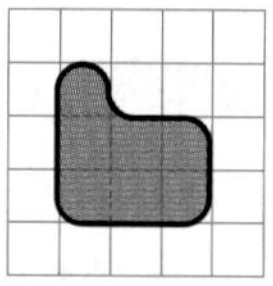
7 square units

6.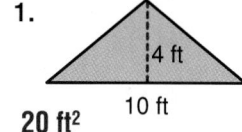
12.5 square units

Lesson 9-7

Find the area of each triangle.

1.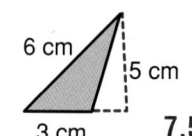
4 ft
10 ft
20 ft²

2. base: 5 in. **22.5 in²**
height: 9 in.

3.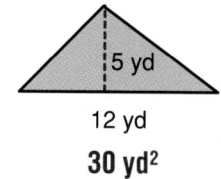
6 cm
5 cm
3 cm
7.5 cm²

4. base: 12 cm **48 cm²**
height: 8 cm

5. base: 25 mm
height: 32 mm
400 mm²

6.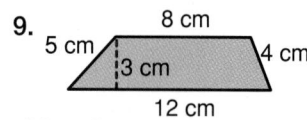
8mm
10 mm
6 mm
24 mm²

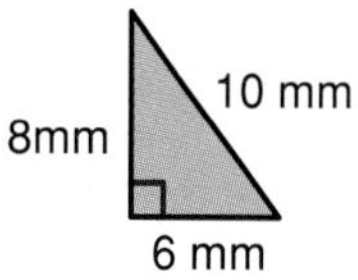

7. base: 3 yd
height: 7 yd
10.5 yd²

8.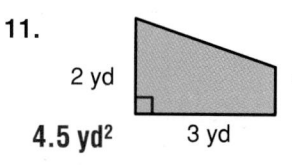
5 yd
12 yd
30 yd²

Find the area of each trapezoid.

9.
8 cm
5 cm
3 cm
4 cm
12 cm
30 cm²

10. bases: 3 cm, 8 cm
height: 12 cm
66 cm²

11.
2 yd
3 yd
1
4.5 yd²

12. bases: 10 ft, 15 ft
height: 12 ft
150 ft²

13. 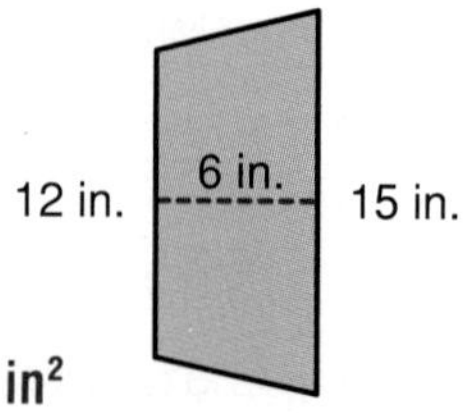
12 in.
6 in.
15 in.
81 in²

14. bases: 5 m, 9 m
height: 10 m
70 m²

Lesson 9-8   Find the area of each circle shown or described below. Round answers to the nearest tenth.

1. radius, 8 in.
   201.0 in²

2.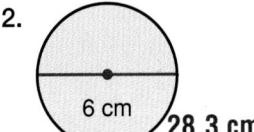
   6 cm
   28.3 cm²

3. diameter, 5 ft
   19.6 ft²

4.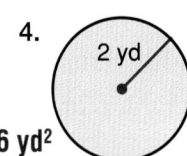
   2 yd
   12.6 yd²

5. radius, 24 cm
   1,808.6 cm²

6.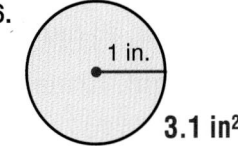
   1 in.
   3.1 in²

7. diameter, 2.3 m
   4.2 m²

8.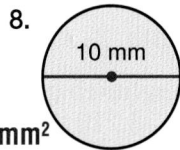
   10 mm
   78.5 mm²

Find the length of the radius of each circle given the following areas. Round answers to the nearest tenth.

9. 15 cm² **2.2 cm**   10. 24 ft² **2.8 ft**   11. 125 in² **6.3 in.**   12. 36 yd² **3.4 yd**
13. 100 m² **5.6 m**   14. 200 mm² **8.0 mm**   15. 72 ft² **4.8 ft**   16. 142 in² **6.7 in.**

Lesson 10-3   Find the surface area of each rectangular prism. Round answers to the nearest tenth.

2. $343\frac{3}{4}$ cm²   156.2 yd²   2,350 mm²

1. length, 8 ft   2. length, $4\frac{1}{2}$ cm   3. length, 9.4 yd   4. length, 20 mm
   width, 6.5 ft   width, 10 cm   width, 2 yd   width, 15 mm
   height, 7 ft **307 ft²**   height, $8\frac{3}{4}$ cm   height, 5.2 yd   height, 25 mm

5.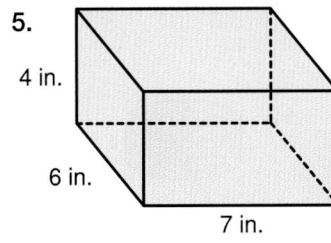
   4 in.
   6 in.
   7 in.
   188 in²

6.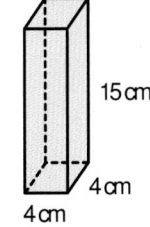
   15 cm
   4 cm
   4 cm
   272 cm²

7.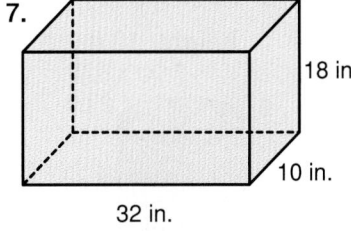
   18 in.
   10 in.
   32 in.
   2,152 in²

Lesson 10-4   Find the surface area of each cylinder. Use 3.14 for π. Round answers to the nearest tenth.

1.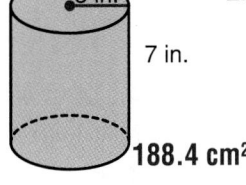
   3 in.
   7 in.
   188.4 cm²

2. 6.5 cm
   2 cm
   107.2 cm²

3. 1.5 m
   6 m
   31.8 m²

4. $\frac{1}{2}$ ft
   $5\frac{3}{4}$ ft
   19.6 ft²

Find the surface area of each cylinder. Use $\frac{22}{7}$ for π.

5. height, 6 cm   6. height, $5\frac{1}{2}$ in.   7. height, 16.5 mm   8. height, 22 yd
   radius, 3.5 cm   diameter, 3 in.   diameter, 18 mm   radius, 10.5 yd
   209 cm²   **66 in²**   **$1,442\frac{4}{7}$ mm²**   **2,145 yd²**

Extra Practice   **593**

Lesson 10-5
Find the volume of each rectangular prism.

1. length, 1.5 in.
width, 3 in.
height, 6 in.
27 in³

2. length, 4.5 cm
width, 6.75 cm
height, 2 cm
60.75 cm³

3. length, 3 ft
width, 10 ft
height, 2 ft
60 ft³

4. length, 16 mm
width, 0.7 mm
height, 12 mm
134.4 mm³

5. length, 18 cm
width, 23 cm
height, 15 cm
6,210 cm³

6. length, $3\frac{1}{2}$ ft
width, 10 ft
height, 6 ft
210 ft³

7. length, 25 mm
width, 32 mm
height, 10 mm
8,000 mm³

8. length, 12 in.
width, $5\frac{1}{2}$ in.
height, $3\frac{3}{8}$ in.
$222\frac{3}{4}$ in³

9.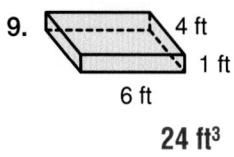
4 ft, 1 ft, 6 ft
24 ft³

10.
8.5 cm, 2 cm, 2 cm
34 cm³

11.
$12\frac{1}{2}$ mm, 3 mm, 4 mm
150 mm³

12.
2 yd, $\frac{1}{2}$ yd, 2 yd
2 yd³

Lesson 10-6
Find the volume of each cylinder. Round answers to the nearest tenth.

1. radius, 6 in.
height, 3 in.
339.1 in³

2. radius, 8.5 cm
height, 3 cm
680.6 cm³

3. diameter, 16 yd
height, 4.5 yd
904.3 yd³

4. diameter, 3.5 mm
height, 2.5 mm
24.0 mm³

5. radius, 8 ft
height, 10 ft
2,009.6 ft³

6. diameter, 12 m
height, 4.75 m
536.9 m³

7. radius, 6 cm
height, 12 cm
1,356.5 cm³

8. diameter, $\frac{5}{8}$ in.
height, 4 in.
1.2 in³

9.
2 cm, 4 cm
50.2 cm³

10.
3 yd, 6.5 yd
45.9 yd³

11.
7.5 mm, 16 mm
2,826 mm³

12.
4.5 in., 1.5 in.
23.8 in³

Lesson 11-1
Express each ratio as a fraction in simplest form.

1. 45 to 15 $\frac{3}{1}$
2. 64:128 $\frac{1}{2}$
3. 12 weeks out of 15 $\frac{4}{5}$
4. 14 to 49 $\frac{2}{7}$
5. 125:25 $\frac{5}{1}$
6. 18 to 81 $\frac{2}{9}$
7. 33 minutes:60 minutes $\frac{11}{20}$
8. 16:40 $\frac{2}{5}$
9. 120 to 180 $\frac{2}{3}$
10. 32:64 $\frac{1}{2}$
11. 10 ft to 8 yd $\frac{5}{4}$
12. 90 to 100 $\frac{9}{10}$

Tell whether the ratios in each pair are equivalent. Show your answer by simplifying.

13. 14 to 77 and 8 to 44 **yes**
14. $\frac{48}{16}$ and $\frac{1}{3}$ **no**
15. 65:13 and 500:100 **yes**
16. 72 to 90 and 20 to 16 **no**
17. 250:100 and 5:2 **yes**
18. $\frac{32}{2}$ and $\frac{3}{48}$ **no**
19. 8 hours to 5 days and 24 hours to 15 days **yes**

See Solutions Manual.

Lesson 11-2   Express each rate as a unit rate.

1. $240 for 4 days **$60/day**
2. 250 people in 5 buses **50 people/bus**
3. 500 miles in 10 hours **50 miles/hour**
4. 18 cups for 24 pounds **$\frac{3}{4}$ cup/pound**
5. 32 people in 8 cars **4 people/car**
6. 3 dozen for $4.50 **$\frac{2}{3}$ dozen/dollar**
7. 245 tickets in 5 days **49 tickets/day**
8. 12 classes in 4 semesters **3 classes/semester**
9. 60 people in 4 rows **15 people/row**
10. 48 ounces in 3 pounds **16 ounces/pound**
11. 20 people in 4 groups **5 people/group**
12. 1.5 pounds for $3.00 **0.5 pounds/dollar**
13. 45 miles in 60 minutes **0.75 miles/minute**
14. $5.50 for 10 disks **$0.55/disk**
15. 360 miles for 12 gallons **30 miles/gallon**
16. $8.50 for 5 yards **$1.70/yard**
17. 24 cups for $1.20 **20 cups/dollar**
18. 160 words in 4 minutes **40 words/minute**
19. $60 for 5 books **$12/book**
20. $24 for 6 hours **$4/hour**

Lesson 11-3   Solve each proportion.

1. $\frac{4}{9} = \frac{x}{3}$ **$1\frac{1}{3}$**
2. $\frac{12}{m} = \frac{15}{10}$ **8**
3. $\frac{36}{90} = \frac{16}{t}$ **40**
4. $\frac{g}{32} = \frac{8}{64}$ **4**
5. $\frac{5}{14} = \frac{10}{a}$ **28**
6. $\frac{k}{18} = \frac{5}{3}$ **30**
7. $\frac{120}{150} = \frac{p}{20}$ **16**
8. $\frac{15}{w} = \frac{60}{4}$ **1**
9. $\frac{81}{90} = \frac{y}{20}$ **18**
10. $\frac{14}{s} = \frac{8}{4}$ **7**
11. $\frac{h}{3} = \frac{36}{9}$ **12**
12. $\frac{44}{8} = \frac{150}{t}$ **$27\frac{3}{11}$**
13. $\frac{42}{8} = \frac{36}{d}$ **$6\frac{6}{7}$**
14. $\frac{125}{v} = \frac{35}{5}$ **$17\frac{6}{7}$**
15. $\frac{u}{72} = \frac{2}{4}$ **36**
16. $\frac{45}{80} = \frac{j}{3}$ **$1\frac{11}{16}$**

See students' work for justifications.

Lesson 11-4   Tell whether each pair of polygons is similar. Justify your answer.

1. 2 cm, 3 cm, 4 cm, 5 cm **no**

2. 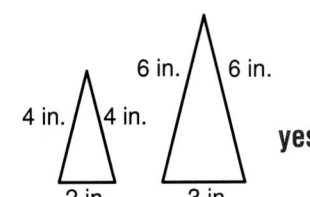 **yes**

3. 3 mm, 3 mm, 7 mm, 7 mm **yes**

Find the value of x in each pair of similar polygons.

4. 2 in., 3 in., 4 in., 6 in., x, 0.5 in. **0.25 in.**

5. 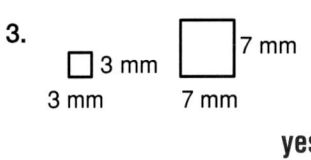 **2.5 cm**

6.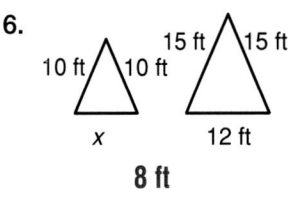

Lesson 11-5 On a map, the scale is 1 inch:50 miles. For each map distance, find the actual distance.

1. 5 inches
250 miles

2. 12 inches
600 miles

3. $3\frac{1}{2}$ inches
175 miles

4. $2\frac{3}{8}$ inches
$118\frac{3}{4}$ miles

5. $\frac{4}{5}$ inch
40 miles

6. $6\frac{3}{4}$ inches
337.5 miles

7. $2\frac{5}{6}$ inches
$141\frac{2}{3}$ miles

8. 8 inches
400 miles

On a scale drawing, the scale is $\frac{1}{2}$ inch:2 feet. Find the dimensions of each room in the scale drawing.

9. 14 feet by 18 feet **$3\frac{1}{2}$ inches by $4\frac{1}{2}$ inches**

10. 32 feet by 6 feet **8 inches by $1\frac{1}{2}$ inches**

11. 3 feet by 5 feet **$\frac{3}{4}$ inch by $1\frac{1}{4}$ inches**

12. 20 feet by 30 feet **5 inches by $7\frac{1}{2}$ inches**

13. 8 feet by 15 feet **2 inches by $3\frac{3}{4}$ inches**

14. 25 feet by 80 feet **$6\frac{1}{4}$ inches by 20 inches**

Lesson 11-7 Express each ratio as a percent.

1. $\frac{32}{100}$ **32%**

2. 48 out of 100 **48%**

3. 25 hundredths **25%**

4. $85\frac{1}{2}$:100 **85.5%**

5. $\frac{16}{100}$ **16%**

6. 23 out of 100 **23%**

7. 58.5 hundredths **58.5%**

8. 67:100 **67%**

9. $\frac{28}{100}$ **28%**

10. 54 out of 100 **54%**

11. 3 hundredths **3%**

12. 89.25:100 **89.25%**

Write a percent to represent the shaded area. If necessary, round answers to the nearest percent.

13. 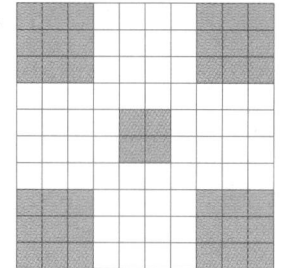 **40%**

14. 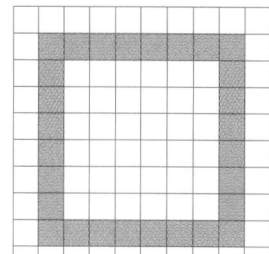 **28%**

15. 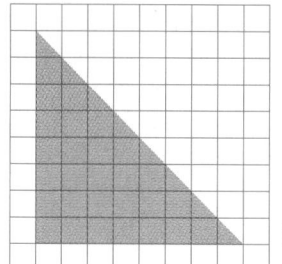 **32%**

Lesson 11-8 Express each fraction as a percent.

1. $\frac{14}{25}$ **56%**

2. $\frac{28}{50}$ **56%**

3. $\frac{14}{20}$ **70%**

4. $\frac{9}{12}$ **75%**

5. $\frac{4}{6}$ **$66\frac{2}{3}$%**

6. $\frac{3}{8}$ **37.5%**

7. $\frac{7}{10}$ **70%**

8. $\frac{17}{17}$ **100%**

9. $\frac{9}{16}$ **56.25%**

10. $\frac{80}{125}$ **64%**

11. $\frac{8}{9}$ **$88\frac{8}{9}$%**

12. $\frac{3}{16}$ **18.75%**

Express each percent as a fraction in simplest form.

13. 32% $\frac{8}{25}$

14. 18.5% $\frac{37}{200}$

15. 89% $\frac{89}{100}$

16. 72% $\frac{18}{25}$

17. $52\frac{1}{4}$% $\frac{209}{400}$

18. $33\frac{1}{3}$% $\frac{1}{3}$

19. 11% $\frac{11}{100}$

20. 1% $\frac{1}{100}$

21. 28% $\frac{7}{25}$

22. 55% $\frac{11}{20}$

23. $26\frac{1}{4}$% $\frac{21}{80}$

24. $3\frac{1}{3}$% $\frac{1}{30}$

Lesson 11-9

Express each decimal as a percent.

1. 0.41 **41%**
2. 0.375 **37.5%**
3. 0.916 **91.6%**
4. 0.09 **9%**
5. 1 **100%**
6. 0.425 **42.5%**
7. 0.895 **89.5%**
8. 0.0455 **4.55%**

Express each percent as a decimal.

9. 67% **0.67**
10. 43.5% **0.435**
11. 2.5% **0.025**
12. $55\frac{1}{5}$% **0.552**
13. 28.3% **0.283**
14. 100% **1.0**
15. 9.05% **0.0905**
16. 39% **0.39**

Replace each ● with $<$, $>$, or $=$.

17. 24% ● 0.024 $>$
18. 0.1 ● 10% $=$
19. $66\frac{2}{3}$% ● 0.66 $>$
20. 0.4525 ● 4.525% $>$
21. 38% ● 0.38 $=$
22. 1 ● 1% $>$
23. 0.695 ● 695% $<$
24. 2.08% ● 0.028 $<$

Lesson 11-10

Express each percent as a decimal.

1. 125% **1.25**
2. 0.045% **0.00045**
3. 895% **8.95**
4. 0.000075% **0.00000075**
5. 200% **2.0**
6. 0.001% **0.00001**
7. 0.01345% **0.0001345**
8. 555% **5.55**

Express each number as a percent.

9. $4\frac{1}{4}$ **425%**
10. $7\frac{9}{10}$ **790%**
11. 3.245 **324.5%**
12. 0.003 **0.3%**
13. 25 **2,500%**
14. 16.74 **1,674%**
15. $2\frac{3}{5}$ **260%**
16. 900 **90,000%**

Replace each ● with $<$, $>$, or $=$.

17. 3.25 ● 325% $=$
18. 2,000% ● 2 $>$
19. 45 ● 4.5% $>$
20. 245% ● 2.45 $=$
21. $24 \times \frac{1}{4}$ ● $24 \times 25\%$ $=$
22. $16 \times 1\frac{1}{3}$ ● $133\frac{1}{3}\% \times 16$ $=$

Lesson 12-1

Use a proportion to solve each problem. Round answers to the nearest tenth.

1. What number is 25% of 280? **70**
2. What number is 32% of 54? **17.3**
3. 90% of 72 is what number? **64.8**
4. Find 45% of 125.5. **56.5**
5. What number is 80% of 500? **400**
6. 12% of 120 is what number? **14.4**
7. Find 68% of 50. **34**
8. What number is 23% of 500? **115**
9. 20% of $58\frac{1}{2}$ is what number? **$11\frac{7}{10}$**
10. Find 75% of 1. **0.8**
11. What number is $33\frac{1}{3}$% of 66? **22**
12. 50% of 350 is what number? **175**
13. Find 80% of 8. **6.4**
14. What number is $37\frac{1}{2}$% of 32? **12**
15. 95% of 40 is what number? **38**
16. Find 30% of 26. **7.8**

Lesson 12-3

Write the fraction, decimal, mixed number, or whole number equivalent of each percent that could be used to estimate.

1. 28% $\frac{1}{4}$
2. 99% **1**
3. 450% $4\frac{1}{2}$
4. 0.09% **0.001**

5. $\frac{3}{4}$% **0.01**
6. 65.5% $\frac{2}{3}$
7. $15\frac{3}{5}$% $\frac{1}{8}$
8. 39.45% $\frac{2}{5}$

9. $8\frac{1}{2}$% **0.1**
10. 48.2% $\frac{1}{2}$
11. 0.009% **0**
12. 287% **3**

Estimate.

13. 50% of 37 **20**
14. 18% of 90 **20**
15. 60.5% of 60 **36**
16. 300% of 245 **600**

17. 0.7% of 200 **2**
18. 1% of 48 **0.5**
19. 7% of 24 **2.4**
20. 400% of 13 **40**

21. $5\frac{1}{2}$% of 100 **6**
22. 40.01% of 16 **6**
23. 70% of 300 **200**
24. 35% of 35 **12**

Lesson 12-4

Write a proportion for each problem. Then solve. Round answers to the nearest tenth.

1. What number is 24% of 60?
$\frac{24}{100} = \frac{n}{60}$; **14.4**

2. 38 is what percent of 50?
$\frac{38}{50} = \frac{x}{100}$; **76%**

3. 54 is 25% of what number?
$\frac{25}{100} = \frac{54}{n}$; **216**

4. What percent of 300 is 50?
$\frac{x}{100} = \frac{50}{300}$; **16.7%**

5. What number is 65% of 200?
$\frac{65}{100} = \frac{n}{200}$; **130**

6. $24\frac{1}{2}$% of what number is 15?
$\frac{24.5}{100} = \frac{15}{n}$; **61.2**

7. 99 is what percent of 150?
$\frac{99}{150} = \frac{n}{100}$; **66%**

8. What percent of 240 is 32?
$\frac{n}{100} = \frac{32}{240}$; $13\frac{1}{3}$%

9. 20% of what number is 6?
$\frac{20}{100} = \frac{6}{n}$; **30**

10. What number is 15.5% of 45?
$\frac{15.5}{100} = \frac{n}{45}$; **7.0**

11. 54 is 40% of what number?
$\frac{54}{n} = \frac{40}{100}$; **135**

12. What percent of 150 is 30?
$\frac{n}{100} = \frac{30}{150}$; **20%**

13. 68 is $33\frac{1}{3}$% of what number?
$\frac{68}{n} = \frac{33\frac{1}{3}}{100}$; **204**

14. What number is 85% of 1,000?
$\frac{85}{100} = \frac{n}{1,000}$; **850**

15. What percent of 450 is 50?
$\frac{n}{100} = \frac{50}{450}$; **11.1%**

16. 42 is what percent of 126?
$\frac{42}{126} = \frac{n}{100}$; $33\frac{1}{3}$%

Lesson 12-5

Write an equation for each problem. Then solve. Round answers to the nearest tenth. **For equations, see Solutions Manual.**

1. 12% of what number is 50? **416.7**
2. Find 45% of 50. **22.5**

3. 38 is what percent of 62? **61.3%**
4. $28\frac{1}{2}$% of 64 is what number? **18.2**

5. 5% of what number is 12? **240**
6. 80 is what percent of 90? **88.9%**

7. $66\frac{2}{3}$% of what number is 40? **60**
8. Find 46.5% of 75. **34.9**

9. 90 is what percent of 95? **94.7%**
10. Find 22% of 22. **4.8**

11. 16% of what number is 2? **12.5**
12. 75 is what percent of 300? **25%**

13. 75% of 80 is what number? **60**
14. Find 60% of 45. **27**

15. What number is 55.5% of 70? **38.9**
16. 80.5% of what number is 80.5? **100**

Lesson 12-6

Use the information in the following charts to make a circle graph.

1.

Car Sales by Body Style	
Style	**Percent**
Sedan	45
Station Wagon	22
Pickup Truck	9
Sports Car	13
Compact Car	11

2.

Favorite Flavor of Ice Cream	
Flavor	**Percent**
Vanilla	28
Chocolate	35
Strawberry	19
Mint Chip	12
Coffee	6

See Solutions Manual.

Lesson 12-7

Find the percent of change. Round to the nearest whole percent.

1. old: $75 **33% decrease**
   new: $50

2. old: 450 **50% increase**
   new: 675

3. old: 3.25 **9% decrease**
   new: 2.95

4. old: $5.75 **9% increase**
   new: $6.25

5. old: 180 **11% decrease**
   new: 160

6. old: 32.5 **35% increase**
   new: 44

7. old: 1.5 **33% decrease**
   new: 1.0

8. old: 450 **11% decrease**
   new: 400

9. old: $1,500 **20% decrease**
   new: $1,200

10. old: 750 **20% decrease**
    new: 600

11. old: $65 **15% increase**
    new: $75

12. old: 380 **16% decrease**
    new: 320

13. old: 0.75 **33% increase**
    new: 1.0

14. old: $3.95 **8% increase**
    new: $4.25

15. old: 350 **20% increase**
    new: 420

16. old: 500 **80% decrease**
    new: 100

Lesson 12-8

Find the sales tax or discount to the nearest cent.

1. $45 sweater; 6% tax **$2.70**   2. $18.99 CD; 15% off **$2.85**   3. $39 shoes; $5\frac{1}{2}$% tax **$2.15**

4. $199 ring; 10% off **$19.90**   5. $29 shirt; 7% tax **$2.03**   6. $55 plant; 20% off **$11**

Find the total cost or sale price to the nearest cent.

$1.70

7. $19 purse; 25% off **$14.25**   8. $150 clock; 5% tax **$157.50** 9. $2 notebook; 15% off

10. $145 coat; $6\frac{1}{4}$% tax **$154.06** 11. $89 radio; 30% off **$62.30** 12. $300 table; $\frac{1}{3}$ off **$200**

Find the rate of discount to the nearest percent.

13. regular price, $45
    sale price, $40 **11%**

14. regular price, $250
    sale price, $200 **20%**

15. regular price, $89
    sale price, $70 **21%**

Lesson 12-9

Find the interest to the nearest cent for each principal, interest rate, and time.

1. $2,000, 8%, 5 years
2. $500, 10%, 8 months
3. $750, 5%, 1 year
4. $175.50, $6\frac{1}{2}$%, 18 months
5. $236.20, 9%, 16 months
6. $89, $7\frac{1}{2}$%, 6 months
7. $800, 5.75%, 3 years
8. $5,500, 7.2%, 4 years
9. $245, 6%, 13 months

1. $800 2. $33.33 3. $37.50 4. $17.11 5. $28.34 6. $3.34 7. $138 8. $1,584 9. $15.93

Find the interest to the nearest cent on credit cards for each credit card balance, interest rate, and time.

10. $750, 18%, 2 years
11. $1,500, 19%, 16 months
12. $300, 9%, 1 year
13. $4,750, $19\frac{1}{2}$%, 30 months
14. $2,345, 17%, 9 months
15. $689, 12%, 2 years
16. $390, 18.75%, 15 months
17. $1,250, 22%, 8 months
18. $3,240, 18%, 14 months

**10. $270 11. $380 12. $27 13. $2,315.63 14. $298.99 15. $165.36
16. $91.41 17. $183.33 18. $680.40**

Lesson 13-1

Make a tree diagram to show all the outcomes in the sample space. Then give the total number of outcomes.

For diagrams, see Solutions Manual.

1. rolling 2 number cubes **36 outcomes**
2. choosing an ice cream cone from waffle, plain, or sugar and a flavor of ice cream from chocolate, vanilla, or strawberry **9 outcomes**
3. making a sandwich from white, wheat, or rye bread, cheddar or swiss cheese and ham, turkey, or roast beef **18 outcomes**
4. flipping a penny twice **4 outcomes**
5. choosing one math class from algebra and geometry and one foreign language class from French, Spanish, or Latin **6 outcomes**

Lesson 13-2

Find the total number of outcomes in each situation.

1. choosing a local phone number if the exchange is 234 and each of the four remaining digits is different **5,040 outcomes**
2. choosing a way to drive from Millville to Westwood if there are 4 roads that lead from Millville to Miamisburg, 2 roads that connect Miamisburg to Hathaway, and 4 highways that connect Hathaway to Westwood **32 outcomes**
3. tossing a quarter, rolling a number cube, and tossing a dime **24 outcomes**
4. spinning the spinners shown below **96 outcomes**

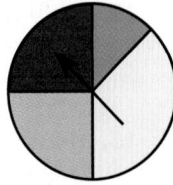 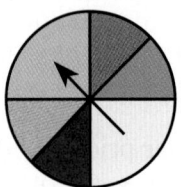 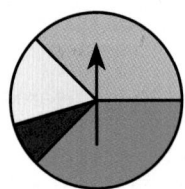

Lesson 13-5   Of 42,000 registered voters, the voting preferences of a random sample of 2,000 are listed in the table at the right.

Candidate	Number of Votes
Brown	540
Kim	380
Andrews	620
Undecided	460

1. How many voters out of the 42,000 might you expect to vote for Kim? **7,980 voters**
2. How many voters out of the 42,000 might you expect to be undecided at election time? **9,660 voters**
3. If the undecided voters choose Brown, how many votes might Brown expect to receive? **21,000 votes**

Lesson 13-6   Find each probability.

1. Two evenly-balanced nickels are flipped. Find the probability that one head and one tail result. $\frac{1}{2}$

2. A wallet contains four $5 bills, two $10 bills, and eight $1 bills. Two bills are selected without the first selection being replaced. Find $P(\$5, \text{ then } \$5)$. $\frac{6}{91}$

3. Two chips are selected from a box containing 6 blue chips, 4 red chips, and 3 green chips. The first chip selected is not replaced before the second is drawn. Find $P(\text{red}, \text{then green})$. $\frac{1}{13}$

4. A blue die and a red die are rolled. Find the probability that an odd number is rolled on the blue die and a multiple of 3 is rolled on the red die. $\frac{1}{6}$

Lesson 13-7   Find the value of each expression.

1. 3! **6**
2. 0! **1**
3. 6! **720**
4. $P(5, 3)$ **60**
5. $P(6, 6)$ **720**
6. $P(10, 2)$ **90**
7. $P(5, 0)$ **1**
8. $P(3, 2)$ **6**

9. How many different five-digit zip codes can be formed if no digit can be repeated? **30,240 zip codes**
10. Eight runners are competing in a 100-meter sprint. In how many ways can the gold, silver, and bronze medals be awarded? **336 ways**

11. In a lottery for which 30 tickets were sold (all to different people), in how many ways can the grand prize, second prize, and third prizes be awarded? **24,360 ways**

Lesson 13-8

Find the value of each expression.

1. $\frac{8!}{3!}$ **6,720**

2. $\frac{4!}{0!}$ **24**

3. $\frac{7!}{6!}$ **7**

4. $\frac{10!}{5!}$ **30,240**

5. $C(5,3)$ **10**

6. $C(9,4)$ **126**

7. $C(3,3)$ **1**

8. $C(10,2)$ **45**

9. List all of the possible combinations of Andrew, Jonathon, Megan, Rebecca, and Jeffrey taken 2 at a time. If all of the combinations are equally likely, find the probability that the combination chosen will consist of 2 males. $\frac{3}{10}$

10. List all the combinations of the digits 1, 3, 5, 7, 9 taken 3 at a time. If all of the combinations are equally alike, find the probability that the combination chosen will contain a 1. **135, 137, 139, 157, 159, 179, 357, 359, 579, 379;** $\frac{6}{10}$ **or** $\frac{3}{5}$

9. Andrew, Jonathan; Andrew, Megan; Andrew, Rebecca; Andrew, Jeffrey; Jonathan, Megan; Jonathan, Rebecca; Jonathan, Jeffrey; Megan, Rebecca; Megan, Jeffrey; Rebecca, Jeffrey

Lesson 14-2

Solve each equation and graph the solution.
For graphs, see Solutions Manual.

1. $3x + 6 = 6$

2. $\frac{p}{4} + 5 = 7$

3. $-10 + 2d = 8$

4. $\frac{3}{5}k + 2 = 8$

5. $12 - 5w = 3$

6. $5t - 4 = 6$

7. $2q - 6 = 4$

8. $\frac{g}{6} + 3 = 9$

9. $15 = 6y + 2$

10. $3s - 4 = 9$

11. $18 - 7f = 4$

12. $13 + 3p = 7$

13. $\frac{1}{2}(x - 3) = 2$

14. $4.2 + 7z = 2.8$

15. $-9m - 9 = 9$

16. $32 + 0.2c = 1$

17. $14 - 5t = 14$

18. $\frac{r}{6} - 4 = 8$

19. $-\frac{1}{4}(r - 2) = 4$

20. $4d - 3 = 9$

21. $16 - 2w = 9$

22. $4k + 13 = 20$

23. $7 = 5 - 2w$

24. $8x + 15 = 14$

25. $92 - 16b = 12$

26. $14e + 14 = 28$

27. $1.1j + 2 = 7.5$

28. $16 - \frac{1}{2}k = 10$

29. $4r + 3 = 25$

30. $16 - 5t = 3$

31. $3.5 + 1.5w = 7$

32. $-\frac{1}{3} + 5s = -\frac{4}{3}$

1. 0 2. 8 3. 9 4. 10 5. $1\frac{4}{5}$ 6. 2 7. 5 8. 36 9. $2\frac{1}{6}$ 10. $4\frac{1}{3}$ 11. 2 12. -2 13. 7
14. -0.2 15. -2 16. -155 17. 0 18. 72 19. -14 20. 3 21. 3.5 22. $1\frac{3}{4}$ 23. -1 24. $-\frac{1}{8}$
25. 5 26. 1 27. 5 28. 12 29. 5.5 30. 2.6 31. $2\frac{1}{3}$ 32. $-\frac{1}{5}$

Lesson 14-3

Find four solutions for each equation. Write your solutions as ordered pairs. **See Solutions Manual.**

1. $y = 3x + 2$

2. $y = -5x - 3$

3. $y = -\frac{1}{2}x - 1$

4. $y = 7x + 1$

5. $y = -3.5x - 0.5$

6. $y = 2x + 8$

7. $y = -2x - 16$

8. $y = -8x$

9. $y = \frac{1}{3}x - 1$

10. $y = -2$

11. $y = x$

12. $y = -5x - 5$

13. $y = 13$

14. $y = 3x - \frac{3}{2}$

15. $y = 4x$

16. $y = 5x + 15$

17. $y = \frac{1}{2}x + 5$

18. $y = -9x + 9$

19. $y = -x$

20. $y = 6x + 2$

21. $y = 6x$

22. $y = -2x + 18$

23. $y = 5x + 1$

24. $y = -8$

25. $y = 4x + 4$

26. $y = -6x + 5$

27. $y = \frac{1}{4}x - 3$

28. $y = 7x + \frac{1}{2}$

29. $y = 12x + 4$

30. $y = 4 - x$

31. $y = 2x$

32. $y = 5x + 100$

Lesson 14-4   Graph each equation. **See Solutions Manual.**

1. $y = 3x$

2. $y = 2x + 3$

3. $y = -x$

4. $y = 4x + 2$

5. $y = \frac{1}{2}x + 2$

6. $y = -x + 3$

7. $y = \frac{1}{4}x + 6$

8. $y = -3x + 6$

9. $y = 5x + 2$

10. $y = \frac{1}{3}x$

11. $y = -6$

12. $y = 3x - \frac{1}{3}$

13. $y = 2x + 7$

14. $y = -5x + 1$

15. $y = 13 + x$

16. $y = 5 - \frac{1}{2}x$

17. $y = x - 6$

18. $y = 5x + \frac{3}{2}$

19. $y = 16 - 4x$

20. $y = 4x + 5$

21. $y = -5x + 7$

22. $y = 13 - 7x$

23. $y = -x - 4$

24. $y = 2$

25. $y = 5 - 2x$

26. $y = 0$

27. $y = 11x + 5$

28. $y = -7 - 3x$

29. $y = \frac{1}{4}x$

30. $y = 14 + \frac{1}{2}x$

31. $y = -7x$

32. $y = 5$

Lesson 14-5   Find the output for each function, given the input and the function rule.

1. $f(x) = 2x + 4$ **0, 4, 6, 14**
   $x = -2, 0, 1, 5$

2. $f(x) = 16 - 3x$ **28, 19, 7, 1**
   $x = -4, -1, 3, 5$

3. $f(x) = \frac{1}{2}x$ **-2, 0, 1$\frac{1}{2}$, 4**
   $x = -4, 0, 3, 8$

4. $f(x) = 5x$ **-30, -20, 5, 35**
   $x = -6, -4, 1, 7$

5. $f(x) = -2$ **-2, -2, -2, -2**
   $x = -10, -5, 0, 6$

6. $f(x) = 1.5 + 3x$ **3, 5.1, 10.5, 16.5**
   $x = 0.5, 1.2, 3, 5$

7. $f(x) = -\frac{1}{3}x - 1$ **0, $-\frac{2}{3}$, $-1\frac{2}{3}$, -3**
   $x = -3, -1, 2, 6$

8. $f(x) = 2.5x$ **-10, -2.5, 7.5, 15**
   $x = -4, -1, 3, 6$

9. $f(x) = 3x - 6$ **-51, -27, 18, 54**
   $x = -15, -7, 8, 20$

10. $f(x) = -x$ **4, -3, -7, -15**
    $x = -4, 3, 7, 15$

11. $f(x) = \frac{5}{4}x + 2$ **-5$\frac{1}{2}$, -3, 5$\frac{3}{4}$, 10$\frac{3}{4}$**
    $x = -6, -4, 3, 7$

12. $f(x) = 0.25x - 0.5$ **-0.875, -0.5625, -0.25, 0.5**
    $x = -1.5, -0.25, 1, 4$

Lesson 14-6   Graph each triangle and its transformation. Write the ordered pairs for the vertices of the new triangle. **For graphs, see Solutions Manual.**

1. $\triangle ABC$ with vertices $A(-4, 3)$, $B(2, -1)$, and $C(0, 5)$ translated 3 units left and 4 units down **A$'$(-7, -1), B$'$(-1, -5), C$'$(-3, 1)**

2. **D$'$(5, -2), E$'$(-1, 1), F$'$(3, -4)**

2. $\triangle DEF$ with vertices $D(5, 2)$, $E(-1, -1)$, and $F(3, 4)$ reflected over the x-axis

3. $\triangle GHI$ with vertices $G(0, 7)$, $H(5, 0)$, and $I(-2, -4)$ translated 2 units right and 3 units up **G$'$(2,10), H$'$(7, 3), I$'$(0, -1)**

4. **J$'$(4, -4), K$'$(-4, -4), L$'$(0, 0)**

4. $\triangle JKL$ with vertices $J(-4, -4)$, $K(4, -4)$, and $L(0, 0)$ reflected over the y-axis

5. Rectangle $PQRS$ with vertices $P(3, 5)$, $Q(-4, 5)$, $R(-4, -1)$, and $S(3, -1)$ translated 1 unit down and 4 units left **P$'$(-1, 4), Q$'$(-8, 4), R$'$(-8, -2), S$'$(-1, -2)**

Glossary

A **absolute value** (254)   The number of units a number is from zero on the number line.

acute angle (297)   Any angle that measures between 0° and 90°.

addition property of equality (225)   If you add the same number to each side of an equation, the two sides remain equal. If $a = b$, then $a + c = b + c$.

additive inverse (265)   Two integers that are opposites of each other are called additive inverses. The sum of any number and its additive inverse is zero, $a + (-a) = 0$.

algebra (28)   A mathematical language that uses letters along with numbers. The letters stand for numbers that are unknown. $10n - 3 = 17$ is an example of an algebra problem.

algebraic expression (28)   A combination of variables, numbers, and at least one operation.

area (243)   The number of square units needed to cover a surface.

arithmetic sequence (136)   A sequence of numbers in which you can find the next term by adding the same number to the previous term.

associative property of addition (204)   For any numbers $a, b,$ and c, $(a + b) + c = a + (b + c)$.

associative property of multiplication (204)   For any numbers $a, b,$ and c, $(a \times b) \times c = a \times (b \times c)$.

average (104)   The sum of two or more quantities divided by the number of quantities.

B **base** (32)   The number used as a factor. In 10^3, 10 is the base.

base (244)   Any side of a parallelogram.

base (383)   The faces on the top and the bottom of a three-dimensional figure.

base (454)   In a percent proportion, the number to which the percentage is compared.

bisect (298)   To divide something into two congruent parts.

C **cell** (36)   Each section of a spreadsheet. A cell can contain data, labels, or formulas.

center (197)   The middle point of a circle or sphere. The center is the same distance from all points on the circle or sphere.

circle (197)   The set of all points in a plane that is the same distance from a given point called the center.

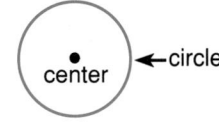

circumference (197)   The distance around a circle.

cluster (101)   Data that are grouped closely together.

clustering (54)   A method used to estimate decimal sums and differences by rounding a group of closely related numbers to the same whole number.

combination (522)   An arrangement of objects in which order is unimportant.

common denominator (164)   A common multiple of the denominators of two or more fractions.

commutative property of addition (204)   For any numbers a and b, $a + b = b + a$.

commutative property of multiplication (204)   For any numbers a and b, $a \times b = b \times a$.

composite number (132)   Any whole number greater than one that has more than two factors.

congruent angles (298)   Two angles that have the same measure.

congruent sides (307)   Sides that have the same length.

coordinate system (259)
Two perpendicular number lines that intersect at their zero points form a coordinate system.

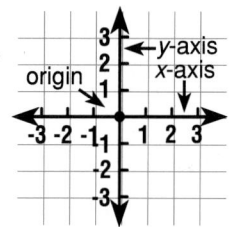

cross products (417)   If the cross products in a ratio are equal then the ratio forms a proportion. In the proportion $\frac{2}{3} = \frac{8}{12}$, the cross products are 2×12 and 3×8.

cup (239)   A customary unit of capacity equal to 8 fluid ounces.

cylinder (388)   A three-dimensional figure with two parallel congruent circular bases.

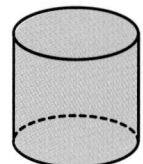

D **data base** (96)   A collection of data that is organized and stored on a computer for rapid search and retrieval.

decagon (304)   A polygon having ten sides.

degree (297)   The most common unit of measurement for angles.

dependent event (511)   Two or more events in which the outcome of one event does affect the outcome of the other event or events.

diameter (197)   The distance across a circle through its center.

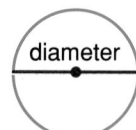

discount (479)   The amount deducted from the original price.

distributive property (205)   The sum of two addends multiplied by a number is the sum of the product of each addend and the number. $a \times (b + c) = a \times b + a \times c$.

divisible (129)   A number is divisible by another if the quotient is a whole number and the remainder is zero.

division property of equality (228)   If each side of an equation is divided by the same nonzero number, then the two sides remain equal. If $a = b$, then $\frac{a}{c} = \frac{b}{c}$, $c \neq 0$.

dodecagon (304)   A polygon having twelve sides.

E **equation** (38)   A mathematical sentence that contains an equals sign, =.

equiangular (313)   A polygon with equal angles.

equilateral triangle (308)
A triangle with three congruent sides.

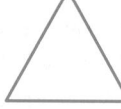

equivalent equations (225)   Two or more equations with the same solution. $x + 3 = 5$ and $x = 2$ are equivalent equations.

evaluate (28)   To find the value of an expression by replacing variables with numerals.

event (157)   A specific outcome or type of outcome.

expected value (201)   The average value that one would expect to get over many attempts.

experimental probability (500)   An estimated probability based on the relative frequency of positive outcomes occurring during an experiment.

exponent (32)   The number of times the base is used as a factor. In 10^3, the exponent is 3.

exterior angle (314)
If you extend a side of a polygon, an exterior angle is formed.

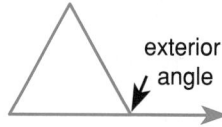

F **face** (383)   Any surface that forms a side or a base of a prism.

factor (32, 129)   When two or more numbers are multiplied, each number is a factor of the product.

factorial (519)   The expression $n!$ is the product of all counting numbers beginning with n and counting backwards to 1.

field (96)   The elements within each record of a computer data base file.

file (96)   A collection of data within a computer data base about a particular subject.

frequency table (93)   A table for organizing a set of data that shows the number of times each item or number appears.

function (547)   A relationship in which the output value depends upon the input according to a specified rule. For example, with a function $f(x) = 2x$, if the input is 5, the output is 10.

Fundamental Counting Principle (497)   If there are m ways of selecting an item from set A and n ways of selecting an item from set B, then there are $m \times n$ ways of selecting an item from set A and an item from set B.

G **gallon** (239)   A customary unit of capacity equal to 4 quarts.

geometric sequence (136)   A sequence of numbers in which you can find the next term by multiplying the previous term by the same number.

gram (78)   The basic unit of mass in the metric system.

greatest common factor (GCF) (145)   The greatest of the common factors of two or more numbers. The greatest common factor of 18 and 24 is 6.

H **height** (244)   The vertical distance from the base of a parallelogram to its other side.

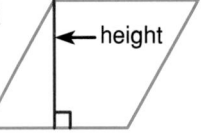

heptagon (304)   A polygon having seven sides.

hexagon (304)   A polygon having six sides.

hypotenuse (344) In a right triangle, the side opposite the right angle is called the hypotenuse.

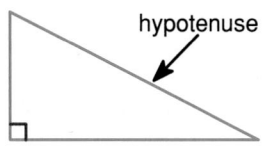

identity property of addition (204)   For any number a, $a + 0 = a$.

identity property of multiplication (204)   For any number a, $a \times 1 = a$.

improper fraction (174)   A fraction that has a numerator that is greater than or equal to the denominator.

independent event (510)   Two or more events in which the outcome of one event does not affect the outcome of the other event or events.

integers (254)   The whole numbers and their opposites. . . . , $-3, -2, -1, 0, 1, 2, 3, \ldots$

interest (482)   The amount charged or paid for the use of money.

interval (98)   The difference between successive values on a scale.

inverse property of multiplication (204)   The product of a number and its multiplicative inverse is 1. For all fractions $\frac{a}{b}$, where $a, b \neq 0$, $\frac{a}{b} \times \frac{b}{a} = 1$.

inverse operation (220)   Pairs of operations that undo each other. Addition and subtraction are inverse operations. Multiplication and division are inverse operations.

irregular figures (351)   Figures that do not necessarily have straight sides and square corners.

isosceles triangle (308)   A triangle that has at least two congruent sides.

L **leaf** (109)   The second greatest place value of data in a stem-and-leaf plot.

least common denominator (LCD) (164)   The least common multiple of the denominators of two or more fractions.

least common multiple (LCM) (161)   The least of the common multiples of two or more numbers, other than zero. The least common multiple of 2 and 3 is 6.

leg (344)   A leg of a right triangle is either of the two sides that form the right angle.

line plot (101)   A vertical graph showing a picture of information on a number line.

linear equation (543)   An equation for which the graph is a straight line.

line symmetry (327)   Figures that match exactly when folded in half have line symmetry.

line of symmetry (327)
A fold line on a figure that shows symmetry. Some figures can be folded in more than one way to show symmetry.

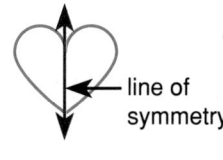
line of symmetry

liter (78)   The basic unit of capacity in the metric system. A liter is a little more than a quart.

mean (104)   The arithmetic average; the sum of the numbers in a set of data divided by the number of pieces of data.

median (104)   The middle number when a set of data are arranged in numerical order. When there are two middle numbers, the median is their mean.

meter (78)   The basic unit of length in the metric system.

metric system (78)   A system of weights and measures based on tens. The meter is the basic unit of length, the kilogram is the basic unit of weight, and the liter is the basic unit of capacity.

mixed number (174)   A number that shows the sum of a whole number and a fraction. $6\frac{2}{3}$ and $8\frac{3}{4}$ are mixed numbers.

mode (104)   The number or item that appears most often in a set of data.

multiplication property of equality (228)   If each side of an equation is multiplied by the same number, then the two sides remain equal. If $a = b$, then $ac = bc$.

multiplicative inverse (204)   A number times its multiplicative inverse is equal to 1. The multiplicative inverse of $\frac{2}{3}$ is $\frac{3}{2}$.

negative integer (254)   Whole numbers to the left of zero on the number line or numbers less than zero.

nonagon (304)   A polygon having nine sides.

obtuse (297)   Any angle that measures between 90° and 180°.

octagon (304)   A polygon having eight sides.

opposite (254)   Two integers are opposites if they are represented on the number line by points that are the same distance from zero, but on opposite sides of zero. The sum of opposites is zero.

ordered pair (259)   A pair of numbers where order is important. An ordered pair, which is graphed on a coordinate plane, is written in this form: (*x*-coordinate, *y*-coordinate).

order of operation (24)   The rules to follow when more than one operation is used. 1. Do all operations within grouping symbols first. 2. Do multiplication and division from left to right. 3. Do addition and subtraction from left to right.

origin (259)   The point of intersection of the *x*-axis and *y*-axis in a coordinate system.

ounce (238)   A customary unit of weight. 16 ounces equals 1 pound.

outliers (101)   Data that are far apart from the rest of the data.

parallelogram (244)   A quadrilateral that has both pairs of opposite sides parallel.

pentagon (304)   A polygon having five sides.

percent (433, 454)   A ratio that compares a number to 100.

percentage (454)   In a percent proportion, a number (P) that is compared to another number called the base (B).
$$\frac{\text{Percentage}}{\text{Base}} = \text{Rate or } \frac{P}{B} = \frac{r}{100}.$$

percent of decrease (477)

$$\frac{\text{Amount of Decrease}}{\text{Original Value}} \times 100$$

percent of increase (477)

$$\frac{\text{Amount of Increase}}{\text{Original Value}} \times 100$$

perfect square (338)   Squares of whole numbers.

perimeter (194)   The distance around a geometric figure.

permutation (517)   An arrangement or listing of objects in which order is important.

pint (239)   A customary unit of capacity equal to 2 cups.

polygon (303)   A simple closed figure in a plane formed by three or more line segments.

population (506)   The entire group of items or individuals from which the samples under consideration are taken.

population density (414)   The population per square mile.

positive integers (254)   Whole numbers greater than zero or to the right of zero on the number line.

pound (238)   A customary unit of weight equal to 16 ounces.

power (32)   A number expressed using an exponent. The power 7^3 is read *seven to the third power*, or *seven cubed*.

prime factorization (132)   A composite number that is expressed as the product of prime numbers. The prime factorization of 12 is $2 \times 2 \times 3$.

prime number (132)   A number that has exactly two factors, 1 and the number itself.

principal (482)   The amount of an investment or a debt.

prism (383)   A three-dimensional figure that has two parallel and congruent bases in the shape of polygons.

probability (157)   The ratio of the number of ways an event can occur to the number of possible outcomes; how likely it is that an event will occur.

proper fraction (174)   A fraction that has a numerator that is less than the denominator.

proportion (417)   A proportion is an equation that shows that two ratios are equivalent, $\frac{a}{b} = \frac{c}{d}, b \neq 0, d \neq 0$.

Pythagorean Theorem (344)   In a right triangle, the square of the length of the hypotenuse is equal to the sum of the squares of the lengths of the legs. $a^2 + b^2 = c^2$

Q **quadrant** (259) One of the four regions into which two perpendicular number lines separate a plane.

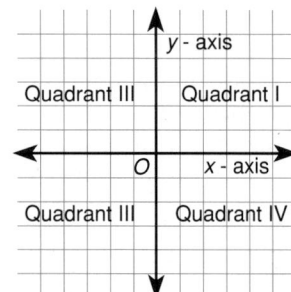

quadrilateral (303)   A polygon having four sides.

quart (239)   A customary unit of capacity equal to 2 pints.

R **radical sign** (339)   The symbol used to represent a nonnegative square root is $\sqrt{}$.

radius (197)   The distance from the center of a circle to any point on the circle.

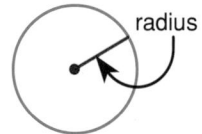

random (157)   Outcomes occur at random if each outcome is equally likely to occur.

random (506)   A sample is called random if the members of the sample are selected purely on the basis of chance.

range (98)   The difference between the greatest number and the least number in a set of data.

rate (414)   A ratio of two measurements with different units.

rate (454)   In a percent proportion, the ratio of a number to 100.

rate (482)   The percent charged or paid for the use of money.

ratio (411)   A comparison of two numbers by division. The ratio comparing 2 to 3 can be stated as 2 out of 3, 2 to 3, 2:3, or $\frac{2}{3}$.

reciprocal (204)   Another name for a multiplicative inverse.

record (96)   The subject or sub unit within a computer data base file.

rectangle (243)   A parallelogram with all angles congruent.

rectangular prism (383)
A prism with rectangles as bases.

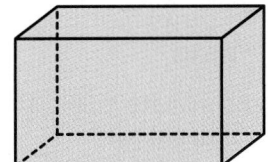

reflection (327)   A mirror image of a figure across a line of symmetry.

regular polygon (313)   A polygon that is both equiangular and equilateral.

repeating decimal (154)   A decimal whose digits repeat in groups of one or more. Examples are 0.181818. . . and 0.83333. . .

rhombus (308)   A parallelogram with all sides congruent.

right angle (297)   Any angle that measures exactly 90°.

S   sales tax (479)   A tax based on the amount received for articles sold.

sample (506)   A small part or piece of anything that shows what the whole is like.

sample space (492)   The set of all possible outcomes.

scale (98)   The set of all possible values of a given measurement, including the least and greatest numbers in the set, separated by the intervals used.

scale drawing (426)   A representation of something that is too large or too small to be drawn to actual size.

scalene triangle (307)   A triangle with no congruent sides.

scientific notation (67)   A way of expressing numbers as the product of a number that is at least 1, but less than 10, and a power of ten. In scientific notation 5,500 is 5.5×10^3.

sequence (136)   A list of numbers in a specific order.

similar polygons (422)   Two polygons are similar if their corresponding angles are congruent and their corresponding sides are in proportion. They have the same shape but may not be the same size.

simplest form (150)   The form of a fraction when the GCF of the numerator and denominator is 1. The fraction $\frac{1}{4}$ is in simplest form because the GCF of 1 and 4 is 1.

solution (38)   Any number that makes an equation true. The solution for $n + 10 = 15$ is 5.

solve (38)   To replace a variable with a number that makes an equation true.

spreadsheet (36)   A computer spreadsheet organizes numerical data into rows and columns. It is used for organizing and analyzing data and formulas.

square (338)   The product of a number and itself. $7^2 = 7 \times 7 = 49$.

square root (339)   One of the two equal factors of a number. If $a^2 = b$, then a is the square root of b. The square root of 144 is 12 because $12^2 = 144$.

stem (109)   The greatest place value of data in a stem-and-leaf plot.

stem-and-leaf plot (109)   A system used to condense a set of data where the greatest place value of the data forms the stem and the next greatest place value forms the leaves.

straight angle (297)   Any angle that measures exactly 180°.

subtraction property of equality (225)   If you subtract the same number from each side of an equation, then the two sides remain equal. If $a = b$, then $a - c = b - c$.

surface area (383)   The sum of the areas of all the faces of a three-dimensional figure.

T **terminating decimal** (154)   A quotient in which the division ends with a remainder of zero. 0.25 and 0.125 are terminating decimals.

tessellation (321)   A repetitive pattern of polygons that fit together with no holes or gaps.

theoretical probability (500)   The long-term probability of an outcome based on mathematical principles.

tiling (321)   Covering a surface with regular figures.

time (482)   When used to calculate interest, time is given in years.

ton (238)   A customary unit of weight equal to 2,000 pounds.

translation (324)   A method used to make changes in the polygons of tessellations by sliding a pattern to create the same change on opposite sides.

trapezoid (307, 355)   A quadrilateral with exactly one pair of parallel sides.

tree diagram (492)   A diagram used to show the total number of possible outcomes in a probability experiment.

triangle (355)   A polygon that has three sides.

U **undecagon** (304)   A polygon having eleven sides.

unit price (414)   The cost of an item and its unit rate.

unit rate (414)   A rate in which the denominator is 1 unit.

V **variable** (28)   A symbol, usually a letter, used to represent a number in mathematical expressions or sentences. In $3 + a = 6$, a is a variable.

vertex (297)   A vertex of an angle is the common endpoint of the rays forming the angle.

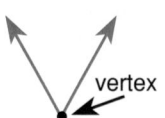
vertex

volume (394)   The number of cubic units needed to fill a space.

X **x-axis** (259)   The horizontal line of the two perpendicular number lines in a coordinate plane.

x-coordinate (259)   The first number of an ordered pair.

Y **y-axis** (259)   The vertical line of the two perpendicular number lines in a coordinate plane.

y-coordinate (259)   The second number of an ordered pair.

Selected Answers

1 Tools for Problem Solving

Pages 6-7 Lesson 1-1
4. 1,609 miles 5. yes 7. 58 tables
9. $191.40 11. 498 miles
13. Sample answer: about 530 million radios

Pages 9-10 Lesson 1-2
4. 1,500 5. 300 6. 1,900 7. 2,000 8. $110
9. 13,000 10. 12,000 11. 600 12. 600
calories 13. 11,000 15. 9,000 17. 15,000
19. $18 21. 9,000 23. 24,000 25. false
26. 20 days 27. 30-ounce bottle; $6 as opposed
to $5 28. no 29. about 10,000 students
31. about 9,200 stations

Pages 12-13 Lesson 1-3
3. 180 4. 16,000 5. 200 6. 160 7. 360
8. 6,300 9. 1,600 10. 3,200 11. 120 12. 200
13. 50 14. 100 15. 800 16. 1,000 17. 2,000
19. 5,600 21. 25 23. 3,200 25. 4,200
27. 250 29. 7,200 31. 16,350 seats 32. 200
tons 33. 9,000 34. 200 campers 35. about
$2,800 37. about 3,000 39. about $750

Pages 15-16 Lesson 1-4
4. no 5. yes 6. yes 7. no 8. no 9. yes
10. $10.00 11. yes 13. no 15. yes 17. no
19. no 21. yes 23. yes 25. no 27. 48 miles
28. about 100 members 29. about 12,000
30. about 3 miles per day 31. about
24 patients 33. yes; $3,000 + 3,000 +
4,000 + 3,000 = 13,000$

Pages 18-19 Lesson 1-5
4. exact 5. estimate 6. estimate 7. exact
8. exact 9. estimate 11. 36 miles per gallon
13. Sample answer for 1, 2, 3, 4, 5: 245×13
15. about 16 cubic miles

Page 19 Mid-Chapter Review
1. Sample answer: 120 pounds $\div 6 = 20$ quarts
3. 4,000 5. 90 7. no 9. 108 meters

Page 21 Lesson 1-6
3. Not enough facts; the cost of each video.
4. $40.95 5. Not enough facts; whether or not it
is a leap year. 7. $1.26 9. Not enough facts;
which socks he bought.

Pages 25-26 Lesson 1-7
4. multiplication 5. addition 6. subtraction
7. addition 8. multiplication 9. addition 10. 23
11. 4 12. 28 13. 24 14. 13 15. 12
17. subtraction 19. multiplication 21. addition
23. 2 25. 8 27. 6 29. 5 31. 7 33. 25 35. 9
37. $(16 + 5) \times 4 \div 2 = 42$ 39. $(36 \div 3 - 9) \div 3 = 1$
41. 3,840 cans 42. about 17,000 43. about 4
44. no 45. yes 47. $48 49.a. 19 b. 20 c. 32
d. 3 e. 12 f. 225

Pages 30-31 Lesson 1-8
4. 8 5. 1 6. 2 7. 18 8. 10 9. 5 10. 12
11. 9 12. 5 13. 6 14. 5 15. 20 17. 21
19. 7 21. 4 23. 16 25. 2 27. 12 29. no
31. 10 33.a. $740m$

Pages 33-35 Lesson 1-9
4. $2 \cdot 2 \cdot 2 \cdot 2$ 5. $7 \cdot 7 \cdot 7 \cdot 7$
6. $12 \cdot 12 \cdot 12$ 7. $9 \cdot 9 \cdot 9 \cdot 9 \cdot 9 \cdot 9$ 8. 6^3
9. 15^4 10. a^6 11. 625 12. 64 13. 256
14. 512 15. $100,000,000 17. $9 \cdot 9 \cdot 9$
19. $n \cdot n \cdot n \cdot n \cdot n \cdot n \cdot n \cdot n \cdot n$ 21. 12^2
23. 49 25. 243 27. 81 29. 81 31. 36
33. 125 35. true 37. true 39. 625 41. 121
43. 128 44. about 30 miles per gallon 45. yes
46. 39 47. 56 pens and pencils 48. 36
49.a. $7y$ b. 84 years old 51. 10^{18}
55. $999,800,000,000

Pages 40-41 Lesson 1-10
4. false 5. true 6. true 7. false 8. 13 9. 41
10. 81 11. 20 12. 7 13. 18 14. 143 15. 44
16. 80 17. 37 18. 50 mph 19. 4 21. 7
23. 18 25. 96 27. 56 29. 86 31. 48 33. 173
35. 112 37. 146

39. 72 41. 22 43. 17 45. 154 46. no
47. $246 48. false 49.a. $75 + ($1)n
b. $120 50. 4⁴ 51. 216,000 seconds
53. 84 cm

Pages 42-44 Study Guide and Review
7. 420 miles 9. 24,000 11. 700
13. 330,000 15. 200 17. 70 19. no
21. no 23. yes 25. 82 27. 89
29. 10 31. 3 33. 78 35. 1,000
37. 225 39. 47 41. 64
43. $20 \times 468 = 9,360$ 45. $30 + 5n$

2 Applications with Decimals

Pages 49-50 Lesson 2-1

4. >
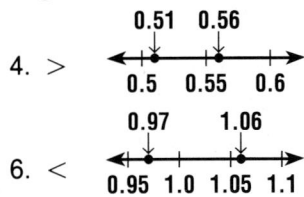

6. <
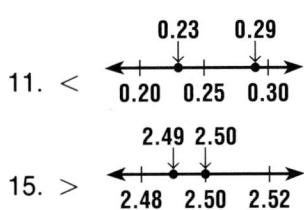

7. > 8. = 9. <

11. <

15. >

17. > 19. = 21. < 23. < 25. <
27. > 29. 5.009, 5.07, 5.13 31. 0.087, 0.901,
1.001, 2 33. $250 34. 485 35. Maria is 18
years old. 36. 86,698 39.a. 19.924, 19,875,
19.837, 19.837 39.b. Daniela Silivas
39.c. Phoebe Mills and Gabriela Potorac
39.d. They are tied.

Pages 52-53 Lesson 2-2
4. 0.3 5. 0.25 6. 7.038 7. 17.5 8. 8
9. 12.13 10. 23 11. 0.24 12. 16.5
13. 0.22 14. 709.1 15. 0.085 17. 0.4
19. 1.0 21. 0.2 23. 15.5 25. 4.530
27. 0.8 29. 60 31. 1.70
33.

34. $730 35. 93 items 36. 64 37. 18
38. 6.32, 8.75, 8.78, 9, 9.15, 10.29 39.a. 9 cm
39.b. 9.2 cm 41. 7.22 in³

Pages 55-57 Lesson 2-3
4. 15 5. 30 6. 28 7. 7 8. 240 9. 60
10. 159 11. 5 12. 12.40 13. 3 14. 25
15. 6 16. 34% 17. $19 19. 10 21. 64
23. 9 25. 600 27. 2,400 29. 200 31. 600
33. 7,200 35. no 36. $500 + 5n$ 37. 15 38. <
39. 5.7 miles 41. about 5 times faster
43. about 12,000 miles

Page 59 Review
1. 6.4 3. 0.24 5. $11.77 7. 1.747
9. 180.75 11. 8.64 13. 11.18 15. 37.632
17. 51.525 19. 13.59 21. 10.72 23. 12.43
25. 28.601 27. 168 29. 3.64
31. 268.3 million people

Pages 62-63 Lesson 2-4
4. 5.28 5. 0.77 6. 19.728 7. 0.28 8. 26.52
9. 0.1845 10. 5.405 11. 0.009 12. 0.53248
13. 1.14 14. 1.26 15. 15.12 17. 0.27
19. 0.0736 21. 1.53 23. 8.814 25. 9.075
27. 21.93 29. 0.0001 31. 0.1053 33. 0.72
35. 0.00589 37. $0.06 38. 32
39.

40. 26 miles 41. 2.21 43. $3.38
45. 4382.88 days

Pages 65-66 Lesson 2-5
3. 234 4. 0.8 5. 2.8 6. 140,000 7. 125.3
8. 605 9. 315.9 10. 20,310 11. 78
12. 1,320 13. 5 15. 2,780 17. 92.5
19. 780 21. 6,894 23. 9,300 25. $73.00
26. 2,000 27. 0.03, 0.3, 0.33, 3, 3.03, 3.33
28. 63 29. 60 mph 31. $12.50
33.a. 1×10^6 33.b. 6.07×10^2
33.c. 3.9256×10^7

Page 66 Mid-Chapter Review
1. > 3. > 5. 6.5 7. 3.1 9. $2 11. 7
13. 0.63 15. 21.812 17. $290

Pages 68-69   Lesson 2-6

3. 8.9×10^2 **4.** 4.3×10^3 **5.** 6.235×10^3
6. 5.2×10^4 **7.** 8.2×10^5 **8.** 1.264×10^8
9. 9,870 **10.** 600 **11.** 17,500 **12.** 23,000
13. 495,000,000 **14.** 570,000 **15.** 7.5×10^3
17. 4.07×10^4 **19.** 4×10^5 **21.** 7.9×10^6
23. 1.6×10^8 **25.** 14,200 **27.** 547,000
29. 27,100,000 **31.** 602,400,000
33. 1.1×10^6 **35.** yes **36.** 13
37. 112 **38.** 18.17 min **39.** 18,700
41.a. Mauna Kea **41.b.** 4,500 feet

Pages 72-74   Lesson 2-7

5. $3.6 \div 4$ **6.** $10.5 \div 7$ **7.** $44 \div 11$
8. $2,940 \div 84$ **9.** $18.9 \div 9$ **10.** $5,040 \div 56$
11. 5 **12.** 3.5 **13.** 1.5 **14.** 8.2 **15.** 63.75
16. 0.35 **17.** $8.2 \div 4$ **19.** $26 \div 13$
21. $14.88 \div 31$ **23.** 8 **25.** 70 **27.** 140
29. 0.91 **31.** 0.046 **33.** 0.5 **35.** 0.088
37. 12 **39.** 3.4 **41.** 0.65 **42.** no **43.** 10
44. $147.27 **45.** 120 **46.** 6.35×10^5
47. 2.6 inches **49.** 1,000 bacteria

Pages 76-77   Lesson 2-8

3. 41.9 **4.** 21.7 **5.** 400.0 **6.** 400,000
7. 10,000 **8.** 300,000 **9.** $1.38 **10.** $11.24
11. $2.13 **12.** 645.65 **13.** 0.26 **15.** 4.36
17. 50,000 **19.** $913.40 **21.** $185.58
23. 4,000,000 **24.** about 30,000 inches
25. 4.25 years old **26.** 30,750
27. $0.05 per ounce **29.** 541 times larger

Page 80   Lesson 2-9

3. 55 **4.** 43,800 **5.** 0.814 **6.** 16,500
7. 5,000 **8.** 32,000 **9.** 89,000 **10.** 67,100
11. 600 **12.** 1,010 grams **13.** 56 cm
15. 580 **17.** 9 **19.** 6.7 **21.** 0.080
23. 73,800 **25.** 8,100 **27.** 0.047 **29.** 70 mL
31. 14,000 mg **32.** 256 **33.** 3.19 **34.** 6.48
35. $42.67 per second

Pages 82-83   Lesson 2-10

3. No, $3,000 \times 7 = 21,000$ **4.** $20 **5.** no
7. 7 miles **9.** 10.8 seconds **11.** 3.5 miles
13. 923 points **15.** 3 quarts **17.** increase of
1.1 million **19.** about 16 times

Pages 84-86   Study Guide and Review

7. 3.04, 3.15, 3.7, 3.9, 4.2 **9.** 0.015, 0.105, 0.149,
0.15, 0.501 **11.** 0.257, 2.04, 2.046, 25.7, 26.04
13. 13.27 **15.** 0.1 **17.** 257.20 **19.** 0.002
21. 350 **23.** 36 **25.** 30 **27.** 0.26
29. 22.725 **31.** 13,700 **33.** 63.7 **35.** 6×10^3
37. 13,700 **39.** 10 **41.** 0.004 **43.** 1,000
45. 2.7 **47.** 0.027 **49.** 6,850 **51.** 160
53. 0.043 **55.** Thomas is lower. **57.** no

3 Statistics and Data Analysis

Pages 91-92   Lesson 3-1

3. 400 thousand women **4.** 1988 **5.** Sample
answer: Yes, until the recession ends.
7. $279.55 **9.** 11 cans **11.** more **13.** 89.6 million

Pages 94-95   Lesson 3-2

3. 1, 5, 10, 1, 6, 3 **4.b.** 25 **5.a.** 30 seconds
5.b. 60 seconds **7.** $93.72 **9.** 16 people
11. Sample answer: 245×13 **13.** 1.5 inches

Pages 99-100   Lesson 3-3

4. 2 to 10, 2 **5.** 1 to 21, 4 **6.** 50 to 70, 5
7. 100 to 160, 20 **8.** 8 **9.** 19 **10.** 50
11. 444 **12.** 5.5 **13.** 10 **15.** 100 **17.** 1,000
19.a. Sample answer: 30 to 150, 20 **20.** $26.00
21. 9.66 minutes **22.** 2,330 m **23.** Range
must remain constant; scale and interval can vary
somewhat depending on an individual's choice.
25.a. Walt Disney

Pages 102-103   Lesson 3-4

14. 570 miles **15.** Sample answer: scale, 0 to
40; interval, 5; range, 33

Pages 106-107   Lesson 3-5

3. 12, 13, 15, 17, 17, 18, 20; 17, 17, 16 **4.** 2, 3, 4,
5, 6, 7, 7, 8; 7, 5.5, 5.25 **5.** 90, 90, 91, 92, 94, 94,
95, 98; 90 and 94, 93, 93 **7.** 65, 65, 65.5
9. 1,755 and 1,805; 1,780; 1,780 **11.** 3.25×10^4
12.

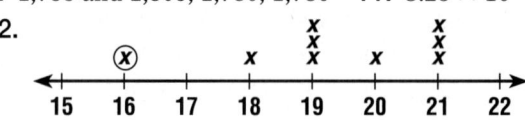

13.a.

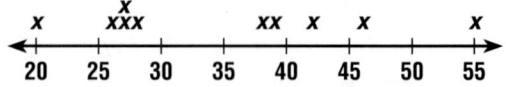

13.b. 27, 33, 34.8   **15.a.** 89, 84, 84.7
15.b. the mode, 89

Page 107   Mid-Chapter Review

1. greater   **3.** 9
4.

```
                        x
              x         x   x
          x   x   x   x  x   x
     x    x   x   x   x  x   x  x x
  ←──┼───┼───┼───┼───┼───┼───┼───┼───┼──→
    11  12  13  14  15  16  17  18  19  20
```

6. Mean, it includes all scores.

Pages 110-111   Lesson 3-6

3. 1, 2, 3, 4, 5   **4.** 0, 1, 2, 3, 4
5. 8, 9, 10, 11, 12, 13

6.a.
```
1 | 6
2 | 3 5 9
3 | 2 5 5 6
4 | 1 5
5 |
6 | 7      1 | 6 means 16 years.
```
6.b. 4   **6.c.** 30's

7.
```
2 | 0 4 7
3 | 4 5 6 6 8
4 | 3 5 7
5 | 3 4 8 8
7 | 8      2 | 7 means 27.
```
9. 36°, 6°   **11.** 110   **12.** $12, $12, $10

13.a.
```
0 | 2 2 3 4 4 6 9
1 | 1 5
2 | 2      1 | 5 means 15 points.
```
13.b. 3   **13.c.** 2 and 4, 5, 7.8; median

Pages 114-115   Lesson 3-7

3. Ana   **4.** about 30   **5.** black   **7.** 21.6, 23, 25.9, 27.4, 30.2

8.
```
6 | 0
7 | 2 5 6
8 | 1 3 6 8
9 | 14     6 | 0 means 60
```
9.a. about 60 million   **9.b.** Sample answer: popularity of baseball compared to other sports.

Pages 117-119   Lesson 3-8

3. A, it makes the scores look higher.   **4.** It starts at 80 instead of 0.   **5.** No, this is not a representative group.   **7.a.** $5, $10, $11.05
7.b. mean   **7.c.** median   **9.** rock

Pages 120-122   Study Guide and Review

15. none, 24, 24.4   **17.** none; 70,500; 74,166.7
21. The 29 brought the mean down, the other six scores were well above 81.6.   **23.** greater
25. $3.90, $3.95, $4.02

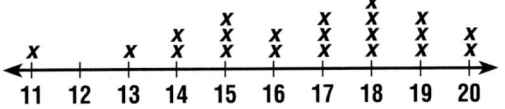

4   Patterns and Number Sense

Pages 130-131   Lesson 4-1

5. no   **6.** yes   **7.** yes   **8.** no   **9.** 2, 3, 4, 5, 6, 9, 10   **10.** 2, 4   **11.** 5   **12.** 2, 3, 4, 5, 6, 9, 10
13. 2, 3, 4, 6, 9   **14.** none   **15.** yes   **17.** no
19. yes   **21.** 2, 3, 5, 6, 10   **23.** none   **25.** 5
27. 10, 20   **29.** 30, 60   **31.** 30, 60   **32.** 10
33. 0.01
34.
```
  ←─●─┼─●─┼───●─┼─●─●─┼───●─┼───●─┼─→
   15  20  25  30  35  40  45  50
```
35. $42,100 is considerably higher than all the other salaries.   **37.** 12 desks

Pages 133-135   Lesson 4-2

6. composite   **7.** prime   **8.** composite
9. composite   **10.** $2^2 \times 3^2 \times 7$ **11.** $2 \times 3 \times 11$
12. $2^4 \times 5 \times 11$ **13.** $2 \times 3^3 \times 5$ **14.** $2^4 \times 3^2$
15. $2^3 \times 11$ **16.** 2×73 **17.** 13×17
18. 2×5^3 **19.** $2^2 \times 3 \times 5^2$ **21.** prime
23. composite   **25.** $2^2 \times 3^2 \times 5 \times 7$
27. $2^2 \times 5^2 \times 13$ **29.** $2 \times 3^2 \times 5$ **31.** $5^2 \times 7$
33. $2^6 \times 5$ **35.** 10   **37.** 78   **38.** 45   **39.** 0.9

40.
```
1 | 9
2 | 5 7
3 | 1 1 2 3 4 6
4 | 1      4 | 1 means 41
```
41. 135 is divisible by 3, 5, 9   **43.a.** $4 = 2 \cdot 2$, $9 = 3 \cdot 3$, $16 = 2 \cdot 2 \cdot 2 \cdot 2$, $25 = 5 \cdot 5$, $36 = 2 \cdot 2 \cdot 3 \cdot 3$, $49 = 7 \cdot 7$, $64 = 2 \cdot 2 \cdot 2 \cdot 2 \cdot 2 \cdot 2$
43.b. Squares of prime numbers have only two factors in their prime factorization.
43.c. The hypothesis holds.   **47.** 3, 5; 5, 7; 11, 13; 17, 19; 29, 31; 41, 43; 59, 61; 71, 73

Pages 138-139   Lesson 4-3

5. arithmetic: 49, 56, 63   **6.** geometric: 162, 486, 1,458   **7.** neither: 21, 28, 36
8. arithmetic: 75, 90, 105

9. neither: 15, 13, 18   **10.** geometric: $\frac{1}{27}, \frac{1}{81}, \frac{1}{243}$

15. geometric: 0.125, 0.0625, 0.03125
17. arithmetic: 5.4, 6.5, 7.6
19. geometric: $\frac{1}{64}, \frac{1}{256}, \frac{1}{1,024}$
21. arithmetic: 55, 66, 77   **23.** neither: 125, 216, 343   **25.** 1, 9, 25, 49: neither   **27.** 21
28. 0.0023 L   **29.** 3, 3, 3   **30.** $2 \times 3^2 \times 5 \times 7$
31. 5, 10, 20, 40, 80, 160, 320;

no, 320 min = $5\frac{1}{3}$ hours

Pages 143-144   Lesson 4-4
3. 1, 1, 2, 3, 5, 8, 13, 21, 34, 55, 89, 144, 233, 377, 610, 987, 1,597, 2,584, 4,181, 6,795
4. number under total = number under number of As + previous number of As
5.a. 1, 0.5, 0.667, 0.6, 0.625, 0.615, 0.619, 0.618, 0.618   **b.** The quotient, rounded to the nearest thousandth, eventually equals 0.618; also, the quotients are alternately greater than 0.618 and less than 0.618.   **7.** 832,040   **9.** 27, 29
11. yes; 1, 144; 1, 8

Page 147   Lesson 4-5
4. 4   **5.** 6   **6.** 11   **7.** 28   **8.** 3, 5; 15   **9.** 3, 3; 9   **10.** 15   **11.** 10   **12.** 6   **13.** 13   **15.** 12
17. 1   **19.** 10   **21.** 1   **23.** 5   **25.** 18   **27.** no
28. about 6
29.

x			x	xx		xx				x		x	
64 66 68 70 72 74 76 78 80 82 84 86 88 90 92 94

30. multiply by 2; 208, 416, 832   **31.** 15
33. No, the factor of any number is not greater than the number.   **31.** 15   **33.** No, it must divide into all numbers.

Pages 151-153   Lesson 4-6
4. $\frac{3}{7}$ **5.** $\frac{3}{7}$ **6.** $\frac{5}{9}$ **7.** $\frac{3}{2}$ **8.** $\frac{9}{10}$ **9.** $\frac{11}{40}$ **10.** $\frac{4}{5}$
11. $\frac{3}{4}$ **12.** $\frac{25}{35}, \frac{15}{21}$ **13.** $\frac{1}{2}$ **15.** $\frac{5}{9}$ **17.** $\frac{9}{11}$
19. $\frac{7}{9}$ **21.** $\frac{7}{16}$ **23.** $\frac{2}{3}$ **25.** $\frac{4}{6}, \frac{6}{9}, \frac{8}{12}$ **27.** $\frac{6}{8}$, $\frac{9}{12}, \frac{12}{16}$ **29.** no   **30.** 2.7   **31.** red   **32.** 18
33. $\frac{7}{15}$ **35.** $\frac{1}{3}, \frac{1}{12}, \frac{1}{24}, \frac{7}{24}, \frac{1}{8}, \frac{1}{12}, \frac{1}{24}$ **37.** $\frac{10}{11}$

Page 153   Mid-Chapter Review
1. no   **3.** yes   **5.** $2^2 \times 7$ **7.** $2^3 \times 3^2$
9. arithmetic: 40, 47, 54

11. geometric: $\frac{1}{256}, \frac{1}{2,048}, \frac{1}{16,384}$ **12.** $\frac{143}{11} =$
13; $\frac{231}{11} = 21$ **13.** 4   **15.** 1   **17.** $\frac{2}{7}$ **19.** $\frac{19}{28}$

Pages 155-156   Lesson 4-7
3. 0.8   **4.** 0.34   **5.** 0.24   **6.** 0.028   **7.** 1.12
8. 0.56   **9.** 0.175   **10.** 1.375   **11.** $0.\overline{7}$
12. $0.\overline{36}$ **13.** $\frac{17}{20}$ **14.** $\frac{5}{8}$ **15.** $\frac{1}{2}$ **16.** $\frac{83}{100}$
17. $\frac{3}{40}$ **19.** 0.55   **21.** 0.12   **23.** 0.875
25. 0.375   **27.** $0.\overline{72}$ **29.** $0.\overline{6}$ **31.** 0.875
33. $\frac{9}{100}$ **35.** $\frac{3}{8}$ **37.** $2\frac{1}{2}$ **39.** $\frac{12}{25}$ **41.** $12\frac{41}{200}$
43. 81   **44.** 0.22, 0.23, 1.6, 2.29, 2.3, 23
45. 63, 63   **46.** 5×7^2 **47.** $\frac{13}{27}$

Pages 159-160   Lesson 4-8
4. $\frac{1}{2}$ **5.** $\frac{1}{2}$ **6.** $\frac{1}{4}$ **7.** $\frac{5}{12}$ **8.** $\frac{2}{9}, 0.\overline{2}$ **9.** $\frac{5}{18}$,
$0.2\overline{7}$ **10.** $\frac{1}{3}, 0.\overline{3}$ **11.** $\frac{1}{6}, 0.1\overline{6}$ **13.** $\frac{1}{4}$ **15.** $\frac{23}{24}$
17. $\frac{1}{24}$ **19.** $\frac{1}{4}, 0.25$ **21.** $\frac{9}{20}, 0.45$ **23.** 2
24. $2.15   **25.** 0.314   **26.** $0.\overline{4}$ **27.** $\frac{2}{9}$
29. an event that will definitely happen

Pages 162-163   Lesson 4-9
3. 60   **4.** 30   **5.** 30   **6.** 300   **7.** 36   **8.** 102
9. 44   **10.** 1,225   **11.** 15   **13.** 180   **15.** 24
17. 900   **19.** 240   **21.** 36   **23.** 2,460
24. 8.19

25.

0	2 5 9
1	0 2 3 6 7
2	3 5 5
3	1 3 | 1 means 31

26. 0.01   **27.** 3 years   **29.** when the smaller number is a factor of the larger number

Pages 166-167   Lesson 4-10
3. 36   **4.** 55   **5.** 26   **6.** 112   **7.** <   **8.** <
9. >   **10.** <   **11.** 30   **13.** 8   **15.** 30   **17.** 68
19. 30   **21.** 21   **23.** >   **25.** =   **27.** <
29. <   **31.** >   **33.** >   **35.** 55   **36.** 1.03×10^4
37.

1.0   1.5   2.0   2.5   3.0   3.5   4.0   4.5

38. $3 \times 5 \times 17$ **39.** 270   **41.** $\frac{4}{6}, \frac{7}{10}, \frac{7}{9}, \frac{9}{11}, \frac{8}{9}, \frac{7}{9}$
45. brass section

Pages 168-170 Study Guide and Review

9. 5 **11.** 2, 4, 5, 10 **13.** none **15.** 2, 3, 6, 9

17. 3 **19.** $2^4 \times 3^2$ **21.** 7×11

23. $2^2 \times 3 \times 5^2$ **25.** $2 \times 5^2 \times 29$

27. geometric: 1,024; 4,096; 16,384

29. geometric: 100,000; 1,000,000; 10,000,000

31. 5 **33.** 3 **35.** $\frac{4}{5}$ **37.** $\frac{2}{3}$ **39.** $\frac{7}{11}$ **41.** 0.4

43. 0.375 **45.** $0.\overline{5}$ **47.** $\frac{1}{2}$, 0.5 **49.** 30

51. 80 **53.** 3,969 **55.** < **57.** < **59.** 2

5 Applications with Fractions

Pages 176-177 Lesson 5-1

4. improper **5.** mixed number **6.** proper

7. improper **8.** improper

9.  **10.**

11. $1\frac{2}{3}$ **12.** $4\frac{1}{2}$ **13.** 3 **14.** $2\frac{1}{3}$ **15.** 1

16. $4\frac{1}{2}$ **17.** $\frac{15}{8}$ **18.** $\frac{11}{4}$ **19.** $\frac{3}{1}$ **20.** $\frac{41}{9}$ **21.** $\frac{41}{3}$

23. mixed number **25.** improper **27.** $1\frac{2}{7}$

29. $2\frac{2}{5}$ **31.** $2\frac{1}{2}$ **33.** 3 **35.** $4\frac{1}{3}$ **37.** $\frac{19}{5}$

39. $\frac{5}{1}$ **41.** $\frac{31}{8}$ **43.** $\frac{35}{8}$ **45.** $\frac{27}{10}$ **47.** $\frac{39}{7}$

49. $9,300 **50.** 17.25 minutes **51.** 0.09

52.

45 50 55 60 65 70 75 80 85 90 95 100

53. 78.125, 195.3125, 488.28125 **54.** $\frac{1}{16}, \frac{1}{2}, \frac{2}{3},$
$\frac{5}{6}, \frac{7}{8}$ **55.** $3\frac{1}{2}$ pies **57.** $2\frac{1}{2}$ pages

Pages 179-181 Lesson 5-2

4. 1 **5.** 0 **6.** $\frac{1}{2}$ **7.** 1 **8.** $\frac{1}{2}$ **9.** 6 **10.** 9

11. 3 **12.** 4 **13.** 7 **14.** $1\frac{1}{2}$ **15.** $\frac{1}{2}$ **16.** 2

17. 11 **18.** $\frac{1}{8}$ **19.** 1 **21.** 1 **23.** 1 **25.** 0

27. $\frac{1}{2}$ **29.** 1 **31.** 4 **33.** 4 **35.** 6 **37.** 9

39. 7 **41.** $\frac{1}{2}$ **43.** 8 **45.** 9 **47.** 11 **49.** 8

51. $\frac{1}{2}$ **53.** 3 **55.** no, 124 **56.** 9 **57.** 10

58. 0.036 liters

59. 0 | 0 1 3 3 4 7 8 9 9
      1 | 0 3 4 5
      2 | 4
      3 | 1   3 | 1 means 31

60. $2^2 \times 3^2$ **61.** $\frac{29}{8}$ **65.** 7,000 pounds

67. about 5 cups

Pages 184-185 Lesson 5-3

4. $\frac{3}{5}$ **5.** $\frac{1}{6}$ **6.** $\frac{7}{24}$ **7.** $1\frac{1}{10}$ **8.** $\frac{11}{15}$ **9.** $1\frac{1}{45}$

11. $\frac{1}{4}$ **13.** $\frac{2}{3}$ **15.** $1\frac{8}{35}$ **17.** $1\frac{7}{18}$ **19.** $1\frac{1}{6}$

21. $\frac{13}{24}$ **23.** $\frac{35}{72}$ **25.** 31, 31.5, no mode

26.
```
    x  x   x  x            x   x  x
 ├──┼────┼────┼────┼────┼────┼────┼→
 0   200  400  600  800  1000 1200
```

27. 80 **28.** $2 \times 12 = 24$ **29.** $\frac{5}{18}$

Pages 187-188 Lesson 5-4

3. 7 **4.** 3 **5.** 8 **6.** 3 **7.** $8\frac{1}{2}$ **8.** $4\frac{1}{2}$ **9.** $1\frac{3}{4}$

10. $17\frac{5}{24}$ **11.** $1\frac{4}{5}$ **12.** $29\frac{23}{40}$ **13.** 3 **15.** 1

17. 11 **19.** 13 **21.** $8\frac{1}{3}$ **23.** $12\frac{1}{4}$ **25.** $2\frac{1}{6}$

27. $4\frac{4}{15}$ **29.** $7\frac{1}{20}$ **31.** $11\frac{17}{40}$ **33.** $3\frac{7}{9}$

35. 9 feet **36.** 30 **37.** 32.5, 35, 37.5

38. 12 hours **39.** $1\frac{1}{2}$ **41.** $1\frac{3}{4}$ inches

Pages 192-193 Lesson 5-5

3. $\frac{3}{10}$ **4.** $\frac{5}{9}$ **5.** $\frac{1}{4}$ **6.** $1\frac{1}{2}$ **7.** $6\frac{2}{3}$ **8.** $\frac{1}{6}$

9. $\frac{1}{10}$ **10.** $1\frac{3}{5}$ **11.** $8\frac{2}{3}$ **13.** $\frac{1}{10}$ **15.** $\frac{3}{10}$

17. $\frac{1}{10}$ **19.** $\frac{2}{7}$ **21.** $\frac{5}{16}$ **23.** $\frac{1}{2}$ **25.** $7\frac{1}{3}$

27. 6 **29.** 6 **30.** It is high because of the
outlier, $49,500. **31.** 2, 3, 4, 5, 6, 10 **32.** $16\frac{5}{8}$

33. 16 inches

Page 193 Mid-Chapter Review

1. $\frac{5}{2}$ **3.** $\frac{10}{3}$ **5.** 1 **7.** 20 **9.** $15\frac{5}{24}$ **11.** $10\frac{1}{9}$

13. $\frac{5}{21}$

Pages 195-196 Lesson 5-6

3. 56 ft 4. $17\frac{7}{8}$ in. 5. $21\frac{3}{4}$ in. 6. 32 feet

7. $3\frac{1}{4}$ in. 8. $2\frac{3}{4}$ in. 9. 50 miles 11. 54 in.

13. 10.4 miles 15. $42\frac{1}{2}$ feet 17. $3\frac{1}{2}$ inches

18. 7,689 pennies 19. $\frac{3}{4}$ 20. $\frac{5}{12}$

21.b. 103 bushels

Pages 199-200 Lesson 5-7

5. 25.12 ft 6. 21.98 m 7. 28.26 yd
8. 37.68 cm 9. 43.96 in. 10. 20.096 m
11. 65.94 in. 12. 20.41 in. 13. 3 meters
14. 15 meters 15. 11 ft 17. 29.83 km
19. 55 mi 21. 9.42 km 23. 38.936 cm
25. $27\frac{1}{2}$ ft 27. 26 feet 29. about 200 cases
30. 1.9, 2.3, 2.6, 3.4, 3.6, 3.8 31. 0.875
32. $50\frac{4}{5}$ feet 33. 200.96 in. 35.a. 6.28, 12.56, 25.12, 50.24, 100.48, 200.96 b. When the diameter is doubled, the circumference doubles.

Pages 202-203 Lesson 5-8

3. $\frac{1}{2}$ 4. $\frac{1}{4}$ 5. $\frac{1}{4}$ 6. $0.75 7. win 9. lose

11. $3.50 13. Coke, Pepsi, Slice

14. $30\frac{9}{14}$ inches 15. $1\frac{1}{2}$ girls

Pages 205-206 Lesson 5-9

3. identity of + 4. associative of × 5. no

6. yes 7. yes 8. yes 9. $2\frac{1}{3}$ 10. $2\frac{1}{5}$

11. $2\frac{1}{8}$ 13. $\frac{8}{7}$ 15. $\frac{1}{3}$ 17. multiplicative

inverse 19. distributive of + over × 21. 11

23. $3\frac{1}{6}$ 24. 65 words/minute 25. 3.5

26. $\frac{5}{36}$ 27. 500 29. $1\frac{1}{6}$ in²

Pages 208-209 Lesson 5-10

3. $\frac{5}{3}$ 4. $\frac{1}{2}$ 5. 3 6. $\frac{2}{9}$ 7. $1\frac{1}{2}$ 8. $3\frac{1}{2}$ 9. $\frac{2}{3}$

10. $\frac{5}{14}$ 11. $\frac{3}{8}$ 12. $5\frac{1}{3}$ 13. $\frac{2}{5}$ 14. $1\frac{1}{2}$

15. $\frac{6}{5}$ 17. $\frac{5}{4}$ 19. $\frac{5}{18}$ 21. $2\frac{2}{5}$ 23. $\frac{2}{3}$

25. $\frac{7}{16}$ 27. $\frac{2}{3}$ 29. $\frac{4}{15}$ 31. $3\frac{3}{8}$ 33. $\frac{2}{3}$

35. $\frac{2}{3}$ 37. $\frac{17}{210}$ 38. 75 39. 10.3 40. $\frac{7}{12}$

41. 241.78 feet 42. $\frac{30}{7}$ or $4\frac{2}{7}$ 43. 16 lots

Page 213 Lesson 5-11

3. 80 4. $2.70 5. $10.65 7. $38

Pages 214-216 Study Guide and Review

9. $\frac{25}{7}$ 11. $15\frac{3}{4}$ 13. $2\frac{5}{8}$ 15. 18 17. $\frac{1}{2}$

19. 90 21. 3 23. $\frac{1}{4}$ 25. $\frac{19}{40}$ 27. $8\frac{1}{4}$

29. $13\frac{9}{14}$ 31. $18\frac{1}{5}$ 33. $34\frac{4}{7}$ 35. $75\frac{13}{21}$ ft

37. $23\frac{9}{35}$ yd 39. $20\frac{26}{35}$ ft 41. $12\frac{3}{4}$ 43. $4\frac{1}{18}$

45. $3\frac{3}{5}$ 47. $5\frac{11}{24}$ cups

6 An Introduction to Algebra

Pages 221-222 Lesson 6-1

4. $5 = 8 - 3$ 5. $9 = 4 + 5$ 6. $m = 19 - 7$
7. $n = 21 + 12$ 8. $5 = 30 \div 6$ 9. $54 = 6 \times 9$
10. $a = 13 \times 2$ 11. $c \div 3 = 14$ 12. $e = 48 \div$
4 13. 8 15. 7 17. 31 19. 114 21. 300
23. 11.6 25. 13.4 27. $1\frac{1}{4}$ 29. 22 31. 9.2
33. 13.4 35. 0.8 37. about $800 38. $8.59

39.
```
0 | 0 2 2 4 5 7 7 9
1 | 0 2 3 3 8 9
2 | 0 3        1 | 2 means 12
```

40. $\frac{3}{4}$ 41. $8\frac{4}{5}$ 43. 98 45. 1.8 kg less

Pages 226-227 Lesson 6-2

5. 25 6. 36 7. 39 8. 9 9. 11.7 10. 21

11. $4\frac{1}{4}$ 12. 9 13. $7\frac{3}{4}$ 15. 16 17. 25

19. 38 21. 73 23. $47\frac{5}{12}$ 25. 127 27. 1.3

29. 10.7 31. $76\frac{1}{15}$ 33. 20.2 34. 9.8×10^3

35.

36. 24 37. 48 39.a. $4\frac{3}{4}$ hours b. $3\frac{1}{4}$ hours

Pages 230-231 Lesson 6-3

4. 5 5. 36 6. 294 7. 7 8. 24.025 9. 6
10. $1\frac{3}{5}$ 11. 864 12. 96 13. 7 15. 13
17. 18 19. 51 21. 44 23. 768 25. 6
27. 32.4 29. 40 31. 243 32. mean = 14, median = 14 33. $2 \cdot 2 \cdot 2 \cdot 3$ 34. $3\frac{5}{12}$
35. 100 37. $3,200 39.a. $9,600 = 4m$
b. 2,400 bits per second

Page 231 Mid-Chapter Review
1. 48   3. 157   5. 68   7. 0.45   9. 306

Pages 234-235 Lesson 6-4
5. $t + 7$ 6. $r + 2$ 7. $p - 8$ 8. $g - 4$

9. $12 + s$ 10. $18 - y$ 11. $\frac{c}{4}$ 12. $3a$

13. $\frac{b}{2}$ 14. $7a$ 15. t minus 10, 10 less than t

16. the quotient of 4 and d, 4 divided by d
17. 10 times n, the product of 10 and n
18. 14 plus h, 14 more than h 19. $y + 5$

21. $2p$ 23. $\frac{a}{3}$ 25. $\frac{a}{6}$ 27. $19 - r$

29. $j + 1,110$ 31. $8 - d$ 33. $\frac{6}{k}$ 35. $s - 8$

37. $x - 15$ 41. $\frac{1}{4}$ 42. Bill   43. 12   44. $\frac{22}{75}$

45. $136.50   47.a. brushing teeth   b. $\frac{t}{2}$

49. 17.3, 26, 40.3, 41.8, 47.3, 56.2, 60.7

Page 237 Lesson 6-5
3. 3   4. 110   5. not enough information

7. $\frac{5}{9}$

Pages 239-240 Lesson 6-6
3. 6   4. 4,000   5. 80   6. 8   7. 3   8. 3
9. 7.5   10. 6   11. 8   13. yes   15. 10,000

17. 10   19. 3   21. 4   23. 5   25. 9   27. $\frac{1}{4}$

29. 9 pints   31. $\frac{1}{4}$ lb   32. 4.5   33. $61.02

34.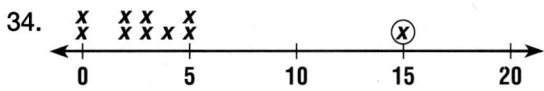

35. $3\frac{7}{12}$ 36. $12 + d$ 39. $68°, 76°$

Pages 244-245 Lesson 6-7
4. 24 in²   5. 14 m²   6. 32.5 ft²   7. 6 in²
8. 216 cm²   9. 40 cm²   11. 28 mm²

13. $19\frac{1}{8}$ m²   15. 414 ft²   17. 142.38 ft²

19. 18 cm²   21. about 210   22. 3,000   23. 32
servings   25.a. yes   b. 126 ft²

Pages 246-248 Study Guide and Review
9. $1\frac{1}{2}$ 11. 0   13. $\frac{3}{8}$ 15. 14.26   17. $6\frac{1}{2}$

19. 63   21. 1.5   23. 8   25. $\frac{5}{6}$ 27. 4

29. 36   31. $x + 5$ 33. $13 - r$ 35. $9 + q$

37. $b - 23$ 39. $\frac{c}{100}$ 41. 80   43. $3\frac{3}{8}$

45. 11.5 or $11\frac{1}{2}$ 47. 45 yd²   49. 36.72 in²

51. $6\frac{1}{24}$ in²   53. no   55. 250 in²

7 Integers

Pages 255-256 Lesson 7-1
5. +4   6. -5   7. +12   8. +6   9. -6
10. +10   11. -5, 5, 5   12. -1, 1, 1   13. -8, 8, 8
14. 8, -8, 8   15. 0, 0, 0   16. 3, -3, 3   17. 1
18. 63°F, -21°F   19. +6   21. +2   23. -25
25. -6, 6, 6   27. -9, 9, 9   29. -1, 1, 1   31. -1
33. no
34.

(number line from 17 to 22 with X marks)

35. $11\frac{1}{9}$ 36. 30,000 ft²   37. 20,320; -282

Page 258 Lesson 7-2
3. >   4. <   5. <   6. >   7. <   8. >
9. -98, -76, -1, 14, 31, 56   11. >   13. >
15. <   17. -91, -76, -9, -6, 2, 18, 32
19. -14, -7, -1, 0, 5, 13   20. $2,245
21. Sample answer: 24, 48   22. 21, 21
23. 21°F   25. -3

Pages 260-261 Lesson 7-3
3. (2, 2), I   4. (5, -2), IV   5. (0, -4), y-axis
6. (-1, 0), x-axis   7. (-3, 1), II   8. (-4, -4), III
9.-14.

(coordinate grid with points L, T, W, P, B, N)

15. (4, 4)   17. (-5, 5)
19. (2, -1)

21., 23., 25., 27., 29.

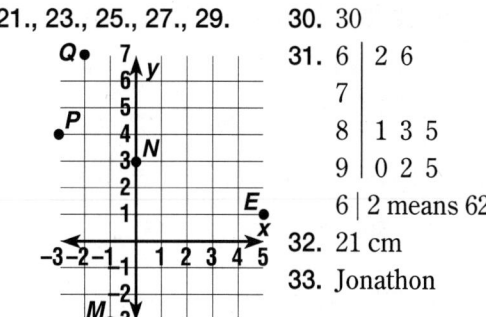

30. 30

31.
6	2 6
7	
8	1 3 5
9	0 2 5

6 | 2 means 62

32. 21 cm

33. Jonathon

9.

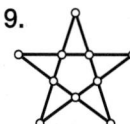

11. $9{,}567 + 1{,}085 = 10{,}652$

Pages 265-266   Lesson 7-4

5. 0 **6.** − **7.** + **8.** + **9.** + **10.** −
11. − **12.** + **13.** -5 **14.** -10 **15.** 11
16. 7 **17.** 0 **18.** 9 **19.** gained 4 yards
21. -4 **23.** 6 **25.** 25 **27.** 100 **29.** -13
31. -6 **33.** 0 **35.** -14 **37.** \$6/pound
39. $\frac{1}{16}, \frac{1}{32}, \frac{1}{64}$ **40.** $t = 8$
41.

B(-4, 4)

(coordinate grid)

43. T + 45 seconds

Pages 269-271   Lesson 7-5

5. 19 **6.** -12 **7.** 27 **8.** -7 **9.** 45 **10.** -8
11. -3 **13.** -27 **15.** -68 **17.** 20 **19.** 0
21. -83 **23.** 0 **25.** 11 **27.** 1 **29.** -18
31. -10 **33.** -4 **35.** -12 **37.** -2 **39.** -6
40. 3,500 **41.** 42 **42.** \$1.40 **43.** $w - 65$
44. -5 **45.** 59°, 840°, 5° **47.a.** normal rainfall
b. -3, -2, -4, 2 **47.c.** August; it has the lowest
rainfall compared to normal **47.d.** There was a
drought this summer.

Page 271   Mid-Chapter Review

1. 15, 15 **3.** 0, 0 **5., 7.**

M(-3, 4)

(coordinate grid)

P(-2, -6)

9. -12 **11.** -7 **13.** 8

Pages 275-276   Lesson 7-6

3. 1 and 3 alternating; 1, 3, 1 **4.** squares of
ordered whole numbers; add 3, 5, 7, 9...
5. 54, 48 **7.** 255 people

Pages 279-280   Lesson 7-7

5. -42 **6.** 20 **7.** -18 **8.** -81 **9.** -45 **10.** 9
11. -18 **12.** -18 **13.** 9 **14.** -108 **15.** -324
16. 54 **17.** 90 **19.** 121 **21.** 36 **23.** -96
25. -68 **27.** -70 **29.** 49 **31.** 189 **33.** 49
35. 150 **37.** -525 **39.** 45 **40.** 1.5
41. 0.375 **42.** $\frac{11}{36}$ **43.** 84 **44.** 87 feet

45. No; at -18 feet the pressure dropped 3(2.7),
so it is 22.8 pounds per sq. in.

Page 282   Lesson 7-8

3. -3 **4.** -10 **5.** 5 **6.** -20 **7.** 17 **8.** -7
9. 31 **10.** 24 **11.** 8 **13.** 4 **15.** -5 **17.** -3
19. -56 **21.** -8 **23.** -8 **25.** -1 **27.** 24
29. 64 **30.** 2.5, 2, 2 **31.** -60 **33.** -2°F

Pages 285-286   Lesson 7-9

5. -4 **6.** -28 **7.** -7 **8.** -12 **9.** 13 **10.** -54
11. -10,100 **12.** 32 **13.** 420 **14.** -8
15. -56 **17.** 43 **19.** -401 **21.** -190 **23.** 46
25. -168 **27.** -5 **29.** 6 **31.** 24.5 cm
32. $\frac{35}{24}$ **33.** 2.5 lb **34.** 40 ft/min
35. 110 feet; $-50 - (-160) = 110$ **37.** 17 cm
39. 24 years

Pages 288-289   Lesson 7-10

3. 0.0003 **4.** 0.6 **5.** 0.00007 **6.** 2×10^{-5}
7. 5×10^{-3} **8.** 9×10^{-7} **9.** 0.000000001
11. 0.7 **13.** 0.00003 **15.** 0.0000008
17. 1×10^{-3} **19.** 9×10^{-1} **21.** 3×10^{-7}
23. 0.00006 **24.** 3 P.M. **25.** $\frac{1}{4} < \frac{2}{7}$ **26.** $\frac{5}{9} < \frac{3}{4}$
27. 32 **29.** 0.002 cm **31.** 0.04 oz.

Pages 290-292   Study Guide and Review

9. 42 **11.** 75 **13.** -5 **15.** -1, 1, 1 **17.** <
19. > **21.** > **23.** I **25.** III **27.** y-axis

23., 25., 27.

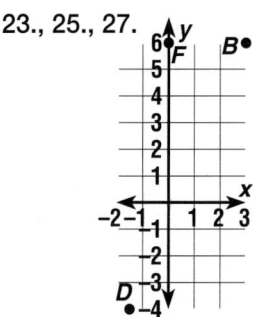

29. 4 **31.** 7 **33.** -25 **35.** -2 **37.** 8 **39.** -6
41. -8 **43.** 9 **45.** -25 **47.** -5 **49.** 6
51. -3 **53.** -5 **55.** -480 **57.** 5×10^{-9}
59. 0.002 **61.** They gained 5 yards.

8 Investigations in Geometry

Pages 299-300 Lesson 8-1
4. obtuse **5.** acute **6.** right **7.** obtuse
8. right **9.** acute **10.** straight **11.** 42°
13. acute **15.** acute **17.** obtuse **19.** acute
21. acute **23.** 20 **25.** 72° **26.** 0.75
27. 1.9 miles **28.** 6×10^{-5} **29.a.** A **b.** C

Pages 304-305 Lesson 8-2
3. No, not closed. **4.** yes **5.** yes **7.** No,
sides do not meet at vertex. **9.** yes **11.** yes
13. 70 **14.** acute **15.a.** 5 **15.b.** 9
17.a. octagon, stop **b.** square, curve
c. triangle, yield **d.** rectangle, speed limit 50

Pages 309-310 Lesson 8-3
4. scalene, right **5.** scalene, obtuse
6. isosceles, acute **7.** parallelogram, rectangle
8. trapezoid **9.** parallelogram, rectangle,
rhombus, square **11.** equilateral, acute
13. scalene, obtuse **15.** scalene, acute
17. parallelogram, rectangle
19. parallelogram, rhombus
21. parallelogram, rectangle, square, rhombus
23. 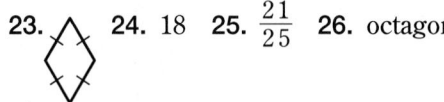 **24.** 18 **25.** $\frac{21}{25}$ **26.** octagon

Pages 315-316 Lesson 8-4
5. No, not equiangular **6.** yes **7.** No, not
equilateral or equiangular **8.** 90°, square
9. yes **11.** yes **13.** 36°, 144° **15.** rhombus
17. 24, 18, 16, 16 **18.** 23 **21.a.** 40

Page 316 Mid-Chapter Review
1. obtuse **3.** parallelogram

Page 320 Lesson 8-5
3. Q, octagon; R, square; S, hexagon **5.** Susan
Sales **7.** about 10 yards **9.** 1, 6, 15, 28; 45

Page 323 Lesson 8-6
3. yes **4.** no **5.** no **7.** no **11.** 1 square,
2 octagons **13.** No, not equilateral or
equiangular. **15.** Use one of each.

Page 326 Lesson 8-7
3.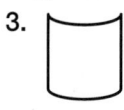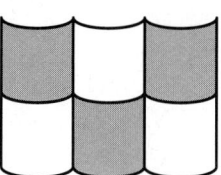

5.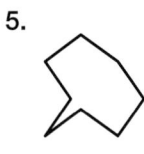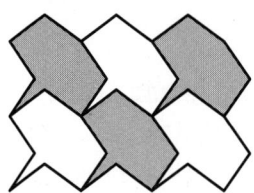

7.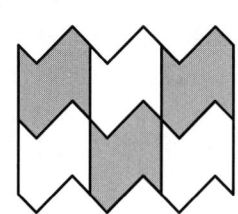

9. No, the patterns on the top and bottom will
not tessellate. **10.** $1\frac{7}{8}$ **11.** no
13. No; no opposite side. **15.** 1.3 miles

Pages 328–329 Lesson 8-8
3.

4.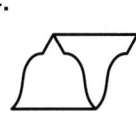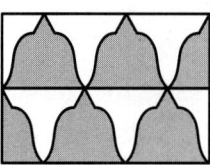

5. 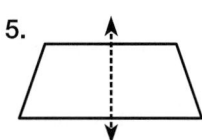 **7.**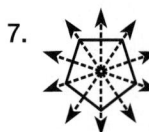

9.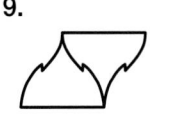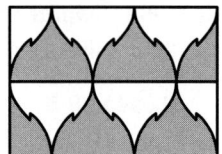

11.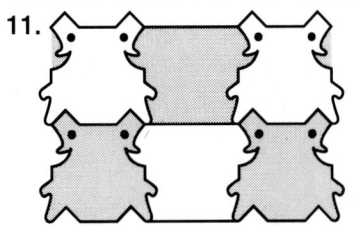

12. 4,500 yd²

13.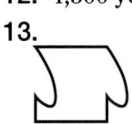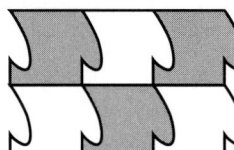

Pages 330-332   Study Guide and Review

9. acute   **11.** straight   **13.** obtuse   **15.** yes
17. yes   **19.** scalene, right
21. parallelogram, <u>rhombus</u>   **23.** No, not
equilateral or equiangular.   **25.** No, not
equilateral or equiangular.   **27.** yes

31.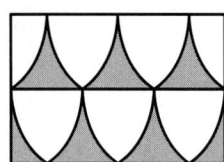

35. isosceles, right

9 Area

Pages 336-337   Lesson 9-1
2. 7 tables   **3.** 45, 62   **4.** 16 years old
5. 2 packages of each   **7.** 24 ways   **9.** b

Pages 339-340   Lesson 9-2
4. 4   **5.** 9   **6.** 49   **7.** 100   **8.** 121   **9.** 144
10. 2   **11.** 6   **12.** 9   **13.** 10   **15.** 25
17. 196   **19.** 400   **21.** 900   **23.** 8   **25.** 12
27. 20   **29.** 40   **31.** 21   **33.** 225 m²   **35.** yes
37. yes   **39.** yes   **40.** about $1,500
41. 14, 12   **42.** 245   **43.** 7.6   **45.** 64 squares

Page 342   Lesson 9-3
3. 3   **4.** 5   **5.** 5   **6.** 6   **7.** 8   **8.** 8   **9.** 10
10. 10   **11.** 3   **13.** 7   **15.** 10   **17.** 12
19. 19   **21.** 27   **23.** $\sqrt{14}$ **24.** 5   **25.** $\frac{19}{20}$
26. 14

Pages 346-347   Lesson 9-4
4. legs 3, 4; hypotenuse 5   **5.** legs 5, 12;
hypotenuse 13   **6.** legs 7, 24; hypotenuse 25
7. $6^2 + 8^2 = c^2$; 10 ft   **8.** $5^2 + 12^2 = c^2$; 13 cm
9. $(9\frac{1}{2})^2 + (4\frac{2}{3})^2 = c^2$; 10.6 m   **10.** $8.2^2 + 15.6^2$
$= c^2$; 17.6 yd   **11.** $10^2 + b^2 = 25^2$; 23 m
12. $12^2 + a^2 = 15^2$; 9 yd   **13.** $5^2 + b^2 = 13^2$;
12 cm   **14.** $15^2 + b^2 = 30^2$; 26 ft   **15.** no
16. yes   **17.** no   **19.** 7.6 in.   **21.** 16.1 ft
23. 20.2 yd   **25.** 16.6 ft   **27.** 12.4 in.
29. 23.7 cm   **31.** no   **33.** no   **35.** no
37. no   **39.** December 31   **40.** $2^4 \times 3^2 \times 5$
41. 75   **42.** 18   **43.** about 3 miles

Pages 349-350   Lesson 9-5
3. 23.6 m   **4.** 16.5 cm   **5.** 11.5 ft   **6.** 9.4 miles
7. about 102.5 ft   **9.** $3/pound   **10.** no

Page 350   Mid-Chapter Review
1. 36   **3.** 484   **5.** ≈4   **7.** ≈12   **9.** ≈18.6 in.

Pages 352-353   Lesson 9-6
3. 28 square units   **4.** 18 square units   **5.** 22
square units   **6.** 52 square units   **7.** 18 square
units   **8.** 56 square units   **9.** 42 square units
11. 63 square units   **13.** 52 square units
17. scalene, right   **18.** ≈29.7 feet
19.a. Alabama, Colorado, Montana, Oregon
b. Maryland, Maine   **c.** Montana, Colorado,
Oregon, Alabama, Maine, Maryland
21. 48 square units

Pages 357-358   Lesson 9-7
4. 12 m²   **5.** 900 ft²   **6.** 27 in²   **7.** 30 ft²
8. 238 in²   **9.** 248.37 m²   **10.** 57 cm²
11. 80 yd²   **13.** 56 km²   **15.** 0.77 in²
17. $2\frac{5}{36}$ yd²   **19.** 150 yd²   **21.** $127\frac{1}{6}$ ft²
23. 25; scale: 5 to 35; intervals of 5   **24.** $7\frac{17}{24}$
25. about 32 square units

Pages 361-362   Lesson 9-8

4. 12.6 ft²   5. 153.9 m²   6. 78.5 in²
7. 1.5 cm²   8. 2.0 cm   9. 2.9 ft   10. 4.9 m
11. 6.0 in.   13. 153.9 cm²   15. 615.4 yd²
17. 754.4 ft²   19. 113.0 cm²   21. 1,962.5 ft²
23. 1,194.0 m²   25. 5.0 m   27. 0.6 km
29. 1.8 yd   31. 5.3 m   33. $2.36
34. -8, -4, -3, 0, 1, 4, 6   35. square, rhombus
36. 60 in²   37. about 706.5 m²

Pages 366-367   Lesson 9-9

3. $\frac{1}{16}$ 4. $\frac{3}{20}$ 5. $\frac{1}{6}$ 7. $\frac{3}{14}$ 9. $\frac{1}{3}$ 11. $\frac{5}{26}$

13. obtuse   14. about 2.83 cm². about 3.46

cm², about 2.54 cm², about 4.52 cm²   15. $\frac{1}{45}$

17. Gulf of Mexico, Sea of Okhotsk, Sea of Japan

Pages 368-370   Study Guide and Review

9. 1   11. 13   13. 100   15. 6   17. 6   19. 20
21. ≈11.2 yd   23. ≈17.0 m   25. ≈5.8 mi
27. 35 square units   29. 60 yd²   31. 30 ft²
33. 254.34 mm²   35. 94.99 yd²   37. $\frac{1}{3}$

39. $\frac{1}{20}$

10 Surface Area and Volume

Pages 379-380   Lesson 10-1

7. 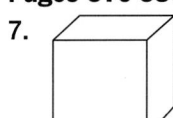   15.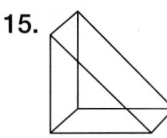

17. Yes, everyone is using the same figures.
There is only one top, front, and side view.

18. 49 sick days   19. 3.68 cm²   20. $\frac{17}{50}$

Page 382   Lesson 10-2

3. 20 in. × 8 in. × 8 in.   4. 5, 3   5. 55 boxes
7. 4 prisms   9. 20 million, $8; 30 million, $10

Pages 384-386   Lesson 10-3

4. 4,200 mm²   5. 94 ft²   6. 192 in²   7. 88 yd²
8. 167.4 m²   9. 310 cm²   11. 181.3 cm²
13. $308\frac{1}{4}$ ft²   15. 784 cm²   17. 3,804 m²
19. 48 in²   21. about $3.00   22. 1   25.a. 252 in²

Pages 389-391   Lesson 10-4

4.a. 12.56 cm²   b. 100.48 cm²   c. 125.6 cm²
5. 125.9768 m²   6. 282.6 ft²   7. 942 cm²
9. 602.9 mm²   11. 324.9 ft²   13. 904.3 m²
15. 415.8 cm²   17. $2,313\frac{1}{7}$ m²   19. $1,168\frac{3}{4}$ yd²
21. 678.24 in²   23. quadrilateral, parallelogram,
rectangle, square   24. 6 ft²   27. 1 can

Page 391   Mid-Chapter Review

3. 88 cm²   5. 71.8432 ft²

Pages 395-397   Lesson 10-5

3. 64 cm²   4. 135 in³   5. 120 mm³
6. 53.24 cm³   7. 150 in³   8. 24 cm³
9. $236\frac{1}{4}$ in³   11. 226.8 ft³   13. 28 in³
15. 350 mm³   17. 1,051.732 cm³
19.a. 343 in³   b. $V = s^3$ 20. 2, 3, 4, 5, 6, 9, 10
21. about 13   22. 196.25 m²   23. $V = x^3$
27. 480 cubic meters

Pages 399-400   Lesson 10-6

5. 100.5 in³   6. 129.8 in³   7. 169.6 m³
8. 183.7 cm³   9. 235.5 in³   10. 37.7 mm³
11. 76 cm³   13. 401.9 cm³   15. 89.5 yd³
17. 282.6 in³   19. 161.9 ft³   21. 39 inches
22. -60   23. 152.88 cm³
27. 132 soft drinks

Page 403   Lesson 10-7

3. 351.68 cm²   4. $27   5. -9   7. 2 yd³
9. No, the box has a surface area of 5,200 cm².

Pages 404-406   Study Guide and Review

7.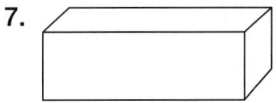

11. 23.9 yd²   13. 195.1 in²   15. 1,406.7 cm²
17. $168\frac{3}{4}$ ft²   19. 9.4 ft³   21. 47.2 in³
23.a. 231 in³   b. about 18 ounces
25. 196.25 in³

11 Ratio, Proportion, and Percent

Pages 412-413   Lesson 11-1

4. $\frac{3}{4}$ 5. $\frac{1}{2}$ 6. $\frac{6}{1}$ 7. $\frac{3}{4}$ 8. $\frac{4}{3}$

9. no, $\frac{65}{100} = \frac{13}{20}$ 10. yes 11. no, $\frac{12}{9} = \frac{4}{3}$

12. yes 13. $\frac{9}{5}$ 15. $\frac{7}{2}$ 17. $\frac{1}{3}$ 19. $\frac{1}{9}$ 21. $\frac{4}{3}$

23. $\frac{16}{7}$ 25. yes, 32:24 = 4:3 and 96:72 = 4:3

27. yes, 4:72 = 1:18 and 12:216 = 1:18
29. no, 6:39 = 2:13 31. 100 32. multiply by
3; 324, 972, 2,916 33. -5, -1, 3, 5

34. 117.75 in³ 35.a. $\frac{6}{8} = \frac{9}{12} = \frac{30}{40}$

35.b. $\frac{3}{4} = \frac{3}{4} = \frac{3}{4}$ 35.c. $\frac{54}{96}$ or $\frac{9}{16}$; $\frac{9}{16} = \left(\frac{3}{4}\right)^2$

Pages 415-416   Lesson 11-2

4. $0.79 per pound 5. 40 mph 6. 2 cups per
pound 7. $1.19 per disk 8. $70 per day
9. 4 people per car 10. 4 pounds per week
11. 30 tickets per day 13. 80 miles per day
15. $1.45 per disk 17. $\frac{1}{2}$ cup per pound
19. 3 people per car 21. 0.003 g 22. $8\frac{3}{4}$
23. hexagon 24. 5:9 25. 47 people per
square mile 27. 305 people per square mile
29. 13,919 people per square mile

Pages 419-420   Lesson 11-3

4. 6 5. 6 6. 15 7. 2 8. 22.5 9. $1\frac{2}{3}$
10. 4.8 11. 16 12. $0.25 13. 12 15. 6
17. 3 19. 75 21. 3 23. 200 25. no, 7 ×
15 = 105 and 8 × 13 = 104 26. 2.0 × 10⁶
28. 25 29. $0.31 per ounce 31. 5.6 pounds

Pages 423-425   Lesson 11-4

4. yes, $\frac{2}{6} = \frac{1}{3}$ and $\frac{3}{9} = \frac{1}{3}$ 5. no, $\frac{10}{5} = \frac{2}{1}$ and
$\frac{12}{7} = \frac{12}{7}$ 6. 8 m 7. 3 in. 8. 125 feet
9. no, $\frac{2}{2} = \frac{1}{1}$ and $\frac{3}{6} = \frac{1}{2}$ 11. no, $\frac{3}{6} = \frac{1}{2}$ and
$\frac{4}{7} = \frac{4}{7}$ 12. yes, $\frac{5}{2.5} = \frac{2}{1}$ and $\frac{8}{4} = \frac{2}{1}$ 13. 2.5 ft
15. 6 m 17. 75 inches 18. about 2 seconds
19. skiing 20. $10\frac{2}{3}$ 21. 74 cm

Pages 428-429   Lesson 11-5

4. 266 miles 5. 114 miles 7. 25 inches
8. $2\frac{1}{2}$ inches 9. $1\frac{13}{32}$ inches 10. 71 inches
11. 480 mi 13. 105 mi 15. 390 miles
17. 30 mi 19. 1.6 cm 21. 9 in. by 6 in.
23. 5 in. by $5\frac{1}{2}$ in. 24. $\frac{4}{5}$
25. 3 points per day 26. no

Page 429   Mid-Chapter Review

1. $\frac{1}{5}$ 3. $\frac{24}{7}$ 5. $1.19 per pound
7. 6 inches per day 9. 12 11. 60
13. $5\frac{1}{4}$ cm 15. $2\frac{1}{2}$ inches

Pages 431-432   Lesson 11-6

3. after 7 stops 4. 10 handshakes
5. 4 T-shirts and 3 gym shorts
7. 1,024 recipes 9. 10 chairs
11. 11 tapes and 33 compact discs

Pages 434-435   Lesson 11-7

5. 45% 6. 37% 7. 13% 8. 18.5% 9. 12.5%
10. 98.5% 11. 42% 12. 30% 13. 50%
14. 28% 15. 60% 16. 79% 17. 22%
19. 98% 21. 11% 23. 62% 25. 40%
27. 25% 29. 36% 30. 125.1 31. $17\frac{1}{2}$

Pages 437-439   Lesson 11-8

3. 90% 4. 45% 5. $33\frac{1}{3}$% 6. $87\frac{1}{2}$% 7. $31\frac{1}{4}$%
8. $\frac{3}{10}$ 9. $\frac{1}{100}$ 10. $\frac{9}{20}$ 11. $\frac{23}{100}$ 12. $\frac{9}{40}$
13.a. 60% b. 40% 15. 86% 17. 40%
19. 30% 21. 25% 23. 12.5% 25. 43.75%
27. 32% 29. $\frac{1}{4}$ 31. $\frac{18}{25}$ 33. $\frac{7}{10}$ 35. $\frac{4}{5}$
37. $\frac{1}{8}$ 39. $\frac{2}{3}$ 41. $\frac{7}{40}$ 43. $\frac{1}{16}$ 45. $\frac{27}{50}$
46. $\frac{15}{24} > \frac{17}{32}$ 47. 5 × 10⁻⁵
48. isosceles triangle, obtuse triangle
49. 8 feet 50. 120 cm³ 51. 34% 53. $\frac{11}{20}$

Pages 442-443   Lesson 11-9

3. 46% 4. 5% 5. 60% 6. 56.5% 7. 0.39
8. 0.04 9. 0.7 10. 0.2325 11. 1.7 13. 75%
15. 32.5% 17. 3% 19. 1% 21. 99.9%

23. 100% **25.** 0.89 **27.** 0.02 **29.** 0.9
31. 0.134 **33.** 0.625 **35.** 1 **37.** > **39.** <
41. = **43.** > **45.** 0.63 **47.** 125
48. $3\frac{1}{2}$ pounds **49.** 21 **50.** 12 **51.** 352 in²
52. $\frac{7}{20}$ **53.a.** 34.4% **b.** about 34 hits

Pages 445-447   Lesson 11-10
5. 4 **6.** 1.8 **7.** 1.3 **8.** 1.45 **9.** 0.0075
10. 0.0024 **11.** 0.002 **12.** 0.00125 **13.** 180%
14. 110% **15.** 0.5% **16.** 0.35% **17.** 925%
18. 750% **19.** 0.92% **20.** 0.116%
21. Yes, people moved to California between 1980-1990 so the population increased.
22. No, he cannot have more goals than shots taken. **23.** 169% **25.** 0.00068 **27.** 2
29. 0.00012 **31.** 0.00032 **33.** 500%
35. 525% **37.** 190% **39.** 28,500% **41.** 0.1%
43. 0.9% **45.** 310% **47.** 400% **49.** =
51. > **53.** =
55. Yes, an antique car can be worth more now than was originally paid for it.
57. No, John can't give away more than all the coins in his collection.
59. Yes, a pine tree's height can increase.
61. $2^2 \cdot 5 \cdot 7$ **62.** 34 in² **64.** 42 cm²
65. 207.24 in² **66.** 0.45 **67.** 309%

Pages 448-450   Study Guide and Review
7. $\frac{5}{2}$ **9.** $\frac{1}{6}$ **11.** $\frac{30}{11}$ **13.** $\frac{7}{1}$
15. 4 cups per person **17.** $4.75 per pound
19. $9.50 per hour **21.** 75 **23.** 1,750
25. yes, $\frac{5}{10} = \frac{8}{16}$ **27.** no, $\frac{4}{6} \neq \frac{7}{14}$
29. 144 km **31.** 360 km **33.** 432 km
35. 3,600 km **37.** 63% **39.** 60% **41.** $\frac{27}{200}$
43. 62.5% **45.** 47% **47.** 0.75 **49.** 99.5%
51. 1.25 **53.** 0.2% **55.** 475%
57. 2,444 people per square mile

12 Applications with Percent

Pages 455-456   Lesson 12-1
5. 93, 100; 200 **6.** $\frac{P}{88}$; 56.3 **7.** $\frac{P}{220} = \frac{40}{100}$; 88 **8.** $\frac{P}{16.5} = \frac{12}{100}$; 2.0 **9.** 140 **11.** 64
13. 72.4 **15.** 28.8 **17.** 8 **19.a.** $9.10
b. $149.10 **20.** 0.78 **21.** 16 **22.** 56.52 in²
23. 0.065% **25.a.** about 47 million
b. about 1,468,750 pounds **27.** 676 immigrants **29.** $224.75

Pages 457-458   Lesson 12-2
2. 18 people **3.** $3,600 **5.** 4 parts **7.** 4

Pages 460-461   Lesson 12-3
3. 36% **4.** 52% **5.** 30% **6.** 100 **7.** 1.2
8. $68 **9.** 0.4 **11.** 2 **13.** 0.1 **15.** 0.01
17. 0.01 **19.** $\frac{1}{8}$ **21.** 24 **23.** 6 **25.** 10
27. 1.1 **29.** 90 **31.** 0.1 **33.** about $3
36. 41 **37.** acute **38.** 560 miles **39.** 720
41. about 25 million Americans

Pages 463-464   Lesson 12-4
4. b **5.** c **6.** a **7.** 27 **8.** 7.5% **9.** 106.7
10. 50% **11.** 20.4 **12.** 125 **13.** 140 students
15. 20%, 18 **17.** 105%, 36 **19.** 30, 15
21. 28.6% **23.** 3.6 **26.** 192 **27.** 31.6
29. 10% **31.** 60 **33.** about $10,800
34. 2, 5, 10 **35.** $\frac{3}{8}$ **36.** 4 **37.** about 48
39. about 12.2% **41.** about 413 books

Pages 466-468   Lesson 12-5
4. 40 **5.** 44% **6.** 5.1 **7.** 25% **8.** 90 **9.** 9.0
10. 30.9 **11.** 47.5% **12.** 42.5 **13.** 65.5%
14. 12.5 **16.** 96.2 **17.** 125% **19.** 2.3
21. 13.6 **23.** 64 **25.** 124 **27.** 500 **29.** 84.7
31. 6.9 **33.** 66.7% **35.** Copying any percent under 100 is reducing. **36.** 6 **37.** 52
38. It is not a closed figure. **39.** 326.56 cm³
40. 76.67% **43.** 16 free throws

Page 468   Mid-Chapter Review
1. $10 **3.** 6 **5.** about 23,018 children **7.** 3
9. 7.8 **11.** 80 **13.** 125 **15.** 33.3%

Pages 472-473   Lesson 12-6

3. $\frac{7}{31}$ 4. $\frac{5}{31}$ 5. $\frac{8}{31}$ 6. $\frac{4}{31}$ 7. $\frac{5}{31}$ 8. $\frac{2}{31}$
9. 83°   10. 58°   11. 94°   12. 47°   13. 58°
14. 22°   19. $2.21   20. no   21. 7

Pages 477-478   Lesson 12-7

4. 50%   5. 20%   6. 50%   7. 37%   8. 10%
9. 18%   11. 20%   13. 41%   15. 19%
17. 100%   19. 59%   21. 50%   22. $w - 6$
23. 405.6 cm²

Pages 480-481   Lesson 12-8

3. $1.40   4. $0.96   5. $5.78   6. $7.50
7. $90.85   8. $186.51   9. $10.60   10. $1.87
11. 17%   12. 20%   13. $2.22   15. $17.33
17. $12.79   19. $4.27   21. 14%   23. 30%
25. $55.12   26. 63   27. 15.7 inches   28. 128
29. 12.8%   31.a. $18.59   b. $2.79
33.a. $507   33.b. $8,307

Pages 482-483   Lesson 12-9

3. $24   4. $61.22   5. $3.23   6. $1,165.50
7. $60.13   8. $171   9. $472.50   11. $43.75
13. $637.20   15. $205   17. $38   19. $28.80
20. 4, 3.5, 3   21. 113 in²   22. 30%
25. $1,120

Pages 484-486   Study Guide and Review

9. 357   11. 352.8   13. 450   15. 30   17. 650
19. 12   21. 5.3%   23. 52.5%   25. 217
27. 750   29. 55%   31. 15%   33. $43.75
35. $16.67   37. $3.75   39. $324
41. 190 days

13 Discrete Math and Probability

Pages 493-494   Lesson 13-1

4. 4 outcomes   5. 12 outcomes
6. 16 outcomes   7. 27 outcomes
9. 9 outcomes   11. 12 outcomes
13. 45, 42, no mode   14. $630
15. 27 numbers

Pages 498-499   Lesson 13-2

4. 30 outcomes   5. 12 outcomes
6. 260 outcomes   7. 16 outcomes
9. 18 outcomes   10. 12   11. 12

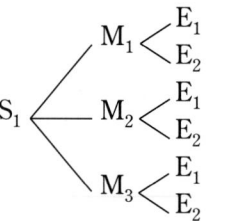 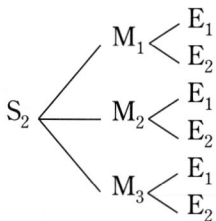

13. *ghn* selections

Pages 501-502   Lesson 13-3

3. $\frac{2}{3}$ 4. $\frac{5}{12}$ 5.a. $\frac{8}{15}$

b. The experimental probability is slightly
greater.   7. $\frac{1}{36}$ 9. 0   10. about 15
11. about 33%   13.a. 0.38   b. no

Page 505   Lesson 13-4

3. 1   4. at least 8 packages   5. at least 6 times
7. $\frac{3}{4}$

Page 505   Mid-Chapter Review

1. 6 outcomes

orange < wheat / rice / corn   apple < wheat / rice / corn

3. $\frac{1}{10}$

Pages 507-509   Lesson 13-5

5. about 22,260 voters   6. about 3,360 voters
7. about 19,740 votes   9. 16%   11. 32%
13. about 11,000 voters   15. Sample answer:
No, because those called may not be registered
voters.   16. 400   17. obtuse, scalene   18. $\frac{1}{2}$
19.a. about 600,000   b. about 900,000
c. about 1,200,000   23. 336 days

Pages 512-513   Lesson 13-6

4. dependent   5. independent   6. $\frac{1}{12}$ 7. $\frac{7}{69}$
8. $\frac{1}{4}$ 9. independent   11. $\frac{1}{15}$ 13. $\frac{1}{6}$
15. $\frac{45}{343}$ 16. $\frac{33}{40}$
17.

18. 39 games   19. 0.3

Pages 519-520   Lesson 13-7

4. 6.   **5.** 1   **6.** 4   **7.** 20   **8.** 6 ways

9. 120 permutations   **10.** 60 flags   **11.** 1

13. 360   **15.** 120 words   **17.** 5,040 ways

19. 27,216 zip codes   **20.** 108   **21.** -18

22. 0.7744   **23.** 6 ways

Pages 524-525   Lesson 13-8

5. 60   **6.** 56   **7.** 15   **8.** 4   **9.** RST, RSU, RSV,

RTU, RTV, RUV, STU, STV, SUV, TUV   **11.** $\frac{1}{14}$

13. 1,680   **15.** 28   **17.** $\frac{1}{252}$

19. permutation; 24 ways   **21.** Sample answer

is: 1.9 million farms, 500 acres   **22.** 1.8

23. 120 signals   **25.** $\frac{1}{20}$ **27.a.** damage is

total, ground becomes wavy   **27.b.** once every

5 to 10 years

Pages 526-528   Study Guide and Review

7. 6 outcomes   **9.** 216 outcomes   **11.** $\frac{3}{10}$

13. $\frac{9}{10}$ **15.** about 2,000 voters   **17.** $\frac{5}{51}$ **19.** 1

21. 720   **23.** 1   **25.** 70   **27.** 6,840 ways

14 Functions and Graphs

Pages 533-534   Lesson 14-1

2. 3 ounces   **3.** Jim, 18; Phyllis, 6; Ed,

10; Matsu, 2   **5.** 30 gallons   **7.** $1.35

11. 2,048 cartons   **13.** 15,132,158.6 times

15.a. mean   **15b.** moved west and slightly south

Pages 538-539   Lesson 14-2

5. 7   **7.** -24

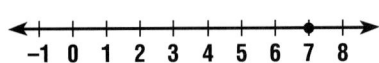

9. -1   **11.** 0.7

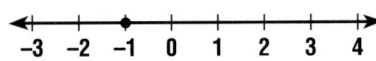

13. $3\frac{1}{2}$ **15.** $3 + \frac{n}{2} = 11; 16$

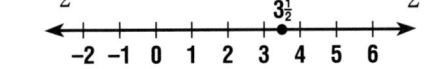

17. -9   **19.** -12

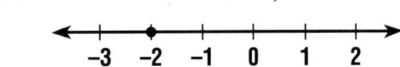

21. -21   **23.** 3.5

25. 56   **27.** -6

29. $4\frac{1}{3}$ **31.** -10

33. 16   **35.** $5x + 3 = -7; x = -2$

37. yes   **38.** -3 **39.** 25%   **40.** 12% decrease

41. 15   **43.a.** 21 miles

b.

Pages 541-542   Lesson 14-3

4.

x	2x + 1	y	
1	2(1) + 1	3	(1, 3)
2	2(2) + 1	5	(2, 5)
3	2(3) + 1	7	(3, 7)
4	2(4) + 1	9	(4, 9)

5.

x	3x	y	
-1	3(-1)	-3	(-1, -3)
0	3(0)	0	(0, 0)
1	3(1)	3	(1, 3)
2	3(2)	6	(2, 6)

6.

x	-2x + 3	y	
-1	-2(-1) + 3	5	(-1, 5)
0	-2(0) + 3	3	(0, 3)
1	-2(1) + 3	1	(1, 1)
2	-2(2) + 3	-1	(2, -1)

7.

x	1.5x	y	
1	1.5 (1)	1.5	(1, 1.5)
2	1.5 (2)	3	(2, 3)
3	1.5 (3)	4.5	(3, 4.5)
4	1.5 (4)	6	(4, 6)

9. {(-1, -3), (0, -2), (1, -1), (2, 0)}

11. {(-1, -5), (0, 0), (1, 5), (2, 10)}

13. {(-1, 2), (0, 0), (1, -2), (2, -4)}

15. {(-1, 4), (0, 2), (1, 0), (2, -2)}

17. {(-1, $\frac{3}{4}$), (0, 1), (1, 1$\frac{1}{4}$), (2, 1$\frac{1}{2}$)}

19. {(-1, -2), (0, -2), (1, -2), (2, -2)}

21. $25 + 35x = y$; {(1, 60), (2, 95), (3, 130), (4, 165)}   **22.** 3.0×10^6 **23.** 0.625   **24.** -13

25.a. $f = g - 18$ **b.** 86, 80, 84, 90

c. (104, 86), (98, 80), (102, 84), (108, 90); (original score, handicap score)

Pages 544-545   Lesson 14-4

4.

x	y	(x, y)
2	6	(2, 6)
1	3	(1, 3)
0	0	(0, 0)
-1	-3	(-1, -3)

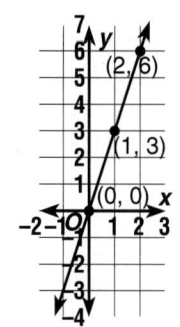

6.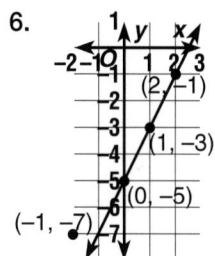

9.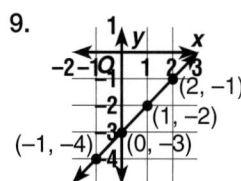

13. 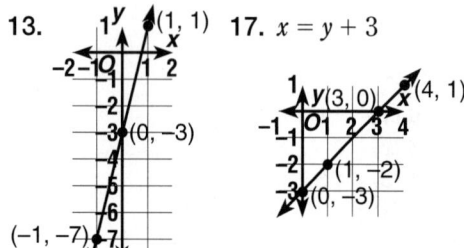   **17.** $x = y + 3$

20. $2\frac{1}{4}$ **21.** 8 m   **22.** (-1, 10), (0, 7), (1, 4), (2, 1)   **23.a.** $y = 6x$

b. 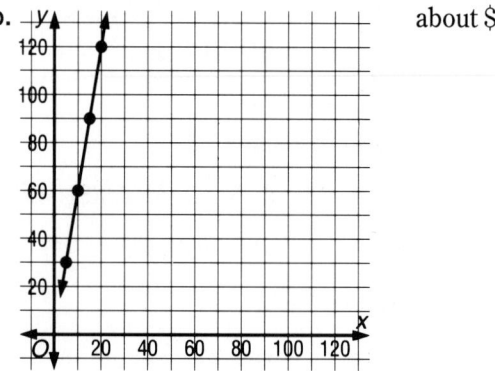   about $45

Page 545   Mid-Chapter Review

1. 6 and 9   **3.** -22

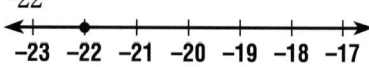

7. (2, 8), (1, 3), (0, -2), (-1, -7)

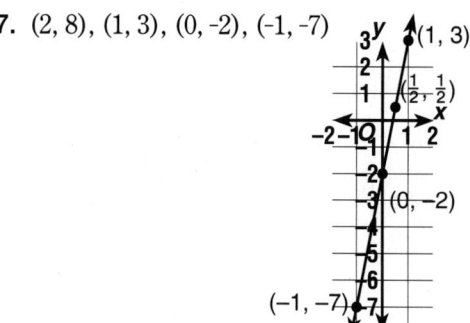

Pages 549-550   Lesson 14-5

4.

x	x + 3	f(x)
-5	-5 + 3	-2
-1	-1 + 3	2
0	0 + 3	3
3	3 + 3	6

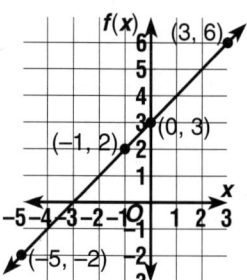

6.

x	-x + 3	f(x)
-2	-(-2) + 3	5
-1	-(-1) + 3	4
2	-2 + 3	1
4	-4 + 3	-1

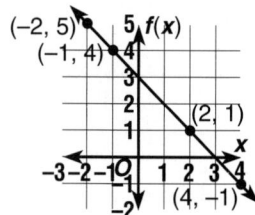

9. -6, 0, 9, 12　**11.** $3\frac{1}{2}$, 4, $4\frac{1}{2}$, 5

13. 5, 2, -1, -4

15. (-4, -3), (0, -2), (4, -1), (8, 0)

17.

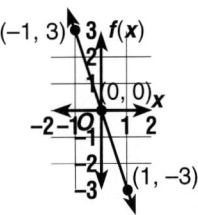

21.

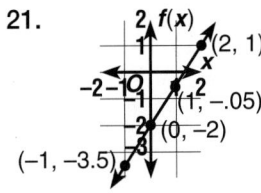

22. $1\frac{1}{2}$ miles　**23.** isosceles, right

24. 36 ways

25.

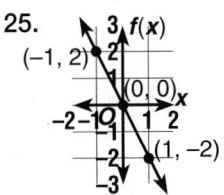

27.a. no negative diameters

b.

d	3.14d	C(d)
1	3.14 (1)	3.14
2	3.14 (2)	6.28
3	3.14 (3)	9.42
4	3.14 (4)	12.56

c.

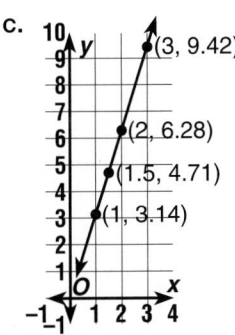

Pages 553-554　Lesson 14-6

4. translation　**5.** translation　**6.** reflection

7.a.

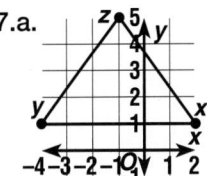

c.

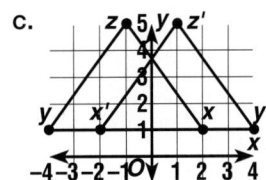

e.

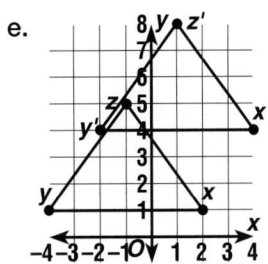

11.

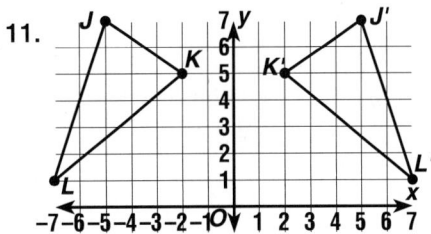

13. 36 m³　**14.** -6, 14, 86

15. on the lid: reflections; on the side: translations and reflections

17.a. translation　**b.** (2, 4)

Pages 556-558　Chapter 14 Study Guide and Review

7. 4

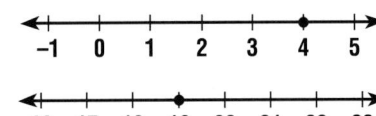

11. 19

13. {(-1, -13), (0, -9), (1, -5), (2, -1)}

15. {(-1, 1), (0, -2), (1, -5), (2, -8)}

17. {(-1, 4), (0, 5), (1, 6), (2, 7)}

19. {(-1, 0), (0, 0), (1, 0), (2, 0)}

21.

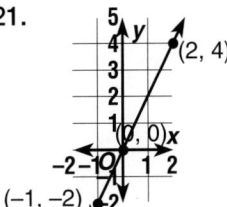

23.

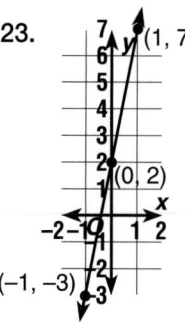

25. 5, 3, 2, 1　**27.** -10, -7, -4, -1

29.

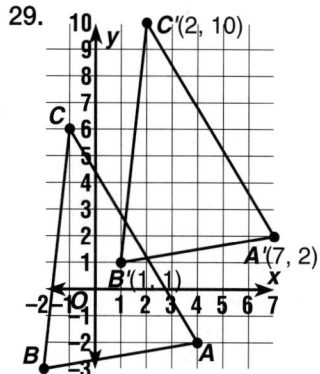

31. Jeff, 27; Fina, 9; Mario, 12; Danielle, 16
33.a. $f(x) = 12.50x$　b. $500

Index

Photo Credits

Cover: (tr) Comstock, (cl) Kevin Morris/Allstock, (c) Stock Imagery, (cr) Glencoe File Photo, (bl) Stock Imagery

iii, Robert Mullenix; **viii,** (t) Konard Wothe/The Image Bank, (b) Aaron Haupt; **ix,** Michael A. Keller/The Stock Market; **x,** (t) Duomo/Rick Rickman, (m) Marti Pie/The Image Bank, (b) Pictures Unlimited, (bkgd) Mark Gibson; **xi,** (t) Caroline Kroeger/Animals Animals, (b) Hank Morgan/Photo Researchers, Inc.; **xii,** (t) Pictures Unlimited, (b) Janet Adams; **xiii,** (t) KS Studio, (b) Mike Luque/Photo Researchers, Inc.; **xiv,** (t) file photo, (b) Brownie Harris/The Stock Market, (bkgd) Glencoe photo; **xv,** (t) KS Studio, (b) Bud Fowle; **xvi,** Skip Comer; **xvii,** Matt Meadows; **xviii,** Matt Meadows; **xix,** Matt Meadows; **1,** Matt Meadows; **2,** (t) Richard Price/Westlight, (b) Reprinted with special permission of King Features Syndicate, Inc.; **3,** (t) Allsport/Vandystadt/Jean-Marc Barey, (b) Robert Mullenix; **6,** Tom & Pat Leeson/ Photo Researchers, Inc; **7,** (t) Ken Frick, (b) ©FPG International, Inc.; **8,** Matt Meadows; **9,** (t) KS Studios, (b) KS Studios; **10,** Alan Carey/Image Works; **11,** Jack Van Antwerp/Stock Market; **12,** Archive Photos; **13,** (t) Randy Trine, (b) Lee Snider/Image Works; **14,** Matt Meadows; **15,** KS Studios; **16,** KS Studios; **19,** Doug Martin; **20,** Skip Comer; **22-23,** J. Messerschmidt/Westlight; **24,** Ken Frick; **26,** courtesy Chrysler Corporation; **28,30,** Ken Frick; **31,** NASA/Science Source/Photo Researchers, Inc; **32,** Skip Comer; (tl) Skip Comer, (tr) Doug Martin, (b) Ken Frick; **36-37,** Skip Comer; **38,** Steve Lissau; **39,** Doug Martin; **40,** Gabe Palmer/The Stock Market; **41,** Doug Martin; **44,** Ken Frick; **46,** (l) courtesy of the Girl Scouts of the United States of America, (r) Historical Pictures Service; **47,** (t) Sobell/Klonsky/The Image Bank, (m) Bob Daemmrich/Stock Boston, (b) The Bettmann Archive; **48,** Doug Martin; **51,** Cincinnati Convention & Visitor's Bureau; **53,** Skip Comer; **54,** Gabe Palmer/The Stock Market; **55,** Ken Frick; **56,** Shooting Star; **57,** Skip Comer; **59,** Duomo/Paul Sutton; **63,** (t) Konard Wothe/The Image Bank, (b) Tim Courlas; **65,** Paul W. Nesbit; **66,** Comstock, Inc.; **69,** Rick Golt/Photo Researchers, Inc; **71,** Scala/Art Resource, New York; **72,** (l) Ken Brate/Photo Researchers, Inc., (r) Duomo/David Madison; **74,** Historical Pictures Service; **75,** Skip Comer; **76,** NASA; **81,83,** Doug Martin; **86,** Skip Comer; **88,** (l) Harald Sund/The Image Bank, (r) Used by permission. Merriam-Webster, Inc.; **89,** (t) George Holton/Science Source/Photo Researchers Inc., (ml) ©David Bartruff/FPG International, Inc., (mr) R.Ian Lloyd/Westlight, (bl) Archive Photos/Lambert, (br) Culver Pictures, Inc.; **90,** Ken Frick; **92,** Doug Martin; **93,** Jon Provost/Movie Still Archives, (b) ©William Read Woodfield/FPG International, Inc.; **103,** Skip Comer; **104,** KS Studios; **107-108,** Doug Martin; **111,** Andy Caulfield/The Image Bank; **112,114,** Skip Comer; **116,** Latent Image; **118-119,** Doug Martin; **122,** MAK-I; **126,** (t) courtesy of the USDA Forest Service, (b) W.Cody/Westlight; **127,** (t) Tom Ulrich/Tony Stone Worldwide, (b) Calvin and Hobbes ©1989, Universal Press Syndicate. Reprinted with permission. All rights reserved., (br) Doug Wilson/Westlight; **129,** MAK-I; **131,** Doug Martin; **132,** Welzenbach/The Stock Market; **134,** MAK-I; **136,** Comstock, Inc; **139,** Matt Meadows; **142-143,** MAK-I; **144,** Joe Towers/The Stock Market; **145,** ©FPG International, Inc.; **147,** (t) Skip Comer, (b) Tim Courlas; **148,** (t,b) Robert Mullenix, (m) Skip Comer; **150,** Doug Martin; **152,** MAK-I; **154,** Dave Hogan/LGI; **157,** Michael Kevin Daly/The Stock Market; **159,** MAK-I; **160,** H. Armstrong Roberts; **161,** Alex Webb/Magnum; **163,165,** MAK-I; **167,** Doug Martin; **170,** MAK-I; **172,** (t) Grant V. Faith/The Image Bank, (bl) Larry Lefever/Grant Heilman Photography Inc., (br) Dr. E.R.Degginger; **173,** (t) Comstock, Inc., (ml) The Bettmann Archive, (mr) C. Ursillo/H.Armstrong Roberts, Inc., (b) courtesy of Texas Instruments; **174,** KS Studios; **177,** Porterfield/Chickering/Photo Researchers, Inc.; **178,** Doug Martin; **181,** (t) B. Bartholomew/Black Star, (b) The Granger Collection; **183,** Ed Hille/The Stock Market; **184,** Turner Entertainment; **186,** Skip Comer; **191,** Comstock, Inc.; **193,** Skip Comer; **197,** Hank Morgan/Photo Researchers, Inc.; **199,** Tom Braise/The Stock Market; **201,** Skip Comer; **203,** (l) MAK-I, (r) Ken Frick; **204,** R.B. Sanchez/The Stock Market; **205,** Margot Conts/Animals Animals; **207,** Doug Martin; **208,** Latent Image; **209,** Skip Comer; **210,** (l) Latent Image, (r) Doug Martin; **211,** Doug Martin; **212,** (t) Skip Comer, (b) Doug Martin; **213,** (l) Pictures Unlimited, (r) Doug Martin; **218,** (t) John A. Sawyer/Profiles West, (b) PEANUTS reprinted by permission of United Features Syndicate, Inc.; **219,** (bl) Robert Mullenix, (br) Rob Mustard; **220,** Comstock, Inc.; **221,** ©Alan Nyiri/FPG International, Inc.; **223,** Doug Martin; **225,** Mary Evans Picture Library/Photo Researchers, Inc; **226,** Latent Image; **228,** Vic Bider/The Stock Market; **230,** Doug Martin; **233,** Flip & Debra Schulke/Black Star; **236-237,** Doug Martin; **238,** Caroline Kroeger/Animals Animals; **239,** Pictures Unlimited; **240,** Don C. Nieman; **242,** Skip Comer; **243,** Ken Frick; **245,** Roy Scheider/The Stock Market; **248,** Doug Martin; **252,** A.J. Verkaik/The Stock Market; **253,** (t) GARFIELD reprinted by permission of UFS, Inc., (m) Comstock, Inc./Stuart Cohen, (b) Comstock, Inc.; **254,** Clark Mishler/The Stock Market; **256,** Johnny Johnson; **258,** Skip Comer; **261,** Werner Stoy/The Image Bank;

TECHNOLOGY ACTIVITIES & DATA BANK

Technology Activities

Data Bank

Objective Evaluate expressions using a graphing calculator.

Time Required

1 day

TEACHING NOTES

- Use the Activity after completing Example 4 in Lesson 1-8.
- Allow students plenty of time to explore the various keys of their calculators. It may be beneficial to have students work in pairs to assist each other in the exploration and discovery.
- Stress that the order of operations will be followed by the calculator. Have students test the calculator by entering the expression 3 + 2 × 2. A calculator that does not use the order of operations will give (3 + 2) × 2 or 10 as a solution. A calculator that uses the order of operations will give 3 + (2 × 2) or 7 as a solution.

TECHNOLOGY ACTIVITY 1:
Evaluating Expressions with a Graphing Calculator

Use with Lesson 1-8, pages 28-31

Graphing calculators observe the order of operations when an expression is evaluated. So there is no need to perform each operation in the expression separately. You can enter the expression just as it is written to evaluate it. The calculators also have parentheses that are used in the same way as in writing to group terms in an expression or to clarify the meaning of the expression. You can also use parentheses to indicate multiplication. For example, 3(2) or (3)(2) can be entered for 3 × 2.

The expression appears as you enter it in a graphing calculator. On TI calculators, the multiplication and division signs do not appear on the screen as they do on the keys. Instead, the calculator displays symbols used in computer language. That is, * means multiplication, and / means division.

You can use arrow keys to go back and correct any error you make by typing over, by using the INS (insert) key, or by using the DEL (delete) key.

Example
Evaluate $3(x - 6) + 1$ **if** $x = 8.$

TI: 3 (8 − 6) + 1 ENTER

Casio: 3 (8 − 6) + 1 EXE

$3(x - 6) + 1 = 5$ if $x = 8.$

If you get an error message or discover that you entered the expression incorrectly, you can use the REPLAY feature to correct your error and reevaluate without reentering your expression. Follow the steps below to use the REPLAY feature.

TI: On the TI-81, press ▲ . On the TI-82, press 2nd ENTRY . The expression is redisplayed below the previous evaluation with the cursor at the end. Use the arrow keys to move to the location of the correction. Then type over, use INS , or use DEL to make the correction. Then press ENTER to evaluate. You don't have to move the cursor to the end.

Casio: Press ⇨ or ⇦ . The answer disappears and the cursor goes to the beginning or end of the expression. Move the cursor using the arrow keys and make changes. Then press EXE to evaluate.

Exercises
Use a graphing calculator to evaluate each expression if $x = 4, y = 7,$ **and** $z = 9.$

1. $12 - z$ 3
2. $x + 9$ 13
3. xy 28
4. $y - 2$ 5
5. $\frac{x}{2} + 12$ 14
6. $2(18 - z)$ 18
7. $\frac{2(z - x)}{(y - 2)}$ 2
8. $14 + \frac{3x}{2}$ 20
9. $x(y + z) - x$ 60

TECHNOLOGY ACTIVITY 2:

Divisibility with a Spreadsheet

Use with Lesson 4-1, pages 129-131

f 96 is divisible by 12, then the quotient of 96 and 12 is a whole number. You can test for divisibility by using a spreadsheet. Enter the spreadsheet below.

Use the spreadsheet to determine whether 96, 57, 108, 36, and 154 are divisible by 12, 14, and 19 by making the following substitutions. A2 = 96, A3 = 57, A4 = 108, A5 = 36, A6 = 154, B1 = 12, C1 = 14, and D1 = 19.

	A	B	C	D
1		B1	C1	D1
2	A2	A2/B1	A2/C1	A2/D1
3	A3	A3/B1	A3/C1	A3/D1
4	A4	A4/B1	A4/C1	A4/D1
5	A5	A5/B1	A5/C1	A5/D1
6	A6	A6/B1	A6/C1	A6/D1

1. 96, 108, and 36
3. If the number is divisible by 12 and by 19.
4. See margin.
5. See margin.

The printout below shows the results of making the substitutions and running the spreadsheet. If any of the results are whole numbers, then the number in column A of that row is divisible by the number at the top of that column. For example, cell B2 contains a whole number. So the number in cell A2, 96, is divisible by the number in cell B1, 12.

Exercises

1. Which numbers are divisible by 12?
2. Which number is not divisible by 12 or 19? 154
3. How could you use the spreadsheet to determine if a number is divisible by 228?
4. Change row 1 of the spreadsheet to test divisibility by 15, 18, and 23. Then change column A to test numbers 90, 253, and 574. Which numbers are divisible by 15, 18, and 23?
5. How could you change the spreadsheet to find the greatest common factor of 18, 45, 90, and 120?

	A	B	C	D
1		12	14	19
2	96	8	6.857	5.053
3	57	4.75	4.071	3
4	108	9	7.714	5.684
5	36	3	2.571	1.895
6	154	12.833	11	8.105

Objective Use a spreadsheet to determine divisibility.

Time Required
1 day

TEACHING NOTES

- Use the Activity after discussing Example 3 in Lesson 4–1.
- Each spreadsheet program has a different way of entering formulas and text into the cells. Consult the User's Guide to learn how to enter information into your specific program.
- You may wish to have students work in pairs to enter the spreadsheet program into a computer.

Answers

4. 90 is divisible by 15 and 18; 253 is divisible by 23.
5. Keep changing the divisibility tests in row 1. You could test every number from 1 to 18. The greatest common factor of 18, 45, 90, and 120 is 3.

Objective
Plot points on the graphics screen of a graphing calculator.

Time Required
1 day

TEACHING NOTES

- Use the Activity after discussing Example 4 in Lesson 7–3.
- If students have had little experience with graphing calculators, they will need help entering the program into the memory. Explain that many of the TI-81 programming commands are found in the menus. Consult the User's Guide for the locations of specific commands.
- You may wish to have students work in pairs to enter the program into the graphing calculator. Have one student read the program while the other enters the lines into the calculator.

TECHNOLOGY ACTIVITY 3:
Plotting Points on a Graphing Calculator
Use with Lesson 7-3, pages 259-261

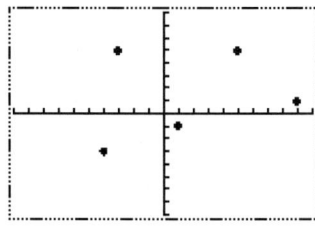

The graphics screen of a graphing calculator can represent a coordinate plane. The x- and y-axes are shown, and each point on the screen is named by an ordered pair. You can plot points on a graphing calculator just as you do on a coordinate grid.

The program below will plot points on the graphics screen. In order to use the program, you must first enter the program into the calculator's memory. To access the program memory, use the following keystrokes.

Enter: [PRGM] [▶] 1

Example

Plot the points (-3, 5), (9, 1), (1, -1), (-4, -3), and (5, 5) on a graphing calculator.

The Program is written for use on a TI-81 graphing calculator. If you have a different type of programmable calculator, consult your User's Guide to adapt the program for use on your calculator.

First set the range. The notation [-10, 10] by [-8, 8] means a viewing window in which the values along the x-axis go from -10 to 10 and the values on the y-axis go from -8 to 8.

Enter: [RANGE] [(−)]
    10 [ENTER] 10
    [ENTER] 1 [ENTER]
    [(−)] 8 [ENTER]
    8 [ENTER] 1
    [ENTER]

```
Prgm 1: PLOTPTS
:All-Off
:ClrDraw
:Lbl 1
:Disp "X="
:Input X
:Disp "Y="
:Input Y
:Pt-On(X, Y)
:Pause
:Disp "PRESS 0 TO QUIT OR
1 TO PLOT MORE POINTS"
:Input A
:If A = 0
:End
```

Exercises

Use the program to graph each set of points on a graphing calculator. Then sketch the graph. See students' work.

1. (9, 1), (-2, 1), (3, 3), (-7, -1)

2. (-12, 1), (15, -5), (-3, -2), (-19, -9)

Now run the program.

Enter: [PRGM] 1 [ENTER]

Enter the coordinates of each point. They will be graphed as you go. Press [ENTER] after each point is displayed to continue in the program.

TECHNOLOGY ACTIVITY 4:
Simple Interest with a Spreadsheet
Use with Lesson 12-9, pages 482-483

S imple interest, *i*, is calculated by finding the product of the principal, *p*, the rate, *r*, as a percent, and the time, *t*, in years. The formula used is $i = prt$. The new account balance is then found by adding the interest to the principal, or $A = p + i$.

A spreadsheet like the one below can be used to generate a simple interest table for various account balances.

	A	B	C	D	E
1	Principal	Rate	Time	Interest	New Balance
2					
3	500	B2/100	C2	A3*B3*C3	A3+D3
4	1000	B2/100	C2	A4*B4*C4	A4+D4
5	1500	B2/100	C2	A5*B5*C5	A5+D5
6	2000	B2/100	C2	A6*B6*C6	A6+D6
7	2500	B2/100	C2	A7*B7*C7	A7+D7

Suppose you are the manager of a local bank. Your bank is starting a "Young Savers" program for children. You want to make a table of the interest that children can earn to show how important saving money is. The current rate on the "Young Savers" account is 5%. Use 2 years as the time period. Substitute the values B2 = 5 and C2 = 2 into the spreadsheet to show how much will be in an account with the different starting balances at the end of 2 years.

1. To change the percent to a decimal.
2. $1,650
4. See margin.
5. B2 = 7, C2 = 0.75; $1,578.75

Exercises
Use the spreadsheet to answer each question.

1. Why is the rate in column B divided by 100?
2. What is the account balance after 2 years if the principal is $1,500 and the simple interest rate is 5%?
3. What is the interest earned in 2 years on an account with a principal of $2,000 and an interest rate of 5%? $200
4. Suppose you wanted to add a new row to the spreadsheet which represents a principal of $3,000. List each of the cell entries (A8, B8, C8, D8, and E8) that you would enter.
5. What entries for cells B2 and C2 would you use to calculate the simple interest on a principal of $1,500 at a rate of 7% for a nine-month period? What is the balance of this account at the end of the 9 months?

Technology Activity 4

Objective Use a spreadsheet to find simple interest.

Time Required
20 minutes

TEACHING NOTES
- Use the Activity after discussing the introductory example in Lesson 12–9.
- You may wish to have students work in pairs. One student can read the lines of the spreadsheet while the other enters the information into the program.

Answer
4. A8 = 3000; B8 = B2/100; C8 = C2; D8 = A8*B8*C8; E8 = A8 + D8

Objective
Graph linear equations on a graphing calculator.

Time Required
30 minutes

TEACHING NOTES
- Use the Activity after discussing the Example in Lesson 14-4.
- You may wish to have students use the graphing calculator as a check to their own graphs. Have students graph an equation. Then graph on the graphing calculator and compare.
- If students have had little experience with graphing calculators, you may wish to have them work in pairs. Have one student read the instructions while the other operates the calculator. Then have them switch roles.

TECHNOLOGY ACTIVITY 5:
Linear Equations on a Graphing Calculator
Use with Lesson 14-4, pages 543-545

A graphing calculator is a powerful tool for studying functions. Any of the graphing calculators will graph linear functions, but the procedure for graphing is slightly different for each one. On any of the calculators, you must set an appropriate range before you can graph a function. A viewing window of [-10, 10] by [-10, 10] with a scale factor of 1 on both axes denotes the values $-10 < x < 10$ and $-10 < y < 10$. The tick marks on both axes in this viewing window are one unit apart. This is called the **standard viewing window**.

Example
Graph $y = 2x + 3$ in the standard viewing window.

Be sure that your calculator is in the correct mode for graphing functions.

Casio fx-7000: MODE +

Casio fx-7700: MODE + MODE MODE +

TI: Press the MODE key. If "Function" and "Rect" are not highlighted, use the arrow and ENTER keys to highlight them. Press 2nd QUIT to return to the home screen.

Now graph the function.
Casio fx-7000: Graph 2 ALPHA X + 3 EXE

Casio fx-7700: Graph 2 X,θ,T + 3 EXE

Exercises
Graph each function on a graphing calculator. Then sketch the graph on a piece of paper. See students' work.
1. $y = -x + 4$
2. $y = 2x - 1$
3. $y = 4$
4. $y = \frac{1}{2}x + 5$
5. $y = 6x - 3$
6. $y = -5x + 2$

TI: Y= 2 X|T + 3 GRAPH

On the TI-82, x is entered using the X,T,θ key.
You will need to clear the graphics screen before you can graph a second function. To clear the screen on a Casio, press SHIFT Cls EXE. On a TI, press Y= and use the arrow and CLEAR keys to clear any functions from the Y= list.

POPCORN, SPORTS, AND SCOUTING

Popcorn Sales (Unpopped)

Year	Pounds
1975	393,000,000
1976	415,000,000
1977	450,000,000
1978	486,000,000
1979	520,000,000
1980	568,000,000
1981	600,000,000
1982	611,000,000
1983	618,000,000

Year	Pounds
1984	630,000,000
1985	670,000,000
1986	700,000,000
1987	741,000,000
1988	807,000,000
1989	872,000,000
1990	938,000,000
1991	1,031,800,000
1992	1,124,600,000

Americans consume 18 billion quarts of popped popcorn annually or 71 quarts per man, woman, and child. Approximately 70 percent is eaten in the home (home popped and pre-popped) and about 30 percent outside the home (theaters, stadiums, schools, and so on). Unpopped popcorn accounts for approximately 90 percent of sales for home consumption.

Almost all the popcorn consumed throughout the world is grown in the United States. Americans consume more popcorn than the citizens of any other country.

Source: The Popcorn Institute, 1993

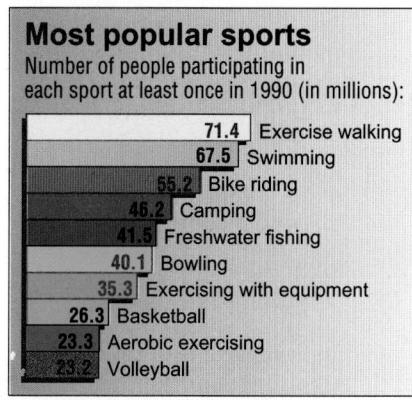

Most popular sports

Number of people participating in each sport at least once in 1990 (in millions):

71.4	Exercise walking
67.5	Swimming
55.2	Bike riding
46.2	Camping
41.5	Freshwater fishing
40.1	Bowling
35.3	Exercising with equipment
26.3	Basketball
23.3	Aerobic exercising
23.2	Volleyball

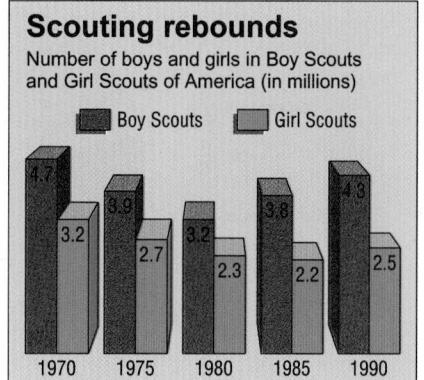

Scouting rebounds

Number of boys and girls in Boy Scouts and Girl Scouts of America (in millions)

Boy Scouts   Girl Scouts

Year	Boy Scouts	Girl Scouts
1970	4.7	3.2
1975	3.9	2.7
1980	3.2	2.3
1985	3.8	2.2
1990	4.3	2.5

Source: Statistacal Abstract of the United States, 1991 (in USA TODAY)

The Data Bank provides students with up-to-date statistical information. Students must refer to the Data Bank to answer questions that appear throughout the text. The following table lists the lessons in which the questions appear.

Data Bank Page	Lesson and Page
p. 649	1–1, p. 7
	2–10, p. 83
	3–1, p. 92
	12–1, p. 456
p. 650	4–4, p. 144
	5–7, p. 200
	8–5, p. 320
p. 651	6–1, p. 222
	7–6, p. 276
	9–1, p. 337
p. 652	10–2, p. 382
	11–6, p. 432
	13–7, p. 520
	14–1, p. 534

FIGURATE NUMBERS AND JUICES

Figurate Numbers

Triangular Numbers	•	△	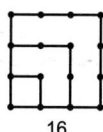	
	1	3	6	10

Square Numbers	•	▢	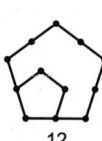	
	1	4	9	16

Pentagonal Numbers	•	⬠		
	1	5	12	22

The Juice We Drink

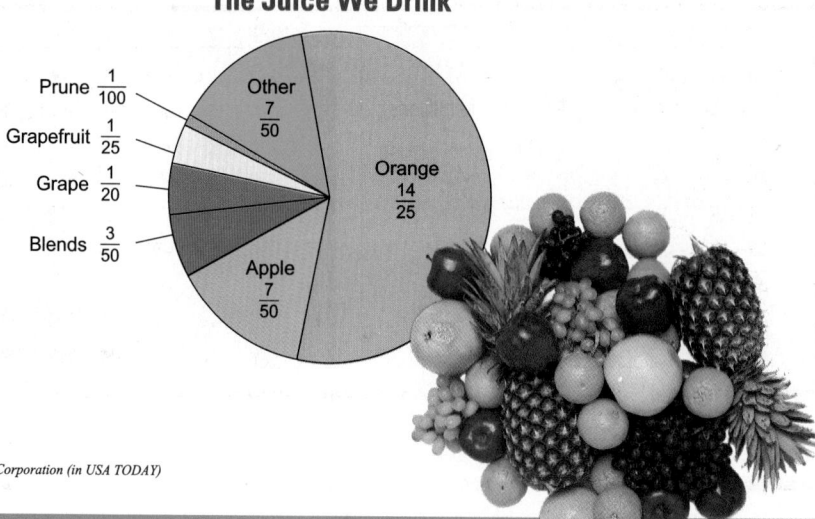

Prune $\frac{1}{100}$

Grapefruit $\frac{1}{25}$

Grape $\frac{1}{20}$

Blends $\frac{3}{50}$

Other $\frac{7}{50}$

Orange $\frac{14}{25}$

Apple $\frac{7}{50}$

Source: Beverage Marketing Corporation (in USA TODAY)

HEIGHTS, WEIGHTS, AND WIND CHILLS

Average Height and Weight for Children

Girls					Boys				
Age	Height		Weight		Age	Height		Weight	
years	ft. in.	cm	lb.	kg	years	ft. in.	cm	lb.	kg
11	4'8"	142.2	77	34.9	11	4'8"	142.2	77	34.9
12	4'10"	147.3	86	39.0	12	4'10"	147.3	83	37.7
13	5'0"	152.4	98	45.5	13	5'0"	152.4	92	41.7
14	5'2"	157.5	107	48.5	14	5'2"	157.5	107	48.5

Source: Physicians Handbook, 1990

Wind Chill Table

The combination of cold and wind make you feel colder than the actual temperature. The table below shows the temperature that you feel at a given actual temperature with the given wind speed. This is called the **wind chill.** For example, when the actual temperature is 15 degrees Fahrenheit and the wind speed is 10 mph, it feels like minus 3 degrees. In the table below, the top line of figures shows actual temperatures in degrees Fahrenheit and the column at left shows wind speeds. Wind speeds greater than 45 mph have little additional chilling effect.

MPH	35	30	25	20	15	10	5	0	-5	-10	-15	-20	-25	-30	-35	-40	-45
5	33	27	21	16	12	7	0	-5	-10	-15	-21	-26	-31	-36	-42	-47	-52
10	22	16	10	3	-3	-9	-15	-22	-27	-34	-40	-46	-52	-58	-64	-71	-77
15	16	9	2	-5	-11	-18	-25	-31	-38	-45	-51	-58	-65	-72	-78	-85	-92
20	12	4	-3	-10	-17	-24	-31	-39	-46	-53	-60	-67	-74	-81	-88	-95	-103
25	8	1	-7	-15	-22	-29	-36	-44	-51	-59	-66	-74	-81	-88	-96	-103	-110
30	6	-2	-10	-18	-25	-33	-41	-49	-56	-64	-71	-79	-86	-93	-101	-109	-116
35	4	-4	-12	-20	-27	-35	-43	-52	-58	-67	-74	-82	-89	-97	-105	-113	-123
40	3	-5	-13	-21	-29	-37	-45	-53	-60	-69	-76	-84	-92	-100	-107	-115	-123
45	2	-6	-14	-22	-30	-38	-46	-54	-62	-70	-78	-85	-93	-102	-109	-117	-125

Source: National Weather Service, NOAA, U.S. Dept. of Commerce

GARDENING, CABLE TV, AND U.S. POPULATION CENTER

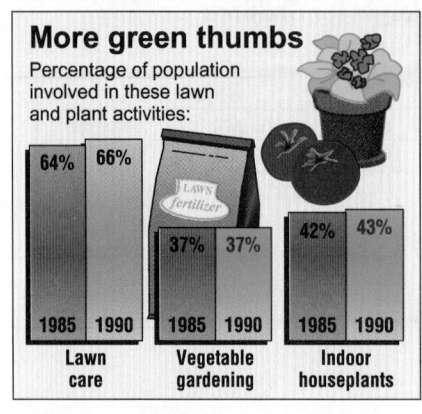

More green thumbs
Percentage of population involved in these lawn and plant activities:

	Lawn care		Vegetable gardening		Indoor houseplants	
	1985	1990	1985	1990	1985	1990
	64%	66%	37%	37%	42%	43%

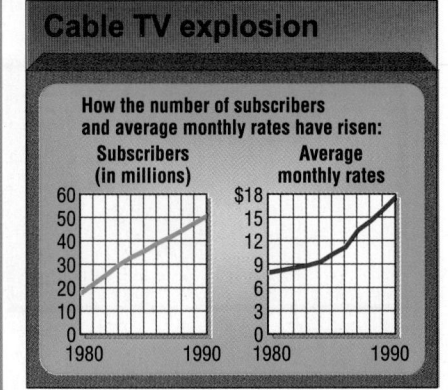

Cable TV explosion

How the number of subscribers and average monthly rates have risen:

Subscribers (in millions): 1980–1990
Average monthly rates: 1980–1990

Source: Statistical Abstract of the United States, 1991 edition (in USA TODAY)

U.S. Center of Population, 1790-1990

The center of population represents the point about which the population is equally distributed. That is, if the U.S. were a rigid plane without weight, and each individual exerted equal weight at the point where he or she resides, the plane would balance on the point considered to be the center of population.

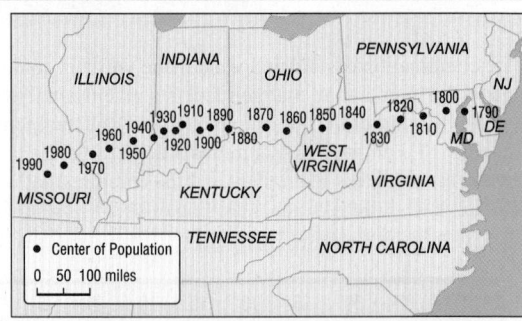

- Center of Population
0 50 100 miles

Year	N. Latitude °	′	″	W. Longitude °	′	″	Year	N. Latitude °	′	″	W. Longitude °	′	″
1790	39	16	30	76	11	12	1900	39	9	36	85	48	54
1800	39	16	6	76	56	30	1910	39	10	12	86	32	20
1810	39	11	30	77	37	12	1920	39	10	21	86	43	15
1820	39	5	42	78	33	0	1930	39	3	45	87	8	6
1830	38	57	54	79	16	54	1940	38	56	54	87	22	35
1840	39	2	0	80	18	0	1950*	38	48	15	88	22	8
1850	38	59	0	81	19	0	1960	38	35	58	89	12	35
1860	39	0	24	82	48	48	1970	38	27	47	89	42	22
1870	39	12	0	83	35	42	1980	38	8	13	90	34	26
1880	39	4	8	84	39	40	1990	37	52	20	91	12	55
1890	39	11	56	85	32	53							

* Includes Alaska and Hawaii.